Letters from a Life:
The Selected Letters of Benjamin Britten 1913–1976

Letters from a Life:
The Selected Letters
of Benjamin Britten
1913–1976

VOLUME THREE
1946–1951

EDITOR-IN-CHIEF: DONALD MITCHELL

EDITED BY
DONALD MITCHELL
PHILIP REED
AND MERVYN COOKE

CO-ORDINATING EDITOR
JILL BURROWS

University of California Press
Berkeley and Los Angeles, California

University of California Press
Berkeley and Los Angeles, California
Published by arrangement with
Faber and Faber Limited
3 Queen Square London WC1N 3AU

ISBN 0–520–24259–9

Phototypeset by Agnesi Text Hadleigh Suffolk
Printed in Great Britain by Mackays of Chatham plc

A CIP record for this book is available from the British Library

Endpaper: Winter storm, Crag Path, Aldeburgh, 1949

10 9 8 7 6 5 4 3 2 1

To the memory of
Eric Crozier 1914–1994
and Nancy Evans 1915–2000

CONTENTS

Index of Correspondents   ix
List of Illustrations   xiii
Editorial Method   xix
Acknowledgements   xxi
Key to Bibliographical Abbreviations   xxv

Introduction: Happy Families?
Donald Mitchell   1

LETTERS

I   Towards *Peter Grimes*   53
     January 1936–October 1945

         The Correspondence   59

         'I love being with you & picking your brains': The Letters of
         Benjamin Britten and Edward Sackville-West, 1942–1945
         Donald Mitchell   109

II   Chamber Opera is Created   135
     January 1946–August 1947

III The Aldeburgh Festival is Launched   311
     September 1947–August 1948

IV   *Spring Symphony*   405
     August 1948–July 1949

V   Towards *Billy Budd*   531
     July 1949–December 1951

     Bibliography   703
     Index of Britten's Works   719
     Index of Other Composers   727
     General Index   731

INDEX OF CORRESPONDENTS

ERNEST ANSERMET *Letters* 541, 545
DR G. A. AUDEN XIX

HERBERT BARDGETT 678
GEORGE BARNES, BBC 573
BBC, *see* GEORGE BARNES, DOUGLAS CLEVERDON,
    VICTOR HELY-HUTCHINSON, JOHN LOWE
DAVID BEDFORD 586, 648
LESLEY BEDFORD 565, 610, 685
MARY BEHREND 531, 558, 607
LENNOX BERKELEY XI, XII, 559, 647, 667, 721
LEONARD BERNSTEIN XIV
LESLIE A. BOOSEY XIII
BOOSEY & HAWKES, *see* LESLIE A. BOOSEY, RALPH HAWKES,
    ERNST ROTH, ERWIN STEIN
HENRIËTTE BOSMANS 588, 604, 626, 652
RUTLAND BOUGHTON XXV, 516
HENRY BOYS 560
BARBARA BRITTEN 526, 548, 661, 686
BENJAMIN BRITTEN *from Peter Pears* 629, 703
EDITH BRITTEN IV
FLORENCE BRITTEN 568
ROBERT BRITTEN 691
PETER BURRA II, III, V, VI, VII
JAMES BUTT XXI

JOHN CHRISTIE 537, 542
JANE CLARK 669
DOUGLAS CLEVERDON, BBC 695, 700
BASIL COLEMAN 637, 705
JOAN CROSS 532
ERIC CROZIER 538, 570, 572, 592, 631, 633, 636, 645, 646, 651, 663,
    664, 673, 679, 697, 719

NORMAN DEL MAR   684
E. J. DENT   582, 722
WILFRED DERRY   613
RALPH DOWNES   606
RONALD DUNCAN   527, 557, 567, 618, 653, 655, 662
PIERS DUNKERLEY   612

DOROTHY ELMHIRST   689
NANCY EVANS   562, 569, 646

HARRY FARJEON   I
E. M. FORSTER   688, 696, 708, 718

ANTHONY GISHFORD   581
ALBERT GOLDBERG   681
PERCY GRAINGER   641

GEORGE HAREWOOD   682, 692, 717
MARION HAREWOOD (*née Stein*)   659, 680, 692, 717
KENNETH HARRISON   671, 704
CLARE HAWKES   534
RALPH HAWKES   517, 528, 534, 540, 556, 575, 595, 616, 627, 632, 672
CHRISTOPHER HEADINGTON   585
VICTOR HELY-HUTCHINSON, BBC   518
IMOGEN HOLST   XXVI, 535, 593, 638, 668, 683, 698
WALTER HUSSEY   519, 550, 578, 665

CHRISTOPHER ISHERWOOD   XVI

SERGE KOUSSEVITZKY   546, 608, 630, 634, 656
SERGE KOUSSEVITZKY *from Ralph Hawkes*   529

JOHN LOWE, BBC   707

ELIZABETH MAYER   533, 539, 543, 571, 601, 619, 694, 699
HERBERT MURRILL, BBC   587

BOYD NEEL   710
JOHN NICHOLSON   675

CARLOS PEACOCK   583
PETER PEARS   X, XXII, 515, 554, 555, 561, 563, 576, 577, 589, 590, 596,
    598, 599, 600, 602, 603, 611, 614, 615, 620, 621, 622, 625, 650, 658,
    660, 676, 690, 701, 702, 706
JOHN PIPER   523
WILLIAM PLOMER   711, 714
JOHN POUNDER   579

JEAN REDCLIFFE-MAUD   544, 551
SIR HOWARD ROBERTS, CLERK TO THE LONDON COUNTY COUNCIL
    693

NED ROREM   654

ERNST ROTH   623

JOAN ROTHMAN   XV

THOMAS RUSSELL, LONDON PHILHARMONIC ORCHESTRA   657

EDWARD SACKVILLE-WEST   536, 552, 566, 635
   see also pp. 111–34 *passim*

GUSTEL SCHERCHEN   521

EDITH SITWELL   639, 716

LEONARD SMITH, THE GRAMOPHONE CO. LTD   564, 591

STEPHEN SPENDER   VIII

ERWIN STEIN   XVIII, XXIII, XXIV, 525, 547, 553, 584, 640, 643, 674, 713

SOPHIE STEIN   674

MARION STEIN (*later Harewood*)   628

REGINA STURMDORF   XVII, XX

ELIZABETH SWEETING   617, 642, 644, 677, 715

JOSEPH SZIGETI   597

EDITOR OF *THE TIMES*   530

JOHN F. WATERHOUSE   IX

DAVID WEBSTER, ROYAL OPERA HOUSE, COVENT GARDEN: 549, 580,
   594, 670, 720

ERIC WALTER WHITE   574, 605, 609, 649, 687, 709, 712

GRACE WILLIAMS   624

JOHN WOOLFORD   524

BASIL WRIGHT   522

SOPHIE WYSS   520

BENJAMIN ZANDER   666

LIST OF ILLUSTRATIONS

PLATE SECTION I
between pages 198 and 199

1 Benjamin Britten in 1947 © Frederick Vogt
2 Peter Pears and Benjamin Britten in 1948 © Maria Austria/MAI Amsterdam
3 Glyndebourne, 1946: *The Rape of Lucretia*, Act I scene 2
   Photo Angus McBean; by permission of the Harvard Theatre Collection
4 Ernest Ansermet and Britten in the Organ Room at Glyndebourne, 1946
5 Ronald Duncan and Britten in the gardens at Glyndebourne, 1946
6 Glyndebourne, 1946: *The Rape of Lucretia*, Act II scene 2
   Photo Angus McBean; by permission of the Harvard Theatre Collection
7 Glyndebourne, 1946: *The Rape of Lucretia*, Peter Pears and Joan Cross
   as the Male and Female Choruses
   Photo Angus McBean; by permission of the Harvard Theatre Collection
8 Glyndebourne, 1946: members of the creative team for *The Rape of
   Lucretia* – Otakar Kraus, Kathleen Ferrier, Peter Pears, Nancy Evans,
   Britten, Eric Crozier and Ernest Ansermet
9 Switzerland, 1947: Lionel Billows, the British Council representative who
   lent his surname to the grande dame of Loxford in *Albert Herring*, with
   Peter Pears
10 Glyndebourne, 1947: *Albert Herring*, Act II scene 1 – Albert (Peter Pears)
   addresses the dignitaries of Loxford © Edward Mandinian
11 Eric Crozier, Britten and Frederick Ashton in the Walled Garden at
   Glyndebourne, 1947
12 John Piper
13 Glyndebourne, 1947: *Albert Herring*, Act II scene 1 in rehearsal
   © Cyril Arnold
14 Switzerland, 1947: Britten at work on *Albert Herring*
   © FotoHänssler, Zurich
15 Glyndebourne, 1947: *Albert Herring*, Act II scene 2
   Photo Angus McBean; by permission of the Harvard Theatre Collection
16 Arts Theatre, Cambridge, 1948: Tyrone Guthrie and Britten
   © Maria Austria/MAI Amsterdam

17   Arts Theatre, Cambridge, 1948: Britten and Tanya Moiseiwitsch
     © Dennis de Marnay/Getty Images
18   Orchestral rehearsal for *The Beggar's Opera*, with Eric Crozier, Britten,
     Ivan Clayton and Hans Oppenheim, Arts Theatre, Cambridge, 1948
     © Maria Austria/MAI Amsterdam
19   Arts Theatre, Cambridge, 1948: Britten and Tyrone Guthrie
     © Maria Austria/MAI Amsterdam
20   Arts Theatre, Cambridge, 1948: *The Beggar's Opera*, Act III
     © Maria Austria/MAI Amsterdam
21   Arts Theatre, Cambridge, 1948: *The Beggar's Opera*
     © Maria Austria/MAI Amsterdam
22   Erwin Stein
23   Humphrey Maud
24   William Primrose
25   Edward Sackville-West   © Cecil Beaton Archive, Sotheby's, London/
     Collection National Portrait Gallery

     PLATE SECTION II
     between pages 550 and 551

26   Tanglewood, 1946: Benjamin Britten and Serge Koussevitzky
     © Ruth Orkin
27   Tanglewood, 1946: Britten and W. H. Auden   © Ruth Orkin
28   Tanglewood, 1946: *Peter Grimes* – the curtain call   © Ruth Orkin
29   On the Meare at Thorpeness, Suffolk, 1950: George and Marion
     Harewood, Peter Pears, George Behrend and Britten
30   Britten the hardy swimmer in the North Sea   © Roger Wood
31   Round the piano at Crag House, Aldeburgh, 1947: Pears, Ronald Duncan,
     Arthur Oldham and Britten
32   Christopher Isherwood, E. M. Forster and William Plomer, visitors to the
     first Aldeburgh Festival in June 1948   © Bill Caskey
33   With friends in the garden at Crag House during the 1948 Aldeburgh
     Festival: Pears, Imogen Holst, E. M. Forster, Britten and Arthur Oldham
     © Kurt Hutton/Getty Images
34   Britten and Pears buying vegetables from Jonas Baggott in Aldeburgh
     High Street, 1948   © Kurt Hutton/Getty Images
35   Aldeburgh Festival, 1948: *Saint Nicolas* in the Parish Church
36   Aldeburgh Festival, 1949: Sammy's bath and the rocking horse arriving at
     the stage door of the Jubilee Hall for the premiere of *Let's Make an Opera*
37   Aldeburgh Festival, 1949: Hugh Gathorne-Hardy with Roguey and Sally
     Welford at a rehearsal for *Let's Make an Opera*
38   Aldeburgh Festival, 1949: members of the audience at *Let's Make an Opera*
     providing an ad hoc chorus
39   Aldeburgh Festival, 1949: *The Little Sweep* in rehearsal
40   Aldeburgh Festival, 1949: *The Little Sweep* in performance
     © Desmond Tripp

41 Aldeburgh Festival, 1949: *The Little Sweep* company in 'The Coaching Song'

42 E. M. Forster, Britten and Eric Crozier working on the libretto of *Billy Budd* at Crag House, Aldeburgh, August 1949 © Kurt Hutton/Getty Images

43 Co-librettists of *Billy Budd*: Eric Crozier and E. M. Forster © Kurt Hutton/Getty Images

44 Royal Opera House, Covent Garden, 1951: *Billy Budd* – Peter Pears as Captain Vere © Roger Wood

45 Royal Opera House, Covent Garden, 1951: *Billy Budd*, Act I scene 1 © Roger Wood

46 Royal Opera House, Covent Garden, 1951: *Billy Budd*, Act IV scene 1 – Billy (Theodor Uppman) in the Darbies *Photo* Angus McBean; by permission of the Harvard Theatre Collection

47 Royal Opera House, Covent Garden, 1951: *Billy Budd*, Act II scene 3 © Roger Wood

48 Britten the conductor in rehearsal © Willi Rudolph, Wiesbaden

49 Britten the conductor in rehearsal © Willi Rudolph, Wiesbaden

50 Amsterdam Concertgebouw, 1949, after the first performance of *Spring Symphony* – Britten and Pears with Jo Vincent, Eduard van Beinum and Kathleen Ferrier

ILLUSTRATIONS IN THE TEXT

page 37 Model of the proposed Festival Theatre, Aldeburgh (1954) *Photo* Henry Lewes

37 Aerial view of Aldeburgh showing the site of the proposed Festival Theatre, Aldeburgh (1957) *Photo* Tudor Photos

77 The manuscript fair copy of *The Ascent of F6*: the opening of the Prelude to Act II British Library Add. MS No. 60622; © Boosey & Hawkes

94 The official notification of the outcome of Britten's Appellate Tribunal on 18 August 1942

108 The opening bars of Purcell's divine hymn 'We sing to him', as it appears in the *Harmonia Sacra* and in the manuscript of Britten's realization Britten's realization © Boosey & Hawkes

110 The first page (Prologue) of the manuscript full score of the *Serenade*, with the dedication to Edward Sackville-West – 'To E.S.-W.' © Boosey & Hawkes

126 *The Rescue*: a page from Britten's annotated copy of the typescript

127 *The Rescue*: the corresponding page from Britten's manuscript full score

145 Programme for the Concertgebouw, Amsterdam, 9/10 January 1946: Pears sings *Les Illuminations*

153 Advertisement for the first Amsterdam recital by Pears and Britten, 11 January 1946

156 'THE WORLD WAITS': the front page of the *Evening Standard*, 7 August 1945

157 The first page from Britten's copy of the typescript of *Mea Culpa* © The Estate of Ronald Duncan

159   Britten's fair copy of the two-piano arrangement of the *Impromptu*,
      in 1945 the newly composed third movement of the Piano Concerto
      © Boosey & Hawkes

164   Auden's draft of his *Anthem for Saint Matthew's Day*
      © The Estate of W. H. Auden

175   *Peter Grimes* comes home: a flyer for a concert in aid of the Suffolk Rural
      Music School, 22 April 1946

179   *The Rape of Lucretia*, Act II scene 2: the final page from Duncan's draft
      libretto, showing the original ending of the opera without the Epilogue
      © The Estate of Ronald Duncan

204   Tanglewood, August 1946: the programme for the US premiere of *Peter
      Grimes*

215   Glyndebourne, 12 and 13 July 1946: the cast lists for the first and second
      performances of *The Rape of Lucretia*

216   Glyndebourne, 1946: pages from the programme for *The Rape of Lucretia*

233   From Ronald Duncan's draft libretto of *Letters to William*, Act I
      © The Estate of Ronald Duncan

241   Britten's diary, 8–21 September 1946

245   'Opera as a Profession', advertisement in the programme for *The Rape of
      Lucretia* at Sadler's Wells, August 1946

247   Programme for the Concertgebouw, Amsterdam, 3 November 1946:
      Britten narrates *The Young Person's Guide to the Orchestra*

249   The cover and contents page from Eric Crozier's paperback copy of
      Maupassant short stories   © Penguin Books

256   *The Rape of Lucretia*, Act II scene 2: Junius' and Collatinus' return to
      Rome and Lucretia's appearance at fig. 81, in the original (1946) and
      revised (1947) versions   © Boosey & Hawkes

258   *The Rape of Lucretia*: Britten's setting of 'the prodigious liberality / Of self-
      coined obsequious flattery'   © Boosey & Hawkes

266   A pair of pages from Britten's 1946 loose-leaf diary on which he works out
      the possible casting of *The Rape of Lucretia* and *Albert Herring*

275   *Albert Herring*, Act III: the Threnody, 'In the midst of life is death', in
      Britten's composition draft   © Boosey & Hawkes

278   Programme for a recital in Copenhagen, 25 February 1947

281   Programme for a 'Concert of English Music', Naples, 30 April 1947

283   *Albert Herring*, Act II scene 1, in Britten's composition draft, with the
      '*Tristan* chord' as Albert drinks his lemonade   Boosey & Hawkes

291   An appeal for War Resisters' International in the programme for a fund-
      raising recital at the Friends House, London, 18 April 1947

293   Glyndebourne, 12 July 1947: the programme for the first performance of
      Albert Herring

307   Tonhalle, Zurich, 19 August 1947: the programme for a concert given by
      the English Opera Group

318   The minutes of the first meeting of the Aldeburgh Festival Executive
      Committee, 27 October 1947

334 Royal Opera House, Covent Garden, 6 November 1947: the programme
     for the opening night of the Guthrie–Moiseiwitsch production of *Peter
     Grimes*

360 Aldeburgh Parish Church, 5 June 1948: the programme for the inaugural
     concert of the Aldeburgh Festival

371 The cover of *Time* magazine, 6 February 1948, prior to the New York
     opening of *Peter Grimes*

394 Polly Peachum's 'The turtle thus with plaintive crying' in Britten's anno-
     tated copy of *The Plays of John Gay*

395 Britten's realization of Polly's 'The turtle thus with plaintive crying'
     © Boosey & Hawkes

398 Arts Theatre, Cambridge, 24 May 1948: the programme for the first per-
     formance of *The Beggar's Opera*

447 The title page of the Suite, Op. 6, for violin and piano   © Boosey & Hawkes

451 The opening of *I saw three ships* (*The Sycamore Tree*), composed in 1930
     Suffolk County Record Office

462 Britten's unpublished *Einladung zur Martinsgans*, composed in 1957

466 Programme for the Continental premiere of *Saint Nicolas*, in Amsterdam,
     6 December 1948

481 Britten's outline synopsis of Melville's *Billy Budd* and his stage sketch of
     the *Indomitable*, with annotations by E. M. Forster and Eric Crozier

482 Forster's first draft of the Prologue of *Billy Budd*: 'I am an old man who
     has experienced much'

513 Palais des Beaux-Arts, Brussels, 6 May 1949: programme for a recital by
     Pears and Britten

515 Jubilee Hall, Aldeburgh, 14 June 1949: programme for the first perform-
     ance of *Let's Make an Opera*

523 Amsterdam, 14 July 1949: programme for the first performance of *Spring
     Symphony*

545 Flyer for Pears's and Britten's New York recital, 23 October 1949

582 Advertisement of the 'Britten Number' of *Music Survey* from the
     programme for the UK premiere of *Spring Symphony*

592 *Lachrymae*: the title page and opening in Britten's composition draft
     © Boosey & Hawkes

593 *Lachrymae*: the final pages in Britten's composition draft
     © Boosey & Hawkes

619 *Billy Budd*, Act II scene 2: Claggart's 'O beauty, o handsomeness, goodness!'
     in Britten's composition draft   © Boosey & Hawkes

626 Britten's sketch for his *Scherzettino 'A.B.'* (1971) to honour Sir Arthur Bliss
     on his eightieth birthday

649 Pages from the programme for the performance by the English Opera
     Group of Monteverdi's *Il combattimento di Tancredi* and Purcell's *Dido
     and Aeneas* in the edition by Britten and Imogen Holst at the Lyric
     Theatre, Hammersmith, 3 May 1951

671 Britten's incomplete libretto synopsis for *The Tale of Mr Tod*

684   Royal Opera House, Covent Garden, 1 December 1951: programme for the
      first performance of *Billy Budd*
688   Britten's composition draft for the sequence of chords at the end of Act III
      (four-act version) of *Billy Budd*   © Boosey & Hawkes
689   The opening of the Epilogue of *Billy Budd* in Britten's composition draft
      © Boosey & Hawkes

*All illustrative material, with the exceptions of plates 2 and 50,
may be found at* BPL.

EDITORIAL METHOD

THE TEXTS OF THE LETTERS

In one regard we have departed from a principle that guided us in our transcription of Britten's letters in volumes 1 and 2. Since Britten's death, it has often been remarked that when he sat down to write a letter or a postcard – and it is important to remember what a substantial proportion of his letters was handwritten, especially in his earlier years – he customarily had to hand an English dictionary, although there must have been occasions when the indispensable dictionary was absent, for instance when he was on his travels. His spelling, as he was himself aware, could be uncertain. Throughout the text that follows there are many examples of his questioning himself, even when he had a spelling correct; these self-doubts we reproduce as they appear in his letters. However, we have silently corrected his mistakes; it seemed needlessly pedantic and distracting not only to reproduce every one of his errors but also to identify it as such, lest, as could all too easily be the case, the mistake might be read as a printing error. We have occasionally retained a mis-spelling but only when it adds something to the character and flavour of what Britten was writing or provokes a smile. (We have found nothing to match the classic entry in one of Britten's diaries when he refers to a 'Bach sweet'.) Likewise, in the case of his sometimes eccentric punctuation, we have added to or adjusted it in order to clarify his intended meaning; often he was writing, it should be emphasized, under pressure and at high speed. While generally more reliable than Britten's, Pears's spelling and punctuation have received similar editorial attention in this volume. In Britten's and Pears's letters, the writers' use of ampersands, 's'-spellings (e.g. 'realise' rather than 'realize') and underscoring have been retained; deletions are shown only when meaningful. In letters and documents by other hands, obvious mistakes have been silently corrected and the presentation of the text conforms to current publishing practice.

FORMAT

The diverse layout of addresses in the original letters has been rationalized, and small capitals indicate a printed letterhead. Dates appear in the format given in the original document. Where addresses have been supplied or dates conjectured, this information appears within square brackets, as does editorial information about the medium of communication, e.g. postcard or telegram. When a complete letter (or a substantial extract) has previously appeared in another publication, this information is also displayed in square brackets. We indicate where letters are typed (as distinct from hand-written) and where handwritten interpolations have been made. Carbon copies of typed letters can be identified by the lack of a signature. All post-scripts are placed after the signature, although Britten, having finished the main text of a letter, would often add an afterthought at the top of the first page, above the date and address.

Opus numbers for Britten's works are not used in the annotations but are included in the Index of Britten's Works (pp. 719–26). Full biblio-graphical information for books cited in the annotations is included in the Bibliography (pp. 703–18).

When referring to specific passages in Britten's scores, we have used the convention of a negative or positive superscript digit to indicate the number of bars before or after a rehearsal figure; e.g. fig. 6^{-6} = six bars before fig. 6, fig.6^{+6} = six bars after fig. 6.

The abbreviation IC1/2 refers to the Index of Correspondents for volumes 1 and 2.

INDEXES

As in the earlier volumes, the index has been divided into three: an Index of Britten's Works, an Index of Other Composers and a General Index. Additional information – for example, a work performed by Peter Pears, tenor, and Benjamin Britten, piano (PP–BB), or both these artists (PP/BB) appearing at different times in a particular location (in Britten's case also perhaps as a conductor); or the location or premiere status of a work – is supplied wherever it would appear to be helpful or of interest to the reader. As both Britten and Pears are constant presences on virtually every page, it has not proved useful or desirable to reference every element of their lives in their individual entries in the General Index, although a number of personality traits and recurring aspects of their lives are listed there. The reader might find it easier to trace a particular event or performance through one of the Works indexes or through an organization or a venue in the General Index.

Where a reference is to a plate or an illustration in the text, the entry appears in *italic* type. **Bold** type is used to show the recipient of a numbered letter and underlining indicates a major biographical annotation. Abbrevi-ations used in the indexes are as follows:

AF	Aldeburgh Foundation	PP	Peter Pears
BB	Benjamin Britten	*pp*	private or domestic performance
c	conductor, conducted by	*sop*	soprano
IOC	Index of Other Composers	*vla*	viola
ms	mezzo-soprano	*vln*	violin

ACKNOWLEDGEMENTS

We thank all those who have so generously placed at our disposal their correspondence with Benjamin Britten and Peter Pears and we are grateful to the owners of Britten or Pears letters – individuals and institutions – for their indispensable co-operation. The names of correspondents are listed on pp. ix–xi.

We owe a special debt to the Trustees of the Britten–Pears Foundation, the owners of the copyright in Britten's letters and diaries, his other writings and unpublished music, and to the Executors of Sir Peter Pears, owners of the copyright in his letters and other writings.

We express our warmest thanks to the staff (past and present) of the Britten–Pears Library, Aldeburgh. Without their invaluable assistance this volume would not have been possible: Dr Christopher Grogan (Librarian), Dr Andrew Plant, Dr Nicholas Clark, Judith Tydeman, Wendy Phillips and Andrea Chamberlain. Particular thanks are owed to Pamela Wheeler and Anne Surfling for their checking of the texts of all letters and other quoted matter. Among former staff we should like to thank: Professor Paul Banks, Dr Jenny Doctor, Dr Elizabeth Gibson, Dr Paul Kildea and Judith LeGrove.

The publishers have given invaluable support to the preparation of this volume, and we salute our Faber and Faber colleagues: Belinda Matthews, Lesley Felce, Ron Costley and Ilsa Yardley.

We wish to thank the following individuals and institutions for the assistance given us throughout the preparation of this volume: Arts Council Archive; Elizabeth Auman (Library of Congress, Washington DC); Don Bachardy; Chris Banks (British Library); Mollie Barnett; Steuart Bedford; George Behrend; the late Eileen Bell; Lady Freda Berkeley; Michael Berkeley; Lionel Billows; Boosey & Hawkes Music Publishers Ltd; Sally Brighton; Alan Britten; Humphrey Burton CBE; the late Isador Caplan; Bridget P. Carr (Archivist, Boston Symphony Orchestra); the late Lord Clark; Basil Coleman; Conservatoire de Genève; the late Joan Cross CBE; the late Eric Crozier OBE; the late Norman Del Mar CBE; Barbara Diana; Professor Peter Dickinson; the late Brian Easdale; Valerie Eliot; Dr John Evans; the late Nancy Evans OBE; Hans Ferwerda (Royal Concertgebouw Orchestra, Amsterdam); Francesca Franchi (Archivist, Royal Opera House); Malcolm Gerratt (London representative, Yale University Press); Johan

Giskes (Gemeentearchiev, Amsterdam); Glyndebourne Archive; Alistair Hardy and Mrs Hardy; Lord Harewood; David Heckels; the late David Hemmings; the late Peter Heyworth; Beris Hudson; Richard Jarman (General Director, the Britten Estate Ltd and the Britten–Pears Foundation); David Fraser Jenkins (Tate Britain); Peter Jones (Fellow and Librarian, King's College, Cambridge); Jacqueline Kavanagh (BBC Written Archivist, BBC Information and Archives); Dr Colin Keen; Andrew Kemp (Head of Copyright, Boosey & Hawkes Music Publishers Ltd); Michael Kennedy CBE; Bruce Kubert; Brigit Lampe (Royal Netherlands Embassy, London); John Lindsay; The London Library, St James's Square; John Lucas; Alan Lyon; Dr Colin Matthews (chairman) and the Board of Directors of the Britten Estate Ltd; David Matthews; Sir Humphrey Maud; Kathleen Mitchell; Professor Edward Mendelson; La Monnaie Archives, Brussels; the late Arthur Oldham; Dr Janet Pennington (Lancing College Archives); Gary Pietronave (EMI Archives); Andrew Porter; Public Record Office; Kara Reed; Eleanor Roberts (Archivist, Hallé Orchestra); the late Stephen Reiss OBE; Bobby Rothman; Dr Martijn Sanders CBE (Amsterdam Concertgebouw); Tom Sutcliffe; Professor Jon Stallworthy; Henriette Straub; Rosamund Strode and the Holst Foundation; the late Beata Sauerlander (*née* Mayer); Professor Claude Tappolet; Dr Richard Thompson; Rita Thomson; Marion Thorpe; Oliver Tims; the late Patrick Trevor-Roper; Janet Waterhouse; Gil Williams; and Judy Young MBE.

We are especially pleased to be able to acknowledge the following copyright holders of letters to Britten, Pears and others included in our annotations; we are extremely grateful for their generous collaboration: Arts Council England; The Executors of the Estate of W. H. Auden; Don Bachardy (Executor of the Estate of Christopher Isherwood); BBC Information and Archives; The Executors of Sir Lennox Berkeley; The Executors of Leonard Bernstein; Boosey & Hawkes Music Publishers Ltd; The British Council; The Executors of Joan Cross; The Executors of Eric Crozier; Fritz Curzon; The Executors of Norman Del Mar; Roger Duncan; Valerie Eliot (Mrs T. S. Eliot); The Executors of Nancy Evans; Mukki Fairchild; excerpts from E. M. Forster's correspondence are copyright © 2004 the Provost and Scholars of King's College, Cambridge; The Estate of John Gielgud; Glyndebourne Archive; Lord Harewood; Lucy Hemmings (Mrs David Hemmings); Holst Foundation; Sir Humphrey Maud; The Executors of Arthur Oldham; The Executors of William Primrose; Winifred Roberts; Royal Opera House Archives; Lady Spender; Marion Thorpe; The Executors of Sir Michael Tippett; Lady Walton; The Executors of Eric Walter White; The Executors of Grace Williams; John and Pauline Woolford. The correspondence of E. M. Forster is held in the Library of King's College, Cambridge, under the reference EMF/18/Britten, and the William Plomer correspondence is reprinted by permission of Durham University Library.

Copyright material from the following newspapers, journals and magazines has been reproduced with permission: *Algemeen Handelsblad*;

Birmingham Post; Cambridge Daily News; Classical Music; Daily Mirror; Daily Telegraph & Morning Post; East Anglian Daily Times; Le Figaro; Guardian; Gramophone; Life; Listener; Manchester Guardian; Il Momento; Monthly Musical Record; Music & Letters; Music and Musicians; Music Survey; Musical Times; National-Zeitung (Basel); *Neue Zürcher Zeitung und Schweizerisches Handelsblatt; New Republic; New Statesman and Nation; New York Herald Tribune; New York Sun; New York Times; New York World-Telegram; Observer; Opera; P.M.* (New York); *People; Die Presse* (Vienna); *Radio Times; Scotsman; Spectator; Sunday Times; De Tijd; Time; Time and Tide; The Times; Times Literary Supplement; De Waarheid; Welt von Heute.*

Copyright material from the following publishers' books has been reproduced with permission: The Bodley Head; Cambridge University Press; Century; Chatto & Windus; Faber and Faber; John Lane; The Kensal Press; Macmillan; Oxford University Press; Philip Wilson Publishers; Phillimore; The Rebel Press; Rockcliff; St Martin's Press; Thames Publishing; Weidenfeld & Nicolson. All titles from which copyright material has been quoted are included, with full bibliographical details, in the Bibliography, pp. 703–18.

Details of all photographic credits and copyrights are given in the List of Illustrations, pp. xiii–xviii, along with all copyright acknowledgement for printed and manuscript music reproduced here.

We have made every reasonable effort to trace copyright owners and shall be grateful to hear from those whom we have been unable to locate or have inadvertently omitted, to whom we extend our apologies.

DM, PR, MC
July 2004

KEY TO BIBLIOGRAPHICAL ABBREVIATIONS

BBMCPR   Mervyn Cooke and Philip Reed, *Benjamin Britten: Billy Budd*
CHB   Christopher Headington, *Britten*
CHPP   Christopher Headington, *Peter Pears: A Biography*
CPBC   Christopher Palmer (ed.), *The Britten Companion*
DHOBB   David Herbert (ed.), *The Operas of Benjamin Britten*
DMCN   Donald Mitchell, *Cradles of the New: Writings on Music 1951–1991*, selected by Christopher Palmer, edited by Mervyn Cooke
DMHK   Donald Mitchell and Hans Keller (eds.), *Benjamin Britten: A Commentary on His Works from a Group of Specialists*
DVDM   Donald Mitchell (ed.), *Benjamin Britten: Death in Venice*
EWB   Beth Britten, *My Brother Benjamin*
EWW   Eric Walter White, *Benjamin Britten: His Life and Operas*, 2nd edition, edited by John Evans
HCBB   Humphrey Carpenter, *Benjamin Britten*
JBBC   *Britten's Children*, documentary film by John Bridcut
MCBFE   Mervyn Cooke, *Britten and the Far East*
MCCCBB   Mervyn Cooke (ed.), *The Cambridge Companion to Benjamin Britten*
PBBG   Paul Banks (ed.), *Britten's 'Gloriana': Essays and Sources*
PBMPG   Paul Banks (ed.), *The Making of Peter Grimes*
PFL   Donald Mitchell and John Evans, *Pictures from a Life: Benjamin Britten 1913–1976*
PGPB   Philip Brett (ed.), *Benjamin Britten: Peter Grimes*
PKBM   Paul Kildea (ed.), *Britten on Music*
PKSB   Paul Kildea, *Selling Britten: Music in the Market Place*
PPT   Marion Thorpe (ed.), *Peter Pears: A Tribute on his 75th Birthday*
PRIM   Philip Reed, *The Incidental Music of Benjamin Britten: A Study and Catalogue of His Music for Film, Theatre and Radio*
PRPP   Philip Reed (ed.), *The Travel Diaries of Peter Pears 1936–1978*
RDBB   Ronald Duncan, *Working with Britten: A Personal Memoir*
RLEC   Eric Crozier (ed.), *The Rape of Lucretia*

TBB   Anthony Gishford (ed.), *Tribute to Benjamin Britten on His Fiftieth Birthday*
TP   *A time there was . . .: A Profile of Benjamin Britten,* documentary film by Tony Palmer
WRMC   Mervyn Cooke, *Benjamin Britten: War Requiem*

The abbreviation BPL is used to indicate the Britten–Pears Library, Aldeburgh, and its collections of printed and manuscript music, books, art and ephemera. Details of the work of the Britten–Pears Library may be accessed on the website www.britten-pears.co.uk

INTRODUCTION: HAPPY FAMILIES?

Donald Mitchell

In loving memory of my parents,
Frederick George Mitchell (1895–1978)
and Kathleen Mary Mitchell (1893–1944)

I am often asked, 'Where is the biography of Britten you were invited to undertake by the composer a few months before he died in 1976?' Or, as it is sometimes put more bluntly: 'Why haven't you written it?'

It is true, as I have recounted elsewhere,[1] that I made the commitment, though even my early outline of a book, talked over with Britten and approved by him, was already perhaps rather distant from the concept of a straight biography. I had mapped out a sequence of creative phases and key works that would be framed by an account of the particular circumstances of and events in Britten's life that were relevant to the creation of the works singled out for attention. I certainly saw this at the time as an integration of 'life' and 'work', though not quite in the sense that fashionable biography is pursued today.

In the event, after Britten's death, which brought with it access to a vast mass of correspondence and auxiliary documentation – Britten had already sent me off in the summer of 1976 with the shoebox in which he kept his pocket diaries for the years 1928–39[2] – it became clear, to me at least, that my original ambitions would best be solved otherwise, by a chronological account of his life extrapolated from his letters, his diaries and other personal statements. This would be amplified, contextualized and, I hoped, illumined, by a scarcely less vast mass of annotations, drawing on the widest range of diverse sources, primary and secondary, an attempt to recover what might otherwise be thought irretrievably lost time. It is indeed, in the spirit of Proust's towering masterpiece, *A la recherche du temps perdu* – a work that has been an influence on my own thoughts and feelings of a scale quite comparable to the music of Britten or Mahler (not to speak of Mozart) – that I have pursued, with due humility, this very text, encouraged by the publication of a biography of Proust, by the leading Proust scholar of

1 See Donald Mitchell and Philip Reed (eds.), *Letters from a Life: The Selected Letters and Diaries of Benjamin Britten 1913–1976*, London: Faber and Faber, 1991; pbk edn, 1998, vol. 1, pp. 55–6. Subsequent references to volumes in this series are indicated by number only.
2 See vol. 1, pp. 3–8.

our time, Jean-Yves Tadié,[3] which, while scrupulously recounting a life that gave birth to the art, no less scrupulously ensures that each keeps its distance from the other.

Proust himself, Tadié makes the point, believed that one of the principal tasks of criticism was to chart a 'spiritual biography', to reconstruct, for example, the particular spiritual life of a writer 'obsessed by [...] unusual realities' such as those of Ruskin, for whom Proust had a profound passion. The artist's inspiration, Proust suggests, 'matches his vision of those realities, his talent re-creates them in his work and his "morality" encourages the instinct that drives the artist to sacrifice his own life to this vision and its reproduction'.[4] I would beg the reader to keep Proust's priorities – inspiration, vision, talent, morality, sacrifice – in mind, and not least these words from Tadié's preface: 'The biography of a great writer is not that of a man of the world, or a pervert or an invalid: it is that of a man who draws his stature from what he writes, because he has sacrificed everything to it, including his lesser qualities.'[5]

Without question, music would be at the heart of the enterprise I have described, and specifically the evolution of Britten's own creative genius and the works in which it was embodied. It is sometimes overlooked that in one important respect composition, writing music, was virtually an immediate presence in the story of Britten's life, something we owe to his prodigiously gifted childhood. It is almost always the case that among composers whose exceptional talents emerge in youth or young adulthood, the very earliest years are the most difficult to render in terms of musical creativity and evolution, so slender are the available materials. With Britten it was quite else; music was abundantly – almost embarrassingly – there, from the start. It was music indeed that was already telling the story of his life; and so it was to continue until his life ended. Thus it was, or so it seemed to me, that the best biographical approach was to assemble an account of a life, mostly in the composer's own words, the telling of which – because of its peculiar dedication to music – had no option but also to function as a powerful illumination of the oeuvre itself. To be sure, analysis, description or interpretation of individual works or periods formed no part of the editorial scheme, though these modes of writing surfaced in the guise of published commentaries generated by first performances. This is not to underrate the importance of independent evaluation and comparative assessment, a still outstanding example of which remains Peter Evans's *The Music of Benjamin Britten* and, in the same vein, though intendedly less comprehensive, Arnold Whittall's *The Music of Britten and Tippett* and

3 *Marcel Proust*, translated by Euan Cameron.
4 Ibid., see pp. 556–8.
5 Ibid., p. xix.

important recent studies by Mervyn Cooke[6] and Philip Reed.[7] Nor should the pioneering and sometimes provocative studies of Philip Brett be overlooked;[8] the volume he edited on *Peter Grimes* (1983), and to which he made major contributions, opened up new areas of debate which he continued vigorously to explore and expound until his untimely death. His masterly entry on Britten in the second edition of the *New Grove* showed him, I believe, at his best. I may not often share his approach to the music but the seriousness of his work and conviction of his own insights never fail to be a source of challenge and stimulus, even if the latter proves to be, finally, a stimulus to disagree. But what the modification of my original commitment to a biography turned out to be, in the shape of the first two volumes of Britten's letters in this series, was an effort to show the interaction between Britten's life and his music which would then form a useful basis for both interpretation and evaluation; and also, perhaps, the basis for punctilious biography.

Since Britten's death there have appeared a number of biographical studies which also incorporated at various levels commentaries on and descriptions of the music, notably by Christopher Headington, Michael Kennedy and Michael Oliver,[9] but it was Humphrey Carpenter's major biography of 1992 (*Benjamin Britten: A Biography*; hereafter HCBB) that effected a fundamental change in much writing about the composer. This was not only due to the fact that Carpenter enjoyed virtually unrestricted access to all the papers – I can think of only insignificant exceptions, and if these were made, then it was at the request of the owners of the materials, not at the request of the Britten–Pears Library or the composer's Trustees – but because he brought to his task exceptional professional skills as a biographer, among them tireless energy and an irrepressible zest for leaving no stone unturned. But somewhere along the way the enterprise was hijacked by the issue of Britten's sexuality, to which it seemed (and seems) to me Carpenter paid an excess of attention. For one thing there proved, ultimately, little to report on Britten's relationships with boys – scarcely, one must remark, the only relationships in his life of importance to him – for another, and more damagingly, the sexual issue, which then became linked with Britten's

---

6 *Britten and the Far East* [MCBFE]; *Benjamin Britten: War Requiem* [WRMC]; *The Cambridge Companion to Benjamin Britten* (ed.) [MCCCBB], and, with Philip Reed, *Benjamin Britten: Billy Budd* [BBMCPR].

7 'A *Peter Grimes* Chronology, 1941–1945' and 'Finding the Right Notes' in PBMPG, and see n. 6 above.

8 See, for example, *Benjamin Britten: Peter Grimes* (ed.) [PGPB] or 'Eros and Orientalism in Britten's Operas', in Philip Brett, Elizabeth Wood and Gary Thomas (eds.), *Queering the Pitch: the new gay and lesbian musicology*, pp. 235–56. (See also Lloyd Whitesell, 'Britten's Dubious Trysts'.)

9 Headington, *Britten*, 1981 [CHB] and 1996; Kennedy, *Britten*, 1981 and 1993, and Oliver, *Benjamin Britten*, 1996.

supposedly sado-masochistic character, was deployed as the chief instrument of interpretation in Carpenter's discussion and description of the
music.

If I use the word 'damagingly' it is not because I think in the longer term
that Britten's music will suffer but, rather, that the quality of the biography
itself will come to be seriously underrated. If one ignores these preoccupations and the simplistic musical commentaries, what remains is a biography
of the composer to which all future biographers must be indebted. It would
be ironic indeed if those parts of the book that I believe to be open to very
serious question, while undeniably gaining it a certain notoriety, may prove
eventually to undermine its genuine importance.

The truth is that the practice – the whole culture – of 'biography' has
radically altered in our time and become an unthinking pursuit of what is
often represented to be the 'dark' side of the biographer's subject. Everyone,
it is assumed, has a 'dark' side that is compulsive, socially unacceptable, and
therefore concealed; and the main task of the biography is to strip away
the wrappings and reveal the dark 'truth'; and the 'truth', need one hardly
add, has become inextricably associated with sex.[10] One should not hold
Carpenter responsible for those who have perhaps been unduly influenced

10   This whole topic of biographical 'truth' and the fashionable pursuit of the 'dark' side of a
     biographer's subject was very interestingly touched on in a long article by Adrian Searle in the
     Guardian (28 August 1998), 'Me, myself and eye', an account of the film by John Maybury,
     Love is the Devil, subtitled 'Study for a portrait of Francis Bacon', who might be regarded,
     writes Searle, 'as the last great European artist-as-existential hero'. He writes:

     > His paintings proclaim as much. His life and personality have come to overshadow all
     > discussions of his work. Or rather, the work has come to be seen as a cartoon strip of the
     > alarming life and times of Francis Bacon, man of extreme appetites, genius painter, drunk,
     > gambler, sado-masochistic homosexual, emotional monster and millionaire who worked in
     > a tiny, squalid Kensington studio which was as much one of the artist's self-dramatizing,
     > theatrical inventions as the work itself.

     Searle ends by quoting the comment of a painter friend: 'This is a movie for people who don't
     like art'; and continues, 'But then what should anyone expect? It is a movie about the art
     world, which is a different thing altogether.'
          That 'different thing' is the life as distinct from the work, the paintings in Bacon's case, the
     music in Britten's. One wonders, however, how many people who have seen the film will read it
     back into their assessment and comprehension of the paintings? (Compare the analogous 'rela-
     tionship' between Visconti's film of Mann's *Death in Venice* and the *Adagietto* from Mahler's
     Fifth Symphony. The film in the public ear has now become installed as an accompaniment
     of the music. See also Philip Reed, 'Aschenbach becomes Mahler', in DVDM, pp. 178–83.)
          As for the 'dark' truth about Bacon, Searle remarks that to attempt to suppress it or
     disguise it is 'futile'. One may well agree with that; but it does not diminish the necessity to
     maintain a distance between the life and the work and not, absolutely not, to mistake one for
     the other. For which reason I sympathize with David Sylvester, the art historian and Bacon
     authority, who 'refused to have anything to do with the film, nor to allow any of Bacon's
     words, recorded [in Sylvester's interviews with the artist] to be used'.

by his emphases and exaggerations and gone on to exaggerate them, copiously, to fantasize about them. However, it says something about the culture of biography that became predominant towards the end of the twentieth century that BBC Radio 3 should have chosen to salute the 50th anniversary of the Aldeburgh Festival by commissioning a radio play, *The Ceremony of Innocence*, by Martyn Wade, first broadcast on 7 June 1998, the central theme – preoccupation – of which was Britten's supposed preoccupation with 'the boys' who, again supposedly, were not only fundamental to his life but also to his creativity. The level at which this 'drama' was conducted, especially when attempts were made to link music and the composer's 'life', can be illustrated by just one example, the reading of a list of boys' names to the accompaniment of the procession of the animals to board ship in *Noye's Fludde*. Or there was the telephone call by 'Imogen Holst' to 'Peter Pears' informing him that Aldeburgh Parish Church was declining to host the premiere of the work because it had 'hundreds of boys' in it. (There had been a precedent of a kind for this event in a drama, *Once in a While the Odd Thing Happens*, by Paul Godfrey, subtitled 'A Play from the Life of Benjamin Britten', commissioned originally by the National Theatre Studio and given its premiere at the Cottesloe, National Theatre, in September 1990. But this was a work serious in intent and ambition, seriously researched and rooted in the main in fact, not fantasy.)

More to the point there is an arresting, if exaggerated, first sentence in a monograph entitled *Benjamin Britten's Operas*, by Michael Wilcox, the intention of which in fact was entirely honourable – to draw attention to the scandalous homophobia of the society in which Britten and Pears lived and worked: it begins 'Benjamin Britten and Peter Pears, two criminals under both English and American State Law on account of their homosexual relationship . . .' It is in the specific context of Wilcox's observation that I reproduce below a document of classic relevance and resonance that appeared in the *People* on 24 July 1955:

MUSIC CHIEF LEADS BIG CAMPAIGN AGAINST VICE

A campaign against homosexuality in British music is to be launched by Sir Steuart Wilson, until last month Deputy General Administrator of the Royal Opera House, Covent Garden. Sir Steuart, 66, told the *People* last night:

'The influence of perverts in the world of music has grown beyond all measure. If it is not curbed soon, Covent Garden and other precious musical heritages could suffer irreparable harm.

'Many people in the profession are worried. There is a kind of agreement among homosexuals which results in their keeping jobs for the boys.'

And Mr Walford Davies, the famous composer and conductor, said: 'Homosexuals are damaging music and all the other arts. I am sorry for those born that way, but many acquire it – and for them I have nothing but contempt. Singers who are perverted often get work simply because of this. And new works by composers are given preference by some people if the writer is perverted.'[11]

The passage of time and growth of more civilized attitudes, public and private, does little to diminish the sense of shame aroused by this eruption of dreadful prejudice from 1955. Nor surely can it be questioned that verbal assault and battery of the kind I quote here exemplifies the hostility to homosexuals that had characterized preceding decades, let alone the 1950s, when it enjoyed a particularly poisonous revival. It would have made an impact on the composer, the degree of which it is difficult to quantify. *Peter Grimes* speaks for itself; and never more clearly than in its articulation of the theme of social rejection and expulsion that is central to the opera's drama, though we should remember how potent a reality persecution was in Europe during the 1930s, a history of which Britten was vividly aware and by which he was often fiercely occupied. While it would be approaching the absurd to suggest that the fact of Britten's homosexuality did not have a significantly determining hand in the creation of *Grimes*,[12] is it not essential to stand back from declaring an equivalence of life and art and instead pursue the evolution of Britten's unique creativity and those positive inter-actions between life and work that led him to explore new areas of feeling and find the forms, words and sounds to match them? These new areas of feeling and above all an appropriate dramatic articulation of them may

11 See Richard Witts, *Artist Unknown, An Alternative History of the Arts Council*, p. 249, and Norman Lebrecht, *Covent Garden: The Untold Story*, pp. 172–6. Wilson himself had first taken up an appointment at Covent Garden as Deputy General Administrator in 1949. Ironically, he would still have been in the post at the time that Britten was invited in 1952 to become Musical Director of the opera house (see p. 47 below). Wilson was a celebrated English tenor – in his youth Britten was an admirer of his performances in the Bach Passions – and was also a dis-tant relative of Peter Pears. In a letter to Wilson's widow, Pears wrote:

> He made a great impression on me and I owe a lot to him; indeed his Evangelist was what started me off [. . .] It was my ambition to follow in his footsteps in the Bach Passions. If I have done something in them, a large part of it is due to Steuart. (PRPP, p. 225)

Wilson was in fact invited to give a lecture at the first Aldeburgh Festival (1948) entitled 'The Future of Music in England'. See also Diary for 22 March 1931, n. 4; Letter 408, and CHPP, pp. 57, 58 and 103.

12 I wonder sometimes, however, if sufficient thought has been given to the chronology of Britten's awareness of hostility to him as a homosexual? What certainly would prove to heighten that hostility was the very success of *Grimes* itself. But some of the most virulent public homophobia to be documented was most of it after the completion of the opera, while one has to remember that from 1939 to 1942 Britten was himself out of England. I raise the question only because the very ferocity of *Grimes*'s impeachment of society would seem to imply a response to a scorching, searing experience of homophobia to which the opera remains chief witness; also it overlooks the profile of politico-social persecution during the periods of the Spanish Civil War and the onset of Fascism in Germany, events that signifi-cantly preceded the composition of *Grimes* but certainly contributed to it. Do we need to be reminded of the juxtaposition of 'German, Jew' that we encounter already in *Our Hunting Fathers* in 1936?

indeed have had their roots in his sexuality but they also constitute an unequivocal acknowledgement of it: as the three Israelites in *The Burning Fiery Furnace* so memorably aver (though little remarked on), 'What we are, we remain . . .' But as always what we experience, what we hear, is not an item of biography but its transformation, if you like, into a musical experience or communication of relevance and importance to us all, irrespective of our sexual orientation.

Grimes, in fact, proved retrospectively to be only the first of Britten's parables about human behaviour in the twentieth century. The point is made by the second of the three Parables proper, *The Burning Fiery Furnace*, which, like *Grimes*, is undoubtedly another parable of rejection. But it brilliantly introduces into its vocabulary of images (if the paradox may be forgiven) specifically racial and cultural conflict (new to Britten, this), the manipulation of a mindless ideology that climaxes in a frightening display of mass hysteria (shades of Nuremberg and its rallies). The *Furnace*, it cannot be missed, has in fact its own (Babylonian) lynching chorus; and there are many other parallels with *Grimes* in terms of preoccupations and protest: intolerance, exclusion, persecution and execution. The parallels are often so telling that one has to remind oneself that the *Furnace* in terms of format, resources and compositional techniques is virtually the diametric opposite of *Grimes* on almost every count. But again like *Grimes*, and many other works of Britten's, the *Furnace* takes significant note of those phenomena in our century that have accounted for huge volumes of human suffering. Since we are what we are and how we have been made to be, it is scarcely surprising that certain preoccupations remain a constant presence throughout our lives, whether mundane or unique. It is self-evident that for Britten the experience of rejection, of expulsion, of social condemnation, however that came to be assimilated and incorporated into his personality, often, though not exclusively, plays an influential role in the dramas that he chose to imagine as parable operas; and I am not thinking here only of the Church Parables. (Is there an opera of Britten's that is not a parable?) But in saying that, one has not really said much about the process of transformation and transcendence which in truth creates our experience in the theatre (whether it be *Grimes*, the *Furnace*, *Lucretia*, *Gloriana* or *Billy Budd*, to choose a handful of titles at random), something quite other, I want to suggest, from re-experiencing – as it were at (musical) second-hand – an experience, however fundamental, that ultimately belongs to the composer's biography. It is of the first importance to move away from the bald system of equivalence in which Britten's sexual orientation 'equals' (that is to say, 'explains') his preoccupation with the idea of social rejection, embodied in the symbolic figure of the nonconformist, the outcast, etc., etc. This may be true at one simplistic level of comprehension but it says nothing about the extraordinary diversity and richness of the musics that Britten summons up to meet the challenges posed by the sheer complexity of his responses, not only to the problems of his own life but to the problems, as he saw them, of the world at large, prominent among them violence, and a later preoccupation, the protection of our earth (perhaps there was early indication of this in his passionate admiration of the coda to the 'Abschied' in Mahler's *Das Lied von der Erde*, 'Die liebe Erde . . .').

As I come to suggest much later, the narrowness of the focus of which I complain has toppled over from the interpretation of the music into accounts of the life itself which, in a comparable sense, can all too easily be bleached of its human, and sometimes all too human, complications and contradictions. Here again, one needs more than one key to unlock the many doors offering access to Britten, not only the Britten who was the pre-determined 'outcast' but the many Brittens who went to make up the social being and serious citizen that he was. I believe it to be essential to achieve a change in emphasis and address how it was that Britten responded creatively to the consequences of 'rejection'. We might then find ourselves talking about the music as distinct from speculating about its psychological origins. Thus it is a different interaction between life and art that it is one of my prime purposes in this introduction to pursue.

We might make a start with the image of the family and its creative significance for Britten. This has often been overlooked, first as a source of inspiration – diverse and contrasting inspiration, it must be said – and secondly as a format: a ready-made community with built-in potentialities for drama. In this latter category, at one extreme we have the ferocious, feuding family of Wingraves (*Owen Wingrave*, 1971); at the other, *Noye's Fludde* (1958), a setting of the Chester Miracle Play that depicts what one might think of as humankind's *Ur*-family. Noye, in particular, anticipates the *Ur*-Father of *The Prodigal Son*, yet to be composed.[13] *Noye's Fludde* was to bear the third and last of Britten's 'family' dedications, in this case, members of his own family: the inscription reads, 'To my nephew and nieces, Sebastian, Sally and Roguey Welford, and my young friend Roger Duncan [the son of Ronald Duncan, and one of Britten's godsons]'. *Albert Herring*

13   In his consideration of 'The Britten Era' (The Proms Lecture, 1997) Philip Brett remarked on Britten's 'preoccupation with authority' while observing that it 'does not always take the same turn of course'. He pointed out in particular that the 'moral and tone of *The Prodigal Son* appear, for instance, to reverse the *carpe diem* anti-Establishment attitudes of *Albert Herring* in favour of reconciliation, finally, to the law of the Father, personified here in an unusual way, almost suggesting wish-fulfilment, as all merciful and munificent, not the Abraham who, in Wilfred Owen's vision incorporated in the *War Requiem*, sends his sons to destruction one by one instead of sacrificing the ram of Pride'. See also Robin Holloway, 'The Church Parables: Limits and Renewals', in CPBC, in particular pp. 221–2.

(1947), too, may have been Britten's only social comedy in music, but there can be no denying the seriousness of Albert's oppression by his Mum, a familiar family situation that gets the serious music it deserves in Act II scene 2 (Albert's great *scena*). A happier domestic context was provided a little later in *The Little Sweep* (1949), the miniature opera that was originally conceived to form the second part of *Let's Make an Opera*; and that musical initiative, an altogether novel enterprise, especially at the time it was written, introduces a notable example of those 'family' works that often had their roots in a family to which Britten was close, to the children in particular: *The Little Sweep* was dedicated to a team of children, the 'models' for their counterparts in the little opera. The dedication reads: 'Affectionately dedicated to the real Gay, Juliet, Sophie, Tina, Hughie, Jonny and Sammy – the Gathorne-Hardys of Great Glemham, Suffolk'. As Eric Crozier himself recollected in his foreword to the libretto: 'We chose Iken Hall for the setting because it was a large rambling farmhouse on a lonely stretch of the river Alde where occasionally we went to visit friends: we took our children ready-made for the sons, daughters and nephews of other friends living at Great Glemham.'

The *Young Person's Guide to the Orchestra* on the other hand is not a piece of music theatre, though from one point of view it is: the instruments and their characters comprise its 'cast'. The work surfaces here because, like *The Little Sweep*, this famous set of variations that started life as an educational film in 1946 was again dedicated to a family to which for a time at least Britten was very closely bonded through ties of mutual affection, to the children especially. Once again the dedication reads: 'This work is affectionately inscribed to the children of John and Jean Maud: Humphrey, Pamela, Caroline and Virginia, for their edification and entertainment'.[14]

Jean Redcliffe-Maud, in response to questions put to her in 1984 by

14 Sir Humphrey Maud has kindly provided us with a copy of a letter from Britten to his mother which was written on 8 January 1947 and dispatched from Zurich. Seeking permission for the dedication to her children 'for their edification & entertainment', it is reproduced here as Letter 544.

It was typical one might think of Britten to unite affection with 'edification', i.e. something 'morally instructive, uplifting'. A comparison of the letter with the published full score shows that Britten's suggested form of dedication was adopted. In a further letter to Jean Redcliffe-Maud dated 10 July 1947 (Letter 551) Britten wrote, 'I've sent Humph a copy of the "Y. Persons Guide" – the first off the press – thought it might cheer him up a bit.' The inscription read: 'For Humphrey & his sisters, with much love from Ben'. In the published inscription, which follows the format in the letter, there are three sisters named. Tragically, Pamela had died of a brain tumour at a very early age, hence Humphrey's reference to 'two sisters' in his conversation with me (see p. 22). Britten nevertheless included Pamela in the dedication, a delicate act of remembrance of a child he had never met that speaks volumes for the closeness he felt to the Redcliffe-Maud family.

It seems appropriate to add here some bare details of the Redcliffe-Maud family, of which for a time Britten was happy to be part. Humphrey Maud (b. 1934), who had been a cellist in the

Elizabeth Sweeting (General Manager of the English Opera Group from 1948 to 1955), remembered Britten's exceptional ways with her own children, whose world – which a little later I am to explore in more detail – he was able to enter it seems without condescension or affectation:

ES   You must be very happy that it was your family who exemplified another one of Ben's notable qualities, and that was his sincere and exciting love of children and young people, because you said that he dedicated the *Young Person's Guide*, and after that of course he wrote *Let's Make an Opera, Noye's Fludde* and so on. So that the early acquaintance with your family made obviously a milestone in their progress.

JRM   Yes, yes. He was absolutely delightful with children and happy with them and they were happy with him in the most unaffected way – I mean, when we went (before he moved to Aldeburgh) to Snape, to the Lighthouse, wasn't it?

ES   The Old Mill.

JRM   Yes, and he enjoyed Humphrey's company very much and Humphrey his. But as I say, later on more and more people got involved, whom we didn't know. And so roughly speaking, there was a time when it really wasn't possible to see much of him.

ES   Indeed, well his life became very peopled and of course the coming and going of so many people with whom he was associated in his work kept him really always in a close community of his own of changing composition.[15]

From a much later date – in 1969 – when Britten and Pears, in the wake of the fire at Snape Maltings, made fund-raising visits to New York and Boston (a brief tour on which I accompanied them), comes a recollection from the American conductor and author Frederik Prausnitz, which once again

---

National Youth Orchestra from 1949 to 1952, joined the Foreign Service and became a distinguished high-ranking diplomat. He was knighted in 1993, the year in which he became Deputy Secretary General of the Commonwealth. He has sustained his musical interests and enthusiasm throughout his life.

His father was John Redcliffe-Maud (1906–1982), who was knighted in 1963. During the Second World War he was Permanent Secretary Ministry of Education. He was also to serve as a high-ranking diplomat, after which he became Master of University College, Oxford, from 1963 to 1976. He was raised to the peerage in 1968. Humphrey Maud's mother, Jean Hamilton (1904–1993), studied at the Royal College of Music, where she was a pupil of Harold Samuel, to whom Britten had gone for private lessons when he was a schoolboy. She continued her studies with Artur Schnabel, Wanda Landowska and Angus Morrison, and during the war gave concerts for CEMA (Council for the Encouragement of Music and the Arts), on occasions with Britten and Pears. She was noted as a pianist for her performances of Bach, Schubert and late Beethoven, and in 1949 gave the premiere of Alan Rawsthorne's Sonatina. (She had earlier played the continuo in performances of the *St Matthew Passion* in which Steuart Wilson had been the Evangelist.) She had helped found the University Musical Society at Oxford in 1932 and continued her support and musical activities there when her husband was Master of University College.

15   The tape and transcript of Elizabeth Sweeting's interview with Jean Redcliffe-Maud in 1984 are available at BPL.

reveals the striking empathy that marked Britten's relationships with children (it was the *immediacy* that was so remarkable, as this occasion suggests):

It began with an unforgettable concert: Benjamin Britten and Peter Pears, in a joint recital in Boston, last stop on their American tour of 1969. The programme included Britten's Thomas Hardy songs [*Winter Words*] and Schumann's *Dichterliebe* [...]

The reception afterwards was in my house. Our rooms were large, connected by wide archways, and with high ceilings and tall windows overlooking Boston Common. It was as well that we had moved tables and sofas to the walls in antici-pation of a crowd, for soon it seemed as if the entire concert audience had come to meet the performers. The film crew which had recorded the Britten and Pears American tour for a BBC documentary[16] had just stashed their voluminous equip-ment on our back stairs when our guests of honour arrived. Much applause. Margaret, my wife, was thrilled to receive an inscribed score from the composer. And that was the last we saw of Benjamin Britten.

Pears was elegantly in evidence as he towered over the noisy crowd. After a while I asked my wife, 'Have you seen Ben?' With a happy gesture to the piano on which rested Britten's gift to her, she replied, 'He's here, of course.' But where? Three rooms and the hall encompassed the social territory of the evening, and it should not have been difficult to locate one of only two men in full evening dress, even in that crush. Nevertheless, a slow and soon somewhat anxious exploration of that densely packed space produced no trace of our composer.

No, Peter had not seen him either, but he would help us to look. He had the advantage of height – to no avail. Then, just as we began worrying in earnest and trying not to look it, as we ploughed once more through the jammed bodies of Boston's celebratory musical elite, the buzz and hum of our party in full swing was topped by happy noises from the far end of the hall, where a corridor led off to the nursery. Peter and Margaret and I hastened along there.

And there he was, in the nursery, giving his second performance of the evening. Benjamin Britten, our son Sebastian aged five, and our old dog Timmy (designated babysitter for the evening), were romping on all fours across the floor, while little two-year-old Maja crowed with delight from her crib. The master, having decided perhaps that he had already given of his best to the lionizing crowd, had discovered the children. While graciously apologetic, he seemed as regretful as his playmates about their interrupted idyll. But a few moments later, once again in the front rooms, Britten was listening smilingly to a succession of his grown-up admirers, every inch the world-famous composer he was expected to be.[17]

It is not for sentimental reasons that I have quoted Jean Redcliffe-Maud's words above or included Prausnitz's revealing memory;[18] and to the Redcliffe-Maud family I shall return. But for the moment I want to stay with the idea of the family, and its possible significance for Britten. There are other manifestations of the family in Britten's dramatic works that I have not yet mentioned, most notably the third and last of the Church Parables, *The Prodigal Son* (1968). Interestingly, it is perhaps only now, after thirty

16 *The Money Programme*, broadcast on 1 January 1970 on BBC2.
17 Personal recollection.
18 For a like reminiscence, see also HCBB, p. 345.

years or so, that the stature of the third Parable has been recognized; and part of its strength, I have come to believe, derives from the powerful appeal the image of the family, in all its diversity – its unities, hostilities, liberations, absences and oppressions – had for Britten, as man and artist.

It was surely no accident that it was the childhood card game of Happy Families that Britten liked to play, when childhood was long behind him. From all accounts, a certain scepticism might occasionally attend this Christmas ritual; and perhaps it is not surprising that, with the exception of *The Little Sweep* and *Noye's Fludde,* those other works in which the 'family' is a defining factor reveal a remarkable complexity of response. *The Prodigal Son* is a particularly interesting case because it embraces both the loss of Innocence and the acquisition of Experience and articulates a whole array of inter-family tensions and jealousies; and yet, at the end, the wheel turns full circle and the Younger Son returns, along with and by means of the music which accompanied his departure. It is this 'travelling' music (the long walk home), in which the solo viola plays a leading part, the characterizing instrument which is the Prodigal Son's (compare its compassionate role as the 'voice' of the Apprentice at the beginning and end of the Passacaglia in *Grimes*), which returns the chastened youth to the B$\flat$ which from the outset of the Parable has represented family, home, integration, stability and, not least, the Father.[19]

I almost wrote 'harbour' instead of 'home'; and in recalling Grimes's 'What harbour shelters peace?', one recalls that Grimes as he is known to us in the opera – in an early draft there was a moment when he is envisaged singing about his father – is a man without a vestige, a shred, of family history: he lives and dies an outsider. So too does the boy Apprentice who shares, with Grimes, ironically, a family history of equal blankness, and comes to share his tragic fate. This absence of any family context makes its emphatic contribution to the intensity of Grimes's tragedy; and I find it of

19 It is interesting to find that this most memorable passage in the last Church Parable is clearly presaged in the slow movement of the Double Concerto in B minor for violin, viola and orchestra, composed when Britten was a student at the Royal College of Music. The comparable passage in the concerto is to be found in the slow movement, four bars before fig. Q to fig. R, conceived as a gradual *accelerando,* gathering vitality as it proceeds and remarkably anticipating the moment when the Prodigal Son picks himself up from the ground to begin the return to his Father (figs. 65–7). It is not only the timbre of the instrumentation – the viola prominent in both passages – that evokes the parallel; note too the 'travelling' bass that accompanies both of these mobile transitions, each occurring at a highly significant formal juncture in each work. See also Donald Mitchell, 'Britten and the Viola', 1997 Aldeburgh October Britten Festival programme book, pp. 12–13, and n. 21 below.

With the recovery of *Plymouth Town,* the ballet score Britten composed while still a student at the Royal College of Music in 1931 and brought to first performance there on 27 January 2004, the significance for him of the viola is already evident. The publication of the score by Faber Music is forthcoming. A note on the work by Paul Banks appears in the programme. See also Diary for 13 July 1931, n. 1; illustrations in vol. 1, pp. 189 and 192–3, and Letter VII n. 1.

some interest at least that even in those operas or Parables where the image
of the family is by no means central, the absence of 'family' – of father and
mother figures especially – makes its own telling point. This is certainly the
chilling case in *The Turn of the Screw*, where the children, like Grimes, have
no parental history – 'Poor babies,' sings the Governess on her way to Bly,
'no father, no mother' – while in *Owen Wingrave*, the opera's protagonist
again is parentless. His father, of course, has gone down in battle; his
mother's miserable history briefly stated: she 'died bereft', we learn, 'bearing
my dead-born brother' (Act I scene 4), after which she is mentioned only
once again, by Mrs Julian in the big ensemble that opens scene 5 – 'Better
dead,' she exclaims. On the other hand, he enjoys what in effect are proxy
parents, in the shape of Mr and Mrs Coyle, whom Britten takes care, musically, to characterize with a sympathy denied to Owen's family proper. (Nor
should we forget that Billy Budd, was a 'foundling . . . found in a basket tied
to a good man's door, the poor old man'.)

Even in *The Little Sweep*, which ends happily, aside and apart from the
cruel practices inflicted on him by his brutal owners, the sweep boy's suffering is intensified by his parentless isolation. (We note, incidentally, that it is
Rowan, the kind-hearted nursery maid, who assumes the (mother's) caring,
quasi-parental role in relation to Sam.) In the ensemble in which the child's
plight finds its fullest expression, 'O why do you weep/Through the working
day?', the response that the boy makes in the shape of a refrain – 'How shall
I laugh and play?' – to his rescuers' comment, 'Father and mother are far
away', projects an image and a situation that recur, albeit in hugely different
musical realizations, throughout Britten's oeuvre; it is the persistence of the
image that unifies the disparate musics it gives rise to – differences, that is,
of style, genre, period and use – and testifies to the powerful role it played
in Britten's imagination. But what impresses, and what, ultimately, must be
the principal concern of those who want to write about Britten is the richness, variety, complexity of the compositional response. Why else bother?

As Britten's music developed and moved towards what proved to be his
last phase, whether or not a work was destined for the theatre, the tendency
to share common techniques, preoccupations and imagery greatly increased;
and I make no apology for isolating one number from the last orchestral
song-cycle, *Nocturne* (1958), as an example of Britten's acute awareness of
the uncertainties and vulnerabilities created by the absence of family. It is
spelled out for us in the third song of the cycle, a setting of Coleridge's
poem, 'The Wanderings of Cain', for harp and strings (shades of Mahler!), in
which the poet describes his vision of a 'Beauteous boy', seen by moonlight:

> Alone, by night, a little child,
> In peace so silent and so wild –
> Has he no friend, no loving mother near?

In which context one cannot overlook what must be the earliest instance of outside/inside imagery in Britten's music, one that is also one of the most remarkable and illuminating. I am thinking of the third of the *Quatre Chansons Françaises* for high voice and orchestra composed in 1928 by the fourteen-year-old Britten, inscribed and dedicated, one notes, to his father and mother on the twenty-seventh anniversary of their marriage. It is a setting of Victor Hugo's 'L'enfance'. Outside the window a child sings and plays. Within there is the 'absent' mother; she lies dying. There is not only an unequivocal outside/inside juxtaposition but also the use of two quite distinct musics to represent the bleak contrast: without, the poet tells us, 'the poor creature sang all day', while within, 'the mother coughed all night'. 'L'enfance' must be reckoned a key document in the evolution of the images of parental absence and loss, of outside and inside, that were to haunt Britten's creative life and provoke some of the most memorable of his feats of invention.

Nor can one help but observe that in a late work, *Curlew River* (1964), the first of the Church Parables, although a family history of the kidnapped boy is vouchsafed as the ferryboat crosses the river, it is above all a story of absences; the boy dies bereft of both his father and mother. For him, in life at least, there was no amelioration of the absence of parents. This deployment of absence as a sometimes defining dramatic presence is, in its own way, and perhaps in a related way, as eloquent and meaningful as Britten's elevation of silence to major status in many of his dramas. One needs to take only one small step further to be able to suggest with some confidence that if absence could constitute a dismaying experience, then exclusion – exclusion from the family – might be no less so. Outsider status is thereby confirmed, not only as an outsider but as an outsider looking in. When Gustav von Aschenbach, the celebrated author, arrives at his hotel in Venice, he is greeted by the Manager with a prediction – 'Signore, outside [N.B.!] your room, but private, unfrequented, you may sit and see the world go by . . .' – the implications of which are almost immediately fulfilled by the gathering of a Polish family in (of course!) the lobby, before dinner: 'Poles, I should think,' notes Aschenbach. 'Governess with her children – a beautiful young creature, the boy.' (However, it is not – this time – a governess who is an important presence in later events but Tadzio's glamorous mother, the extravagantly named 'Lady of the Pearls'.)

Death in Venice is 'about' many things; but one of them certainly is exclusion, and specifically the impossibility and impracticality of Aschenbach becoming an integral part of the family that rivets his attention at the very start of his visit to Venice. His own isolation is intensified by what he observes of the boy's relationships with his sisters and, not least, with his especially beautiful mother.

Like Grimes before him, Aschenbach is virtually a man without a history. Clues are few and far between but for rhetorical statements like 'I, Aschenbach, famous as a master-writer . . .'; while any kind of domestic context for himself is confined to his single mention of the 'death of a wife and marriage of an only daughter'. As for Tadzio, is he not, as I have suggested elsewhere, entirely a creature – a creation – of Aschenbach's imagination? His only 'voice' is in fact the composer's, that is to say, Aschenbach's; and his music is exclusively how Aschenbach 'sees' him, obsessively longs for him, feels about him.[20]

In this respect Tadzio in *Death in Venice* has even less of a voice of his own than the silent Apprentice in *Peter Grimes*, for whom Britten himself speaks up in the Passacaglia between Scenes 1 and 2 of the opera's second act. The composer's explicit compassion (viola) endows the boy with a felt human image, eloquent of his suffering.[21] Tadzio (vibraphone) on the other hand does not have any feelings of his own to be reported.

Even this brief digression is, I hope, suggestive of the exceptional wealth of nuances that *Death in Venice* unfolds by means of an elaborate performing apparatus and accumulation of late-style techniques drawn from Britten's encounter with non-Western musics. The very complexity of the compositional processes involved, and one's own tentative speculations about the 'meaning' of them, emphasizes again the need to look to the work and the composer's oeuvre as a whole for 'explanations' and illuminations, not to a cartoon-like representation of the life.

We find, then, even in *Death in Venice*, the subtext of family persisting. Who can doubt that it was of real importance to Britten creatively, scattered as it is both positively and negatively throughout his dramatic output and surfacing on occasion in other genres? And that would be the reason for drawing attention to parallels in the life that are clearly of specific relevance to the materialization and characteristics of specific works, not to 'explain' them (or as some would wish, explain them away) but to show what Britten makes of his materials, at which point the autonomy of the making asserts itself and the biographical parallels, such as they are, cease to have much significance.

It was surely a heavy blow to Britten that he had lost both of his parents by his mid-twenties, but during his formative years of infancy and childhood

---

20 See Donald Mitchell, '*Peter Grimes*: Fifty Years On', in PBMPG, pp. 162–3, and Philip Rupprecht, *Britten's Musical Language*, pp. 245–96.

21 Mitchell, '*Peter Grimes*: Fifty Years On', but see especially n. 30 on p. 162. Edward Sackville-West was the first commentator to make an explicit connection between the apprentice and the viola theme in the *Passacaglia*. In his essay '*Peter Grimes*: The Musical and Dramatic Structure' in Eric Crozier (ed.), *Benjamin Britten: Peter Grimes*, p. 44, he describes the 'desolate, wandering motif depicting the workhouse boy [. . .] who does not know how to deal with Grimes's sudden changes of mood and so [. . .] takes refuge in silence'.

his parents had been a constant and loving presence; it would be hard to attribute that painful awareness of loss, absence, rejection, conflict and abandonment, which was so often to take shape as distinctive music, to events or parallels in his early life. That his childhood was happy, stable and, yes, successful, was as amply documented as was possible at the time when the first two volumes of letters and diaries in this series were completed.

What had become a generally held assumption – 'idyllic' was a word Pears often used to describe Britten's childhood – was subjected to later scrutiny by Carpenter in his biography, who comes up with disquieting recollections from two of Britten's closest friends and librettists, Eric Crozier and Myfanwy Piper. Crozier claimed that he had been told by Britten that he had been 'raped' as a boy, supposedly at preparatory school, and Piper that she had been told by Britten himself that his father had an 'interest' in boys. It is not my purpose to rehearse all over again here what is carefully and indeed cautiously documented by Carpenter in his biography,[22] but to remind readers that this was information that was not available to us when compiling volumes 1 and 2, and – possibly of greater significance – that, to my knowledge, absolutely no further evidence to substantiate or verify these matters has emerged in the interim.[23] Of their very

---

22 See HCBB, pp. 19 and 25.

23 'A classic instance of surmise *ex silentio*': I quote this phrase from a brilliant review essay by Professor Brian Vickers (Zurich), 'All rising to great place is by a winding stair: The difficulties of being fair to Sir Francis Bacon', published in the *Times Literary Supplement* (10 June 1998), pp. 12–14. (See also my reference to Ray Monk's biography of Wittgenstein on p. 19.) His words are peculiarly relevant to Crozier's document, the existence of which was made known to me by the kindness of Humphrey Carpenter, not by Crozier himself. I don't complain about that; but it was most unfortunate that during the period between Crozier writing his account and giving Carpenter access to it, those whose opinion of its possible veracity would have been most valuable, even conclusive – e.g. Peter Pears – had died. A silence was imposed on it by Crozier's wayward temperament and by his own death in 1994. In the obituary notice I wrote for the *Guardian* (8 September 1994; see also Letter 529 n. 2), I attempted a description of his problematic personality while at the same time recognizing his very considerable importance and achievements:

Peter Pears, whose association with Crozier was a long one, would often remark that his old friend was a man of 'difficult temperament', an observation the truth of which was surely confirmed by the strangely dislocated character of Crozier's career. Here was a man of exceptional gifts which he might have applied consistently to more than one of the areas of activity and creativity which he had at his command. But some flaw in him meant that he never wholly achieved what his talents promised: too often there was a bewilderingly abrupt cessation of relationships with colleagues, friends and institutions, which seemed to put an end to longer-term collaborative enterprises. A case in point was his friendship with Benjamin Britten which regrettably ended with powerfully negative feelings on Crozier's part.

These found expression in a remarkable memorandum which he wrote about his relationship with the composer, part of which Humphrey Carpenter made use of in his recent biography of Britten. We owe it to Carpenter, in fact, that this sometimes savage text surfaced. The truth of Crozier's far from flattering portrait of Britten will no doubt continue

nature, of course, the character of such events would preclude 'documentation' as we would normally understand it, but recognition of that does not prevent me from having uppermost in my mind a wise remark made (I think) by Ray Monk, the biographer of Ludwig Wittgenstein, who pointed out how difficult it was in principle to prove that something that had not happened, had not happened.

If Britten's own family life was as stable and relatively unclouded as it seems to have been – and I am not overlooking the tension that was undoubtedly part of his relationship with his father – then perhaps it is not surprising that the idea of 'family' in his work was often a real presence, nor that throughout his life relationships with families – belonging – mattered a lot to him; hence, no doubt, the dedications of *Let's Make an Opera* to the Cranbrooks and the *Young Person's Guide* to the Mauds, in which affection and, not least, inspiration were combined.

We have read above how Jean Redcliffe-Maud, in 1984, recollected Britten's particular gift with children, her children, that is – Humphrey, Pamela (see n. 14 above), Caroline and Virginia. This particular idyll was not to survive; and for a description of the manner in which it did not survive – a longer and fuller account than he has given hitherto – I am indebted to the very Humphrey who was one of the original dedicatees. His memories, it seems to me, are of such outstanding interest that it is worth quoting from them at unusual length.[24] I have chosen excerpts that specifically illumine Britten's relationship to a family and one particular member of it, who was born in 1934 and whose recollections belong principally to the period 1943–49, when he was between the ages of nine and fifteen and was himself, it is important to understand, a very musical child. He begins by relating an 'absolutely typical occasion' when Britten and Pears

---

to be debated. What was odd though, and typical, and perhaps a shade disconcerting, was Crozier's keeping this small explosive device ticking away under wraps until such a late date; releasing it indeed when most of those who might have authenticated it (or otherwise) were dead, and locating it, one must suppose, where it could result in maximum damage.

No doubt there were many temperamental clashes, grievances and resentments on both sides, but this secretive act of demolition speaks volumes for Crozier's appetite for destruction not only of his old friend's reputation but also, reluctantly one may come to feel, of his own.

But what was a bad end to a friendship should not blind us to what the two men achieved while they continued to like each other: *Saint Nicolas*, *Let's Make An Opera*, *Billy Budd* and above all the brilliant comedy of *Albert Herring*, for which Crozier wrote a vernacular libretto of an astonishing originality, the virtuosity of which is still not generally recognized. Marvellous words, marvellous music, which in every performance celebrates Crozier's unique contribution to the history of musical theatre in our time.

24 The tape and transcript of Donald Mitchell's original interview with Humphrey Maud, 11 September 1998, are available at BPL.

came down to Eton for lunch and stayed for tea and supper and the night, because there was so much to talk about. And I think that my mother would have been a very welcome interlocutor of his because [Ben] having been away out of Britain since 1939, there would have been so much to catch up on, though of course he had [had] constant correspondence with Beth [Welford, Britten's sister] and other members of his family.

[...] I have a very vivid recollection of him because, being a mere child, a sort of add-on to the family party, I was very conscious that he took a great deal of interest in me and listened to what I had to say, which little boys don't often have, particularly from a great man like that. And we struck up a strong friendship between a grown-up and a boy of a very natural kind, which then blossomed in my case into something which became very much closer, and didn't involve my parents, save that it was they who agreed to his kind invitations that I should join them [Britten and Pears] on various school holidays [...]

He continued:

Well, as I say, I think he clearly had a lot of sympathy for young children, and one sees this in the wonderful skill with which he writes for children's voices, not only boys' voices, though he had a wonderful aptitude for that. I think there was a side to his personality which hadn't ever grown up. There was a kind of boyishness about him which gave him great pleasure in boyish activities, like playing tennis, for instance. I remember playing quite a lot with him. He coached me quite purposefully. The games were fun but they were also serious. I remember him saying, 'Get your first serve in, hit the first serve with a flat face and then when you have a second serve, cut it with a fiendish spin.' Which of course *he* did, in a most hideous fashion. He liked to win. When he was playing with me it was extremely enjoyable but rather purposeful singles, and he thought that I could indeed be a good deal better than I was, and so gave me some ideas about that.

If tennis was, in its own way, seriously pursued, much more so was music:

I suppose [Ben] was the first person, other than a few schoolmasters and music teachers that I'd had – but not in any comparable sense – with whom I'd had serious musical conversations. And this went on till I suppose about the age of fifteen, because I saw him really pretty often. So, as one was discovering on the old 78 [r.p.m.] records, particularly when I went to Eton where they had a wonderful music library and record library, I would as it were test out my reactions to particular bits of music on him, and he always listened extremely sensitively. He never contradicted one. He often had a very different view; I remember for instance my enthusing about Beethoven and quoting particular bits of music, or movements or bits of movements that I particularly liked, and he listened, but had a sort of reflective smile on his face and said, 'Well, actually I don't go for Beethoven at all now. I find that he shouts, that he's too obvious: it's all too' – as we would say these days – 'in your face' (he'd probably not have used such a phrase). 'But,' he said, 'when I was your age I couldn't have enough Beethoven. The house was full of little plaster busts of him.[25] I was always playing his music on the piano. I played all the sonatas, I played all the symphonies, and would play through the scores.' I remember him

25 See PFL, plate 70, where one of these busts (were there more?) can clearly be seen in the photograph (1934) of Britten's bedroom at 21 Kirkley Cliff Road, Lowestoft.

saying, incidentally, how when he was a schoolboy, when other boys would take a book to read in bed before lights out, he would take a musical score and this was just as lively, just as vivid for him as the boys who were reading Rider Haggard or Buchan or whatever it was the others read.

I had a very powerful personality in my mother, and music was very much in the household from my earliest recollection, and indeed this was one of the great strengths that I recall in the friendship between her and Ben. They played together for CEMA during the war. But she had been a pupil of Schnabel's, as had Curzon; and Ben, I remember him talking about, in rather a different sense from what I was saying earlier about Beethoven, how he regarded Schnabel as being *the* Beethoven pianist, and having very technical discussions with my mother about how he taught, and his interpretations, chiefly, of course, of the Beethoven sonatas, but also works like the Schubert B♭ Piano Sonata. This was a great bond between them, and I would as it were eavesdrop on this conversation without of course knowing the detail of what they were talking about. But I was so struck by the fact that he would answer all of my impertinent questions without any sort of hesitation; and that encouraged me to speak in a very spontaneous way to him about my own musical interests. On one occasion, when we were staying outside Cliveden, the Astors' place, and my parents had a little cottage there, Parr's Cottage, I remember I hadn't been able to bring my cello over, back from Eton, and so we drove over, Ben and Peter and I, and picked it up, so we could play. And I remember from quite an early age playing with him whatever it was that I was learning at the time; the last occasion that this ever happened must have been in the 1960s, when we played the Shostakovich Sonata all the way through. I made a recording of this, and of course it got mislaid. In any case it was only made by sitting the tape recorder on top of the piano, so it was full of distortion and everything, and anyway I was lamentably out of practice – I remember kicking myself round the block for being so. But even so it was he who said, 'What are we going to play?'

So really over that period, on and off quite consistently up to, as I say, about the age of fifteen or so, and then later on a more occasional basis, we would meet and play; and I was very conscious of what a wonderful pianist he was, technically, and of course how he accompanied in a very discerning fashion, and how music represented a kind of unity. There were two instruments and the goal of the performance was achieved by two people. But there is no separation between the two – or at least there shouldn't be. No sense of independence at all. And he conveyed this to me at a very early age; and since I have played a lot of chamber music since then, it has been for me one of the fundamental lessons, particularly when playing the cello.

Basically, I remember him as a sort of wonderful boy's companion. There was one occasion, I remember, when he and I went upstairs after supper. We got into a conversation of some sort and I suppose talked for really quite a long time, perhaps an hour or two in the evening, and on my return my mother said something to the effect of 'flying the nest' or 'Good, good that you should spread your wings, Humphrey' – some sort of remark like that – and in a way this was absolutely right.

But as I say, although we had lots of interesting people coming to our house, musicians and people from all sorts and conditions, Ben was someone to whom I felt I could say anything, and who treated everything I said seriously, whatever value it may or may not have had.

I can recall asking who the main influences on him as a writer of opera were, and he said without any hesitation, 'Mozart and Verdi.' And he talked about

Tchaikovsky; and indeed with Pears took me to hear *The Queen of Spades* at Covent Garden later on, you know, when I was a schoolboy, and that was absolutely marvellous. A marvellous piece of music but equally, to go *with them*, and listen and to hear Ben then comment on the music – I mean one just *learnt* so much, one's ears were so to say enlarged whenever one was in his company, and everything he said I have an absolutely accurate recollection of. It really went in, as something which has stuck. For instance, he took the view that people these days 'didn't know how to play slowly'; I was very intrigued by the lovely recording that he and Slava [Mstislav Rostropovich] had made of the Schubert 'Arpeggione' sonata, which is quite eccentrically slow. It is a unique performance; and I did immediately make that particular link with his saying that it is jolly difficult to play slow and 'that's why lots of people don't bother to do so'. That was certainly one of his observations.

And then there was the family:

Whenever we were there, when my two sisters were there, it was all, you know, a jolly family holiday. I think that Ben had a special affinity, to put it that way, with young boys as embodiments of his own self, the boyish side of his character. But I remember him being very sweet to Caroline, my next sister, and very sympathetic about the last one, Virginia, who was a diabetic, and has since died of that [in 1992]. But every time there were family visits or family expeditions, all the children were made equally at home and very happy. I think at a trivial level he enjoyed being a family favourite. I mean whenever he came to stay it was always: 'Oh *great*! What train's he coming on? Shall we go and meet him?' He was a welcome member, and I certainly think he loved that. And he would play up to the children and play games and tease them, tease us, and be as it were one of us; but I think that particularly where the parents were visibly extremely close – even though, in the case of my parents, they were very, very different personalities and characters – I think that he felt there was a kind of structure there within which he was made very welcome: he could come in and out, as it were, he could befriend now one, now another member of the family, and this was very reassuring for him, and made us particularly welcome as guests, as we so often were.

And then the unexpected rupture:

Let me tell you all that I can recall about this. We were, as I say, very close, Ben and I, and I was not at all the only one of those young boys with whom Ben had a close rapport. Michael Berkeley was saying the other day that he too was always made to feel completely at home by Ben. Ben enjoyed his company and we indeed found that we had had just the same sort of responses, and that this had been a very formative influence both on Michael and on me.

But when I was about fourteen or fifteen, my parents knew very well a man called Bobbie Shaw. He was Nancy Astor's son by her first marriage to Robert Gould Shaw II. He was always around at Cliveden, an extremely funny man, homosexual, and making no secret of it.[26] But he took my father on one side, it seems, and said, 'I think you should know that Humphrey is known to be an intimate friend of

26 In 1931, it seems, he had served a prison sentence. See also James Roose Evans (ed.), *Joyce Grenfell Darling Ma: Letters to her Mother, 1932–1944*, p. 42, where Grenfell writes of Shaw, 'His conversation is so tinged with bitterness and his cynicism is so poisonous that it pervades and fouls the atmosphere.' (He was Grenfell's cousin.)

Benjamin Britten' and that he [Shaw] thought that I might be at risk because Ben, being a practising homosexual who enjoyed the company of others of that ilk, was not for that reason entirely to be trusted. My father and I never discussed this, neither then nor afterwards. But he suffered real agony about this, because he knew that I greatly enjoyed Ben's company and Ben enjoyed mine, and that this had been going on for years and there had been absolutely no problem. That's the sad thing. If Pa had asked me, I would have been able to put his worry at rest, and offset this well-intentioned but utterly misguided bit of advice. However, he did decide that it was in a sense his moral duty as my guardian to bring to an end something which involved a risk to me as his only son. My father, who was high-minded – not old-fashioned exactly, but still perhaps very much a son of the Manse – had never, I may say, uttered any kind of warning about homosexuals.

So it was that he asked Ben to come and call on him at the Ministry of Education where he was Permanent Secretary, and said that our friendship, formally – I don't know in what terms he said it – but, basically, it must have been that he didn't want me to go on going and staying with Ben. I know that Ben was absolutely shattered by this. And the more one understands Ben's nature, the more one can see why he would have been, because it was a gross affront to what had been a long-standing friendship of the most innocent kind, and innocence misunderstood or affronted, it's a theme that of course goes through his operas – 'The ceremony of innocence is drowned', for example.

I think in a word that it was a dreadful mistake on my father's side, and I remember my younger sister, Ginny, also being absolutely outraged by it, speaking of it in later life, as something that was completely unnecessary. Happily, it didn't mean that his and my friendship was for that reason completely switched off: I think my father meant that Ben shouldn't go on inviting me to spend summer holidays with him and Peter. But my parents went on meeting them and they came down to Oxford, and with my mother in particular they continued the strong musical bond, when my parents were at University College, Oxford, where they were from 1963 onwards. My mother ran the Friends of the Radcliffe Hospital, and outraged the local musical establishment in Oxford by successfully inviting Ben and Peter to come and give a recital at the Town Hall when others had tried and failed. I remember them staying at the Lodgings, and indeed that may have been the time when we played the Shostakovich Sonata together.

I remember too that when I was posted to the British Embassy in Madrid in 1961, I asked Ben to come and visit us there. But he said he didn't think he would be allowed to enter the country, having signed so many letters and declarations against Franco.[27] But the implication was that he would have liked to do so had this been possible, which I think was a mark of the strength of our continuing friendship.

I asked Humphrey Maud about his reaction to the rupture in 1949:

In a way, I barely noticed it. You know, I was busy growing up. In holidays I had different things to do and one stayed with other friends but didn't have this kind of concentrated experience of, you know, improving one's tennis, playing new works with Ben, which would have been lovely to have. And then one came through it; and I did National Service and Cambridge. I well remember them coming up to

27 See also Donald Mitchell, 'Violent Climates', in MCCCBB, and particularly pp. 211–16, 'Epilogue: prohibited immigrants'.

Cambridge to perform *The Turn of the Screw* and I went I think to all of the performances there and had, again, you know, a perfectly happy and friendly relationship with them both. I had always got on very well with Peter, too. We had perhaps rather the same kind of sense of humour.

It is not hard to imagine the pain caused to Britten by this seemingly entirely unforeseen and arbitrary severance of a valued family relationship and valued friendship with Humphrey (reciprocated, as we have read above, on the boy's part). One has no wish to rake over what are now distant unhappinesses; it is, after all, the *Young Person's Guide* and its dedication that will be remembered and constitute their own testament to a remarkable alliance. Moreover, the family friendship, though it may have temporarily faltered, was to continue. Britten's later letters to the Mauds bear witness to this. We find him writing to Jean Redcliffe-Maud on 7 May 1967, 'Thank you all for your great kindnesses to us last week – it was a great joy to be with you & John and the dear Family again' – one cannot but note the capitalization – after which he adds – and again one cannot but sense a charge of emotion colouring what is otherwise a perfectly conventional form of words – 'it was as if no time had gone by since those lovely early days'. None the less, the sorry tale of the imposed breach makes its own point about the homophobic fears that, under pressure, could be released in the 1940s even among some of the most civilized, courteous, gifted, intelligent and warmly admiring of the composer's friends.

This bruising rebuff, however politely and reluctantly it may have been put, must have seemed to Britten like a fall from grace, and undeniably lends substance to the point that Michael Wilcox makes; not only because of the embargo peremptorily imposed on a friendship that meant a great deal to Britten but because suddenly, and without warning, he found himself (or felt himself) expelled from a family that had generously welcomed him and in a sense become his own. Tom Sutcliffe, in his article 'Parental Concerns',[28] is perceptive in suggesting that Britten 'felt his personal exclusion from natural parenthood as the most regrettable and painful aspect of his homosexuality'; hence, 'when his collaborators had families he revelled in the chance to be *in loco parentis*'. In fact it was not only the opportunity to be *in loco parentis* that Britten welcomed. In one significant instance and

28 This appeared in the programme book for a production of *The Turn of the Screw* at Théâtre de La Monnaie, Brussels, in 1998. A further and longer article by the same author was published in the programme book for the Welsh National Opera production of the opera in 2000, 'Haunting parallels between life and art', pp. 30–33. The text is important in itself but also for a further reason. It ends (pp. 34–7) with the first publication of four letters from David Hemmings, the original Miles, to Britten written in 1954 and 1955 (the originals are held at BPL). The letters are of unquestionable interest and vividly confirm the character of the relationship as described in his later memories. (See pp. 25–8.) See also John Bridcut, 'The boys who loved Britten', *Daily Telegraph* (29 May 2004), pp. 8–9, and JBBC, in which Hemmings is interviewed and Britten's relationships with children are examined in depth.

in a unique context, he was able to assume the role of full-fledged father figure.[29] David Hemmings, who as a boy created the character of the fatherless Miles in *The Turn of the Screw*, delivered the text that follows as an introduction to the production of the opera by Scottish Opera shown on BBC2 on 13 August 1994. It is not widely known and is of particular interest, perhaps just because of the 'infatuation' to which Hemmings himself refers. This in itself tells us something about Britten's relationship with him, though he (Hemmings), it seems, was unaware of it, or at least not troubled by it, at the time:

1953: A very small boy stood on the stage of La Scala Theatre in London and sang [Handel's] 'Where e'er you walk', and a voice came from the back of the auditorium saying, 'Thank you; thank you very much.' It was Benjamin Britten's.

I've no idea to this day why I got the role, but from that moment my energies were dedicated to the English Opera Group and the process that was to become *The Turn of the Screw* – perhaps *the* finest British opera since Purcell's *Fairy Queen*.

[...]

Benjamin Britten was born in Lowestoft and he made his home in Aldeburgh where he spent with Peter Pears the most significant, creative part of his life.

[...]

I went to stay with Britten in this wonderfully claustrophobic atmosphere and he cared for me, he developed my voice and he was a deeply considerate father figure. It was only later that I learnt that he was very much infatuated with me and that caused some problems between himself and his long-time companion, Peter Pears. In all of the time that I spent with him he *never* abused that trust. My parents, I suppose, were effectively banished, so I spent most of my time sitting at the piano listening to him play wonderful, wonderful music, Peter Pears singing cadenzas with extraordinary clarity, powerful and thrilling, an ever-recurring theme that as I began to know Britten and his work seemed so synonymous with the two of them.

As a composer, pianist, and conductor, sometimes revered, sometimes deeply misunderstood, he remains one of the most significant creators of twentieth-century British music. I had the good fortune to know him well, to sit by him and listen at his piano and share in some of the creative moments that went into this score; and I suppose it was frightening that the intensity of Aldeburgh somehow became entangled with Bly [the country-house setting of *The Turn of the Screw*].

For my own involvement I can only say that at the premiere, at the Fenice Theatre in Venice in 1954, the curtain fell to a miraculous, terrifying silence.

The Governess had just reprised the simple Latin lesson that I as Miles had sung to her in Act I. Now it was not a lesson, it was a reassurance. She had saved this poor sagging child into her care. She had made him whole. His – perhaps their – ghosts, she thought, were gone.

She clutched me tighter and she gasped, 'Miles, what is it? What is it?' There were

29 I write here and in the immediately ensuing text about David Hemmings (who died in 2003), whose relationship with Britten, like that of Humphrey Maud, had a highly significant musical dimension to it. There was another parallel case, though music perhaps was not at the heart of it. A detailed account of his quasi-adoptive 'sharing' of Roger Duncan, with his father, Ronald Duncan, the librettist of *Lucretia*, is to be found in HCBB, pp. 366–8, and in RDBB, pp. 131–3. 'My young friend, Roger Duncan' was among the dedicatees of *Noye's Fludde* and was to become one of Britten's godsons.

only breaths, and *then* she showed the realization of the price that she had paid, and there was a sudden burst of vocal energy which haunts me – and Peter Quint – to this day:

> Malo, malo, I would rather be
> Malo, malo, than a naughty boy
> Malo, malo – what have we done between us?

Never in my career have I ever felt that strength and moment when the audience applauded us, as they did beyond all measure, never have I ever known a moment that told me this was a very special thing to call yourself a performer.

And when I listen to *The Turn of the Screw* now, I remember that moment, and it is perhaps one of the best gifts that anybody could *give* anyone, and I thank Benjamin Britten for that because no one else could have given it to me – particularly at eleven years old.[30]

But there is more to the recollections of the original Miles than I have so far suggested. Indeed, one might think they rather pointedly expose the danger of merging – confusing – life with art. If the chronology of the opera's composition had been otherwise, how convenient it would have been to have a ready-made 'infatuation' as an 'explanation' for its existence. But Miles, in fact, was a creature of Britten's (and James's) imagination, without a specific human model; while the very nature of the later relationship with the boy who in fact had brought to musical life the Miles whose only begetter was the composer himself, is itself revealing of the complications of the feelings involved in Britten's own acted-out imagination of himself as Father. That this bit of his biography post-dated the opera does not mean that it is therefore of no relevance to the opera. On the contrary, it simply testifies to the complexity and richness of the sources, deep in the composer's psyche, from which the opera was born, an act of creation that, for sure, was related to the composer's personality – how could it be otherwise? – but which no single biographical event or personal relationship or stretch of time can account for, can 'explain'.[31] The work *is* its own 'explanation'. It requires no other.

30 See also HCBB, pp. 357–8. In the recollections of Hemmings reported there he says, 'Of all the people I have worked with, I count my relationship with Ben to have been one of the finest [. . .] And it was never, under any circumstances, threatening [. . .] Did I feel that he was desperately fond of me? I suppose I did, but I thought far more in a sort of fatherly fashion [. . .] But there is no man in my entire life that has been more influential on my attitudes than Ben.' To Tom Sutcliffe (see n. 28) he remarked, 'I had a marvellous relationship with Ben as a surrogate father.'

31 The *Screw* itself was composed with extraordinary speed between March and September 1954 when it was given its premiere at La Fenice in Venice. Compositional revisions had continued up to and beyond the very last minute. (See Donald Mitchell, 'Britten's Revisionary Practice: Practical and Creative', in DMCN, pp. 393–406. This article first appeared in an issue of *Tempo* in 1963. I had to approach Britten to seek his permission to use and publish discarded drafts. He readily agreed. It was the first time he had been asked to allow earlier stages in the evolution of a work to be made public.) Henry James's story, as most now know, had been floating

about in Britten's mind since he had first heard it, in the shape of a play, broadcast by the BBC on 1 June 1932. He followed this up by reading the tale on the 6th and 7th, writing in his diary 'Finish the "Screw". An incredible masterpiece.' Then began the long germinating period of some twenty-one years – long even by Britten's standards – that eventually culminated in Myfanwy Piper undertaking the libretto. The idea of the opera had already been under consideration for the repertory of the English Opera Group by May 1951, with a view to its premiere at the Venice Biennale of 1952. But the composition of *Gloriana* (1952–53) intervened and later an attack of bursitis which meant that the *Screw* did not finally reach the stage until September 1954. In the meantime, doubtless, as was his practice, Britten was clarifying the composition of the work in his mind, which – the libretto done – he began to get down on paper at the very end of March 1954; and in 1952 and 1953 auditions were held to find a treble for the role of Miles, when Britten first encountered David Hemmings. Although not a note of the opera had been written, Britten would have had a pretty clear concept of the role and what it would demand of the singer. Basil Coleman, who staged the premiere, remembered that 'the auditions were disappointing. One of the few boys brought back for a second hearing was a very shy but quite personable little twelve-year-old, with a true but very small voice. Despite this it was decided to risk casting him, in the hope that the voice would develop and grow during rehearsals – the boy was David Hemmings.' (Basil Coleman, 'Staging first productions 2', in DHOBB, pp. 40–43.) The contribution made by Hemmings's unique performance to the success of the *Screw* cannot be overestimated. However, the making of the long-contemplated Miles whom Britten brought to life in his opera, aided by his good fortune in finding the boy who could be trained to meet the role's exacting technical demands, was one thing. Quite another was the ironical turn in events that led him to fall in love, it seems, with the boy who himself so admirably brought to life the Miles who had been created in the first place by the composer's own imagination.

A participant in this same audition was another boy soprano, Michael Ingram, now celebrated as the actor, singer and entertainer Michael Crawford. In his autobiography, *Parcel Arrived Safely: Tied with String* (p. 42), Crawford writes of the occasion, 'the pure terror of stage fright overcame me [. . .] and my voice left me completely. I couldn't sing a note. David Hemmings won the role, which marked his debut as a performer.' This albeit unsuccessful first audition was, it seems, remembered by Britten, and Crawford later alternated with Hemmings in the 1955 production of *Let's Make an Opera* at the Scala Theatre in London, conducted alternately by Norman Del Mar and Charles Mackerras. Like Hemmings, who went on to record the work in the same year, his memories of the composer are warm and untroubled. In his book he outlines the circumstances of his first encounters with Britten: a neighbour, it seems, read that

[. . .] the English Opera Group was looking for boy sopranos to play in a production of Benjamin Britten's *The Turn of the Screw* [. . .] So I went along to join the hundreds of other children who auditioned. I sang 'Early One Morning' and recited a poem about a donkey, Walter de la Mare's 'Nicholas Nye', managing quite painlessly to get through that audition, and several more, until it got down to the last four boys. But the pure terror of stage fright overtook me at that last audition and my voice left me completely. David Hemmings won the role, which marked his debut as a performer [. . .] He had a very fine, very strong voice, much stronger than mine, and he was certainly far more suitable for the role than I would have been. Both he and that production of *Turn of the Screw* enjoyed well-deserved success.

I must say something here about Benjamin Britten – indeed, I cannot say enough about the kindness of that great man. I was twelve when I met him, and he was at the time by far the poshest person I'd ever seen [. . .] Benjamin Britten was the pre-eminent British composer of his time and he had a wonderful patience and affinity with young people. He loved music, and loved youngsters caring about music [. . .]

From the very start he showed me enormous consideration and tolerance. I remember an incident when, in the midst of the studio recording of *Let's Make an Opera*, the engineers began to pick up a crunching sound on one of the mikes. Everything stopped until

This is not an approach, a mode of understanding, that finds much favour with Carpenter, even when writing about a work, the *Young Person's Guide,* that one would have thought was a fairly straightforward exercise in the education ('edification', as Britten had it) and entertainment of young people; it was, too, only one of the many manifestations of Britten's fascination with Purcell in this same period. Carpenter, however, trivializes the genuine importance and innovations of the *Guide* by creating the impression that the work was all 'about' the eleven-year-old Humphrey Maud, the 'particular young person' he claims that Britten 'had in mind while writing it'; 'Britten became especially friendly with Humphrey, who played the cello'. Hence – of course – the 'passage for solo cellos, which has a Mahlerian tenderness that stands out from the rest of the work, may be another mark of dedication'. For good measure, in 'the exuberant simplicities' of the *Guide* Carpenter hears the composer 'restoring his faith in life by impersonating a lost innocence'.[32] Phew!

The note of exasperation must be excused. To whom, one wonders, is the tender melody of the solo oboe addressed in Variation B, manifestly more *espressivo* to my ears than the melody for cello (Variation G) and twice marked *largamente*? Or the violas' variation (Variation F), marked successively *dolce e commodo* and *espressivo*? Events and contexts of genuine musical and creative significance which we can safely presume *were* vitally involved in the making of the *Young Person's Guide* should make us cautious

---

the technicians could figure out what it was or where it was coming from. An engineer finally discovered the source of the problem off in a corner – me cracking chestnuts. As I wasn't singing I thought it was perfectly all right to eat, never realizing it was all being picked up on the studio microphones. Mr Britten never scolded – the humiliation alone was enough to make me never do it again – but only gave a kindly word of advice about appropriate studio behaviour, which in its way was far more effective.

It is perhaps of some interest to note that Crawford's vocal and theatrical potentialities were first discovered by his taking the role of Sammy in *The Little Sweep* at his prep school in South London (as it happens, conducted by Donald Mitchell), while it was Hemmings's debut in *The Turn of the Screw* that brought his very striking talents to the fore. For a time at any rate Britten's music often performed the then novel function of revealing and encouraging musical gifts at a very early stage. Crawford was to sing the role of Jaffet in the 1958 premiere of *Noye's Fludde.* One should add that while Crawford's recollections lack nothing in colour and exuberance they are not always wholly reliable in factual detail. But they constitute a valuable documentation of the impact Britten, both the man and his music, made on young lives, talents and voices in the 1950s. This is vividly borne out in a paragraph of a letter from Hemmings to Britten written in November 1954:

I certainly have tried not to forget my singing and acting, and I certainly miss working with members of the *Screw.* Lately I have, on successive Saturdays, won two cups in music festivals, and I am shortly to be in our new school house plays. I want to go all out now to make a recording. And so, working hard at both Mrs Brookes and Mr Kimble [his teachers], I hope to achieve my aim.

of attributing its existence to Humphrey and his cello; it would have happened without him. I hope he won't take this amiss; indeed he has no need to: as he himself observed, the dates don't work, in that his friendship with Britten took root in music-making only significantly later. (In fact, he started his cello lessons only in 1945 at the age of eleven.) Think, for instance, of the specific aesthetic that was the *raison d'être* of the work, the education of young people, a thrust already firmly rooted in Britten's compositional character (e.g. *Friday Afternoons, Simple Symphony*, etc.); indeed, the educational factor, and its evolution, was something that he owed to his own family, and in particular the career in teaching of his elder brother, Robert, while by the time Britten came to compose the *Guide* he had behind him the years he had spent collaborating with John Grierson and the GPO Film Unit in the creation of documentary film, a form of film-making that was also an innovative form of social education and (above all) information. We should not forget that it was as soundtrack of a film (*Instruments of the Orchestra* (1946)) that the *Guide* was originally conceived.[33] It is scarcely surprising that the work came to be so famously linked with a family in which the composer had not only found talent and happiness but also a fortuitous combination of music and education, the latter personified in the figure of Humphrey's distinguished father, John Redcliffe-Maud. The family bond, the encouragement of a communal musical experience, is implicit in the aesthetic of the *Guide*. As Humphrey interestingly observed to me in his recollections from which I have already extensively quoted, the *Guide* helped parents 'introduce their children to music. After all, apart from school, we were probably brought to our first concerts by our parents. I think that is often so.' Times change, of course, and have changed radically since 1946 when the *Guide* was first heard and seen. Worth remembering, therefore, that it was addressed to the broad swath of generations that the family comprises. A piece of its period undoubtedly, but all its other excellencies apart, its communal, supragenerational appeal has guaranteed it a frequent and popular presence in the concert hall.

Even this bit of history, both biographical and musical, is suggestive of the complicated interaction between the life of an artist and his art; and the better the artist, the more complicated the relationship. To pretend that Britten's sexual orientation tells us anything useful or revealing about the *Young Person's Guide* seems to me to get us nowhere. On the other hand the Maud 'story' powerfully illumines the role of the family both in his creative imagination and in his day-to-day life, a role in a continuous state of transition *between* life and art. This illustrates once again the danger of drawing parallels between the supposed chronologies of a composer's life and his

33 See Letter 522 n. 2.

creations. Or, as P. N. Furbank – himself an admirable biographer of E. M. Forster – has written when reviewing a biographical study of Virginia Woolf, subtitled, needless to add, the 'hidden life' of that author:

> I think [. . .] that Leaska's book has certain weaknesses. The first relates to the problem of writing the Life of a writer and the (to my mind) fatal theory that knowledge of the life will help one to respond to the works.
>
> [. . .]
>
> What we are encountering here is a causal theory, a matter of explaining, by biographical causes, how a given work of art came to take the shape it did; and I am with Wittgenstein in thinking that causal explanations have no rightful place in aesthetics. One can indeed extend this objection and say that biographers (like historians) might do well to eschew causal explanations in general, for – the events they are studying being non-repeatable – such explanations can only ever be pure guesswork. They might be better left to the reader.[34]

A later story, once again with a 'family' dimension to it, though not of a scale comparable to the earlier experience, belongs to 1970–71, to the period that immediately followed the rebuilding of the Maltings at Snape after its destruction by fire in 1969. The events I go on to describe were eventually to lead to the resignation of Stephen Reiss, the then General Manager of the English Opera Group and General Manager of the Aldeburgh Festival, a resignation attended by much tension and bitterness. It was undoubtedly a *cause célèbre* among those close to Britten and Pears, to Reiss, and to those involved in managing the activities of the Festival, the English Opera Group, and the use of the Maltings.[35]

I was fortunate to have the opportunity to talk at length to Reiss himself, before he died in 1999,[36] during the course of which there was an exchange that centred on a feature of the breakdown in his personal relationship with Britten. Reiss had described it thus to Carpenter:

---

34 *Times Literary Supplement* (11 December 1998), p. 9, a review of Mitchell Leaska's *Granite and Rainbow: The hidden life of Virginia Woolf.*

35 With the Aldeburgh Festival's growth in extent and ambition, the available venues, including the Jubilee Hall in Aldeburgh itself and a number of local churches, proved inadequate to stage opera satisfactorily or cater for the increasing audiences. The conversion of the Maltings at Snape – a building that Britten had looked out on from his balcony at the Old Mill in the late 1930s and even then imagined as a concert hall or opera house – was to provide a near-ideal space and acoustic. The building work was funded by public appeal, grants from the Arts Council and the Gulbenkian Trust, and donations from the Decca Record Company and Britten himself; the building was opened by Queen Elizabeth II at the start of the 1967 Aldeburgh Festival. After the first night of the 1969 Festival, the concert hall was destroyed by fire. The generosity of Britten and his friends and the superhuman efforts of the builders meant that a rebuilt and slightly redesigned concert hall was ready for the 1970 Festival, when the Queen returned to take part in a repeat opening ceremony.

36 The tape and transcript of my interview with him on 18 July 1998 is available at BPL, together with a later addendum in the shape of a letter dated 7 September. Some minimal editing of the excerpts reproduced here have been made in the interests of clarity. Reiss was appointed General Manager of the Aldeburgh Festival in 1955 and of the English Opera Group in 1958.

We decided that we had to have a full-time caretaker at the Maltings, and Ben and Peter were very keen that I shouldn't engage the person myself, but it ought to be a collaborative effort, a collective decision. Anyway, we engaged this chap before reopening in 1970. He was an absolute disaster, but he had this very, very beautiful son, who was athletic to boot – he was practically an England international. I think he was more or less the prototype for the boy in *Death in Venice*. Ben and Peter were crazy about him.[37]

Reiss was obliged to sack the caretaker, an event that brought to an end what had been a period of spectacular development at Snape and Alde-burgh under Reiss's – perhaps sometimes reluctant – management; the end, too, of a long-standing and productive friendship between Reiss (and his wife, Beth) and the composer and Pears.[38] After the breach, he was never to exchange a further word with Britten. However, in the light of my 1998 conversation with Reiss, not to speak of my later (1999) and extensive interview with some of the principal participants in the 'caretaker' affair, on which I report below, I began to wonder whether the implications of the account he gave Carpenter might not be rather differently interpreted if looked at from another angle.

Let me make a start by questioning the notion that the 'very, very beautiful' boy was the 'prototype' for Tadzio in *Death in Venice*, because it can be answered and, I believe, disposed of, on a factual basis. What it represents,

---

37 See HCBB, p. 524. The chapter (pp. 514–31) is entitled 'Under the lash'.

38 It should not be forgotten that Britten dedicated *A Midsummer Night's Dream* to Reiss, who was kind enough to send me a copy of the handwritten inscription in the study score of the opera, of which Britten had made him a gift. The printed dedication – 'Dedicated to Stephen Reiss' – was crossed out and the following substituted: 'For Stephen, with much gratitude & admiration for so many things over so many years! – with love to both you & Beth from Ben. Feb. 1961'. The note accompanying the score read: 'My dear Stephen – Better late than never, & gloriously full of mis-prints! With love, Ben.' The premiere of the opera had taken place as part of the 1960 Aldeburgh Festival. In his interview with me Reiss had this to say about the thinking that attended the legendary production of the opera in the Jubilee Hall:

> SR [Ben and Peter] wanted to have their own place, and they felt the limitations of the church [at first Blythburgh] partly on account of the artistic character, because certain secular works were not *really* right for it; for the sake of argument, Tchaikovsky, or Haydn's *The Seasons*, and [similar?] large-scale secular works. They felt they must have their own place.

> DM Their own theatre, their own concert hall?

> SR Yes, yes. And the opera – I mean [they] were not pressing now so much for opera as they were for secular concerts. But we had meantime, of course, advanced the Jubilee Hall, in 1960 you know, as a prelude to doing *Midsummer Night's Dream*. We bought the house next door, and that enabled us to enlarge the Jubilee Hall, and we enlarged the stage, we enlarged the orchestra pit, we added dressing rooms and we had the space next door for rehearsals and drinks in the interval and so on. And we had – originally it was only one entrance, and the whole thing was – well, it was just a village-hall situation, but we did improve it. But even so, Ben [was] not happy with that. It was better, but not good enough. And so the pressure rose to develop Snape.

DATE	EVENTS	OWEN WINGRAVE	DEATH IN VENICE	OTHER WORKS
1950/1960s			Britten's copy of Mann's text probably acquired	
1965			'It seems . . . that *Death in Venice* was well in mind by 1965 at the latest.'[39]	
1967 2 June	Maltings Concert Hall opened			
1968 22 April				*The Prodigal Son* completed
Spring		Work starts on libretto of *Owen Wingrave*		
10 Nov.				*Children's Crusade* completed
1969 April		Begins composition of *Wingrave*		
7 June	Maltings Concert Hall burns down			
Summer				*Who are these children?*
1970 Feb.–August		Completes composition and full score of *Wingrave*		
1 May	New caretaker appointed			
5 June	Maltings Concert Hall reopens			
Sept.			Opens discussions on *Death in Venice* with Myfanwy Piper	
Nov.		*Wingrave* recorded for BBC TV in the Maltings over 9 days		

Date	Events	Recordings & Broadcasts	Death in Venice	Works
Dec.		Records *Wingrave* for Decca in Kingsway Hall, London		
1971				
Jan.–Feb.			Further discussion of *Death in Venice* with Pipers on holiday in France. On return Myfanwy begins drafting libretto	*Canticle IV*
Feb.–March				*Suite No. 3*, for cello
16 May		TV premiere of *Wingrave* (BBC2, in collaboration with twelve European, Scandinavian and N. American broadcasters)		
1 June			Premiere of *Death in Venice* announced for September 1972	
5 July	Caretaker informs Britten that he has been dismissed			
Sept.			Work on libretto of *Death in Venice* resumes	
Oct.	Britten and Pipers visit Venice			
Dec.			Draft for Act I of libretto completed	
1972				
Jan.–Feb.			Premiere of *Death in Venice* announced for June 1973	
July			Britten (at Aldeburgh, then in Germany at Schloss Wolfsgarten) begins work on composing opera	
17–24 Dec.			Composing of opera resumed	
1973			End of opera reached (and revised)	
16 June			*Death in Venice* premiere at Snape (not attended by BB)	
12 Sept.			Private performance at Snape for BB	
18 Oct.			London premiere at Covent Garden (attended by BB)	

however, is a classic example of an immediate and, after a moment's reflection, patent mis-identification that even as experienced a biographer as Carpenter does not doubt or pursue: the assumed equivalence between life and art he has so vigorously expounded has taken so strong a hold that any thought of submitting the proposition to sceptical scrutiny is repressed. At the same time the very fact that Reiss himself casually, one must suppose, introduces the equivalence into his recollections, shows how easy it was, without any help from Carpenter, to slip into matching up quite unrelated persons and creative events.[40] One might well think that even on the grounds of probability alone, so sophisticated, elaborate and innovatory a work of the character of *Death in Venice*, with its roots in a key text by one of the most complicated of twentieth-century European authors, was unlikely in any serious sense to have had anything much to do with matters relating to the caretaker and his son, which in any case are not supported by the chronology of the opera's composition. Britten had had this in mind for many, many years – the seeds of the opera date back to the 1950s or 1960s, when he made his first acquaintance with Mann's novella – before embarking on the project. (One cannot help but recall in this context Mann's remarks to his son, Golo, that, if asked, the composer he would have chosen to 'realize' the imaginary music of Leverkühn in *Dr Faustus* would have been Britten;[41] hardly surprising, perhaps, that an initiative – a film? a play? – that might have prompted the invitation to be put to him never materialized. If it had done, Schoenberg would certainly have been surprised by Mann's choice.)

I think the table on pp. 32–3 spells out the point I am trying to make: in the account that Reiss gave Carpenter, the sequence of incidents he describes simply does not fit the creative facts (i.e. the relevant dates). In particular, it is difficult, to say the least, to see how it could be thought possible that the new caretaker's son, who would have surfaced presumably

39 [*See Table on page 32*] See Rosamund Strode, 'A *Death in Venice* chronicle', in DVDM, pp. 26–44. This Cambridge Opera Guide contains much information about the pre-history and evolution of the opera. This table shows only the specific works Britten was writing during a period of hectic activity in many other areas. Strode describes in detail the 'punishing schedule' characteristic of these years, which the table illustrates.

40 A reason for scepticism, my scepticism at least, would have been the improbability of an infatuation, on this scale and of this intensity – for so it was represented to be – with a seventeen-year-old youth. It was chiefly pre-pubescent boys to whom Britten was attracted and for one of whom, some sixteen years or so earlier, there had been an unequivocal infatuation (see pp. 25–6 above). It is necessary perhaps to remind ourselves that the beautiful child who was the model for Mann's Tadzio was in fact just that: not an adolescent but a pre-pubescent boy. That the role of the boy in the opera demanded a young dancer old enough and skilled enough to fulfil the composer's elaborate compositional needs is a telling example of a work of art superseding supposed 'biography' and dictating its own creative and technical agenda.

41 Golo Mann reported this conversation to Donald Mitchell while he and his mother Katia were visiting London in 1973 to see *Death in Venice* during its run at Covent Garden.

around May 1970, was the 'prototype' for Tadzio in *Death in Venice*, a project that Britten had already been pondering for some years. However, that this mis-identification[42] could be made so readily is itself of no little interest, an issue to which I shall return.

It is clear, I think, that the work that was Britten's active creative pre-occupation at this time was *Owen Wingrave*, his penultimate opera. The need to complete *Wingrave* was lent extra urgency by the destruction of the Maltings. The fee he received for his first and only opera for television (£10,000 if my recollection is correct; the equivalent of about £95,000 in 2004), he allotted in its entirety to the rebuilding fund – 'to help get the roof on', as he told me. He embarked on *Death in Venice* just as soon as the TV commission was done and the recording made in the resurrected Maltings. The 'authentic' Tadzio – that is to say, the creature of Britten's imagination – had in fact been waiting in the wings since the 1960s to make his debut. (Similarly Owen who, be it noted, had been in Britten's mind since at least 1954. The *Screw* had hardly been completed and first performed when the composer wrote to Eric Walter White (5 November 1954), 'By the way, do you know another short story of James' called "Owen Wingrave" with much the same quality as the Screw?' Fifteen years were to elapse before *Wingrave* was written, a typical example of the long period of gestation that in Britten's creative process so often preceded a work's birth.)

If all of this were just a question of tidying up the chronologies, why on earth make a fuss about it? To which my response is this: that the very readi-ness with which the assumption was made – the speed if you like, with which the reference, the equation, the identification of the 'prototype', was established that the caretaker's son = Tadzio – is striking evidence of the culture, predominant today, in which the artist's biography and his or her work of art have become inextricably locked in a far from productive embrace.

The contemporary culture of biography, and in particular that sector of it preoccupied with sexual orientation, has itself responded to – indeed reflected – the relatively recent liberalization of attitudes to and discussion of homosexuality, the onset of which Britten, in later life, both witnessed and, it is often forgotten, profoundly welcomed; and to which, it might be argued, his own work and life – lives, rather – as composer and performer, significantly contributed.[43] All the more ironic that one of the consequences of this entirely to be applauded liberalization should be to empower the

---

42 It is not only mis-identification that we encounter when giving an account of *Death in Venice* and its sources but also on occasion *self*-identification, in which an element of wishful think-ing seems to figure. See, for example, HCBB, pp. 538–9, though I doubt if much time need be spent on considering the credibility of the claim (if that's the right word).

43 See Donald Mitchell, *Memories, Commitments, Communication*, p. 16–18.

casual use of an artist's sexual orientation as a prime retrospective means of interpreting his works. This, to use the jargon emblematic of the last decade of the last century, is dumbing-down with a vengeance. (Ironic too, one may think, that the period should itself have invented a description of one of its leading characteristics of a peculiar appropriateness.)

In his dialogue with me, Stephen Reiss had something to say about an issue that was prominent during the years under discussion and which, I believe, had a bearing on the story of the caretaker, George Hardy, and his family: Britten's and Pears's 'vision' of what the Maltings might ideally become. (It is perhaps of some significance that in the Festival Programme Book for 1971, p. 4, Hardy is listed as 'Maltings Concert Hall Warden'.)

Reiss, as the excerpt below shows, repeated again what he had said to Carpenter about the dismissal of the caretaker, though with a new twist to it at the end, that his own – Reiss's – dismissal at Britten's hands fulfilled the need for a 'sacrifice'. But what had preceded it was mention of a 'theatre project' for Aldeburgh in 1957:

SR   [In 1954 Ben] had got a model made and everything; it was going to be on the high grounds above the Wentworth [Hotel] [. . .] and [Lord] Harewood – there was a preface to the [1957] programme book – I mean great celebrations – this was [something that was] going to happen.[44] He [Britten] hadn't arranged it with Elizabeth Sweeting [then General Manager of the Aldeburgh Festival, and Reiss's predecessor] or anybody. They [Britten and Pears] simply threw it out on to Aldeburgh, and it was turned down. And it was the sort of snub or the indignity of it which infuriated Ben. It did make him very angry that he should be –

DM   – rejected –

SR   – treated like that, you see. Now the same thing –

DM   – and did he blame Sweeting for that, do you mean? Or that it brushed off on you? –

SR   Well no, I mean that blood had to be drawn; I mean, there had to be *some-thing* –

DM   – sacrifice? –

SR   Some sacrifice; exactly. There had to be a sacrifice. That's the only way he could sort of recover his sense. And over this – the real truth of it, over this Tadzio thing, this boy, was that he had invested quite a lot in the family. He

44 The Programme Book for the 1957 Aldeburgh Festival included a Foreword by the Earl of Harewood (then President of the Festival) in which (p. 9) mention is made of 'plans for the new theatre'. H. T. Cadbury-Brown, the architect involved, contributed an article 'Notes on an Opera House for Aldeburgh' (pp. 10–11), while among the illustrations is an aerial photograph of Aldeburgh on which has been superimposed an outline indication of the site of the proposed Festival Theatre. Another important item and source of information in regard to the evolution of the Maltings is the brochure issued in 1974 by the Aldeburgh Festival–Snape Maltings Foundation and entitled 'Snape Maltings Concert Hall – the next step'. There is a specific reference to two exhibition galleries, one for pictures and one for 'crafts'.

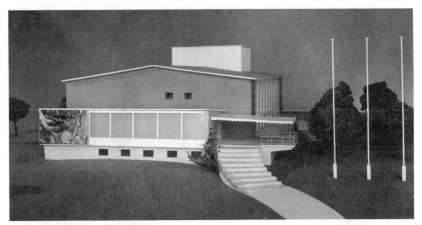

Model of the proposed Festival Theatre (1954), which was on view during the 1954 Aldeburgh Festival. A flyer headed 'A New Theatre in Aldeburgh' indicates that the venue would seat between 600 and 700 people, and that it would be situated 'behind Aldeburgh Lodge, on high ground, with an uninterrupted view over the marshes, and near enough to the sea for interval promenading'.

Key 1 Auditorium   2 Stage   3 Dressing rooms   4 Foyer   5 Open-fronted loggia
6 Forecourt and approach from Alde Lane   7 Enclosed garden   8 Approach from town

Aerial view of Aldeburgh showing the site of the proposed Festival Theatre (1957). This scheme, apparently more ambitious than the 1954 proposal, sited the theatre in the heart of the town on land south of the Parish Church.

was fond of the father, fond of the mother, fond of the boy. They'd made a big fuss of him. As soon as I gave him [the caretaker] the sack, in effect he immediately came to Ben, talked to Ben here in Horham,[45] in fact (I think he lived quite near here), and it was a kind of [*pause*] it was a kind of slap in the face to Ben. D'you follow what I mean? It wasn't the romantic thing [the Tadzio 'connection'], it was a slap in the face to Ben that here he'd invested in the – you know –

DM   – in the family –

SR   – they were his friends – in the family; they were friends and they were nice to him, and he'd made a fuss of them, they'd made a fuss of him, he'd made a fuss of them; they'd done – they were at his service, doing everything for him when he was abroad and everything and it wasn't – it wasn't – Ben didn't like it. [*After a long pause*] I think that's really what it was.

DM   So in this case, *you* were the sacrifice.

SR   Yes [. . .] I was put on the bonfire.

In the event this theatre project did not materialize, but it gives us a glimpse of the objectives and ambitions that Britten and Pears had in mind, eventually to be realized in the building of the concert hall at Snape. It is important, I believe, to bear in mind their ideas about the possible further evolution of the Maltings, post-1970, when the new caretaker was appointed, which may have added a complicating factor that goes unmentioned by Reiss. (It is this possible extension of Snape into an arts and crafts centre which Mrs Hardy interestingly mentions in her interview with me (see p. 41 below), in which context the name of Sidney Nolan, the distinguished Australian painter, whose work often took shape as a significant form of 'collaboration' with Britten's music, seems to have cropped up. There was, it seems, to be a 'Nolan Gallery'.)

It seemed worthwhile to me to approach the surviving participants in the drama, Mrs George Hardy (the caretaker's widow) and her son, Alistair, and attempt at least to document *their* side of the story. This was one area that the normally indefatigable Carpenter, it appears, did not explore; and, as our very long conversation progressed,[46] some surprises did surface. For example, until the occasion of my interviewing them, the Hardys seem to have been totally unaware that Reiss had been actively involved in the uproar leading to George Hardy's dismissal and that his ultimate judge-

---

45 The remote house ('Chapel House') in Suffolk, near Eye, purchased by Britten and Pears in 1970 as a 'hideaway' from the ever growing pressures of Aldeburgh and Britten's 'public' life. (They had it in mind eventually to retire there.) After Britten's death Pears retained the house until 1979 when it was acquired by Donald and Kathleen Mitchell, in whose possession it remained until 2003.

46 A complete recording and transcript of this conversation, which took place at Horham on 10 April 1999, is available at BPL. The excerpts I use here have been minimally edited.

ment of the caretaker's competence, like that of his Festival colleagues, was unequivocally negative. Mrs Hardy's recollections were pretty clear on this one point:

DM   You must know that Stephen [Reiss] considered that your husband was not up to the job, that the job didn't work out successfully and therefore he had to be asked to resign, and that *really* upset Britten –

MRS H   Yes.

DM   – and as a result of what he thought was an arbitrary dismissal of your husband –

MRS H   Yes.

DM   – in the end Stephen himself had to go.

MRS H   Oh, I hadn't heard that, you see, because we were all – I mean my husband was very upset about it all, but I think perhaps it was – I mean, it was nothing to do with Stephen or Ben you know and my husband directly; I think it was other – other people involved, who were –

DM   Really?

MRS H   Yes, you know, not – nothing to do with musicians or Ben and Peter. I think it was various other people who had some connection with the actual Maltings and Festival.

'Other people' it seems from these recollections of the Hardys, not – it seems – Reiss; or at least that is how they remember the crisis. It was a point I returned to, wearingly, more than once, but always got more or less the same response, e.g.:

I didn't realize there was such an upheaval. No, I had no idea that there was any connection whatever [with Reiss].

or

I always thought it was someone putting pressure on Stephen.

or

I don't know really whether he [George Hardy] fell out with someone or upset somebody and they complained about his attitude at one of their committee meetings or what, but it wasn't anything like, where *Ben* was involved, I don't think, at all, because it came, it seemed to be a complete shock to him when George [was dismissed].

That last comment of Mrs Hardy's at least confirms one feature of Reiss's account, the 'shock' Britten experienced on learning of the caretaker's dismissal. It remains curious, however, that the Hardys remained, it seems, so unknowing about Reiss's own dissatisfaction with George's performance. Indeed, Alistair even went on to say, 'People handle situations in the most appropriate way, and it's possible that Stephen Reiss handled it in – shall we say – in the most appropriate way.' But then he added, 'But my recollection of it was that Stephen Reiss was entirely *against* it.' A comment that introduces a yet further enigmatic complication.

Complications, in fact, abound, not only with regard to the act of dismissal but elsewhere too. Reiss, as we have read above and in the account he gave Carpenter, was explicit about Britten's 'investment' in and dependence on the Hardy family: 'He was fond of the father, fond of the mother, fond of the boy. They'd made a big fuss of him [. . .] they were friends and they were nice to him, and he'd made a fuss of them, they'd made a fuss of him; they were at his service, doing everything for him when he was abroad', etc. This would seem to imply a pretty constant flow of association and commitment; how else could 'doing everything' get done? But when one comes to understand that the caretaker was dismissed even before the accommodation that was being prepared for the family had been completed; that Mrs Hardy had a job and was working at Ipswich –

I would go to [Ipswich] station and pick up wigs for an opera or anything like that [. . .] And I would go [to the Maltings] and help [. . .] they used to set up a small bar at the other end of the hall you know, so that people could get their drinks and I would go and help and went to all the concerts.

– and that in the meantime the Hardys lived at Yoxford (about seven miles north of Snape), as Mrs Hardy explained, 'in the coach house of my parents' place', one begins to be a shade sceptical about the practicality of a relationship of this supposed order of intensity having been sustained with a family which in addition had other commitments and responsibilities (a daughter as well as a son).

This is not to suggest that there was not fondness on both sides – Britten is remembered still with affection and respect by the Hardys – but it is hard to gather from their collective recollections much sense of the disproportional emotional investment that Reiss describes, though it is clear too, given Britten's predilection for acquiring families, his own loss of the family when the father lost his job would undoubtedly have caused him genuine dismay.

It is a somewhat disconcerting feature of the Hardy affair that the principals involved so often found it hard to recall what, in Reiss's memory, had played such a vivid role – for example, the occasion when the caretaker failed to turn off the stopcock and the pit at Snape was 'flooded', a few hours before a concert was to begin. Mrs Hardy remembers her husband being at the Maltings 'late one night, and it was something to do with water'. On the other hand if it had been the case that this was a key incident leading to the caretaker's departure, she would have expected to remember her husband saying, 'I've done a dreadful thing'; and that she evidently doesn't remember. 'It does seem odd', was Alistair's comment, 'that we didn't know about that [. . .] I thought there was a little more responsibility to the job, other than switching taps off – and you know it seems odd that if you made a mistake and left a tap on, which anyone can do – the matter would have perhaps been brought to a head, discussed and then, immediately, action would have been taken.'

All of this may strike some as banal and trivial but in fact the pursuit of how, if, and why a stopcock was not turned off led to a further surprising illumination, this time of the character and personality of the caretaker himself. What Mrs Hardy had to say about her husband I found of particular interest:

There was an advertisement, I think, for a job at the Maltings. And as he was interested in music and – actually at that time *there was a concept of having people involved with various arts and crafts,* but it was all going to become – it was all going to *belong* to the Aldeburgh Festival; and so my husband was going to be involved with that. [My emphasis.] The hall of course had been destroyed by fire [. . .] Well, of course it was rebuilt and they then realized they'd got to – they needed to be very sure of no further chance of fire, so they had to have someone there on the premises who would be knowledgeable of the building and have – liaise with the fire brigade, but also he would have other duties, you know, connected with the concerts. I mean, for instance, if a grand piano was coming, he [George] would be there, whatever was happening, to do with the Festival. And of course he was there every day while he was working there and so he would often see Ben and chat to him and Ben would play things, you know, on the piano in the actual hall and say, 'What d'you think about this?'; and you know it was really very nice. And of course he had the Tannoy system in his office, so that when the concerts were on he could hear every bit of the concert and – the involvement was – I mean, to be quite honest, I don't know *all* the things he did, but he was very familiar – he became familiar – with all the people from the English Opera Group. He used to come home and say, you know, 'So-and-so's doing so-and-so.' He didn't mind what he was doing there, because all the time he was surrounded by music and could hear it all the time.

Mr Hardy, it seemed, 'although he had had no musical training whatever', was able to play the piano 'by ear'. 'He could play little bits of all sorts of things. He went to see the film *The Glass Mountain*, when he was working away from home, once. When he came back he sat down and played it.' It was a gift, it seems, that, together with the proximity of pianos at Snape, resulted in musical encounters, on one occasion the caretaker at the keyboard, on another perhaps the composer.

This is just the kind of 'bond', if that's not too strong a word, that would have amused Britten and that he would have enjoyed, and it formed a significant part of what the Hardy family's recollections clearly suggest to me, a genuine and unusual rapport between Britten and his caretaker at the Maltings, the rupture of which would certainly have been a matter of sorrow to him. Furthermore, and perhaps of greater significance, it is clear from Mrs Hardy's memories that the appointment of her husband (who had formerly held senior positions in the construction industry) was in tune with Britten's and Pears's concept of the Maltings as an accommodating centre for the arts, not just music but 'people involved with various arts and crafts'. It was provision for those activities, a yet further expansion of the Maltings, with which Reiss was very possibly not wholly in sympathy; after all, he already had enough on his hands and very few other hands to render assistance. George Hardy could well have been not the right pair of hands to play the required role, whatever that was. But his caretaking competence is not at all what I am attempting to assess. It is, rather, to adumbrate what may have been the much more complex and intriguing matters involved in the caretaker's story than had previously been imagined; and that the friendship of Britten and Hardy, with its idiosyncratic musical dimension, may have been more fundamental to the strength of Britten's feelings about the unhappy affair than has been made clear elsewhere.

Alistair Hardy, for his part, when I put to him Reiss's description of his family's relationship with Britten commented, 'I don't think it's fair to say that we were aware of this extreme relationship as you describe; but then again you must understand that Ben was, of course, busy. He was pressured by other people [. . .] He was preoccupied, so it's not as if one felt that you could sit down and have a quiet moment.' But he went on to add, 'I think Britten saw my father's *sincerity* about the things that were being done and achieved and I think probably Ben, being at the centre of this thing, did get undivided attention; and you know if he said, "This is what I want to happen" – this is what happened.'

As for Alistair's participation – he was seventeen at the time – it was limited, by his own account, to the role of driver, a part-time job 'which covered a few [six to eight?] weeks during [. . .] the year [1970] that *Owen Wingrave* was filmed [for BBC TV at the Maltings]'. He continued:

Well, I suppose it was because I was young and not doing anything in particular, and I suppose Ben must have said to Father that he perhaps needed somebody to drive him from the Red House to the Maltings as and when required, and Peter was sometimes there also, of course – depending on who was doing what. And it was just very simply that.

His duties chiefly comprised 'running errands: going places in the car to pick things up. I *might* have picked other people up but it's bad memory. I can't actually remember.' And there was the provision of a jar of peppermints, always to be kept in the car: 'If he got frustrated he would ask for the peppermints and I would have to run down the hall and get them. Yes. That's what he did. He would crunch them and get a little bit stroppy with everyone.' (Philip Reed has observed that in some of the publicity photographs of Britten conducting the rehearsals of *Wingrave* the ubiquitous jar of peppermints is clearly visible.)

It was Alistair, incidentally, who gathered holly and ivy from the moat at Snape to decorate the windows of Paramore for the TV production of *Wingrave* in the Maltings. I asked him if he were aware of Britten taking an interest in him, in what his future was to be. He replied:

Oh yes, I think he did. I think it's fair to say that I probably didn't – you know, wasn't very worthy of the advice at the time in that I, you know, I was young and not *sure* in which direction I was going and he was, as *you* said, quite a good father figure; inasmuch – and indeed because he wasn't a father, he, you know, he was probably listened to a bit more too. He took an interest, yes. Yes, we did talk about that sort of thing. I mean, I had supper there with him and Peter Pears, at least once if not twice and, you know, it was a great experience really to be – you know. He *did* take an interest and actually he, on one occasion, just before I went off, before the whole thing stopped and – but it was only ever going to be a temporary arrange-ment – Ben said, 'Look, I'm really sorry to see you go, that this has to come to an end.' He said, 'Can I – would you like to borrow some money to start a business of some description? [. . .] Can I help you? Can I give you some money so that you can start – something?'

He added a little bit later:

I think he was concerned that I was going to go off without a job and be off the rails. I didn't notice that at the time. Isn't that extraordinary? How stupid. So I wasn't worried, but perhaps other people were. Perhaps he was one of them. I must have given him cause for concern, I think.

And on the more general relationship with the family:

I'm sure somebody in his position could at times feel isolated because of his fame and his position and his not being able to go out and just have a chat in the pub with somebody. Doesn't happen. So perhaps people like myself, were the sort of people that, you know, perhaps *could* go to the pub and have a pint.

There exists at BPL a very slim file of letters exclusively consisting of con-ventional recommendations of Alistair by Britten to various prospective employers.

Alistair was certainly not alone in his experience. There were other young men – sons of parents who were themselves friends of Britten and Pears – who similarly made themselves useful; their help was generously acknowledged and sometimes accompanied by concern about their futures. Once again we encounter Britten in fatherly guise. For the rest, the central image of the 'family' apart, there are more divergences than parallels when one juxtaposes the Maud and Hardy histories. Both ended unhappily, though in 1971 there was no one about to play the role of Bobbie Shaw in 1949. On the other hand, when scanning the diverse recollections of those involved I sometimes sensed the uncomfortable presence of a seam of older-generation homophobia among some who were close to Britten and Pears and the affairs of the Festival and the hall, a deep-seated, prejudiced assumption that, albeit unconsciously in some – perhaps most – cases, none the less directly influenced how the Hardy debacle was 'read' and conclusions arrived at, that the caretaker's son, for example, about whom, inevitably, Britten and Pears were 'crazy', must have been the model for Tadzio; while, at a later stage, this preoccupation with Britten's homosexuality, observed and commented on, often critically, in his life as symptomatic of his life, has been transformed into a blunt instrument of interpretation.[47]

Before rounding off this extraordinary tale, and as a result of my own scrutiny of the Hardy file, I want to introduce a final and important perspective, this time taking account of another and very different 'family' altogether, of which Britten (along with Pears) was a member: the Management Committee of the Aldeburgh Festival.

In his letter to Britten (see entry for 5 July 1971 in the table above) George Hardy, seeking a meeting with the composer, wrote 'On Friday last Stephen Reiss informed me that Aldeburgh Festival no longer required my services [. . .] [He] also told me that the reason for my dismissal was due to a lot of people had complained that they could not work with me [. . .] Now we are high and dry, without a word of warning, I am without a job and without a home.' Hardy's letter forms part of a file at BPL inscribed in Britten's own hand 'Affaire G.H.'. This was clearly made available to Carpenter who gives his own account of Reiss's resignation in his biography. The missing dimension there is the Hardys' chronicle of the fracas, and it is that, along with a calculation of its significance, that I have tried earlier to provide.

A letter to Britten from Reiss, dated 6 July, followed on the heels of Hardy's; Britten and Pears were on the vacation they always took after the end of the Aldeburgh Festival, on this occasion at Horham, and were apparently inaccessible. Reiss wrote, 'I do hope that you will understand about George Hardy. Apart from the fact that everyone encouraged me to take immediate action [. . .] there were personal reasons [i.e. Hardy's preparations to move with his family into a flat at the Maltings] which made it virtually impossible not to disclose my views to George.' Reiss informed him, so the letter runs, that he was going to recommend to the [Festival's Management] Committee that 'he would have to go. In fact this is all that I did. I did not dismiss him; I simply said that I was bound to tell him of the report that I was going to make.' (It is a somewhat fine distinction, one might think, that Reiss was drawing.) He then goes on to say, 'I was fully

47   In this particular respect one cannot but reflect on the impoverished state modish commentators pursuing this line of approach would find themselves in if it were not for the rich legacy of Britten's operas – relatively easy game for those with an almost obsessional drive to prove that the composer's sexuality was a virtually dominant conditioning factor. The long list that comprises Britten's orchestral and chamber music – genres that include some of the most significant works he was to produce – are paid relatively scant attention.

aware, of course, that if it had been merely a matter between him and me the choice [as to who should be asked or compelled to resign, Hardy or Reiss] might perfectly well have gone the other way. But, in fact, right up to the end, I have always been the only one (at the administrative level) to defend him.' That last remark makes entirely comprehensible Alistair's remark, 'But my recollection of it [his father's dismissal] was that Stephen was *against* it.'

I have already insisted that it has not been my intention to debate the question of Hardy's competence. However, from letters addressed to Britten by members of the Management Committee, it is clear that there was widespread dissatisfaction with his performance (it seems that the 'water' incident had led to the pit at the hall being twice flooded). But Hardy, efficient or inefficient, was not the real issue. It was Reiss's own future that had come under scrutiny and increasing strain, that had become inextricably enmeshed by a strange quirk of fate with the Hardy affair, and was now itself at stake. It was his 'dismissal' of the caretaker (in whatever form it took) that led to a climactic eruption, the scale of which can be judged by Britten's and Pears's threat to resign from the Management Committee, which would have effectively and publicly dissociated them from the Festival and its management. A handwritten, four-page letter of 8 July to Rosamund Strode registers the exceptional anger and disillusion that seems to have fuelled Britten's response to the turmoil he describes:

We have had some nice days in Horham, but unfortunately the affaire George Hardy, with all its quicksand feeling of ungraspable tensions, has rather coloured it. We have been backwards & forwards here, with each visit [to Aldeburgh] producing a new letter or telephone call. However, I have decided to cut out of all Management concerns now – P.P. will go on, but generally the Red House will do much less, & let'm stew in their own juice! I'm hoping Sue [Phipps, Pears's niece, at the time Britten's and Pears's agent] will take on more of the go-between stuff between us & them (& I've made a new plea for a music editor for the [programme] book) – but it makes me feel sick even to write about it; we'll talk a bit about it when we are back from our Henley–Sussex–London trip (it's good to be getting away in spite of Horham being heavenly in glorious weather).

[...]

Sorry about the green ink – it matches my mood!

One cannot but remark on the image he introduces of 'us and them', with its powerful echo of the concept of outside(r)/inside(r) which I have earlier suggested to be one of the main preoccupations of Britten's since his youth. It would have been hard, none the less, to predict that during the closing years of his life it would have surfaced in the context of the 'family' that was Aldeburgh and its Festival: 'let'm stew in their own juice' makes this letter unique of its kind.

The resignation was, of course, withdrawn, but for Reiss, despite his protestations to Lady Cranbrook, the Chairman of the Aldeburgh Festival Council in 1971, that he 'fully realized [Britten and Pears] were fed up' with him, and that he 'did awfully want to get on' with them both, there was, he came to realize, finally no other option but for him to resign; which he did. It is thus that a curiously ironic, even tragi-comic bit of Aldeburgh history was brought to an end, a history that yet again prompts the question: Happy Families? – whether it is Britten and the Hardys one has in mind, or the 'family' of friends and colleagues who managed the Festival. What it does demonstrate undeniably, and above all if considered in the light of the factual account of Britten's hectic creativity that the table above represents, is the daunting, seething chemistry of the interaction between an artist's life and work, which denies all possibility of simplistic explanations.

A last word: in the file of letters inscribed 'Affaire G.H.', there is no mention of Alistair; and a letter that Britten wrote in reply to George Hardy's letter to him of 5 July, from which I have quoted, seems to be lost. That no copy exists suggests that it must have been handwritten. Mrs Hardy's comment on it was brief but revealing: 'Yes, . . . puzzled . . .' At Christmas, after her husband's departure, there was a card from Peter Pears (a photograph of Snape and the estuary). 'How are things going?' he asked. The rest was silence.

If I have accomplished nothing else, I hope that I may have brought retrospective recognition to a rapport between the composer and his caretaker in the early 1970s that perhaps should not have been cast into oblivion for ever, and which for me was memorably – if haltingly – remembered in 1999 by Mrs Hardy:

MRS H He would sometimes play to my husband and then say, 'What do you think?' [. . .] They were really – That's why he loved [the job] so, you know. They seemed to be alone a lot, you see. I mean he'd be at the concert hall often when it was empty and my husband was the only one there.

DM You mean, Britten would try something out on the piano?

MRS H Yes [. . .] and then, he would [say to George], just someone without any knowledge or anything [. . .] 'What do you think?'

Towards the end of my dialogue with Stephen Reiss – the relevant excerpt appears on pp. 36–8 above – I found myself discussing with him the idea and image of obligatory 'sacrifice'. If there were one person with whom it might be meaningfully associated, it would have to be Britten himself, whose life, from the start to its ailing end, was sacrificed to music. Nothing, ultimately, was allowed to stand between him and his compulsive creativity, not himself, nor the demands or needs even, of others.

That there were 'sacrifices' of others along the way is indisputable; Reiss himself is an example, one who one might think merited, at the very least, a more considerate exit. Likewise, Basil Douglas, Reiss's predecessor as

General Manager of the English Opera Group.[48] There is no question that those colleagues of Britten's and Pears's who filled crucial posts in organizations such as the English Opera Group or Aldeburgh Festival were vulnerable to what may appear to have been exceptionally arbitrary severance or dismissal. The longish list of departures and attendant unhappinesses – of varying degrees of intensity – speaks for itself, and it is certainly not my intention indiscriminately to 'defend' Britten from the accusations of bad faith that have sometimes been aimed at him (amply documented in HCBB and elsewhere), nor excuse the hurt that was sometimes done.

On the other hand, having said that, I think none the less that one has to remember – the more easily, of course, if one has not been personally involved – that the performing arts have never been less than an area of high risk, high temperature and extreme volatility. These perils were scarcely unique to Aldeburgh. On the contrary, long before Britten was born or the Aldeburgh Festival thought of, an extensive international history – think only of Mozart and Salzburg, Wagner and Bayreuth, Mahler and Vienna, Stravinsky and more or less anywhere – confirms that abrupt explosions, exits and embarrassing confrontations are integral to the performing arts, and as much the source of success as failure. The rows, ejections, separations, disappointments and recriminations continue to resound, even in the wake of a long stretch of historical time. But was it not ever thus in the arts, that the hot seat occupied by administrators, without warning or the proprieties of a trial, can suddenly assume the function of an electric chair? (In this context it is ironic to recall that in 1952 Britten was invited to take on the job of Music Director at Covent Garden.) In short, it seems a shade unrealistic to expect an ineffable placidity to characterize an organization that had the good luck to be guided by a man of genius.

When heads rolled there was undoubted anguish, and Stephen Reiss was certainly not alone in thinking of himself as having been 'sacrificed'. In the shorter term, or on the shorter view, perhaps there is some justification for the use of that image to match an unpalatable succession of exits. 'Signore, it is the time of departure,' the Hotel Manager remarks in the final scene of *Death in Venice*, words that might well serve as a rubric for that still unwritten chapter in the history of Aldeburgh dedicated to the Festival and the English Opera Group, along with the Hotel Porter's preceding observation, 'First one goes, then another goes, then five go – *é vero, capo*?' But in the longer term, and on an altogether broader view, the concept of 'sacrifice' in the context of Britten's own life and work takes on a meaning somewhat removed from domestic or organizational strife. It was recognized by very

---

48 See Maureen Garnham, *As I Saw It: Basil Douglas, Benjamin Britten and the English Opera Group, 1955–1957*.

many of those who worked closely with him throughout his life that it was his creativity to which he wholly subordinated himself and which ultimately defined the trajectory of the life of which biography seeks to give an account. The totality of the dedication bears witness to the uncompromising truth of that often quoted remark of Britten's made in reply at a tennis party to an acquaintance enquiring about his future: What, he was asked, was he going to be when he grew up. 'A composer,' he replied. 'Yes, but what else?' the interrogator insisted.[49] The subsequent career and life's work were to provide the answer: absolutely nothing else, though in the light of Britten's eventual multiple musical activities – festival and opera-company director, conductor, accompanist – perhaps it should be slightly differently expressed: composition was always to take precedence. The self-sacrifice was total, and if it involved the sacrifice of others, then sacrifices there had to be.

If there were one person who would have hated the premise on which this part of my text is based, it would have been Britten himself; talk of sacrifice he would have found unbearably pretentious. But keenly though I feel his reproving presence as I write, none the less I shall pursue the point because I believe it can help us to understand his attitude to – his assessment of, if you like – his own gifts. His letters amply document the famous work ethic that was a predominant feature of his life; that, for sure, would have been his preferred way of putting it. On the other hand, while the general principle of working hard is admirable in whomever it may be found, one cannot overlook in Britten's case the quite exceptional gifts with which, from childhood, he was prodigiously endowed and to the development and exploitation of which he made an unreserved, life-long commitment. It is as if, quite objectively, his finding himself to be in possession of rare talents placed upon him a conscious obligation not only to bring them to the maximum pitch of which he was capable – it is the already evident compulsion to refine, explore and exploit his gifts through ceaseless composition that makes the huge array of his so-called juvenilia so fascinating to study – but also to protect them.

This idea of protection surfaces, memorably, in the recollection of a fellow schoolboy at Britten's Lowestoft preparatory school, South Lodge, from the cricket pitch:

Ben and I became friends, being of the same age, added to the fact that I was Captain of the cricket side with Ben as my Vice. (I appear wearing the cap in the group photograph No. 35 in your book [PFL].) I was invited on occasions to his home for tea, when he and his mother might have a musical session [. . .] at the piano. Even at that tender age his talent was accepted with the expectation then that he would become a concert pianist. For this reason he always had to field in the

49   See EWB, p. 37.

deep and when a high ball was hit towards him the Headmaster, Captain Sewell, fearing for his fingers, would shout from the boundary, 'You're not to catch it, Britten! You're not to catch it!'!![50]

Captain Sewell and his school have had something of a bad press since Britten's death – though here again Carpenter[51] is cautious in the conclusions he draws – for which reason it is perhaps refreshing to read of an incident in which Sewell emerges in a role other than that of an enthusiastic flogger. If that were indeed the case, one has to remember that the culture of beating was prevalent in British prep and (most) public schools in the 1920s and 1930s to a degree that today is hard to imagine. But while I am happy to be able to show that there was, it seems, a caring side to Sewell's character, what is of greater interest, in relation to the course Britten's life was eventually to take, is Mr Lyon's own explanation of Sewell's warning shout, which reminds us that at this early stage Britten's promising future was expected to be that of a successful 'concert pianist'. But in fact the boy's inner life was already set on another course altogether, albeit one that did not manifest itself on the cricket field, and inevitably and understandably went largely unrecognized, except by his family and friends: composition. In retrospect, that commitment is already made explicit in Mr Lyon's cherished autograph album where what represented his cricketing friend is a tiny composition, signed by the composer and author of the text. The composer as a working, functioning entity was already, so to say, in place.

There is something a shade ironic about Captain Sewell's anxiety about Britten's hands in relation to his piano playing; for, as things turned out, there was a very real sense in which as his life progressed, Britten the composer had to protect himself from the demands of his own multiplicity of gifts, confining his activities as a pianist to those partners – across the whole span of his life – with whom he had a creative relationship, pre-eminently Pears, but also Joan Cross, Clifford Curzon, Nancy Evans, Kathleen Ferrier, Dietrich Fischer-Dieskau, Sviatoslav Richter, Mstislav Rostropovich, Galina Vishnevskaya, Sophie Wyss, etc., etc.: these partnerships in which Britten sat at the keyboard were tied in, often profoundly so, with his composing.

Likewise Britten the conductor, who was rarely permitted to encroach on Britten the composer, and then principally in the context of the Aldeburgh Festival or English Opera Group. This is not to underestimate the remarkable insights he brought to his interpretations (of other composers' music besides his own) or the power he had at his command to achieve his

50 Personal communication (24 October 1996) from Mr Alan Lyon, of Bristol, who has in his possession an album to which Benjamin Britten contributed a composition with words by C. B. Dacam, 'a young master at South Lodge', and Robert Britten, the elder brother, a pen and ink drawing.

51 See HCBB, pp. 21–2.

interpretative ends, a power all the more remarkable because so outwardly undemonstrative.[52]

It was indeed a multiplicity of gifts with which he was endowed, though, from a very early stage, there was little doubt in his mind about which 'gift' it was that he was to commit himself. I sometimes wonder if Captain Sewell's injunction did not continue to resonate in Britten's mind. Sewell could not have foreseen that it was a composer his vice-captain of the cricket team was to become, not a career pianist. But it was perhaps the idea of 'protection', of protecting his gift(s), that had its origins in Britten's early youth and was to take root and persist. It was a duty laid upon him, just as it was a duty, by means of incessant hard work, to develop the gift that he had been 'given'. I am far from suggesting that there was something mystical about this.[53] I am certain none the less that Britten's belief in the importance and benefits of exploiting Man's creativity – making the most of his spiritual life – was a profound one. If one were lucky enough to find oneself in possession of a creative gift, then it was also one's duty to protect it, a duty one owed one's fellows. Nor do I doubt that this idea of protection, whether consciously or unconsciously (Britten never spoke of it in my experience), had a role to play in the evolution of his pacifism and the fierce conviction with which he held it.

At the same time, I believe, he came to be conscious that because of his absolute opposition to violence, and thus his non-participation in the war of 1939–45, he had excluded himself from the immediate experience of events that shaped the post-war world and the lives and imaginations of countless of its inhabitants. This topic surfaces in an interview I undertook with Yehudi Menuhin in 1979,[54] when I was asking him specifically about

52 We are fortunate now in having access to a major series of performances conducted by Britten issued on CD in 1999 by BBC WorldWide ('The Britten Edition') and the further series ('BBC Legends' and 'Britten at Aldeburgh') released by the BBC and Decca in 2000 and after. Many, I think, will be surprised by the extent of his repertory and the stature of his conducting.

53 Or perhaps more specifically 'religious'. Britten's submission in 1942 to the wartime Tribunal for conscientious objectors (see Letters 375, 382 and 397) opened with the words, 'Since I believe that there is in every man the spirit of God', and then continued, 'I cannot destroy, and feel it my duty to avoid helping to destroy as far as I am able, human life.' There is little doubt – and this was my experience too – that Tribunals found it hard to accept a submission that lacked a conventional reference to Christian doctrine; and it may well have been that Britten was so advised and complied with the advice, which makes it the more striking (and courageous) that he went on to say, or had said on his behalf, that he did not believe in the Divinity of Christ and had not attended church for the previous five years, while reiterating (in his written submission), 'The whole of my life has been devoted to acts of creation [. . .] and I cannot take part in acts of destruction.' It could well have been that the unequivocal denial of belief in Christ's Divinity was responsible for the Tribunal on the first submission rejecting his application for exemption from call-up. His appeal, however, in which he argued that the Tribunal had 'failed to appreciate the religious background [sic] of my conscience, trying to tie me down too narrowly to a belief in the divinity of Christ', succeeded, and he was granted unconditional exemption. See also Letter XVI n. 6 and p. 94.

54 The interview took place during the filming of A Time There Was . . . , Tony Palmer's docu-

his visit to the concentration camps – Belsen and elsewhere – in 1945, when Britten had travelled with him, at his own urgent request, as his accompanist. He had in fact virtually insisted on displacing Gerald Moore who had originally been chosen to partner Menuhin.[55] I had asked Menuhin if he thought that this might not have been a way in which Britten were able retrospectively to share in the experience of the war. To which he responded:

I think so. I think so. I think he felt that he had denied himself as a British man, as one living in that era, had denied himself an essential experience which was part of his nation, was part of his people's experience, and by taking it as it were in one fell swoop, it wasn't spread over many years – it came with a terrific power. I think that must have been a part of the motive, I'm sure.

And continued, after exchanging a few words about the 1945 premiere of *Peter Grimes*,

Yes, yes, I'm sure that the theme [I had mentioned the opera's preoccupation with the theme of 'conflict and the tragic destiny of man'] engaged his mind and his heart . . . since he was a child, probably, because that was Ben. [. . .] His compassion was tremendous, but he had to have somehow *the reality, the physical evidence of it as well. I think he needed it.* [My emphasis.]

I am not for one moment proposing that once the war was over Britten suddenly started regretting that he had not taken part in it. But I find it extremely interesting, characteristic and revealing that while in no way modifying his stand against war, as expressed in his submission to the Tribunal for conscientious objectors – 'I cannot destroy, and feel it my duty to avoid helping to destroy, as far as I am able, human life' – he none the less felt compelled to acquaint himself with the reality of it, and as it happened, one of the most awful realities of it.

At the same time, I would suggest it was perhaps the confrontation with the reality of Belsen that finally generated the very long list of post-war works (of which *War Requiem* was of course a notable but by no means solitary example) in which and by which Britten saw to it that his creativity, which had enjoyed protection, was passionately dedicated to the cause of non-violence and peace.[56] It was thus, I believe, that he both guarded his gifts and discharged his obligations to humanity.

Protection of the 'gift' was not an issue of self-preservation or evidence of lack of courage but an affirmation of his belief that creativity had to take

---

mentary film of 1980, but no part of it finally was used. The omitted materials from the film have been generously given by Mr Palmer to BPL. The transcript of the Menuhin interview was made by Pamela Wheeler and Anne Surfling, to whose skills I am much indebted, likewise for the indispensable transcriptions of the interviews with Sir Humphrey Maud, Stephen Reiss, and with Alistair Hardy and Mrs Hardy.

55 See Letter 504 n. 4 and Letter 505.

56 In my contribution, 'Violent Climates', to MCCCBB, pp. 188–216, I have tried to give an account of all the music both pre- and post-war in which was manifest Britten's preoccupation with acts of violence, whether committed by individuals, the community or the state.

precedence over destruction and violence, on the longest view perhaps the only possible, albeit improbable, resolution of the world's ills. It is in no trite spirit, nor lack of awareness of others' suffering in and from war, that I believe that Captain Sewell's protective 'You're not to catch it, Britten! You're not to catch it!' is worth more than a moment's amused reflection. Is it not in fact a perfect example of the authentic – that is to say, unpredictable, unforeseeable, immeasurably intricate and often undocumented – interaction between life and art that I believe this volume of letters, annotations, and interpolations of oral history, like its predecessors, uniquely affirms, and in so doing, *temps perdu* – transformed – becomes *temps retrouvé*?

London – Basel – Horham – Bangkok – Brigueuil – London
July 1998–March 2004

I TOWARDS *PETER GRIMES*

JANUARY 1936–OCTOBER 1945

In the fourteen years since the publication of the first two volumes of *Letters from a Life*, a further 96 letters to 36 correspondents, spanning the period from 1932 to 1945, have come to light and now form part of BPL. These letters offer valuable new information and insight into Britten's life and compositional development during this period. Many of them are addressed to correspondents already represented in the first two volumes of the series: for example, Lennox Berkeley, Edith Britten, Peter Pears and Erwin Stein; others are to recipients entirely new to the collection, notably Leonard Bernstein, Peter Burra and Christopher Isherwood. Most significant of all is the wholly extraordinary collection of letters to the critic and writer Edward Sackville-West.

We have selected approximately one-third of the total number of new letters available to form a bridge from volumes 1 and 2 to volume 3, the principal text of which comprises letters for the period from 1946 to 1951. The first half follows the convention of letter text with accompanying editorial annotations; the second, however, breaks with this convention and is devoted to a detailed exploration of the previously little-known relationship between Britten and Sackville-West by Donald Mitchell, the text of which incorporates many quotations from their correspondence.

In Part 1 we have indicated the location of the new letters in relation to volumes 1 and 2 in square brackets below the correspondent's name. To maintain the continuity of this chronological sequence, we have repeated the three Britten letters from the Addenda to volume 2 (to Harry Farjeon, Stephen Spender and Rutland Boughton; see pp. 1334–6).

CHRONOLOGY 1913–1945

YEAR	EVENTS	COMPOSITIONS
1913	*22 November*: Born in Lowestoft	
c. 1919	First music lessons with his mother	First compositions
c. 1921	Piano and music theory lessons with Ethel Astle	
1922–23		Early piano compositions and songs
1923	Enters South Lodge Preparatory School, Lowestoft, as a day boy	
c. 1923	Viola lessons with Audrey Alston	
1925		Songs and piano music
1926	Passes finals (Grade VIII) Associated Board piano examinations with honours	
1928	Begins composition lessons with Frank Bridge; Enters Gresham's School, Holt; Begins piano lessons with Harold Samuel	Chamber and orchestral music *Quatre Chansons Françaises*
1929		*Rhapsody*, for string quartet, 'The Birds'
1930	Wins open scholarship to the Royal College of Music, London; Composition lessons with John Ireland; piano lessons with Arthur Benjamin	*Quartettino, A Wealden Trio, A Hymn to the Virgin, Elegy, Two Portraits, The Sycamore Tree* (*I saw three ships*)

YEAR	EVENTS	COMPOSITIONS
1931	First performance of *A Hymn to the Virgin* and *I saw three ships* (Lowestoft Choral Society); Wins Ernest Farrar Prize for composition	*Christ's Nativity* (*Thy King's Birthday*), Twelve Variations, String Quartet in D, *Plymouth Town*
1932	Cobbett Prize for *Phantasy* in F minor; First performance (Macnaghten–Lemare concert) and publication of Three Two-part Songs	*Phantasy* in F minor, Three Two-part Songs, Double Concerto, *Sinfonietta*, Op. 1, *Phantasy*, Op. 2
1933	First performance of *Sinfonietta* (Macnaghten–Lemare concert) and broadcast (BBC); First broadcast of *Phantasy* in F minor and *Phantasy*, Op. 2; Conducts *Sinfonietta* at RCM; BBC tries out *A Boy was Born*; Wins Ernest Farrar Prize; Passes ARCM and leaves RCM	*A Boy was Born*, Op. 3, Two Part-songs, *Alla Quartetto Serioso*
1934	First performances of *A Boy was Born*, *Simple Symphony* and *Holiday Diary*; Attends ISCM Festival in Florence, where *Phantasy*, Op. 2, is performed; Father dies after a long illness; Travels in Europe with mother and meets Erwin Stein in Vienna	*Simple Symphony*, Op. 4, *Te Deum* in C, *Jubilate Deo* in E♭, *Holiday Diary*, Op. 5
1935	Begins association with GPO Film Unit and Group Theatre; Meets W. H. Auden	*Two Insect Pieces*, Suite, Op. 6, *Friday Afternoons*, Op. 7; Films include *The King's Stamp* and *Coal Face*
1936	Signs exclusive publishing contract with Boosey & Hawkes, London; Joins permanent staff of GPO Film Unit	*Russian Funeral*, *Our Hunting Fathers*, Op. 8, *Soirées Musicales*, Op. 9, Two Ballads

YEAR	EVENTS	COMPOSITIONS
	Attends ISCM Festival in Barcelona, where Suite, Op. 6, is performed; First performance of *Our Hunting Fathers* at Norwich	*Temporal Variations*; Films include *Night Mail*, *Peace of Britain*, *Love from a Stranger*, *The Way to the Sea*
1937	Mother dies; Friendship with Peter Pears begins; Buys the Old Mill, Snape; *Bridge Variations* performed at Salzburg Festival; First performance of *On This Island*	*Variations on a Theme of Frank Bridge*, Op. 10, *On This Island*, Op. 11, *Mont Juic*, Op. 12 (with Lennox Berkeley); Theatre includes *The Ascent of F6*, *Pageant of Empire*, *Out of the Picture*; Radio includes *King Arthur*, *The Company of Heaven*, *Hadrian's Wall*
1938	Moves to 43 Nevern Square sw5 with Peter Pears and to Old Mill, shared with Berkeley; Attends ISCM Festival in London and meets Aaron Copland; First performance of Piano Concerto at Proms with composer as soloist	Piano Concerto, Op. 13, *Advance Democracy*; Theatre includes *On the Frontier*; Radio includes *The World of the Spirit*
1939	First performance of *Ballad of Heroes*; Moves to 67 Hallam Street w1 with Pears; *29 April*: leaves UK with Pears for North America; *9 May*: arrives in Quebec; *27 June*: travels to New York; *21 August*: Britten and Pears take up residence with the Mayers; *3 September*: Second World War begins; First performance of *Young Apollo*	*Ballad of Heroes*, Op. 14, *Young Apollo*, *A.M.D.G.*, Violin Concerto, Op. 15, *Les Illuminations*, Op. 18, *Canadian Carnival*, Op. 19; Theatre: *Johnson over Jordan*; Radio: *The Sword in the Stone*

YEAR	EVENTS	COMPOSITIONS
1940	First complete performance of *Les Illuminations* in London; First performance of Violin Concerto, in New York; Ill with streptococcal infection; Britten and Pears move to 7 Middagh Street, New York	*Sinfonia da Requiem*, Op. 20, *Diversions*, Op. 21, *Seven Sonnets of Michelangelo*, Op. 22, *Introduction and Rondo alla Burlesca*, Op. 23 No. 1; Radio: *The Dark Valley*
1941	First performances of *Sinfonia da Requiem*, *Paul Bunyan* and String Quartet No. 1; Visit to Escondido, California; Encounters poetry of George Crabbe; US enters Second World War	*Paul Bunyan*, Op. 17, *Matinées Musicales*, Op. 24, *Mazurka Elegiaca*, Op. 23 No. 2, String Quartet No. 1 in D, Op. 25, *An American Overture*, *Scottish Ballad*, Op. 26
1942	First performances of *Diversions*, *Michelangelo Sonnets*, *Hymn to St Cecilia* and *A Ceremony of Carols*; Commission by Koussevitzky Foundation of *Peter Grimes*; Britten and Pears return to UK and register as conscientious objectors	*Hymn to St Cecilia*, Op. 27, *A Ceremony of Carols*, Op. 28, *Folk Song Arrangements* vol. 1 British Isles, *Folk Song Arrangements* vol. 2 France
1943	First performance of *Serenade*; Moves to St John's Wood High Street; In hospital with measles	*Serenade*, Op. 31, *Prelude and Fugue*, Op. 29, *Rejoice in the Lamb*, Op. 30, *The Ballad of Little Musgrave and Lady Barnard*; Radio: *The Rescue*
1944	Begins work on *Peter Grimes*	*Festival Te Deum*, Op. 32; Radio: *A Poet's Christmas*
1945	First performances of *Peter Grimes*, String Quartet No. 2 and *Donne Sonnets*; *May*: VE Day; Concert tour with Yehudi Menuhin of German concentration camps	*Peter Grimes*, Op. 33, *The Holy Sonnets of John Donne*, Op. 35, String Quartet No. 2, Op. 36, *The Young Person's Guide to the Orchestra*, Op. 34; Theatre: *This Way to the Tomb*; Radio: *The Dark Tower*

THE CORRESPONDENCE

1 **To Harry Farjeon**[1]
[vol. 1, p. 408; after Diary for January 1936]

Flat no. 2, West Cottage Road, West End Lane, N.W.6.[2]

Jan 6th 1936

Dear Mr Farjeon,

Thank you for writing to me about my 'Boy was Born'. I am glad you liked the work; I think it was a good show that evening.[3]

I cannot promise that I shall go on 'like that' – as you say – always. One grows up, I find. And even now after four years or so I find that there is a lot in the work one wouldn't do nowadays.

However – I hope you won't be disappointed!

Yours,

BENJAMIN BRITTEN

1 English composer (1878–1948). Farjeon was a pupil of Landon Ronald and later studied with Frederick Corder at the Royal Academy of Music, London, where he was eventually to teach harmony and composition. Among his works were three operettas. He wrote many piano pieces for young players, and his sister Eleanor (1881–1965) was the well-known children's writer.

In *Friday Afternoons*, Britten had set a poem by Eleanor Farjeon, 'Jazz-Man' (No. 10): the song was written on 15 November 1933. She later attended the first performance of *Peter Grimes* and wrote to the composer to thank him for it. Later still, in 1965, at the age of eighty-four, she wrote again with some recollections of a meeting at Sadler's Wells during an interval in the second performance of the opera:

[. . .] on getting back my breath after the first Act [I] stumbled downstairs and booked for all the other performances. I seem to remember [your] stammering 'Is it all right?' when I reintroduced myself. I stammeringly suggested that it was.

The letter ends: 'Thank you for filling my old years with joys and wonders.'

2 The flat that Britten shared with his sister Beth and their family friend Kathleen Mead from autumn 1935 (see Letter 71 n. 9).

3 17 December 1935, on which date Britten's set of choral variations *A Boy was Born* received its first concert performance. Britten's diary entry is quoted in Letter 72 n. 2.

II To Peter Burra[1]

[vol. 1, p. 427; after Letter 82]

Biltmore, Pole Barn Lane, Frinton-on-Sea[2]
June 22nd 1936

Dear Peter,

I am very sorry not to have answered your letter before this. But I am working very hard here – slaving against time to get a work finished.[3]

I liked the photo & I am very glad to have it. Mine have also come out pretty well.[4] When I get to town next week I'll have the best developed & send them to you.

I hope you enjoyed your further stay in Barcelona.[5] I suppose you are very fluent in the tongue now.

I have been here for about a month now – working very hard. I have got a hut in Cornwall[6] for July where I am going to bury myself. A pleasant thought.

We couldn't have had a worse evening for listening to 'Jonah'.[7] As well as the extreme unpleasantness of the atmospherics we were in great danger of being struck by lightning, by continuing to use the aerial. However we survived to enjoy it a lot.

Hope you are well.

Yours,

BENJAMIN BRITTEN

1 Peter Burra (1909–1937), writer and critic, a close friend of Peter Pears (they were at school together; see PFL, plate 87). He died in an aeroplane accident on 27 April 1937; his death and the sorting out of his effects cemented Britten's and Pears's friendship. See also Diary for 13 March 1937, n. 1, and the obituary in the *Lancing College Magazine* (June 1937), p. 47, in which the anonymous writer quotes from a letter that appeared in *The Times* shortly after Burra's untimely death: 'He was a man of great personal charm, infectious enthusiasm, and considerable artistic discernment.'

Burra contributed a review of Rupert Doone's Group Theatre production of *The Agamemnon of Aeschylus* in the translation by Louis MacNeice to the *Group Theatre Paper* (November 1936), p. 2. Of Britten's incidental music he writes that it 'seemed [. . .] completely successful – homogenous, unobtrusive but adequate and thoroughly appropriate'. A complete run of the short-lived *Group Theatre Paper* (June 1936–January 1937) is held at BPL.

2 The house to which Britten's mother had moved in February 1936 after the death of her husband two years earlier. See also Letter 74 n. 6.

3 *Our Hunting Fathers.* The orchestral song-cycle was due to receive its first performance that autumn in the Norfolk and Norwich Triennial Music Festival. See also Diary for 25 September 1936.

4 Britten's photograph album from this period includes eight pages of images taken in Barcelona. One of the snaps is of the folk dancers at the 'Mont Juic Festival' (see Letter VII n. 1). Three of the photographs Britten took while in Barcelona (see n. 5 below) are reproduced in PFL, plates 82–4; plate 83 includes Burra and Berkeley.

5 Britten, Burra and Berkeley all met for the first time at the ISCM Festival in Barcelona, which Burra was covering for *The Times* and the *Monthly Musical Record*. In 'The Barcelona Festival', *Monthly Musical Record*, 66 (June 1936), pp. 107–8, Burra wrote:

> Only two English composers were included in the Festival, but they represented us well: Lennox Berkeley and Benjamin Britten. Evidently neither of them is particularly interested in being English and they are equally far from looking for their inspiration in theory. In fact their work belonged to the small body which seemed to have its roots in genuine individual character [...]

6 Britten spent the summer of 1936 staying in a hut in the grounds of Ethel Nettleship's home at Crantock, Newquay (see Letter 84 n. 1), where he continued to work on *Our Hunting Fathers* and studied Beethoven and Mahler. Lennox Berkeley was his guest for two weeks.

7 Lennox Berkeley's oratorio, composed 1933–5, the first performance of which had been given at Broadcasting House, London, by Joan Cross (soprano), Jan van der Gucht (tenor) and William Parsons (bass), and the BBC Chorus and Orchestra conducted by Clarence Raybould, and broadcast by the BBC on 19 June. Among those present in the audience was Peter Burra, for whom Berkeley had obtained a ticket.

Berkeley sent Britten a score on 18 June in readiness for the following day's premiere to which Britten listened while staying in Frinton:

> [...] after dinner & then in spite of a colossal thunderstorm nearby, try & listen to Lennox' Jonah from B.B.C. From what one could tell (& having score of course) there are some very good things in it. To its advantage it is under Stravinsky's influence of course, but the harmony is extremely personal. A weakness is a comparative dullness in the vocal line. Some of the choral writing is extremely beautiful – especially at the end.

Britten attended a further performance at the Leeds Festival on 7 October 1937: see Letter 112 n. 1. See also Peter Dickinson, *The Music of Lennox Berkeley*, 2nd edn, pp. 28–33. Professor Dickinson's assessment of the oratorio includes a previously unpublished letter from Berkeley (23 June 1936) in response to one from Britten which is now lost.

III **To Peter Burra**
[vol. 1, p. 432; after Letter 84]

Quarryfield, Crantock, Newquay, Cornwall
July 10th 1936

Dear Peter,

Here are the photos I promised. Some didn't come out very well –
something also wrong with my shutter – but these are the best of the
bunch.

I came down here to work last Sunday, & it is frightfully quiet – just
what I wanted – but the weather has been appalling – hail & wind & rain
practically all the time. However as it isn't much inducement to go out, it
is probably a good thing & I have done a tremendous amount of work.

Lennox[1] may come down here for a few days later on. I saw him once
or twice when I was in town – but it was only for a short time. I shall be
back there in September when we must definitely meet.

Yours ever,
BENJAMIN BRITTEN

1 Lennox Randal Francis Berkeley (1903–1989), English composer, educated
at Gresham's School in Norfolk and at Oxford University, and a student of
Nadia Boulanger in Paris, 1927–32. He was knighted in 1974. See also Letter 86
n. 2; IC1/2; Peter Dickinson, *The Music of Lennox Berkeley*, 2nd edn, and
Michael Berkeley, 'We lived in a secret, intoxicating world', *Guardian* (10
February 2003). In 2003 Lady Berkeley and the Lennox Berkeley Estate
deposited the Berkeley Family Papers on loan at BPL.

Britten and Berkeley first met in Barcelona in 1936 and became close
friends, a relationship that was consolidated by their work together on a
joint composition, *Mont Juic* (see Letter VII n. 1) and by their shared occupancy of the Old Mill at Snape from 1938. That same year Britten dedicated
his Piano Concerto to Berkeley, while Berkeley reciprocated by dedicating
his *Introduction and Allegro* for two pianos to Britten. Post-war they
remained close, with Berkeley's music frequently performed at Aldeburgh,
while the English Opera Group gave three of Berkeley's operas – *A Dinner
Engagement* (1954), *Ruth* (1956) and *Castaway* (1967) – as well as the *Stabat
Mater*.

During the 1920s and 1930s, Berkeley had several homosexual relationships and it is clear that during 1936 and 1937 he saw himself as a potential
partner of Britten's. When Berkeley left Crantock on 30 July 1936, Britten
noted in his diary:

He is an awful dear – very intelligent & kind – & I am very attached to him, even
after this short time. In spite of his avowed sexual weakness for young men of my age
& form – he is considerate & open, & we have come to an agreement on that subject.

The following year, when staying with Berkeley in Gloucestershire, Britten
recorded in his diary for 11 April:

He is a dear & I am very, very fond of him; nevertheless, it is a comfort that we can arrange sexual matters to at least _my_ satisfaction.

In 1937 Berkeley set two poems of Auden's – 'Lay your sleeping head, my love' and 'Night covers up the rigid land' – both of which he dedicated to Britten, whose diary reveals a picture of Berkeley as pursuer and Britten as the pursued. The second of these two poems was also set by Britten in 1937.

The crisis in the relationship came in the autumn of 1938, a few months after they had begun to live together at Snape. Berkeley's declaration of love for Britten would seem to have been precipitated by Britten's close attachment to Wulff Scherchen (see Letter xvi n. 4), itself at its height during the summer and autumn of 1938. Berkeley was deeply affected by Britten's rejection. This is borne out by his many letters to Britten from the end of 1938 and throughout 1939.

iv To Edith Britten [1]
[vol. 1, p. 435; after Letter 85]
[*Postcard: Porth Johe, Cornwall*]

[Quarryfield, Crantock]
[Postmarked 16 July 1936]

Everything is still going well here. I'm enjoying life a lot & the scoring is leaping ahead (half done already!) so I shall be – with luck – beautifully free in August for you. I hope you are enjoying Stroud[2] – Just had a letter from Lennox Berkeley from there – Isn't it tragic about our flood in Hampstead?[3] Poor old Beth.[4] I'll write a letter later but funnily enough there's so little time! Love to Flo.

Much Love
BENJ

Write occasionally please!

1 Edith Rhoda Britten, née Hockey (1872–1937), Britten's mother. See also Letter 1 n. 1 and 1c1/2.

2 Britten's aunt, Florence Hay Britten (1875–1956), his father's elder sister, lived at Whiteshill, near Stroud, Gloucestershire. See also Diary for 27 May 1931, n. 1.

3 Britten's Diary for 14 July 1936: 'Beth writes to say there's been a tank leak in the flat & gives a lurid description of ceiling's falling – carpets up etc. in the sitting room. It is hard for her to have to cope with it alone [...]'

4 Charlotte Elizabeth (Beth) Britten (1909–1989), Britten's sister. She married Kit Welford on 22 January 1938. Her memoir, *My Brother Benjamin* (EWB), was published in 1986. See also Letter 1 n. 1 and 1c1/2.

v To Peter Burra

[vol. 1, p. 443; after Diary for 19 September 1936]
[*Postcard*]

[Flat 2, West Cottage Road, West End Lane, London, NW6]
[Postmarked 20 September 1936]

Thank you for your letter – sorry I haven't answered it before but I have been off my head with work! Very glad to hear you are coming to Norwich, next Friday[1] – but the outlook is black for me at the moment. I had an abominable rehearsal last night,[2] & only 1½ more to come. Things may change, but I am doubtful. Come & see me on Friday & condole with me if necessary! I saw Dorothy[3] the other day & she said she'd been with you. Let me know if you want names of hotels etc. in Norwich. I might be able to find something.

BENJAMIN

1   For the premiere of *Our Hunting Fathers*. Britten's programme note for this performance and the preview from the *Eastern Daily Press* are reproduced in Diary for 21 September 1936, n. 1 (and see PKBM, p. 359). Press notices for the song-cycle are reproduced in Diary for 26 September 1936, n. 1.

Berkeley, who was in Paris at the time of the premiere of *Our Hunting Fathers*, wrote to Burra on 13 October:

I had a long letter from Benjamin about a week ago – he seems to have been pleased with the performance at Norwich, though he does not think the work was understood on the whole. Of course that was to be expected; although I have never heard it, I know the work fairly well, and having studied the full score I like it immensely, especially the beginning and the slow movement (Messalina), but I admit that it wouldn't be easy to follow at first hearing, and Auden's words, beautiful as they are, don't make it any easier to understand for the uninitiated.

He had already written admiringly about the work in two previous letters to Burra. On 16 July 1936:

I saw Benjamin before I left London – he played me his new work which is to be done at the Norwich Festival in September. I think it is extremely good, and far the most important thing he has done so far.

And on 2 August, following his stay with Britten in Cornwall:

I spent a very pleasant few days with Benjamin. [. . .] I am more than ever impressed by his talent which I think is very great, and his technical proficiency is extraordinary. I have read his new work – I think it ought to make rather a sensation. It is not only exciting but a lot of it is very beautiful. We played some of it as a duet from the full score on an awful old piano!

From Paris, on 22 October 1936, Berkeley wrote to Britten:

Many thanks for your letter and for the copy of [the vocal score of] *Our Hunting Fathers* which I have read and played to myself a lot. I like it all, but I like best the slow parts in the opening, Messalina, and the last movement. The funeral march is grand music. The whole thing is full of feeling and life, and no English composer, to my way of thinking, can do anything as good – or if there is one, he is keeping it very dark! I have lent my copy to Nadia Boulanger who is very keen to read it, having heard of you but never seen or heard a note of your music.

2   Britten's description of this rehearsal appears in Diary for 19 September 1936.

3   Dorothy Wadham, Secretary of the ISCM, with whom Britten had travelled to Barcelona. He had first met her in 1934 in connection with the performance of his *Phantasy* quartet at the Florence ISCM Festival.

VI   To Peter Burra

[vol. 1, p. 483; after Diary for 15 March 1937]
[*Postcard*]

[559 Finchley Road, London, NW3]
[Postmarked 16 March 1937]

The Forster article[1] is <u>first-rate</u>. I haven't had time to read the other yet. Christopher Ish.[2] was here last night until very late, & we had a grand time. Told me a lot more about E.M.F.[3]

I hear from Dorothy that you enjoyed the romp last night. Hope you didn't feel too sad.

My leg is getting on well,[4] but I haven't been out today. I <u>may</u> see you tomorrow night – not sure yet. Anyhow keep Sunday evening for Left Theatre revue.[5] Is it too bourgeous [*sic*] to say thank you for a <u>lovely</u> weekend?

Love,
BENJ

1   This was probably Burra's essay 'The Novels of E. M. Forster', which had been published in *The Nineteenth Century and After*, 116 (1934), pp. 581–94. Burra's other essay might have been about the Oratory of All Souls (the Sandham Memorial Chapel) at Burghclere, the chapel decorated with murals by Stanley Spencer; Britten had visited the chapel while spending the weekend with Burra: see Diary for 14 March 1937. Burra's drafts and typescript of this essay were purchased by BPL in 1991.

2   Christopher Isherwood (1904–1986), English novelist and writer, a friend of Britten from the 1930s and a collaborator with W. H. Auden on a number of plays and other literary projects for which Britten wrote incidental music. Isherwood emigrated to the US in 1939 with Auden and took US citizenship in 1946. For the last thirty years of his life he lived in Santa Monica, California, with his partner, the portrait painter Don Bachardy. Bachardy's drawing of Peter Pears (November 1976) is reproduced on the jacket of TPP.

Isherwood is probably best remembered for his autobiographical Berlin stories written in the 1930s (e.g. *Mr Norris Changes Trains* and *Goodbye to Berlin*), which formed the basis of the play and the film *I am a Camera*; this in turn was adapted in 1972 as the highly successful musical (and film) *Cabaret*. In later years he became interested in Eastern philosophies. See also Letter 35 n. 1; the *Times* obituary (6 January 1986); Stephen Spender, 'The Secret of Issyvoo', *Observer Review* (12 January 1986); Donald Mitchell's account of a visit to Isherwood in 1978, 'Down There on a Visit: A Meeting with Christopher Isherwood', *London Magazine*, 32/1–2 (April/May 1992), pp. 80–87, reprinted in DMCN, pp. 441–9, and Peter Parker, *Isherwood*.

In his Diary for 15 March 1937, Britten writes: 'Christopher Isherwood comes to dinner – a grand person; unaffected, extremely amusing & devastatingly intelligent.' Isherwood and Britten remained friends right until the end of the composer's life, though, with Isherwood residing in California and Britten in Suffolk, they saw each other only occasionally. In an article published in the *Guardian*, 'Christopher's jungle book: Christopher Isherwood discusses his autobiography with Christopher Ford' (30 March 1977), p. 10, Isherwood recalled their final meeting, in the summer of 1976:

Last summer David Hockney, Don Bachardy, and I went for a drive, up to the north of Scotland, and one of the places we stopped off at was Aldeburgh. I knew Ben was ill, but I didn't know how ill he was. Any emotion was bad for him. He was so moved at seeing us again that he could hardly trust himself to speak. The others left us, and Ben and I sat in a room together, not speaking, just holding hands.

3 E. M. (Edward Morgan) Forster, the English novelist who was to collaborate with Eric Crozier on the libretto of *Billy Budd*. For Isherwood and his generation of writers, particularly those who, like Forster, were homosexual, Forster was a literary hero and role model. When Isherwood was publicly criticized for remaining in the US after the outbreak of war in 1939, Forster was one of his principal supporters. Isherwood supervised the posthumous publication of Forster's novel *Maurice* (1971), which has a pronounced homosexual theme. See also Letter 571 n. 9.

4 Britten had sprained his ankle playing squash two days earlier; see Diary for 14 March 1937.

5 Montagu Slater's satirical sketch *Pageant of Empire*, for which Britten had contributed the incidental music, was included in the Left Theatre revue which had opened at Collins' Music Hall, London, on 28 February 1937. In his letter to Burra, Britten refers to a performance of the revue on 21 March. However, as the next letter to Burra (Letter VII) reveals, this performance was postponed until 25 April, when Britten writes in his diary:

Beth & I [...] go to the Left Revue – to which I did the music of Montagu Slater's little Pageant of Empire. I feel that this is the best form of propaganda – guying the other side – especially when as most of tonight it is hilariously funny. A little discretion might be added here & there (such as regards length & overstatement), but the talent was very obvious throughout.

VII **To Peter Burra**
[vol. 1, p. 846; after Letter 99]

BILTMORE, POLE BARN LANE, FRINTON ON SEA
April 4th 1937

My dear Peter,

I am very very sorry but next weekend must be off. The Left Theatre show on the Sunday is postponed until 25th (I think) – & they've only just let me know. And I have been held up from going to Lennox until Monday (tomorrow) & I must get a clear week with him.[1] I am naturally sorry about Saturday afternoon, but I hope you will go all the same & enjoy yourself. I have had a hectic time here – trying to work & to sort out stuff – furniture & books etc. – as well, which has been a hell of a business.[2] Everything has gone smoothly, otherwise we could never have got things done in the time. What have you been doing? Any work? What have you decided about the Listener[3] – or heard anything yet?

I shall be back in town permanently about the 15th – & therefore, please let me know when you are coming to town.

Nothing decided about the cottage yet.[4] But as soon as I have a free weekend and got a car – I want to bring a sister down to have a look.

How goes the motorbike?[5] I hope your ecstasies are continuing.

Things [*text missing owing to damaged document*]

Much love – sorry about the weekend. Be good.

BENJAMIN

1 Britten and Berkeley spent a week together in Gloucestershire working on *Mont Juic*, their jointly composed suite of Catalan dances for orchestra. See Letter 122 n. 2. Later in April, while Britten was completing his contribution to *Mont Juic*, news reached him of Burra's death in an air accident on the 27th.

While working on *Mont Juic*, Berkeley consulted a former collaborator of Britten's, Violet Alford (1881–1972), who had a specialist knowledge of Basque folksong and dance; see Diary for 13 July 1931, n. 1. Berkeley wrote to Britten on 30 September 1937:

I have just written to Violet Alford – I have written out all the tunes for her, so I hope that having duly cogitated she will be able to throw some light on the problem. Otherwise we shall have to invent names ourselves!

Berkeley and Britten wished to identify the melodies they had taken down at the performance of folk-dancing they attended in Barcelona in 1936 and subsequently used in their suite. Berkeley does not refer to Alford again in his correspondence with Britten, and the tunes remain unidentified in the published score.

It was Violet Alford who had provided Britten with the scenarios for two ballets in the early 1930s: *Plymouth Town* (1931), and another on a Basque theme (1932); see Diary for 13 July 1931. While the latter remained unfinished,

Plymouth Town was not only completed but submitted to the Camargo Society (see Diary for 15 November 1931, n. 4) on 6 December 1931, on the advice of the Society's secretary, Montagu Montagu-Nathan (see Diary for 15 November 1931, n. 2). The Society rejected the ballet, and it remained unperformed until 2004, when the RCM Sinfonietta, conducted by Michael Rosewell, gave the first performance at the Royal College of Music, London, on 27 January.

In a little-known article published in the *Radio Times* (31 July 1953), p. 29, Montagu-Nathan documented the history of Britten's submission to the Camargo Society and recalled his first meeting with the composer:

The party, which was at a flat in the purlieus of Earls Court, turned out to be, like the house-maid's baby in *Mr Midshipman Easy*, only a little one, consisting as it did of less than a dozen people. After formal introduction of the very late arrival and the acceptance of a beverage which, like the above-mentioned infant, was quite unwanted, I found myself sitting alongside a young fellow of about eighteen years and of the most modest mien. My hostess, having made the usual mumbled communication as to his name, informed me that my new acquaintance was 'musical'. I naturally took steps to institute a 'probe', for long experience had rendered me suspicious of that adjective. Eventually I enquired whether his condition of musicality comprehended an addiction to ballet. His reply, couched in tones as though the question had related to bicycling or gardening, considerably astonished me. He had written a ballet! Indeed? Well, my Society was contemplating a season and was looking for novelties likely to impress its subscribers. Among them, I explained, were such people as Lady Oxford, Lord Rothermere, the Bernard Shaws, Lady Cunard, H. G. Wells, Augustus John, Samuel Courtauld, Lord Berners, and Rex Whistler. Why not send the ballet to me for the Committee's consideration? He promised to do so.

[. . .] And so, on the arrival of my young man's ballet I at once sent it round to [Edwin] Evans with a request to vet the work and, having done so, to pass it on to our conductor, Constant Lambert. Our Savoy season, which included the production of Vaughan Williams's *Job*, ran its appointed course – terminating, as this kind of effort so often does, in the loss of some thousands of pounds for our noble band of guarantors. Among those who had co-operated in our productions had been [Lydia] Lopokova, Ninette de Valois, [Alicia] Markova, Marie Rambert, [Anton] Dolin, Frederick Ashton, Walter Gore, William Chappell, and a very special importation from Paris in the person of [Olga] Spessivtseva.

But what of my young friend's ballet? While busily engaged in cleaning up the financial mess and endeavouring to respond to claims somewhat difficult to satisfy I received a letter asking for its return. It was signed Benjamin Britten.

I cannot remember enquiring of either Evans or Lambert what was their opinion of the submitted score, and judging by what has since happened to its composer it seems charitable to suppose that neither had opened the parcel. A little later, feeling that I had perhaps let the tyro down, I wrote offering to use my best endeavours in the advancement of his career and received a grateful reply.

2 Britten's mother had died on 31 January 1937 and the family was clearing her home at Frinton. In his diary Britten writes:

30 MARCH

We settle down in morning – the four of us [i.e. Britten and his brother, Robert, and their sisters, Barbara and Beth] – & in afternoon too, to dividing all the furniture & things in the house. Picking one thing in turn starting from Barbara. It all goes very amicably, & there is no disturbance or even discussion – people being extremely unselfish – which is a blessing. We all get good things – me of course with an eye to the future – cottage & flat of course – Beth to marriage & Robert for school – Barbara sticks principally to smaller things. It is a relief to get it done – but oh what an accursed thing to have to break up this charming little home after only a year.

31 MARCH

We spend the morning doing the Books – dividing them between us four; this arouses some bitterness, for I think none of us can bear to be parted from any of the books that have surrounded us all our lives. I get some of my special wants tho'.

3 It would seem possible that Burra had been offered a position – as music critic? – on the *Listener*, a weekly periodical devoted to discussion and debate about broadcasting published by the BBC.

4 Having been left a little under £2000 in his mother's will, Britten was planning to buy a cottage; his diary entry for 29 June 1937, quoted in Letter 104 n. 2, refers to his 'cottage quest', which began while he was staying with Burra at his cottage in Bucklebury Common on 13 March: Britten viewed 'a charming little cottage nearby – which I'm thinking of taking as it is such a heavenly part of the country'. His search was to end when he bought the Old Mill at Snape in July 1937.

5 In his Diary for 15 March 1937, Britten describes Burra's motorbike as 'his new toy [. . .] which symbolises his craving for the normal or "tough" at the moment'.

VIII **To Stephen Spender**[1]
      [vol. 1, p. 557; after Letter 132]

                                                           43 Nevern Square, s.w.5.[2]
                                                           May 26th 1938

Dear Stephen,

    Thanks a lot for the letter & for sending the poem.[3] I think it is grand, & have some ideas for setting it. I think it might go very well for Hedli[4] – sung half-dramatically with backcloth or something – together with Wystan's old dictator poem.[5] Perhaps the Unity [Theatre] might be interested in them as interludes in a show or revue? This is all very much in the air & I haven't thought at all about details.[6] I am <u>fearfully</u> busy at the moment – I have a concerto down for the Proms.[7] & the thing's not nearly done yet. There's your Danton play[8] – Wystan's & Christopher's[9] – & a Ballet for Sadler's Wells[10] – & possibly one for de Basil (with Sitwell (O) (!)[11] – to be thought about.

However the Mill (apart from domestic ructions at the beginning) is peaceful.[12] You must see it.

I heard from Wystan this morning – they seem to be having an exciting time.[13]

˜Yours,

BENJAMIN

1 Stephen Spender (1909–1985), English poet and critic, who was much influenced by his friend W. H. Auden whom he first met while at Oxford. From 1970 Spender was Professor of English at University College, London. See also Letter 380 n. 1; Addenda to vol. 2: Letter 397 n. 2; John Sutherland, *Stephen Spender: The Authorised Biography*; and obituaries by Frank Kermode, 'Grand Old Man of Letters', *Guardian* (17 July 1995), Peter Porter, *Independent* (18 July 1995) and in *The Times* and the *Daily Telegraph* (both 18 July 1995).

2 Britten's and Pears's first joint home. They had moved in on 16 March 1938.

3 Spender had written to Britten on 11 May:

> I enclose a poem I have written which might be suitable for a song. Let me know if you would care to write music for it. I shall be home in a week.
> I heard from Wystan and Christopher today. They seem to have had a very interesting time. They'll be in America by the end of this month.

Although the enclosure has not survived and Spender, when asked in 1990, did not recall the poem sent to Britten, it is known from other sources that Britten set at least two poems of Spender's: 'Not to you I sighed. No, not a word' and 'Your body is stars whose millions glitter here'. The former, distinctly remembered by Wulff Scherchen (see Letter 165 n. 2 and the addendum to this note in vol. 2, p. 1337), is lost; an incomplete setting of the latter survives at BPL.

4 Hedli Anderson (1907–1990), English singer and actress. She sang in a number of theatre and radio productions with music by Britten, including Auden's and Isherwood's *The Ascent of F6*, Edward Sackville-West's *The Rescue* (see pp. 123–8) and *The Dark Tower* by her husband Louis MacNeice. Britten composed his Cabaret Songs with her in mind. See also Letter 126 n. 2 and Donald Mitchell and Philip Reed, '"For Hedli": Britten and Auden's Cabaret Songs', in Katherine Bucknell and Nicholas Jenkins (eds.), *W. H. Auden: 'The Language of Learning and the Language of Love'*, Auden Studies 2, pp. 60–68.

5 Professor Edward Mendelson confirms that this must have been Auden's poem 'It's farewell to the drawing room's civilised cry'. Britten was to use this text in his *Ballad of Heroes* (1939). See Letters 92 n. 2 and 167 n. 4.

6 This project seems not to have materialized.

7 The Piano Concerto was due to receive its first performance at the BBC Promenade Concert on 18 August 1938.

8 *Danton's Death*, a translation by Stephen Spender and Goronwy Rees of Georg Büchner's play, first published in 1939. The outbreak of war in September 1939 prevented this Group Theatre production from taking place.

An advertisement in the programme for the Group Theatre's revival of Auden's and Isherwood's *The Ascent of F6* at the Old Vic in June 1939, furnishes us with some information about this aborted production. It was to have been directed by Rupert Doone and Rollo Gamble, with scenery and costumes by Robert Medley and John Piper. At the time of writing to Spender Britten evidently intended to provide the incidental music, but the advertisement in the *F6* programme promises 'Music by Lennox Berkeley and Brian Easdale'. Britten's departure to North America in the spring of 1939 made it impossible for him to collaborate on *Danton's Death*.

9 *On the Frontier*, first performed, with Britten's incidental music, by the Group Theatre at the Arts Theatre, Cambridge, on 14 November 1938. See also Letter 155 n. 3.

10 Britten considered a number of dance projects at this period; see Letter 120 n. 2.

11 This otherwise unidentified and unrealized project must have given rise to Pears's reference to Osbert Sitwell (1892–1969) in Letter 134: 'Exciting about Osbert. Make him do a Tenor Cantata!!' Colonel Wassily de Basil (1888–1951) founded the Ballets Russes de Monte Carlo in 1932 and was later sole Director of the original Ballets Russes from 1939 to 1948.

12 The Old Mill was Britten's principal home between 1938 and 1947: see Letter 104 n. 2 and vol. 2, plates 49a and 49b. He listed the crises in Letter 130: 'sacking of a complete family working here : reorganising of whole house : notice of housekeeper : pacifying of ditto : Andoni [Barrutia, a Basque refugee boy who stayed briefly at the Old Mill; see Letter 131 n. 2] is going – which bleeds my heart but it is better on the whole : And the moods & temperaments connected with all these. It's been h—l.'

13 Auden and Isherwood were in China (January–July 1938), a trip that led to the publication of their joint account of their travels, *Journey to a War*. Auden had written to Britten, probably from the British Consulate, Hankow, in mid-April:

Dear Benjamin,

It was nice to hear from you. You can't imagine how we long for letters. So glad about H.M. [unidentified], the [piano] concerto, and the Mill.

We have just come back from a month of wandering in the north including a visit to to the front line. When we watched a bombardment and drank a lot of tea. Most of the Chinese soldiers look about 15 years old. We also saw a dog eating a spy.

I have two albums of Chinese opera records for you, but I hope they won't influence you *too* much.

I wonder how you, who are keen on trains, would appreciate the Zanghai railway. (This runs from Suchow to Sian.) The train stops for days on the way, but
there was a carboy who gave us his photograph.

C. is very well and sends his love. Letters received to date from Cambridge highly
satisfactory.

best love,

WYSTAN

The reference to the 'highly satisfactory' news from Cambridge probably
concerned arrangements for *On the Frontier*.

In *Journey to a War*, some of the events mentioned in Auden's letter are
detailed:

On a waste plot of land beyond the houses a dog was gnawing what was, only too
obviously, a human arm. A spy, they told us, had been buried there after execution
a day or two ago; the dog had dug the corpse half out of the earth. It was rather a
pretty dog with a fine, bushy tail. I remembered how we had patted it when it came
begging for scraps of our supper the evening before. [rev. edn, 1973, p. 102]

The liveliest of them [the car-boys] was called Chin-dung; his long floppy hair
framed a charming, flat-nosed, impudent face. Chin-dung was exceeding vain: he
was eternally combing his hair or admiring his figure in the glass. He wore a thick
rubber belt, like a bandage, which squeezed his pliant body into an absurdly
exaggerated Victorian wasp-waist. [. . .] Chin-dung presented us with a signed
photograph of himself looking loutish and rather touchingly ridiculous in his best
holiday suit of clothes. The other car-boys soon joined him, bringing with them a
portable gramophone which played wailing opera-airs. We both began to feel that
we had lived in this compartment for the whole of our lives. [ibid., p. 112]

IX To John F. Waterhouse[1]

[vol. 1, p. 595; after Letter 155]

THE OLD MILL, SNAPE, SAXMUNDHAM, SUFFOLK

Oct. 17th 1938

Dear Waterhouse,

I have hurriedly written out an Introduction to Act 2 for you.[2] I was
rather at sea as to what was wanted – but Wystan said over the 'phone,
that the motive might as well be 'Doom' or 'Mountain' – so I have used
the Tibetan chant[3] & concocted something, I hope, sufficiently striking
to start the act in a suitable manner. I've not had time to copy out [the]
percussion part. Would you please oblige – ?

If I can, I am going to have a shot to get to Birmingham next week to
see the show.

Excuse incredible haste,

Yours,

BENJAMIN BRITTEN

1   John F. Waterhouse (1904–1989), English academic and music critic, who
     was Reader in English at the University of Birmingham in 1938, and who
     left academia post-war to succeed Eric Blom as music critic of the *Birming-*
     ham Post. He knew both Auden and Louis MacNeice at Oxford in the 1920s.

     Waterhouse contributed to the *Birmingham Post* ('Soirée Musicale',
     18 November 1963) an illuminating account of an evening spent in the
     company of Britten and Auden, some time during the winter of 1937–38:

     One morning the poet W. H. Auden, whom I had known since Oxford years in the
     1920s, rang up from his parents' house in Harborne to say that Benjamin Britten
     was staying with him and could he bring him round that evening? I had never met
     Britten, though I knew some half-dozen of his compositions directly or from score.
     In those days I was not a music critic, so had no dreary professional scruples about
     meeting practitioners. Needless to say Auden's suggestion was enthusiastically wel-
     comed, and some sort of supper hastily planned.

     I remember that when the two of them arrived I had the gramophone playing an
     early Duke Ellington record called 'Echoes of the Jungle', and that Britten's first
     words within earshot of it were an approving identification of 'the Ellington line'.
     He looked much younger than twenty-five, as he still looks much younger than
     fifty. At first, except momentarily, on Ellington, he was quiet and unforthcoming,
     and Auden did most of the talking anyway.

     What eased Britten's shyness, I think, was my wife or I for some reason recalling
     at table a rhyme about a greedy teddy-bear from a children's picture-paper (it
     began: 'Tea! Tea! Plenty of sugar for me!') and Auden proposing that we should try
     it out as a sort of spoken, or rather shouted, four-voice 'round'; which we did, with
     much hammering of spoons.

     Across the end of our bit of garden, from wall to wall, was a big wooden studio
     erected by our predecessors in the flat. It was backed by a pocket of slum, long since
     demolished, near the corner of Bromsgrove Street. It housed, among other things,
     two pianos, also recently united in wedlock: my wife's grand and my upright,
     neither of them very good, and both in some need of mutual tuning.

     The upright still survives, if only just, in our present household: as a mere
     'instrument of reference' in the attic study of one of our sons. It got wet during the
     war, and has never recovered. But on its deathbed, so to speak, it cherishes a proud
     spot of memory: for at it, that evening, Britten pencilled a few emendations into
     the score of his Opus 10, his *Variations* on a theme of his master Frank Bridge,
     which he had with him and which he would then be preparing for publication. It
     had recently had its first performance at Salzburg.

     Yet apart from Auden's persuading him to show us those dazzlingly brilliant
     Variations, Britten's talk, so far as it concerned music, always avoided his own. I
     recall enthusiastic discussion of Stravinsky's *Apollo musagètes*, of which I admired
     a recent recorded interpretation that he thought unworthy of the music (and he, of
     course, was right); and I remember his pointing out some of the beauties of Berg's
     Violin Concerto, with which I was just beginning to make acquaintance from a
     borrowed violin-and-piano copy. But the high spot of the evening came when,
     looking at the two pianos, he suddenly said, 'Let's play the Tchaikovsky Concerto!'

     I'm afraid that my eyebrows must have registered a 'shock of mild surprise'.
     Tchaikovsky was at that time very far from being an OK composer in musical fash-
     ion, and I simply could not have believed that a rising young modern would have

any truck with him. But Britten, again of course, was right and I note with interest (and no longer surprise) that, in Murray Schafer's recent *British Composers in Interview*, he names Tchaikovsky among his eight favourites, along with Mozart, Purcell, Schubert, Bach, Verdi, Mahler, and Berg – not Stravinsky, now, but perhaps he was limiting himself to composers of the past.

Well, I unearthed an old copy of No. 1 in B♭ minor, with orchestra arranged for second piano; and, at the upright, proceeded to bumble most abominably through the 'orchestra'. Britten, at the grand, despite its limitations and the still more obstacular ones of his accompaniment, produced from memory and *con* evident *amore* what I still regard as one of the most masterly and revealing performances of the solo part I have ever heard. I knew pretty well for sure that he was going to be a great composer; but I had had no idea that he was already a great pianist.

Donald Mitchell recalls that when he invited Britten to talk informally to music students at Sussex University, the composer's immediate choice of subject was Tchaikovsky's ballet music and, more specifically, 'the perfection of his small forms'. It proved impossible, alas, to find a space in Britten's hectic schedules when the event might have taken place.

2 Entitled 'Prelude to Act II', this 47-bar *Lento maestoso* introduction to the second act of *The Ascent of F6*, scored for piano duet and percussion, was composed at Waterhouse's request for a production of Auden's and Isherwood's play given at the Birmingham Repertory Theatre for two weeks from 22 October 1938 (see Letter 125). The production was directed by Herbert M. Prentice. Among the cast was Waterhouse's wife, Elspeth Duxbury, in the role of Lady Isabel Welwyn; Britten's music was performed by pianists Marjorie Hazelhurst and Michael Mullinar (no percussionist is credited in the programme). Sally Brighton, Waterhouse's daughter, has a clear recollection that Britten sent his new Act II prelude by return of post. This music did not feature in the original Group Theatre production of 1937. The production had already been presented by the Birmingham Repertory Theatre at the Princes Theatre, Manchester, in the week beginning 4 July 1938, when Waterhouse was himself one of the pianists. It was presumably after participating in the Manchester production that Waterhouse decided to approach Britten for a prelude to the second act.

In March 1939 Waterhouse was involved in a production of Auden's and Isherwood's most recent play, *On the Frontier* (see Letter 155 n. 3). He was in touch with Britten about the music in January, evidently attempting to dispense with the trumpet parts. Britten wrote to him on 29 January:

Re the Frontier play – I am afraid that the two trumpets are a very integral part of the score – so many fanfares off, which help to characterise the two countries [the fictional Ostnia and Westland] (on different sides of the stage). The trumpet parts are not by any means virtuosi parts – but need good playing certainly.

3 The chant for male chorus in Act II scene 1, 'Go Ga, morum tonga tara'.

The manuscript fair copy of *The Ascent of F6*: the opening of the Prelude
to Act II, composed in October 1938 at the request of John F. Waterhouse

x **To Peter Pears**[1]
[vol. 1, p. 608; after Letter 164]
[*Postcard: Maison du Roi, Bruxelles*]

Brussels[2]
[Postmarked 5 January 1939]

Having a v. good time as you could imagine with Wys[3] & Chrys (&
Jackie!)[4] about the place. F. André was very good at the rehearsal this
morning – hope ditto tonight. Shall be back <u>mid-day</u> SATURDAY at flat.
If away – please leave telephone number.

Love,

B.

Hope audition[5] was success.

1 Peter Pears (1910–1986), English tenor, partner and musical collaborator
   with Britten for nearly forty years; creator of numerous operatic roles and
   first performer of many concert works written for his voice by Britten and
   others. See also Letter 113 n. 1; IC1/2; CHPP and PRPP.

2 Britten was in Brussels to give a performance of his Piano Concerto with the
   Belgian Radio Symphony Orchestra conducted by Franz André (1893– 1975).
   See also Letter 164 n. 2.

3 Wystan Hugh Auden (1907–1973), poet, and a profound influence on
   Britten's convictions and creativity. They first met in 1935 and worked
   together at the GPO Film Unit. Britten set several texts written or devised
   by Auden, including the film *Night Mail*, the song-cycle *Our Hunting
   Fathers*, the operetta *Paul Bunyan*, and *Hymn to St Cecilia*, as well as lyrics
   such as 'Underneath the abject willow', 'Tell me the truth about love' and
   'Out on the lawn' (*Spring Symphony*), and incidental music for *The Ascent
   of F6* and *On the Frontier*. See also Letter 71 n. 3.

4 At this time Christopher Isherwood was living in Brussels, where he was
   joined by his friend Jackie Hewit (1917–1997), described by Britten as 'a
   dear, nice creature'. After a brief liaison with Isherwood, Hewit returned to
   London and his former lover, the spy Guy Burgess. At the outbreak of war
   Hewit joined the army but he was soon seconded to MI5. See also Letter 164
   n. 1; Miranda Carter, *Anthony Blunt: His Lives*; Duncan Fallowell, 'The Spies
   Who Loved Me', *Sunday Times Magazine* (8 April 1991), pp. 18–22; and obituaries in *The Times* (3 January 1998) and *Daily Telegraph* (8 January 1998).

5 This was most probably an audition with the BBC to be accepted as a solo
   artist; we do not know if Pears was successful on this occasion.

XI **To Lennox Berkeley**
[vol. 1, p. 618; after Letter 170]

THE OLD MILL, SNAPE, SAXMUNDHAM, SUFFOLK
March 30th 1939

My dear Lennox,

Thank you for your letter. I have done all that is to be done re license &
registration card, & everything is going well with the car[1] – I did 85 in her
on Saturday just to show that the wheels were going round properly. But
don't worry I'm very careful! It was on the Newmarket road which is nice
& straight. I'm leaving her at Wesby's for an overhaul this weekend, before
taking her away for Easter when I go down to the Bridges.[2] It is grand to
have such a car to drive! But it's useless to say thank you! you can't say
thank you for a car – or should I say the permission to drive one – Which
reminds me – Beth had a son[3] on Sunday – & we're all excited. She has
been frightfully good & plucky – & luckily hasn't had too bad a time, but
it can't be pleasant. But she was asking for a cigarette (& had it!) about an
hour after the event. I'm going up tomorrow to see her & kid – I couldn't
go before because I've been ill with (a) a concert in Ipswich[4] (b) 'flu – con-
currently with concert – unpleasant this – however the Mangeots'[5] brandy
kept things going (c) a foul cold (d) the score of that something Ballad of
somethings.[6] But all that being now behind me – I'm going tomorrow.

I am sorry this letter's a bit distrait (distré, distrai? – pity you aren't here
to help with my French!)[7] – but I've been endeavouring to listen to Bartók
& Bizet all done by Beecham, & then a funny man afterwards[8] – & the
telephone's rung incessantly – & all of which is not good for concentrating –
especially when one's feeling slightly gooey after a week of baby-births, &
the aforementioned troubles – (a), (b), (c) & (d). – & so what.

My love to José – & Marc – when you see him – & John[9] when you
write. Vally's[10] well but has been absent for a long time yesterday & today –
& was Mrs Hearn cross! It's awfully difficult talking to her about him –
because we have continually to leave blanks in our conversations – 'if he
does – every night, he's so exhausted' – 'if you'd had him – er – done – it
would have been all right'! He's too male for her liking – I think she'd have
liked the place litter'd with kittens & then I'd have had to do the drowning.

I must off to bed now – & do some packing – I've got to catch the early
train. Had a nice recital with Michel Cherniavsky[11] on Saturday among all
the girls at St Felix[12] – but they were all plain & terribly unattractive en
masse & so they didn't convert me exactly –

Well – my dear – hope you're feeling better now – see lots of Marc (you
dare!!) – & come back a new man –

Love,
BEN

1 An Acedes coupé, which was on loan to Britten from Berkeley. See also vol. 1, plate 28a.

2 Frank Bridge (1879–1941), English composer and conductor and Britten's first and pre-eminent composition teacher, and his wife Ethel (1881–1961); see also Letter 11 n. 2. Britten had become virtually a surrogate son of the couple. This visit to the Bridges' Sussex home, where Britten had stayed many times over the previous ten years, would be his last before sailing to Canada in April.

3 Thomas Sebastian Welford, known as Sebastian, b. 26 March 1939.

4 A concert on 27 March 1939 promoted by the Ipswich Chamber Music Society, in which Britten joined the International String Quartet in a programme that included the piano quintets by Franck and Dvořák.

5 André Mangeot (1883–1970), French-born violinist and chamber musician who studied in Paris and settled in London after the First World War, becoming a British citizen.

   Britten had many connections with Mangeot in his early life. Mangeot had led the Norwich String Quartet, of which Audrey Alston, a friend of the Brittens and the Bridges, had been a member, and he had also taught Anne Macnaghten, co-founder of the Macnaghten–Lemare concerts. As leader of the International String Quartet he had taken part in the first broadcast performance of Britten's *Phantasy* quartet in 1933, and in the following year had played concertos by Haydn and Vivaldi (according to Britten, 'v. badly') in the same concert that saw the first performance of Britten's *Simple Symphony*. While in Barcelona in 1936, Britten and Mangeot had broadcast a recital of sonatas by Purcell, (?Henry) Eccles and Michael Festing – 'Pretty bad', wrote Britten, 'and very under rehearsed.'

6 *Ballad of Heroes*, due to receive its first performance on 5 April 1939, at the Festival of Music for the People at the Queen's Hall, London. See also Letter 167 n. 4.

7 Berkeley's command of French was complete and he had lived in Paris for five years.

8 Sir Thomas Beecham (1879–1961), English conductor; see also Diary for 31 January 1932, n. 1. Britten listened to part of the broadcast of Beecham's concert with the London Philharmonic Orchestra from the Queen's Hall, London, the programme of which included Bartók's *Music for Strings, Percussion and Celesta* and Bizet's Symphony in C. The 'funny man' billed in the *Radio Times* was 'Professor Billy Bennett introducing his "Almost an Academy"'.

9 José = Berkeley's Corsican friend José Rafaelli, with whom Berkeley shared a flat in Paris, and to whom Berkeley dedicated his Five Short Pieces, Op. 4, for piano. In 1938 he and Berkeley had visited Britten in London and Snape.

During the war Rafaelli was killed while working for the French Resistance.

Marc remains unidentified. John = John Davenport, to whom Berkeley dedicated his *Serenade*, Op. 12. When Berkeley ceased living at Snape in 1940 he moved in with Davenport and his wife.

10 Evidently a highly sexed tomcat owned by the housekeeper, Mrs Hearn.

11 Michel Cherniavsky (1893–1982), Russian-born cellist and sometime chamber music partner of Antonio Brosa.

12 St Felix School, Southwold, Suffolk.

XII To Lennox Berkeley

[vol. 1, p. 618; following Letter xi, after Letter 170]

THE OLD MILL, SNAPE, SAXMUNDHAM, SUFFOLK

April 16th 1939

My dear Lennox,

Thank you for your (a) postcard from Belgium (b) wire (c) letter (d) card. Sorry not to have answered them before but I have been unconscionably (however you spell it!) busy – & anyhow I have only just been able to make plans for the near future. This has now been done – & Peter & I sail for <u>Canada</u> on April 29th – so as there is a bit to get settled <u>and</u> I'd like to see you before you go off – you'd better come back a few days before. This next weekend I think the Bridges will be here – but, as we've got that double-bed it'd be all right for you to be here – wouldn't it? Anyhow – if you don't come, don't forget to listen to the new Rimbaud songs[1] this Friday 1.15 from National – there's this Britten programme from Birmingham.

The Ballad went quite well & was a great success – & I've never had more consistently good notices[2] – & headlines in each paper! But it's infuriating for such a sketchy little work.

I'm glad the 'cello work's[3] going ahead. You must tell me what Eisenberg says.

No time for more, my dear. Let me have a card to say when you're coming.

Love,

BENJAMIN

1 'Marine' and 'Being Beauteous', two songs that were to form part of the song-cycle for high voice and string orchestra, *Les Illuminations*. See also Letter 170 n. 1.

2 A selection of the reviews is reproduced in Letter 167 n. 4.

3 Berkeley's Cello Concerto (1939) composed for the German-American cellist Maurice Eisenberg (1900–1972). It would seem that Eisenberg, who had been based in Paris during the 1930s, returned to America at the outbreak

of war. Berkeley told Britten in a letter of 5 January 1940 (by which time Britten himself was in the US): 'I think in some ways [the Concerto] is the best thing I have done, but it's still so far from what I hope some day to do that I can't get very keen about it really.' The war disrupted plans for the premiere and the Concerto was not first performed until 1983. See Peter Dickinson, *The Music of Lennox Berkeley*, 2nd edn, p. 42.

XIII **To Leslie A. Boosey**[1]
Boosey & Hawkes
[vol. 2, p. 815; after Letter 263]
[*Typed*]

c/o Dr. W. Mayer
The Long Island Home, Amityville, N.Y.[2]
May 23rd, 1940

My dear Mr Boosey:

Thank you very much for your letter and for the enclosure of the assignments in respect of "LES ILLUMINATIONS",[3] which I return to you duly signed.

I was very pleased to get your letter and to hear your news. I am afraid things with you must have slumped again seriously since you wrote, but I do hope that you are able to carry on still.[4] Everyone here is terribly worried over the situation but hope has not been given up yet that things will turn out the way we all want them to.

In the meantime I try to go on writing music which, as you can guess, is not always very easy under these circumstances; but more than I can say I am grateful for the encouragement that you and Ralph[5] have always given me. Although this country is passing through a phase of chauvinism, people are being kind to me musically and I have had quite a lot of work.[6] But I cannot feel it any more than a temporary period, and with all my heart I look forward to the time when we can all be working together again under normal circumstances.

With kindest regards,
Yours sincerely,
BENJAMIN BRITTEN

1 Leslie Arthur Boosey (1887–1979), English music publisher. He had been Chairman of Britten's publishers, Boosey & Hawkes, since 1930. See also Letter 110 n. 1 and 1C1/2.

2 The home of William Mayer (1887–1956) and his wife Elizabeth (1884–1970). Dr Mayer was Medical Director at the Long Island Home, a psychiatric institution. The Mayer family provided generous hospitality and profound emotional support for Britten and Pears throughout their time in the US. See also Letter 194 n. 1 and 1C1/2.

3   *Les Illuminations* was composed between March and October 1939. 'Marine'
    and 'Being Beauteous' had received individual performances and broad-
    casts, while the complete cycle was first performed by Sophie Wyss and the
    Boyd Neel Orchestra, conducted by Boyd Neel, in January 1940. Peter
    Pears's first performance of the cycle, which was also the US premiere,
    was to be broadcast over the CBS network from the ISCM Festival in
    New York on 18 May 1941, an off-air recording of which was released on
    CD (NMC D030 Archive Series) in 1995. Boosey & Hawkes published the
    full score and miniature score in 1940 and the vocal score in 1944 (see below,
    pp. 129–30).

4   Leslie Boosey had written to Britten on 25 April 1940, enclosing the assign-
    ment in respect of *Les Illuminations* and describing the situation in London:

The world over here is a funny one, as I expect many of your friends have written
and told you. The musical activities slumped to nothing at the outbreak of war,
then reappeared gradually like a lot of rabbits who had been frightened into their
holes by the sound of a gun. The Norwegian campaign was another bang and back
they have all gone again but I suppose if nothing else startling happens, they will
begin to peep out once more in a few weeks' time.

Life appears to go on very much as usual but, of course, there is a tense atmosphere about everything, which affects everybody in different ways. I am afraid the
musical fraternity has been as hard hit as anyone: in our own case, as Ralph
[Hawkes] has probably told you, our business is rather like the famous curate's egg
'good in parts' but anything but good in other parts. However, that is much better
than being completely addled, as many are.

He responded to Britten's letter on 6 June 1940, expressing his personal
feelings about the war:

Yes, of course, things have slumped away here terribly and the anxiety of the last
month is something which I never dreamed I should experience in my lifetime.
The last war was nothing at all beside it. It is true I was in the firing line but one had
no responsibility beyond the military ones and one's attitude was 'let's eat, drink
and be merry, etc.' Now I am too old to fight but too young to feel that I can look
on. My responsibilities to my family, to the business, etc. weigh terribly heavily on
me but I know that I must carry on here and do nothing foolish. There are a great
many people who are dependent upon Boosey & Hawkes for their livelihood and if
the heads of the firm go rushing off on quixotic jobs what is to happen to the
others. If I were free of these responsibilities, my decision would be quite different.
[. . .]
I hope, with you, that the world may one day regain its sanity.

5   Ralph Hawkes (1898–1950), English music publisher and a director of
    Boosey & Hawkes. He had offered Britten an exclusive contract with the
    firm in 1935 and had been unfailingly encouraging and supportive of him
    ever since. At this time he was running the company's New York office. See
    also Letter 49 n. 2 and 1C1/2.

6   In his letter of 25 April Leslie Boosey had written:

I have been watching your progress in America with much interest and was very pleased to hear of the success of your Piano Concerto. Ralph also sent me your article that appeared in the papers about America and American Music ['A Visiting Composer Looks at Us', *New York Times* (24 March 1940), reprinted as 'An English Composer Sees America', *Tempo*, American Series, 1/2 (April 1940); see PKBM, pp. 24–7], which I read with much interest and with which I fully agreed. America has always been a place which had a great attraction for me. I think the more one is in the United States, the more one becomes impressed with that feeling of limitless opportunity which has been so lacking over here. If only there were a United States of Europe, instead of 20 squabbling countries, what a marvellous place it would be. Who knows, perhaps this is the good that may come out of the present evil, though if one starts to think about it, one is appalled by the insuperable difficulties which appear to confront one.

Since reaching the United States, Britten had completed his Violin Concerto and *Les Illuminations*. The concerto was premiered by the violinist Antonio Brosa, with the New York Philharmonic Orchestra conducted by John Barbirolli, in New York in March 1940. At the time of writing to Leslie Boosey, Britten was working on his *Sinfonia da Requiem*; his first song-cycle for Pears, the *Seven Sonnets of Michelangelo*, and the operetta *Paul Bunyan*.

XIV To Leonard Bernstein[1]

[vol. 2, p. 913; after Letter 310]

7 MIDDAGH STREET, BROOKLYN, N.Y.[2]
Main 4.9079
April 28th 1941

Dear Lenny,

Please forgive the lateness of this – but I have been working all day & night for the last three weeks on the score of the operetta[3] & I haven't had a moment for letters.

I was very, very pleased that you liked the Sinf. da Req.[4] Judging by your remarks you certainly 'got' what I wrote, & it was extremely nice of you to take the trouble to write & say so. I am sure that it's the 'best so far' – and as it's the last, that is as it should be. I might argue with you about one or two of your remarks about my earlier masterpieces – but may be there is something in what you say. The only thing is, maybe those particular vices are less vicious than some others I can think of – such as inhibitions, sterility, self-conscious ideas of originality – but we won't go into that now!

How are you? I saw you were conducting on the Radio on Saturday[5] – how did it go? When do you come to New York? I shall be around until June 1st or thereabouts. Give me a call when you get here. How are your chamber concerts going? As you probably know – the Bowlesesses[6] departed for Mexico.

The Operetta is chaotic. Goberman[7] is not doing it – Hugh Ross[8] has taken it over – & although he has the right mentality for training choruses, (entre nous) he is not so hot on orchestras. However – we shall see.

Thank you again for your note. You ask how the others liked the symphony – all the ones I respect were pleased – including Aaron,[9] Chavez,[10] Colin,[11] Lincoln[12] et all –

Best of luck,
Yours ever,
BENJY B.

1 American composer and conductor (1918–1990); see also Letter 205 n. 3. Bernstein studied at Harvard and the Curtis Institute, and was much influenced by friendships with Aaron Copland and Serge Koussevitzky, whose assistant he became at Tanglewood and to whom he remained devoted. He was appointed Artur Rodzinski's assistant at the New York Philharmonic Orchestra in 1942, and his conducting career was spectacularly launched the following year when he deputized for the indisposed Bruno Walter. In 1958 Bernstein was the first American to become Music Director of the New York Philharmonic, a post he held until 1969. As a composer he wrote both for the popular theatre – *On the Town* (1944), *Candide* (1956) and *West Side Story* (1957) – and for the concert hall – three symphonies, the second of which, 'The Age of Anxiety' (1949), is based on Auden's poem of the same title; *Chichester Psalms* (1965), commissioned by Walter Hussey, and *Mass: a Theater Piece for Singers, Players and Dancers* (1971), in memory of President Kennedy. From the 1930s onwards Bernstein had left-wing sympathies (he directed Marc Blizstein's *The Cradle Will Rock* while at Harvard), was a friend of many leading Democrats, including the Kennedys, and was involved in the civil rights movement in the 1960s; in 1970 he courted controversy by holding a fund-raising meeting for the Black Panthers at his home. See also obituaries by Edward Greenfield, 'Everyman's musician', *Guardian* (16 October 1990), Peter Dickinson, *Independent* (16 October 1990), and in *The Times* (16 October 1990).

Britten probably first met Bernstein through their mutual friendship with Copland; in an interview for TP, Bernstein recalled visiting the Middagh Street house on only one occasion. Following his conducting of the US premiere of *Peter Grimes* at Tanglewood in 1946 (see Letter 529 n. 1), Bernstein and Britten were rarely in touch. As Bernstein's biographer Humphrey Burton notes, 'perhaps Britten did not warm to his flamboyant interpreter' (*Leonard Bernstein*, p. 153). Prompted by Burton's description, Donald Mitchell remembers Britten telling him that, on one occasion, travelling together by cab down Fifth Avenue he became so exasperated by a show of Bernstein's undeniably flamboyant personality – he could not remember exactly what it was that so irritated him – that he punched him in the chest in an effort to shut him up. It was the only time, Britten claimed, 'that I have ever punched anybody'.

An undated letter (probably written in 1960) survives at BPL in which

Bernstein writes, 'I've deeply missed seeing you all these years: but I've been hearing you & reading about you with enormous pleasure.' In April 1973 he sent a telegram to wish Britten well for his forthcoming heart operation; Britten's response has not apparently survived, but Bernstein's answer (18 May) to Britten's note has:

I can't tell you how moving your note was to me. It seemed to put something right – to heal – something undefined that has been awry for years. You are among the few composers whose work I cherish, in the most personal way; and that is why I cherish your words equally dearly.

Two telegrams from Harry Kraut (Bernstein's manager) to Britten from September 1974 survive at BPL; these indicate that Bernstein had been invited to conduct at the 1975 Aldeburgh Festival. When this proved impossible for Bernstein, the 1976 Festival was proposed, but this also came to nothing. It was through this renewed contact between them that Bernstein was given permission by Britten to make the first recording of the *Suite on English Folk Tunes*. The recording, in which Bernstein conducted the New York Philharmonic, was released in 1977 (Columbia M–34529) under the title *A Tribute to Benjamin Britten*, the composer having died in December 1976; the other works on the disc were the *Four Sea Interludes* and *Passacaglia from 'Peter Grimes'*.

Humphrey Burton (p. 152) documents that, at the very end of his life, Bernstein was planning to make a complete recording of *Peter Grimes*.

In TP Bernstein spoke revealingly of Britten's musical character:

[...] it's strange because on the surface Ben's music would seem to be decorative, positive, charming and it's so much more than that [...] there are gears that are grinding and not quite meshing, and they make a great pain inside, so that when you hear Britten's music you become aware, if you really hear it, not just listen to it superficially, you become aware of something very dark, very pained.

2 Britten's and Pears's New York home from November 1940 until the summer of 1941. The building was owned by the writer George Davis and the bohemian household was presided over by W. H. Auden. The floating population at this period included Gypsy Rose Lee, Louis MacNeice, Carson McCullers and Erika, Golo and Klaus Mann. See also Letter 291 n. 2.

3 *Paul Bunyan*, which was to receive its first performance on 5 May 1941 at Columbia University. For its press reception, see Letter 311 n. 3.

4 The *Sinfonia da Requiem*, which had been commissioned to mark the 2,600th anniversary of the Founding of the Japanese Empire but which did not form part of the celebrations, ostensibly because of its overtly Christian content, had been first performed at Carnegie Hall, New York, by the New York Philharmonic Orchestra conducted by John Barbirolli on 29 March 1941. The second performance, the following evening, had been broadcast by CBS. An off-air recording of this broadcast (see Letter 390 n. 2) was issued on CD (NMC D030 Archive Series) in 1995.

5 This was Bernstein's first broadcast appearance as a conductor, a performance of Brahms's Serenade in A, Op. 16, with the Orchestra of the Curtis
Institute. See Burton, p. 90.

6 Paul Bowles (1910–1999), American writer and composer, and his wife Jane
(1917–1973), also a writer, tenants of the Middagh Street house. See also
obituaries by Gary Pulsifer, *Guardian* (19 November 1999); John Calder,
Independent (19 November 1999), and in *The Times* (19 November 1999).
While living in Mexico, Bowles collected Latin American folk music.

7 Max Goberman, American conductor and, with Bernstein, a student of
Koussevitzky's at Tanglewood. He later conducted the first New York performances of Bernstein's *On the Town* and *West Side Story*.

8 Hugh Ross (1898–?), English-born American choral conductor and organist, who conducted the first production of *Paul Bunyan*. According to Olin
Downes in the *New York Times* (6 May 1941), 'Mr Ross conducted with
authority and animation, showing a talent for stage music as well as choral
and orchestral manifestation.'
   Ross studied at the Royal College of Music and at New College, Oxford,
as well as privately with Mengelberg (conducting) and Vaughan Williams
(composition). In 1921 he took up a post in Canada before moving to New
York in 1927 to become conductor of the Scola Cantorum, a post he held
until 1971. (The New York Scola Cantorum took part in the first production
of *Paul Bunyan* in 1941.) From 1941 until 1961 he was Chairman of the
Choral Department of the Berkshire Music Center at Tanglewood. In
October 1965 at the UN General Assembly Hall, New York, Ross conducted
one of the simultaneous triple premieres of Britten's *Voices for Today*, an
anthem commissioned by the United Nations to mark its twentieth
anniversary.

9 Aaron Copland (1900–1990), American composer, pianist, conductor,
teacher and writer on music. Both Britten and Bernstein regarded him as a
paternal figure, Britten referring to him as 'my cheery "Father"' and
Bernstein as a 'substitute father'. See also Letter 138 n. 5 and 1c1/2.
   Britten and Copland had first met at the ISCM Festival in London in
June 1938, following which Britten invited his American colleague to spend
a weekend at Snape (see Copland's 'A Visit to Snape', in TBB, pp. 71–3), when
Copland played through his 'play-opera' *The Second Hurricane* to Britten,
who played through his recently completed Piano Concerto. Soon after
their arrival in the United States in 1939, Britten and Pears spent most of
July and August in Woodstock staying with Copland. Throughout his stay
in the United States, Britten remained in close touch with Copland.
Although in later years they saw far less of each other, Copland was among
the audience at Tanglewood for the US premiere of *Peter Grimes*, and they
met when Copland visited England (for example, in 1949, when Copland
noted in his diary, 'Benjie's charm is still potent and derives from a combination of severity and boyishness' (see Aaron Copland and Vivian Perlis,

Copland Since 1943, p. 145), and again in 1950 and 1958). When Britten and Pears were in the United States in the autumn of 1949 Copland recollected that he

sang the songs [the *Old American Songs*] for Peter Pears and Ben Britten [. . .] promising to send them on to England when I finished them. Peter told me, 'I like them *very much* indeed – we shall do them first at Aldeburgh June 17 [1950], then Amsterdam June 30th; then again here in July; probably Edinburgh Festival September 3rd, & in London in October – So you see! They will, as singers say, prove a most useful addition to my repertoire! I am still a little inclined to make the cat say 'fiddle *my* fee' [as opposed to 'fiddle-eye-fee']! [Copland and Perlis, p. 167.]

Pears and Britten made the first recording of Copland's *Old American Songs* in 1950, which was released the following year (DA 7039).

Although Copland did not come to Aldeburgh for the premiere of his *Old American Songs*, he did spend time at the Festival in 1960:

I travelled there with composer Harrison Birtwistle and conductor John Carewe. We were put up in rooms without baths or telephones (I always have felt slightly uncomfortable in a room without a phone). My Piano Quartet was performed and the Society for the Promotion of New Music sponsored a program at which I spoke. Jack Kennedy [a former student and friend] met me as planned and caught me up on all the news from home. We were invited to tea chez Benjamin Britten, and it was very posh with the Prince of Hesse and Earl of Harewood present. I was to conduct a new piece at the Aldeburgh Festival, but it was not finished yet; instead, I conducted *Two Pieces for String Orchestra*, *Quiet City*, and *In the Beginning* at the Blythburgh Church. [Copland and Perlis, p. 293.]

Movie footage of Copland in the Red House garden during the 1960 Aldeburgh Festival survives at BPL. In 1974 Copland attended the New York Metropolitan Opera premiere of *Death in Venice* with Pears as Aschenbach.

In *Copland Since 1943* (p. 213) Copland recalls:

I once asked Ben Britten what he thought was the most important requisite in composing opera. I was sure he would say a sense of drama, ability to indicate the meaning of a scene musically in a matter of seconds. What he said was that the most important thing a composer must have is the ability to write many kinds of music – chorus alone, chorus with orchestra, soloists separately, soloists in ensemble, and so on. The needs are so varied that one must have terrific facility to handle them all.

10   Carlos Chávez (1889–1978), Mexican composer. See also Letter 265 n. 3.

11   Colin McPhee (1901–1964), Canadian-born American composer and ethno-musicologist. McPhee had been a patient of William Mayer and was responsible for introducing Britten to Balinese music. See also Letter 312 n. 12.

12   Lincoln Kirstein (1907–1996), American writer and ballet director. He founded the School of American Ballet in 1934 with George Balanchine (1904–1983) and was co-founder of the American Ballet a year later. He established the Ballet Society in 1946, which was soon to become the New York City Ballet, of which he was General Director from 1948. See obituaries by

Dale Harris, 'New York's lord of the dance', *Guardian* (6 January 1996) and
Marilyn Hunt, *Independent* (6 January 1996), and in the *Daily Telegraph*
(8 January 1996) and *The Times* (11 January 1996).

In 1940 Britten orchestrated Chopin's *Les Sylphides* for Kirstein's company;
it was first performed on 11 February 1941 in New York. Britten's instrumentation is lost: see Letter 310 n. 2. Britten completed his composition of
the Rossini suite *Matinées Musicales* for Kirstein's American Ballet Company in June 1941. With the earlier *Soirées Musicales* it formed the score for
the ballet *Divertimento*, which was choreographed by Balanchine. See also
Letters 178 n. 2 and 315 n. 4.

xv To Joan Rothman[1]

[vol. 2, p. 980; after Letter 340]

Escondido, California[2]
Sept. 15th 1941

Dear Joan,

Please forgive me for not having answered your nice letter before, but,
as you can guess, I have been just as busy as possible these last few months,
and the only kind of letters I have been able to write have been horrible
business ones!

Anyhow, thank you very much for it. I was very interested to hear about
your doings at camp. You seem to have had a swell time, and done some
exciting things. I am glad you avoided being 'dunked' in the lake – that
sounds very unpleasant! I have had a nice time out here – I have worked
very hard, but also had some nice trips to the ocean (with swimming) and
into the mountains all around, which are very high and beautiful.

I have just written a piece for 2 pianos and orchestra which Bartlett &
Robertson, the piano-duo, who are our hosts here, are going to play next
season.[3] The other day we went to a music store and played it on 3 pianos
(I played the orchestral part on another piano) – you cannot imagine how
much noise we all made banging away together. How was the composing
contest? – and how is the 'Fantasie-Impromptu' coming along?

Give my love to all the family, including that 'rapscallion' of a brother of
yours[4] – if he knows what that means! And lots of luck to you this term at
school.

Your friend,
BENJAMIN BRITTEN

1 One of the daughters of the Rothman family, friends of Britten and Pears
on Long Island. Her father David ran a hardware store at Southold on Long
Island. His wife played the piano and Joan was a talented pianist. See also
Letter 219 n. 4.

2 Britten and Pears spent much of July and August 1941 in Escondido, staying
   with the piano duo Ethel Bartlett (1896–1978) and Rae Robertson (1893–
   1956). See vol. 2, plate 47a.

3 *Scottish Ballad*, for two pianos and orchestra, based on a number of
   Scottish melodies, including the psalm tune 'Dundee', 'Turn Ye to Me' and
   'Flowers of the Forest', an acknowledgement of Robertson's Scottish
   roots. The work was premiered on 28 November 1941, at the Music Hall,
   Cincinnati, with Bartlett and Robertson, and the Cincinnati Symphony
   Orchestra conducted by Eugene Goossens.

4 Bobby Rothman (b. ?1928), to whom Britten dedicated his arrangement of
   the Somerset folksong 'The trees they grow so high'. See PFL, plate 127;
   vol. 2, plates 42a and 42b; and Letters 351 n. 1 and 388 n. 1.
      In an interview with Donald Mitchell and Philip Reed (23 October 1992),
   Bobby Rothman shared his memories of his friendship with Britten on
   Long Island during the period 1939–42. Despite Britten's writing to him in
   1942 about the dedication of 'The trees they grow so high' (see Letter 388),
   Rothman evidently forgot all about it until many years later when a singer
   neighbour happened upon it and brought it to his attention. Rothman
   recalled that when Britten was composing,

   my father liked to drive him around the area where the birds were flying along the
   water and the seagulls; I still remember him telling me that he was looking to give
   him inspiration to write music, and finally, when Ben got Father out of his sight, he
   looked at me and said, 'That's not music. It's very pretty, but not music.'

   When Britten stayed with the Rothman family, he shared a room with the
   thirteen-year-old Bobby:

   [...] many an evening we used to spend [...] a lot of time just really talking, he in
   the bed next to me [...] His fondness for me was something that was beyond my
   normal social connections, and I was a little overwhelmed that someone should be
   so fond of me [...] I can still remember us talking late at night one time, and finding when it was really time to call it quits and go to sleep [...] he said, 'Bobby,
   would you mind terribly if, before we fell asleep, I came over and gave you a hug
   and a kiss?' It was just one of those touching moments [...] And I've got to say I
   really did not know what to do except say, 'no, no I don't mind', and he gently got
   up and gave me a gentle hug and kiss and said goodnight.

   In recalling the occasion, Rothman emphasized that he was unaware of the
   strength of Britten's feelings towards him at this time:

   He *was* very fond of me, but there was never any words, any activity, any suggestion
   on his part, and this is all very clear to me that this [never] extended any further
   than plain fondness for another individual in a very social way [...] It was a relationship that was just admiration, far more on his part for me, although I enjoyed
   his company. He was rather just a friend or a playmate [...] in my life and at that
   age. I didn't appreciate his expertise in the field of music.

xvi To Christopher Isherwood

[vol. 2, p. 1025; after Letter 369]
[PBMPG, pp. 23–4 (extract)]

123 Louden Avenue[1]
AMITYVILLE, LONG ISLAND, N.Y.
March 10th 1942

My dearest Christopher,

Please forgive me for not having answered your letter[2] nor acknowledged Crabbe before, but I have been horribly busy & worried the last
weeks I am afraid. Well, things are coming to a head at last, thank God –
and there is something tangible to face, instead of Consuls and Draft-
boards & Exit permits. We have a boat, leaving sometime next Monday.[3]
The Brit. Consul is gloomy about the sailing, i.e. that there hasn't been a
more unpleasant time – but, honestly I don't worry about it now. I am,
and have been in an acute work crisis these last 6 months, and I truly
believe that if I am intended to do something worthwhile I'll get thro',
and if I'm not – well, it's a painless way out. Peter I know will – he is the
kind of person who develops late in life, and he hasn't yet done what he's
got to do.

I'm not really happy about the other side. It'll be lovely to see my family,
& Wulff,[4] and all again; but I am more & more (especially after reading
Morgan's Dickinson)[5] convinced that I cannot kill, so it'll be a tribunal,[6]
& I am scared stiff of judges & all that. But, pray for me, my dear.

I can't pretend that I wasn't disappointed that you can't do Grimes with
me. But I understand of course. I know that as it stands, P.G. is no more
than a rather bloodthirsty melodrama; but it has the elements of what I
want in an opera, and we are slowly but surely getting nearer to a serious
plot. Incidentally a lot of your hints dropped that Saturday afternoon[7]
have proved useful – thank you!

I saw Wystan – minus tooth and very cheerful. He gave me a loud &
intimate lecture on my 'It'[8] in a small coffee shop. True but embarrassing.

Do write my dear, as much as you can. It'll be such a help to know
you're thinking about us. Let us know how you fare, and if & when you
have to move. I am so glad to hear Pete[9] is with you – you liked him so
much I know. I am sorry not to have seen more of Harvey,[10] because I
really am fond of him, & we always get on so well. But I go to New York so
seldom – for financial reasons, I'm afraid, and always when I go I have to
charge around doing business things. But I'll try to see him before I go.

All my love, Chris dear, perhaps we'll meet again sooner than we think,
from Peter too.

BENJY

P.T.O. [*Text missing*]

1   The private address of the Mayer family in the Long Island Home complex.

2   Isherwood had written to Britten from Haverford, Pennsylvania, on 18
    February 1942:

    I'm sorry, but I don't see any possibility of collaborating with you and Peter on the
    Peter Grimes libretto. I have thought it over carefully: it surely is good melo-
    dramatic material, and maybe something more than that: the setting is perfect for
    an opera, I should think. But the real point is that I am quite sure I shan't have the
    time for such work for months or maybe years ahead; and frankly, the subject
    doesn't excite me so much that I want to *make* time for it; I mean, to use every
    available spare moment out of a life like the one I lead at present, or in a work
    camp, or somewhere even more strenuous. Also, I doubt very much if collaborators
    can work so far apart as we seem likely to be. So let's drop it, regretfully but finally.
       I wish we weren't going to be parted by so much water and so many U-boats. Of
    course, I may quite possibly come to England; you never know. I don't have to say
    that I wish you both every kind of success and happiness. If you really leave within
    ten days and can't get down here, we shan't meet again; as I simply cannot leave
    right now. Glad you saw Harvey. Wish you could have seen more of and been more
    to him. Maybe you are the only one who could help.
       God bless you both. I'll be thinking of you very often.
       Crabbe returns under separate cover.

    The commission from the Koussevitzky Foundation to compose *Peter
    Grimes* had been confirmed in February 1942. Although Britten and Pears
    had done some preparatory structural work on the opera, carving out a
    narrative from Crabbe's *The Borough*, a series of character portraits and
    anecdotes, it was not until after their return to the UK that Montagu Slater
    was engaged as librettist.
       In Donald Mitchell's 'Montagu Slater (1902–1956): who was he?', PGPB,
    p. 36, Isherwood is quoted as saying (in 1981), 'How fortunate that I *didn't*
    attempt to write the opera! I was absolutely convinced that it wouldn't
    work. And, when I saw it on stage, I was astonished – I mean, of course, as
    a dramatic piece – I never doubted that Ben, as a composer, could rise to
    any occasion!' In conversation with Philip Brett in 1977 Isherwood 'admit-
    ted that he found the story homophobic': see Brett, '*Peter Grimes*: The
    Growth of the Libretto', in PBMPG, p. 56, n. 8.

3   Britten and Pears had endured a stressful wait for a passage back to Europe,
    finally leaving the US on 16 March. The impact of the war had now spread
    across the globe: America had entered the war on 8 December 1941;
    Rommel had launched a new offensive in the Western Desert on 21 January
    1942, and Singapore had fallen to the Japanese on 15 February.

4   Wulff Scherchen (b. 1920), the son of the conductor Hermann Scherchen.
    Britten and Scherchen had shared an intense friendship, having first met at
    the 1934 ISCM Festival in Florence. In 1938 Wulff and his mother Gustel
    had settled in Cambridge, with Hermann continuing his conducting career
    from Switzerland. During the war Wulff changed his name to John

Woolford. See Letter 136; IC1/2; JBBC, and John Bridcut, 'Britten's real young Apollo', *Daily Telegraph* (31 May 2004), p. 19.

5 E. M. Forster's biography of the humanist, historian and philosophical writer Goldsworthy Lowes Dickinson (1862–1932).

6 Tribunal for the Registration of Conscientious Objectors. As a pacifist refusing to engage in military activity, Britten was required to go through this legal process. See also Letter 340 n. 4. Britten's Local Tribunal took place on 28 May 1942 (see Letter 375): its unanimous decision was that he be registered 'as a person liable under the Act to be called-up for service but employed only in non-combatant duties'. Britten's appeal to the Appellate Tribunal, heard in London on 18 August (see Letters 381 and 382), decided that he 'shall without conditions be registered in the Register of Conscientious Objectors'.

7 Isherwood's move to Pennsylvania (see Letter 340 n. 4) gave him the opportunity to visit New York occasionally and see his friends there. Britten's reference to 'hints dropped that Saturday afternoon' may refer to discussions between the two men (or among three, with Pears) in Pennsylvania in late September/early October 1941 and January 1942, or to a more recent meeting in New York. In his diary for Friday, 16 January 1942, Isherwood writes about attending the first performance of Britten's *Diversions*, for piano (left hand) and orchestra, given by Paul Wittgenstein and the Philadelphia Orchestra conducted by Eugène Ormandy, at the Academy of Music, Philadelphia:

> To Benjamin Britten's concert. Benjy and his friend Peter Pears met me afterwards. They are leaving soon for England, where Benjy has decided to register as a C. O. We all got sadder and drunker and drunker.

See Katherine Bucknell (ed.), *Christopher Isherwood: Diaries, Volume One 1939–1960*, p. 206.

8 Auden was prone to analyse his friends; it was only a few weeks earlier, on 31 January 1942, that he had sent Britten a challenging assessment of his creativity and sexuality (Letter 364). Here he appears to have held forth on Britten's sexual attractiveness.

9 José Martinez (real name Pete Stefan), Mexican ballet dancer. In 1942, while waiting to be called up for military service, Martinez worked with Isherwood at the Quaker-run refugee hostel in Haverford, Pennsylvania.

10 Harvey remains unidentified. See Isherwood's letter to Britten quoted in n. 2 above.

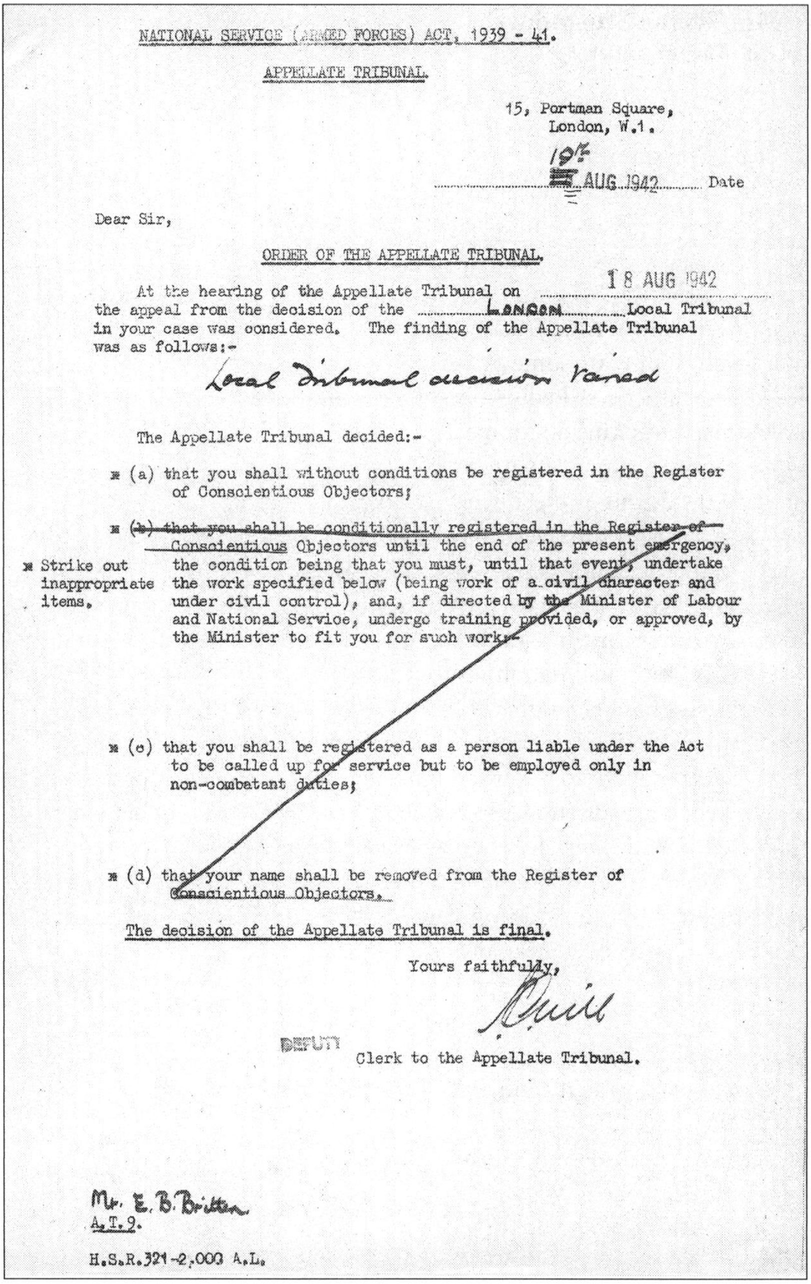

NATIONAL SERVICE (ARMED FORCES) ACT, 1939 - 41.

APPELLATE TRIBUNAL.

15, Portman Square,
London, W.1.

19th AUG 1942 Date

Dear Sir,

ORDER OF THE APPELLATE TRIBUNAL.

At the hearing of the Appellate Tribunal on 18 AUG 1942 the appeal from the decision of the London Local Tribunal in your case was considered. The finding of the Appellate Tribunal was as follows:-

Local Tribunal decision varied

The Appellate Tribunal decided:-

x (a) that you shall without conditions be registered in the Register of Conscientious Objectors;

x ~~(b) that you shall be conditionally registered in the Register of Conscientious~~ Objectors until the end of the present emergency, the condition being that you must, until that event, undertake the work specified below (being work of a civil character and under civil control), and, if directed by the Minister of Labour and National Service, undergo training provided, or approved, by the Minister to fit you for such work:-

x Strike out inappropriate items.

x (c) that you shall be registered as a person liable under the Act to be called up for service but to be employed only in non-combatant duties;

x (d) that your name shall be removed from the Register of Conscientious Objectors.

The decision of the Appellate Tribunal is final.

Yours faithfully,

[signature]

DEPUTY Clerk to the Appellate Tribunal.

Mr. E. B. Britten
A.T.9.

H.S.R.321-2,000 A.L.

The official notification of the outcome of Britten's Appellate Tribunal on 18 August 1942

xVII To Mrs Regina Sturmdorf[1]

[vol. 2, p. 1069; after Letter 387]

11 Tryon House, Mallord St, s.w.3.[2]

June 24th 1942

My dear "Grandmother",

What a lovely letter I have just received from you! Thank you so much for it. I am very pleased and touched that you haven't forgotten all about me – because I feel so very isolated over here, so far away from all my dear friends in America, & I am so very keen not to lose touch with you all. Of all my lovely stay in America, my memories of Southold, of you, & David & his lovely family, are some of the very warmest. Thank you for being so nice, & sympathetic, & loving – in these very dark days it is a great help to know you are thinking about me.

I have written a long letter to young Bobby, in answer to one of his, telling all the details of the journey, & one's impression on arriving in England again after three years of war, so I won't bother you with all those, & also I want to get this off to-day – besides if I don't finish this soon I don't know <u>when</u> I shall have the opportunity. This is only a quick note to say thank you for writing – & to ask you to write again whenever you have the opportunity & inclination – and let it be soon!

Of course it has been rather a shock getting back here. It has been wonderful to see all one's family again (my sister has a fine child aged 3, who is a great delight to his proud uncle!) and all one's dear friends. All the nice people are just as nice as ever. But the whole place is rather shabby & dejected, which is certainly not surprising, but nevertheless rather disturbing. Things seem very well organised, & the food & transport, though not luxurious (& nothing like the memories of the States!) are really quite adequate. I haven't been near any bombs yet, although there have been quite a lot of 'alarms'! I do hope so much that you all will be spared that kind of thing – it is very unpleasant! Peter has had a really great success in opera, & is now touring the country in the Tales of Hoffmann, & singing the hero[3] – making a great hit, both by his singing, and by his acting & looks! If he knew I was writing I know he'd send lots of love. Please forgive this scribble, my dear, only I just wanted to say 'hullo'.

Keep fit, take care of yourself, & I'm sure we'll meet again sooner than we expect – this can't go on for ever, & then I'm coming rushing back to Southold!

With much love,

BEN

1 Regina Sturmdorf was the aunt of David Rothman's wife Ruth. This letter was enclosed with one to Bobby Rothman (Letter 387).

2   For a few months from May 1942, Britten used his sister Barbara's flat as his London base.

3   Pears sang the role of Hoffmann in Offenbach's opera for the first time on 6 May 1942 at the Strand Theatre, London, in a production by George Kirsta for Albion Opera Limited, conducted alternately by Walter Susskind and Hans F. Redlich.

XVIII   To Erwin Stein[1]

[vol. 2, p. 1140; after Letter 421]

Old Mill, Snape, Suffolk
March 31st 1943

My dear Erwin,

I haven't been terribly thorough over these proofs,[2] I am afraid, but I have found enough mistakes for the engraver to carry on with for the moment! Could you check the instrument headings & key signatures, please? On the whole it looks very good I think – & although one or two pages are a bit of a scramble I don't see what else could be done about it. It is nice to see it engraved – what a world of difference there is between engraving & any sort of makeshift, however good![3] I have made one or two small changes in dynamics – would you get someone to check the parts? One matter – I think it is simpler in the score if we keep the 2 B♭ Clarinets separate & make Bass Clarinet change to E♭, don't you? The parts can be written the other way round if you wish, but I think it better in the score.

I quite agree about St Cecilia – I have listened quite a lot to the records, & altho' they are far from ideal, I don't see how, short of getting another choir, they would get better.[4] O – these performers – I have just had a very self-satisfied letter from Sophie Wyss[5] about the Gallery concert, & a show yesterday of the Illuminations! A little more modesty, & a little more musical ability might improve matters. T. B. Lawrence[6] wrote me a snooty letter saying should he send back the Carols as you asked – & I replied that since you'd paid for them I think you ought to be allowed to have them if you want!

The work on the nocturnes[7] has fallen off a bit – what with the proofs, & the awful hullabaloo over Goehr[8] & all (I can't be bothered with musical politics!), the rather unpleasant air-raids we've been having, & general lack of congenial atmosphere – but they will progress, & anyhow I'm getting stronger & quite enjoying being lazy. I expect to get back to town towards the end of next week, & am looking forward to seeing you & Mrs Stein again soon – & some more good talks!

With best wishes,
Yours,
BEN

1   Austrian-born conductor, editor, publisher and writer (1885–1958). After
    the *Anschluss* Stein and his family came to London in 1938 when he worked
    as an editor at Boosey & Hawkes, becoming one of Britten's closest col-
    leagues and influential musical advisers. When the Steins' flat was
    destroyed by fire in November 1944 Britten and Pears invited the family –
    Erwin, his wife Sophie and daughter Marion – into their St John's Wood
    flat where they lived until the summer of 1946. See also Letter 59 n. 9 and
    1C1/2.
        In a letter to Dr P. Gradenwitz of Tel Aviv (4 May 1945), Stein gives his
    frank opinion of Britten:

    Britten stands here in the centre of musical interest, and not only in this country, but
    also in such European cities with which we have made renewed contact during the
    last few months [. . .]
        I personally think that Britten is one of the living composers who count. I admit
    to have been puzzled at his works at the beginning. Having a profound admiration
    for Schoenberg – whose pupil I am – and having followed the development of music
    since Mahler's late years at very close quarters, I was startled to meet here a young
    composer who seemed to have little connection with the immediate past, although I
    realized at once his enormous gifts. Actually these connections were close enough,
    and Britten knows the musical literature, new and old, better than any other English
    composer I have met. His favourite composers are Mozart, Schubert, Verdi, Mahler
    and Berg. You may guess from this queer combination that his musical mind is work-
    ing differently from what were accustomed.

2   Stein had sent Britten the proofs of the full score of *Sinfonia da Requiem* for
    checking.

3   The first edition of the full score of *Sinfonia da Requiem*, published in the
    US, had been a facsimile of the composer's manuscript.

4   The Decca recording (K1088–9) of *Hymn to St Cecilia* by the Fleet Street
    Choir, which was thought below par by Britten and his publishers. Ralph
    Hawkes had written to Britten on 23 March 1943:

    It appears that permission has been given for the recording and, therefore, legally,
    I could not stop their issue [. . .]
        Stein feels the same as I do – one can always pick holes in this sort of work and
    under these circumstances but as I do not feel that the Fleet Street Choir will do any
    better, I think that we should accept the fact that they have done their best and in
    any event we shall get a lot of performances of the records; in all probability we
    may get some human performances as a result, which are much better.

    See also Letter 420 n. 1.

5   Swiss soprano (1897–1983) who settled in England in 1925. She had given
    the first performances of *Our Hunting Fathers*, *On This Island*, and *Les
    Illuminations*, of which last she was the dedicatee. The three works were
    composed with her voice in mind, as were Britten's French folksong
    arrangements. See also Letter 88 n. 3.
        Britten had written to Stein on 30 March: 'Thank you for your letter &

comments on the Nat. Gallery concert – they didn't surprise me. Anyhow, Peter & I will do them properly for you soon!' Wyss and the pianist Gerald Moore had performed Britten's voice and piano arrangement of *Les Illuminations* at the National Gallery on 26 March. Stein told Britten that, while he had enjoyed the concert, Wyss was 'not too good' and Gerald Moore 'did not quite get the right tempis'.

6 Conductor of the Fleet Street Choir. Britten had written to Stein on 30 March: 'Don't believe T. B. Lawrence – he <u>had</u> the full scores of No. 7 (Winter) & 9 (Deo Gratias) [i.e. Nos. 8 and 10 of the revised version of *A Ceremony of Carols*] – but I suppose others can be made – but he <u>is</u> a nuisance. I hope he's sent everything back to you now.'

In April 1943 Boosey & Hawkes was anxious to make progress with the publication of *A Ceremony of Carols* now that Britten had revised the work, adding two numbers (No. 4a, 'That yongë child', and No. 7, the *Interlude* for harp) to the original sequence (see also Letter 374 n. 5). Britten wrote to Stein in early April:

Here at long last are the Carols complete, & I <u>don't</u> think there will be any alterations, except perhaps in the words, which I must consult Louis MacNeice about when I get back to town. But that won't be much, so go ahead with the printing if you want.

7 *Serenade*. Given the texts' concentration on aspects of night, Britten's working title for the song-cycle was 'nocturnes'. From Snape Britten had reported to Stein in an undated postcard (received at Boosey & Hawkes on 23 March): 'I am having a nice lazy time here – I've done nearly three of the horn songs since I got here.'

8 Walter Goehr (1903–1960), British conductor of German birth. There had been an unfortunate clash between Boosey & Hawkes's plans to schedule the first performance of *Serenade* in the firm's series of concerts at the Wigmore Hall and Britten's offer to Goehr to premiere the work in one of his concerts at the same venue. The matter was finally resolved by the publishing house engaging Goehr to conduct the first performance, on 15 October 1943, for its concert series.

XIX To Dr G. A. Auden[1]

[vol. 2, p. 1158; after Letter 433]
[*Typed*]

[c/o BOOSEY & HAWKES LTD, 295 REGENT STREET, LONDON]
July 21st 1943

Dear Dr Auden,

Please forgive me for not having answered your kind letter[2] with the enclosure before this, but I have been most terribly busy. I was very interested to see Blom's comments on the Sonnets.

I wonder if you have yet heard or seen my setting of Wystan's St Cecilia Ode. It is having quite a few performances and many people think the words some of the loveliest he has ever written.

I had a letter from him about a month ago, but it did not say much about him, except that he was still at Swarthmore[3] and seemed very cheerful. He is working hard which is the main thing.

It may amuse you to know that when I was at Wellington[4] two weeks ago I gave a lecture to the Sixth [form; pupils aged from sixteen to eighteen] on Wystan and his work which was very popular. He is still one of the most widely read of the poets there, and that goes for many other schools too, I hear.

Unfortunately, I have not had time to work on the Oratorio yet,[5] and anyhow it is the kind of task that one cannot hurry over. I, personally, find the script very exciting, but, of course, being written for music it probably will not seem quite clear until publicly performed.

It seems possible that in the not too distant future I may be coming to Birmingham. If so, I should very much like to meet you again if you have the time.

With kind regards,
Yours sincerely,

1   George Augustus Auden (1872–1957), W. H. Auden's father. He was a doctor of medicine; in 1908 he had been appointed Birmingham's first School Medical Officer.

2   Dr Auden had written to Britten on 18 May 1943 enclosing Eric Blom's review of 'Seven Sonatas [sic]' and 'St Cecilia'. (Blom had described the Fleet Street Choir's recording of *Hymn to St Cecilia* as 'unbelievably perfect' in the *Birmingham Post*: see Letter 431.) He also enquires about performances of the 'Oratorio'. The most recent letter Dr Auden had received from his son, who was still in the US, was dated 30 November 1942, but several had, apparently, failed to arrive.

 Pears and Britten had given the first performance of the *Seven Sonnets of Michelangelo* on 23 September 1942 at the Wigmore Hall. Press reviews, though not that by Eric Blom, are reproduced in Letter 391 n. 2. *Hymn to St Cecilia* had received its first performance (and broadcast) on St Cecilia's Day, 22 November 1942. Auden acknowledged receipt of his copy of the score in a letter to Britten of 23 March 1943: 'Have just got *St Cecilia* and think it is *lovely*. Thank you, my dear.'

3   Auden had taken up an appointment at Swarthmore, a private liberal arts foundation with Quaker associations, in the autumn of 1942. He had initially felt isolated and dissatisfied there and had discussed with friends the possibility of joining the Merchant Marine for the duration of the war.

4 Wellington College, where Kenneth Green (1905–1986), the Suffolk-born
   artist and stage designer, was art master. He was to design the costumes and
   sets for the first production of *Peter Grimes* in 1945. See also Letter 443 n. 10.
   There is evidence to suggest that Britten remained in touch with a small
   group of Wellingtonians both during their time at the College – see Letter
   434 where Britten thanks Walter Hussey for 'being so good to my young
   Wellingtonians' – and after they had left. In June 1945 one of this group,
   'David', was offered some secretarial work by Britten.

5 The history of Auden's text 'A Christmas Oratorio' ('For the Time Being'),
   which he wrote in what proved to be the ultimately disappointed expectation of Britten setting it, is set out in Letter 397 n. 2.

xx **To Mrs Regina Sturmdorf**
    [vol. 2, p. 1182; after Letter 446]

                                              The Old Mill, Snape, Suffolk
                                                          Jan. 11th 1944

My dear Mrs Sturmdorf,
     I ought to have written to you ages ago to thank you for your letters
which give me such a great deal of pleasure, including giving me a picture
of the family circle that means so much to me, & that I remember with so
much affection and nostalgia. I also wish you the season's greetings, very
belatedly, for all the best in 1944 and for many years to come. And may all
our prayers be answered that this year will see the end of this ghastly
carnage, and deterioration of the behaviour of the so-called civilised man.
I hope that you yourself are well, and enjoying life as you have done so
fully always. I wonder if you can get into New York ever to hear music, or
does the gasoline shortage prevent that? I'm sure if it is physically possible,
David [Rothman] would manage it for you! We go on well here – we have
most of us had our dose of 'flu, as I believe you have over your side, but it
hasn't been a serious kind, only terribly depressing. Both Peter & I are
working overtime – he singing better than ever, & has had an acting
succès fou with Vašek in the Bartered Bride,[1] playing everyone else off the
stage! I go on writing, & getting commissions – playing a lot too, and
occasional conducting which I enjoy. But the chief occupation of the
moment is the writing of an opera for Koussevitzky,[2] which I think will be
done at the Berkshires this summer. What a lark if you could get there to
hear it!? I am enjoying doing it enormously – in fact I feel that opera is
my real métier. I am spending most of the time here in the country, where
my sister and her children are living – most gay little creatures, aged nearly
five and one year![3] I find their conversation (such as it is) suits well my
mental level! So in spite of everything, you see my life isn't at all bad –
true, we all have our ups & downs, but I am very fortunate. Let me have

some news of you, my dear – & forgive only this short scrawl but I wanted
to send you my love & every good wish, from your very devoted,

BEN

1 Pears first sang Vašek in Smetana's opera on 10 November 1943 in a Sadler's
   Wells production in London directed by Eric Crozier and conducted by
   Lawrance Collingwood. See Philip Reed (compiler), 'Peter Pears and *The
   Bartered Bride*', 1995 Aldeburgh October Britten Festival programme book,
   pp. 14–16.

2 Serge Koussevitzky (1874–1951), Russian-born American conductor of the
   Boston Symphony Orchestra from 1924 to 1949. He championed Britten's
   music in the US and was responsible for the commissioning of *Peter
   Grimes* and *Spring Symphony*. See also Letter 174 n. 3 and IC1/2.
       In the event *Peter Grimes* was premiered in London, at Sadler's Wells, in
   May 1945. It was performed at Tanglewood in 1946.

3 Beth Welford's daughter Sarah Charlotte, known as Sally, had been born on
   13 January 1943. Pears was her godfather.

XXI To James Butt[1]
[vol. 2, p. 1190; after Letter 455]

[London]
3rd April 1944

Dear Jim,
       I enjoyed meeting your parents yesterday, and feel that you should start
more advanced serious study of composition as soon as possible.
       I shall be returning to the mill at Snape, tomorrow, where I shall be
closeted for the next six weeks working on 'Peter Grimes'.
       I would like you to come and stay with myself and Beth for a few days,
so that I can begin to teach you about counterpoint, if you would do
some copying for me in exchange.
       If you ring me at Snape after the 5th, I will find out the times of the
best trains for you.

Yours sincerely,
BEN

1 English composer, pianist and conductor (1929–2003). Butt received composition lessons from Britten in return for working as his assistant at this
   period. He studied composition with Erwin Stein and Mátyás Seiber, and
   piano with Franz Osborn. Following National Service, Butt completed his
   studies at Dartington under the supervision of Imogen Holst (see Letter
   638). See also Letter 485 n. 1 and John Howard, 'Respects paid to Suffolk
   composer', *East Anglian Daily Times* (6 March 2003), p. 14.

XXII **To Peter Pears**
[vol. 2, between pp. 1229 and 1240]
[*Postcard: views of Aldeburgh*]

Old Mill
[November 1944]

I forgot to say in my other letter that I've heard the new Serenade 'takes'[1] –
& they are terrific. The Dirge[2] especially is a really super bit of singing, &
Orch: & Dennis[3] are also fine. I'm a bit worried about the matching tho'.
Erwin's flat has been drenched as the house caught fire, but luckily the P.G.
score is safe. Thanks for your letter – I'm glad about A.K.H![4] Sing nicely.

Love,

B.

1 On 25 May 1944, Pears, Dennis Brain and the Boyd Neel String Orchestra
   conducted by Britten had recorded the *Serenade* for tenor, horn and strings
   for Decca (AK1151–3). There had been an additional recording session on
   8 October.

2 The fourth song of the *Serenade*, a setting of the anonymous fifteenth-
   century 'Lyke Wake Dirge'.

3 Dennis Brain (1921–1957), for whom the horn part in the *Serenade* had been
   conceived; see also Letter 392 n. 2.

4 A. K. Holland (1892–1980), English critic and writer, who was music critic
   of the *Liverpool Daily Post*. On 12 October Holland's wife had written on
   her husband's behalf to apologize for a review in which he had claimed that
   a performance of the *Michelangelo Sonnets* at the Services Quiet Club, presumably in or close to Liverpool, had been the premiere.

XXIII **To Erwin Stein**
[vol. 2, between pages 1246 and 1252]

[Friston Field, Sussex][1]
[?May 1945]

Dear Erwin,

Here is the note.[2] Could you please get it typed & send it with the note
on the Kermesse[3] to the Cheltenham chap? If you could please write an
explanatory note, saying why we have decided on that rather than the
Dances,[4] I think it would carry more weight than if I wrote.

We're having a lovely time here – lovely food, & sleep & weather. That's
why I'm writing in pencil!

Love from us both to you all,

BEN

The Cheltenham chap is: G. A. M. Wilkinson Esq, Spa Manager, Town Hall, Cheltenham.

1   Britten was staying with Ethel Bridge.

2   Britten attached the following note:

Interludes from "Peter Grimes"

"Peter Grimes", an opera in 3 Acts and a Prologue, was written in 1944. Commissioned by Serge Koussevitzky in memory of his wife Natalie Koussevitzky who died in 1942, it was intended to be given first at the Berkshire Festival in New England last year. Wartime conditions however prevented this, & the first performance was given on June 7th by the Sadler's Wells Opera, at their own theatre, the principal singers being Joan Cross & Peter Pears & the conductor Reginald Goodall. The opera deals with life in a small fishing town on the East Coast of England, and it is different aspects of this seascape that the interludes describe. They are played without a break but in character they are quite distinct.

I, played before Act I scene one, is a grey cold morning. Everyday work is going on, but there is an ominous feeling beneath the deep swell of the brass.

II introduces Act II. It is a brilliant Sunday morning. Church bells ring, and the sunshine glitters on the waves.

III, played before Act III, describes a beautiful summer night, with a full moon, and only the slightest movement in the dark sea.

IV links scenes one & two of Act I, and introduces one of the typical March gales on the East Coast which do so much damage, eating away that much eroded coast. It is in rondo form, with ever increasing vigour, except for a lyrical episode, which describes the ecstasy of Peter Grimes, the central character, whose existence is a solitary one & whose soul is stimulated by such a storm as this.

3   *Canadian Carnival* (*Kermesse Canadienne*), for orchestra, composed November–December 1939; see also Letter 180 n. 4. The performance at Cheltenham on 13 June 1945, given by the London Philharmonic Orchestra, conducted by Britten, was the work's first concert performance. This same concert included the first performance of the *Four Sea Interludes from 'Peter Grimes'*; see also Letter xxv n. 2.

    The note on *Canadian Carnival* that appeared in the Cheltenham Festival programme book reads as follows:

The word Kermesse is a corruption, familiar in French Flanders, of the German Kirchmesse (Church Mass) indicating the fair held in association with the anniversary of the consecration of the parish church, from which its meaning has been broadened to include almost any popular festivity.

    The work, composed at Amityville, Long Island, New York, in the last months of 1939, is a rhapsody on French-Canadian folk tunes which Britten had heard in the Province of Quebec. Against a background suggesting the Canadian landscape gradually coming to life on the morning of the great day, Britten evokes a number of Canadian tunes. The fair grows boisterous, but after some climaxes it dies down, the villagers disperse, and all is again quiet and peaceful.

4   Perhaps a projected orchestral suite to be derived from the dance in the Moot Hall, *Peter Grimes* (Act III scene 1) in which the sequence of dance numbers – including a hornpipe and a ländler – is played by an offstage band.

xxiv   To Erwin Stein

[vol. 2, p. 1278; after Letter 508]

Old Mill, Snape, Suffolk
Aug. 18th 1945

My dear Erwin,

Lovely to hear all your voices & to know that you've enjoyed your holiday.[1] What a bore that it was so short.

This is only a note to return your P.G. article[2] & to say how much I liked it. Peter & I have queried one or two expressions which are either not clear or not too "good English!" But it is fine, & I'm very proud that you feel that way, my dear – you know what I feel about your opinions and tastes.

The other enclosures are just bores – but after dictating 30 (!) letters to a nice girl-secretary down here, I couldn't face these three, & didn't see why I should do these people's work for them. If you feel they should be coped with, could you please – otherwise, our old friend the Waste-Paper-Basket –

I hope you'll like the Donne sonnets[3] – I've done eight, & at the moment think they're O.K. – but they're difficult & rather odd.

Love to you all,
BEN

1   The Stein family, joined by violinist Winifred Roberts (see n. 3 below), had taken a holiday in Devon near Ronald and Rose Marie Duncan. Winifred Roberts remembers Erwin Stein working on some proofs; these would have been the vocal score of *Peter Grimes* (see PBMPG, p. 193).

2   Stein's article, 'Opera and *Peter Grimes*', *Tempo* (old series), 12 (September 1945), pp. 2–6, which was subsequently reprinted in Stein's *Orpheus in New Guises*; part of the article appeared in DMHK, pp. 125–31.

3   *The Holy Sonnets of John Donne*, for high voice and piano, composed 2–19 August 1945, immediately on Britten's return from his concert tour of German concentration camps (see Letter xxv n. 3). By the date of this letter Britten had composed the entire cycle with the exception of the ninth and final song, 'Death be not proud', which was written on 19 August. The cycle

was dedicated to Pears. Britten had been considering Donne for at least a year: in August 1944 (Letter 473) Pears told Elizabeth Mayer that 'Ben talks of George Herbert & John Donne (the Sacred Sonnets perhaps)'; and dating from the American years there is an incomplete setting of 'Stay, O sweet, and do not rise'. (With reference to Herbert, see p. 122.)

The first performance of the *Donne Sonnets* was given on 22 November 1945 (Britten's thirty-second birthday) at the Wigmore Hall, London, by Pears and the composer. Winifred Roberts reported in a letter to Antonio and Peggy Brosa (11 November 1945) that Pears and Britten had included one of the *Donne Sonnets* in a private recital at a party to celebrate Stein's sixtieth birthday on 7 November:

[. . .] we had a jolly party with Ben, Peter and Ronnie Duncan. Ben and Peter sang, and Marion [Marion Thorpe, Stein's daughter] and I played a Schubert piano duet, and a Mozart violin and piano sonata, and Ben, Peter and I played Mozart's *Sinfonia concertante* (Ben playing the viola). Ronnie Duncan wrote a greetings poem in honour of Mr Stein. Ben set it, & Peter sang it. I also heard one of Ben's new settings of Donne's holy sonnets.

The setting of Duncan's 'greetings poem' is *Birthday Song for Erwin*, which did not resurface until the mid-1980s when Marion Thorpe was sorting out some of her father's papers. The song was published in the collection *The Red Cockatoo & Other Songs* by Faber Music in 1994.

xxv To Rutland Boughton[1]
[vol. 2, p. 1277; after Letter 507]

Old Mill, Snape, Suffolk
Aug. 29th 1945

Dear Rutland Boughton,

Your kind & moving letter[2] has lain very long unanswered. I am very sorry, actually since it arrived I have been either abroad, or down here sick with the result of my <u>first</u> vaccination![3]

So I'm afraid my correspondence has got hopelessly behindhand. Please forgive my apparent rudeness.

I was very pleased that you got pleasure from Peter Grimes. I was very nervous about my first operatic venture, I admit, but I am rather encouraged by the kindness so many people have expressed about it. I take it as a real compliment that such an experienced opera composer as yourself approve of it. I am afraid that there won't be any performances in London in the near future: there has been a big bust-up in the company, & the Governors of the Wells have sided with the "opposition" to Grimes, & so it doesn't seem likely that it will be revived there. But happily there seems to be possibilities of other homes for it.

I note your criticism of the final lighting. Actually the lighting generally was erratic, since the electricians had laws unto themselves – such was the chaos in the company! – so what you saw was probably not the intention of the producer. There should have been a spot on Peter all through the scene.

Thank you again so very much for your letter. I was really most happy to get it.

Yours sincerely
BENJAMIN BRITTEN

1 Rutland Boughton (1878–1960), English composer, principally of opera. See also Diary for 10 September 1931, n. 7.

2 Boughton had written to Britten on 3 July 1945:

Hearing the interludes from *Peter Grimes* at your Cheltenham rehearsal [for the first concert performance of the *Four Sea Interludes* at the Cheltenham Festival on 13 June 1945], I was compelled to run down to town for the complete work, and I rejoice in it even though my old ears cannot always accept your dissonances, though my 3 days at Cheltenham give me hope that they (my ears) are still capable of Education. I am ordering the vocal score of *P.G.* from B. & H. in the hope of a more real understanding of the work. The relation of voices to orchestra I thought was completely satisfactory, and the scene with the fog-horn very fine [Act III scene 2].

Don't you think the lighting might be increased with advantage in some of the other scenes? It is only on a *very* dark night that one cannot see much better than your producer seemed to think.

He added in a postscript:

Is there likely to be a London performance soon after Sep. 1? On that day I am lecturing on opera at the Regent St Polytechnic, and would like to refer to *P.G.* if those references could be followed up by a performance.

3 At the end of July 1945 Britten had toured German concentration camps as Yehudi Menuhin's accompanist. On Britten's return, his doctor insisted on his having a vaccination (see Letter 509), probably for typhoid and para-typhoid, to which he had an adverse reaction and was ill for several weeks.

XXVI To Imogen Holst[1]
[vol. 2, p. 1283; after Letter 511]

The Old Mill, Snape, Suffolk
Oct. 2nd 1945

My dear Imogen,

As Peter has probably told you, since the great surprise, your most lovely present, arrived at St John's Wood, we have been travelling around, giving concerts & working very hard. I have had therefore to wait till I got back to the peace of Snape to write to you, & to give you my hopelessly inadequate thanks. My dear, the Harmonica Sacra[2] [sic] is quite the most lovely & moving present I have ever had. It was a most touching gesture, & one Peter & I will never, never forget. You know how much Purcell means to us, & to have this superb edition of some of his most phenomenal works is of untold value. Reading it & playing from it one realises how much this beautiful engraving adds to one's real understanding & love for the music (& also, incidentally, how poor modern engraving is in contrast to it) – and there are many little differences from the accepted modern editions which are fascinating & instructive. Thank you a thousand times for your generosity. The fact that your sweet action had something to do with the "Holy Sonnets of John Donne" make it all the more moving & exciting to me.

We hope to come down before too long & give you a more adequate show of them.[3] There are many spots in both music & performance which need brushing up. After we have done them a few times, I think they ought to 'settle down' – but they are very difficult.

It was lovely seeing you. I hope your work, your splendid & valuable work, goes on as well as always. How are the pieces for female voices?[4]

Please forgive these hopelessly meagre lines – but I cannot possibly convey my thanks for the Harmonica Sacra [sic].

With love,
BENJAMIN B.

1   English composer, conductor, teacher and writer (1907–1984). At this period she was the Director of Music in the Arts Department at Dartington. She worked as a music assistant to Britten from 1952 until 1964 and was an Artistic Director of the Aldeburgh Festival from 1956 to 1977. See also Letter 436 n. 1, 1C1/2 and Peter Cox and Jack Dobbs (eds.), *Imogen Holst at Dartington*.

2   Imogen Holst had given Britten and Pears a volume containing the first and second books of Purcell's *Harmonia Sacra: or, divine hymns and dialogues: with a through-bass for the theorbo-lute, bass viol, harpsichord, or organ*. The first book is a copy of the third edition (1714); the second book is a copy of the second edition (1714). The volume is inscribed by Imogen Holst: 'For Ben and Peter, with love and gratitude. September 1945'.

On 21 and 22 November 1945, the 250th anniversary of the death of Henry Purcell was commemorated with two concerts at the Wigmore Hall, including a number of Purcell works, some realized by Britten, and the first performances of Britten's Second String Quartet, written in homage to Purcell, and *The Holy Sonnets of John Donne*. See also Letter 514 n. 3.

3   Imogen Holst must have attended a private run-through of the *Donne Sonnets*.

4 Probably Imogen Holst's *Welcome Joy and Welcome Sorrow*, six settings of
John Keats, for female voices and harp, which received their first performance at the 1951 Aldeburgh Festival.

The opening bars of Purcell's divine hymn 'We sing to him',
as it appears in Britten's and Pears's copy of *Harmonia Sacra*
and in the manuscript of Britten's realization

'I LOVE BEING WITH YOU & PICKING YOUR BRAINS!'

Letters of Benjamin Britten and Edward Sackville-West 1942–45

Donald Mitchell

The first page (Prologue) of the manuscript full score of the *Serenade*, with the dedication to Edward Sackville-West – 'To E.S.-W.'

On 17 April 1942, Benjamin Britten and Peter Pears returned home from the United States, where they had lived and worked since 1939. As soon as they had been granted exemption from military service both men plunged into hectic and often independent musical activities, substantial parts of which were in fulfilment of the conditions imposed by the Tribunal that had heard their cases. Britten resumed living at the Old Mill, Snape, and also, together with Pears, acquired a London address: the first, in July 1942, 104A Cheyne Walk, SW10; the second, from February 1943, at 45A St John's Wood High Street, NW8, which remained their London base until 1946, and into which they invited Erwin Stein[1] and his family after a fire at their own home. A prominent feature of the months that immediately followed their relocation in England was the number of important premieres of Britten's music, for example, of the *Sinfonia da Requiem* at a Prom in July (first performance in the UK), a BBC broadcast premiere of *Hymn to St Cecilia* (22 November), and, most importantly, the first public performance of the *Seven Sonnets of Michelangelo*, the cycle Britten had completed in the US, was given at the Wigmore Hall (Pears and Britten) on 23 September.

Among those present at the Wigmore Hall was the remarkable figure of Edward Sackville-West (1901–1965), whose friendship with Britten, in particular during the crucial years 1942–45, has been relatively little examined. Sackville-West's biographer, Michael De-la-Noy,[2] found it not possible 'to pin down' when Sackville-West and Britten first met and conjectures that it seems 'reasonably certain [. . .] they knew each other well enough before the war to have collaborated on *The Rescue*[3] within months of Britten's return from America in April 1942'. It seems more likely to me that their friendship – its consultative character above all, which led to the dedication

---

1   See Letter XVIII n. 1.

2   Many of De-la-Noy's working papers and Sackville-West material gathered in the course of writing his biography, *Eddy: The Life of Edward Sackville-West*, are held at the British Library (MS Add. 68904–68921).

3   See Letter 416 n. 5 and pp. 123–8 below.

of the *Serenade* for tenor, horn and strings to Sackville-West apparently for the advice he gave Britten in making his final choice of poems – was generated by their mutual and professional involvement in the wartime BBC, where Sackville-West from 1939 was a prominent member of the Features and Drama Department. He was conspicuously literate, innately musical and himself a highly accomplished pianist. In addition he was an imaginative writer of some distinction and also a writer on music, a critic – he wrote for the *New Statesman* – whose views and enthusiasms were often markedly different from those prevailing in British musical culture in the 1930s and 1940s. It is hardly surprising that Sackville-West himself developed strong links with BBC colleagues active in the arts, among them many with whom Britten was to establish sympathetic relations on his return to the UK. What should not be overlooked is the need Britten had, after gaining his exemption from military service, to find employment, in which context we should remember that, although still in the relatively early stages of his career – the impact made by *Peter Grimes* was still to come – he had behind him a record of impressive experience and achievement in the area of film and incidental music; indeed this was something of which the Tribunal was aware: that he should continue to write incidental music for broadcast programmes of an appropriate, non-military character was one of the conditions to which Britten agreed, to help secure his exemption. In some of these programmes broadcast in 1942 and 1943 Louis MacNeice,[4] himself since 1941 a member of the BBC Features and Drama Department, was author and producer. It must have been a moment of singular ignition when Britten encountered Sackville-West ('Eddy') and his ambition to create specifically for radio a drama that, with genuine seriousness, attempted to integrate text and music: *The Rescue* (after Homer's *Odyssey*) reflected, in Sackville-West's own words, 'victory – and with it the liberation above all of France and Greece – for the first time in sight'.[5]

It has been difficult, until now even impossible, to attempt an assessment of the true significance of the relationship between Sackville-West and Britten: there was access to Sackville-West's side of what proved to be a substantial correspondence but it was only comparatively recently that

4   Irish poet and playwright (1907–1963). His translation of Aeschylus' *Agamemnon* and his own play *Out of the Picture*, both with incidental music by Britten, were produced by the Group Theatre in 1936 and 1937 respectively. From 1941 to 1961 he worked with great originality and distinction for the BBC Features Department and again collaborated with Britten in three wartime propaganda programmes in the series *Britain to America* (1942; see Letter 375 n. 2) and *The Dark Tower* (1946; see Letter 514 n. 6). See also Letter 320 n. 3 and, for information on Britten's setting of 'Sleep, my darling, sleep' and other projected settings of MacNeice, n. 22 below. MacNeice married Hedli Anderson in 1942.

5   See p. 124.

Britten's letters to Sackville-West were unexpectedly found and generously handed over to the Britten–Pears Foundation. (De-la-Noy had had to write his biography without knowledge of them.) I need hardly add that my account of them is necessarily brief and selective, but am confident that what follows will encourage a fresh estimate of what turned out to be a friendship with – as will be seen – unique features.

As early as October 1942, in a letter to Sackville-West, Britten responds very positively to his *New Statesman* review of the premiere of the *Michelangelo Sonnets*[6] while at the same time enquiring after what progress is being made on the script of *The Rescue*, again in highly enthusiastic terms:

I have just been shown this week's New Statesman, & believe me, it has done more towards my recovery than any of these horrible little pills or red medicines (that I usually forget to take). I have been laid up here for just a week with a particularly virulent form of 'flu bug, and have been more than usually down in the dumps, but your note on the Sonnets has bucked me up enormously. You have been so sympathetic towards them since Peter & I first did them for you,[7] but that you should go so far as to say what you have this week I never really expected. So very rare is it that critics have the courage to go the whole hog & say exactly what they feel without some qualification or other. But I shouldn't class you as a 'critic' (how I hate the parasitic race) & that is perhaps the explanation! If Peter were here he would I know join in my thanks, for actually you are the first person to write anything drawing attention to his great gifts &, I think, astounding performance. Your 'learned friend & colleague' G.A. [Gerald Abraham (1904–1988)] in the Observer made me sick (literally – because I did go down with this germ within an hour after reading him!!) – dismissing him as 'rumbustious'. Don't they want good voices around? Luckily the article was so badly written as to draw more attention to G.A.'s lack of talent than Peter's or my lack.

I like the beginning of your draft script [*The Rescue*] very much. It has quite a terrifying atmosphere, & grand opportunities for juicy music! How is the rest going?

[...]

Once again – thank you very much, more than I can say, for your article. It is one I shall always keep, because it has touched me so much.

So far so (relatively) straightforward. But in December of this same year

6 This review is quoted in Letter 391 n. 2; Sackville-West describes the cycle as 'the finest chamber songs England has had to show since the seventeenth century, and the best any country has produced since the death of Wolf'. On 16 November 1942, shortly after the premiere, James Lees-Milne, in his diaries for 1942–45, *Ancestral Voices and Prophesying Peace*, p. 113, documents a unique occasion taking place in Whistler's House, 96 Cheyne Walk, when 'Eddy [Sackville-West] and young Benjamin Britten played on two pianos Schubert and Chopin, and a tenor, Peter Pears, sang extremely competently the *Dichterliebe* of Schumann as well as *Seven Sonnets of Michelangelo*, composed by Britten himself'. (Presumably Pears would have been accompanied by Britten.) Here the importance of contemporary diarists, Lees-Milne, for example, and Frances Partridge, as invaluable sources of information and illumination is revealed. To date these have received little attention in Britten studies.

7 In private, one must assume, and in advance of the public premiere.

Britten was to receive a letter from Sackville-West (undated, but internal details establish that it was written on 2 December 1942), which must have come as something of a surprise:

Dear White Child.[8]

I am sitting here in the interval between two broadcasts – T. S. Eliot's *Little Gidding* and *And So To Bed*[9] – and because I think of you always and am so lonely without you, I must just talk to you on paper.

The Rescue seems (but again it may be an illusion) to be getting a move on, and from what I can hear, it will almost certainly be done. So begin thinking of the music ... Oh Benjie, I do so want this to happen – I have never wanted anything so much in my life. With your music – if you really take trouble – it should be something remarkable.

How foolish I am to be writing to you like this! how foolish ever to have told you how much – how unspeakably I love you! For I know from experience how unwelcome and how embarrassing it is to be loved by someone for whom you cannot care. But I am a born burner of boats and am past caring how pathetic a picture I make.

You see – I have always loved people inferior to myself in every way (except once, and he died); so it is a new experience to love someone whom I regard as a heavenly genius and potentially the greatest composer of the new era. It is wonderful to have come up against you at the moment when, your long apprenticeship over, you are at last launching into a series of masterpieces.

Let nothing distract you from this – neither the war nor people nor any outward circumstance whatever. This is the great moment in your life and if you hold on to it you will have twenty years at least at the height of your powers. But don't, oh don't! get led astray by Success or Money or what some fool may tell you is your duty to the world. You know in yourself what you have to do and that it is supremely worth doing and that, where you are concerned, nothing else matters.

Here I am talking about you again, instead of about myself, which I had meant to do in this letter. But my shyness and pride get in the way of self-expression nowadays, and I always shut up – or shut other people up – I live alone. To share another's life – I have dreamed of and longed for this so long, and it has always eluded me, because of the immitigable rondo that has been my private life.

Goodnight, my dear love,

EDDY

8 Sackville-West's term of endearment has its roots in a passage from W. H. Auden's text for Britten's *Hymn to St Cecilia*:

O dear white children casual as birds,
Playing among the ruined languages,
So small beside their large confusing words,
So gay against the greater silences
Of dreadful things you did: O hang the head,
Impetuous child with the tremendous brain,
O weep, child, weep, O weep away the stain,
Lost innocence who wished your lover dead,
Weep for the lives your wishes never led.

9 *And So To Bed* became a famous wartime late-night programme in 1942 when Sackville-West took charge of it, choosing not only the poems and prose excerpts but also the readers. On 5 July 1943 Britten participated in one of these programmes, reading extracts from Mozart's letters to his wife.

One should bear Sackville-West's later candid self-analysis in mind – 'Unrequited love is the only relationship in which I have ever been able completely to realise my capacities as a human being'[10] – while trying to make sense of so extravagant a declaration of love and remembering too something of which Sackville-West would have been fully aware, that since 1939 Britten had been in a deeply committed relationship with Peter Pears.[11] This love letter was first published in Michael De-la-Noy's biography in 1988 but has never found its way into Britten studies; and it is only now, with the recovery of what we believe to be the majority of Britten's letters to Sackville-West, between 1942 and 1959, that we can publish Britten's response, written a week later, on 9 December:

I haven't answered your letter before simply because things have been too much in a whirl to have even considered sitting down & writing letters; & now I am afraid this can only be the shortest note before I have to dash out again.

In so many ways your letter has made me very, very happy. I have been from the beginning so fond of you, & I respect & admire you so much that it is wonderful for me that you feel as you do. It is also a great relief for me that you don't, as I always imagine all exceptionally intelligent people must, feel bored stiff with being with me. (I go through life feeling singularly inadequate!) So it is pleasant, because I love being with you & picking your brains! But also, for these very reasons, I was worried by your letter. Since you are so damnably sensitive, I am afraid that this may spoil our friendship & that is the last thing I want to happen. Surely we can manage it? We have much too valuable a relation to throw [it] away so easily. It is perhaps more difficult for you than for me, because you are that much more proud & sensitive than I am, & it will be so easy for me to hurt you. But I want you to give me the benefit of every doubt – if I say I can't do this or that, the reasons will be genuine & never because I don't want to see you. I do want to see you a lot, & you behave so well that I never get any sense of strained atmosphere. I go away tomorrow until Sunday, but next week we must meet. I will call you when I get back – unless you call me . . . ?

Much love, my dear. This is a hopeless letter; but my only excuse is the usual one of inadequacy in dealing with words, & please believe that it is real affection which makes me write.

BEN

P.T.O.
I am awfully glad about the Rescue. I hope they'll give us lots of time to get a really good show ready.

I have said definitely 'no' to Dorian Gray & I am now trying to think of a good biblical story instead.[12]

In the days that passed after receiving Sackville-West's letter Britten must

10 Diary entry for 12 February 1953, quoted in De-la-Noy, p. 262.
11 Britten's and Pears's commitment to share their lives had been made in Toronto in June 1939; see vol. 1, pp. 20–21.
12 *The Picture of Dorian Gray* (1890) by Oscar Wilde, a possible ballet commission from Sadler's Wells Ballet, and a projected ballet, *The Mark of Cain*, to a scenario by Montagu Slater and the subject of much discussion between Britten and Sackville-West: see also Letter 415 n. 3.

have asked himself what the reality was of his relationship with Sackville-West. But his reply, when committed to paper, was exemplary, calming down the torrent of feeling and torrent of rhetoric released in Sackville-West's letter and showing an impressive patience, and generosity of spirit. All of this while collaborative work on *The Rescue* had not even begun!

Sackville-West replied by return of post, on the 10th, and it is quite clear that the tone the composer adopted had had a soothing influence on his impulsive, unpredictable friend:

Your sweet letter was a great relief to me. I thought you were never going to speak to me again ... The fact is, I am quite easy to deal with as long as I *know* when I am going to see you again, or if I can be sure that if you are busy – or I am busy – you will at least give me a ring and say hullo. What I can't bear is silence and uncertain absence. So, if you love me, you must try for my sake never to let the rally stop. Once the ball is allowed to fall to the ground and run away into the long grass, I begin to feel the snow falling round me, cutting me off ... So, this week, until this morning when your letter came, I went through an extreme of misery such as I had hoped never to be able to feel again. I can't help imagining things, and then I tear myself slowly into long strips ... I know it is all unreasonable and very hard on you; but after the betrayal, the cheat, the wicked cruelty I endured six years ago,[13] I have to re-learn confidence in the good will of others.

There was not to be any comparable exchange in the remaining correspondence, and from September 1943 'My White Child' was finally abandoned and 'My dear Ben' restored.

For both men this was undeniably a critical moment in their relationship. But in fact the friendship survived – if we might introduce a musical analogy, the dynamics henceforth were notably reduced – and that it did so was largely due to Britten's wisdom; and so too did the creative relationship, which was to have by no means marginal consequences for the composer. Fascinatingly, it is in the very continuation of the letter from which I have just quoted that Sackville-West quits the world of fantasy and reveals the serious and positive mutualities that formed the basis of the friendship:

[...] I am not such a fool as not to know my luck in possessing your affection. And what is all that nonsense about being a bore and inadequate?! Why, I consider you one of the most consistently intelligent people I have ever met. You never say a dull thing and your mind – your outlook – is endlessly sympathetic to me. I never tire of talking to you, – whatever the subject, – and of walking with you, or making toast, or playing 2-handed [*sic*] Mahler (even if I do look cross when you play loud while I am playing soft), or just sitting reading when you are composing. It is just your presence – your *continuous* companionship – that I need to remake my life, so that I may be reasonably happy and get on with my work. And since friendship means giving as much as taking, I will say what I believe you know: that I have a good deal to give you – particularly at this most important point in your career.

13 Sackville-West refers to his long and unhappy relationship with Sir Paul Latham: see De-la-Noy, pp. 156–9, et seq.

That glimpse of what Sackville-West viewed as an ideal domesticity – talking, walking, continuous companionship, playing the piano – cannot but
remind one of the companionship that Britten and Pears had only just
established and achieved in the US after their commitment to share their
lives and musical gifts, made only a year or two before this letter was written.
Recourse to piano arrangements of Mahler was certainly one of Britten's
and Pears's favoured relaxations when living with the Mayer family on
Long Island from 1939 to 1940 and again from 1941 to 1942, and I find it
impossible not to wonder if at some level Britten was not responding sympathetically to features of Sackville-West's personality that were akin to
Pears's.

I am not suggesting that Britten even momentarily thought of Sackville-
West as playing a role in his life in any way comparable to that played by
Pears; and yet the fact remains that, as Sackville-West himself remarks to
Britten, 'I will say what I believe you know: that I have a good deal to give
you – particularly at this moment in your career.' And there, surely, he
spoke – or wrote – the truth.

If one looks at the brief period when his friendship was creatively at its
most active, one cannot but conclude that Sackville-West's knowledge,
both literary and musical, made a highly significant contribution to a
number of the specific works on which Britten came to be engaged. The
collaborative venture of *The Rescue* speaks for itself, and Britten's letters to
Sackville-West are peppered with enquiries about the progress being made
on the completion of the text. The broadcast premiere I shall come to a
little later, but there is no doubt to my mind that Sackville-West had stimulated Britten to compose a major orchestral score between his completion
of the *Serenade* (Op. 31) and that of *Peter Grimes* (Op. 33), the significance
of which is perhaps still not adequately recognized today, though William
Mann, a former music critic of *The Times*, wrote a pioneering account of
the work for the Mitchell–Keller *Commentary* (DMHK) of 1952, the first
perhaps to acknowledge the ambition of *The Rescue*. In conclusion he was
to observe that the work was 'such an achievement that we looked forward
with optimism to Britten's opera *Peter Grimes*, then already being planned'
(p. 303).

None the less, for many years it has been Sackville-West's supposed and
widely assumed influence on the choice of Britten's texts for the *Serenade*
that has seemed to tell us what we needed to know about the character and
importance of the two men's relationship. In fact, as I believe and hope to
show, the relationship was also rather broader and more diverse, perhaps
even more interesting than that, though the *Serenade*, by its very nature,
must remain central to any account of it. Ironically, however, whatever
Sackville-West's involvement may have been, it is the least documented of

their exchanges or conversations about texts with which Britten was often preoccupied during these years and when he frequently sought Sackville-West's advice; in short, 'picking his brains', as he was memorably to put it in a letter in 1942.[14]

Britten seems to have started work on the concept and content of the *Serenade* by taking his copy of the Quiller-Couch *Oxford Book of English Verse*, awarded him as a school prize in 1930, and – under the title 'Night' (before 'Serenade' was adopted Britten referred to his new songs as 'Nocturnes') – proceeded to list on the back flyleaf those poems in the anthology that caught his attention, no fewer than sixteen in all. Among these were No. 184, 'Hymn [to Diana]' (Ben Jonson); No. 381, '[Lyke-Wake] Dirge' (Anon.); No. 638, 'Sonnet [to Sleep]' (Keats); No. 704, 'Nocturne' ['The Splendour Falls'] (Tennyson), and No. 705, 'Now sleeps the crimson petal' (Tennyson).[15] It is of no little interest that of these five texts, all of which, finally, were set by Britten, the last, No. 705, was to be discarded (though published independently in 1989), for musical reasons no doubt but also perhaps because so overt an affirmation of the composer's love for his soloist might have generated problems in the early 1940s.[16] Thus it is that at this stage the tally of poems initially chosen by Britten himself and later used in the work itself amounted to four texts. This left only two poems still to be found and selected: Cotton's 'Pastoral' ('The Day's grown old; the fainting Sun . . .') and the crucial choice of Blake's 'O Rose, thou art sick . . .'; neither poem is to be found in the edition of the anthology of English poetry in which Britten inscribed his list of texts for later consideration.

Every aspect of this particular issue is shrouded in uncertainty, and as Britten himself was a passionate consumer of English poetry from an early age it must have been the case that he would have known the Blake, if not the Cotton. However the fact remains that these did not figure in his extensive first list of nocturnal poems, and I believe it is possible that it was exactly here where Sackville-West may have stepped in, perhaps with more suggestions among which were Blake's and Cotton's texts. On the other

14 See p. 115.
15 The texts listed but not included in *Serenade* were: No. 93, Sir Philip Sidney, 'His Lady's Cruelty'; No. 174, Thomas Campion, 'Winter Nights'; No. 262, Robert Herrick, 'The Night-piece: To Julia'; No. 298, William Habington, 'Nox Nocti Indicat Scientiam'; No. 459, William Collins, 'Ode to Evening'; No. 491, William Blake, 'Night'; No. 521, William Wordsworth, 'Evening on Calais Beach'; No. 600, Lord Byron, 'She Walks in Beauty'; No. 609, Percy Bysshe Shelley, 'The Moon'; No. 612, Shelley, 'Night'; No. 617, Shelley, 'Remorse'; and No. 666, Thomas Lovell Beddoes, 'If thou wilt ease thine heart' (see also n. 21 below).
16 In a letter to Britten probably dating from March or April 1943, Lennox Berkeley wrote: 'I am rather excited about your setting "Now sleeps the crimson petal" – curiously enough it is right for you to set; I see that very clearly. I think that the kind of words any composer sets have nothing to do with period – his kind probably exists in every period.'

hand it is also possible that there may have been earlier discussion between Britten and Sackville-West as a result of Britten showing Sackville-West his pencilled list before he himself had begun to make the choices that eventually came to comprise the work we now know. Britten would have needed no help from Sackville-West in articulating the form of the work once the texts were established. But if it was Sackville-West who came up with some final propositions that in effect brought the cycle into being, then the tradition of crediting him with helping the composer with his choices is explained, as is the work's dedication, coloured though this is by a strange ambiguity.

Why, one wonders, did it take shape only as initials, 'E.S.-W.', instead of the full name of the dedicatee? This is the only instance in all of Britten's dedications of a major work – and the *Serenade* was certainly that – where this abbreviated format was adopted. (I am aware of course that while *Les Illuminations* in its entirety was unequivocally dedicated to Sophie Wyss,[17] its first soloist, each of three songs was dedicated to an individual who is identified by his and her initials: 'K.H.W.S.', Wulff Scherchen;[18] 'E.M.', Elizabeth Mayer;[19] and 'P.N.L.P.', Peter Pears.) There was good reason for each dedication but why the format of initials was used for the major dedicatee even while its conventional placing at the head of the score was retained remains a puzzle. In an edition of the score published by Boosey & Hawkes in 1999, however, Sackville-West's full name was at last spelled out.

Britten, throughout his life, chose his dedicatees with almost as much care as he chose his texts, and it remains a puzzle why Sackville-West's name was not spelled out. I myself have no doubt that the dedication can be read, for all its singularity of expression, as acknowledgement of help and encouragement that had been rendered. This was surely in Britten's mind when, in a note from Snape of 11 May 1944, he wrote, 'Thank you most awfully for the sweet letter[20] about the Serenade. I am terribly glad you like the piece, & I can't think of anyone I would rather have given it to.' As the work was first published in 1944 (the vocal score was made by Erwin Stein) it seems reasonable to guess that Britten's note to Sackville-West was prompted by the latter's response to receiving from him an inscribed(?) copy of the score.

As soon as one begins to put the relationship in context, in the unfolding chronology of Britten's life and works, it begins to take on genuine significance. Though it was probably the case that Sackville-West and Britten did not meet until after Britten's return from the States, we know

17 See Letter xviii n. 5.
18 See Letter xvi n. 4.
19 See Letter xiii n. 2.
20 This seems not to have survived.

that Sackville-West's enthusiasm for his music was initiated by his hearing an early part-performance of *Les Illuminations*, an off-the-air recording of which was in his possession.[21] This usefully reminds us of the role that W. H. Auden had played in steering Britten in the direction of poets whom Britten would then set. It was Auden who introduced him to Rimbaud, and who may possibly have had a hand in interesting him in Michelangelo. As for Auden himself, for an appreciable period he functioned as a major poetic source, as poet-in-residence so to speak; and it was Auden who was still about and at hand when he and Isherwood and Britten and Pears had all crossed the Atlantic.

But after Britten's return to the UK in 1942 there was, so to say, a gap. For sure, Pears and Britten had embarked on their life together, and Britten had already embarked on the creative relationship with Pears's voice which was to be fulfilled over the coming decades. But Pears's role as principal adviser on Britten's choice of texts – and sometimes adventurous instigator of his choice of poet (William Soutar, for instance, the poet of *Who are these Children?* (1969) is a case in point) – had hardly developed to the degree that today, when considering this matter of choice, brings Pears immediately to mind.

In the chain of command, Auden was the dazzling and brilliant first representative; but for the period roughly from 1942 to 1945, a critical period in both Britten's and Pears's lives – the return from America, their Tribunals as pacifists, their each pursuing significantly independent lives and activities, Britten as composer, Pears as itinerant performer – Britten found himself, I suggest, without anyone to follow in Auden's magisterial footsteps; and there can be little doubt, if one looks at the whole picture of Britten's life, that what finally took shape as Pears's indispensable advisory function had been already from the 1930s onwards an important and obligatory component of Britten's creativity. Thus it was, surely, that when Britten found himself deprived of Auden and without easy access to Pears – a glance at the substantial correspondence between Britten and Pears (see vols. 1 and 2) reveals the hyperactivity of both men in the 1940s – his finding himself thrown into close contact with Sackville-West must have seemed especially welcome, the more so as the latter had already shown himself to be a perceptive critic of Britten's music.

It is possible, then, to recognize that in his person, and given the unique circumstances of the period, Britten found a continuity of advice – albeit short-lived, and subject to the many eccentricities of Sackville-West's temperament and the sensitivities of Britten's – that bridged the gap between Auden and Pears. Another – and, for Britten, welcome – distinction of Sackville-West's would have been his espousal of Mahler, not only at the

21 See also pp. 128–30.

piano but in print. At this most barren of times in the culture of music criticism in England, Sackville-West was notable for being one of the very few
writers who ventured publicly to support and praise that composer. It is
perhaps of some interest to record that when I organized the first number
of *Music Survey* (in 1947: Hans Keller was to join me in 1949) my intention
was to redress, as I saw it at the age of twenty-two, a prevailing musical
culture in England that was unashamedly opposed to the influence of
European music as it had developed in the later nineteenth century and in
the first decades of the twentieth. Bearing in mind the intensity of Britten's
dedication to Mahler in the late 1930s and his determination in the US to
make the case for Mahler by whatever means at his disposal, Sackville-
West's already established Mahlerian credentials must have provided
another reason for the flowering of the friendship in the 1940s, another
instance of Mahler acting as a kind of bond. It was likewise in Britten's
relationship with Stein: the recognition of a shared and influential musical
culture.

There can be no doubt at all that the consultation of Sackville-West in all
manner of ways was prominent at this time. Here, for example, is a typical
passage from a letter of Britten's to Sackville-West dated 5 March 1944:

> Peter Grimes goes ahead well – I have completed Act I, &, except for one or two bad
> bits, it seems good to me. I long to play it to you, & I wonder what you'll say of my
> operatic style. Certainly it has come surprisingly easily considering that it's my
> first 'go'!
> What I have been meaning to ask you for ages is – can you think offhand of a
> good source I can go to for words for a song-cycle?[22] Peter & I have done the

22 Sackville-West was to respond with two suggestions: Thomas Beddoes (1803–1849) and
Frederic Prokosch (1906–1989). Sackville-West devised a sequence of Beddoes's poems for
Britten's consideration and, in a covering note, explained the thinking behind his suggested
arrangement as describing 'the arc of romantic love, from its inception to its early grave. The
theme is illustrated by the progress from earliest dawn to midnight.' In the event the suggestion was not taken up. This manuscript is at BPL.
It is of some interest that in March 1944 – the same month that Britten invited suggestions
from Sackville-West – Pears gave Britten a copy of *The Works of Thomas Lovell Beddoes*. On
the back flyleaf Britten lists five poems under the heading 'Dreams': p. 237, 'A Crocodile';
p. 169, 'The Masque in the Moon'; p. 110, 'Dream-Pedlary'; p. 242, 'A Dream', identified by
Britten as 'Thou pale Cupid'; and p. 248, 'Dream of Dying'. This annotation may date from
any period in Britten's life after March 1944, but the subject-matter of these poems bears a
strong relation to the theme of *Nocturne* (1958).
Britten had in fact already set two poems by Beddoes ('Song on the Water' and 'Dirge for
Wolfram', retitled 'Wild with Passion' and 'If thou wilt ease thine heart' respectively) in April
1942 on his return journey to the UK. Both settings are included in *The Red Cockatoo & Other
Songs*, and were first performed on 15 June 1992 by Lucy Shelton (soprano) and Ian Brown
(piano).
In the mid-1970s Britten planned a 'Sea Symphony', a large-scale work for soloists, chorus
and orchestra, setting a number of poems by a variety of writers, one of which was Beddoes.
What appears to be a near-final scheme includes Beddoes's 'Song from the Ship' ('To sea! To

Michelangelo until we're nearly crazy and if the demand for recitals from us continues as it is we've got to have a new big work from me for future seasons. Louis MacNeice has done me a lovely song-cycle,[23] but unfortunately it's for a woman and unless the attitude of society alters radically to you know what, Peter can't possibly sing it! What would be ideal would be some fifteen or twenty very short lyrics, in different metres, with some story to give dramatic impulse running thro' it. I've looked at the Donne love poems,[24] but there's not enough plot in those, heavenly tho' they are. The Herbert[25] I want to save for a bit, & anyhow they wouldn't do for the purpose I have in mind. 'Maud'[26] I can't face frankly. Is there an English equi-

---

sea! the calm is o'er') opening the second movement, probably a scherzo. Also listed in Britten's index of 'Sea poems' in one of his notebooks (BPL) is 'Song on the Water' ('Wild with Passion').

23 The cycle was entitled *The Revenant*, the concluding number of which, 'The nearness of remoteness like a lion's eye', was included in MacNeice's *Collected Poems* (1949) and identified as the 'last lyric from a Song Cycle: a girl speaks to her dead lover' (who has lost his life in war). The copy of the cycle that MacNeice sent Britten has not been found, but Jon Stallworthy, MacNeice's biographer, very kindly procured for us a copy of the complete cycle which was in fact published for the first time in Ireland in 1975 on the initiative of Hedli Anderson (see Letter VIII n. 4), who introduced the extensive cycle of twelve 'songs' and eleven 'interludes', as follows:

> Louis and I were married on 1 July 1942. [. . .] shortly after our marriage, while on a walking tour in Northern Ireland, Louis casually remarked that he would write a song-cycle for me. Equally casually, while we were guests of Mercy MacCann in a cottage in County Down, he sat down and wrote the poems of his song-cycle, and turned them over to me.

Anderson then goes on to list some of the approaches she made to composers who she thought might undertake the setting of the cycle, though without success. Oddly enough she makes no mention at all of Britten, despite her very close and long association with him. His letter to Sackville-West, dated 5 March 1944, from which I quote above, reports receipt of the 'lovely song-cycle' that MacNeice had done for him, words that suggest the cycle of songs and interludes had been conceived specifically for him, which it clearly was not. The cycle had already been put together in the latter half of 1942. No less oddly, and despite the fact that Britten raises the issue of the cycle's conception 'for a woman' – hence the problem of Pears's performing it – there is no mention at all of Anderson, who at this very time herself would have been preparing for her participation in the premiere of *The Rescue* (November 1943). A minor puzzle here undoubtedly. Who or what prompted MacNeice to send *The Revenant* to Britten in 1944?

While still in the US, Britten had embarked on a setting of a poem by Louis MacNeice, 'Sleep, my darling, sleep' (as 'Cradle Song'), to which he returned, probably in the autumn of 1942, by which time he was collaborating with MacNeice at the BBC. See prefatory note by Rosamund Strode to *The Red Cockatoo*.

We are much indebted to Professor Stallworthy for his assistance and information.

24 It was not Donne's love poems but his devotional verse that Britten was to set, as the cycle *The Holy Sonnets of John Donne*, in August 1945. However, he had started a setting of 'Stay, O Sweet, and do not rise' while in the US; see also Letter 507 n. 2.

25 At Christmas 1943 Britten had been given by Sackville-West *The Works of George Herbert*, edited with a commentary by F. E. Hutchinson. His only setting of Herbert was in 1956, *Antiphon*, for choir and organ. Britten thanked Sackville-West on 8 January 1944: 'I do really love it – you couldn't have given me anything I wanted more & it is a miracle that you could find it – I have looked everywhere for it without success. Thank you, my dear, more than I can say.'

26 The best-known setting of Tennyson's sequence of poems was by Sir Arthur Somervell in

valent of the Heine cycles, or Müller (was it he who wrote the Schubert cycles?)? Sorry to bother you, my dear, but if you have a brainwave do send me a P.C.

I believe that text admirably both characterizes and summarizes the dialogue that was sustained between the two men. The references to *Peter Grimes* and Pears – 'Peter & I have done the Michelangelo until we're nearly crazy' – brings to mind another letter of Britten's, this time to Pears, dated 11 March 1943 (Letter 416) in which, remarkably, Sackville-West is mentioned as a possible candidate to take on the libretto of *Grimes* if Montagu Slater fails to come up to scratch, though the suggestion is hedged around with doubts and qualifications on Britten's part which continued to surface again and again throughout the relationship. A line or two further on, Britten is telling Pears of 'quite a promising suggestion' from Sackville-West about the *Scottish Ballad* for two pianos and orchestra. And, it is this same letter that reveals that, Sackville-West's advisory role apart, Pears was kept informed of the complexities of his personality: 'I have just had a sweet letter, with no complications!, from Eddy.' Britten's exclamation mark, one might think, says it all. But the quotation makes clear that Pears had been kept informed by Britten of the 'complications' that had been introduced by Sackville-West's paroxysm of 2 December 1942.[27] *The Rescue* was yet to be completed and first broadcast (on 25 and 26 November 1943), a month or so in fact after the famous premiere of the *Serenade* had taken place at the Wigmore Hall.

I have already mentioned the absence of any precise indication of Sackville-West's influence on Britten's choice of poems, which makes all the more fascinating a comment Pears makes in a letter to Britten, written in late March 1943, when the completion of the work was under way. Pears writes (from Blackpool), 'How are the songs? I do hope I didn't damp your poor old enthusiasm too much about them – Don't be discouraged. Don't forget, my darling, that I am only as critical as I am because I have high standards for you.'[28] To which Britten replied on 1 April, '[. . .] don't worry, the Nocturnes [*Serenade*] will be worthy of you by the time I've finished!' If nothing else, this comment of Pears's might well mean that he himself had not been involved in the choice of the poems, though it is also possible that he was responding to a sight of the songs Britten had composed or perhaps even a run-through.

Hard on the heels of the *Serenade* followed the broadcast premiere of *The Rescue*, its two ninety-minute episodes broadcast on two successive

---

1898. The BBC Home Service had broadcast a reading of 'Maud' by Robert Harris on 16 October 1942. The *Radio Times* billing acknowledged 'incidental music selected by Edward Sackville-West'; the programme was produced by Stephen Potter.

27 See p. 114.
28 Letter 422.

nights.[29] Sackville-West's own highly intelligent introduction to a new production of the work, broadcast in the Third Programme, again in two parts, on 13 and 14 September 1951,[30] sets out very clearly his original intention and usefully reminds us of the historical context of its 1943 premiere:

Europe still occupied by the Germans, but victory – and with it the liberation above all of France and Greece – for the first time in sight; so intoxicating a relief from the strain and anxiety of the three preceding years coincided in my own mind with a dream I had long nourished – that of extending the scope of radio drama by combining words and music in a more thorough-going manner than had hitherto been attempted. A varied experience in 'Features and Drama' had convinced me that the rough and ready methods we had been pursuing in this field were worse than useless. Music was far too freely and loosely employed as a substitute for stage lighting, for the production of 'atmosphere', or merely to fill gaps in the script; meanwhile the characters and events remained obstinately invisible. It seemed to me, then, that music should not be used at all where words alone were sufficient, but that when needed it should take the place of gesture and movement, paint the landscape, characterize the persons of the play, and above all replace 'sound effects' – at the best a very rudimentary and ambiguous accessory. Only thus, I came to feel, could the listener's imagination be caught and held, so that he would have the impression of *seeing* what was happening, very much as the reader of a novel forms his own vision from the novelist's discursive method [. . .] My admiration for the genius of Benjamin Britten was an additional spur to me in shaping the text of *The Rescue*. He had been in on the idea from the first and needed no instruction from me to grasp every opportunity I gave him. The result is a kind of radio opera, for to my mind Britten's magnificently beautiful and adroit score is as important a part of *The Rescue* as the text itself.[31]

It was Walter Goehr, who had launched the *Serenade* in October 1943,

29 Stephen Potter, in 1943 a leading member of the BBC Features Department, had hoped to produce the first broadcast of *The Rescue*. (In the event, John Burrell took responsibility.) He admired the text – 'Read Eddy's new Homer masterpiece and find it fascinating' (Potter's diary for 18 October 1942) – and attended the first run-through with the orchestra on 23 November 1943, noting in his diary: 'The orchestra are not too Bolshevistic. These scraps of new music by a young composer often using only a very few instruments are hell. There are some grim smiles and a big rush for tea. "Yell of pain from the orchestra" is one of the stage directions in Eddy's script. If any of them troubled to read the script – unlikely – what a joke for them.'
    He was an attentive listener when *The Rescue* was broadcast a few nights later: 'Part II of *The Rescue* was a thrilling poetic and artistic and dramatic experience. Part I last night I listened to critically. But this time, influenced partly by P's [i.e. his wife Mary Potter's] boundless enthusiasm for it, I listened without script – and was completely carried away and moved to complete silence for 10 minutes after it was over.' See Julian Potter, *Stephen Potter at the BBC: 'Features' in War and Peace*, pp. 152–6.
    Julian Potter also documents his father's involvement in a programme entitled *The Living Spirit of France*, 'a compendium with music chosen by Lennox Berkeley and readings by Raymond Mortimer' which Potter and Sackville-West produced in August 1943. Britten also played a role in selecting the music for this programme, in which he and Pears performed. See Julian Potter, pp. 110 and 151.
30 The second of four productions (1948, 1951, 1956 and 1962) of *The Rescue* by Val Gielgud.
31 'A melodrama based on The Odyssey', *Radio Times*, (7 September 1951), p. 6.

who was also to conduct the revival of 1948; and this time it was the producer of its first broadcast, John Burrell, who provided a perceptive note
that focused on the music rather than the text. Of course he was writing
post-*Grimes, Lucretia* and *Herring*, and the point he makes may strike us
now as obvious; but it is exactly for that reason that we should take note of
it and recall that *The Rescue* (with the exception of the then unknown,
discarded and inaccessible *Paul Bunyan*), pre-dated the first public and
critical awareness of Britten's compositional methods in opera. What
Burrell wrote in 1948 takes on a renewed significance in the light of the
degree to which Britten was eventually to take the identification of character
and instrument in his late theatrical works: in this respect *The Rescue*
already anticipates, say, the Church Parables of the 1960s. Hence its importance in the evolution of Britten's operatic language. Burrell begins:

[. . .] Sackville-West describes it as a melodrama – taking his definition from the
Oxford English Dictionary – 'a play usually romantic and sensational in plot and
incident, in which songs are interspersed and in which the action is accompanied by
orchestral music appropriate to the situations'. There could be no better description.
  Music appropriate to the situations – ! Here is where Britten and Sackville-West
collaborated with such startling and successful results. Through the association of
a single instrument with a particular character (for instance, strings for Odysseus,
a saxophone for Penelope, a trumpet for Athene, a xylophone for Irus, the traitor
pimp) the music contributes to the characterization, in addition to its other
functions of setting the scene and time, and representing action. The killing of the
suitors by Odysseus is one of the most exciting examples of action in sound I know.
Suspense is clearly developed in the scenario, words provide the scene-painting,
and the music launches the dramatic and highly emotional climaxes.
  Music and speech and speech and music are integrated in the dramatic structure
as closely as in the dramatic picture. And the most elusive and fascinating element
of all the ingredients required in any work of art – style? Here is where so much
music in radio drama offends. Here is where integration between speech and music
is so often absent. Here in production is where musical syntax is so often abused.
But in *The Rescue*, I hope you will agree with me that above everything Britten has
found a musical style that is one with Sackville-West's style of writing – that is as
modern in its expression as it is classical in its derivations.[32]

The conflict in Europe, however, was not the only conflict that coloured
the premiere of *The Rescue* in 1943. There was also the farcical business at
the BBC, a combination, one guesses, of hostility to Britten's pacifism and
his homosexuality, which led to his standing down from conducting the
broadcast premiere.[33] The result was a performance that left the composer
less than satisfied. He wrote to Sackville-West on 12 December:

I ought to have written ages ago to thank you for all the copious details of the
Rescue performance, which I was glad to get. [. . .] I am glad the show went so well –

32 'A Landmark in Radio Creation', *Radio Times*, (27 February 1948), p. 3.
33 See Letter 437.

- 18 -

PENELOPE: Ah! I see you have lost hope. I suppose all of you have, - if I only knew. You no longer tell me the truth.

Music to background and hold

Ah! Eurynome! You have never known
The heavy weight of love,
The burden of it, like
A sick body.
On the day he left me -
Long,
So long ago - a day sunk deep in the furthest ebb of
memory -
Artemis sped an arrow into my breast,
And an obstinate bead of blood oozes from the wound
Every day that I live.
The hours drop to the ground,
Like tired leaves,
And decay,
And sink into the earth and become part of it.
And I sit here and listen,
Listen for each tiny sound - the chirr of a cricket
astray on the broad step of the house,
the gurgle of the lamp when the oil is
giving out, the ticking of my needle,
the footstep that seems to approach in
the distance of the house... and then
dies away into
The deepening silence of those who listen
No longer to the voice of their hearts.
The goddess too
Is silent; but
I listen to that silence.
Eurynome! Eurynome!
It is so hard to strive

Opposite The Rescue: a page from Britten's annotated copy of the typescript;
note the composer's pencil markings, 'Harp & / Strings (pizz)' and lower down
the page '+ Oboe solo', and his precise timings for the required duration
of the music

Above The corresponding page from Britten's manuscript full score.
Penelope's theme (No. 19) was originally intended to be played by the solo oboe;
however, when Britten came to write this number he jettisoned his earlier idea
(see the typescript) and allotted this melody to the alto saxophone.

I endeavoured to listen to it all, but the set was so awful, the reception so poor, & I so 'fluey that I didn't really make much sense out of it, words or music. From what little I could hear, I gathered that Tony[34] had picked up the right tempi & had managed to din them into Raybould's[35] head – with one awful exception in Part II, when the brass fugue was miles too fast & all the peaks came in the wrong places! Also, the Hermes scherzo seemed a flop because of unimaginative singing & a completely inaudible orchestra! – but perhaps that wasn't as bad as my 'flu made me think. I'm glad you were pleased with the cast: I liked Hedli, her voice came over well to us in Devon,[36] but there wasn't much Mediterranean feeling in Arundel,[37] whom I was surprised to learn you liked! [. . .] I am so glad people seemed to like the music & thought it went well with the words & that you were pleased with it yourself. Considering the atmosphere it was written in I am surprised that it came out so well!

Britten had intended to attend a playback but in the event was unable to be present. Moreover, it was now the completion of *Peter Grimes* that was uppermost in his mind: on 12 April 1944 he wrote to Sackville-West, 'after nearly a week's chewing my pencil and kicking my heels, I have at last got back to work on Grimes – ahead with the 2nd Act, and doing some unpicking in the 1st'. His comments that follow show that Sackville-West, for all the 'complications', was still a confidant to whom Britten could express himself freely about musical matters:

I quite agree with what you say about the setting of the piece – in fact that is the point that Eric Crozier, the young man who's going to produce it with Guthrie,[38] has been hammering at all the time. It mustn't look pretty – & neither must the music sound it either. That may be the trouble with some of Act I – but I don't feel it's a chronic trouble, & can easily eradicate it. I don't really agree with you about Ellen's Aria[39] – I feel you can't quite have got the point of it in that awful gabble-through – but there's plenty of time before it goes to print or on the stage, & every inch of it will come under the microscope over & over again.

The 'awful gabble-through' must have been a play-through to which Sackville-West had been invited, for good reason since it was to him that Britten was to entrust the writing of a major text on the new opera. There had, in fact, been a precedent, in connection with *Les Illuminations*, which work, as I have already suggested,[40] was one of Sackville-West's earliest

34 Antony Hopkins (b. 1921), English composer, pianist and educator. In later years he became a popular broadcaster with his radio series *Talking About Music*. See also Hopkins's autobiography, *Beating Time*.

35 Clarence Raybould (1886–1972), English conductor, composer and accompanist. He was Chief Assistant Conductor of the BBC Symphony Orchestra from 1938 to 1945. See Letter 99 n. 1.

36 Britten was staying with Christopher and Cicely Martin. Christopher Martin (1902–1944) was the Administrator of the Arts Department at Dartington Hall, 1934–44.

37 Dennis Arundell (1898–1988), the actor who played Odysseus.

38 Crozier (see Letter 529 n. 2) was sole producer of the opera at its premiere. Tyrone Guthrie (1900–1971) produced the opera at Covent Garden in 1947. In 1948 Guthrie was to produce the premiere of Britten's realization of *The Beggar's Opera* at Cambridge. See Letter 416 n. 6.

39 'Let her among you without fault cast the first stone . . .', Act I scene 1.

40 See p. 120 above.

encounters with Britten's music, if not the first, and his response was immediate and admiring. Hence, no doubt, when a performance of the cycle was planned in 1944, it was to Sackville-West that Britten turned for a programme note. It would be my guess that the composer himself was asked to provide it and unsurprisingly invited Sackville-West to fulfil the invitation. In any event, when he had received and read the text, this was his reply of 2 February:

The programme note has just arrived – and is really excellent. It was sweet of you to bother to do it, but I knew you'd do it so well, & I didn't want anyone else to – it has got in all the points that I wanted, and I think the bit about <u>understanding</u> the verse couldn't be better. The only small point that could be mentioned is, whether you couldn't say a bit more about 'J'ai seul la clef –'? Where you talk about him alone holding the clue to the meaning – could you say something about the point in the music of the recurring phrase – that possibly it wasn't only the <u>meaning</u> that he held the key to . . What do you think?

And the letter concludes with a mention of the *Serenade*: 'The proofs [. . .] are here & I'd like to show them to you.'

Later in this same year, the vocal score of *Les Illuminations* was published, an unusual feature of which was the inclusion of a prefatory note by Sackville-West, the only example I can think of when one of Britten's works was introduced by an independent albeit insightful critic. There is not space here to reproduce the preface in its entirety but if one bears in mind Britten's comments at the start of his letter – fascinating in themselves – and then reads Sackville-West's highly sophisticated text one cannot but conclude that the 'programme note', for whichever occasion it was intended,[41] revised possibly but in essence unchanged, now served as preface to the first publication of the vocal score. These are the last two paragraphs of Sackville-West's text:

Those who insist upon knowing what a poem *means* (in the narrower sense) cannot in this case be satisfied. All these short pieces must be considered in the light of (1) the title, which makes play with two meanings: the medieval illuminated manuscript and the sense of casting light upon a specified scene; (2) Rimbaud's expressed intention of searching for a new use of language in which words and phrases should be used like notes and harmonies in music. The first meaning is justified by the sharpness and exactitude of the images; the second by the way in which they are juxtaposed. Rimbaud in fact suppresses the simile: the word 'like' has no place in the vocabulary of his later work; the thing and that with which it is compared, become a single image, the meaning of which has to be felt, rather than apprehended, like a phrase of music. Yet it is always a picture, not an idea, that is evoked, and Britten's settings have rightly the sharp outlines and vivid colours of a missal. This point is important, for these poems are only obscure in the sense that, as Rimbaud says, the ultimate key to them is in his keeping alone. Taken separately, they explain, or rather express themselves, like elliptical entries in a diary.

41 It has not proved possible to identify this performance.

The composer's choice was evidently governed, at least to some extent, by what would set effectively. Yet, as the final episodes indicate, the guiding thread is the transition from one phase of life to another – as it were from the reckless experiments of adolescence (*Villes, Phrases, Being Beauteous*) to the disillusioned, but clarified intentions of maturity: 'Departure amid fresh love and fresh sounds.' So this is the opposite of nostalgic music: it looks forward, with the microscopic vision and the ruthless energy of discovered power.

It is clear that Sackville-West, by no means superficially, takes up the issue of 'meaning', one that Britten too touches on in his letter. It is exceptionally interesting that the programme note that Britten and Pears wrote for the first American performance of *Les Illuminations* on 18 May 1941 as part of the ISCM Festival in New York, when Pears was the soloist and Britten conducted, made specific mention of the 'arrogant cry' from 'Parade', 'J'ai seul la clef . . .';[42] and as we find in Sackville-West's introduction he addresses it in his comment that 'these poems are only obscure in the sense that, as Rimbaud says, the ultimate key to them is in his keeping alone'. This exchange about Rimbaud – about whom Sackville-West at the instigation of Virginia Woolf had written a pamphlet published in 1927 – allows us a glimpse at least of the intellectual dimension Sackville-West manifested in his relationship with Britten, on occasion perhaps too prominently even for the composer. In a letter of 5 March 1944 from which I have already quoted,[43] he returns to the topic of the note for *Les Illuminations*. 'I hope', he writes, 'Erwin Stein has not bothered you too much about your note [. . .] It was merely that the addition seemed to me a little too erudite for the people likely to have it to read, & to spoil slightly the excellence of the original note. What have you done about it? – but please don't worry.' What is reproduced above is taken from the preface to the published vocal score. Britten's loose terminology may well have blurred the distinction between a 'programme note' and a 'preface'.

As for the later text on *Peter Grimes*, this was to be published in 1945 as the third in the series of Sadler's Wells Opera Books and Sackville-West's long essay, 'The Musical and Dramatic Structure' (pp. 32–54), was one of four. The other contributors were E. M. Forster and Montagu Slater, while it was Britten who contributed a now famous introduction: 'One of my chief aims is to try and restore to the musical setting of the English language a brilliance, freedom, and vitality that have been curiously rare since the death of Purcell' (p. 8).

Since their first encounter in 1942 Britten of course had been constantly aware of Sackville-West's literary and critical presence, often manifesting itself in enthusiastic accounts of his music. So it is unsurprising perhaps

42 See Letter 313 n. 4 and PKBM, pp. 366–7.
43 See p. 121–3.

that he should have been asked to write what has to be regarded as the first serious study of Britten's opera. Moreover, there can be no doubt Sackville-West had the advantage of discussions with the composer about the opera, even while it was being written. It is this that lends a particular importance to his text.[44] For example his account of the Passacaglia for the first time identified the significance of the viola solo, which opens the interlude, which he describes as the 'centre-piece of the whole opera':

Interwoven with the development of the Passacaglia, the theme of which represents the obdurate will of Grimes himself, is a desolate, wandering motif depicting the workhouse boy who, accustomed no doubt to a steady lack of kindness, does not know how to deal with Grimes's sudden changes of mood and so – as children often do – takes refuge in silence. This theme (in which Grimes sees, not only the solitary boy beside him, but also the innocent child out of which he himself has grown) is heard first as a viola solo, accompanied only by the Passacaglia theme, *pizzicato*, with brief timpani rolls. [p. 44.]

This was not common knowledge in 1945, and the source of it could have been only the composer himself. Indeed, that Britten must have read a draft of Sackville-West's text and, while approving it, suggested additions or amendments, is precisely what lends it a special importance. Reading the text now, inevitably, one is struck by the familiarity of it all, and perhaps too by the somewhat pedestrian character of Sackville-West's literary style, something Britten became increasingly aware of even as the *Rescue* project was in train. But *déjà vu* would be an unjust conclusion; much of what Sackville-West wrote in 1945 was musically informed, fresh and arresting, and later generations of critics and students owe him a genuine debt.

A significant parallel is provided by Erwin Stein's 1945 piece on *Grimes*,[45] which was published after the premiere of the opera, unlike Sackville-West's, which preceded it. Here again the writer had Britten's ear (and vice versa), and we know that Stein's text met with the composer's approval: on 18 August 1945 he wrote, 'This is only a note to return your P.G. article & to say how much I liked it. Peter & I have queried one or two expressions which are either not clear or not too "good English!" But it is fine, & I'm very proud that you feel that way, my dear – you know what I feel about your opinions and tastes.'[46] (It was to Stein, in 1924 and 1926, that Schoenberg entrusted the first published accounts of his new compositional methods, in the first of which Stein wrote, 'For modern composition, the old keys are dead.' I sometimes wonder if Stein recalled that sentence when embarking on his *Grimes* article? Here was a scholar and critic whose work

---

44 See also Letter 416 n. 4; Philip Reed, 'Finding the Right Notes', and Donald Mitchell, '*Peter Grimes*: Fifty Years On', respectively chapters 5 and 7 in PBMPG.
45 See Letter XXIV n. 2.
46 Letter XXIV.

spanned some of the most eventful decades in the history of twentieth-century music.)

It is interesting that Stein too makes a point about the viola's solo at the beginning of the Passacaglia, much the same point as Sackville-West in fact but approached from a slightly different and more far-reaching perspective. The Passacaglia, writes Stein, 'is a set of variations on a new theme, played by the solo viola. Fragments of the variations appear in the following scene between Peter and the boy, forming, as it were, the only utterances of the unhappy child. The viola theme is repeated in its entirety, but with inverted intervals, at the end of the act after the boy's death.' (Oddly, neither Sackville-West nor Stein mentions that the viola was Britten's own personifying instrument, but Stein was perhaps the first to spell out quite so precisely that what we hear on the viola is not simply descriptive of the suffering child but represents his otherwise totally absent voice.)

Sackville-West's participation in the Sadler's Wells Opera Book of 1945 was to mark the end of his creative – advisory, consultative, critical – relationship with Britten. Inevitably, after the launching of the opera on 7 June and its phenomenal success, Britten's compositional career took on an altogether different character. Of no less importance was the end of the war in Europe in May 1945, which in itself radically revised the practicalities, both musical and personal, of Britten's and Pears's life together. In short Britten now would have had no need of Sackville-West's advice. That their friendship had a genuinely creative dimension to it in the peculiar circumstances of the hectic years from 1942 to 1945 cannot, and should not, be doubted or underestimated. If one simply runs through the list of Britten's works to which Sackville-West made contribution in a variety of ways and to differing degrees of involvement, it is clear that this was a relationship, a friendship, created though it may have been by the altogether exceptional historical circumstances of the time, that should not be ignored.

The works in question were *Rejoice in the Lamb*, *Serenade*, *The Rescue*, *Peter Grimes* and two items, *A Shepherd's Carol* and *Chorale after an Old French Carol*, both with texts by W. H. Auden and originally forming part of the *Christmas Oratorio*, a projected collaboration between Auden and Britten that was ultimately abandoned. It was for a BBC Home Service Features programme of Sackville-West's, *Poet's Christmas* (24 December 1944), that Britten composed the two settings.[47] They were then withdrawn until he authorized their performance in 1961 and their eventual publication. Pears aside, there would not have been many people to whom Britten would have shown Auden's incomplete oratorio.

47 In addition to Britten's two Auden settings, Sackville-West commissioned Tippett to set Edith Sitwell's 'The Weeping Babe' and Lennox Berkeley to set Frances Cornford's 'There was neither grass nor corn'.

But while the dialogue may have run its course, the friendship survived, generating still from time to time the unnecessary tiffs, slights and imagined insults that had always been a feature of it. But there is little point in spending time on the trivia except to remark that while undoubtedly Sackville-West was happy at the enormous success of *Grimes* and took pride in it, he may have found it difficult to come to terms with a protégé who had become, so to say, public property. Sackville-West was not without a sense of humour and when he himself was remarking on a typical instance of a suspected slight in a letter to Britten (27 June 1945) he added this postscript: 'Our respective biographers will have fun with this little episode. "At this time there appears to have been a slight coolness" – then a footnote (by your man) referring to other instances of my notorious touchiness, and one (by mine) animadverting on the egotism of genius.' But the coolness in fact normally dissipated. The letters (on Sackville-West's side at least) did not diminish in quantity and he continued to follow Britten's career and attend first performances of new works.

For the most part these were very warmly and encouragingly received by Sackville-West, though by no means with indiscriminate enthusiasm. His comments after the premiere of *Lucretia* in 1946[48] typically did not please the composer. But he had made an insightful response to the Second String Quartet, enjoyed *Herring* and the *Spring Symphony*, was passionate about *Billy Budd*, much of which he had heard played by Britten himself, and had admiring things to say about *Gloriana*. In 1953 he visited Aldeburgh and returned in 1954, for what proved to be his last visit. He was hoping, he wrote in a note to Britten of 13 May, that 'you will sometime find an opportunity to play me some or all of *The Turn of the Screw*, of which I expect great things'.

At the end of 1945 Britten himself had visited for the first time Sackville-West's home at Long Crichel House in Dorset, the co-residents and owners of which were Eardley Knollys,[49] the music critic Desmond Shawe-Taylor,[50] and Sackville-West, to be joined later by the writer and critic Raymond Mortimer, literary editor of the *New Statesman* from 1935 to 1947. On Britten's return, he wrote a thank-you letter (19 December) from the Old Mill at Snape:

My dear Eddy,
I arrived back last Sunday in London to find a nice bunch of crises waiting for me

48 See Letter 536 n. 1.
49 British artist (1902–1991), known particularly for his colourful treatment of his native Hampshire landscape. From 1942 to 1957 Knollys was the National Trust representative for South-West England. It was he and Desmond Shawe-Taylor who had discovered Long Crichel House for Sackville-West. See also obituaries in *The Times* (13 September 1991) and by Michael Parkin, with a further contribution by Frances Partridge, *Independent* (11 September 1991).
50 See Letter 602 n. 2.

(mostly over the opera company).[51] The result is that I am only just arrived down here with leisure enough to write to you & thank you for a most lovely four days. Thank you, my dear, more than I can say. You couldn't have given me a lovelier present than that luxurious rest, & I feel a new person after it, & not at all guilty that I ate so much, slept so much, and did so little work! It is a most lovely happy home that you have, & I am delighted to be able to think of you there. Please thank Desmond too for the way he looked after me – he couldn't have been more thoughtful or kinder. I hope his car didn't develop any more alarming internal troubles on the return journey after the great dash to Salisbury! I was going to write him a note too, but since I got so involved in London I am more than ever behind-hand with my BBC homework,[52] & am a bit scared as to what the head-prefect (Louis [MacNeice]) or even the house-master (Laurence Gilliam)[53] may say if I don't show up with it soon. I was also going to write a Serenade for Topaz for Christmas – but that will have to wait too.

Much love to you, my dear, & many many thanks again, & best Christmas wishes to you all three,

BEN

There were upsets yet to come – with Shawe-Taylor for one, author of a review to which Britten once again took exception – but the warmth of the letter reflects, I like to think, a genuine gratitude for a singular relationship at a highly critical period in Britten's life. As for Topaz, this was surely a reference to a household pet. The name in fact crops up again in the post-script to a letter to Britten from Sackville-West dated 1 March 1946 in which he writes, 'Desmond and Eardley send their love. Topaz, faint from lack of food, contributes a moo.' I am not sure that this puts beyond doubt a correct identification of the pet itself (dog? cat?), but the probability that it was a dog is confirmed by a reminiscence of Frances Partridge of her first impressions of the household at Long Crichel. She recalls as a 'counterbase' to the hospitality of her hosts (Sackville-West, Shawe-Taylor, Mortimer, Knollys), 'an overlapping series of large, soft, affectionate labrador dogs who rushed to give visitors a gratifying enthusiastic welcome, filled the hearthrug with their outstretched, golden bodies, or fixed one with doe-like eyes pleading for a walk'.[54] Whether it was Topaz, or a successor, who was among the groups we cannot be sure. But of one thing we can be absolutely certain: that it could never have been anything other than a 'Serenade' that Britten had in mind to compose for Eddy's household pet. After all, there had been a distinguished precedent.

Special thanks are due to: Philip Reed, the Britten–Pears Library (Nick Clark, Anne Surfling and Pamela Wheeler), Jill Burrows, John Evans, Andrew Porter, Jon Stallworthy, and the late Patrick Trevor-Roper.

51 Britten refers to current problems at Glyndebourne (where *Lucretia* was to be forthcoming in 1946), which finally led to the birth of the English Opera Group.
52 Britten's music for the radio drama *The Dark Tower*, text by Louis MacNeice, first broadcast in the BBC Home Service on 21 January 1946. Among the ensemble were Richard Walton (trumpet) and James Blades (percussion), and the conductor was Walter Goehr.
53 Producer in the BBC Drama Department (1904–1964).
54 Frances Partridge, *Diaries 1939–1972*, p. 164.

II CHAMBER OPERA IS CREATED

JANUARY 1946–AUGUST 1947

CHRONOLOGY 1946–1947

YEAR	EVENTS AND COMPOSITIONS
1946	
9–12 January	Concerts in Amsterdam, The Hague and Brussels, including first Dutch recital with Pears
21 January	First performance (BBC broadcast) of *The Dark Tower* (MacNeice)
23 January	Begins composition of *The Rape of Lucretia*
7 February	*Peter Grimes* revived at Sadler's Wells
2 March	Boston: Koussevitzky conducts US premiere of *Four Sea Interludes* and *Passacaglia from 'Peter Grimes'*
21 March	Stockholm: Swedish premiere of *Peter Grimes*
28 March	Supervises music recording of *Instruments of the Orchestra*
3 May	COMPOSITION *The Rape of Lucretia*
6 May – 9 June	In Switzerland with Pears for holidays, concerts and opera performances, including *Peter Grimes* in Basel and Zurich
10 June	To Glyndebourne for rehearsals of *The Rape of Lucretia*
2 July	Cheltenham: First performance of the revised version of Piano Concerto
12 July	Glyndebourne: First performance of *The Rape of Lucretia*, conducted by Ernest Ansermet
29 July – 28 September	*The Rape of Lucretia* toured to Manchester, Liverpool, Edinburgh, Glasgow, London (Sadler's Wells) and Oxford
31 July – 10 August	Visits US for Tanglewood performances of *Peter Grimes*, conducted by Leonard Bernstein (US premiere: *6 August*)
26 August	Moves to new London address, 3 Oxford Square, London W2
late August	COMPOSITIONS Theatre: *The Duchess of Malfi* (Webster); *The Eagle Has Two Heads* (Cocteau, trans. Duncan)
14 September	COMPOSITION *Occasional Overture*
18 September	COMPOSITION *Prelude and Fugue on a Theme of Vittoria*

20 September	Providence, Rhode Island, US: First performance of *The Duchess of Malfi* with Britten's music
21 September	St Matthew's, Northampton: First performance of *Prelude and Fugue on a Theme of Vittoria*
29 September	BBC Third Programme: First performance of *Occasional Overture*
October	*The Rape of Lucretia* toured to the Netherlands COMPOSITION Folk Song Arrangements, Vol. 3, British Isles
11 October	First UK broadcast of *The Rape of Lucretia*
mid-October	Crozier working at libretto for *Albert Herring*
15 October	Liverpool: First performance of *The Young Person's Guide to the Orchestra*
26 October – November	Concerts in the Netherlands with Pears, including *Young Person's Guide* (narrated by Britten) at Concertgebouw, Amsterdam
November	UK concert tour with Pears
29 November	Empire Theatre, Leicester Square, London: first screening of *Instruments of the Orchestra*
December	Begins work on *Albert Herring* English Opera Group founded

1947

January – February	In Switzerland composing *Albert Herring*; concerts with Pears in Switzerland, Belgium, the Netherlands, Sweden and Denmark
22 March	Hamburg: German premiere of *Peter Grimes*
Spring	COMPOSITION Revisions to *The Rape of Lucretia*
April	COMPOSITION *Albert Herring*
26 April – 5 May	Concert tour of Italy with Pears
5 June	Basel: Swiss premiere of *The Rape of Lucretia*
20 June	Glyndebourne: First performance of *Albert Herring*
7 July	Glyndebourne: First performance of revised version of *The Rape of Lucretia*
16–19 July	Supervises abridged HMV recording of *The Rape of Lucretia*, conducted by Reginald Goodall
22–30 July	EOG tour of *Lucretia* and *Herring* to Holland Festival
12–19 August	Lucerne: EOG performs *Lucretia* and *Herring*, and gives first performance of Berkeley's *Stabat Mater*
26–30 August	With Pears records *Donne Sonnets* for HMV
late August	Moves from Old Mill, Snape, to Crag House, 4 Crabbe Street, Aldeburgh

515　To Peter Pears

> Old Mill, Snape
> Jan. 24th 1946

My honey darling,

Well – I've taken the plunge and old Lucretia is now on the way. I started last night and I've now written most of the first recitative before the drinking song. I think it'll be all right but I always have cold feet at this point.¹ It is loathsome starting pieces – I always regret that I'm not a coal heaver or bus-driver and not have to depend on things you can't control. Perhaps it's as well you won't be coming here this weekend, when I should badger you for encouragement that perhaps you wouldn't feel up to giving! Now I shall have to rely on myself – always a risky business. Esther² was here last night – & was very sweet & helped Beth with her W.I.³ problems a great deal. She is a really sympathetic & intelligent person, & I'm devoted to her. She got on well with Beth, who thoroughly approved of her! Of course we talked a lot about you (my favourite pastime), & she, like me, is nicely prejudiced which makes it so easy.

I'm afraid I talked to her a bit about Park Crescent (knowing that you'd once talked to her about a similar problem), & she confirmed my feeling that, ideal as the place may be, we must be very cautious – unless we want yet another move in six months time after a quarrel which would be a thousand pities. Couldn't Joan⁴ have that maisonette, & we go across the road? But I'll trust you absolutely, old thing, do what you feel – but do it with your eyes open.⁵

I miss you just enormously, & get crashingly bored with myself.

Still it's got to be, & I've got to get on with the piece. How goes Grimes?⁶ Do take care, & if you have a vestige of temperature – go straight to bed.

> All my love, my darling, I love you,
>
> B.

Please don't forget my sleeping pills – necessary companions at this moment!

1　Britten refers to the Prologue from *The Rape of Lucretia* ('Rome is now ruled by the Etruscan upstart') for the Male and Female Chorus, sung in the first production by Pears and Joan Cross.

　　Ronald Duncan, the librettist of *Lucretia*, wrote of the Prologue: 'First we decided to write a vocal overture to be sung by the chorus. As soon as I had written this, Britten set it and played it over to me several times. Then we pulled it to pieces, cutting out two or three lines of verse here, and putting in two or three there, in order to improve the flow and coherence of the whole' (see RDBB, p. 62). Britten's pencil composition draft for this passage, however, betrays none of the rewriting that Duncan suggests took place.

See also Margaret S. Mertz, *History, Criticism and the Sources of Benjamin Britten's Opera 'The Rape of Lucretia'* (PhD dissertation, Harvard University, 1990).

2 Esther Neville-Smith, the wife of H. A. N. Neville-Smith, a master at Lancing College, Sussex, and a friend of Pears from his schooldays. See also Letter 221 n. 7.

3 W.I. = the Women's Institute, founded in 1915.

4 Joan Cross (1900–1993), English soprano, and of the first importance to Britten as artist, colleague, collaborator and friend. As Director of Sadler's Wells Opera in 1945 she took the bold decision to stage *Peter Grimes*, herself taking the role of Ellen Orford. She also created the roles of the Female Chorus in *The Rape of Lucretia*, Lady Billows in *Albert Herring*, Elizabeth I in *Gloriana*, and Mrs Grose in *The Turn of the Screw*. See also the following obituaries: Frank Granville Barker, 'A leading role in the opera', *Guardian* (14 December 1993); Elizabeth Forbes, *Independent* (14 December 1993); *Daily Telegraph* (14 December 1993); *The Times* (15 December 1993), and Colin Graham, 'Joan Cross – "so rare a soprano"', *Opera* (February 1994), pp. 164–9, which also includes a personal tribute by Ava June (pp. 169–70). See also Letter 417 n. 2. A copy of Cross's unpublished autobiography may be consulted at BPL.

5 Britten and Pears were evidently looking for a new London home, a search that was to end in spring 1946 when they discovered 3 Oxford Square, W2, moving there in August. Park Crescent, W1, lies at the north end of Portland Place. There was perhaps some proposal whereby Britten, Pears and Joan Cross were to share a home. The 'similar problem' to which Britten alludes may be the domestic difficulties he and Pears experienced when renting part of Ursula Nettleship's home, 104A Cheyne Walk, London, SW10, in 1942: see, for example, Letter 403.

6 Pears was rehearsing the first revival since the summer of 1945 of the original Sadler's Wells production of *Peter Grimes*. The revival opened on 7 February, with Joan Cross as Ellen Orford and Reginald Goodall conducting. The company gave ten performances between February and May (see Letter 514 n. 9). Pears and Cross appeared as guest artists, having resigned from the company in 1945 following the dissension that ironically accompanied the opera's phenomenal success.

Frank Howes reviewed the revival for *The Times* (8 February 1946):

> The opera on its revival last night showed the several and separate strands more clearly, and proved the strength of its structure as the strands are woven together. The performance still left a little to be desired in the articulation of the words, and the chorus had not the last degree of discipline. A better balanced orchestra would enhance the many very striking features of the score. But its psychological power was proved again to be such that in this respect it can compare with any opera in the repertory. Every musical device – figuration, instrumentation, harmony,

contrapuntal forms – everything, except perhaps strongly characterized melody, is used to produce the unique powers of music, drama, and discharge it at the audience from the stage.

The cast was the same with two small exceptions as at the original production, and the characterization was therefore the sharper, from Mr Peter Pears as the schizophrenic fisherman downwards to the small sketches of figures in the life of the Borough. Mr Agnus Digney effectively took the part of Bob Boles, the Methodist, at short notice. Miss Catherine Lawson made a motherly licensee of the Boar, but really needs a more incisive vocal edge for the part. Miss Joan Cross again provided the motif of pathos as the widow in a good piece of characterization that would have been still further improved with clearer delivery of her important words. Mr Roderick Lloyd as Balstrode and Miss [Valetta] Iacopi as the seedy widow effectively touched the springs that set off the catastrophe. Mr Reginald Goodall was in command and once more showed his ability to unleash and control the forces that move through this powerful score.

Desmond Shawe-Taylor, who had greeted the opera's first performance with a pair of reviews (see Letter 502 n. 2), returned for the revival and wrote about it in the *New Statesman and Nation* (16 February 1946):

Last week's revival of *Peter Grimes* at Sadler's Wells was marked by scenes of extraordinary enthusiasm [. . .] There was only one important change in the Sadler's Wells cast, and that was not an improvement. Miss Catherine Lawson, the new landlady of the Boar, lacked her predecessor's loud voice, rolling eye and Hogarthian aspect [. . .] Several points in the stage management had been clarified, and to the general effectiveness there is now only one serious exception: the climax of the second act [. . .] quite misses fire [. . .] not only was the boy's scream inaudible (it ought to freeze the theatre), but Mr Pears failed to convey the horror of the moment for Grimes. Indeed, well as Mr Pears sang, I felt rather too frequently the conflict between his own amiable personality and the daemonic character he was attempting to impersonate [. . .] an air of benevolence hampers Mr Pears in his more violent outbursts. If only, one couldn't help thinking, Mr Laurence Olivier happened to be a tenor, what an elemental Grimes we should witness!

It is perhaps for the same reason that I am beginning to find the unaccompanied 'mad scene' in the last act tedious: it demands in the performer a combination of dramatic virtuosity, musicianship, variety of tone-colour and sheer animal magnetism which few operatic tenors are likely to possess. The idea of the scene is excellent; and if the intended effect is perhaps unrealizable, it is almost a solitary error of judgement; otherwise, each rehearing of the score increases our admiration for the composer's workmanship, his sense of the stage, and the boldness and fertility of his musical invention.

To introduce the BBC live broadcast of the opera on 13 March from Sadler's Wells, Pears wrote an article for the *Radio Times*, 'Neither a Hero nor a Villain' (8 March 1946), p. 3, reprinted in PGPB, pp. 150–52, in which he sets out the opera's main dramatic themes, concluding that

Grimes is not a hero nor is he an operatic villain. He is not a sadist nor a demonic character, and the music quite clearly shows that. He is very much of an ordinary weak person who, being at odds with the society in which he finds himself, tries to overcome it and, in doing so, offends against the conventional code, is classed by society as a criminal, and destroyed as such.

The broadcast also engendered further press comment on the work: Robert L. Jacobs contributed an introductory article to the *Listener* (7 March 1946), 'The Significance of *Peter Grimes*', and in a later issue of the same periodical (21 March 1946), Dyneley Hussey reviewed the occasion from the point of view of opera broadcast direct from the theatre rather than the studio. Evidently there were technical problems that prevented all the subtleties of Britten's orchestral detail from making their fullest impact, but Hussey reserved his loudest complaints for a BBC production matter:

Will it be believed by those who did not hear the broadcast that the statement of the theme of the passacaglia was obliterated by the 'narrator's' voice telling us what any intelligent listener could perceive – that this music embodied the whole of Grimes's tragedy? [. . .] the listener should hear that first statement so that he may understand how the music develops. In the final scene the narrator was also too garrulous, interrupting the most lovely and poignant passages with such remarks as, 'they are putting up the shutters'.

Similar complaints were voiced by Ernest Newman in his review, '*Peter Grimes* and After – I', in the *Sunday Times* (24 March 1946):

Will someone who has a bit of influence at Broadcasting House break it gently to all parties concerned in this kind of thing that an orchestral episode like the passa-caglia in *Peter Grimes* is just as vital a part of the drama as anything that Auntie or Ned Keene has to say, and allow the commentator to keep his gob shut, as they would say in refined Lancashire circles, while this splendid and significant music is in process?

In response to Newman's comments, the BBC's Director of Music, Victor Hely-Hutchinson, wrote to the Editor of the *Sunday Times* on 5 April 1946 stating the BBC's policy in respect of radio broadcasts of opera. Copies of his letter were sent to Newman and Britten; the latter's copy survives at BPL:

When an opera is broadcast, the absence of stage action must be compensated for if the broadcast is to be intelligible to listeners who do not know the plot. It follows that in the case of an opera with continuous music either the music must occasion-ally be obscured or interrupted by an explanatory announcement, or the probability must be accepted that the plot will not be clear for lack of explanation. Either course has its disadvantages; but the BBC's policy is to do its utmost to make the plot clear, even if this means accepting periodical interruption or masking of the music. But in the case of a living composer this policy is only followed subject to the composer's own wishes.

In the case of *Peter Grimes*, the 'commentary' was originally prepared by Mr Britten himself, together with Mr Crozier, and the first draft was substantially reduced in consultation with my own colleagues. In connection with the *Passacaglia* itself, I have Mr Britten's authorization to say that he himself was most insistent that the significance of the *Passacaglia* in the story should be emphasized by an announcement at its opening.

516 To Rutland Boughton

Old Mill, Snape, Suffolk
Jan. 26th 1946

Dear Mr Boughton,

Thank you for your kind letter.[1] I am glad you enjoyed the Dark Tower. I was too involved in the production to realise how it was coming over; & so I am glad to hear from you that it was successful.

I should of course be extremely happy to meet you (& discuss all the vicissitudes of opera!) when you come up for Peter Grimes.[2] I shall not always be there for the performances this season, so perhaps you could let me have a card in advance which one you'll be coming to, & if possible we might have a meal together?

With best wishes,
Yours sincerely,
BENJAMIN BRITTEN

1   Boughton had written to Britten on 22 January, the day following the first broadcast, in the BBC Home Service, of Louis MacNeice's radio play, *The Dark Tower*, for which Britten had composed incidental music:

Again my thanks to you – this time for your contribution to Child Roland – a subject which seems to me even more suited to music than *Peter Grimes*, though in the shorter work your part was smaller. It's the first time I've ever been reconciled to the association of music and the speaking voice. Is it possible that the author of Child Roland might collaborate with you in an opera?

The cast of the original production included Cyril Cusack (Roland), Olga Lindo (Mother), Mark Dignam (Tutor) and Lucille Lisle (Sylvie), with an unnamed orchestra conducted by Walter Goehr; MacNeice himself was the producer. The BBC has mounted four subsequent productions, each with Britten's music, in 1950 and 1956 (both again produced by MacNeice), 1966 and 1973. The 1973 production was broadcast in honour of Britten's sixtieth birthday. On its publication in 1947 (*The Dark Tower and Other Radio Scripts*), MacNeice dedicated the text to Britten. See also Barbara Coulton, *Louis MacNeice in the BBC*, pp. 77–83, Antony Curtis, 'BBC MacNeice', *Financial Times* (24 May 1980), and Jon Stallworthy, *Louis MacNeice*, pp. 334–44. According to Professor Stallworthy, MacNeice had originally suggested Antony Hopkins be engaged to write the music but that after reading the script Laurence Gilliam, MacNeice's Head of Department, had a copy sent to Britten. See also p. 134.

2   Boughton had written:

Would it bore you to discuss with an old and old-fashioned man the whole subject of opera? I believe you have it in you to do much (perhaps most) for English opera, if you don't do *too* much. (The first much refers to quality, the second to quantity).

If such a talk would amuse you, perhaps we could meet when I come up to hear *Peter Grimes* again.

See also Letter xxv.

517 **To Ralph Hawkes**

45A St Johns Wood High St, N.W. 8[1]
Feb 4th 1946

My dear Ralph,

Thank you very much for your nice long letter. I am glad that you both are well & that things are going so excitingly for you! You seem to be getting around the place quite a bit! I envy you your flight to Vancouver – that must have been an experience. Please give my regards to Arthur Benjamin[2] when you write, or see him. I am always glad to hear news of him. He seems to have made a tremendous place for himself out there. I can imagine that the new set-up in New York must be giving you a great deal of work – but I am sure that the split with 23rd St was a good thing. The difference in point-of-view was too fundamental. I am certain that B & H will eventually fill as big a place in the American musical world as it does in the English.[3]

Things here too are buzzing. I was away in Snape for ten days, & in spite of the 'flu epidemic (Beth & the kids both had it badly), managed to finish the first scene of the Rape of Lucretia! The plans for the opera are going ahead well. Sadler's Wells Governors finally rejected, after having wooed, us – but luckily Bing of Glyndebourne came to our rescue and we are likely to open there in July for a fortnight, before 4 weeks in London, some three or four in the provinces, & a short tour on the Continent (Paris, Amsterdam, & Brussels are angling for us).[4] We have a remarkable collection of singers. Apart from Joan & Peter, Kathleen Ferrier,[5] Roy Henderson,[6] Nancy Evans,[7] Owen ('Swallow')[8] are joining us; & so, we ought to be able to produce quite a good show – if the opera itself is any good! I'm hopeful at the moment – but things may easily go wrong! We are of course an independent company – nothing to do with the Glyndebourne Summer Festival (or Beecham!)[9] – but Bing[10] is the Business Manager, & Christie[11] one of the directors. All the artistic things are in our own hands. Reggie Goodall is going to be our musical director, I think.[12]

Thank you for being so understanding about the Contract. I felt an ass writing all that about it – but I am simple as regards money matters![13]

Peter & I had a really exciting time in Amsterdam, made real friends and had a really big success. Münch did a wonderful accompaniment to Les Illuminations for Peter, & the audience rose at it.[14] That brings me to your most kind & tempting invitation for next year. Maggie Teyte[15] would

CONCERTGEBOUW

AMSTERDAM

WOENSDAG
9 JANUARI
1946 - 8.15 UUR

DONDERDAG
10 JANUARI
1946 - 8.15 UUR

ABONNEMENTSCONCERT

SERIE A EN B

HET CONCERTGEBOUWORKEST

dirigent: CHARLES MÜNCH
solist : PETER PEARS, tenor

PROGRAMMA

W. A. Mozart 1756—1791	SYMPHONIE D GR. T., K.V. NO. 385 „HAFFNER" Allegro con spirito Andante Menuetto Finale: Presto
Albert Roussel 1869—1937	DERDE SYMPHONIE G KL. T., OP. 42 Allegro vivo Adagio Vivace Allegro con spirito
	PAUZE
Benjamin Britten geb. 1913	* „LES ILLUMINATIONS", OP. 18 voor tenor en strijkorkest
Maurice Ravel 1875—1937	TWEEDE SUITE UIT HET BALLET „DAPHNIS ET CHLOÉ" Lever du jour Pantomime Danse générale

* eerste uitvoering
Partituur en orkestpartijen zijn verkregen door wendelijke bemiddeling van The British Council.

Programme for 9/10 January 1946, the Concertgebouw, Amsterdam:
Pears sings *Les Illuminations*, with the Concertgebouw Orchestra
conducted by Charles Münch

certainly launch the Illuminations in New York in no uncertain manner &
I am very pleased that she has considered doing it, and a link with Peter &
me in a recital might prove a good start for us in New York. But we really
agree that the time is not quite ripe for that. However, the crucial point is
simply – time. We have now enquiries from Italy, Greece, Sweden, Prague
& we feel we must go back to Holland, Belgium & France who want us so
much. I have had to cut down my concerts in this country to one month
only so as to be able to do some of these countries – but above all so that
I shall be able to do some writing, which remains my chief job! But that I
should choose these European countries rather than America isn't really
surprising. Peter & I have found, without any doubt, that our work is
exportable eastwards; and my music is going so well in that direction, that
my sympathies rather naturally lie there too. Besides, once having tried
the American Way of Life, I feel, inspite of its silly muddles, really a part
of Europe.[16]

I'm sorry, Ralph, about this. It must be difficult to understand living as
you are in U.S.A., and having so much sympathy with it. I do appreciate
your difficulties in building me up out there – but I have a hunch that as
far as publicity goes, waiting doesn't matter.

Thank you & Clare[17] so much for the parcels. They have made a great
difference to our menus, so inclined to be without variations! It is really
sweet of you to think of us.

I had a word with Mrs Mayer on the telephone the other day – most exciting after all these years. She sounded well.

I'll let you know how Lucretia gets along. The libretto's fine, I think.

With love to you both,

Yours ever,

BEN

1 Britten's and Pears's London home from February 1943 until August 1946: see Letter 410 n. 3.

2 Australian-English composer and pianist (1893–1960). He had been Britten's piano teacher at the Royal College of Music from 1930 to 1933; see also Letter 25 n. 6.

Between 1938 and 1945 Benjamin was the conductor of the CBC Symphony Orchestra in Vancouver, one of the four principal orchestras maintained by the broadcasting authority at that time. On his return to the UK, Benjamin was once again in touch with his former pupil whom he had not seen since before the war. He attended a performance of *Lucretia* conducted by Britten, following which he wrote to the composer:

I was so moved by *Lucretia* that I could not tell you, not having the control over my emotions that I had in my youth!

I am convinced that in you this country has found the 'universal' British composer. By which I mean one who will be understood and acclaimed by all the world. I feel that all that the others have done has been leading up to you as a peak, and I should be very humbly proud if I were to be considered as among them.

All of which is very badly put, and may sound to you to be a bit hysterical or just a bit of 'fan-mail'.

But take it as being sincere.

Britten responded on 19 August:

My dear Arthur,

Your most moving letter reached me just as I was leaving for the States [for *Peter Grimes* at Tanglewood], & I am only just recovered enough from the trip to be able to answer it! It was sweet & generous of you to write it. I am delighted that you like "Lucretia". Your opinion means a great deal to me – especially since your arriving here after some years away enables you to have a fresher & more objective judgement. Incidentally may I say how delighted I am that you are back. We need you here greatly.

I shall be in London for most of September. Cannot we meet and talk sometime? I will tell you the story of P.G. in Tanglewood – quite a saga!

Thank you again for your letter.

With best wishes in haste,

BENJAMIN B.

3 Britten refers to a division of Boosey & Hawkes's activities in New York. From around this time, the offices in 23rd Street were to house the Boosey & Hawkes Artists Bureau, with the publishing wing of the operation,

now under Hawkes's direct management, moving to 668 Fifth Avenue. At the same time, Hawkes was launching an arm of the firm's instrument-manufacturing business in the US, as well as opening a small office in Los Angeles where Stravinsky, a recently acquired Boosey & Hawkes composer, had settled.

4   Following the premiere performances at Glyndebourne (see Letter 531 n. 2), *Lucretia* toured to Manchester (Opera House, 29 July–3 August), Liverpool (Royal Court, 5–10 August), Edinburgh (Royal Lyceum, 12–17 August), Glasgow (Theatre Royal, 19–24 August), London (Sadler's Wells Opera House, 28 August–21 September), and Oxford (New Theatre, 23–28 September). In October, six performances were also given in Amsterdam followed by further performances by the second cast at The Hague. (A proposed tour to Paris appears not have materialized.) According to Eric Crozier, the opera received 83 consecutive performances between July and October (see 'Staging First Productions 1', in DHOBB, p. 28).

One of the Dutch performances, from the Stadsschouwburg (Municipal Theatre) in Amsterdam, on 4 October, with Kathleen Ferrier in the title role and the remainder of the first cast, was broadcast live; a complete recording of this performance is held by Dutch Radio Sound Archives (Ref. EM–HM–0030) and excerpts were first issued in 1981 by Educational Media Associates on IGI 369. Although Britten is named on the record sleeve as the conductor of this *Lucretia* performance, Paul Campion has suggested that this is incorrect and that Hans Oppenheim was in charge on the evening of the 4th (see *Ferrier – A Career Recorded*, pp. 13–17); a surviving programme for the 4th confirms Oppenheim as the conductor. According to Campion, Britten conducted only the first of the Dutch performances, on 2 October.

The first UK broadcast of *Lucretia* was given live from the Camden Hippodrome on 11 October 1946 in the BBC Third Programme. With the exception of Edmund Donlevy (Junius), who was replaced by Frederick Sharp from the second cast, the cast was the same as the Dutch broadcast but with Goodall conducting. Lord Harewood recorded the broadcast off-air on to acetate discs. Not all of the performance survives, but the extant sections can be heard at the National Sound Archive (British Library), London.

5   English contralto (1912–1953) who, with Nancy Evans, created the role of Lucretia. Britten conceived the contralto parts in his *Spring Symphony* and *Canticle II: 'Abraham and Isaac'* for Ferrier. See also Letter 462 n. 5 and Christopher Fifield (ed.), *Letters and Diaries of Kathleen Ferrier*.

According to Ronald Duncan (RDBB, pp. 90–91):

Ben was so impressed by Kathleen Ferrier's performance in *Lucretia* – not only by her voice but by the true innocence and purity of her character – that almost immediately after the first night he told me that he would like to write something especially for her. Our first idea was a cantata, not an opera. I came up with the idea of *Hylas*, and suggested to him that there were possibilities for him in *Echo*. He was enthusiastic. So I wrote the libretto almost at once. Ben liked it. But he could not get down to set it because the Christies asked him to write another opera. He saw this as something for Kathleen. *Hylas* was never set. Eliot published the text in *The Mongrel*.

Among Duncan's papers at the Harry Ransom Humanities Research Center, Austin, Texas, are two drafts of *Hylas (a canzone)*, one in a notebook also containing part of his play *Stratton* (see Letter 534 n. 2). Duncan published a version of *Hylas* in *The Mongrel and Other Poems*. T. S. Eliot (see Letter 557 n. 3) was Duncan's editor at Faber and Faber, the London publishers with whom Eliot worked for forty years from 1925 until his death in 1965.

6 Scottish baritone (1899–2000) who studied at the Royal Academy of Music, 1920–25. Henderson sang Count Almaviva at the inaugural performance at Glyndebourne in 1934, and other Mozart roles there subsequently. He was also a distinguished oratorio singer, in particular as Elijah and Christus (*St Matthew Passion*), and a noted interpreter of Delius (*Sea Drift* – the nineteen-year-old Britten had heard and admired a 1929 broadcast with Henderson as soloist – *Mass of Life* and *Idyll*) and Vaughan Williams (*Sea Symphony* and *Dona nobis pacem*). He was the soloist in the first performance of Vaughan Williams's *Five Tudor Portraits* in 1936, at a concert that also included the premiere of Britten's *Our Hunting Fathers* (see Diary for 25 September 1936). Henderson was Kathleen Ferrier's principal teacher from 1943, and later pupils included John Shirley-Quirk and Norma Proctor. As the conductor of the Nottingham Oriana Choir in the 1940s, he invited Britten to compose a work for Ferrier and four-part female chorus; the commission, however, was not accepted by the composer. See also Andrew Green, 'Twentieth-century voice', *Independent* (2 July 1999) and obituaries in *The Times* (17 March 2000) and by Elizabeth Forbes in the *Independent* (17 March 2000).

   Although Britten seems confident of Henderson's participation in *Lucretia*, the baritone wrote to the composer on 19 February 1946 to withdraw from the production, arguing that he would have to take a break from singing during the summer (when the performances of *Lucretia* were scheduled) if he were to be fully prepared for the 1946–47 winter season. As a consequence, Henderson did not take part in any of the original performances or in any subsequent English Opera Group productions.

7 English mezzo-soprano (1915–2000) who had studied with the conductor John Tobin in her native Liverpool and with Maggie Teyte. She created the roles of Lucretia (with Kathleen Ferrier), Nancy (*Albert Herring*), Polly Peachum (in Britten's realization of *The Beggar's Opera*) and Dido in Britten's realization of Purcell's opera (she had already recorded Dido at the age of twenty, in 1935, the first complete recording of the *Dido and Aeneas*, conducted by Constant Lambert). In 1952, she sang the role of Lucinda Woodcock in the English Opera Group's production of the eighteenth-century ballad opera *Love in a Village*, in a new version by

Arthur Oldham. Britten wrote his *A Charm of Lullabies* for her in 1947 (see Letter 562 n. 1), and she performed regularly at the Aldeburgh Festival from its inception in 1948 until 1955. She also worked with Poulenc (in 1948, she broadcast the *Trois Poèmes de Ronsard* accompanied by the composer), Lennox Berkeley, Copland, Honegger and Stravinsky, and sang frequently for Vaughan Williams. Malcolm Williamson's *Six English Lyrics* were written for her, and she gave the first performance, with the composer, in 1966. Two years later she created the role of the Poet and seven other characters in Williamson's chamber opera *The Growing Castle*. She was a regular broadcaster for the BBC for over thirty years and made appearances at thirteen consecutive BBC Proms seasons.

After her retirement from singing, she taught at the Colchester Institute, and from 1973 at the Britten–Pears School for Advanced Musical Studies as Co-Director of Singing Studies with Pears (whom she first met in the Glyndebourne Chorus in 1938: see Letter 134 n. 3), 1979–86, and as Director, 1986–90; Director Emeritus, 1991–2000.

She was married first to Walter Legge (see Letter 431 n. 1), for whom she did much work for ENSA (Entertainments National Services Association) in the war years (including a ten-month run of *The Merry Widow*, and *Top of the World* with the Crazy Gang, a show that was abruptly halted by the 'Blitz', the concentrated air-raids on London in 1940), and in 1949 to Eric Crozier (see Letter 529 n. 2). Both she and Eric Crozier received the OBE in the 1991 New Year's Honours List.

See also John Evans, 'Profile: Nancy Evans', *Aldeburgh Soundings*, 2 (spring 1985), p. 2, and the serialization of Crozier's and Evans's autobiography, 'After Long Pursuit', *Opera Quarterly*, 10/3–11/3 (1994/95). See also obituaries in *The Times* (23 August 2000), the *Daily Telegraph* (23 August 2000), by John Calder in the *Independent* (22 August 2000) and Jim McDonald in the *Guardian* (24 August 2000), and Alan Blyth's liner note to 'Nancy Evans: "The Comely Mezzo"' in Dutton's 'Singers to Remember' CD series (Dutton Laboratories, CDBP 9723, 2002). In his *Independent* obituary John Calder writes: 'As an artist Nancy Evans had a warm, vibrant natural voice, remarkable for its clear diction, while her sparkling personality brought charm and vitality to all her roles.'

8   Owen Brannigan (1908–1973), English bass, who was a member of the Sadler's Wells Company (1943–48, 1952–58) where he sang with Pears and Joan Cross in a number of notable productions, including *The Bartered Bride* and *Così fan tutte*. A specialist in Mozart and *buffo* roles, he also created several important Britten roles: Swallow (*Peter Grimes*, 1945), Collatinus (*The Rape of Lucretia*, 1946), Noye (*Noye's Fludde*, 1958), and Bottom (*A Midsummer Night's Dream*, 1960), all of which, except for Collatinus, he recorded with the composer. Malcolm Williamson and John Gardner also created operatic roles for Brannigan. In the late 1960s Brannigan took part in performances and a subsequent Decca recording, conducted by Britten, of the concert version of Purcell's *The Fairy Queen*

devised by Pears and edited and realized by Britten and Imogen Holst.

9 Sir Thomas Beecham approached John Christie at Glyndebourne, having
   failed to be appointed as Music Director at Covent Garden, and plans were
   made to produce three operas in the 1946 season – *The Magic Flute* (in
   English), *La Bohème* and *Carmen* (a project first mooted for the abandoned 1940 season: see Letter 221 n. 8), the latter with Kathleen Ferrier in
   the title role. Beecham, however, was not prepared to use Ferrier as she
   possessed no stage experience and was not vocally or temperamentally
   suited to the role, and it was Britten's *The Rape of Lucretia* that was finally
   performed. Beecham conducted Mozart and Haydn concerts at Glyndebourne with the Royal Philharmonic Orchestra (the resident Glyndebourne
   orchestra until 1963) in 1948 and 1949, and, in 1950, gave performances of
   the first version of Strauss's *Ariadne auf Naxos* – his only Glyndebourne
   operatic performances – at the Edinburgh Festival. See also Wilfrid Blunt,
   John Christie of Glyndebourne, pp. 244–53, and Spike Hughes, *Glyndebourne:
   A History of the Festival Opera Founded in 1934 by Audrey and John Christie*,
   pp. 153–5 and 164–6.

10 Rudolf Bing (1902–1997), Vienna-born British opera impresario, who
   worked in Berlin during the 1920s before acting as Carl Ebert's assistant at
   the Hessian State Theatre, Darmstadt, 1928–30, and then as Assistant to the
   Intendant of the Charlottenburg Opera, Berlin, 1930–33. Bing became
   General Manager of the Glyndebourne Festival Opera in 1935, a post he
   held until 1949. As a consequence of Glyndebourne's wartime closure,
   Bing's activities as an impresario were interrupted and he worked in the
   Peter Jones department store in London's Sloane Square, rising through the
   ranks to Assistant to the Manager. (By a curious coincidence, David
   Webster, who was, post-war, to be General Director at Covent Garden, was
   working at a department store in Liverpool at the same time.) In 1947 Bing
   helped found the Edinburgh Festival – he was, for example, responsible for
   reuniting Bruno Walter and the Vienna Philharmonic for the first time
   since the *Anschluss* – and was Artistic Director for three years. From 1950
   until 1972 Bing was General Manager of the New York Metropolitan Opera
   where he was influential in raising the standards of performance and production. His autobiography, *5000 Nights at the Opera*, which includes on
   pp. 81–3 references to *The Rape of Lucretia* and *Albert Herring* at
   Glyndebourne, was published in 1972. Bing became a British citizen in
   1946 and was knighted in 1971. See also obituaries in *The Times* and the
   Daily Telegraph (4 September 1997), and Daniel Snowman, *The Hitler
   Emigrés: the Cultural Impact on Britain of Refugees from Nazism*, pp. 60–65
   and 216–19.

11 John Christie (1882–1962), English opera enthusiast and founder of the
   Glyndebourne Festival Opera, near Lewes, Sussex. He built an opera house
   in the grounds of his home at Glyndebourne, which opened in 1934 with a
   fortnight's festival comprising Mozart's *Le nozze di Figaro* and *Così fan tutte*

conducted by Fritz Busch (see Letter 138 n. 2). Thereafter Mozart, and the da Ponte operas in particular, became the backbone of Glyndebourne's repertoire, although in 1938 Verdi's *Macbeth* (with Pears in the chorus) received its British premiere there. Glyndebourne has always been noted for the highest musical and production standards, achieved by extended and intensely concentrated rehearsal periods.

In 1931 Christie married the soprano Audrey Mildmay (see Letter 537 n. 5), who sang in a number of early Glyndebourne productions.

Although Christie had been prepared to finance the Glyndebourne English Opera Company in 1946, the relationship between him and Britten was hardly ever more than courteous at best and by the following year, when Britten and his associates appeared at Glyndebourne as 'visitors', there was open hostility between them. At the opening night of *Albert Herring*, Christie allegedly greeted the audience with the words: 'This isn't *our* kind of thing, you know.' The animosity between the two men and the rivalry between their two opera companies continued for the remainder of their lives, although we note that in 1962, the year of Christie's death, Moran Caplat, Glyndebourne's General Manager (who had acted as Bing's Assistant in 1946–47), invited Britten to compose an opera for Glyndebourne's 1967 season: 'A modern equivalent of *Figaro* would be marvellous, or Jane Austen?' (In suggesting Jane Austen to Britten, had Caplat subconsciously remembered Britten's projected opera of *Mansfield Park* (*c.* 1946)? See Letter 534, n. 2.) The same letter indicates his intention to revive one of Britten's operas at Glyndebourne, a project that remained unfulfilled until 1981 when a new production of *A Midsummer Night's Dream* was staged. In 1966 Britten's edition of Purcell's *Dido and Aeneas* was used at Glyndebourne.

See also Wilfrid Blunt, *John Christie of Glyndebourne.*

12   Reginald Goodall (1905–1990), English conductor. His association with Britten began when he conducted the orchestral version of the *Te Deum* in C major in 1936. He conducted the first performance of *Peter Grimes* on 7 June 1945 and shared the first production of *The Rape of Lucretia* with Ansermet at Glyndebourne in 1946. See also Letter 392 n. 3.

Bing had invited Goodall to undertake the Musical Directorship of the new opera company in a letter dated 7 January 1946, although it is clear from the same letter that Britten and Crozier had already approached Goodall informally. (A letter from Bing to Audrey Christie, dated 21 December 1945, indicates that Britten and Crozier had two possible conductors in mind for the new company: Goodall, whom they knew very well through his work on *Grimes* at Sadler's Wells; and Peter Gellhorn.) By mid-February Britten had told Goodall there was a possibility of Ernest Ansermet becoming involved, and a second scheme was hatched in which Goodall would share the conducting at Glyndebourne with Ansermet and act as his assistant, and be responsible for performances on tour in the UK and in the Netherlands. A letter from Bing to Audrey Christie (15 January) makes it clear that Bing (and therefore Glyndebourne) held strong reservations about Goodall's abilities:

I met Reginald Goodall yesterday and as a personality was not in the least impressed by him. I am afraid he is what John [Christie] would call 'a little man'. This may be of course an unfair judgement but one cannot help forming an opinion if one talks to a man. I said so to Britten over the telephone this morning and I cannot help feeling that for this particular work, and with the lack of other really suitable conductors, Hans [Oppenheim] would be by far the best choice. This is not a great dramatic opera like *Don Giovanni* or *Carmen* but is very much on chamber music lines and will require more than anything else superb coaching and superlative workmanship, and of all musicians now available in this country only Hans can do it. As he is a great admirer of Britten I feel sure that Britten would be able to inspire Hans to do what he (Britten) would want.

[. . .] We have agreed that it is mainly Britten's responsibility to decide on a choice of a conductor, but I don't want him to be in a position afterwards if things go wrong to say 'there was no other choice'. If he insists on having Goodall [. . .] that is the end of it and we must hope for the best, but I will resist for all I am worth [. . .]

(In the same letter Bing also reports: 'I am lunching with Fergus Dunlop tomorrow. He is head of the European Section of the British Council. I want to discuss with him the possibility of a continental tour of the Britten opera.')

Three weeks after sending this letter to Audrey Christie, Bing was still pressing Oppenheim's suitability with Britten in spite of his having already invited Goodall to be the Musical Director of the new company. Bing reported to John Christie (6 February 1946):

Opposition [to Oppenheim] seems severe. Britten still feels that in the circumstances Goodall is the best choice and both he and Peter Pears think that under better conditions [a reference to the hostile atmosphere at Sadler's Wells] he could do infinitely better; up to a point that was always your argument.

A meeting at Glyndebourne on 11 February between Britten, Crozier, Bing and the Christies was most probably the occasion when Ansermet's participation was first mooted. Ansermet's involvement would have appeased Glyndebourne's doubts about Goodall and would give the season a conductor of international stature whose high profile would doubtless have reassured the nervous Christies. It clearly would have been imprudent of Britten to have resisted Arnsermet's participation in favour of Goodall and a happy compromise was found. An entry in Britten's pocket engagement diary on 14 February, three days after the meeting at Glyndebourne, reads: 'Ansermet 5.0 [p.m.]'.

Once the second scheme was in place (i.e. with both Ansermet and Goodall sharing the conducting at Glyndebourne), Goodall was asked to assist Bing and the composer in securing orchestral players. A further letter from Bing to Goodall (27 February) indicates that he was to receive £12 per week during the rehearsal period (10 June–12 July, approximately) and thereafter £25 per week during the run of performances.

Arrangements were set in hand to find a suitable Assistant for Goodall once Ansermet had departed: Bing's letter of 27 February nominates two candidates, Peter Gellhorn (Britten's suggestion) and Michael Mudie. Evidently, Mudie was approached but was unavailable. Britten, on the recommendation of John Amis (see Letter 458 n. 4), suggested Norman Del Mar, but in the event it was Bing's original choice, Hans Oppenheim (in 1946 Head of Music Staff at Glyndebourne), who worked alongside Goodall.

See also John Lucas, *Reggie: The Life of Reginald Goodall*, pp. 107–10.

13   See Letter 514 (to Ralph Hawkes, 19 December 1945), in which Britten wrote:

I wonder if you would mind if I went back to the original method of only receiving what I earn, & when I earn it. You see, Ralph, I am scared of receiving the large sum you mention (£600 per annum) & then (by evil chance) having to pay some back at the end of three years. If I needed a large sum now I should have to accept the advance method, but I don't & I'm old-fashioned enough not to feel easy about receiving more than I actually earn.

In a letter of 28 January 1946 Hawkes agreed to Britten's request.

14   Charles Münch (1891–1968), French conductor and violinist; see also Letter 487 n. 4.

Pears sang *Les Illuminations* with the Concertgebouw Orchestra in Amsterdam on 9–10 January, and in The Hague on the 12th. 'Music in the Making', *Tempo*, 1/14 (March 1946), p. 15, reported that during this European tour Britten and Pears visited the Netherlands, where their recital at the Concertgebouw on 11 January 1946 included Britten's *Michelangelo Sonnets*, and Belgium, where they broadcast *The Holy Sonnets of John Donne* on Brussels Radio. In an unpublished interview with Peter Heyworth (London, 17 January 1984), Pears recalled this trip to Holland:

My first visit to Amsterdam in January 1946 was very memorable. I realized at the time that I would never see the city like that again. There was virtually no traffic. I can't remember whether there were any trams running. If so, there were only a few,

CONCERTGEBOUW-KAMERMUZIEK
Concertgebouw   —   Kleine Zaal
Vrijdag 11 Januari 1946 - 8.15 uur

Engelsche Liederenavond

PETER PEARS tenor - BENJAMIN BRITTEN, piano
Werken van: John Bartlet, Dowland. Purcell. Britten

Toegangsprijs f 2.—, verh. m. rechten en vestiaire
Kaartverkoop er plaatsbespreking van Woensdag 9 Januari a.s. af, van 10—3 uur in het Concertgebouw, telefoon 27300

Advertisement for Pears's and Britten's first recital in Amsterdam, 11 January 1946

and there were almost no cars at all. Benjamin Britten and I were put up in the Victoria Hotel near the station. For the rehearsal we found one of those very rare cars to take us to the Concertgebouw. But in the evening – it was 9 January – we were collected by a horse and carriage. Snow was still falling gently and we crossed an absolutely deserted Amsterdam. All we heard was the plop, plop, plop of the horses. It was romantic beyond words. It might have been Russia in Tchaikovsky's day. It was adorable. And very exciting. I had, of course, never sung there before, and the audience was greeting someone new, who was also a representative of their Allies and all that. The performance of Britten's *Les Illuminations* was really quite good. The orchestra was obviously marvellous and Charles Münch was sympathetic, although a little eccentric [. . .] He was a perfectly good conductor and a nice chap. The hall has very good acoustics and it all went very well. For me, the only painful memory is of the entrance to the platform: the artists have to enter high up and descend a long, steep staircase.

15   English soprano (1888–1976); see also Diary for 17 February 1932, n. 4. There had already been a proposal in 1943 for Teyte to record *Les Illuminations*: see Letter 248 n. 6.

16   For an assessment of Britten's European, rather than American, orienta- tion, see Donald Mitchell's Introduction to vols. 1 and 2, pp. 38–9 ('The American Dream'). Britten's identification with Europe and his misgivings about the United States were to lead him to make only two concert tours to the United States in future years: in 1949 (see Letters 640–45), and in 1969 when he and Pears undertook a hastily arranged recital tour to raise funds for the rebuilding of Snape Maltings Concert Hall. See also MCCCBB, pp. 211–16, where Britten's and Pears's status as 'prohibited immigrants' is discussed.

   Hawkes was, as ever, generous in his disappointment over Britten's deci- sion not to come to America in 1947, recognizing that a delay would allow him more time to prepare the ground for when he and Pears actually would tour. He concluded, 'I agree with you about Europe – you couldn't do better than to follow your success there – acceptance on the Continent means a very great deal and I'm so glad it's come early' (letter to Britten, 11 February 1946).

17   Hawkes's second wife, Clare Zollner (née Watson) (1906–1989).

518   To Victor Hely-Hutchinson[1]
      BBC
      [*Typed*]

                                        45A, St John's Wood High St, London N.W.8
                                                             25th February, 1946

Dear Dr Hely-Hutchinson,
      Thank you for your letter about any possible new works which I might have for your future programmes.
      I am afraid the only new works which will interest you which look like

being complete in the near future, are the Oratorio "Mea Culpa"[2] and a
new version of my first Piano Concerto.[3] The new version of the Piano
Concerto will be given fairly soon both at Cheltenham and on the continent, but if you would like it for the "Proms", that would probably be the
first performance in London.[4] Mewton Wood[5] is playing it at Cheltenham.
The scoring is as before and the timing now reduced by 2 minutes.

With best wishes,

Yours sincerely,

BENJAMIN BRITTEN

1   South African-born composer, conductor, pianist and administrator
    (1901–1947); Director of Music at the BBC, 1944–47. See also Diary for 22
    December 1932, n. 1.

2   The oratorio *Mea Culpa* was conceived by Ronald Duncan and Britten as a
    post-Hiroshima and Nagasaki protest. In August 1945 Duncan was working
    in the Features Department of the BBC. Following the dropping of the first
    atomic bomb on Hiroshima, he sent a memorandum to his Head of
    Department, Laurence Gilliam, proposing a programme that would be a
    response to the appalling devastation in Japan. He ends his note, 'Benjamin
    Britten is enthusiastic for the above, and I am sure would write a valuable
    Cantata on this theme.'
        In RDBB, pp. 54–5, Duncan recalled:

    After I'd been sitting in Rothwell House for a couple of weeks or so the first atomic
    bomb was dropped on Hiroshima on my birthday in 1945. It made me feel sick and
    depressed at first, I then became violently angry and indignant.
        [. . .] Here, I realized, was a supreme opportunity: humanity was now anaes-
    thetized with shock and was, as it were, lying prostrate ready for music and poetry
    to perform a major operation on it.
        [. . .] I went to Ben. 'We must immediately write an oratorio about this,' I said,
    'something as artistically painful as the burns we've inflicted on the Japanese.'
        'Of course we must. [. . .] Let's go for a walk and work something out.'
        By midnight we had sketched the plan for an oratorio in three parts. It was to
    be a full-scale work with chorus, soloists and symphony orchestra, almost like
    the *Messe des Morts* in scope, with a pastoral symphony which Ben insisted should
    be in the first part. [. . .] We planned a big contralto part, and a soprano role for
    Joan Cross.

    On 14 September Gilliam handed on the project to Hely-Hutchinson,
    with his full support; just over a month later, on 17 October, Duncan sent
    copies of the typescript of his libretto to Gilliam and Hely-Hutchinson,
    telling the latter that Britten had approved it and was ready to begin setting
    the text in December on his return from Europe. (According to Duncan in
    RDBB, p. 55, 'I wrote quickly [. . .] Within two days I had the nine pages com-
    pleted. Ben said he was ready to go.')
        Duncan's typescript (Britten's copy is at BPL), with the dedication 'For

TUESDAY, AUGUST 7, 1945

Evening Standard

37,719   24-HOUR FORECAST: Cool; fair; local rain.   MOON: Rises 4.25 a.m. Sets 8.49 p.m. LIGHTING-UP TIME: 9.38 p.m.   ONE PENNY

FINAL NIGHT EXTRA

TOKYO NEXT: *The Japanese are warned by radio*

THE WORLD WAITS

Dust still hides Hiroshima: Tokyo says it is 'massacre'

ATOM BOMB 'DROPPED BY 'CHUTE'

A tense and breathless world still waits for detailed news of Hiroshima, the Japanese city on which fell the first Atom Bomb thirty-six hours ago.

The city covered twelve square miles; it had 300,000 people. It is probably now a mass of rubble. But no-one will know exactly until the great clouds of smoke and dust have cleared and reconnaissance airplanes have been able to observe the effect of the Bomb.

The Japanese Cabinet is in session. The first Jap comment was that in the attack the Americans used "a new type of bomb," there was "considerable damage" and train services in Hiroshima had to be cancelled.

Later a Japanese broadcast said the Bomb was dropped by parachute and exploded before reaching the ground. Added the broadcast:—

"Investigation is still going on into result of the wanton attack a considerable the extent of the damage wrought by the number of houses in the city were demolished, while fires were started at enemy's new tactics. several points.

"By employing a weapon designed "The Japanese authorities are already to massacre innocent civilians the Americans have shown their sadistic nature to the world. effective, will eventually lose its power

"The destructive power of the new weapon cannot be disregarded. As a nullify its effect.

Unless the Japanese surrender Tokyo may be the next on the list for Atom Bomb destruction.

Powerful radio transmitters all along the Pacific coast and at Allied bases in the Marshall Islands are beaming the news to Japan that the Allies have the new weapon which will change the history of the world. Super Fortresses are expected to scatter millions of leaflets throughout the Japanese homeland within the next few hours warning the people of the awful devastation that lies ahead.

How they dropped it

Evening Standard Air Reporter

Except for the fact that it was dropped from a United States Army Air Force aircraft, no official details have yet been given about how the Atom Bomb was sent down to its target.

First Japanese reports say it was dropped by parachute. No details of the bomb itself have been released; but it has been said—unofficially—that the bomb is ten times smaller than a 4000lb. "block-buster" used by the R.A.F.

Whether this is in size or weight, or both, is not known. But from this report it would seem that the new weapon, capable of doing the same damage as all Bomber Command raids on Hamburg during five years, is somewhere about the size of a five hundred pounder bomb.

From 30,000 feet

This would mean that a single Super-Fortress or an R.A.F. Lincoln, the newest type of British bomber now in preparation for the Far East war, could carry whole sticks of Atom Bombs, sufficient with only a handful of aircraft to wipe out all the industrial cities of Japan.

Experts to-day suggested that the single bomb was carried to Hiroshima in the bomb-rack of a heavy bomber and dropped like any other bomb, the bomb-aimer sighting his target through the bomb-sight.

It was probably dropped from a great height—it may have been as high as 30,000 feet—to give it its unparalleled blast effect.

Invasion plans unchanged

BUT JAPANESE MAY COLLAPSE

Allied plans to invade Japan have not been changed. Mr. H. S. Basset, Assistant Secretary of the U.S. Navy, who is making a survey of Navy supply problems in the Pacific, said to-day, according to a Reuter despatch from Brisbane: "I am optimistic that Japan will collapse before she is invaded. But all our plans are made to carry the fight right to Japan. None has been altered."

Vatican view

'Absolutely opposed'

An authoritative Vatican source told the Associated Press to-day that the Vatican is "absolutely opposed to the atomic bombing of Japan."

The Catholic Church has equal pity for all subjected to atomic bombing, and cannot make any distinction between the victims, the source said.

The discovery of the Atom bomb has caused an unfavourable impression in the Vatican because the use of the Atom bombs might be the first link in a chain of unpredictable violence.

A greater thing than discovery of electricity

By TUDOR JENKINS

Sir John Anderson told me to-day that he regards the discovery of how to use the energy set free by splitting the atom as the greatest ever made in the realm of physical science.

Sir John was appointed by Mr. Churchill as the Cabinet Minister responsible for the research; he himself is a Fellow of the Royal Society.

I was discussing with Sir John Anderson the prospects of the peace-time uses of the discovery.

"It opens up endless possibilities," he said.

"We have been able to harness this tremendous energy in a small bomb. That is for use in war. The first thing now is for the scientists to discover how they can harness it for the benefit of peace; it will be a long job."

In Sir John's opinion the new discovery is of far greater

◀ Back Page, Col. Two

MOSCOW

No comment

Moscow radio gave President Truman's statement on the atomic bomb in full, including the warning to Japan.

The statement was given at dictation speed for the benefit of provincial newspapers in Russia. No comment was broadcast.

Germans timed atom bomb for October

The Germans had an atom bomb which would have been ready by October.

A colossal blast effect was uncovered four months ago, when an Allied search party walked into a small silk factory at Celle, north of Hanover.

The German atomic plant was uncovered four months ago, very close to Britain the same day.

This man, with others, had been working on the Atom bombs for months. The Nazi Government apparently had not asked for immediate results.

◀ Back Page, Col. Three

BRITISH PLANES BOMB TOKYO

Super Forts and other bombers are scorching wide areas of the Japanese islands on the Allied "death lists," which now contain the names of 31 towns which are to be wiped out.

British airplanes raided the Tokyo region to-day, according to a Japanese broadcast picked up in New York.

This report said: "A force of industrial town of Tarumizu, on Mushima Isl., by a Japanese bombed and strafed south-western districts Tokyo and the Yokohama district announced as the most success for an hour.

◀ Back Page, Col. Three

SO OPENS A NEW ERA FOR MAN

By JAMES STUART

Scientists all over the world were discussing to-day the harnessing of Atomic energy and its implications.

Uranium is in this village

August 6, 1945—day on which the Japanese city of Hiroshima was destroyed by a force of nature controlled by man—will live as an historic date in the world's story.

On that day began the greatest revolutionary change in history.

The Cornish village of Grampound Road (pop. 419), six miles south-west of St. Austell, finds this eyes of the world on it to-day.

For here, in a derelict copper mine called South Terrace, are believed to be Britain's biggest deposits of uranium, important component of the Atom Bomb.

The work of extracting copper from South Terrace stopped nearly 20 years ago, and the mine is now flooded; but a mining expert told me to-day that with the aid of modern pumping machinery it could be brought back into production fairly quickly.

Uranium is usually associated with copper deposits, but it is known to be present in some tin mines also. In them, are traces of copper. Generally, the temperatures at which the ore was formed decades ago were too high to allow of the formation of uranium.

In other mines

There are small quantities of uranium in the East Foot tin mine near Redruth, which is still being worked. It is known to be present in the Cononia Mine and Glen Mine, both near St. Ives.

Cornish uranium was the raw material from which was made the radium used by Mme. Curie in her experiments in the 1900s.

Uranium is also used in the making of decorative glass and in

◀ Back Page, Col. Three

Peep into future

Those are a peep into the future (perhaps not so distant) are some of the possibilities of controlled atomic energy in war and peace.

The end of armies, navies and air forces as we know them today—tons rockets and enormous destructive power, probably tremendous propulsive speed; energy, will undoubtedly take the place of airplane-dropped Atom Bombs in any way of the future.

These would hurtle through the skies at the touch of a switch; they may become a permanent fountain of world prosperity.

Peace possibilities

In peace the possibilities are equally staggering.

Mr. Stimson, U.S. War Secretary, has said that it will be ten years before atomic energy can be converted into useful power. But he also said: "We are on the threshold of a new industrial era which will bring easy riches and enough expenditure of money to develop."

What shall we say to that era? Certainly the end of coal and oil as fuels.

Atomic energy would supply all power needs. It would drive motorcars and airplanes and trains; it would keep factory machinery turning.

When that day comes it will no longer be necessary for factories to have great chimneys blowing out clouds of smoke.

If it does not, itself take the place of electricity, atomic power would keep the generators going in place of the oil or coal fuel of to-day.

TRUMAN NEARS HOME

The United States cruiser Augusta, bringing President Truman home from Potsdam, is nearing the American coast, said the United States.

"GRAND SLAM"

10 tons

AVERAGE MAN

ATOMIC BOMB   400 lb.   *Reported weight. Destructive power more than 20,000 tons.*

'THE WORLD WAITS': the front page of the *Evening Standard*, 7 August 1945

PART I.

TENOR (accompanied rec.)

God saw everything he had made and it
was good. But there was not a man to till the ground.
And the Lord God formed man of the dust of the ground,
and breathed into his nostrils the breath of life, and
man became a living soul. Where there is life it is His
Life.

TENOR (air)

How slowly the earth revolves
So heavy it is with fruit;
How softly the night descends
Fearing to disturb the day;
Unwillingly the sun ascends
Raised from the thighs of night.

Chorus

Wherever we throw our seed
There is a harvest;
Our fields are fat.
And the generous earth
Lets down its treasure
(like a fresh cow with a full udder).

SOPRANO (acc. rec.)

Our roses bleed into the darkness
And the falling moon is held with the scent of jasmine.
Till the earth wears the sun as a dress
And the black panther night recalls its litter of tired stars.

DUET (Soprano and Tenor)

What tree is there as straight as man?
What beast is there as strong as man?
What fire is there as warm as love?
What flower is there tender as her passion?

PASTORAL SYMPHONY

Chorus

Homesick, the waves compete to reach the shore;
And glad, the petals fade and fall upon the floor;
Where man and leaves once lay before
Creation weaned them from their mother.
O Earth! We are in love with thee.
As with a woman we are in love with thee.

BASS (acc. rec.)

All is at peace; and man can
ride the high places of the earth again.
Everything grows; our women
Have male sons and our calves are all heifers.

BASS (air)

God made the mountains
So that I may climb them;

The first page from Britten's copy of the typescript of *Mea Culpa*, the projected
oratorio he planned with Ronald Duncan in response to the dropping of atomic
bombs on Japan

an unknown child whose severed hand lay like a glove on the floor', is sub-titled 'A Libretto for Cantata'. It is divided into three parts – I The Garden; II The Wrath; III The Choice – and conceived for four soloists (SATB), chorus and orchestra. The text itself is laid out with designations such as accompanied recitative, air, duet, trio, quartet, fugue and funeral march, as well as indicating the position of the 'Pastoral Symphony' requested by Britten. (The text, preserving this format, appears in Duncan's *The Mongrel and Other Poems*, pp. 76–85, where it is described as a 'Libretto for Benjamin Britten'.) Preserved with Britten's typescript is a copy of the *Evening Standard* (7 August 1945; see p. 156) reporting the atomic attack on Japan, the event that provoked the work, under the banner headline, 'THE WORLD WAITS Dust still hides Hiroshima'.

On 21 December 1945 Britten's publisher Leslie Boosey was organizing terms with Hely-Hutchinson for a BBC premiere the following year. According to Duncan, 'Boosey and Hawkes advised Ben not to start com-posing till they had negotiated a contract for him with the BBC. The BBC meanwhile intimated to his publishers that they would consider giving a contract for the work when he had submitted it. These negotiations con-tinued over twelve months.'

The project seems to have foundered partly because Britten had moved on to different and more pressing work such as *The Rape of Lucretia* (with a libretto by Duncan), though *Mea Culpa* makes a final appearance in the correspondence in January 1948 (see Letter 567). The themes of pacifism and humanitarian causes are a striking aspect of *Mea Culpa*, which link it directly with three works from the 1960s: *War Requiem*, composed for the Coventry Cathedral Festival of 1962; *Voices for Today*, commissioned for the twentieth anniversary of the United Nations in 1965; and *Owen Wingrave*, composed for BBC Television in 1969–70 and first broadcast to a worldwide audience of millions on 16 May 1971.

3 In 1945 Britten replaced the original third movement, *Recitative and Aria*, with a newly composed *Impromptu* based on a theme taken from his inci-dental music to *King Arthur* (1937; see Letter 99 n. 4). Although it was to be Noel Mewton-Wood who would give the premiere of the revised Piano Concerto (see nn. 4 and 5 below), it was another pianist, Clifford Curzon (see Letter 525 n. 23), who played a seminal role in persuading Britten to revive and revise the work. On 1 September 1945, after receiving Britten's autograph manuscript of the *Impromptu* (laid out for two pianos), Curzon wrote enthusiastically to Britten:

It has just arrived & is exquisite: I can't tell you how delighted I am. [. . .]

I have only read it through twice (I have no piano) & I don't think it could be better in any way – and beautifully as it will slip in between the other movements, it is lovelier than anything you would have written at the time.

The Tema one can *steal* in with, just as one can the opening of a Mozart slow movement. The interspersed cadenzas keep the *freedom* of the old movement, but as a *whole* this has a unity the other hadn't. Just at a glance all kinds of things excite

Britten's fair copy of the two-piano arrangement of the *Impromptu*, in 1945 the newly composed third movement of his Piano Concerto. The orchestra's music has been arranged by the composer for a second piano. This copy belonged to Clifford Curzon.

me about it: the ghostly passage in 3rds, a premonition of a heftier one to come in the last movement: the retaining of the little marionette waltz (12/8) which is so much more satisfying in this context: the stretta near the end, with the delicious 'Rückblick' of all the couplets, through the wrong end of the telescope – preparing the last movement so perfectly. I'm so glad to have indications of scoring – it all looks masterly, and thank you endlessly. [. . .]

I'm really thrilled by the prospect of playing the Concerto.

Curzon added in a postscript: 'E[rwin Stein] seems to think *Birmingham* is owed *1st* performance – but surely it was *London*? Stoll [Theatre]? It doesn't really matter because we shall have a *first London performance* anyway.'

By November 1945, however, Curzon was forced to cancel the proposed first performance of the revised Piano Concerto, due to take place at the Royal Albert Hall in February 1946. The cancellation centred on Britten's unwillingness to assign to Curzon an exclusivity agreement. As Curzon explained to Leslie Boosey (of Boosey & Hawkes) on 27 November 1945:

I telephoned Ben about a month ago to see whether we could not make some reciprocal arrangement of mutual benefit [. . .] To my surprise (since there had been no previous disagreement in the matter), Ben made it impossible for me to get into touch with him, and finally disclosed the fact, through Mr Stein, that he did not intend to deal directly with me in the matter. [. . .] On Saturday Mr Stein telephoned suggesting the rights of performance for a short time in England only, which, as I explained to him, were of little use, as this would still mean my giving up the large amount of time and work the Concerto demands, with an agreement covering only the engagements I was certain to have in any case, but with no guarantee either of any performances abroad, or of a first recording (which is also in the publisher's hands). He asked for a further two days in which to consider the matter, and promised to telephone me on Monday morning at the latest, also saying that Ben was writing me over the weekend. [. . .] I was holding up both Albert Hall and BBC Concerts (the BBC having asked me for a first broadcast on February 27th), and so on Monday night, having heard nothing further, I was forced to notify those concerned of what had happened.

Curzon concluded:

I much regret that the matter had to end in this way [. . .]; the more so as the difficulty began, not by any demand for 'exclusivity', but only by my attempt to arrange the reasonably expected degree of collaboration with the composer.

A letter from Curzon to Britten (28 November) responds to one from the composer (now lost) in which many of Curzon's arguments for withdrawing are once again gone over. One new piece of information, however, is offered in Curzon's letter: that Britten wished to drop the proposed conductor of the Albert Hall performance – Sydney Beer (1899–1971; see Letter 381 n. 4) – in favour of Ernest Ansermet. (Ansermet was to conduct the premiere of *The Rape of Lucretia* at Glyndebourne in 1946, but Britten was apparently already trying in November 1945 to attract Ansermet's interest in his works.)

The rift between pianist and composer was only temporary and their friendship survived. As far as can be ascertained Curzon did not perform the original version of the concerto in public. He was a frequent performer at the Aldeburgh Festival, and eventually performed the revised Britten Concerto on 11 August 1952, as part of the Proms at the Royal Albert Hall.

4   The first performance of the revised version of the Piano Concerto was given at the Cheltenham Festival on 2 July 1946, with Noel Mewton-Wood as soloist and the London Philharmonic Orchestra conducted by the composer. A notice of the performance appeared in *The Times* (3 July 1946):

> Upon a fine melody he has constructed a beautiful aria and well-scored piece which makes the remainder of the concerto sound immature and impudently smart. The hall is not primed to loud orchestral tone, but one felt that Mr Britten, in his capacity as conductor, might have attempted to tone down the noisiness of the orchestration, which often made the details inaudible [. . .]

'Our Music Critic' concluded:

> Mr Mewton-Wood surmounted the formidable difficulties of the solo in Britten's work with brilliant success. A good deal of the music calls for no more than percussive dexterity, but where expressiveness is required in the new movement the pianist amply met the demand.

(*The Times* noted 'the programme was also to have included the *Passacaglia from 'Peter Grimes'*, but this had to be omitted because of lack of time for adequate rehearsal'.)

On 2 August, at the Concerto's London premiere at the Henry Wood Proms in the Royal Albert Hall, Mewton-Wood was again the soloist with the London Symphony Orchestra conducted by Basil Cameron. The date of the European performance mentioned by Britten has not been ascertained.

5   Noel Mewton-Wood (1922–1953), Australian pianist who studied at the Melbourne Conservatory, at the Royal Academy of Music and with Artur Schnabel. He made his debut in 1940 at the age of seventeen and was thereafter highly regarded, particularly in twentieth-century repertoire which included the concertos by Busoni, Stravinsky, Bliss and Britten, and Tippett's First Piano Sonata. In the early 1950s he became Pears's 'second' accompanist (when Britten was unavailable), taking part in the first performances of Alan Bush's *Voices of the Prophets* and Mátyás Seiber's *To Poetry* (both 22 May 1953, Royal Festival Hall) and recording Tippett's *Boyhood's End* and *The Heart's Assurance* (Argo RG 15). Mewton-Wood appeared at three consecutive Aldeburgh Festivals (1951–53) in repertoire that included Bartók's Sonata for two pianos and percussion, Bridge's Piano Quintet, Gerhard's Piano Concerto, Hindemith's Horn Sonata (with Dennis Brain) and *Kammermusik No. 2*, and Saint-Saëns's *Carnaval des animaux* (with Britten as the second pianist). In 1952 he also gave a recital with the violist William Primrose which included Britten's *Lachrymae*.

His suicide in 1953, according to John Amis the result of Mewton-Wood blaming himself for the death of his partner, Bill Fedricks, but also because he felt a lack of career success, came as a heavy blow to both Britten and Pears. A memorial concert was organized by Amis at the Wigmore Hall, London, on 28 January 1955 (postponed from 4 December 1954 because of Pears's indisposition), at which were given the first performances of Alan Bush's two pieces for horn and piano, *Autumn Poem*, Op. 45 ('written as a tribute to the memory of Noel Mewton-Wood') and *Trent's Broad Reaches*, Op. 36; Bliss's *Elegiac Sonnet* (words by Cecil Day-Lewis), for tenor, string quartet and piano, and Britten's *Canticle III: 'Still falls the Rain – The raids, 1940, Night and Dawn'*, for tenor, horn and piano (words by Edith Sitwell). The programme also included Britten's *Lachrymae*; Benjamin Frankel's Sonata, Op. 13, for solo violin; 'Remember your lovers', the last song from Tippett's *The Heart's Assurance*, and a song composed by Mewton-Wood at the age of fifteen, *As ye came from the Holy Land* (words by Walter Raleigh), for tenor and piano. Among the artists paying tribute to Mewton-Wood were Pears and Britten, horn-player Dennis Brain, Alan Bush and the Zorian String Quartet. In a note in the programme for the concert, 'Noel Mewton-Wood: A Recollection', Edward Sackville-West wrote:

Noel had in him the makings of a great pianist and would, I feel, have become one, if he had lived only a little longer. The necessity of pushing ahead with his career perhaps made him in too much of a hurry to realize his assets – a miscalculation that seems almost inevitable in these days. But at no time did he belong to the world of good, reliable, second-rate pianists: he played either magnificently or downright badly, with a jarring ferocity that seemed designed to hurt himself as much as the music; and in both cases he played with the energetic aplomb that distinguished everything he said or did.

[. . .] For his deep understanding of a contemporary idiom, and the musicianship that enabled him to form a perfect duo with another artist of the same calibre, we cannot do better than listen to the admirable recording of Michael Tippett's two works for tenor and piano [*Boyhood's End* and *The Heart's Assurance*], in which he accompanied Peter Pears.

Although Britten had intended to present the autograph fair copy of *Canticle III* to Mewton-Wood's mother at the time of the memorial concert, he in fact did not do so. He and Dulcie Mewton-Wood continued to keep in touch while she remained in England; in 1963, ten years after her son's death, by which time she had returned to Australia, Mrs Mewton-Wood wrote to Britten requesting a handwritten extract from the piece as a memento. Realizing his omission, Britten promptly forwarded the complete manuscript. The fair copy of *Canticle III* returned to BPL in 1989 when it was purchased at auction.

See also John Amis, *Amiscellany*, pp. 209–14.

519   To Walter Hussey[1]

45A, St J. W. H. St
Feb. 26th 1946

My dear Walter,

This is only a scribble (just ain't no time these days) to say Wystan
Auden has sent me direct already part of the St Matthew anthem, & it is
very very lovely.[2] Have you seen it yet? But, Walter, you blighter you never
told me that it meant more homework for me! You'll have to wait, I'm
afraid – because what with Lucretia and the Oratorio with Duncan my
schedule is filled for quite some time; Auden's stuff is desperately hard to
set, & can't be done over night. Still if you have patience – ?

You blighter!

How are you?

P. is not over-well these days – but sends his love.

So do I.
BEN

1   The Very Reverend John Walter Atherton Hussey (1909–1985), Vicar of St
    Matthew's, Northampton, 1937–55, and Dean of Chichester, 1955–77. For
    over forty years Hussey encouraged Church patronage of the arts and was
    responsible for commissioning a number of distinguished visual artists
    and composers, beginning with Britten and *Rejoice in the Lamb* in 1943. See
    also Letter 421 n. 2.

2   Letter 500 gives the first indication that Hussey was prepared to offer a
    commission to Auden and Britten for a new work to celebrate St Matthew's
    Day, 1946. Britten wrote to Hussey (postmarked 13 May 1945), 'Auden
    turned up the other day on his way [home] but [. . .] he'll be back soon &
    we'll tackle him then,' and two months later, on 13 July, Hussey reminded
    the composer, 'If you get a chance, you won't forget a word in the ear of
    W. H. Auden when you see him, will you?' On 30 January 1946 Auden sent
    to the composer the two stanzas of his 'Anthem' for Britten to set (and see
    Letter 500 n. 2), the same day he wrote to Hussey agreeing to write some-
    thing. Auden concluded his letter to Hussey: 'As to fee, I will leave the fig-
    ure to you but I would like to make two demands: a) It shall be a bit more
    than you can afford, b) You shall donate it to any fund for the relief of dis-
    tress in Europe which does not intentionally exclude the Germans.' Hussey
    made a £25 donation to Oxfam, the familiar abbreviated name of the
    Oxford Committee for Famine Relief, which had been established in 1942
    to exert pressure on the British government to allow essential supplies
    through the Allied blockade of Nazi-occupied Greece and to raise funds for
    war refugees and displaced people across Europe, later widening its remit
    to include 'the relief of suffering arising as a result of wars or other causes
    in any part of the world'.

Anthem

Praise ye the Lord.

Let the whole creation give out another fragrance,
Nicer in our nostrils, a novel sweetness
From its cleansed creatures in accord together
As ~~my~~ feeling fabric, flushed and intact of
~~phenomena~~ and ~~in~~ numbers announcing in one
Multitudinous oecumenical song
Their grand givenness of gratitude and joy,
Peaceful and plural, their positive truth an
Authoritative This, an unthreatened Now
Where in love and in laughter each lives itself
For the pattern is complex; their places safe,
System and order are a single glory.

———

Bless ye the Lord.

As we wander and weep He is with us always.
Minding our meanings, the least matter dear to Him
Though our bodies too blind or too bored to demand
What sorts excite them are slain interjecting
Their childish 'Ows', and in choosing how many
And how much they will love our minds insist on
Their own disorder as their own punishment,
His question disqualifies our quick senses,
His Truth makes our theories historical sins,
It is where we are wounded that is when He speaks
Our disconsolate tongue, concluding His children
In their mad unbelief to have mercy on them all.

———

Auden's draft of his *Anthem for Saint Matthew's Day*, sent to Britten in January 1946

On 16 February Hussey wrote to Britten:

I am delighted to be able to tell you that W. H. Auden has written to say that he will be 'very pleased to try and do something for the Patronal Festival in September'. What he suggests is 'a special litany for St Matthew's Day followed by an anthem' [...] I have explained the length of Rejoice in the Lamb, and suggested that anything sung at the end of the service should not probably be very much longer than that. Do you agree?

I told him, as you most kindly said I might, that if he wrote something you would be willing to set it to music. So, if it comes along, do you think you could find the time ... would you be willing ... ?

After a weekend visit to Northampton, probably in April, Pears wrote to Hussey (postmarked 6 May): 'I am thankful to be enclosing my pencil (but I hope legible) copy of the Auden.'

Britten never set the Anthem and the poet's 'Litany and Anthem for Saint Matthew's Day' was read by Valentine Dyall on 21 September 1946 as part of the 'Festival of Holy Music and Poetry' held at the church in the afternoon. The programme also included Britten's Rejoice in the Lamb and Te Deum in C major. At that morning's Solemn Eucharist Britten's Prelude and Fugue on a Theme of Vittoria for solo organ received its first two performances; Vittoria's 'Ecce Sacerdos Magnus', on which the Prelude and Fugue is based, was sung by the choir.

John Ireland's Service in C was also sung at the morning service. On the back of the service sheet he sent to Britten, Hussey wrote: 'Sorry about this! But the number of possible settings is so small. I hope before long we shall be able to substitute one by the Composer we really want!!' The hope that Britten might one day compose a complete Anglican Service was to become a recurrent theme of Hussey's correspondence with the composer in later years, as was his unfulfilled wish that Britten might make a setting of the Mass (see Letter 578 n. 2). See also Walter Hussey, Patron of Art: The Revival of a Great Tradition among Artists, pp. 83–7.

520 To Sophie Wyss

45A, St Johns Wood High St, N.W.8
Feb. 26th 1946

My dear Sophie,

At last the French Folk-songs are coming out in print. The delay is of course because of the shortage of labour & paper – I hope it hasn't inconvenienced you.[1]

The dedication is 'to my young Friends Arnold & Humphrey Gyde'[2] – I hope they'll be pleased. It gives me great pleasure to do this, because I am so fond of them.

We are both in our individual ways so busy that it seems we shall never meet – but I do hope that that isn't the case, because I should love to see you.

With love to you all.

Yours ever,

BENJIE

1   Britten's set of eight *French Folk Song Arrangements*, for high or medium
    voice and piano, was composed at Snape in December 1942. The published
    edition includes English translations prepared by Pears's friend Iris
    Holland Rogers. In May 1943 Wyss and Britten recorded five of the settings,
    only two of which – 'La belle est au jardin d'amour' and 'Le roi s'en va-t'en
    chasse' – were released by Decca (M 568, 78rpm). The other three – 'Voici le
    printemps', 'Fileuse' and 'Quand j'étais chez mon père' – remained unissued
    until 1993, when they were released by EMI (CMS 7 64727 2) under licence
    from Decca. See Philip Reed's accompanying liner notes for the EMI
    recording, 'Britten's Folk Song Arrangements', pp. 27–31.

    Britten later made orchestrations of six of the French folksongs, five of
    which – 'La belle est au jardin d'amour', 'Eho! Eho!', 'Fileuse', 'Quand j'étais
    chez mon père' and 'Le roi s'en va-t'en chasse' – were premiered by the
    French baritone Martial Singher (1904–1990), the son-in-law of Fritz Busch.
    Busch conducted the first performance at Chicago, on 23 December 1948,
    with the Chicago Symphony Orchestra. See also Letter 597. The sixth song
    to be orchestrated – and the only one to survive in the composer's auto-
    graph manuscript at BPL – was 'La noël passée' ('The Orphan and King
    Harry'). The manuscript of this arrangement was written by Britten left-
    handed, probably in the autumn of 1953 when he was severely affected by
    bursitis in his right arm and was obliged to rest it for several weeks. Britten
    returned to 'La noël passée' in the 1960s when he made another arrange-
    ment (unpublished and unperformed) for solo voice (tenor?) and chorus.
    See also Philip Reed, 'Britten's Folk Song Arrangements: Documentation',
    notes to the Collins Classics recording of the complete Britten Folk Song
    Arrangements (Collins Classics 70392, 1995). For a discussion of the rela-
    tionship between 'Quand j'étais chez mon père' and Act III of *Peter Grimes*,
    see Donald Mitchell, 'Peter Grimes: Fifty Years On', in PBMPG, pp. 135–51.

2   Sophie Wyss's children; Humphrey (b. 1936) was Britten's godson.

521 **To Gustel Scherchen**

Old Mill, Snape, Suffolk
March 27th, 1946

My dear Gustel,

Your sweet letter about "P.G." gave me great pleasure. I am so happy
that you have liked it. It is a great pity that John won't be able to see it, as
there is no performance while he is on leave.[1] Perhaps he can get to

Switzerland or Belgium to see it. It has just been successfully launched in Stockholm, but that is too far, I suppose.[2]

I am sorry that there was that fracas with Dent – but he has behaved so mischievously that I don't want to have any contact with him – not that I have ever had any, really.[3]

It was a pity we saw so little of you in Cambridge.[4] Peter & I are coming over to fetch Joan Cross (singing in the Messiah) on Easter Saturday – perhaps we could meet for lunch?[5]

Excuse shortness of this, but I'm hard at work at opera 2! – & I just wanted to send my love –

BEN

1   John Woolford (formerly Wulff Scherchen) had not yet been demobilized from the Army but had been home on leave, 11–20 March, visiting his mother in Cambridge during the weekend of the 16th and 17th.

2   Performances of *Peter Grimes* were given in Basel (23 May) and Zurich (1 June): see Letters 525 and 526. The Belgian premiere of *Grimes* (sung in Flemish) was given in Antwerp on 25 May; according to a letter of 23 June 1946 from Britten to Desmond Shawe-Taylor, who had sent the composer reviews of the Antwerp production, 'Eric Crozier went over earlier to give advice on the production. They obviously did as well as a small opera house could possibly do – just as Basel did. Rough but extremely ready. Zurich was another matter. A superb performance in every way.' The Swedish premiere, the opera's first production after the Sadler's Wells original and the first outside the UK, took place in Stockholm on 21 March 1946.

Britten did not attend any of the rehearsals or performances in Stockholm, probably because he was too preoccupied with the composition of *Lucretia*. However, some evidence has come to light in a letter of 2 October 1945 to the composer from Ernst Roth of Boosey & Hawkes, which suggests that Britten may have been unable to attend any of the Stockholm performances as it would have breached a clause in his contract with the Municipal Theatre, Zurich, in which he undertook not to be present 'at any performance of his opera in other theatres before the Zurich perfomances'. A draft of this contract is attached to Roth's letter of 2 October, in which he argues the objections to such a restrictive clause: 'You certainly could not be bound not to go to Basel if you wished to do so and to hear your opera there. Besides that, the wording is by no means clear and could be construed that you would not be allowed to hear your opera either in Stockholm or in Antwerp. Please let me know what your opinion is.' Britten's response has not survived, but in the event it was the composer's most trusted associate Erwin Stein who was dispatched to Sweden to attend the final rehearsals and the first two performances. He wrote to Britten from Stockholm on 22 March:

Your *Peter Grimes* has stood up here in full size under conditions which were almost completely the London ones inverted. Every plus there was a minus here and vice versa. This of course refers particularly to the main figure and to the orchestra. But the astounding [?thing] is that even [Set] Svanholm [in the title role] represented some figure, although he cannot sing any melody, and certainly not in the right tempo. He has a big voice which sometimes sounds very lovely and the phrase 'and God have mercy upon me' was very good indeed. One critic declares Grimes to be one of Svanholm's best roles. You see how little idea the people have. But the consolation is that you can send your child into the big world without fear that it perishes.

The orchestra was a feast, although the music can certainly be played still better. [Herbert] Sandberg [the conductor] says the musicians like playing it tremendously. The storm was terrific, the 'Moonlight' [Interlude] most beautiful [...] Sandberg is very good indeed and most enthusiastic.

[Inga] Sundström [who played Ellen] was better than I imagined at the dress rehearsal. She is leaner than Joan, she is no full-weight Ellen, and the embroidery aria ['Embroidery in childhood was a luxury of idleness', Act III scene 1], though beautifully sung, lacked Joan's intensity and maturity. But she has at least an idea of phrasing and understands what it is all about. Balstrode, Sigurd Björling, was at long last himself. His voice is a match to Svanholm's and his whole appearance gave the duet [for Grimes and Balstrode in Act I scene 1, 'And do you prefer the storm to Auntie's parlour and the rum?'] more weight. Auntie [played by Brita Ewert] was very good, Mrs Sedley less pointed than [Valetta] Iacopi [who sang the role at Sadler's Wells], Boles [played by Gösta Björling] very much better, the Nieces very sweet with much better voices than in London. The terzetto in the last act [for the Nieces and Swallow, 'Assign your prettiness to me'] sounded magnifique. Swallow has a good voice but not Brannigan's humour [Owen Brannigan sang the role at Sadler's Wells]. Also Keene [played by Arne Wirén] was lacking in character, but has a real voice.

Apart from the circular horizon, the visible sea and the spacy shore, the pictures are not as good as in London. Nor is the production. Yes, the lighting is much better and the people have ample room for moving. But André [the director], although he knows the music by heart, is not very sensitive. He gets the broad effects, but he has often the people moving when and where they shouldn't. [...] The applause at the first night was very good and lasted long. Usually the people applaud very little here and what happened was considered a great success.

3 Edward J. Dent (1876–1957), English musicologist, a friend of Gustel Scherchen, had been elected the first President of the ISCM in 1923 and was Professor of Music at Cambridge University from 1926 to 1941. He attended the Sadler's Wells performance of *Peter Grimes* on 26 February and wrote to Britten the next day:

I'm afraid you didn't quite understand what I said to you last night [...]; I dare say I expressed myself badly in the hurry of the moment (and you didn't give me much chance!).

I have taken seats for all the performances of *P.G.* this season, and I enjoy the opera more and more every time I see it. I find it quite unlike any other opera I have ever seen; I study it at home too, and I find new things in it every time. A great deal of it is extremely beautiful music and grows upon me more and more, and certain moments are profoundly moving.

As to reminiscences – you can find hundreds of them in Mozart, Verdi and Wagner, Gluck too – to take only the really great opera composers, that is, if you are intimately acquainted with their predecessors. Myself I find that study of that kind is a great help to the understanding and enjoyment of those men's own great works. In actual performance I don't notice them at all, any more than I do when I see *your* opera on the stage. I hope I succeed in seizing it as a whole.

When I said I saw places which reminded me of Massenet and Liszt I meant it as a compliment; perhaps I ought to have said that I thought Massenet and Liszt (who were extremely serious musicians and men of very deep artistic sensibility towards music not their own) would have particularly appreciated those moments.

The ordinary 'critics' [. . .] are generally more interested in performers than in composers; my outlook on music is just the other way. Perhaps when this season's performances are all over I may feel inclined to write something about *P.G.* [. . .]

Dent continued:

I am sorry you don't feel satisfied with the Sadler's Wells performances [. . .] The performances have certainly improved steadily all along, and they really are making the whole thing clearer as a whole, even if details go astray. [. . .]

However, don't be ungrateful; no English composer has ever had such chances before, except perhaps Balfe and Wallace; and I don't think any composer in the world has ever had so much outward success with a first opera – except Humperdinck with *Hänsel and Gretel*.

[. . .] The former Mrs Scherchen was at S.W. last night and had supper with Miss Scott and me afterwards. They were both most enthusiastic, and of course Mrs Sch. will write to Hermann about it.

Britten, however, was not to be pacified by Dent's letter of explanation; he had been wounded by Dent's comments at the theatre and his letter of response (14 March) demonstrates that he was not readily prepared to forgive him:

Thank you for writing to tell me you'd changed your mind about Peter Grimes – although it would be difficult to measure the harm that was caused to some fine people & some important ideas by your first opinion.

Why you & your young critics bother yourself about 'reminiscences' I cannot understand. That is the easiest & most provincial form of criticism. As Brahms said 'any fool can see that'.

But anyhow, thank you for your good wishes for the opera and for Peter Pears abroad.

In a contribution to the programme (edited by Philip Reed) for English National Opera's 2002 production of Mozart's *Così fan tutte*, 'The Truth About *Così*', Donald Mitchell recollected an amusing story about Professor Dent, told to him by Britten. The anecdote concerns the moment in *Così* when Don Alfonso's multiple deceptions are revealed to Dorabella and Fiordiligi by quoting music that has been previously associated with the elaborate charades, not least of which was Ferrando's and Guglielmo's new personae as 'Albanians'. As Donald Mitchell observes, 'Ferrando, still in part disguise as an "Albanian", greets Fiordiligi. The only problem here is the "quote" he seems to be making cannot be identified [from earlier in the opera; it refers to something that Mozart must have subsequently deleted].'

Britten told Mitchell that 'he, too, when young had been struck by Mozart's puzzling omission [. . .] It so happened that he ran across E. J. Dent, the then renowned Mozart scholar of his day, and shyly asked him for his explanation of the paradox. There was a pause for reflection, after which Dent confessed that he had never noticed it. For Britten this was a moment when his faith in musicology was irretrievably shaken, never to return.'

For Dent's further comments on *Grimes* (and *Lucretia* and *Albert Herring*), see Letter 502 n. 2.

4 On 10 February, as part of the Cambridge Arts Theatre Trust's Sunday Concert Series, Joan Cross, Pears and Britten gave a recital of music by Purcell and Britten at the Arts Theatre. The programme included Britten's realization of Purcell's 'Mad Bess' (dedicated to Joan Cross) and excerpts from *Peter Grimes*. E. J. Dent wrote afterwards to the composer (27 February), 'Cambridge was also delighted with your concert. I hope Peter is not over-straining himself.'

During the week beginning 4 February the Arts Theatre had presented the original Mercury & Pilgrim Players production of Ronald Duncan's 'Masque with Anti-Masque', *This Way to the Tomb*, with incidental music by Britten under the direction of Arthur Oldham. The play was directed by E. Martin Browne and designed by Stella Mary Pearce. Apart from training and conducting the Tenison Singers, Oldham also played percussion in the Anti-Masque; the pianists were John Lindsay and Henry Vincent. The programme included the following statement about Britten's incidental music:

Benjamin Britten has scored his music in the Masque for a four-part choir, using the Latin words of Psalm 69 and of a Franciscan hymn quoted in the play. In the Anti-Masque he uses four hands at the piano and jazz percussion, returning to the choral music at the end. Julian's songs are accompanied by muted piano. In achieving a unity with means so diverse he has completed the similar achievement of his friend the author. This is his first new work since *Peter Grimes*.

See also Letter 456 n. 1.

The Cambridge performances were given under the auspices of the Company of Four, a theatrical venture sponsored by the Cambridge Arts Theatre Trust, Glyndebourne Productions Ltd, Tennent Plays Ltd and the Arts Council of Great Britain. According to the programme, the new Company's objects were:

To provide an outlet in London for new authors, designers and theatre technicians.
    Offer scope to established people of the theatre in experimental work.
    Ensure a regular flow of new productions with the original casts to selected theatres in the provinces.

Productions were toured each week to Cambridge, Bristol, Cardiff and Brighton, before being given for four weeks at the Lyric Theatre, Hammersmith. The programme states that 'all casts and staff are recruited, wherever possible, from members of the profession recently returned from service with the Forces'.

Several items from Britten's incidental music for *This Way to the Tomb* have been revived in recent years: the setting of Psalm 69 for unaccompanied chorus, 'Deus in adjutorium meum', was published by Boosey & Hawkes in 1983 and first recorded by the Choir of Westminster Cathedral, conducted by David Hill, in 1986, on Hyperion CDA6220; the 'Boogie-woogie', in an arrangement by Daryl Runswick, was first performed at the Jubilee Hall, Aldeburgh, on 8 June 1990, as part of Runswick's *Britten's Blues* and subsequently recorded on Unicorn Kanchana DKP(CD)9138 in 1992; and Julian's three songs were published by Boosey & Hawkes in 1988 under the title *Evening, Morning, Night* and first recorded by Ian Bostridge (tenor) and Graham Johnson (piano) for Hyperion CDA66823 in 1995.

The BPL is in possession of three unpublished discs of music from *This Way to the Tomb* (*Deus in adjutorium meum*, and what is described on the label as 'Soprano songs'), recorded at the Mercury Theatre, London, by the Pilgrim Players under Arthur Oldham's direction on 12 November 1945 and broadcast as part of an abridged version of Duncan's play on the BBC Light Programme on 14 November; the programme was repeated on 18 November. The *Radio Times* identifies the pianists as Mark Langley and Anthony Dodd, and the percussionists as Arthur Oldham and Eric Shilling (who also took the role of Julian). An unspecified extract from Britten's incidental music – most probably *Deus in adjutorium meum* – was broadcast on 10 April 1946 by the Con Moto Choir under Oldham's direction.

5   Easter Saturday was 20 April. Letter 524 makes it clear that Britten did meet Gustel Scherchen.

522   **To Basil Wright**[1]

Old Mill, Snape, Suffolk
April 1st 1946

My dear Basil,

Thank you for your sweet note. Thank you for all your patience in the long wait of months before the piece was delivered.[2] I am glad that the Min. of Ed. chaps approve – or so I gather from talking to Shaw[3] this morning. I never really worried that it was too sophisticated for kids – it is difficult to be that for the little blighters! But we must stop the Doctor from talking nice Brains Trust to them.[4] What we want (I should think) is nice facts.

It was sweet of you to be there all that long & tiring day – nice moral support!

Excuse brief scrawl, but Lucretia is patiently waiting to be raped – on my desk.[5]

Much love,
BEN

1   English documentary film-maker and producer (1907–1987). He had
    worked with John Grierson at the GPO Film Unit (where he brought
    Auden and Britten together for the first time for *Coal Face*); at the Realist
    Film Unit, which he founded in 1937 and where he produced *Advance
    Democracy* with music by Britten; during the war for the Ministry of
    Information, and between 1945 and 1946 for the Crown Film Unit (the
    GPO Unit's successor). See also Diary for January 1936, n. 2.

2   Britten refers to his music for the Crown Film Unit/ Ministry of Education
    film, *Instruments of the Orchestra*, known in its concert version as *The
    Young Person's Guide to the Orchestra*. Wright had written to the composer
    on 28 March, the day of the music recording:

> This to say Thank You for the lovely work you gave us today. To me it is the exact
> job we were all hoping and looking for; and (with suitable control over Sargent) I
> know we shall now have a really remarkable film which will also be a pioneer in the
> musical-film field.
>
> I hope the day was not too much of an interruption to *Lucretia*.

Michael Gordon recalled (in 1991) the recording session for *Instruments of
the Orchestra*, a memory that qualifies Norman Del Mar's account (see
Letter 514 n. 7):

> It was recorded in the first place by Malcolm Sargent; he recorded at Wembley
> Town Hall and then his sound track was used; Muir [Mathieson] directed the
> film – he didn't record anything. Sargent's sound track – his recording with the
> Philharmonia [*recte*: London Symphony Orchestra] was played back to the musi-
> cians who were actually performing in the film studio, so it was that way round.
>
> What the editor told me was that it was great fun at Wembley Town Hall when
> it was first recorded because Britten was sort of jumping about and laughing with
> pleasure at hearing what he'd done.

Further documentation concerning *Instruments of the Orchestra* came to
light at BPL in 2003, including a draft typescript scenario/script entitled
'The Orchestra and its Instruments', dated 24 February 1945, which, almost
a year before a note of the music was to be written, already incorporates
many of the principal characteristics of the film and Britten's score (though
not, it would seem, that it would follow a theme and variations structure):

> The Orchestra plays a simple theme (written specially for this film). The Con-
> ductor explains that this is a Symphony Orchestra and that he conducts it, men-
> tioning what a Conductor has to do. He then shows that an Orchestra consists of
> three groups of instruments:–
>
> (1) Instruments which are blown – wood and brass
> (2) Instruments which are hit – percussion
> (3) Instruments which are 'scraped' – strings
>
> Each group is 'broken down' to show (and hear) the instruments in that group.
> Then the harp makes an appearance as one of several 'occasional' instruments. The
> Theme heard at the beginning is then played in fugue-form bringing in all the

instruments of the Orchestra section by section until the whole Orchestra is playing the grand climax.

Throughout, the Orchestra will be playing, the music being scored specially to
'spotlight' the sections and groups in turn.

Britten's loose-leaf pocket diary for this period (March 1945–May 1947)
includes a reference to a meeting with Malcolm Sargent at the Ministry of
Information on 22 January 1946 and the following draft outline for the film
in Britten's hand:

The Orchestra
Titles – Tuning Up
Orchestra – full view – Theme

Flute	Var. 1
Oboe	2
Clarinet	3
Bassoon	4
Horns	5
Trumpet	6
Trombone	7
Tuba	8
Timp	9
Percussion	10
Violins (& II)	11
Violas	12
Cellos	13
Bass	14

Orchestra full view Theme again

(Flute) Introduction – Here is a flute

It can go high ＼ low

It is very agile

(In this orchestra are two flutes, the second of which often plays
the piccolo, a smaller flute, much higher, but with the general
characteristics of the flute.)

Notable is the absence from this draft of any statements of the theme by
the sections of the orchestra (woodwind, brass, percussion, strings), the
lack of a variation for harp but the inclusion of distinct variations for timpani and percussion (they are combined in the final version). Moreover,
the order of the variations differs from the final sequence – where the individual variations for the strings appear after the woodwind, not after the
brass – and there is no indication of the fugue which 'reassembles' the
entire orchestra.

As noted in Letter 514 n. 7, Britten completed the score on 31 December

1945, the next day playing it through to Basil Wright, then producer-in-charge at the Crown Film Unit, who had commissioned the music. Montagu Slater, who took final responsibility for the film's script (but see below), wrote to Britten on 25 February 1946, 'Basil was very excited about the music for the film. I'm longing to hear it.'

Also surviving at BPL is a 'Note of a Meeting held in Mr Slater's Room, M.O.I. [Ministry of Information] at 5.30 pm on 8th March 1946 to discuss details of the C.F.U. [Crown Film Unit] Film "Orchestra"'. These minutes note that two orchestras were under consideration to appear in the film – the London Symphony Orchestra (Sargent's preference) and the National Symphony Orchestra (Britten's first choice); it was the LSO that eventually took part. Intriguingly, the minutes record that Britten 'should write the commentary, so that it should be revised by Dr Sargent'. Is perhaps the incomplete draft in Britten's pocket diary – it breaks off abruptly – the composer's attempt at writing the script? It is, however, Montagu Slater who is credited with writing the script. Did Britten fail to deliver what was needed – he was, after all, working intensively on *Lucretia* throughout the first months of 1946 – thus providing an opportunity for Slater, an experienced professional writer, to step in with his contribution? (Slater, after all, had been involved with the project for some time and had a clear idea of what was required.) The minutes also note that the music was to be recorded at Watford Town Hall (not Wembley Town Hall, as Michael Gordon erroneously recalled), with Ken Cameron, the Crown Film Unit's head of sound, supervising, while the actual shooting of the film at Denham Studios was to take place 14–17 May (Britten was unable to attend as he was Switzerland). The order of the recording sessions, music then visuals, concurs with Gordon's recollection.

3 Alexander Shaw (1910–?), English film producer, who began his career in the mid-1930s with the GPO Film Unit. He subsequently worked with Paramount–British Productions and Alexander Korda's London Films before spending a year as film adviser to the Indian Government. He returned to the UK in 1942 to work as a producer with Strand Films (London) and in 1945 took up a position with the Crown Film Unit where he was the producer of *Instruments of the Orchestra*.

4 The Doctor = the British conductor, Dr Malcolm Sargent (1895–1967): see also Diary for 25 January 1931, n. 1, and Letter 514 n. 7.

   The Brains Trust was a popular BBC radio programme in which a panel of experts from different disciplines (including Malcolm Sargent and from its beginning the combative philosopher C. E. M. Joad (1891–1953)) addressed listeners' questions, which then formed the basis for discussion. Joad was Head of the Philosophy Department, Birkbeck College, London, from 1930 to 1953.

5 This remark suggests that Britten had reached Act II scene 1 in his composition draft.

"PETER GRIMES," Benjamin Britten's first Opera, is set in Aldeburgh in about 1830.

Britten was born in Lowestoft in a house directly facing the sea and his life has been strongly coloured by his experience of the fierce storms which drive ships on to the sandbanks, and eat away whole stretches of coast and cliff. In his own words: "In writing "Peter Grimes," I wanted to express my awareness of the perpetual struggle of men and women whose livelihood depends on the sea." The libretto is written by Montagu Slater, based on a story in "The Borough," by George Crabbe, the Aldeburgh poet, who was born here in 1755.

The scenes of the opera take place in the Moot Hall, where the fishermen are gathered mending their nets; the inside of the Boar Inn; Peter Grimes' hut, made from an up-turned boat; these and the music express the life of the Borough, the breaking of the waves, the cry of the sea gulls, the brawls in the tavern, the storms at sea, the jovial gatherings. Against this background stands the strange character of Peter Grimes, in whom good and evil, sanity and madness are persistently and violently at war.

The story tells of his uneasy life in Aldeburgh. He lives alone, visionary, ambitious, impetuous, poaching, fishing without caution or care of the consequences, and with only one friend, Ellen Orford, the widowed school-mistress. He is determined to make enough money to ask her to marry him, though too proud to ask her until he has lived down his unpopularity and his poverty. He fishes with the aid of an apprentice, bought according to the custom of the time from the Workhouse. His first apprentice dies at sea and Grimes is called as chief witness at the inquest in the Moot Hall. The verdict is accidental death, but the people are suspicious and Grimes is boycotted. He gets a second apprentice, whom Ellen goes to fetch for him and promises to care for. Later she discovers that he has been using the boy cruelly. She accuses him of this and they have a violent quarrel, which is overheard by several townspeople. Led by the Rector, the men go to his hut to investigate. He hears them coming, and drives the boy down the scar of a recent landslide. The boy slips and falls to his death. When this is discovered a hue and cry from the Borough pursues Peter, who driven mad by fear and misfortune, rows out to sea in the small hours of the morning, scuttles his boat and goes down with her himself.

At this concert, Peter Pears (Grimes) and Joan Cross (Ellen Orford) will sing arias and duets from their original parts. Benjamin Britten will play his piano version of the orchestral score and Eric Crozier, the producer of the Opera, will tell the story.

ALL ALDEBURGH PEOPLE WILL HAVE A PERSONAL INTEREST IN THIS CONCERT.

The Suffolk Rural Music School

announces

A CONCERT

IN THE

JUBILEE HALL, ALDEBURGH,

On MONDAY, April 22nd,

1946 —————— AT EIGHT P.M.

Artistes—

JOAN CROSS - - (Soprano)

PETER PEARS - - (Tenor)

BENJAMIN BRITTEN - (Piano)

PROGRAMME.

1. SONGS - - by Purcell.
2. Selections from "PETER GRIMES"
   Benjamin Britten's Opera about Aldeburgh, now being performed at Sadler's Wells Theatre, London. Joan Cross and Peter Pears will sing arias and duets from their original parts, and Benjamin Britten will play his piano version of the orchestral score. Eric Crozier, the producer of the Opera, will tell the story.
3. Folk Songs arranged by Benjamin Britten.

PRICES OF SEATS: 5/-, 3/6, 1/6

obtainable from Miss Stephenson, Jeweller, High Street, Aldeburgh (Tel. Aldeburgh 431) from 9 - 1 and 2 - 5 (excepting Wednesday afternoons) and at the door.

Proceeds in aid of the SUFFOLK RURAL MUSIC SCHOOL.

(P.T.O.)

Peter Grimes comes home: flyer for a concert in aid of the Suffolk Rural Music School, Jubilee Hall, Aldeburgh, 22 April 1946

523   To John Piper[1]

Old Mill, Snape, Suffolk

April 25th 1946

My dear John,

This is only a note to explain why you are probably receiving new bits
of 'Lucretia' from Boosey & Hawkes. They are the Interlude from Act II,
& the new Epilogue – the first one replacing the Interlude in your present
copy.[2] Ronnie & I thought they might give you ideas about the costumes
for the Choruses, & possibly the new Curtain Eric is suggesting for Act II.[3]

I am up Friday & Saturday next week & can play you the music then if
it's convenient for you – (would you like to come to Grimes' (last) matinée
on Saturday?)[4] – in case you want any more 'impressions'.

I can't say how pleased & excited I was by your models for the sets. I
think they are absolutely masterly.[5]

Excuse scribble – but I'm racing against time trying to get the score done.

Yours ever,

BENJAMIN B.

1   John Piper (1903–1992), English painter, stained-glass and stage designer,
who, from *The Rape of Lucretia* onwards, was to be one of Britten's most
constant artistic collaborators, designing the majority of the composer's
theatrical works. Piper's second wife, Myfanwy (1911–1997), was to write the
librettos for *The Turn of the Screw* (1954), *Owen Wingrave* (1970) and *Death
in Venice* (1973). Britten gave John Piper the composition draft of *Albert
Herring* in 1947 on the day of the opera's premiere, inscribing the manuscript, 'For dear John P. / with affection, & admiration lots of it, / & everlasting thanks for his / great work on Albert Herring / Benjamin Britten /
June 20th 1947', and dedicated his Hardy cycle *Winter Words* to Piper and
his wife in 1954. Piper was a tremendous supporter of, and contributor to,
the Aldeburgh Festival, with many exhibitions of his paintings and photographs as well as contributions to the programme books. He was generous
in giving pictures for auction in aid of the Festival and in allowing the sale
of various souvenir items, including, in 1954, an Aldeburgh Festival calendar to which he, Mary Potter and Prunella Clough each contributed four
lithographs.

When Britten first met the artist in 1937 on the occasion of the Group
Theatre conference at the Pipers' farmhouse on the edge of the Chilterns
(see Letter 89 n. 2), Piper was at the height of his early abstract and con-
structivist phase, a member of Ben Nicholson's 7 & 5 Society (among whose
other members were the sculptors Barbara Hepworth and Henry Moore)
and a regular contributor to *AXIS*, 'a Quarterly Review of Contemporary
"Abstract" Painting and Sculpture', edited by Myfanwy Evans, who was to
marry Piper in 1937. (As well as being a contributor, Piper was also responsible for the magazine's striking cover design.)

While Piper drew much from the discipline of abstraction, his over-riding fascination for topographical English architecture took hold – already in the early 1930s he had painted subjects on the South Coast – and was to dominate his painting, which became increasingly romantic and representational in style, for the remainder of his life. His passion for architecture was further strengthened when John Betjeman, who became a close friend, enlisted Piper's help with the *Shell Guide to Oxfordshire* (1938); when Betjeman relinquished his role as series editor, it was Piper who took over, and many of the Shell Guides were enriched by photographs taken by Piper. It was to Betjeman that Evelyn Waugh confessed that Piper was the inspiration for Charles Ryder in *Brideshead Revisited*, who on leaving Oxford becomes a successful architectural painter.

Piper did not become an official War Artist until 1944, but already in the early 1940s he had been commissioned by the Pilgrim Trust for its *Recording Britain* project, and his paintings from this period include bombed churches in London, Bristol and Coventry, as well as the House of Commons, a series of watercolours of Windsor Castle (commissioned by Kenneth Clark) and Renishaw Hall in Derbyshire (commissioned by Osbert Sitwell).

Piper first designed for the theatre in the 1930s – the 1938 Group Theatre production of Spender's *Trial of a Judge* (see Letter 89 n. 2) – and this was to be an area of his work that would expand. In addition to the major sequence of designs for Britten's operas, Piper's stage designs include the front cloth for the 1942 revival of Walton's *Façade* and the ballet *The Quest* (Sadler's Wells Ballet, 1943), Vaughan Williams's 'masque for dancing', *Job* (Sadler's Wells Ballet, 1948), *Don Giovanni* (Glyndebourne, 1951), *The Pearl Fishers* (Sadler's Wells, 1954, directed by Basil Coleman), *The Magic Flute* (Covent Garden, 1956) and Ronald Duncan's *Abelard and Heloise* (Arts Theatre Club, 1960). Other spheres into which Piper ventured with considerable success were stained-glass design (realized by Patrick Reyntiens), tapestry and ceramics. Among his notable stained-glass commissions are the vast Baptistry Window at Coventry Cathedral (1958–59), the cathedral for which Britten composed *War Requiem*, and the Benjamin Britten Memorial Window (1979) in Aldeburgh Parish Church. The subject of the Britten window is the three Church Parables, none of the productions of which Piper had designed.

See obituaries in *The Times* (30 June 1992); the *Daily Telegraph* (30 June 1992), including a further appreciation by Henry Thorold; 'All England: paint, set and ceramics' by James Richards and John Russell in the *Guardian* (30 June 1992), with an additional contribution from John White (*Guardian*, 8 July 1992); and by Colin Amery, 'The Master of Pleasing Decay', *Financial Times* (6 July 1992). See also the catalogue prepared for the retrospective exhibition at the Tate Gallery in 1983.

See plates 3, 6, 7, 10, 12, 15 and 44–7.

2 Britten refers here to two new passages of text for *Lucretia*, both for the

Male and Female Chorus. The Interlude for Act II (between scenes 1 and 2)
had read in Duncan's first complete draft libretto:

MALE CHORUS
Like a great pine tree man
Stands in the wind of woman's love;
And reaches for the light,
From his roots of night;
His limbs lean into her suppleness,
His loins anoint her smoothness,
As he climbs towards the sun
Seeking the womb luminous
From which he came from; thus
With his passion poised like a dart
At the heart of woman
Man becomes a god
Making himself again
In the dark loins of pain.
  Taking thus, he gives
  Giving thus, he lives.

FEMALE CHORUS
As an unending river
Woman flows for ever
Slaking the fierce thirst of man
With her love generous as water.
Man from her own muscles, torn
Man from her own thighs is born.
Man her child, man her master.
Man the thirst, she the river
Flowing on and never
Being of herself, but always of the river
Flowing to the thirst of man she gives.
  Yielding thus, she takes
  Taking thus, she lives.

This was replaced by four stanzas in which Christian imagery, which was to
prove so controversial, is introduced for the first time in the opera:

FEMALE AND MALE CHORUS
Here though this scene deceives
  Spirit's invincible
  Love's unassailable;
All this is endless
  Crucifixion for Him.

Nothing impure survives,
  All passion perishes,
  Virtue has one desire
To let its blood flow
  Back to the wounds of Christ.

She whom the world denies
  Mary, Mother of God,
  Help us to lift this sin
Which is our nature
  And is the Cross to Him.

She whom the world denies
  Mary most chaste and pure,
  Help us to find your love
Which is His Spirit
  Flowing to us from Him.

Britten's composition draft uses a slightly different version of this text, a draft of which survives at BPL in Britten's hand. The opening stanza was later rewritten by Duncan.

The second additional passage mentioned by Britten is the new Epilogue. Duncan's draft had ended with Lucretia's suicide and everyone singing the lines 'So brief is beauty. / Is this it all? It is all! It is all!' Duncan's Epilogue, added at Britten's request, reveals a Christian interpretation of Lucretia's tragedy.

BIANCA LUCIA	She lived with too much grace to be Of our crude humanity. For even our shame's refined By her purity of mind. Now place the wreath about her head And let the sentinels of the dead Guard the grave where our Lucretia lies. So brief is beauty. Why was it begun? It is done.
FEMALE CHORUS	Beauty is the hoof of an unbroken filly Which thundering up to the hazel hedge Jumps into the sun And is gone So brief is beauty. Why was it begun? It is done.
MALE CHORUS	They have no need of life to live; They have no need of lips to love; They have no need of death to die; In their love all's dissolved In their love all's resolved. They have no need of life to live; They have no need of lips to love; They have no need of death to die. What is there but love? Love is the whole. It is all!
OMNES	So brief is beauty. Is this it all? It is all! It is all! - C U R T A I N -

The Rape of Lucretia, Act II scene 2: the final page from Duncan's draft libretto, showing the original ending of the opera without the Epilogue

3   A design for the Act II Interlude cloth, as well as other set and costume designs by Piper, can be found in DHOBB, p. 131, and in RLEC, where Angus McBean's photographs of the original Glyndebourne production can also be found; and see plate 7. In his article in RLEC, 'The Design of *Lucretia*', John Piper wrote about the Act II front cloth (p. 71):

> [It] was the last item of scenery to be designed. The rest of the designing scheme had reached a pretty final form on the model and much of it was already constructed and painted when Britten and Duncan produced the chorale in Act II which demanded a setting that would bear its weight and importance in the whole work. The Christian moral must be given its scenic equivalent. It was a poser, and I spent a long time wondering how the equivalent could be found. As in most moments of doubt, I turned to remembered experiences, and thought of English stained glass of the thirteenth and fourteenth centuries in country churches that I had copied in water-colour, and I began to think again of how wonderfully early glass tells a story by intensity of colour and simple formal means. Our Lord in Majesty is one of its favourite subjects. I have no intention of going far in verbal explanation of this cloth; but its colour bears definite relation to the colour of all the other scenes and the costumes, and it contains no hidden symbolism or realism – so far as I know – whatever. It is an attempt to find a suitable scenic equivalent, at this stage of the work, for Benjamin Britten's music.

> An exhibition of Piper's 'Stage Designs for Benjamin Britten's Opera *The Rape of Lucretia*' was held at the Leicester Galleries, London, during October and November 1946. The exhibition catalogue indicates that twenty-three costume and stage designs were on display, including five earlier attempts at the Act II cloth and a set model (lent by the Victoria and Albert Museum).

> In *John Piper: The Forties*, p. 45, David Fraser Jenkins notes that Piper's 'sets for *The Rape of Lucretia* were largely designed under the shadow of Tryfan in his Welsh cottage', Pentre, in Bethesda, Bangor, North Wales, from where Piper was to write to Britten on 29 August 1946:

> I am proposing to show the designs for sets and costumes at the Leicester Gals. in October. Do you remember the drawing you had in the bottom of a suitcase at Glyndebourne of the Act II cloth? I thought it would be a good idea to show all the evolving drawings for that cloth; if you've still got it *could* you send it along here? I fear this is a bore, but don't bother about packing it flat or elaborately, as I will flatten it out and repaint it if necessary, when it arrives.

4   The last of the Sadler's Wells performances with members of the original cast.

5   One of Piper's models is illustrated in DHOBB, p. 131.

524 To John Woolford

Hotel Baren, Sigriswil, Switzerland[1]
(as from: Old Mill, Snape, Suffolk)
May 8th 1946

My dear John,

I am afraid I have neglected you badly recently – but as I've had no time at all for letter writing you are in the same boat as many others! However now Peter & I are having a week's holiday at this heavenly spot up in the Bernese Oberland – preparatory to giving recitals here & attending Grimes in Zurich & Basel, there is a bit more time & I can answer your letters.[2]

As you probably heard – we had no luck in getting Folk-song records for you – when they come back into print you'll be sent a copy – but as always at the moment supply is a good deal less than the demand.[3] I am afraid that it wasn't true that Grimes is coming to Germany for the B.A.O.R. When the Sadler's Wells Opera Co. went last year, they decided that Grimes was too highbrow for the troops.[4] It is just possible that the new opera (Rape of Lucretia) may be coming over at the end of October, & if that does Peter can certainly do the Serenade for you (if you can find a horn player good enough for the part! – but I forgot, Germany is always swimming in horn players).[5]

I am awfully glad that you are doing your present job, & obviously enjoying it. It must be better than the other dreary ones were. How much longer will you have to stay out there, or will you make it a permanent thing?[6] How is the family – steadily increasing? I must meet them sometime – maybe in London in September – any chance of that?

I saw your mother for a moment in Cambridge this Easter – she seemed well & was cheerful. We went over to fetch Joan Cross who was singing there for John Lowe.[7] She is a good singer – have you heard her. She is also coming out here to do Grimes[8] – both Peter & she are singing it in German – a pretty good effort – don't you think! I hope to see your father when we go to Winterthur at the end of this month.[9] We shan't be able to stay long there unfortunately as the rehearsals in Zurich will be in full flight then.

This is an incredible spot. Do you know that lake of Thun at all? Peter & I went to the top of the Jungfrau yesterday, & ate hard boiled eggs looking down a glacier!

I hope you are well, my dear. Is Trevor Harvey[10] still with you in Hamburg. If so – give him Peter's & my love – & to yourself too.

Yours ever,

BEN

1 On the shores of the Thunersee.

2 See Letter 525 for the composer's account of the performances and
   rehearsals of *Grimes*. Britten's 1946 engagement diary suggests that he and
   Pears arrived in Switzerland (at Geneva) on 6 May and holidayed until the
   11th. On the 14th they were in Berne, and on the 15th–16th in St Gallen.
   Their recital on the 16th was shared with organist Karl Grenacher and the
   St Galler Kammerchor who performed Britten's *Festival Te Deum*, while
   Pears and Britten contributed Purcell's Divine Hymn, 'We sing to him', and
   The Holy Sonnets of John Donne. On the 17th they travelled to Zurich.
   Britten noted in his diary that rehearsals for the Zurich *Peter Grimes* would
   take place between the 18th and 30th. They were in Schaffhausen (north of
   Zurich, near the Swiss–German border) on the 19th and in Basel between
   the 20th and 23rd where they attended a performance of *Grimes*. They gave
   a broadcast concert for Zurich Radio on the 26th entitled *An Hour with
   Benjamin Britten*, a programme of Britten's Purcell realizations and folksong arrangements, as well as the two-piano pieces, *Introduction and Rondo
   alla burlesca* and *Mazurka Elegiaca*, in which Britten was joined by
   Dorothea Braus. Two days later, on the 28th, at the Tonhalle, Zurich, Britten
   conducted the Tonhalle Orchestra in a performance of his *Sinfonia da
   Requiem*. After the Zurich *Grimes* at the beginning of June, Britten and
   Pears visited Winterthur (on the 2nd) and Lugano (on the 6th), returning
   to London on the 9th by way of Geneva.

3 Woolford had asked Britten for the recording of 'The Salley Gardens'
   (Decca, 1945) as he wished to include it in a 'Personal Favourites' radio programme for the British Forces Network.

4 B.A.O.R. = British Army of the Rhine. Britten refers to the ENSA
   (Entertainments National Services Association) tour by the Sadler's Wells
   company, organized by Walter Legge: see Letter 506 n. 4.

5 Woolford had written from Hamburg on 10 April, where he was Assistant
   Musical Director of the British Forces Network radio station: 'We played
   your *Serenade* records this afternoon, and as a result the Modern Music
   Department are all agog to record the work over here. What are the chances
   of this, and could Peter be induced to play the main part?' As far as is
   known, Pears did not record the *Serenade* in Germany; *Lucretia* was toured
   to Holland but did not reach Germany. Woolford was probably influential
   in broadcasting the first German performance of *Sinfonia da Requiem*,
   with the North-West German Radio Symphony Orchestra conducted by
   Trevor Harvey in August 1946 (recording made on 23 June).

   In an interview with Donald Mitchell (15 September 1989), Woolford
   recalled:

   [I] found myself, just after the war, in Brussels and later on in Germany, always
   following Benjamin around, just missing the performances he'd been giving in
   various places, because by the time I'd found out that he was somewhere, he'd
   already moved on somewhere else.

In a letter to Britten (27 January 1946), he told the composer:

I have been meaning to tell you for a long time how sorry I was that I missed the Britten–Menuhin recital at Bad Oeynhausen last summer. When I got to the Rhine Army that was an event people were still discussing in awed voices. The most annoying thing about it all was that at the time of the recital I was with Intelligence Rear H. Q. only ½ hr run away from it all, but didn't know you were there.

The recital to which Woolford refers was part of the tour undertaken by Menuhin and Britten in the summer of 1945, which included a recital at Belsen (see Letter 505 n. 5, Letter xxv n. 3, and pp. 50–51).

6 Woolford's wife, Pauline, was to write to Britten on 18 November 1946 that her husband had been 'very badly let down':

It seems that an intrigue which has been going on for some time last week found expression in Wulff [i.e. John] being told by the Programme Director that owing to the cutting down of the establishment his services were no longer required by the broadcasting section.

This was a double blow as Woolford had hoped to take over the running of the Music Department of Radio Berlin in 1947.

7 English radio producer, administrator and conductor (1906–1996). In the mid-1940s Lowe was Director of Music at Homerton College, Cambridge, and Conductor of the Cambridge Philharmonic Orchestra and Chorus, for which organization Joan Cross must have been singing. (Among Lowe's most distinguished Cambridge performances was Bach's B minor Mass with Kathleen Ferrier and Pears.) Lowe was a music producer for the Third Programme (1946–51, in charge of Music for the Third from 1947) and subsequently became Head of Midland Region Music, in which capacity he conducted the BBC Midland Chorus in the first broadcast performance of Britten's *Five Flower Songs* in 1951 (see Letter 707 n. 1) and the first performance, also a broadcast, on 7 March 1954 of the *Choral Dances from 'Gloriana'*. During his time in Birmingham, he collaborated closely with Rudolf Schwarz, then Conductor of the City of Birmingham Symphony Orchestra.

Lowe had first been in touch with Britten in March 1945, when he requested a theme from the composer on which the French organist–composer Marcel Dupré (1886–1971) might undertake a broadcast improvisation. Britten obliged with two themes – one for a prelude, the other for a fugue – which were published in *Tempo*, 12 (1945), p. 15. The improvisation was broadcast by the BBC on 24 July 1945 from St Mark's, North Audley Street, London (see also Letter 87 n. 1). One of Lowe's innovations at the Third Programme was the institution of two song recitals per week, starting in the summer of 1947. Lowe instructed Basil Douglas, the producer in charge, who was later to become General Manager of the English Opera Group (see Letter 600 n. 3), to make 'plenty of use of Pears – plus Britten whenever possible and Ferrier' (see Humphrey Carpenter, *The Envy of the*

World: Fifty Years of the BBC Third Programme and Radio 3, 1946–1996, p. 55). Britten was also among those composers approached by Lowe – the others were Tippett, Vaughan Williams, Walton, Rawsthorne, Patrick Hadley, Poulenc and Strauss – to write pieces to mark the first anniversary of the launch of the Third Programme. Britten was too committed elsewhere to accept and, as Humphrey Carpenter notes (pp. 62–3), none of the others accepted the commission with the exception of Poulenc whose *Sinfonietta* (1948) originated from Lowe's initiative.

   After leaving the BBC, Lowe worked as a freelance artistic adviser and festival administrator. He was the Artistic Director of the 1962 Coventry Cathedral Festival and therefore responsible for the commissioning of Britten's *War Requiem*. As Festival Director of Liverpool's Commonwealth Arts Festival in 1965, he invited Britten to compose a new work to mark the opening of the Roman Catholic Cathedral the following year. Britten, however, declined the invitation.

   See also the obituary in *The Times* (27 January 1996).

8   According to Britten's engagement diary, Joan Cross arrived in Zurich on 17 May.

9   Woolford's father, the conductor Hermann Scherchen (see Letter 35 n. 7), had an intermittent association with the Winterthur Musikkollegium between 1922 and 1947. According to Britten's engagement diary Britten and Pears visited Winterthur on 2 June, but we do not know if they met Scherchen. Dent, however, gave Britten news of Scherchen in his letter of 27 February:

> Hermann Scherchen is at Zurich, but at the Radio Beromünster, not at the opera. I am sure he will be extremely keen to see *Peter Grimes* and to see you personally; he has a genuine and very sympathetic understanding of English music. He is also a very friendly character, and his present (Chinese) wife is charming.

10 English conductor (1911–1989). He was working (as a conductor) at the British Forces Network in Hamburg, where he was in charge of the Music Department. See Letter 172 n. 2.

525   To Erwin Stein

HOTEL BELLERIVE AU LAC, ZURICH
May 24th 1946

My dear Erwin,[1]

   Peter, Joan, Iris[2] & I have spent an hour of the afternoon on the lake, in a motor boat – I had to return for a lightning rehearsal at the theatre (they all went shopping) & I have now about half an hour to spare before we eat before going to Orpheus[3] in the evening, & an orchestral rehearsal of Illuminations after![4] So you see why I haven't written before. Every day has every moment engaged, & nothing is done save eating & working. Still we are all enjoying ourselves madly, & work is going very well. Everyone

is very nice & interested in us & P. Grimes. We went over to Basel last
evening (hiring a taxi there & back, there being no late train) & it was
very interesting.⁵ Everyone is amazed at what that theatre has achieved.
It seems only a small establishment of no great repute; but their Grimes
is quite something, & it's all due to the terrific efforts & devotion of
Krannhals,⁶ who is really gifted. The Grimes himself is remarkable &
a real personality – but for my taste, far too dotty, & not sympathetic
enough – nor enough singing.⁷ After all the emotions in opera should be
conveyed in singing – but, after seeing one Act of Arabella the other day,
that idea seems a bit forgotten.⁸ The Chorus is good – Ellen, poor⁹ –
Balstrode Excellent¹⁰ – sets ordinary, production – well, as you said before
Eric is a good producer, isn't he?¹¹ Terrific reception – much bigger than the
Wells – after being given laurels(!), & bowing from the box, I was literally
hauled onto the stage (I had refused to do this because of my Zurich
agreement¹²), & carried around in quite an embarrassing manner – but
very touching. It was interesting to see that the opera came off even with
quite another (& wrong) kind of Peter – but mostly because the orchestra
was adequate. Here, on the other hand, the orchestra is magnificent.
Denzler,¹³ after a slow start, is really taking great trouble, & showing considerable understanding. Peter & Joan have a great deal of personal success,
& they all admire their voices, skill & simplicity, more than they can say.
Of course there are the blasé ones – the Swallow¹⁴ who prefers to sing
Boris Godunov – but 99% of the chaps are good (Balstrode, Keene,
Auntie first rate)¹⁵ & immensely keen. Production is not over-imaginative,
but very efficient, & very co-operative.¹⁶ But I wish you could hear it if
only for the Interludes, & the hut-scene which with Peter is most moving.
The little boy is very pathetic, & a good actor, but not quite the figure that
Leonard was. He screams himself, & very effectively.¹⁷

We had a good time with recitals. Everyone marvels at Peter. He is
obviously a continental rather than an English singer, judging by the
terrific notices & receptions. We heard an appalling John Passion in
Schaffhausen.¹⁸ Arabella is a nightmare, but Strauss is extremely popular
still here, & so is still that appalling method of barking & yelling instead
of singing, of no vocal line, & of a perpetual lush elaboration in the
orchestral pit. I'd forgotten all about that kind of thing & am horrified
at its continued existence. The singers, most of whom have good voices,
have no legato & no technique at all (that is why the Hut scene &
Embroidery aria at Basel were so awful). But it is interesting to learn from
a young Swiss composer Sutermeister,¹⁹ that I am considered shocking
(because of the emphasis on the voice, & prosody & 'lack' of orchestral
support) by Honegger & the older generation, & considered the leader as
I thought. He made one interesting remark: "So Ansermet is conducting

Lucretia? He'll find it very difficult, because he's only used to Stravinsky & Hindemith!"[20]

My dear Erwin, I must stop this ramble. It'll be lovely to see you & to chat about it all. A pity you're not coming out. Thank Marion[21] for her nice long letter. I'm glad Schnabel[22] can still play Schubert – it used to be wonderful. Have you met Clifford[23] around at all? I've recommended that he should come out here & play for the British Council[24] (as long as he plays the right notes, & interesting programmes!).

Peter's enclosing a note about the house. Sorry to leave you with all that bother.[25] We adored Sophie's letter. Our German fliesst, but I found rehearsing the orchestra in German quite a teaser!

Much love to you,
See you soon,
BEN

1   Stein was the dedicatee of *Lucretia*. Eric Crozier wrote to Stein on 17 April 1946, from Stratford-on-Avon:

> I heard this morning that Ben will dedicate *Lucretia* to you, and I couldn't feel better about anything. It is so right that he should do so – but Ben has an uncanny habit of being right.
> I hope you won't mind my sending you warmest congratulations, but I feel very happy at the news – and I think anyone who has a love for Ben's music, and who also knows you, will feel exactly the same pleasure as I do about this.

2   Iris Holland Rogers (d. 1982), a friend of Pears and a talented linguist; see also Letter 169 n. 6, CHPP, pp. 70–71, and CHPP, plate 4 (which is incorrectly captioned: for Harley Place read Charlotte Street).

3   Gluck's *Orfeo ed Euridice*, with Elsa Cavelti (Orfeo), Monika Huber (Euridice) and Lisa Della Casa (Amor), conducted by Robert F. Denzler and produced by Hans Zimmermann. In a radio broadcast given by Lionel Billows from Basel, 5 August 1947, about the work of the English Opera Group, Billows mentions that 'Since seeing Gluck's *Orpheus* in Zurich last year, Britten is determined to include that in the repertory [of the EOG] as soon as possible.'

4   No details of the performance of *Les Illuminations* have come to light, except that Pears was the soloist (see Letter 527 n. 10). Britten probably conducted.

5   The German language premiere of *Peter Grimes* had been given in Basel on 6 May 1946 (Montagu Slater's libretto was translated by Herberth E. Herlitschka). A notice in the *National-Zeitung (Basel)*, 205 (7 May 1946), described the scene in the theatre on the first night:

> The auditorium was decked with lights, flowers and flags and the audience, just as festively turned out, followed the performance with intense concentration and

empathy, despite its challenging nature, its extremes of emotion and the austerity of the score. The applause seemed to go on for ever and a mountain of flowers built up on the stage. It was particularly gratifying to see members of the chorus being presented with bouquets as well as the principals. The entire government were guests of honour and the composer's native country was also officially represented [...] Herr Milville, a member of the cantonal authority, in a brief statement in the programme, pointed to the special significance of the performance within the context of this first international arts festival and announced the theatre administration's intended policy of international artistic exchange, leading to the growth of understanding between nationalities.

The London *Times* (7 May 1946) reported that the performance, 'a gala one in connection with the Basel Trade Fair', had taken place, and that it 'began with the playing of the British National Anthem and was broadcast by the Swiss Radio'.

6　Alexander Krannhals (1908–1961), German conductor, who held appointments in Lucerne, Ghent, Strasbourg, Mulhouse and at the Théâtre des Champs-Elysées in Paris. From 1949 Krannhals was the Director of the St Gallen Concert Society and from 1955 until his death was the General Music Director of the Staatstheater at Karlsruhe. He also taught conducting at the Basel Conservatory and was vice-president of the Swiss conductors' society.

　　The reviewer of the *National-Zeitung (Basel)* thought that in *Grimes* 'Krannhals proved himself as an orchestral conductor with well above average qualities. He had obviously worked in untiring and resolute dedication with the orchestra which excelled itself; he was able to raise it to its highest achievement.'

7　Grimes was sung by Bislaw Wosniak.

8　Richard Strauss's three-act comedy, conducted by Victor Reinshagen and directed by Karl Schmid-Bloss, with Maria Cebotari (Arabella), Lisa Della Casa (Zdenka) and Paul Schoeffler (Mandryka), had been given at the Stadttheater, Zurich, on 22 May.

9　Sung by Annie Weber.

10　Sung by Marko Rothmüller (1908–1993), Croatian baritone and composer who had studied in Zagreb and in Vienna with Berg. He made his debut in 1932 and soon established himself as one of the most promising baritones of his generation. He was a member of the Zurich Opera (1935–47) where he took part in the premiere of Hindemith's *Mathis der Maler*. Post-war he joined the Covent Garden Company (1948–52), where he sang the title role in the first staged performance of Berg's *Wozzeck* in England (1952), and sang at Glyndebourne. At the 1954 Aldeburgh Festival, Rothmüller sang the role of Tarquinius in Basil Coleman's production of *The Rape of Lucretia*, conducted by Norman Del Mar. Subsequently he sang with the Metropolitan Opera, New York.

11 The production was directed by the German actor and director Egon
    Neudegg (1891–1957), who was Director of the Stadttheater, Basel, 1932–49,
    and designed by Ludwig Kainer (1885–1967), the German painter, illustrator
    and set designer, who had worked for the Ballets Russes and the Berlin Opera.
        E. J. Dent had already warned Britten of what might be in store for him
    in Switzerland in his letter of 27 February:

    > I fear too that you may have trouble with German producers, unless you are taking
    > Eric with you everywhere! The first idea of a German producer is to upset the
    > entire scheme of production and do something entirely different. Things may have
    > changed in the last ten years, but I doubt it, and you will probably find Zurich and
    > Basel obsessed by the German styles of ten or fifteen years ago.

    On musical matters, Dent added:

    > Zurich ought to give you a really good performance; they have a large modern
    > stage, and are accustomed to all the most modern things and modern technical
    > methods. Basel will probably have a fair orchestra and clever producers and designers,
    > but indifferent singers. [. . .] I hope you have got good translations, for I should
    > imagine that the libretto will be very difficult to translate and that much alteration
    > of rhythms (especially in German) will be necessary. I fear that with the best will in
    > the world foreign singers will find your music exceedingly difficult, even if they
    > have tackled *Wozzeck* and *Lulu*; it is a matter of rhythms rather than of notes. [. . .]
    > And I don't think you will find any chorus as intelligent as Sadler's Wells.

12 See Letter 521 n. 2.

13 Robert F. Denzler (1892–1972), Zurich-born Swiss conductor and composer.
    After studying at the Zurich Conservatory and working as a répétiteur at
    Cologne and Bayreuth, Denzler became Director of Music at Lucerne in
    1912 and two years later Director of the Zurich Opera. In the 1920s he was
    Guest Conductor of the Orchestre de la Suisse Romande, and between 1927
    and 1932 was Chief Conductor at the Berlin Städtische Oper. Denzler
    returned to the Zurich Opera in 1934; in 1937 he conducted the premiere of
    Berg's *Lulu* (two-act version) and in the following year the first perform-
    ance of Hindemith's *Mathis der Maler*. After 1947 he gave up the opera
    house in favour of conducting concerts only. He was renowned as an inter-
    preter of classical opera, contemporary music and Wagner.

14 Sung by Lubomir Vischegonov.

15 Sung by Andreas Boehm, Heinz Rehfuss and Magrit von Syben respectively.

16 *Grimes* was directed by Hans Zimmermann, with decor by Max Röthlis-
    berger.

17 Grimes's apprentice was played by Freddy Stubenrauch. Leonard =
    Leonard Thompson who played the role in the first production at Sadler's
    Wells (see Letter 497 n. 3) and who evidently did not himself vocalize the
    Apprentice's offstage scream in Act II scene 2.

18 Britten's diary for 19 May contains the entry: 'Bachfest Schaffhausen'.

19 Heinrich Sutermeister (1910–1995). After studies in philology in Basel and
    Paris he became a pupil of Carl Orff at the Munich Hochschule für Musik
    (1932–34). Orff and the Italian repertory (in particular Verdi's *Otello* and
    Falstaff) provided the models for Sutermeister's work and he achieved an
    international reputation as an opera composer during the 1940s with, for
    example, *Romeo und Julia* (Dresden, 1940).

20 Ernest Ansermet (1883–1969), Swiss conductor, who was to become an out-
    standing Britten interpreter; see Diary for 27 January 1932, n. 2, and Claude
    Tappolet (ed.), *Ernest Ansermet: Correspondances avec des compositeurs
    Européens (1916–1966)*, vol. 1, pp. 45–77. Ansermet had close friendships
    with several composers, most notably Debussy, Ravel and Stravinsky. It was
    on Stravinsky's recommendation that he became principal conductor for
    Diagilev's Ballets Russes, and he conducted the premieres of *L'histoire du
    Soldat*, *Pulcinella* and *Renard*.
        Britten presented Ansermet with the composition draft of *The Rape of
    Lucretia* on the occasion of the opera's premiere. The manuscript is
    inscribed:

    To <u>Ernest Ansermet</u>. / Please accept this souvenir of Lucretia at Glyndebourne,
    with / my most sincere thanks for your wonderful collaboration, / and your unfailing
    patience & sympathy / Benjamin Britten / July 12th 1946

    The dedication and first page of music from the draft are reproduced in
    Tappolet, pp. 46–7.

21 Marion Stein (b. 1926), Stein's daughter, an intimate friend of both Britten
    and Pears from 1944. She gave up her career as a concert pianist on her
    marriage to the Earl of Harewood in 1949 (marriage dissolved 1967). In 1973
    she married the Rt Hon. Jeremy Thorpe (b. 1929), Leader of the Liberal
    Party from 1967 to 1976. She was appointed a Trustee of the Britten–Pears
    Foundation in 1985, in which year she compiled and edited PPT, and
    became a Trustee Emeritus in 2002. See also Letter 418 n. 7.

22 Artur Schnabel (1882–1951), Austrian pianist and composer who became an
    American citizen. He was married to the contralto Therese Behr who
    taught Pears in the United States during 1940 (see CHPP, pp. 98, 312–13).
    Schnabel was a renowned interpreter of the classical repertory, in parti-
    cular Beethoven and Schubert. William Glock – at one time a pupil of
    Schnabel's – wrote of his teacher: 'In Schubert he managed to combine
    lyrical expression with a rhythmic élan and discipline that gave everything
    a new intensity [*Notes in Advance*, p. 23].'
        As a young man Britten heard Schnabel on two occasions, recording the
    events in his diary:

    8 MAY 1933
    Listen to Schnabel playing Brahms B♭ [Concerto], in London Musical festival, after

dinner. Wireless bad – unable to judge much. Technique seemed excellent & the idea of the work as a whole. But many details annoyed & irritated me.

14 FEBRUARY 1934
[. . .] Schnabel is rather disappointing in Brahms D min concerto – tho' the slow mov. was mostly beautiful.

23   Clifford Curzon (1907–1982), English pianist, who had studied with Artur Schnabel and Nadia Boulanger. He had a long and important musical friendship with Britten, though there were occasional differences, especially when, in Curzon's view, a matter of professional principle was involved (see, for example, Letter 518 n. 3). He performed and recorded a number of Britten works and in later years was known particularly for his distinguished interpretations of Mozart and Schubert. See also Letter 388 n. 2.

Curzon presented to BPL in 1979 the autograph manuscripts of the *Impromptu* from the Piano Concerto (see p. 159) and *Holiday Diary* (both gifts from the composer). In addition, Britten's autograph manuscript of his unpublished cadenzas for Haydn's Harpsichord Concerto in D major (H. XVIII:11), composed for Curzon's wife, the harpsichordist Lucille Wallace, and non-autograph copies of the *Introduction and Rondo alla Burlesca*, for two pianos, and *Lachrymae*, for viola and piano, formed part of the gift.

The British Library holds a major collection of Curzon's annotated scores, student compositions and papers (BL Add. MSS 64966–65087), which includes several important items reflecting his long association with Britten. Among the composer's works are copies of the published scores of *Holiday Tales* (subsequently renamed *Holiday Diary*), with a programme note for the piece in Britten's hand (see Letter 56 n. 2); the *Introduction and Rondo alla Burlesca*, with a dedication from Britten on the title page ('For Clifford, / who has made it his (or at least ½ of it), / with affection (& deepest admiration too) / Ben / March 1945') and the *Mazurka Elegiaca*; and a photocopy of the composer's autograph manuscript of the two solo parts and piano reduction of the orchestral parts of *Scottish Ballad*, with corrections and annotations in Britten's hand. (Curzon and Britten had given the first broadcast of *Scottish Ballad* on 16 February 1943, with the BBC Orchestra (Section B) conducted by Clarence Raybould, and the first UK performance on 10 July 1943 at the Royal Albert Hall, with the London Philharmonic Orchestra conducted by Basil Cameron.) Also among the British Library's Curzon Collection is the published two-piano score of the original version of the Piano Concerto, together with an autograph manuscript of eleven bars of the solo part, from fig. 18 in the first movement, as they appear in the revised version of 1945, with a list of queries in Curzon's hand concerning the printed score.

Among the scores, other than those by Britten, is a copy of Debussy's *Six épigraphes antiques* for piano duet, with annotations by Curzon, Britten and Nadia Boulanger (Curzon and Britten gave a performance of this work at the 1962 Aldeburgh Festival), and Fauré's A minor Barcarolle, Op. 26, with a dedication from Britten: 'Clifford / – a present from Paris / March 1945 / with love / Benjie'.

A performance of Mozart's Sonata in D (K. 448) for two pianos, given at the 1960 Aldeburgh Festival by Curzon and Britten, was released on CD by BBC Legends (BBCL 4037–2) in 2000. For an assessment of Curzon's artistry, see Max Loppert's note to *Clifford Curzon: Decca Recordings 1949–64*, vol. 1 (Decca Original Masters, 2003).

24 The government-funded organization, founded in 1935 'to promote abroad a wider appreciation of British culture and civilization'. From 1946 onwards Britten and Pears were to undertake many foreign tours under the auspices of the British Council. See also Seymour Whinyates, 'Music and the British Council', *Tempo*, 44 (summer 1957), pp. 7–10.

25 In March 1946 Pears had begun to negotiate through Isador Caplan, his and Britten's solicitor, the purchase of the leasehold of 3 Oxford Square, London, w2. The transaction of what was in effect Pears's first home of his own was completed on 12 June. In his absence abroad Pears had evidently been forced to ask Stein for assistance with the arrangements about the new home. Christopher Headington describes the accommodation in CHPP (p. 138):

The house was spacious, with a basement kitchen and a large first-floor living room, and he shared it with Britten and no less than six other people including his [Pears's] parents, whom he invited to occupy a small flat behind the dining room on the ground floor. There were also his and Britten's friends Erwin and Sophie Stein and their pianist daughter Marion (who had already shared their flat and were 'almost second Mayers', as Britten put it); they had two bedrooms on the second floor. The two men had another on the same floor, and Eric Crozier lived in a third floor 'attic' (as he called it), another bedroom on this upper floor being occupied by the living-in housekeeper, Mrs Hurley; it seems to have been a fairly happy household.

In a private communication to Philip Reed (1990), Marion Thorpe comments:

The mixed household of Britten, Pears, the Steins and the old Pearses was not always easy and Mrs Pears was I think jealous of my mother, who ran the house, and to whom Pears perhaps sometimes paid more attention than to his mother. When in London, Pears and Britten usually had meals with the Steins.

Eric Crozier described the house and its occupants in his and Nancy Evans's autobiography, 'After Long Pursuit' (quoted in HCBB, p. 260):

It was in a district of huge early-Victorian houses [. . .] In theory, the plan was a good one. Peter had two elderly parents who needed somewhere to live: so what could be better than for them to make their home with him and Ben, plus, of course, the Erwin Stein family, and for Sophie to manage the housekeeping? [. . .] But Sophie, a courageous and cheerful woman, was run off her feet trying to manage the house and to conjure up three meals a day from the antediluvian kitchen in the basement [. . .] Mr and Mrs Pears, a stiff-necked and rather arrogant couple, did not like the Steins. They objected to the food, they criticized Sophie, and they went out of their way in general to make mischief. They strongly objected, too, to Marion's piano playing. She was now eighteen or nineteen, a pretty girl who had recently begun studying the piano in earnest, and she had a basement room where she used sometimes to practise four or five hours a day. The elderly Pears hated it [. . .] so did the old man who lived in the enormous house next door [. . .] He used to hammer violently on the party-wall [. . .]

526 To Barbara Britten[1]

c/o Stadttheater, Zurich

May 25th 1946

My darling Barbara,

I ought to have written ages ago to thank you for your sweet letter. But it arrived just as we were leaving Sigriswil and since then every moment of every day has been full, & this is only a scribble before dinner & going to the opera to see 'Entführung',[2] & then supping with a member of the cast after!

I was very happy that Bethley liked Grimes. Actually since then Peter & I have met her & Hansi & talked a bit.[3] She was looking very lovely, & was sweet to us. We haven't yet had time to see little Barbara,[4] but we hope to go back & spend some time there with them at the beginning of June. I have got them tickets for the first performance here.

I seem to be inundated with friends of my early childhood. In Bern I met some one who taught me French at Miss Astles![5] And opposite the Theater here is a tea-shop called Carmen owned by one Pauli Dietwieler who stayed with the Evans at the same time as when Bethley & Lisel were in Lowestoft.[6] She seems awfully nice (taking us for a long drive tomorrow) & has an amusing book of photos of all of us & the Hardies & Mrs Black![7]

This is a lovely town, & we are having a terrific time. The opera rehearsals are going well – good singers & a wonderful orchestra – & if the success is anything like Basel it will be O.K. There I was literally carried on to the stage, & had laurels presented to me – all very romantic! The people are very pleasant – seem to admire Joan very much, & have taken to Grimes all right. The conductor is excellent – Denzler; but we work very hard – every morning, starting at 9.30 & most afternoons & some evenings. They certainly know how to work here.

It is a lovely country – beautifully organised. The perfect place for a holiday. I am awfully glad you're coming out here for your holiday. You'll adore it – & it'll be lovely seeing Bethley again. She really is a sweet person & so is Flansi. She hasn't changed a scrap – looks just like she did in Lowestoft.

Well, my dear – I must go now. We're back on June 9th – but I don't think I'll be able to come to Snape – I must be in Glyndebourne on 10th.[8] But we'll meet somehow & tell you all the gossip.

Please give Helen[9] my love – & say how sorry I am about Mrs Heinson.[10] I hope she & you are both well – lots of love from both of us. Peter's well – but Zurich is bad for his hay fever.[11]

BEN

1 The elder Britten's two sisters (1902–1982): see IC1/2.

2 A performance of Mozart's singspiel, *Die Entführung aus dem Serail*, given at the Stadttheater, Zurich, conducted by Eduard Hartogs and directed by Karl Schmid-Bloss.

3 Bethley Kauffman-Meyer and her husband, Hansi. Bethley was a friend of Barbara who had visited Lowestoft in Britten's childhood. In EWB (p. 77) Beth Welford writes: 'Two Swiss girls who had stayed with us in the summer of 1920, Lisel and Bethley, both lived [in Basel] and through them I had had an exchange with a young friend of theirs, Yvonne Clar.' (See PFL, plate 43, where Yvonne Clar is erroneously described as the 'Swiss au pair'.) Barbara visited Bethley in Basel in August 1933, and the following year, in September, Bethley was once again in England; Britten's Diary for 3 September 1934 reads: 'I see Bethley Kauffman-Meyer (Swiss, who stayed with the Hardies & us, over 13 years ago) husband, & niece at Royal Court – Sloane Square, where they've been staying near Barbara.' Later in 1934, Britten and his mother were to stay with Bethley and her family in Basel (see Letter 57). According to Britten's Diary for 28 October 1934, Hansi was nicknamed 'Flansi' by Barbara.

4 Presumably the Kauffman-Meyers' daughter, called Barbara after her English namesake Barbara Britten.

5 Britten was in Bern on 14 May. Miss Astles = the pre-preparatory school, 'Southolme', in Lowestoft, run by Ethel Astle (1876–1952), Britten's first piano teacher, and her sister; see also Letter 4 n. 1.

6 Evans = Dr Harold Evans, the Britten family doctor, and his family; see also Letter 14 n. 1. Lisel = Lisel Suter-Schlotterbeck, mentioned by Beth Welford (see n. 3 above). When visiting Basel in 1934, Britten and his mother dined with Lisel on 18 October.

7 Hardies = Revd Hardie, the Vicar of St John's, Lowestoft, and subsequently Bishop of Jamaica, and his family. Mrs Black was a neighbour of the Britten family from Kirkley Cliff Road; see also Diary for 29 April 1931, n. 2.

8 To commence rehearsals of *The Rape of Lucretia*.

9 Helen Hurst (1887–1981), Barbara's partner. She was a social worker and had first met Barbara when the latter came to work as a health visitor in Peckham, London.

10 Unidentified.

11 A recurrent problem for Pears.

527 To Ronald Duncan[1]

c/o Stadttheater, Zurich
May 31st 1946

My dear Ronnie,

This is only a hasty note written in the middle of rehearsals – I hope you got the St Gallen greetings all right.[2]

I've seen Heinsheimer (of Boosey & Hawkes),[3] who saw the French Author Society chap in Paris, & Roth,[4] who'd had your agent's letter – & thrashed out again this Obey business.[5] He's certainly got us stymied – because of these Droits Morales,[6] & because the work is <u>written</u>. You & I know how little it owes to him, but there <u>are</u> coincidences which to a court of law would seem obvious. Anyhow two things to me seem clear – (i) That we must <u>avoid</u> a court-case; I personally would prefer to give up any little money I might earn over the piece than to waste time, energy & worry in court. (ii) that the performance <u>cannot</u> be postponed. We have got a first-rate company together on goodwill, & if that failed they'd never come again. The experimental character of the work makes the difference – if it were just another opera, or even a new song, we could postpone or substitute another work – which we can't in this case.

So p<u>lease</u>, don't let your agents bully us – I will talk over the financial side of the affair when I come back – but I promise you, you personally won't lose by it – it can be all adjusted. I personally think that Obey is not being exactly helpful over the matter; but he has too many weapons, & after all he can't be expected to like us very much!

<u>Please</u> write to your agents at once & say this. I know it's a bore, but we've made a mistake & we've got to swallow our pride (I'll swallow the financial loss!). After all, for the future, anyone can read Obey & Duncan, & decide for themselves whether 25% is fair – & I haven't much doubt what the verdict will be.[7]

Much love to you & to Rose Marie.[8] How is she? I shouldn't hesitate to bring her out here – it's a divine country.

See you soon. We saw Huis Clos[9] last night – I thought it stank – & there was quite an anti-demonstration in the theatre.

Grimes goes ahead – it ought to be pretty good.[10] I saw the Basel show which was wild – but very creditable.

Much love,
BEN

1 Rhodesian-born poet, playwright and publisher (1914–1982). His friendship with Britten, partly rooted in their shared pacifist convictions, dated
   from the mid-1930s. The most significant of the Britten–Duncan collaborations were *This Way to the Tomb* (1945) and *The Rape of Lucretia*. See also
   Letter 116 n. 1 and 1C1/2.

2 Britten and Pears were at St Gallen, south of Lake Constance, on 15–16 May.
   Britten sent a postcard of the interior of the cathedral to Duncan on 26 May:

   This is where we were last week – but only, alas, for one night so we didn't see much
   of the place. But the cathedral we did see & it is terrific. Lovely to see some decora-
   tion – the rest of the Calvinistic churches are as dull as ditchwater. The library is
   absolutely amazing. Do you remember anything of it! This is a lovely country & we
   are enjoying every moment – but we're very busy! How's everything with you &
   Rose Marie?

3 Hans W. Heinsheimer (1900–1993), German-born American publisher and
   writer on music, who had been head of the opera department of Universal
   Edition when Britten had visited Vienna with his mother in 1934 and met
   him. He emigrated to New York in 1938 where he worked for Boosey,
   Hawkes, Belwin, Inc., and G. Schirmer, Inc., which again brought him into
   contact with Britten. See also Letter 59 n. 8.

4 Dr Ernst Roth (1896–1971), English music publisher of Czech birth. He
   worked first with Universal Edition in Vienna and, following the *Anschluss*,
   was employed by Boosey & Hawkes in London, becoming Chairman in
   1963. Strauss dedicated his *Vier letzte Lieder* to him. See also Letter 450 n. 1.

5 André Obey (1892–1975), French actor-manager and dramatist. Many of
   Obey's works were produced by the French experimental theatre company
   the Compagnie des Quinze (founded by Michel Saint-Denis, c. 1930), including *Le Viol de Lucrèce* (1931) which treats the story of Lucretia's rape in the
   manner of Greek tragedy, with chorus and commentators. It was this play that
   formed the basis for Duncan's libretto for *The Rape of Lucretia*. In a note
   enclosed with a copy of Obey's text now at BPL, Eric Crozier writes:

   I gave my copy of this play to Ben in November or December 1944, as a possible
   subject for his next opera after *Grimes*. I had seen performances by the Compagnie
   des Quinze while I was still at school, and I admired them so much that I ordered
   copies of Obey's texts and translated two of them – *Lucrèce*, and *Loire* – into
   English.

   (In his article 'Benjamin Britten's Second Opera: *The Rape of Lucretia*',
   Tempo, 1/14 (March 1946), pp. 11–12, Crozier makes no acknowledgement of
   Obey as a source for Britten's *Lucretia*.)
       Obey was clearly protesting about Duncan's and Britten's use of his work
   for their new opera. In RDBB (p. 81), Duncan writes:

   Out of the blue came a letter from André Obey's agents claiming that we had
   infringed the copyright on his play and demanding a part of our royalties. I pointed
   out that the theme was hardly anybody's invention. The French agents replied that

our use of a male and female chorus contradicted this. Again, I indicated that the use of a chorus framing the work as commentators had been a well-used convention since Euripides and Sophocles. To this his solicitors threatened to apply for an injunction to prevent *The Rape of Lucretia*'s opening performance.

Duncan responded to Britten on 3 June in a letter which sets out further details of this difficult situation:

Erwin has just read your letter out to me over the phone. I cabled you immediately. For, as you must know, I am in entire agreement with everything you say. From the outset I instructed my agent that he must, as far as I was concerned, accept Obey's claims rather than risk injunctions, etc. But he said that since Obey's claim was made against us both he was not authorized to accept for you and that the matter must be referred back to Switzerland. He also took me to some solicitor who is an expert in copyright and who'd read the libretto and Obey. This chap had come to the conclusion that Obey had no claim. But he pointed out that that might not prevent an injunction being brought. And so I left instructing everybody that as far as I was concerned they could have my pants as well as my coat rather than risk the production being cancelled. The next thing I heard was a phone call from [Moran] Caplat who, in a panic, said that Roth had told him that I was refusing to negotiate with Obey! I told Caplat to cable you to clarify this.

This morning I have again phoned my wretched agent and told him that he must accept whatever you decide – or whoever it is who is actually in touch with Obey's minions. I suppose it is Hertseimer [i.e. Heinsheimer] or whatever.

A pity this business has come up but it really cannot spoil *Lucretia* or in anyway take away from the *fun* of writing it with you. What we have written we have written. Now let the Obeys do their worst or whatever they like. All those are secondary and trivial considerations. And ten years from now will count as less than nothing. I hope you've not been too worried about the whole business, it's a pity if you have. I must admit it's been a pest. However, all that is part of doing anything.

Duncan continued:

Henry [Boys] came here last week and played over the 1st act to Rose Marie's delight. By the way, one error in the score is amusing . . . I wrote Virgil Book II – *two* – and you've set that as *eleven*. I don't know whether Virgil wrote eleven books. Anyhow, let's leave it for the musicologists and literologists to find. It will give them pleasure to prove us illiterate. [. . .]

Have you made up your mind re Epilogue? [. . .]

Tell Eric I've done the essay for his book though it was hard going. I've cribbed from your introduction – which, incidentally Eliot has corrected here and there for you! He is a pedantic but lovable aunt. He's now in US and gone to see Ezra [Pound].

(Duncan's contribution to the symposium on *The Rape of Lucretia* was entitled 'The Libretto: the Method of Work' (pp. 61–6); Britten contributed a characteristically brief 'Foreword' (pp. 7–8), which Duncan's friend and publisher, the poet T. S. Eliot, had evidently seen and modified.)

Duncan added an amusing postscript to his letter of 3 June:

By the way, I dreamt last night that Obey challenged me to a duel. You were my second and we rode to the meeting place like Don Quixote and Sancho. But when we arrived there was M. Obey dressed in full armour – the cad! You handed me a very frail-looking sword which immediately bust on his armour plating. Whereupon you went to a violin case and took out a huge tin opener and attacked him with that.

See also Christopher Smith, 'André Obey and Benjamin Britten', in Christopher Smith (ed.), *Aldeburgh and Around*, pp. 69–78.

6 Duncan's letter of 3 June (see n. 5) to Britten clearly reflects an issue that would have been raised quite properly with Boosey & Hawkes by those representing the copyright interests of the playwright André Obey. This would undoubtedly have involved the Société des Auteurs Compositeurs et Editeurs de Musique (SACEM), founded in 1851, which in ensuing decades was to lead Europe in establishing 'moral rights' ('droits morales') in copyright law.

   In the case of *Lucretia* the issue was settled by Britten in effect conceding Obey's case. The composition of the work had already reached a creative stage when he would have found it impossible to run the risk of a conflict. Most of the succeeding operas were either out of copyright (e.g. *Noye's Fludde* and *A Midsummer Night's Dream*) or their librettos were the work of his chosen collaborators. On occasion, however, certain categories of independent rights (e.g. film or theatre) had been acquired even in the absence of copyright in the original work (e.g. *Billy Budd*) and these involved renegotiation. There was too the rare instance when his expression of interest in an already published work, e.g. *The Tale of Mr Tod* (Beatrix Potter) was abandoned when he was confronted with the excessive demands made by the copyright owners. An exception was his last opera, *Death in Venice* (1973), which raised all manner of unforeseen copyright problems. A fascinating tale in its own right, which must await its telling in a later volume.

7 Britten's suggestion prevailed: the publishing assignment for *Lucretia* was signed on 19 October 1946 in which it stipulated that Obey was to receive 25 per cent of all the royalties and fees payable to Britten and Duncan. An agreement between Obey and Boosey & Hawkes had been signed on 6 September.

8 Duncan's wife, who was recovering from tuberculosis.

9 *Huis clos* (variously translated as *In Camera*, *No Exit* and *Vicious Circle*), a one-act play by Jean-Paul Sartre (1905–1980), French Existentialist philosopher, novelist and dramatist, about 'three characters in a stuffy second-empire room which represents for them hell, since within it they are destined to torture each other endlessly without issue' (John Russell Taylor, *The Penguin Dictionary of the Theatre*, p. 239). 'Hell in this play', according to E. Martin Browne (Introduction to *Three European Plays*), is 'the negation of individual human freedom by means of the permanent incursion of other human beings [. . .] "Hell is other people."'

10 The first night of *Grimes* in Zurich was the following day, 1 June, when it was given as part of the Zurich Festival of Theatre. The anonymous critic of the morning edition of the *Neue Zürcher Zeitung und Schweizerisches*

Handelsblatt (3 June 1946) wrote a lengthy appraisal of Britten's opera and a detailed critique of this performance, concluding:

The performance was an event in itself, as befits the famously high standards of the Zurich Opera Festival. The audience was indeed international with many – often distinguished – British and American visitors and might truly bear comparison with first-night audiences from the days of *Lulu* and *Mathis der Maler*.

Earlier, he wrote:

Denzler's light, sure hand, his exquisite tone and his insistence on accurate intonation and rhythmic precision ensured a performance it was difficult to imagine bettered in terms of dramatic tension and exactitude. [...] He created the brief intense moments that are so vital to this work as powerfully as he constructed the architecture of entire scenes and interludes. The chorus was more than adequate and if, on occasion, the thrilling chorus scenes did not quite achieve the desired impact, they still made a significant contribution to the overall effect. Max Röthlisberger's design created a subtle and sombre atmosphere, and a vivid evocation of the sea.

Producer Hans Zimmermann brought the crowd scenes alive and structured them effectively while maintaining a powerful stillness around the principals with eerie and tightly focused lighting.

As for the principals, the two British guest artists [Cross and Pears] deservedly attracted most attention [. . .] The tenor, whose interpretation of Britten's *Les Illuminations* was recently admired here, has a particularly close association with the opera. This Peter Grimes will be long remembered, even though the singer was somewhat inhibited by the unfamiliar language (the British had no qualms about singing in German in front of a German audience!) and the brisk articulation in the animated recitatives defeated him.

528 To Ralph Hawkes

45A St Johns Wood High St, N.W.8

June 30th 1946

My dear Ralph,

There are two matters which we never seem able to discuss fully – either because there are more pressing matters which crowd them out, or there are other persons present who cramp our style somewhat! So I take the opportunity to write about them. The first is this vexed question of our Glyndebourne company's visit to Switzerland.[1] I say "our" deliberately because it was Eric's, & my (& Joan's & Peter's) scheme originally, & although Christie put the money up and Bing manages it, it remains "our" company & its policy is directed by us. As you know I am passionately interested in it – I am keen to develop a new art form (the chamber-opera, or what you will) which will stand beside the grand opera as the quartet stands beside the orchestra. I hope to write many works for it, & to be interested in this company for many years. I am proud that we have got off to such a good start (whatever the critics or public will say), & I

1 Benjamin Britten in 1947

2 Peter Pears and Benjamin Britten in 1948

3 *The Rape of Lucretia*, Glyndebourne, 1946: Lucia
(Margaret Ritchie), Lucretia (Kathleen Ferrier)
and Bianca (Anna Pollak) in the spinning scene
(Act I scene 2)

4 Conductor Ernest Ansermet and Benjamin Britten work on *Lucretia* in the Organ Room at
Glyndebourne
5 Librettist Ronald Duncan and Britten in discussion in the gardens at Glyndebourne

6 *Lucretia*, Act II scene 2: Bianca (Catherine Lawson), Lucia (Lesley Duff), Lucretia (Nancy Evans) and Collatinus (Owen Brannigan)
7 Peter Pears and Joan Cross as the Male and Female Choruses

8 Members of the creative team for *Lucretia*: *back row* Otakar Kraus (Tarquinius), Kathleen Ferrier (Lucretia), Peter Pears (Male Chorus) and Nancy Evans (Lucretia); *front row* Britten (composer), Eric Crozier (director) and Ernest Ansermet (conductor)

9 Switzerland, January 1947: Lionel Billows, the British Council representative who lent his surname to the grande dame of Loxford in *Albert Herring*, with Peter Pears

10 *Albert Herring*, Glyndebourne, 1947: Act II scene 1, Albert (Peter Pears) addresses the dignitaries of Loxford, including Lady Billows (Joan Cross), Mr Gedge, the Vicar (William Parsons), Miss Wordsworth (Margaret Ritchie) and Mr Upfold, the Mayor (Roy Ashton), with Harry (David Spenser)

11 Librettist Eric Crozier, composer Benjamin Britten and director Frederick Ashton in the Walled Garden at Glyndebourne

12 John Piper, designer for *Albert Herring* and an Artistic Director of the English Opera Group. Piper also designed the premiere productions of *The Rape of Lucretia* and *Billy Budd*

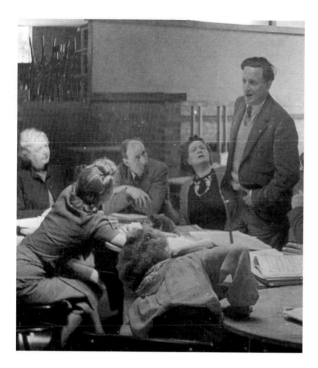

13 The Marquee scene (see opposite) in rehearsal: Gladys Parr (Florence, Lady Billows's house-keeper), Norman Lumsden (Superintendent Budd), Betsy de la Porte (Mrs Herring) and Peter Pears (Albert), with Anne Sharp and Lesley Duff (Cis and Emmie)

14 Switzerland, January 1947: Britten at work on *Albert Herring*

15 Act II scene 2: Albert (Peter Pears), inside the shop, overhears Sid (Frederick Sharp) and Nancy (Nancy Evans), outside the window

16 *The Beggar's Opera*, Arts Theatre,
Cambridge, 1948: director Tyrone Guthrie
with Benjamin Britten
17 Designer Tanya Moiseiwitsch
demonstrates the set model to Britten

18 Orchestral rehearsal for *The Beggar's Opera*: Britten with Ivan Clayton. Eric Crozier sits
behind them on the left and Hans Oppenheim, a member of the EOG music staff, on the far right.

19 Britten and Guthrie in rehearsal for
The Beggar's Opera
20 The Newgate scene, Act III: Polly Peachum
(Nancy Evans), Macheath (Peter Pears) and
Lucy Lockit (Rose Hill). Polly: 'But hark! I
hear the sound of the bell!'

21 *The Beggar's Opera*

22 Erwin Stein, Britten's publisher and editor at Boosey & Hawkes, London
23 Humphrey Maud, a dedicatee of *The Young Person's Guide to the Orchestra*, in his Eton uniform, *c.* 1947/48

24 William Primrose rehearsing at Crag House for the first performance of *Lachrymae* at the 1950 Aldeburgh Festival
25 Edward Sackville-West, writer and music critic, the dedicatee of Britten's *Serenade*

am passionately keen that the continent will see what we in England can do (with four exceptions the company of thirty is entirely British), & also to see what this new kind of opera can accomplish. (It is ideal for towns with only small opera houses.) That is why I asked you months ago (& you granted) for European rights for a year. I want this thing to get going in the right manner. Also in Roth's own words, he didn't want another opera to fight P. Grimes yet, & also he saw no future for the large opera houses for an opera without chorus & with an orchestra of twelve players. So I got a shock when I learned your attitude to our visit to Switzerland.[2] What I wanted, & still want, is for our company to go to Zurich and Geneva for three performances. I don't see how this can affect (except for good) the future of the work there. It is after all a special performance in English. I am willing to waive the exclusivity for Switzerland, so as not to stand in Krannhals's way in Basel[3] – but I do want you not to word your letters to Schmid-Bloss[4] & Billows[5] in such a way as to discourage them from having us (if they want to – which of course isn't yet known).

The other matter is Covent Garden. As you know I am keen to write an opera for it. But when we will discuss agreements and terms (will we?), it must be clear that I have the veto on performers & producer & conductor. I have no faith in an organisation which has Lambert[6] as assistant conductor, & on the Committee behind it – Walton[7] & Dent. After all remember what happened about the Fairy Queen, which after all I was invited to be concerned in just as clearly as I am now invited to write an opera.[8] If you want to tell the Committee this, do – I am not frightened of them; I have now other stages to take my works if they don't like my conditions! Please don't take this wrong, Ralph – you know I trust you – but there are others not so reliable.

The orchestral rehearsal yesterday of Lucretia was most exciting. Ansermet was excellent, & I was pleased with the resultant noises![9]

Love to you & Clare,

Yours ever,

BEN

1　A scheme originally suggested by Ansermet, and no doubt encouraged by the extraordinary success of not only the two recent Swiss productions of *Peter Grimes* but also Pears's and Britten's recital tour.

2　Lionel Billows (see n. 5 below) had written to Britten from Bellerivestrasse 38, Zurich, on 22 June:

> I have just had a letter from Ralph Hawkes headed '*The Rape of Lucretia*' saying: 'It does not now appear that the Glyndebourne Company will be coming to Switzerland and in these circumstances, therefore, we shall proceed to make arrangements with Basel, Bern or Zurich for presentation there in German during this coming

winter. I shall be grateful, therefore, if you will not go ahead with any arrangements regarding touring, which you may have contemplated and I will keep you advised of any developments.

'You will appreciate the difficulty in which we find ourselves here regarding the first performance of this new work, in view of the position Britten has in Switzerland, for all three of these houses want the premiere. Any premature discussions or promises would aggravate this situation considerably as far as we are concerned.'

If this conflicts at all with the facts and you feel obliged to take it up with Ralph Hawkes, please tell him simply that I have informed you that in view of a letter from him, I am taking no further action with regard to the question of a tour of the Glyndebourne Company. I have written confidentially to Miss Whinyates [Seymour Whinyates, Director of the Music Department at the British Council, 1943–59] asking if she thinks the Council can sponsor a tour by the company and telling her of Willie's [William Walton's] wiles [. . .].

3   *The Rape of Lucretia* was given in Basel for the first time on 5 June 1947, when it was sung in Elizabeth Mayer's German translation.

4   Karl Schmid-Bloss (1883–1956), German bass-baritone and Director of the Stadttheater, Zurich (1932–47), whose productions of *Arabella* and *Die Entführung aus dem Serail* Britten had seen while in Zurich. See also Marianne Zelger-Vogt and Andreas Honegger (eds.), *Stadttheater Opernhaus: Hundert Jahre Musiktheater in Zürich*, pp. 25–6 and 32–9.

5   Lionel Billows (b. 1909), at this time the British Council's Assistant Representative in Switzerland. He remained a friend of the composer, writing to him infrequently but regularly until 1974. He later held similar British Council posts in Ankara (1948–51), Madras (1952–60) and Cologne (1961), following which he joined the Faculty of Education at Makerere University College, Kampala (1962–70). For ten years from 1970 Billows held a variety of academic positions in West Germany. A gifted linguist, Billows was a pioneer in the teaching of English as a foreign language. As an amateur singer, he sang the solo tenor role in Britten's *Saint Nicolas*.

The surname of Lady Billows in *Albert Herring* was taken from Lionel Billows, as he recalled in a British Council report for August 1947:

One of the numerous private jokes in *Albert Herring* intended for his [Britten's] friends to enjoy quietly among the general laughter was his taking from me, his host in Switzerland, my good name and giving it to the central female character, an elderly, benevolent local tyrant who gives a large cash prize for virtue. I haven't seen the opera yet, but the first act was played through for the first time on my piano, with the unexpected result that my neighbours who live in the flat underneath gave notice to the landlord the next day; I was able to enjoy many of the other jokes more spontaneously while Britten was writing the music and talking over the libretto with Eric Crozier [. . .]

In a private communication to Philip Reed (26 August 1993), Billows commented:

The use of the name Billows for the character Lady Billows [. . .] came to my notice towards the end of the summer of 1946, I believe. We could never get Ben to say what he had in mind in choosing the name, whether he saw June [Billows's first wife] as a masterful harridan, or whether I was somehow seen in some sort of aspect of the character; we speculated, [but] found no answer. Probably he wanted some other name than Jones or Smith, and my rather unusual name came to his notice.

6 Constant Lambert (1905–1951), English composer, conductor and writer. Britten and Lambert were never close friends but their careers coincided at various points; see also Diary for 10 September 1931, n. 4.

7 William Walton (1902–1983), English composer. The relationship between Britten and Walton was on occasion full of respect and warmth; at other times there was a degree of mutual wariness and, according to Walton's wife Susana, on Walton's part, rivalry. See also Diary for 9 September 1931, n. 1, Malcolm Hayes (ed.), *The Selected Letters of William Walton*, and Humphrey Burton and Maureen Murray, *William Walton: The Romantic Loner*.

Walton's lack of support for the proposed British Council-sponsored recording of *Peter Grimes* in the autumn of 1945 (see Letter 504 n. 2 and PBMPG, pp. 212–14) was the source of much friction between him and Britten during the first months of 1946. Britten learned of Walton's opposition to the recording (though perhaps not the reasons for it) and was acutely hurt by this action. Two letters from Walton to Britten concerning this episode came to light at BPL in 2003. (They were not available to Malcolm Hayes when compiling his edition of Walton's correspondence.) The first was written from Ashby St Ledgers, Rugby, on 10 March 1946:

Dear Benjamin,
    This is a difficult, and though I sincerely trust not, also a probably futile letter to write. It would seem, as I understand it from Jane [Clark, wife of Kenneth Clark], that things have gone too far, and that on your part at any rate, you and I (I learn for the first time) are neither on speaking or meeting terms.
    To me at least, this seems a disastrous situation, since under these conditions how can the damage be ever repaired?
    I have more than an inkling what it is about – the proposed recording of *Peter Grimes* by the British Council. If so, to give a full and lucid account in writing is beyond my powers, involving as it would, breaches of confidence, libel actions and other distressing repercussions. But I am sure that if we could meet I could so enlighten you about it, that though you might not approve, you would also not misconstrue the attitude I took up. I willingly admit that in the heat of the moment I uttered some harsh, almost unforgivable things, but if you realized the background of intrigue involved you might understand why I was so provoked into saying them. Some or all of this doubtless reached your ears and that being so I can fully understand how you feel and only blame myself.
    You may remember that I wrote you about *P.G.* saying, if I recall correctly, that it was the most extraordinary achievement and that you had the future of British opera in your hands etc. [See Hayes, pp. 153–4, and Philip Reed, 'A *Peter Grimes* Chronology, 1941–1945', in PBMPG, pp. 46–7.] Though you may consider my attitude mentioned above to be, to say the least, inconsistent with that letter I nevertheless still believe what I wrote you then.

I can only add that I am most profoundly sorry that anything I have said should have caused you pain and hurt. I am sorry – indeed very sorry – because nothing would, or would have pleased me more than to be your friend – a great friend of yours, but thinking it over, there never seemed much chance of that – we hardly ever met and everything and everyone, to me at any rate, seemed to conspire, if anything, to set us at loggerheads and try and create rival factions.

I realize that all this is slightly undignified for me to write and embarrassing for you to read but there seems no alternative if the situation is, as I hope, to be remedied. So I do beg you to accept this olive branch and that we can meet sometime in the near future and make it up. If you won't there is nothing I can do except be sad and deplore that it should ever have occurred.

I'm not in London a great deal but shall there from the 19th to the 24th and if you would have lunch or dinner with me I should be delighted, or at any other time you like.

Well, bless your heart,

Yours,

WILLIAM WALTON

Britten's reply has not survived, but Walton answered on 3 April 1946:

Dear Benjamin,

I am touched to tears at receiving your letter and it has taken a great load off my mind.

I think you are right about *Grimes* and let us drop the whole murky business connected with it, though as a final word I should like you to know that it was I who proposed at the B.C. that it should be recorded provided that a really first-class cast etc. could be found. Save for Joan Cross and Peter Pears that was one reason why I thought it should wait, since it would hardly have been a shining example of British operatic prowess.

That decision I believe still stands though, as you know, the Interludes are being done in any case [see Letter 564]. But they ought to have been recorded commercially long ago and I would prefer to see the 2nd quartet done instead sponsored by the B.C. I heard it the other week on the radio and regard it as your high-water mark.

If you have any views about this let me know and I will put it to the committee. After all Decca are bound to do the Interludes on their own, but perhaps might be inclined to jib at the quartet. What do you think?

As for myself, after a frightful period of dejection, inferiority complexes, etc. (more than a year of it) and feeling all my works past and present and future to be quite hopeless, I seem to have snapped out of it and be settling down to a quartet [completed in 1946] but it is rather like starting all over again at the beginning and it may well be that it never sees the light of day.

My London tel. no. is Hamp. 4747 if by any chance you happen to be there. I look forward to our meeting, whenever it happens to be.

I hope the new opera progresses favourably and thank you again for your very kind and understanding letter.

Yours ever,

WILLIAM

P.S. I heard this morn. from Stockholm of the great success of *P.G.* there. This sentence from the letter may amuse you, '. . . I could love even Hitler if he had written *Peter Grimes.*'

8 When the announcement was made in June 1946 that Karl Rankl had been
   appointed Music Director of the new Covent Garden Company, it was also
   revealed that the Company intended to mount a production of Purcell's
   The Fairy Queen, to be conducted by Constant Lambert, in November of
   that year. At the same time it was also announced that *Peter Grimes* would
   be included in the repertory for the first season (although it was, in fact,
   not staged there until 1947). The first performance of Purcell's semi-opera
   was given on 12 December 1946. The sets and costumes were designed by
   Michael Ayrton (after Inigo Jones), and the director was Malcolm Baker-
   Smith; Frederick Ashton choreographed, and the cast included Margot
   Fonteyn, Robert Helpmann and Michael Hordern. See also Harold Rosenthal, *Two Centuries of Opera at Covent Garden*, p. 566; Andrew Motion, *The
   Lamberts: George, Constant and Kit*, pp. 232–3, and *Purcell's The Fairy Queen
   as presented by The Sadler's Wells Ballet and the Covent Garden Opera.*
       The Board Minutes of the Royal Opera House, 9 May 1946, indicate that
   Britten had 'expressed himself', in conversation with David Webster, 'to be
   keenly interested in the idea of doing a reorchestration' of *The Fairy Queen*,
   but that E. J. Dent 'felt that Constant Lambert should be asked to undertake
   the work'. (In fact, Dent and Gordon Jacob collaborated with Lambert on
   the instrumentation.) At their next meeting (22 May) it was resolved that
   the 'Trust would be better served by an original work' from Britten, 'and
   that Mr Hawkes should invite him on behalf of the Trust to prepare a new
   work for the 1947/48 season'. At this same meeting Lambert's arrangement
   of *The Fairy Queen* was approved. See also Michael Burden, '"Gallimaufry"
   at Covent Garden: Purcell's *The Fairy-Queen* in 1946', *Early Music* (May
   1995), pp. 268–84.
       On behalf of Rankl and the Opera House Trustees, David Webster
   (General Administrator) was to write to Britten on 15 November 1946
   (quoted in Lewis Foreman, *From Parry to Britten: British Music in Letters*,
   pp. 271–2):

   This is just a note on our conversation and not in any way a formal letter, although
   immediately after our next conversation I will write to you formally at least on the
   points of our desire to have you do an Opera for us in the 1947/48 season. [. . .]
       I can confirm that all the details of the casting, designing and production would
   be in the hands of Karl and myself in consultation with you.

   This same letter touches on Webster's proposal to stage seven performances of *Peter Grimes*, beginning on 3 June 1947, with an autumn tour also.
   Webster was, naturally enough, keen to secure Pears and Joan Cross, but
   their involvement in the first English Opera Group season at Glyndebourne precluded their taking part. Consequently, *Grimes* was postponed
   to November 1947 (see Letter 547).

9 Probably the first orchestral rehearsal. Britten had written to the critic
   Desmond Shawe-Taylor, on 23 June: 'Lucretia is flourishing. It is certainly
   an ideal place to work in – Ansermet is proving ideal too.'

The Berkshire Music Center

SERGE KOUSSEVITZKY, *Director*

Presents the first American performances of

PETER GRIMES

An Opera in Three Acts and a Prologue
derived from the Poem of George Crabbe

Words by Montagu Slater

Music by BENJAMIN BRITTEN
Op. 33

All the Performers are Students of The Berkshire Music Center

Conductor: Leonard Bernstein
Stage Directors: Eric Crozier and Frederic Cohen
Stage Designer: Richard Rychtarik
Choral Director: Hugh Ross
Director of the Opera Department: Boris Goldovsky

Scene: The Borough, a small fishing town on the East Coast.

Time: Towards 1830.

Prologue: A room inside the Moot Hall, arranged for
a coroner's inquest.

Act   I   *Scene 1:* The Borough beach and street, the Moot Hall, The
Boar Inn, Keene's Shop, and Church porch are all
visible.

Scene 2: Inside "The Boar" — the same night.

Act II   *Scene 1:* The village street and beach (as before).

Scene 2: Peter Grimes' hut (an upturned boat).

Act III   *Scene 1:* The village street and beach a few nights later.

Scene 2: The same scene — some hours later.

Tanglewood, August 1946: the programme for the US premiere of *Peter Grimes*.
Not shown is the orchestra list, which included Julius Katchen (celesta) among its
members. In 1954 Katchen was to record Britten's *Diversions* for piano (left hand)
and orchestra, with the composer and the London Symphony Orchestra.

CHARACTERS (Performance of August 6)

PETER GRIMES, a fisherman.....................*William Horne*
BOY (JOHN), his apprentice.....................*Frederic Zighera*
ELLEN ORFORD, a widow, schoolmistress of the
    Borough ....*Florence Manning*
CAPTAIN BALSTRODE, a retired merchant skipper........*James Pease*
AUNTIE, landlady of "The Boar"...................*Ellen Carleen*
NIECES, main attractions of "The Boar".......*Mildred Mueller and*
                                        Phyllis Smith
NED KEENE.....................................*Robert Gray*
BOB BOLES, a fisherman and Methodist...............*Paul Franke*
SWALLOW, a lawyer.............................*Leonard Treash*
MRS. (NABOB) SEDLEY, a rentier widow of an East India
    Company's factor ....*Frances Lehnerts*
REV. HORACE ADAMS, the rector....................*Paul Knowles*
DR. THORP.....................................*Byron R. Kelley*
HOBSON, carrier...............................*Matthew Lockhart*
Chorus of townspeople and fisherfolk

CHARACTERS (Performance of August 7)

PETER GRIMES, a fisherman.....................*Joseph Laderoute*
BOY (JOHN), his apprentice.....................*Frederic Zighera*
ELLEN ORFORD, a widow, schoolmistress of the
    Borough ....*Frances Yeend*
CAPTAIN BALSTRODE, a retired merchant skipper........*James Pease*
AUNTIE, landlady of "The Boar"...................*Ellen Carleen*
NIECES, main attractions of "The Boar".......*Mildred Mueller and*
                                        Phyllis Smith
NED KEENE.....................................*Robert Gray*
BOB BOLES, a fisherman and Methodist...............*Robert Long*
SWALLOW, a lawyer.............................*Duane W. Crossley*
MRS. (NABOB) SEDLEY, a rentier widow of an East India
    Company's factor ....*Irene Jordan*
REV. HORACE ADAMS, the rector....................*Paul Knowles*
DR. THORP.....................................*Byron R. Kelley*
HOBSON, carrier...............................*Matthew Lockhart*
Chorus of townspeople and fisherfolk

On August 9 the cast will be the same as on August 7, except that the part of Bob Boles will be sung by Paul Franke, the part of Mrs. Sedley by Frances Lehnerts, the part of Swallow by Leonard Treash.

529   To Serge Koussevitzky
From Ralph Hawkes
[*Typed*]

BOOSEY & HAWKES LIMITED
295 REGENT STREET, LONDON W1
July 4th, 1946

Dear Dr Koussevitzky,

I confirm the various cablegrams that have passed between us as set out hereunder and also our conversations on the telephone:[1]

Your cable June 26th

WOULD ERIC CROZIER[2] BE AVAILABLE EARLIEST POSSIBLE TIME
TO COME TANGLEWOOD TO STAY. PETER GRIMES MAY NEED HIS
ASSISTANCE. PLEASE CABLE. REGARDS

My reply June 27th

BRITTEN CROZIER ANXIOUS COMPLY YOUR WISHES ATTEND
TANGLEWOOD BUT OWING PRODUCTION BRITTEN SECOND OPERA
RAPE OF LUCRETIA ON JULY 12TH GLYNDEBOURNE AND AT
MANCHESTER JULY 29TH IMPOSSIBLE FLY BEFORE 30TH. BOTH
HAPPY DO THIS IF NOT TOO LATE. AM ENDEAVOURING ARRANGE
RESERVATIONS NOW IN ANTICIPATION YOUR AGREEMENT BUT WOULD
LIKE CABLE CONFIRMATION. THEY WOULD HAVE TO RETURN BY
AUGUST 9TH. REGARDS

Your cable June 27th

GRAF[3] DEFINITELY OUT ABSOLUTELY NECESSARY TO HAVE ERIC
CROZIER OR SOMEONE EQUALLY QUALIFIED FOR GRIMES STAGING.
PLEASE TAKE IMMEDIATE STEPS. ADEQUATE FEE. LIVING AND
TRAVELLING EXPENSES WILL BE PAID. ARRIVAL HERE NOT LATER
THAN JULY 15TH. PLEASE INFORM BERNSTEIN. URGENT CABLE REPLY.
REGARDS

My cable June 28th

CONFIRMING TELEPHONE CONVERSATION. CROZIER FLIES PAN
AMERICAN 19TH JULY. CAN YOU PICK HIM UP NEW YORK. BRITTEN
FLIES 31ST. BOTH SHOULD RETURN ABOUT AUGUST 9TH. CROZIER
HAS TO GIVE UP PRODUCING JOB HERE AND WOULD LIKE
SUGGESTION REGARDING FEE. GLAD TO HAVE BEEN HELPFUL.
LENNY FULLY INFORMED. BEST REGARDS

Your cable July 1st

THANK YOU. WONDERFUL NEWS. WOULD LIKE MEET CROZIER TERMS.
PLEASE SUGGEST WHAT YOU CONSIDER RIGHT OFFER PLUS EXPENSES.
GREETINGS

My cable July 2nd
WOULD SUGGEST ONE THOUSAND DOLLARS FOR CROZIER PLUS
EXPENSES. WRITING. REGARDS

Your reply July 3rd
TERMS ACCEPTABLE. SHALL MEET CROZIER NEW YORK. REGARDS

All appears now to be settled and I am very pleased that we were able to arrange this for you; I fully realize the difficulty in which you found yourself when Graf had to pull out. Crozier should arrive on the morning of the 20th in New York by Pan American and will, of course, be prepared to go immediately to Tanglewood to commence work. I take it that you will arrange accommodation for him. I do not anticipate trouble with his visa and all will be completed by the 16th.

It is regrettable that he cannot come earlier but he is at present engaged day and night on the production of "The Rape of Lucretia" at Glyndebourne and cannot get away from there until after the premiere, which is on Friday, July 12th. It will be necessary for him to stay on for a day or so after this in order to touch up any alterations in the production that may be necessary, in view of its departure to Manchester on the 28th; where it will be done on a much larger stage.[4]

Benjamin Britten will be flying with us on the 31st July and will, of course, come straight to Tanglewood.

With Best Wishes,
Believe me to be,
Yours very sincerely,
RALPH HAWKES

1   This letter spells out the arrangements that brought Crozier and Britten to the US for the American premiere of *Peter Grimes* at the Berkshire Music Center, Tanglewood, where three performances were given by two casts – on 6, 7 and 9 August – conducted by Leonard Bernstein. The production was directed by Crozier and Frederic Cohen; Hugh Ross, who had conducted *Paul Bunyan* in 1941, was the chorus master. See also PFL, plates 205–9.

To secure a US premiere for *Grimes*, Ralph Hawkes had arranged three private performances of excerpts from the opera in association with the singing teacher Clytie Mundy (see Letter 589, n. 9). The first took place at the Mundys' New York apartment on 27 November 1945, at which representatives from Tanglewood were present. Elizabeth Mayer also attended and told Britten in a letter of 6 January 1946:

The singing at the Mundys' was rather odd, and not very satisfactory, but well meant of course. It is going to be repeated [. . .] with more singers [. . .] Ralph will be probably back at that time. He made the introductory speech at the first reading, and seems very keen on 'promoting' you here.

Hawkes himself informed Britten of the subsequent private performances, in a letter of 28 January 1946:

We have two further private readings on a somewhat better scale than the first one,
at Clytie Mundy's apartment on Sunday [3 February] and Tuesday [5 February]
next. Koussevitzky, Graf, Dowling and others will be present. This time we are
having a chorus – small but good. All is set for the Tanglewood performance[. . .]
Graf, who will produce, is going to Switzerland to see the production in Zurich.
Should Peter like to come, he could, of course, do it by flying here and back but I
hesitate to ask this.

Though illness had prevented Mrs Mayer's attending, she reported to
Britten on 7 February: 'I know that Wystan [Auden] wrote you some days
ago, and I hope he told you about his impression of *Peter Grimes* or the
fragments he heard at Clytie's lately [. . .] Cl. had her chorale group from
Philadelphia, and the soloists too, and W. said, that everything was ever so
much better than the first time only he was not so satisfied about the
tempi.' Hawkes himself wrote to Britten about the occasion on 11 February:
'*P.G.* had a fine private reading last week – Koussy, Lennie Bernstein, Graf,
etc. etc. all there and the little chorus trained by Clytie M did awful well.
We had a fine Swallow, Auntie and Nieces but P.G. wasn't so hot and of
course Joan had spoiled us for Ellen. Still it went over fine [. . .]'
    Auden had written to Britten from New York on 30 January 1946: 'I went
to Mrs Mundy's to hear scraps of *Peter Grimes*, and loved what I could hear.
Heinsheimer has given me a piano score so I can begin to get to know it
before Tanglewood.'
    Leonard Bernstein had been in England during June 1946 fulfilling con-
ducting engagements with the London Philharmonic Orchestra when he
had been invited by Ralph Hawkes to visit Glyndebourne, attend rehearsals
of *Lucretia* and meet Britten. While at Glyndebourne Bernstein took the
opportunity to talk with Britten about *Grimes* in preparation for the forthcoming US premiere (see Humphrey Burton, *Leonard Bernstein*, pp. 149–
53). In conversation with Burton, Eric Crozier recalled meeting Bernstein at
Glyndebourne (*Remembering Bernstein*, Aldeburgh Festival, 10 June 1991):

A shadowy figure appeared during this time. It was a young man in a white
mackintosh who hung about – we had none of us time to spare – we couldn't be
sociable or chat. It was Lenny Bernstein who'd made his decision to come down
and see Benjy. (Lenny was the only person I ever heard call Ben, 'Benjy'.)
    After a few days he said to me, 'I have a message for you from Koussevitzky. He's
asked me to say, "We're doing *Peter Grimes* at Tanglewood next month. Will you
come and direct it?"' I thought this was impossible: to leave the production of
Lucretia which I'd only just put on and which still needed work, but Ben was very
eager for me to go as I'd directed the opera the year before – the premiere – and
he'd like me to be there to make sure [. . .]
    My first experience of Tanglewood was of Lenny taking a rehearsal of the two
orchestras of students who'd come from all over the United States. He had them –
one vast orchestra in front of him – and at the back the two casts of young singers

doing their best to make themselves heard over that amount of noise. In those days Tanglewood was a shambles: there was no union labour allowed on the site; there were no electricians; there were no scene-painters. There was a young student I knew [. . .] from Los Angeles, a student of Schoenberg. He arrived and was given a paintbrush and told to paint the scenery. That applied to everyone. My electricians were young girls who were string-players [. . .] – they were doing madrigals before breakfast. A whole day long they were wasting their energies instead of concentrating on this difficult opera which they had to stage in about two to three weeks.

I went to Aaron Copland, who was Koussevitzky's assistant, and I said, 'Look – something has to be done about this.' He couldn't help me, so I demanded to see Koussevitzky [. . .] I said to the great man, 'I'm very sorry, but unless everyone connected with *Grimes* is told that they are to concentrate on that from now on, I'm leaving straight away. It's not worth the trouble.' He agreed, orders were given and things improved a little; but not enough and I felt unhappy about Ben coming out from England with Ralph Hawkes for this not very good production. So I went down to Lenox to the Western Union Office and I cabled Ben and said, 'For God's sake, stay where you are.' I went back to rehearsal and there was Lenny and I thought I must own up. I said, 'Lenny, I'm very sorry. I've just been and cabled Ben and asked him not to come because he won't enjoy it.' I thought he would be furious with me, but he said, 'Oh Eric, I'm so glad you've done that. I wouldn't want Bengy coming all this way out here and upsetting my tempi!' [Although Crozier's cable to Britten has not survived, a telegram message from him to Joan Cross, dated 1 August 1946, does: 'CONDITIONS HERE INDESCRIBABLE. HOW IS LUCRETIA FAMILY. MUCH LOVE TO YOU ALL. LONGING TO RETURN.']

Unfortunately, Ben read my telegram as a frantic appeal for help and came out with Ralph Hawkes and saw that what I'd said was pretty true. Any way we did our best. The performance was not of a high standard [. . .]

My last memory of Tanglewood concerns the last night of *Grimes*. It's the only time I saw Ben so upset. At the end there was big applause. We were standing backstage and Ben had to go on stage, and he was so upset he said, 'For God's sake, give me a cigarette.' I'd never seen Ben smoke. He hated it. But he took a cap from a hatstand, pulled it down as if to disguise his full appearance and had the cigarette in his mouth. Then we went on and took our call.

The American premiere of *Grimes* was reviewed by many of the New York newspapers. Olin Downes ('Britten's *Grimes* unveiled at Lenox', *New York Times*, 7 August 1946), who, like many of the other critics, had reviewed most of the Britten premieres during the years 1939–42, wrote:

Peter Grimes, [. . .] designated by Serge Koussevitzky before the curtain as the opera that came 'first after *Carmen*,' was given its American premiere by the students' orchestra, chorus and soloists of the Berkshire Music Center this evening in the Opera Concert Theatre at Tanglewood.

[. . .] Mr Britten had said to Dr Koussevitzky: 'This opera is yours.' Dr Koussevitzky related his reply: 'No, this opera belongs to the world.' He said finally that he had been asked to remind the audience that the performers at this premiere were students. [. . .]

The performance of a modern and very difficult score was astonishingly brilliant on the part of the orchestra, the chorus and, in the sum of it, the gifted and intelligent solo interpreters, whose sincerity was contagious.

[...] the score is astonishing, first in its integrated, over-all structure, of which no part is a mere accessory of the main idea. The motives or phrases of chorus, principals and orchestra are all bound together, sometimes in free symphonic fashion, but more often in ways that are singularly classic and formal in design. To the orchestra, to be sure, is given a freer role, especially in the four [*sic*] symphonic interludes [...].

This is more music than theatre, though it amounts to dramatic expression by a composer who knows well his Mussorgsky, Berg and Sibelius, whose technic is dazzling and so brilliant that one is never precisely sure, at first hearings of the music, where the technic ends and the genuine and expression of feeling begins.

[...] It must be admitted that the lyrical phrase, which exposes character or feeling as they are instantaneously and unforgettably expressed for example by the opening phrase of *Tristan* or the motive of just seven notes in which Bizet in *Carmen* lays bare the jealousy of José's soul, are mostly conspicuous by their absence. It is an eclectic, highly organized modern score. The harmonic bite and the vivid colors of the orchestra, sometimes black, sometimes wild and shrill, and now and again of prismatic brilliance, go far toward supplying the sonorous accentuation that the situations need, and there is more than intimation of the sounds and terrors of the sea.

[...] this opera is a prodigious advance, in form, technic and integration of its elements, over the one work of his in dramatic form, the chamber opera, *Paul Bunyan*, that was heard in 1941 in New York. *Peter Grimes* is the work of a composer, 33, still at the threshold of his powers, whose latest opera, *The Rape of Lucrece* [*sic*] is mentioned from authoritative sources as a further conspicuous advance. A young composer who can go so fast and so far so soon is one to be watched respectfully.

Irving Kolodin ('*Peter Grimes* opera is heard', *New York Sun*, 7 August 1946):

[*Peter Grimes*'s] first American performance here last night suggested, at its best, the young Englishman's writing transcends what is ordinarily heard from orchestra and chorus in an opera house, but in its minute-by-minute progress it is more often a drain on the attention, and a trial to the patience.

[...] For, with all the skill of Britten in handling a large orchestra, chorus and numerous solo voices, it is precisely in the realm of melodic interest that the work is deficient. At a first hearing there was more that possessed promise of durability in the orchestral 'Interludes' that dot the work. [...]

A problem that plagued William Horne, who sang the part of Grimes (and which will probably pursue more of his successors) is the high range of the part [...] Horne acted his part with stock dramatic gestures, and when he was not pressed too hard by the cruel requirements of music, sang it capably.

Easily the most compelling performance on the stage was that of James Pease, who carried himself well as Capt. Balstrode and also sang eloquently. [Pease was to record the role in Britten's Decca recording of *Grimes* in 1958.] The principal female role of Ellen Orford was admirably interpreted by Florence Manning [...] The composer was present in a seat adjacent to Koussevitzky's and seemed pleased with what he heard.

A review of *Grimes* in *Time* (19 August 1946) mentions a projected Broadway production:

The most unimpressed member of the Tanglewood audience was Composer Britten himself. Said he stiffly: 'There's no use pretending it was professional . . . It was a very lively student performance.'

[. . .] At Tanglewood he glumly watched rehearsals wearing a pearl-grey jacket, a yellow tie and strap sandals.

After the first two performances, Britten emplaned for England, where his new opera *The Rape of Lucretia* opened last month and got even better notices than *Peter Grimes*. For the US première of *Lucretia*, Britten would like to 'bring over the original British company.' Actor-producer Eddie (*The Glass Menagerie*) Dowling hopes to produce *Peter Grimes* on Broadway since Manhattan's starchy Metropolitan Opera has shown no real interest so far.

Dowling's proposal to stage *Grimes* on Broadway remained unachieved. Letter 514 makes reference to it; Dowling was misidentified in n. 8.

Life magazine (26 August 1946) published an impressive series of photographs of the Tanglewood production as well as a brief interview with the 'curly-haired [. . .] lean and bashful' composer:

Unlike most composers, Britten believes it possible to make a living by composing. He has proved his theory mainly by writing music for radio, movies and such plays as *The Ascent of F6* by his friend W. H. Auden. 'Hack work will never hurt your integrity,' says Britten, 'if you do your best on every commission.' Before the war he was commissioned to do a symphony for Japan's celebration of 2,600 years of Japanese dynasty only to have the work rejected as 'unsuitable [. . .] partly because of its Christian nature.'

[. . .] He studied at the Royal College of Music and was once regarded as a promising pianist. But his playing has deteriorated, partly because of the time he spends sailing in Suffolk. 'Now,' Britten says, 'I play like Chico Marx.'

[. . .] After receiving the toasts of outstanding US musicians, Britten hurried back to London where his second opera, *The Rape of Lucretia*, recently was given a much-praised premiere. His third opera, says Britten, will depart from somber themes and be a 'comedy of manners.'

Among Britten's friends who attended the Tanglewood premiere were W. H. Auden and Aaron Copland (see plate 26 and PFL, plate 206). Of Tanglewood, Auden wrote to his friend Rhoda Jaffe, 'It was fine to see Benjy Britten again. The performance was terrible but the work made an impression just the same' (quoted in Charles Osborne, *W. H. Auden: The Life of a Poet*, p. 222).

Although Bernstein conducted the stage premiere, Koussevitzky had conducted the first performance in the United States of the *Four Sea Interludes* and the *Passacaglia* in Boston on 2 March 1946. Hawkes telegraphed Britten: 'KOUSSEVITZKY GAVE WONDERFUL PREMIERE INTERLUDES TODAY. WILL REPEAT NEW YORK MARCH THIRTEENTH.' The performance at Carnegie Hall afforded the New York press their first opportunity to hear the orchestral interludes.

Robert Bagar ('Bostonians Give Britten Opera [Interludes] Fine Performance', *New York World-Telegram*, 14 March 1946):

The *Passacaglia* section started right off winning friends and influencing people, and the *Four Interludes* – 'Dawn', 'Sunday Morning', 'Moonlight', and 'Storm' – went on doing additional good deeds along those lines. [. . .]

The composer has invented themes that are immediately striking contrasts. Cleverly wrought stunts catch the ear as the music progresses, things like glisses, quaint and curious sounds in the rhythm section, sudden bursts and weird tinklings. All of these are mood makers.

The piece was beautifully played by the Bostonians, though, not knowing the score, I wonder if on occasion there was not a fluff here and there in the rhythm or the dynamics or the notes themselves.

Olin Downes ('Opera [Interludes] by Britten heard at concert', *New York Times*, 14 March 1946):

The score has a pervasive and tragical mood, and a genuinely individual utterance. The fact that the composer uses with complete readiness and ease the modern vocabulary of his art is not in itself conclusive; what moves us here is not merely the sounds but their emotional significance. [. . .]

How the opera, when it is performed, stands as a work for the theatre cannot be told. It could easily prove that in its symphonic pages the composer had delivered the essence of his message. There may be theatrical weaknesses in his work. Enough that last night one was aware of music of uncommon tension and psychological suggestion; music by a composer who may not himself be a simple man.

Irving Kolodin ('New English music by Koussevitzky', *New York Sun*, 14 March 1946) noticed some of the influences on the work:

The most impressive of last night's excerpts was a *Passacaglia*, which occurs between two scenes of the second act. It is masterfully constructed, with a content that is expressive as well as adroit. Along with the *Four Interludes* which completed the Koussevitzky selection, it suggested that Britten's model may well have been operas of the unconventional type of *Pelléas* and *Wozzeck* [. . .] One interlude, depicting Sunday morning, suggested that church bells sound much the same in an English village as they do in the Kremlin that Moussorgsky imagined in *Boris*; in another, contrariwise, Britten whipped up an angry storm which avoided most of the clichés found in the two standard musical storms – Beethoven's 'Pastoral' and Rossini's *William Tell*. The orchestral colors are deftly applied throughout, and it is hardly necessary to say they were thoroughly revealed by the penetrating clarity of the orchestral playing.

See also the documentary film *A Tale of Tanglewood: Peter Grimes Reborn* about two productions of *Grimes* at Tanglewood, in 1946 and 1996.

2   English director, librettist and translator (1914–1994). He directed the first productions of *Peter Grimes* (Sadler's Wells, 1945) and *The Rape of Lucretia* (Glyndebourne, 1946), and provided Britten with the texts for *The Young Person's Guide to the Orchestra* (1946), *Albert Herring* (1947), *Saint Nicolas* (1948), *Let's Make an Opera* (1949) and, with E. M. Forster, *Billy Budd* (1951). In 1956 Crozier provided the libretto for Lennox Berkeley's *Ruth*, and his translations of the standard operatic repertory include *The Bartered Bride*, *Otello*, *Falstaff* and *La traviata*. He was a co-founder of the English Opera Group in 1947 and the Aldeburgh Festival the following year. In

1949, he married the mezzo-soprano Nancy Evans (see Letter 517 n. 7).

See also Letter 496 n. 3, and obituaries: John Calder, *Independent* (8 September 1994); Philip Reed, 'Let's make an opera', *Guardian* (8 September 1994), with an afterword by Donald Mitchell, quoted in the Introduction, pp. 18–19; the *Daily Telegraph* and *The Times* (both 9 September 1994), and Alan Blyth, *Opera* (November 1994). Crozier's daughter Blake wrote to the *Guardian* following the publication of Mitchell's 'Afterword'. Her letter was published on 10 September 1994:

My father Eric Crozier died on Wednesday. Before his body was cold you published a vengeful addition by Donald Mitchell to the obituary written by Philip Reed. Whatever opinions Mr Mitchell has of my father, I find it offensive he should use your obituary column to publish his personal grievances, thus causing great distress to my father's family and others.

3   Herbert Graf (1904–1973), Austrian-born American opera director and administrator, who worked at the Metropolitan Opera, New York (1936–60) and was subsequently Director of the Zurich Opera (1960–62) and the Grand Théâtre, Geneva (1965–73). He also taught at the Curtis Institute, Philadelphia (1950–60), and was a faculty member at Tanglewood.

4   *The Rape of Lucretia* was given at the Manchester Opera House between 29 July and 3 August.

530   **To the Editor of** *The Times*[1]

Glyndebourne, Lewes, Sussex
July 8 [1946]

Sir, –

Two leading members of the Arts Council[2] have now stated that Glyndebourne is 'lending' or 'letting' its opera house for the production of *The Rape of Lucretia*. This is a complete misrepresentation of the facts. When some eight months ago the Glyndebourne management became aware of my plans for opera I was approached by Mr Bing, Glyndebourne's general manager, and was offered the production of my new opera at Glyndebourne for the reopening of the Glyndebourne festival – an offer which I gladly accepted. The engagement of all artistic personnel, and the whole organization of the production, carried out in closest collaboration and agreement with myself, was and is in the hands of the Glyndebourne management, who are presenting the opera and are financially and otherwise solely responsible for it.

The purpose of this letter is to inform the Arts Council, who from the start were asked to collaborate, and those who may be interested in the vicissitudes of English opera of the facts.

Yours faithfully,
BENJAMIN BRITTEN

1 This letter, a rare example of Britten writing to the press, appeared in *The Times* (11 July 1946). In June 1946 the Arts Council had offered Glyndebourne a limited guarantee against loss of £3000 for the nine-week tour of *Lucretia*; in 1945 a figure of £5000 had been discussed and apparently promised. Britten's letter to *The Times*, according to Paul Kildea written at the instigation of John Christie, was a response to the reduction in the guarantee. See also PKSB, pp. 81–2, where a letter (16 July 1946) from Britten to the Music Director of the Arts Council, Steuart Wilson, is quoted.

2 Founded in 1945, the Arts Council of Great Britain was the successor to the wartime Council for the Encouragement of Music and the Arts. Its role, then as now, was to administer subsidies awarded by the state to the arts. For analysis of Britten's relationship to the Arts Council, see PKSB, chapters 3, 4 and 5.

531 To Mary Behrend[1]
From Peter Pears

Glyndebourne
[22 July 1946]

My dear Mary –

Thank you so much for your two letters.[2] I am so glad "Lucretia" moved you – I find it enthralling and moving in the simplest & most direct way possible. All this ignorant & juvenile criticism of the libretto passes me by. There are no doubt phrases which irritate some people but the whole is clearly remarkable, & the music of it all (history lessons included) is astonishing. Ernest Newman yesterday was simply puerile – I thought.[3] I seem to be singing on only one Saturday matinée in London – & that is September 14th[4] – with Joan Cross & Kathleen Ferrier. It will be much better when we are rid of this embarrassingly long interval.[5]

Much love to you both and to George[6] –
from PETER

1 Mary Behrend (1883–1977) and her husband John Louis ('Bow'; 1881–1972) were friends of Pears, through whom they were drawn into Britten's circle, from the mid-1930s. They were patrons of the arts, in particular of Stanley Spencer, and generous supporters of the Aldeburgh Festival and the English Opera Group. Britten dedicated his Second String Quartet to Mary Behrend. See also Diary for 14 March 1937, n. 1, and IC1/2.

2 The letters from Mrs Behrend have not survived. The first performance of *The Rape of Lucretia* had been given at Glyndebourne on 12 July, with the first cast conducted by Ansermet; the second cast, also conducted by Ansermet, gave the second performance, on 13 July.

THE GLYNDEBOURNE OPERA
Lessees : GLYNDEBOURNE SOCIETY LTD.
General Manager : Rudolf Bing.

FRIDAY, JULY 12th, 1946, at 6.15 p.m.
GLYNDEBOURNE PRODUCTIONS LTD.
PRESENTS
THE FIRST PERFORMANCE OF
THE RAPE OF LUCRETIA
An Opera in Two Acts
Music by
BENJAMIN BRITTEN
Libretto by
RONALD DUNCAN
Conductor :
ERNEST ANSERMET

Producer :   Designer :
ERIC CROZIER   JOHN PIPER

Male Chorus - - - - - - -	PETER PEARS
Female Chorus - - - - - -	JOAN CROSS
Collatinus - - - - - - - a Roman general	OWEN BRANNIGAN
Junius - - - - - - a Roman general	EDMUND DONLEVY
Tarquinius - - - - - - an Etruscan prince	OTAKAR KRAUS
Lucretia - - - - - - wife of Collatinus	KATHLEEN FERRIER
Bianca - - - - - - nurse to Lucretia	ANNA POLLAK
Lucia - - - - - - maid to Lucretia	MARGARET RITCHIE

ACT I
Prologue
SCENE I: The Generals' tent in the camp outside Rome.
Interlude: The Ride to Rome.
SCENE II: Lucretia's house in Rome, the same evening.

ACT II
SCENE I: Lucretia's bedroom, the same night.
Interlude: A chorale.
SCENE II: Lucretia's house, the next morning.
Epilogue.

Dinner Interval after Act I.

THE GLYNDEBOURNE OPERA
Lessees : GLYNDEBOURNE SOCIETY LTD.
General Manager : Rudolf Bing.

SATURDAY, JULY 13th, 1946, at 6.15 p.m.
GLYNDEBOURNE PRODUCTIONS LTD.
PRESENTS
THE RAPE OF LUCRETIA
An Opera in Two Acts
Music by
BENJAMIN BRITTEN
Libretto by
RONALD DUNCAN
Conductor :
ERNEST ANSERMET

Producer :   Designer :
ERIC CROZIER   JOHN PIPER

Male Chorus - - - - - - -	AKSEL SCHIØTZ
Female Chorus - - - - - -	FLORA NIELSEN
Collatinus - - - - - - a Roman general	NORMAN WALKER
Junius - - - - - - a Roman general	FREDERICK SHARP
Tarquinius - - - - - - an Etruscan prince	FRANK ROGIER
Lucretia - - - - - - wife of Collatinus	NANCY EVANS
Bianca - - - - - - nurse to Lucretia	CATHERINE LAWSON
Lucia - - - - - - maid to Lucretia	LESLEY DUFF

ACT I
Prologue
SCENE I: The Generals' tent in the camp outside Rome.
Interlude: The Ride to Rome.
SCENE II: Lucretia's house in Rome, the same evening.

ACT II
SCENE I: Lucretia's bedroom, the same night.
Interlude: A chorale.
SCENE II: Lucretia's house, the next morning.
Epilogue.

Dinner Interval after Act I.

Glyndebourne, 12 and 13 July 1946: the cast lists from the programmes for the first
and second performances of *The Rape of Lucretia*

3   Newman contributed two extensive reviews of *Lucretia* to successive issues
of the *Sunday Times* (21 and 28 July 1946). Duncan's libretto absorbed
Newman on 21 July:

There can be no actual comparison, of course, between two operas so different
both in subject and in form as *Peter Grimes* and *The Rape of Lucretia*; but for all
that I must register my impression that Mr Britten's second opera does not fulfil all
the expectations set up in us by his first, and most of the blame for this I would lay
on the libretto. The dramatic technique of dispensing with virtually all the usual
stage action by leaving it to a 'Chorus' (in the antique sense of the word) to describe
for us the course of events, a Chorus which, standing as it does outside space and
time, has the privilege of commenting philosophically on not only the before but
the after of the events, was put to great use in André Obey's drama *Le Viol de
Lucrèce* (1931). Mr Ronald Duncan's procedure runs parallel to a great extent with
that of his predecessor in this field, and a comparison of the two works where they
resemble each other is not generally to his advantage.

I hasten to add that his text is in several respects excellent; and those of us who
have suffered in the past from the strange jargon known as 'librettists' English' are
delighted to find that opera composers are at last going to men of letters for their
material. The trouble with Mr Duncan, as I see it, is that, being over-conscious of
the fact that he is a man of letters, he feels himself under the constant necessity of
being 'literary'. Many of his carefully carpentered images creak as we read them;
they creak still more when they are sung, for the heightening of our sensibilities by
music makes us much more critical of a dubious line in song or opera than we are
when it is only read or spoken.

THE GLYNDEBOURNE OPERA

Director and General Manager:
RUDOLF BING

Artistic Director:
CARL EBERT

GLYNDEBOURNE FESTIVAL 1946

Conductors:
ERNEST ANSERMET REGINALD GOODALL

Producer: ERIC CROZIER   Designer: JOHN PIPER

Associate Conductor and in Charge of Musical Studies:
HANS OPPENHEIM

Musical Assistant:
JAMES ILIFF

Assistant Manager: MORAN CAPLAT   Catering Manager: A. H. BROWN

Stage Director:
A. HUNTLY GORDON

Stage Manager:
P. D. MACCLELLAN

Engineer:
W. J. THORPE

Chief Electrician:
C. SALVAGE

Stage Foreman:
R. W. GOUGH

Head Gardener:
F. HARVEY

THE ORCHESTRA

1st Violin: Emanuel Hurwitz
2nd Violin: Peter Schidlof
Viola: Kenneth Essex
Violoncello: Martin Lovett

Double Bass: C. Haydn Gray
Flute: John Francis
Oboe: John Butterworth
Clarinet: Stephen Waters

Bassoon: Edward Wilson
Horn: Neil Sanders
Harp: Enid Simon
Percussion: H. J. Wilson

Reginald Goodall and Anna Pollak appear by permission of The Governors of Sadler's Wells
Hans Oppenheim appears by permission of The Dartington Hall Trustees

Scenery built and painted by AMBASSADORS SCENIC STUDIOS
Dresses and Costumes executed by the JOHN LEWIS PARTNERSHIP.
Fabric Adviser: SCOTT SLIMON.
Wigs by NATHANS.
Plastic headdresses by RALPH SCHORR STUDIO.
Jewellery by BEATRICE DAWSON.

London Box Office (Manager: Miss E. NEWBOULD), c/o Messrs. Dean & Dawson, Ltd.,
81 Piccadilly, W.1. GROsvenor 3333.

THE GLYNDEBOURNE FESTIVAL PERFORMANCES

LE NOZZE DI FIGARO   OF   DON GIOVANNI
COSÌ FAN TUTTE

have been recorded complete by "HIS MASTER'S VOICE" for
THE MOZART OPERA SOCIETY
98 Clerkenwell Road, E.C.1

Ask your dealer for full particulars or write to the Secretary, Mozart Opera Society,

---

THE RAPE OF LUCRETIA

After the play "Le Viol de Lucrèce" by André Obey and based on the works of Livy, Shakespeare, Nathaniel Lee, Thomas Heywood and F. Ponsard.

CHARACTERS

THE MALE AND FEMALE CHORUS frame the tragedy, but do not participate in the scenes themselves, yet comment on them. Outside of time they are able to anticipate the actions of the characters and interpret their thoughts to the audience. The tragedy is set in Rome 500 B.C., but the chorus comment on it as Christians:

> "While we as two observers stand between
> This present audience and that scene,
> We'll view these human passions and these years
> With eyes which once have wept with Christ's own tears."

In a prologue before the curtain rises the Chorus describe the historical background to the tragedy, then the actual scene on the stage.

In the first Interlude the Male Chorus observes Prince Tarquinius as he rides to Rome.

The second Interlude is in the form of a chorale. In this the chorus perceive a significance in the rape which is greater than itself. They see it as a symbolic act in which virtue is defined by man's nature and is the Cross to Him

> "Here though this scene deceives
> Spirits invincible,
> Love's unassailable,
> All this is endless
> Crucifixion for Him."

The tragedy finally drives the female chorus in the Epilogue to ask whether "this old world grows old in sin alone" and whether "this is it all?" The Male Chorus answers her that "it is not all . . . for now He bears our sin and He, stoned with our doubt, turns round and then forgives us all . ." The opera ends with an "exergue" sung by both the chorus:

> "Since time commenced or life began
> Great love has been defiled by Fate or Man;
> Now with worn words and these brief notes we try
> To harness song to human tragedy."

COLLATINUS, a Roman General of great spiritual nobility. He tries to reconcile Tarquinius' quarrel with Junius; neither fearing the former nor suspecting the latter. He is a man of trust and devoid of ambition. His marriage with Lucretia is the complete fulfilment of love.

PRINCE TARQUINIUS, son of the Etruscan tyrant, Tarquinius Sextus. He is unmarried, a profligate whom Junius challenges to prove Lucretia's chaste. He is a man at the mercy of his own virility.

JUNIUS, an ambitious Roman General, who is jealous of the spiritual qualities of Collatinus and the physical virility of Tarquinius. By challenging Tarquinius he deliberately seeks to reduce both to his own level and thus make political capital out of the tragedy.

LUCRETIA, the chaste and beautiful wife of Collatinus.

BIANCA, Lucretia's nurse since childhood. She is as a mother to Lucretia.

LUCIA, Lucretia's maid. She is innocently flirtatious.

THE RAPE OF LUCRETIA

PROVINCIAL TOUR

OPERA HOUSE, MANCHESTER
JULY 29th–AUG. 3rd
ROYAL LYCEUM, EDINBURGH
AUG. 12th–17th

ROYAL COURT, LIVERPOOL
AUG. 5th–10th
THEATRE ROYAL, GLASGOW
AUG. 19th–24th

NEW THEATRE, OXFORD, SEPT. 23rd–28th

LONDON SEASON

SADLER'S WELLS OPERA HOUSE, AUG. 24th–SEPT. 21st
to be followed by performances in
AMSTERDAM, THE HAGUE and PARIS

Glyndebourne, 1946: from the programme for *The Rape of Lucretia*

I must confess my astonishment that Mr Britten, with his generally superfine sensitiveness in these matters, did not foresee the effect that some of Mr Duncan's lines would have on us when we heard them sung. We feel, even when we read them, that such flowers of speech as 'So will my little vase contain / The sun's exuberance slaked with rain' or 'So will my pretty vase enclose / The sun's extravagance which is the rose' are not really poetry but only shop samples of 'poetic diction'; but when they are sung by a couple of servant girls as they arrange Lucretia's flowers we cannot repress a smile. And the smile is apt to become a titter, as it did all around me at Glyndebourne the other evening, when the self-same damsels, forgetting their laboriously acquired literary manners, drop into such colloquialisms as 'Oh! What a lovely morning! . . . It's going to be hot, unbearably hot. And I daresay it will thunder.' [. . .]

This scene, indeed, should be recast. It is not merely that it reminds us, to its disadvantage, of the famous scene between Madam Butterfly and Suzuki; it was handled with such naïveté of technique at Glyndebourne that everyone was amused, and there should be no provocation to amusement in a tragedy like this.

If we want to see how far Mr Duncan can sometimes fall behind his French confrère we have only to compare the different manners of the two when the Male and Female Chorus make an excursion into history. [. . .]

M. Obey it will be seen, not only manages to quote Livy and Shakespeare without setting up any sense of incongruity in us but relates it all poignantly to the drama. What Mr Duncan gives us [. . .] in the prologue to his second act [. . .] is a University Extension lecture [. . .]

[. . .] Once more I ask myself what had become of Mr Britten's sense of the theatre and his sense of the theatre and his feeling for his tragic subject when he allowed things of this sort to go into the libretto.

Newman returned to his dissatisfactions with the libretto the following week (28 July):

After a brief summons by Junius Brutus to the people to bear Lucretia's body through the city, Mr Duncan wanders off into a rhapsody on beauty that is marred by such pseudo-poetic purple patches as 'Beauty is the hoof of an unbroken filly, / Which thundering up to the hazel hedge / Jumps into the sun / And is gone.' Then he writes an Epilogue in which the Male and Female Chorus previse the Crucifixion. Here his piety, or his love for easy effect, seems to me to have got the better of his dramatic sense: lines like these at the end of an opera on the subject of Lucretia – 'For us did He live with such humility: / For us did He die that we might live, and He forgive / Wounds that we make and scars that we are. / In His Passion is our hope, Jesus Christ, Father. / He is all! He is all!' – which have no real connection with what has been occupying us until then. [. . .]

Even Mr Britten's great talent, which no one admires more than I do, has not enabled him to find music that can elevate some of Mr Duncan's preciosities to its own sphere. I must confess also that there is far too much *Sprechgesang* and not enough music in the opera for my liking. When Mr Britten really gets into his stride the results are magnificent – the orchestral suggestion of Tarquin's ride, for instance, or, what is perhaps the most remarkable piece of writing in the whole work, the music that accompanies so subtly and so suggestively the episode of Tarquin's reception in the house of Lucretia. I make bold to say that the young man who can, on occasion, be at once so musical and so dramatic as this is potentially capable of rising to almost any height in opera.

I look forward, then, to the day when Mr Britten will give us an opera that is all music. But to do that he will have to find the right libretto, and he must shed some of his present enthusiasm for recitative at the expense of music. This has now landed him in a blind alley; the sooner he retraces his steps the better for himself and for us.

Frank Howes, the traditionally anonymous critic of *The Times*, 'Glyndebourne Opera' (13 July 1946), also attacked Duncan's libretto:

Mr Ronald Duncan [. . .] specializes in modern morality plays, and the text with which he has provided the composer draws an element from the medieval mystery. Indeed, it draws too much, for the end of the opera, with its Christian moral tacked on to the close of a drama already completed, strikes a false note and spoils with anti-climax the great *ostinato* with which the composer resolves the tragedy. But apart from this grave dramatic error the draft on the past has created a new form in which the age-old balance of music and drama is struck anew. [. . .]

This is the most important thing about the new opera, which creates dramatic tension surely if a little slowly in the first act and powerfully and swiftly in the second. Britten has music for every situation – again, as in *Peter Grimes*, the significant figure, the long-limbed cantilena, the discovery of orchestral effect to emphasize, occasionally to smother, the words. The purely lyrical element, that normally uses formal, even strophic, melody as its vehicle, is not allowed to break away from the *unendliche Melodie* of the declamation, even in a flower song or the song of a summer morning, though by way of counterpoise the musing of the female chorus upon the sleeping Lucretia is sung over an extremely beautiful orchestral lullaby.

The opera is classical in feeling as well as neo-classical in form, for it has few characters, a chamber orchestra for accompaniment, extreme simplicity of texture which always prefers unison to part-writing in its ensembles, a statuesque kind of production with swift strokes when the action moves as in Greek tragedy, and a complete avoidance of everything that could be called romantic. Its economy and consistency are its strength.

The performance had all the advantage of the care which is traditional in Glyndebourne productions. A contralto heroine is unconventional, but in Miss Kathleen Ferrier the opera had a protagonist who was able without strain to present tragedy with a splendid voice and great dignity of bearing. Mr Owen Brannigan lacked the latter quality in the role of her husband, though his voice is of the sympathetic quality that is needed. Tarquinius needs, and in Mr Otakar Kraus received, something rougher. Mr Edmund Donlevy's characterization of Junius, the mischief-maker of the piece, was deft and telling.

The long commentaries of the two choruses were sung by Miss Joan Cross and Mr Peter Pears, with full appreciation of their reflective nature. The two smaller female parts, well sung by Miss Margaret Ritchie and Miss Anna Pollak, contributed high lights to a predominantly sombre picture. The words of all the singers came over pretty well, though the composer is not always as careful as he might be in their disposition over their accompaniment. The sets of Mr John Piper were simple in design and rich in effect. Mr Ernest Ansermet conducted and played the piano for passages of *recitativo secco* which Britten has reintroduced in a modernized form into an operatic score.

Howes returned to *Lucretia* in *The Times* the following week, on 19 July, when it was reviewed in connection with the ISCM Festival, which was

being held at that time in London (ISCM delegates attended Glyndebourne on 15 July, 'by invitation of the London Festival Committee'):

Now it so happened that Britten's new opera, *The Rape of Lucretia*, had its first performance during the festival week, and foreign delegates have been able to hear it.
Britten is no doctrinaire, but he has immense fertility, and he has absorbed all that
he needs of bitonalism and the other '-isms' of the experimentalists. [...] It may be
doubted whether the new opera will have the dramatic compulsion and wide
appeal of *Peter Grimes*. The plot is too simple and short, and so has to be expanded
and built up by means of a device that is always rather a bore, whether it be the
platitudinous chorus of Greek tragedy or the mumbo-jumbo of Wagner's Norns.
Mr Duncan's libretto, too, is tiresome in the way it hands out half-truths in
aphorisms that from their form pretend to have the authority of proverbs. But in
this opera Britten is carrying farther his search for a new type of vocal line, new
forms of vocal ensemble that will lift opera out of the dead end in which it has been
stuck since the death of Puccini. Hindemith's is the only other serious attempt to
render this grand historical service to contemporary music.

(Howes found an opportunity to criticize Duncan's libretto on a third
occasion when he reviewed the vocal score of *Lucretia*, 'Words for Music!
Operatic Experiments', *The Times* (8 November 1946).)

Feruccio Bonavia, for the *New York Times*, 'New Britten opera heard in
England' (13 July 1946), almost alone among his fellow critics, found the
Christian conclusion of *Lucretia* comprehensible:

The share of the chorus is important. The two choristers are imagined as outside of
time. While the tragedy takes place five centuries before the Christian era, the
chorus views these errors and passions 'with eyes that once wept with Christ's own
tears.' One has only to remember Alkestis and her three-day purification after coming to life again to see that the blending of Christian sentiment with a pagan tale is
not as far-fetched as it seems.

But the most striking feature in the new Britten opera is the widening of range,
the deepening of sympathy suggested by music that is at times quite as fierce and
robust as anything in *Grimes*, and also more exquisite and more delicately beautiful than the finest page of the earlier opera.

[...] The opera ends on a note of sadness that in the hands of a less able composer might have become an anti-climax. In Mr Britten's treatment it becomes
fitting and dignified.

In his notice for the *Daily Telegraph* (20 July 1946), Bonavia concluded
by making reference to discussions then taking place about the formation
of a national opera company at Covent Garden: 'Much has been heard
recently about English opera. At Glyndebourne Mr John Christie is giving
us opera in English and English opera. The company he has assembled –
with a hint or two about stage deportment – will do well as the foundation
of a national opera.'

Cecil Gray, writing in the *Observer* (14 July 1946), was critical of the 'sen-
tentious neo-catholic moralizing' of the libretto:

There is a feeling of pastiche, in which moreover, the elements do not coalesce.
The music shows the same characteristics. In the same way that the libretto is an

ingenious and effective mixture of disparate elements, so the composer alternates continually between incongruous styles [. . .] He is certainly well aware of this stylistic inconsistency; it is obviously part of a deliberate intention to escape from the obsessive individualism which marked the art of the immediate past, and to achieve a catholic, inclusive, impersonal form of expression; but in following this admirable ideal he is apt to fall into mere eclecticism. In this Britten greatly resembles Meyerbeer; he is in fact the Meyerbeer of our time, but in saying that, one wishes to imply a compliment, for Meyerbeer is a very greatly underrated composer. Like him, Britten does everything supremely well, and with a genuine dramatic feeling, but one seeks in vain for any central core of personality.

[. . .] A special word of praise [. . .] is due to the superb sets designed by John Piper, who here shows himself to be in the first rank of contemporary stage designers.

Philip Hope-Wallace, 'Opera at Glyndebourne', *Manchester Guardian* (15 July 1946):

Musically it is a work of extreme ingenuity and much interest, written throughout with a strongly marked personal style and in a more than usually rarefied form, exhibiting every characteristic, good and bad, of this much-gifted composer. It contains several highly effective strokes of operatic craftsmanship and some notably beautiful lyrical episodes [. . .] The composer never seems at a loss, as easily creating the tension for 'Tarquin's ravishing stride' as for Lucretia's impending death. [. . .] he sets the words in such a way that almost any portion of the work isolated could – as far as ingenuity goes – hold its own with the subtlest chamber music or lieder in the concert hall. Yet paradoxically the total result, considered as opera, or, indeed, as any sort of dramatic entertainment, is far from being an unqualified success.

The libretto, by Ronald Duncan, who wrote the play *This Way to the Tomb*, is largely to blame. It tries but fails to make the best of many styles, and though drawing extensively for its ideas on the French play of the same name by Obey uses them poorly. Here also the two male and female chorus figures comment on the action, but instead of intensifying the drama they continually tend to dissipate it and to reduce it to the status of oratorio, an impression not lessened by the Christian moralizing which here supplies a frame and an anticlimax to the pagan drama. For a work of such musical facility and wit the total effect is strangely heavy and lifeless.

Eric Blom, *Birmingham Post* (15 July 1946), attended the second performance with the alternative cast, on 13 July; like Bonavia, he was untroubled by Duncan's libretto:

The Rape of Lucretia is not a flawless work, much less an indisputable work, but it is decidedly a masterpiece in its way. Like any other good opera ever written, it is not exclusively a composer's masterpiece [. . .] Much of the interest and fascination the opera displays is due to Ronald Duncan's libretto, a curious but successful blend of poetry, psychology, realism and formality [. . .]

Of course, *The Rape of Lucretia* is modern in conception all round, but its theme justifies constant reference, scenically and musically, to artistic procedures of the past. The author makes use of the Greek chorus [. . .] But the device is modernized by often letting these personages take part in the concerted music, without, however, addressing the characters or ever being noticed by them. Among the musical traditions not so much followed as revivified by Britten are the chorale sung by the chorus in one of the interludes, the set pieces into which the music shapes itself, the general scheme of formal musical patterns succeeding each other, the recitatives connecting them, sometimes accompanied by a piano in the old manner but with new matter, and so on.

All this results in a certain stylistic mixture, it must be admitted. But one is hardly ever made to think of past styles. [...] Britten's score [...] is rich, allusive, imaginative and above all unmistakably individual. The music may not go very deep, but how many great operas are there in the world in which it does?

One of the most thoughtful reviews was written by Desmond Shawe-Taylor, *New Statesman and Nation* (20 July 1946):

Between Benjamin Britten and the average 'good composer' of our day a gulf yawns. *The Rape of Lucretia* may not be a flawless masterpiece, but it is a work of genius, not of talent [...] One difference between Britten and most of his contemporaries is that, in the process of composition, his imaginative 'inner ear' is listening, all the time and at full stretch, to what he is doing; fascinating as his music looks on paper – for he is a master of figuration and of every kind of musical device – I feel tolerably sure that his ideas never occur to him as anything but sheer sensuous sound, and that it is to this fact that they owe the force and freshness with which they strike the listener's ear. [...]

The libretto, with its taut structure, its lyrical episodes and its few but clearly defined characters, is well adapted to the purpose of music. But it contains one or two questionable features. For example, the commentators are saddled with a certain amount of historical exposition which is unnecessary and distracting. In setting these passages to *recitativo secco* Britten has shown prodigious skill in the management of intractable material, but not even he can reconcile us to the opening of the second act. Here the librettist deliberately adopts the style of an encyclopaedia, putting into the mouth of the Female Chorus such phrases as 'All authorities agree that the Etruscan conquest of Rome dates from 600 B.C. – that is, approximately.' At this point the audience giggles – and is presumably meant to; but why, why, why? I implore librettist and composer to make the simple cut which would remove this blot on the integrity and keeping of their work.

A larger problem is posed by the final interpretation of the tragedy in terms of the Christian faith. In spite of the majestic and consoling musical structure upon which this transformation is accomplished, I cannot help thinking it to be an artistic error. The incompatibility of Lucretia's story, culminating in a 'noble' suicide, with the ideas of Christendom emerges all too clearly in the episode in which the 'Christianizing' Choruses attempt to restrain Collatinus from the impulse to 'forgive' Lucretia. There is a whole world of confusion here. A Roman might pity Lucretia, but he would no more 'forgive' her than one 'forgives' a tablecloth for an ugly stain: whereas to the Christian not only does forgiveness rank among the highest virtues, but there can be in this particular instance nothing to forgive.

This second act contains musical and dramatic beauties of the highest order; among them the moving C major *lullaby* sung by the Female Chorus to the sleeping Lucretia, the approach of Tarquin announced by the Male Chorus in a whispered *parlando* accompanied by muffled, stealthy drum-beats; and the whole of the last scene, from the lyrical *aubade* with which it opens to the measured catharsis of its close. But the act is a little flawed by the incongruities I have mentioned; and in particular by the curious failure to make a great musical climax of the central episode of the story – a failure which is part of the price paid for the introduction of the Christian *motif*. One does not, of course, demand a crude Straussian representation of the lustful crime, but the violence of rape must surely be matched by some sort of musical violence, and I cannot think that this was the moment to launch the two commentators on a figured chorale.

The first act, however, is an unquestionable masterpiece; a great arc of tension stretches over the whole hour of its course. As soon as the inner curtain reveals the silent camp beneath the heavy, thunderous night (and you can imagine how John Piper's brush reinforces the atmosphere!), we perceive that with eleven solo instruments and percussion Britten can command effects even more intense and evocative than those of *Peter Grimes*. Everything is magically, classically clear: the moments of lyrical melody captivate, the harmony moves in that absolutely logical manner which was so marked in the Second String Quartet, and the instrumentation is a chain of ravishing subtleties. In spite of the slender resources, the effect is anything but small; here and there we are even reminded of Britten's enormous admiration for Verdi. But it would be absurd to describe the music as derivative; on the contrary, it is all unmistakably in that style which we have come to know and love as Britten's own – the heart-easing melody of friendship given later in the first scene to Collatinus, the tremendous excitement of the Ride to Rome (above all the wonderful moment when horse and rider plunge glowing into the Tiber), the lovely *ensemble* for the women as the linen is folded away, and the solemnity, tinged by foreboding, of the long chain of 'good-nights' which bring the incomparable act to a close. [. . .]

The first two performances were both conducted by Ernest Ansermet, with perfect musicianship and in particular, a most delicate realization of the piano accompaniments to the recitatives. The two casts, however, were entirely different, though in each case *ensemble* and attention to detail were of the standard one has come to expect of Glyndebourne. Peter Pears and Aksel Schiøtz alternate as Male Chorus: Pears's ringing and impassioned declamation ranks among the finest things he has done, while Schiøtz, who is a Dane, deserves special commendation for the clarity and purity of his English. Joan Cross and Flora Nielsen vie with one another in the excellence of their interpretations of the Female Chorus. Neither Tarquin, however, is altogether ideal: Otakar Kraus, who looks magnificent, because of the pronounced 'beat' in his powerful baritone; Frank Rogier, who has a brighter, smoother voice, because of his inexperience as an actor. Of the two Lucretias, Kathleen Ferrier looks the more Roman, but her fine contralto has a touch of oratorio-plum-in-the-mouth from which Nancy Evans is wholly free. Among the smaller parts (none is really small) I must mention the floating, silvery high notes of Margaret Ritchie's Lucia, Owen Brannigan's richly sung Collatinus, and the Junius of Edmund Donlevy, impeccable both musically and dramatically. Eric Crozier's production and John Piper's scenery raise the dramatic tension as surely as they delight the eye; how strange that we should have had to wait all this time to see a stage decorated by so evidently dramatic a painter! It is good news that the whole production is to tour this country [. . .] and thereafter the Continent, for it is of a quality of which we may well feel proud in any capital in the world.

Britten must have taken some pleasure in reading the anonymous letter to the Editor of the *Manchester Guardian* from a member of the audience in Manchester, a letter that Joan Cross carefully preserved in one of her scrapbooks, now at BPL:

Sir, –

I went to hear Mr Benjamin Britten's new opera, *The Rape of Lucretia*, on Saturday night and received the surprise of my life. First, the Opera House was far from full, though this was by any standards the most exciting musical and theatrical production which Manchester has seen for ten years – or twenty for all I know. I am told it has been the same each night. Secondly, the opera itself is in every way more beautiful than the critics (and I have read most of them) have led us to imagine. To be sure the libretto has obvious weaknesses (what libretto has not?), but it also contains passages of genuine poetry, which has so far gone almost unmentioned. To be sure the music is difficult, but it contains songs of the most haunting beauty, of which again, for some reason, few critics have bothered to tell us. To my way of thinking – and to judge from the applause at the end I was not alone – this was one of the finest artistic experiences offered to us in recent years.

Two composer friends of Britten expressed strong views to him by letter. Michael Tippett, who attended a dress rehearsal on 11 July 1946, wrote on the 14th:

I hope I wasn't too abrupt on Thursday. I was so pleased about the music that I rushed rather hastily to the attack on the other. I think I can make it clearer by discussion of one scene: the arrival of Junius and Collatinus in the morning [Act II scene 2]. Here you have various degrees of knowledge among the characters. Coll. knows that something is probably astray, but not the fact of Junius' perfidy. Jun. knows himself the fact of the rape but not the circumstances and imagines the servants know more than they do. The servants know the fact of Tarquin's visit but [only one of them] has a guess at the dreadful consequences. Lucretia knows all, in a sense, but knows also nothing of the wager etc.

Well! that is a classic operatic situation. I do not think it was artistically used up, so to speak: the dramatic qualities never really put *all* the characters or all the *character* of the characters into play (let alone the conscious artistry of playing with the extra knowledge that the audience has). Thus the banality of Collatinus' remark 'Why didn't you tell me this before?' is not merely in the banality of the words, it is *really* in the banality of the response to the situation. 'Can this be the sort of man who has a wonderful love life with Lucretia?' It gives us two aspects of the same character which can't join in the schoolboy-witted soldier and the tender sensitive lover.

Then again – we are taken into the almost secret atmosphere of this love out of which happens the suicide. Afterwards we get a similar jolt over Junius. This Iago-like character suddenly brandishes a dagger and declares death to the tyrant. Is this the real Junius 'come clean', or the old Junius 'jumping on the bandwagon'? We do not know.

You have written a preface, I gather, which I haven't seen yet. But you hinted to me that you thought high-thinking and good poetry were an aid to libretto(s). Maybe that these things are a value to the present stage – I wouldn't like to say – it isn't my province. But the most striking thing lacking in English librettos is the knowledge of how to present emotions and characters in terms of dramatic situations and gestures, whereby the words they actually sing withdraw a bit into the background. Arthur Waley wrote me a letter a little while back in which he gave his ideal of a libretto: 'one which we are not aware of, so that we come out of the theatre and say later "I suppose there *was* a libretto."' [. . .]

I spoke to Glock after he'd been twice and like me he thinks the music an improvement. I'm glad.

I have told you a lot of good things in this letter. Fruits of a great deal of discussion and meditation about this problem. I don't suppose they'll all get over to you, because our mental processes are so different. But I should feel lacking in friendship if I didn't hand over to you all I have, as far as I can. You will write a lot of operas and something said to you now may work through unconsciously.

I shall be starting my own opera soon [*The Midsummer Marriage*] – but I shall not face all the problems I have outlined above, because the subject is so pantomimic.

Grace Williams, to whom Britten had been close in the 1930s, wrote, probably in July 1946:

Thank you very much for last night's *Lucretia*. The A cast is in every way vastly superior to the B and it is a pity they can't always function. On Monday, believe it or not, I heard hardly a word in the first scene – yet last night it was all perfectly clear.

The music – ça va mon vieux – though I didn't think it did after first hearing and even last night it was so bound up with the drama that I felt I wasn't concentrating on it enough – yet today, YES – *except* for the pre-rape Tarquinius music which I thought was wrong dramatically and humanly. A rape surely must build itself up urgently and swiftly – it can't suddenly lag and contemplate – and then get going again – now can it? Let your libertine have his moments of lyricism – but not *those* moments.

Apart from this it's all quite excellent drama of course. Whenever I looked at the Chorus I sort of caught my breath – and Lucretia – Ah —— (but *couldn't* her hair be braided – or whatever it was that Roman women did to their hair at night – during the rape scene? – the slightly tousled loose hair is un-classical and somehow rather unchaste (dishevel *any* woman and you'll make her look like a bawd).

Just one more thing which worried me – and that was a shadow bang in the middle of John Piper's magnificent back-cloth. What was it? The Male Chorus refers to Tarquinius' passing the bust of Collatinus in the hall – was it that?? But wasn't there a bust of Collatinus in the bed-chamber itself?? All I know is that my eyes found it a distracting blot – all I wanted to see was the roving shadow of Tarquinius – a *brilliant* piece of stage craft.

The libretto: why in heaven's or the devil's name drag in Jesus Christ? Who on earth wants a New Testament interpretation of Classical drama? Can't classical drama speak for itself? Of course it can – Wholesomely and completely. The *music* of chorus contra orchestra is splendid indeed – all you need is Exit J.C. written across the libretto *before* he puts in an appearance. In spite of these minor criticisms (which of course you will reject because of course you have faced up to all these problems long ago and must have very good reasons for doing as you have done – nevertheless I just can't resist having my say) – yes in spite of these things *Lucretia* is another winner.

4   *Lucretia* was performed at the Sadler's Wells Theatre between 28 August and 21 September.

5   A reference to Glyndebourne's practice of having an extended dinner interval, still a feature of their performances.

6   The Behrends' son (b. 1922), who in the late 1940s and 1950s occasionally helped out at Aldeburgh and who was Britten's and Pears's driver when on tour. See PPT, pp. 8–9, and plate 29.

532 **To Joan Cross**
From Eric Crozier, Benjamin Britten,
and Clare and Ralph Hawkes
[*Telegram*]

[Tanglewood], Lenox, Mass
1946 AUG 8

PETER [*Peter Grimes*] VERY NEARLY SUFFERED AWFUL FATE LUCRETIA.[1]
MURDER MOST FOUL IT WAS[2] BUT VERDICT UNANIMOUS ACQUITTAL.

LOVE
ERIC BEN CLARE RALPH

1 See Letter 536.

2 A near-quotation from *Peter Grimes*, Act III scene 1, when Mrs Sedley
sings, 'Murder most foul it is / Eerie I find it.'

533 **To Elizabeth Mayer**

Old Mill, Snape, Suffolk
August 20th 1946

My darling Elizabeth,
    It was wonderful to catch those glimpses of you – tantalising that they
weren't longer! It was fine that you were looking so well – & William in
such good form too. You were both sweet to me, and I am sorry if I
behaved in any way selfishly – but really the whole thing was such a rush,
& I felt very much dazed by the quickness of the travelling, & the strange-
ness of everything. Neither Eric nor I were properly "all there" all the
time, I'm afraid. Looking back on those mad days the impression is of a
bad nightmare illuminated by flashes of pure bliss, which was the being
with you at Douglaston.[1] One of the worst & most nightmarish bits was
the hanging around in that appalling heat waiting, literally from hour to
hour to leave. Do you know we actually didn't leave until 11.0 pm. on the
Saturday [10 August]? I didn't call you, because we had no idea how long
it was going to be, & Victor & Andrée[2] kept us going with cooling drinks
& by washing our shirts as they became impossible! (All our clothes were
at the airport all the time). The journey back was pretty nasty – definitely
not the way to travel, I feel; unless absolutely necessary. We went straight
up to Edinburgh,[3] arriving on Monday evening & as you may imagine,
Peter & I didn't stop talking about you for the whole week! He was so
jealous of my seeing you, & greedy for news of you. Then I came here on
Sunday [18 August], & the same thing all over again with Beth; but I don't
get tired of talking about you!

I talked with Ronald Duncan about the Lucretia translation. The man Vogel here hasn't turned out very satisfactory; so we've decided the best thing to do is for you to go ahead, with a collaborator of your choice if you want; & then when you are finished with the sketch to come over here & we can all work it out together.[4] You will get all this officially of course from Ralph or Heinsheimer – & they will give you an idea of when it should be ready by; but it really (quite seriously!) is essential for you to come over here, as we should discuss the possible musical changes that you will want to make, & some will be essential I know. Apart from two short periods in Holland, Peter & I will both be around this country until Christmas. I suggest October as the best month. Do you think that will be possible?[5] Beth is longing for you to come & stay with her. She'll be in her new house then;[6] but I'll be here still, & so we'll have to share you! We move into 3 Oxford Square, w. 2. on Monday next; the house is still in a bit of a mess, but eventually will be nice, we hope. Mr & Mrs Pears are there already.

Please tell Wystan that I'll send the Malfi music as soon as it is done – but there's quite a bit of it, & I feel very much in the dark about the whole matter. Still, I can cable I suppose if there are any major difficulties.[7]

I am so sorry that I had only that glimpse of Christopher, & none at all of Beata & Michael.[8] But next year I hope there'll be more chance. There seems quite a chance of Lucretia Company coming over in the Fall[9] – that I hope will wash out the memory of Grimes in Tanglewood!!

Much, much love to you my dearest & many thanks for everything you did.

Your loving,

BEN

Beth was thrilled by the stockings; & the hot-water bottle was a great success too. Thank you so much! I hope you're enjoying Pemaquid Point. Remember me to Maine![10]

1 Mrs Mayer had originally suggested that Britten should stay with her and her husband, William, when she learned that Britten would be crossing the Atlantic for the Tanglewood performances of *Peter Grimes*. She wrote on 3 July 1946:

When I opened the newspaper yesterday, I found amidst all the nauseating news, a little note, saying that Eric Crozier is coming to Tanglewood to be stage director for *Peter Grimes*, and that 'the composer will be present'. All the little black letters started to dance frantically in front of my eyes. Is it true? or just a rumour? it would be just *too* beautiful to be true. When I was rather sick at the beginning of 1946 I thought just a moment I would never see you again in my life – and it hurt terribly. Ben, my dear, I love you very much. The idea that I may close you once more in my arms, seems just at the moment almost too much for me. Do come! We shall be in our summer-commuting house in Douglaston, just 30 minutes drive from our town-apartment, so that you can have that for the two first weeks of August or the two last of July, however early you come. And I can take care of you once more a bit! It is all very small and crowded with things, but the best place I can imagine, in New York. Now also I can hope to get to hear *Peter Grimes*. I had given up all hope as I never got any answer from Tanglewood, or from Koussev.'s secretary.

Three days later, on 6 July, she wrote once again:

Clytie [Mundy] just called me, saying it was *certain* that you would come here with the Hawkes! Is it? I am quite shaken at the news – it will be wonderful, even if I should only get rare glimpses of you – I do hope to get in after all. I hope it won't be too much work for you – Clytie seems so worried about the Grimes part. If only Peter could take over!

In a night letter telegram sent to Mrs Mayer on 29 July from Manchester (where *Lucretia* was on tour), Britten indicated his plans:

LEAVING PAN-AMERICAN 31ST ARRIVAL TIME UNCERTAIN. PLEASE CONTACT HEINSHEIMER OR PAN-AMERICAN NEW YORK. DESPERATELY KEEN TO SPEND DAY WITH YOU BEFORE GOING TANGLEWOOD

On arrival Britten sent a telegram to Pears in Manchester (of which a pencil draft survives):

JUST ARRIVED. GOOD JOURNEY. STAYING NIGHT WITH ELIZABETH. GOING TANGLEWOOD LENOX MASSACHUSETTS TOMORROW. THINKING OF YOU ALL

A letter from the Friends of the Berkshire Music Center (3 July 1946) indicates that Dr and Mrs Mayer, their friends the lawyer Metcalfe Walling (see Letter 341 n. 1) and his wife, and Auden all attended a performance at Tanglewood together.

2 Victor = Victor Kraft, Aaron Copland's secretary and friend; see Letter 265 n. 2. André = Andrée Vilasse, who, according to Eric Crozier, was a woman friend of Copland's. Britten and Crozier camped out in her apartment for three days because of an unforeseen delay in their flight home.

3 Where *Lucretia* was on tour, 12–17 August. The tour obviously prevented Pears from taking part in the Tanglewood *Grimes*.

4 Correspondence between Erwin Stein and Mrs Mayer (held at BPL) indicates that Mrs Mayer worked on her German translation of *Lucretia* during the autumn of 1946. She was paid $400 for her work and delivered the completed draft by 1 November, in time for it to be entered into vocal scores intended for use in the forthcoming production in Basel (see Letter 539). The translation appears in the 1947 edition of the vocal score and in the published full and study scores (1949 and 1958). The identity of Vogel has not been established.

5 Mrs Mayer did not, in fact, come to England to discuss her translation. All its various refinements, including the revisions Britten and Duncan made

in 1947, were undertaken by letter. The precise dates of Britten's two trips to Holland cannot be determined exactly: his pocket engagement diary suggests that the first trip was made between 30 September and 10 October (this included the Dutch tour of *Lucretia* as well as recitals in Dordrecht and Entschede, and an orchestral concert in Utrecht). Erwin Stein described this tour to Elizabeth Mayer in a letter of 10 October, two days after his own return from Holland:

> It was very exciting there, a huge success, Ben was feted – in a word, we had a grand time. It was a pity you could not listen in [to a broadcast of *Lucretia*]. The performance which was broadcast was one of the best, but Joan Cross told me just now on the telephone that the Saturday performance, which took place after my departure, was still better.

The dates of the second trip are even less certain – the diary indicates that there were changes to the plans – but probably it ran from 26 October until 3 November. See Letters 538–40 for an account of this visit.

6   Beth had moved to The Shrubbery, at Hasketon, near Woodbridge, Suffolk. In EWB, p. 191, she writes:

> Kit and I had for some while been house-hunting in the Woodbridge area. We had bought a [general] practice in the village of Otley and Kit had been commuting from Snape to Otley, which became impossible for him, especially for night calls. Finally we had to be content with a very large run-down house near Woodbridge, which had been occupied by the army [. . .] So rather sadly I had to leave Ben and Snape in September 1946 and our life together came to an end.

Kit = Christopher ('Kit') Welford (1911–1973), Beth's husband and a doctor in general practice.

7   An adaptation of John Webster's *The Duchess of Malfi* was begun by Bertolt Brecht and H. R. Hays in the spring of 1943. Auden joined this collaboration in December of that year, following which Hays withdrew. During the next two years work progressed, with Brecht and Auden producing several versions. In 1946 Paul Czinner mounted a production of the adaptation as a vehicle for his wife, the actress Elisabeth Bergner. In the *New York Times* ('British director signed by Czinner', 22 August 1946) it was announced that George Rylands – 'thoroughly acquainted with *The Duchess*, having directed John Gielgud's London presentation' – was to direct the production. At Rylands's insistence, the adaptation was dropped in favour of Webster's original with some minor appendages by Auden alone. Outraged to discover the adapted version had been jettisoned, Brecht subsequently withdrew his name from the production.

    Auden probably approached Britten in the spring of 1946: Mrs Mayer writes to the composer on 27 March 1946, 'Yesterday Wystan told me that he is trying to get you over here, and that he talked with Ralph [Hawkes] about it. He will have written you about the music to *The Duchess of Malfi*, performed here in fall with Bergner.' No letter from Auden survives, but they must surely have discussed the incidental music when they met at

Tanglewood in August 1946. Already on 6 July, Elizabeth Mayer had reminded Britten that: 'Wystan is very happy that you come – he wants you also for the music to the *Duchess*.' Sam Zolotow reported in the *New York Times* (28 August 1946), that Britten 'is composing the overture and incidental music for *The Duchess of Malfi* [. . .] Paul Czinner, producer of the Elizabethan horror play confirmed the report.' Hawkes wrote to Britten on 9 September: '*Malfi*: I cabled about this for they want it at the end of next week since they open out of town on the 23rd of September [but see below]. I think I have been able to secure $1,250. for you and as there is no withholding tax, you will not suffer the 30% deduction.' Britten's pocket engagement diary contains the single entry 'Malfi' for 24 September.

The production, however, opened on 20 September 1946 at the Metropolitan Theatre, Providence, Rhode Island, from where it was toured to Boston (week of 23 September), Hartford (30 September and 1 October), New Haven (2–4 October), and Princeton, New Jersey (7–8 October), before reaching New York, where it played at the Ethel Barrymore Theatre from 15 October until 16 November. Brooks Atkinson, in the *New York Times* (16 October 1946), records that the incidental music by Britten was 'arranged by Ignatz Strasfogel' but makes no further mention of it in his notice. (Strasfogel's involvement remains unclear – he may have been the company's musical director.) Of Auden's adaptation Atkinson comments: 'W. H. Auden has revised the script to keep the duchess as the central figure straight on to the conclusion. But it still leaves the duchess as a weak figure among brutish men, and limits Miss Bergner's radiance to individual scenes.'

Britten's score for *The Duchess of Malfi* is lost. A royalty statement from Boosey & Hawkes, Inc., New York, suggests that the music was abandoned during the run of New York performances; the document reads: '*Duchess of Malfi*, Incidental Music / 11/4/46 [i.e. 4 November 1946]. Total of $950.00 received from Dr Paul Czinner after withdrawal of music from play.' Elizabeth Mayer gave Britten an account of the performance she had seen in a letter dated 4 March 1947:

They [Bergner and Czinner] are an awful lot, and Wystan can tell you a story about his experience. The whole performance was unbelievably bad, and also got unanimously bad notices. It was really an outrageous performance, everything falsified and mutilated, and your music was nowhere to be heard, only the Dirge was sung (not too badly even) by a singer in monk's habit who crossed the scene before the Duchess' execution.

The 'Dirge' may have been an adaptation of the 'Lyke-Wake Dirge' from the *Serenade*. Mrs Mayer had further cause for complaint in respect of Czinner and Bergner: they had borrowed her gramophone records of the *Serenade*, perhaps to listen to the 'Lyke-Wake Dirge', 'kept them for several weeks and then lost, broke or misplaced them: just the thing she *would* do, or her unreliable husband'.

However, the Czinners' borrowing of the *Serenade* 78s may be misleading in this context: Webster's text contains a celebrated dirge of its own, in

Act IV scene 2 – 'Hark, now everything is still, / The screech-owl, and the whistler shrill . . .' – which may well be the 'Dirge' referred to by Mrs Mayer. Until Britten's score comes to light, we cannot be certain. Edward Mendelson, in his edition of Auden's and Kallman's *Libretti and Other Dramatic Writings by W. H. Auden, 1939–73*, p. 461, notes that in Auden's and Brecht's 1946 version they interpolated Cornelia's dirge for her dead son from Webster's *The White Devil*, 'Call for the robin red-breast and the wren', as an interlude between scenes 3 and 4 of Act I. Professor Mendelson also notes Auden's and Brecht's interpolation of a song from George Peele's *The Old Wives' Tale* – 'When as the rye reach to the chin, / And chopcherry, chopcherry ripe within . . .', a text that was, coincidentally (or was it?), to be set by Britten in his *Spring Symphony* in 'The Driving Boy' (see Letter 602).

See also Letters 534 and 540; Humphrey Carpenter, *W. H. Auden: A Biography*, p. 338; PRIM, pp. 558–60; William Mann, 'The Incidental Music', in DMHK, p. 307; Eric Walter White, 'Britten in the Theatre: a Provisional Catalogue', *Tempo*, 107 (1973), pp. 2–8; Ronald Hayman, *Brecht: A Biography*, pp. 271–2, 279, 300–304; James K. Lyon, *Bertolt Brecht in America*, pp. 141–50; John Willett, *Brecht in Context*, pp. 35–6, 59–72, 120–21, and 216–18, and John Willett and Ralph Manheim (eds.), *Bertolt Brecht Collected Plays*, pp. 331–443.

8 William and Elizabeth Mayer's children; see also Letter 195 n. 1.

9 This proposal remained unfulfilled. Britten did not visit the US again until the autumn of 1949.

10 Britten and Pears had spent time at the Owl's Head Inn in Maine in August 1940 (see Letters 278–84) and found themselves staying in the same hotel as Kurt Weill ("awfully nice and sympathetic") and Maxwell Anderson. Pemaquid Point was where the Mayers usually took their annual summer holiday.

534 To Ralph and Clare Hawkes

Old Mill, Snape, Suffolk
August 22nd 1946

My dear Ralph & Clare,

I am afraid this is the first moment of quiet that I've managed to get since I got back – that is why you haven't heard from me before. I expect Eric told you that we finally didn't get away until 11. p.m. on the Saturday? It finally became a matter of endurance, & Victor and Andrée stuck it out magnificently, – washing our shirts, giving us cooling drinks, taking us to the Marx Brothers & generally coping with our jaded tempers through all the false alarms – I think there were five that day! Finally when we took off we could scarcely believe it. The journey back was rapid, & easy, only uncomfortable when we went too high. The arrival at Heathrow was at 11.0 pm. which was remarkably quick – 19 hours. We went straight up to Edinburgh the next day. Joan, Peter & Kathleen all meet us – they were

delighted with the presents, the chocolates, whiskey & ties. Joan hasn't
seen the bag yet – we're saving it for her birthday on Sept. 7th! The customs were cruel hard on us for it – but it is a beauty & well worth it. We
left the ham behind with heavy hearts[1] – we had already a good deal over-
weight, & the extra 33 dollars to pay that, with the doubt of getting it
through this end (coupled with the fact of our money getting very low)
were too much for our fading spirits. I'm afraid it is too heavy to send, &
you'll have so much to bring back with you – still, it was a nice idea &
thank you for it. Thank you, too, for everything you did for us – for all the
meals, taxis, & presents galore – & above all for your most sympathetic
understanding through a most trying experience. Both of us know that it
would have been wellnigh impossible to stick if you hadn't been around.
I hope you feel that the interest aroused hasn't been dampened by the
execrable performance. It was certainly most unfortunate, & seemed to
me to kill the work stone dead. But I hope I'm wrong. Anyhow it makes
me feel doubly cautious about the start of Lucretia. Every one is terribly
keen for the company here to come over complete. I feel that with my new
one, & the Purcell evening (Dido & the other), it will make an attractive
programme.[2] The discussions here are going well on them all – Ebert[3] is
stimulating & wise, & if we can get over some slight differences of opinion
on the managerial side, all seems set. The tour here isn't going too well.
Entre nous, Bing isn't too hot on touring, & the whole tour is being kept
a firm secret from the public. However the notices are fine, & by the end
of the week the audiences pick up. I don't think enough publicity is made
about our singers – after all, in the North my name & Glyndebourne's are
pretty unknown, whereas Joan, Peter, & people like Ferrier & Kraus[4]
(because of Messiahs, & all) are great drawers. However it's a good start,
& I'm glad we've done it, if it doesn't discourage Christie too much!

I got down here on Sunday, & am in the middle of the BBC overture,
but with no great enthusiasm, I'm afraid.[5] My heart is in the opera &
Koussey's Symphony (which is exciting me a great deal!!).[6] Still, it's got to
be done, & it probably isn't as lame as I feel it is now – & then there is
[*The Duchess of*] Malfi to be coped with, & there is more in that than I
had expected. I feel a bit at sea with that too – no real ideas of what they
want from me. But they'll have to put up with what they get from me, &
at this late date they'll be lucky if they get anything!

I've talked with Ronnie about the translation of "Lucretia". He isn't
happy about the man here – Vogel – & suggests that Elizabeth find her
own collaborator in U.S.A. & then come over when it's done & discuss it.
I think that's the most satisfactory scheme.

We move in to 3 Oxford Square on Monday, Beth & her family into
their new mansion near here on Sept. 7th, leaving me with half this place

empty. So furniture is quite an item on our agenda now. If we sent some detailed lists of small things, Clare dear, do you think you could, at your leisure, cope with some of them – i.e. if my royalty account can stand it!! – not dining room tables, but really small things!

I envy you Bermuda. The weather is atrocious – we haven't seen the sun recently. But you deserve the rest, so enjoy it!

With much love & many thanks again.

Yours ever,

BEN

1 A reminder that there were still difficulties in obtaining some foods in the UK for some time after the end of the war. Rationing was also to continue for a number of years to come.

2 The programme for the first performance of *Lucretia* had carried an advertisement for the 1947 Glyndebourne Festival, to be held 4–26 July: *Lucretia* was to be revived, and Purcell's *Dido and Aeneas* 'edited by Benjamin Britten together with a new Contemporary Opera'. In RDBB (p. 84), Ronald Duncan recalls that

While we were rehearsing *Lucretia* John Christie invited Ben and me to write a new opera which he promised to present the following year. Ben agreed and said he wanted to write a comedy. This put our idea of writing an opera on Abelard and Heloise [see Letter 464 n. 6 and Letter 572] out of the question, and since the new opera in Glyndebourne was to be a chamber opera, *The Canterbury Tales* [see Letter 478 n. 4 and Letters 490 and 496] wasn't suitable either. During *Lucretia* rehearsals Ben had decided he wanted to write a work for Kathleen Ferrier.

It was Joan Cross who eventually produced a subject for us by suggesting *Mansfield Park*. She went off to Brighton especially to buy me a copy of the novel so that I could re-read it. As usual Ben was excited by the idea especially because the story was suitable for Kathleen, with a good part for Joan too. They were both anxious to get Jane Austen's elegant urbanity on to the operatic stage [. . .] We had settled on the title *Letters to William*. The Christies were delighted, mainly because Ben had said there would be a part for Audrey's pug.

Elsewhere in RDBB (pp. 91–2), Duncan writes:

I was writing my second verse play, *Stratton* [. . .] but with Ben's insistence, I dropped my play and went back to Devonshire and immediately continued to write the libretto of *Mansfield Park* entitled *Letters to William*. The reason for this change of title was that he wished to write a letter-scene. Perhaps this wish was something to do with Tchaikovsky's letter-scene in *Eugene Onegin*? [. . .]. [Pears's synopsis for *Letters to William* includes the note: 'Big letter scene for Fanny'. Britten was in fact to compose a letter-scene in 1954 in *The Turn of the Screw*, Act II scene 3.]

Then a couple of months later I went to London on some other business and Marion [Stein] told me that Ben was already working on another opera, *Albert Herring*, with Eric Crozier [. . .] I was dumbfounded. Ben could easily have told me of this change of plans. We had frequently spoken on the telephone. He knew that I had put my play *Stratton* aside half-written, to work on *Letters to William*.

From Ronald Duncan's draft libretto of *Letters to William*, Act I

I now confronted Ben. He admitted the position, looked sheepish but gave no explanation.

The precise chronology of these events is unclear, but a letter from Elizabeth Mayer to Britten (19 November 1946), mentions the Jane Austen opera:

Do you already work at the next opera? who is going to do the libretto? I wish you would take *once* John Betjeman [see Letter 561 n. 5] as a librettist. I have been reading many of his poems, and think that he is adorable – form and contents – and just the light touch, *Mansfield Park* f.i. [for instance] would need. But you have probably decided already.

The BPL possesses a draft libretto of Act I of *Letters to William* in Duncan's hand, as well as an annotated copy of Jane Austen's novel (a Macmillan edition of 1926), one of a set of Austen's novels originally belonging to Pears, accompanied by some notes on the characters and a synopsis in Pears's hand. The copy of *Mansfield Park* contains annotations by the composer, including a draft cast list with the names of possible singers who might play the roles:

Sir B. [Sir Thomas Bertram]	Owen [Brannigan]
Lady B. [Bertram]	Mabel [Ritchie]
Mrs Norris	Joan [Cross]
Mary C. [Crawford]	Nancy E [Evans]
Henry C. [Crawford]	?
Fanny	Kathleen [Ferrier]
Maria	?Anna [Pollak]
Edmund	Peter [Pears]
Rushworth	?

Small characters
    Dr & Mrs Grant

In 1981 Duncan had in his possession a synopsis of the opera in Britten's hand (RDBB, p. 6).

Among the other annotations in the *Mansfield Park* volume is a two-bar sketch for the A major second subject of the *Occasional Overture*, composed in September 1946; see n. 5.

The idea of a 'Purcell evening' – the work intended to complement *Dido and Aeneas* remains unidentified – demonstrates unequivocally how important Purcell had become for Britten since 1945. As with *Letters to William*, this project was laid to one side; it was not until 1951 that Britten was finally to make an edition of Purcell's opera (see Letter 698 n. 3).

3   Carl Ebert (1887–1980), German, naturalized American producer and administrator. Ebert trained as an actor under Max Reinhardt at a school attached to the Deutsches Theater, Berlin. After working as an actor (1915–27) he was appointed General Administrator and Producer of the Landestheater, Darmstadt, where his first opera, *Figaro*, was produced and in 1931 he joined the Berlin Städtische Oper where he remained for two

years. After the Nazis came to power in 1933 he left Germany, working in Salzburg, Florence and South America; in 1934 Ebert and Fritz Busch inaugurated the Glyndebourne Festival where he was Artistic Director, 1934–39, and again 1947–59. He subsequently worked in the US, and was General Administrator of the Städtische Oper, West Berlin, 1954–61.

Ebert is chiefly remembered for his productions of the operas of Mozart and Verdi, but all his productions were noted for their sharpness of detail and intensive rehearsal periods. See also Spike Hughes, *Glyndebourne: A History of the Festival Opera Founded in 1934 by Audrey and John Christie.*

4 Otakar Kraus (1909–1980), British baritone of Czech birth, who created the role of Tarquinius in *The Rape of Lucretia.* Kraus studied in Prague and Milan before making his debut in Brno in 1935, and was a member of the Bratislava Opera, 1936–39. After emigrating to England in 1940 he sang with the Carl Rosa Opera, and subsequently worked at home and abroad with the English Opera Group: Lockit (*The Beggar's Opera*) and Mr Gedge (*Albert Herring*). He was chosen by Stravinsky to play Nick Shadow in the premiere of *The Rake's Progress* in Venice in 1951 (see Letter 713). A member of the Covent Garden Company, 1951–68, Kraus took part in the British stage premiere of *Wozzeck* (1952) and created the roles of Diomede in Walton's *Troilus and Cressida* (1954) and King Fisher in Tippett's *The Midsummer Marriage* (1955). Other Britten roles in his repertory at Covent Garden included Cecil (*Gloriana*) and Balstrode (*Peter Grimes*).

5 The *Occasional Overture* in C, composed to mark the opening of the BBC's Third Programme, their new cultural channel which sought to offer the very best of music, drama, poetry and talks. The overture, billed in the *Radio Times* as 'Festival Overture', was first performed at the opening concert of the Third Programme, a live broadcast from the BBC's Maida Vale Studios, by the BBC Symphony Orchestra conducted by Sir Adrian Boult. Other works in the programme included Vaughan Williams's *Serenade to Music* and Bliss's *Music for Strings* (conducted by the composer), and works by Purcell, Handel and Parry. See Humphrey Carpenter, *The Envy of the World: Fifty Years of the BBC Third Programme and Radio 3, 1946–1996,* pp. 29–31, and PKSB, pp. 70–71.

Britten was approached by Etienne Amyot, a programme planner with the new channel, in June 1946; they met on 1 July. Amyot reported to George Barnes, Controller of the Third Programme:

It was a very sticky dinner until drink made both of them [Britten and Erwin Stein] a little more amiable. The first half of the dinner was a tremendous attack against the BBC by Britten which threatened at moments to become quite hysterical. He said he had no faith in the new programme and that, though we might for a week or two spend a lot of money and time in trying to get the things we wanted, the Service, like the Home and the Light, would disintegrate by Christmas and be indistinguishable from either A or B. I found the real difficulty with Britten was that he spoke not so much his own thoughts as the thoughts of Mr Stein, who is obviously his Svengali [. . .] But towards the end of the evening he was infinitely more amenable, and I found, by ignoring Stein completely and concentrating entirely on Britten, that I was able to change his point of view; so much, that he said he would very much like to write a Festival Overture for our opening concert on 29th September. My own impression of Britten is that he is charming and that I can always get on with him. I think Stein is a stumbling block and at the moment seems to control with an iron hand all Britten's movements.

Victor Hely-Hutchinson wrote to Britten on 6 July to say how pleased he was that Britten had agreed to write the overture. Britten replied from Glyndebourne on the 17th:

I will do my best to write a Festival Overture for your third programme in October. As time is rather short and I have to dash around the world before then, I am afraid I cannot guarantee a very long and weighty opus, but I am sure I can do something suitably festive for you!

Please let me know as soon as possible the actual date of the performance and the deadline for delivery of the score.

The score was required by 4 September to allow for orchestral parts to be copied in time for the concert on the 29th. The manuscript full score is dated 14 September 1946. Britten attended a rehearsal of the overture on 28 September at 6 p.m. at the BBC's Maida Vale Studios before departing for the Netherlands later that evening. According to Michael Kennedy, 'there was trouble over inaccuracies in the parts' (*Adrian Boult*, p. 206), and a letter was sent from Eric Thompson (of Boosey & Hawkes) to Boult, the day after the broadcast, explaining that the BBC had been entirely responsible for the production of the orchestral parts and asking Boult to make it clear to the orchestra that any inaccuracies were not the fault of the publishers. Boult responded: there were no inaccuracies in the orchestral material, but difficulties had been encountered because some of the parts (which had been photographically reproduced) were rather too small. (Boult's comments are borne out by the original orchestral material, now held at BPL.)

A brief notice of the first performance appeared in *The Times* (1 October 1946):

It [the opening concert of the Third Programme] began with a new Festival Overture specially commissioned from Benjamin Britten. This appeared to be rich in invention and bright-lived in texture, as well as festive in mood, though it is impossible to assess critically from the uni-dimensional reduction of it given by radio hearing.

Although it has generally been believed that Britten withdrew the *Occasional Overture* immediately after the premiere, this now appears not to have been the case. A tape recording of another performance conducted by Boult, this time apparently with the Boston Symphony Orchestra, was given to BPL in the mid-1980s. Perhaps this was the performance of which Elizabeth Mayer writes on 9 December 1946:

Last night I could just have a vague impression on the Radio of your Festival Ouverture [*sic*], but it did not come over very clear, in spite of the cold – cold weather which has come over us with the usual vehemence.

The work was withdrawn and not revived until after Britten's death, when it was given by the Chicago Symphony Orchestra conducted by Raymond Leppard on 28 April 1983. The *Occasional Overture* was published by Faber Music in 1984, the year in which it was first recorded by the City of Birmingham Symphony Orchestra conducted by Simon Rattle (EMI EL 2702631).

6 To become *Spring Symphony*, commissioned by the Koussevitzky Foundation and dedicated to 'Serge Koussevitzky and the Boston Symphony Orchestra'. Koussevitzky proposed the commission for the symphony to Ralph Hawkes, who wrote to the composer from New York on 14 March 1946:

> Koussey has asked me whether you'd be interested in accepting a [$]1000 commission from the K. Fdn for a symphony with voice – the voice to be an integral part of the orchestration and it is to be for Carol Brice – mezzo voice (see enclosure). He said he would write to you direct and I stated that I'd no idea how you would consider it but I knew you were plenty busy. He might want it by Jan–Feb 1947 (???).

The 'enclosure' was a page from *Time* (11 March 1946) containing a report of the Boston debut of twenty-seven-year-old black American singer Carol Brice. The report states: 'Koussevitzky's current ambition: to commission a symphony with a contralto obbligato part for her, so that she can tour with the orchestra.' Koussevitzky no doubt discussed the symphony during Britten's visit to Tanglewood. As Letter 546 makes apparent, it was a work that Koussevitzky hoped to premiere at Tanglewood in 1947. The Carol Brice suggestion was not pursued.

535 To Imogen Holst

Old Mill, Snape, Suffolk
Aug 22nd 1946

My dear Imogen,

Your sweet letter about Lucretia has been so long unanswered – but I have had to spend some miserable time in U.S.A. with Grimes, & to tour a bit with the Glyndebourne Company, in the meantime, & I've only just got here to the first peace & quiet for many months! Your appreciation and understanding of my work, of Lucretia especially, gives me great pleasure, & great encouragement. Coming from someone whose personality & mind I admire as much as yours, it is really valuable to me. Especially the manner in which you approach the Christian idea delighted me. I used to think that the day when one could shock people was over – but now, I've discovered that being simple & considering things spiritual of importance, produces reactions nearly as violent as the Sacre [Stravinsky's *The Rite of Spring*] did! I have never felt so strongly that what we've done is in the right direction, & that the faded "intellectuals" are dangerously wrong![1]

I was so sorry not to see more of you during the time you were in Glyndebourne. But the rehearsals were all absorbing I'm afraid – but it was a pity, because I do so enjoy talking with you. If you ever come up to London – do let me know, & perhaps we could have a meal together. Peter & I move to 3 Oxford Square, W.2., next Monday. The opera is at Sadler's Wells for three weeks from next Wednesday, & I shall be round about most of the time. Forgive this letter – I write it late at night, after a hard day at an overture for the BBC which I am not too interested in – ! What are you writing? I hope your students don't take all your energies, but it is a very worthwhile work you're doing.

Many thanks for your great understanding & kindness,
Yours ever,
BEN

1 Imogen Holst had written to Britten from Dartington Hall, Totnes, in Devon, where she was Director of Music in the Arts Department, on 15 July:

This is to try and thank you for allowing me to listen to the rehearsals of *Lucretia*. There are no words to tell you how grateful I am for having had such a wonderful opportunity to learn something about the work. It became more and more exciting at each hearing, and now that I am back in Dartington it is continuously in my mind, to the detriment of my pupils' harmony and counterpoint excersizes [*sic*].

Those of us who know your music were expecting a miracle, but I don't think we anticipated *such* a miracle. It is a miracle to have packed so much intensity into a couple of hours and to have achieved such a perfect balance of changing moods and to have used your material so amazingly economically that the mind can grasp the form and hold it even at a first hearing.

And *what* a miracle the instrumentation is! The sheer volume of tone from those dozen players was astounding: surely there can be no doubt that it will still sound full even in a large opera house. As for the things you ask them to play! – I am still suffering from suppressed heart attack from the excitement of listening to the surging of the river at the end of the ride and the high glittering shimmer halfway through the spinning song. But more than any exciting detail it is the wholeness of the thing that remains in the mind: I was conscious of this in *Grimes*, but to a far greater extent in *Lucretia*.

It is so seldom that dramatized tragedy emerges from its own four walls and its own half-dozen characters:– you have made it the one thing that matters to everybody, and no one who has listened to the 'It is all' scene will ever be quite the same person afterwards. It is a 1946 B minor mass and it is what we have all been wanting and waiting for, whether we realized it or not.

We were all thinking of you on Friday night. It was hard to have to come away before your first night: I came back to a rehearsal of Bach's *Jesu meine Freude*, and as it happened it was one of the few pieces of music in the world that was *just* right after a week of *Lucretia*.

Thank you again for the unforgettable privilege of hearing the rehearsals, and thank you as always for the music you write.

536 To Edward Sackville-West

Old Mill, Snape, Suffolk
August 23rd 1946

My dear Eddy,

Your nice letter about "Lucretia"[1] arrived just before I set off for U.S.A.
to see what a wit over there aptly named my Opera III[2] – "the Rape of
Peter Grimes". The moment I got back I had to go up to Edinburgh to see
how "Lucretia" herself was faring, & I've only just been able to get here &
have a little peace, much overdue too.

I am glad that on the whole you approve of the new piece. You certainly
say some gratifying things about it. What surprises me a little, my dear, is
a rather marked lack of <u>faith</u> that you show in me. Given that you approve
of my talent generally, isn't it possible that, if there are some passages that
you find confusing and/or inadequate, it is because you yourself aren't
familiar enough with it to see what I am aiming at? You dismiss the beginning of Act II as a history lesson; but isn't it fairly obvious that it is a history
lesson with a fairly unusual atmosphere; there are plenty of reasons why
you might have missed the point of this scene (such as the long dinner
interval, for one), but what I ask for is the benefit of the doubt! How you
fail to receive Lucretia's 'point of view' in the rape scene is beyond me; but
I hope that when you get the score you will change your mind about this.
Of course it doesn't matter in a letter (apart from making one a little
cross); it is when it happens in reviews that it may be harmful. One expects
it with the critics who quite genuinely loathe one's work (in the case of
Lucretia, at least 25%), but with those who profess to sympathise – remarks
such as: I like the work, but why on page . . . does the composer . . . ? upset
& mislead potential audiences of the work. My own feeling about works
of artists whom I love & trust, is that when there are passages I don't like
or understand, that it's my fault, & that if I work hard enough or love
enough then one day I shall see the light! But, then we probably disagree
about the function of critics – I only want the John the Baptist kind, &
have no use for the Herod type!

It is a long time since we met – I am sorry to have been so elusive
recently. I hope that the next three weeks or so when I shall be more or
less anchored to London that we can meet & chat; I have lots of things to
tell you. On top of a pressure of work & travelling, my domestic affairs are
undergoing a change – Beth moves out of here soon, & I have to cope
with the place alone, & we move in London to 3 Oxford Square, W.2. And
you haven't yet seen my new car – that'll make you laugh, but I have a
hunch that it will be your cup of tea.[3]

I expect you have by now got rid elsewhere of the Frigidaire – & it
serves me right too. But anyhow the power question was doubtful, & with

all this furniture buying, car expense, & moving I simply couldn't have afforded it. So perhaps it's a good thing. But thank you for being so patient about it.

I hope you are well, my dear. I hope to see you soon.

With love,

Yours,

BEN

1   Sackville-West had written to Britten on 15 July 1946:

Having now heard *Lucretia* twice (I am going again on the 25th) I want to tell you what very great pleasure most of it gave me. On the first night I failed to make much of the first scene, but in the second it made at least twice as much impression on me; indeed the whole of the first act seems to me to succeed to admiration. I think your handling of the orchestra and voices quite masterly and inexhaustibly fascinating to listen to. I do not see how the actual drama could have been heightened – except in the scene of the rape, where the music somehow failed to make me feel Lucretia's emotion. My fault, perhaps, but I can't help thinking that the subsequent chorale – beautiful as it is in itself – does not really carry through the situation as it should. You will not have expected me to like the historical introduction to act 2, and I didn't; also it does not prepare one for the scene that is to follow.

Apart from these two points I have nothing but admiration for the opera, and personally I like the last scene of all the best – from Lucretia's return (that cor anglais solo was a great inspiration) to the end. I think there is some confusion arising from your attempt to meld the two moralities together – but that is a purely intellectual criticism and in no way affects the music of the epilogue, which is quite lovely.

It is a work I shall, I feel sure, want to hear again and again. From an artistic point of view I am sure it is an advance on *Grimes* and in every way one of the very best things you have done. [. . .] I do congratulate you on a most wonderful achievement and a quite unique operatic experience. Your musical imagination is really astonishing [. . .]

I think John Piper did you proud, too. Lovely sets.

Sackville-West responded to Britten's letter on 31 August, defending his integrity as a critic and arguing with Britten on the role of criticism. He concludes his letter:

However much one admires an artist – and you of all people, my dear Ben, cannot reasonably doubt my admiration for your work – one cannot just be his tame cat. [. . .] I hope my remarks, which made you so cross, will not have blotted out in your mind the very great admiration which I expressed (and feel) for *Lucretia*. I shall continue to go and hear it, in the hope that repeated hearings may change my opinion of the rape (the history lesson is another matter: I could never like that). And once again – I *have* faith in you, as everything I have ever written or said about you has made abundantly clear to everyone except yourself! Indeed, I am generally regarded as hopelessly prejudiced in your favour – as of course I am!

Sackville-West ends his letter by inviting Britten to Long Crichel (see pp. 133–4).

2 To the Americans, who would have known of Britten's 1941 operetta, *Paul Bunyan*, *The Rape of Lucretia* was indeed Britten's third stage piece.

3 Britten had recently purchased a 1929 Rolls-Royce Shooting Brake (see PFL, plate 239), which he kept until 1964. Humphrey Carpenter writes: 'Eric Crozier says that soon afterwards Vaughan Williams turned up at an orchestral rehearsal in a Rolls, countering the players' surprised comments with: "Well, why shouldn't I? Ben Britten's got one!"' (HCBB, p. 240).

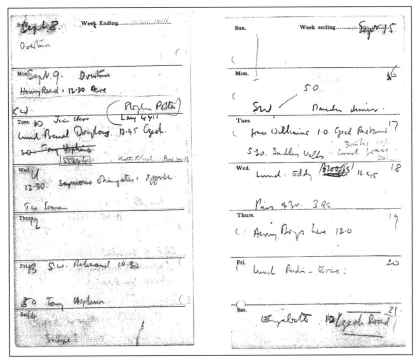

Britten's diary, 8–21 September 1946. Among the entries can be seen:
'Overture' [i.e. rehearsals for Britten's *Occasional Overture*] (8th and 9th);
'Stephen Potter' (9th); 'Grace Williams 1.0. Czech Restaurant' (17th),
and 'Lunch: Eddy [Sackville-West] Brooks 12.45' (18th).

537 To John Christie[1]
From Eric Crozier, with Benjamin Britten
[Typed][2]

The Old Mill, Snape, Suffolk
October 19th, 1946

Dear John,

At our meeting last Tuesday with Mr Edwards[3] and Rudi Bing you explained to me that you would not be able to undertake financial responsibility for the English Opera Group next year beyond the actual Glyndebourne Festival. You were also not certain whether the name of Glyndebourne should be used by the Group in future for touring, because of the poor conditions of work in provincial theatres, and the consequent drop in the quality of performances.

I have discussed both these points thoroughly with Ben. Both of us sincerely regret your financial loss from the past season, and appreciate your inability to risk so much again on activities outside Glyndebourne. But we feel strongly that our work must include touring as an essential part of our policy.

Neither of us is happy about the suggestion from your side that G. [Glyndebourne] should present us for a short Festival season, and that we should then tour under our own financial organisation. This brings a division of control that will not work out well either in administration or artistic direction. It seems clear to us that whether we may or may not tour in future under the name of Glyndebourne, there is a fundamental difference in interest between your view of touring and our own.

After consideration, Ben and I have reached this decision. We intend immediately to set up a non-profit-making company of our own, and to collect private capital for the launching of our next season. We shall finance the production of the new opera ourselves, and would like to consider buying the production of "Lucretia" from G. if C. [Christie] will sell it to us. The new company will be administered by a Board of Directors.[4] Ben and I will serve as joint executive managers, and we shall appoint a General Manager to handle all our financial affairs.

If Glyndebourne would like to present us next season, we shall naturally be delighted to stage both the new opera and "Lucretia" there for two or three weeks, as we had originally planned. You will appreciate that both the administration and the artistic direction of the new company will be our own responsibility. You may not wish, of course, to have an independent group at Gly. – but if you should care to engage us for 1947, we shall be happy to discuss your suggestions.

As for the production of the new opera, you will remember that we agreed – against our own opinion – to your definite wish that Charles [sic]

Ebert should do it, because this was an implicit obligation on your part towards him in any G. sponsored venture. Under the new arrangement we do not feel that this obligation holds, and we shall revert to our original intention that Eric should produce. We shall write to Charles about the radical change in our plans, and enclose a copy of this letter to you.

The whole purpose behind our change in plans for next year is towards creating an organisation that can best develop and extend the particular conception we have of contemporary opera. We are enormously grateful to Audrey[5] and to yourself for the courage you have shown and the vital part you have played in helping to crystallise our ideas into a first season of performances during 1946. We feel, however, that the idea itself is of greater scope than a limited G. Festival, and must have a kind of organisation that will cater for performances wherever there is an audience for them.

Yours sincerely,
sgd   Eric Crozier
Benjamin Britten

1   An important letter in which many of Britten's and Crozier's dissatisfactions with their association with Glyndebourne are spelled out, and in which Britten and Crozier map out the basic principles of their new opera company, the English Opera Group. For a detailed account and analysis of the formation of the EOG, see PKSB, chapter 3, but especially pp. 74–86.

2   Abbreviations in the text and the use of 'Charles' for Carl Ebert suggest this might be a record made for Britten's files of a possibly handwritten original.

3   W. E. Edwards worked for John Christie between 1920 and 1953. Although Christie always referred to him as his accountant, he was in fact much more than this and advised Christie on all matters concerned with the administration of the family estates and business enterprises, including the Festival Opera.

4   The Board of Directors of the English Opera Group, founded in 1946, comprised Rt Hon. Oliver Lyttelton (1893–1972, Chairman), Sir Kenneth Clark (Baron Clark; 1903–1983), Tyrone Guthrie, Ralph Hawkes, Hon. Mervyn Horder (1910–1997), Denis Rickett (1907–1997), Hon. James F. A. Smith and Erwin Stein; Britten and Crozier were joined by John Piper as Artistic Directors.

The public announcement of the Group's formation, a document dating from early 1947 (PFL, plate 212), sets out its artistic policy:

We believe the time has come when England, which has never had a tradition of native opera, but has always depended on a repertory of foreign works, can create its own operas. Opera is as much a vital means of artistic expression as orchestral music, drama, and painting. The lack of it has meant a certain impoverishment of English artistic life.

We believe the best way to achieve the beginnings of a repertory of English operas is through the creation of a form of opera requiring small resources of singers and players, but suitable for performance in large or small opera houses or theatres.

A first essay in this direction was the writing and staging of Britten's *The Rape of Lucretia* in 1946. *Lucretia* was an experiment towards finding a flexible and sensitive operatic form built on the collaboration of small numbers of singers, musicians and other artists. *Lucretia* was given 80 performances in 1946 – more performances than any other British opera has had in its first season, with two exceptions, since the beginning of the century.

The success of this experiment has encouraged the three persons chiefly involved – Benjamin Britten, the composer; Eric Crozier, the producer; and John Piper, the designer – to continue their work as a group by establishing, under their artistic direction, a new opera company to be known as THE ENGLISH OPERA GROUP, incorporated on a non-profit-making basis. This Group will give annual seasons of contemporary opera in English and suitable classical works including those of Purcell.

It is part of the Group's purpose to encourage young composers to write for the operatic stage, also to encourage poets and playwrights to tackle the problem of writing libretti in collaboration with composers.

Benjamin Britten is now writing his third opera – *Albert Herring*, a comedy about life in a Suffolk village. It is scored for 12 singers and 12 players. Its first performance, and a revival of *The Rape of Lucretia*, is planned for the Group's first season this year, which will open at Glyndebourne on June 20th. The Group hope to give a short season at the Royal Opera House, Covent Garden in early October. There will be a provincial tour, and visits to Continental festivals are under discussion.

The Group are assured of the support of many leading singers and players, and the cast for this year's season will include Joan Cross, Peter Pears, Margaret Ritchie, Nancy Evans, Otakar Kraus and Flora Nielsen. The small orchestra of leading chamber music players will include Joy Boughton, John Francis and Stephen Waters. The producers of the two operas will be Carl Ebert and Eric Crozier. [In the event, Ebert was not involved: see Letter 545 n. 4.] The sets will be by John Piper and the conductors will be Benjamin Britten and Reginald Goodall.

The Arts Council has already generously promised financial assistance, which cannot however be expected to cover the Group's initial requirements. To enable the Group to begin work, a total sum of £12,000 is urgently needed as working capital. Of this, the sum of £2000 has already been generously given by a private subscriber.

The British Council will sponsor any Continental tour undertaken by the Group, but owing to other commitments is unable to give financial assistance this year.

The anonymous 'private subscriber' who donated £2000 was Dorothy Elmhirst, who had originally made an offer of considerable financial support to Britten and Crozier late in 1945 before Glyndebourne had become involved in the plans for the production of *Lucretia*. A letter from Rudolf Bing to John Christie (7 February 1946; Glyndebourne Archive) makes it clear that Mrs Elmhirst felt that her support was made redundant by the Christies agreeing to stage *Lucretia* at Glyndebourne, and that both she and her husband, Leonard Elmhirst, felt 'acute disappointment' that Britten's and Crozier's scheme would not now be presented at Dartington. Bing's account of this matter does not accord with that of Leonard Elmhirst, who, following a meeting with Crozier on 6 January 1946, wrote to Britten: 'Please don't worry for one minute about those castles in the air we built around a possible season in Dartington. How we should have enjoyed having you all for rehearsals and an opening in the Barn theatre – wonderful for us and Dartington and we had hoped, for you too – but for the idea, not so good really.'

5 Audrey Mildmay (1900–1953), English soprano and wife of John Christie. After studying in London and Vienna, she sang a number of roles with the Carl Rosa Opera before her marriage in 1931 to Christie, with whom she helped found the Glyndebourne Festival Opera. Mildmay sang at Glyndebourne, 1934–36 and 1938–39, where she was, in Carl Ebert's words, 'an unforgettable Susanna and Zerlina as well as the heart and spirit of Glyndebourne'. Post-war, she assisted Rudolf Bing in the founding of the Edinburgh Festival.

OPERA AS A PROFESSION

A COURSE OF LECTURES AND PRACTICAL DEMONSTRATIONS
TO BE HELD AT TOYNBEE HALL LONDON E.I.

SEPTEMBER 18th—22nd inclusive   Lecturers will be :

JOAN CROSS   BARBARA WARD   PETER PEARS   ERIC CROZIER
TYRONE GUTHRIE   HANS OPPENHEIM

If the response is encouraging a POST-GRADUATE STUDIO FOR OPERA will be established in connection with GLYNDEBOURNE
Further details from
THE GLYNDEBOURNE OFFICES, 66, GREAT CUMBERLAND PLACE, LONDON, W.I

'Opera as a Profession': this advertisement appeared
in the programme for *The Rape of Lucretia*
at the Sadler's Wells Theatre, August 1946

538 To Eric Crozier

American Hotel, Amsterdam
October 27th 1946

My dear Eric,

I hope that this note will find you happily installed at 3 Oxford Square – it can't be 'comfortably' yet I'm afraid, but we'll get that right in time![1] I also hope you're feeling better & that your giddynesses didn't develop into serious troubles in your 'duodenum'. If so, follow Peter's advice – take it to a doctor.

Things are going fairly well here. The journey over was exceedingly rough & uncomfortable – we took some time to settle down after it, & poor Peter's throat is being a nuisance again. However with massaging (& soft & oily drinks) administered daily by a throat chap, he's managing to get through (with the usual hymns of praise in the press whenever he opens his mouth!).

Peter Diamand[2] is his usual efficient & charming self, & everything is organised to a T. He's very relieved that we've made our great decision, & very hopeful about the future here. I think he ought to come over as soon as possible & talk to us & Brit. Council. Any luck with Business managers? I hope that the Christies & Bing aren't being too vile – try & put meetings off till I get back on Monday to help you! I was going to write a nice note to Audrey but on second thoughts I'll wait till I get back & discuss it with you. Everyone sends lots of love to you – Cronheims[3] & all. They were thrilled with their bicycles. We send love to you & all near & dear to you. (I'm speaking your commentary to the Y.P.'s Guide with the Concertgebouw next Sunday – – – !!!!).[4]

> Much love – don't worry.
>
> BEN

(P.P.P.S. How's Albert?)[5]

1 Crozier had two rooms in the uppermost storey of Pears's London home.

2 Dutch-naturalized administrator of Austrian birth (1913–1998) and Britten's and Pears's European agent at this period. (Diamand first suggested he might act for them in March 1946.) After having been forced by the Nazis to abandon his law studies at Berlin University, Diamand was Artur Schnabel's secretary, 1934–38. He spent the war years in Holland; subsequently, he was Assistant to the Director of the Netherlands Opera (1946–48), and was appointed First Secretary to the Holland Festival in 1947 – it was launched in 1948 – and later Artistic Director, remaining in post until 1965. He succeeded Lord Harewood as Artistic Director of the Edinburgh Festival and in 1978 became General Manager of the Royal Philharmonic Orchestra. There can be no doubt that it was Diamand who encouraged both Britten and Pears to visit the Netherlands in the immediate post-war years and later, and who, through the Holland Festival and his contacts elsewhere in the Dutch and European musical communities, provided a bridgehead for their work in Europe. See also obituaries in the *Daily Telegraph* (19 January 1998), *The Times* (20 January 1998), by John Calder, 'A diplomat at the festival', *Guardian* (19 January 1998), and by Richard Demarco, *Independent* (21 January 1998).

In a broadcast interview with John Drummond (BBC Radio 3, 17 August 1992), Diamand recalled his earliest meetings with Britten:

I met, in 1946, Britten and Pears when they came to Amsterdam for their first concert [...] it was dreadful at this time: there was no food; there was no heating; there was no light; they stayed in a miserable hotel. I had heard quite a lot about Britten, and I wanted to meet him, so I just went there and said can I say hello to you; and they were pleased to see anyone there. There was very good contact. They were received tremendously warmly in Holland [. . .] their recitals were absolutely a revelation. I worked for some time – for a couple of years – until I joined the Holland Festival, as their personal representative in Holland and quite a number of European countries. That was wonderful.

I went to Glyndebourne (I knew Rudi Bing quite well), at the rehearsals of *The Rape of Lucretia*, and heard Kathleen Ferrier. I was absolutely bowled over by her. I wanted to introduce her to Holland. Her agent told me that this was a very, very primitive idea which I should give up as quickly as possible. She was [he claimed] a typical English oratorio singer; already *The Rape of Lucretia* taxed her beyond her possibilities.

3 Paul Cronheim (1893–1975), Director of the Netherlands Opera in Amsterdam.

4 Britten's *A Young Person's Guide to the Orchestra* was the opening work in a concert given by the Concertgebouw Orchestra conducted by Eduard van Beinum in Amsterdam on the afternoon of 3 November. A Dutch translation of Crozier's commentary was printed in the programme.

HET CONCERTGEBOUWORKEST

dirigent : **EDUARD VAN BEINUM**
soliste : **EILEEN JOYCE**, piano

PROGRAMMA

Benjamin Britten geb. 1913	*VARIATIES EN FUGA OP EEN THEMA VAN PURCELL, OP 34 (The Young Person's Guide to the Orchestra) *De verklarende tekst wordt door den Componist uitgesproken*
Peter I. Tsjaikofsky 1840—1893	TWEEDE CONCERT G GR. T., OP. 44 voor piano en orkest Allegro brilliante e molto vivace Andante non troppo Allegro con fuoco *eerste uitvoering*

PAUZE

Maurice Ravel 1875—1937	MOEDER DE GANS Vijf Kinderstukjes Pavane van de Schoone slaapster Klein Duimpje Laideronette, Keizerin van de Pagoden Gesprek tusschen het Meisje en het Monster• De Toovertuin
Maurice Ravel	SPAANSCHE RHAPSODIE Voorspel tot den Nacht Malaguefia Habanera Feria

Steinway Concertvleugel van de fa. Kettner & Duwaer

Programme for 3 November 1946, the Concertgebouw, Amsterdam:
Britten narrates his *Young Person's Guide to the Orchestra*, with the
Concertgebouw Orchestra conducted by Eduard van Beinum

The critic of *De Waarheid* (4 November 1946), reported on the weekend concert, which had included Eileen Joyce playing Tchaikovsky's Second Piano Concerto and a performance of Ravel's *Mother Goose Suite*:

Some of the more senior Concertgebouw subscription holders might have been surprised by composer Benjamin Britten addressing them as if they were children last Sunday afternoon. Britten composed his *Variations and Fugue on a Theme of Purcell* a year ago for a film commissioned by the Ministry of Education demonstrating in turn all the instruments of the orchestra. [...] Before each variation was played the composer identified the instrument concerned and described what we were to hear. The work is witty and easy to follow and is a splendid way of introducing young people to orchestral instruments. The Concertgebouw audience appeared to enjoy its music lesson.

'P.T.' in the *Algemeen Handelsblad* (4 November 1946) wrote:

Britten's musical ideas are delightful and he brings off a number of amusing effects. But this set of variations crowned with a magnificent fugue can claim its place in the concert-hall repertoire without its accompanying narration.

However, in an article entitled 'From Pedagogy to Art', 'L. H.' in *De Tijd* (4 November 1946) commented:

The work, which is clearly designed for educational purposes, is straightforward and intelligent in conception and certainly appropriate for young people. The composer received an ovation, just as if he had unveiled a musical masterpiece, which is obviously beyond the ambition of the work. [...] After the interval the tedium of the classroom was set aside and then there was the making of music.

5 Britten's new opera, *Albert Herring*, with a libretto by Eric Crozier after Maupassant's short story *Le Rosier de Madame Husson*. Crozier has recalled how it was the influence of the wartime Sadler's Wells performances of Mozart's *Così fan tutte* (with Joan Cross as Fiordiligi, Margaret Ritchie as Dorabella and Pears as Ferrando, all of whom took part in *Herring*) and Smetana's *The Bartered Bride*, in which Pears sang the role of Vašek, that led him to suggest to Britten the idea of writing a comic opera for the newly formed English Opera Group to perform in 1947. Crozier, a committed Francophile, proposed Maupassant's short story *Le Rosier de Madame Husson* (*Madame Husson's Rose King*), and lent Britten a 1940 Penguin edition (now at BPL), translated by Marjorie Laurie. The volume contains an inscription written by Crozier when the volume was given to the BPL in the 1980s: 'On our return from Holland in October 1946, I gave Ben this volume to read, and suggested that the last story *Mme Husson's Rose King* would make an excellent companion-piece to *The Rape of Lucretia* and also provide splendid parts for Joan Cross and Peter Pears.' For his part, Britten gave Crozier a copy of Boito's libretto for Verdi's *Falstaff* as an encouragement to, and a model for, his librettist, inscribed, 'Eric, a present from Amsterdam, very confidently, Ben'. Pears recalled (in an interview with Donald Mitchell from the unedited soundtrack of TP) another influence:

CONTENTS

	PAGE
BOULE DE SUIF	7
THE DOWRY	52
THE PATRON	59
ROSE	65
THE NECKLACE	72
HAPPINESS	82
VENDETTA	89
THE MINUET	95
FEAR	100
THE CHAIRMENDER	108
THE WILL	116
IN THE COUNTRY	122
HIS SON	129
A DEAL	140
AN EVENING PARTY	147
HIS CONFESSION	157
MADAME HUSSON'S ROSE-KING	165

The cover and contents page from Eric Crozier's paperback of Maupassant short stories, which he lent to Britten. On the contents page there are pencil markings against three of the stories: 'A Deal', 'An Evening Party' and 'Madame Husson's Rose-King'.

'We'd all seen the film [*The Virtuous Isidore* (France, 1932), directed by Bernard Deschamps] with Fernandel and were very much taken by it and thought it would turn into a nice opera.' As Crozier recollected in 'Staging First Productions 1', in DHOBB, p. 29), instead of approaching another librettist as Crozier expected, Britten invited him to write the text:

We began, as always, by drawing up a list of essential characters and voices. Then we blocked out the action in three acts, and listed the probable contents of each scene. Britten went carefully through these lists with me, to establish what musical forms he would like to use at each point – plain or accompanied *Recitative*, *Arioso*, *Aria*, *Duet*, *Trio*, or *Ensemble*. Once we had decided the overall shape of each act, in terms of dramatic development and musical exposition and contrast, and once we were agreed about the voices (and in some cases the personalities) of each performer, it was time for me to make the imaginative leap from Gisors to Loxford and begin writing.

This last remark refers to Crozier's relocation of the story from Maupassant's Normandy to Britten's rural Suffolk, placing the opera in the imaginary village of Loxford, a name clearly derived from Yoxford, a few miles north of Aldeburgh.

Crozier also discussed the writing of *Albert Herring*, but in particular
how he chose the names of the characters, in an extract from his and Nancy
Evans's autobiography, 'After Long Pursuit: The English Opera Group and
Albert Herring', *Opera Quarterly* 11/3 (1995), pp. 3–16:

Ben and I had already agreed upon the scenario for a lyrical comedy in five scenes
and three acts. To this I had added a fairly lengthy description of each character,
clothing their bare bones with touches of individuality, personal characteristics,
and obvious mannerisms. Most important, I had found names for them: until that
was done, we were working with shadows. Albert Herring took his name from the
owner of a grocery store at Tunstall [near Snape, Suffolk]; Lady Billows's surname
came from a rather pompous friend of ours in the British Council [Lionel Billows];
Florence the housekeeper shared her Christian name with Joan Cross's *bonne à tout
faire*; Nancy from the bakery was, of course, Nancy [Evans]; Mr Gedge was the
vicar of a poor South London parish who had provided us with the original
apprentice in *Peter Grimes*; Miss Wordsworth had begun life as Miss Welford, the
name of Ben's married sister; Harold Wood was a railway station on the Liverpool
Street line; Cissie Woodger was a girl in Snape for whom Ben had once bought a
ticket for a CEMA concert (when asked next day how she had enjoyed herself, she
replied, 'Oh, I didn't mind it at all!'). So with all the other characters – only when
they had names could one begin to imagine how they would act, speak, and, above
all, *sing*.

In an illuminating sequence of letters to Nancy Evans, the first Nancy in
Herring and Crozier's future wife, Crozier documents much of his progress
on the libretto and Britten's on the music. On 20 October 1946 he wrote
from Snape, 'The libretto of *Albert* is roughly knocked into shape and now
it only has to be written'; on 3 November, from Woburn Abbey, 'I must go
down and borrow a vegetable catalogue from the head gardener here, to
provide material for *Albert*. There's so much I want to read and look up
before I start writing, but time presses hard'; and from 3 Oxford Square, on
20 November, 'Ben's being awfully nice about *Albert*. He's rather glum
about things generally, and says the only exciting thing of the moment is
how well the libretto is shaping and that I must write more.' (That same
evening Crozier noted that the conductors Eduard van Beinum and Rafael
Kubelik had dined with Britten and Pears.)

The correspondence continued from Snape in December:

MONDAY
Ben and I have done some final revisions on scene 1 (including putting Lady
Billows's speech into verse), and he is going off for a long walk this afternoon to
think, before actually sitting down to begin writing the music. We've made drastic
decisions about scene 2 and are going to have all the *récits* in verse. So I have to
rewrite virtually the whole thing in the next two days. But I'm sure it's right to do
this – and it simplifies many problems for me.

TUESDAY
The rewriting goes along steadily this morning, though I am not feeling awfully well
[. . .] I have just re-done the Nancy–Sid scene [in Act I scene 2] in verse and shall
see what Ben thinks when we meet at lunch. On the whole, it's going fairly fast.

WEDNESDAY

Ben was awfully keen to play me the opening of the opera. It starts off with a terrific rush of energy (Florence bustling about doing tidying-up) and I found it made me roar with laughter just at the music. He's done as far as the entrance of the Committee Members.

THURSDAY

Another two little scenes and Act I will be ready for typing in final shape. I'm much relieved. I see now what Ben means about having me here to consult with. There are dozens of tiny points he comes to ask about while he's setting the text – minor problems keep cropping up. It's exciting actually to see some of it in score already – like seeing one's child in party clothes for the first time. We think of calling the work *King of the May* instead of *Albert Herring*. Do you like that for a title?

SATURDAY

Ben was merciless yesterday. We talked all morning, walked after lunch (me under protest), and then set to for three hours' good work between tea and dinner. I was exhausted and lay down for half an hour to rest before writing and was forcibly awakened three hours later to eat dinner by a sceptical Ben. But oh! I'm so pleased with the results of his work on *Albert*: tonight we've been going through all he has composed till now – the first 20 minutes. I find it excellent and am really excited by it. It will either be a great success or a great failure – I think there's a strong chance of success. His setting of words is remarkable: he transforms them in a curious way, and it's very fascinating when the words are one's own, like seeing them suddenly in colour after black-and-white. I spoke to Ansermet by telephone this morning, and arranged to dine with him next Friday and discuss plans. He suggests we go to the Lucerne and Geneva Summer Festivals with the operas. I shall try to get a copy of the two Auden songs from Ben [perhaps from Britten's and Auden's *Cabaret Songs* (1937–39)]. They are not printed, but he thinks he might have a proof copy [probably a dyeline copy of the manuscript] somewhere. I think he will be very pleased if you do some of his songs in your concerts.

Later in the month he wrote:

Act I is finished and typed out, and today and tomorrow I shall make as much of an attack on Act II scene 1 as I can.

And in a subsequent letter that month:

We are going over to Ipswich for shopping later this morning: so I can only write a wee note as Ben is catching me up dangerously fast and will finish scene 1 this morning. I have got stuck in a mental rut at the High Tea scene: the harder I struggle to arrive at the last ensemble, the deeper I dig myself in. So I must make a big effort to break out in the two hours that are left of this morning. [. . .]

   Now for work – at the Mayor's speech for the umpteenth time. (I have persuaded Ben, by the way, to go back to *Albert Herring* as our title – thank you!)

The following day:

Ben finished scene 1 this morning – he played it through, and it lasts exactly half an hour: quite a good length. I can't wait for you and Peter and Joan to hear it and know how you all feel. *We* like it! I've broken out of my rut, and can get on towards the end of Act II scene 2 by tomorrow evening.

Erwin Stein wrote to Elizabeth Mayer on 3 February 1947:

Ben played me the first scene of the first act of the new opera before he left [for Switzerland on 1 January 1947]. It is quite different again from anything before, but unmistakable Britten. It is most exciting. I think Ben's rarest gift is the enormous range of his expression. I think it is a gift which only great composers possess.

In a letter of 30 December 1946, Crozier explained a reference in Auden's poem set as 'Nocturne' by Britten in the cycle *On this Island*, which Nancy Evans must have been performing:

A *succuba* is a female nightmare creature who castrates young men: a *succubus* her male equivalent attacking young women. So perhaps it's not surprising we didn't recognize him! Ben knew about it, and it made a great impression on him at one time in his youth: he told Auden about it and hence its presence in the poem. He says the tempo should be a slow saraband kind of movement – he marked it *Allegretto* because *Andante* would have suggested something too slow, for the actual phrase must move.

See also Eric Crozier, 'Foreword to "Albert Herring"', *Tempo*, 4 (summer 1947), pp. 10–14; Donald Mitchell and Philip Reed (eds.), 'An *Albert Herring* Anthology', 1985 Glyndebourne Festival programme book, pp. 114–15; Donald Mitchell, 'The Serious Comedy of *Albert Herring*', 1986 Glyndebourne Festival programme book, pp. 105–11, reprinted in DMCN, pp. 352–64; Rosy Sinden-Evans, *'The Making of a May King' or The Creation of* Albert Herring: *a Comic Opera by Benjamin Britten and Eric Crozier* (MMus dissertation, University of London, 1995), which includes a discussion of the significance of the film adaptation *The Virtuous Isidore* to the opera; and PKBM, pp. 67–74, the transcript of *An Opera is Planned*, a fascinating discussion between Britten, Crozier and Piper, written and produced by Stephen Potter, broadcast in the BBC Third Programme, 19 June 1947.

Potter wrote about this important feature programme in a sequence of three of his diary entries:

5 JUNE 1947
At Glyndebourne, spend night with Crozier and Peter Pears at Bishopstone Manor. John Piper is also there and Mr Lee, who takes down our talk.

Glyndebourne very cold, with harsh wind. Piper shows us a wonderful pub on the coast corner of Seaford – beautiful decorations of boats. They are all deeply enjoying themselves. The music is most insinuatingly pretty in a lasting way. Ben is the complete boss, without slightest pomposity or hardness – just because he is working very concentratedly. As with the ballet programme, they are polite to me but I am obviously a queer fish to them, so utterly removed from their world.

Piper is the nicest. No drinks till 6 and then they do make moderate use of the cocktail bar. Ben's old open Rolls used for transport.

Christie, in a white jacket, rather avoided by everybody, which seems a shame. But he is alleged to be a little bit of a boring buttonholer, and he did so to me, asking me to take care over the balance between orchestra and voices. 'We work for months to get every detail exact, you see.' I thought Christie, rather unspoken to in the canteen, a sad figure, for all his wonderful possessions and enlightened use of them.

16 JUNE 1947
Recordings, in morning, for opera programme. They all come up. Piper – I like his
dry voice. Crozier – too incisive and well educated and clear. Britten – sounds, as he
says, like Noël Coward. He improves under production (not so Crozier). 'I suppose
there's a lot to be learnt about talking into the mike,' he says. He likes the records.

19 JUNE 1947
Fitting together extracts from rehearsals, studio discussion recordings, Glyndebourne recordings, James McKechnie's narration – all into a 44-minute programme. Very much enjoying the music, once more.

See Julian Potter, *Stephen Potter at the BBC: 'Features' in War and Peace*,
pp. 192–3.

39 To Elizabeth Mayer

American Hotel, Amsterdam
Oct. 28th 1946

My darling Elizabeth,
    I am very sorry not to have written for so long, or to have expressed
before this my infinite gratitude for your great work on my Lucretia[1] but I
know you understand the hopeless condition of one's life: always behind-
hand & pleasant things of life (such as writing to you) always having to
give way to sordid work! Anyhow, this is a scribble from Amsterdam in
the midst of Peter's & my second round of concerts in Holland this season –
(Peter is now such a favourite here that he's coming back no less than five
times this season!)[2] – from this very beautiful & friendly city, that I am
getting so fond of – Anyhow although I haven't written before – we have
been in the closest contact all these weeks – with your almost daily letters
to Erwin, & perpetual discussion of your work. I do think that it is amazing
what you are doing – I, of course, with my very limited German, find it
difficult to appreciate the finest points, but Erwin, who is a hard & ruthless critic, is <u>delighted</u> with it, & really even I can see how good it is. Thank
you, my dearest. There remains the problems of my future revision of the
work – which Erwin has mentioned to you, I think. There are two scenes,
& a few phrases here & there, that I want to reconsider before performances next year in England (the ones in Switzerland, Belgium etc. will be
played in the present version).[3] I shall not have time to settle down to
them before the New Year, but when I do, I am afraid your presence will
be imperative! I am writing to Ralph about this so that he can make plans
re fare etc. The alterations I am going to make are so subtle that it really
will need your actual company! The changes which I want Ronald
Duncan to make I expect you will already be conscious of – i.e. the scene
between Junius & Collatinus Act I – Collatinus nowhere in the opera

comes out as a sufficiently big or noble character, or his relationship with Lucretia as sufficiently a 'legend' in Roman life for the tragedy to make its effect.⁴ Similarly, his final entrance "Tell me, what is it" – he appears too much like a silly deceived husband. All this I want to change, & some small points besides.⁵ So, if it can be arranged, you will come, if only for a few weeks, my dear, won't you? Before the German edition goes in to print, it must be perfect.⁶ And that can only be done with you actually here.

I am afraid our connections with Glyndebourne are to be broken. They didn't understand what we were after, and Bing couldn't stand for Eric being our director, which was essential for us to continue. So we shall set up on our own – take a London theatre, & tour Europe & England as before. Of course it all means extra thought & worry, but the position before was too compromising.

I must go now to see a rehearsal of Entführung – the producer is the one who's going to do Grimes here in Spring.⁷ Much love, my dearest – & to William, Beata, Michael, Christopher – I am so glad about his staying on this year.⁸ Thank you more than I can say. Peter (at present with a masseur!), sends his love.

BEN

1   Mrs Mayer was to write to Britten on 19 November:

> [...] your good letter from Amsterdam made me very happy – every word of it. Yes, I have been living in very close touch with you, doing the translation. I am so glad you are pleased – Erwin writes me always so nice and encouraging notes, and I regret that we could not do the whole thing from the very beginning together. [...] If I only had heard the whole work once. Ralph tells me that he'll soon have the recordings here, and play them to me.

   The recording to which Mrs Mayer refers must have been privately made from the BBC broadcast on 11 October 1946 (see Letter 517 n. 4).
   Mrs Mayer continued:

> The other day Bernstein did your Violin Concerto with his orchestra – the solo played by Werner Lywen, the first fiddler [...] who did a good job. The orchestra, all young people whom B. trained, did very well too [...] The Concerto was played on two evenings, and very enthusiastically received. I went both times, as I loved to hear it again – it is a most astonishing work. Of course we all missed Toni's beautiful strong noise – the whole interpretation was on a rather lyrical, ethereal level – but sounded lovely nevertheless. Anyway – I am so glad to hear it played again – at last! Tonight I am going to a concert [...] where Desi Halban (who sings the himmlischen Freuden on a recording with Bruno Walter of the Mahler symphony [No. 4]) is going to sing three of the *Michelangelo Sonnets*.

2   Among the concerts given during this second trip to the Netherlands were two recitals in the Kleine Zaal of the Concertgebouw in Amsterdam, on 25 and 31 October, Arnhem on the 29th and Maastricht on the 30th. The

Amsterdam programmes included songs by Purcell, Schubert, Mahler, Britten (*The Holy Sonnets of John Donne*, 'Let the florid music praise' from *On This Island*, and 'Fish in the unruffled lakes'), and folksongs arranged by Britten. Pears was later to return to the Netherlands in November (*Les Illuminations* and Purcell arrangements at Leeuwarden) and in March 1947 (three performances of Bach's *St Matthew Passion* in the Concertgebouw conducted by Eduard van Beinum).

3   The Swiss première of *Lucretia* was given in Basel on 5 June 1947, a production that had been postponed from January in order to allow Elizabeth Mayer more time to complete her German translation. *Lucretia* was first given at the Théâtre de la Monnaie, Brussels, on 25 April 1947 in a French translation by Georges Dalman. The production, by M. G. Dalman, was designed by Olivier Picard and conducted by M. C. de Thoran.

4   It would seem that Britten did respond positively to some of the criticisms of *Lucretia* made by friends, perhaps especially those outlined by Michael Tippett, see Letter 531 n. 3.

5   The revisions to *Lucretia* were made in the spring of 1947 in time for the revival at Glyndebourne that summer. Numerous minor alterations to the libretto were made following the premiere in 1946, as shown by the issue of two different corrigenda slips to accompany the first edition of the libretto. The changes were presumably introduced during the run of performances at Glyndebourne and the subsequent tour. Britten's principal musical revisions to the opera in 1947 comprised: a replacement arioso for Collatinus and the exchange that follows in Act I scene 1 (figs. 26–34); the recomposition of a section of the Female Chorus's introduction to Act II scene 1 (fig. 1^{-2} – fig. 4^{+1}); the interpolation of an arioso for Lucia in Act II scene 2, 'I often wonder whether Lucretia's love is the flower of her beauty' (fig. 67^{+20} – fig. 67^{+37}); and the rewriting of Collatinus' and Junius' arrival in Rome in Act II scene 2 (fig. 80^{+17} – fig. 81). Britten wrote to Duncan on 19 March 1947: 'Any chance of you being in London 17th–20th April [when the revisions were probably finalized]? and in the meantime if you'd have a moment to re-think the last entry of Collatinus & Junius, it might save time.' See also Margaret Mertz, *History, Criticism and the Sources of Benjamin Britten's Opera 'The Rape of Lucretia'* (PhD dissertation, Harvard University, 1990), pp. 26–81, 242–3, and 297–301.

Donald Mitchell recalls that in 1969, in preparation for the complete Decca recording of *Lucretia*, Britten sent a brief schedule of his proposed amendments of the text to Ronald Duncan for his approval. It so happened that Mitchell was with Britten when Duncan's reply (14 November 1969) was received. Britten smiled when reading over this passage:

I am not unaware of several verbal infelicities . . . mea culpa . . . I am at the moment thinking of 'the prodigious liberality of self-coined obsequious flattery'!! This silly mouthful was, as I've confessed somewhere (if not to you?) a sort of tease when I wrote it (you'd been telling me that even a telephone directory could be set) and so

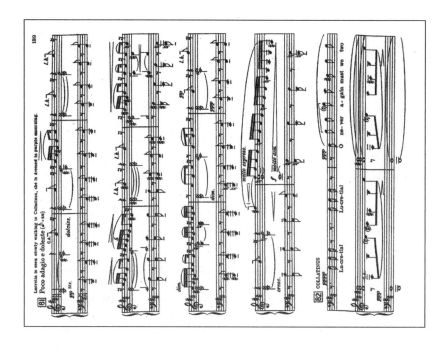

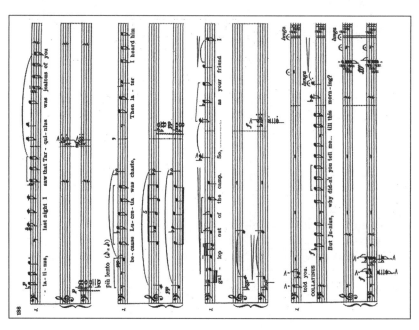

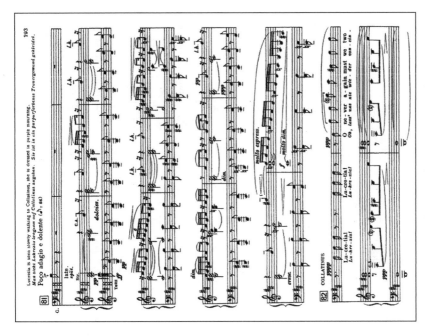

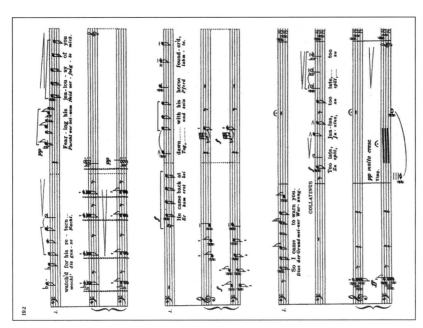

The Rape of Lucretia, Act II scene 2: Junius' and Collatinus' return to Rome and Lucretia's appearance at fig. 81 (with Britten's Bachian cor anglais solo) in the original (1946; p. 256) and revised (1947; p. 257) versions

I wrote those lines as a challenge expecting you to throw them out. To my dismay, you weren't tripped up at all and later Peter coped with them too – and the 'joke' rebounded in my own face. But perhaps I've been hanging on this hook of my own making long enough? Would you consider cutting both 'prodigious liberality' and 'self-coined'? Then the line would read 'pay his way with obsequious flattery'. But don't worry if this change upsets your musical fabric; I'll have to wear my own red nose.

At this Britten shook his head, remarking gently that it was typical of 'dear Ronnie' that he would want to get rid of a setting that had certainly taxed his ingenuity but of which he remained 'proud'. In his reply to Duncan of 18 November, he put it slightly otherwise: 'I will discuss with Peter about the "prodigious liberality etc." – but I've got rather fond of it, & he does it very convincingly! But I note your point [. . .]'

Mitchell doubts if any such discussion took place. Pears indeed as much relished the challenge of singing the famous phrase as Britten of setting it. It remains to this day, neither revised nor omitted.

6   The German edition of the libretto prepared for the Basel performances.

7   This proposed production appears to have fallen through.

8   Christopher Mayer was studying at Yale. In her letter of 19 November, Elizabeth Mayer writes that Christopher 'is working well, and has got over the last months, looking much better'.

540 To Ralph Hawkes

3 Oxford Square, w. 2
Nov. 7th 1946

My dear Ralph,

I am so sorry to have neglected you so badly these last weeks – but it has been a hell of a time! We were abroad with Lucretia, & a great time we had, & since then Peter & I have been all over Holland giving loads of concerts (I even "orated" in the Y. Person's Guide with the Concertgebouw!), & we are only here for a few days before touring this country for about three weeks.[1] So it is all pretty hectic. I've found some time to do some work too – done a Purcell Suite for Voice & orchestra (5 songs)

which Peter did in Holland,[2] & some more Folk-songs.[3] The new opera
(which Eric is writing for me) is being planned ferociously & I hope to get
down to the actual notes in December. I believe Erwin told you of our
difficulties with Glyndebourne. Most unfortunately they have become
very great, if not insuperable. We are about to form our own company
(with Eric, Piper & me as artistic directors & own business manager &
capital) which, we are advised, will have strong Arts Council & British
Council support (& in which Covent Garden also seem very interested!) –
to do, as last year, touring in England & the Continent, & a London season.
Whether Glyndebourne will accept us for a season there remains to be
seen, but we fear not. Ralph, please don't think that we have broken
irresponsibly; the differences were fundamental. If they can take us back
as an independent company, that's fine (& we are very grateful for what
they did last year); but independent we <u>must</u> be.

About Peter's & my tour of U.S.A. for you next season, I cannot yet say
definitely, I'm afraid, altho' I cannot be very hopeful.[4] Peter Diamand (our
continental manager) comes over here next week & we'll work out dates
with him; but both of us feel that U.S.A. is so far away (both physically &
spiritually! – & no more of that flying business either) that only if it can
be done easily & with great financial gain is it worth doing. Besides, with
Peter's incredible success in Europe (when U.S.A. hears of it), perhaps the
longer we wait the better. But we'll write definitely in a week or so.

I was so glad to hear from Erwin that things are going well with you
over there. You must be having a wild time! How's Clare? I hope she's
enjoying herself. When I get back to Snape (all installed with a new housekeeper!),[5] I will write what little things are still missing & unobtainable
here – thank you so much. What is always welcome is sweets – & soap!

Eric is now temporarily installed here – & seems happy. He, Peter, the
Steins & I send lots of love to you both.

Yours ever,
BEN

P.S. How was [*The Duchess of*] Malfi – did she ever occur, did the music
arrive? I never heard a word?

The enclosed from Utah – I pass on to you. I suppose it's not very good.
How's Lincoln, & his plans?[6]

In haste,
BB

1 Their tour of sixteen recitals in twenty-one days ran from 9 November
   until the end of the month and included two BBC broadcasts in the Third
   Programme: on the 18th Britten and Pears performed Schubert lieder and
   the *Michelangelo Sonnets* (the same recital also included Britten's *Phantasy*

quartet from Leon Goossens and the Carter String Trio); and on the 21st they took part in a thirty-minute programme in the series entitled *Music in Miniature* produced by Basil Douglas, with John Francis (flute), the cellist Maurice Gendron, and the Zorian String Quartet. Britten probably attended a St Cecilia's Day Concert given by Morley College at Central Hall, conducted by Michael Tippett and Walter Goehr, which included the first London performance of the *Prelude and Fugue on a Theme of Vittoria* (Geraint Jones, organ), *Rejoice in the Lamb*, Mozart's concert aria *Misero! O Sogno* (K. 431) (sung by Pears), and Purcell's *Ode to St Cecilia's Day 1692* (among the soloists were Margaret Ritchie, Alfred Deller and Pears).

2 The 'Suite of Songs', for high voice and orchestra, Britten's arrangements of 'Let sullen discord smile', 'Why should men quarrel?', 'So when the glittering Queen of Night', 'Thou tun'st this world', and ''Tis holiday – Sound Fame thy brazen Trumpet'. The first performance of the suite was given by Pears in Leeuwarden on 7 November 1946, with the Groninger Orkestervereeniging conducted by Jan van Epenhuysen. In a letter to Nancy Evans (Snape, 2 October 1946), Eric Crozier noted, 'Ben is hard at work scoring and arranging a suite of Purcell songs for first performance next week [*sic*] in Holland. Wonderful songs they are, too.'

3 The precise chronology of Britten's folksong arrangements is difficult to establish. It is clear, however, that among the new arrangements from this period are 'Sweet Polly Oliver', 'O Waly, Waly' and 'Come you not from Newcastle?', all of which had been included in recitals during Britten's and Pears's recent visit to Holland.

4 See Letters 573 n. 12 and 575.

5 Barbara Parker: see also Letter 543. She continued working for Britten when he moved to Aldeburgh in 1947. Humphrey Carpenter writes (HCBB, pp. 260–61):

> Britten engaged a live-in housekeeper, whom Crozier describes as 'a middle-aged, pleasant, but highly strung lady who suffered from severe alternations of mood and would sometimes seem almost distraught with anxieties'. Her social position caused problems, since she was 'too ladylike to be relegated to the kitchen'. She ate with Britten and his friends, but was not expected to take a lead in the conversation, and Crozier says that 'her awareness of not being wanted except as a servant' aggravated her instability. Elizabeth Sweeting describes her as 'possessive about Ben'; like all women, she 'wanted to take him over'. Why did he put up with this? Elizabeth Sweeting answers: 'He looked for a surrogate mother in every relationship.'

6 Lincoln Kirstein had proposed to Ralph Hawkes that his Ballet Society, an organization founded in 1946 to produce important new works of dance and music theatre, would include *Lucretia* as part of its autumn 1946 season of dance and opera. While recognizing that the Ballet Society might

be a valuable means of introducing *Lucretia* in the United States, Hawkes cautioned Britten about allowing Kirstein to proceed, principally because there was a proposal for Glyndebourne to visit the States in the autumn of 1947, presenting not only *Lucretia* but *Albert Herring* also. As Hawkes's discussions with Kirstein progressed, the proposed Ballet Society production of *Lucretia* was moved to February 1947, at the Hekscher Theatre, New York, with further performances on tour. Britten cabled Hawkes on 19 September 1946:

LUCRETIA STYLE TOO NEW AND DANGEROUS. GENERALLY FEEL KIRSTEIN PRO-
DUCTION MIGHT PREJUDICE. EXPERIENCE WITH GRIMES [at Tanglewood]
STRENGTHENS THIS FEELING. GLYNDEBOURNE VISIT IN FALL MORE IMPORTANT
FOR FUTURE PERFORMANCES OF BOTH LUCRETIA AND MY NEW COMEDY. SUG-
GEST CONCENTRATE NOW ON GRIMES. HOPE NEGOTIATIONS WITH OLIVER
SMITH PROCEEDING. LOVE TO BOTH

Britten's encouragment to Hawkes to concentrate on *Grimes* refers to his publisher's lobbying of the Metropolitan Opera to mount a production, which took place in 1948. The reference to 'negotiations with Oliver Smith' concerns a proposal for a twenty-minute ballet (never written) entitled 'Harvest Reel', to be ready by March/April 1947. Little information has emerged about this ballet project, though we note that its title – 'Harvest Reel' – has an affinity with the 1936 documentary film *Around the Village Green*, with incidental music by Britten, the alternative title of which was 'Village Harvest'. Moreover the title music of this film, made for the Travel and Industrial Development Association, was recorded in 1937 by the Charles Brill Orchestra conducted by Charles Brill for Decca, under the title *Irish Reel*. The latter was first published by Faber Music in 1996.

The reference in Britten's telegram to Hawkes to Glyndebourne's 'visit in the fall' concerns a proposed tour to the United States by the company which had to be abandoned when the composer and John Christie went their separate ways.

541 To Ernest Ansermet
[Tappolet, pp. 52–3][1]

3 Oxford Square, w.2
Nov. 8th 1946

Cher ami,

Your letter was very touching & welcome. I was very glad to have news of you, and to know that you are now better in your health, & able to work again. The rumours of your illness worried your many friends here greatly. The Summer, with the Rape, your festivals, & Conference in Geneva,[2] must have been very exhausting for you. Please take care of yourself – you are very valuable!

I am so sorry that you have been put in this very embarrassing position between us & Glyndebourne.[3] It is too long a story for me to tell here, but I know you will understand (because you saw the beginning at Glyndebourne before the first night!), that the differences of opinion that have arisen are not petty, nor that of only temperament, but are fundamental. Briefly – we have demanded to become an independent company with Crozier, Piper & myself as directors (having our own business manager, & capital). We would tour England & the Continent, & have a London season (in which Christie had informed us he was not interested & for which he would give us no facilities, nor even the name Glyndebourne); but also, because we thought we owed it, offered ourselves to perform again Lucretia & another new Comedy which I'm writing for Glyndebourne. (The question of whether Eric Crozier or Ebert produces the new one scarcely arises because he (Ebert) is not here to discuss the production, & cannot arrive, I think, till April.)[4]

This position has upset Glyndebourne, & they indicate that they cannot accept it; & so we presume they are trying to collect their own company for some kind of season, independent from us. We are going ahead with the formation of our own company, but this takes time & nothing is yet fixed. What we should ask, cher maître, is that if possible you could put off a definite reply till you come to England in December, when our negotiations will have progressed & the whole situation be clearer. As you can imagine it has been a horrible time – all of us have many other things to do & to use up our energies – but we believe so strongly in the importance of our new operatic style, that we feel the trouble to be worth while!

We had an enjoyable time, & a really great success in Amsterdam – and we hope to extend our tour further into Europe next season.

Please give my kindest regards to Madame Ansermet, & for yourself the loving gratitude of all of us, singers, players & creators!

Yours very sincerely,
BENJAMIN BRITTEN

1 First published in Claude Tappolet (ed.), *Ernest Ansermet: Correspondances avec des compositeurs Européens (1916–1966)*. In Part II (pp. 45–77) Tappolet includes the complete extant correspondence between Britten and Ansermet.

2 Ansermet had given concerts at Scheveningen and Salzburg. Between 2 and 14 September he had participated in an international conference held in Geneva on the theme of 'European Spirit', during which he spoke on the subject of music as an essentially European phenomenon (see Tappolet, p. 201 n. 16).

3 In a letter to Britten from Geneva, dated 3 November 1946, Ansermet had

explained to Britten his predicament. He had originally been asked to reserve a period the following season for work at Glyndebourne, and had subsequently been told of the disagreement between Britten and Christie in respect of the situation between Ebert and Crozier. According to Ansermet, Bing had invited him to conduct a revival of *Lucretia* and 'another work to be designed [*recte*: directed] by Ebert'. Because of Britten's and Christie's differences Ansermet was placed in a difficult situation: he did not want to relinquish work at Glyndebourne but at the same time did not wish to offend Britten. As he reminded the composer, in his idiosyncratic English, 'I was introduced in Glynde by you and I am gone there for you and your work.' Ansermet proposed that he would do nothing until he had an opportunity to meet Britten in person when in London the following month.

In the same letter Ansermet writes:

I have just written an article on the *Rape* for a Swiss weekly – and I will send it to you when it appears – and on this occasion, I have read again the score, after months of abandon. Now, you cannot imagine how ravished I was in reading it again. After this new contact, I feel more convinced than ever from the absolute value of that work. I understand that the amazing simplicity of means in this music makes that its qualities of substance escape to the majority of its hearers. But, have confidence [...] I thank you very much for the sending of the printed [vocal] score and its very charming dédicace.

Ansermet's article, 'Benjamin Brittens zweite Oper', first appeared in *Welt von Heute* (4 December 1946), and was subsequently reprinted in the *Revue Musicale Suisse*, 6 (June 1947), pp. 230–32.

Ansermet's article concludes:

After the vividness, the epic grandeur, the brilliant colours of *Peter Grimes*, the austerity of this new opera comes as something of a shock. However, beneath the apparent simplicity and spontaneity, there is an even greater musical depth. Undoubtedly what dumbfounds not audiences but many musicians in this work is its blending together of different styles. [...]

We must accept it: a horror of aestheticism has hung over music these last thirty years. Matters of style have seemed to absorb the best creative minds among our composers. Britten, of a younger generation and swept along by the extraordinary abundance of his gifts, has escaped this. When faced with the task in hand, he reaches straight for the expressive means that will best serve his desired ends, and whatever has become available through recent experimentation he makes his own. Such an undertaking could not be achieved without sacrificing something of prevailing aesthetic disciplines. But its value to us is the creation of living art, utterly human and shining with promise.

4   See also Letter 542.

542 To John Christie

From Benjamin Britten and Eric Crozier

[*Typed*]

3, Oxford Square, w.2

November 10th, 1946

PERSONAL

Dear John,

Thank you for your reply to our letter. Although you address yourself only to Ben, we prefer to make a joint answer, and shall try to explain our position as clearly as it can be explained at this moment.

The chief point of misunderstanding between us seems to be about the position of Charles [Carl] Ebert as artistic director of Glyndebourne and as producer. Your letter states that you have engaged him to come to England in January. The last news he gave us when leaving for Turkey was that he would not return to England until April, but would spend February in Switzerland (where we were to try and visit him) and go to Milan to produce in March. Which of these plans is correct?

It is clear to us that you cannot accept anything for Glyndebourne unless it is fully under his direction. This loyalty we appreciate and admire. But by April the production of the new opera will be largely settled: costumes and scenery will be making [being made]: music finished: singers cast and contracted. Charles may return to <u>rehearse</u>, but not – in any real sense – to produce. The only possible arrangement here would be to accept the reality of a joint equal production between him and Eric Crozier, and announce it as such.

Other points of misunderstanding are less apparent, but perhaps more fundamental. It is as well to speak frankly and without prejudice about them.

We regret that Rudolf Bing's admirable devotion to the interests of Glyndebourne should make him so little confident in our own integrity and purpose. We cannot work well with him, for he sums up the mistrust of Glyndebourne for any enterprise that it does not itself mould and con-trol. Glyndebourne is so anxious to have only the very best in opera that it cannot be patient with beginners like ourselves. This mistrust withers the good in its actual struggle to become better. It creates an atmosphere that is inimical to the creation of new work, by insisting on standards and methods that can only reasonably be applied to the reproduction of accepted classical works.

Like all general statements, this over-simplifies – but please try to understand it as an attempt to state one fundamental reason that urges us to independence and freedom of artistic judgment. We need these for the continuance of our work, and are hesitant about too zealous a control from Glyndebourne. We appreciate your great generosity towards our first steps in 1946. Now we must learn to walk by ourselves: impatience about our inability to run will be merely discouraging!

Both Glyndebourne and we ourselves are aiming at the same target: our disagreement is about the method and pace of reaching it. You can envisage only one method – that your own experienced hands should take full control, and direct our energies. We can see how essentially right this must appear to you, but since our group includes the creator of new operas and his collaborators, we believe it will be better that you should allow us complete independence, even if you are doubtful about our capacity to make the fullest use of it.

Briefly, this is our practical plan:

1) We shall appoint a General Manager to form a new non-profit-making company for us. This will have a board of five trustees and an assessor from the Arts Council, if they will collaborate with us. Our manager will organise the collection of capital to launch our 1947 season.

2) The management of the new company will be in the hands of –
   Music Director   –   Benjamin Britten
   Artistic Director –   Eric Crozier
   Scenic Director   –   John Piper

3) Next summer, we shall stage <u>Albert</u>, a new comic opera, and <u>Lucretia</u> – the latter certainly on the Continent, and in England either before or after October 1st., according to Glyndebourne's decision about the exclusive rights which they hold till that date.

4) We should like to negotiate with you for the loan or purchase of the <u>Lucretia</u> production. Alternatively, we may build the production afresh for our company. There will be extensive alterations to the music and text of the opera before its next production.

5) Our work in 1947 will include a Continental tour, a London season and a short provincial tour. It could also perhaps include an opening season at Glyndebourne if you wished to preserve an association with us, and if an arrangement could be made that would satisfy the artistic and financial demands both of Glyndebourne and of our new company.

This is as clear an outline as we can give of immediate policy and aims. We shall be interested to know your views.

On the question of 'Collins's',[1] we will not join issue. We are not ungrateful. You invited us to Glyndebourne as equal collaborators in a joint enterprise, not as guests. Both you and we were offering something of substantial value. We know that our achievement could have been, and

will be, greater, but we are not ashamed of our contribution to the past
season, or conscious of having failed in obligation towards you.[2]

Yours sincerely,

BENJAMIN BRITTEN

ERIC CROZIER

1 Possibly Collins's, the former music-hall on Islington Green, which might
   have been considered as a possible London venue.

2 Christie rejected Britten's and Crozier's analysis of the situation. Britten
   was to write to him again on 23 November, indicating that the newly
   formed, though as yet unnamed, English Opera Group, would forge ahead
   with its arrangements for the 1947 season without Glyndebourne. Crozier
   told Nancy Evans in early December,

   The Glyndebourne offer is poor enough. They offer us ten days' performances after
   Orfeo [Gluck's *Orfeo ed Euridice*] and before rehearsals begin for Edinburgh, with
   one lighting rehearsal and *one* dress rehearsal in their theatre. Hopeless! Their tone
   has changed from complaint to something approaching courtesy, but we shall
   obviously not be able to accept on such skimped terms as they offer.

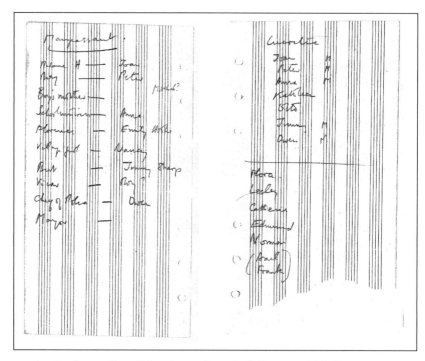

A pair of pages from Britten's 1946 loose-leaf diary on which the composer
is working out the possible casting of *Lucretia* and *Albert Herring* (called
'Maupassant'). This must date from a very early stage in the genesis of *Herring*:
Lady Billows, Albert and Nancy are all referred to by their names in Maupassant's
story; 'Bert' would become Sid and the 'Chief of Police' Superintendent Budd.

543   To Elizabeth Mayer

Old Mill, Snape, Suffolk
Dec. 18th 1946

My darling Elizabeth,

Your sweet letter came yesterday, & I was happy to get it – except to read about poor William's illness. What a worry for you, my dear; but he is so strong that I am sure that once he is over the shock of it, he'll be quite himself again. Please give him lots of love from me, & say how sorry I am, & "please get well quick."[1]

Well, here I am at the old place again. Peter & I had the wildest time careering round Holland, & then three mad weeks (6 concerts a week!) all over England & Scotland (some of it in the Rolls!). Luckily his voice held out, but it was hectic, & we didn't enjoy it much. Now he's up North – singing the Messiah – & I am in the middle of Act I of Albert Herring! Eric, who is writing the libretto, is up & down to London. The libretto is really fine – he's doing a grand job, and it ought to be extremely funny. I'm pleased with music so far – but one cannot judge by emotions at this stage.

My housekeeper, Miss Parker, is installed – & it is all going nicely. She is very efficient, altho' I miss Beth & family. However I see them quite often, & we had a shopping excursion to Ipswich together last Monday. I am sending a Lowestoft calendar to you, but I'm afraid it'll be very late – forgive me my dear – but I've been working so hard, & no time for letter-writing, or shopping or any of the nice things that Christmas demands!

It is exciting that in a matter of months you'll be here! Beth wants you for sometime of course, & so do the Steins & Pears in London – but I'm going to have you here my dear! Can you not come too late – preferably in March? Peter & I have to go to Italy for a few weeks on April 15th[2] – & I don't want to be away for a day when you're here! We'll have lots to do & talk about . . .!

How is Wystan? I am glad he's got his apartment now.[3] I hope he wasn't too upset by the mad Malfi business. It was an impossible thing. Did you see it? I've been re-reading a lot of him recently, & love it more & more. I can't wait to see the new piece.[4] I loved the Northampton one.[5] One day, in a matter of years, I am going to get down to the Christmas Oratorio. That has got to be set, even if no one performs it. It'll probably last three evenings![6] I wonder what you thought of "A boy was born", & how Shaw[7] did it. I haven't heard it for ages, but I must admit that at the moment I rather like early Britten – quite a lot is being dug up now, & it's quite amusing![8]

My dearest – it is terribly late & I'm sleepy (as this letter shows) because I've been "at" it so long to-day. But I wanted to send you my best love, Christmas greetings, and every good wish for the New Year (Peter & I'll be in Switzerland for Jan. 1st).

We are all well. I do hope your invalids are all quite themselves now. Love to them all. Rose Marie Duncan is still doing well – a miracle![9] (Ronnie c/o Fabers is best for "This Way to the Tomb")[10]

Love to Wystan too – & lots to yourself – see you very soon – <u>how</u> lovely that will be.

Your loving
BEN

No Lucretias yet fixed for Germany (only Switzerland & Belgium) – but Grimes in 5 places I think – Hamburg, Berlin, Hanover, ???, but I'm not certain.[11]

1 Mrs Mayer had reported to Britten in a letter dated 9 December 1946:

> William's sudden attack was short but a bit more serious and disturbing. He collapsed in his office after a strenuous day, was just for a second unconscious [. . .] he had completely lost his memory for everything that happened before his collapse [. . .] the next day W. recovered most of his memory, but that one day is completely blacked out, and he puzzles (as a neurologist) and worries, but much less than I feared.

2 Pears and Britten undertook a recital tour of Italy at the end of April 1947, giving concerts in Florence (26 April, as part of the tenth Maggio Musicale), Rome (28th), Naples (30th), Turin (3 May), Verona (4th) and Milan (5th). Programmes for two of their recitals – in Florence and Naples – have survived: they include songs by Morley, Dowland and Purcell, as well as (appropriately enough) Britten's *Michelangelo Sonnets*. The concert programme in Florence notes that it was Britten's Italian debut. See also Letter 546 n. 2.

3 Mrs Mayer had written on 9 December:

> He [Auden] has an apartment at last, in the 'Village' [i.e. Greenwich Village, New York] very small but quite cosy, and at last he got his furniture, bed, chairs and a plain table for writing. His address is 7 Cornelia Street, N.Y. 14 (if you don't know it already). We are going tomorrow together to a party for Cyril Connolly who is here. I heard that E.M.F. [E. M. Forster] is also expected here soon – and I am look-ing forward to meeting him.

See also Humphrey Carpenter, *W. H. Auden: A Biography*, p. 346.

4 Auden's poem *The Age of Anxiety* (1944–47) was first published in the United States in 1947 by Random House, and in England by Faber and Faber the following year. It received a Pulitzer Prize in 1948.

In her letter of 9 December 1946, Mrs Mayer wrote to Britten, 'I am just reading the proofs [of *The Age of Anxiety*], and talking a lot with Wystan about it.' The following April she was to write, 'Wystan's new long opus is in print. You'll be surprised. I wish I could some time talk with you about him – as we both love, and respect him.'

5 The 'Litany and Anthem for St Matthew's Day': see Letter 519 n. 2.

6 A reference to Britten's continued interest in setting *For the Time Being*, a project that had been active intermittently since 1942. See also Letter 397 n. 2.

For the Time Being was first published in 1947, subtitled 'A Christmas Oratorio', and dedicated 'In Memoriam Constance Rosalie Auden, 1870–1941' (Auden's mother). The volume comprised two independent parts, the 'Oratorio' and 'The Sea and the Mirror', Auden's wholly remarkable 'Commentary' on Shakespeare's *The Tempest*. During the period it was written Auden and Britten were in close touch (Auden was teaching at Swarthmore) and it is probable that thoughts about *The Tempest* would have arisen in meetings or conversations between the two men. Early seeds of this kind so often proved to flourish significantly later in Britten's creative mind and, as is widely known, a *Tempest* project surfaced at different stages of his life; alas, it was never to be realized (see Letter 672 n. 3).

An important edition of *The Sea and the Mirror, A Poem* was edited by Arthur Kirsch in 2003. It is essential reading, as is a brilliant review of it by Peter McDonald in the *Times Literary Supplement* (2 January 2004). Particularly fascinating is this passage from McDonald's review which opens with his comment, 'Death, as the thing beyond art's reach, is Auden's most consistent subject in *The Sea and the Mirror*' and ends with a quotation of the final stanza from Chapter II, 'The Supporting Cast' (Miranda): 'One link is missing, Prospero,/My magic is my own;/Happy Miranda does not know/The figure that Antonio,/The Only One, Creation's O/Dances for Death alone.'

That juxtaposition of 'dance' and 'death' is a reminder of how central to Britten's music was the concept of the Dance of Death. It was especially prominent in works from this very period, e.g. the *Dies irae* from *Sinfonia da Requiem*, which Auden may well have heard, or at the least heard *about*, was first played in New York in 1941, and earlier there was the explosive orchestral interlude from *Dance of Death* in *Our Hunting Fathers* (1936), a work Auden had himself devised with Britten. (See also Donald Mitchell, 'Violent Climates', in MCCCBB, pp. 198–205.) The creative interpenetration of two minds, albeit in different arts, working in such close proximity in a clearly defined period is remarkable enough in itself. While the relationship of *The Tempest* to Britten and Auden must remain speculative – was it at some stage a joint interest or arrived at by means of an independent route in each case? – the fact remains that for both the composer and the poet Shakespeare's last play provided a common and rich source of inspiration.

In the light of all this, perhaps it is not so surprising – and it seems not to have been allotted the significance it merits – that on the title page of Auden's ensuing publication of *The Age of Anxiety* (1947/48) – which it might be realistically claimed drew a line beneath the years of Britten's and Auden's mutually stimulating activities and discussions – Auden quotes the stanza beginning 'Lacrimosa dies illa . . .' from the original text of the 'Dies irae' attributed to Thomas of Celano (d. 1250). Might Auden – consciously or unconsciously – have remembered the astonishing evolution of a form and imagery that he had jointly launched in 1936 in the *Dance of Death* of *Our Hunting Fathers*?

As Edward Mendelson makes clear in *Later Auden*, pp. 259–61, *The Age of Anxiety* reveals the 'depth and complexity of Auden's religious interests at the time'. Auden's quotation from Celano also interestingly suggests that henceforth, so far as the 'Dies irae' was concerned, composer and poet were to pursue independent paths. The text allowed Auden to consider human responsibility and guilt in a traditional Christian context, while Britten continued to identify it not simply with God's wrath but with human violence. This is expressed nowhere more powerfully or explicitly than in *War Requiem*, in which the *Dance of Death* of *Our Hunting Fathers* and the 'Dies irae' of *Sinfonia da Requiem* come to full philosophical realization.

7 Robert Shaw (1916–1999), American conductor and founder Conductor of the Collegiate Chorale, New York (1941–54). He was Director of the Choral Department at Tanglewood (1945–48) and founder Director of the Robert Shaw Chorale (1948–66). Mrs Mayer wrote to Britten on 4 March 1947 about Shaw's apparently abbreviated performance of *A Boy was Born*: 'The Collegiate Chorale is deteriorating a bit – these things do not hold here in this country – R. Sh. has become a bit affected, and has lost the view of the whole in working out finicky details, exaggerating dynamic things and so on.'

8 Britten's comments about his own early compositions may have been prompted by a BBC broadcast of his *Phantasy* quartet as part of a recital in which he and Pears took part, on 18 November 1946.

9 A reference to Rose Marie Duncan's convalescence after tuberculosis.

10 Mrs Mayer had written on 9 December: 'The Yale Dramatic Workshop would like to do *This Way to the Tomb* with your music (Hindemith [to] conduct.) They have asked me about it. Should they get in touch with R.D. or with whom?' Hindemith was Visiting Professor of Music Theory at Yale, 1946–53. A search through the archives of the Dramatic Workshop has yielded no further information about this proposal, and it would seem that it never materialized.

11 *Peter Grimes* was given at Hamburg (its first performance in Germany) on 22 March 1947 and in Berlin on 23 May 1947. No performances, however, have been traced in Hanover during this period. *The Times* (20 March 1947) noted that, for the Hamburg performance, 'the German rights of the opera have been acquired by the British Control Commission under a quadri-partite scheme to facilitate the production of plays and compositions that the Nazis would not sanction. Other performances of the opera have been arranged in the Anglo-American zones.' The Berlin performance at the State Opera was given 'as prelude to a series of concerts of British chamber and symphonic music' (*The Times*, 26 May 1947).

544 To Jean Redcliffe-Maud[1]

c/o Lionel Billows Esq.,
Bellerivestrasse 38, Zurich
Jan. 8th 1947

My dear Jean,
      A scribbled note from the snows of Zermatt . . .[2]
The proposed dedication of the Y.P's G. to the O. . . .

> "This work is affectionately inscribed
> to the children of
> John & Jean Maud
> Humphrey, Pamela, Caroline & Virginia,
> for their edification & entertainment."
> ????[3]

If there are any comments and/or complaints could you please ring
Erwin Stein at Boosey & Hawkes (Langham 2060) & tell him because the
thing's got to go to print. If you & John don't want to be mentioned – we
could cut out that bit & add H . . P . . . C . . . . & V . . . Maud, but I would
like it in, if you don't mind – (and senza title, but if you feel strongly
about this of <u>course</u> put it in).
      Peter & I are having a grand time. We've fallen (literally) for ski-ing
which we do passionately & erratically. But we work of early mornings &
late nights to keep the conscience clear.[4]

Love to you all,
Yours ever,
BEN

1 Known also by her professional name (she was a concert pianist), Jean
   Hamilton: see Letter 508 n. 1, and pp. 11–12, n. 14.

2 In the Swiss Alps, near the Matterhorn. Lionel Billows's address was being
   used as a *poste-restante*. Britten's engagement diary for 1947 suggests that
   he and Pears arrived in Switzerland on 1 January, staying there until mid-
   February. Billows, his future wife Johanni, and Britten and Pears spent a
   working/ski-ing holiday together in Zermatt, about which Billows wrote in
   a private communication to Philip Reed (August 1993):

   The four of us travelled by train to Zermatt. The hotel we stayed in was modest and
   clean [. . .] not too expensive, and the people friendly; but after a few nights Ben
   couldn't stand the piano and the drum that played morosely and with mechanical
   monotony in the lounge downstairs, every evening. It disturbed Ben's musical
   thinking. So Johanni went out into the village, and was able to find the top half of
   a chalet, that people didn't occupy in winter, so we moved in, and Ben was able to
   get on with writing the composition [*Albert Herring*] he was on. He didn't seem to
   be disturbed by conversation going on round him, and seemed not to be listening,
   though he would throw in a remark from time to time.

[. . .] [Johanni] got on extremely well with Ben and Peter, so that when I had to leave after a fortnight to go back to my work in Zurich, she stayed on to keep house for them for another fortnight.

See also Letter 528 n. 5.

The play-through of the first act of *Albert Herring*, the composition of which occupied Britten at this period, must have occurred after the visit to Zermatt.

3 Jean Redcliffe-Maud replied on 18 January:

I think the dedication is quite perfect and glow with pride to feel that the work is semi-mine. The children love it; the other day Virginia listened to it sitting on my knee, & when it came to the drum entry, the pom pom pom pom, she turned round and said seraphically 'come in'.

It was Christopher Headington who first drew attention to the fact that *The Young Person's Guide to the Orchestra* is also an *in memoriam* piece: the Mauds' daughter, Pamela, had died five years earlier (see CHB, p. 83) but is included in the dedication. The family's own copy of the score is personally inscribed: 'For Humphrey and his sisters with much love from Ben'.

4 Britten was working at the composition draft of *Albert Herring*; see Letter 545. Britten wrote to Erwin Stein on 8 January, 'I'm doing a bit of work too & enjoying it. Hope to finish the act soon – but I can't start the score till the MS paper you said you'd send out arrives.' The essential manuscript paper appears not have reached Britten: a month later, on 4 February, Britten wrote, 'Did I ask you about the MS. paper in my last letter? – if not, could you send 2 quire to Billows' Zurich, for me of the same size?'

545 To Ernest Ansermet
[Tappolet, pp. 54–5]

Felsennest, Zermatt, Switzerland
Jan. 12th 1947

Mon cher maître,

As you see from this address I am already in Switzerland – but, alas, far from Geneva! Peter Pears & I arrived in Zurich by air, but we were so tired from all our numerous concerts, travelling & work that we came almost immediately up to the mountains, & it wasn't possible to come to Geneva to see you & Madame Ansermet as we had hoped. It is glorious up here and we are able to get in some ski-ing as well as the work on the new opera. Act I is now finished (complete sketching, but not the score yet) & I am quite pleased with it. It is a much <u>broader</u> piece (naturally) than Lucretia, but I have been careful not to go outside the natural limits of style that the small cast & orchestra dictate. It has many ensembles, & is more <u>horizontal</u> in texture than Lucretia,[1] but for some reason (perhaps

you can explain!) that is always the way with comedy. I look forward to
showing it to you, before too long!

Meanwhile in London the matters of the Opera Company progress
only slowly, but in the capable hands of Anne Wood[2] & Eric. They are in
close contact again with Bing & the Christies, & it seems possible that a
season at Glyndebourne may after all take place – but you may imagine
with considerable concessions on either side. I am not happy about this,
but in this hopelessly uneconomic world of opera, especially considering
who owns the rights & scenery of Lucretia, I suppose it's necessary.[3] Ebert
hasn't yet agreed to produce "Albert Herring" (the new one), but Bing
expects him to, & that is a condition on which the Christies insist.[4]
Apparently their own plans for Orpheus have gone too far to give up – &
so the season may be an uneconomic one of 3 operas (with one company
idle when the other performs) & corresponding rise in prices.[5] But this is
for business managers to fight out – if I do any more arguing there won't
be a new opera to perform! One thing I want very badly, & that is for you,
cher maître, to look after & deliver to the world the new piece, Albert
Herring. I shall never forget the loving care which you gave to Lucretia,
& it is my warmest desire, & that of John Piper, Eric, Peter & Joan Cross
(who are so closely connected with it too), that the new one should be
equally fortunate.

The financial side will have to be worked out, & dates too, but by the
aforesaid business managers. None of our group has the slightest idea of
what you were paid last year, & we are, frankly, a little nervous about it.
But we are relying on your good heart, & also on the fact that we understand that you may also conduct Orfeo, which will make your visit worthwhile.[6]

Forgive this long letter – but I wanted to tell you how things stood at
the moment. I shall be here till the beginning of February – then concerts
in Switzerland (alas not Geneva),[7] Belgium, Holland & Scandinavia, &
home again March 2nd.[8] When are you next in England?

I do hope Madame Ansermet is better now, & that you are well too.
Please give her Peter's & my love – & to yourself too the greetings of all
of us.

Yours ever,

BENJAMIN BRITTEN

1   Britten's remark about the texture of Herring – 'more horizontal' than
    Lucretia's (might not 'linear' be the more appropriate word?) – is borne out
    by even the most cursory scrutiny of the score. Counterpoint abounds but
    of an extraordinarily various nature, some manifestations indeed making
    their first major appearance in Britten's music. (Which is not to say that
    Lucretia is without its linear inspirations, for example the brilliant and

savagely dissonant chorale (the Act II Interlude) that follows – comments on – the rape.)

The picture becomes yet more complicated when, which is undoubtedly the case, Britten uses certain types of counterpoint, certain forms, to characterize events and personalities on stage, in short to characterize his characters. A case in point occurs almost immediately in Act I, 'We've made our own investigations', when the Superintendent of Police plus other village worthies participate in an exuberant but intendedly conservative fugue, counterpoint in the service of local pomp and circumstance. Here we have an established form of counterpoint, the impact of which is – or should be – ironic. (Britten was ever consistent, and when the 'investigations' prove fruitless the hitherto fuguing invigilators combine in a dispirited but wholly appropriate canonic quartet, 'My mind has scoured the parish through'.)

But this is scarcely where the innovative linear thinking has its origins in *Herring*, which makes its first appearance not all that long after 'tradition' has been affirming itself. What we hear in fact (at fig. 32) is a texture compiled out of the free, seemingly unrelated combination of the individual thoughts and comments of the characters who make up the diverse social classes of Loxford: something very different from the uniformed (Superintendent Budd et al.) counterpoint of that first big ensemble. This novel concept of linear textures derived from the amalgamation of vocal characterizations evolves throughout the opera and in fact leads to what must be considered the stunning climax of the opera, the all-encompassing cadenza that rounds off the great Threnody in Act III, 'In the midst of life is death', in which all the characters (Albert excepted) participate in an elaborate polyphony built out of their own thoughts and feelings, uttered freely in their own characterizing music.

This is certainly a triumph of the linear, appropriately located, but there are still one or two significant aspects of Britten's 'horizontal' preoccupation which must at least be touched on, among them the remarkable interludes for orchestra alone, and perhaps especially that linking scenes 1 and 2 of Act II. One could hardly get anything more linear than the two-part invention (*Lento e tranquillo*), a nocturne for alto flute and bass clarinet alone (remarkably anticipating an identical texture in the night scene of *The Turn of the Screw*), which magically takes over from the *Allegro* first part, itself another bit of virtuoso counterpoint which has its roots in the preceding celebratory 'Albert the Good' chorus but eschews any kind of conservatism of spirit or style.

There is one other example of *Herring*'s linear thinking: the music for the two lovers, Sid and Nancy. Their mutual passion and union to come is affirmed in their very first duet in Act I, 'We'll walk to the spinney', by the elaborate canon that forms the orchestra's accompaniment of their unison melody (another demonstration of unity!), and again in Act II, in their second duet, 'Come along, darling', of which canon and imitation are pronounced features. *The Beggar's Opera* (1948), as Britten himself recognized,

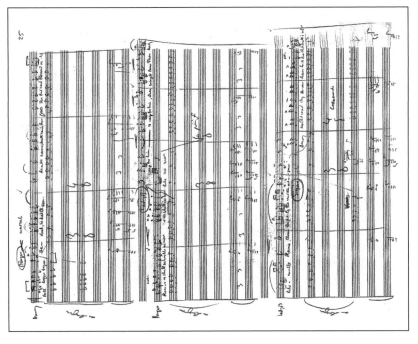

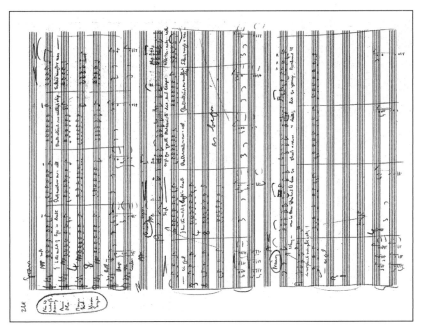

Albert Herring, Act III: the Threnody, 'In the midst of life is death', in Britten's composition draft

was to continue to deploy canon as a prime compositional technique. Fascinatingly, evidence of what was to become his later preoccupation with canon surfaced in the folksong arrangements, including 'The Ash Grove' (1941) and 'Sweet Polly Oliver' (1945). There were of course earlier conspicuous precedents, for example in *A Ceremony of Carols* (1942–43), 'This little Babe', and *Friday Afternoons* (1935), the traditional round, 'Old Abram Brown'.

In his late years, Britten's contrapuntal thinking was hugely influenced by heterophony, which he had first encountered in the early 1940s through Colin McPhee, who introduced him to the indigenous music of Bali. There is undoubtedly a real relationship between heterophonic and canonic practice, which makes it less surprising perhaps that in his final period the canonically inclined Britten pursued heterophony so extensively. Mahler was to follow precisely this evolutionary path from 'Frère Jacques', the traditional round which forms the basis of the slow movement of his First Symphony, to the heterophony of his late style (*Das Lied von der Erde*). Canon, so to speak, was the forerunner of heterophony, which had indeed already been anticipated in the Prologue of *Paul Bunyan*, figs. 11–12, where Britten uses heterophony to convey the shock of the moon turning blue.

2 English contralto (1907–1998). She was a friend and colleague of Pears in the BBC Singers during the 1930s (see PRPP, chapter 1). In 1936 at the Grotrian Hall, London, she gave the first performance of a now lost song by 'Luard Pears' (Pears used one of his middle names for his few compositions), a setting of Robert Nichols's 'When within my arms I hold you', and in the same year she and Pears were soloists in a recording of Peter Warlock's *Corpus Christi Carol*, with the BBC Singers conducted by Leslie Woodgate. She took part in the first broadcast of Britten's *The World of the Spirit* in 1938 (see Letter 132 n. 1). Post-war, she was active in the creation of the English Opera Group of which she was General Manager (1947–48); in 1949 she became an Artistic Director of the EOG, joining the original triumvirate of founders, Britten, Crozier and Piper. In 1948, with Joan Cross, she founded an 'Opera Studio' under the aegis of the EOG 'on a permanent and independent basis as the only school of opera in the country', from which subsequently emerged the National Opera School. In 1965 she founded and managed Phoenix Opera. For a period in the 1960s Britten and Pears had a flat on the top floor of Wood's London home.

An accomplished singer of oratorio and frequent broadcaster, Wood also took part in a number of important first performances, including the UK premiere of Britten's *Spring Symphony* in 1950 (see Letter 643 n. 6) when she sang the part originally conceived for Kathleen Ferrier. See also obituaries by Alan Blyth, 'Opera champion', *Guardian* (23 June 1998); in *The Times* (24 June 1998), and by Rodney Milnes, *Opera* (August 1998), pp. 921 and 953.

3 It was Glyndebourne, not the EOG, that owned the scenery, costumes and props for *Lucretia*. As Britten's letter suggests, Glyndebourne would also

have appeared to hold the rights to Crozier's production of the opera. Had the EOG been unable to reach agreement to perform at Glyndebourne in 1947, presumably the company would have been obliged to purchase the scenery, etc., and the rights to Crozier's production in order to stage *Lucretia* at another venue.

4   While Crozier was in Switzerland, writing the libretto of *Albert Herring*, he reported to Nancy Evans (undated letter) that he had received

A long letter from Ebert tonight – quite stupid – talking about Act I of *Albert* and how the production must express the 'social criticism' of the comedy, and the 'mendacious prudery' of the characters. Oh God! All so off the point . . . Now I must write a long letter back in words of one syllable, explaining that this isn't an Expressionist or Trotskyist attack on the upper classes of a decadent England, but a simple lyrical comedy.

Perhaps one should not too readily assume that Crozier's views at this relatively early stage in the evolution of the work also represented Britten's. It is possible, of course, that Britten too may at the outset have thought of *Herring* as a 'simple comedy'. But what is surely fascinating is the fact that as the composition itself developed, so did hitherto unsuspected levels of drama and psychological sophistication not only emerge but in fact determine the very character of the opera's evolution, exploring areas that almost certainly were not envisaged at or from the start. This manifestation of a work asserting its own right of development is often overlooked even to this day.

On 28 April Ebert announced his withdrawal from the production; the following day a meeting was held between Ebert and the EOG management. Crozier wrote to Evans later that day:

A meeting with Ebert that went on for a long time, and ended with his insistence on withdrawing from *Albert*, tho' we pressed him hard not to. He says he will help in any way he can, but the upshot is that I am now in sole charge of production, with his collaboration when collaboration is possible.

[. . .] I have decided to ring Ben in Italy tomorrow and ask if he will accept Tyrone Guthrie as producer, if I can get him. I really am too tired to take the job on lightly at the present time – and if Tony would accept, he would produce it brilliantly, and leave me free to deal with all the many general problems of the Group's present and future. If he won't or can't, then somehow I must do it myself.

It was Frederick Ashton, not Guthrie or Crozier, who directed the first production of *Albert Herring* at Glyndebourne in 1947.

5   In its 1947 season, Glyndebourne Festival Opera itself presented nine performances of Gluck's *Orfeo ed Eurydice* in which Kathleen Ferrier and Ann Ayors sang the title roles, with Zoë Vlachopoulos (Amor), and the Southern Philharmonic Orchestra conducted by Fritz Stiedry; Carl Ebert produced. A 'concise' version of this production was recorded by Decca in June 1947. See Spike Hughes, *Glyndebourne: A History of the Festival Opera Founded in 1934 by Audrey and John Christie*, p. 159; Maurice

Leonard, *Kathleen: The Life of Kathleen Ferrier*, pp. 94–5; and Paul Campion, *Ferrier – A Career Recorded*, pp. 19–22.

6   It was, in fact, ill health that prevented Ansermet conducting at Glyndebourne; see Crozier to Nancy Evans (12 February 1947), Letter 548 n. 1.

7   Ansermet lived in Geneva.

8   The BPL does not possess information about all the concerts from this European tour, but it is known that Pears sang Mozart's concert aria *Misero! O sogno* (K. 431) and Britten's *Serenade* (with Werner Speth, horn), at the Tonhalle, Zurich, on 11 February, with Britten conducting (the programme also included *The Young Person's Guide to the Orchestra*, but the performance may not have been conducted by the composer); on 12 February, in the Stadthaussaal, Winterthur, Pears sang the Mozart and Britten as before, but with Hermann Scherchen conducting (and Hans Will, horn); on 14 February, in Zurich, Pears was the soloist in a concert that included music by Purcell, Eccles and Muffat, given 'under the patronage of the British Council'; in Diligentia, Holland, on the 17th, Pears and Britten gave a recital that included the *Michelangelo Sonnets*, a programme that was repeated in Stockholm on the 21st; and in Copenhagen, on the 25th, their recital included Purcell's *The Queen's Epicedium* (realized by Britten), songs by Schubert and Mahler, and Britten's 'Let the florid music praise' (from *On This Island*), 'Fish in the unruffled lakes' and folksong arrangements.

A recital in Copenhagen, 25 February 1947, which included four songs by Mahler

546   To Serge Koussevitzky

as from: 3 Oxford Square, W.2

Jan. 12th 1947

My dear Dr Koussevitzky,

I hope that you have already received my messages from Ralph Hawkes, but I want to write to you personally & explain my position. First of all, please accept my profound apologies for not having written before, but my life of work, concerts & travelling has been more than usually hectic, & letter-writing incredibly difficult!

I expect Mr Hawkes has told you of our considerable operatic plans in England & in Europe for this summer. We are forming a new company, independently, to perform during the summer months, & I am the musical director & am in the middle of writing an opera for it to perform. I am afraid that this makes it quite impossible for me to come to Tanglewood for the School. It is very disappointing, because I should have enjoyed the experience greatly, & would have loved to be with all my friends for that time. Perhaps another year, when the new Company is running smoothly, & can be left to itself. But, thank you from the bottom of my heart for your kind & flattering invitation.[1]

The opera plans also affect the Symphony position slightly. As you know, I am desperately keen to do it for you, & I have elaborate & exciting ideas for it! But all the same I am keen not to do it in a hurry; I want it to be my biggest & best piece so far. I shall be working on the opera for a few months more, & after a short tour in Italy in April,[2] I hope to get down to the Symphony early in May. If it will be ready in time for the Berkshire Festival it is impossible to say. If all my ideas work out easily, perhaps; but if not, as I said, I am particularly keen not to hurry it, as I want it to be good! I think the best thing is to let you know how it progresses, & so that you can make your plans accordingly. By the way, I am planning it for chorus & soloists, as I think you wanted; but it is a real symphony (the emphasis is on the orchestra) & consequently I am using Latin words.[3]

Dare I ask if there is still a chance of your orchestra coming to Europe this Fall? That would be a great event for us!

I hope you are in the best of health. I am spending a few weeks in the mountains of Switzerland, in Zermatt, working and ski-ing. After a very busy season in England it is a grand rest to be here and to think quietly & look at the Matterhorn.

Please forgive the rather "negative" tone of this letter, but believe that it is only because I have such a great love & respect for your work that I feel very cautious!

My love & best wishes to you & to my dear friends in your circle,

Yours ever,

BENJAMIN BRITTEN

1   In spite of his evident admiration for Koussevitzky and his work at Tangle-
    wood, Britten never attended the summer school in subsequent years.

2   Britten and Pears sent Eric Crozier a postcard from Florence, postmarked
    3 May 1947: 'This is a superb country – & we're enjoying it hugely. Concerts
    go very well too.'

3   This is the only reference among the extant correspondence mentioning
    Britten's intention to set a Latin text in his proposed symphony for
    Koussevitzky – to become *Spring Symphony* – but little evidence has come
    to light at BPL to suggest what kind of text Britten had in mind during
    this formative stage of the work's evolution. In the event, the text of *Spring
    Symphony* was compiled by the composer in the shape of an anthology of
    English, not Latin, poems on the subject (see Letter 584 n. 4).

    In 'A Note on the *Spring Symphony*', *Music Survey*, 2/4 (spring 1950),
    p. 237, reprinted in PKBM, pp. 374–5, Britten writes:

    I wrote the *Spring Symphony* in the Autumn and Winter of 1948/9, and finished the
    score in the late Spring of 1949. For two years I had been planning such a work, a
    symphony not only dealing with the Spring itself, but with the progress of Winter
    to Spring and the re-awakening of the earth and life which that means. Originally
    I had wanted to use mediaeval Latin verse and had made a selection of fine poems;
    but a re-reading of much English lyric verse and a particularly lovely Spring day in
    East Suffolk, the Suffolk of Constable and Gainsborough, made me change my mind.

    Tellingly, the cover of the first edition of the vocal score of *Spring Symphony*
    reproduced a detail from a Constable landscape.

    The second sentence of Britten's brief article importantly emphasizes the
    totality of the narrative that *Spring Symphony* articulates. The eventual
    celebration of spring is indeed fundamental but it is 'the progress of Winter
    to Spring and the reawakening of the earth and life' as Britten puts it – a
    clear spelling out of the life–death–renewal cycle (cf. Mahler's *Das Lied von
    der Erde*, a work Britten much admired) – that is still insufficiently appre-
    ciated, with adverse consequences for the work's performance.

    A libretto for the abandoned Latin text has not survived; however, a
    small number of volumes of Latin verse from Britten's library, two of which
    contain interesting pencil annotations in the composer's hand, may be
    relevant to the earlier concept for the symphony. These are: C. E. Bennett
    (ed.), *Horace: the Odes and Epodes* (1934); and G. Rostrevor Hamilton's
    compilation, *The Latin Portrait* (1929), given to the composer by Peter
    Pears in March 1943. The latter includes annotations that suggest that
    Britten was considering two anonymous Latin poems, 'De rosis nascenti-
    bus' and 'Pervigilium Veneris', while on the inside front cover of the former
    are page references, inscribed in Britten's hand, to a number of odes includ-
    ing three specifically about spring. None of these poems, of course, is
    'mediaeval Latin verse' as mentioned by Britten in his *Music Survey* article,
    but it would seem quite plausible that they may be related to the symphony
    project. Britten's copy of *The Oxford Book of Medieval Latin Verse* (1946

impression), although dating from the period when the symphony was being planned, is unmarked. A separate edition of 'Pervigilium Veneris' ('The Vigil of Venus'), translated by Cecil Clementi (1911), was purchased by Britten in Boston, Massachusetts, in 1946, when visiting Tanglewood for the US premiere of *Peter Grimes*. It was during this trip that Koussevitzky first proposed commissioning a symphony from Britten.

'Concert of English Music': a recital in Naples, 30 April 1947, which included Britten's *Michelangelo Sonnets*

547 To Erwin Stein

Felsennest, Zermatt
Jan. 21st 1947

My dear Erwin,

Thank you for your nice long letter, which I was happy to get. I will try
to answer all the points in order! I must confess that the non-arrival of
the M.S. paper has been a major nuisance – it still hasn't come, but I
expect that it'll be here by the time you get this (otherwise you'll have got
a cable from me!). I haven't been able to start the score as a result, & it'll
make the work a considerable rush, since I could have done a lot in these
3 weeks. Everything else seems to have arrived all right (including the
French Folk songs); so it remains a mystery, or otherwise sabotage by
some rival composer! I enclose the cheques signed for Mr Newman; and
one or two letters if you could please forward for me. (I must say I miss
Nicholas[1] sometimes!)

About Lucretia – If Ronnie & I do revise her, it certainly won't be in
time for America or Basel, so I think things had better stand as they are,
even the printed libretto. But I think we ought to revise if possible for
Glyndebourne – if only the last big recitative.[2] I hope to go to Basel at the
beginning of February. Lionel Billows is in touch with them.

I have had various documents about the Opera Company meetings
from Anne. She's very efficient. Have you yet met the possible chairman?[3]
The Arts Council news is good.[4] But I admit that every bit of news alarms
me slightly as Albert progresses so slowly! The Act II Scene I is a big problem,[5] & I'm hard at it now – in between ski-ing, which is energetic &
exhausting!

So very glad about Karl's triumph.[6] He deserves it. Now he really must
get the production side of the Garden put in order. I don't think it matters
at all Peter Grimes waiting – no good at all with the producers and
designers they are getting now – much better wait till that's changed, &
Piper & Eric are free. I don't know what to say about Peter – best wait till
after Albert there – I think he'll come round.[7] At the moment he's quite
obsessed by the Matthew Passion; & then there's Schöne Mullerin, &
Albert, & plenty else, so I don't think it's wise to bother him. But I should
love to have it done with him & Karl & that Chorus. Please talk to Karl
about postponement. I've suffered enough from bad singers, & bad décor
& production in that piece.

Well, my dear, I must stop this & post. Life is quiet & pleasant here.
We're both well & enjoying the mixture of sun, snow, ski-ing, working,
eating, sleeping enormously. Wish it could last longer! Love to Sophie &
Marion & lots to yourself.

BEN

Albert Herring, Act II scene 1, in Britten's composition draft. At the close of this scene Albert drains his glass of spiked lemonade to the ironic accompaniment of the '*Tristan* chord' from Wagner's *Tristan und Isolde*.

1   Nicholas Choveaux, an employee of Boosey & Hawkes who had acted as an
    occasional secretary for Britten.

2   Collatinus' and Junius' arrival in Rome, Act II scene 2: see Letter 539 n. 5.

3   The Rt Hon. Oliver Lyttelton (1893–1972) first Chairman of the English
    Opera Group. Lyttelton was a Member of Parliament from 1940 until 1954,
    and served as a member of Winston Churchill's War Cabinet in various
    capacities from 1940 to 1945. He was created 1st Viscount Chandos in 1954
    and served as Chair of the National Theatre Board from 1962 to 1971. The
    Lyttelton auditorium of the National Theatre, on the South Bank, is named
    after him.

4   A recommendation from Steuart Wilson to the Arts Council that the EOG
    should 'be awarded a grant of not less than £3000 and closer to £5000'
    (PKSB, p. 86). As Paul Kildea reports, the EOG received £3000, a grant that
    was, by the end of 1947, to prove insufficient.

5   The scene of Albert's May King coronation, at the close of which he drinks
    the *Tristan*-spiked glass of lemonade.

6   Karl Rankl (1898–1968), British conductor and composer of Austrian birth,
    who had known Erwin Stein in Vienna. Rankl had studied with Schoen-
    berg and Webern, and in the pre-war years had combined the activities of
    conductor and composer. He was Klemperer's assistant at the Kroll Oper,
    Berlin (1928–31), and in 1937 was appointed Director of the Neues Deutsches
    Theater in Prague where he conducted the first performance of Krenek's
    Karl V.
        At the outbreak of war he came to Britain and subsequently took British
    citizenship. In 1946 he became Musical Director of the Covent Garden
    Opera Company where he remained until 1951. In 1947 he conducted the
    company's first production of *Peter Grimes* (see Letters 558 n. 1 and 559 n. 3).
    His opera *Deirdre of the Sorrows* (based on J. M. Synge's play) won an Arts
    Council Prize for the Festival of Britain in 1951, but has never been pro-
    duced. See also Norman Lebrecht, *Covent Garden: the Untold Story*, pp.
    48–127 *passim*, and Daniel Snowman, *The Hitler Emigrés: The Cultural
    Impact on Britain of Refugees from Nazism*, pp. 208–13.
        Rankl's first Covent Garden production was Bizet's *Carmen*, word of
    which – 'Karl's triumph' – had reached Britten in a letter from Erwin Stein
    dated 15 January 1947:

    Carmen yesterday was a great triumph for Karl and it was well deserved. Purely
    musically the performance was first rate, everything emanated from the conductor,
    every single phrase of the singers, of the chorus and the orchestra. He did not dis-
    appoint me, on the contrary, the way he enforced *piano* and *pianissimo* on the stage
    and in the orchestra was really a great achievement. The chorus is excellent: Karl
    says it is better than it was at the Berlin Opera: the orchestra played astoundingly:
    the singers were a mixed bag but among the young ones there are some with
    considerable possibilities if not yet achievements [. . .] About the visual side I had

better not talk: it was at the best ordinary, but in many respects below. Anyhow, a good producer and a designer's imagination and style could produce together with Karl a very fine Opera [...]

By the way, as an opera *Carmen* is rotten of course. I should like to talk to you about this some time.

7   Stein had written to Britten on 16 January in connection with *Grimes*:

I deeply regret the difficulties of *Peter Grimes*. I very well understand that Peter cannot do it at present, but I hope the opportunity will arise. After what I heard yesterday [*Carmen*], I madly would want to hear the music of *Peter Grimes* played by Rankl and sung by his chorus [...] The way Karl keeps the orchestra down is astounding [...] We need not be in the least afraid for putting *Lucretia* and *Albert* on this stage. Anyhow, you will hear for yourself and I guess Peter will gain much more confidence with the acoustics of the house, once he heard an opera under Rankl.

Stein's last remark and Britten's response to him on 21 January suggest that Pears was doubtful about the effectiveness of the size of his voice against the orchestra in the larger space of Covent Garden; he had, to date, sung *Grimes* only in relatively small theatres (Sadler's Wells Theatre and the Zurich Stadttheater). *Grimes* was, indeed, postponed at Covent Garden until the autumn of 1947, when it opened on 6 November.

548   To Barbara Britten

Felsennest, Zermatt
Jan 29th 1947

My darling Barbara,

Lovely to get your letters – thank you so much for being so nice & writing so often! I am sorry not to have written properly, but I know you realise what holidays are, especially holidays when in every free moment an opera has to be written![1] This even can't be a long letter as Peter & I have to catch the morning train up to the mountains to do some ski-ing – one can ski down here, there are many & good nursery slopes, but it is much more fun to go for long runs up above, among all the mountains with the Matterhorn looking down on one. I have got a bit behind with my ski-ing, since I strained a muscle last week & had to have three or four days off (which meant that the opera caught up!), but I enjoy it enormously. Of course one starts very slowly & wobbly at one's advanced age, but as long as one doesn't mind falling down & looking undignified one can get an awful lot of fun out of it.

Yes, we had to move from the hotel – but this is far nicer. It is a wooden chalet just above Zermatt, & we have a flat in it. Wonderful food & much cheaper than the hotels; & much nicer people, more real peasants, & real houses than down in the village, which in spite of its beauty is just a bit

too English & Hotelly. The English people are rather a bore – just the type
one can't bear; very rich, snobbish, blasé, & for all their skill in ski-ing
(they've been out every year, & for most of the year, when they're not
hunting) rather bored. But we don't see anything of them except in trains
& occasionally in restaurants.

My dear, I am so sorry that the fuel & food situation is so dreary.[2] It
makes one feel so bad-tempered, & lazy. Do go as often as possible to
Oxford Square for a good square meal! They've got loads of food, I'm
sure. Barbara Parker <u>has</u> my ration book; I insisted on that. And I think
Sophie has sent a lot of Peter's rations to Germany;[3] which is a good thing.

I hope to go to Basel to see about Lucretia sometime & shall write to
Bethley [Kaufmann-Meyer] & hope to see her. Probably in about a fortnight. We go down from here next week, start concerts on the 8th, & then
pretty full-speed till we get back (for one night only) on March 1st. But I'll
be around later that week. I hope the weekend with Beth is nice. Give my
love to her if this letter arrives in time – & to the kids & Kit.

And to Helen [Hurst] & lots to your self, old dear,

BEN

1 Work on *Albert Herring* had proceeded apace, with Britten in Switzerland
   writing the music and Crozier in England drafting the libretto. Crozier's
   sequence of letters to Nancy Evans (see also Letter 538 n. 5) reveals much of
   the opera's genesis. From 3 Oxford Square, London, on 3 January 1947, he
   wrote:

   I have broken out of my *Albert* troubles this morning and I am halfway through the
   Sid and Nancy scene, with a sympathetic duet led by Nancy about to emerge on to
   paper – about the problems of early love [Act II scene 2, 'Come along darling, come
   follow me quick!']. A subject on which I may or may not be qualified to write, but
   I shall do my damnedest. I certainly feel great sympathy with her in the whole
   matter, and I would like her to sing with such tenderness and warmth that her
   words will do not only for the under-twenties, but also for those ripe middle-agers
   of thirty and over.

   On the 21st:

   I've managed to write one scene already, which isn't too bad (you and Mrs Herring
   [Act III]), and I'm desperately anxious to get on and finish the act quickly. It's not
   a bit easy to do: it mustn't get too funny or too serious, but has to preserve its
   balance on a tightrope somewhere betwixt and between.

   I think writing seriously is easier than writing comedy in some ways. The music
   seems to come into verse more easily when it's in earnest – which perhaps explains
   why there is so much more good serious verse than comic in English.

   In early February Crozier joined Britten and Pears in Switzerland. (On
   the 4th Britten told Stein, 'It is lovely having Eric here, & we are doing a lot
   of work & he is even ski-ing a bit. The score is going well, & I hope to send

a large bit back with him.') Crozier wrote to Nancy Evans on the 3rd:

They [Britten and Pears] want me to go up with them on the funicular tomorrow, but I am staying here to finish work on *The Happy Journey* [a play by Thornton Wilder which Crozier was to direct] and rewrite some bits of Act II [of *Herring*]. Ben has finished scene 1, but there are many things to correct and whole chunks to be redone before he can be satisfied with it. Scene 2 won't present nearly so many difficulties.

In a second letter on the 3rd, Crozier raised two further projected collaborations with Britten which were evidently under discussion at this time:

Ben likes the idea of the children's opera very much, and wants us to do it! Hooray! If we come together to Switzerland in autumn, I will write it then. He keeps talking, too, of *our* next opera for Covent Garden in 1949 [. . .] We discussed who Albert should be dedicated to, and he rather felt it should be to our singers who have remained faithful, which I should awfully like. I hope he doesn't change his mind.

Britten did change his mind: *Albert Herring* was dedicated to E. M. Forster; he was, however, to dedicate *The Turn of the Screw* 'to those members of the English Opera Group who took part in the first performance'.

On the 6th Crozier wrote:

Ben asked plump out today if I would like to write the next opera with him for the Garden. I said of course, I'd love to but wouldn't hold him to it until after we'd seen how *Albert* came out in rehearsal and performance. He wants us to do the children's opera on a Bible story – a good idea, I think.

The children's opera (1949) was to be *Let's Make an Opera*, the second half of which is entitled *The Little Sweep*. While Britten was not to write a children's opera based on a story from the Bible at this time, in 1957 he did compose *Noye's Fludde*, a setting of the Chester Miracle Play which dramatizes the Old Testament story of Noah's Ark.
    Further work on *Albert Herring* preoccupied Crozier on the 7th:

I haven't done all the tidying for Act II yet. It's rather a tricky job, and more difficult than writing new verses – especially the bits where Ben has already done the music and I have to write verses to fit. This is hellish to do.

He subsequently reported:

Your telegram was the spark needed to set me off again working on *Albert*. I had been trying hard enough, but it was heavy, fruitless going, like walking through wet clay. Your telegram came at six last evening, and by ten I had done a whole new section of Act III – lots of verses, including the lament [i.e. the Threnody] over Albert's wreath found on the road to Ipswich. Whether Ben will approve remains to be seen – he and Peter won't be back from Lugano till this afternoon.

On the 9th: 'I have got on well these two days, and now have only Albert's final big aria to do, and a trio for him, you and Sid. By Wednesday these should be finished.' He then returned to the subject of the proposed opera for Covent Garden:

We all seem to have agreed among ourselves, without even talking it over much, that Cromwell and the Civil War period will be the setting for the next big opera. Peter is sitting across the room reading *England Under the Stuarts* [the standard work on the subject by George Macaulay Trevelyan, first published in 1904]. In preparation . . . I must begin reading history, too, when *Albert* is finished, and looking for a subject. Ben wants a big part for Joan as mother of a family split by the Civil War – thinking, I imagine, that this may be her last opera. The Murray Guides will come in useful now [Crozier and Pears, aided by John Piper, had begun assembling a collection of these red-covered handbooks for travellers originated and published by John Murray III (1808–1892), the son and successor of Byron's publisher, John Murray II (1778–1843)] – they have lots of interesting notes and stories about the Civil War period. It will be thrilling if I really *do* have the job of writing the libretto – especially as we shall have plenty of time, and it won't be produced till 1949.

Crozier added the following note to his later transcription of this letter: 'The projected "Civil War opera" with a "big part for Joan" was clearly prompted by Brecht's *Mother Courage*, which Ben and Peter had seen in Switzerland with Theresa Giehse in the leading role.' This project was subsequently abandoned.

On the 11th he could tell Nancy Evans:

I've got to Albert's last song (I have done his recitative which is long and elaborate) ['I can't remember everything'] and hope to finish tomorrow when the boys go to Winterthur. What I am to do for your final trio ['Albert's come / Back to stay'] I don't know – but it must be terribly good to end with.

The next day Crozier wrote from Zurich:

The opera [libretto] is all finished except for rewrites! I got to the end of Act III yesterday morning. We celebrated with a glass of Genever from a bottle Theresa Giehse had sent the boys, and Ben said would I devote the rest of my life to writing libretti for him? He suggested, too, we should write a musical film together to earn lots of money, so I could have leisure to concentrate on more writing – and then we had a long talk about the next (Civil War) opera and how we should set about it [. . .] Act III [of *Albert Herring*] is better written than I or II – I'm learning by practice to be sharper and clearer and to use less words to say what has to be said.

Some bad news yesterday. Ansermet is not well and cannot come to us this summer [to conduct the EOG] because he must rest. We rang Geneva and talked to him and he was very sweet, but his heart is giving him trouble. Second blow – the British Council, after verbally promising £7000 for our tour abroad, had changed its mind and won't give us a penny. Damn them! But somehow we *must* still find a way – I have two possibilities in mind and shall try all I know to keep the Continental tour alive.

A contract with Glyndebourne is being drawn up at the moment for our season there – Ebert will arrive in England in two weeks. Ben will be at Snape throughout March and the first week of April, finishing the opera, so I shall have to go to him for an odd week to continue adjustments as he goes along.

On 24 March, Crozier wrote from London to Nancy Evans: 'Ben is coming to Sid & Nancy in Act II, scene 2, and said on the phone this morning how much he is enjoying getting back to the young people. I think he feels as warm-hearted towards them as I do, and that they are very real for us both.' Three days later, now staying with the composer at Snape, Crozier told Evans that Britten had played through all of *Herring* that he had so far written – the whole of Act I and forty-five minutes of Act II. Within only three more days Act II was finished, and Act III was composed during April. (It was while working on this act that Britten realized he would need extra verses for the scene between Nancy and Mrs Herring.)

While Britten was working at his composition draft and full score, Henry Boys was making the vocal score from which the singers would learn their parts. By 30 March the first forty pages had been circulated, and by 23 April the vocal score had reached Act I scene 2: 'I got some more pages of score today, stopping short just at the bar before your entry' (Crozier to Nancy Evans, 23/24 April 1947).

Music rehearsals commenced in May: Anne Wood wrote to Joan Cross on 5 May, 'Mr Britten wishes to go through Act I with complete cast on Saturday May 10th at 3 Oxford Square at 10.15 a.m.'

See also Crozier's 'Foreword' to the libretto of *Albert Herring*, reprinted in DHOBB, pp. 137–8; Donald Mitchell, 'The Serious Comedy of *Albert Herring*', and Rosy Sinden-Evans, '*The Making of a May King*' or *The Creation of* Albert Herring: *A Comic Opera by Benjamin Britten and Eric Crozier* (MMus dissertation, Goldsmiths College, University of London, 1995).

2 A reference to the fuel and food shortages brought on in the first instance by a strike of road haulage workers. On the day this letter was written chaos and power cuts spread throughout the United Kingdom as freezing weather gripped the country and the crisis intensified. The situation was not to be alleviated until early March.

3 In the immediate post-war years the German people suffered severe deprivation, in particular food shortages. Presumably Sophie Stein was sending food parcels to relatives in Germany.

549 To David Webster[1]
Royal Opera House, Covent Garden

> AMERICAN HOTEL, AMSTERDAM
> Feb. 18th 1947

Dear David,

So sorry that I couldn't wait to meet the Arlberg[2] on Saturday night. Peter & I had to catch the midnight to Brussels, & daren't risk being late with those customs & affairs – Basel being worse organised than every-where else, I think. I hope you got your sleeper – the British Council chap really did his [best] possible to get you one with Cook's Agent[3] – but the situation did not look hopeful.

The enclosed note which Ralph gave me for you will be out of date now – but I send it for your files – I would like to have had a moment's talk with you – to hear your news & views. I'm so glad Manon has been a success,[4] & that Karl has also had generally such a good reception. The position now must be very difficult – but the winter & the crisis cannot last for ever, but you must be at your wits' end. Peter & I are just off to Scandinavia, a bit alarmed by the cold which is intense even as far North as this. We're back first week of March – & I'd love to see you for a moment. I feel that unless everything falls into place unexpectedly neatly that a postponement of P. Grimes until November is much the best – I do hope you can see your way to this.

Excuse haste & scribble

Yours ever,

BEN (BRITTEN)

1 British musical administrator (1903–1971), General Administrator of Sadler's Wells (subsequently Royal) Ballet and of Covent Garden (subsequently Royal) Opera companies, 1945–70. Webster began his career in commerce, as the manager of two department stores in Liverpool, and served on the board of the Liverpool Philharmonic Society. Webster established Covent Garden in the late 1940s and was responsible for policies in which British artists became part of the international scene. He was knighted in 1961. On Webster's retirement from Covent Garden, Britten composed *A Fanfare for D.W.* for brass (unpublished) which was first performed at a concert in Webster's honour (in aid of the Royal Opera House Benevolent Fund and of the Snape Maltings Foundation), held at the Royal Opera House on 30 June 1970. The *Fanfare* was conducted by Georg Solti. Britten prefaced his score with the following note:

This fanfare was written specially for today's occasion. It is based on a series of rising fifths, which celebrate the Royal Opera House (C – – E – – G – – – – –) and its retiring General Administrator (DA – – – – EB – – E –). Over these are scraps of nine of Sir David's favourite operatic tunes, with one [from *Peter Grimes*] thrown in for historical reasons.
No prizes are offered for their identification.

See also Montague Haltrecht, *The Quiet Showman: Sir David Webster and the Royal Opera House*; Norman Lebrecht, *Covent Garden – the Untold Story: Dispatches from the English Culture War, 1945–2001*, and John Tooley, *In House: Covent Garden – 50 Years of Opera and Ballet*.

2 Probably the name of a boat train.

3 The long-established British travel agency founded by Thomas Cook (1808–1892).

4 Massenet's *Manon* was the second of the season's new productions at

Covent Garden, where it opened on 30 January, in a production directed by Frederick Ashton and conducted by Reginald Goodall (his first opera at Covent Garden). In fact, the production (which Britten had not seen) was unsuccessful at the box office and not received with much enthusiasm by the critics. See also John Lucas, *Reggie: The Life of Reginald Goodall*, pp. 114–15.

APPEAL

This concert is given in aid of the funds of the War Resisters' International. It is a token of the respect in which we hold its late Chairman, George Lansbury, and the regard we have for its present President, Laurence Housman.

The War Resisters' International was founded twenty-five years ago. Then, the refusal to fight was contemptible to most of our fellow-countrymen, and to most of the people of the world it was cowardice and escapism. But the days when the order "pistols for two and coffee for one" was universally recognised as the rational and honourable way of settling an individual dispute, have long passed. And more recently the peoples of the earth have come to doubt whether the order "tanks and bombers for two and low rations for all" is a rational and honourable way of settling international disputes.

For more than a quarter of a century the W.R.I. has championed those people in all countries who have said "No" to war. Since Napoleon first cursed the world by introducing military conscription, growing numbers of young men, and lately, young women too, have refused to become the tools by which war has brought the world to its present sorry plight. Hundreds of thousands of young men with this common purpose have been found by the W.R.I. in sixty-eight different countries of the world. Many of them have stood fast in isolation, others in small local or national groups, whilst in other countries there are large and well-organised war resisters' movements. It is very hard to stand alone—through the International, no one to-day is compelled to stand alone.

Pacifism is not a new doctrine, but it is still the most revolutionary of them all. It calls for a new social order and a world-wide patriotism. In the atomic age it has become, not an alternative to war, but the only possible way leading to a world order where there shall be no more war, but "Freedom of Speech, Freedom of Worship, Freedom from Want, and Freedom from Fear." Please help the W.R.I.

It has an extensive relief work, the rational practical expression of its ideals. Please help it as much as you can. Gifts and enquiries to The Secretary, War Resisters' International, 11 Abbey Road, Enfield, Middlesex.

PETER PEARS and BENJAMIN BRITTEN

Friends House, London, 18 April 1947: Pears and Britten gave a performance of Schubert's *Die schöne Müllerin* in aid of War Resisters' International. This appeal appeared in the programme.

550 To Walter Hussey

[*Postcard: View from Snape Bridge*]

Glyndebourne
[Postmarked 25 June 1947]

Dear Walter,

Thank you for your note.[1] "Herring" went off splendidly, & audience reaction all we hoped for – wish we could say the same of the critics – but it is the old story.[2] <u>One</u> day we will meet again, but this life is hectic.

Love to you,

BEN

1 Probably Hussey had heard the BBC Third Programme broadcast of the premiere of *Albert Herring* on 20 June and had written to the composer to offer his congratulations.

2 Part of a letter from Eric Crozier to the conductor Hans Oppenheim, written the day following the first performance, gives a vivid impression of the work's reception from the point of view of one of *Herring*'s creators:

The dress rehearsal had great spirit and a warm, appreciative audience, who responded quite simply and laughed loud and long at all the things they were intended to think funny – much to Mr Christie's disgust, who said they were a very *vulgar* audience. We didn't think so – we liked them, and their encouragement was a great help to the singers.

Then came last night – when the audience was less simple, less willing to be amused, more careful in what they allowed themselves to laugh at! They were rather heavy going in the first act, and this made the singers' job more difficult. There were some stupid little mistakes in the singing from sheer nervousness. Acts Two and Three warmed up a great deal, however, and there was a feeling of considerable enjoyment from the audience, and a good reception at the end of the evening.

Now – this morning! – the critics! *The Times* hates the opera, calls it *a charade*, and complains of the lack of music that 'goes to the heart'. Frank Howes (who telephoned his notice to London immediately after the performance) says Ben is wasting his time writing for a small orchestra, and is going up a blind alley. The *Telegraph* (Richard Capell) says it was a performance of sheer brilliance – wasted on a work which amounts to no more than a snigger! The *News Chronicle* [Scott Goddard] liked everything – music, libretto, performance, scenery, production, and says so enthusiastically.

The general conservative impression seems to be that *Lucretia* (which they reviewed badly last year) is a beautiful work – and *Herring* an ugly, common one. But as this is based on only one hearing and seeing, perhaps they may not be entirely right. It seems to me impertinent to dismiss an entire opera by any serious composer on the strength of *one* hearing only, especially when it is done by anyone like Frank Howes, who is clearly prejudiced by the *kind* of subject of *Albert*. He says of the libretto – 'it is adapted from a salacious French story'!

We'll wait and see what comes from the weeklies – who have more than half-an-hour to consider their verdict.

THE ENGLISH OPERA GROUP

First Season 1947

Artistic Directors:
BENJAMIN BRITTEN   ERIC CROZIER   JOHN PIPER

Conductors: Assistant Conductor:
BENJAMIN BRITTEN, REGINALD GOODALL   IVAN CLAYTON

Designer: Producers:
JOHN PIPER   FREDERICK ASHTON, ERIC CROZIER

Musical Assistants:
ALAN MELVILLE   NORMAN FRANKLIN   HENRY BOYS   DOROTHY ERHART

Stage Director: Stage Manager:
ERIC CROALL   ALICE LIDDERDALE

THE ENGLISH OPERA GROUP CHAMBER ORCHESTRA

1st Violin—Jack Kessler.   *Flute*—John Francis.
2nd Violin—David Wolfsthal   *Oboe*—John Wolfe.
Viola—Bernard Davis.   *Clarinet*—Stephen Waters.
Violoncello—George Roth.   *Bassoon*—Edward Wilson.
Double Bass—Robert Meyer   *Horn*—David Burditt
Harp—Enid Simon.   *Percussion*—Herbert Wilson.

Frederick Ashton and Reginald Goodall appear by permission of the Administrator of the Covent Garden Trust.

Scenery built by the AMBASSADORS SCENIC STUDIOS and painted under the supervision of Charles Bravery.

Women's costumes, hats and flowers executed by the JOHN LEWIS PARTNERSHIP.

Men's costumes by C. I. SAMUELS and EDWARD H. SPARROW.

Wigs by GUSTAVA.

Shoes by ANELLO AND DAVIDE.

Properties made by E. D. WILSON and by WILLSON and HOPPER.

THE GLYNDEBOURNE FESTIVAL PERFORMANCE
OF
ORFEO

THE DECCA RECORD CO. LTD. have pleasure in announcing that they are making a "ffrr" recording of a concise version of Orfeo, with Kathleen Ferrier, Ann Ayars, Zoë Vlachopoulos, the Southern Philharmonic Orchestra conducted by Fritz Stiedry, and the Glyndebourne Festival Chorus in the Glyndebourne production by Carl Ebert.

GLYNDEBOURNE

Lessee: GLYNDEBOURNE SOCIETY LTD.

Artistic Director: Carl Ebert   Director and General Manager: Rudolf Bing

FIRST NIGHT, FRIDAY, JUNE 20th, 1947

THE ENGLISH OPERA GROUP LTD.

WHO COME AS VISITORS TO GLYNDEBOURNE, PRESENT

in association with THE ARTS COUNCIL OF GREAT BRITAIN

ALBERT HERRING

A Comic Opera in Three Acts

Music by   Libretto by   Designed by
BENJAMIN BRITTEN   ERIC CROZIER   JOHN PIPER

Conductor: Producer:
BENJAMIN BRITTEN   FREDERICK ASHTON

Lady Billows an elderly autocrat	JOAN CROSS
Florence her housekeeper	GLADYS PARR
Miss Wordsworth Head Teacher at the School	MARGARET RITCHIE
Mr. Gedge the Vicar	WILLIAM PARSONS
Mr. Upfold the Mayor	ROY ASHTON
Superintendent Budd	NORMAN LUMSDEN
Sid butcher's shophand	FREDERICK SHARP
Albert Herring from the greengrocer's	PETER PEARS
Nancy from the bakery	NANCY EVANS
Mrs. Herring Albert's mother	BETSY DE LA PORTE
Emmie } Cis tiresome village children Harry	LESLIE DUFF ANNE SHARP DAVID SPENSER

The scene is Loxford, a small market town in East Suffolk, in the year 1900 -

ACT ONE (April).—Scene I: The morning room of Lady Billows' house.
     Interlude: The Village Children.
     Scene II: Mrs. Herring's greengrocer's shop.

ACT TWO (May Day)—Scene I: A marquee in the Rectory garden.
     Interlude: May Day Feast and Nocturne.
     Scene II: The greengrocer's shop.

ACT THREE (May the Second)—The greengrocer's shop.

Dinner Interval after Act One.

Glyndebourne, 20 June 1947: the programme for the first performance of *Albert Herring*

Apart from the work itself – the performance is, I think, a good one. Ebert said he had the impression it must have been rehearsed for six months. Freddie Ashton has done an excellent production and the sets look delightful.

Ashton's earliest ideas for the production, however, did not receive Britten's and Crozier's total approbation. Julie Kavanagh reports that 'Ashton's approach verged on caricature' – the opera's creators wanted it played absolutely 'straight' – and that Ashton, unnerved by their disapproval and consequently lacking confidence, offered to resign (*Secret Muses: The Life of Frederick Ashton*, pp. 337–40).

Erwin Stein gave his view of the opera in a letter to Elizabeth Mayer (26 June 1947):

The first performance of *Albert Herring* was most exciting. It is a most brilliant and also most moving work, with some of the loveliest music Ben has written. I saw also a technical progress in his musical treatment of the stage, particularly in the recitatives which are a feast in themselves.

As Crozier indicated in his letter to Oppenheim, the national press was less enthusiastic than the Glyndebourne audience for Britten's new opera. Frank Howes, *The Times* (21 June 1947), had written that

The animation of the comedy does not communicate itself to the listener because the music does not engage his heart. Mr Britten is still pursuing his old problem of seeing how much indigestible material he can dissolve in music. Last year in *The Rape of Lucretia* he tried ancient history as a sermon; this year he essays French farce and psychological caricature. A salacious French story of Maupassant is translated by Eric Crozier into a rustic English comedy of the way a bumpkin kicks over the traces, and the result is a charade.

Britten has a musical comment for every turn of the dialogue, but except for a few notable *ensembles* he has put too little music into it. Nor is the idea of an orchestra of solo instruments, which he employed with a measure of success in *The Rape of Lucretia*, a satisfactory medium for accompanying voices. Without the soft texture of a string foundation the rough edges of his wind and percussion instruments impinge on the singers' vocal lines with harm to the delivery of the words. That the method itself and his brilliant uses of it are original is beyond question, but it seems to be leading him up a blind alley.

Richard Capell, *Daily Telegraph* (21 June 1947), described the music as

of the cinematograph school, lightly flickering, fancifully resourceful, above all witty in its transitions, and bitterly frivolous. And all these talents have gone to no more purpose than the raising of a snigger. *Albert Herring* represents a miscalculation. But the composer, conducting, was given an ovation.

William McNaught, *Manchester Guardian* (23 June 1947), commented:

What it comes to now is that every opera by Benjamin Britten is first-class news before it is performed. This gratifying réclame works a trifle unfairly upon *Albert Herring*, which the English Opera Group produced at Glyndebourne on Friday, for this comedy claims only to be a diverting piece on the second plane, a pleasant trifle that keeps the ball rolling, like another *Much Ado*, between one substantial work and the next. Viewed in that dimension it is a clever and successful entertainment whose faults can be readily passed over.

Although McNaught took issue over aspects of Crozier's libretto, he was positive in his appreciation of Britten's music:

Albert Herring is an evening to be keenly enjoyed, especially by those for whom music comes first. Britten's phenomenal invention works at a great pace, and never fails of something spicy and witty and original, or lovely, or even thrilling. And the many laughs are well earned. A clever cast sees to that with many touches of delightful character acting.

News of the opera reached Britten's and Pears's New York friends as quickly as those in England, as a review by Dyneley Hussey appeared in the *New York Times* (21 June 1947):

During the performance one was continually fascinated by the sheer cleverness with which all manner of operatic tricks and conventions were used to provide a witty commentary upon the characters and action.

Although the opera is a burlesque it is more than a pastiche. As in *The Rape of Lucretia* [. . .] Mr Britten used an orchestra of only twelve players [. . .] In addition, he makes use of *recitativo secco* accompanied on a piano. This gives lightness to the scoring and assures swiftness of movement. At the same time it entails a heavy sacrifice of the advantage of supporting the voices, especially in concerted pieces, with a full string tone. It also mercilessly exposes any failure on the composer's part to maintain his musical invention and there are certain pages, especially in the interludes, that seem to betray hasty composition.

This is not a charge that can be brought against the central figure of the opera. Albert Herring's character has been carefully thought out and skilfully drawn in the music. Perhaps exploration of his psychology has really been too thorough for such a figure of fun, and the long monologue in which he bewails his lot and finally decides to kick over all traces seems too serious for the farcical situation.

For a moment we seem to be back in *Peter Grimes*, an illusion strengthened by the fact that it is the same singer, Peter Pears, who now takes the part of Albert. Pears's thin tone suits the character well and he acts with an appropriate gaucheness.

Charles Stuart, *Observer* (22 June 1947), wrote:

Britten has never given us a lovelier, wittier or defter score than *Albert Herring*, which makes the perfect pendant to *Peter Grimes* and comforts many who had diagnosed a falling-off in *The Rape of Lucretia*. [. . .]

Mr Crozier's text is provocatively prosaic, sometimes admirably so. But whether Butcher Boy Sid (Frederick Sharp) sings about a bike puncture or Mr Mayor (Roy Ashton) about urban district councils, Britten's music is always pointed, iridescent, and redeeming. After a single hearing of so rich a score one's memory is a tumult. From the general welter I pull out the things that happen to be uppermost. The Vicar sings so angelically about Virtue in the first act that one forgets to smile at William Parsons's bland characterization. This lifting and transmuting of character and situation by the sheer loveliness of the music happens often in *Herring*. We take excursions into a rarer world, with the earthiness of comic opera left behind and below. [. . .]

Miss Wordsworth, the schoolmarm (Margaret Ritchie), precise and prim according to music-hall convention, has birdlike little outbursts of song that are quickly checked or quenched. Here again laughter is stayed: the music suddenly makes us see the schoolmarm as the poor, imprisoned creature she is.

Balancing the schoolmarm we have Nancy from the baker's shop (Nancy Evans), a fine blaze of warbling young-womanhood. Which leads to the reflection that the musical portraiture of *Herring* is wider of span and more adroit than anything Britten has essayed before, *Grimes* not excluded. Another forward step: the 12-piece orchestra to which *The Rape* inducted us is handled with greater resource and subtlety. I have never heard more new and enchanting noises in a single evening. Flutter-tonguing for flute accounted in part for some of them.

Ernest Newman made the briefest of comments in the *Sunday Times* (22 June 1947) which included a derogatory remark about Crozier's libretto – 'There is some remarkable music in the score; but once more it is evident that even Mr Britten cannot make good all the defects of a libretto' – to which he returned in two subsequent full-length notices during the following weeks, 'Mr Britten and *Albert Herring* – I' (29 June) and '*Albert Herring* – II' (6 July):

In Mr Britten I see a first-rate opera talent going partly to waste because of a failure to find the right libretto, a failure due in the first place, I suspect, to an insufficient perception on his part of where his real strength lies, and in the second place to a certain confusion as to what is and what is not worth doing in opera today. A good deal of the text of *Albert Herring* is in a true-to-everyday-life vein that of necessity sets the composer trying to find quasi-musical equivalents for the baldest speech. Much of what Mr Britten achieves in this line is very clever. But most of it seems to me wasted cleverness; and it is becoming more and more a mystery to me why a composer of his remarkable gifts should squander his energies in the theatre on futilities of that sort.

[. . .] In his latest opera there are scores of deft little touches in the orchestral tissue that go straight to the mark; while in the lament [i.e. Threnody] of the nine characters after Albert's supposed death Mr Britten has given us a truly great piece of music. Why then, I keep asking myself, cannot a composer who has so much music of the finest quality in him go all out for a subject and a text that will give full scope to what is best in him, instead of frittering away his time and ours on a musical 'pointing' of verbal commonplaces that only leaves us with a mournful sense of talent wasted?

The talk between Mr Britten, Mr Crozier and Mr Piper (the stage designer) on the evening before the first performance – one of the best things of the kind the BBC has ever engineered – showed us that the composer and his collaborators had done a good deal of hard thinking in the process of hammering out a composite work in which the necessity for all sorts of reciprocal compromises crops up at every turn. [*An Opera is Planned*, with extracts from rehearsals, was broadcast in the Third Programme on 19 June; see Letter 538 n. 5 and PKBM, pp. 67–74.] In particular we saw the composer holding fast, by silent implication rather than in set terms, to the central doctrine that what finally matters in an opera is the music, and persuading the librettist to change a line here and there that might be right enough by itself into something that will give the music more rope. Why then has all this conscientious thinking not resulted in something better than certain parts of *Albert Herring*?

Newman concluded his first piece on *Herring* with advice for Britten:

What I am certain of is that he, as composer, should take more complete charge of his next opera from first to last, insisting that his librettist shall provide him with a text that in the first place is potentially musical, in the fullest sense of the word, in every fibre of its being, and in the second place does not lapse into the banalities upon which music throws so cruel a light. *The Rape of Lucretia* was really more musical in essence than *Albert Herring*. The main trouble with it was a sham poetic diction that made the listener alternately writhe and laugh. The problem of finding the right subject and the right text is one that Mr Britten will have to solve for himself, preferably by some rather less expensive method than the present one of trial by error.

Newman returned to his criticisms of Crozier's libretto and Britten's setting of it in his second article:

In the BBC broadcast of a few evenings ago [Britten] said something about the problem of fixing the accents and inflexions of ordinary speech in music. This, I am afraid, is becoming a dangerous obsession with him. He did some rather dreadful things in this line in *The Rape of Lucretia*. In comic opera, of course, more latitude can be allowed the composer in this direction. But Mr Britten goes too far. There are one or two imitations of speech in music that are quite natural [...] But when we come to the many attempts in [*Albert Herring*] to sing words virtually as they would be spoken I find myself compelled to part company from him [...] the one thing we really cannot endure is the attempt which makes so many moments of *Albert Herring* a sore trial to the listener, to make the musical line an exact reproduction in another medium, which is governed by its own different laws, of the rises and falls of the spoken line. The thing simply can't be done successfully: the result is neither fish, flesh, fowl nor good Albert Herring. Mr Britten would do well to think again before he tries to gather any more fruit from that barren tree.

A similar critical line was taken by some of the weeklies and monthlies when they appeared. Martin Cooper in the *Spectator* (27 June 1947) considered *Herring*

a very well played burlesque [...] The characters are largely conventional skits on figures of village life, and their antics caused titters rather than laughter. Comedy demands humanity in the librettist and the composer, and it is not enough to create flat, cardboard figures of fun and then proceed to laugh at them. The musical interest was thin, except in occasional moments of apparently intense seriousness which seemed out of place – Nancy Evans's Mahler-like song [Act III: 'What would Mrs Herring say?'] and the concerted lament in Act 3. An expense of spirit in a waste of brittle giggling – I could not see much more in *Albert Herring* than that.

William McNaught returned to *Herring* for the *Musical Times*, 'Opera at Glyndebourne' (July 1947), pp. 234–5, where, a few minor criticisms of Crozier's libretto apart, he asserted that

of Britten's three librettos that of *Albert Herring* is the best. It is vivaciously written and versified, full of witty give-and-take, excellently characterized (with one exception), and well provided with those incidents, whether quick exchanges or lengthy ensembles, that are the breath of opera.

It was for the role of Albert that McNaught held some reservations:

For one reason and another the principal character did not fully shape himself in the text. Nor did he on the stage. Peter Pears – we know what he is good for – did his amiable and ardent best; but the character he presented was that of Peter Pears trying to look and sound like somebody else (whereas he had been wholly Peter Grimes).

In conclusion, McNaught wrote:

The piece is first-rate operatic entertainment, especially for those who by constitution and habit listen to the music first and all the time. Britten's invention never ceases to throw off pungent and significant ideas of his own extremely individual character [. . .] A good deal of the score is pleasantly irrelevant – Britten having games with his orchestra of twelve soloists. But one cannot recall that his games caused any special interference, whereas they certainly gave rare pastime to the ear. Modernisms [. . .] are served up in plenty; with Britten they are idiomatic. But a score of times one rejoiced in pretty or succulent things that came wearing everyman's harmony. There were episodes that stood out by their ingenuity and beauty [. . .]

Desmond Shawe-Taylor, writing in the *New Statesman and Nation* (28 June 1947), p. 473, considered that much of the opera's success was the responsibility of the 'skill and comic invention' of Crozier's libretto.

The crowning of a May King in Suffolk may sound an unlikely proceeding; but the events, as we watch them unfold, remain well within the limits of comic licence, just as the characters, even those which are most evidently stock types, never descend into the merely facetious. From these dangers both librettist and composer are saved by their feeling for the charm and poetry of life in a small East Anglian market town in the halcyon days of 1900 [. . .] an aroma of good humour [. . .] arises from text and score alike.

Throughout the three acts Britten's musical invention remains brilliantly resourceful. He can distil music out of anything – children playing ball, street-corner whistling, an attack of the hiccups. At his most successful moments, fun and musical invention are completely fused. [. . .] On the other hand, though the flow of musical ideas is unflagging, each one of them is apt to be short-winded. No doubt the composer deliberately accepted this restriction in order to ensure a rapid and fluid action; and in this he has been entirely successful, for the acts, though long for comedy, pass like a flash; nevertheless the ear sometimes wishes for more of those sustained and cumulative musical structures which have always been the glory of comic opera. The only serious drawback in a delightful evening's entertainment is the frequent inaudibility of the text.

William Glock wrote in *Time and Tide* (28 June 1947):

Albert Herring is a work of even more astonishing talent than *The Rape of Lucretia*. There is hardly anything in the text that Mr Britten does not reproduce in his music, from the whirring mechanism of the clock striking the hour, to the most daring translations of atmosphere or character. Yet *Albert Herring* is hardly an opera at all in the ordinary sense; it is rather a play with an extremely animated musical surface. The listener hangs on every word, and is distressed if he misses a single sentence [. . .]

Albert Herring would be a better opera if it were half an hour shorter. The material is spun out to an impossible length. One reason for this is that Britten cannot resist exercising his extraordinary gift for characterization. If the situation gives him the smallest excuse for painting a few portraits, even of people who have sat for him only forty minutes earlier, he will get out his easel and hold up the action until he has finished. One of the most enchanting moments in *The Rape of Lucretia* is when the three women say 'Goodnight' to Tarquinius, each in succession singing a short phrase that is perfectly in character. In *Albert Herring* this technique has been applied on a grander scale. It is delightful where the three children present their bouquets in Act 2, Scene 1; extremely successful in the opening scene when the various members of the committee suggest candidates for May Queen; but when the same members indulge in a succession of speeches at High Tea one begins to long for the first few minutes of *Don Giovanni*: for concentration.

Perhaps this new opera was too hastily written. There are signs of this in certain moments which struck me as mistaken in tone – moments when the music suddenly shifted from authentic Britten to a kind of generalized operatic world of sentiment. And the Nocturne may be another example, for it resembles too closely the music for Lucretia sleeping 'as a rose upon the night'. The best scene, not in inventiveness but in the sense it gives of dramatic unity, is Act 2, Scene 2, where Albert comes home from the tea party, hears Sid and Nancy outside the shop window, and decides to go on the loose himself. Even so it is a little too long.

Yet *Albert Herring* remains a work of great interest, deserving a much more careful analysis than I have been able to give it after a single hearing and without having seen a note of the score. It was very well performed. [. . .]

Albert Herring is an entertainment in which music, designs, and production are equally important and equally imaginative.

It is remarkable that amid the torrent of words about the libretto, whether praise or blame, there was no significant appreciation of its successful integration of vernacular diction.

551 To Jean Redcliffe-Maud

THE ENGLIGH OPERA GROUP LTD
295 REGENT STREET, LONDON, W.1
[Glyndebourne]
July 10th 1947

My dearest Jean,

This is only a madly rushed note – written in a Lucretia rehearsal![1] – but I wanted to thank you for your sweet note. So sorry you & John couldn't manage Lucretia – but I hope you'll see her when she comes to London in October.[2] She went nicely – but will be better later, I think.

I am afraid, my dear, there isn't much hope in the immediate future for a piano & string piece. I am so busy with the opera excepting for September, when I <u>must</u> do my Lancing commission[3] & think about poor old Koussevitzky's piece [*Spring Symphony*] which will have to be written in December & January. But, I promise, I <u>will</u> do you a nice piece – & it'll be the better for waiting too – I think slowly nowadays.[4]

I've sent Humph a copy of the "Y. Person's Guide" – the first off the press – thought it might cheer him up a bit.[5]

Love to you both, & lots of apologies for being so difficult about the piano piece – but have patience!

Love,

BEN

1   The English Opera Group presented performances of the revised version of *The Rape of Lucretia* at Glyndebourne on 7, 9 and 11 July, all of which were conducted by Reginald Goodall. Kathleen Ferrier returned in the title role, while Richard Lewis sang the Male Chorus, his first role with the EOG.

2   *Lucretia* and *Albert Herring* were given by the EOG at the Royal Opera House, Covent Garden, in October 1947. *Lucretia* was heard on the 10th (Nancy Evans as Lucretia), and the 14th and 17th (Ferrier as Lucretia); all three performances were conducted by Stanford Robinson. *Herring* was given on 8, 11, 13, 15, 16 and 18 October, with the composer conducting all the performances with the exception of that on the 13th, when Ivan Clayton conducted.

3   The cantata *Saint Nicolas* (words by Eric Crozier), composed in December 1947 (see Letter 562) but not completed in full score until 31 May 1948 (see Letter 581). It was commissioned by Esther Neville-Smith for the centenary celebrations of Lancing College, Sussex, where Pears had been a pupil in the 1920s. In the summer of 1947 plans were being laid for the school's centenary the following year. Britten and Pears often stayed at Lancing with Esther Neville-Smith (the wife of a member of staff), and when the composer showed interest in writing a new work for the occasion she offered £100 as a commissioning fee. It was another member of staff, Basil Handford (Lancing's historian), who proposed a 'hymn to St Nicolas', perhaps modelled on Britten's *Hymn to St Cecilia*. Nicolas is the patron saint of children, seamen and travellers, but, more importantly in this context, of Lancing itself. Britten, however, recognized that the stories surrounding the saint's life could be more effectively related in a cantata structure. Handford relates in *Lancing College: History and Memories*, p. 255:

We explained [to Britten] that it would be performed by the joint choirs of Lancing, Hurst, Ardingly and St Michael's with perhaps contingents from other schools. This is why there is a special part for female voices, to be sung from the western gallery, lamenting the murder of the three boys in the legend [No. VII 'Nicolas and the Pickled Boys'], and in another movement [No. VIII 'His piety and marvellous works'] the Choir is divided into several sections so that each school could have its own short section to sing.

Although *Saint Nicolas* was performed twice during the first Aldeburgh

Festival in June 1948 with the permission of Lancing College, the first official performance took place under the composer's direction at Lancing on 24 July 1948. Pears sang the title role. (The other works in the programme, all of which had been specially composed for the occasion, were a Chorale Prelude for strings by Jasper Rooper, and Geoffrey Bush's Oboe Concerto.) Esther Neville-Smith wrote to Pears on 21 June 1948:

On the 5th and the 12th [of June, the dates of the Aldeburgh Festival performances of the cantata] we all said to each other 'S. Nicolas today' and thought very hard about you. The thunder on the night of the recorded broadcast of the concert made reception very bad [. . .]
     Our practices of *Saint Nicolas* are going ahead. My goodness! Ben has produced a little masterpiece. It is so *lovely*. Isn't he pleased with it himself? The boys are getting very keen about it, but it does need Ben himself.

A notice of the Lancing premiere appeared in *The Times* (26 July 1948), 'Lancing College Centenary: Britten's Cantata', which concluded:

Both in subject matter and its treatment the work [*Saint Nicolas*] was wholly apt for the occasion, and it testified yet again to the composer's genius for securing the most telling effects by the simplest of means. Mr Peter Pears gave a sensitive interpretation of the solo part of Nicolas, while from his younger performers Mr Britten obtained lively singing.

Charles Stuart, '[Vaughan] Williams and Britten', *Observer* (1 August 1948) wrote:

The keynote is gaiety. Nicolas's birth evokes an adorable waltz, with vamped accompaniment, for women's voices. Why not? Must musical piety always pull a long face? The only weak episode in a swiftly moving score is the longish tenor–bass unison which narrates Nicolas's voyage to Palestine. There is a slight odour of banality here. But the storm music which follows I shamelessly enjoyed, especially the chromatic wails of sopranos and contraltos in the organ loft.

Desmond Shawe-Taylor contributed a lengthy review, 'Lancing and *Saint Nicolas*', to the *New Statesman and Nation* (31 July 1948):

This is an occasional piece, eschewing any great complexity in choral writing, and including two familiar hymns for congregational singing. Like an eighteenth-century composer, Britten enjoys working to a commission, and here he has produced something always perfectly adapted to the occasion, though uneven in point of quality. The first three episodes are meltingly beautiful. The invocation of the saint, with a solo violin climbing and soaring around the vocal line, is followed by a playful description of the young Nicolas's innocent precocity which is one of those small things which single out this composer from his contemporaries; one of those moments in which he seems serenely, almost casually, in possession of the secret of goodness and happiness. How on earth does he do it? A quick waltz in A major, with a single treble piping 'God be glorified' at the end of each stanza: could anything sound, in description, more trivial? – and yet few things could sound, in fact, more heavenly.
     At this point I fancied that *Saint Nicolas* would prove to be a little masterpiece of

the same order as *A Ceremony of Carols* or *Rejoice in the Lamb*; and there were later scenes [...] of great beauty: the dedication of Nicolas, the moment after his stilling of the storm, and the penultimate section describing 'his piety and marvellous works', in which the brief successive instances of these are cunningly embedded within the varied framework of a string *ritornello* based on the idea of a dropping and rising fifth – an effect curiously suggestive of a text meandering through the illuminated border of a medieval Book of Hours. To expect this standard to be maintained throughout is to ask much – and yet no more than Britten has done before. But whatever the cause, the total effect seemed to me patchy. At some moments the naivety sounded assumed rather than spontaneous; others suggested a too ready acceptance of the first idea which occurred (for example, is not the trochaic unison chorus descriptive of the voyage to Palestine unworthy?); at others again the composer seems to have been betrayed, as so often before, by his excessive passion for unaccompanied (or almost unaccompanied) recitative. Nicolas's prayer in the storm scene consists wholly of declamatory, non-melodic phrases, accompanied only by a roll on the kettle-drum; notwithstanding all the skill of Peter Pears, there simply isn't enough going on in such passages to excite or sustain the interest. Though it may be presumptuous say so, I feel strongly that what Britten needs at this moment is a rest from occasional commissions, a rest from concert-giving and accompanying, a rest from peripatetic chamber opera, and a long period of renewed exploration into the depths of his extraordinary genius.

4   This promise remained unfulfilled.

5   Presumably the first issue of the miniature score, published by Boosey & Hawkes. See also Letter 544.

552   To Edward Sackville-West

3 Oxford Square, w.2
July 17th 1947

My dear Eddie,

I was delighted to get your letter about Albert Herring, to know that you got pleasure from it.[1] It went awfully well with the audiences at Glyndebourne (inspite of that mischievous old mad-man J.C. [John Christie]!), & they were nice & big in spite of the notices. So we aren't dreading the provinces too much,[2] & are looking forward to going abroad at the end of the week. We are now in the midst of Lucretia recording – hectic, but it is going well, & it'll be nice to have nearly ¾'s of it on wax.[3]

This can't be more than just a note of thanks to you, but I do hope we shall meet when we get back – at any rate when we come to Bournemouth.

Lots of love to you, & Desmond,
Yours ever,
BEN

1   Sackville-West had written on 27 June 1947:

My dear Ben –

With the exception of Scott Goddard and Desmond the critics appear to me to have dealt most unfairly with *Herring*. They all go on as if it were meant to be deadly serious – not one of them even implied that the whole performance is uproariously funny – and committed the (to my mind) vile heresy of comparing incomparables – in other words expecting of you the same musical depth as they got in *Grimes* and in parts of *Lucretia*.

It will be a thousand pities if this enchanting little comedy is killed by priggish reviews. I loved it personally and thought the acting miraculous. Joan was so exactly like my grandmother (who incidentally had no 'purity' mania, but was just as domineering) that I could see hardly any caricature in her performance. Eric seems to me to have done a very clever job indeed, and of course Freddie was exactly the right producer because he prevented the actors from getting in each other's way – as so often happens in that kind of comedy.

As for the music I found the third act the most *beautiful* – as no doubt you intended it to be. But the whole opera is full of delightful characterization: those horn flourishes in Lady Billows' speech in the tent are a wonderful picture of Self-Importance! And I particularly liked the interlude in act I – a delicious piece of poetry.

Anyway, it was thoroughly worth doing: of that I am convinced. I wonder what you will do now . . . Speaking personally, I hope for some purely instrumental works, for a change.

I shall be coming to *Lucretia* on the 7th, with my cousin Vita Nicolson [i.e. Vita Sackville-West], whom I think you have never met. Perhaps we shall see you, if you are not conducting. I am much looking forward to hearing the work again – especially now that you have revised it.

In any case we all look forward to seeing you and Peter here [Long Crichel House] after the Bournemouth week in September.

Ever

yours affectionately,

EDDY

2 *Albert Herring* and *The Rape of Lucretia* were toured to Newcastle upon Tyne (29 September–4 October), Bournemouth (20–25 October) and Oxford (27 October–1 November).

3 An abridged recording of *The Rape of Lucretia*, representing about two-thirds of the opera, was made by the English Opera Group, conducted by Reginald Goodall, under the supervision of the composer, for HMV at its Abbey Road studios, London, 16–19 July 1947. An additional recording session was to take place on 19 October. The cast was Peter Pears (Male Chorus), Joan Cross (Female Chorus), Norman Lumsden (Collatinus), Denis Dowling (Junius), Frederick Sharp (Tarquinius), Nancy Evans (Lucretia), Flora Nielsen (Bianca) and Margaret Ritchie (Lucia).

In a postcard of 1 August addressed to the Redcliffe-Maud family Britten was to describe the recording as 'an appalling job'. It was made under the auspices of the British Council, whose Music Advisory Committee (Chairman: Arthur Bliss) discussed a proposal from the Gramophone Company (HMV) to record 'eight double sides' of the opera at their meeting on

23 April 1947. In fact, the Gramophone Company had already expressed interest in recording *Lucretia* in 1946, immediately after the Glyndebourne season. The project foundered at this time as Britten wanted Ansermet, Ferrier and Pears for the recording, but all three artists were under contract to Decca. By 1947, when HMV revived the project, Pears's contract with Decca had ended and he had signed up with HMV; Ferrier and Ansermet were still with Decca, so it was decided to proceed with Nancy Evans as Lucretia and Goodall conducting. The draft minutes of the Music Advisory Commitee (23 April 1947) indicate that opinion among the committee's members was divided. The proposal found strong support from Jack Westrup (Professor of Music at Oxford), who favoured a complete rather than an abridged recording, and from Arthur Bliss, who was anxious to see a Britten work included among the British Council's sponsored recordings. Bliss's feelings may have been prompted by the Council's singular failure to secure a recording of anything from *Peter Grimes* (see Paul Banks, 'Bibliographic Notes and Narratives', in PBMPG, pp. 211–20), while from as far back as April 1943 suggestions for a recording of Britten's *Les Illuminations* and *Sinfonia da Requiem* had been submitted to the Committee by Dame Myra Hess and Decca. William Walton, who had so fervently opposed the *Grimes* recording in 1945 (see Letter 528 n. 7), while not as hostile to the *Lucretia* project, supported a view (initiated by Bliss out of financial considerations) that only four sides be recorded. (In the end, six sides were agreed.) A suggestion from the Assistant Secretary (Mrs E. M. Donald) that Britten's views should be taken into consideration prompted Walton to retort 'that the composer is not always the best judge of his own work'.

The draft minutes of a further meeting of the Music Advisory Committee on 18 June 1947 reveal that Britten and Crozier had been approached in respect of the extent of the cuts to the opera and that, in fairness to the work, eight sides was the minimum amount of music that could be recorded. Boosey & Hawkes had agreed to cover 40 per cent of the total cost of the recording, and it was their financial support that tipped the balance of the committee, which was already agreed on the artistic merits of *Lucretia*, in favour of supporting the project. On this occasion Walton was absent, but his views were conveyed by W. H. Montagu-Pollock who reported 'that he had spoken with Dr Walton on the subject of this recording, and that Dr Walton had said that he was not in favour of the work being done'.

The recording was released in March 1948 on HMV C 3699–706 and deleted in 1956. In 1969 it made a brief appearance on LP (MFP 2119) before its withdrawal the following year. The recording was reissued on CD, with the addition of one previously unreleased excerpt, by EMI in 1993 on CMS 7 64727 2, with liner notes by John Lucas, 'Goodall and Britten, *Grimes* and *Lucretia*'. See also Lucas, *Reggie: The Life of Reginald Goodall*, pp. 112–13, and PKSB, pp. 209–10.

The recording received widespread press attention on its release in 1948.

While both *The Times* (30 March 1948) and the *Monthly Musical Record* (May 1948) lamented the fact that the recording represented an abridged account of the opera, all the notices recognized that it was a most welcome addition to the Britten discography, none more so than Alec Robertson's extensive review for *Gramophone* (March 1948) which concluded:

> Both the recording and the presentation of this opera are very well done. The work has evidently been thoroughly rehearsed and one never has the disturbing vision of a bunch of singers gathered round the microphones, anxiously waiting cues. The balance with the voices is, in general, excellent and details of the orchestration tell clearly. Chamber opera is, obviously, ideal for recording purposes and I hope we may have more of it. I should add a word of praise here for Reginald Goodall's fine handling of the orchestra, under the supervision of the composer.

After the British Council's inept handling of the project, it is ironic to read in *The Times* (30 March 1948) that 'this set of records has been prompted by the British Council, who need them as representative of English music to send abroad. They certainly show Britten's genius [. . .]'

553 To Erwin Stein

as from: Friedheim Hotel, Hergiswyl, Lucern[1]
August 8th 1947

My dear Erwin,

I ought to have written you ages ago – but you know how these things are – first of all the incredibly hectic Holland period[2] – then the long & tiring journey here, & the collapse into a small mountain hotel, the walks & the general laziness! However we all go off to Lucern today, so if I don't drop you a line now I shan't have any time till I reach Oxford Square again – & that's not much use!

So glad you managed to get to Snape – & hope you had a nice time a bit. It is a sweet place, & one part of me regrets leaving it – but you know how I am about the sea, & really that Crag House is pretty nice, I think![3]

Well, I suppose Anne has told you about Holland. It was all pretty good – Amsterdam better than Scheveningen – the latter is really only a concert hall, & the action was too dispersed. But the audiences reacted well, & were big & happy. They laughed hugely at Albert – as much if not more than Glyndebourne – Amsterdam. The music sounded fine in A. – at last a decent theatre. Lucretia was bad in Amsterdam, alas – the singers rather poor, & Reggie in a bad mood – aggressive rather than consolatory, & the singers panicked a bit. The acting too was poor. The truth of it is that we haven't got enough good singers to do two operas with different casts 100% well. That fact must influence our next year's plans. Luckily on Tuesday for Lucretia we'll have Joan, Peter, & Mabel[4] so it'll be more satisfactory, but I wish I didn't have to conduct!

Incidentally, it's nice to have Albert taken seriously by critics! I expect you'll see all the notices – I'm told that even the ones who had doubts in Scheveningen all came again to Amsterdam, & the second performance removed these doubts! Charles Münch[5] came to the 1st Albert, very tired, but couldn't leave although he had meant to! Freddie Goldbeck[6] was sent from Paris for Figaro & very sweet about it.[7] Münch did a good Illuminations with Peter, tho' the orchestra was poor & under rehearsed.[8] He is a nice man, really gifted – if he can only keep his balance musically.

So, now, you are off to Ireland? That sounds nice. Hope Sophie is enjoying her rest, now she's got used to the idea!

I called to see Harper[9] before I left, but he was out & I'm afraid it slipped my mind. Oct. 5th is no good as I shall be in Newcastle. I've sent him a card.

Everyone sends their loves. The drive here was exciting, moving & depressing by turns. Some beautiful things, madly hot, & much terribly destroyed – especially France, quite dejected. Luxembourg horrible – a provincial Brussels, which itself is bad enough. Nancy most beautiful – in fact I think Alsace the loveliest part of France I've seen – the only bit I really like. Now Switzerland, pretty, comfortable, bourgeois, cute & tidy. Perfect for a holiday; desperate for anything serious.

Love to you all – so glad Marion's enjoying her performing – that's half the battle.

BEN

1 Britten and Pears, accompanied by Nancy Evans and Eric Crozier, had travelled to Lucerne in Britten's open-top Rolls-Royce driven by George Behrend.

Under the auspices of the British Council, the EOG had been engaged to present two performances each of *The Rape of Lucretia* (12 August, conducted by Britten; 14th, conducted by Goodall) and *Albert Herring* (15th and 18th, both conducted by Britten) at the Stadt-Theater, Lucerne, as part of the Lucerne International Music Festival.

On 16 August members of the EOG took part in a concert at Basel Radio (no details of the programme have emerged); and in the Kleiner Saal of the Tonhalle, Zurich, on the 19th, they gave a concert of English music from the sixteenth and seventeenth centuries and works by Bax (the Nonet), Britten (excerpts from *Lucretia*), and the first performance of Lennox Berkeley's *Stabat Mater*, Op. 28, for six solo voices and chamber orchestra, conducted by the composer. The EOG concluded their tour by giving a concert at Zurich Radio on the morning of the 20th.

Berkeley's *Stabat Mater* was composed between April and May 1947 for the EOG's concerts and dedicated to Britten. Its first UK performance was given by the EOG under Britten's direction at a 'Concert of English Music'

TONHALLE ZÜRICH   KLEINER SAAL

Tuesday, August 19th, 8.15 p.m.

CHAMBER CONCERT

The Tonhalle-Gesellschaft in conjunction with The British Council present

"The English Opera Group"

Conductor:
Benjamin Britten

Singers:

Soprano: MARGARET RITCHIE - FLORA NIELSEN - LESLEY DUFF
Alto: NANCY EVANS - JOAN GRAY
Tenor: PETER PEARS, RICHARD LEWIS
Bass: FREDERICK SHARP, NORMAN LUMSDEN

Instrumentalists:

JACK KESSLER (1st Violin) - DAVID WOLFSTHAL (2nd Violin)
BERNARD DAVIS (Viola) - GEORGE ROTH ('Cello)
ROBERT MEYER (Doublebass) - ENID SIMON (Harp)
JOHN FRANCIS (Flute) - JOHN WOLFE (Oboe)
STEPHEN WATERS (Clarinet) - EDWARD WILSON (Bassoon)
DAVID BURDITT (Horn) - HERBERT WILSON (Percussion)
MILLICENT SILVER (Harpsichord)

The first Performance of "Stabat Mater" will be conducted by the Composer,

LENNOX BERKELEY

PROGRAMME

Ballets, Canzonets, Canon and Duets for Accompanied and Unaccompanied Voices:

THOMAS MORLEY (1557—1603)
a) "Sing we and chant it", Ballet for 5 Parts
b) "Leave now mine eyes lamenting"
c) "I go before, my darling", Canzonetta for 2 Voices

WILLIAM LAWES (1602—1645)
"Shee weepeth sore in the night", Canon for 4 Voices

THOMAS WEELKES (1575—1623)
"Strike it up tabor", Madrigal for 3 Voices

HENRY PURCELL (1658—1695)
a) "Shepherd leave decoying" Duet for 2 Sopranos
b) "Lost is my quiet", Duet for Tenor and Bass
c) "Sound the trumpet", Duet for 2 Tenors

Instrumental Fantasias:

ORLANDO GIBBONS (1583—1625)
a) Fantasia in 4 Parts for Strings
b) Fantasia in 3 Parts for Strings

THOMAS MORLEY (1557—1603)
2 Fantasias for Flute and Oboe

HENRY LAWES (1596—1662)
Fantasia for 2 Violins, 'Cello and Harpsichord

HENRY PURCELL (1658—1695)
Ode for St. Cecilia's Day
"Welcome to all the pleasures" for Voices, Strings and Harpsichord

INTERVAL

ARNOLD BAX (born 1883)
"Nonet" for Harp, Flute, Oboe, Clarinet, String Quartet and Double Bass
Molto moderato — Allegro

LENNOX BERKELEY *) (born 1903)
"Stabat Mater" for 6 Solo Voices and Chamber Orchestra
First Performance

BENJAMIN BRITTEN (born 1913)
Excerpts from "THE RAPE OF LUCRETIA"
a) The Ride to Rome
    Male Chorus: PETER PEARS
b) "Within this frail Crucible"
    Tarquinius: FREDERICK SHARP
c) The Flower Duet
    Bianca: FLORA NIELSEN
    Lucia: MARGARET RITCHIE
d) Funeral Chaconne
    Male Chorus: RICHARD LEWIS
    Lucia: MARGARET RITCHIE
    Bianca: JOAN GRAY
    Junius: FREDERICK SHARP
    Collatinus: NORMAN LUMSDEN

*) Conducted by the Composer

Programme for a 'Chamber Concert', which included the first performance of Berkeley's *Stabat Mater*, given by the English Opera Group in the Kleiner Saal of the Zurich Tonhalle on 19 August 1947

presented at Friends House, London, on 26 September 1947, with a broadcast performance in the Third Programme the following day. Members of the EOG also gave a performance of the work at the 1953 Aldeburgh Festival, conducted by Norman Del Mar, to mark Berkeley's fiftieth birthday.

The performance of *Lucretia* at Lucerne on 14 August was Reginald Goodall's last appearance with the EOG. Although Britten had wanted him to conduct the performance of *Herring* on the 18th, Goodall had already accepted engagements with Covent Garden in Glasgow, including his first *Turandot*. John Lucas (*Reggie: The Life of Reginald Goodall*, p. 112–13) reports Goodall's recollection of this time: 'Ben thought I should have stayed with him [. . .] but joining Covent Garden was a big thing for me. I didn't want to abandon it.' According to Lucas, it was Britten's recommendation that had helped secure the position at Covent Garden for Goodall. After this break Goodall was not invited to conduct the premiere of any of Britten's later operas, although he conducted successful revivals of *Peter Grimes* at Covent Garden and distinguished performances of *Gloriana* on tour, as well as the recording of excerpts from *Grimes* (see Letter 591). Lucas further relates Goodall's opinion of *Herring*, which partly explains his reluctance to conduct the opera: he found it 'silly – that's the word, silly; that prissy Englishness would have been knocked out of Ben if he had studied abroad. His entourage persuaded him to do that sort of thing, you know.'

2   Under the auspices of the British Council, the English Opera Group gave performances of *The Rape of Lucretia* and *Albert Herring* in the Kurzaal, Scheveningen (22, 25 and 26 July), and at the Stadsschouwburg, Amsterdam (28, 29 and 30 July). Britten conducted four performances of *Herring*; Reginald Goodall conducted two performances of *Lucretia*.

3   Britten was to leave the Old Mill, Snape, later that month, having purchased Crag House, in Aldeburgh, a substantial three-storey house on Crag Path overlooking the shingle beach and the North Sea. Two years earlier, during the summer of 1945, he had contemplated buying the Rectory at Iken, on the river Alde, but had eventually abandoned the idea (see Letter 510). On moving to Aldeburgh, Britten did not immediately sell the Snape mill but leased it to tenants for some years. Crag House remained his and Pears's home until November 1957 when they moved a mile or so inland to the Red House in Golf Lane. See plates 31 and 33, Letters 554–6, and HCBB, pp. 257–8.

4   Margaret (Mabel) Ritchie (1903–1969), English soprano was a member of the English Opera Group and created the roles of Lucia in *The Rape of Lucretia* and Miss Wordsworth in *Albert Herring*, roles that were composed by Britten with her particular vocal personality in mind. Britten realized Purcell's *The Blessed Virgin's Expostulation* for her and dedicated it to her. She knew Britten and his family in the 1930s when she sang for the Lowestoft Musical Society: see Diary for 11 February 1931 and 13 October 1931.

5 French conductor Münch was to succeed Koussevitzky as Chief Conductor of the Boston Symphony Orchestra. See Letter 487 n. 4.

6 Frederick Goldbeck (1902–1981), Dutch music critic, who had settled in Paris in 1925. He contributed reviews to several journals, including *Le Figaro* and the *Revue Musicale*. Between 1946 and 1952 he was the editor of *Contrepoints* and published a book, *The Perfect Conductor*. Britten and Pears remained on friendly terms with Goldbeck and his wife, the French pianist Yvonne Lefebure (1900–1986), over the years. Lefebure appeared at the 1958 Aldeburgh Festival in a recital on 17 June, in which she was partnered by Britten in Debussy's *En blanc et noir* and which concluded with a performance of Janáček's Concertino for piano and chamber orchestra. Britten and Pears also knew Goldbeck's mother, Celine, from their many appearances in the Netherlands during the immediate post-war years. After her death in the early 1960s they wrote to Goldbeck: 'She seemed an integral part of our work in Europe since the war – Holland was never the same after she left.' Goldbeck made a contribution to 'Evaluations and Comparisons' (25 November 1973), a BBC Radio 3 tribute to Britten on his sixtieth birthday presented by John Amis.

7 Goldbeck contributed an extensive notice of *Albert Herring*, 'Comment l'esprit vient à un Parsifal de sous-préfecture', to *Le Figaro* (2 August 1947):

Far from despising them, Britten adores his characters. He treats his world – old trouts and scarlet women, flirts and thoroughly bad lots, mayor, vicar and constable – like an enchanting tribe of savages who are performing an initiation rite for a young chap who is no more innocent than you or me. All the elements of a conventional opera are present: arias, ariosos, ariettes, songs, ensembles, finales, recitatives for one or more of the singers. The opera takes on board the essential qualities of tradition, innocence and parody. Here we have the aesthetic of *Falstaff* and *L'Heure espagnole*, a game of allusions and knowing winks. It requires a knowledgeable audience to pick up all the quotations [. . .] an audience that knows its Verdi and is familiar with the classical and romantic operatic repertoire in general, who will then be delighted by the allusions and references. This approach does not always succeed in avoiding jeopardizing the overall arch of the composition, particularly when Britten and his gentle librettist allow the details, the social nuances, the incidents to pile up one on top of another. But Britten has a sure instinct when it comes to setting a text, to knowing what makes a scene work [. . .]

Britten has a gift for swift and economic stylization, for placing the entirely new alongside the perpetually familiar. A single accidental and his musical language acquires a startling tonal colour; a note or two added to a chord and immediately the aural perspective deepens and darkens. From his modest orchestra of a dozen players he draws all the volume and variety he needs. This reduced orchestration brings instruments and voices into an equal balance and Britten seizes the opportunity to extend and vary the polyphony and to achieve a more profound relationship than is usually possible between stage and pit, with singers and players challenging and stretching each other. [. . .]

But, above all, Britten's creativity is rooted in his affection for his characters. This is a quality rarely given to artists of such dexterity and virtuosity; usually they are too busy playing the seducer to fall in love. But Britten's music has a delicious freshness, an exquisite precision and a marvellous sense of passion.

Goldbeck discussed Britten in the context of an article on contemporary British music, 'L'Angleterre qui fut privée longtemps de compositeurs originaux a aujourd'hui ses jeunes maîtres', in *Le Figaro* (23 August 1947):

His speedy acquisition of a wide variety of styles and means of expression should not be taken as an indication of indecisiveness but rather, in his case, of vitality. He is not following the line of least resistance but the trajectory – one might almost say the whirlwind – of his own insatiable musical imagination. He is extremely intelligent and has marshalled his musical forces with a sure hand from the outset. For him there is something dramatic in this musical quest, in the whole creative process. For Britten, counterpoint is not simply a technical device but the interaction, the dialogue, on a number of levels, between melodic units. [. . .] His individual style is born of the struggle between his favourite musical masters, filtered through his own musicality, which is itself startlingly original.

8 Pears and Nancy Evans appeared in a concert with the Residentie Orkest under Münch's direction in the Kurzaal, Scheveningen, on 25 July. While Britten's letter makes it clear what Pears sang, no information has come to light to indicate the nature of Nancy Evans's contribution.

9 Britten had been invited to participate in a concert of his works at the opening of the Music Teachers' Association Assembly on 5 October.

III THE ALDEBURGH FESTIVAL IS LAUNCHED

SEPTEMBER 1947–AUGUST 1948

YEAR	EVENTS AND COMPOSITIONS
1947	
early September	Composing *Canticle I*, and planning *Spring Symphony* and *Saint Nicolas* Pears at inaugural Edinburgh Festival singing *Les Illuminations* (4th) and Mahler's *Das Lied von der Erde* (11th and 12th)
12 September	COMPOSITION *Canticle I: 'My Beloved is Mine'*
1 November	London: first performance of *Canticle I*
6 November	Covent Garden, London: first night of new production of *Peter Grimes*
9 November	Broadcasts Bridge's *Phantasy* in F♯ minor for piano quartet and Piano Trio (1929)
19–30 November	UK concert tour with Pears
early December	Holidaying in Dublin with Crozier
17 December	COMPOSITION *A Charm of Lullabies* Begins composition draft of *Saint Nicolas*
18 December	COMPOSITION Radio: *Men of Goodwill*
25 December	BBC: first performance of *Men of Goodwill*
1948	
3 January	The Hague: first performance of *A Charm of Lullabies*
8 January	Completes composition draft of *Saint Nicolas*
27 January – 5 March	European concert tour with Pears (Switzerland, Italy and the Netherlands). During this tour begins work on *The Beggar's Opera*

12 February	Metropolitan Opera, New York: *Peter Grimes*
28 March – *2 April*	Concert tour in south-west England
12 April	Conducts BBC studio performance of *Albert Herring*
May	COMPOSITION *The Beggar's Opera*
mid-May	Scoring *Saint Nicolas*
24 May	Arts Theatre, Cambridge: first performance of *The Beggar's Opera*
31 May	COMPOSITION *Saint Nicolas*
5–13 June	First Aldeburgh Festival, which includes first performance of *Saint Nicolas*
25 June – *1 July*	English Opera Group tour of *The Beggar's Opera* to the Holland Festival
24 July	Lancing College, Sussex: first official performance of *Saint Nicolas*

554 To Peter Pears

~~THE OLD MILL, SNAPE, SAXMUNDHAM, SUFFOLK~~
Crag House, Aldeburgh
Sept 4th 1947

My darling,

It is a heavenly day – the wind has gone round to the West, & the sea is as still as a mill-pond. I'm sitting in the study (?) – upstairs, right in the window in the hot sun. I have to go round to the bank with Barbara [Parker] to arrange about accounts, & to the electricians to see about the removal of all those pimples all over the ceiling in the big room, in a few moments – but I wanted to get a note off to you by the weekend to remind you of the things you already know so well.

Little David[1] went off yesterday morning – rather sadly, poor little thing. His home life is hell, but I think his existence has been made a little brighter by being treated properly for a few days. Barbara was sweet to him, & he poured his heart out to me – rather self-consciously, but the old feelings were genuine, I'm sure. Eric came last night, & it's lovely having him here. We've already bathed twice – cold sea, but wonderfully clean & refreshing after those stuffy Swiss lakes. I've also got Lionel [Billows], & his mother & three pathetic sisters installed in boarding-houses all over the town – but eating at that nice Crabbe house[2] where we had that party last year.

I saw Marjorie[3] yesterday afternoon – she isn't well, bad lumbago – but I think the "Festival Idea" has cheered her – she thinks it the idea of the century, & is full of plans & schemes.[4] We haven't yet been over the Jubilee Hall, but I'm full of hopes. Do you know she got 390 in for our concert last year?[5] Even if we have to cut it to 300, that isn't quite so hopeless economically as we feared.

Beth comes over today for lunch with kids. I'm afraid this sounds horribly like just a holiday – but it isn't so really, because I'm getting down to the Quarles[6] & planning the Symphony, talking over St Nicolas & Herring with Eric etc. etc., quite like work – but everything in this place is pleasurable. It must sound beastly to you – but I hope Edinburgh isn't being too nasty for you, & that there aren't too many functions which you have to attend which are boring or embarrassing.[7]

I suppose Illuminations is today – & then just the Mahler & then – Aldeburgh! I can't wait to get you here! Lots of decisions on curtains, paints, furniture to be made. I'm afraid this weather can't last – but it probably had better not, if we're to get any food at all next winter.

If you see the Mauds – give them my love – we can probably arrange to see Humphrey before he goes to school on 18th or 19th. Poor kid – I'm sorry for him, what a nightmare new places are.

I've already been to see the nice friendly town clerk about making our address Crabbe Street – I think it can be managed![8] Everyone is all of a titter to have us here – & I think it's going to be fairly sick-making if we don't take a strong line about not seeing chaps & going out. Barbara is being pestered with invitations to bring Mr Britten to tea to meet dear Mrs so-&-so who's *so* musical. But she's being very firm.

All my love, my dearest. Sing nicely – don't let Walter[9] worry you by his slop.[10] My love to Kathleen. Don't try & sing too loudly.

Come here quick, because I *think* you'll like it.

Your devoted

B.

1 David Spenser (b. 1935), who, when he was thirteen years old, played the part of Harry in *Albert Herring* at Glyndebourne and on tour. Spenser had already gained some experience as a child actor in radio and occasional West End productions and came to the attention of Nancy Evans through a broadcast of Honegger's *Jeanne d'Arc au bûcher*. Although he had received no vocal training, he successfully auditioned for the EOG.

  HCBB, pp. 341–6, includes extracts from an interview Spenser gave to Humphrey Carpenter in July 1990, a discussion that centres on Britten's attraction to and affection for Spenser. Spenser recalled this visit to Aldeburgh shortly after Britten had moved into Crag House: 'Peter wasn't there. Ben was alone, and that was the reason we had to share the same bedroom, because the house wasn't ready. He said that Peter might come back during the night, and might need his own room, so we shared the double bed in Ben's room.' Spenser confirmed that nothing untoward occurred then or at any other time he was with Britten, whose interest in the youth had caused some concern among members of the EOG. Later he stayed with Britten and Pears at Crag House: '[Peter] was always terribly nice – he went out of his way to be really sweet. Peter was much jollier with me than Ben was, a very boisterous companion – it was more altogether party time.'

2 Crabbe House, 2 Dial Lane, Aldeburgh.

3 Margaret (Margery) Spring-Rice (1887–1970), grand-daughter of Newson Garrett who built The Maltings, Snape, in the mid-nineteenth century. Margery Spring-Rice was active in women's rights, particularly in the field of family planning. For twenty years from 1935 she lived at Iken Hall, Snape, where she was a neighbour of Britten's, and subsequently in Aldeburgh. Her musical interests were wide ranging. She was involved in the establishment of the Suffolk Rural Music School and was, as Britten's letter makes clear, active in the founding of the Aldeburgh Festival on whose Executive Committee (later Council) she served from 1948 until 1964.

4 The 'Festival Idea' was, of course, the planning of the first Aldeburgh Festival, which took place between 5 and 13 June 1948 and which has been an annual event in June ever since. According to Eric Crozier, the idea for an Aldeburgh-

based festival sprang from the EOG's experience of touring to the Netherlands and Switzerland during the summer of 1947. Although the EOG was
warmly received at all its European performances – more so than it had
been at some of its UK venues – the tour was to lose £3000 (a sizeable sum
in the 1940s) despite substantial financial support from the British Council.
As Crozier noted in the 1948 Aldeburgh Festival programme book, 'It was
exciting to represent British music at international festivals, but we could
not hope to repeat the experiment another year.' It was Pears who, with
remarkable perspicacity, suggested creating their own festival at Aldeburgh: 'A modest Festival with a few concerts given by friends? Why not
have an Aldeburgh Festival?'

The suggestion was fully discussed while the EOG was in Lucerne and, as
Crozier relates, if the stage of Aldeburgh's Jubilee Hall proved commodious
enough to present opera, then the idea would be pursued further. On
Britten's return to Suffolk, an approach was made to several prominent
local citizens to gauge how sympathetic they might be to the festival
proposal; among them was Margery Spring-Rice. She wrote to Britten on
7 September 1947:

Do you think it would be a good thing to get a few people together here [Iken Hall,
Snape] to discuss your plan for an Aldeburgh Festival, I mean the people who
either might be able to serve on whatever sort of committee you think is necessary,
or who would be able to advise and express a competent opinion about what
should be done, or both?

[. . .] I would suggest the Cranbrooks [. . .] and possibly a few others whom you
or I may think of.

An Executive Committee under the chairmanship of the Countess of
Cranbrook was formed, and in January 1948 a public meeting held at the
Jubilee Hall to promote the Festival and to seek subscriptions in the form
of guarantees against loss. Excellent pre-Festival ticket sales (more than a
quarter of all the available tickets were sold within a week of the box office
opening) and the support of the Arts Council both contributed to reducing what was a very considerable financial risk.

Within the broader perspective of the remarkable burgeoning of the arts
in the United Kingdom in the post-war era, itself a development of the genuine enthusiasm for the arts that was fostered during the war years through
the work of organizations such as CEMA, Aldeburgh continues to play a
significant role in national and international musical life largely owing to
the exemplary standards set by its founders, Britten, Pears and Crozier. Like
Cheltenham (founded in 1946) and Edinburgh (founded in 1947), of both
of which Britten and Pears had knowledge and experience before launching Aldeburgh in 1948, the Aldeburgh Festival has passed through the naive
optimism of the immediate post-war years to the harsh economic realities
of mounting international music festivals of competing excellence and
individual character in the twenty-first century. Aldeburgh, almost uniquely
among music festivals world-wide, has always taken its artistic direction
from musicians, and while this has on occasion precipitated worrying

Aldeburgh Festival.

A meeting of the Executive Committee was held at Thellnam Lodge. Aldeburgh at 2:30 pm on Monday 27th October 1947.

Present:—
Lady Cranbrook (in the chair)
Lady Eddis
Mrs Galsworthy
Mr Goldfinch
Rev. R.C.R. Godfrey
Miss Matthews
Mr Pitt
Mrs Spring Rice
Mrs Welford.

Also present was Miss Anne Wood, representing the English Opera Group.

1. Name.

It was AGREED that the Festival be called "The Aldeburgh Festival," but the question as to whether the words "Music" and/or "Drama", and a reference to the Britten's name be included, was left open. Miss Matthews was asked to seek advice as to the drawing up of a simple Constitution.

2. Finance

Miss Wood reported that the directors of the English Opera Group could not undertake financial responsibility for the Festival, & she recommended that on the basis of certain figures, a local guarantee amounting to at least £1,000 (one thousand pounds) would be necessary in order to place a festival on a firm basis. Various ways of attempting to raise such a figure were discussed & it was AGREED that the Chairman should send a personal letter to certain prominent people, business firms & individual undertakings. Miss Wood stated that Mr Benjamin Britten

Mr Peter Pears, Mr Eric Crozier, Miss Nancy Evans had each promised a guarantee of £25 & Mrs Spring Rice promised £100 on similar terms & stated that she was willing to make this sum available immediately in order to assist in meeting certain minor expenditures. Mrs Galsworthy promised a further guarantee of £50. Miss Wood was of the opinion that the Arts Council of Great Britain might give a guarantee of between £200 & £300 which was a generous sum in consideration of amounts guaranteed to other organisations of a similar kind. Miss Wood also thought that the arrangements might be made for this sum to be paid into the Bank without delay to finance immediate expenditure.

Consideration was given to a statement setting out the proposed scale of charges for seats & it was AGREED that the suggested prices were generally rather too low. It was considered advisable that these rates be scaled up to achieve the present figure for takings of £1,500 at two-thirds capacity.

It was stated that the Bishop had made a ruling that 200 free seats must be made available at every performance taking place in the church & that no performance of any kind might be held in the church on a Sunday. Adjustment of prices for seats in the church must therefore cover these decisions & it was suggested that 200 seats be priced at 7/6 & 300 at 5/-

The question of a Treasurer was considered & it was AGREED to invite Mr Gilchrist to undertake this office.

3. Sale of Tickets. Publicity.

A letter was read from Seafolk's Agency containing certain proposals for undertaking the sale of tickets, making arrangements for transport etc., & for the opening of a branch

The minutes of the first meeting of the Aldeburgh Festival Executive Committee, 27 October 1947

administrative and financial difficulties (and even artistic tensions and disagreements from time to time), it continues to place artistic considerations
at the top of the agenda. Musicians providing active artistic input to the
programming over the fifty-plus years of the Festival's existence have
included Thomas Adès, Steuart Bedford, Oliver Knussen and Mstislav
Rostropovich, while composers-in-residence have included Birtwistle,
Carter, Dutilleux, Henze, Lutoslawski and Takemitsu.

See also PKSB, pp. 148–93; Judith LeGrove, 'Aldeburgh', in MCCCBB,
pp. 306–17; Jenni Wake-Walker (compiler and editor), *Time & Concord:
Aldeburgh Festival Recollections*, pp. 1–14, and Elizabeth Sweeting, 'Let's
Make a Festival!', unpublished memoir, at BPL.

5   A concert in aid of the Suffolk Rural Music School had been given by Joan
Cross, Pears and Britten in the Jubilee Hall, Aldeburgh, on 22 April 1946 (see
p. 175). The programme comprised music by Purcell, extracts from *Peter
Grimes* (introduced by Eric Crozier) and folksong arrangements by Britten.

6   The English poet Francis Quarles (1592–1644), whose poem 'Ev'n like two
little bank-divided brooks', partly based on words from *The Song of
Solomon*, Britten set as his *Canticle I: 'My Beloved is Mine'*, for high voice
and piano. It was the first work Britten was to complete in his new home:
the manuscript draft is dated 'Aldeburgh / September 12th 1947'. Britten
found the poem in Horace Gregory (ed.), *The Triumph of Life: Poems of
Consolation for the English-Speaking World*, a volume given to him by Eric
Crozier to whom the canticle was originally to have been dedicated.
(Annotations elsewhere in the copy suggest that Britten used this anthology as a textual source for other works, notably *Canticle IV*, the setting of
T. S. Eliot's 'Journey of the Magi' composed in January 1971.)

As the published score declares, *Canticle I* 'was written for the Dick
Sheppard Memorial Concert on 1 November 1947, when it was performed
by Peter Pears and the composer'. The concert had been arranged at the
Central Hall, Westminster, to commemorate the tenth anniversary of the
death of Dick Sheppard, who was among the founders of the Peace Pledge
Union in 1936. The concert also included Purcell's *Evening Hymn* and a
group of Britten's folksong arrangements performed by Pears and Britten,
Mozart's A major Piano Sonata (K. 331), Franck's *Prelude, Aria and Finale*
(Colin Horsley, piano), and Byrd's *Ave Verum* and Vaughan Williams's *The
Valiant for Truth* sung by a 'special choir' conducted by Michael Tippett;
readings were contributed by Clifford Evans.

The Times (3 November 1947) reviewed the concert. Of Britten's new
canticle, the anonymous critic (Frank Howes) wrote:

It is a setting of a six-stanza poem of Francis Quarles in which the composer pushes
on with his search for a new, non-metrical and wide-ranging line. Some of the
word painting seemed a little obvious at first, but by the time the song ended the
listener had been forced into a mood of willing acceptance; the impressive end
throws a retrospective significance upon all that goes before.

7   Pears was participating in the first Edinburgh International Festival of
    Music and Drama held from 24 August until 15 September. The Festival's
    Director was Rudolf Bing. On the morning of 4 September in the Free-
    masons' Hall, Pears sang Britten's *Les Illuminations*, with the Jacques
    Orchestra conducted by Reginald Jacques, and on 11 (also broadcast) and
    12 September he and Kathleen Ferrier were soloists in celebrated perform-
    ances at the Usher Hall of Mahler's *Das Lied von der Erde*, with the Vienna
    Philharmonic Orchestra conducted by Bruno Walter.

    Pears wrote to his mother from the Caledonian Hotel, Edinburgh:

    It is really lovely up here – and most exciting. They have managed to stir up the
    proper Festival feeling of excitement. Everything is going well. All the concerts
    and theatres are sold out and the whole thing is a terrific success. There are many
    foreign journalists here to see what it is like and they are v. impressed.

    I have been rehearsing with Bruno Walter and have been very nervous about it.
    I didn't sing very well at first but now I hope it's better – anyhow he's very kind.

    In the *News Chronicle* (12 September 1947) Scott Goddard noted that, in
    'Mahler's baffling work' (a conventional British attitude to Mahler at that
    period), Walter 'made things clearer than ever. For instance in the heavy
    scoring of the first scene [*recte*: song], through which Peter Pears's voice
    shone splendidly, [and] Kathleen Ferrier's singing had terrific quality that
    was a delight to hear.'

8   Crag House lies between Crag Path and Crabbe Street. Presumably when
    Britten purchased the property the address located Crag House on Crag
    Path. Britten's and Pears's association and admiration for the Aldeburgh-
    born poet George Crabbe (1754–1832), author of *The Borough* in one of
    whose 'letters' the story of Peter Grimes is told, presumably made them
    want to adopt Crabbe Street as the official address of their new home.

9   Bruno Walter (1876–1962), German conductor, who worked under Mahler
    in Hamburg and Vienna. After Mahler's death, Walter conducted the first
    performances of *Das Lied von der Erde* and the Ninth Symphony, and his
    recordings of these works in the 1930s, both of which Britten knew
    intimately (see Letter 103 n. 2), did much to foster interest in Mahler's
    music in the UK. Britten and Pears were to encounter Walter in Vienna, in
    November 1955: see PRPP, p. 21.

10 It is hard to match up this disconcertingly dismissive comment on Walter
    with Britten's unique enthusiasm for the two Walter recordings of *Das Lied
    von der Erde* and the Ninth Symphony. All the odder when one takes into
    account the relatively positive response Pears had to working with Walter
    on this specific occasion at Edinburgh. Donald Mitchell remembers that
    Britten sustained this suspicious attitude to Walter and suggests that it may
    have been bound up with a certain reluctance on Britten's part to giving
    way – or whatever the appropriate phrase might be – to an unrestrainedly

expressive style. He further recalls in a late conversation about Mahler, Britten remarking that, while his admiration for the music remained undiminished, there were days when he simply could not bear to listen to a note of it. Some evident tension here between unqualified enthusiasm and the remorseless intensity of the emotional demands that the music makes and of which there is no avoidance. Maybe it was Walter's total (and in Mitchell's view inspired) submission to the detail of Mahler's expressive demands that on occasion caused Britten to switch off. But to Mahler's music he continued ardently switched on to the end of his life. In any event, as Letter 556 suggests, Britten's musical misgivings did not prevent him from getting on with Walter at a personal level.

555 **To Peter Pears**

~~THE OLD MILL, SNAPE, SAXMUNDHAM, SUFFOLK~~
Crag House, Aldeburgh
[between 4 and 11 September 1947]

My darling,

It was heavenly, and a great relief after these long days of silence, to hear your voice last night. I am very glad you are enjoying yourself quite a bit, more at any rate than you thought. I am glad also that the festival is being such a success – congratulate Rudi from me. Next year he must engage us properly, & the Group too![1] Don't worry about the Mahler – I hope you'll get lots of rehearsal & get used to the excitement of singing with the orchestra, because if you <u>do</u> relax I'm sure you can get it over perfectly. I'll listen, all ears, to it. I hope to goodness it comes over well.

I've been working all the morning, although the sea's looking tantalising – there's quite a stiff breeze, & the waves look grand in the sun, & the swimmers very pretty! But as I'm going to Lesley's[2] tomorrow I have to get some work on the Quarles done. I wonder how it will turn out.

Eric has started S. Nicolas & it looks good[3] – I think he's developing well as a poet – & very settable. I've given him the Creation[4] as a model – a good one, I think.

I'm writing this scribble because it is so difficult to phone at that house – small room, smell of cooking, & people overhearing. But all the same I'll telephone when I get back from the Broads to see how you are & tell you about it all!

Barbara P. [Parker] says that we can use almost any size or shape or colour of curtain, if you're buying 2nd hand complete curtains. But if you're buying <u>new</u> stuff to go in the big room (the most urgent need!) – she'll put in some measurements to guide you at the end of this. The colour of the carpet at the moment in there (a new one B. bought) is a lightish blue. The walls will be white with an offness of pink. The greatest need otherwise is lampshades, table lamps & above all standard lamps, as the lighting system now is dotty.

Much love, my darling – longing to hear you, but above all to see you next week & to be with you . . .

I miss you, most dreadfully.

Your devoted

B.

1   Rudolf Bing did not engage Britten, Pears or the English Opera Group for the 1948 Edinburgh Festival.

2   Lesley Duff (1907–1987), English soprano, mother of the composer David Bedford (see Letter 580 n. 1) and the conductor and pianist Steuart Bedford (see Letter 580 n. 4). A member of the EOG from its outset until 1949, she created the roles of Lucia in *The Rape of Lucretia* (shared with Margaret Ritchie), Emmie in *Albert Herring*, and Mrs Vixen in Britten's realization of Gay's *The Beggar's Opera*. In an interview with Humphrey Carpenter (10 October 1990), Anne Wood recollected the difficulty of Lesley Duff play-ing the juvenile role of Emmie at a time when she looked too old for the part: 'It was grotesque. And it suddenly came to the point when Ben saw that it was grotesque. And he could not, he *could not* make up his mind to say anything to her. I had to do it. And she was distraught.' (See HCBB, p. 321.)

The Bedford family had a cottage at Snape from the late 1940s, and Britten, as a family friend, would occasionally visit them there or invite them over to Aldeburgh. Britten and Crozier joined the Bedford family for two days' sailing on the Norfolk Broads on 8–9 September.

3   The libretto of *Saint Nicolas*, about which Crozier wrote from Crag House, Aldeburgh, to Nancy Evans on 8 September:

He [*Nicolas*] is going gently forward, but each line costs me a groan – and I don't really like anything I have written yet. Some of it just does; but nothing is exciting or fresh. I am counting on feeling my way through the whole thing, fixing its shape, then beginning at the opening again and rewriting the parts in relation to the whole. It's more difficult than a libretto, for there aren't any characters to suggest ideas for themselves.

The next day he told her:

I've been terribly concerned with *Nicolas* and began to feel the task was beyond me and that I had better admit it at once so that Ben could find another writer. But we have had a long work this morning and *Nicolas* has begun to unfreeze. I've done the first two little sections: the *Introduction* and the *Childhood* [i.e. 'The Birth of Nicolas'] – the first rather formal, the second a lively ballad. Both can be improved later or maybe rewritten entirely, but it cheers me to have made some sort of begin-ning. [. . .]

Ben is setting a long and fine poem by Quarles for voice, with a refrain from the Song of Songs [. . .]. After dinner he plays the piano and I turn over – Schubert sonatas, Bach preludes and fugues, Buxtehude and so on – which is a splendid way of finishing the day.

On the 12th Crozier wrote:

I'm in my usual state of tangle with *Nicolas*, whose mere name begins to give me a funny feeling in the tummy. Ben assures me it's going well, but I feel as if I am faced with a hill too steep to climb. It's *astonishing* how slow progress is [. . .]

[. . .] Ben's *very* pleased with the aria I have written this morning – three verses for Nicolas about giving everything up to serve God ['Nicolas devotes himself to God'] – and he says it's a beautiful piece of writing. It's not as good as that, but I'm glad he approves, because it was one of my really bad patches of being stuck.

He also played me his new piece (not quite finished yet) for voice and piano, which is profoundly moving and very fine indeed. I look forward so much to hearing Peter sing it.

By 28 November Crozier had finished the text of *Saint Nicolas*. When he and Britten were in Dublin together at the beginning of December, they discussed the libretto. As Crozier told Evans (6 December): 'There are very few alterations to be made in *Nicolas*, but I must have peace to do them. It's very lucky how well Ben agrees with the general plan and the working-out of the whole thing.' On the 7th he wrote again to Evans: 'Great, great trouble with my afterbirth. Oh dear! twice today I nearly lost my temper and tore *Nicolas* to shreds. But I didn't quite! About one third of him has to be rewritten and it's very hard to do.'

Back in Aldeburgh on 17 December, Crozier reported to Evans that

Ben began *Nicolas* this morning and has done a surprising amount already. We are writing letters this afternoon and will work again after tea, I on a new section about the little boys who were rescued from pickling. Then there is only one big and difficult section to do before I am finished.

On 3 January 1948 he wrote to Evans:

Ben has been working like a beaver at *Nicolas* and tonight has finished all but the last section [in composition draft], the Death. He will finish it before I come [to the Netherlands] and Peter will help him to copy out all the chorus parts for printing immediately, so that it can be learnt. I showed the script today to Tony Guthrie, who made small criticisms of words and so on, but said he liked the whole character and treatment very much indeed.

4   Haydn's oratorio, composed in 1797–98, of which Britten conducted a memorable performance at the 1966 Aldeburgh Festival.

556   To Ralph Hawkes

~~THE ENGLISH OPERA GROUP LTD~~
~~295 REGENT STREET, LONDON, W.1~~
Crag House, Aldeburgh, Suffolk
[9 September 1947]

My dear Ralph,

This is my first letter from the new house, & very excited I am about it too! We all got back from Lucerne at the beginning of last week; I spent a few days recording up at H.M.V. with Peter[1] & then on Sunday came down here. Barbara Parker had in the meantime moved the things over from Snape & got it already looking rather good, & now we are at any rate installed. The painting & distempering, & a few minor alterations are being done around us (the licence came thro' without difficulty) – but it is already comfortable and immensely promising. The view is indescribable, & the house the makings of being comfortable & charming. It is more elaborate than Snape of course – but I shall gradually shift my focus from London to here, incidentally good for composition too! Thank you, Ralph, more than I can say for making it possible for me to come here. We must talk the business side of the matter over thoroughly when you come back; but I hope you're not worried about that![2] Incidentally our new life here was made much easier by the arrival of the food parcels from Clare & you – thank you more than I can say for the thought & the deed! As you know the food situation is harder, especially where there are only a few people in an establishment such as here. But these parcels are really a treat & a great help – thank you both ever so much.

You will have heard all about Scheveningen, Amsterdam & Lucerne from Tony Gishford[3] I think. Whatever the financial result may be – & we had a sticky moment in Lucerne (nearly becoming a company of "destitute" persons!) – it was wonderfully worth doing for the press & public success of it. After the cool notices in England it was heartening to us all to have real "raves" most of the time. Willi Schuh[4] did us proud, saying that the Group as an idea is so important & fine. We took the old Rolls across, motoring from Holland to Lucerne & then back to the Hook again – in all nearly 5000 miles, without a spot of trouble! She is a wonderful old thing – carrying Eric, Nancy, Peter & me & a young friend of mine who did most of the driving & paperwork [George Behrend] – & luggage for all for six weeks. Perhaps her present enforced rest cure (without basic petrol) is a good thing!

I went down to see Pascal[5] with Eric on Saturday about this wild Grimes scheme,[6] & honestly I don't think now, after seeing him, that it is so wild. He seems to know a lot about it; his ideas are definitely interesting

& serious. He wants to do it as an <u>opera</u> (no or little cuts), with a good
Italian director (Galoni??)[7] who has already made opera films in Italy
(Traviata, Rigoletto etc) & should know the problems. I think he would
like to consult Eric & Guthrie a lot about it – I told him how exciting the
latter's plans for Covent Garden were, & they are too – most exciting (I've
worked with him & Tania Moiseiwitsch[8] (whose sets are very promising)
this last week quite a bit on it).

I don't know at all about the financial side – how sound he is – he
sounds most plausible. But if he is also doing St Joan, & Androcles & the
Lion,[9] I should think he's all right – (Shaw being (even at 92) a very sound
businessman!).[10] I think that there should be some clause about me
having an artistic veto in the contract, but I hope that can all wait till
you get back.

Thank you for your letter – I hope to see Koussevitsky on his way
through London; my plans are developing for his piece. Peter and I are
now wavering a bit about next autumn,[11] the dollar situation influencing
us slightly. If we come to another decision before you come back we'll
wire you at once. He's now up at the Edinburgh Festival, doing Das Lied
von der Erde with Walter. He doesn't like doing that particular piece
much – it's heavy going – but Walter seems delighted. I chauffeured the
old man across London on Sunday – he seems nice.

The Festival is a roaring success altho' I gather they've had difficulties,
& some of the performances I hear are poor (Figaro on the radio was a
disgrace).[12] But the audiences are terrific. Rudi asked Peter & me to do the
Schöne Müllerin but I had to refuse because of desire to do some writing.
I'm fairly well represented with Y.P.'s Guide, Illuminations (Peter) & P.G.
Interludes.[13]

I hope that the weather has cooled a bit with you – it's been Europe's
hottest for 50 years – the heat across France was a nightmare. Here there
is a serious drought – in East Anglia particularly, & the farmers are desperate. God isn't being kind to us – but I suppose we deserve it all . . .

I must stop this ramble now. I look forward a lot to your return. Will
you have everything settled at the office by the time you leave? It has been
an upset for you – but I suspect all for the good eventually.

Lots of love & many thanks again for the lovely parcels to you both,

Yours ever,

BEN

P.S. It seems a little mad that Stiedry[14] shouldn't do Grimes at the Met,
considering I worked the whole thing through with him. I leave it to you
whether you should put this point of view to Johnson[15] – I don't know
how well Busch would do it – but he's a fine disciplinarian of course.[16]

1   Britten and Pears undertook recording sessions at HMV's Studio No. 3 at
    Abbey Road between 26 and 30 August. The repertoire was Britten's *Holy
    Sonnets of John Donne* (DB 9348–50), which was not completed satisfac-
    torily until an additional session was held on 12 December, three folksong
    arrangements, 'The Plough Boy', 'Come you not from Newcastle?' and 'The
    Foggy, Foggy Dew' (DA 1873), and Britten's realization of Purcell's *The
    Queen's Epicedium* (DB 6763). In addition, Britten and Pears recorded four
    of Britten's other Purcell realizations – 'There's not a swain on the plain',
    'Sweeter than roses', 'If music be the food of love' (first version) and 'I'll sail
    upon the Dog-star' – none of which was issued. However, test pressings of
    the unreleased recordings survive at BPL.

2   Hawkes, Britten's publisher for over a decade, must have advanced the
    composer a substantial sum against future royalties in order to facilitate the
    purchase of Crag House. It would have been a typically generous act on the
    part of Hawkes, and an indication of his confidence in Britten.

3   Anthony Joseph Gishford (1908–1975), English music publisher. Gishford
    was related to Ralph Hawkes, for which reason, no doubt, Gishford himself
    joined Boosey & Hawkes, becoming a director in 1951.
        He was educated at Westminster and Wadham College, Oxford, and
    during the Second World War served in the Intelligence Corps and finally
    in the Grenadier Guards. Although he was a man of conservative views,
    appearance, lifestyle and opinions, he was a warm and generous character
    and a sensitive and skilful negotiator. Britten responded positively to
    Gishford, while recognizing his musical limitations. He enjoyed his friend-
    ship, his unfailing support and the hospitality he extended in his elegant
    Highgate house, which he shared with his partner, Sir Campbell Stuart.
        Gishford played an important role at Boosey & Hawkes, which itself was
    by no means free of internal tensions, tensions that eventually were to lead
    both to Gishford's departure and Britten's (see HCBB, pp. 427–8). It was
    undoubtedly because Gishford foresaw the possibility of an impending
    conflict of major dimensions that he tried to take steps to ease Britten's
    misgivings and objections to company policy. (These were largely generated
    by his unhappy relationship with the then Chairman of Boosey & Hawkes,
    Ernst Roth (see Letter 527 n. 4).) One of Gishford's attempts at mitigation,
    Donald Mitchell recalls, led to Mitchell's appointment as a consultant with
    special responsibility for liaison with prospective performers of Britten's
    works and the acquisition of new composers for the catalogue. Gishford, as
    editor of the Boosey & Hawkes house journal, *Tempo*, which he guided
    from 1947 to 1958, had come to know Mitchell through his writings on
    Britten. In earlier years Gishford had shown himself sceptical of the
    provocatively enthusiastic critical opinions voiced in DMHK and it speaks
    for his independence of mind and judgement that he came to revise his
    views. It was the abrupt dismissal of Mitchell by Roth that precipitated
    Britten's exit from Boosey & Hawkes, and the formation of Faber Music,
    Britten's publishers since 1964. Gishford joined the board of Faber Music in
    1966. From 1960, he was Chairman of the English Opera Group and in 1963

he edited TBB. After Britten's operation for diverticulitis in February 1966, it was Gishford Britten chose as companion on a brief convalescence in Morocco in April (Pears was otherwise engaged). Gishford kept an account, now at BPL, of the trip to Marrakesh. It is entirely typical of his studiously accurate but uninformative self.

Volume IV of Britten's *Folk Song Arrangements, Moore's Irish Melodies*, composed in 1947 and published in 1960, was dedicated to Anthony Gishford.

Gishford had been appointed an Executor of Britten's will, but predeceased the composer. He was replaced, with the approval of the composer and the existing Executors (Peter Pears, Isador Caplan and Leslie Periton) by Donald Mitchell, to whom Britten remarked, 'I'm afraid you'll find there'll be an awful lot of work to do. Are you sure you want to do it?'

See also obituaries in *The Times* (25 January 1975) and by 'J.H.A.' (John Andrewes) in *Tempo* (March 1975), p. 50.

4 Swiss critic and musicologist (1900–1986), who was music critic of the *Neue Zürcher Zeitung* from 1928 and music editor from 1944 until 1965. His carefully prepared reviews, with an emphasis on analysis and evaluation, did much to enhance the standing of Swiss musical life. As a musicologist, his many publications include several on Richard Strauss who chose Schuh as his biographer.

5 Gabriel Pascal (1894–1954), Hungarian-born film producer and director, who won the esteem of George Bernard Shaw and was entrusted with filming several of his plays: *Pygmalion* (1938), *Major Barbara* (1941), *Caesar and Cleopatra* (1944), a notoriously extravagant production for which Britten was invited, but declined, to write the music (see Letters 415 n. 2 and 456), and *Androcles and the Lion* (1951). See also Michael Holroyd, *Bernard Shaw: Volume 3: 1918–1950: The Lure of Fantasy*, pp. 386–93, 436–7 and 473–8, and Valerie Pascal, *The Disciple and his Devil*.

6 Pascal's proposal to make a film of *Peter Grimes*, about which much correspondence emanated from the Boosey & Hawkes office at this time. Apart from the artistic possibilities such a scheme offered, Britten and Crozier were attracted by the financial arrangements – an advance of £10,000 on account of Britten's share of the royalty on the gross takings was agreed by Pascal on 29 September – as a means of placing the EOG on a firm financial footing, particularly in the face of the sizeable deficit incurred on the Group's recent European tour. The forthcoming launch of the Aldeburgh Festival, the financial risk of which Britten was all too aware, might also have motivated their interest in the proposal.

The minutes of the Directors' Meeting of the EOG, 13 October 1947, note that Britten proposed to invest his share of the film rights of *Grimes* in the EOG, and that Pascal was 'interested to obtain the option on the rights of all Mr Britten's operas'. By the next Directors' Meeting, on 17 November, Ralph Hawkes had to report that 'he did not think the agreement with Pascal would go through. Nothing had been heard from Pascal for some time.' It was further noted that 'Mr Lawrie and Mr Hawkes agreed that

Pascal was probably insufficiently capitalized for such a big venture as film-ing an opera'. Pascal's reputation for overspending – *Caesar and Cleopatra* had failed to recoup its considerable production expenses – had gone before him.

Pascal's project was by no means the only film proposal under consider-ation at this time. As the EOG Minutes of 13 October 1947 reveal, 'This Modern Age' Film Unit, which had already undertaken a day's shooting of *Albert Herring* at Glyndebourne for a film provisionally entitled 'Booming Culture', wished to make a forty-minute film of the opera, and Michael Balcon, 'an independent producer but connected with the J. Arthur Rank organization', was offering to undertake the whole or part of the EOG's forthcoming production of *The Beggar's Opera*, in return for an option on the film rights; see also Letter 572. The *Albert Herring* film was never made. 'Booming Culture', however, was released under the title *This Modern Age: The British: Are They Artistic?* and contains a brief but fascinating sequence from the original production of *Albert Herring*. A copy of the film is at BPL.

7 Carmine Gallone (1886–1973), Italian film director and a pioneer of opera on film. His opera films include *Madama Butterfly* (1939), *Manon Lescaut* (1940), *La traviata* (1947), *Rigoletto* (1947), *La forza del destino* (1951) and *Tosca* (1956).

8 Tanya Moiseiwitsch (1914–2003), English designer, daughter of the concert pianist Benno Moiseiwitsch. After an apprenticeship at the London Old Vic in the 1930s, Moiseiwitsch was invited by Tyrone Guthrie to collaborate with him at the Liverpool Old Vic, a theatrical partnership that continued in the post-war years in London at the Old Vic and Covent Garden, and at the Shakespeare Memorial Theatre at Stratford and elsewhere. In 1948 Moisewitsch designed Guthrie's EOG production of *The Beggar's Opera* (see Letters 581–2). In his authorized biography of Guthrie, James Forsyth writes of the 'rare understanding' between designer and director, 'He would scribble rough sets and costumes on backs of envelopes, sides of scripts, etc., and she would go to work from then on, completely trusted by him. All debates would be very open, remarkably unstrained' (*Tyrone Guthrie: A Biography*, p. 209). See also Rosie Runciman, 'Gordon Craig, Moiseiwitch and Chagall', *Opera Now* (September/October 1998), pp. 76–9, and obituaries in the *Daily Telegraph* and *The Times* (both 20 February 2003); by Alan Strachan, *Independent* (22 February 2003), and by Raymond Ingram, *Stage* (27 February 2003).

9 *St Joan* (1923) is one of Shaw's most performed plays. *Androcles and the Lion* was first produced in 1913.

10 George Bernard Shaw (1856–1950), the Irish playwright and polemicist.

11 Britten did not, in fact, go to the United States: see Letter 575.

12 Carl Ebert's production of Mozart's *Le nozze di Figaro* was given by the

Glyndebourne Opera at the King's Theatre, Edinburgh, throughout the first Edinburgh Festival. Although Georg Szell had been engaged on Bruno Walter's recommendation, a disagreement with the management caused Szell to leave and Walter Susskind stepped in at the last moment. According to Spike Hughes, one or two performances were conducted by Renato Cellini (see Hughes's *Glyndebourne: A History of the Festival Opera Founded in 1934 by Audrey and John Christie*, pp. 160–61). *Figaro* was broadcast on two separate occasions from Edinburgh: on the Third Programme on 30 August; and on the Home Service (but without Act III) on 3 September.

13 *The Young Person's Guide to the Orchestra* was heard on 5 September at the Usher Hall as part of a programme given by the Liverpool Philharmonic Orchestra conducted by Malcolm Sargent. (The concert was also broadcast in the Third Programme.) In the same hall, two days later, the Scottish Orchestra conducted by Walter Susskind performed the *Four Sea Interludes from 'Peter Grimes'*. Characteristically, Sargent had *The Young Person's Guide* billed in the souvenir programme book as 'Variations and Fugue on a Theme of Henry Purcell': see Letter 514 n. 7.

14 Fritz Stiedry (1883–1963), Austrian-born American conductor, who began his career in Dresden after a recommendation from Mahler, and became Kapellmeister at the Berlin Opera (1914–23). Stiedry succeeded Felix Weingartner at the Vienna Volksoper (1924–28) and Walter at the Berlin Städtische Oper (1928–33), where he and Carl Ebert led the German renaissance of Verdi. Stiedry also conducted the first performances of Weill's *Die Bürgschaft* and Schoenberg's *Die glückliche Hand*. The Nazi regime caused him to emigrate, first to Russia and then, in 1937, to the United States. Between 1946 and 1958 he conducted frequently at the Metropolitan Opera, New York, where he was the principal Wagner conductor. For the brief period when Boosey & Hawkes took on the publication of the scores of certain Mahler symphonies from Universal Edition (a consequence of Nazi prohibition) it was Fritz Stiedry, now an immigrant himself, who was invited to contribute analytical notes of no little distinction. Stiedry had probably worked on *Peter Grimes* with Britten during the composer's 1946 visit to the US.

15 Edward Johnson (1878–1959), Canadian tenor and opera administrator, who was General Manager of the Metropolitan Opera, New York, from 1935 until 1950. He steered the Met through the difficult war years and fostered an impressive company of young Americans. See R. Mercer, *The Tenor of his Time: Edward Johnson of the Met*, and Irving Kolodin, *The Story of the Metropolitan Opera 1883–1950: A Candid History*.

16 In the event, neither Stiedry nor Busch conducted the Metropolitan premiere of *Grimes*. The production, which was to open on 12 February 1948, was conducted by Emil Cooper (1877–1960). See Letter 575.

557 To Ronald Duncan

3 OXFORD SQUARE, W.2
[after 9 November 1947]

Dear Ronnie,

Many thanks (a) for sending the Quarles[1] (b) for writing about the
curious Cochran suggestion![2] (a) I am enjoying looking at & reading a
lot. Ask for it back when you want. My Canticle goes nicely now & I'm in
love with the form. (b) is quite mad, & even if we all had the time or the
inclination I don't think we could make a success of it. <u>Whatever</u> does
T.S.E.[3] think!

Excuse the hurry of this, but I'm up to my eyes in work & worry. Really
grand opera is too much of a strain – the organisation of the Garden is nil –
our opera group is a rest cure compared. Tony Guthrie[4] has some fine
ideas of production, but on the whole, I'd rather have Eric.

Love to you & Rose Marie, & kids,

BEN

1 Duncan had sent Britten a copy of Francis Quarles's *Emblems*, a copy which
was on loan from the London Library, in response no doubt to learning of
Britten's setting of 'My Beloved is Mine' as his *Canticle I*, the first performance of which had been given at the beginning of November. Duncan was
not to write to Britten until October 1948 to ask for the book's return.

2 Duncan had written on 9 November 1947:

> That tycoon C. B. Cochran wants us to write a show for him together & with T.S.E!
> Yes, I know all three of us are too busy to do anything about it but I'm bound to
> pass the offer on. Perhaps some day our inclination – or our pocket – may make
> this more interesting. Meanwhile we can keep it up our sleeves.

The English impresario C. B. (Charles Blake) Cochran (1872–1951) was
renowned for his revues, which included Noël Coward's *On with the Dance*
(1925) and *This Year of Grace* (1928): the latter was the first to feature
Cochran's famous 'Young Ladies'. Although his association with Coward
was close, Cochran was also responsible for bringing to London many plays
and players from abroad. He was knighted in 1948. See Vivian Ellis's entry
on Cochran in *The Dictionary of National Biography, 1951– 1960*, pp. 232–5,
and James Harding's biography, *Cochran*.

An exchange of correspondence between Duncan and Eliot (kindly made
accessible by Mrs Valerie Eliot) explains something of the project's history.
Duncan wrote to Eliot on 1 November 1947:

> When I was last in Town I made some remark to my agent, Margery Vosper, about
> our once having an idea of writing a revue together. You may remember a dinner
> we had about a year ago at the Etoile [a notable French restaurant in Charlotte
> Street, w1, which still exists today] to discuss the matter? Now it appears that the

news of this has reached C. B. Cochran who is very interested and wants to know whether we would really write such a piece with Ben to set it.

What do you feel about it? For my part, I've not thought about the matter much since we left Christopher Fry [b. 1907, playwright] to produce an idea to which we could contribute. But I gather from [E.] Martin [Browne (1900–1980), director] that he has done nothing towards it.

I suppose it would not be impossible for us to do something better than Sir A.P.H. [Sir Alan Patrick Herbert (1890–1971), humorist and politician]; but, what worries me is that we might be expected to do something worse. Personally, I can think of nothing so grim as his humour. Perhaps Cochran has tired of *Punch*? But there it is, he is now most interested that we should do something & is wanting to hear what we have in mind. Perhaps you'll let me know what you feel about this?

Eliot replied on 4 November:

I am rather staggered by being taken notice of by a tycoon like Mr C. B. Cochran, though I doubt whether he would consider me seriously except in collusion with you and Ben Britten. But if I was puzzled to know what part I could take in such an enterprise when it was on a modest scale of a cosy entertainment for the Mercury Theatre, I am still more bewildered now. I've been waiting for several years for the opportunity to try to write another play [*The Cocktail Party*, 1949] and as things are I don't see how I can get down to it until after Christmas. If I get involved in a big musical show my hopes of writing a play would have to be postponed to a remote future indeed. At present I happen to want the time more than the money and the temptation to make money out of a Cochran production is more than quenched by the thought that at best it must be something ephemeral. If it happened to fall in a period when there was nothing else one wanted to [do] even then it would be great fun, but as it is I think I must leave you and Ben to make up your own minds and deal with your own scruples quite apart from me. As it is Martin wants a play, but I can't confidently promise him one in time for next summer.

Duncan responded to Eliot on 8 November:

I really am glad to hear that you are thinking of writing another play. Forgive me for distracting you with the Cochran bait – it probably had a hook in it anyhow. But I felt bound to pass the offer on.

As it is, Ben and I had better follow your example and let the matter ride for a year or so when we might all review the idea. Heaven knows we've both got enough to do.

Cochran's interest in Britten may have been stimulated by Laurie Lister's 'intimate revue', *Tuppence Coloured*, which ran at the Globe Theatre in London's West End, during October 1947, for which Britten gave permission for a choreographed version of his folksong arrangement 'Sweet Polly Oliver' to be used. Joyce Grenfell, one of the principal performers of *Tuppence Coloured*, recalled in her volume of autobiography, *Joyce Grenfell Requests the Pleasure*, p. 230:

I was involved in *Tuppence Coloured* from the beginning, and I should think it was a classic example of revue-making. Outside advice came from all sides: 'Beware of artiness.' 'Don't let in too much Beauty.' 'Insist on strong direction.' Yes, I said, of course; and hoped for the best in fluctuating moods of gloom and optimism. We aimed high and decided to ask Benjamin Britten to contribute a song. He kindly asked me to tea and wasn't very tempted by the idea but allowed us to have his arrangement of 'Sweet Polly Oliver'.

Angus Menzies sang the folksong in the revue, and Sheila Nicholson's choreography was danced by Silvia Ashmole, André du Guay, Julia Falls and John Heawood.

3   T. S. (Thomas Stearns) Eliot (1888–1965), poet, playwright, critic, editor and publisher, who was probably the most influential writer working in the English language during the twentieth century. Britten's and Eliot's paths did not frequently cross. Apart from the Cochran revue mentioned in this letter, Britten had suggested Eliot in 1944 as a possible collaborator on a 'Christmas show' for the Sadler's Wells Company (see Letter 500 n. 3); in March 1946 Eliot had invited Britten to contribute 'a short general article on the problems of the small opera' as a preface to Faber and Faber's proposed publication of Duncan's libretto for *The Rape of Lucretia*, and the composer invited Eliot to participate in the 1949 Aldeburgh Festival, an invitation Eliot was obliged to turn down because of other engagements. According to Valerie Eliot, her husband was delighted by the founding of Faber Music in 1964 to publish Britten (see PFL, plates 328 and 330). After Eliot's death in 1965, Britten took Eliot's place in the Order of Merit, a distinction conferred by the Sovereign personally and restricted to twenty-four holders at one time.

  Britten's admiration for Eliot's poetry found expression in the last two canticles, *Canticle IV* (1971), a setting of 'Journey of the Magi', and *Canticle V: The Death of Saint Narcissus* (1974). After receiving an inscribed copy of *Canticle IV* in 1973, Valerie Eliot wrote to the composer (10 February):

  I wish my husband could have known of your setting for he admired your work. Once when we were listening to *Les Illuminations* and *Serenade* he said, 'I dislike my poems put to music, but I should be pleased if Britten cared to do it.'

In an interview with Alan Blyth, 'Britten returns to composing', *The Times* (30 December 1974), p. 5, Britten remarked of the period of his convalescence following his heart surgery in May 1973:

  While I have been ill, one of my greatest consolations has been reading, especially music (Haydn's symphonies) and poetry, above all Eliot, for the clarity and security of his language. I don't understand all his poems but I find them very absorbing. And 'The Death of St Narcissus', a beautiful, strange poem, was one in particular that I liked.

This poem was published in 1967 in a volume of Eliot's juvenilia entitled *Poems Written in Early Youth* (Faber and Faber) given to Britten by Donald Mitchell to read during his convalescence.

4   Sir (William) Tyrone Guthrie (1900–1971), director and theatre designer, whose work as Director of Plays at the Old Vic and Sadler's Wells did much to raise theatrical standards. In 1947 he became a Director of the English

Opera Group and directed the first Covent Garden production of *Peter Grimes*. The following year he directed Britten's realization of *The Beggar's Opera* for the EOG (see Letter 581 n. 1). See also Letter 416 n. 6.

558 To Mary Behrend

3 OXFORD SQUARE, W.2

[?10 November 1947]

My dear Mary,

Thank you for the lovely goose. It has been a great boon & a pleasure this week to us – especially as poor Peter hasn't been well (this horrible fog) – but the good food has helped him back to health & voice, & I hope he can sing tomorrow, better than ever – because of the goose!

Also, thank you for your note about Grimes. I am glad you feel reassured about the piece – & got enjoyment from it. No – I don't feel as badly as you do about the production – partly because it wasn't given a chance under the circumstances – & partly because I think a piece like Grimes can stand a different – non-realistic production. Certainly, on Thursday, a lameness of acting, combined with a lameness of musical performance, was on occasions nearly fatal to the piece! But, quite generally I was miserable on Thursday evening[1] – the whole set-up at Covent Garden is lamentable. Whether it has always to be like that in a large opera house I don't know – but anyhow it more than confirms my feeling that the small opera is the thing – in spite of the nice noises one can make with an orchestra of 85 & chorus of 60!

Please give my love to George & thank him for his nice letter and tell him I shan't forget to have the battery "topped-up"!

Lots of love & thanks again to you and Bow. It was lovely to see you in Oxford.

Yours ever,

BEN

1 A reference to the first night (6 November 1947) of Guthrie's new production of *Peter Grimes* at Covent Garden, with designs by Tanya Moiseiwitsch. Pears and Joan Cross returned to the roles originally created for them, and Karl Rankl, Covent Garden's Musical Director, conducted. There were further performances on the 11th and 13th (conducted by Reginald Goodall) and on the 28th (conducted by Rankl, but with Richard Lewis replacing Pears). (A scheduled performance on 8 November was replaced by Puccini's *Turandot*.) Further performances in the 1947/48 season were all given with Lewis and Doris Dorée as Grimes and Ellen, with Rankl conducting on 9 December, 6 January 1948 and 22 May, and Goodall on 13 December 1947 and 1 January, 12 and 17 March, 26 April and 6 May 1948. The production

Thursday, November 6th, 1947

CAST

Peter Grimes, a fisherman .	PETER PEARS
Ellen Orford, the Borough schoolmistress .	JOAN CROSS
Auntie, Landlady of the Boar .	EDITH COATES
Her Nieces {	BLANCHE TURNER / MURIEL BURNETT
Captain Balstrode, a retired sea captain .	TOM WILLIAMS
Mrs. Sedley, a widow .	CONSTANCE SHACKLOCK
Swallow, lawyer and magistrate .	OWEN BRANNIGAN
Ned Keene, apothecary .	GRAHAME CLIFFORD
Bob Boles, a Methodist fisherman .	HUBERT NORVILLE
The Rector .	DAVID TREE
Hobson, the village carrier .	RHYDDERCH DAVIES
The Boy, Peter Grimes' new apprentice .	DEREK NORTH

THE AUDIENCE IS ASKED TO REFRAIN FROM APPLAUSE DURING THE
INTERLUDES BETWEEN SCENES AS THE MUSIC IS CONTINUOUS

THE ROYAL OPERA HOUSE, COVENT GARDEN
Sole Lessees: BOOSEY & HAWKES, LTD.

House Manager: PETER WALLER
Box Office Manager: A. M. WOLSTENHOLME

THE COVENT GARDEN OPERA TRUST
(General Administrator: DAVID L. WEBSTER)

present

PETER GRIMES

An Opera in Three Acts and a Prologue
Derived from the poem of George Crabbe
Words by Montague Slater
Music by Benjamin Britten
Scenery and Costumes by Tanya Moiseiwitch

Conductor   -   KARL RANKL
Producer   -   TYRONE GUTHRIE

THE COVENT GARDEN OPERA CHORUS
Chorus Master   -   DOUGLAS ROBINSON

THE COVENT GARDEN ORCHESTRA
Leader   .   JOSEPH SHADWICK

The Covent Garden Opera Trust works in full association with the
Arts Council of Great Britain

Royal Opera House, Covent Garden, 6 November 1947: the programme for the opening night
of the Guthrie–Moiseiwitsch production of *Peter Grimes*

was toured abroad in June 1948, with two performances in Brussels (7th, Rankl conducting; 8th, Goodall) and Paris (11–12th, Rankl).

559 To Lennox Berkeley

3 OXFORD SQUARE, W.2

[c. 15 November 1947]

My dear Lennox,

So very glad to hear your news – I'd be honoured & delighted to be godfather to the infant when it arrives.[1] Please give my love to Freda[2] & tell her how pleased I am.

Forgive this scribbled note, but I'm up to my eyes & Grimes is being more than usually tiresome. The dear old critics follow along three or four years behind as usual – what bores they are![3]

I'll see Christopher Headington[4] if there's time – but I'm a bit doubtful.

In the meantime – love to you both – let me know how things go. How superb it must feel to be creating a real live symphony! Lucky things.

Love as ever,

BEN

1 Berkeley's first child, Michael (b. 1949), who has become, like his father and godfather, a composer. He has been a Trustee of the Britten–Pears Foundation since 1996 and was Director of the Cheltenham Festival for a decade until 2004.

2 Berkeley's wife (b. 1923), whom he met while working as an orchestral programme planner at the BBC (1942–45). They married in 1946.

3 Neville Cardus's notice in the *Manchester Guardian* (12 November 1947) was extremely positive:

Peter Grimes at Covent Garden will give deep satisfaction to all who have for many years suffered the hopes and disappointments of the cause of English opera. Here, at last, are a work and a production fit to stand four-square anywhere in the world – and not because of lofty emulation of a foreign masterpiece. *Peter Grimes* is English through and through, without trustful resort to folklore. It is English in spirit, in its atmosphere of constricted communal life, where gossip is fateful; it is English in its direct tough humours, which so swiftly turn to spite amongst neighbours; it is English in its inhibited passion and blunt changes from rude animal strength to tenderness. The theme of the 'borough' took charge of Benjamin Britten, possessed him in all his imagination, and left him no time, for once, for fussy cleverness. The music comes from the libretto as water from a rock, or – to choose a more promising metaphor – it runs devouringly like fire along the combustible texture of a gripping drama. Yet it does not burn the libretto to ashes; only at the moments of emotional crisis, or when the stage-picture calls for it, or when the curtain is down, does Britten take full charge. With a rare discretion he suits the action of the orchestra to the words; the treatment of the court scene is a model of apt dialogue and pointed, significant orchestral accompaniment. The charge against Grimes is read, and when the question is put to him whether he has anything to say the vocal part rises interrogatively, while low brass sounds a bodefulness that has foreknowledge in the harmonies.

But the dominating characters and forces of the opera are not Grimes and Ellen, or frustrated love and egoism. The sea and the chorus generate the power. Not since *Boris Godunov* – and now in an entirely different way – has an opera chorus been elevated to the function of protagonist as in *Peter Grimes*. The repetitions of Grimes's name during the man-hunt, vocal harmonies in the distance, are as terrific as the knockings at the gate in *Macbeth*. And the music rises, as the story gathers the momentum of malice and pitiful doom, like the sea. It fills the air, and at the climaxes bursts over the stage even as the storm bursts open the door of the 'pub'.

The orchestral interlude depicting the raging of the elements is the most overwhelming accumulation of orchestral sequences that I can recall in all music. The fury is the more impressive because Britten composes here – as elsewhere in this score – with reserves in hand; there is no waste, no mere rhythmical assertiveness; the music is always being developed. In fact, the score is a remarkable fertilization by drama of recognized music-forms, which are brought into unusual contrasts that quicken the tension. Possibly there is a lack of truly original melody, though here and there Ellen and Grimes sing phrases of much lyrical curve and eloquence.

The voices of the soloists are borne about by the surge and rise and fall of the sea and the wind of chorus and orchestra. The regional atmosphere is caught magically, as during the scene where Ellen talks to the boy 'apprentice' on a Sunday morning, while the church service sings its antiphonies close at hand. It is a pity that in this superb production we are not allowed to see the church; the congregation and the parson are only heard; and we feel, for an irreverent moment, that some popular out-of-door Sabbath meeting is taking place up on the cliffs. Another doubtful change in the setting is the hut of Grimes, which in this Covent Garden production is poised in mid-air, amongst the rocks, like a mountaineer's dwelling; there is something funicular about it and it is very small.

Grimes is not a strong enough character, not psychologically realized. For this reason the opera cannot strike the authentic tragic note. We are more frequently excited in our imagination, or made to feel suspense, than we are internally moved. But to hear and to see any English opera that is an organic and powerful conception is a consummation worth the long time we have had to wait for it. Peter Pears, as Grimes, is the greatest English actor-vocalist since Frank Mullins. Joan Cross, as Ellen, gradually thaws an excess of spinsterishness to some womanly warmth and pathos. All the other characters are alive and kicking, though we could occasionally wish for a clearer articulation of words. Karl Rankl conducts strenuously and well, sometimes riding the storm like a jockey who needs to use his whip; and on this course (forgiving the mixed metaphor) he need not. The genius of the work is a complete fusion of composer, librettist, and producer: it is an ensemble opera, not to be missed.

Frank Howes in *The Times* (7 November 1947) continued the positive attitude to the work that he had expressed back in June 1945 (see Letter 502 n. 2):

The revival of *Peter Grimes* at Covent Garden last night proved three things: that it is a great opera, that its success is deserved and inevitable, and that its successors from the same pen are by comparison progressive aberrations after mistaken ideals.

In *Peter Grimes* Britten puts his immense talent at the service of dramatic truth: there is no striving for originality, no absorption in problems that interest him but bore or offend the listener, no fascinated experiments in word setting and word painting. Its drama lets loose all the malign powers of the sea and the herd instinct, and in scene after scene, which have been cleverly set in effectively contrasted juxtaposition by the librettist, the heart of the listener misses a beat and at the great climactic moments stops still. The composer has been content to accept the forms and conventions which two centuries of operatic experience have handed to him, and he has filled them with what is new, original, true, and powerful.

The new production by Mr Tyrone Guthrie with sets and costumes by Miss Tanya Moiseiwitsch is not all gain. We miss the church and the inn – the Saturday night jollification is almost unintelligible without the town hall and the pub facing one another across the street. The bar parlour is not so cosy nor its fug such a contrast with the storm outside on the larger stage. But we gain the sea and space for well-contrived movements of the crowd. The chief parts are mostly taken by those who created them. In the name part Mr Peter Pears has made the division in the mind of Grimes much more convincing, and Miss Joan Cross conveys the courage and tenderness of Ellen Orford, though not as many of her words as are needed for the elucidation of the plot detail. The Captain Balstrode of Mr Tom Williams is an excellent character sketch and Mr Owen Brannigan as Swallow is, if not a model magistrate, at any rate a model of operatic articulation and acting. The orchestra, conducted by Dr Karl Rankl, is not yet at home with its difficult music. The lighting was somewhat traduced by the fog but seemed too much a thing of beams and pools. But neither this nor that affects the dramatic sweep of the opera.

4   English composer, pianist and writer (1930–1996), who studied at the Royal Academy of Music and privately with Berkeley. He taught at Lancing College (1954–64), and after a year at the BBC became a tutor in the Department of Extramural Studies at Oxford University until 1982. His many writings include a short biography of Britten (CHB) and a biography of Pears (CHPP). In the late 1940s, he received encouragement from Britten, when he was commissioned by the EOG to compose a Latin psalm, *Qui habitat*. This was dedicated to Britten; and among Headington's many other compositions will be found *The Healing Fountain*, for medium voice and orchestra, written in 1979 for Britten *in memoriam*. He died following an accident while on a ski-ing holiday. See also obituaries in *The Times* (25 March 1996) and by Philip Reed, 'A friend of Aldeburgh', *Guardian* (1 April 1996).

Britten was to write to Headington on 25 January 1948:

I am sorry not to have written you the nice long letter of criticism I promised, but (a) I have been rushed off my head with work (b) I realised the impossibility of saying all the things I wanted to say on paper. I am now off abroad for 5 or 6 weeks. When I get back in March we will meet and have a good talk about things. In the meantime I am taking your MS up to London. If you want them call at 3 Oxford Square & pick them up.

560   To Henry Boys[1]

3 OXFORD SQUARE, W.2
Nov. 24th 1947

My dear Henry,

I was very touched that you remembered my birthday – I feel that I have
neglected you so badly recently that I don't deserve it! But one so often
gets one's deserts in this world, it was nice for a change – not to! Thank
you so very much for the Gide.[2] I have already looked at a lot of it –
it is a fine book, & worthy of a great man & endlessly interesting &
instructive.

Actually, Peter <u>has</u> a copy of the Einstein Mozart,[3] & I am afraid I don't
admire it much. Of course there is great experience in it – but a lot of
extremely loose thinking, & a particularly cheap approach – I feel, but we
can talk about this, sometime.

I am so sorry not to have seen you recently, but my life has been hectic.
Our own season was quite worrying, but finally went well, we felt. The
Covent Garden Grimes was a grave disappointment; only the great art of
Joan & Peter, some moving conducting by Reggie, & some fine concep-
tions of movement from Guthrie saved it from complete mediocrity. A
great bore – & I lost my temper over & over again, an exhausting & useless occupation! Since then Peter & I have been dashing over the country
giving recitals, a far finer & more rewarding way of making music.[4]

How are you & your wife? Let me have a note sometime to say how you
are, and what you are doing. If you ever want to talk about the proposed
book[5] do come down to the new house at Aldeburgh. I shall be there most
of December & January, & if you'd like to come down you are always
welcome. The house isn't yet completely furnished, but becoming nice &
comfortable gradually – & the position is incredible!

My love to you both, & very many thanks & much love,

BEN

1   English critic, composer and teacher (1910–1992), dedicatee of Britten's
    Violin Concerto, and a contemporary of Britten's at the Royal College of
    Music where they first met on 17 July 1933. They remained friends through-
    out the 1930s and 1940s, united at first by their shared enthusiasm for the
    music of Mahler and Berg. Boys was responsible for one of the earliest and
    most important articles on Britten – 'The Younger English Composers V:
    Benjamin Britten', *Monthly Musical Record*, 68 (October 1938), pp. 234–7 –
    and contributed a 'Musico-dramatic analysis' to the symposium on *The
    Rape of Lucretia*, edited by Eric Crozier. He was responsible for the vocal
    scores of *Lucretia* and *Albert Herring*, and in 1947 was Musical Assistant
    to the English Opera Group. See also Letter 74 n. 2, 1C1/2, and the tape and
    transcript of Boys's interview with Donald Mitchell (November 1986) at BPL.

2   André Gide (1869–1951), French novelist, essayist and playwright, who was
    awarded the Nobel Prize for Literature in 1947. We have been unable to
    identify which of his works Boys gave the composer for his thirty-fourth
    birthday.

3   Alfred Einstein's *Mozart: His Character, His Work*. Pears's copy was a first-
    night gift for *Albert Herring* from Lord Harewood. See also Letter 220 n. 4.

4   On 9 November Britten and members of the Zorian String Quartet had
    broadcast in the Third Programme Frank Bridge's *Phantasy* in F♯ minor for
    piano quartet and his Piano Trio (1929); Britten introduced the concert
    (see PKBM, pp. 75–7 for a transcript of Britten's text, and Philip Reed,
    'Britten, Menuhin and Gendron play Beethoven, Mozart and Bridge', liner
    notes to BBC Legends CD (BBCL 4134–2, 2003)). It was a programme that
    Britten himself had offered to the BBC. On the 19th Pears and Britten gave
    a recital at the Huddersfield Music Club of music by Purcell, Britten
    (*Donne Sonnets*), Bridge and Berkeley ('Eia Mater' from the *Stabat Mater*);
    and on the 20th, a recital at the Chester Music Club of Purcell, Schubert
    and Britten. On the 24th, the day of Britten's letter, they were to be heard in
    the Third Programme in a joint recital with the Zorian String Quartet, in
    which Pears and Britten performed songs by Mahler ('Ich atmet' einen
    linden Duft'; 'Der Tamboursg'sell'; 'Rheinlegendchen'; 'Um schlimme
    Kinder artig zu machen') and two of Britten's realizations of Purcell ('If
    music be the food of love' (3rd version) and *The Queen's Epicedium*).
       The days immediately following this letter to Boys were no less busy. On
    the 26th Pears and Britten broadcast a programme entitled *Songs of
    Benjamin Britten*, in which *On This Island* was followed by the first broad-
    cast performance of *Canticle I*. The following day they were in the Guild-
    hall, Cambridge, for a recital of Purcell, Schubert, Britten (*On This Island*)
    and folksong arrangements. On the 29th they participated in a broadcast con-
    cert of duets and cantatas from the seventeenth and eighteenth centuries,
    with Max Meili (tenor), David Martin and Neville Marriner (violins),
    Eileen Grainger (viola) and Bernard Richards (cello). The programme
    comprised: Schütz's sacred concerto *Der Herr ist mein Licht* (SWV 359), for
    two tenors, two violins and continuo; Buxtehude's cantata *O fröhliche
    Stünden* (BuxWV 84), for tenor, two violins and continuo; three duets by
    Monteverdi, including 'Zefiro torna'); an aria from Handel's *Ode for Saint
    Cecilia's Day* (1739); and two duets by Purcell in realizations by Britten –
    'When Myra sings' and 'Sound the trumpet'. On the 30th Pears and Britten
    gave a recital in Cranleigh of music by Purcell, Schubert, Britten (*Donne
    Sonnets*) and folksong arrangements.
       The number of BBC broadcasts in which Britten and Pears were
    involved in November 1947, three in less than a week between the 24th and
    29th, was the cause of concern among some members of the BBC music
    staff, including the Assistant Director of Music, Herbert Murrill, who
    raised the matter with the Music Booking Manager.

Apparently oblivious of any internal petty wranglings, George Barnes, Controller of the Third Programme, was to write to Britten on 1 December: 'I thought your Concert on Saturday with Peter Pears and Max Meili was one of the loveliest experiences I remember in broadcasting.'

See also PKSB, pp. 71–2, for subsequent complaints from Murrill concerning the over-exposure of Britten's music by the BBC.

5 Boys was evidently planning a book on Britten's music. Britten wrote to Boys on 25 January 1948, following an attempted meeting, 'I hope the book's going well, & that you're saying lots of trenchant things!' Boys's study of Britten, unfortunately, was never written. He was an innovative writer and thinker, ahead of his time in many of his views and enthusiasms.

561 To Peter Pears

Buswell's Hotel, Dublin[1]
[early December 1947]

My darling –

I hope this will catch you in between journeys, at any rate before the weekend. But I'm not sure, because I'm certain that Irish Posts are as dotty & casual as everything else here – & letters may take ages.

I've been thinking lots about you – wondering how you are getting on – how the Messiah feels after all this time,[2] & whether you stayed in York, or Lincoln, & if you got a decent hotel to stay in. We have found this simple, pleasant place thro' Reggie Ross Williamson[3] – friend of John P. [Piper] & Lionel [Billows] – who is attached to the Ministry, Legation, or whatever, here – it is immediately opposite the Dail – you'll probably remember. We had a pretty stinking journey over – no heating in train to Holyhead – when we arrived hours late (at 3.45) & a fearsomely rough crossing, when I was not sick, but sleep was impossible because one was so knocked about. But it was worth it, & we're spending quiet days, walking around, looking at bookshops, gossiping & oh – how we eat! Jaumet's is on top of its form, tho' expensive – & the Dolphin (where we ate once when we were here before – do you remember) gave us a terrific lunch. We stay here till Saturday & then we go down to near Arcklow, Shelton Abbey Hotel, which is a converted private house owned by one Lord Wicklow,[4] friend of John P. & John Betchiman [sic].[5] It seems to be a nice spot, & Reggie R. W. is going to drive us down on Saturday morning.

Life here seems much the same as it was – shops filled with things, & prices lower than in England. Poverty seems enormous; I'd forgotten what real rags on people look like, & find it heart-bleeding. The infinite number of dirty & charming small boys is moving – do you remember? – selling papers, violets, or God-knows-what. If we can buy things to bring back, we don't yet know, but I believe the customs are strict to a degree. Dismal as life is in England now, I find this terrific difference between rich & poor (& the rich are now very rich, because of the boom in visitors) even more dismal – very old fashioned.

My dearest old thing – I hope all goes well with you, that the voice is functioning as it should, & that you don't find sitting thro' Messiahs, or coping with lousy conductors too tiring. Give my love to Dr John I.,[6] & sing his indulgences lusciously for him[7] – you'll be giving him the thrill of his life, I know. Let him talk to you after, it'll give him fun, & be amusing besides . . . . . !

Don't be depressed about the Schöne Müllerin. It wasn't bad, & I'm sorry I was so stinking to you.[8] Let it be a lesson to us, not to work in these conditions again. One programme – wider spaced-out. Let's think again about the Holland & other programmes; let's be firm about them. But please, just because I'm a nervy, & upsetting bedfellow, don't give me up & take to J.I. or H.S.;[9] I think in my wasp manner I'm good for you in some ways, & if conditions are better we can do really good performances, not just serious & tasteful ones. By-the-way, Eric suggests we get Meili[10] in for one of our Wigmore recitals. What do you think? Did you see, lying around, the charming note from George Barnes[11] about our programme with him?

All my love, my darling – sing nicely. Give my love to Humph & Jean if you see them. And to Boyd[12] too.

We should get back fairly early on Tuesday morning, so don't lock up the front door. Lovely as this holiday is, I yearn to get back to you again – & miss you most dreadfully. We scarcely have a meal without saying – "what a pity Nancy & Peter aren't here!"

All my love & my self,

B.

1 Britten had travelled to Dublin in the company of Eric Crozier.

2 As Letter 563 makes clear, Pears was engaged to sing more than one performance of Handel's *Messiah*, a work he had not sung since January 1944. No information about these 1947 performances has come to light, though Britten's letter would suggest that Boyd Neel was conducting.

3 Reginald Ross Williamson (1907–1966), British diplomat, who was UK Press Attaché at the British Embassy, Dublin, 1943–53.

4 The Earl of Wicklow (1902–1978), a friend of John Betjeman from their Oxford days in the 1920s.

5 John Betjeman (1906–1984), English poet, broadcaster and writer on architecture, who was on the periphery of Britten's circle through his friendship

with William Plomer and John and Myfanwy Piper. (Betjeman and Piper were founding contributors to the famous Shell County Guides.) He was knighted in 1969 and created Poet Laureate in 1972.

6 John Ireland (1879–1962), English composer, pianist and teacher, who taught at the Royal College of Music, 1923–39. Britten studied composition with Ireland throughout his years at the College, but it was an uneasy relationship. Their paths crossed very little in later years, though in the 1950s when Ireland took a strong interest in Britten's new works they were occasionally in touch. See also Letter 26 n. 14.

7 Pears gave a broadcast recital in the Third Programme of Ireland's song-cycle *The Land of Lost Content* and five other Ireland songs ('Love and Friendship'; 'Hawthorn Time'; 'I have twelve oxen'; 'The Trellis'; 'My true love hath my heart') on 8 December 1947, with the composer at the piano. In 1964 Britten and Pears recorded *The Land of Lost Content* and other Ireland songs for Argo (ZRG 5418).

8 It has not been possible to trace this performance of Schubert's song-cycle.

9 Humphrey Searle (1915–1982), English composer, whose *Put away the flutes*, a setting of the poem by W. R. Rodgers, for high voice, flute, oboe and string quartet, was composed in July–August 1947 and dedicated to Peter Pears. (The autograph manuscript is at BPL.) Arthur Oldham (see Letter 590 n. 5), Britten's composition pupil, wrote to his friend John Lindsay on 28 December 1948, 'Do you remember Humphrey Sole [*sic*] wrote a piece for Peter called *Put away the flutes* – well, Ben says, "He ought to have called it, *Put away the score*."'

    Searle had studied with Webern in Vienna from 1937 to 1938 and compositionally was much influenced by Schoenberg and his twelve-note method. However, Britten was to invite Searle to contribute to the so-called *Variation on an Elizabethan Theme* for string orchestra, a collaborative venture which formed part of the 1953 Aldeburgh Festival's tribute to the Queen's Coronation. His *Nocturne (Adagio)* was the penultimate number. The first concert performance on 20 June 1953 of the *Variation*, with Britten conducting, was recorded by Decca (LXT 2798). Britten also attended a rehearsal of Searle's full-length opera *Hamlet* prior to its performance at Covent Garden in 1969.

10 Max Meili (1899–1970), Swiss tenor, who established himself in the 1930s as an early-music specialist, associated particularly with Monteverdi and Schütz.

11 The English broadcasting director (1904–1960). He joined the BBC in 1935, was appointed Director of Talks in 1941 and four years later Controller of Talks. He was made Controller of the newly created Third Programme in 1946, setting the highest possible standards. In 1948 Barnes joined the BBC's Board of Management as Director of the Spoken Word, and in 1950

was appointed to the post of Director of Television. He was knighted in 1953. Barnes left the BBC in 1956 to become Principal of the University College of North Staffordshire (later Keele University).

12 Louis Boyd Neel (1905–1981), English conductor, who founded the Boyd Neel Orchestra in 1933. He first met Britten in 1936 when he invited him to compose the incidental music for the feature film *Love from a Stranger* (Britten's only score in this genre). This has been recorded by the BBC Symphony Orchestra conducted by Jac Van Steen on NMC D073. The following year Neel and his Orchestra were invited to the Salzburg Festival, for which occasion he approached Britten for a new string orchestra work: Britten's response was the *Variations on a Theme of Frank Bridge*. To celebrate the tenth anniversary of the Boyd Neel Orchestra in 1943, Britten composed his Prelude and Fugue, for 18-part string orchestra. Boyd Neel contributed a chapter – 'The String Orchestra' – to DMHK, pp. 237–44. See also Letter 106 n. 3.

562 To Nancy Evans

THE ENGLISH OPERA GROUP LTD,
295 REGENT STREET, LONDON, W.1
[17 December 1947]

Nancy darling

– Here, at long, long last . . . so very sorry, but I'm sure you won't find them difficult.[1] If you can arrange to come down, we can work at them together . . . ! The title, thought up by Eric & me, is only provisional; do you like it!

In haste – looking forward lots to the Broadcast[2] – sing nicely as you always do.

With lots of love,
BEN

1 Britten's song-cycle *A Charm of Lullabies*, for mezzo-soprano and piano, composed in December 1947 for Nancy Evans, the cycle's dedicatee, who gave the first performance with Felix de Nobel (piano) in The Hague on 3 January 1948. This letter accompanied Britten's autograph fair copy which remained in Nancy Evans's possession until 1992, when it became part of the collection at BPL. Britten found the texts for the cycle – a sequence of poems by Blake, Burns, Robert Greene, Thomas Randolph and John Philip – in an anthology edited by F. E. Budd, *A Book of Lullabies 1300–1900*, a volume that might have been purchased while Britten and Crozier were in Dublin (Crozier to Evans, 4 December 1947: 'We are off looking for more lullabies in the 2nd-hand bookshops.'). The same volume also furnished the composer with texts for two additional songs (the

manuscripts are at BPL) which did not find their way into the cycle: 'Come, silly Babe' (Nicholas Breton); and 'Somnus, the humble god' (Sir John Denham). In a private communication to Philip Reed (8 February 1996) Nancy Evans wrote: '[. . .] of about ten broadcasts of the "Charm" which I did, I don't think any have survived, which is disappointing for Archive material.'

Crozier also wrote to Nancy Evans on 17 December:

Ben copied out all five songs this morning and we shall post them now to Huddersfield [. . .]

I long for your next letter, to have your feelings about the songs. Not that you will have had time to play them, but I think the title-page will please you (it did *me*!) and that you will be excited by them. Ben played them all straight through to me before we carried them cheerfully to the Post Office [. . .]

 2 Possibly a reference to a Third Programme transmission of Handel's *Messiah* on 19 December in which Nancy Evans was a soloist, or to a broadcast from Hilversum on 1 January, of songs by Mahler and Debussy, the first of a series of engagements in the Netherlands.

563 To Peter Pears

THE ENGLISH OPERA GROUP LTD,
295 REGENT STREET, LONDON, W.1
Dec. 18th 1947

My darling,

Well – all my chores are done – the BBC have got their score,[1] & yesterday we posted off to Nancy a "Charm of Lullabies" (??) all nicely washed & brushed, & quite charming & successful I think now – five of them. And yesterday Eric & I went over to Ipswich & talked in the middle of Mabel's Rural Music Concert[2] – I for about 3 minutes (quite accomplished, my dear, with even a little humour ("laughter" according to the E.A.D. Times))[3] & Eric for about 10 about the Festival, so that's off my chest. And now, I am beginning St Nicolas, & enjoying it hugely. It'll be difficult to write, because that mixture of subtlety & simplicity is most extending, but very interesting. I have just got the details of the choirs from Jasper,[4] & it looks quite hopeful. I think St Michael's will have to be relegated to the galleries (where anyhow all girls should be in Church), because they are obviously the most efficient, & their breathy voices are obviously most suited to the wind noises & so forth.[5] Yes, writing's all most exciting & interesting, but it doesn't get any easier.

How are you, my dear? I hope the Messiahs are going nicely. I wish you were broadcasting it because I'd love to hear you do it again. I wonder what you're doing about next Monday[6] – let me have a card to say, will you? but then I suppose as usual the Third Programme will be quite impossible.[7] I shouldn't feel over-inclined to be nice to Columbia after the Interlude Record scandal,[8] but if you're committed – I suppose that's that. If you want me to ring you any time Saturday or Sunday wire me.

The enclosed note from Schouwenburg[9] is peeving – but I don't feel inclined to go over P. Diamand's head, although I'm feeling peeved with him at the moment (it seems the cancelling of Theo's date[10] was his fault, & I've had a most creepy-crawling letter from him about it). What do you think? Drop me a line (a long one, too) & I'll answer whatever you want. I must write too to Schouwenburg about this Concertgebouw Jubilee piece muddle[11] – he's not an attractive character.

Mabel sang most beautifully last night – her performance of the Shepherd on the Rock[12] with Steve Waters[13] was really remarkable. And yet she doesn't seem to get the audience; it's a mystery. She also sang some of our Purcell most finely – If Music (3rd) & B.V.'s Exp.[14] – which she must record.[15] I don't know a more accomplished singer today (altho' I know a greater).

The house is lovely – really quite warm, beginning to look more furnished with pictures an' all. Looking forward immensely to your coming, which will complete the furnishing –

Talking of Mabel – she's quite a lot thinner, & looked lovely last night. But, alas, Tony G's [Guthrie's] reaction to her as Polly was fatal, also to Kath – but still I don't feel hopeless about persuading him.[16]

I must go now – poppetty – darling – love you lots & lots – & come home quickly. Take care of yourself.

All my love & self,

B.

1   Britten's incidental music to *Men of Goodwill: The Reunion of Christmas*, broadcast in the BBC's Home and Light Services on 25 December 1947. Described by the BBC as 'a Christmas journey across the world', this programme brought together goodwill messages from around the globe and immediately preceded the King's Christmas Day message to the Commonwealth. It was compiled and produced by Laurence Gilliam and Leonard Cottrell; Laurence Olivier acted as narrator, and Britten's music was played by the London Symphony Orchestra conducted by Walter Goehr. There was a rehearsal and a stand-by recording of the music on 19 December, and the music was broadcast live on Christmas Day. The score comprises a set of short orchestral variations on the traditional carol 'God rest ye merry, Gentlemen'; a fugal finale, marked 'new last section' in the full score, was jettisoned in the original broadcast. On 31 December, a week after the transmission, Walter Goehr wrote to Britten: 'I hope that we performed your music satisfactorily. It was praised by everybody and I liked it very much indeed. I do hope you will make a little Suite of these Variations ...'

Britten did not respond to Goehr's invitation to contrive a suite and *Men of Goodwill* was not published until 1982 by Faber Music.

2   A concert given by Margaret Ritchie under the auspices of the Suffolk Rural Music Schools Association in the Christchurch School Hall, Ipswich.

3   'Arpeggio', 'Music Festival at Aldeburgh: Plans announced at Ipswich concert', *East Anglian Daily Times* (18 December 1947), reported:

> Mr Benjamin Britten, the eminent Suffolk composer, and Mr Eric Crozier, Artistic Director of the English Opera Group, spoke of their plans for the new festival of music and the arts, which they are promoting at Aldeburgh next summer, during the interval of a concert given by the Suffolk Rural Music School (of which Mr Britten is the music adviser) [...]
>
> Mr Britten, having affirmed his affection for the county in which he was born, said that Aldeburgh seemed to him to be the ideal place for the type of festival he had in mind. The festival he liked was not the kind which concentrated everything on music, but the sort of thing 'where one can wander about'. For several years past, he said he had been writing large-scale musical works, not a single one of which had ever been performed in Suffolk. In these days of universal suffering, he did not see why this should be so. (Laughter.)
>
> [...]
>
> It was hoped that the Aldeburgh Festival, once instituted, would steadily expand, and in ten years' time, perhaps, it might be possible to build a Suffolk Opera House in Aldeburgh. [See pp. 36–8.]

4   Jasper Rootham (1898–1981), English composer and Director of Music at Lancing College (1926–49); see also Letter 487 n. 8. The participating choirs from the Southern Division of the Woodard Schools were St Michael's, Petworth, Ardingly College, Hurstpierpoint College and Lancing College.

5   A reference to the two-part semi-chorus of girls' voices in *Saint Nicolas*, which is situated away from the main performers. One the most effective uses of the girls' voices is during the storm in No. IV, 'He journeys to Palestine'.

6   Pears was one of the soloists in a performance of Schütz's *Christmas Story*, with the BBC Singers and the New London Orchestra conducted by Steuart Wilson, broadcast in the Third Programme on 22 December.

7   The first of several references in Britten's correspondence to the difficulties of achieving satisfactory reception of the Third Programme in Aldeburgh. See also Letters 590 and 593.

8   See Letter 564. It remainds unclear what was Pears's commitment to Columbia Records (a division of HMV to whom he was contracted).

9   The Dutch banker J. W. de Jong Schouwenburg (1906–1981), Vice-President of the Concertgebouw Orchestra. His note to Britten has not survived.

10 Possibly the Dutch violinist Theo Olof (b. 1924) who gave the first per-

formance in the Netherlands of Britten's Violin Concerto. He performed the work at the 1947 Cheltenham Festival, with the Hallé Orchestra conducted by John Barbirolli. (It was Barbirolli who had conducted the premiere of the Violin Concerto in 1939.) Olof recorded the Concerto for HMV – the original version; the revised version was not made until 1950 – with the Hallé and Barbirolli in April 1948, a performance that was not released at the time. It was first issued by EMI Classics in 1997 (CDM 5 66053 2). See also Michael Kennedy's liner notes to this recording.

11 A letter of 16 January 1948 to Britten from Rudolf Mengelberg, nephew of the conductor Willem Mengelberg and a director of the Concertgebouw Orchestra, 1935–54, explains the situation:

> Referring to the tentative proposal to you by our Vice-President, Mr J. W. de Jong Schouwenburg, to compose a new work on the occasion of the diamond jubilee of the Concertgebouw, I wish to express to you our deep appreciation of your promise to do so.
>
> We herewith take the liberty to repeat and confirm our invitation. We would be very glad if your name could be connected with the Concertgebouw on the occasion of its 60th anniversary, after your works have brought so many marvellous and new impressions to the Dutch musical audiences these last years.
>
> We have the intention to invite you to conduct the first performance of your new work personally and this performance could take place, if possible, in the first part of the next season, i.e. in the months of October or November 1948.

The 'muddle' Britten found himself in was presumably because Schouwenburg and Mengelberg were of the opinion that he had agreed to write a new piece for the Concertgebouw, whereas the composer believed this not to be the case. In the event no new work was written by Britten expressly for the diamond jubilee season of 1948–49. However, *Spring Symphony*, commissioned by the Koussevitzky Music Foundation, was to receive its premiere at the Concertgebouw, Amsterdam, with the Concertgebouw Orchestra conducted by Eduard van Beinum, in July 1949 as part of the Holland Festival. Were the circumstances of this premiere a substitute for the piece Britten did not have time to write? See also Letter 575 n. 10.

12 Schubert's *Der Hirt auf dem Felsen* (D. 965), for soprano, clarinet and piano.

13 Stephen Waters (1914–1989), English clarinettist and a member of the English Opera Group Orchestra from its inception. Until 1958 Waters also appeared regularly in chamber music concerts at Aldeburgh Festivals, including performances of Mozart's E♭ Trio (K. 498) and Berg's *Four Pieces* for clarinet and piano, with Britten at the piano. He was married to the mezzo-soprano Catherine Lawson. See also the obituary by Mark Sellen, *Independent* (25 July 1989).

14 Britten's realizations of Purcell's 'If music be the food of love' (3rd version) and *The Blessed Virgin's Expostulation*. The latter was published by Boosey & Hawkes in 1947.

15 Ritchie recorded Britten's realizations of *The Blessed Virgin's Expostulation* and 'Evening Hymn', with George Malcolm, on Nixa NLP 921.

16 In the event, the role of Polly Peachum in Britten's realization of *The Beggar's Opera* (1948) was sung by neither Margaret Ritchie nor Kathleen Ferrier, but by Nancy Evans.

564 To Leonard Smith[1]
The Gramophone Co. Ltd

THE ENGLISH OPERA GROUP
295, REGENT STREET, LONDON, W.1
4 Crabbe Street, Aldeburgh
Dec. 18th 1947

Dear Leonard,

Thank you for sending along the new records of the Peter Grimes Interludes, & for your letter.[2] I must frankly say that I was surprised that the records were the finished pressings, & not tests, which I had understood from our telephone conversation would be the case. It would have been nice of you if you had let me hear them before they were issued. It is therefore, I presume, too late to do anything about a set of records which are most disappointing. They show every mark of having been done in great haste – poor playing (ragged ensemble as well as slips), lack of understanding in the interpretations, & in one case (side 3) ludicrously bad balancing.[3] I should certainly fear for the reputation of the pieces had not Decca simultaneously released a fine set of the same pieces (but including the Passacaglia which makes more sense) by the Concertgebouw Orchestra.[4] Sorry to be so frank, but I think the situation warrants it.

Yours sincerely,
BENJAMIN BRITTEN

1 A member of the Columbia label's Artistes Department (b. 1907).

2 Smith had written to Britten on 5 December 1947, enclosing a set of Columbia's recording on two 78 rpm discs of Britten's *Four Sea Interludes from 'Peter Grimes'*, with the London Symphony Orchestra conducted by Malcolm Sargent (Columbia DX 1441–2): 'Laurie [Lawrance Collingwood], Malcolm Sargent and myself are enchanted with them. They are most exciting, and I believe will become very popular records with the public.' He would have been unprepared for Britten's total dismissal of the venture; moreover, the recording would have undoubtedly confirmed Britten's misgivings about Sargent's abilities as a conductor.

3 Side 3 contained the atmospheric 'Moonlight' interlude.

4 The first of Eduard van Beinum's two recordings with the Concertgebouw
   Orchestra of the *Four Sea Interludes* and *Passacaglia from 'Peter Grimes'* was
   made in September 1947, and released that year by Decca (K1702–4). Writing in the Discography to DMHK, p. 353, Desmond Shawe-Taylor compared
   Sargent's and van Beinum's accounts:

   > Of the two [. . .] versions, the Decca is easily the superior; not only because it
   > includes the great *Passacaglia*, but because both recording and performance reach a
   > higher level. Indeed it is unlikely that any English audience, whether in the theatre
   > or the concert hall, has heard certain passages so splendidly realized as in this
   > recording by the Concertgebouw Orchestra under van Beinum; among its more
   > notable features are the strong, resonant tone of the high unaccompanied violins at
   > the opening of the first interlude, and the frenzied, yet controlled, brass outburst at
   > the climax of the *Passacaglia*.

   It says much for Britten's reputation – and that of *Grimes* – that a major
   European orchestra under its principal conductor *and* a leading British
   orchestra with a fashionable conductor were both to make recordings of
   what, in 1947, was still a very new piece.

565 To Lesley Bedford

[late December 1947]

My dearest Lesley,

   What a lovely book – thank you so <u>very</u> much for it. A lovely period of
people & a charming example is Sir T.B.[1] You <u>do</u> chose beautifully! The
enclosed book is for the boys. Sorry I couldn't get presents separately, but
Nicolas takes all my time! Give 'em my love & say I'll find a way <u>somehow</u>
of playing them ping-pong.

   Your father's sheep[2] look lovely on our wall here – I like it a whole heap.

   Will Leslie[3] be back? – If so, please include him in my best Christmas
love to you all.

BEN

1 Sir Thomas Browne (1605–1682), English physician and author of a number of meditations on the mysteries of death, including *Religio Medici* and
   Hydriotaphia.

2 *Sheep in a Meadow*, a characteristic pastel by John R. K. Duff (1862–1938)
   owned by Britten and Pears. An exhibition of work by this English artist,
   who particularly favoured watercolours, pastels and etchings, was held at
   the 1984 Aldeburgh Festival.

3 Lesley Bedford's husband.

566 To Edward Sackville-West

~~THE OLD MILL, SNAPE, SAXMUNDHAM, SUFFOLK~~
4 Crabbe St, Aldeburgh
Jan. 8th [1948]

My dear Eddy,

I am <u>delighted</u> with the new book. Thank you so much for having it sent to me. It has lots of things, most fascinating things, in it which I'd never met before. It is an extremely good collection.[1]

This is only a note in haste as I'm up to my eyes in work. St Nicolas[2] is just on finished, & I have to get down to the new Beggar's Opera[3] – an exciting thing to do, but as usual not enough time – I'm turning over a new leaf in that direction now, a New Year's Resolution not to do so much!

The new house is lovely – I hope you'll come & see it sometime.

Lots of love to you, & many thanks again,
Yours ever,
BEN

1   *And So To Bed*, compiled by Edward Sackville-West, inscribed on the fly-leaf: 'For Ben / with New Year love / from Eddy / 1/1/48'. (See p. 114.)

2   Crozier wrote to Nancy Evans from Aldeburgh on 6 January 1948: 'Strange that *Nicolas* is so near an end. He is on his death-bed now and Ben may finish him tomorrow, though tidying up will probably take a day or two more.'

3   Britten's realization of John Gay's and John Christopher Pepusch's ballad-opera of 1728, composed during the first months of 1948 and first performed by the EOG under Britten's direction, with Pears as Macheath and Nancy Evans as Polly Peachum, at the Arts Theatre, Cambridge, on 24 May 1948 (see Letters 581 n. 1 and 582 n. 4). Tyrone Guthrie, who collaborated with Britten on the adaptation, directed the production, which was designed by Tanya Moiseiwitsch. See plates 16–21. See also Norman Del Mar, 'The Chamber Operas III: *The Beggar's Opera*' in DMHK, pp. 163–85; Donald Mitchell, '*The Beggar's Opera*: An Introduction', and Donald Mitchell and Philip Reed, 'Documents' and 'A commentary on the music', all CD liner notes for the first recording of Britten's realization (Argo, 436 850–2, 1993), and Eric Roseberry, 'Old songs in new contexts: Britten as arranger' in MCCCBB, pp. 297–300.

67 To Ronald Duncan

THE OLD MILL, SNAPE, SAXMUNDHAM, SUFFOLK
4 Crabbe St, Aldeburgh
[mid-January 1948]

My dear Ronnie,

First of all thank you for the terrific present. The Steins all came down to Aldeburgh for the festival [the Christmas and New Year holidays] & we all together tucked eagerly into the butter, which was enormously enjoyed.

Thank you also for the letter.[1] I am sorry about Father Patrick; but I told R.H. [Ralph Hawkes] I wouldn't accept any more commissions for 20 years (or thereabouts), because I am so sick of having too much to do & not being able to do it properly. I will try & do Mea Culpa sometime but I daren't tie myself at the moment. I'll write to him & explain, & hope he won't be upset. As an example of this ghastly rush – I've just had to write a complete cantata on St Nicolas for Lancing College in less than three weeks, & haven't started Beggar's Opera yet – altho' I'm off to the Continong in 2 weeks for 6 weeks![2] It's a bloody nightmare.

How's Rose Marie? Give her lots of love from me, & say Peter & I are longing to come down at Easter time. We'll let you know exact details later – is that O.K.?

The Lucretia records are nice, & should be out soon.

Love,
BEN

1 In an undated letter Duncan had written to Britten:

After our 'discussion' at Marion's party about *Mea Culpa*, I told Father Patrick that you were prepared to accept the commission but 'couldn't possibly promise it before end of 1949' – and would require £500. He was delighted and immediately busied himself on the Bishops' Committee bringing a few recalcitrant mitres to heel and eventually got their approval. Whereupon I advised him to approach Ralph Hawkes. Which he did and to his dismay received the enclosed [which has not survived]. Can you please untangle this by speaking to Ralph; and perhaps, write a note to Father P. The poor little man is so upset.

Father Patrick remains unidentified.

2 Britten and Pears were to leave on 27 January for Zurich, where they gave two concerts and another in Basel before embarking on a short concert tour of northern Italy (7–12 February). From Italy, they travelled to the Netherlands where they gave concerts and broadcasts until their return to the UK on 5 March.

568   To Florence Britten

~~THE OLD MILL, SNAPE, SAXMUNDHAM, SUFFOLK~~
4 Crabbe St, Aldeburgh
Jan 20th 1948

My dear Aunt Flo,

I simply don't know how many birthday, & Christmas presents there
are that I owe you letters for . . . Beth always seems to hang on to them for
such ages, & then produces them for the wrong Festival!

However, thank you very much for the extremely useful handkerchief,
& scarf – very smart indeed. It is sweet of you to remember me – it is
such ages since we met that I can't think why you haven't forgotten my
existence altogether!

Perhaps some day when you come down to see Beth you will come over
here & see the house – very nice now, all painted & furnished complete. I
am delighted with it, & don't really regret the Old Mill at all. I have always
felt most at home by the sea!

My love to you, & many thanks again. I hope you are keeping well, &
warm & getting enough to eat. I am just off abroad for six weeks, but I
don't look forward to travelling in this weather.

Your loving nephew,
BEN

569   To Nancy Evans

~~THE OLD MILL, SNAPE, SAXMUNDHAM, SUFFOLK~~
4 Crabbe St, Aldeburgh
Jan 23rd 1948

My dear Nancy,

I was <u>delighted</u> to see from the notices what a good success you have
had in Holland.[1] It is really most encouraging that they have taken you so
to their hearts, for they are a most discriminating public, I know! You must
have sung the Charm most beautifully, for it to have had that success. I
look forward to hearing you do it, now that you know it so well.

Eric has been here you know, & I have had to break some disappointing
news to him, which I am afraid has upset him a bit. That is this . . .

Peter you know has spent his holiday here, & hasn't been at all happy
that he couldn't work anywhere in the house without disturbing me (I'm
silly about music being audible when I'm writing), & has said that in
these kind of lazy working holidays, he <u>must</u> have somewhere to work, or
else will have to go elsewhere for them, or have again some larger London
establishment than we intend to have, after getting rid of Oxford Square.
Now obviously that is wildly expensive & inconvenient. The only room

possible is the top back room – your prospective kitchen. Also he feels he must have a separate bedroom. I agree too, instead of crowding in with me. I think it is important, especially as we plan to have more time to work together in the future, that he has this pied-à-terre in Aldeburgh. So what I suggested to Eric was that when you were married we should try & buy a small cottage (there are two now for sale here) & let you have it all to yourselves, for whenever you want, the oftener the better! Of course, before that happy date (!), the position is the same as now – Eric lives here; and even after if he wants he can live (and/or eat) here, if he wants to.[2]

I do apologise most warmly for this change of plans, & hope most sincerely that you will accept this bona fide offer, if we can find the cottage you like – which I'm sure we can. I forgot to say, that if <u>ever</u> in the meantime (including the Festival) you want to come here, you are always welcome.

I'm afraid Eric has taken it rather to heart – p<u>lease</u> try & persuade him that it doesn't mean much change. Only I have a feeling that, in the long run, with possible expansions of family, it is the best arrangement!

My love, & apologies, & congratulations to you, as ever,

BEN

1 Nancy Evans had undertaken a recital tour of the Netherlands from 1 to 12 January 1948, the programmes of which included the earliest performances of Britten's *A Charm of Lullabies*.

2 Crozier was at this time living at Crag House with Britten. It is clear from this letter that this convenient arrangement had evolved into a scheme whereby he and Nancy Evans, once married, would occupy the top floor of Crag House in what would be converted into a self-contained flat. Britten's cancellation of this proposal, which may have been prompted by past difficulties when sharing properties (see Letter 515 n. 5), was replaced by a most generous offer typical of the concern he could show for the well-being of his close friends and colleagues. In fact, Crozier did not take up Britten's suggestion, but found instead a cottage in Southwold where he lived from 1949 and where he wrote the libretto of *The Little Sweep*.

70 **To Eric Crozier**

38 Bellerivestrasse, Zurich
Feb. 3rd 1948

My dear Eric,

Thank you for your long letter.[1] I am so desperately sorry that you & Anne [Wood] have had this extra beastly worry – really this whole idea seems more trouble than it is worth. I don't mean that really because I do feel that we must go on for at least one more year if physically possible. Perhaps next year some other scheme of consolidation may seem best to us, or a token season in conjunction with the school,[2] but that is only possible I feel if we are that much more established. Peter & I both agree with your proposals. It is a pity to drop Lucretia[3] – especially because of this new F. Commentator [Female Chorus]. But your figures are unanswerable – unless the miracle of a financial godmother turns up, which seems as ever unlikely.

It must have been maddening for you & Anne to have to bury yourselves in these obstinate figures, especially as you want to get on with other things. But having made this curtailing decision I hope you can leave things a bit & get away. Of course I'll do the conducting with Ivan.[4] It won't be all that heavy, & interesting to do too. Peter is quite up to tackling all the performances, but I think Richard[5] may have to help with the Cambridge Alberts, altho' I should prefer to find an adequate cover for Macheath who can take over when Peter could do Albert. Is that a possibility or have you fixed with Richard? We go on to Italy on Saturday for a week[6] – after which you can get us c/o Peter Diamand in Amsterdam.

Things went finely at the much dreaded concert,[7] beyond hope. It is good to have that worry over. Please tell Anne I hope to send a big batch of Beggar's Opera at the end of this week.

We saw M. Vincent[8] the new Fresnay[9] film you talked about. Coming on the top of Gandhi's death[10] it was overwhelmingly moving. He's a fine actor, & it's a most serious film.

My love to you & Anne, & to dear Nancy too. I do hope her throat's better now.

Love from us both,
BEN

1 Crozier had written to Britten from 3 Oxford Square, London, on 30 January 1948, with anxious news about the EOG's financial prospects for the forthcoming season:

Anne and I have had to face a large financial crisis during the last two days, and I feel that you should know the decisions we fear must be made to meet it. We have been estimating the probable cost of our summer season as it is planned at present, and find that by doing Beggar's Opera, Herring and Lucretia, we shall lose at least five thousand pounds in addition to our present debt of nine thousand. Fourteen thousand altogether, after allowing for Balcon's £3000 [see Letter 556 n. 6] & the Arts Council £5000! [...]

There is only one solution to the problem [...] This is to reduce our planned programme in scope and length, to reduce our company, and to ask our singers to work harder for the same money. [...]

By this plan, our loss will be kept down to about three thousand on this season.
See also PKSB, pp. 91–7.

2 A reference to the 'Opera Studio' founded by Joan Cross and Anne Wood in

1949 under the aegis of the EOG, from which the National Opera School subsequently emerged.

3 *Lucretia* was indeed dropped from the EOG's 1948 season, during which the company gave thirty-seven performances of *The Beggar's Opera* and eighteen of *Albert Herring*.

4 Ivan Clayton (1913–1966), English conductor, who studied at the Royal College of Music (he was a pupil of Arthur Benjamin, and a fellow student with Britten in Basil Allchin's aural class) and at the Conservatorium Mozarteum, Salzburg. After a year as a répétiteur in Germany, Clayton was appointed Musical Director of the Anton Dolin Ballet and conducted at the Carl Rosa Opera Company. Further spells as a répétiteur at Covent Garden (1936–39) led to his appointment as Musical Director of the Sadler's Wells Theatre Ballet (1946–47). Clayton conducted a single performance of *Albert Herring* for the EOG as part of the Covent Garden season in October 1947 and then undertook further performances of *Herring* as well as *The Beggar's Opera* for the EOG in 1948. He was one of the pianists in the Aldeburgh Festival premiere of *Saint Nicolas* in June 1948. The following year he had to yield the direction of a performance of *Albert Herring* to Britten because of illness and subsequently never appeared again with the EOG: his promising career was tragically curtailed by the onset of multiple sclerosis. Jennifer Vyvyan was prominent among a group of friends who organized nursing care for Clayton by inviting former colleagues to covenant relatively small amounts of money annually. Britten and Pears both contributed substantial sums towards the costs of Clayton's care.

5 Richard Lewis (1914–1990), English tenor who made his debut in 1941 with the Carl Rosa Company. In 1947 he sang the Male Chorus in *The Rape of Lucretia* with the EOG at Glyndebourne and at Covent Garden, and shared the role of Grimes with Pears in Guthrie's Covent Garden production in 1947, appearing again in the role the following year (see Letter 580 for Britten's reaction to Lewis's performance). His only other Britten role was Captain Vere in *Billy Budd*, which Lewis sang in the first staged performances of the revised, two-act version of the opera at Covent Garden in January 1964. (He subsequently sang the role in productions in Chicago (the two-act version's US premiere) and San Francisco.) A well-loved singer at Glyndebourne, Lewis sang numerous roles there, including Idomeneo and Tom Rakewell, the latter in the UK premiere staging of Stravinsky's *The Rake's Progress* at Edinburgh in 1953. At Covent Garden he often specialized in contemporary opera, and his roles included Troilus in Walton's *Troilus and Cressida* (1954), Mark in Tippett's *The Midsummer Marriage* (1955), Achilles in the same composer's *King Priam* (1962), and Aron in Schoenberg's *Moses und Aron* (1965). In addition to his operatic work, Lewis was a noted concert singer and a fine exponent of the tenor parts in Elgar's *The Dream of Gerontius* and Mahler's *Das Lied von der Erde*.

Humphrey Carpenter reports that, while a member of the EOG, Lewis experienced difficulties with Britten. In an interview with Carpenter, Anne Wood recalled that Britten 'would *not* rehearse with him, he would *not*'. Wood considered that it was because Lewis possessed a stronger upper register than Pears: 'I think Ben, on Peter's behalf, was jealous of it. Richard would come to me and say, "I've still not had any rehearsals with Ben. I can't understand – can't he find time?"' (HCBB, p. 320). Although Lewis sang with the EOG for two successive seasons (1947 and 1948), the records show that he sang only two performances of *Albert Herring* under Britten's direction, all his other EOG performances being conducted by Reginald Goodall or Ivan Clayton.

See also obituaries in *The Times* (14 November 1990); Elizabeth Forbes, *Independent* (14 November 1990); Edward Greenfield, 'A very British hero-tenor', *Guardian* (16 November 1990), and Alan Blyth, 'Richard Lewis (1914–1990)', *Opera*, 42/1 (January 1991), pp. 33–6.

6 Britten and Pears travelled to Italy on 7 February, gave a recital in Milan (10th), visited Venice (11th), and gave a recital in Trieste (12th), the day after which they journeyed to the Netherlands via Zurich. No programmes or press reviews survive at BPL for these Italian recitals.

7 This refers to the concert of the Collegium Musicum, Zurich, conducted by Britten, with Pears as soloist, on 30 January 1948; the programme comprised Purcell's Chacony in G minor, the *Suite of Songs* from *Orpheus Britannicus*, and the Overture from the *Ode for St Cecilia's Day* (1692) – all realized by Britten – and Britten's *Sinfonietta*, *Les Illuminations* and the Prelude and Fugue for 18-part string orchestra. While in Switzerland Pears participated in two further concerts: on the 4th, again in Zurich, he sang in a programme of music by Bach; and in Basel, on the 6th, he gave a performance of the *Serenade* with the Basel Kammerorchester conducted by Paul Sacher.

8 *Monsieur Vincent* (France, 1947), Jean-Bernard Luc's and Jean Anouilh's life of the seventeenth-century St Vincent de Paul.

9 Pierre Fresnay (1897–1975), French stage actor who made numerous films and played the title role in *Monsieur Vincent*.

10 Mohandas Karamchand Gandhi (1869–1948), universally known as 'Mahatma' ('great soul'), had been assassinated by a Hindu extremist on 30 January. He dedicated his life to the betterment of the Indian people, and through a sequence of campaigns of non-violent civil disobedience proved crucial to the granting of India's independence from the British in 1947. In his lifetime, he became a worldwide symbol of pacifism, tolerance and spirituality, qualities that commended him to Britten, who almost immediately was to consider writing a 'requiem' in Gandhi's memory: see Letter 575 n. 4.

571 To Elizabeth Mayer

38 Bellerivestrasse, Zurich
Feb. 4th 1948

My dearest Elizabeth,

Please forgive the long, long silence. Writing letters is one of the greatest problems with me, I am afraid. Because when one actually does stop working, the eyes or the fingers or the brain are so tired that letters <u>can't</u> be coped with! And, I know you know, one doesn't stop working very often! But, with you my dear, letters aren't a necessity. You are in our thoughts continually, & actual contacts occur so often – even after a concert here last week a young American (whose name I didn't catch) came up to me & said he'd spent an evening recently with you & William, & we had a long talk about you! So even without writing letters we aren't so cut off! It is lovely to have the Mörike book[1] – it is a beauty, & very tender & moving reading. We are doing some songs of his & Wolf in Holland[2] quite soon, & I find him a most moving poet too. Do you remember 'Im Frühling'? I love the little St Cecilia notebook too. Always on my desk in front of the sea. The new house (with its lovely 4 Crabbe Street address!) is turning out a great success. I had in a way outgrown the Mill. I still have it – friends from Switzerland have rented it[3] – but I wanted something simpler, bigger, & above all in front of the sea as before! It is next door to the Grimes "Moot Hall" too, like this.

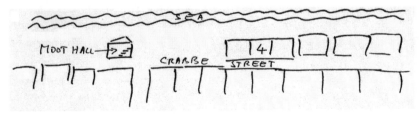

Aldeburgh is a sweet little town, & the beach & sea full of fishing-business – not at all "quaint" though. Our plans for a Festival in June are going ahead with great enthusiasm. We are planning 3 performances of "Albert Herring"[4] – many concerts in the Church (including, Peter & me,[5] Clifford Curzon,[6] two choral concerts including my new St Nicolas Cantata etc.),[7] lectures[8] (including E. M. Forster,[9] Kenneth Clark, Guthrie), exhibitions of modern paintings as well as the local painters Constable & Gainsborough![10] & Popular concerts,[11] & bus excursions around the district, as well as a Festival dance![12] Can't you & William consider making a little excursion across then? You could also see the new Beggar's Opera production in Cambridge with Peter as Macheath – as well as see the new house, and <u>at last</u> Beth & the children & our many,

many by now mutual friends! I don't want to tempt something which may
be quite impossible – but we do so long to have you over here; it has had
to wait so long. I know we're coming in the Fall, but concert tours are so
exhausting, & one has never time to sit & gossip & drink coffee!

We go on to the North of Italy from here (alas, we can't get south to
Rome) & then for 3 weeks in Holland. It is exciting doing these concerts
& to find people reacting so warmly to our rather humble music &
performance! Europe is sad & worried now, but very friendly & beautiful,
& excessively moving.

We are giving up 3 Oxford Square now – we were never there much,
& it was incredibly expensive. We shall probably have just a room in the
Steins' new flat,[13] & concentrate on the Aldeburgh house.

Peter has taken a great interest in the house & has many ideas re furn-
ishings & curtaining – but these are very, very difficult & expensive these
days. Still we manage – & with our new Constable & Turner, & several
John Pipers we feel very grand![14]

I do so hope that your worries with the family & their health are over
now, & that life goes on quietly & smoothly with you all. Write tiny notes
when you can, & I'll try to do the same. Peter joins with me in all this –
he'd write a note, but he has a strenuous Bach programme tonight & is
resting.

With all our love, my dearest, to you all & every good wish,

your devoted
BEN

The date of the Festival is June 5–13 – do come!

1 Eduard Mörike (1804–1875), German poet, much admired by Hugo Wolf
whose fifty-three settings of *Mörike-Lieder* (1888) did much to broaden the
appeal of Mörike's verse. The 'Mörike book' Britten refers to was a copy of
Mozart on the Way to Prague (1855), Mörike's fictional account of Mozart's
journey to Prague for the premiere of *Don Giovanni*. Mrs Mayer had sent
Britten a copy of Walter and Catherine Phillips's recently published English
translation for his thirty-fourth birthday, which she had inscribed: 'To my
dear Ben / with birthday wishes, / remembering Nov. 22, 1939, / and B.B.
"On the Way / to Fame". / E'.

2 For example, in Leiden, on 16 February 1948, Pears and Britten were to perform three Wolf lieder in their recital programme, including 'Im Frühling'
from the *Mörike-Lieder*. Wolf featured regularly in their recital programmes
over the years, including their last recital together at Snape Maltings in
September 1972 (which included 'Im Frühling'). Although they never
made any commercial recordings of Wolf lieder, after Britten's death two
gramophone recordings of archival material appeared: their final Snape

recital (AF 001), and recordings drawn from the BBC Sound Archive (REGL 410). In 1999 BBC Legends released on CD archival recordings of further Pears–Britten performances of Wolf lieder from a recital at Snape Maltings on 4 June 1972 (BBCB 8015–2), and 'Three Christmas Songs' from a recital at Snape on 26 June 1971 (BBCB 8011–2). The latter CD also includes Wolf's *Three Poems of Michelangelo* performed by John Shirley-Quirk (baritone) and Britten from the same 1971 recital. See also the liner notes for both these important recordings: Graham Johnson, 'Benjamin Britten – The Unwilling Accompanist' (BBCB 8011–2), and Roger Vignoles, 'Empathy and Understanding: A Britten–Pears Song Collection' (BBCB 8015–2). In the former, Johnson recalls Britten saying that 'Wolf's talent was quite extraordinary but that, unlike Schubert, he was not a composer one wanted to listen to every day'.

3 Britten had leased the Old Mill to June Billows, who was by then estranged from her husband Lionel.

4 The EOG, including many from the original Glyndebourne cast, gave performances of *Albert Herring* in the Jubilee Hall, Aldeburgh, as part of the first Aldeburgh Festival, on 7, 9 and 11 June 1948, all of which were conducted by the composer.

5 Pears and Britten, with George Roth (cello), gave a recital in Aldeburgh Parish Church on 8 June 1948. The programme included songs by Dowland, Handel, Maurice Greene, Schubert, Purcell (*Job's Curse*), Britten (*Canticle I*) and folksong arrangements.

6 Curzon was engaged to give a recital in the Aldeburgh Cinema on 6 June 1948, the programme of which was to have included music by Schubert, Lennox Berkeley (Sonata), Ravel, Chopin and Liszt (Sonata in B minor). Curzon was, however, indisposed on the day of the concert and his place was taken by Noel Mewton-Wood, who performed a different programme: music by Bach, Schumann (*Davidsbündler*), Purcell, Constant Lambert (Sonata) and Debussy (*Suite pour le piano*).

7 A programme of choral and orchestral music in the Parish Church opened the first Aldeburgh Festival on 5 June, and was repeated a week later on the 12th. A chamber orchestra led by the principals of the EOG Orchestra, conducted by Leslie Woodgate, performed Purcell's Chacony in G minor for strings, Handel's Organ Concerto, Op. 7 No. 4 (Ralph Downes, organ) and, with the Aldeburgh Festival Choir (Ursula Nettleship, chorus master), gave the first performances of *God's Grandeur* – Martin Shaw's setting of Gerard Manley Hopkins, commissioned by the Aldeburgh Festival for the occasion – and Britten's *Saint Nicolas* (Peter Pears, tenor).

8 Lectures were given each weekday afternoon in the Baptist Chapel, beginning on 7 June with E. M. Forster who spoke on 'George Crabbe and *Peter Grimes*' (subsequently published in Forster's *Two Cheers for Democracy* and

THE PARISH CHURCH

A CHORAL AND ORCHESTRAL CONCERT

SATURDAY, 5TH JUNE, AT 2.30 P.M.   SATURDAY, 12TH JUNE, AT 2.30 P.M.

With

PETER PEARS (*Tenor*)

RALPH DOWNES (*Organ*)

HANS OPPENHEIM AND IVAN CLAYTON
(*Pianoforte*)

THE ALDEBURGH FESTIVAL CHOIR
(*Chorus Master*: Ursula Nettleship)

CHAMBER ORCHESTRA
led by
JACK KESSLER (*1st Violin*)

HANS GEIGER (*2nd Violin*)   GEORGE ROTH (*'Cello*)
BERNARD DAVIS (*Viola*)   ROBERT MAYER (*Doublebass*)
HERBERT WILSON (*Percussion*)

CONDUCTED BY LESLIE WOODGATE

CHACONNY IN G MINOR FOR STRING ORCHESTRA   *Henry Purcell*

This is one of the finest examples of the ancient form of the Chaconne. The theme of eight bars is incessantly repeated, mostly in the bass, but occasionally ascending to the other instruments. On the theme, as basis, a great variety of melodic and harmonic structures is erected, which keep the music in steady flow. To the last entry of the theme, Purcell has added the word 'soft'. Otherwise, there are no expression marks, although the music undoubtedly demands a great flexibility of performance.

ERWIN STEIN

ORGAN CONCERTO (*Op. 7. No. 4*)   *George Frederick Handel*

Adagio — Allegro — Allegro

Handel's Organ Concerti, first played as interludes during his oratorio performances in 1735, with Handel as soloist frequently improvising the organ part, appeared subsequently as Opus 4 (1738) and Opus 7 (1760): a third set, mostly arranged from the Concerti Grossi, appeared in 1740. All except one were composed for an organ without pedals:* the instruments on which they were played were small, but of clear and brilliant sonority. Opus 7, No. IV, is distinguished by its noble grandeur, which the instrumentation further enhances.

* Only the organ in St. Paul's Cathedral possessed this luxury.

14

Aldeburgh Parish Church, 5 June 1948: the programme for
the inaugural concert of the Aldeburgh Festival.
(The concert was repeated a week later, on 12 June.)

Only the Finale appears to have been used before, in 1712 in the Overture of 'Il Pastor Fido', in 1720 as part of the third Suite for harpsichord, and again in 1729, in Concerto Grosso, Opus 3, No. VI.

Interpretationally, the present performance will follow the eighteenth-century tradition, but the *ad libitum* passages (left blank by Handel), are being composed by Benjamin Britten.   RALPH DOWNES

GOD'S GRANDEUR (First performance)   *Martin Shaw*

This setting of the poem by Gerard Manley Hopkins is scored for chorus, strings, drums and organ, and was specially composed for the Aldeburgh Festival.

After a short instrumental prelude on a sustained low pedal D the chorus enters in unison. 'The world is charged with the grandeur of God . . .' The tempo quickens. 'Why do men then now not reck his rod? Generations have trod . . .' Man, with his toil and trade has made a mess of things—'bleared, smeared.' He has lost touch with the earth. 'Nor can foot feel, being shod . . .'

But 'nature is never spent' a high solo voice proclaims. 'There lives the dearest freshness deep down things.'

A solo violin carries on the note of hope, which is taken up and transmuted into certainty by the chorus. For nature is not all. After the dark . . . 'Morning . . . springs Because the Holy Ghost broods with warm breast and with ah! bright wings.'

MARTIN SHAW

SAINT NICOLAS   Words by *Eric Crozier*. Music by *Benjamin Britten*

This Cantata was written at Aldeburgh during the early winter of 1947-8 for first performance at the Centenary Celebrations of Lancing College in July 1948. The period of its composition coincided with the planning of the first Aldeburgh Festival, and the Lancing Centenary Committee generously allowed the work to be included in the Festival programme for two performances before its official first performance in Lancing College Chapel. In return for this kindness, it is asked that the two Aldeburgh performances shall be regarded as privileged occasions, and that public criticism of the Cantata shall be reserved for the Centenary performance at Lancing College on July 24th, 1948.

The Cantata is written for tenor, mixed choirs, string orchestra, pianoforte and percussion, and includes two great familiar hymns for congregation and choirs, *All People that on earth do dwell* and *God Moves in a Mysterious Way*.

Nicholas was born at Patara, in Asia Minor, and spent most of his life in ministering to the physical and spiritual needs of the Christian community of Lycia, his native country. His memory is celebrated in many legends, from which it is hard to sift positive facts. This Cantata endeavours to bring the little that is known of him as a man into imaginative harmony with the Saint whose life and miracles are revered in all Christian countries, and who has been identified in the West with the vague, homely figure of Santa Claus.

No attempt is made to rationalize the miraculous qualities in the legends of the Saint. These are described by the chorus with the simple faith that has preserved them in the hearts of generations of believers, while Nicolas himself expresses the anguish of the struggle for faith that all good men must experience in a world corrupt with sin, despair and lack of grace.   ERIC CROZIER

15

reprinted in PGPB, pp. 7–21). On the 8th William Plomer discussed Edward Fitzgerald, and on the 9th Tyrone Guthrie gave a talk entitled 'The Theatre Today'. On the 10th Steuart Wilson (see pp. 7–8) spoke on 'The Future of Music in England' and on the 11th, the anniversary of Constable's birth, Sir Kenneth Clark lectured on 'Constable and Gainsborough as East Anglian Painters'.

9   E. M. (Edward Morgan) Forster (1879–1970), English novelist and man of letters who, while closely associated with the Bloomsbury group in London, at the same time managed to preserve a certain detachment from it.

   After studies at King's College, Cambridge (1897–1901), Forster travelled extensively in Italy and Greece, countries that meant much to him and symbolized a lifestyle that he juxtaposed with the puritanism of northern Europe. Short stories were among his earliest publications, to be followed by his first novel *Where Angels Fear to Tread* (1905), in which the character Philip Herriton is modelled on Forster's friend at King's, the eminent musicologist E. J. Dent. Three further novels followed in rapid succession: *The Longest Journey* (1907), *A Room With a View* (1908) and *Howards End* (1910). His intimate knowledge of India – Forster was for a time the private secretary of the Maharaja of Dewas State Senior – provided the background for his *A Passage to India* (1924). This novel proved to be his last major work in the genre, but he continued to lecture, write essays and criticism, and to give broadcast talks, which were published in two collections – *Abinger Harvest* (1936) and *Two Cheers for Democracy* (1951). The latter appeared in the same year as Britten's *Billy Budd*, the libretto of which Forster had written in collaboration with Eric Crozier. Although Forster was to live for almost another twenty years, *Billy Budd*, based on Herman Melville's novella, proved to be his last piece of major writing, and one that, with his profound love of music, gave him in the main immense satisfaction.

   Forster first encountered Britten during the Group Theatre production of Auden's and Isherwood's *The Ascent of F6* in February–March 1937, for which Britten had composed incidental music. (Forster told Isherwood in a letter of 27 February, 'How good the music is.') While their paths occasionally crossed during the remaining few years before the war, once Britten was in the United States (1939–42) contact between them ceased. It was Forster, however, who in 1941 unwittingly played a key role in Britten's decision to compose an opera based on part of the Aldeburgh-born poet George Crabbe's *The Borough*. In California during the summer of 1941, Britten happened on a copy of the *Listener* (29 May 1941) which contained the text of a broadcast talk by Forster entitled 'George Crabbe: The Poet and the Man'. The article not only provided an immediate catalyst for *Peter Grimes* but also perceptibly influenced the composer's decision to return home. See also Letter 328 n. 3.

   Once back in England, the former association with Forster revived and blossomed into a warm friendship: the two men frequently corresponded and met. While comparatively few of Britten's letters to Forster survive, over two hundred from Forster to Britten are extant at BPL (see Mary Lago (compiler), *Calendar of the Letters of E. M. Forster*, pp. 28–31). Forster's early letters to Britten reveal an enthusiasm for each of his new works, although he was not indiscriminate in his praise. For example, he saw *Lucretia* at Glyndebourne in 1946 when he found much to admire but was disturbed by the 'Christian enhaloing' of the story. On its publication, *Albert Herring* was dedicated to Forster whose own copy bore an inscription from the composer – 'For my dear Morgan / a very humble tribute to a very great man / Benjamin B. April 1948' – to which Forster responded:

What a present! I am quite overwhelmed. And *what* an inscription. It makes me feel a little strange! What are any of us doing with greatness? I do feel very proud, but proudest of your affection.

The relationship was not always easy, and at least on one occasion during the composition of *Billy Budd* Forster overstepped the mark with Britten (see Letter 679 n. 1). However, in spite of occasional blemishes the friendship endured to the end of Forster's life, and he made frequent visits to Aldeburgh, staying with Britten, or at the White Lion Hotel, or with the fisherman Billy Burrell (see Letter 688 n. 4). Britten contributed an unusually elaborate essay – 'Some notes on Forster and music' – to the *Festschrift* compiled by Oliver Stallybrass, *Aspects of E. M. Forster*, to celebrate Forster's ninetieth birthday, reprinted in PKBM, pp. 316–20.

See also BBMCPR, pp. 42–73; P. N. Furbank, *E. M. Forster: A Life*, and Mary Lago and P. N. Furbank (eds.), *Selected Letters of E. M. Forster*.

10   An exhibition of oil paintings, watercolours and drawings by Constable from the collection of Dr H. A. C. Gregory was mounted at Sandhills and Prior's Hill, Aldeburgh. No paintings by Gainsborough were exhibited, although the Festival brochure advertised that Gainsborough would be one of the artists to be shown. Two other exhibitions were organized for the first Aldeburgh Festival: an exhibition of photographs, stage models and designs for *Peter Grimes*, including those by Kenneth Green and Tanya Moisiewitsch, was held at the Moot Hall, Aldeburgh, and at Alde House there was an exhibition entitled *Contemporary Painting by East Anglian Artists*, the selection committee for which included John Nash and John Piper.

In his autobiography, 'After Long Pursuit', ff. 158–60, Eric Crozier was to recall the circumstances surrounding the Constable exhibition.

11   The 'Aldeburgh Serenade Concert', a 'musical entertainment' arranged and compèred by Basil Douglas, was given by members of the EOG at the Jubilee Hall, Aldeburgh, on 12 June, and repeated the following day. As the Festival programme book states, 'These Aldeburgh Serenade Concerts present a remarkable group of singers and instrumentalists in a variety of popular music ranging from the eighteenth century to the present day [. . .]

The centrepiece of the concert is Liza Lehmann's song-cycle *In a Persian Garden'*. Other music performed included songs by Ethel Smyth and Roger Quilter (who, according to the annotated programme book at BPL, took part), as well as folksong arrangements by Britten, Moeran and Vaughan Williams.

12 A 'Grand Festival Dance' was held at the White Lion Hotel on 12 June.

13 After the deaths of Pears's mother in October 1947 and of his father early in 1948, Pears no longer needed to maintain such a substantial London home. As Britten suggests in his letter to Mrs Mayer, he and Pears were to sub-let two rooms from the Steins at 22 Melbury Road, off Kensington High Street.

14 We cannot be absolutely certain which paintings by Constable and Turner Britten is referring to, although it seems likely that the Constable is either *Suffolk Landscape with Cottage*, purchased by Pears in 1947, or a storm scene (*c.* 1820) given to Britten by Dr Gregory. Pears owned an oil entitled *Coastal scene* which was attributed to Turner. Research undertaken in 1993 suggests that the painting is in fact a copy, not executed by the artist, of a watercolour by Turner (source: Ian Warrell, British Collection, Tate Gallery, London).

One of the most recent acquisitions to Britten's and Pears's collection of paintings was by John Piper, specially commissioned as a present to Britten. In 'After Long Pursuit', f. 157, Eric Crozier recalled:

Just before the first performance of *Albert Herring* at Glyndebourne in 1947, I took the lead in collecting donations towards the commissioning fee for a painting by John Piper, as a gift for Ben. It was a version in oils of the drop-scene for the Act Two Interlude, handsomely framed in gold, for which I paid £50: it now hangs in the Britten–Pears Library at Aldeburgh. We presented it to Ben on stage during the first-night dinner-interval – an occasion marred by the fact that the electricians had hurried off to their meal, leaving the stage in almost total darkness.

See also Paul Banks and Philip Reed, *Painting and Music: Exhibition Catalogue*, pp. 7–8.

572 To Eric Crozier

American Hotel, Amsterdam
Feb. 19th 1948

My dear Eric,

Thank you for your sweet letter.[1] I must confess I was a bit shocked to hear your news, because of the great unhappiness which it must bring you & Nancy at any rate for the time being. But I trust your judgement, & my love & prayers go with you whatever you decide, as you know. Please don't say thank you for the little we may have done. It is nothing compared to the immense trouble, energy & gift you have spent on work for us & me in particular. It has been in every way a sickening period for you. One goes on hoping that things will clear for you & that you can get down to the work you want – it surely will come one day. Anyhow, you _must_ be a little pleased with Nicolas. I think it looks fine, & it is (at any rate from you, my dear) a first rate piece of work. I think you are developing excellently as a poet, as Heloise[2] shows too. Peter is writing one or two observations on the first bit – but we both like it a lot.[3]

I have written to Leslie Boosey – yesterday, actually, immediately on receipt of his letter. I _don't_ frankly want a _debt_ of £1000 round my neck & told him so. I have not signed a specific agreement about the B's O. but there _may be_ a clause in my general agreement with B & H about film-rights. (My copy is at Aldeburgh, but Miss Jackson will have a copy, I think.) What I suggested to him, is that he should let the E.O.G. have the £2000 at once, & leave the £1000 until I get back. But since writing him I have had this idea ... When first discussed, the money was to be an _insurance_ against a film (nothing to do with rights). When the rights question came up later, surely it was not mentioned what _proportion_ of the money was rights, & what proportion remained the old insurance? Isn't that therefore a way to get round the B & H problem of not wanting to put up more money for theatrical enterprises? – let's call it £2400 insurance – £600 rights: – E.O.G. gets £2800, & B & H £200 ... ?? Think over that one with Anne ...[4]

I also put forcibly that I didn't want him to spread rumours of my dissatisfaction about existence of E.O.G. & pointed out that B & H had got something out of it already!

Peter is a bit better, but still a bit under the weather. We shall try the concert tonight,[5] I think. Anyhow I've had a chance to get on with B's O. a bit. But, by the way, Erwin tells me they're planning to _engrave_ the vocal score right away. Is that wise? I may make hundreds of radical changes, right up to the 1st night. After all I shan't see Tony [Tyrone Guthrie], _with the music_, till March 8th. I'll see him for a moment here next week, I think, but only can discuss most general outlines.

I've had the letter from Steve[6] – not at all unreasonable. I feel he may come round – especially when he knows there is no bass clarinet in Beggar's Opera. I shall write a friendly note, but rather vague, because in the meantime I shan't know what Anne has said, nor what the position about having an extra player for broadcast & important first nights would be. It is awfully necessary to have him, especially with the Aldeburgh & Cheltenham concerts in view.[7] Peter & I have discussed this programme question – it's a little difficult from a distance. Did you plan for a soloist? ... I don't know _what_ could be done if you wanted, say, Joan. Perhaps she knows a bit she could sing. I should otherwise like to make the centrepieces the Schubert Octet & the Ravel Septet. Those would use fl., cl., horn, bassoon, harp & all strings. Then either the Bridge Divertimenti[8] – or there is a fine big piece by him "There is a willow grows aslant a brook", which is nearly the right combination for the whole group (I could adjust the differences). The rest could wait till we get back, but if we need a new piece I suggest we ask E. J. Moeran[9] (lived for ages in Norfolk) to write a piece for all instruments or something starring the oboe, or oboe & bassoon. Or Arthur [Oldham] could write a short piece perhaps – Michael[10] won't have time, & there's already Lennox's Sonata.[11]

Enormous interest in the Aldeburgh Festival out here – I'm plugging it hard in interviews.

I must dash now, but I'm afraid I've left out all the important bits. But you can always wire or ring up (we're in practically <u>every</u> morning).

Peter & I are sending a cable to Ralph cancelling the American tour – I can't face it, & I've got loads of music wanting to come out, & I can't let my subconscious revolt & get the better of me. Afraid he'll be cross.[12]

Love to Biddy & the kids, & to Anne too,
Your devoted
BEN

P.S. We saw Otto [Otakar Kraus]– he's <u>most</u> keen to come with us – but thinks it's the 26th April that he's needed. It might be difficult for him to leave before especially with broadcast[13] . . but when he's here for that, we could do some work on B's O.[14] – & he's very sound musically.

1   This letter does not survive at BPL, but it must have conveyed news to Britten that a divorce between Crozier and his first wife, Margaret Johns (known as 'Biddy'; d. 2004), who had fallen into what Crozier was to refer to in one of his subsequent letters to Britten (5 May 1950) as a 'condition of depressive hopelessness (sometimes bordering on insanity)', had been postponed for the foreseeable future.

2   Crozier was writing the text of a cantata on the story of Abelard and Héloïse, which Britten intended to set for Pears and Nancy Evans. It was a subject that Britten had considered for operatic treatment as early as 1944 and had discussed with Ronald Duncan after the composition of *Lucretia* (see Letter 464 n. 6, and RDBB, pp. 99–102). Crozier had written to Britten on 16 February 1948, 'I have tried to do a first section of the *Héloïse* piece, which I enclose for you to see – but don't bother to return it.' In the event, the cantata was never composed. Crozier's text has apparently not survived.

3   Pears wrote to Crozier on the same day as Britten with detailed comments on the draft of *Abelard and Héloïse*:

   I enjoyed your Héloïse (La plus nouvelle Héloïse!) very much, and because I did &

because there were some things which seemed to me could be better, Ben encouraged me to put down my points on paper. I do hope you don't mind? Anyway disregard them in the biggest way if you want to.

verse 1. Doesn't somehow the 3 'cold's seem one too many – the repetition of the 2nd line is v. nice but isn't the 1st one somehow a give-away?

verse 2. Excellent.

verse 3. To me a long way the weakest. Surely a pity <u>not</u> to repeat the 2nd line as in all other verses.

Last line surely <u>not</u> good. 'Down' is only a syllable put in. Don't like kneeling – knees.

The direct appeal to Abelard (let ... beg ...) doesn't ring quite true with the rest of the poem with its fine monumental stone quality – may be it <u>could</u> be done, but I don't think that verse does it.

I feel verse 4 should come at the end of the poem. It is much more a final verse – the appeal to Mary too is right, at the end.

Do you think "could condemn" would be better than "might condemn"? 'Might' seems to me to be weakish, & 'could' would be another alliteration which I think you use most skilfully in the poem.

To my ear, 'fault' should be 'faults' – merely musically.

Not sure about 'raging' – not dead sure about 'towering': – two "–ing"s right? I like the echo of the hawk – v. good.

But I like the whole poem enormously. It has a very strong atmosphere – & is most moving.

4   Crozier had written to Britten on 16 February 1948 concerning Michael Balcon's interest in the film rights of *The Beggar's Opera* (see Letter 556 n. 6):

I have just had a talk with Leslie Boosey about *B.O.* He is writing to you himself, but I want to make one point as well. Boosey thinks £3000 a fair price for a version for films, but points out that while *you* may want to give your share to the EOG, £1000 of that sum is the property of Boosey & Hawkes, by your agreement with them. (Have you, in fact, signed an assignment of *B.O.* to them yet? If you haven't, surely they have no legal claim yet on that £1000?) He is prepared to recommend to his Board that they either lend or give that £1000 to the EOG – but suggested it might be repayable by you to them from future royalties! This is *impossible*! And as EOG we would not accept the £1000 on such terms, because it would be monstrously unfair to you.

May I suggest that if *Beggar's Opera* is *not* included in your general contract with B. & H., but has still to be assigned, you should reserve for yourself the film rights, sell them to Balcon for £3000 and let the Group have this sum without further obligation to B. & H.

Leslie Boosey is anxious to do what you want, but has recently expressed the opinion to Anne and the legal adviser of Ealing Films that if the EOG collapsed, it would rid you of a distraction and you'd write more music! This is one point of view, but I don't think it is really his business to propagate it, and I nearly lost my temper when he tried it on me twenty minutes ago. Not that he is malicious – but he *is* stupid.

See also PKSB, pp. 93–4.

5 In The Hague.

6 Stephen Waters had written to Britten on 14 February expressing his unwillingness to double on clarinet and bass clarinet in the forthcoming EOG season. For the Aldeburgh Festival performances of *Albert Herring*, Waters played clarinet and Wilfred Hambleton bass clarinet.

7 The EOG Orchestra was to give a chamber concert at the Aldeburgh Festival on 13 June 1948, conducted by Britten and Arthur Oldham, and repeated at the Cheltenham Festival on 4 July. The programme comprised Schubert's Octet in F, Frank Bridge's *There is a willow grows aslant a brook* arranged by Britten (the unpublished arrangement is at BPL), the first performance of Oldham's *Variations on a Carol Tune* (conducted by the composer), and Ravel's *Introduction and Allegro*.

8 For flute, oboe, clarinet and bassoon, composed 1934–38.

9 Ernest John (Jack) Moeran (1894–1950), English composer of Irish descent, who had studied at the Royal College of Music and later with John Ireland. The son of a Norfolk clergyman, Moeran, like Britten, was much influenced by his East Anglian origins. The Britten and Moeran families were friendly in the mid-1930s, and Moeran and his mother were among the group of Britten's friends who attended the premiere of *Our Hunting Fathers* at Norwich in 1936. It was Moeran to whom Britten turned for assistance in sourcing some of the folksongs used in music to the documentary film *Around the Village Green* in 1936; see Letter 90 n. 3.

Moeran did not write a piece for the 1948 Aldeburgh Festival. As n. 7 above makes clear, Arthur Oldham's *Variations on a Carol Tune* filled the gap in the programme.

10 Michael Tippett (1905–1998), English composer, who first met Britten and Pears in 1942 on their return from the United States. They remained warm friends and colleagues. Tippett composed two song-cycles for Pears and Britten – *Boyhood's End* (1943) and *The Heart's Assurance* (1950–52) – and dedicated his Concerto for Orchestra (1963) to Britten to mark the latter's fiftieth birthday. Britten reciprocated by dedicating *Curlew River* to Tippett in honour of the latter's sixtieth birthday. See also Letter 430 n. 4; Michael Tippett, *Those Twentieth Century Blues: An Autobiography*; Meirion Bowen (ed.), *Tippett on Music*, pp. 66–72; and obituaries by Paul Driver, *Independent*; Meirion Bowen, *Guardian*; Andrew Clark, *Financial Times*, and in the *Daily Telegraph* and *The Times* (all 10 January 1998), and by Nicholas Kenyon, *Observer* (11 January 1998).

While Tippett was not invited to contribute a new piece for the 1948 Aldeburgh Festival, he was represented by his String Quartet No. 2, which was performed by the Zorian String Quartet on 10 June.

11 Berkeley's Piano Sonata was originally included in Clifford Curzon's recital programme for 6 June 1948. Curzon's cancellation, however, meant that the

Sonata, along with the rest of the planned programme, was not played (see Letter 571 n. 6).

12   A draft telegram to Ralph Hawkes in Pears's hand survives on the verso of a letter from Leslie Boosey to Britten (17 February 1948):

~~AM FEELING VERY STRANGE ST[OP]~~ MOST URGENTLY WISH PLEASE CANCEL AMERICAN TOUR TO START NEW LARGE SCALE WORKS NEEDING SEVERAL MONTHS UNINTERRUPTED CONCENTRATION. VERY MUCH REGRET CAUSING TROUBLE BUT FEEL THIS MOST STRONGLY. COULD PERHAPS POSTPONE VISIT TILL SAME TIME NEXT YEAR BEN BRITTEN AMERICAN HOTEL AMSTERDAM

See also Letter 575.

13   Probably a reference to a studio performance of *Albert Herring* given by the EOG under Britten's direction, broadcast in the Third Programme on 12 April 1948. Rehearsals took place on the 7th–8th, 10th and 12th. Otakar Kraus sang the role of Mr Gedge, the Vicar.

14   Kraus was to take the role of Lockit in *The Beggar's Opera*.

573   **To George Barnes**
       BBC

                                              American Hotel, Amsterdam
                                                       Feb. 23rd 1948

My dear George,

   Please forgive my delay in answering your letter,[1] but as you probably have gathered we have been travelling around the continent & it took ages to catch up with us.

   I don't see how I could manage to fit in this Opera talk with Walton & Michael T. for quite a time. I shan't be back from here for a week or so, & then I must go down to Aldeburgh & work. After that I've got another series of concerts[2] & then the opera rehearsals start in grim earnest. Perhaps when we are in London April 11–26 rehearsing[3] we could have a lunch together & talk over the subject, but frankly I am not hopeful about the result. We are such different people, & the differences in our actual operatic experiences might be rather embarrassing![4] I will, at any rate, telephone you round about that period if you really think the idea is worthwhile pursuing.

                                              With every good wish,
                                                       Yours ever,
                                                       BENJAMIN B.

1   Barnes had written to Britten on 29 January 1948:

As a follow-up to the discussion between you and Crozier and Piper which we did last May [*recte*: June; *An Opera is Planned*], would you be willing to discuss at the microphone with Walton and Michael Tippett the difficulties and opportunities that you find in writing opera? I have spoken to both the others and they would be happy to do it if you could be persuaded [. . .] This must be the first occasion in British musical history when our leading composers have been engaged in the writing of opera [. . .]

Britten did not participate and, as far as can be ascertained, the proposal was dropped.

2   Pears and Britten gave recitals at Dartington (28 March), Tiverton (29 March), Weston super Mare (31 March), Bridgwater (1 April) and Bideford (2 April), before returning to Amsterdam for a recital at the Concertgebouw on 4 April. On the 9th they broadcast live from the BBC's Maida Vale Studios a recital for the Third Programme of lieder by Schubert and the UK premiere of Frank Martin's *Sechs Monologe aus 'Jedermann'*. Two notes in Britten's pocket engagement diary on the date of this broadcast – 'Martin here 1.15' and 'Martin' – suggest that Frank Martin met Britten and Pears to advise on the performance of his work.

3   For *The Beggar's Opera*.

4   Walton's and Tippett's first operas – *Troilus and Cressida* and *The Midsummer Marriage* respectively – had yet to be completed.

574   To Eric Walter White[1]

American Hotel, Amsterdam
[Postmarked 24 February 1948]

Dear Eric,

Please forgive this hurried note on an odd piece of paper – I am away till beginning of March, & then in Aldeburgh working like a mad thing on Beggar's Opera. If you'd like me to read the first section[2] then, I could certainly do it, & then we could meet in London early April – or will that be too late? I don't see that there'll be much chance for more than a telephone conversation on March 5–6 when I go thro' London.

So glad it's going so well! After Time's monstrous vulgarities & inacarracies [*sic*], it'll be nice to have something cool & sensible written about one![3]

We're having a rushed, & hectic tour. Peter caught a cold between Milan & Zurich (the trains were boiling hot) & had to cancel 2 concerts; but he's back singing now, & Amsterdam as usual is at his feet . . . !

With best wishes, & in haste,
Yours ever,
BEN

The cover of *Time* magazine, New York, 6 February 1948.
Peter Grimes opened on 12 February.

1   English writer on music, arts administrator and poet (1905–1985). White
began his career as the English tutor in the household of a cultured banker
and patron of the arts in Potsdam, where he got to know the publisher of
Thomas Mann and Bertolt Brecht, and the film-maker Lotte Reiniger, with
whom he subsequently collaborated as composer and librettist on two of her
silhouette films; see Letter 609 n. 3. He published an essay on Reiniger –
Walking Shadows – in 1931. He worked as a translator for the League of
Nations in Geneva (1929–33) before returning to London to work for the
National Council for Social Service (1935–42). In 1942 he was appointed
Assistant Secretary to CEMA and continued in this post when CEMA
became the Arts Council in 1946, remaining there until 1971. For the last
five years of his period at the Arts Council, White also served as its first
Literature Director.

     As a writer he not only contributed much to the early development of
serious Britten studies (see n. 2 below), but also wrote important studies of
Stravinsky (*Stravinsky: The Composer and his Works*) and English opera (*A
History of the English Opera*). White's major and notably early writings on
both Britten and Stravinsky testify to the challenging independence of
his musical judgement. As he himself wrote in the first edition of his
Stravinsky volume (1966), 'I [. . .] felt certain that, despite the great weight
of hostile criticism currently directed against his music, particularly in
Great Britain, he was one of the great composers of all time.' Critical
hostility and suspicion were still prevalent in the late 1940s and after, but
this time the target was often Britten, one typical example of which White
singles out himself when correcting the history of the first edition of his
Britten monograph (see Letter 627 n. 6).

     White's *Tippett and His Operas* is valuable not least for its inclusion of
many letters from Tippett to the author. White commissioned Tippett's
cantata *Crown of the Year* for the centenary of his daughter's school in 1958.
See also Douglas Cleverdon's obituary in *The Times* (17 September 1985).

2   A reference to White's biography and study of the composer, first published
as *Benjamin Britten: eine Skizze von Leben und Werk* – it had been commissioned and translated by Martin and Bettina Hürlimann, the directors of
the publishers, Atlantis Verlag – and subsequently published in English by
Boosey & Hawkes. White was the first to write a full-length study of
Britten's life and works. A revised edition appeared in 1954, and a reworked
version entitled *Benjamin Britten: His Life and Operas* appeared in 1970
under the imprint of Faber and Faber, with a second edition, edited by
John Evans, in 1983 (EWW).

3   Britten was evidently annoyed by the anonymous profile, 'Opera's New
Face', *Time* (16 February 1948), pp. 62–8, coinciding with the premiere of
Peter Grimes at the Metropolitan Opera. Among the inaccuracies that
would have irritated the composer were the reporting of the wrong year for
his father's death, a shared occupancy by himself and Montagu Slater of the
Old Mill at Snape, and the remark that 'he doesn't answer letters'.

75 **To Ralph Hawkes**

American Hotel, Amsterdam
Feb. 27th 1948

My dear Ralph,

Eric, lecturing here for the British Council, brought your second wire[1] with him. I have just cabled our considered reply to it, & as I said on it I am writing to give you some details. I was anyhow going to write in reply to your first wire & letter, to thank you from both of us for your extremely sympathetic, understanding reaction to our decision, for we understand only too well what a nuisance & embarrassment the cancellation must be to you. The facts are these: as you know I have been planning several big works for some time: the fourth opera,[2] the Koussevitzky piece,[3] to say nothing about an infinite number of small pieces which have been at the back of my mind. Added to this list, is now another major piece. As you probably guessed, the death of Gandhi has been a great shock to one of my strong convictions, & I am determined to commemorate this occasion in, possibly, some form of Requiem, to his honour.[4] When I shall complete this piece I cannot say, but I have had recently a strong revulsion against <u>having</u> to complete a work in a given time (e.g. every piece I've written in the last four years!). What I want desperately, and have decided I must take, is a long period off to think quietly about all these works, to write some of them, & think about music in general. This can only happen in the second half of this year – apart from a few scattered opera performances in September,[5] I shall have nothing to disturb me now from the middle of July till Christmas!

In future I am planning only the shortest concert trips with Peter, a week or two here & there. This trip, altho' it has been exciting & most successful, (Switzerland especially was a real conquest), I have felt much too long. The American one, even in the curtailed version your 2nd wire suggested, would have been much longer. 6 weeks, or 2 months more, away entirely without work is now unthinkable. I am so very sorry, Ralph, and apologise for having changed my mind at such a late date. Please tell all this to Dick Leech.[6] We very much hope to be able to arrange something later if we are still wanted. Peter agrees with me in all this; he has been sweet about it. He is of course disappointed, but also, frankly, the idea of two months off to work quietly & rest is attractive to him.[7] He sends you his best wishes, & regrets too.

Thank you for the notes about the Met. Grimes.[8] It does seem to have been catastrophic! I am only too thankful that I wasn't there . . . ! I've only seen one notice, that of Olin Downes, & that was, honestly, just what I expected.[9] It is fantastic how much separated general American & European artistic (if not otherwise as well) ideas are today. The enormous sympathy one feels for one's ideas on the continent, even compared with England, is most moving. Albert Herring is talked about with bated breath out here! I am sorry for you, Ralph, though – because I realise what a disappointment it has been, & how very hard you have worked about it. I am conceited enough to believe that it will come round in the end, though! The "Time" publicity I am sure was grand, although not exactly to my taste!

Please give Clare my love – & from Peter too. We think about you both a lot. Things seem to be going all right with plans in England now. I hope to be able to work something out about the Beggar's Opera film problem with Leslie when I get back. He's being very helpful about it.

> Greetings to all my friends – & to yourself,
>
> Yours ever,
>
> BEN

The Concertgebouw & Venice Festival[10] have both asked me for pieces, but I have had to tell them that unless something miraculous suddenly pours from my pen it isn't any good, & I cannot at the moment tie myself.

1 Hawkes's telegram, dated 25 February 1948, reads:

I AM GREATLY EMBARRASSED BY CANCELLATION AMERICAN TOUR. I AM PRESSED ASKING RECONSIDER FOR MONTH NOVEMBER ONLY SINCE TWELVE DATES BOOKED APPROXIMATE GROSS VALUE TEN THOUSAND. CAN I PRESS YOU BOTH PERSONALLY PLEASE FOR THIS SHORTENED PERIOD. REGARDS RALPH HAWKES

2 Eventually to be *Billy Budd.* Hawkes comments in a letter to Britten, 3 March 1948: 'Eric says that he feels he will have to complete the libretto by March 1949. I feel that production of this work need not take place till the winter of 1950–51 and I think Covent Garden will probably pre-empt it through the Arts Council for the great Exhibition Year.' The premiere of *Billy Budd* was given at the Royal Opera House, Covent Garden, on 1 December 1951: see Letter 718 n. 2.

3 Hawkes writes in his letter to the composer, 3 March 1948:

I saw [Koussevitzky] on Friday and he is of course ready and willing to accept this piece when you deliver it. My understanding is that there is a commission of $1,000.00 for it, but as this is not in writing I cannot very well say that it is so. He says that if you can let him have the score by about March 1949 he will produce it in Boston at the end of the season and do it again at Tanglewood that summer. I feel that this date is quite possible for you and in view of your 'revulsion' as you put it in your letter, against having to complete a work at a given date, I hesitate therefore to ask for any date on this piece.

4 Hawkes writes in his letter of 3 March:

I know how close to your heart this whole business must of course be, and I did not realize the regard that you had for Gandhi. I think the idea is terrific and I am sure you will give of your very best for this work. Time will not matter over this for it is bound to be a major work and will involve a great deal of preparation.

Crozier wrote to Nancy Evans at this time from Amsterdam:

It's perhaps not strange that Ben and I both had the idea separately of a work in memory of Gandhi – and Ben has cancelled the American tour very largely so that he can settle down to write it. He wants it to be a Requiem, using the traditional Latin words of the Requiem Mass, with linking interludes that I think he will ask me to write for him. And he has some idea of possible first performance by the Concertgebouw Orchestra and the Amsterdam Tonkunst Chor. He's on fire with the whole idea and says it will really be his Opus 1.

On 28 February, having attended a performance of Bach's *St Matthew Passion* in Rotterdam in which Pears was the Evangelist, Crozier told Nancy Evans: 'I have never heard it through before – and Ben specially wanted me to and got me a score, because of the interest it has for the planning of the Gandhi *Requiem*.'

It was surely Bach's complex interweaving of different musical and narrative elements in the *St Matthew Passion* that Britten must have recognized as a possible model for his own requiem in memory of Gandhi. Although the 'Gandhi Requiem' was never written, Crozier's description of it – 'using the traditional words of the Requiem Mass, with linking interludes' – is striking in its similarity to the form of *War Requiem*, in which Britten juxtaposes the timeless words of the liturgy with settings of Wilfred Owen's poems reflecting the horrors, brutality and wastefulness of the First World War. See also Letter 645 n. 3, and Philip Reed, 'The *War Requiem* in progress', in WRMC, p. 20.

5   Britten conducted three performances of *The Beggar's Opera* (6, 15 and 18 September) and three of *Albert Herring* (8, 10 and 13 September) with the EOG, at the Sadler's Wells Theatre, London. Britten does not mention to Hawkes that he was engaged to conduct three performances of *The Beggar's Opera* (27 and 30 September, 2 October) and one of *Albert Herring* (1 October) at the Alexandra Theatre, Birmingham, and three further performances of *The Beggar's Opera* (11, 14 and 16 October) at the People's Palace, London.

6   Unidentified.

7   In fact, Pears did visit the United States in the autumn: see Letters 589–603.

8   Hawkes must have sent Britten press notices of *Peter Grimes*, which had been given at the Metropolitan Opera, New York, on 12 February 1948. The title role was sung by Frederick Jagel, Ellen Orford by Regina Resnik, and Balstrode by John Brownlee. Emil Cooper conducted and the director was Dino Yannopoulos. Hawkes returned to *Grimes* in his letter of 3 March:

Grimes is certainly the talk of the town whatever the Met did with it and I hear that there is something going on in Canada that may indicate a radio performance of a concert version. It is to be played in Los Angeles on the Met tour, April 16th, and as a result the picture folk will undoubtedly realize that you exist.

9   Olin Downes's notice, 'Opera by Britten in premiere here', appeared in the *New York Times* (13 February 1948):

Had it been heard last night in a theatre of intimate character much that could not have been understood either by words or stage business might have been clear. But this did not prevent the warm welcome of Mr Britten's score.

We say 'score' because a musical composition skilfully put together, with effective instrumentation and an interesting rhythmical and contrapuntal scheme, would seem to be the main reason for the considerable degree of acclaim that has met this work. Its story is a grim one, and in itself potential of powerful drama. But the libretto is foggy and in the main both undramatic and untheatrical.

This story is told in rhythmed and high-falutin' verse – verse of a symbolic, pseudo-philosophic and undramatic sort, in which there is little emotional reality. The theme is a man against nature and fate, and the opinion of his community. If there were a moral to the tale it would be 'There but for the grace of God – .' But the tale is not told in terms genuinely of the lyric theatre.

[. . .] The action is for the most part lugged in, to give some semblance of real dramatic life to the picture. The one real character is Grimes. The motivations of the characters are neither seen nor felt; nor are they provided by the actual nature of the music. The composer thinks of his chorus as Moussorgsky uses his chorus in *Boris Godunoff*. Grimes is one man, against the people. Nature herself he defies, and since the fine noises of the orchestra, depicting wind and storm, are among the most graphic pages. Mr Britten knows his Berg, and builds much of his score upon the foundation of old forms – fugues, canonic imitations, and all that, and a passacaglia on a theme associated with Grimes for one of the best of his orchestral interludes which bind scenes together.

But one does not hear, in a single individual part, the song which naturally and inevitably characterizes the person and the moment. Not that characterization is forgotten by the composer, or that he fails carefully to ticket each personality and some of the symbolic forces of his drama with motives! This is skillfully and intellectually done. For all that it is artificial and exterior. The melodic outburst of unmistakable feeling and genuineness, revealing character and emotion in a flash, is not there.

So the opera, for us, is only the façade of an opera. The choruses are oratorio choruses, not operatic. Like oratorio, they are appropriate for the concerted expression of collective feeling, to verse of general sentiments, philosophies, etc. The orchestration is one of the strongest features of a virtuoso score.

But in essence this is instrumental, not lyrical music – music thought throughout as if for instruments. It cannot be very grateful to the singers, though often in the principal parts, especially that of Grimes, it is difficult to sing. The worst feature of the performance was the very poor and indistinct English. Why? We echo the question. Why is it that with much clamor for opera in English; with an opera that particularly requires distinct enunciation and the diction of the best; with American singers singing in their own tongue, the English language suffers as no other language does on the Metropolitan stage?

As for the performance, or the few particulars about it that can be recounted now, we do not feel that Mr Jagel was equal as singer or actor, or type, to the part of Grimes.

Miss Resnik had a dead part to begin with. Her vocalism was not of the best, but no one could have done very much with the straw figure of Ellen, or found anything very convincing to deliver in her music. Mr Brownlee's Balstrode was a competent job. The smaller parts were taken care of properly, and with Jerome Hines' Swallow one of the most outstanding. Mr Cooper conducted vigorously and in masterful fashion. The scenery was a little cluttered, but not without imagination. The stage was certainly cluttered with too many people, too much of the time. But the chorus, which has to be big, was brilliantly effective in a hard job.

Virgil Thomson contributed a notice of *Grimes* to the *New York Herald Tribune* (13 February 1948):

Benjamin Britten's *Peter Grimes*, which was added last night to the repertory of our Metropolitan Opera, is a success. It always is. Given in any language, in a house of any size, it always holds the attention of an audience. As given last night 'the works,' so to speak, which is to say, the full mechanism, musical and scenic, of a mammoth production establishment, it still held the attention.

This is not to minimize the excellences of the present production, which are many, or the care that has gone into it, which is considerable. It is merely to point out that the steam-roller processing that our beloved Met, geared to Wagner, puts any new work through is one of the severest tests known for the strengths of theatrical materials. If Mr Britten's work came out scarcely in English, vocally loud from beginning to end and decorated in a manner both ugly and hopelessly anachronistic, it also came through the ordeal with its music still alive and its human drama still touching.

Make no mistake about *Peter Grimes*. It is varied, interesting and solidly put together. It works. It is not a piece of any unusual flavor or distinction. It adds nothing to the history of the stage or to the history of music. But it is a rattling good repertory melodrama. And if the executant artists, beginning with Emil Cooper, who conducted, going on through Frederick Jagel and Regina Resnik, who sang the tenor and soprano leads, to the smallest rôle in a large cast and even including the chorus, treated the work with no consideration for its special or poetic subject-matter, but rather as disembodied, or 'pure,' theater, just 'wow' material, that is exactly what the composer himself has done, what his score invites and asks for.

There is everything in it to make an opera pleasing and effective. There is a trial scene, a boat, a church (with organ music), a pub (with drinking song for the full ensemble), a storm, a night club seen through a window (with boogie-woogie music off stage and shadow play), a scene of flagellation, a mad scene and a death. There are set pieces galore, all different, all musically imaginative and mostly fun. And there are a good half-dozen intermezzos, most of which are musically pretty weak, but expressive all the same.

The musical structure of the opera is simple and efficient. Everything and everybody has a motif, a tune or turn of phrase that identifies. The entire orchestral structure and most of the vocal is pieced together out of these, in the manner of Italian verismo. The harmony is a series of pedal points broadly laid out to hold together the bits-and-pieces motif continuity. There is no pretense of musical development through these motifs, as in Wagner. They are pure identification tags

[. . .] The music is wholly objective and calculated for easy effect. That is why it works.

It works even in spite of its none too happy handling of English vowel quantities. It sacrifices these systematically, in fact, to characteristic melodic turns, as if the composer had counted from the beginning on translation. A good part of the obscurity that was characteristic of last night's diction, in spite of the singers' visible effort to project sung speech, was due to the deliberate falsity of the prosodic line. Mr Britten is apparently no more bothered about such niceties than he is by the anachronisms of an almost popishly High-Church service in an English fishing village of 1830 and an American jazz band in the same time and place. He has gone out for theatrical effects, got them, got his success. So did the Metropolitan. And still his opera is not a bore.

Louis Biancolli, 'Met Bravely Sounds Bleak *Peter Grimes*', *New York World-Telegram* (13 February 1948):

Nobody needs reminding at this point that the 34-year-old Britten is one of the outstanding names in current music history. The vigorous, daring idiom he uses is all his own, and he knows how to vary his colors and move about the orchestra like a master.

What he also knows how to do is write for chorus. In this respect he belongs in the great tradition of Britain's great oratorio writers, and, in fact, some of the most gripping moments of *Peter Grimes* are those in which the chorus comments passionately on the action.

My attention was also rivetted last night on the orchestra. There Mr Britten was enacting a kind of drama within a drama, a story of fierce, rasping action, of sardonic queries and waspish replies, of seething horror and shrieking suspense. The orchestra was the thing last night.

Had Britten paralleled in stage action what he projected through symphonic color, *Peter Grimes* would have been as fascinating to watch as to hear. As it is, he chose a bleak story out of the Suffolk coast of the 1830s and cluttered it with all kind of fisherfolk using an often opaque English to communicate with one another.

The character of Peter Grimes, a surly fisherman suspected of murder and hounded by suspicion of a second murder into flight and suicide, never stands out too clearly. And the reason is that he is an idea, rather than a human being, a puppet of protest against a harsh social milieu.

Still, Mr Britten and his librettist Montagu Slater have managed to build a concentrated atmosphere of doom around Grimes. One senses the two forces – Grimes' brooding surliness and the narrowing circle of tragic compulsion – grappling through the whole fabric.

The Metropolitan has done everything in the way of evocative sets and smooth direction to give *Peter Grimes* the look of real opera. The fishing village on the east coast of England is vividly suggested, and the crowds are maneuvered with purpose and animation for a change.

But the final impact of dramatic action is lacking, despite the taut episodes of crisis in Grimes' tragedy. Perhaps one way of explaining it is that Mr Britten seemed too intent on a subjective conflict of ideas, and his librettist too concerned with literary patterns.

Irving Kolodin, 'An Impressive *Peter Grimes* at the Opera', *New York Sun* (13 February 1948):

The Metropolitan took its courage in hand last night and challenged the intricacies of Benjamin Britten's *Peter Grimes*, which has had performances in eight countries and half a dozen languages since 1945. For their pains, the performers could remember today a patter of applause after the first act, something more substantial after the second and a respectable salute at the finish. None of this approached a demonstration, however.

[...] Nevertheless, the experience left with this listener (who was not at all taken by the work as given in its American premiere in Tanglewood in August, 1946) a feeling of profound respect for the musical capacities of Britten and admiration for the industry of performers. Emil Cooper's direction had a decisive grasp of the large outlines of the score, if more than a little roughshod disregard for subtleties. The superb orchestral interludes which hold the work together were technically adroit, but hardly as imaginatively phrased as they can be.

The Grimes of Frederick Jagel was a credit to the intelligence of this singer and his power to create a dramatic image, but the part asks for a special kind of high tenor voice which he doesn't have. Regina Resnik's Ellen Orford, thoroughly artistic, was a little soft and comely for the widowed schoolmarm, who seeks to save Grimes from the doom within his character. Some of her quieter moments were beautifully, and a little prettily sung. John Brownlee didn't make enough of Capt. Balstrode's lines intelligible to atone for his lack of vocal power. A better choice for this part might have been Jerome Hines, who did a superb Swallow – vocally potent and cleanly understandable. Martha Lipton as Mrs Sedley sang well, though looking much younger than the 65 years noted in the text, and Claramae Turner's Auntie, as well as the nieces of Paula Lenchner and Maxine Stellman, were a little conventionally operatic for their unconventional trade. Unquestionably the best work was done by the chorus trained by Kurt Adler, which performed with assurance and fine musicality.

That the performance created as much mood as it did is a tribute to the force of Britten's writing, since the production was channeled into conventional operatic lines by Stage Director Dino Yannopoulos and Designer Joseph Novak. The realistic intent of Britten was ill-served by the oversized chorus, the static direction and stylized groupings which might well have been the seaside of Ponchielli's *La Gioconda*. Nor did it seem reasonable that the 'nieces' should have been as coquettish about their ancient profession as they were in Act III. For another detail, the first act was poorly lit, to the detriment of the illusion in Britten's writing.

The sum of the matter is that the Metropolitan has added to its repertory a work of great imaginative power and theatrical force, which is not so musically self-sufficient that it can absorb the liabilities of preparation inherent in this production. The foundation is sound enough, but it requires a good deal more careful architecture for justice to Britten and the personnel involved.

Robert A. Hague, 'The Met Does Poorly By Britten's *Grimes*', *P.M.* (15 February 1948):

Faced with the challenge of a modern work requiring some amount of adroitness, originality and imagination in its presentation, the Met has fallen down badly. It has staged *Peter Grimes* as though it were a cross between *La Gioconda* and *Die Meistersinger*; cast it indifferently and in many cases unsuitably; and provided it with a clutter of old-fashioned picture-book settings made up of pasteboard houses and flickering projections of Wagnerian cloud effects on wrinkled backdrops. Here was an opera which cried out for simplicity and directness, for stylization or at least a unity of style, in its acting and its production. It got nothing of the sort. That it got across at all – and it did hold the attention and was well received by its initial local audience – is a tribute to the sound theatrical values of its libretto and the pungency, expressiveness and power of its music.

[. . .] Mr Britten has given it skillful and viable musical expression. The recitatives, set-pieces, choral and orchestral interludes, which make up the score, animate the story and carry it forward to its tragic conclusion. Though the words and phrases of the English text are not always gracefully or aptly set, and are sometimes difficult to sing, the essential thought and meaning are generally well enough conveyed. Music of considerable inventiveness, individuality and persuasiveness, whether dissonant or consonant, it is always arresting to the ear; it is highly atmospheric and evocative of mood, especially in its orchestral seascapes and storm sequences; and often it is quite powerful in its projection of emotion.

Given a first-rate production, *Peter Grimes* should be first-rate musical theater [. . .]

As Grimes, Frederick Jagel has neither the physical presence nor the acting skill to bring the role off with complete success; and though he sang much of the music admirably, the always taxing and often cruelly high part would seem to call for a fresher and more lyric voice. Miss Resnik's Ellen was believably and affectingly acted, but sung with a voice that was often edgy and strident. Miss Lipton did her best to hide her youthful good looks as Mrs Sedley – the village gossip, troublemaker and dope addict – and made her a striking stage figure, though hardly the characterization it should have been. Many of the minor roles were better cast and sung, among them the Swallow of Jerome Hines, the Ned Keene of Hugh Thompson and the Rev. Adams of John Garris.

Mr Cooper conducted with more forcefulness than discretion. The chorus sang loudly and with considerable effect, though their movements were often erratic and ill-timed. There was much running about, and concerted waving of arms, in the climactic choral numbers, which gave the impression they had been staged for the finale of a 1920 musical comedy.

Opera News, 12/21 (8 March 1948), published by the Metropolitan Opera Guild, was largely devoted to Britten and the new Met production of *Peter Grimes*.

10 Hawkes writes in his letter of 3 March, 'I am sorry in a way that you are not doing a *Concertgebouw* piece. We really badly need an 8–10 minute orchestral work from you and the orchestras are constantly asking for it. Possibly a miracle will occur and will "pour from your pen" as you put it.' See also Letter 563 n. 11.

Mention of the Venice Festival in Britten's letter may be the first indication of the commission that eventually produced *The Turn of the Screw* in 1954.

576 To Peter Pears

~~THE OLD MILL, SNAPE, SAXMUNDHAM, SUFFOLK~~
4 Crabbe Street, Aldeburgh
March 17th 1948

My darling old thing,

Only a note to tell you that (as you probably have guessed) I'm thinking about you all the time, & being with you in spirit through all the big
things you must do this week.[1] I'll listen all over the continent on Sunday
in case it's to be broadcast.

Things are going quite well here. The booking started on Monday for
the Festival, & by midday today about ¼ – ⅕ of the tickets were all sold,
which is a good beginning I think. Elizabeth[2] is up to her eyes, but little
Miss Parker is doing well, & Mrs Galsworthy[3] is standing by all the time,
with Margery [Spring-Rice] near! We had a committee yesterday which
was rather wild – too many people, & Fidelity[4] not too skilful at control-
ling them. She & Margery stayed to dinner afterwards & we talked "Pfaff"
till a late hour, which is quite a business. Barbara [Parker] wasn't too
pleased, as it turned out (too late to change plans) that it was her birthday,
& would have liked a ceremony, I think. Still, I'm taking her & Elizabeth
out to dinner tonight, which ought to put things right!

Beth & Sally[5] were here for the night. Sally – <u>very</u> sweet, & considerably
better away from her difficult brother & charming sister.[6] It was nice having
them, & Beth was very dear.

The work goes well, & pretty fast. I'm enjoying this bit, & allowing
myself a bit of space to develop the music. But I must stop myself too
much "canonizing" of the music, which is probably more entertaining to
write than to listen to![7]

I look forward to hearing your "Evangelist" again – if only to get Eric
Greene[8] out of my head! I was really disgusted at the sloppiness of his actual
singing – it was really 'faked' singing I felt, – at the hopeless word distortion (the Je-<u>sers</u> all the time). And the embarrassing 'big moment' of
Peter's going out – I admired the way at Rotterdam[9] that you gave this
moment its importance, but yet kept it in the <u>style</u> of the whole. I <u>loathe</u>
the long pauses there, as if the "<u>going-out</u>" of Peter were the climax of the
whole terrible story of the Crucifixion[10] – You're a very great artist, honey.

I've written a note to Basil [Douglas], & am doing so to Jasper
[Rooper]. Any more to do? Did you tell Emmie[11] we don't need hospitality
at Tiverton?[12]

I hope the Hotel is nice – but go & have a drink at the American & give
the small things my love – esp. Willi!![13] Your room's beginning to look
nice without the awful black paint.

Lots of love my dear – take care of yourself. Sing nicely.

Love to all the friends . . .

BEN

1   Pears had returned to Amsterdam to sing the role of the Evangelist in two
    performances of Bach's *St Matthew Passion* (20 and 21 March) and a public
    rehearsal (18th), with the Concertgebouw Orchestra conducted by Eduard
    van Beinum (see Letter 577). In addition he sang in a concert of Bach can-
    tatas with Musica Antiqua on 17 March.

    Pears wrote to Britten on the 17th:

I had a rehearsal with van Beinum this morning – very nice & slightly boring. Ernst
Haefliger (Swiss tenor) was there, singing tomorrow instead of [Frans] Vroons –
not very impressive but nice. Vroons very nervous in Bach!

Pears described the public dress rehearsal of the *St Matthew Passion* in a
letter to Britten of 19 March:

Last night I had the public rehearsal of the Matthäus, it was all right but a bit dull
and a bit depressing! I don't know. Van Beinum really doesn't know it & has no idea
of 18th century music nor have the players, I believe. I don't think Bach is really
supposed to sound quite like that – but never mind [. . .]
   The Christus is better this year (Laurens Bogtman) I think – [Dora van Doorn-]
Lindeman is a bit disappointing the others much the same. Haefliger was good but
not a knock-out. Voice rather similar to mine I should think. The performance is
being broadcast, that nice blond radio man was there yesterday testing it.

In an unpublished interview with Peter Heyworth (17 January 1984), a
complete transcript of which is at BPL, Pears recalled performing the Bach
Passions in the Netherlands, expanding his comments to Bach performance-
style in general:

I went to Holland every season for seventeen years to sing in the *St Matthew
Passion*. The *St Matthew Passion* has a very special place in Dutch musical life; it's
performed there much more often than it was then in England. It was something I
looked forward to very much. For the first four years I sang under van Beinum. His
performance was traditional and musically sound within that tradition. He used a
full orchestra throughout. Though he was a devout man his performances were – I
think 'routine' would be the word. [. . .] The dancing elements in the music were
not very light. But of course with a huge chorus it was bound to be heavy and
rather slow.
   [. . .] During the years I went to Amsterdam I always did two performances of
the *St Matthew Passion* in Rotterdam. They were very different, on a much smaller
scale, though the chorus was still a fair size. The conductor was [Bertus] van Lier.
[. . .] One of the features of the Rotterdam performance was that it was given in a
church. I used to sing from a high pulpit in the east end. It was as though one were
delivering the Gospel to everyone below. I think that's a good way of doing it.
   The Evangelist that I used to admire very much and hear a lot was, however,
Steuart Wilson. His voice had been more or less blown away in the First World War.
But I was really taken by the way he sang the notes and even had a brief lesson or
two. He made the text the most important thing. What I reacted against was the

English edition he used by Elgar and Atkins. It was based on the Authorized Version and Bach's music just had to get along with it as best it could. I prefer singing it in German. On the other hand I also believe in singing it on occasions in the vernacular. In fact I've done an English version of *St John* myself and it's available; the *St Matthew* I haven't quite finished. But I don't care for the Authorized Version as a libretto! Provided that the story's not changed, the main thing is to fit in all Bach's notes.

See also Wolfgang Dinglinger et al., *De Matthäus-Passion, 100 Jahr Passie-traditie van het Koninklijk Concertgebouworkest*. An edition of the *St John Passion* edited by Benjamin Britten and Imogen Holst with an English version by Peter Pears and Imogen Holst, is available on hire from Faber Music.

2 Elizabeth Sweeting (1914–1999), English arts administrator, who was General Manager of the Aldeburgh Festival from its inception in 1948 until 1955. Educated at London University, Sweeting began her career as a teacher, first at Birmingham's King Edward Grammar School for Girls and later at University College, London. During the war she decided to change tack and began working as an assistant stage manager at the Arts Theatre Club based at the Lyric, Hammersmith. One of her earliest contacts with Britten's music was through the revue *Tuppence Coloured* (see Letter 557 n. 2), but it was in 1947, while she was on the staff at Glyndebourne, that Sweeting first came into personal contact with Britten and Pears. The composer asked her to join the English Opera Group as an assistant to Anne Wood, and subsequently invited her to become the first General Manager of the Aldeburgh Festival.

 After her departure from Aldeburgh – officially, financial difficulties were given as the reason for 'dispensing with the services of a professional general manager' (but see also HCBB, pp. 368–9) – Sweeting became the highly successful Administrator of the Oxford Playhouse and General Manager of its resident company, Frank Hauser's Meadow Players. She remained in Oxford for twenty years, teaching English Literature at St Catharine's College in addition to her responsibilities at the Playhouse. From 1976 until 1981 she was the first Director of the Arts Council of South Australia. A pioneer in arts administration, Sweeting wrote two studies, *Theatre Administration* and *Beginners Please: Working in the Theatre*, and was active in the establishment of the first course in Arts Administration at the Polytechnic of Central London in 1970.

 See Sweeting, 'Let's Make a Festival!', unpublished memoir, at BPL, and obituaries by Paul Iles in the *Guardian* (11 December 1999) and David Freud in the *Independent* (17 December 1999).

3 From time to time Miss Parker (not to be confused with Barbara Parker) also helped Britten with his correspondence (see, for example, Letter 590). A Mrs W. H. M. Galsworthy appears in the list of Festival guarantors on page 47 of the 1948 Festival programme book.

4 Fidelity Cranbrook, the Dowager Countess of Cranbrook (b. 1912), who

was the first Chairman of the Aldeburgh Festival (1948–1981) and pro-
moted the cause of the Festival and the Britten–Pears School for Advanced
Musical Studies for over forty years. In 1949, Britten and Eric Crozier used
the names of of Fidelity Cranbrook's five children – Gathorne, Juliet,
Sophia, Christina and Hugh – as the names of the children in *The Little
Sweep*, together with those of two cousins, Jonathan and Samuel. The opera
was 'affectionately' dedicated to them, 'the Gathorne-Hardys of Great
Glemham, Suffolk'. In 1963, Britten was to dedicate his *Cantata Miseri-
cordium* to Fidelity Cranbrook.

5 Sally Welford, Britten's niece.

6 Beth's third child, Elizabeth Ellen Rosemary (known as 'Roguey'), had been
   born on 21 April 1945.

7 Britten refers to his realization of *The Beggar's Opera*, in which he developed techniques – but in particular canons – previously explored in his
   many folksong arrangements. See, for example, No. 1 ('Through all the
   employments of life'), No. 11 ('A fox may steal your hens, sir') and No. 34
   ('Cease your funning'). See also Letter 545 n. 1.

8 Eric Greene (1904–1966), English tenor, noted for his interpretation of the
   role of the Evangelist in the Bach Passions. Greene had been a member of
   the New English Singers with Pears: see PRPP, plate 1 and pp. 1–15. Greene
   had been the Evangelist in a performance of Bach's *St Matthew Passion* at
   the Royal Albert Hall, on 14 March, in which Pears sang the tenor arias.
   Britten had evidently heard the broadcast of Part I in the BBC Home
   Service. The other soloists were Elsie Suddaby (soprano), Kathleen Ferrier
   (contralto), William Parsons (bass) and Harold Williams (Christus), with
   the Jacques Orchestra and the Bach Choir conducted by Reginald Jacques.
   Four days earlier, Pears had sung the role of the Evangelist in the *St John
   Passion* under Jacques's direction at the Royal Albert Hall.

9 While Britten and Pears were in the Netherlands, Pears had sung the role of
   the Evangelist in the *St Matthew Passion* in two performances in Rotterdam
   on 27 and 28 February, with the choir and small orchestra of the Rotterdam
   Volks-Universiteit conducted by Bertus van Lier. Eric Crozier wrote to
   Nancy Evans from Amsterdam on 28 February:

   We left for Rotterdam at 5 yesterday afternoon and arrived back at 1 this morning,
   having had no food since lunch, and having sat through the whole *Matthew
   Passion*, uncut and with all repeats, with only one 15-minute interval. It took exactly
   four hours, and was wonderful but too exhausting. Peter is a magnificent
   Evangelist, and the soprano and alto were good – but the other soloists were poor.
   But what a work it is!

   Pears returned to Rotterdam and Amsterdam to participate in van Lier's
   annual performance of the *St Matthew Passion* almost every year until 1965,
   and in 1950 extended an invitation to van Lier and his Rotterdam forces to

mount the first complete German performance of the work to be heard in the UK, as part of the 1950 Aldeburgh Festival. See also Letter 647 n. 3.

10 Britten refers to Nos. 38a–38c of the *St Matthew Passion*, which ends with Peter's denial of Christ and the remarkable arioso passage for the Evangelist at the words 'Und ging heraus und weinete bitterlich' ('And he went out, and wept bitterly').

11 Emmie Tillett (1897–1982), Managing Director of Ibbs & Tillett, the artists' agents who acted for Britten and Pears at this time.

12 Pears and Britten were to give a recital at Blundell's School, Tiverton, on 29 March 1948. A note in Britten's pocket engagement diary suggests that he met Ethel Astle (see Letter 4 n. 1), his former piano teacher from Lowestoft, who was living now at Tiverton. Pears and Britten did not require any accommodation to be arranged for them as they had been invited to stay with Ronald Duncan, who lived nearby.

13 In a letter to the composer of 16 March, Pears contrasted his accommodation at the Hotel des Pays-Bas with that provided by the American Hotel, where he and Britten usually stayed:

Here I am – arriven – back again in Omsterdom – but a different hotel – first impression is faintly disappointing. Small (and alas! single) room ohne bad [without bath] – but quiet and no trams at all going round the corner quickly at all hours. However I'm not going to judge it too harshly until I've had a meal which I expect to be super terrestrial. There is no superabundance of youthful charm – not to compare with Willi and the rest, but also there is no middle-Indonesian-Emma-period hall with gamelan-type chandeliers, and that's a blessing.

Pears presumably refers here to the glassy jingling of the chandeliers set in motion by a draught.

77 To Peter Pears

~~THE OLD MILL, SNAPE, SAXMUNDHAM, SUFFOLK~~
4 Crabbe Street, Aldeburgh
[21 March 1948]

My darling –

You finished the Passion about ten minutes ago – it came over beautifully (altho' I missed ½ hr of it because you said 11.30!), & your voice sounded full & beautiful.[1] It was a most thoughtful & moving performance from you, it gets better & better, altho' I can imagine a lot of it irritated & bored you as much as it did me. Of course much of it "came off" very well because of really remarkable wind playing, & the choir sounded good too. But my feelings about the soloists hasn't changed (over the radio Dora van D.L.[2] sounded unbearable above E, hard & cold & no vowels apart

from 'ah'). I wasn't enamoured of the Christus[3] either who was very sentimental. They all _emote_ so terribly, & pull the music around. Of course it
all comes finally from lack of technique – they want to express something,
but all they can do is to slur up or down or sing louder. That's what you
needn't do, & thank God you don't – & so the extraordinary dignity of the
work, & its heartbreaking controlled pathos came over in spite of all the
blemishes. I _like_ Annie Hermes'[4] (?) voice; it has real edge to it – but I
wish she wasn't so insecure & sloppy. Poor Vrons[5] – but it might have
been worse – he sounded as scared as a rabbit! The Peter bit came over
wonderfully – it is an _extraordinary_ conception, & you do it incredibly.
How were the other performances? The thing that struck me so particularly today (the orch. being so good) was the three different levels of
approach to the "scourging". 1st – the direct narration of it – then the

translation of it into agonised protest – then in the aria the same ♩♩

sublimated into the highest blessing (the aria wasn't so well done – too
fast for poor Annie[6]). It reminded me strongly of the agonised marked
body in the Colmar altar,[7] & then the serene head above it.

   Thank you for your sweet letters. I hope you'll get this before you leave.
A pity that the Pays Bas is a disappointment – mind we go back to the
American next time! Have you seen Mrs Goldbeck?[8] I had a sweet letter
from her full of your praises. Love to Peter & Maria[9] & all the Cronheims.
Dashing to post now.

All my love, & congratulations,
Your devoted
B.

1 Pears wrote to Britten on 22 March, before having received Britten's letter
   of the 21st:

   I wonder if you heard yesterday. It _was_ broadcast, and I hope you got my letter
   telling you so in time. Saturday had been all right bei mir [with me] vocally until
   towards the end when I began to feel old – I had caught a cold behind the nose on
   Friday. After the performance on Sat., I went round to Peter's for tea and sand-
   wiches etc. and though the speaking voice was all right, the whole [voice] box felt a
   bit aged. And yesterday morning it really felt 100, so I went (you'll never guess) to
   Dr de Vivere! and he dropped on to my cords, and that was a bit better – and actually I think it went rather well didn't it honey? Just one or two A's I would have
   'dared' a little more open and loud, if I'd felt quite certain. It has been terribly
   useful doing it. Performances are really the only sure way of getting to know a
   work, even though it may take many years to get it quite right. Van B. isn't really _any_
   good at Bach. The whole performance was depressing. None of the voices were _too_
   good. Tempi were dotty, the whole solo arias not enough rehearsed, ensemble
   terrible often, and the sweet harpsichordist at one time apparently fell into her
   keyboard. Organ too loud – and oh! the Alderman and the Minister of Fine Arts

and Mr and Mrs de Jong Schouwenburg and all the stiff audience in black – trying
to hope it was better than that old Nazi Mengelberg, and yet missing him and longing for him. [Pears refers to Mengelberg's unhappy association with the forces of
the German occupation during the war.] I made one or two tidyings up in the long
recitatives which I think improves it and keeps it going. 'Peter weinete' not too
good I'm afraid – coldy and nervy. Van Beinum plans doing it in London next
spring! His wife (!) hoped I would do it with him. He's a funny one. Had lunch with
Mrs Goldbeck [the critic Frederick Goldbeck's mother] in the interval. She's getting awfully deaf, and is inclined to shout her opinions on the bad performance all
over the artist's room and the restaurants!

2   Dora van Doorn-Lindeman, who premiered Bertus van Lier's *The Song of
    Songs*, with Pears and Hermann Schey, in Amsterdam's Oude Kerk on 12
    July 1949.

3   Sung by Laurens Bogtman.

4   Annie Hermes (1906–1995), Dutch contralto, who made a considerable
    reputation in her own country as an interpreter of Bach's *St Matthew
    Passion*.

5   Frans Vroons (1911–1983), Dutch tenor, who in 1945 became a member of
    the newly founded Netherlands Opera and sang with them for almost
    twenty years. Vroons was an excellent actor and was, according to Elizabeth
    Forbes in *New Grove*, a particularly convincing exponent of the role of
    Grimes.

6   Britten refers to the scourging of Christ as portrayed in the *St Matthew
    Passion*: the Evangelist's account (No. 50e), 'Da gab er ihnen Barabam los';
    the alto soloist's arioso (No. 51), 'Erbarm es Gott!', in which Bach depicts
    the scourging by means of a constantly repeated dotted rhythmic motif,
    and the alto soloist's aria (No. 52), 'Können Tränen meiner Wangen nichts
    erlangen'.

7   The Isenheim altarpiece by Matthias de Grünewald (?1480–1528). It com-
    prises nine paintings in the artist's vibrant colours with his characteristic
    use of physical distortion to express suffering. Grünewald is the Mathis der
    Maler of Hindemith's opera.

8   Pears reported to Britten on 19 March:

    As I am a grass-widower here (alas!) I'm going a bit social. Today: 1.0 lunch with the
    Frank Martins. 5.30(!) dinner with the Dora Lindemanns. Sunday: lunch with Mrs
    Goldbeck: evening chez Diamands. Monday: lunch Henriëtte Bosmans, evening
    my two Dutch queer admirers. Tuesday evening: Nicholas Roths. So you see! Some
    duty, some pleasure. Some mixture. I ought to try & fit in a visit to Ré Koster too I
    suppose, oh dear!

9   Maria Curcio (b. 1929), Italian pianist and teacher. Curcio studied with
    Alfredo Casella and Nadia Boulanger before becoming a pupil of Artur
    Schnabel. It was when studying with Schnabel that she first met Peter

Diamand, whom she married in 1948. She was in Amsterdam when war broke out and remained there during the German occupation, working secretly for the Resistance movement. Ill-health – she contracted tuberculosis during the war – prevented her from embarking on a major international career, although post-war she gave concerts in the Netherlands and in 1956 appeared at the Aldeburgh Festival. In 1965 she moved to London to concentrate on teaching. See also Simon Mundy, 'Curcio in Camera', *Classical Music* (11 March 1989), p. 49, and Michael Church's interview with Maria Curcio, '"My task is to liberate pianists"', *Independent* (2 February 2001), in which he writes, 'The most formative musical friendship in her life was with Benjamin Britten, with whom she often played piano four-hands.'

578   To Walter Hussey

~~THE OLD MILL, SNAPE, SAXMUNDHAM, SUFFOLK~~
4 Crabbe St. Aldeburgh
March 22nd 1948

My dear Walter,

The wicked, wicked bottle arrived when Peter & I were on the Continent, we are not long back & since we arrived I've been up to my eyes in accumulated businesses & other horrors, hence the long silence! But, my dear, you <u>shouldn't</u> have done this, or rather you shouldn't have done it because you thought I was in any way estranged from you! I shouldn't enjoy it half as much if I thought that was the reason for your sending it to me – in fact I should be tempted to send it back; but that is a temptation I should never fall to, because Pernod is (perhaps?) my only real weakness, and the pleasure I'm going to get from it is going to be pretty enormous whatever your reasons for sending it – ! Thank you, my dear Walter, for the thought & the generosity, & for the forgiveness, because deep down in my much scarred conscience I'm aware of having behaved like a beast, firstly for having been stupidly touchy, & then out of sheer slackness not doing anything to prevent that impression from growing. Please forgive me, & try to believe that it isn't only the welcome presence of some highly seductive liquid in a pretty green bottle which prompts this confession!

Whenever shall we meet again? Northampton seems the other end of the world. I haven't yet seen more than reproductions of the really magnificent-looking Sutherland.[1] Perhaps this Summer I can get down. I suppose there's no chance of your coming to London in the second half of April when I shall be solidly in London rehearsing? If there is, do send a card, & we could have lunch or something.

I haven't forgotten the Mass.[2] When my chores are all done, it will materialise, & I hope then I'll be a better composer & less unworthy of the task.

My love to you, & many, many thanks,

BEN

1   Graham Sutherland (1903–1980), English artist, whose *Crucifixion* had been commissioned in 1944 by Hussey for St Matthew's, Northampton. Sutherland's most famous contribution to ecclesiastical art is probably his immense tapestry, *Christ in Glory in the Tetramorph*, designed between 1954 and 1957, which hangs in Coventry Cathedral. See Walter Hussey, *Patron of Art*, pp. 49–66, and Allan Doig, 'Architecture and Performance: Dean Walter Hussey and the Arts', *Theology*, 94/787 (January/February 1995), pp. 16–21. It may have been the composer's admiration for Sutherland's *Crucifixion* which led to its use on the original box cover for his Decca recording of Bach's *St John Passion* in 1971 (SET 410-1).

2   Although Britten was to compose his *Missa Brevis* in D in 1959, for George Malcolm and the boys of Westminster Cathedral Choir, he never made a setting of the Mass for Anglican use. It was, however, a project that was occasionally to resurface in his correspondence with Walter Hussey, notably in 1970–71.

579   To John Pounder[1]

3 OXFORD SQUARE, W.2

May 3rd 1948

My dear John,

Thank you for your sweet letter, just arrived. I was really desperately sorry not to be able to lunch with you on Sunday, but I was feeling too hellish I'm afraid – I couldn't even have toyed with Czech food! But it was nice to catch a glimpse of you & your sweet fiancée. I am so very glad about it, John. Of course I don't know her at all yet, but the first impressions were most favourable, & I somehow feel she is right for you, my dear. But, speaking generally, I cannot say how happy I am that you are getting married. I think I know how empty your life has been these last years, & it has worried me considerably – Of course, living in this dotty existence I have done as usual nothing about it, but I fancy you know how often you've been in my thoughts.

But it is splendid that you've met the right person at last, & had the intelligence & courage to realise it!

Do try & get over to Cambridge – or if not that, to Aldeburgh – or best to both. I think you'll enjoy the Beggar's Opera which is coming on very well.

Please forgive the scribble, but it's fearsomely late & I'm just off to bed.
Love from Peter, & lots from your devoted

BEN

(And to Madeleine)

1   John Ward Pounder (1915–?), a schoolfriend of Britten's from South Lodge.
He had accompanied Britten on his trip to the ISCM Festival in Florence in
1934 and during 1938 lived for a time at Britten's and Pears's Nevern Square
address. Pounder, who was a solicitor, remained in touch with Britten until
the end of his life. See also Letter 5 n. 4, 1C1/2, and the tape and transcript
of Pounder's interview with Donald Mitchell (June 1989) at BPL.

580   To David Webster
Royal Opera House, Covent Garden
[*Typed*]

Festival Theatre, Cambridge
15th May 1948

Dear David,
Thank you for your letter. I am so sorry I have not answered it before but
we have been up to our eyes rehearsing all day and large parts of the night.
I am afraid I was distressed by your letter, since I feel negotiations with
Paris and Brussels must have been progressing for many weeks and the
whole position between you and me would have been infinitely easier had
you told me about it, especially about the dates concerned.[1] What perhaps
you do not realise is how authoritative an air these performances will have
since I am an Englishman and Covent Garden has the reputation of being
the English National Opera.
I went to Covent Garden to see a performance of "Grimes" recently
and I must frankly say I was shocked by it, and I feel that to take the work
abroad in this condition would be to its detriment and, incidentally, to
the detriment of English Opera itself. The reasons, I think, are three:
1. Under-rehearsal; 2. A disregard of dynamics and expression marks that
has grown up; 3. Miscasting (which might have been avoided if the
discussions we had in the summer of last year had proved fruitful). If
Richard Lewis had been approached last summer, as I wished and to
which you did not agree, he could have been thoroughly trained and
could, I think, have performed the part adequately. As it is, I feel he is
quite unsatisfactory in character and voice – so much so that the story
makes no sense. I feel greatly distressed about Dorée[2] who makes an
unsympathetic character both in voice and acting. It is a disaster for the
work that these performances, which may well set a tradition in France

and Belgium, will take place with neither Joan Cross nor Peter Pears singing these two desperately important roles. Richard, I feel, could be improved; Dorée is quite obviously temperamentally unsuited for the part. Have you no one else to suggest for Ellen?

Boles and Mrs Sedley are quite hopeless.[3] Auntie[4] now scarcely sings at all. The rest of the characters need thorough rehearsing which also applies to the Chorus, which I admit is now sure of its notes whereas it was not when I heard the third performance in November. The fact that the performance might be said to have "come off" was due to the untiring energy of the conductor – Goodall.[5]

To sum up: What I feel is that thorough rehearsing could make a possible performance, with the exception of the three bad cases of miscasting. Alas, you have let Tyrone Guthrie and myself know your dates so late that it is highly unlikely that we can attend any of the rehearsals. I should be happy to discuss many of these points with the conductor and yourself if we can arrange the time and place.

I hate to say this, but I feel that unless you can do something about the performance I shall feel strongly inclined to put pressure on my publishers to make the tour impossible. You see I am not so anxious to have "Grimes" given under <u>any</u> circumstances since it has already been given with effect in Antwerp[6] and is, I believe, scheduled for Strasbourg this Autumn.[7]

Yours sincerely,

BENJAMIN BRITTEN

1   Britten refers to a forthcoming short tour by the Covent Garden Opera Company, who presented performances of *Peter Grimes* in Brussels (7–8 June 1948) and Paris (Palais Garnier, 11–12 June). Despite Britten's misgivings about performance standards at Covent Garden, the composer was to receive a letter from Webster (14 June 1948) reporting that '*Peter Grimes* and the Company have had a great success both in Brussels and in Paris. The Queen of the Belgians was at the first performance.' (Quoted in Norman Lebrecht, *Covent Garden: The Untold Story*, p. 96.)

2   Doris Dorée (1909–1971), American soprano, who played Ellen Orford. She made her debut at the Metropolitan Opera, New York, in 1939, joining the New York City Opera in 1945. From 1947 until 1951 she was among the leading sopranos at Covent Garden.

3   Boles was played by Hubert Norville. The English mezzo-soprano Constance Shacklock (1913–1999) played Mrs Sedley. She had joined the Covent Garden Opera Company in 1946 (her first role was in Purcell's *The Fairy Queen*), remaining with the company for a decade. In 1953 she shared the title role of Britten's *Gloriana* with Joan Cross, a performance described by

Alan Blyth in his *Guardian* obituary (1 July 1999) of Shacklock as a 'power-ful assumption, acted with the intelligence and attention to detail that characterized all her work'. After leaving Covent Garden she forged a new career in musicals, most significantly in the long-running London produc-tion of *The Sound of Music*. See also Alan Blyth's obituary in *Opera* (September 1999), pp. 1044–5.

4   Played by the English mezzo-soprano Edith Coates (1908–1983), who had created the role in the original Sadler's Wells production in 1945. Coates had been a member of the Sadler's Wells Company from 1931 until 1947, when she joined the Covent Garden Opera Company with whom she created the role of the Housewife in Britten's *Gloriana* in 1953.

5   Reginald Goodall, who travelled to Brussels ahead of the rest of the Covent Garden Company, to rehearse the Monnaie orchestra, gave a report to the composer of their progress in a letter dated 2 June 1948:

> I arrived here early this morning to commence the rehearsals for *Grimes* – only last night they gave *Albert Herring* at the Opera which unfortunately I missed – but I thought you would like to know of the great success it had and the intelligent appreciation and love of your music.
>
> I had a talk with the man who had translated *Albert Herring* – he likes the music of it even more than *Lucretia* – he finds it more 'spirituel' and at the same time more 'tonal' for the public – instancing the C major fugue (is it a Fugue? – but you wouldn't know, would you!) also he finds the orchestration fuller as the piano is more integrated with the orchestra than in *Lucretia*.
>
> I had my first rehearsal with the orchestra and was very surprised and pleased that they played it so well and with such understanding – the strings are particularly good with glowing tone – but unfortunately the trombones are weak – the 2nd and 3rd especially so – and that makes it difficult to get a right sonority in all the brass passages – the 1st bassoon has a lovely vibrato – he sounds like a saxophone – you can imagine it in 'I had to go from pub to pub' we fairly lurch along.
>
> Please remember [me] to Peter – I wish he was singing it here.

See John Lucas, *Reggie: The Life of Reginald Goodall*, p. 117.

6   *Grimes* was first given in Antwerp on 25 May 1946, in a Flemish translation.

7   *Grimes* was not to reach Strasbourg until 24 March 1949, when it was sung in a French translation by Roger Lalande.

581   To Anthony Gishford

Festival Theatre, Cambridge
May 20th 1948

My dear Tony,

I am really delighted with the Aldeburgh print. It is a real beauty & I love it dearly for what it is & what it represents! Thank you more than I can say for the extremely kind & generous thought! It cheered a parti-

cularly worrying patch of life, overwork & depression, which is happily
lifting now. The Beggar's Opera has been a real b–gger to get done & on.
I think it's better now, & since I have at last finished the music I can be
a little more objective & panicky! Will you be able to see it? It's a most
exciting production & I think the cast is turning out fine.[1]

Please excuse this brief note, as the scoring of Nicolas[2] is behindhand
(I wish I didn't give birth to quite so many unruly children); but I wanted
to let you know how much I love the picture, & to thank you enormously.

With best wishes,

Yours ever,

BEN

1   The first performance of Britten's realization of *The Beggar's Opera* was
     given by the English Opera Group, conducted by Britten, on 24 May 1948,
     at the Arts Theatre, Cambridge, in a production by Tyrone Guthrie, with
     designs by Tanya Moiseiwitsch. The cast included Pears as Macheath,
     Nancy Evans as Polly Peachum, Rose Hill as Lucy Lockit, George James as
     Peachum, Flora Nielsen as Mrs Peachum, Otakar Kraus as Lockit and
     Gladys Parr as Mrs Trapes.

     Britten contributed the following note to the programme (reprinted in
     PKBM, pp. 373–4) for the first night:

     The tunes to which John Gay wrote his apt and witty lyrics are among our finest
     national songs. These seventeenth and eighteenth century airs, known usually as
     'traditional tunes', seem to me to be the most characteristically *English* of any of
     our folksongs. They are often strangely like Purcell and Handel: may, perhaps, have
     influenced them, or have been influenced by them. They have strong, leaping inter-
     vals, sometimes in peculiar modes, and are often strange and severe in mood.

     A definitive arrangement of them can never be achieved, since each generation
     sees them from a different aspect, but I feel that most recent arrangements have
     avoided their toughness and strangeness, and have concentrated only on their
     lyrical prettiness.

     For my arrangements of the tunes I have gone to a contemporary edition of the
     original arrangements by Dr Pepusch. Apart from one or two extensions and repe-
     titions I have left the tunes exactly as they stood, except for one or two places where
     the original seemed confused and inaccurate. Three of them have had to be omit-
     ted because of the excessive length of the whole for performance in our time, but a
     far higher percentage of the sixty-nine tunes will be in this version than in any
     other recent one.

     Tyrone Guthrie also contributed to the programme:

     This production will aim to stress the fact that this is indeed a *Beggar's* Opera – the
     expression of people made reckless, even desperate by poverty, but in whose
     despair there is none the less a vitality and gaiety that the art of elegant and
     fashionable people too often misses. Indeed the whole work is a satire of the
     elegantly absurd conventions of fashionable romantic entertainment.

     The beautiful melodies offer a curious contrast to the satirical bitterness of the

(handwritten annotation) Short i dyprinti end

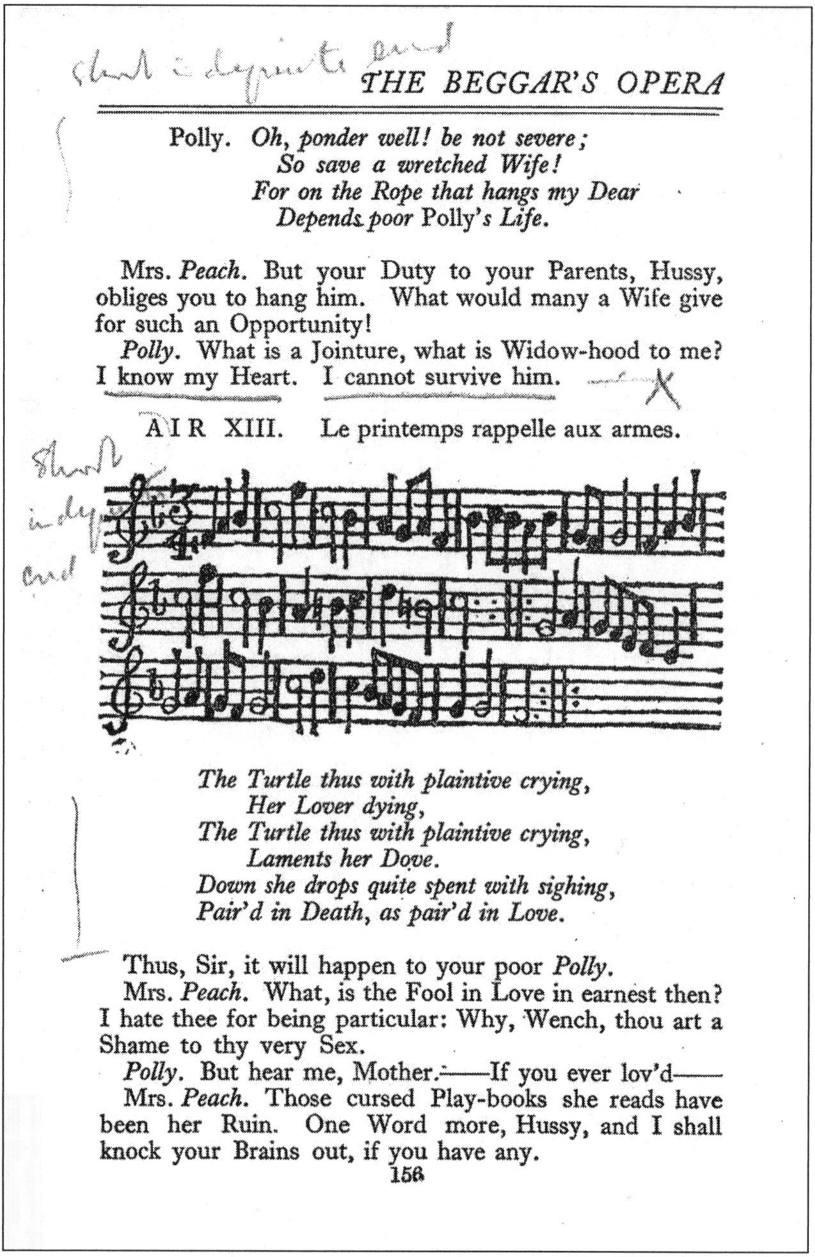

THE BEGGAR'S OPERA

Polly.   *Oh, ponder well! be not severe;*
So save a wretched Wife!
For on the Rope that hangs my Dear
Depends poor Polly's *Life.*

Mrs. *Peach*. But your Duty to your Parents, Hussy, obliges you to hang him. What would many a Wife give for such an Opportunity!
Polly. What is a Jointure, what is Widow-hood to me? I know my Heart. I cannot survive him. ⟶ ✗

AIR XIII.   Le printemps rappelle aux armes.

(handwritten annotation) Short in dy end

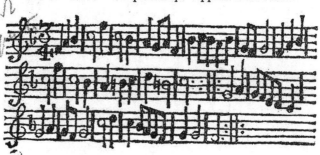

The Turtle thus with plaintive crying,
Her Lover dying,
The Turtle thus with plaintive crying,
Laments her Dove.
Down she drops quite spent with sighing,
Pair'd in Death, as pair'd in Love.

Thus, Sir, it will happen to your poor *Polly*.
Mrs. *Peach*. What, is the Fool in Love in earnest then? I hate thee for being particular: Why, Wench, thou art a Shame to thy very Sex.
Polly. But hear me, Mother.——If you ever lov'd——
Mrs. *Peach*. Those cursed Play-books she reads have been her Ruin. One Word more, Hussy, and I shall knock your Brains out, if you have any.
156

Polly Peachum's 'The turtle thus with plaintive crying' in Britten's copy of *The Plays of John Gay*, vol. 1, published in 1923, annotated by him while making his realization of *The Beggar's Opera*

Britten's realization of Polly's 'The turtle thus with plaintive crying', No. XIII

text, and they also typify what is still true – the 'country-town' quality of London – the fact that though it is a great cosmopolitan city, it is at the same time an agglomeration of typically English villages.

2 Although Britten completed the composition draft of *Saint Nicolas* before he and Pears left for their European tour in January, he was evidently unable to undertake the scoring of the cantata until work on *The Beggar's Opera* was completed.

582 To E. J. Dent
[*Typed*]

4 Crabbe Street, Aldeburgh, Suffolk
16/6/48

Dear Professor Dent,

Thank you for your extremely kind letter about the Beggar's Opera.[1] Praise from you is indeed great praise, since you know so well the enormous problems of this masterpiece.[2] My only regret is that you saw the production at the beginning of the week – because it had generally improved 300 per cent by the time we left Cambridge and will, I hope, continue to improve as long as we perform it this season. We take it abroad to the Amsterdam Festival next week.[3] It will be interesting to see how they react to this performance, but I should imagine they will not have the pretty general prejudice against this handling of the work that exists in England since their memory will be closer to Brecht–Weill than the Lyric Hammersmith.[4]

We have just come out from a most interesting experimental Festival here, in Aldeburgh; hundreds of people came – and Albert Herring was received with joy in the Jubilee Hall! What we seem to have proved without a doubt is that local people react strongly and encouragingly to this kind of local festival. It is a pity that you could not be here because I suppose you will have been to the Festival in Amsterdam. I hope that went well.

May I add that I think it is disappointing that the English branch takes such a dim view of my pieces – not only for my sake, but, perhaps, for others too![5]

Thank you again for your sympathetic letter and for troubling to write.

Yours sincerely,
BENJAMIN BRITTEN

1 Dent's letter has not survived.

2 Dent had prepared his own edition of Gay's ballad opera.

3 The EOG gave performances of *The Beggar's Opera* at the Holland Festival
   in Amsterdam (25 and 28 June), Utrecht (26 June), Rotterdam (29 June)
   and Scheveningen (30 June and 1 July).

4 The London theatre where Frederic Austin's version of *The Beggar's Opera*
   was first presented on 5 June 1920 and ran for 1,463 performances. In 1928
   Bertolt Brecht made a celebrated adaptation of Gay's work, with music by
   Kurt Weill, entitled *Die Dreigroschenoper* (*The Threepenny Opera*).

   The EOG production was widely reviewed in the national press. Frank
   Howes, in *The Times* (25 May 1948), compared Britten's realization with
   that of Dent:

   Oxford beat Cambridge by 10 days in staging new versions of *The Beggar's Opera*.
   Actually, however, the contest is unequal, for Oxford's was an amateur production,
   whereas that given here at the Arts Theatre tonight [24 May] was the work of the
   English Opera Group, whose aims and ideals it suits very well.
   Both nouns in the title are given their full weight: it is an opera and it is a beggars' opera. Mr Tyrone Guthrie, instead of taking the Beggar as a theatrical excuse
   for the satire of the play, places the action in a room at St Giles's which by day was
   used as a wash-house – this is the scene throughout. It is a possible if rather literal
   use of the convention, neither better nor worse than any of the many other frames
   that had been provided for the action.
   Mr Benjamin Britten has seen to it that the music is the main business, whereas
   in Professor Dent's Oxford version the tunes got lost in the drama. Some of the
   tunes get lost in Britten's clever and elaborate settings, but on the whole he has
   preserved their character and built up from them some wonderfully effective
   miniature *ensembles*. He has also contrived some fascinating sounds from his 12-
   piece orchestra, though in a few songs the words are obscured, as before, by a too
   brittle sound-texture. The satirical drama, such as it is, keeps up its end by virtue of
   a hundred and one happy touches of the producer's art.
   The most striking piece of characterization was Miss Flora Nielsen's Mrs
   Peachum, less loud and more individualized than most. Her husband was also a
   well-studied interpretation by Mr George James. Miss Nancy Evans was not too
   ingenuous a Polly; Mr Peter Pears's was a skilful though external presentation of
   Macheath rather than a heart-felt impersonation from within. The Ladies of the
   Town were nicely differentiated in only one sense of that adverb. The whole opera
   was played and sung slickly and with a high degree of finish.

   Howes returned to *The Beggar's Opera* in a later notice ('Beggar's Operas
   and Odious Comparisons', 28 May):

   Mr Britten is nothing if not ingenious, and his way of expanding the tunes by
   distributing their phrases among different singers, or by harmonizing them for
   singing offstage, or by supporting them on some instrumental figure as apt as it is
   unexpected, made the music take pride of place, as it did in Austin's version. So that
   in fact it was opera, not interrupted drama, as in the Oxford performance. Sometimes the listener might think he was having too much of a good thing, that the
   tunes were being a little obscured by too rich a setting, but for the most part the
   conversion of a simple strand of melody into a tiny concerted ensemble showed
   what bottomless depths of inspiration are to be found in those hard-worn tunes.

THE BEGGAR'S OPERA

Cast:

Macheath: PETER PEARS

Polly: NANCY EVANS   Lucy: ROSE HILL

Peachum: GEORGE JAMES

Mrs. Peachum: FLORA NIELSEN

Lockit: OTAKAR KRAUS

Mrs. Trapes: GLADYS PARR

Other characters by:

LESLEY DUFF	CATHERINE LAWSON	LILY KETTLEWELL
ROY ASHTON	DENIS DOWLING	JOHN HIGHCOCK
ELISABETH PARRY	ANNE SHARP	JENNIFER VYVYAN
NORMAN LUMSDEN	NORMAN PLATT	
MILDRED WATSON	MAX WORTHLEY	

THE ARTS THEATRE OF CAMBRIDGE

Licensee and Managing Director: Norman Higgins, M.B.E.
Box Office open from 10.30 a.m. to 8 p.m.

MONDAY 24 MAY 1948   FOR SIX DAYS
Monday & Tuesday at 6.30   Wednesday to Saturday at 8
Matinee on Saturday at 2.30

THE ENGLISH OPERA GROUP

(in association with The Arts Council of Great Britain)

presents

the first performances of a new musical version of

THE BEGGAR'S OPERA

realised from the original airs by
BENJAMIN BRITTEN

Produced by   Scenery and Costumes by
TYRONE GUTHRIE   TANYA MOISEIWITCH

with

THE ENGLISH OPERA GROUP CHAMBER ORCHESTRA

(Leader: Jack Kessler)

Conducted by

BENJAMIN BRITTEN and IVAN CLAYTON

Arts Theatre, Cambridge, 24 May 1948: the programme for the first performance of *The Beggar's Opera*

In a letter to Britten of 18 June 1948, Dent – referring to Howes's notices – writes:

I agree with you entirely about the stupidity of our critics about *The Beggar's Opera* & can't understand how Howes, a specialist in folksong! should consider the Austin version as the one & only original B.O.

'H.H.H.', 'Virtually a New *Beggar* – But Not Quite So Gay?', in the *Cambridge Daily News* (25 May 1948), contributed an extensive notice of the opera:

As shown to a large and enthusiastic audience last night, the English Opera Group's production of John Gay's *The Beggar's Opera* is, musically at any rate, virtually a new work.

True it is that most of Gay's original airs are there, but their treatment by that remarkable and brilliant young composer Benjamin Britten is such that the opera has been given a 'New Look', which, paradoxically enough, is claimed to be nearer Gay's conception than that of some previous productions. Whilst these other versions had by no means overlooked the work's coarse frankness and wry humours, they did provide a certain charm which, if it did rather glamorize the subject, proved very attractive.

[. . .] The present composer has produced a brilliant and occasionally intricate score in which the opera's grim drama is the principal highlight, so that the tale's air of stark coarseness invests even those tunes which by themselves have a certain melodic charm. Few will deny that the score admirably matches the producer's conception of the work – the tolling bell effect produced orchestrally is only one of its strikingly imaginative features – or that the attempt to weld together music, action and atmosphere has been brilliantly achieved; but those who expect to bask in the warmth of elegant and charming melody will be frequently disappointed.

[. . .]

Whilst the acting, taken as a whole, was, perhaps, a trifle uneven, the singing was uniformly good, no mean feat with a score in which unconventional treatment predominates.

Leading the way in brilliant style both vocally and histrionically was that operatic expert Peter Pears, whose Capt. Macheath had all the bravado and amorous weaknesses to be associated with the 'gallant' highwayman. Singing and acting were beautifully wedded, too, by Rose Hill as Lucy Lockit, and the same may be said of Nancy Evans's Polly Peachum. And the way in which these three combined in the prison scene provided one of the most satisfying features of the production.

George James sang well the part of Mr Peachum, and Otakar Kraus well pointed the dramatic side of Lockit. Flora Nielsen had a good shot at the part of Mrs Peachum and there was a nice touch of unconscious comedy from Gladys Parr as the beggar author of the opera.

The Ladies of the Town and the Macheath gang brought respectively an amorous and rough liveliness to some of the scenes, and the whole production was a notable one for Tyrone Guthrie and his designer, Tanya Moiseiwitsch.

The orchestra, naturally, has a role comparable in importance with that of the actors, and the present ensemble, conducted last night by Mr Britten, rightly shared in the audience's ovation.

Charles Stuart contributed a notice to the *Observer*, 'Britten in Newgate' (30 May 1948):

At dinner after the Cambridge Arts Theatre premiere of *The Beggar's Opera* in Benjamin Britten's version, a minor Musical Eminence when asked his opinion of the score gave an unknowing wink and pronounced it devilish clever.

People used to say this of Britten's music in 1936 or thereabouts. How ungum so inane a label? When a dog walks on two legs; when Mr Squawk (tenor) persuades Mr Spry (impresario) to renew his contract; when Mr Void (composer) charms the Dupetown Festival Committee into producing his latest lump of unleavened atonality, all three are, in the average acceptance of the phrase, being as devilish clever as you please.

But what are we to say of music whose tenderness and felicity, in number after number, bring a tear of delight to the eye? To talk in public about one's tear ducts goes against the grain. Yet I have no choice. At Cambridge the tear was undeniably there. I adduce it in evidence. It is Britten's Exhibit A. To evoke a tear from so sceptical a duct as mine demands rather more than Cleverness, however Devilish. Let me cite its efficient causes.

The fond, foolish Filch comes up to the footlights and, with his head on one side, sentimentally sings about the charms of the Sex ('' Tis woman seduces all mankind') to a naive air which Britten has set in a melting and pellucid style, something between Haydn and Mozart, with the harp continuously prattling in octaves. The Haydn–Mozart echo italicizes, not cancels, the individual stamp and savour of this number. The purity and simplicity of it are unforgettable. In 'Cease your funning' the bass lags canonically behind the voice: the adored melody casts its shadow wheresoever it walks, so to say. Again, the harmony is simple as two-and-two-make-four. Britten's treatment sounds pre-ordained. Like all good music, it has the air of having been around ever since music and time began. [. . .]

I am obliged to admit that Britten occasionally takes the liberty of being ingenious. 'How happy could I be with either', cast in 7/4 time, is combined with 'I'm bubbled, I'm troubled' in 27/8! What makes this trick more reprehensible is that it comes off brilliantly.

Here I am at the end of my tether with most of the score's beauties unhailed. Perhaps I have said enough, however, to damn the Devilish Clever judgement. This is exquisitely a musician's piece. But I fancy I see in it also great popular potential. Crowd favour bloweth where it listeth; but I shall be surprised if Mr Britten and the English Opera Group's latest does not have a vogue and something more.

Edward Sackville-West, writing in the *New Statesman and Nation* (5 June 1948), greeted not only Britten's arrangement but Guthrie's production:

I shall expect Britten's 'realizations' of the songs to meet with resistance in some quarters. It is not only that many people know and love their Frederick Austin too well to put up with so wholly different a treatment, but that even more people are apt to think of that version as in some obscure sense 'traditional'. Yet Austin's tactful and charming score is harmonically no nearer to the High Baroque style than Grieg's *Holberg Suite* or many another nineteenth-century pastiche. Britten has in fact stuck close to Pepusch's basses, and after only one hearing I can think of none of the tunes which did not move naturally and with ease among the eloquent images, the puns and astonishing hyperboles, of the orchestral accompaniment (brilliantly played). Although seldom angular and never out of style, the harmony is markedly individual and you may listen in vain for 'perfect' cadences and the many other properties usually associated with tunes of this date. Those who have heard Britten's folksong arrangements will know what to expect. As in the best English cooking, the material tastes of itself and not of some sauce or other; yet it would be difficult to exaggerate the variety and ingenuity with which the dishes are dressed. Britten's wonderful musicianship is evident on every page of a score which has not a dull moment in it; but amid so much that is fresh and surprising, one cannot fail to notice that the unflagging quality of this entertainment arises from a texture which has all the air of being as continuous as that of a 'through-composed' opera. As often as not the orchestra acts as a kind of ramp up which the speaking voices mount gradually into the air; the songs seldom come to a full close and sometimes end in a foreign key – which proves, a few minutes later, to be that of the next song. Benjamin Britten has included far more of the original numbers than Frederick Austin did, and has occasionally supplied passages of poetically appropriate melodrama which assist the continuity and throw the characters into relief.

Mr Tyrone Guthrie's production stresses the sinister fantasy, the squalor and pathos, of the underworld which stretches unbroken from Dekker, through Hogarth, Cruikshank and *Oliver Twist*, to the minor black markets of today. Miss Tanya Moiseiwitsch's immense rag-and-bone shop makes a most imaginative setting, eminently suitable to the rudimentary changes of scene. Among a large cast the Lockit of Otokar Kraus was outstanding: a Scarpia of the slums. Peter Pears's admirable singing, the wit and gaiety of his acting, triumphed over some natural unsuitability to the part of Macheath (not to mention an unfortunate wig). As Polly, Miss Nancy Evans looked as pretty as can be and sang with touching sweetness. As her foil, Miss Rose Hill quite rightly played Lucy Lockit for the uncontrolled fury that is in the part; but she should resist a tendency to overdo it. As Mrs Trapes, Miss Gladys Parr made the very most of her one great scene; and Miss Flora Nielsen's Mrs Peachum had some admirable moments in the first scene. I should have liked to hear rather more of the words – especially in the songs; but the acoustics of the Arts Theatre are notoriously woolly, and the cast may be counted upon to improve in this respect, as they settle into their parts.

5 Dent responded to Britten on 18 June 1948:

As regards the ISCM and the London Jury, I have no influence and I am no longer active president of the ISCM, thank goodness! The tendency is still (as in 1922) rather towards the Schoenberg school and I was amused to read in a German magazine that *Peter Grimes* was influenced by Schoenberg! I hope we may be able to have something of yours at Palermo in April 1949. There is no Englishman on next year's Jury. I remember agreeably meeting you for the first time at Florence in 1934 and taking you and Arnold Cooke out for a long walk to Grassina for the Good Friday procession!

For an account of Britten's visit to the 1934 ISCM Festival, see Letter 46.

583   To Carlos Peacock[1]

THE ENGLISH OPERA GROUP LTD
295 REGENT STREET, LONDON, W.1.
August 8th 1948

Dear Carlos

– Forgive official note-paper but I have run out of the ordinary sort. Thank you very much for arranging about the Constable – I picked it up at Saxmundham, all intact, & it is now gracing our wall in the big room downstairs, looking superb in its beautiful birthday-suit, stripped of all its false brown clothing! Thank you for your help in the cleaning. I am glad beyond measure that we decided to have it done, & thankful that Drowns didn't find just nothing under the big brown tree. I feel at the moment an honour & thrill to have taken part, even in a tiny way, in the rediscovery of a great work of art. Will you let me know if you had to pay anything for the dispatch of it – or will that go on Drowns's account?

I hope you are well. We are slowly recovering from our months of over-work. The weather is far from kind, but perhaps if it were sunny we should be rushing around swimming sailing & all, & I feel this enforced laziness indoors is perhaps more effective!

With many thanks for your great help, & best wishes,

Yours ever,
BENJAMIN B.

1   Art historian and curator at the Tate Gallery, London, who had played a part in the Constable exhibition shown at the first Aldeburgh Festival (see Letter 571 n. 10). Among Peacock's publications are *John Constable: the man and his work*, which the author dedicated to Britten, and *Samuel Palmer: Shoreham and after*, copies of which he sent to Britten. Peacock remained in occasional touch with Britten throughout the 1950s and 1960s, sending him, it would seem anonymously, drawings of Aldeburgh and pictures by Constable and Palmer. For example, on 30 April 1952 Britten wrote to thank Peacock for the gift of Constable's portrait of his eldest son, John Charles Constable:

It seems now that the evidence we can collect, but that isn't much, points to the fact that it was you who put that lovely little Constable portrait in the post for me last Christmas. Is that correct? – will you confess? If so, & I'm sure it is so, please accept my warmest thanks. It is a thing I shall treasure greatly, not only for its remarkable beauty, & originality, but because also it makes such a lovely companion piece to the other one, of the same young man when a boy [*recte*: a portrait of Constable's second son, Charles Golding Constable, purchased by Pears from the Leicester Galleries in 1950; at the time, the portrait was misidentified as Constable's eldest son]. I love them both dearly, & not less because the boy meant so very much to Constable at the end of his life. One can see from the tenderness & romance with which the paintings are done how much the father loved him. Thank you so much for the sweet thought & your generosity.

In 1966 Britten was once again thanking Peacock:

I cannot get over the great generosity of your gifts. I was sorry that I was deep in work when you came, & wasn't able to thank you personally. But the Palmer etching & watercolour are ravishing, & it is a great pleasure & privilege to have them. What a little beauty the 'Sleeping Shepherd' is! – & the charming watercolour too [*View of Lynmouth, Devon*, originally thought to have been by Palmer]. Did you realise that protecting the latter was another nice drawing (I can't quite read the name of the artist, who is unknown to me, I think)? Was this a mistake, & do you want it back? It is too nice to be just anonymous!

IV *SPRING SYMPHONY*

AUGUST 1948–JULY 1949

YEAR	EVENTS AND COMPOSITIONS
1948	
17–28 August	E. M. Forster stays with Britten at Aldeburgh to discuss possible subjects for an opera. During autumn 1948 Melville's novella *Billy Budd* is chosen
6–18 September	Conducting EOG in *The Beggar's Opera* and *Albert Herring* at Sadler's Wells Theatre, London
21 September	BBC broadcast of *The Beggar's Opera* from the Camden Theatre, London
18 October	Pears leaves for New York, returning to UK in mid-November
19 October	Begins composition of *Spring Symphony*
late October	Publication of the symposium on *The Rape of Lucretia* (RLEC), edited by Eric Crozier. Discussions about a possible 'film-opera' for the Ministry of Education and a children's opera with Crozier
30 October	Presents small collection of early music manuscripts to Lowestoft Public Library
November	Publication of Eric Walter White's *Benjamin Britten: eine Skizze von Leben und Werk*
6–9 December	Amsterdam: conducts *Saint Nicolas*, with Pears as soloist (6 and 9 December); recital in Concertgebouw (7 December)
mid-December	Ill with exhaustion and depression, cancels all engagements and postpones work on *Spring Symphony*
1949	
mid-January	Forster and Crozier in Aldeburgh to discuss adaptation of *Billy Budd*
21 January–12 February	Holiday with Pears in Italy, staying mainly in Venice

March	Recommences composition of *Spring Symphony* following illness
3–15 March	Forster and Crozier in Aldeburgh to work on first draft of *Billy Budd* libretto
15 March	Composition draft of *Spring Symphony* completed
April–May	COMPOSITION *The Little Sweep*
16 April–21 May	Recital tour with Pears in Italy and Belgium
June	COMPOSITION *Spring Symphony*
10–19 June	Aldeburgh Festival, which includes first performance of *Let's Make an Opera* (*The Little Sweep*) on 14 June, conducted by Norman Del Mar
14 July	Amsterdam Concertgebouw: first performance of *Spring Symphony*, conducted by Eduard van Beinum

84   To Erwin Stein

4 Crabbe Street, Aldeburgh
August 24th, 1948

Dear Erwin,

No time for more than a note to thank you for yours – we are up to our eyes in doing nothing, the best possible occupation. So glad you enjoyed Bryanston[1] – I long to hear all about it, & what you said. We've had a lovely month (in spite of consistently villanous weather) – lots of nice people here,[2] & we've sailed & bathed & played tennis. Peter had a bad throat (but it didn't matter!) for a day or so, but otherwise everyone's been well.

Perhaps I ought to see the vocal score of Nic. before it goes to the engraver,[3] but surely it can wait till next week? We come up on Tuesday early.

I've done no work, only a few letters – but I've had a wonderful time planning things, & reading possible poems for the Spring piece.[4] I'm just getting excited about it – it's in the exciting stage & I haven't got to worry about finding the right notes – that comes later! It is also possible that E. M. Forster (who's staying here now) will collaborate with Eric & me on the next opera[5] – opera needs a great human being like him in it – which is a dazzling prospect.

I gather Marion's having a time & a half![6]

Love to you & Sophie. Hope you're well & see you soon.

In haste,
Love,
BEN

1   Bryanston Summer School of Music, established in 1948 at Bryanston School, Dorset, under the direction of William Glock, at which Stein had delivered a series of lectures, including two on the music of the Second Viennese School. He had written to Britten: 'Bryanston was fun. I enjoyed speaking (five lectures!) and I think I was all right.' The idea for the summer school had originated with Gwynn Jones, a friend of the pianist Artur Schnabel, whose chief idea was to celebrate the classical piano repertoire. For which reason, Schnabel was invited to the 1948 summer school. Other members of the teaching staff included Paul Hindemith, Nadia Boulanger and the Amadeus String Quartet. In his autobiography, *Notes in Advance*, p. 52, Glock recalls that

the syllabus at Bryanston was more didactic than later at Dartington [Summer School]. Lectures filled the whole of each morning, and every week there were special subjects that were discussed in these lectures and illustrated at concerts [...]

One aspect of the Bryanston summers [...] was the importance given to talks on literature, the theatre, philosophy, and the visual arts.

E. M. Forster had also appeared at Bryanston during that first summer
school, delivering a lecture entitled 'The *Raison d'être* of Criticism'.
He mentioned the occasion in a letter to Britten (9 August 1948), who
responded on the 11th: 'Bryanston sounds gloomy if worthy. Schnabel is a
great man – but little Schnabels have most of the weaknesses & few of the
strengths – & are nearly always unattractive. But it was good of you to go.'

2 Among the visitors to Crag House during August 1948 were Kathleen
   Ferrier, Lesley Bedford and her family (whom Britten joined for a few
   days on the Norfolk Broads), Humphrey Maud, Bob Buckingham and
   E. M. Forster.

3 The vocal score of *Saint Nicolas* had been prepared by Arthur Oldham,
   whose manuscript copy was evidently about to be engraved. The first edition of the vocal score was published by Boosey & Hawkes in October 1948.

4 By this point in 1948, Britten had abandoned his original scheme for *Spring
   Symphony* (see Letter 546 n. 3) and adopted a new plan using English lyric
   verse. Many of the poems that found their way into *Spring Symphony* – in
   particular all but one from Part I of the piece – were found in Norman
   Ault's anthology *Elizabethan Lyrics from the original texts*, a second-hand
   copy of which Britten had purchased on 19 August 1932 from the Lowestoft
   Library. Other textual sources that can be identified in BPL are Auden's
   'Out on the lawn', to be found with Britten's annotations, in *Look, Stranger!*,
   the collection of Auden's verse that had furnished Britten's song-cycle *On
   This Island* in 1937, and Barnfield's 'When will my May come that I may
   embrace thee', taken from *The Poems of Richard Barnfield*.

5 Forster, accompanied by Bob Buckingham, visited Crag House between 17
   and 22 August, during which time he and Britten must have aired their
   views about potential subjects for a future operatic collaboration. Forster
   had already stayed at Crag House during the Aldeburgh Festival in June,
   when the possibility of writing a libretto for Britten was first discussed. On
   his return to Cambridge after the Aldeburgh Festival, Forster wrote to
   Britten on 20 June: 'I shall be very glad dear Ben to discuss the libretto
   question.' The two men met in Cambridge during July when Forster and
   Kenneth Harrison (like Forster, a Fellow of King's College, Cambridge)
   hosted a lunch party in their adjoining rooms for members of the EOG.
      Forster's inexperience of such a specialized medium as libretto-writing
   led to the involvement of Crozier, who was by this time highly skilled in
   this area. Crozier recalled that he and Forster held 'one or two meetings to
   discuss the project. He was most enthusiastic, but hampered – as I was – by
   lack of a story' ('The Writing of *Billy Budd*', p. 12). At one stage in October
   1948, Richard Cobbold's *The History of Margaret Catchpole: a Suffolk Girl*
   (1845), the story of a servant girl's fatal relationship with a smuggler, was
   under consideration, and Crozier recollects that he and Britten had first

thought that Forster might be attracted to writing a social comedy. Forster, however, had other ideas, and made known his wish for grand opera. It was not until early November that Britten suggested the possibility of Herman Melville's last work, the novella *Billy Budd, Foretopman*. In a letter of 11 November to Britten, Forster asserted, 'I *have* read *Billy Budd*, and did once broadcast on it.' (Forster had also discussed *Billy Budd* in his 1927 Clark Lectures, delivered at Cambridge, and first published that same year under the title *Aspects of the Novel*. In a BBC Third Programme discussion about the opera, Britten recalled that it was through *Aspects of the Novel* that he first encountered Melville's novella; see PKBM, pp. 194–207.) The subject for Britten's next major opera had been found and in March 1949 (see Letter 625 n. 2) Forster and Crozier stayed at Crag House for their first serious working session on the libretto. See BBMCPR, pp. 44–6.

6 Marion Stein was on holiday with a cousin in Austria and Italy. It was her first trip to Europe of any significant duration since the end of the war.

585 To Christopher Headington

3 OXFORD SQUARE, W.2

[September 1948]

Dear Christopher,

I am up to the old eyes in rehearsals, performances, & meetings because of our season at Sadler's Wells[1] so I can't, alas, do more than send you a scribbled line of best wishes for your, I am afraid, rather dreary immediate future.[2] I hope that you will get some time to go on working, & to hear some music, & I hope above all that you will find some nice chaps you can talk to. Let me know from time to time where & how you are. The best address is always Aldeburgh for me.

So glad you did a piece for Northampton,[3] but maddening that you can't get there to hear it. I'd like to see it – perhaps Walter Hussey will send me a copy.

With best wishes always to you,

Yours ever,

BENJAMIN B.

1 The EOG presented a two-week season of *The Beggar's Opera* and *Albert Herring* at London's Sadler's Wells Theatre from 6 to 18 September. Britten shared the conducting with Ivan Clayton.

2 Headington was about to embark on his two-year period of National Service. After basic training, he was posted to the British Army of the Rhine and joined the Music Department of the British Forces Network in Hamburg

where, shortly before his military service came to an end, he was the soloist in the first performance of his *Variations* for piano and orchestra, with the Hamburg Symphony Orchestra.

3 Headington had written to Britten earlier in September:

[. . .] I wrote an Anthem for Northampton, which should be done on Sept. 21st. They are also doing it with something of yours (*Te Deum?*) on October 10th, according to Dr Hussey's plans. Unfortunately, I suppose I won't be able to be there.

Headington had been approached by Walter Hussey at Britten's instigation.

586 To David Bedford[1]

3 OXFORD SQUARE, W.2
September 15th 1948

My dear Dave,

Thank you for your nice letter. I am very glad you enjoyed Albert Herring.[2] I enjoyed your cake too – you are very clever to be able to cook – I can't, at all.

I hope to see you before you go back to school.

How's your opera going?

Give my love to Peter[3] & Steuart,[4]

With love,
BEN

1 English composer (b. 1937), who studied with Lennox Berkeley at the Royal Academy of Music and in Venice with Luigi Nono. He taught music in London secondary schools from 1963 and his output includes several works for children. Bedford composed two works for Pears: *The Tentacles of the Dark Nebula*, for tenor and chamber ensemble, first performed by Pears and the London Sinfonietta under the composer's direction in 1969; and *Because he liked to be at home*, for tenor (with treble recorder) and harp, first performed at the Snape Maltings Concert Hall on 14 June 1974 by Pears and Osian Ellis as part of the Aldeburgh Festival.

2 David Bedford had presumably attended one of the EOG's performances of *Albert Herring* at Sadler's Wells, given on 8, 10 and 13 September.

3 Peter Lehmann Bedford (1931–2001), English singer who sang with the English Opera Group during the late 1960s; brother of David and Steuart Bedford.

4 English conductor and pianist (b. 1939), and brother of David and Peter Lehmann Bedford, Steuart Bedford has long been closely associated with Britten's music. After studying at Lancing College, Sussex, and the Royal Academy of Music, he became organ scholar at Worcester College, Oxford.

While at Oxford he made his conducting debut in University Opera Society productions of *Albert Herring* and Menotti's *The Consul*. In 1965–66 he was a member of the music staff at Glyndebourne, and in 1967 joined the EOG as a répétiteur and made his conducting debut with the company at Sadler's Wells in Britten's realization of *The Beggar's Opera*. During the next decade he conducted several Britten operas for the EOG as well as the premiere of John Gardner's *The Visitors* (1972), Mozart's *Idomeneo* (1973; Bedford had acted as Britten's assistant when Britten conducted the opera in 1969), and Holst's *Sāvitri* and *The Wandering Scholar* (1974).

Bedford acted as an assistant to Britten during the BBC Television recording of *Owen Wingrave* in 1970 and conducted the stage premiere of the work at Covent Garden in 1973, as well as the first performances of *Death in Venice* (1973) at Snape and Covent Garden, the *Suite on English Folk Tunes* (1975), *Phaedra* (with Janet Baker, 1976), and the revised version of *Paul Bunyan* (1976). He was an Artistic Director of the Aldeburgh Festival from 1973 to 1998. As Artistic Director of the Collins Classics 'Britten Edition', he has made a significant contribution to the interpretation of Britten's works on disc. Bedford has written about his long friendship with Britten and Pears: see 'The Struggle with the Word', in PPT, pp. 5–7, and 'Composer and Conductor: Annals of a Collaboration', *Opera Quarterly*, 4/5 (autumn 1986), pp. 60–74.

587 To Herbert Murrill[1]
BBC

4 Crabbe Street, Aldeburgh
October 6th 1948

Dear Herbert Murrill,

I am afraid I cannot accept the BBC's kind invitation for me to write a work to mark the birth of Princess Elizabeth's child.[2] Up to & including November, I am completely snowed up with other commitments. I regret though that you did not give me more notice since it would have been a happy commission for me.

Yours sincerely,
BENJAMIN BRITTEN

1 English composer and musical administrator (1909–1952). He was Musical Director of the Group Theatre from 1933 to 1936, in which year he joined the BBC. See also Diary for 18 November 1935, n. 3. In 1948, Murrill was Assistant Head of Music at the BBC.

2 Murrill had written to Britten on 1 October with an invitation for a new work, to be ready by November, 'in the nature of a serenade', to celebrate

the birth of the first child of Princess (later Queen) Elizabeth and the Duke of Edinburgh. When Britten declined, Murrill approached Michael Tippett, whose *Suite for the Birthday of Prince Charles* (Suite in D) received its first performance on 15 November 1948, the day after Prince Charles's birth, in a BBC Third Programme broadcast by the BBC Symphony Orchestra, conducted by Sir Adrian Boult. See also Ian Kemp, *Tippett: The Composer and His Music*, pp. 296–8.

588   To Henriëtte Bosmans[1]

4 Crabbe Street, Aldeburgh
October 8th 1948

My dear Jetty,

You will think yourself mad when you read these words; 'it <u>can't</u> be a letter from that hopeless Ben', you'll say! No, I am truly sorry to have left you neglected so long – it is simply that time for <u>nice</u> letters, not for those dreary kind of business letters which must be written every day, just doesn't exist, & anyhow you know how lazy I am! Anyhow, it isn't that we don't think of you, enquire after you, drink your health in fine Geneva [*recte*: Genever], & eat your health in lovely chocolate (when those exciting packages arrive!). We were so sorry to hear from Peter D. [Diamand] that you had been so ill, & then glad to hear from Otto Kraus that you were better. We were thrilled that you heard the old Beggar's Opera, & approved of the way it sounded – it delighted us that you should have sent a telegram too.[2] Thank you my dear from the bottom of our hearts for all these kindnesses & many others, & forgive our ingratitude & apparent thoughtlessness. It is wonderful to have such a devoted friend – & one so intelligent that the friendliness <u>means</u> so much!

We have nearly finished our Opera Season now – only one week more & then I come back to Aldeburgh for a nice long work on a big new piece (the Spring Symphony (?)[3] for Chorus, Soloists & Orchestra which I have been planning for such ages) & Peter goes off to America for 4 weeks – & then we come to Holland for St Nicolas![4] Will you be there Dec. 4–10? – I do hope so. We are doing several concerts besides St Nicolas in Rotterdam and the Kunstkring.[5]

The new house here in Aldeburgh is lovely as ever – the sea, in front of me now – is looking wonderful, big waves & lots of sun. Next year you must make <u>the</u> great effort & come over for our great Festival – June 9–19! Keep the dates, & begin getting used to the idea that you will be coming. Nice programmes – A. Herring, Lucretia, Bach & Purcell Cantatas, Mozart & Schubert Quintets, S. Nicolas, Handel Oratorio, some of our best writers to lecture, & lovely pictures[6] . . . there, doesn't that tempt!

Thank you, once again, my dear for the lovely presents. They have been much enjoyed – & forgive your penitent friend who never writes letters.

Lots of love, from Peter,
and from
BEN

Coda

I of course have forgotten, typically, to answer any of your questions about the piano Concerto – (i) Although it is such a baby piece (1938!) I do like it played especially, & only in (ii) the new version which I can assure you is the last! (iii) Materials can only be hired, through British Council (?), or direct from Boosey & Hawkes – this applies to (iv) no full-score published yet, so conductors will have to take it on trust – scoring (as far as I can remember) is ordinary 2 fl, 2 ob, 2 cl, 2 fg, 4 horns, 2 trts, 3 trb, tuba, harp, perc., strings – & never thick – why, I can make myself heard in it, & I am not all that tough!

(((P.P.S. (pp [pianissimo])I do hope you play it!)))[7]

1   Henriëtte Bosmans (1895–1952), Dutch pianist and composer, a pupil of Willem Pijper. Bosmans was a highly accomplished performer of her own music and that of her Dutch contemporaries. As a composer, she produced a great deal of vocal music. 'Jetty' was Britten's and Pears's pet name for her. See Helen Metzelaar, *Zonder muziek het leven onnodig. Henriëtte Bosmans (1895–1952) een biografie*; chapter 11 (pp. 159–73) is entitled 'Benjamin Britten and Peter Pears (1948)'; and Metzelaar, 'Who sent Benjamin Britten hundreds of eggs from Holland?', *Keynotes* (September 1997), pp. 17–21.

2   Bosmans had sent a telegram to Britten on 25 September, after hearing a broadcast of *The Beggar's Opera*:

THREE CHEERS FOR THE BBC AND A GREAT BRAVO TO THE BEGGARS THE ORCHESTRA AND TO THE CONDUCTOR COMPOSER HIMSELF. WITH ONCE MORE GREAT ADMIRATION AND LOVE

3   The first occasion in the extant correspondence in which Britten, albeit with some uncertainty, uses what proved to be the work's final title.

4   Pears was the soloist in the European premiere of *Saint Nicolas* at the Zuiderkerk, Amsterdam, on 6 December (St Nicolas's Day) 1948, with the choir of the Volks-Universiteit of Rotterdam, conducted by the composer.

5   Pears and Britten gave a recital in the Kleine Zaal of the Concertgebouw, Amsterdam, on 7 December; Pears took part in a concert in Utrecht with the Leyden Orchestra on the 8th, and a second performance of *Saint Nicolas* was given in Amsterdam, at the Lutherskerk, on the 9th under the auspices of the Amsterdam Kunstkring. Britten returned to Aldeburgh – and to the

composition of *Spring Symphony* – on the 11th. Pears gave a performance of the *Serenade* with the Concertgebouw Orchestra, conducted by Eduard van Beinum, at the Concertgebouw on 19 December.

6   The second Aldeburgh Festival was held from 10 to 19 June 1949. It opened with the EOG production of *The Rape of Lucretia*, conducted by Norman Del Mar (repeated on the 13th), and included two performances of *Albert Herring* (15th and 18th), conducted by Ivan Clayton. Not mentioned by Britten in his letter to Henriëtte Bosmans were the first performances of *Let's Make an Opera*, to be conducted by Del Mar on the 14th and 17th. Britten conducted two programmes of 'Sacred Music and Poetry' (14th and 16th) which included cantatas by Bach (Nos. 151, 156, 159 and 161) and Purcell's *My Beloved Spake* and *Saul and the Witch at Endor*. Mozart's Quintet in E♭ (K. 452) for piano and wind was performed by members of the EOG, with Britten at the piano, on 15 June; Schubert's String Quintet was not, however, to find its way into the final programmes. Handel's *Ode for Saint Cecilia's Day* was given on the 18th, conducted by Leslie Woodgate, and *Saint Nicolas* was revived on the 11th, with Pears in the title role and the composer conducting. Among the distinguished lecturers were the author Arthur Ransome and the actor Robert Speaight, and the exhibitions included drawings by the Suffolk-born artist Thomas Gainsborough.

7   Bosmans broadcast Britten's Piano Concerto on Radio Hilversum on 20 October 1948, with the Radio Philharmonic Orchestra, conducted by Albert van Raalte. See Letter 590.

589   To Peter Pears

4 Crabbe Street, Aldeburgh
Oct. 18th 1948

My darling Peter,

Your sweet & comprehensive wire[1] has just arrived, & I am put out of my agony! Judging by the fact that it arrived about 7 p.m. (<u>our</u> time), you can't have been very late in arriving, which is immensely relieving, because my worry was more that you would be detained & bored to desperation than have an accident (which I was sure you wouldn't have). You must be now happily with Elizabeth [Mayer], & talking, talking . . . . ! I long to get a note about the journey; how it was, whether boring and/or frightening & uncomfortable.[2] I loathed, more than any moment of my silly life, leaving you. Thank God I was with Lesley [Bedford], because I made a fool of myself in the car. I caught the 4.50 easily, but walked to it across Liverpool Street in a dream, only being aroused by a man's shout that I had dropped a packet of £5 notes on the ground – I hadn't bothered to put them in my pocket properly!

Beth met me, & was infinitely sweet & understanding! I loved being
with her & Sally & Roguey. Sally's now very sweet, but Roguey not well –
very pale & thin. Kit was quite human too. Beth took me to Ipswich this
morning – I tried on my new suit, which will be quite becoming I think,
tho' the tailor is a bit pompous. My visit was spoiled by seeing half a
headline on an Evening Paper ". . . . . believed lost" – & immediately feared
the worst. My heart only got back to normal beating when we arrived
back at Hasketon! She brought me over here for tea-time, plus Annie the
new temporary Swiss girl who seems nice. We had tea – Barbara very
cheerful, because they seem to have had a whale of a time in Amsterdam.
She & Beth got _very_ fond of each other, which is immensely satisfactory –
altho' Aimy Nichol[3] seemed to have been rather scared & damping. Then
your wire arrived, Beth went back, (slightly Bols-tiddly), we had supper,
& now I am waiting to hear Nancy do the Lullabies.[4] I'll finish this in the
morning to tell you how they were, & then I'll send it off quick, with
my love.

Good night – my darling.

Tuesday morning . . . .
     The 3rd programme was up to its tricks, & we heard the lullabies thro' a
mixture of Latvian Brass-bands, & Viennese Commentary – so there wasn't
much atmosphere! But the tempi seemed O.K.
     It is a heavenly morning – sunny, cold & incredibly beautiful. I shall
write letters, go & pay in some cheques, see gas company about radiation
here, & then walk – think of the Spring piece, which I hope to start
tomorrow.[5] I'll send you a packet of selected correspondence when there
are enough to bother with; so far only cheques & a sweet note from
Ursula.[6] I had one from Jetty B. this morning – she is broadcasting the
piano concerto tomorrow from Hilversum[7] & adores it (see how love is
blind!). She says _why_ do you go to U.S.A. You couldn't sing better![8]
     Lots of love to Elizabeth, William, Beata & all – & Clytie,[9] John,[10] Meg[11]
& young John[12] too, and Ralph & Clare – do hope the money business
isn't embarrassing – Blast the silly Treasury.[13]
     All my love, dear heart – take care of yourself – come back soon and safe.

Till then,
Your B.

Lots of love from Barbara (P.) & from Beth.

1 The telegram has not survived.

2 Pears was to write to Britten on 19 October from 240 East 49th Street, New
   York, the Mayers' home, soon after his arrival, and after making what was
   his first Atlantic crossing by air:

The aeroplane is a great modern invention, of great use in dragging one rapidly from latitude to latitude. It is not wholly uncomfortable and Flight No. 151 of A.O.A. [American Overseas Airlines] was entirely safe and ever so hospitable. The hostess was graciousness itself, the sherry was fair, the steak at Shannon was enormous, the nightcap soothed (the Seconals [sleeping tablets] helped). Bright shone the moon over the Atlantic, even Gander was faintly glamorized – but best of all, I had sitting by me in the plane an American who didn't open his mouth for 19 hours – ! Perhaps this was the main reason for thinking that the trip was really very easy and I wasn't frightened at all – not at all.

It's lovely to be with Elizabeth, who is exactly the same, and we talk – all yesterday & all this morning we have talked. I went to see Clytie last night [. . .] I start work with her tomorrow morning. [. . .] I'm having dinner with Ralph & Cardelli tomorrow night.

Giovanni Cardelli (see also Letters 590 and 598), was one of the financial backers of the forthcoming Broadway production of *The Rape of Lucretia*.

3   Unidentified.

4   Nancy Evans and the pianist Ernest Lush gave the first broadcast performance of Britten's *A Charm of Lullabies* as part of a BBC Third Programme concert, shared with the Aeolian String Quartet and Ruth Cummings (viola), on 18 October 1948.

5   The composition draft. Britten had been planning the work since 1946 (see Letters 534 and 546).

6   Ursula Nettleship (1886–1968), singing teacher and choir trainer. She first met Britten when he was staying in her sister's (Ethel's) house in Crantock in 1936 and she lent Britten and Pears her London home on their return from the US in 1942. She is the dedicatee of *A Ceremony of Carols*. She advised on the formation of a local choir for the Aldeburgh Festival and acted as choir trainer for the 1949 Festival; a footbridge at the Snape Maltings site is named in her memory. See also Letter 118 n. 1 and IC1/2.

7   The location of the headquarters of Dutch public service broadcasting.

8   Pears had gone to the United States to have singing lessons with Clytie Mundy, who had taught him during 1940–41.

9   Clytie Hine Mundy (1887–1983), Australian-born singer and teacher. See also Letter 307 n. 6 and CHPP, p. 98.

10 John Mundy, Clytie's husband, principal cellist in the Metropolitan Opera Orchestra.

11 The Mundys' daughter, the soprano Meg Mundy, who had been a member of the Elizabethan Singers, of which Pears was also a member in 1941. See also Letter 307 n. 5.

12 Meg Mundy's son.

13 Treasury restrictions on the amounts of sterling currency that could be
    taken abroad were still in force at this period.

590 **To Peter Pears**

4 Crabbe Street, Aldeburgh
October 22nd (?Friday) [1948]

My darling Peter,

I am longing to have a note from you saying how you are, & how the
journey was, & if & when the lessons are started . . . etc. etc. With luck
there may be a note tomorrow; I've counted out the days on my fingers to
see when it is possible to get a letter by airmail . . . ?!

It all goes peacefully here. Weather a bit overcast, & a beastly depressing
West wind which I hope will turn into a healthy Easter soon. I work all
day, except in the afternoon when little Miss Parker comes & we wade
thro' letters together, gradually catching up on the dreary pile! Then I
walk, & work after tea till a latish dinner & then listen to the Radio (which
is intolerably interfered with now) or correct proofs[1] till a lonely bed . . .
The work started abysmally slowly & badly, & I got in a real state. But I
think it's better now. I'm half way thro' the sketch of the 1st movement,[2]
deliberately not hurrying it, fighting every inch of the way. It is terribly
hard to do, but I think shows signs of being a piece at last. It is such cold
music[3] that it is depressing to write, & I yearn for the Spring to begin, &
to get on to the 3 Trumpets & Tenor solo![4]

I listened to Jetty Bosmans playing the piano concerto – some of it not
bad, but pretty heavy & clumsy the 1st two movements. She hasn't got
much sense of rhythm, & obviously minds too much about what she's
playing! The reception as usual was awful – Hilversum. Tonight, Arthur[5]
is here & we are going to try to get Wozzeck[6] from Hamburg, but I'm not
hopeful. He is getting on with Norah[7] like a house on fire – she says he's
the model guest, which I'm sure he is. He is working madly, has finished
one, & half done two sonnets for you already.[8] I'm looking forward to
seeing them. Barbara is well, happy I think, & the Swiss girl is splendid –
but there may be some legal snag about keeping her; it would be a bore if
she had to go, as she's intelligent & charming.

And you . . ? I wonder how it is all seeming. I hope the Russian Bogey[9]
doesn't obscure everything. Here it seems more dormant, tho' the Times
& all agitate it pretty frequently. There is no mail to speak of for you,
except some bills, the urgent ones of which I've paid, & some receipts. The
enclosed nice one from Ursula may please you! There has been a bite for
the house,[10] & Caplan[11] is dealing with it, Erwin says – let's hope it comes
off. The telephone is half-in, has been for the week. When it succeeds I

may give myself the pleasure of a transatlantic call, if the gnaw gets worse. Still a month is not for ever, & there's a lot to be done in the month!

<u>Saturday morning</u>

As usual, the reception last night was hopeless, & Arthur got a very strange impression of the work. Actually the performance was very poor, only Wozzeck having any idea of character <u>or</u> pitch. We were lucky if Marie was within a fourth of her notes! You must get us to imitate the small boy singing 'hop-hop' at the end. Arthur was quite bewildered, even with the score, perhaps <u>because</u> of it, because really it makes the simplest passages look like Chinese. I alternated between mad irritation at the ridiculous excesses of it, with the ludicrous, hideous, & impossible vocal writing, and being moved to tears by the incredible haunting beauty of lots of bits of it. If <u>only</u> he [Berg] could relax in the relaxed bits!

Your sweet note has come this morning[12] – my morale, sagging all the week, has soared again! I am relieved the journey was easy & good, & I am praying the return one will be similar. So sorry about Clytie;[13] give her lots of love from me. It is lovely to think of you with Elizabeth, William, Meg & all; if only the traffic were normal I wouldn't worry a bit! Please, darling, remember to look <u>left</u> when stepping off pavements (is that correct

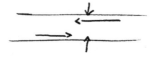

. . . yes, I think so)

Don't feel you've got to do too much Ralph-ing & Cardelli-ing. Have a rest from business matters, & <u>don't</u> try & sell you or us too much. It doesn't matter really whether we go to Indiana University or Saskatchewan, <u>really</u>![14]

My very best, & only love to you. Take the greatest care of yourself, my darling.

Lots of greetings to friends, & write <u>often</u> please – You mustn't practise <u>all</u> day!

Thine own,

B.

1   Of *Saint Nicolas*.

2   The 'Introduction', 'Shine out, fair sun, with all your heat' (Anon., sixteenth century), which forms the first setting in Part I of *Spring Symphony*.

3   Britten evokes the poem's wintry imagery by means of stark intervals of the

fourth and fifth, a percussion (with harp) 'refrain', bare contrapuntal textures, and – perhaps most effective of all – a juxtaposition of the chorus, which sings *a cappella* throughout this number, with the orchestra. Britten deliberately denies the chorus the 'warm', generous cushion of support from the orchestra, thereby evoking a most striking sound world, made all the more so when heard in the context of the rest of the piece.

4 'The merry Cuckoo' (Edmund Spenser), for tenor and three trumpets, whose fanfares dispel at once the bleak mood of 'Shine out' and herald the arrival of spring.

5 Arthur Oldham (1926–2003), English composer, pianist and chorus master. He had been Music Director of the Ballet Rambert from 1946 to 1947. He was one of Britten's very few composition pupils and made the vocal scores of a number of his works. See also Letter 481 n. 2, Letter 511 and obituaries by Tim Bullamore, *Independent* (13 May 2003), by Conrad Wilson, *Guardian* (14 May 2003) and in *The Times* (23 May 2003).

   Oldham's autobiography, *Living With Voices*, pp. 20–31, includes an account of his association with Britten, which began in 1944 when he acted as the composer's assistant, preparing the full score manuscript pages of *Peter Grimes* by ruling in the bar lines and adding the clefs and key signatures, and continued through the 1960s and 1970s when Oldham was responsible for various choruses involved in performances and recordings conducted by Britten.

   Throughout the years of his closest association with Britten (1944–49), during which Oldham lived in Suffolk, acted as Britten's amanuensis and was, for a time, his pupil, Oldham maintained a frequent and lively correspondence with his friend, the pianist John Lindsay (see Letter 596 n. 3). This correspondence, a copy of which is at BPL, provides numerous insights into the Britten–Oldham relationship, not least of which is the account below – unique in Britten documentation – of a composition lesson Britten gave to his young colleague in April 1948. Oldham wrote to Lindsay on 29 April:

My session with Ben tonight was the most wonderful one I've ever had. I had tea with him, and then we went into the studio (on our own all the time) and began to talk about variations in general – and my piece in particular. For the first time I was able to talk easily to him, on the same level. He wasn't tired, or pressed for time; everything was perfect. He asked me to describe what I'd done and my plans for the piece [*Variations on a Carol Tune*; see Letter 572 n. 7], in detail and then asked me to play them. And (again for the first time and to my intense delight) I was able to play them calmly, and just as I do to you; pointing out the good bits as I went along, and with Ben agreeing and looking as pleased as me with a right chord. He likes what I've done very much; and made some excellent suggestions which I agree with completely. He wants the theme lengthened by repetitions because the later variations are longer and complete pieces in themselves. Then he played me the Mozart Variations on 'Ah vous dirai-je, maman' [K. 265] with great poetry and intelligence. He asked me if I had a score of *The Young Person's Guide* – and, because I hadn't, gave me one 'with my love'. All the time [we] were talking and I told him how highly I rated his work – that I thought 'On the First of May' (the concerted item in the first scene of *Herring*) was on a par with the Mozart operas. He at once said that he could never believe that himself and gave me his reasons: all of which were perfectly honest. He rates his work well below Mozart's; but said how terribly happy it made him to hear such a thing said about his work by a person 'of such tremendously promising gifts and very great sensitivity'. I convinced him that I really *did* believe what I had said; and it also pleased him because he himself feels there is nothing at all in the particular piece of which to be ashamed and he felt it was a promising sign that I had singled it out.

Don't get the idea that this was a mutual admiration society! Not at all; it was just a completely honest talk which has given me enormous personal help and confidence. Ben says that from now on I will [find] it easier to compose – because I know more of what I'm doing – although he warned me of some very gloomy days that are bound to come always. They did to Mozart and they do to him. Just before I went he asked if *he* could play *me* (!!!) his new Scena from *The Beggar's Opera*; with Greensleeves [No. 53 'The Condemned Cell']. I found out something he dislikes (which I'd suspected all along). He hates apologies. At one point I apologized for my ignorance over some detail in the Variations and he at once made it plain that one *shouldn't* apologize for things. Altogether I was with him for about two hours. [. . .] He asked me how I felt, hearing my piece at Saturday's concert. I told him I loathed every minute of it; and he said *he* does too, with his own pieces – 'That's why I can never bear to go and see *Grimes*.'

Oldham and Lindsay were enthusiastic about each new Britten work, and on many occasions in the letters Oldham is eager to share with his friend some technical detail of Britten's current work. For example, following a radio broadcast, he wrote to Lindsay on 10 April 1947:

I had two marvellous inspirations this week – one was hearing Nancy Evans singing three Britten songs – two from *The Rape of Lucretia*. And the other was hearing Peter sing a Bach Cantata – so he's back, and I presume Ben must be also. The *Lucretia* songs were extremely interesting harmonically – perhaps that is where his strongest line of development will be. He seems to be heading toward a new and original purity – constantly fining everything down to essential rightness, discarding even his own earlier idiomatic little touches altogether in some cases. Stravinsky must have worked along similar lines, although the length of time between the publication of one new work and the next makes it less possible to see the joins.

His and Lindsay's shared musical enthusiasms included Stravinky, whose scores Oldham was proofing for Erwin Stein ('Stymny' in Oldham–Lindsay parlance) at Boosey & Hawkes, who were Stravinsky's as well as Britten's publishers. On 19 December 1947 Oldham wrote to Lindsay:

I saw the Stravinsky scores of both *Oedipus* and his noo ballay *Orpheus and Eurydice* and had a very inspiring chat with Stymny about them both. The great fount of knowledge also confirmed what I'd heard about the new opera [*The Rake's Progress*] he's writing. Stravinsky's manuscript is perfect man! absolutely beautiful and very clear. He obviously writes more slowly than Ben and takes great pains to make each page look neat: he takes stacks of room for everything.

It was to Stein that Oldham turned for clarification on Schoenberg's influence on *Grimes*, writing in the same letter to Lindsay:

I told Stymny that I'd read an article by Humphrey Sole [i.e. Searle] which declared that, had Schoenberg never lived *Grimes* could not have been written! But Sty. of course found an explanation for it by quoting the interlude in the very last act of *Grimes* (after the huge choruses 'Grimes ... Grimes ...') [between Act III scenes 1 and 2] which certainly does show a marked influence of Berg. But Sole is a stupid sod to exaggerate that into such a sweeping statement; if, indeed, that is what he bases it on.

The letters also include some vignettes of Britten's and Pears's domestic life. In the summer of 1949, when staying at Crag House, Oldham wrote to Lindsay on 4 August:

I spent a very pleasant week with Ben and Peter at their house recently. We talked and played music endlessly, bathed and had a lovely time. Each day, after lunch, Ben would play a Mozart piano concerto with Peter at the other piano. He played lots of Fauré and together they played Debussy's *En blanc et noir* for two pianos – a marvellous piece of piano writing and very powerful. Peter also sang Grieg and Hugo Wolf.

6   In 1934 Britten had listened to the first broadcast performance in the UK of *Wozzeck* (also distorted by poor reception). He wrote in his Diary for 14 March 1934:

Only the third Act (& bits of second) were intelligible. The music of this is extra-ordinarily striking without the action, while that of the first isn't – except for the exciting march & beautiful little lullaby. The hand of Tristan is over a lot of the intense emotion, but Berg emerges a definite personality.

For Britten's attitude towards Berg in the 1930s, see Letter 73 nn. 6 and 8.

7   Oldham writes in *Living With Voices*, p. 24:

Ben very kindly arranged with one of his Suffolk neighbours, Norah Nichols, widow of the poet Robert Nichols, [for me] to stay at her house for a month, during which I completed my composition. Norah was a kind and discreet hostess, well accustomed to existing alongside the artistic temperament, and our friendship matured and blossomed. I was to use her home as a base for composing for the next six years.

8   Oldham was working on his *Summer's Lease*, seven sonnets of Shakespeare, for tenor and string orchestra, first performed at Chelsea Town Hall on 28 March 1949, with Pears as soloist and the Boyd Neel Orchestra conducted by the composer. Britten had helped Oldham secure this performance but, as Oldham writes in *Living With Voices*, p. 24,

Ben was critical: perhaps, I suspect, because it was a rather blatant attempt on my part to rival the success of his own *Seven Sonnets of Michelangelo* [...] Ben, in spite of being disappointed with the piece, continued to encourage me [...].

9   A reference to the investigations of the House Un-American Activities

Committee of the US Congress, whose belief in the 'Red Menace' of Communism was to develop into a full-scale witch-hunt under the direction of Republican Senator Joseph McCarthy. The 'Russian Bogey' was to leave its mark on both Britten and Pears; see MCCCBB, pp. 211–16.

10 3 Oxford Square.

11 Isador Caplan (1912–1995), Britten's and Pears's solicitor and legal adviser from the mid-1940s, who was later to become an executor of both Britten's and Pears's estates and a senior Trustee of the Britten–Pears Foundation. Caplan also served on the board of the EOG from 1951.

After studying at Fitzwilliam College, Cambridge, and qualifying as a solicitor in March 1937, he became a partner in the distinguished London firm of Forsyte Kerman that same year. It was here that he met his wife, Joan Bray (1915–1997), whom he married in 1938. During the war Caplan and his family moved into a flat in the same building as Erwin Stein and his family, and it was through this connection that he first met Britten and Pears and began to act for them on legal matters.

Caplan soon established himself as an indispensable member of the professional team on which Britten and Pears relied, and who subsequently became close friends of his. (Their accountant, Leslie Periton (see Letter 636 n. 2) was another.) Britten invited Caplan to be one of the four executors to oversee his affairs after his death – with Pears, Periton and Donald Mitchell. Caplan played a key role in the establishing of the Britten–Pears Library in 1973, and, after Britten's death, the negotiations with the Treasury led to the offer to the nation of a pre-eminent collection of Britten's autograph manuscripts – the list of specific works was devised by Donald Mitchell – in lieu of capital gains tax. Caplan's skill as a lawyer, coupled with his unshakeable belief in Britten as a creative artist, led to an agreement being reached in which this manuscript collection could remain on permanent loan to BPL and thus preserve the integrity of the autograph legacy as a whole. The precedent of this innovative settlement with a private library was in fact to lead to a change of legislation.

Caplan's political and humanitarian beliefs – he was a lifelong member of the Labour Party and a committed pacifist – were very much in tune with the composer's own values, and led to the dedication to Caplan and his wife of *Owen Wingrave* in 1971. See also obituaries by Donald Mitchell in the *Independent* (23 January 1995) and Marion Thorpe in the *Guardian* (10 February 1995), and Caplan's own 'Recollections of Benjamin Britten', an informal talk given in Richmond on 24 October 1993, transcript at BPL.

12 See Letter 589 n. 2.

13 In his letter to Britten of 19 October, Pears had told the composer that Clytie Mundy was unwell – 'very tired & low (or high) blood pressure'.

14 One of Pears's tasks while in the US was to arrange with Ralph Hawkes dates and venues for Pears's and Britten's 1949 tour.

591 To Leonard Smith
The Gramophone Co. Ltd
[*Typed*]

Crag House, Aldeburgh, East Suffolk
22/10/48

My dear Leonard,

Please forgive the long delay over my comments on the Peter Grimes records.[1] I was always hoping that we could have a quiet lunch and chat about them, but London is never 'quiet' for me and whenever we met it was on formal occasions and unsuitable for frank conversation.

Actually one of my greatest difficulties in selecting from these records has been finding a suitable instrument on which to hear them. My old H.M.V. machine has developed strange troubles and the new one lent to me by Pye has similar jitters on approaching the centre of each record. But at last using my friends' machines I have come to these conclusions. Here they are:

Peter's Pub and Hut scenes[2] are both very satisfactory; and also Joan's first act aria.[3] Which takes of these I leave to the singer concerned.

The Church scene[4] is a much more complicated affair. The playing on Side 1 is not wonderful but I fear that with that particular orchestra it cannot be better.

The perspective of the "off-stage" is very disappointing, as in all the records the organ is much too loud. Why I passed this in the Studio is beyond me but I can only feel that this must have been changed in the reproduction since only a lunatic could have allowed the organ so to overweigh the singer!

The second side of this scene suffers most and is, I fear, unusable.

Of the other side I prefer the following takes:–

Side 1. No. 1.

    "   3. No. 1. (in spite of the blob)

    "   4. No. 2.

Peter's part in the Mad scene[5] is terrific and there is little choice between the takes. On the whole I prefer No. 1. of 307 and No. 2. of 306. Alas, the only take (No. 1.) of the preceding interlude,[6] is unusable. The horns came to grief seriously in the middle and generally the playing is poor.

Embroidery Aria.[7] Joan is not happy about this; neither am I. It is an exceptionally difficult piece to record and I am sure, and she is sure, that she can do better. Incidentally, she is quite upset that she has never been sent a copy of the takes concerning her, and has been able to hear them but once, and then surreptitiously. Perhaps you can put this straight with her.[8]

Summing up this long letter, in order to have a good set of records, and I hope you agree with me in what I say, we have already waited so long that an extra month or two is immaterial. We should try to repeat the Embroidery Aria in the second recording of the Church scene and the interlude preceding the Mad scene.

Peter puts in plea to be able to re-do the Hut scene since he feels that he can now do it very much better. I hope you will give him this chance.

Please do not take these comments as meaning to be difficult, but these are the first vocal extracts of the opera to be recorded and therefore have the air of authenticity. Please let us get them then as good as possible.[9]

With best wishes,
Yours sincerely,

1   During sessions held at No. 1 Studio, Abbey Road, London, on 12, 14, 16 and 17 July 1948, the BBC Theatre Chorus and the Orchestra of the Royal Opera House, Covent Garden, conducted by Reginald Goodall, recorded the following extracts from *Peter Grimes*:

   1   Act I scene 1: 'Whatever you say . . .'. Ellen Orford (figs. 27^{+13}–29^{+5}). Matrix No. CAX10298.

   2   Act I scene 2: 'Now the Great Bear and Pleiades'. Peter Grimes (figs. 74–77). Matrix No. CAX10297.

   3   Act II scene 1: Interlude III – 'Glitter of waves' – etc. Ellen Orford, The Rector, Peter Grimes (Opening to fig. 18^{-2}). Matrix Nos. CAX10296; CAX10303–5.

   4   Act II scene 2: 'In dreams I've built myself some kindlier home'. Peter Grimes (figs. 60–65^{+2}). Matrix No. CAX10300.

   5   Act III scene 1: 'Embroidery in childhood'. Ellen Orford (figs. 23^{-4}–25^{+2}). Matrix No. CAX10299.

   6   Interlude VI – Act III scene 2. Peter Grimes, Ellen Orford (figs. 44–53). Matrix No. CAX10306–8.

The soloists were Pears (Grimes), Joan Cross (Ellen Orford) and Tom Culbert (The Rector), all repeating their original roles. All the other solo parts – for example, Ned Keene, Auntie and the Nieces in the extract from Act I scene 2 – were omitted.

2   Nos. 2 and 4 in the list of extracts in n. 1.

3   No. 1.

4   No. 3.

5 The second part of No. 6.

6 Interlude VI, the first part of No. 6.

7 No. 5.

8 Britten's plea for Joan Cross to be allowed to hear test pressings was heeded. She wrote to Britten (undated letter: late 1948/early 1949?):

> I had a gay session with Leonard Smith and Laurie [Lawrance Collingwood, the producer of the recording] (I was 'officially' invited to hear the *Grimes* recordings – following your letter, of course) and over lunch Leonard agreed and is at once preparing and making tentative plans to *re-record 4 sides*. I hope you will think this suitable.
>
> 1. The Embroidery area (as your secretary wrote in Leonard's letter from you!)
> 2. The Hut scene, if Peter still desires, and the 2nd and 4th sides of the Church scene. I wouldn't like that 4th side to go out with that miserably shaky intonation on my part.
>
> Leonard is also arranging to re-do the prelude to the 'Mad' Scene [Interlude VI] ...

9 Although Joan Cross's letter to Britten quoted in n. 8 makes it clear that arrangements were in hand to re-record the unsatisfactory sides of the recording, no further documentation has come to light to explain why the extra sessions were not arranged, thereby causing the project to lapse. None of the eleven recorded sides appeared at the time. In 1972, with Britten's and the artists' permission, eight sides were issued as part of a boxed set of recordings entitled *Stars of the Old Vic and Sadler's Wells* (RLS 707), and in 1993 all eleven sides were issued in digital transfers by EMI (CMS 7 64727 2). See also John Lucas, 'Goodall and Britten, *Grimes* and *Lucretia*', CD liner notes to the 1993 EMI recording, and Paul Banks, 'Bibliographic Notes and Narratives', a detailed account of the history of this and all other *Grimes* recording projects involving the composer, in PBMPG, pp. 211–28.

592 To Eric Crozier

4 Crabbe Street, Aldeburgh
Oct. 24th 1948

My dear Eric,

It's hard to say an adequate thank you for the Lucretia books,[1] both for the sweet thought of sending them, & above all for the trouble & skill you put into the really remarkable production. It is an extraordinary success I feel, & in quickly glancing thro' the letter press, I don't feel it so far below the wonderful pictures as I feared – indeed, I think your essay on the situation, remarkably clear & true, & very significant today as in 1946! It's nice to have that in circulation.

I shouldn't worry about Morgan. I haven't heard either from him, but I am sure he'll reply in a day or so.[2] His mind works slowly, & he probably has other absorptions.

The NUTG sounds wild[3] – I am sorry you had to go thro' the interview with them, joyless they certainly sound! I feel if they won't commission good & proper we won't do it – after all they'll have to pay the orchestra & the Albert Hall, & they won't get the electricity for nothing either. It was stupid of them to raise the matter with you.

Wandering Scholar.[4] My feeling is that we should do it with the small orchestra (his [Holst's] boiling down) which means just our band. The parts will have to be copied, possibly by B & H if they will be interested in publishing it. But there's no great hurry (it's not a long job) & I'd like to talk it over with Erwin & Imogen if we could all meet when I come up in the middle of November. Casting is not easy. Peter, yes; George[5] yes; Rose,[6] if possible – Jennifer[7] could sing but never act it. The husband is a snorter – a sort of Roy Henderson when younger. Jimmy Sharp[8] is the best bet – I don't [know] whether Denis[9] could, & there's not character yet enough in High Cocks'[10] voice. I'll think about it. (Rehearsals look adequate.)

Yes, let's go on with the Film-Opera[11] – but keeping 1950 as the sort of earliest date. I'm sorry I show my feelings so much that [Alexander] Shaw reacted as he did – nice of you to comfort, though.

I hope Nicolas broadcast position is clear now.[12] No promises made by me to Morley – but that whole position is incredibly vague; is 28 Dec. fixed?

Dear Eric, this letter is a horribly scrappy scribble, but I'm trying to catch the post, & not forget anything. The work is progressing slowly & painfully, & I'm bad company (poor Barbara). But I suppose it'll come right one day.

Love to you, & to Nancy. The second broadcast of the Charm[13] was even more confused than the 1st – I was furious. I've now listened to 4 broadcasts in one week, & every single one was interrupted, & impossible to hear clearly.

Peter doesn't seem wildly happy in U.S.A., but I hope will get good work done, & have a nice rest.

Best of luck with Nicolas – I do look forward to seeing what you do with it.[14]

Lots of love & many, many thanks again,

In haste,

BEN

P.S. Please thank Nancy for her sweet note – & say how sick I was about last night.

1 The symposium on *The Rape of Lucretia* (RLEC), which Crozier had edited

(although he is not identified as the editor on the title page). Crozier wrote
to the composer on 21 October:

> Here are two copies of the *Lucretia* book for you, and I do hope that it does at least
> suggest a little of the admiration and love that all those who know the opera well
> feel for it – and for you. I wish we could have a similar book for each of your operas.

The volume's contents comprise: 'Foreword' by Britten, 'The Libretto' by
Ronald Duncan, 'Lucretia: 1946' by Eric Crozier, 'The Libretto: The Method
of Work' by Ronald Duncan, 'The Design of Lucretia' by John Piper (the
volume was illustrated with eight colour plates of Piper's costume and set
designs), and 'Musico-Dramatic Analysis' by Henry Boys.

2 Crozier's letter to Forster is lost, but it was evidently concerned with the
search for a story suitable for adaptation as Britten's next full-length opera.
Forster's reply to Crozier (24 October 1948; at BPL) reads:

> Unluckily I have not got my mind on to a subject yet, which is the real feebleness of
> this letter. I must write to Ben also. My feeling is that you ought to start and do the
> thing – calling on me to look over your shoulder when you will. There seems to me
> good reason that Ben should not yet write again about the sea. I was attracted to
> Margaret Catchpole at first.

It was to be only a few more weeks before Britten proposed Melville's final
novella, *Billy Budd, Foretopman*. See also BBMCPR, p. 45.

3 Crozier wrote on 23 October 1948:

> I went to see the Secretary of the Union of Townswomen's Guilds and Kathleen
> Merritt [Music Adviser]. We discussed in general terms the subject for a cantata for
> them, length, and possibilities of rehearsal, without arriving at any definite deci-
> sions, and I collected some literature (very dull, too) about the NUTG. The only
> positive thing that happened was that they wanted to discuss the cost of the com-
> mission, which I said I couldn't discuss without you, and finally they pleaded
> poverty, and asked whether it need be a commission at all, and wouldn't the sale of
> copies, etc., be payment enough. I referred them to Boosey & Hawkes, not wishing
> to get involved in the matter [. . .] their main idea was that the cantata should
> express the general idea that woman had now arrived at her full adulthood, but I
> felt that they saw 'woman' and 'adulthood' and 'female suffrage' and all those fine
> things through a pair of iron-rimmed spectacles spelling NUTG, and were con-
> fined by an excessive enthusiasm for their own small furrow. [. . .] The next move
> is with them – to make some suggestions about particular subjects, and to
> approach B & H. They want the cantata to begin rehearsing in autumn, 1949.

Kathleen Merritt had first approached Britten in September 1948 with a
view to his not only composing a new piece for the NUTG, but, moreover,
arranging an unspecified choral work by Purcell for their anniversary concert in September 1949. Britten suggested Imogen Holst might be able to
arrange the Purcell work (presumably for women's voices), although in fact
she was unable to undertake the task. As late as July 1949, Kathleen Merritt
still hoped for a cantata from Britten but the project foundered because of the

NUTG's unwillingness to accept the need for a proper commissioning fee.

4 Gustav Holst's one-act chamber opera, *The Wandering Scholar*, Op. 50 (H. 176), with a libretto by Clifford Bax, 'founded on an incident in Helen Waddell's *The Wandering Scholars*', which was composed in 1929–30 and first performed in 1934. The EOG was to broadcast the opera in the BBC Third Programme on 5 January 1949 (repeated on the 11th), with Pears (Pierre), Margaret Ritchie (Alison), Frederick Sharp (Louis) and George James (Father Philippe); Ivan Clayton conducted and Eric Crozier was the director. See also Letter 595.

Imogen Holst notes in *A Thematic Catalogue of Gustav Holst's Music*, p. 179:

The first performance [of *The Wandering Scholar*] was only a few months before [Holst's] death, and he was too ill to go to it. He had no chance to revise the work. There are pencil queries in the margins of his vocal score, such as 'Tempo?', 'More?', 'More harmony?'.

Britten and Imogen Holst therefore prepared a new edition of the score, first performed at the Cheltenham Festival on 9 July 1951, which

answered these queries by making some alterations in speeds and dynamics [. . .] Britten adapted Holst's own suggestions for cueing-in for single wind, and wrote new parts for harp and percussion so that the work could be performed by the English Opera Group's orchestra.

Imogen Holst wrote to Britten the day after the broadcast in January 1949:

Last night was a wonderful experience. I do hope you managed to hear it reasonably clearly. It was, I'm afraid, a terrific strain for Clayton as he was feeling so ill – but I thought he did magnificently. Eric's additions [revisions made by Crozier to Clifford Bax's libretto] are just right – the whole thing sounds truly comic – much more so than I was prepared for. And the singers were *superb*: – I'm completely converted to George James – the part couldn't have been better. As for Peter, he made it sound as if the part had been specially written for him, and I kept on thinking it *had* been!

Your orchestral alterations I knew would sound right, but OH how much *more* than right they were. Bless you for what you have done [. . .]

The 1949 broadcast was undoubtedly mounted with a view to reviving the opera on stage and thereby completing a definitive edition of the score. At the Cheltenham Festival performances the cast was: Roderick Jones (Louis); Gladys Whitred (Alison); Max Worthley (Pierre); and Ian Wallace (Father Philippe). Norman Del Mar conducted, and Basil Coleman was the director. The vocal score of Britten's and Imogen Holst's edition was published by Faber Music in 1968, with a full score following in 1971. See also Imogen Holst's 'Introduction: *The Wandering Scholar*', in Gustav Holst, *Collected Facsimile Edition of Autograph Manuscripts of the Published Works*, vol. 1: Chamber Operas, pp. 77–8.

5 George James, English bass-baritone, who sang the roles of Peachum (*The Beggar's Opera*, 1948) and Collatinus (*The Rape of Lucretia*, 1949).

6 Rose Hill (d. 2003), English soprano and comedienne, who created the role of Lucy in Britten's realization of *The Beggar's Opera* in 1948, a role she took again in 1950 and 1954. Rose Hill was also well known as a singing actress, particularly in West End revues. In the 1980s she was a member of the cast of the popular BBC Television series *'Allo, 'Allo*. See also the obituary by Anthony Hayward, *Independent* (1 January 2004) and afterword by Elizabeth Forbes, *Independent* (5 January 2004).

7 Jennifer Vyvyan (1925–1974), English soprano. Following studies at the Royal Academy of Music and privately with Roy Henderson and Fernando Carpi, Vyvyan joined the English Opera Group in 1948 to sing Jenny Diver in Britten's realization of *The Beggar's Opera*, subsequently playing Nancy (*Albert Herring*) and the Female Chorus (*The Rape of Lucretia*). She quickly became a valued colleague of Britten, and her position as one of the leading members of the EOG was confirmed by her creating two major Britten roles: the Governess in *The Turn of the Screw* in Venice in 1954, a remarkable performance perfectly captured in the 1955 Decca recording under the composer's direction; and Tytania in *A Midsummer Night's Dream* at Aldeburgh in 1960. At Covent Garden she was the first Penelope Rich (*Gloriana*). Her final Britten role was Mrs Julian in the BBC television production of *Owen Wingrave*, a role that Vyvyan was too ill to re-create by the time *Wingrave* reached the stage (Covent Garden, 1973). Vyvyan was also a noted concert singer. She sang the soprano solo role in *War Requiem*, and participated in Britten's recordings of *Spring Symphony* and Purcell's *The Fairy Queen*.

8 Frederick ('Jimmy') Sharp (1911–?), English baritone, who studied at the Royal College of Music. Sharp shared the role of Junius with Edmund Donlevy in the first production of *The Rape of Lucretia* at Glyndebourne in 1946, and returned there the following year to create the role of Sid in *Albert Herring*. Although he became a principal baritone with the Sadler's Wells Company in 1947, Sharp returned to sing with the EOG in 1954 (*Love in a Village* and *A Dinner Engagement*).

9 Denis Dowling (1910–1996), New Zealand baritone who sang prinicipally with Sadler's Wells Opera (later English National Opera) from 1939 until 1984. He was a member of the English Opera Group from 1947 until 1948, singing Junius in *The Rape of Lucretia*, Sid in *Albert Herring* and Ben Budge in *The Beggar's Opera*. He returned to the EOG in 1971 to sing Merlin in Purcell's *King Arthur*. See also obituaries by Alan Blyth, 'From farmyard to Figaro', *Guardian* (24 September 1996); by Elizabeth Forbes, *Independent* (25 September 1996); in the *Daily Telegraph* (26 September 1996), and by Alan Blyth, *Opera* (December 1996).

10 John Highcock, English bass, who sang with the EOG from 1948 to 1950 (*The Beggar's Opera* and *Let's Make an Opera*).

11 Crozier wrote to Britten on 23 October 1948:

Alexander Shaw came to see me yesterday. He says Grierson is all for the opera-film, and suggested a length of about 40 minutes, the film to be produced by himself (Shaw) and directed by Muir Mathieson. I said that you could not be ready with such a film until spring 1950: he accepted that, and thought the film should appear for the 1951 Festival [of Britain].

Shaw also asked whether you and I could work with himself and Mathieson as a unit on this kind of project, as he had the impression you didn't much like him or Muir. I told him I thought this was an exaggeration [...]

He now wants me to write again to Grierson, and to try and see John [Redcliffe-] Maud [...]

This 'opera-film' project, which united Crozier and Britten with John Grierson, a colleague of Britten's from the documentary film world of the 1930s, and with some of those who had been responsible for *The Instruments of the Orchestra*, was evidently bound up with Britten's and Crozier's intention to compose a children's opera. Crozier wrote to Britten on 2 August 1948:

After seeing the two films at the Ministry of Education the other day, I think we are probably mistaken in aiming to combine an opera-film for children with a children's opera for the stage. The problems in each medium are immensely different, and the *most* important difference seems to me that on film an hour's experience is expressed in about twenty minutes of screen time. I was very much struck with this fact in the Ballet film, which lasted eighteen minutes, and was in three parts [...]

I think that if you would like to do the third short film in this series that the Min. of Ed. would very much wish to have, on Opera, it should be constructed and written only for film use. And the first question is: does one do what the other two films have done – explain the ordinary methods and performance of opera by using a stage and a group of singers to illustrate the component parts? – or keep off direct explanation, keep away from the stage, and create a *film-opera*, that would be good enough in itself to attract children with the possibilities of the medium, and expand the idea of 'opera' in their minds.

A possible subject for this kind of film-opera might be to take two villages, like those we saw when we drove round the Framlingham district [...] Each village of two–three hundred inhabitants, with a keen rivalry between their teams of bell-ringers and their choirs of boys, and with an annual competition organized by their respective vicars for bell-ringing, singing and sports, which could include every-thing from darts in the local pubs to a miniature Oxford–Cambridge boat-race (in complement to the vicars) between the village choirs on the river joining the two places. And the prize an outdoor supper given by the losing village to the winning one. I suggest this subject just as a starting-point for discussion; – as one suitable for a great variety of treatment both visually and musically, and into which a story could be woven that might lend itself to gay and simple operatic treatment.

Crozier goes on to outline what proved to be the 'entertainment', *Let's Make an Opera*, composed in 1949:

For the children's opera for the stage, I think our idea of doing two acts (I) prepa-ration, and (II) performance, is right. And it seems to me the main thing is to estab-lish our limitations in order to use them for making a good story. Supposing our cast were

(1) Four young grown-ups (Sop. Ten. Alt. Bass)
(2) Three boys (Gathorne, Johnny, Sammy)
(3) Two girls (Juliet, Sophie)
(4) A mixed chorus of boys and girls from a particular school.

The three principal boys and two girls would have to be over fifteen, to avoid tiresome restrictions and legal bothers. The chorus could be any ages, provided it was properly supervised by its schoolmaster. And we would probably have to see that a chorus was prepared locally in each place we went to perform, which would mean keeping all the chorus-work (music and stage) pretty simple [. . .] I will try to have some kind of a story for the stage-opera roughed out before we meet again.

In an undated letter (?August 1948), Crozier told Nancy Evans:

I had lunch with Ben yesterday, when we hit upon a good and sound idea for the children's opera. I spent until late last night writing it out in story form and took the results to him this morning. It will use three adults and eight children, in three short scenes, and most of the plot is carried by the children themselves, with a small share for the adults. It concerns a group of children kidnapping and concealing a wretched little chimney-sweeper's boy and restoring him to his parents. The opera proper, about 45 minutes long, will have a preface in play form, showing the business of writing, rehearsing and staging it.

In the event, Britten did not accept the commission for the film-opera project.

12 The first UK broadcast of *Saint Nicolas* was given in the BBC Third Programme on 6 January 1949, preceded by an introductory talk by Eric Crozier. The broadcast was repeated on 9 January. Pears sang the title role, with Margaret Schofield and John Wills (piano duet), Geraint Jones (organ), the gallery girls' choir directed by Ursula Nettleship, choristers of the London Choir School, the BBC Choral Society, and the Jacques String Orchestra conducted by Leslie Woodgate. Although the *Radio Times* describes this as the first broadcast performance, this had already taken place on 9 December 1948 from Hilversum. There evidently had been some confusion about who – the BBC's own forces, or Morley College under Michael Tippett – was going to have the opportunity to broadcast *Saint Nicolas*.

13 Britten refers to the repeat broadcast on 24 October of the performance already transmitted on the 18th.

14 Crozier's *The Life and Legends of Saint Nicolas, Patron Saint of Children*, illustrated by Douglas Rolf. The BPL's copy is inscribed by Crozier: 'For Ben and Peter with gratitude from Eric. October 1949'.

593   To Imogen Holst

4 Crabbe Street, Aldeburgh
Oct. 27th 1948

My dear Imogen,

How are you? We are both all right – Peter in U.S.A. (but hating it) & me here (sitting in front of a roaring sea & loving it!).

I listened to the Planets[1] last night, & in spite of a shocking reception (all radios are impossible now) & a worse performance[2] I really enjoyed lots of it. Of course I do see the weaknesses, the problems not really solved, but there is such musicality there & above all a really wonderful imagination I do now want to get to know Egdon Heath,[3] which must I feel have the same quality together with a greater discipline & a higher, more consistent level of ideas. Tell me, is Neptune[4] really balanced, in form I mean? Of course Sir A.B.[5] did nothing to balance the orchestra, to blend the colours, to make the tempo live – but even then, is it musically digested? I like so much of it so much that I was wondering . . .

About Wandering Scholars – we are now settled about the early January broadcasts as you probably know. As we are regarding these largely as pre-rehearsals for the Summer season I should like to try out the reduced scoring (probably adding the percussion & harp as I suggested in London) – but if you feel strongly that it should be done with the original, as it is virtually a first performance, I shall absolutely agree! When we have decided this point we shall have to go into the matter of material. I <u>did</u> mention the matter to Hawkes who was very interested in publication – if you agree, & they make up their minds then that settles the problem of copying. Otherwise we'll have to think of someone, or something else. About casting – Peter for the Scholar, George James for the Priest – is that all right? I have suggested Frederick Sharp for the husband (a high baritone?) – if we can get him – otherwise it may have to be Dennis Dowling – Kraus is too heroic, & none of our other baritones is good enough vocally. Or have you suggestions? (always bearing in mind the <u>stage</u> production). I want Rose Hill for the wife, if you agree – she has such character, & if you can take the rather hard little voice, sings awfully well. Otherwise it is very difficult; most of our young singers are too inexperienced (& I feel that Mabel Ritchie would be a bit too skittish & old for the part on the stage, but she would sing it charmingly – if on the light side). Would you be an angel & let me know what you feel about all this?[6] – After all you know it so much better than I, & you know your father's ideas too. About conductor – Susskind[7] may be coming as our regular conductor next year, & I'd like him to do it. But dates are difficult as he's up in Scotland all the winter, in which case I shall have to do it myself – Any objections?

Another dreary business matter – is March 19–20 fixed for Peter & me at Dartington? (19 – Nic.; 20 – Schöne Müllerin),⁸ because otherwise we are wanted abroad for that weekend. We'd <u>much</u> rather come to you if we can – but otherwise if it has fallen thro' could you let us know, & we'll absolutely understand. There are one or two young musicians, possibly for your course, that I want you to meet over Christmas.

Please excuse scribble – but Spring Symphony calls! –

With love,
yours ever,
BEN

1 Gustav Holst's suite for large orchestra, *The Planets*, Op. 32 (H. 125), composed 1914–16 and first performed (privately) in September 1918, at the Queen's Hall, London, by the New Queen's Hall Orchestra conducted by Adrian Boult.

2 A live broadcast in the Home Service of the BBC from the Royal Albert Hall, London, with the BBC Symphony Orchestra conducted by Sir Adrian Boult. Another instance of Britten's continuing disappointment with Boult's conducting.

3 Gustav Holst's 'Homage to Thomas Hardy', *Egdon Heath*, Op. 47 (H. 172), was composed in 1927 and first performed in February 1928 at the Mecca Auditorium, New York, by the New York Symphony Orchestra conducted by Walter Damrosch. In 1957 Imogen Holst gave Britten Holst's sketches for this work. Four years later, at the 1961 Aldeburgh Festival, on 6 July in Orford Parish Church, Britten conducted the London Symphony Orchestra in a performance of *Egdon Heath*. This performance was released on CD by BBC Legends (BBCB 8007-2) in 1999, where it is described in Paul Kildea's liner notes ('Three 20th-century English Masters') as 'bleak and uncompromising'.

4 'Neptune, the Mystic', the seventh and final movement of *The Planets*, which adds an offstage, wordless female chorus to the orchestral sonority.

5 Adrian Boult (1889–1983), English conductor, knighted in 1937. He was Chief Conductor of the BBC Symphony Orchestra from 1930 to 1950. Although Britten was not alone in his unenthusiastic view of Boult's conducting, the persistence of his negative attitude might be seen as somewhat idiosyncratic. Boult showed little enthusiasm for Britten's music, but did conduct a number of his works, including, in 1937, *Our Hunting Fathers*, when Britten commented after a rehearsal that 'he doesn't really grasp the work – tho' he is marvellously painstaking'. See also Diary for 22 March 1931, n. 1.

6 Imogen Holst's response to Britten's letter has not survived. However, in a later letter (12 December 1948), she writes, 'Under separate cover I'm

sending you the MS full score of *The Wandering Scholar* – it's meant for you to keep as a thank you, but I can't give it you properly until I've found a publisher.' The manuscript full score is at BPL.

7   Walter Susskind (1918–1980), British conductor of Czech birth. After studies in Prague, Susskind became George Szell's assistant at the German Opera, Prague. After the German Opera's closure in 1938, Susskind went to England where he worked as a pianist until he was able to resume his conducting career. From 1943 until 1945 he was Music Director of the Carl Rosa Opera Company, and from 1946 until 1952 Music Director of the Scottish (later Scottish National) Orchestra. A two-year spell in Australia was followed by nine years as Music Director of the Toronto Symphony Orchestra. He was Director of the Aspen Festival, 1962–69, and Music Director of the St Louis Symphony Orchestra, 1968–75.

   Susskind did not take up an appointment with the EOG at this time or any later date.

8   These dates had, indeed, fallen through. The performance of *Saint Nicolas*, with Pears as soloist, was given in the Great Hall, Dartington Hall, on 2 April 1949, with Dartington forces conducted by the composer. It was preceded by Weelkes's 'Hosanna to the Son of David', Purcell's Chacony for strings, and Gustav Holst's 'How mighty are the Sabbaths'. Pears and Britten had planned to perform Schubert's song-cycle, *Die schöne Müllerin*, at Dartington the day following *Saint Nicolas*, but because this recital was their first after several months' break, a less taxing programme of early English songs, Schubert lieder, songs by Frank Bridge, Gustav Holst and Britten ('Let the florid music praise' and 'Fish in the unruffled lakes'), followed by the customary group of folksong arrangements, was given instead. The suggestion for the change of programme appears to have come from Imogen Holst.

594   To David Webster
Royal Opera House, Covent Garden
[*Typed*]

4 Crabbe Street, Aldeburgh, Suffolk
27/10/48

Dear David,

   Thank you for your letter[1] which I have waited until I came down to the peace and quiet of Aldeburgh before answering.

   I appreciate highly your kind gesture about the new opera for 1951. I certainly intend to write a big new one[2] which should be ready, if everything goes to plan, by that year but I am afraid I can in no way commit myself about a first performance until it has at least begun to materialise. Then I shall have to see if your Company includes the kind of people I should want for the opera, and above all whether you and Karl [Rankl] could agree my demands.³

Please do not think that I do not understand at least a few of your problems in casting, but as you know our views on this matter differ so strongly that before I commit myself to any production of a new work at Covent Garden I shall have to be very strongly assured that my demands will be met.

I hope that Peter Grimes is going well although I am afraid my suggestions with regard to Ellen, Boles and the Rector have not been followed.⁴ However, I suppose I must be grateful for the one performance with Joan and Peter in January.⁵

I am afraid I shall be away from London for some weeks now and so there will not be an opportunity for us to meet.

With best wishes to you all in spite of our differences,

Yours sincerely,

BENJAMIN B.

1   Webster wrote to Britten on 7 October 1948:

I have been waiting to write to you in the hope that we would know something official about the recommendations that the Opera Panel made through the Arts Council to the 1951 Exhibition people suggesting certain official approaches to composers, and needless to say your name was the first mentioned.

These things however appear to be taking much longer than I expected and I think it is high time we wrote you officially to say that whatever steps the 1951 Exhibition take about operas, and they may decide of course not to act at all, we here would welcome a new opera from your pen as soon as you have it ready.

I personally would welcome at your leisure a very preliminary discussion about our joint attitude to the problem, and I look forward to hearing from you some time in the near future.

The '1951 Exhibition' was the Festival of Britain, designed to celebrate the arts and culture of the country as it regained its confidence and exuberance on emerging from the economic gloom and deprivations of the post-war years. It also echoed the Great Exhibition of 1851, the brainchild of Prince Albert, which was held between May and October 1851 in Hyde Park, where the Crystal Palace had been specially constructed to house it. The income generated by the 1851 Exhibition was applied to the advancement of cultural, educational and scientific learning, embodied in the new museums in South Kensington, the Albert Hall, the Royal College of Music and Imperial College of Science and Technology.

Webster, like so many others, had been enormously impressed by *Peter Grimes* in 1945, and wasted little time in mounting a new production at Covent Garden in November 1947. In fact, as a letter Webster wrote to the composer on 15 November 1946 shows, Covent Garden was not only prepared to stage *Grimes*, but was most anxious to commission a new opera from Britten for the 1947–48 season. But Britten, at that time exploring the possibilities of chamber opera – *Lucretia*, *Albert Herring* and the realization of *The Beggar's Opera* – was not to be drawn by their offer, though for a time in early 1947 he was considering an opera set in the period of the English Civil War which was intended for Covent Garden (see Letter 548 n. 1). Webster was also willing for the EOG to come under Covent Garden's administrative umbrella after the demise of the relationship with Glyndebourne. (Although *Albert Herring* was premiered at Glyndebourne in the summer of 1947, the EOG appeared there only as 'visitors'.) See also Lewis Foreman, *From Parry to Britten: British Music in Letters*, pp. 271–2.

According to his biographer, Montague Haltrecht (*The Quiet Showman*, pp. 122–3), Webster turned to Arthur Bliss after Britten's refusal of a commission; Bliss's opera *The Olympians*, with a libretto by J. B. Priestley, received its first performance at Covent Garden on 29 September 1949. See Arthur Bliss, *As I Remember*, pp. 170–82.

But the premiere of *The Olympians*, as Bliss and Priestley subsequently admitted, was not a success, partly owing to the ambition of the enterprise which the fledgling Covent Garden company could not fully realize. In his autobiography (p. 179), Bliss recalled:

When the work was advertised for future performances I received a cable from America, signed by Benjamin Britten and Peter Pears, wishing me 'Good Luck' and intimating that I should probably need it. In truth, I did.

The Olympians, like *Billy Budd*, is an example of a collaboration between an established composer and a major author. Both Priestley and E. M. Forster were interested in and knowledgeable about music, and Priestley, whose experience as a dramatist one might think would give him the edge over Forster as a librettist, had a developed sense of what role music might play in the theatre. For example, his 'modern morality', *Johnson over Jordan* (1939), with incidental music by Britten (see Letter 160 n. 2), sustained an impressive fusion of music, dance, mime, scenery and lighting along with Priestley's own idiosyncratic concept of time to produce a memorable and moving theatrical event.

Britten was away in the United States when *The Olympians* was given at Covent Garden, but Forster attended. E. J. Dent reported to Bliss, on 3 November 1949: 'I met Forster in the foyer, keenly interested; but he said he was unable to buy a libretto at the bookstall.' No doubt Forster the librettist was taking a proper professional interest. He wrote to Crozier on 1 December:

I have been several times to Covent Garden, including *The Olympians*, which was much better than the critics suggested. But I came away from my season possessed of one painful truth: *the words of a 'grand opera' are not audible.*

2   *Billy Budd.*

3   Britten at first intended that the premiere of *Billy Budd* should be presented by the Sadler's Wells Company (which had given the triumphant first per-

formances of *Peter Grimes* in 1945), at the 1951 Edinburgh Festival, and both Ian Hunter (Director of the Edinburgh Festival) and Norman Tucker (Director of Opera at Sadler's Wells) worked hard to make this happen. However, disagreements over financial matters could not be satisfactorily resolved and Sadler's Wells was forced to withdraw. Hunter was reluctant to relinquish such an important premiere and therefore approached Glyndebourne, oblivious to the discomforts and distrust Britten had experienced there during 1947. See Michael Kennedy, 'How Albert became our kind of thing', Glyndebourne Festival Opera programme book 1990, pp. 121–7.

Budd was, of course, eventually to be premiered at the Royal Opera House, Covent Garden, in December 1951. See Letter 718 n. 2.

4 See Letter 580, although there is no criticism of the singer playing the part of the Rector.

5 This isolated performance of *Peter Grimes*, given on 14 January 1949, was conducted by Karl Rankl. Apart from Pears and Cross, the cast included Owen Brannigan (Swallow), Tom Williams (Balstrode) and Edith Coates (Auntie). A review appeared in *The Times* (15 January 1949) describing it as a 'very mixed achievement':

The prologue and first act began the opera well and brought out immediately the dramatic tension which the composer has skilfully varied and sustained throughout. The second act disintegrated, partly because Miss Joan Cross, whose authority in confronting the crowd had strengthened the first act, was unintelligible and ineffective when pitted against the congregation in church. Also there was a disastrous prelude through which the orchestra floundered without so much as a decisive beat from Dr Rankl to rescue them. But when the crowd once more resumed its function as protagonist in the last act, matters mended. Mr Peter Pears's study in schizophrenia might be criticized on the ground that the brutal side of Grimes is overbalanced by the dreamer, but since no one is to say that the two alternating personalities are exactly equal and opposite, it can be granted that he retains the audience's sympathies by a well-conceived and finely executed conception of a difficult part [. . .]

595 To Ralph Hawkes
[*Typed*]

4 Crabbe Street, Aldeburgh
27/10/48

Dear Ralph,

As you probably have heard from Peter, I am now hard at work at Aldeburgh slowly ploughing ahead with the Spring work. The condition of the piece is not yet advanced enough to be able to say whether it will be ready in time for the Boston [performance] in April,[1] but I have not yet given up hope and will report later when I can see my way more clearly.

Thank you for the suggestion of Rodzinski[2] for the Group. I am afraid he really is too grand a person to be able to work with us in the quiet way we need. At the moment we are negotiating [with] Susskind which will be in every way ideal if dates can be managed.

Our plans next year are going ahead well and the economic strain has been greatly relieved by the arrival of the Balcon money.³ We expect to revive Lucretia and Herring in the first part of the season with a new Children's Opera⁴ – if I can find time to write it. Then add, in the second part of the season, The Beggar's Opera to Holst's "Wandering Scholar" and a new makeweight – yet to be decided on.⁵ We expect to have one or two try-out broadcasts of the Holst early in January. It is an interesting little piece and should be a useful addition to our repertory.

Peter reports to me that your negotiations about our tour progress.⁶ He tells me about the projected Los Angeles concert, which I agree to in principle (i.e. conducting the whole concert) but I am not yet convinced that the programme is quite right. But I daresay there is no hurry about this.

I expect the Lucretia production in New York takes up a great deal of your time. I am immensely relieved that you were able to complete the scenery negotiations so well.

I was sorry not to be able to do the extra French Folk Song arrangement that I had hoped to. I hope the stupid selection that I made will not greatly embarrass the show.⁷

Would you please remember to ask [*handwritten*: Peter to ask] Peter Diamand whether Kathleen Ferrier would be free to sing at our Aldeburgh Festival Lucretias on June 10th and 13th?⁸

New York must seem quite European these days with all of you around.

My best wishes to all my friends and my love to Clare – and the best of luck in all your ventures,

[*Handwritten*:] Yours ever,

BEN

[*Handwritten*:] P.S. The enclosed plea arrived from Columbia [University] this morning, & so all I can do is to pass it on! Of course I leave these things to you, & if you think a 'pre-view' at Columbia would prejudice the piece, I agree.⁹ I haven't the <u>happiest</u> memories of the place!¹⁰

1 Hawkes had written to Britten on 13 October 1948:

Any news on the Koussevitzky piece? I am sure to be asked in the next week or two if any date is yet available. Apparently he has no objection to the Dutch performance taking place before, but would this be so if it is ready by April?

Arrangements for the premiere of *Spring Symphony* at the Concertgebouw, in Amsterdam, were already in hand.

2 Artur Rodzinski (1892–1958), Polish-born American conductor. He had been Conductor of the Cleveland Orchestra from 1933 to 1943, when he succeeded Barbirolli at the New York Philharmonic. In 1941 Britten had

written an overture for him. This was originally entitled 'An Occasional Overture' and given the opus number 27, which was subsequently allocated to *Hymn to St Cecilia*. When the manuscript was rediscovered in 1972 at the New York Public Library, the work was renamed *An American Overture*, to avoid confusion with the *Occasional Overture* of 1946, which was commissioned by the BBC for the opening concert of the Third Programme. See also Letter 343 n. 2.

3 See Letters 556 n. 6 and 572 n. 4.

4 *The Little Sweep*: see Letter 632 n. 7.

5 In the event, the 1949 EOG season comprised performances of *Albert Herring*, *The Rape of Lucretia* and *Let's Make an Opera*, the 'entertainment' that incorporated *The Little Sweep*.

6 In an undated letter from New York, Pears wrote to Britten:

Ralph is beginning to get busy on our tour! madly keen of course! I am trying slowly & diplomatically to softpedal it all & to keep it on a small scale, but it takes time! 1st: he wants to know your reaction to this:– [Alfred] Wallenstein offers us the Los Angeles Orchestra for three concerts, same programme at each; it would mean you taking over the whole programme: Purcell–Britten perhaps. What d'you think? The fee is very good – $3000. It would mean a week there rehearsing & doing these 3 concerts. I myself am rather for it – as it would mean a whole week in one place on one programme trying to improve it. But of course it entirely depends on you being willing & able to cope with a whole evening's conducting: eg. Chaconne, Orpheus Brit [Britten's Purcell arrangements for high voice and orchestra, *Suite of Songs from Orpheus Britannicus*], Sinfonia da Requiem, Serenade, Grimes' Interludes. And if you can't face it, then you have only to say so! really my darling! Ralph of course is trying to edge more days in each end – he wants us to catch Q. Eliz. on Oct 15th. I try to push it off to Q. Mary on Oct 22nd. He wants us to stay till December 3rd; I try to keep it November 30th. Well, we may have to give in at one end but not both! I'm trying to keep it to New York & East as much as possible, with just Chicago on the way to the West Coast perhaps. [...] You've no idea the prestige P.G. at the Met. has given you! They are doing it again this season!

7 See also Letter 520 n. 1. The additional folksong orchestration, not achieved at this time but completed in the autumn of 1953, was probably 'La noël passée'.

8 Ferrier was not free for the 1949 Aldeburgh Festival and the role of Lucretia was sung instead by Nancy Evans.

9 The letter from Columbia University has not survived, but it evidently concerned a preview of *The Rape of Lucretia* prior to the sequence of performances on Broadway. No evidence has come to light to suggest that the preview took place.

10 A reference to the first performances of *Paul Bunyan*, given by the Columbia Theater Associates of Columbia University, New York, at the Brander Matthews Hall, in May 1941. See Letter 311 n. 3.

596   To Peter Pears

4 Crabbe Street, Aldeburgh
[28 October 1948]

My darling Peter,

This is only a scribbled note to tell you we're now on the telephone
Aldeburgh 323. It is in Barbara's room – they haven't yet put in the
extension to the dining room, but that'll be along soon. So, if you feel
<u>particularly</u> lonely, ring, of an evening – but it's safer to wire before, just
<u>in case</u> I should be out! I won't ring you unless there's something terrifi-
cally important, or I get similarly lonely. But while your sweet letters
continue to arrive so regularly I think I prefer them to a hectic 3 minutes
with fading, & not daring to say what I really feel . . .

The work is at last progressing, & is on the whole very good I think. I've
done, roughly, three movements including the Nashe[1] – lots of things not
right yet but coming along slowly. I hope you'll be pleased, but you're so
very severe a critic that I daren't hope!

A terrific sea today, most wonderfully beautiful; big racing clouds, lots
of bright sun, & the gigantic waves all white. Don't be jealous, because
you'll be home soon, & anyhow I expect by now you'll have settled down
& feeling easier, & are adoring the work with Clytie. Of course I do see
how tied you must feel, & I expect you're irritated by the provincialism
of so many of the people you meet. I hope by now you have restored
contact with sweet Elizabeth [Mayer] & the family. Nice to see Aaron![2] It
sounds a wild party. I wrote to R.H. [Ralph Hawkes] yesterday, & incidentally said I would agree to the Los Angeles Show – after all I shan't have
been conducting all the summer – I hope!

No particular news – nor letters. We go on evenly from day to day.
Barbara [Britten] & Helen [Hurst] come for next weekend & we all go
over to Lowestoft on Saturday – Arthur & John[3] (coming to Norah
[Nichols]'s for weekend) & Norah will probably come too. Doris Brown[4]
came in. Elizabeth [Sweeting] was here for last weekend, & young Jim
[Butt] for a lesson (very depressed by R.A.F.).

But how I miss you, my darling. I'm planning to come up to London
on 15th (most <u>urgent</u> business!). Be careful. Keep safe & well –

your devoted

B.

(Love to all).

1   The setting of Thomas Nashe's 'Spring' ('Spring, the sweet spring, is the year's
    pleasant king'), which forms the third setting in Part I of *Spring Symphony*.

2   Pears described his encounter with Copland in an undated letter to Britten:

Yesterday morning Ralph & Clare & Betty Bean & I went to a Young person's concert at Hunter College, where they played the Y.P.G. [*Young Person's Guide*]. Too
small an orchestra, and a dreary commentator through a loud speaker, and a dim
conductor called Thomas Scherman. Then we all drove in Ralph's handsome Buick
up to Aaron's house about 15 miles up the Hudson. It was terribly nice to see Aaron
again – I'm really very fond of him. Victor [Kraft] was there too – a bit of a tubby
celestial coal-heaver! and a new girl hanging around. Lots of love to you from
Aaron & he is coming to Europe next spring & will be in England for the Aldeburgh
Festival so I've insisted he comes down! Isn't that exciting? Couldn't he lecture? on
American music?!!
   After lunch Harold Shapero came over & played his piano sonata to Ralph who
is interested. (He was the boy who played his trumpet sonata at Tanglewood in '40
[see Letter 282] d'you remember?) A dreary piece just like Beethoven! My! What
next! Then Aaron played a bit on records of his new Clarinet Concerto for Benny
Goodman. Just Aaron – competent & a bit dull. Then I sang 2 or 3 of the
Michelangelo with Aaron! Very funny! & then we all drove back – & spent a quiet
evening here! William getting up & turning the radio on and off every 8½ minutes!
He's just the same, fidgety as ever – rather a worry to them all because of dizzy &
fainting spells he had a year ago, & he won't relax and take it easy.

Copland did not lecture at the Aldeburgh Festival until 1960, when he spoke
on the subject of 'Music in the Twenties' at the Jubilee Hall on 22 June.

3   John Lindsay (b. 1926), English pianist and a friend of Arthur Oldham,
    with whom he had been a fellow student at the Royal College of Music in
    the early 1940s. It was during Lindsay's student days that he first met
    Britten, when the composer had been invited by Oldham to hear his Piano
    Trio performed at the Cobbett Prize concert. While still at the RCM
    Lindsay and Oldham played to Britten the latter's arrangement of *Simple
    Symphony*, a two-piano version made for the Ballet Rambert. Lindsay was
    one of the pianists in the first production of *This Way to the Tomb* (1945)
    (see Letter 521 n. 4), an engagement that incurred the displeasure of the
    RCM authorities. He was refused permission by the RCM to participate in
    the production. In an interview with Donald Mitchell (10 July 1990; tape
    and transcript at BPL) Lindsay recalled:

You just can't accept ultimatums like that. I thought, 'I'll jolly well give up the
College and blow it.' So I did and Arthur said, 'Well, Ben could do something to
help. Perhaps he'd have some influence with the authorities', and put in a good
word for me. Of course, he wasn't liked at the College at all, so that didn't help.

   After Lindsay's departure from the RCM, Britten did what he could to help:

'Oh, John,' he said, 'I'm going to make a very dazzling offer.' If I left the College he
would continue to pay for me to have my lessons privately with Frank Merrick,
and then he sent me subsequently to Franz Osborn whom Marion Stein was studying with and he thought was very good, and to Erwin [Stein]. I was with Erwin for
about four years, doing this, that and the other.

   As a pacifist, Lindsay registered as a conscientious objector when he was called up for National Service in 1946. Britten introduced him to Stuart Morris (see Letter 381 n. 1), who had represented Britten and Pears at their Tribunals in 1942; Lindsay's appeal, however, was turned down and he served four months in prison, an event that prompted Britten to write with compassion to Lindsay's mother (22 September 1946):

I was shocked & disgusted to hear of John's cruel sentence. But he is a brave boy, & I am sure this dreadful experience will not harm him, but give him added courage & conviction. Am I allowed to write to him? If not, perhaps you would give him my love & tell him that when he comes out there will be great things waiting for him [...]

I know your great sympathy has made all the difference to John. I know that you are suffering nearly as much as he. You have my warmest thoughts.

After working as a répétiteur with the Ballet Rambert, Lindsay eventually settled into a teaching career and his association with Britten faded.

In his 1990 interview, Lindsay provided a fascinating description of Stein's and Britten's abilities as teachers:

Stein was wonderful, because although he wasn't a great pianist himself he taught me so much about music. You know, it just opened so many doorways into what music was all about – so it didn't matter what I took to Stein, he would give me great insight on it.

I went to have a lesson on the Chopin Fourth Ballade and Stein wasn't there [at 3 Oxford Square], and Ben was in. He said, 'I'll help you with it.' And I played this through to Ben and he was absolutely wonderful about it. He just made you feel music wasn't to do with dots on paper; it was to do with an experience in time, and [how] it would sound – it was quite a revelation to see the music from a composer's point of view – how much more insight. Ben was wonderful at seeing the architecture of a piece. I felt I just understood the whole thing after Ben had been through it. He talked about the little bit at the end about being the angels. There's little soft chords come descending down – 'When you get to the angels, you do this.' So that was wonderful.

In answer to a question about Britten's personality, Lindsay replied:

Very warm-hearted – and full of fun and impishness and sort of childishness, this sort of nice childlike nature seemed to bubble out of him. Very bubbly sort of personality and *quick*, very perceptive, as though he had clear sort of flashes of what everything was about all of a sudden. And about his compositions, he *loved* to be told that they were good, even though it was coming from someone who perhaps didn't know very much about it, but if you'd enjoyed his work he just loved to hear you tell him that; and he'd go quite boyish, as though he knew that he deserved the praise but he wanted to be a little bit coy about it. And that was a very nice trait in his character, that he welcomed this being liked so much. I think he did a lot of things because he wanted to be loved and liked.

Turning to Pears's character, Lindsay remarked:

Peter seemed to sort of control Ben. I think he had a lot of influence on whom Ben was going to help and support and like and be interested in working with and who he wasn't. You couldn't get so friendly with Peter as with Ben. Peter was always like the schoolmaster. He was ready to correct you and censor you from a lofty point of view. Ben was a friend who was genuinely wanting to bring out whatever there was in you, not push it down and say it wasn't right or anything. You felt a freedom with Ben, that music was a great adventure; it wasn't something that you did right or wrong, but within limitless opportunities of expression.

Donald Mitchell recalls that when they were walking together through Central Park, New York, in October 1969, Britten remarked to him that on occasion he could be quite fearful about revealing to Pears new ideas he might have in mind for future works, fearful – or perhaps reluctant might be the better word – because he could sometimes be easily disconcerted by Pears's unsympathetic or even hostile reaction, which he found difficult to overcome. (Note Britten's description of Pears as 'so very severe a critic', above.) However, he did not mention any specific instance of a project he had felt compelled to abandon because of Pears's opposition or scepticism. He simply had to be wary about how he aired new proposals.

4   Unidentified.

597   **To Joseph Szigeti**[1]
[Typed]

4 Crabbe Street, Aldeburgh, East Suffolk, England
28/10/48

Dear Mr Szigeti,

I hear from Mr Stein that you are going to play my violin suite next season.[2] I need not say how much I appreciate the honour that you give me by so doing. My only regret is that I shall not be in America to hear one of your performances but I am sure you must be coming to Europe before long and perhaps I shall have the good fortune to hear you play it then.

It gives me particular pleasure that you are playing this piece. Although I wrote it when I was young, it is a work for which I feel considerable affection and which I think is complete in an unambitious way. The four notes on the cover, which should by the way be read without a clef (i.e. it is the pattern not the pitch which matters) are really the thematic basis for the whole work. It is not of any importance really, but may have given me a discipline which I was looking for at that time.[3]

By the way, I have never played the violin; the nearest approach to it were some scattered viola lessons when I was at school; but I have that kind of mind which amuses itself by thinking up 'tongue twisting' as you say, string passages.

You make one or two queries about the tempi of the last movement. There are no misprints here and the metronome marks are I think accurate. Personally to me "comodo" need not necessarily mean slower and in this case means slightly faster – it means 'comodo' in the sense of being without heavy accents and therefore being able to flow along more easily.[4]

I do hope this makes it clear for you. If there are any other queries the above address will find me for many weeks to come. In the meantime my very best wishes to you and many thanks for the honour and pleasure you are giving me.

Yours sincerely,
BENJAMIN BRITTEN

1 American violinist of Hungarian birth (1892–1973), who had been a child prodigy but whose career did not flourish until he was in his mid-thirties. Szigeti was particularly noted as an exponent of Bartók's Second Violin Concerto and gave the premiere of Bartók's *Contrasts*. He was a tireless advocate of Berg, Milhaud, Ravel and Stravinsky.

   Britten had heard and admired Szigeti's playing on several occasions during the 1930s, including a performance of Bartók's First Rhapsody at the 1934 ISCM Festival in Florence. Through Alberto Cavalcanti, a colleague at the GPO Film Unit, Britten was introduced to Szigeti in June 1935, on which occasion Britten showed him some of his music, including the Suite.

2 Szigeti wrote to Stein on 1 September 1948:

   Will you please give my greetings to Britten and tell him that I am going to play his Suite, Op. 6, practically everywhere next Season (I will be playing the Britten at Carnegie in February [1949] and in about twenty cities) and that I am hoping and praying not to get a stroke or something while 'negotiating' that devilish passage in the *Moto Perpetuo*:

   It's about the hardest violinistic equivalent to a 'tongue twister' I've ever encountered! Would Britten write a few lines about the piece, about how it came about (with whom did he study the violin?), what those four notes on the cover refer to etc. [. . .] Am I right in thinking that he showed it to me in MS in the mid-1930s?

3 Britten uses a similar motto device in his *Quartettino* (1930).

4 Stein wrote to Britten on 21 October:

   I had another letter about your Violin Suite and he [Szigeti] refers in particular to some instances in the *Waltz*. He writes: 'Would you be good enough to ask Britten about those misleading tempo indications in the *Waltz*? If *Vivace* ♩. is 67–76, the *più comodo* can't be ♩. 84–88, and *Animato molto subito* again 84–88!! There must be some misprint there!' Szigeti is probably under a misapprehension concerning the meaning of the word 'comodo' which need not mean 'slower'. Unfortunately, the meaning of the tempo expressions has become stereotyped and they represent for few musicians what they really should be – indications of character.

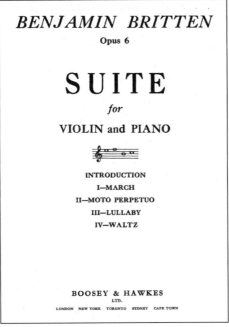

The title page of the Suite, Op. 6, showing the four-note motto.
Despite Britten's comments to Szigeti (Letter 597), the pitches
have been fixed by the inclusion of a treble clef.

598 To Peter Pears

Aldeburgh
[?28/29 October 1948]

My darling –

This is only a scribbled note – Miss Parker has been here taking horrible
official notes, & I am just off on a "thinking walk",[1] but I want just to send
you my love & thanks for your sweet note (no. 2) arrived this morning. I
do hope by now you will have got at least one of mine – this post is terribly
slow: I think the hold-up is between here & London – Also, I hope you're
feeling happier. I think most of the cause of your depression was physical –
it's that damned journey – much more exhausting than it seems, even if it
goes smoothly! Don't work too hard, or see too many people. I hate to
think of you wasting your time on the Betty Beans[2] of this world – or the
R.H's & Cardellis, for that matter![3] I must say the Lucretia project sounds
dotty, but I presume they have got their eyes open. Is Novotná[4] having
a gusset let in to enable her to sing the part? What a dreadful pity about
Aksel[5] – whatever happened? Or are the New Yorkers insensitive to that
kind of singing – for all his weaknesses, he is a cultured & sensitive person,
& artist.

Are you still looking both ways crossing the street? Lesley has had her op. [on her neck] successfully & without complications. Send her a p.c. if you've time – to the Westminster hospital. There is a large photostat of a J. C. Bach aria from Brit. Mus. – do you want it sent?

Much love, my darling – I'm living for Nov. 16th!!

XXXXXX BEN

Long letter from Humps,[5] who sends loads of love to you. (a wonderful letter .. he says "his Classics beak is a stinking good man"!!)

1   Britten's daily habit of breaking his two periods of work at his desk by taking a walk in the first part of the afternoon, during which he would plan out compositions in his head.

2   American music administrator and publisher (1917–2002), who worked in the New York office of Boosey & Hawkes as director of promotion, press and public relations. In 1949 she accompanied Pears and Britten on their coast-to-coast recital tour of the US (see PFL, plate 242) and subsequently remained in touch with them both. In the early 1970s she was director of press and public relations for the New York Philharmonic Orchestra. See also Pears's diary 'The New York *Death in Venice*', in PRPP, pp. 181–200.

3   Pears wrote to Britten on 21 October 1948:

> Last night I was at Ralph's & Clare's flat to meet Mr Cardelli – quite a nice young man who adores Lucretia – but their plans for Broadway production make it sound like – to me – a certain flop. But any way why on Broadway? Because the Met's dead anyway etc. Betty Bean was there – not too bad & very keen and helpful.

4   Jarmila Novotná (1907–1994), Czech soprano who made her American debut in San Francisco in 1939 and went on to appear at the Metropolitan Opera from 1940 to 1956.

5   Aksel Schiøtz (1906–1975), Danish tenor who, after his debut in 1938, refused to sing during the German occupation of Denmark. A noted Mozart and lieder singer, he toured Sweden and Norway in 1945, and broadcast for the BBC. In 1946 he shared the role of the Male Chorus with Pears at Glyndebourne, and in 1948 toured the United States. His career was interrupted by a brain tumour in 1950, following which he had to relearn to speak and sing before resuming his career as a baritone. His final years were mainly spent teaching.

     Pears reported in his letter to Britten of 21 October: 'Poor Aksel had his first concert last night & I gather that it was all rather distressing and tragic.'

6   Humphrey Maud (b. 1934), English diplomat, the son of John and Jean Redcliffe-Maud, and one of the dedicatees of Britten's *The Young Person's Guide to the Orchestra*. See pp. 19–24.

99   To Peter Pears

4 Crabbe Street, Aldeburgh
Sunday [31 October 1948]

My darling Peter,

I am so sorry that I haven't written for a day or two, but I have been awfully busy with other drearier sorts of letters, mostly dictating to little Miss Parker – she is quite good, but alas getting deaf, & we have difficulty in agreeing on the number of s's. Life has been ticking over, each day nearer to your return, thank God.

Barbara & Helen have been here this weekend, sweet people, & nice to have them. We went over to Lowestoft for the day yesterday, with Norah Nichols, Arthur & John. It was a grey, misty kind of day, perfect for the Herrings & that mysterious kind of drab beauty of the Markets. We saw them unloading, & Scotch Girls gutting, & some remarkably fine-looking fishermen & boys, terrifically tanned & strong, in their curiously attractive clothes.[1] You'd have loved it! The day also had its depressing side, of the cemetery[2] & meeting sad older friends. I had a nice little reception at the Library, a deputation to meet me, & I made a little speech presenting them with some priceless (you know in which sense I use the word!) manuscripts.[3] It is quite touching & slightly exaggerated!

I went for a nice long, marsh, walk with Barbara this morning – she is a sweet creature, devoted & sympathetic. It is nice that she & Helen now are considering retiring to a house in this part of the world. I wonder if it will come off. This afternoon, Beth & the three kids have come over to see them, & are now banging at the piano downstairs.

My work has been truculent; it is just the difficulty of finding the right notes (and of knowing what one wants!). 3 pieces are more or less satisfactory; the rest are bothersome. But I refuse to hurry them.

I had a long talk with Lesley on the phone today – she is out of hospital, & at home with Leslie & all the boys around her! Scarcely peaceful – but she seems fine. As soon as she is ready to travel Leslie will drive her down here for some days to recuperate. Morgan may come next week too, which will be nice. Eric has rented a house in Southwold! He seems to be coping all right, but I somehow feel guilty that he's so close & yet not actually here. But I had to be quiet for this work, & having him means Group planning, & Festival discussions.

And you, my darling? Wie gehts? [How are things going?] Better – I hope. I hope there'll be a letter tomorrow, saying that you're well, enjoying yourself, working well, resting a lot, & longing to come home . . . . !

I must post this now & entertain the family. I wanted to send you my Sunday love, & you know you have every other day's love too.

I hope Clytie's better – my love to her & Elizabeth too & all the family.

Your devoted

B.

1   Comments on the Lowestoft herring fleet and fish market frequently
    appear in Britten's diary from 1928 to 1938, and, as this reference in the
    letter to Pears makes clear, the fishing industry remained powerfully evoca-
    tive of Britten's childhood and home town. On 27 October 1937, he writes
    in his diary:

    In the afternoon we go (Beth & I are taken by Mrs W. [Welford] in her car) over to
    Lowestoft & have a lovely time watching the fishing, smelling the sea & the kippers,
    & watching the Scotch girls gutting the herrings – all of which makes me homesick
    in the extreme.

    Britten not only enjoyed smelling the Lowestoft kippers but eating them.
    Donald Mitchell remembers that when on a visit to the composer well
    towards the end of his life he was asked to drive him to a favourite fish shop
    in Southwold to purchase kippers (or was it bloaters?) for consumption the
    next day.

2   Britten and his sister Barbara visited their parents' graves.

3   On 9 August Britten had replied to a letter from A. V. Steward, Borough
    Librarian of the Lowestoft Public Library, announcing the decision of the
    town's Libraries Committee to maintain a 'Benjamin Britten Collection':

    It will give me great pleasure to know I am so adequately represented in the library
    of my home town. Alas, I have not a duplicate set of my works which I could present
    to the library, but I shall look out a decent & (I hope) legible MS of one of them
    which I shall be happy to present to the library – if the Committee will accept it.

    It was not until 30 October, however, that he was able to visit Lowestoft and
    deliver the promised manuscripts to Mr Steward. He made a gift of the
    composition draft of *Holiday Diary*, fair copies of *A Hymn to the Virgin* and
    I saw three ships (*The Sycamore Tree*) and a few items of juvenilia including
    the 'Grand Sonata No. 4' (1925), the manuscripts of which remain in the
    ownership of the Suffolk County Record Office, who placed them on loan
    at BPL in 1987.

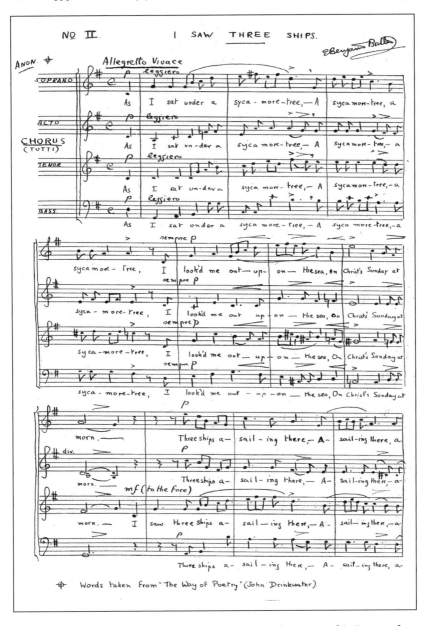

The opening of *I saw three ships* (*The Sycamore Tree*), composed in Lowestoft in September 1930. This manuscript was presented by Britten to the Lowestoft Public Library in 1948.

600 To Peter Pears

Aldeburgh
Nov. 2nd 1948

My darling,

Your two letters have arrived today, one by each post so I feel <u>very</u> spoiled. It is sweet that you write so often, but I am really depressed that you are feeling homesick, & hating New York so. Is it just tiredness, or <u>is</u> the place as hopeless as I feel it is! Your letters reflect so clearly what I remember of it that I get depressed by it, too. Still – it is not so long now – when you get this there'll be not much more than a week left – ! I am planning a little excursion for that weekend. Esther [Neville-Smith] has written to Beth suggesting that she should go & see the school, so I propose to drive her (either direct to Lancing, or leave the car in London, all depending on the petrol situaggers)¹ spend Sunday night at the school, & then meet you on Tuesday morning! I will find the time of the plane from the London office. That is something to live for . . .

I was <u>horrified</u> to hear your news about the Decca records.² That is maddening of them, and quite against agreements & law. I rang up Erwin & Roth about it, & they are consulting together now – they may even get in touch with Ralph. I feel it rather lets us out of doing Illuminations, if we want to . . . It <u>is</u> a bore, because I remember how poor those records were.

The enclosed note came from Basil³ – would you write to him if you think it ought to be changed? I've written him a note saying I'm not happy about the plan of it, but not suggesting anything, till my Lord & Master gives <u>his</u> opinion. (My darling – I <u>hate</u> you being unhappy – it makes me wretched too.)

All the other letters for you are from business, & dull people & can easily wait. No news yet about Oxford Square, alas. The Steins move next week,⁴ I think. I may ring Caplan to see, the next day or so –

My work goes slowly on – I'm fairly sure of the first 3 movements, but not happy about the next two yet.⁵ The formal problem is a corker. But I like the plan of the work, & its atmosphere, anyhow. I've got some sweet poems. I can't wait to show it to you – and it <u>isn't</u> so long now, really it isn't – when you get this letter it won't be. I hope you can get your stuff in London done in time to get down here by Wednesday evening – then you'll have a clear week, I hope. We've got a lot to do – of every kind of thing!! Have you had time to work at the Amsterdam programme⁶ – memorising, etc? I've looked at the Mozart a bit. This isn't a nice tidy letter like yours, my darling, but as usual I'm rushing to post it. Miss P. comes after lunch for letters, & it usually takes most of the afternoon till I'm done, & then I have to rush for the post.

Barbara is well, & is writing herself, I think. I go to Fidelity

[Cranbrook] tonight for dinner. Marjory [Spring-Rice] comes back today, too, so I'm not too cut off.

But I miss you, most dreadfully. Come home quick, & safe & sound.

Your devoted

B.

Love to all Mayers, of course & the friends you see.

1 Petrol rationing, introduced during the war, was not to end until 1950. The addition of '–aggers' was a slang style of the day, later popularized by the cricket commentator Brian Johnson.

2 Pears wrote on 29 October 1948:

I'm furious to discover that Decca have issued "Sweet Polly" "Ash Grove" "Bonny Earl" and "Hey ho!" – quite without our permission! They have recently been sold here & have had wonderful reviews (for what that's worth). But I played "Ash" & "Polly" & they won't do (although the recordings themselves are good). What can we do about it? I'll bring a copy back perhaps. Ralph of course doesn't mind, as the reviews are good & presumably people will buy them, and that's all he wants.

Britten was to write to Harold Sarton at Decca on 19 November, a few days after Pears's return from the United States:

Peter Pears has now returned from America and I have had an opportunity of talking the whole matter of the issue of the Folk Songs in America with him, and have come to the following conclusions.

We are both quite clear that we never passed these records for issue anywhere: and are sure that Mr Gibbs must have known this. We have been again listening to the records and we are convinced that we were right in coming to this conclusion.

The whole matter is very regrettable and we trust that you will not issue them in any other country. This also applies equally strongly to D.R. 992 and the double-sided Schubert record.

Mr Pears is not enthusiastic to have the Faust Aria [of Gounod] issued since the record was made so many years ago; but he agrees that at the time he did pass it.

As to the recording of Les Illuminations; I should feel much happier if this could be done with the Concertgebouw Orchestra. But if this condition would delay too much the making of the records, then I suggest the best alternative would be to use the Boyd Neel Orchestra, augmented, and to record it in a good-sized hall so as to avoid the chamber music effect which spoilt the previous trial record.

If it could be arranged, we think there will be some free dates for us late in May. When we know exactly what these are we will write to you again.

Britten and Pears had recorded 'The Ash Grove' for Decca in January 1944, 'The Bonny Earl o' Moray' and 'Heigh-ho! Heigh-hi!' in June 1945, and 'Sweet Polly Oliver' and 'There's none to soothe' in January 1946. Also recorded in January 1946 were three Schubert lieder, 'Am See', 'Die Forelle' and 'Nacht und Träume'. It has not been possible to trace any information

concerning Pears's recording of an aria (or arias) from Gounod's *Faust*.
Sarton replied to Britten on 13 November:

> I have checked up the outstanding records that have so far not been issued and I
> find we have still the D.R. 992 'There's none to soothe', the double-sided Schubert
> record and the two Operatic Arias.
>
> My impression is that one of the latter was passed, viz. 'All Hail Thou Dwelling
> Pure and Lowly'. Would you kindly confirm that this is in order as I would be very
> sorry to see any further records issued if they had not your approval.
>
> I would like to take this opportunity of reminding you that we are still contracted
> for a record of *Les Illuminations* with Peter Pears and I think it would be a good
> idea if we could set a date in 1949 for this recording to take place. The last conver-
> sation we had on the matter was I think that you decided the Concertgebouw
> Orchestra should do the orchestral part but you finally decided that you approved
> the London Symphony Orchestra making it.

No recording of *Les Illuminations* was made at this period with the
Concertgebouw or London Symphony Orchestra. Pears was later to record
Les Illuminations on two occasions: in 1954, with Eugene Goossens and the
New Symphony Orchestra (Decca LXT 2941); and in 1966, with the English
Chamber Orchestra under the composer's direction (Decca SXL 6316).

3 Basil Douglas (1914–1992), Scottish music administrator and agent, whose
   early aspirations to be a professional singer were brought to an end by ill
   health. During the 1930s Douglas shared a flat with the conductor Trevor
   Harvey and Pears. He was a member of the BBC music staff 1936–51, where
   he originated the popular series *Music in Miniature*. (It is probably to a
   request to participate in one of these programmes that Britten refers in his
   letter to Pears.) In 1951, at Britten's invitation, he became General Manager
   of the English Opera Group, remaining until 1957. (For a detailed account
   of Douglas's time with the EOG, see Maureen Garnham, *As I Saw It: Basil
   Douglas, Benjamin Britten and the English Opera Group, 1955–1957*.) He
   subsequently founded an artists' agency. See also Letter 372 n. 5; Andrew
   Green, 'Rites of Passage', *Classical Music* (22 August 1992), p. 27, and an
   obituary by Maureen Garnham, *Independent* (10 November 1992).

4 To 22 Melbury Road, London W14, where Britten and Pears were to have
   rooms until 1953.

5 'The Driving Boy' (George Peele – John Clare) and possibly 'The Morning
   Star' (Milton), the two movements that round off Part I of *Spring Symphony*. But see Letter 602 where Britten sets out what he has successfully
   sketched.

6 Pears and Britten were to give a recital in the Kleine Zaal of the Concertgebouw on 7 December. The programme included an 'Alleluia' by Purcell,
   arias by Handel, lieder by Mozart, and Frank Martin's *Sechs Monologe aus
   Jedermann*, as well as a group of English songs by Bridge and Holst, the 'Eia
   Mater' from Berkeley's *Stabat Mater*, Britten's 'Fish in the Unruffled Lakes'
   and folksong arrangements by Grainger and Britten.

601 To Elizabeth Mayer

4 Crabbe Street, Aldeburgh
Nov. 5th 1948

My dearest Elizabeth,

Your most lovely parcel has just arrived. My love & great thanks for it . . .
lovely socks, the kind I simply love to wear (especially in this time of cold
East winds) and of course the <u>Thin Mints</u>[1] – what they do to my Muse,
only you know! My dear – thank you so very much.

Peter is so loving being with you, and it is sweet of you to be so good &
kind to him. I am afraid he was a bit tired & worried when he arrived, but
his letters show now that he's now really more relaxed – <u>and</u> enjoying your
lovely food! His work is really good with Clytie, & it is excellent that he
made the decision to do it – <u>I</u> feel. Have you heard him sing yet, properly
I mean, not only mi-mi-mi's? I wonder what you think of the voice, now.

He will have told you all our news – it is so much more satisfactory
than by letter. Now you must really manage to come over next year and
see all the result of our labours. I feel so very sorry that you have only
seen parodies of performances of Grimes,[2] &, judging by what Ralph
Hawkes writes, Lucretia will be no better. I <u>wish</u> I were good enough to
write fool-proof music!

Peter will have told you all about this house – it is a real pleasure to
us, & every day becomes more appreciated. The view as I sit at my desk
writing is beyond description – a deep blue-green sea, flat as a pond, with
big ships out at sea, & small fishing boats being launched from the beach
& fishing right along-shore, with all the seagulls hovering around them.
Not a striking breathtaking view which distracts, but a part of one's life,
like eating & sleeping! Morgan Forster has got to love it too – he comes
in a day or so again. You must get to love it too!

I must post this now. My love, my dearest, & many – many thanks.
Greet all my friends

– your loving

BEN

1 Peppermint continued to be a favourite flavour; see p. 42.

2 At Tanglewood in 1946 and at the Metropolitan Opera earlier in 1948.

602 To Peter Pears

4 Crabbe Street, Aldeburgh
Friday [5 November 1948]

My darling Peter,

This is only a rushed note because I want to get one off before the weekend – I have to go to Ipswich with Margery [Spring-Rice] this afternoon, & there won't be time for letters tomorrow. Your sweet note came this morning. I am glad it seemed a bit more cheerful than the others – I hope it means you're relaxing a bit more. It is certainly exciting about the voice . . . keep it up my dear! I promise you not to write any E♭'s in the Spring Symphony, but don't let it get about, because Webster'll be wanting you for I Puritani,[1] & then won't the Shaw-failures[2] love you!

It is really heavenly here, & I can't wait for you to enjoy it with me. The weather is perfect today – sea looking like a pond, & really warm sun. I sit here at my desk, watching the fishing boats go out, do their stuff, and come back all full up with sprats & herring. We've had some big seas too, which were most thrilling to watch, & to feel the spray. The windows got thick with salt.

My work is going better, but I'm up against quite a snorter of a formal problem now. I've sketched out six already – the Winter one (Orch. & Chorus), the Spenser (3 trumpets & you!), the Nashe (everyone), the Clare driving-boy (with soprano solo), a Herrick Violet (for Kathleen),[3] and a lovely Vaughan one about a shower for you.[4] And now . . . well, we'll see – lots of possibilities; I'd got it all neatly planned, but it's coming out different, bigger (& I hope better!).

I had a nice dinner with Jock[5] & Fidelity the other night – quiet, relaxed, & gay. I'm very fond of those two, especially in that mood. I go off to a wretched R. Music School do in Ipswich with Margery after lunch – a bore, but I must help the poor dear in a rather measly situation.

The enclosed note will amuse you – a typical family reaction – only writing to complain about things, seldom to praise – & what a complaint (not even daring to mention the title, or perhaps he'd forgotten. I suppose it's the F–F–D (sh–sh–sh!).) Dirty old man. Which is he?[6]

I'm taking up the matter about Decca with them here – they mustn't do that kind of thing. I'm quite ashamed to let those records be heard.

Could Jennifer [Vyvyan] do Lucy? For Belgium in March (that is all fixed now)?[7] It doesn't seem likely that Rose can manage it. Eric is pressing for Mabel to do the Holst – it'll probably make you cross, but I can't see an alternative at the moment. The Holst & new piece (Easdale[8] & Guthrie are getting together)[9] must be cast out of Herring crowd.

My dear – it'll only be a week when you get this – unbelievable, but quite long enough. Beth & I will probably motor up to the airport from

Lancing that morning, if there's time. Come back safe & sound, & we'll
have a blissful week together in this sweet house.

Much, much love,

Your devoted

B.

(Lots of love from Elizabeth [Sweeting] who's just rung up)

1 A reference to Bellini's final opera, *I Puritani* (1835), in which the role of the
  principal tenor, the cavalier Lord Arturo Talbot, sings in a high tessitura.
  Perhaps *I Puritani* was in Britten's mind following his own scheme for an
  opera set in the time of the English Civil War.

2 Desmond Shawe-Taylor (1907–1995), Anglo-Irish music critic, who wrote
  for the *New Statesman* (1945–58) and was subsequently chief music critic of
  the *Sunday Times* (1958–83) in succession to Ernest Newman. With Edward
  Sackville-West and Eardley Knollys, Shawe-Taylor occupied Long Crichel
  House, near Wimbourne, in Dorset, where they were later joined by
  Raymond Mortimer, literary editor of the *New Statesman*.

    Shawe-Taylor was an enthusiastic reviewer of Britten's new works, of the
  operas especially, as well as an early devotee of Berg, the premiere of whose
  Lulu he welcomed in 1937, and Janáček, whose operas he admired long
  before they had become established repertory in the UK. His enthusiasm
  however was often found wanting by Britten; hence his ironic version of
  Shawe-Taylor's name. With Sackville-West, he wrote the influential *Record
  Guide* (1951), while it was Shawe-Taylor who contributed the 'Discography'
  to DMHK. He was appointed CBE in 1965. See also obituaries by Patrick
  O'Connor, *Guardian*; Michael De-la-Noy, *Independent* (both 4 November
  1995) and David Cairns, *Sunday Times* (5 November 1995), and in *The
  Times* (3 November 1995).

3 'Welcome, Maids of Honour', destined to be the first movement of Part II
  of *Spring Symphony*.

4 'Waters above', the second movement of Part II.

5 John ('Jock') David Gathorne-Hardy, 4th Earl of Cranbrook (1915–1978),
  whose wife Fidelity was the first Chairman of the Aldeburgh Festival (see
  Letter 576 n. 4). Lord Cranbrook contributed 'The Suffolk Countryside' to
  TBB, pp. 21–38.

6 Pears's uncle, Steuart Pears (1859–c.1951), sometime Superintendent–
  Engineer of Public Works in Madras, had written to his nephew concerning Britten's arrangement of the folksong 'The foggy, foggy dew':

  I confess that some of your 'modern' utterances are beyond me, possibly my fault
  or misfortune. But I heard last night a recorded song of yours which made me
  distinctly sorry. You will probably know which one I mean without my describing
  it in detail. I heard it some months ago, but I thought you were then actually

singing it and I hoped it would be soon forgotten. But now that I know that you
have had it recorded I cannot help writing to ask whether on serious consideration
you do not agree with me that it would be much better stopped if possible, by
destroying the record or otherwise . . . now that the record is bound to reach hundreds or thousands of places where it will be heard by innocent and susceptible
boys and girls there can hardly be two opinions but that it must do immense harm.
'It is impossible but that offences must come' (I quote from memory) 'but woe
unto him through whom they come.' Do think about it and do what you can.
[Quoted in CHPP, p. 145]

The reference is to St Matthew 7:50, 'It must needs be that offences come;
but woe to that man by whom the offence cometh!'

7   The performance(s) of *The Beggar's Opera* did not materialize.

8   Brian Easdale (1909–1995), English composer and pianist, who studied at
     the Royal College of Music with Armstrong Gibbs. During the 1930s he
     composed music for documentary films, including several for the GPO
     Film Unit (it was in fact Britten who brought him into contact with the
     Unit), and acted as musical director for various theatres, notably the Group
     Theatre. In the 1940s he composed the scores for two celebrated
     Powell–Pressburger films: *The Red Shoes*, for which he won an Oscar, and
     Black Narcissus. He and Tyrone Guthrie wrote the opera *The Sleeping
     Children* for the English Opera Group. See also Letter 148 n. 1; Kevin
     Macdonald, 'The composer who scored', *Guardian* (20 March 1992); and
     obituaries by Kevin Macdonald, with contributions from Moira Shearer
     and Blue Johnson, 'Music with a touch of magic', *Guardian* (31 October
     1995) and in *The Times* (18 November 1995).
          In an interview with Donald Mitchell (22 July 1992; tape and transcript
     at BPL), Easdale recalled making the published two-piano arrangements of
     Britten's *Soirées Musicales* and Piano Concerto, attending the first perform-
     ance of *Our Hunting Fathers* ('I remember having lunch with Vaughan
     Williams, Jack Moeran and Ben'), and Britten introducing him to Mahler's
     Das Lied von der Erde in the 1936 Bruno Walter recording. Mahler was not
     their only shared enthusiasm, for Easdale remembered attending Marx
     Brothers films with Britten, who was – and remained – a great fan. For a
     time from October 1937, Britten rented a room as a London pied-à-terre in
     Easdale's house at 38 Upper Park Road.
          During the war Easdale was conscripted and served in India. After
     Easdale's demobilization, Britten was once again in touch with him. When
     they met, Easdale recollected, 'He said, "I heard you've been in India.
     Would you write [. . .] something based on India?" And I did this – I called
     [it] *Bengal River* [. . .] and I went up that summer to conduct it at the
     Festival in Aldeburgh. The first performance of the chamber orchestra
     version of *Bengal River* was given in the Jubilee Hall on 12 June 1949.

9   Brian Easdale's one-act opera *The Sleeping Children*, with a libretto by
     Tyrone Guthrie, was to receive its first performance at Cheltenham on

9 July, in a double-bill shared with Holst's *The Wandering Scholar*.
Both operas were produced by Basil Coleman and conducted by Norman
Del Mar.

603 To Peter Pears

4 Crabbe Street, Aldeburgh
Nov. 9th 1948

My darling Peter,

This may or may not reach you before you leave – I am rushing it off to
post just in case I'm lucky & the posts work as they should. It is <u>thrilling</u>
that you're coming a day or so early. I hope very much to be at the airport
to meet you, but if there are terrific delays, or eccentricities of arrival, I
<u>may</u> miss you, in which case, you'll find me at Oxford Square.

I'm not sure whether the Lancing thing will work or not as a result this
weekend – Beth may go alone, or if you felt inclined we might all drive
down. But I think you'll probably not want to go, especially if the journey
is delayed or difficult. Don't worry, we'll leave this till you arrive.[1] I can't
<u>wait</u> for the arrival of the plane, my darling – you'll hear a great rattle as
you land, & it will be my heart beating.

Much, much love,
Your в.

1 Pears had written to Britten the previous day telling him of his plans. The
   letters had crossed in the post:

> I <u>do</u> hope this won't upset your plans with Lancing too much. Don't bother to meet
> me – & I'll come down too to Lancing! I'm longing to see you again. New York has
> definitely seemed a great deal more tolerable now that the end is in sight – ! We had
> a quiet weekend with William and Elizabeth – drove up to the Wallings [the lawyer
> Metcalfe Walling and his wife] for lunch – nice to see them again – & I went last
> night to Poulenc & Bernac's first recital here & after to Doda Conrad's for a party.
> They were well received & have very good notices but there was a fatal lack of
> warmth and colour in the performances – Schubert! Nacht & Träume! Uh uh!

604 To Henriëtte Bosmans

4 Crabbe Street, Aldeburgh
Nov. 9th 1948

My dear Jetty,

Welcome to England . . . . ! I am so sorry not to be able to greet you in
person – I am here, working madly and dare not leave while the new
"masterpiece" (!) is in a precarious state. I do hope you will enjoy your
stay here, & have nice concerts.

I am sorry not to have written to you before, but the Piano Concerto broadcast was such a disappointment.[1] It was <u>terribly</u> difficult to hear anything; stations kept butting in and there is enough happening in the work itself without an Italian Opera, or a French musical comedy at the same time! You seemed (what little I could hear) to have understood the piece very well, my dear; I realise what you said about the conductor. It does need more brilliant & lively playing & the second movement quicker & more of a waltz – but y<u>ou</u> couldn't do anything about that. The last movement seemed to be going well – but it was impossible to tell, I am afraid – so disappointing. But my thanks for spending so much time & gift on my baby piece!

I will do (eventually!) what you ask for Bertus van Lier,[2] & look forward lots to seeing you in December!

No – my dear, I am NOT at all rich! My mother left me enough money to buy a little house, & otherwise I live entirely by pushing this old pen, & being a nice background for P. Pears to sing against! So don't throw me up because of idle gossip – pl<u>ease</u>!

Love, & best wishes for a lovely concert – & see you soon.

BEN

1 Henriëtte Bosmans had broadcast Britten's Piano Concerto on 20 October, on Radio Hilversum, with the Radio Philharmonic Orchestra conducted by Albert van Raalte (see Letter 590).

2 Dutch composer and conductor (1906–1972), who had studied composition with Pijper and conducting with Scherchen. As a conductor he was particularly admired for his annual performances of Bach's *St Matthew Passion* in Rotterdam, in which Pears was a regular participant for many years (see Letter 576 n. 1). In 1949 Pears was to be the tenor soloist in van Lier's most significant composition, *Het hooglied*, based on *The Song of Songs*, for soloists, chorus and orchestra.

Van Lier had requested from Britten a short article on *Saint Nicolas*.

605 To Eric Walter White

4 Crabbe Street, Aldeburgh

Nov. 9th 1948

My dear Eric,

I am so very sorry not to have acknowledged your letter, & the wonderful book[1] before. I had to go away the day they arrived, & I am only just back.

I have glanced thro' the book, which is wonderfully impressive. I must really write a note to Hürlimann[2] to congratulate him too. I cannot really judge the translation, as my German isn't really stylish – but it (my

German) will be much improved by reading the exciting things you say about me & about [*word missing*]! I do thank you, Eric, for the tremendous amount of work you have given to a rather difficult & trying job! It is difficult indeed to write about a chap when he's still conscious, especially a touchy one like me, & who is changing so much as I am. I think you have done a fine job, & as far as I am concerned a most sympathetic & understanding one. I am looking forward to our celebration dinner. Most unfortunately it cannot be the (Jan) 1st – since Peter is up north that day, & I am already committed for that night (E. M. Forster's 70th birthday). Would (Dec.) 28th (Tuesday) be possible? Perhaps you'd let me know.³

I'll write a Joggy, Joggy Dew one of these days⁴ – if only to make you bring out a new edition of the book. The title suggests endless possibilities!

With many thanks & congratulations,
Yours ever,
BEN

1 See Letter 574 n. 2. Britten's copy is inscribed on the half-title page: 'E. W. WHITE [to] BENJAMIN BRITTEN [in friendship & with the greatest admiration. Eric W. White / Nov. 11, 1948]'. The words enclosed within [ ] are handwritten. If the date of the inscription is correct, then Britten must have received an earlier copy of the book, perhaps direct from the Swiss publishers.

2 Martin Hürlimann and his wife, Bettina Hürlimann-Kiepenheuer, were directors of Atlantis Verlag, Zurich, the publishers who had commissioned White's biography of Britten. The book is dedicated to Bettina, one of its translators into German. In 1957 Bettina Hürlimann invited Britten to make a setting of a poem from *Des Knaben Wunderhorn* for her husband's sixtieth birthday: the result was *Einladung zur Martinsgans*, an eight-part canon for voices and piano (see p. 462), which remains unpublished. See also Bettina Hürlimann, *Seven Houses: My Life with Books*, translated by Anthea Bell. In 1973, when Britten was awarded the Ernst von Siemens prize, it was Martin Hürlimann who made the speech in honour of the composer (subsequently published in 1976 as *Laudatio auf Benjamin Britten*).

3 The proposed meeting is confirmed in Britten's diary for 28 December by the entry 'Eric White'. There is no mention of E. M. Forster, however, for the night of 1 January 1949, presumably because illness forced Britten to cancel; see Letter 610. P. N. Furbank reports in his biography of the novelist, *E. M. Forster: A Life*, vol. 2, p. 283, that it was William Plomer and Joe Ackerley who organized the seventieth birthday party at a restaurant in Soho. Furbank lists the guests: Britten's name does not appear. Britten had responded to Plomer's invitation on 21 November 1948, before his illness:

I have made myself free for the evening of Jan. 1st – because I couldn't bear to miss such an occasion. But Peter alas has to be up in the North that night – singing the

Britten's unpublished *Einladung zur Martinsgans*, composed in 1957.
The voices in this eight-part canon enter at two-bar intervals.

Messiah, & those engagements are horribly sacred, & booked ages ahead, so he cannot get out of it. He is very sorry.

4   Britten refers to an amusing misprint. On p. 132 of White's monograph, in the Chronological List of Works, for the year 1948, the item entitled 'Folksong Arrangements: (Book III, British Isles)' contains the following entry for the fifth song: 'The Joggy, Joggy Dew'. It should, of course, have read 'The Foggy, Foggy Dew'.

606   To Ralph Downes[1]

[*Typed*]

4 Crabbe Street, Aldeburgh, Suffolk
11.11.1948

Dear Ralph Downes

I am very excited that it is you who have been appointed Consultant to the L.C.C. [London County Council] for the new organ in the proposed Southbank Concert Hall.[2] It will be wonderful to hear the results of your scheme because, as you know, you are one of the few organists (dare I say [*handwritten*: the] only one [*handwritten*: !]) whose playing and registration I whole-heartedly admire. What I am sure we shall get is something miles away from Wurlitzer organs one is so tired of hearing in our major Cathedrals and Concert Halls – but something which is worthy of the great music written for the noble instrument.

Heartiest congratulations and with every good wish,
Yours sincerely,
BENJAMIN BRITTEN

1   English organist (1904–1993), who exerted a considerable influence on organ design in the UK from the 1950s onwards. After studies at the Royal College of Music and Oxford, Downes initially pursued his career in the United States before returning to London in 1936 on his appointment as Organist of the Brompton Oratory, where he remained until 1977. A distinguished recitalist and ensemble-player, he appeared at the first Aldeburgh Festival in 1948 and maintained an unbroken run to 1976; he returned for three memorable recitals in the early 1980s. Downes's innate musicality made him a superb accompanist, and he established himself as Britten's preferred organist throughout the 1950s and 1960s. At the composer's request, he prepared the ad lib. organ parts of *A Boy was Born* (1955 revision) and *Voices for Today* (1965). He published an informative and often amusing account of his life entitled *Baroque Tricks: Adventures with Organ Builders*. See also obituaries in the *Daily Telegraph* (30 December 1993) and by Marc Rochester, *Independent* (1 January 1994).

2   Downes had been appointed design consultant for the new organ to be

installed in the Royal Festival Hall (apparently known in 1948 as the 'Southbank Concert Hall' because of its location on the south bank of the Thames). The instrument he and the builders provided, while controversial, signalled a refreshing change in organ design in the UK, particularly in its favouring of baroque-type sonorities. The organ's inauguration in 1954 was an occasion for which Britten had intended to compose an Organ Concerto, with Downes as soloist. Britten's bursitis during the autumn of 1953 prevented his meeting the deadline and, reluctantly, he was forced to withdraw. He was to write to Downes on 2 December 1953:

I only want to add to you personally how deeply sorry I am that I cannot do the piece for you, but I hope it will only be [a] postponement, and that one day we may work on the concerto together.

The project, however, was never revived.

607 To Mary Behrend

4 Crabbe Street, Aldeburgh
Nov. 25th 1948

My dear Mary,

Thank you for the lovely box of fruits. They have been the greatest of successes, & have considerably added to the festive spirit of the last few days.[1] Thank you & all of you for the kind thought, & welcome gift! Peter has been here for a few days – not long enough to relax completely after the strain of the U.S.A. visit. But strain that that may have been, it was very worth while, and he has benefited greatly from his lessons. He is off to Switzerland on Saturday,[2] & I meet him in Holland next week. By the way, he gave me that Spenser Gore[3] for my birthday! I think he mentioned it to you) – & it is a most lovely picture – as fresh & spontaneous as one could imagine. It stands up proudly besides the little Constables & Turner, & the big Piper.[4] The Boudin is a joy as ever – & we always think of you when we look at it![5]

My new piece [*Spring Symphony*] progresses slowly – it is an enormous work; perhaps the most involved & serious I have ever done. I look forward to your reactions when you hear it.

Our love to you all as ever – & thank you for the sweet present.

With love,
BEN

1   Britten celebrated his thirty-fifth birthday on the 22nd.

2   Pears was to take part in a performance of Britten's *Serenade* at the Théâtre Municipal, Lausanne, with Edmond Laloir (horn) and the Orchestre de la Suisse Romande, conducted by Paul Sacher.

3 Spencer Gore (1878–1914), English artist, who trained at the Slade under, among others, Philip Wilson Steer. It was, however, his association with Sickert and Pissarro that contributed more decisively to his development as an artist. Pears gave Britten Gore's *The Haystacks, Richmond* (1913). In September, Pears had written to Mary Behrend about his intention to buy a picture for Britten:

> I am more & more inclined to buy a Spencer Gore – I want to have another look at the landscape I have in mind. John Minton I am not awfully attracted by, though I admit his character & skill. Lowry I know not – I will enquire about him & see. There are quite a number of <u>agreeable</u> young painters – but I should like to find something more than that. Anyway it's fascinating looking about. I only wish I had more time to spend on it.

See also Paul Banks and Philip Reed, *Painting and Music*, p. 16.

4 Britten refers to the oil of John Piper's *Albert Herring: Drop cloth of Loxford* (1947), which was specially painted for presentation to Britten during the interval of the first performance of *Herring* at Glyndebourne in 1947. A similar design was used as the cover of the vocal score of *Herring* published by Boosey & Hawkes. See also Banks and Reed, p. 16.

5 Eugène Boudin (1824–1898), French painter, who had a profound influence on Monet. Britten refers to Boudin's watercolour *Les Crinolines* (1865), which Pears owned until it was sold in 1985 at Sotheby's in aid of the Aldeburgh Appeal to raise money for the Aldeburgh Festival and the Britten–Pears School.

608 To Serge Koussevitzky
[*Telegram*]

[Aldeburgh]
[December 1948]

PLEASE FORGIVE DELAY. HAVE BEEN ABROAD. MUCH HONOURED BY KIND INVITATION TO TANGLEWOOD NEXT SUMMER BUT SINCERELY REGRET COMMITMENTS IN EUROPE PREVENT IT.[1] SYMPHONY WELL ON WAY TO COMPLETION.

GREETINGS
BENJAMIN BRITTEN

1 Koussevitzky wrote to Britten on 29 November 1948, inviting him to join the teaching faculty in the Composition Department at Tanglewood the following summer. Koussevitzky also asked Britten if he would conduct the proposed performance of *Spring Symphony*.

Volks-Universiteit te Rotterdam

CONCERT

OP MAANDAG 6 DECEMBER 8 UUR, Nw. ZUIDERKERK

PROGRAMMA

1e GEDEELTE

Uit te voeren door V.U.-Koor en -Orkest
onder leiding van Bertus van Lier

1. 2e SUITE in b voor strijkorkest en fluiten
   J. S. Bach   (1685—1750)
2. AVE MARIA voor a capella koor
   Josquin des Prez   (1450—1521)
3. AVE VERUM voor koor en strijkorkest
   W. A. Mozart   (1756—1791)
4. „WAS MEIN GOTT WILL, DAS G'SCHEH' ALLZEIT"
   Koraal voor koor en strijkorkest
   Heinrich Schütz   (1585—1672)
   (bew. Bertus van Lier)

2e GEDEELTE

Continentale première van
BENJAMIN BRITTEN'S CANTATE SINT-NICOLAAS

Medewerkenden:
> V.U.-KOOR en -ORKEST
> JONGENSKOOR van de H. Willibrorduskerk
>   (door bemiddeling van P. de Keyzer)
> Tenor-solo: PETER PEARS (St. Nicolaas)
> Organist: PIET VAN DEN KERKHOFF
> Pianisten: LILLY VAN SPENGEN en GERT VAN DER STEEN

Het geheel onder leiding van de Componist

> Tekst van ERIC CROZIER
> Vertaling van HANNO VAN WAGENVOORDE

Gaveau Concertvleugel - Vertegenwoordiger: Rijken & De Lange

Omslag: Beeldje van G. Héman.

PRIJS *f* 0.50

Programme for the Continental premiere in Amsterdam of *Saint Nicolas*
on 6 December 1948, appropriately the saint's feast day

609 To Eric Walter White

4 Crabbe Street, Aldeburgh
[early December 1948]

My dear Eric,

Thank you so much for sending "The Little Chimney Sweep"[1] – it looks charming, & what a coincidence! Also a coincidence that Eric C. had not either read Kingsley,[2] although I was brought up on him & am still devoted. I do remember vividly the Reiniger[3] Film but I had no idea that you had made it into such a nice book. Our story is quite different – but do you think we should change our title so as to avoid confusion?

I shall be replying to your other, formal note, but not before I get back from Holland I'm afraid (end of next week) as it is a difficult letter to write.[4] I have already had an awkward, & abortive, correspondence on the same subject with D. Webster.[5]

In haste & with thanks,
Yours ever,
BEN

1   White had written to the composer on 24 November:

> Seeing that you and Eric Crozier are working on an opera called *The Little Sweep*, I thought it might amuse you to hear of a work of mine called *The Little Chimney Sweep* which was published in 1936. Unfortunately the book came out in a limited edition, and no spare copies seem to be available. I am therefore sending you a set of the proofs; and from this you will see that *The Little Chimney Sweep* arose out of a commission Lotte Reiniger received to make a silhouette film about London Street Cries. Curiously enough – it seems hardly credible, I must admit – I had at that date not read *The Water Babies*!

The proofs of White's book are at BPL.

2   Charles Kingsley (1819–1875), whose fairy-tale *The Water Babies* (1863) was an important source for Britten's *The Little Sweep*, tells the story of Tom, a chimney-sweep, who runs away from his employer, the bullying Mr Grimes, falls into a river and is changed into a water-baby. Britten, *c.*1916, had taken part in a dramatized version at the Sparrow's Nest Theatre, Lowestoft, in which his mother played Mrs Do-as-you-would-be-done-by. In the speech Britten made on receiving the Freedom of Lowestoft (28 July 1951; reprinted in PKBM, pp. 108–11), he recalled that he was 'dressed in skin-coloured tights, with madly curly hair, trying desperately to remember the lines spoken by Tom the water-baby'. See PFL, plate 15.

3   Lotte Reiniger, German-born film-maker (1899–1981), and inventor of the animated silhouette film. It was for her 1935 GPO Film Unit 'film ballet', *The Tocher*, that Britten composed his 'Rossini Suite' (see Letter 100 n. 2). It has not been possible to identify the 'silhouette film about London Street Cries' mentioned by White, but might a page of musical sketches in

Britten's hand, headed 'Street Cries' at BPL be connected with Reiniger's film? See also Rachael Low, *Documentary and Educational Films of the 1930s*, pp. 149–50.

4 Neither White's 'formal note' nor Britten's response have survived, but they must surely have concerned the commission of what in the event was to be *Billy Budd*. (White was currently a prominent member of the Arts Council.)

5 See Letter 594.

610 To Lesley Bedford

Aldeburgh
[Postmarked 16 December 1948]

My dear Lesley,

I am so very sorry not to have written before, but as you might imagine Holland was a tremendous rush, & since I got back life has been very complicated. The trouble is that my tummy went all wrong again – even on the journey over! I had to cancel one concert, & only staggered thro' the others – Poor Peter, singing beautifully all the time, had a very worrying time. Anyhow, here I am, back in Aldeburgh in bed – & the Doctor warns me that it may be three months of just lying around this time.[1] I am X-rayed tomorrow so I shall soon know the worst – but I believe that even if it isn't serious, the rest will be enforced. What a bore! At least I can go on writing, but all our concerts & tours abroad to go – I could kick myself! And I shan't see your kids in the holidays, now nothing!

Please tell Leslie that I don't know when I shall be able to go over & see about that boat[2] – hope there's no hurry! Is he well? Give him lots of love from me – & the kids when they get home. I hope you have a rip-roaring Xmas.

Thank you so much for being so nice to me before I went off – I loved being with you.

I hope the neck is absolutely well now – how goes the singing? I hope you didn't go to Aberdeen, & enjoyed Dave's performance – & Stewy's![3]

Lots of love – please forgive pencil.

BEN

1 Britten was at first believed to have a stomach ulcer but further examination revealed this not to be so, though he remained exhausted and depressed for several more weeks to come.

2 Britten was thinking of buying a boat and wanted advice from Leslie Bedford, who was a keen yachtsman.

3 Presumably Lesley Bedford's sons were involved in an end-of-term concert at Lancing.

511   **To Peter Pears**

Aldeburgh
[mid-December 1948]

My darling,

I am so very sorry that I was beastly on the 'phone last night – selfish
& unsympathetic. Only excuse is – it's a bit of a shock all this business, &
I got _madly_ depressed. It is one thing thinking gaily about a possible free
time, & another being ordered to rest for 3 months, & to have to forgo all
the things with you, my darling, to have to be separated too, for so long
from you at times when I thought we'd be travelling & working together –
& I _do_ adore working with you, & think we really achieve something
together. My only way of coming sane thro' this miserable time is to think
that this will make it possible for us to continue working together in the
future, & if I _didn't_ rest we might have had to cut it out altogether –
because I was physiologically unsuited for it. Which I know I'm not!

Here are the few letters – I'll send on any others that arrive. Take care of
yourself, my darling – you are so precious, not only to me, but to so many
many people. I wish you were broadcasting on an audible wavelength –
because then I'd be able to enjoy you – but at any rate I shall be able to
hear that you are well.

All my love, my angel. You are very sweet –
too sweet to me,
B.

P.S. I'll let you know definitely when I hear about length of time from
Dr Acheson.[1] Only we'd better say now – nothing till end of Jan. Could
you tell Peter D. [Diamand]? Give them my love, if you see them.
(ALCI??)[2]

1   Britten's Aldeburgh doctor.

2   A reference to Agenzia Lirica Conartistica Internazionale, Britten's and
Pears's Italian agents for their recital tour of Italy in April 1949.

612   **To Piers Dunkerley**[1]

4 Crabbe Street, Aldeburgh
Ben Ald 312   Peter 347
Dec. 23rd 1948

My dear Piers,

It was very nice to get your letter; I often wondered what you were up
to, & where.[2] I am glad that on the whole the kind of life you lead seems
to please you. I certainly envy you getting to know lots of new places –

not seeing them as I usually do, just for a night or two & then passing on. Malta doesn't sound so attractive as Hong Kong, but the sailing must be terrific. My puny sailing on Suffolk rivers & Norfolk Broads must be tame in comparison though one can get great fun out of it. I hope to have a boat round here soon – which reminds me, as you see by the address, I have left the Mill at Snape & am now living in a nice house, bang on the sea in Aldeburgh. Do you remember Aldeburgh Lodge,[3] where we used to come to play matches from South Lodge? It is a small fishing town, very charming, with nice people. I can't spend much time usually here, as I have so much travelling to do – but now, as it happens, I shall see almost too much of it, because I've been ordered a three months' complete rest by the doctors, & shan't be allowed to stir from the place. I have been overworking (so they say!) & have got to relax a bit. The result is that I'm crotchety, & take it out on my friends! But I hope very much to be up & around if you get back for some spring leave. I've got to be in Italy & elsewhere sometime,[4] but let me know when it is to be, & if by any happy chance I'm down here you must come & inspect the place.

Peter is well, immensely successful, & consequently terribly busy. I expect him down here tomorrow just for Christmas. Beth & her three kids also thrive, the eldest Sebastian is at a prep-school near here. Barbara is hoping soon to be able to leave London & come & live nearer Beth & me – Beth, I don't know if you remember, lives near Woodbridge, where Kit is a prospering doctor, & I am coped for by a housekeeper, quite adequately. That seems all the general news. I write lots of music, which some people like & some hate – just as before, though perhaps a bit more so! I personally think the music is getting better – there is one new opera I think would please you a lot, called Albert Herring, in which Peter & Joan Cross are extremely funny. Perhaps it'll be on when you are in England next year.

I hope this will get you at least by New Year, for which you have my very best wishes. Please greet your family when you write to them – & don't forget to let me know when you're coming back, because it would be nice to see you indeed –

Yours ever,

BEN

1   Piers Montague Dunkerley (1921–1959). While Dunkerley was a pupil at South Lodge, Britten's preparatory school, and later at Bloxham School, Oxfordshire, he enjoyed a close friendship with Britten, who was then in his early twenties. Although, on Britten's side at least, there would seem to have been a degree of sexual ambivalence in the relationship, Britten assumed the role of mentor and surrogate father to the fatherless boy. During the war Dunkerley served as a captain in the Royal Marines, was

wounded and taken prisoner. After the war he continued his service career, returning to civilian life in the 1950s. Difficulties in adjusting to life outside the forces and in his relationship with his fiancée (he had invited Britten to be his best man) appear to have led to his suicide by seconal poisoning. Britten included him as one of the dedicatees of *War Requiem*, an indication that he viewed him as a casualty of war. See also Diary for January 1936, n. 1.

2 Dunkerley was currently stationed in Malta. It was a life that was, as he described it to Britten, 'very dull, a glorified Cook's tour, with the occasional event to mark its progress'.

3 A preparatory school in Aldeburgh during the 1920s and 1930s.

4 Britten and Pears were in Italy from 21 January until 12 February 1949.

613 To Wilfred Derry[1]

4 Crabbe Street, Aldeburgh
Jan. 1st 1949

My dear Wilfred,

Thank you for your nice letter – yes everything <u>is</u> rather a bore, & this all takes a bit of getting used to . . . I'm not the type that takes resting & relaxing easily.

I was a little jealous to hear of your "monster" carol service, all taking place there without me enjoying it too. But I am comforting myself that I may have the chance at the end of my fallow period to get down to Lancing & see you all. It is disappointing that I can't get up to Nicolas next week – but Eric is going to do what he can about getting you & the chaps into the studio (it's suddenly become very difficult and strict), & will ring or wire you to this effect.[2] I don't think it'll be nearly as nice a performance as <u>we</u> all gave! A score <u>should</u> be coming for you in a day or so . . .

I know what you feel about John Alston[3] – I've known him for ages, since we were scruffy little boys together. He can be insensitive, but it is mostly a feeling of insecurity & inadequacy (he hasn't <u>quite</u> lived up to his promise), & I'm hoping that Esther's [Neville-Smith], yours, & Lancing's influence may smooth & civilise him. I'm glad that he overlaps with Jasper too – that ought to show him that other things are important besides clockwork & O.T.C. discipline – what a <u>dreary</u> thing that Corps can be, & how much I prefer your Scouts! I hope you get to Finland.[4] Most interesting. Peter & I have schemes of getting into Russia, which may be possible – but difficult since I have personally been singled out as the "bad" composer![5] Anything rather than accepting tacitly this dreadful

curtain – I feel anyhow a much more iron-like curtain down the Atlantic
... but that's another story!

Every good 1949 wish to you & love
from
BEN

1 The Reverend Wilfred Derry, Chaplain of Lancing College, Sussex.

2 Derry had told Britten that he had written to Pears to enquire whether
   it might be possible for some Lancing boys to attend the BBC studio
   performance of *Saint Nicolas* on 6 January 1949.

3 John Alston (1914–1996) was the son of the viola-player Audrey Alston, a
   family friend of the Brittens in Lowestoft, who first introduced Britten to
   Frank Bridge. See Diary for 16 February 1931, n. 3; Diary for 17 November
   1932, n. 1, and Donald Mitchell's interview with John Alston (20 June 1988;
   tape and transcript at BPL). In 1948 Alston succeeded Jasper Rootham as
   Director of Music at Lancing College, a post he held until his retirement in
   1974. Derry had written to Britten on 29 December 1948:

   I can't reconcile myself to Jasper's leaving us, & what little I have seen of John
   Alston doesn't incline me to more reconciliation, but perhaps it will be all right in
   the end. Anyhow he is going to have a bedroom in Esther's house so [she] can
   indoctrinate him during the next 2 Terms [...]

   See also the obituary by J. F. Bell in *Lancing College Magazine* (Advent
   1996), pp. 21–2.

4 Derry's scout troop had received an invitation to Finland for the summer
   of 1949.

5 The Soviet composer Tikhan Nikolayevich Khrennikov (b. 1913), who came
   to prominence for his musico-political wholesale condemnation of
   Prokofiev, Shebalin and Shostakovich in 1948, also turned his attention to
   Western composers who were 'infected with formalistic defects, sub-
   jectivism, and mysticism, and bereft of ideological principles'. According to
   Khrennikov, Britten's music, as well as that of Berg, Hindemith, Krenek,
   Messiaen, Menotti and Stravinsky, displayed 'a conglomeration of wild
   harmonies, a reversion to primitive savage cultures ... eroticism, sexual
   perversion, amorality, and the shamelessness of the contemporary bourgeois heroes of the twentieth century'. Khrennikov's remarks are quoted in
   Boris Schwarz, *Music and Musical Life in Soviet Russia, 1917–1970*, p. 225;
   Schwarz notes that the full text of Khrennikov's speech is to be found in
   Nicolas Slonimsky, *Music Since 1900*, pp. 691–9.
      No information has come to light concerning Britten's and Pears's
   'schemes' for visiting the Soviet Union at this time, and it might therefore
   be assumed that his denouncing by a representative of the Soviet authorities effectively prevented any visit being made. It was not until 1963 that

Britten and Pears made the first of several trips to the Soviet Union, encouraged by their friendships with Rostropovich, Vishnevskaya and Shostakovich himself. See also PRPP, pp. 151–2.

614 To Peter Pears

as from: 4, Crabbe Street, Aldeburgh
Jan. 4th 1949

My darling,

I am writing this from Beth's – seated in the nursery before a nice fire watching Sebastian make obscure-looking "Slag Dump Catchers" or what not, with his Meccano. Beth has gone in the Morris [car] & pouring rain to Ipswich to meet Robert & John[1] to come to stay today, & this afternoon I beat a (not too) hasty retreat when Jock fetches me & I go to Glemham till Thursday; then back to Aldeburgh. Rather contrarily Barbara P. [Parker] hasn't gone away as planned – not till tomorrow & won't be back till Monday when Eric & Nancy & Barbara B. [Britten] will be leaving – but I feel it's all actually best that way. Don't worry about that situation, my dear, it has got on to quite a discussable (I won't exaggerate & say "unemotional" quite!) level, & will be solved amicably I am sure, for us all.[2]

I was relieved to see that you were spared Sargent on Sunday – probably only a negative advantage, but anyhow an advantage, I expect.[3] I hope the rehearsals go well in London now, & that Ivan [Clayton] comes up to scratch. He's got quite a mouthful to chew, especially as regards the orchestral side. I hope they play well & co-operate with him. I'll listen, but I have no hopes of hearing anything recognisable.[4] Perhaps the Cranbrook wireless will be better. One or two things about Old Nic. Try & bully Woodgate[5] into the right tempi, please (& Ursula – especially don't let her take the Gallery Girls in the Pickled Boy section too quick). I've been thinking about the difficulty you have in number III.[6] I feel it all will be better if done with a more nasal coloured tone – 'specially the Heartsick phrases – don't try & do them too big, but accentuate the

two notes (𝄞) & I think that will give you the agonising quality.

Don't worry about the crescendo on the G at (11) on "Still"; leave it to the orchestra, even taking the note off earlier if you want. I've marked it thus in the score. Above all don't worry about it! In the last number[7] – don't let Leslie get too slow in the middle section – drag him on. If the chorus doesn't make enough noise in the crescendo, let the tenors go up an octave at "Glory be" as we did in Holland.[8] Sorry, dear heart, that this letter is all instructions, but I feel a bit worried about not being there. Ring up if there are any queries – Rendham 24.

I hope you are well, & not getting wet in this filthy weather. How was the party? – I expect Sophie was in a state of nice excitement, especially as Harewood[9] was there!

I'm getting better my dear, but don't think work will really be possible until later after we've been away, perhaps. I can't wait till that moment. Have you any suggestions <u>where</u> we can go?

– Darling, you have just rung so most of this letter has become super-fluous. But I'll send it because so little love can come over the telephone wire! – especially when people are listening. Please give my love to all the chaps in the shows, orchestra & singers <u>&</u> to Grace Williams[10] if she's there – and a kiss!

Lots of love,
Your devoted
B.

1   Britten's elder brother, Robert (1907–1987), and his son John, Britten's nephew (b. 1932). The composer had already suggested to Pears that Robert's arrival at Beth's might precipitate his own removal to the Cranbrooks. The relationship between the two brothers was often difficult and testy.

2   In letters from January 1949 Eric Crozier reports to Nancy Evans that relations between Barbara Parker and Britten had reached a crisis and that she would have to leave. Crozier told Evans (17 January 1949), following an 'explosion' between the housekeeper and her employer:

> It really is most essential that Barbara Parker should go away, for she is becoming a millstone round Ben's neck by the obscure struggle for the centre of attention that lies, I think, at the root of her troubles. Sorry though one is for her in her difficulties, it does seem wrong that Ben should be exposed to constant and sapping emotions when he most needs repose.

3   Presumably Malcolm Sargent had cancelled an engagement in which Pears was singing. No further details have come to light.

4   See Letter 590 n. 6.

5   Leslie Woodgate (1902–1961), English conductor and chorus master. He was Chorus Master of the BBC Choral Society from 1934 to 1961. He was associated with Britten's music from the 1930s, when he conducted the first performance (a broadcast) of *A Boy was Born* (see Letter 42 n. 2) in 1934 and the first broadcast performances of the Two Part-songs and *A Hymn to the Virgin* in 1935; in 1939 he directed the incidental music for *The Sword in the Stone* (see Letter 175 n. 1). Following Britten's return to the UK in 1942, Woodgate conducted the first performance (a broadcast) of *Hymn to St Cecilia* (see Letter 374 n. 4) and the following year the first broadcast

performance of the revised version of *A Ceremony of Carols*. Woodgate also conducted the musical contributions, including those by Britten, to *A Poet's Christmas* (1944) and the first performance of *Saint Nicolas*. See also IC1/2.

6 'Nicolas devotes himself to God'.

7 No. IX, 'The Death of Nicolas'. The 'middle section', in which the chorus intones the Nunc Dimittis, begins at fig. 61.

8 It was a change Britten adopted in the published score of the cantata.

9 George Lascelles, 7th Earl of Harewood (b. 1923), English operatic administrator and writer, a grandson of King George V and Queen Mary, and a first cousin of Queen Elizabeth II. Harewood began contributing opera criticism to the *New Statesman* and *Ballet and Opera* in 1948, and two years later founded *Opera*, which he edited until 1953. He held posts at the Royal Opera House, Covent Garden, from 1951 until 1960, and again between 1969 and 1972, before becoming the influential Managing Director of Sadler's Wells (later English National) Opera from 1972 until his retirement in 1985. He was Artistic Director of the Leeds Festival, 1958–74, and of the Edinburgh Festival, 1961–65. He has edited four successive editions of *Kobbé's Complete Opera Book* (1954, 1976, 1987 and 1997).

   Harewood first met Britten in 1943 through Joan Cross, but was drawn more closely into the composer's circle through his marriage to Erwin Stein's daughter, Marion, in 1949. In 1952 he contributed an important biographical 'portrait' of Britten – 'The Man' – to DMHK, pp. 1–8. He remained a close and trusted friend, adviser and confidant of Britten's throughout the 1950s and early 1960s (he and his wife were the joint dedicatees of *Billy Budd*; see Letter 717), but after the breakdown of his marriage Britten and Pears effectively brought to an end their friendship with him; they were by no means alone in ostracizing Harewood, who has written extensively of his friendship with Britten – and his sadness at its collapse – in his memoirs, *The Tongs and the Bones*.

10 Welsh composer (1906–1977). She studied with Ralph Vaughan Williams at the Royal College and privately with Egon Wellesz. She and Britten had shared an important friendship before the war, strengthened by their association with the Macnaghten–Lemare concerts, and remained in touch in the post-war period. See also Diary for 11 July 1932, n. 2, and IC1/2.

615 To Peter Pears

4 Crabbe Street, Aldeburgh
Jan. 9th, 1949

My darling,
     Eventually your sweet letter arrived – almost one whole week after you wrote it – but it couldn't have arrived more opportune-like, because I was

at the bottom of the well, & it was the best bucket & strongest rope to lift me out of it! It was a darling letter, quite a vintage one, & I won't tell you exactly whereabouts on me I carry it, in case it'll make you blush.

Eric, Nancy & Barbara are here – it is nice having them, & Annie is coping splendidly. She is a grand cook, & I can't think what Barbara P. was making all that fuss about. We help all a bit of course. Peter Diamand came down for the night, but he's staying at the Wentworth.[1] It is nice to hear all his news, very amusing & hair-raising about U.S.A. – but dear, o dear, <u>how</u> I hate the thought of it all . . . You cannot imagine the inanity of all those Lucretia notices;[2] they still arrive, almost by every post – what an ass Ralph is to send them!

I'm feeling <u>heaps</u> better, my dear – & the rum did no harm, honestly it didn't. If I hadn't had it, probably much greater & chronic harm might have been done – at least to the furniture & wireless, if not to me! So in future, I don't think I shall try to listen to wireless at all – try & forget that it is all happening. After all I know Old Nic (& Leslie!), & I've heard the Holst & can't anyhow hear P.G. How's that going? – I at least hope that Rankl gets your tempi right. I'm so glad that you bullied Leslie about the Nic one, now you can do the same with Karl! Isn't it strange how one's sympathies have all gone over to Webster & Rankl in this silly Beecham business?[3] Nancy suggested that we should club together & send a muzzle to the silly doddering old fool!

Beth & Robert & John are coming over to tea this afternoon – it'll be nice for the latter two to see the house & sea & all, but I can't pretend I look forward to it.

I gather, you secretive old thing, that you <u>have</u> had the furniture moved from Oxford Square! I am so glad, because now at least you'll have a quasi home to go to with all your things. It's so nice that it has turned out better than I at least feared.[4]

I must <u>really</u> get up now & entertain my guests. So goodbye for the moment, my darling. I can't bear to think that it is still a week longer – but I suppose I must. Next week has sorted itself out neatly – the Mauds on their own initiative have suggested coming on Friday (which leaves us free for the following one!), & Morgan is coming on Monday week.

By the way, if you want a cheque just let me know how much – I hope to get Egypt news[5] from Fidelity [Cranbrook] soon.

<u>Enormous</u> & glorious parcel from Elizabeth [Mayer] – loads of food – very sweetly done up. Nice letter from Clytie [Mundy] – <u>if</u> you had a moment do write to her; she wants to hear from you, darling.

All my love, my everything, my darling,

Take care of yourself.

Your devoted

B.

1   One of the sea-front hotels in Aldeburgh, often patronized by musicians appearing at the Festival.

2   The following are among the reviews surviving at BPL. Olin Downes, 'At the Theatre', *New York Times* (30 December 1948), wrote:

Opera, in the truly modern sense of the word, blossomed last night on Broadway. The effect of the production of *The Rape of Lucretia* in the Ziegfeld Theatre was as revolutionary as it was exhilarating. The text of Ronald Duncan is not only sing-able, despite certain artificialities and some high-falutin', but is an effective dramatic vehicle. The score is far and away the most mature, flexible and distinguished composing that Benjamin Britten has yet done for the lyric theatre. It runs thin in places, but is never inexpert; at climactic moments it supplies the indispensable atmosphere and stimulus.

Then we come to the casting, the stage direction and the superbly unified elements of the presentation. There was a cast, singularly well appointed, of which the members were not only personable to the eye, but capable of intelligent acting as well as of song. There was not a bad voice in the lot. There were several exceptional ones. Vocal virtuosity, where it was appropriate, was not lacking. The orchestra of twelve players gave a finished performance under Paul Breisach. The settings and costumes, creations of John Piper, were simple yet rich in color and imaginative suggestion.

The stage direction was by a dancer, Agnes de Mille. In her stylized groupings and pantomimes she made an effect singularly appropriate to the subject, if per-haps we accept the superfluous activity of the male and female proponents of the Greek chorus, who in the original production of the opera at Glyndebourne remained in their niches at each side of the stage, always apart from the action, reading from the book of fate as the drama went on its way. [...]

All of this was first-class musical theatre. What of the intrinsic values of the score? There will be later occasion to discuss it in detail, and with further perspec-tive. It is, at least, extremely accomplished in craftsmanship and accentuation of the stage. Sometimes it becomes a musical organism in itself and thus more than a highly dexterous comment upon the dramatic development. Seldom, in the last analysis, does it rise to the greatest heights of musical revelation. Sometimes it falls short. Thus Lucretia's soliloquy with the wreath becomes wordy and melodically repetitious. The vocal phrase which pierces direct to the heart of an emotion is seldom sounded. Highly compensatory is the dramatic feeling and sensibility with which the composer uses his material. It is on that basis, and that of the splendid interpretation, that the opera reaches its mark. As a modern score, and operatic presentation, it makes history.

Cecil Smith contributed a notice to *New Republic* (24 January 1949):

Whether *The Rape of Lucretia* is a good music-drama or not – and I belong to the party of those who think it is – it is a real landmark in local theatrical and musical history. Except for [Menotti's] *The Medium*, which undoubtedly helped break the ice for the present more ambitious project, we had never before seen a contem-porary opera professionally mounted, costumed and lighted as effectively as a Broadway musical; directed by a good craftsman (Agnes de Mille) who under-stands American taste and who was given enough rehearsal time to realize the purposes of her direction; and performed by a cast chosen because every member of it could act as well as sing.

As a production, *The Rape of Lucretia* is a miracle of intelligent planning and an object lesson to every opera-producing organization from the Metropolitan down, or up, to the New York City Opera Company. The scenery and costumes designed for the English production by John Piper, and borrowed for the occasion, suit the tone of the piece exactly, with a sort of poetic literalism that corresponds to the texture of both Duncan's libretto and Britten's score. Miss de Mille has visualized the action in a fusion of realistic gesture, miming and choreography – and with just about the right number of Roman touches – that is right in essence, even if some of the passing details seem a bit studied. [...]

If I were to offer an extended opinion on *The Rape of Lucretia*, I should merely be repeating myself, since I expressed a page of satisfaction with the work when it was given its American premiere in Chicago in 1947, and found no reason to alter my state of mind nineteen months later. Two fairly frequent objections of New York reviewers I cannot understand: I do not think that the plot wanders, even though the accompanying text is handed back and forth between the actors and the Male and Female Chorus; and I do not think that the vocal parts are unsingable or that the prosody (most of the time) is clumsy.

On the same day as his letter to Pears, Britten wrote to Elizabeth Mayer in New York:

[...] I am so keen that you should see & hear Lucretia as she was meant to be, in surroundings sympathetic to her, & not on Broadway. It has been hard knowing what was happening to her in New York & being able to do nothing, & hard to read all the inane press notices (sent by misplaced kindness of Ralph!). I have no respect for criticisms anywhere, but these (even the friendly ones) touched a bottom that even England cannot surpass! I feel hideously disinclined to come over in the Autumn, but only do it because it will be a chance to see you, my dearest, & show you a little what we can do.

Mrs Mayer responded on 18 January:

We four Mayers, William, Michael and Chris who saw it together, were so furious – even the boys, who did not really know the work and the intention, as I know it. But they immediately sensed that everything was done in the wrong way, that each role was miscast, etc., etc. I am happy to say that more people, I saw afterwards, felt the same way; I had had my misgivings and did not follow an invitation for the Preview, and even did not go to the first performance but to the second as I did not want to meet people involved in the production. The only one I know is Cardelli who has, I confess, behaved well, protested in many ways (when it was too late) and introduced the work on the Radio twice, the week before, once with some singers of the cast singing bits, and once with the whole recording of the English Opera Group! We now have that recording and enjoy it immensely; it is beautiful, and has completely obliterated in our minds and ears the ghastly performance. But the settings by John Piper!! how exquisite they are: we are so happy to have seen them. They were standing there, expressing so much of the true style of the whole, like a silent reproach for the bungling that went on beneath.

3   During his address to the annual conference of the Incorporated Society of Musicians on 5 January, Sir Thomas Beecham had denounced the administration and Musical Director at Covent Garden. A report in the *New York Times* (6 January 1949) claimed that Beecham, in discussing the

members of the Covent Garden Trust, had said 'that the first most noticeable feature was that there was not a single person who knew anything
about opera or had practical experience of it and "whose opinion is worth
a brass farthing"'. He capped this with offensive remarks concerning
Karl Rankl:

> The appointment of an alien, and one bearing a German name, was so incredible
> that he had to remind himself from time to time that it had actually happened and
> was not some fantastic dream. 'It must be, I think,' he continued, 'because ignora-
> muses and nitwits who brought this about – this disaster – were under the impres-
> sion that the functions of a musical director in an opera house were of such exotic,
> intricate and profound a nature that only a person of the sublime intelligence of a
> Teuton could grasp and manipulate them.'

See also J. D. Gilmour (ed.), *Sir Thomas Beecham: Fifty years in the 'New
York Times'*, pp. 139–41.

4   Pears had moved the furniture and his and Britten's other belongings to
    22 Melbury Road, London w14, the Steins' home, where Britten and Pears
    would maintain a pied-à-terre until 1953.

5   Britten and Pears were considering Egypt as a holiday destination.

616   To Ralph Hawkes

4 Crabbe Street, Aldeburgh
Jan. 20th 1949

My dear Ralph,

I am afraid this can't be as long a letter as I should have wished – I can't
write much at the moment, but anyhow we had that nice talk on the
phone on Sunday when I think the main points were settled. You will by
now have received my cable about Koussevitzky's kind new invitation for
Tanglewood.[1] I am afraid well or ill I cannot accept that, in the first place
I have commitments here – in the second, fond as I am of him, I don't feel
Tanglewood is the place to rest, & anyhow teaching is not a thing that
I can do easily & would be an immense strain. I will let you all know if I
can get on & finish the Symphony when I get back from Italy in February;
I have hopes of getting it ready for Tanglewood, but I feel chary now
about making any promises!

Everyone here is being extremely nice about taking things off my
shoulders. Erwin & Roth at B & H are very helpful of course – Eric &
Elizabeth Sweeting are being most efficient about the E.O.G. & the
Aldeburgh Festival! They are well on the way to being able to find the
young conductor to take over my job.[2]

I haven't been either entirely inactive artistically, because E. M. Forster
has been here for a few days & the plans for the libretto of the big opera

for 1951 are going ahead. I hope before long to be able to give you details of them. They are most exciting I think.[3]

Please forgive this not being a longer letter, but I will write later to tell you how things go, abroad & back here.

I am afraid you will have been disappointed about Lucretia – but I honestly feel it was wrong for Broadway, & had no chance of succeeding, especially this quiet kind of work (because it is essentially that). I feel certain its day will come in U.S.A. – perhaps when certain prejudices are dead! (I was amused by the Volte Face of O. Downes!)

Please give my love to Clare, & the very best wishes for 1949 for you both.

Yours ever,

BEN

P.S. I was very nearly finishing this letter without thanking you for the magnificent Christmas presents – the Ham & the Champagne. It was extremely kind of you to send them. Both, I was able to partake of – even in my dubious internal state! – and they have added considerably to the gaiety & ease of the household. Thank you very much indeed, from Peter & myself, & also, the many friends (all the Mauds included!) who have shared in them!

1   Koussevitzky's modified invitation was discussed by Elizabeth Mayer in a letter to the composer of 18 January 1949: '[Ralph Hawkes] told me of Koussi's wish to have you in Tanglewood in summer (teaching, but he had said that that part would be a negligible matter, just occasional informal talks) [...]'

2   Norman Del Mar (see Letter 617 n. 8), who was to join the EOG later in 1949.

3   Forster, Crozier and Britten had met at Crag House for a few days in mid-January to thrash out the possibility of adapting Melville's *Billy Budd, Foretopman*. Three documents survive from this first working session: a preliminary stage sketch of the *Indomitable*, a list of characters, and a breakdown of the basic events of the story. Several matters concerning the operatic adaptation were also decided, including the allotting of the principal tenor role (to be sung by Pears) to Vere, and the framing of the action by a Prologue and an Epilogue in which Vere would be seen in old age. A synopsis of an opera in five scenes was made by Crozier as the basis for future discussions. Shortly after this working session, Forster sent Crozier what he described as a 'rough-out for Vere's opening speech', a draft that is very close to the final version. See BBMCPR, pp. 47–51.

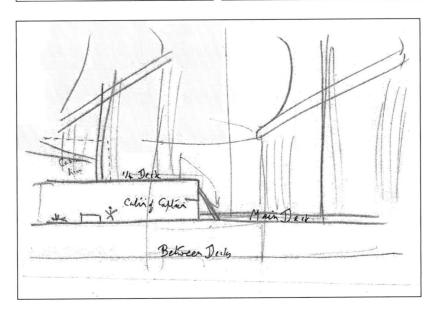

Britten's outline synopsis of Melville's *Billy Budd* and his stage sketch
of the *Indomitable*, with annotations by Forster and Crozier

Scene I   Vere as Chorus

                          much

I am an old man who has experienced . I have been a man of action and fought for my King and Country at sea. I have also read books and studied and pondered and tried to fathom eternal truth.

     Much good has been shown to me and much evil. The evil has sometimes been absolute. And the good has never been perfect. There has always been some flaw in it, some defect, some imperfection in the divine image, some stammer in the divine speech, some fault in the angelic song. So that — I am an old man now — it seems to me that the Devil must have has his part in this make up of ours. God grant that it be a small part.

     On sea as on land that struggle fight between good and evil continues. And my mind goes back to the ~~something~~ summer of 1797, to the French wars, to the difficult and dangerous days after the Mutiny of the Nore, to the days when I, Edward Fairfax Vere, commanded the <u>Indomitable</u>.

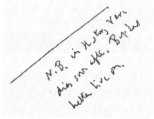

N.B. in the story Vere dies after the Battle while Billy lives on.

'I am an old man who has experienced much': Forster's first draft
of the Prologue of *Billy Budd*.

617 **To Elizabeth Sweeting**

22 MELBURY ROAD, KENSINGTON, W.14
Jan. 22nd 1949

My dear Elizabeth,

This is only a scribbled note. We're off tomorrow, everything seems fixed & now I'm really looking forward to it[1] – largely owing to a fairly clear conscience due to your help yesterday – thank you very much for all you did, my dear.

I hope today's concert[2] has been a success & that enough people came to enjoy it, & to make Jacques[3] & Joan enjoy it too, & for you to enjoy it (at least from a financial angle!). I was sorry to miss it. Did Fidelity & Juliet[4] come – I hope you gave the latter my love if she did.

I enclose a letter (overdue like most of the posts nowadays) from J. Ireland which is a blow. Would you be an angel & acknowledge it & say please 1950?[5] I suggest that under the circs. that Dr Thomas Wood[6] had better be approached for a short piece, if he can do it in the time, with suitable apologies & all. I don't really like his music, but Moeran, whom I. [Ireland] suggests, would be so slow & might produce something very difficult for the choirs to learn in the time. I'm writing a note to Anne [Wood] (whom I've not been able to see) to this effect – perhaps you could get in touch with her, & concoct a letter together or she (who I believe knows him) might even see him. I suggest a piece for choir, strings, organ (& percussion if he wants it), about 5–10 minutes.[7]

I have talked with Peter & Erwin a great deal about Norman Del Mar,[8] whom the latter recommends strongly. Steve [Waters], if you remember, wasn't very anti – only slightly! Anyhow he is the only English hope, & is enthusiastic & a good musician. The question to be decided is:– can we afford Sacher[9] for the 3 weeks of Festivals – & then, if so, what happens if there is an Autumn season? Would Sacher, an international figure (not terribly well known), be an asset for publicity at these Festivals?[10] Certainly a chap like Del Mar would be a longer term policy, & might rise to the occasion with responsibility. Suggest he might do Lucretia, Ivan [Clayton] (if well enough) Albert. Anyhow, talk it over with Eric & Anne – & I do strongly suggest that someone soon talks to Del Mar. Erwin will speak to Eric this weekend.

A tiny chore – please, dear; could you possibly go to Crag House, & copy the words of some Bach Cantatas for us, & send them to Anne? Not much. You'll find them all in Vol. 32 of the Bach Gesellschaft (the innumerable red volumes in the sitting-room bookcase); & what we want, please, are the words of the CHORALES each of Nos. 151, 156, 159 – the CHORALE in each case is the last movement of each Cantata. About 4 lines each. If there's a doubt, Eric will be down on Monday evening & can help you. We must get new translations made, & I'm writing to Anne to suggest whom.[11]

You will have written to Parikian?[12] I gather the orchestra are a little impatient about the autumn season dates, but I know the difficulty there . . . but I hope within a day or so that can be settled.

We haven't yet decided where after Venice yet – but we'll send post-cards, but I hope very much that things can go smoothly for you without my august personality to advise you! Sorry I've been useless, & querulous, but I promise to come back on terrific form, & play (at any rate) squash with speed & venom!

Thank you again for helping so much – forgive scribble & haste,

with love

BEN

1   Britten wrote to Ronald Duncan on 19 January: 'Peter's taking me away to Italy on Sunday for three weeks, & if that doesn't cure me I feel nothing else will!' The first two weeks were spent in Venice from where they visited Torcello, Chioggia and Padua, followed by a week in Portofino, before returning home on 12 February. In an undated postcard to Mary Behrend, Pears declared, 'It's all quite wonderfully beautiful [. . .] What a place!' On 1 February Britten sent a postcard to Crozier:

> This place is as lovely as you could imagine, & I am already feeling <u>heaps</u> better, eating like a trojan, walking miles every day looking at astounding things, & getting brown in the lovely sun. We haven't yet decided where we go to from here, or even whether we shall move at all, it's so lovely. Thank you for sending Billy Budd so promptly – I'm thinking about it quite a bit – but mostly <u>sub</u>-conscious, I'm afraid!

2   An 'Aldeburgh Festival Winter Concert' probably held in Aldeburgh Parish Church. Music by Bach and Handel (soloist: Joan Cross), Corelli, Mozart and Moszkowski was performed by the Jacques Orchestra conducted by Reginald Jacques.

3   Reginald Jacques (1894–1969), English organist and conductor, who was appointed Conductor of the London Bach Choir in 1931, a post he held until his enforced retirement through ill health in 1960. Jacques did much to establish the tradition of the annual performance of the St Matthew Passion by the Bach Choir, with whom he recorded the work in 1949. He founded the Jacques Orchestra in 1936, an ensemble that appeared both with the Bach Choir and independently, notably at several early Edinburgh Festivals. From 1940 until 1945 Jacques was the first director of CEMA.

4   Juliet Gathorne-Hardy, one of the Cranbrook daughters.

5   Ireland must have been approached by Britten, his former pupil, for a new work to be included in the 1949 Aldeburgh Festival; evidently he declined and suggested instead that he might write something for the 1950 Festival. However, no new work emerged and the only Ireland pieces included in

the 1950 Festival were the piano piece *Amberley Wild Brooks* and the song 'I have twelve oxen'.

6 English composer and writer (1892–1950), who had settled in Essex in 1928 after spending a period teaching at Oxford and elsewhere. In 1949 he was appointed Chairman of the Arts Council's Music Panel. His autobiography, *True Thomas*, was published in 1940.

7 In the event, Wood did not provide a new piece along the lines suggested by Britten, who was to write to Elizabeth Sweeting on 3 February:

> I hope all prospers with you, & that Festival & Group matters go easily. I've had a long & sweet letter from Anne about this & that, & gather you've also talked similarly with her. I think she's probably right about Thomas Wood, but anyhow you may have made up your mind by now one way or another. It would be nice to have a new work by an East Anglian, but time is short & I'm afraid we can expect only less than a masterpiece from him. After all we can do him in the Serenade concert. But if you've written to him, don't worry, & we'll talk it over soon. If you've not written, the 2 programmes can be (i) Holst, Psalm [86] (for chorus & orchestra) – Nic. [*St Nicolas*]; (ii) Holst, Psalm – Handel, Ode [for St Cecilia's Day]; & we can fill in the rest later.

Britten had evidently intended that there should have been a commissioned work from an East Anglian-based composer in the choral and orchestral concerts presented in Aldeburgh Parish Church on 11 and 18 June 1949. As he notes in his letter to Elizabeth Sweeting, some of Wood's part-songs for men's voices concluded the 'Serenade Concert' in the Jubilee Hall on 11 June.

8 English conductor, composer and writer on music (1919–1994), who in 1949 was appointed Principal Conductor of the EOG, a post he held until 1954. Del Mar studied horn and composition (the latter with Vaughan Williams) at the Royal College of Music, and later privately with Mátyás Seiber. He was a member of the RAF Central Band during the war, where he came into contact with Dennis Brain; post-war, Del Mar played second horn to Brain's principal in Beecham's Royal Philharmonic Orchestra. Del Mar's conducting career began in 1944 when he founded the amateur Chelsea Symphony Orchestra and the Croydon Symphony Orchestra, with whom he explored much repertory hitherto unknown in England, including music by Strauss, Hindemith and Poulenc, as well as Busoni's Piano Concerto and Mahler's Second and Ninth Symphonies. With reference to the latter, Del Mar was one of the band of British Mahler enthusiasts – Britten himself was another – who contributed much to the reassessment and rehabilitation of Mahler in the UK. An associate conductorship with the RPO in 1947 led to Del Mar's professional debut in the Strauss Festival that same year, held in London in the presence of Strauss himself. After working with the EOG and at Aldeburgh Festivals in the 1950s, and at Sadler's Wells Ballet and with the Yorkshire Symphony Orchestra, in 1960 Del Mar was appointed Conductor of the BBC Scottish Orchestra, a post

he held for five years. He subsequently held appointments in Sweden and Denmark, with the Academy of the BBC (a training orchestra for young professionals), and taught conducting at the RCM, 1972–90. His scholarly writings are crowned by his three-volume study of Richard Strauss and his *Anatomy of the Orchestra*. He also contributed studies of *Lucretia*, *Herring* and *The Beggar's Opera* to DMHK, pp. 132–85.

Although he conducted a wide range of music – Berlioz, Mahler and Strauss were all great favourites – he will perhaps be best remembered as an unflinching champion of British music, in particular Britten and Tippett (Del Mar's 1963 BBC broadcast of *The Midsummer Marriage* rescued Tippett's opera from oblivion), as well as Lutyens, Rawsthorne, Gerhard and Maw.

His collaborations with Britten began at Aldeburgh in 1949 when Del Mar conducted the first performance of *Let's Make an Opera* at the Jubilee Hall, where his generous physique, warmth of personality and lively wit made him the most successful of conductors at rehearsing many a reluctant audience in its contribution to the piece. He conducted *Lucretia*, *Herring* and *The Beggar's Opera* for the EOG, as well as Holst's *The Wandering Scholar*, and the premieres of Easdale's *The Sleeping Children* and Oldham's realization, *Love in a Village*. The skills that made Del Mar such a success in *Let's Make an Opera* were again put to good use when conducting performances and the recording of *Noye's Fludde* at Orford in 1961. In 1957 Britten invited Del Mar to devise a suite of dances from *The Prince of the Pagodas*, which received its first performance in December 1963, given by the BBC Scottish Symphony Orchestra conducted by Del Mar. It was published as *Prelude and Dances from 'The Prince of the Pagodas'* in 1980. A significant collection of Del Mar's conducting scores, mainly of works by Britten, is now at BPL.

In an interview with Humphrey Carpenter, Del Mar recalled two stories about the composer and his relationship with him:

On occasion, he would take me for a long walk, and it would emerge that, for example, I had not been quite strict enough in this or that respect. You could go wrong without knowing it [HCBB, p. 277].

During an EOG tour:

I blotted my copybook inadvertently because I started reading one of the crits in the interval to Ben and Peter and Joan. And I hadn't read the crit ahead, and it said that I'd conducted it as well as Ben, and that didn't go down at all well. And I suddenly realized that I had put my foot in it without meaning to. The silence was rather awful. I mean, all right, I was Ben's conductor, but that I should actually be able to challenge him on his own territory – no, that didn't do' [HCBB, p. 320].

See also Richard Alston, *Norman Del Mar*, chapter 2; John Amis, *Amiscellany*, pp. 94–100, and obituaries by Robert Ponsonby, *Independent*, Edward Greenfield and Alexander Goehr, *Guardian*, and in the *Daily Telegraph* (all 7 February 1994).

9   Paul Sacher (1906–1999), Swiss conductor and an influential patron of the
    arts. After studying at the Basel Conservatory with Weingartner, Sacher
    founded the Basel Chamber Orchestra in 1926 with the expressed intention
    that it should concentrate on the pre-classical period and contemporary
    repertories. He commissioned and premiered numerous compositions,
    including Bartók's *Music for Strings, Percussion and Celesta* and *Diverti-
    mento*, Hindemith's *Die Harmonie der Welt*, Honegger's Second and Fourth
    Symphonies, Martin's *Petite symphonie concertante*, Strauss's *Metamor-
    phosen*, Stravinsky's Concerto in D and *A Sermon, Narrative, and a Prayer*,
    and Tippett's *Divertimento on Sellinger's Round*. From Britten, Sacher com-
    missioned the *Cantata academica, carmen basiliense*, first performed under
    Sacher's direction on 1 July 1960. To celebrate Sacher's seventieth birthday
    in 1976, Britten composed, at Rostropovich's request, his *Tema: 'Sacher'*.
    The original intention (Mstislav Rostropovich's idea) was that each of the
    tributes, all of them to be composed for solo cello, should be a variation on
    Britten's theme. But in the event each contributor pursued his own individ-
    ual inspiration. These salutations were published under the collective title
    Hommages à Paul Sacher.
        Sacher had given an early performance of Britten's *Variations on a
    Theme of Frank Bridge* and had got to know both Britten and Pears in the
    immediate post-war years when they made occasional appearances with
    the Basel and Zurich orchestras. Sacher made two appearances at the
    Aldeburgh Festival: in 1956, with the Aldeburgh Festival Orchestra and
    Francis Poulenc (piano) in Poulenc's *Aubade* and Milhaud's *La Création du
    monde*, and in 1961, when he conducted a programme of works by Martinů,
    Honegger and Martin. See also *Dank an Paul Sacher*, and *80 Jahre Paul
    Sacher: Erinnerungen an den Geburtstag*.

10 Sacher was not engaged by the EOG at this time, nor in the future.

11 Cantatas 151 and 159 were performed at an Aldeburgh Festival concert on
    14 June 1949 in Aldeburgh Parish Church, conducted by Britten. Cantata
    156 (together with Cantata 161) was performed two days later, also under
    Britten's direction. The new English translations were by Iris Holland
    Rogers.

12 Manoug Parikian (1920–1987), British violinist of Armenian origin, who
    was leader of the Liverpool Philharmonic Orchestra (1947–48) and the
    Philharmonia Orchestra (1949–57) before fully establishing himself as a
    soloist and chamber-music player. As a solo violinist he gave the premieres
    of works by Rawsthorne and Seiber, and concertos by Crosse and Goehr.
    He led the EOG Orchestra between 1949 and 1951, and participated in
    Aldeburgh Festival concerts, chamber, orchestral and operatic. In 1951 he
    was the violin soloist in a performance of Mozart's *Sinfonia concertante* in
    E♭ (K. 364), conducted by Britten; the violist was William Primrose. In 1954
    Parikian assisted Britten in revisions to the solo part of his Violin Concerto,
    composed in 1939 for Antonio Brosa.

618 To Ronald Duncan

From Benjamin Britten and Peter Pears

[*Postcard: Palazzo della Ragione, Padua*]

Venice

[Postmarked 4 February 1949]

Dear Ronnie

Greetings from the most lovely city we know. Venice has done the trick, spiritually & physically for me I think – what with all this beauty, food & sun. Actually the weather is cold now & we move across to Mediterranean tomorrow. We were here (Padua) yesterday – also fine. How are you?

Love to you all,

BEN

Is Roger[1] being good? Rose Marie, you should [bring] Briony[2] here. They love blondes.

Much love to you all,

PETER

1 Roger Duncan (b. 1943), the son of Ronald and Rose Marie Duncan. Britten's and Roger's friendship began in 1954, when Roger was eleven years old. According to Ronald Duncan, Britten asked him if he might 'adopt' Roger, 'give him presents, visit him at school, and let him spend part of his school holidays' with the composer. Roger's father agreed to this arrangement and, as he recollected, 'For the next ten years Ben was a second father to my son, giving him affection and advice as he grew up' (see RDBB, pp. 132–3). Britten and Roger began a regular correspondence with one another; in particular, the letters Britten sent to Roger during his Far East trip in 1955–56 constitute a remarkable account of the experience. Roger was one of the dedicatees of *Noye's Fludde* in 1957.

In an interview with Humphrey Carpenter, Roger Duncan recollected that Britten was 'extremely warm, and extremely loving, and generated those genuine feelings', but added, 'they weren't physical' (HCBB, p. 368). On Britten's part, the platonic friendship allowed him to be *in loco parentis*, fulfilling his need to play a paternal role. Although Roger married soon after graduating from Cambridge and emigrated to Canada, he continued to keep in touch with the composer and saw him on one occasion at the end of Britten's life. He was also interviewed for JBBC.

A portrait of Roger Duncan (*c*. 1956) by Mary Potter is at BPL.

2 The Duncans' daughter.

619 To Elizabeth Mayer

Portofino Mare
February 7th 1949

My dearest Elizabeth

This is just a line of greetings from Italy, from the Mediterranean! We go back to England on Saturday, & shall find the North Sea different from this amicable piece of water, no doubt, but lovely in its way. Peter & I have had nearly three weeks of this heavenly country, & the beauty of it all, the warmth of the sun (on the whole most kind to us), the satisfying & wholesome food has really worked the trick with my beastly nervy inside, & I am feeling a new person, impatient to get back to work, for the first time for months! Peter's choice of Venice for the first two weeks was perfect. We drifted from galleries to churches, round the Lagoon in boats, & can really say that we have got to know the town a bit – certainly caught its flavour. Do you know it well? It is so quiet, man seems definitely in charge – no cars, or bicycles even, to escape from, only the noise of people walking & talking, church bells (how many!), & ships & gondolas. It was extra pleasant to be there out of season too, because nothing was crowded, & people seemed to be living a natural life, & not only as touts to tourists. We struggled with the language, Peter succeeding far better than I, but perhaps his lyric repertoire helped him! What a beautiful language tho' – I'd love to be able to speak it well. The weather turned cold on us, & so then we took a sleeper & came over this side of the country, to the considerably warmer west coast. This is a small village, fishing, near Rapallo, not far from Genoa. Very peaceful – nothing to do but walk up the mountains, but that in a way is a rest after the excitements of Venice, & it is nice to be able to digest some of the wonders we saw there. We stay till Friday, then to Milan, where we shall catch a plane on Saturday to England, London & Aldeburgh.

Ralph Hawkes will have told you my decision about Tanglewood. It was sweet of you to offer to put me up there, & in order to be with you for a holiday, I'd love to have accepted. But if I'm well, which I shall be, I have too many commitments here, work to do, the Opera Group to help with, Holland Festival, & it now looks as if Peter will be singing Titus in Salzburg[1] & I'd love to pop over & hear it. Another reason: at the moment my plate is so full that I cannot add teaching (except in special individual cases) & lecturing to it, & if I could face starting this frightening branch of the art, I think I'd better do it over here, among my own kind, people whom I understand & who understand me. As you know, I'm not happy in musical circles in the States.

I'm still hoping against hope that you'll be able to get to the Aldeburgh Festival. If it is too early for William to come, couldn't you come alone & he follow later in the summer? You know, there's no need to say, that the Aldeburgh House is longing to welcome you whenever & however long you're here – if I can tear you away from Beth who demands you too! But I won't bore you with pressure.

My love to you, my dear, & all of your dear ones. I hope there'll be news of you when we get back to England.

Your devoted

BEN

1 The proposal to sing the title role in Mozart's *La clemenza di Tito* came to nothing. It was a role that Pears was never to tackle. See also Letter 621 in which another Mozart tenor role for Pears – Belmonte in *Die Entführung aus dem Serail* – is mentioned.

620 To Peter Pears

Aldeburgh

[after 19 February 1949]

Darling P –

Perhaps after all we'd better NOT telephone, because we always get cross – ! But somehow even getting cross, or feeling you're cross with me is better than silence, so perhaps after all we'd better keep it up! Anyhow, thank you very much for ringing.[1]

This is only to send on two little notes. I must say I think your "Coz" is very attractive, and gay. And also intelligent. Could you at least, think, about the Vellain one – she was the nice secretary, wasn't she? And answer it when we think about programmes in general?

Dr Acheson has just been – he's a nice kind man. He says my depression is natural, & I mustn't worry about it! By the way, in the bottom of the well last night, I started putting on records – Ponselle,[2] a very good singer, not perfect musically, but lovely voice & extraordinary technique, Gigli[3] & Schipa[4] – & feeling very dissatisfied with the latter two, I put on your record of Nacht & Träume[5] & do you know, poppetty, that there's nothing they've got you haven't – the quality of your voice (& it's a bad record too) is much lovelier than theirs. What they've got, which isn't the fashion today, is this extraordinary worked-out quality, even with all the exaggerations that it means: a pause really is a pause, louds are loud, & crescendos & dims are immensely strong & long. Of course the latter two (G. & S.) nearly always do it in the wrong places, & are shockingly unmusical. I think what you have got to work to is this immense "effect-ness", & with the musicianship you've got, & all the technique & voice advantages – you can lead them by miles. It was an interesting (& gratifying!) contrast.

All my love, darling,

take care of yourself,

B.

1   Britten wrote to Pears on 19 February:

> I am sorry I was so gloomy yesterday, but it was the bottom of the well for me.
> Work was impossible, & I felt absolutely desperate. I think it was the reaction after
> Italy, & especially coming back to the hopeless realities of the E.O.G. financial crisis!

2   Rosa Ponselle (1897–1981), American soprano, whose voice was, according
    to *The New Grove Dictionary of Opera*, 'generally regarded as one of the
    most beautiful of the century'. Britten and Pears owned Ponselle's 1920s
    recording of 'Casta diva' from Bellini's *Norma* (HMV DB 1280).

3   Beniamino Gigli (1890–1957), Italian tenor. Britten and Pears owned the 78s
    of Gigli's 1940 recording of Leoncavallo's *Pagliacci* (HMV DB 7760–8).

4   Tito Schipa (1888–1965), Italian tenor, who is described by Desmond
    Shawe-Taylor in *The New Grove Dictionary of Opera* as 'the outstanding
    tenore di grazia of his generation'. It has not been possible to identify which
    of Schipa's recordings Britten listened to on this occasion.

5   Pears's and Britten's 1946 Decca recording of Schubert's song, which was
    not authorized for commercial release.

621   To Peter Pears

4 Crabbe Street, Aldeburgh
[2 March 1949]

My darling,

   Here is the first batch. Hope they all arrive O.K. I had a look at Seraglio[1]
before I packed it – what a lovely, lovely piece! I wish I could hear you do
Belmonte some time – how nice if you could do it at Salzburg next year!
Or Geneva.

   It's a heavenly day, rather oppressed by bad Group financial news, but it
can't spoil the wonderful light on the sea – rather like the Chioggia trip,
but perhaps not quite so blue. My memories of the three weeks grow
lovelier & lovelier – but unlike most memories they don't make me
unhappy or nostalgic, only contented & looking forward. Lovely as
Venice, Bellini, the little Carpaccio boys, Mimosa and the wine-dark sea
off Portofino were, my happiest & most treasured memory is of the
wonderful peace & contentment of your love & friendship. Love, such as
I felt we had in those 3 weeks, is a rare thing – as beautiful and luminous
as this sea outside, & with endless depths too. Thank you, my dearest.

   I saw Mr Robinson,[2] the footman this morning & liked him immensely.
But I must talk some things over with Beth, & then talk over the 'phone
with you. But I think he'll do.

   My love to everyone; hope Erwin is better. When you've seen Morgan, if
you can, & we know his plans, I'll ask him down here, perhaps?

All my love, my dearest,

BEN

1   Britten must have forwarded to Pears his vocal score of Mozart's *Die Entführung aus dem Serail*. Belmonte is the principal tenor role.

2   Employed by Britten at Crag House to replace Barbara Parker, who left Aldeburgh in mid-February. Robinson's appointment did not last as he showed signs of mental instability.

622   To Peter Pears

[Aldeburgh]
[after 7 March 1949]

My darling –

Two letters, both a little unpleasant – so sorry!

We had a nice day with Cecily & Walter[1] & they were really charming to us. You must really manage to pay them a visit – Cecily is devoted to you – & you'd like to see all the chaps & the lovely house & position. We then went back to Ipswich & heard 37 children for the opera! Some, happily very promising, & one poppet of a tough small boy![2]

Hope you are well & working – writing any letters . . . ?? !!

I had a good morning's work – tra-la, trala.

All my love, my darling,

B.

1   Pears's sister and her husband, Walter Smithwick.

2   Britten and Crozier were auditioning for the cast of *Let's Make an Opera*, to be given its premiere at the 1949 Aldeburgh Festival. Britten wrote to John Redcliffe-Maud on 7 March:

I heard 37 Ipswich children, possibles for the Festival Children's opera on Monday, & was enormously impressed. It was all organised by the Co-op, & all sorts & conditions of children turned up. But the combination of skill & assurance was staggering. I feel the next generation of Britons is going to be a knock-out, in the best sense too! Most encouraging.

Eric Crozier was to write in the *Radio Times* (30 September 1949), in an introduction to the opera which was broadcast on 7 October:

The Co-operative Society Choir of Ipswich produced no less than thirty-seven children between the ages of twelve and fifteen for us to audition. The level of their accomplishment was so high that we were able to choose our entire cast of children and a set of understudies from this one source.

623 To Dr Ernst Roth
Boosey & Hawkes
[*Typed*]

4 Crabbe Street, Aldeburgh, Suffolk
9th March, 1949

Dear Dr Roth,

I have before me: (1) a translation of the letter you wrote to Mr Ravizza on October 15th (just passed on to me by Keith Falkner[1]), and (2) an article from 'Il Momento' which quotes a reading of this letter at a reception given in Rome by the British Council.[2]

I am so horrified and made so furious by these two documents that I have immediately written to Keith Falkner describing the opinions made public (purporting to be arrived at after "lengthy consultations with Mr Britten") as perhaps 2% mine, the rest "a misleading, inaccurate and distorted elaboration . . .". It wholly misrepresents my true feelings about 'Dido' and Purcell.[3]

In your letter you have built up, on a sentence or two of my own opinion, a monstrous edifice of inaccuracy and half-truths which gives the falsest impression of my real ideas about Purcell and opera in general. And now excerpts from this silly nonsense have been given to the Press in Rome, of all places, which I shall be visiting for concerts next month. A nice impression to have circulated of one in a city where 'Dido' has been a success and 'Lucretia' somewhat of a flop!

It means that I have had to ask Keith Falkner to explain to the Italian Press that I am not quite such a fool or a prig as they think I am.

How can you have been so irresponsible as to give the impression that I held all those opinions? You are supposed to represent me, not to misrepresent me. I should mind having those opinions said to any one person, but to be passed on to official people as my official reasons – it is monstrously tactless. I am exceedingly annoyed.

In the future, please, I should like to make it quite clear that when my opinions are quoted in a letter I shall expect to have a copy of that letter immediately sent to me, so that I may examine it to see whether I am misrepresented.

Yours sincerely,

1 English bass-baritone (1906–1994), particularly known as a soloist in oratorio. Falkner was Music Organiser for the British Council in Italy, 1946–50 and Director of the Royal College of Music, 1960–74. See also Diary for 22 March 1931, n. 6; Julia Falkner, *Keith Falkner: 'Ich habe genug'*, and obituaries by Elizabeth Forbes and Michael Gough Matthews, *Independent* (3 June 1994) and in *The Times* (20 May 1994) and the *Daily Telegraph* (27 May 1994).

2 Roth's letter to Ravizza of 15 October 1948 has not survived among the composer's files. However, the translation of the offending article from *Il Momento* (7 February 1949) has:

> After supper Falkner [. . .] read some notes on the operas *Dido and Aeneas* by Purcell and *The Rape of Lucretia* by Britten. As had been duly announced, there was to have been an evening dedicated to English music during the 1948–49 season. But it has not been possible to celebrate this 'wedding' of Purcell and Britten on the stage of the Rome Opera just because Britten has not wished to consent to this. Dr Roth explains the reasons in a long letter after having 'discussed at great length with Britten'. This latter asserts that 'the English public who go to the opera no longer can stand Purcell on the stage' and considers his work 'terribly tiring, not to say boring'. Presenting both operas in one evening beginning, as would be logical, with *Dido*, Britten thinks that the public 'would be so tired and bored as not to be in the mood to appreciate properly the performance of *Lucretia*'.

3 Britten's letter (9 March 1949) to Keith Falkner reads:

> Ronald Duncan has passed on to me the translation of the report in "Il Momento" about the 'Dido' and 'Lucretia', and also the translation of Dr Roth's letter of October 15th, 1948. I must say at once that I do wish that you had not felt obliged to quote Dr Roth's letter to the Rome Press; surely it could have been done rather more abstractly, as it were, or could you not have confirmed these opinions from me?
>
> On the other hand I quite appreciate that his letter reads like a convincing expression of opinion, but I wish to make quite clear, here and now, that that expression of opinion is his entirely and of the opinions expressed perhaps 2% may be considered as mine. The rest is a misleading, inaccurate and distorted elaboration, and it wholly misrepresents my true feelings about 'Dido' and Purcell.
>
> Purcell is the king of English music. I love him enough to be making a large edition of his works and am only longing for the time when the English Opera Group can stage a worthy production of this gem of English opera (we have actually long ago published our intention to do so). It is true that the 'Fairy Queen' was not a great success opening Covent Garden's 1946 season, but Purcell is not to be blamed for that. It is also true that 'Dido and Aeneas' has not been seen on a London stage for (I think) over ten years, but let us rather blame the Managements for that.
>
> My true feeling about the coupling of 'Dido' and 'Lucretia' springs simply from the fact that I do not think it good programme building because it would not make a balanced evening's music. The stories are too similar in setting and denouement and not dissimilar in musical treatment. And, quite simply, in my opinion, the evening would be too long and then both operas (and incidentally the cause of English music) would suffer. In fact, what has happened seems to be the perfect solution – 'Dido' with Stravinsky's 'Orpheo' [the ballet *Orpheus*] makes a fascinating programme, and 'Lucretia' by itself is quite long enough. Admittedly we do not have a monstrous "Gala Evening" which is a pity; well, perhaps there may be another chance of that.
>
> In the meantime I should like to make it clear to the Italian press and its readers that neither the English public (nor least of all I) find 'Dido' "terribly tiring, not to say boring", that I think Purcell's theatre music when properly treated has great possibilities of success, that 'Dido' should be in the English repertoire (though it is

not) just as I think 'Ulysses' and 'Poppaea' [Monteverdi's *Il ritorno d'Ulisse in patria* and *L'incoronazione di Poppea*] should be (but are not) in the Italian repertoire.

I am sending a copy of this letter to Seymour Whinyates because I do not want these mistakes to get circulated further in the British Council.

Falkner responded on 15 March:

I am quite offended however that you could think I should be so indiscreet as to quote anything Dr Roth had said about these two works to the Press. I am indeed surprised that Ronald Duncan did not inform you of the true position. I made it quite plain to him that the translation of Dr Roth's letter and *Il Momento* article were things over which we had no control, as I am sure you are now aware the critic of *Il Momento* got his information direct from the Rome Opera House. Indeed we had to use the utmost tact after Dr Roth's letter arrived to enable the two works to be performed at all.

It makes one's working exceedingly difficult if one's actions are continually to be misinterpreted.

624 To Grace Williams

4 Crabbe Street, Aldeburgh
March 11th 1949

My dear Grace,

Your very welcome letter has lain unanswered for nearly a month – I am so sorry; but I have got (owing to this horrible illness-business) very behind-hand with everything. I was happy to know that you liked the Sinfonia,[1] as it is a piece that I have a special feeling for – written as it were in a crisis, & for all its inadequacies it reflects that crisis. It was impossible to tell (the 3rd programme is all but inaudible here) whether it was a good performance, but I'm sure it made sense as Ansermet knows it well & sees what it's all about.

You are right about one's life, but you are a nice one to talk having been banished for the same reason![2] Actually mine didn't actually develop into the ulcer-class, only every symptom was heralding it and the doctors were firm with me. It wasn't only endless touring which caused it – every kind of pressure of work, responsibility, domestic as well – in fact like 90% of the world today! But I'm fine again now, & after three months' inability am just down to work again. I hope you'll approve of the result – a Spring Symphony, full chorus, orchestra, soloists & God-knows-what – indulging myself properly in every kind of extravagance! I'm also planning another full-scale opera (with E. M. Forster) – so you can't reproach me any more for neglecting the Symph. Orch. It is merely that I like to write for what is handy & don't call one performance every five years under Boult or Sargent "handy" – do you? Are you writing? What happened to those Welsh folk-songs?[3] Would they be suitable for Peter & me?

I hope you get really well. Let me know when you & I might converge on London & perhaps have a lunch.

Yours ever,

BEN

1   Grace Williams wrote to Britten on 17 February 1949 after hearing a BBC Third Programme broadcast of *Sinfonia da Requiem* by the BBC Symphony Orchestra conducted by Ernest Ansermet.

2   A reference to Williams's return to Wales, a move that, according to her letter to Britten, restored her to full health.

3   Williams's folksong arrangements *Six Welsh Oxen Songs* had been much admired by Britten in 1934 (see Letter 55 n. 2): 'they are by far the best arrangements of any folk-songs I know' (Britten to Williams, 25 September 1934). In 1950 she arranged *Three Traditional Welsh Ballads* for tenor, flute, oboe and string quartet, the first performance of which was given under the aegis of the EOG by Pears and members of the London Harpsichord Ensemble, at Friends House, Euston Road, London, on 14 November 1950.

625   **To Peter Pears**

[Aldeburgh]

[before 18 March 1949]

My darling

This is only to say good morning & to say I love you, & miss you, & long for you to come back on Friday, & how I hope that you've had a lesson today, & that it was a nice one & pleased you & Madam[1] too, & that the opera libretto is pounding ahead with Morgan still at full steam & irrepressible,[2] and that I like the Spring Symphony, apart from one still beastly bit that I <u>can't</u>, <u>can't</u>, <u>can't</u> get right, but I suppose I shall one day, and how are you, and are you taking your blood-pressure pills, & if not, why, & hadn't you better go & see the Doctor again, & tell him what's the matter with them, and to ask you what train you think you'll be on on Friday, & that it doesn't seem likely that we will be able to come to Ipswich because Eric's got to be in London for a Directors' meeting (did you see or talk with Anne [Wood] – a bit important) & to send you my love, & my love, & my love, & kisses & my love –

Your

B.

1   Pears had embarked on a series of singing lessons with Eva de Reusz.

2   Forster and Crozier had stayed at Crag House from 2 to 15 March to work

at the first draft libretto of *Billy Budd*. See BBMCPR, pp. 52–4. Crozier's letters to Nancy Evans chart the librettists' progress:

3 MARCH 1949
[. . .] Morgan is champing keen to work on *Billy*! We began at 10.00 this morning, and it seems that all our days will be spent on the opera, which worries me because of other jobs and responsibilities that are on my mind. But I can't discourage Morgan's great enthusiasm and show myself unwilling; so there it is. The sooner we get on with Billy, I suppose, the sooner I shall be free for other things, and I should not forget how lucky I am to be working with Morgan and Ben at all.

4 MARCH 1949
We are immersed in *Billy Budd* like two Trappist monks. Morgan comes to my room straight after breakfast, we pull chairs as close over the fire as possible, and there we sit until lunch, endlessly discussing, suggesting, rejecting and scribbling, in a welter of technical terms as we try to imagine what life can have been like on a man-of-war. After two days we have sketched out the bones of the first scene, and it will take another week to finish all scenes. After that we must look for answers to many questions before trying to write actual words. The collaboration seems to go well. Morgan is the careful, wise mind who will write most of the text and dialogue: I am the technician and will write what is needed in the way of songs and shanties, but there will not be many of those. Once our drudgery of the next week is over, the actual writing of the text will not take terribly long, for we are making clear what will need to be said, as we go along.

[5 MARCH 1949]
Poor Ben is in a wretched state these last days. Something is worrying him, spoiling his temper, jamming his work, and throwing his tummy out of gear. I can't make out what is the cause: [. . .] perhaps it's the symphony and its great problems: even, I begin to suspect, it may be that he does not really want to do *Billy* as an opera, but feels he can't withdraw now that Morgan and I are so earnestly at work. [. . .]

[. . .] [Morgan] has been writing a draft of one of our first scenes (the first arrival of Billy on the man-o'-war) to show Ben and me tomorrow, and for us to turn into libretto form together.

6 MARCH 1949
I was right in my guess about Ben's wretchedness. He was going through a period of revulsion against *Billy Budd*, from a misunderstanding about the purpose of the story, and he wanted to give the whole thing up. But now he has come through and sees that his feeling was muddled, and with the change everything has improved – health, temper, outlook, work on the [*Spring*] symphony, and spirits.

Morgan and I have been working for two hours since breakfast, and now he is making a draft of the scene we have been planning, on the other side of the table [. . .] Occasionally he interrupts for advice on special points, or asks for suggestions, and Ben has just been in for two minutes to join us at elevenses, but has gone back to his study now to get on with his last movement [of *Spring Symphony*], which is running well after weeks of doubt and indecision.

FRIDAY [11 MARCH 1949]
The work goes surprisingly well at present, with great speed and ease, and Morgan and I have reached a state of agreement in which we can guess how the other's

mind is working and save time by talking shorthand. I am becoming an expert on technical ship matters and have got much help from a book published by someone named C. N. Parkinson of Liverpool University. Morgan is in charge of the drama, I am in command of the ship, and we share matters out between us. It is going to be a stupendous opera. Like *Grimes* – with a much better story, a fine libretto and a classical shape.

14 MARCH 1949

Ben has very nearly finished the symphony: Morgan and I are rapidly nearing the end of the second act, and the third is only a short one [at this stage *Budd* was envisaged as a three-act opera]: my head is stuffed with details of ships and sailing. When we began ten days ago, Morgan wrote and I provided technical fodder. Now we collaborate much more closely and sometimes I write a whole scene myself, or draft a scene to provide a skeleton for him to clothe. It's a fascinating experience, and I hear from Ben that he [Morgan] said the other day that I could have written the libretto alone, but he couldn't possibly have written it without me. Typically generous of him, for he's a most kind man.

15 MARCH 1949

We have come to a point where I must type the whole libretto so far as it has gone, which will be a day's work.

Morgan insists, Ben tells me, that I shall be announced as joint author with him. Isn't that splendid! If we also share in the proceeds I shall be well off, for a big opera is highly profitable [...]

626 To Henriëtte Bosmans

4 Crabbe Street, Aldeburgh
March 18th 1949

My dear Jetty,

Many, many apologies for the long silence – you must have given me up for lost or dead! Afraid I have been up to my eyes in crises since I got back from Italy – crises of work, domestic ones, personal ones, & sea crises! However they are all (with the exception of the last one, which is I suppose permanent) being solved now, & so I am able to send you a word of thanks for the lovely eggs, and a word of how I am – much better, thank you, and with only very occasional lapses into the old troubles. Italy was really wonderful. I was well enough to enjoy it thoroughly, and we had most beautiful weather. We were in Venice for 2 weeks, & then a week on the Riviera in Portofino (near Rapallo & Genoa). Both Peter & I felt most relaxed & refreshed after it, and if only it could have been much longer ...! But money difficulties, & Peter's work brought us back, & I came almost straight down here. I wasn't perhaps so cured as I'd felt, & hoped, & back to everyday life things weren't quite 100%. But your eggs & sweet letters helped, & I now have good domestic help, & work is progressing once again (after terrible weeks of anxiety & difficulties). My

Spring Symphony is now fully sketched & I am happy with it. It is a big piece, about 45 mins – full chorus, soloists, orchestra – with many movements. I think it'll be done in Amsterdam in July,[1] so I hope you will hear it, & like it too! In the meantime work on the libretto of the new big opera progresses fast. We (Eric & I) have the invaluable aid of England's greatest novelist, E. M. Forster – who is also an angel, & lovely to work with. I'll tell you the subject when we meet; it is provocative, but great.

And – the sea! . . . What problems! We have had terrible storms, & a lot more of the beach & front has been washed away – the house is much nearer to danger, & in fact was flooded in the cellars! I hope that they will do something about walls or breakwaters soon, or we may have to take to living in the upper floors! The sea was really big & frightening though.

And you – ? – I hope are well. So very glad about your good piano recitals. When do you broadcast? – let us know, because although we cannot get <u>English</u> programmes, we can occasionally get <u>Dutch</u> ones!

We are in Holland at the beginning of May for a few days.[2] So we can meet & gossip then.

Peter is well, & singing very well. His voice is growing all the time.

With many thanks again, & much love,
BEN

1 See Letter 634 n. 1.

2 Britten and Pears broadcast from Hilversum on 10 May and gave a recital in The Hague on the 14th.

627 To Ralph Hawkes
[*Typed*]

4 Crabbe Street, Aldeburgh, Suffolk
24th March, 1949

Dear Ralph,

I am afraid I have neglected you terribly these last months. My excuse, as usual, is pressure of work and this time, if ever, is that excuse justified.

I hope, in the meantime, that you have had a good holiday and have returned to the office feeling thoroughly refreshed. Did you ski as usual in your grand manner, and did you persuade Clare to like it as well? There are so many things to say that I scarcely know where to begin, but the tour is as good a start as any.

1. Thank you for your letter of February 27th about the tour.[1] Everything seems to be extremely well organised by you. I hope by now that you will have received Peter's letter from Italy (which seemed to take an

unconscionable time to arrive). I cannot say that there are any outstanding queries unanswered, but, anyhow, I know that you know our tastes and will be able to decide any problems for us.

Peter in London, I think, is coping with booking the passages. I cannot pretend I look forward to it, but at any rate it will be very nice to see you and Clare and our good friends in the U.S.A.

By the way, I will do what I can about an "a cappella" chorus for California,[2] but my composition plate is so full at the moment that I dare not guarantee anything. That leads me to subject 2:

2. <u>Louisville Philharmonic Society</u>. I was delighted with John Woolford's letter,[3] but I am afraid my reaction is as usual – some day I want to write a piece for Kathleen, but I do not see how I could do it by the time, nor, if I did, how the concert could be fitted into our schedule. Would you please give him my good wishes and say that "one day – or perhaps"!

3. <u>Spring Symphony</u>. I have at last good news for you. Apart from one movement I have now completed my sketches;[4] indeed, I have also copied from them the chorus parts, which Erwin is having engraved immediately. The extra piece, when it is done, will have to be copied separately and added later. I hope after our spring tour (Switzerland, Italy, Vienna, Belgium, Holland) to get down to the scoring, which I think we had better have photographed immediately and sent to you in time for the Tanglewood Festival.[5] I am writing to Koussevitzky direct about the piece, with which I am happy at the moment, although I have gone through considerable agony of body and spirit through it. It became, in some way, connected with my illness and I was incapable for months of restarting work on it but the illness and the work now seem to be completed together.

I shall also ask Dr Koussevitzky whether he will mind the Holland Festival performance taking place, that is, on July 15th. I am passionately keen that this should be so, since, with all my commitments, much as I should like it, I shall not be able to hear the Tanglewood performance. If I miss this opportunity of hearing it in Holland it will be at least a year before I hear the work, and that will be a considerable disadvantage in my preparation for the opera which is subject number 4:

4. <u>New big opera</u>. I will send you in a few days time an authoritative little paragraph about this. At the moment the wording of this, including the title of the work, is giving us trouble.

I think you know some of the details already. E. M. Forster and Eric are joint librettists and the subject is a short story of Herman Melville. The libretto is astonishing. Forster has been staying here for the last three weeks and has sketched out practically the complete work. He is at the height of his form and most people will consider that that is without rival today. Eric has been helping considerably and has in fact done all the research into naval behaviours of 1797 – a considerable subject.

As usual I am afraid the subject and the treatment will be controversial, but I know you are used to that! I am truly excited and hope very much to start work on it this summer when subject number 5 is finished.

5. The Children's Opera. Eric has written a charming little libretto for a one-act children's opera[6] and is in the process of writing an introductory act in play form showing the preparation by the children of this one-act piece. The cast consists of five professional singers and six children, and the audience constitutes the chorus (a neat device for saving money, don't you think?) I have left myself ten days for composing this, but I do not anticipate any difficulties arising.[7]

The first performance will take place in Aldeburgh, in the Aldeburgh Festival in June, then in Wolverhampton and Cheltenham, and we are hoping to arrange a tour in the autumn. We have already picked some startlingly good children to take part. They all come from Ipswich, where they are at various schools.

6. The English Opera Group. You will soon be receiving the details of our latest financial crisis, perhaps the most acute to date, caused largely by the Arts Council reducing our grant, but we are fighting with amazing energy for our existence and I feel certain that we shall succeed.

As you know, this is no whim of mine. Too many people now acknowledge our importance and the successes of last year have confirmed us in the public favour. I am afraid we may not be popular in B & H, I think principally because I always feel that Dr Roth's view is a short-term policy and ours a long. Probably if we perform in a foreign country it may put off for a year or so a potential performance (although that is arguable) but I think our exploits have shown that this kind of opera is more inclined to be misunderstood than a normal full-scale piece; and therefore I think it is important for the success of the works that wherever possible we should show our own productions to set the style. Hearing yours, Ansermet's, Elizabeth's and Clytie's opinions, to say nothing of the grotesque newspaper criticisms, I am convinced that if the production in New York had been modelled on ours the understanding of Lucretia would have been infinitely greater. Apropos of this, it would be lovely if Ashton[8] can go to Tanglewood to supervise the Herring production.[9] Without him or his advice I feel the production is doomed to failure, as it was in Brussels,[10] where we should have been with our own production recently, had it not been for some very unhappy interference which I believe you know about, which, alas, leads me to subject 7.

7. <u>Lucretia and Rome</u>. I enclose a letter that I have had to write to Falkner recently [see Letter 623 n. 3]. It is to do with the proposed double per-formance of Dido and Lucretia in Rome recently. Dr Roth, with my full agreement, opposed this but, unfortunately, he wrote a long letter to Carisch[11] which was then given publicity and which contained his own exaggerated and mad views on the dullness of Dido, attributing these to myself. Knowing that, I think the letter is self-explanatory. I dipped my pen in vitriol to Roth himself, and had an equally vitriolic reply but that was a fortnight ago and I hope tension has relaxed again!

In the meantime, Falkner is giving publicity to my denial of these opinions because I really cannot let people in Rome, where we are to go so soon, think I am quite such a fool or a prig.

I am sure I have forgotten to say lots of things, but I will write again as soon as I am back from a tiny tour (including a performance of Nicolas at Dartington next weekend).[12]

[*Handwritten:*] Thank you again for another delicious ham, which arrived in splendid condition. It is most generous and thoughtful, Ralph, of you, because with all the comings & goings to do with the new opera, & endless Group, Festival & Symphony business the strain on the house-keeping is considerable! Thank you, from all who have participated in it, for a most delicious treat!

My love to both of you,
& best wishes,
Yours ever,
BEN

1 Hawkes's letter of 27 February has not survived; it was clearly a follow-up letter to one sent by him to the composer on 11 January in which details of Britten's and Pears's forthcoming North American tour were discussed.

2 Details of this proposal must appear in Hawkes's letter of 27 February: the unaccompanied chorus was presumably intended for the concert at the University of Southern California, Los Angeles, on 30 November. No such work was composed.

3 John R. Woolford, Manager of the Louisville Philharmonic Society, and formerly John Barbirolli's secretary, wrote to Hawkes on 14 February to try to interest Britten in writing an orchestral song-cycle for Kathleen Ferrier, to be premiered in the orchestra's 1949–50 season. Britten had composed the role of Lucretia and the contralto part in *Spring Symphony* with Ferrier's voice in mind. In 1952 he was to compose *Canticle II: 'Abraham and Isaac'* for Ferrier and Pears.

4 On the same day as this letter, Britten also wrote to Henriëtte Bosmans: 'I

have finished the sketches of the Spring Symphony (except that I <u>may</u> after all add another movement!!).' It is not clear whether Britten did write an additional movement, nor, if he did, can its identity be determined.

5 See Letter 635 n. 2.

6 Writing from his cottage in Southwold, Crozier charted the progress on the libretto of *Let's Make an Opera* in a sequence of letters to Nancy Evans, beginning with an undated letter probably written in January 1949:

[...] I have been planning out the children's opera. Although I shall leave the First Part [i.e. the play] to be written last, it is necessary to sketch the action and the characters before I tackle the opera itself. I have done only a little so far, but hope to complete it by the time I go to bed and to have the foundations dug so that actual building can begin.

1 FEBRUARY 1949
I have begun *Let's Make an Opera* with very peculiar results so far. Everything takes an inordinate time and when I have tailored a verse I haven't the least idea whether it's good or ghastly. This is the old problem of using simplest words and ideas, with, for me the catastrophic example of [Holst's] *The Wandering Scholar* poking its head through at every instant.

3 FEBRUARY 1949
I have written and partly revised Scene One of the opera. Two more scenes to write and still more revision. The general shape seems not too bad, but the details hold me up. I have foresworn all near-rhymes and sometimes fret for an hour seeking an exact one. Especially difficult, because many of them are double-rhymes, of which English has infinitely fewer than other languages. I am feeling very canny about the whole undertaking, for writing *Albert* and *Nicolas* has at length taught me what a slipshod writer I often am, and watching Morgan [Forster] at work [on *Billy Budd*] has shown me how hair-splittingly exact a good writer must be. It is hard to combine natural exuberance and fussiness in the right proportions, but I hope eventually to find a true balance.

17 FEBRUARY 1949, FROM 4 CRABBE STREET, ALDEBURGH
Ben likes the children's opera text, thank goodness; but I am still badly stuck in the middle of Scene 2 and the Arts Council makes me despondent about whether it will ever get done, though I hope, even if the Group collapses, that the Festival plans will continue. [The Arts Council had reduced the EOG's grant from £5000 to £3000.]

23 FEBRUARY 1949, FROM ALDEBURGH
At last I have finished sketching out the children's opera, after what seems interminable weeks of trying without result. This moment I have typed the last page. There will be lots of alterations to make, but the main shape is established, and it's never so hard to alter things as it is to have the despairing feeling that something should exist and doesn't.

In this letter Crozier goes on to mention Britten's progress with *Spring Symphony* – 'He is having a stiff time with the Choral Symphony and cannot get the shape of the whole thing to come right' – and describes his and Britten's daily routine:

We live a quiet life. Up at eight, breakfast and post (and delicious letters from you to start the day well), work all morning and throughout the day except for meals, or a daily game of squash instead of a walk. Ben is demonic at squash. Almost championship standard and as full of tricks as a cartload of monkeys. He usually beats me nine–love; but twice I have beaten him, to both our surprises.

The letter continues:

There was a hateful attack on Ben in a *TLS* [*Times Literary Supplement*] review of E. W. White's book [see Letter 605]. Really beastly and Dyneley Husseyish, but unsigned. [Dyneley Hussey was the music critic of the *Listener*.] So I have written a ferocious letter to the Editor, which he will probably not dare to publish. I am tired of our malevolent critics and feel it is time to go into attack against them when they are more than usually malicious in their scribbles. It may at least encourage editors to treat their venom with more caution.

In a later letter (4 March 1949), Crozier reports: 'Letters from Tony Gishford and E. W. White about my *TLS* letter, both approving and both having followed my example by protesting to the Editor. I must get tomorrow's copy, in case Hussey has been roused to an answer.'

The anonymous review of Eric Walter White's *Benjamin Britten* appeared in the 19 February 1949 issue of the *Times Literary Supplement*:

Every religion at an early stage in its development becomes possessed of a canon of sacred writings, acceptance of which is sooner or later regarded as one of the tests of orthodoxy. The phenomenon is familiar and has repeated itself in our own days with the writings of Karl Marx and Mrs Baker Eddy: no self-respecting sect can afford to be without its scriptures. It was, therefore, to be foreseen that the latest and most flourishing of our musical sects would furnish itself with a written account of the life and works of its hero, a neat and unpretentious gospel discreetly combining the qualities of hagiography with those of a modern publicity agency.

Mr White's small book possesses both qualifications. To the converted, who see in Mr Benjamin Britten a special vessel of election with no compeer among modern composers and few among the great names of old, Mr White's almost unqualified admiration will seem both natural and proper. The rest of the world, which recognizes in Mr Britten a composer of quite exceptional natural gifts in great danger of being spoiled by too-easy success, and the victim of adulation rather than of misunderstanding, will nevertheless find many interesting things in this book. The account, for example, of Mr Britten's early experience of writing music for films throws a new light on his operatic technique, and the formidable list of early unpublished or virtually forgotten works combines in an unusual manner great facility with great industry.

Mr White's thorough description of Mr Britten's two main operas, *Peter Grimes* and *The Rape of Lucretia*, goes far towards exploding the current myth that the composer has hitherto been badly served by his librettists. He quotes Mr Britten's own words to show that he had, at all stages, a large say in the fashioning of the text and that he regards this as 'one of the secrets of writing a good opera'. He therefore assumes more than the usual responsibility for both virtues and deficiencies. *Peter Grimes* is one of the most remarkable first operas by any composer; and, considering that the composer had no native operatic tradition upon which to draw, his instinctive solution of many of the problems amounts almost to genius. The great weakness of the work lies in the insufficiency of the story to stir emotions or to move sympathies. Mr White describes Grimes as 'a maladjusted aggressive psychopath', but he apparently sees nothing incongruous in making such a figure the central character, and indeed the hero, of the work. In casting a Byronic aura round this man, whose only claim to our interest is that he has been involved in the death of several small boys and is therefore an object of suspicion and dislike among his neighbours, composer and librettist seem to be attaching some mystical value to the mere fact of being in opposition to society.

The majority of the inhabitants of the Borough, according to Mr White, are 'prejudiced bigots', but their prejudice was against certain cruelty and probable manslaughter, their bigotry consisted in refusing again to trust a child to the care of a man with so unsavoury a past. In fact, the Borough represents the normal and healthy instincts of society, expressed in a crude and primitive way. The absence of any feminine figure, except the purely maternal schoolmistress and the cardboard caricatures of femininity in its most unpleasing or ludicrous forms, accentuates the extraordinary emotional unbalance of the whole plot. It is only in the descriptive music and the episodes – set pieces not more than incidentally connected with the central theme – that Mr Britten's music is wholly effective. [. . .]

In *The Rape of Lucretia* Mr Britten again chose a subject luckily on the border line of normal experience; but he chose to set it in a formal framework of apparently Christian sentiment which clashes violently with the purely pagan denouement of the story, namely, Lucretia's suicide. Some extraordinarily pretentious verbiage of the librettist, Mr Ronald Duncan, is lightheartedly quoted by Mr White, 'Just as fertility or life is devoured by death, so is spirit defiled by Fate. Lucretia is, to my mind, the symbol of the former, Tarquinius the embodiment of the latter.' And a further quotation provides a neat commentary on his literary approach. 'The poet', he writes, 'must drive his metaphor to the point of clarity and contain in one image the condensation of a mood.' The reader of Mr White's book is seldom driven quite to this point of exasperation; but the author's image of the composer springs from a mood too uncritically admiring to satisfy any readers except those belonging to the small but powerful sect which threatens to kill with kindness one of the most naturally gifted of contemporary British composers.

Eric Crozier's riposte was published on 26 February 1949:

Sir, – Your critic fears that Benjamin Britten will be spoiled by 'too easy success' and by the adulation of 'a small but powerful sect of admirers', of whom I have the honour to count myself one.

A creative artist is less easily spoiled by success nowadays than by the sedulously cultivated malice of a small but powerful sect of critics. At least one of these critics has earned my unwilling admiration during the last five years by the pertinacity of his attempt to discredit Britten's music on every possible occasion, through the columns of one English daily newspaper, two English weekly papers, one American daily paper, and one Government-subsidized magazine. Such monopoly of criticism is not only damaging to the artist, but is equally harmful to the public, whose opinions the critic seeks to form.

The opening paragraph of the review entitled 'Words and Music' is perhaps less informative about Mr White's book than about your reviewer, whose prejudice it epitomizes.

In the 5 March 1949 issue, Eric Walter White's letter to the editor spelled out the genesis of the book:

The commission to write this book came to me shortly after the war from a Swiss publishing house, Atlantis Verlag of Zurich [see Letter 605 n. 2]. When I accepted I expressed the wish that in addition to the original German edition there should be an English edition in this country, and I left arrangements for this in the hands of Atlantis Verlag. Their choice fell on Boosey & Hawkes, who accordingly published the English edition last November, a few days after the German edition had appeared in Switzerland. Boosey & Hawkes are also publishers of Britten's music. The fact that your reviewer specifically refers to my monograph as possessing certain 'modern publicity agency' qualities is likely not only to mislead persons who are ignorant of the above circumstances but also to do less than justice to what, I submit, is a striking example of Swiss interest in contemporary British music and of Swiss initiative in commissioning the first book to appear in any country on Benjamin Britten and his work.

The anonymous reviewer, now writing under the pseudonym 'Bene Latui' ('Well Concealed'), had his letter to the editor denying Eric Crozier's imputation that he was Dyneley Hussey published on 26 March:

The anonymity of your columns protects me from Mr Crozier's wrath but I am unwilling to take advantage of this protection to the extent of seeing an innocent man suffering in his reputation for what are wholly my misdemeanours.

The reviewer is now known to be Martin Cooper.

7 *The Little Sweep* was to be composed at the beginning of April. Britten wrote to Pears on the 8th:

I am pushing on terrifically with the children's opera, not stopping to think what I'm doing or how it is – because I have to deliver some of the score on Monday to Erwin! I think anyhow that it's gay enough, altho' possibly not very distinguished – and also it's <u>easy</u>, which is something! It's funny writing an opera without you in it – don't really like it much, I confess, but I'll admit that it makes my vocal demands less extravagant!

To Nancy Evans, Eric Crozier reported on Britten's progress with *The Little Sweep*:

7 APRIL 1949, FROM ALDEBURGH
[...] I have seldom seen Ben so cheerful as he is these days. He is loving writing the children's opera and goes about with a beaming smile. So far he has written four numbers – as simple as can be and great fun.

11 APRIL 1949
Ben is getting on so fast through the score that I am kept busy rewriting and altering, and shall not be able to begin the play until next week. You should hear his waltz for the Bathing of Sammy [the Interlude between scenes 1 and 2, the audience song 'The kettles are singing/Like midsummer larks']. It's as gay as anything could be and even more infectious than the *Nicolas* waltz. He has set the words brilliantly, and I don't think anyone will ever forget it after a first hearing. With a sparkling

string accompaniment on top, like spray blowing from the tops of waves on a sunny, windy day. Later in the scene, he repeats it in the minor key for a general song pitying Sammy.

16 APRIL 1949

Ben is working furiously hard at *Let's Make an Opera*, composing all day, and scoring at night. He has written nearly half and aims to finish by Thursday [21 April]. I am eager for you to hear it – it gives me great pleasure, and the simple tunes are incisive and memorable. Luckily I have at last finished the Programme Book [for the 1949 Aldeburgh Festival] today, and can concentrate tomorrow on writing a song for Anne Sharp [who played Juliet] to replace one I don't like and have torn up. Then on Monday I must settle to the play [i.e. the first part of *Let's Make an Opera*], which will take about two weeks.

8 Frederick Ashton (1904–1988), English dancer and choreographer, founder–choreographer of the Royal Ballet, of which he was Principal Choreographer, 1933–70, and Director, 1963–70. He was knighted in 1962. He produced the premiere production of *Albert Herring* at Glyndebourne in June 1947 and choreographed the movement and ballet sequences for *Death in Venice* in 1973. See also Letter 138 n. 3, and Julie Kavanagh, *Secret Muses: The Life of Frederick Ashton*.

9 The US premiere of *Albert Herring* was given at Tanglewood on 8 August 1949, in a production conducted by Boris Goldovsky, with a cast led by David Lloyd (Albert) and Ellen Faull (Lady Billows). James Pease sang the role of the Vicar, Mr Gedge.

10 The Théâtre de la Monnaie in Brussels had presented *Albert Herring* in June 1948: Letter 580 n. 5.

11 Unidentified.

12 A performance of *Saint Nicolas*, with Pears as soloist, was given at Dartington on 2 April. The following day Pears and Britten also gave a recital there.

628 **To Marion Stein**

4 Crabbe Street, Aldeburgh
April 7th 1949

My dear Marion,

I have been thinking so much about you these last few days, & wishing that I could have been around with you in your considerable quandary! I do so sympathise with you, but I feel that absolutely nothing should weigh in importance beside whether you really love him, & feel you'd like to spend your life with him.[1] It isn't of the slightest importance that I personally like him a lot; only you can answer that question. Don't worry about, or let people exaggerate to you, the difficulties which may arise owing to his position. After all, they might not arise; if they do they'd only be for a short while, & after all you've got some pretty good friends around you who'd stand by you through thick & thin!

Forgive the avuncular advice, but I wanted you to realise that you've got my love & confidence in whatever you decide, & I know that goes for Peter too.

In the meantime don't forget about the Mozart Fantasy[2] – I hope that goes well too?

My children's opera shoots ahead, & is rather fun. I went riding yesterday, & my new breeches behaved beautifully.[3]

Lots of love – come down if you want to –
BEN

1   Marion Stein had written to Britten to seek his advice about her relationship with Lord Harewood.

2   At this period Marion Stein was pursuing her studies as a concert pianist.

3   This activity was not sustained.

629   To Benjamin Britten
From Peter Pears

American Hotel [Amsterdam]
Monday A.M. in bed
[?11 April 1949]

My own honey darling –

Your adorable letter has just arrived, brought up by the scruffy little pageboy, & so I'm writing straight off to you waiting for my breakfast to come. I was terribly happy to have your wire last evening. I got it when I came back from the Diamonds where I had tea after the Passion[1] – Jetty [Bosmans], Pam H. J., Hazel[2] & one or two others very sweet. I've been rather a neurotic voice-conscious old tenor this week – Wolverhampton & Birmingham were pretty dreary – the weather was awful – pouring showers & B'ham with the shops shut – the only relief was that I found a copy of "Curious Relations"[3] & yelled with laughter for 2 days. What a funny book. Then the car journey to London was no fun & the flight was all right except for last 10 minutes which were bumpy – & then it was boiling sweaty hot in the Concertgebouw for Thursday's general probe[4] – & I thought my voice had gone – I really did. So I stayed in bed all Friday & inhaled & fussed & saw no one – & same on Saturday – & I thought "I can probably make tonight but what about Sunday?" & then I made Saturday all right & went straight back to bed & inhaled etc. oh dear! & then Sunday was all right after all! What a fool I am! but thank goodness you weren't here all the same – I couldn't have borne to see your nervous little look in the eyes – ! Honey-bee!

So now it's Bertus [van Lier] & his do – I hope that'll be all right. It'll be lovely to see Nancy [Evans]. She's staying at Rotterdam.

I'm glad you liked the Passion & that it came over well – I am getting to know it better (with, I hope, certain advantages) but so is van Beinum[5] – & I'm afraid that has its disadvantages. All those choruses that will accelerate in the last 2 bars – & the ensemble & tempi in the arias – & "Wahrlich dies war Gottes Sohn!"[6] – terrible. They get wilder with the years.

Haefliger's[7] voice is really excellent, though he's not a sensitive musician. What did you think of Jo?[8] First of all, she's a darling! Then, though she sang flat in the "Aus Liebe",[9] I thought she sang the G major 6/8 Aria[10] nicely – & I do think all things considered she is the right person for Spring [*Symphony*]. Her voice is cool – but has character & I find charm. She would sing the Driving boy nicely I think & also our Duet,[11] which is not heavily scored. Apparently above A according to Jetty she has difficulty – but what is there above A? I can't remember.

So glad the Children's Opera is going so well.

You are an old poppet & I do love you very very dearly – & am longing for next weekend!

By the way, a dozen bottles of assorted sherries should be arriving from Harvey's of Bristol, also a lot of nice dishes for oven + table combined – from W'hampton.

> All my love – honey-bee – my boy –
>
> P.

John Nicholson[12] is looking thin. I'm worried about him. The sweet pageboy asked tenderly after you. They are sorry for me being alone!

The Bach arrived incredibly quickly! On Thursday evening! v. many thanks. P.

1 Pears was in Amsterdam to take part in van Beinum's annual performances of Bach's *St Matthew Passion*. The public rehearsal took place on Thursday, 7 April, with performances on the 9th and 10th.

2 Unidentified.

3 A collection of family anecdotes and stories written by Anthony Butts and edited, under the pseudonym William D'Arfey, by William Plomer. The book sold well when published in 1945 in the UK and 1947 in the US. Anthony Butts, a friend of Plomer, had committed suicide in 1941 while suffering from terminal cancer.

4 *Generalprobe* (Ger.) = dress rehearsal.

5   Eduard van Beinum (1901–1959), Dutch conductor who succeeded Willem
    Mengelberg as Principal Conductor of the Amsterdam Concertgebouw
    Orchestra in 1945, having been Second Conductor (from 1931) and later
    Associate Conductor. He was also Principal Conductor of the London
    Philharmonic Orchestra (1949–51) and Music Director of the Los Angeles
    Philharmonic Orchestra from 1956. See K. Ph. Bernet Kempers and Marius
    Flothuis (eds.), *Eduard van Beinum*, and Wolfgang Dinglinger et al., *De
    Matthäus-Passion, 100 Jahr Passietraditie van het Koninklijk Concertgebouw-
    orkest.*
         Van Beinum was an early champion of Britten's music in Europe,
    recording the *Four Sea Interludes* and *Passacaglia from 'Peter Grimes'* for
    Decca in 1947 (see Letter 564 n. 4) and conducting the premiere of *Spring
    Symphony* in 1949. An off-air recording of the latter was issued by Decca on
    CD in 1994 (Decca 44 063–2). Like Mengelberg before him, van Beinum
    preserved the traditional Passiontide performances of Bach's *St Matthew
    Passion* at the Concertgebouw, adding Pears to his pool of soloists.

6   The setting of the Centurion's words, 'Truly, this was the Son of God', which
    Bach allocates to the chorus in the *St Matthew Passion*, Part II, No. 73.

7   Ernst Haefliger (b. 1919), Swiss tenor, noted for his interpretation of the
    Evangelist in the Bach Passions and of Schubert's *Die schöne Müllerin* and
    Die Winterreise.

8   Jo Vincent (1898–1989), Dutch soprano, the leading concert soprano of the
    Netherlands until her retirement in 1953 and a favourite of Mengelberg,
    who liked the purity of her sound in Bach, Beethoven and Mahler. She
    published her memoirs, *Zingend door het leren*, in 1955. Vincent was the
    soprano soloist at the first performance of Britten's *Spring Symphony* in
    1949. Britten, however, was not at first convinced that she would be an
    effective soloist. In a letter to Henriëtte Bosmans (11 January 1949) he wrote:

    I did hear Jo Vincent [on the radio], thanks to your information. Of course she
    wasn't helped by the conductor's drab, colourless & indefinite performance, but I
    was really worried by her lack of authority, & felt that if she was so unsure about
    Bach, how could she perform Britten with conviction? Also there was nothing
    high she had to sing, & my part goes (lightly) quite high. I reluctantly feel she won't
    do – which is a thousand pities, as I am sure in character & charm she is perfect.

9   *St Matthew Passion*, Part II, No. 58.

10 'Ich will dir mein Herze schenken', *St Matthew Passion*, Part I, No. 19.

11 'Fair and fair' (George Peele), from Part III of *Spring Symphony.*

12 The son of the Britten family's solicitor (1914–1975) remained a lifelong
    friend of Britten from their days at South Lodge preparatory school; see
    also Diary for 18 April 1931, n. 4.

630   To Serge Koussevitzky

4 Crabbe Street, Aldeburgh
April 19th 1949

Dear Dr Koussevitzky,

Ralph Hawkes has just forwarded to me a copy of your letter to him about the Spring Symphony. I am so very sorry that you feel as you do about the proposed Holland Festival performance, but I quite understand – and certainly my long silence has not in any way helped matters![1] The truth is that, with my illness, the work has become somewhat of a bogey – and there was nothing to write to you but doubts and miseries! But now it is finished (although I still have plans to add a new movement),[2] I think I can be more cheerful about it. But the "doubts & miseries" are the reasons for my wanting to hear the work as soon as possible. As you know I should have dearly loved to have come to Tanglewood for your performance, but the fact of my commitments here (intensified by the illness) and my later tour in U.S.A. preclude that, & I just have to agree to the Dutch performance (otherwise it would be Spring 1950 at least before I heard it). But under the circumstances I absolutely understand if this will make you revise your Tanglewood plans; but, with your permission, I should like to retain the proposed dedication,[3] hoping to hear one day a performance of unequalled brilliance & understanding, by yourself.

Perhaps there will be a chance of meeting you when I come in October? I do hope so.

With warmest greetings, and deepest apologies!
Yours ever,
BENJAMIN B.

1   Koussevitzky's letter to Hawkes has not survived, but it must have contained a negative response to Britten's request for the first performance of *Spring Symphony* to take place in Amsterdam. Koussevitzky himself had intended to premiere the work at the Tanglewood Festival that summer. In the light of this letter from Britten, he relented and relinquished his claim to the first performance.

2   See also Letter 627 n. 4.

3   The published dedication reads 'For Serge Koussevitzky and the Boston Symphony Orchestra'.

631   To Eric Crozier

American Hotel [Amsterdam]
[before 15 May 1949]

Dear Eric,

Only a scribble, with a query or two. I've sent off the last bit of score[1] to Erwin, so I hope it won't be too long before the chaps & children get the rest of it. I wasn't sure about the words of the Finale, so I concocted something in the rhythm I thought we agreed on (my <u>version</u> isn't serious, only an indication. . . ! ! !). The rhythm I've used for the verse is always the same, i.e.

$$\cup/{-} \cup\cup/{-} {-}/{-} \cup\cup/{-} {-}/$$
$$/{-} \cup\cup/{-} \cup\cup/{-} \cup\cup/{-}/^{2}$$

Perhaps you'd have a word with Erwin about the words before they're reproduced.

I've suggested that after 1st 2 verses the other children come back, & after 4th verse all the other characters. Perhaps you've an idea how this can be managed. I think it's important, to have all the sound on the stage we can. Also, I suggest that the stage should sing the refrain with the audience.[3]

I think that's all. I hope all is going well. We didn't enjoy Brussels[4] much – too tired. I do hope Nancy's throat's better. She must get some rest.

I'm writing to Elizabeth [Sweeting]. I hope to goodness the orchestral situation is settled now. Back on Sunday.

Lots of love & to Basil [Coleman] too from us both,

BEN

1   Of *The Little Sweep.*

2   The rhythm of the first two lines of each stanza from the 'Coaching Song' observes this rhythm, e.g.

The horses are champing, eagerly stamping,
Crack! goes the whip as the coachman lets slip.

3   Crozier wrote to Nancy Evans on 12 May: 'I am still trying to get the last song in the Children's Opera right, but I find it obstinate because of the alteration Ben has made in my original. It must go off today for engraving, after which it will be unchangeable for all eternity.' In the same letter Crozier announced to Evans:

I have decided that I must withdraw from *all* practical complications of production and administration in order to be free for concentrated writing and I have taken the first step by writing to offer my resignation [from the EOG] from the end of the Cheltenham Festival, after which I must be a writer and nothing but a writer.

4   Britten and Pears had given recitals in Brussels on 6 and 7 May 1949.

★ SOCIÉTÉ PHILHARMONIQUE DE BRUXELLES ★

Récital de Chant et Piano

DONNÉ PAR

Peter PEARS

ténor

ET

Benjamin Britten

pianiste et compositeur

★ VENDREDI 6 MAI 1949, A 20 HEURES ★

Prix : 5 Frs

SOCIÉTÉ PHILHARMONIQUE ★ PALAIS DES BEAUX-ARTS ★ BRUXELLES

PALAIS DES BEAUX-ARTS ★ BRUXELLES ★ SOCIÉTÉ PHILHARMONIQUE

PROGRAMME

1. a) If Music be the food of love .   Henry PURCELL
   b) I'll sail upon the Dog-star .   »
   c) There's not a swain . . . . .   »
   d) Divine Hymn : Job's Curse .   »

2. a) Auf der Bruck . . . .   Franz SCHUBERT
   b) Am See . . . .   »
   c) Im Fruehling . . . .   »
   d) Der Musensohn . . . .   »

INTERRUPTION

3. Seven Sonnets of Michelangelo   Benjamin BRITTEN

4. Folk Songs . . .   arranged by   Benjamin BRITTEN
   a) Sally Gardens (Irish)
   b) The Bonny o'Moray (Scottish)
   c) Little Sir William (English)
   d) Troupiaux ! Troupiaux ! (French)

Palais des Beaux-Arts, Brussels, 6 May 1949: programme for a recital
by Pears and Britten

632   To Ralph Hawkes

4 Crabbe Street, Aldeburgh
May 29th 1949

My dear Ralph,

Your very kind & sympathetic letter about Eric Crozier arrived at the
end of Peter's & my strenuous but very successful tour over Europe,[1]
& since I got back here hard work on the score of the Symphony, &
rehearsals & details of the great Festival,[2] have occupied my time to the
entire exclusion of letter-writing!

Briefly, what I feel is this, & I am writing at Leslie's request the same to
him (L.A.B. [Leslie A. Boosey]). I am satisfied with E.C.'s work within
certain limits. He has provided me with neat libretti, & has developed a
good technique of writing for the stage, which has been invaluable for his
collaboration with E. M. Forster over "Billy Budd". But if you decide to
give him this guarantee against future royalties, I <u>cannot</u> feel myself
bound always to use him as my librettist. I must pick & choose according
to my ideas. As it happens the two vocal works I shall probably write in
the next two years <u>will</u> concern him – "Billy Budd" & possibly a work for
the Townswomen's Guild[3] (which they want to commission) – but after
that, I cannot say. If you think that his past works for me, plus these next
two would warrant such a guarantee – all well & good; but I must make
it clear that in the future artistic demands must dominate my choice of
librettists rather than a personal loyalty to him, or to his tie with B & H.

I hope this doesn't sound harsh towards him, or too much like throwing the ball back to you (!), but it's a fair statement of my case, I think.

About his family life, I can't be any more helpful. It seems ludicrous that he cannot make a sounder financial arrangement with his ex-wife. I have been agitating for this for ages, as you know, but without success. I feel strongly, like you, that until this happens his work must suffer, until the poor man has a securer background – in other words.

[after 19 June 1949]

My dear Ralph –

This was all written nearly a month ago, when I didn't have a chance to complete it – then I heard of your illness,[4] & I waited till I had a moment to add a word of sympathy (<u>and</u> advice!). I am so very sorry Ralph that it has happened, but you <u>must</u> take care & follow the doctors' advice <u>to the letter!</u> It will mean a great boredom for you, but you are far too precious to many many people, & your ideas are too valuable to go playing around with your health. So please take my advice. Give lots of my love to Clare, & say how much I'm thinking of her in her worries.

In the meantime, too, I had written the above about Eric to Leslie who acted accordingly. I must however say that Eric put me in an embarrassing position, by his request to you – which he did without consulting me at all, as a matter of fact; and, hard as it was, I am relieved that L.A.B. came to that decision. The effect on Eric has been disastrous; he has left the Group (although we are keeping his name on as Director), & has indicated that his only interest in the future can be in making money (!) – which in his circumstances I can well understand – but, how I wish these circumstances would change! But, as before, we can do nothing about that.[5]

The Aldeburgh Festival went, like last year, with a bang. Lots of people came, & I think financially it ought to have been sound again. We did excellent performances of Herring & Lucretia – the latter in a new production by Basil Coleman,[6] & conducted by Norman Del Mar, both great finds. And the children's opera was a great success – even with a good press!!![7] The first part, the play part, needs tidying & shortening, but the opera is quite a little winner, & the Ipswich kids tough & charming. When it is improved, which we are working on now, we are going to try for a short London season, in the school holidays, for instance.[8]

I must stop this rigmarole now, because you mustn't tire yourself with dreary business matters! Do get someone to write how you are, because it is worrying not to know.

With lots of love, & from Peter to you both,
(& take care!)
Yours ever,
BEN

The

Aldeburgh Festival

of Music and the Arts

JUNE 10–19 1949

In association with the

Arts Council of Great Britain and the English Opera Group

THE

ENGLISH OPERA GROUP

presents

Artistic Directors:

Benjamin Britten, Eric Crozier, John Piper, Anne Wood

LET'S MAKE AN OPERA!

An Entertainment for Young People

by

BENJAMIN BRITTEN

Libretto by ERIC CROZIER   Designed by JOHN LEWIS.

Produced by BASIL COLEMAN

FIRST PERFORMANCE

in the Jubilee Hall

Tuesday, June 14th at 7.30 p.m.

PART ONE: THE PLAY.   PART TWO: THE OPERA.

Mr. Chaffinch	sings Black Bob, the sweep	NORMAN LUMSDEN
Max Westleton	„ Clem, his son	MAX WORTHLEY
Sammie Fisher	„ Sam, the new sweep-boy	JOHN MOULES
Mrs. Parworthy	„ Miss Baggott, the housekeeper	GLADYS PARR
Gay Parworthy	„ Gay Brook (aged 13)	BRUCE HINES
Annie Dougall	„ Juliet Brook (aged 15)	ANNE SHARP
Sophie Stevenson	„ Sophie Brook (aged 11)	MONICA GARROD
Elisabeth Parrish	„ Rowan, nursery maid to the Brook children	ELISABETH PARRY
John Chaffinch	„ Johnnie Crome (aged 14)	PETER COUSINS
Hugh Lark	„ Hughie Crome } Twins	RALPH CANHAM
Christina Chaffinch	„ Tina Crome } aged 8	MAVIS GARDINER

The Orchestra:

HANS GEIGER, *First Violin*   CECIL ARONOWITZ, *Viola*
MANOUG PARIKIAN, *Second Violin*   GEORGE ROTH, *Violoncello*
CATHERINE SHANKS and MARION STEIN, *Pianoforte*
HERBERT WILSON, *Percussion*

Conducted by NORMAN DEL MAR

PART ONE: The stage shortly before a dress rehearsal.
Time: the present.

PART TWO: The children's nursery at Iken Hall, in January, 1810.

Scene One: Mid-morning.
Scene Two: Afternoon.
Scene Three: Next day.

There will be one interval of fifteen minutes.

Coffee may be obtained during the interval at The Copper Jug, Crag Path (between the lifeboat and the lookout station). A bell will be rung five minutes before the end of the interval, and you are courteously requested to return promptly to your place so as not to delay the performance.

No Smoking, please.

SCENERY built by Herbert Copley in the English Opera Group Workshop, Aldeburgh, and painted by John and Griselda Lewis.

COSTUMES executed by Flora Kandy, Joan Jefferson Farjeon and Maureen Copley.

PROPERTIES made by Rita Burr, and lent by residents of Aldeburgh.

Staff of the English Opera Group:

General Manager	::	Elizabeth Sweeting
Secretary	::	Elizabeth Butcher
Stage Manager and Electrician	::	Ronald Thomas
Assistant Stage Manager and Property Master	::	Rita Burr
Scenic Supervisor and Stage Carpenter	::	Herbert L. Copley
Wardrobe Mistress	::	Maureen Copley

Jubilee Hall, Aldeburgh, 14 June 1949: programme for the first performance of *Let's Make an Opera*

1 Britten and Pears gave recitals in Milan (23 April), Rome (25th), Genoa (28th), Turin (30th), Vienna (3 May), Brussels (6th and 7th) and The Hague (14th).

2 The 1949 Aldeburgh Festival was held from 10 to 19 June.

3 See Letter 592 n. 3.

4 The first signs of the heart condition that was to lead to Hawkes's tragically early death from a heart attack the following year.

5 These events were eventually to put an end to Crozier's personal and professional relationship with Britten. See p. 18 n. 23.

6 English director of opera, theatre and television (b. 1916), who worked extensively with the English Opera Group during the 1940s and 1950s – for Tyrone Guthrie he was to coach the cast of *The Beggar's Opera* in the spoken dialogue – and was to collaborate with Britten on the first stagings of *The Little Sweep*, *Billy Budd*, *Gloriana* and *The Turn of the Screw*. Coleman's relocation to Canada in the mid-1950s for a decade suspended his professional links with the composer, but on his return to the UK he became involved in the 1966 BBC Television production of *Billy Budd*. Although Coleman had wanted to produce *Peter Grimes* for television, he was full of misgivings about Britten's insistence on abandoning the double-studio method of recording (in which the cast and set are in one studio, and the conductor and orchestra in another) and instead recording the opera at Snape Maltings. Coleman strongly believed that the constraints imposed by filming away from the studio would result in sub-standard televisual results, and he withdrew. A further casualty of this was Coleman's projected involvement in *Owen Wingrave*, Britten's television opera. The composer in fact came to regret that he had not heeded Coleman's advice about recording at Snape, especially in respect of *Wingrave*, and offered a conciliatory hand to him which Coleman was generous enough to accept. In the 1980s Coleman worked alongside Pears and Steuart Bedford in several productions of Britten operas with students from the Britten–Pears School for Advanced Musical Studies, including a notable *Owen Wingrave* in 1984.

   Coleman has written about his association with the composer in 'Staging first productions 2', in DHOBB, pp. 34–43. See also Alan Blyth, *Remembering Britten*, pp. 111–16. The tape and transcript of Donald Mitchell's interview with Basil Coleman (29 October 2000) is at BPL.

7 Frank Howes contributed the following notice to *The Times* (15 June 1949):

   Once upon a time there lived an unhappy little boy called Sam. His cruel master used to send him up chimneys to sweep them, but one day he got stuck in the nursery chimney at Iken Hall. The children heard his cries, pulled him down, and hid him in the toy cupboard till it was safe to smuggle him away in a trunk so that he could live happily ever after.

   But that is only what happens in the second act of Benjamin Britten's delightful new entertainment for young people, *Let's Make an Opera*, which had its first performance in the Jubilee Hall at Aldeburgh last night. It is, in fact, only the little opera which the children have written themselves, and in the first act we are allowed to watch them rehearsing so that we can learn all the things we ought to know about an opera: what an aria is, and an ensemble, and most grown-up of all, a number seven gelatine in a spot frame. During this rehearsal, too, Mr Norman Del Mar, the conductor, with great patience and kindliness and humour, teaches us four songs so that we in the audience can also play a part in the performance.

On several past occasions Britten has ministered to children with instinctive understanding of their needs, but in *Let's Make an Opera* he surpasses his previous efforts. The most striking and original effects are once again produced with the simplest and most economical of means, particularly where the small orchestra of string quartet, two pianos and percussion is concerned, and the work is thoroughly deserving of a long and happy life.

Later performances, at the Cheltenham Festival, were reviewed by other critics. Desmond Shawe-Taylor, *New Statesman and Nation* (23 July 1949):

As we enter we are given sheets, some containing the words only, and some the music, of four 'audience songs'; we eye these, and our neighbours, apprehensively. The songs don't look at all easy: one is in 5/4 time, another has some tricky stretches of cross-rhythm, a third contains queer simultaneous bird-noises. Lights out; curtain up; no music. Where are we? An invisible man on the stage and an invisible small boy in the audience call out to each other; it's a rehearsal, an opera, some sort of children's opera. Two grown-ups are seen dealing with a hundred last-minute emergencies; half-a-dozen children unconcernedly wander in and out. Awkward bits are tried over; we learn the elementary principles of staging and opera-writing; we find that our opera is about a chimney-sweep, an enchanting small boy called Sammy. Meanwhile, the conductor, Mr Norman Del Mar, turns up, and coaxes us with all kinds of ingenious flattery into trying the choruses; they're not so hard after all, in fact quite infectious. By this time, what with the singing, and the queer bird-noises, and above all the Aldeburgh children, a wave of English good humour has spread all round the house.

An interval. Amusement in the foyer: chaffinches compare notes with owls, herons with turtle doves. Part Two consists of the children's opera itself, *The Little Sweep*; the orchestra is small, even for Britten: a string quartet, two pianists at a single piano, a percussion man. The audience provides its own overture with the 5/4 'Swee–ee–eep!' song; on the rise of the curtain the tune is taken up, with alterations, on the stage. The action is *Peter Grimes* in miniature: another bullied child, but no ambiguity this time about the character of the bully. Date, 1810; the nursery of a large Suffolk manor house; a poor shivering little sweep, sold to wicked Black Bob, is about to be sent up his first chimney. The humanitarian children are shocked; they conceal him in a toy cupboard, give him a bath, finally contrive his return home and future happiness. All this is conveyed in three brief scenes, separated by the audience-choruses. Enchanting musical episodes flash past; one in particular, when all the children in turn wish Sammy good morning, and with his shy and serious smile that engaging urchin replies: 'Morning, morning!' – one upward interval, and one downwards, a tiny example of the charm and ingenuity with which Britten can conjure music out of the simplest ingredients. The art displayed in *The Little Sweep* is like that of his folksong arrangements: small, clean and perfect. And the ending is unforgettable: the rescued Sammy riding homewards in a coach. In ten seconds, without a curtain-drop, the carriage is improvised – out of nothing, with twirling parasols for wheels and little Sammy in front on the rocking horse, while stage and audience sing together the last and simplest and most ravishing little tune of all, the Coaching Song: 'The horses are champing, eagerly stamping ... the gravel is churning, look! they are turning ... they swing from the bye-road on to the high road ...' A magical moment of pure happiness. Not a soul in the house but wanted an encore; wanted to keep the pretty and absurdly touching little tableau in front of his eyes a little longer, and in his ears the frosty D major jingle with its faint, clear clip-clop along the January roads of childhood.

Of course it's all very slight, an occasional piece, so occasional that it may not survive the dispersal of the present company. But there's more real music in a few bars of it than in some of the pretentious 'symphonic poems' of the previous week; and even those who regret the amount of time and energy spent by Britten on the ephemeral can hardly fail to enjoy this delicious morsel. What has been going on, all this while, in the depths of his musical personality we shall know better when we have heard the first performance of his big *Spring Symphony* broadcast from the Holland Festival.

J. F. Waterhouse in the *Birmingham Post* (8 July 1949):

It was interesting to visit Cheltenham's pretty Opera House tonight and see how *Let's Make an Opera* would succeed in a real two-gallery theatre: a very different matter from the informal and family atmosphere of the Jubilee Hall at Aldeburgh where it was born. It succeeded very well; though it was hard to judge the four audience songs from a seat well back in the dress circle, among some reasonably competent 'herons'. The 'chaffinches' up aloft sounded rather an anaemic and scruffy lot. But the energy and bonhomie of Mr Norman Del Mar (conductor) could turn even the Albert Hall into some sort of aviary.

Howes returned to the piece in *The Times* (9 July 1949):

To *The Rape of Lucretia* and *Albert Herring* is now added that new, light-fingered 'entertainment for young people' *Let's Make an Opera*, which is so designated because it is both more and less than an opera. Its originality of form consists in the fact that the audience has to provide the overture, the entr'actes, and finale. It learns its part at the rehearsal which forms Act I of the entertainment; it duly performs its four songs when the tiny opera about Sam, the chimney-sweep, is actually presented in Act II. To mark the distinction the conductor, Mr Norman Del Mar, wears flannels in Act I, tails in Act II. But whatever his vestment, he successfully induces the children on the stage and the young people of whatever age in the audience to play their respective parts with verve. The tunes are catchy, but they have catches in them: it is surely characteristic of a composer, who began by writing a *Simple Symphony*, to write deceptively simple songs for unison singing that always avoid the obvious by some ingenious trick of rhythm. The whole conception is indeed a fantastication of the simple and is full of happy surprises as each dramatic corner in the slenderest of plots is turned. Mr Eric Crozier's book is this time quite free from those occasional miscalculations or infelicities of phrase that have elsewhere caused the composer a momentary indigestion, and his final tableau is a triumph in which we all gaily ride off behind Sam, mounted on the nursery rocking-horse, into the land of the happy-ever-after.

See also Jenni Wake-Walker (compiler and editor), *Time & Concord: Aldeburgh Festival Recollections*, pp. 15–21.

8 The EOG was to present a season of *Let's Make an Opera* at the Lyric Theatre, Hammersmith, from 15 November 1949 until 14 January 1950. In the 'Britten issue' of *Music Survey*, 2/4 (spring 1950), three young people were invited to review performances of *Let Make an Opera* during its London run. Sixteen-year-old Elizabeth Mullan (pp. 237–8) wrote:

Before I went to see Britten's children's opera, *The Little Sweep*, I knew nothing at all about opera. Now I know that opera sets out to tell a story, supplementing the words with music which, as one of the actors said, brings to the surface and emphasizes all the exciting, romantic things lying beneath ordinary, everyday happenings. I think that this was illustrated very well in the opera where Miss Baggott is on the verge of opening the toy room cupboard and discovering the little chimney-sweep. The music screws you up to a point of quite nerve-racking tension which would be very difficult to achieve in an ordinary play.

The scenes before the actual opera gave this fundamental explanation, introduced us to the story and helped to make the opera a more personal affair, but I think that these scenes could have been used more profitably. The title was 'Let's Make an Opera' but, although it was very interesting to hear the children's adventures in finding a hip-bath, and to watch the scenery put up and hear some of the songs beforehand, we did not learn very much about how the opera was actually *made*. For instance, we were told that one of the aims of an opera-writer was to try to vary as much as possible the different combinations of voices, but we never learnt how the different combinations were chosen for the various songs.

Most of the songs I liked, particularly the one which the children sang when they held a consultation in the nursery about what was to be done with the Little Sweep; I think the music to the little chimney sweeper's plea, 'Please don't send me up again', is rather moving. That is an example where, however well the actor had spoken, words alone could never have expressed all that the music did. The only part of the opera I did not enjoy was the part where the children pulled the little boy down the chimney. The firm way in which they pull the rope and the way the song matches their actions – gently first, now a little harder, now a tug – is so effective that it is horrible. I shuddered to think how painful it must be to be stuck in a chimney and pulled down with such difficulty.

It was great fun singing the songs arranged for the audience. I thought at first I should hate this since I am generally very embarrassed at that kind of thing, but the songs were so irresistible and Mr Norman Del Mar created such a friendly atmosphere among the audience that it was perhaps the pleasantest part of the afternoon.

By the end of the opera, when all the actors ran back on to the stage and sang the stagecoach song, I was really excited and this last song seemed to harmonize exactly with this excited feeling. It trotted first, then – 'Let me see you canter, canter, canter/Good brown mare' – then the song galloped, but everything must come to an end as we realized when the song slowed down to a walk and finally stopped.

I am not musical, and I never thought music could excite me so much. I used to think opera was quite beyond my sphere and suspected that I should find it rather dull. Now I have changed my mind and want to hear more opera. *The Little Sweep* has at least removed my indifference.

633   To Eric Crozier

4 Crabbe Street, Aldeburgh
[late June 1949]

My dear Eric,

It's most unfortunate for me that we've started communicating by letter – nice for you, so handy with a pen, but difficult for inarticulate & uneducated me. Let me say, anyhow, how desperately sorry I am that you've got into this beastly financial jam. It isn't surprising when you've been handing over to Biddy[1] 5/4's of what you've been earning – & the Group not being in a position to pay you more. We all realise that what you've given to us in enthusiasm, energy & talent is worth far more than the few shillings you've been paid, but that that is the automatic result of starting something new, & people like Elizabeth, Anne, Nancy & Peter & others have also given up lots for very little except the satisfaction of aiming at something worthwhile. But I do hope now that you can find a job which will give you the necessary money, & also be more mentally compatible for you.[2] Please don't think that we are any of us unsympathetic with your great troubles in this respect – I realise fully what lack of confidence [i.e. shortage of funds] means. Let's hope & pray that when you are happily married, & in a job that you really like & feel suited to, that you will regain what is the essential commodity of creative & administrative work. I hate to write like an uncle, but after all it's an affectionate one, but please Eric, force Biddy to see that she cannot go on draining you like this. You are being wrecked by it, & so is dear Nancy. The children are strong, & we can ask Barbara[3] to keep an eye out to their physical condition, to see that they're not neglected nor ill-treated. I know it's hard for you, but it's going to be increasingly hard for both Nancy & you if you go on like this, & will result in disaster after disaster – & you are both too valuable to let that happen.

Now, dear Eric, please tell me in future what will be happening to you, & what you're thinking & planning – after all we want to keep Billy Budd going, & Elizabeth Fry,[4] don't we? We can't afford, personally or professionally, to let these "iron curtains" interfere![5]

Much love, and confidence,

BEN

1   Crozier's first wife and mother of his two daughters.

2   Crozier was appointed as part-time Artistic Director of Bournemouth's contribution to the 1951 Festival of Britain in December 1949. He resigned in March 1950 after his proposals for reorganization were rejected by the Festival Finance Committee. See 'Town's Festival Director Resigns', *Star* (Bournemouth; 17 March 1950). See also Letters 645 and 646.

3   Britten suggests his sister Barbara in this context because of her experience
    as a social worker.

4   The identity of this work concerning the prison reformer Elizabeth Fry
    (1780–1845), an ancestor of Peter Pears, has not been established. Might it
    have been a suitable subject for the Townswomen's Guild piece that Britten
    and Crozier were planning at this time?

5   Crozier wrote to Nancy Evans on 7 July 1949:

> About Ben, darling – I think he and you are right in believing such things cannot
> be settled by letter-writing. Either the affection and the will to work together are
> still there, despite temporary difficulties, or they are not. We must accept the
> situation as it turns out to be, and if we cannot work together any longer, at least we
> can be grateful for the many productive and happy years of work we have shared
> till now.

Later that summer, in an undated letter (?July) to Evans from Aldeburgh,
Crozier wrote:

> He [Britten] has sometimes told me, jokingly, that one day I would join the ranks
> of his 'corpses' [i.e. those hitherto close colleagues who found themselves aban-
> doned, as they saw it, when Britten's creativity led him into new fields], and I have
> always recognized that any ordinary person must soon outlive his usefulness to
> such a great creative artist as Ben. When that happens, the only thing to do is to
> accept it, and not to make matters worse by clinging to a relationship that is out-
> worn. I have known since early this year that Ben was done with me, and that we
> could not work together again – for some years, anyway.
>   [...] Perhaps, during the leisure of August, there may be a chance of talking with
> Ben in greater freedom, and the air may clear a bit.

See also Introduction, p. 18 n. 23.

634   To Serge Koussevitzky
[*Telegram*]

[Amsterdam]
[15 July 1949]

DELIGHTED TO TELL YOU SYMPHONY GREAT SUCCESS IN HOLLAND.[1]
EVERYONE MOST GRATEFUL FOR YOUR GENEROUS PERMISSION.
LOOKING FORWARD TO YOUR REACTIONS.

GREETINGS
BRITTEN

1   The first performance of *Spring Symphony* took place in the Concert-
    gebouw, Amsterdam, as part of the Holland Festival, on 14 July 1949 (not
    9 July as incorrectly reported in the 1963 and 1973 editions of the Britten
    Catalogue of Works, prepared by the composer's publishers), with Jo
    Vincent (soprano), Kathleen Ferrier (contralto) and Peter Pears (tenor),

the Boys' Choir of St Willibrorduskerk, Rotterdam, the Dutch Radio Chorus and the Concertgebouw Orchestra, conducted by Eduard van Beinum. See also plate 50.

A private off-air recording of the premiere, which was broadcast live in the BBC Third Programme, exists at BPL and at the National Sound Archive (a copy formerly owned by Lord Harewood); the NSA copy was issued by Decca in 1994 (440-0632-2 DM), with a liner note entitled 'The First Performance of the *Spring Symphony*' by John Steane. The liner note also gives the incorrect date of 9 (not 14) July for the first performance. A repeat performance was given at Scheveningen on 15 July.

Piet Tiggers in the Amsterdam *Algemeen Handelsblad* (15 July 1949) was one of several Dutch critics to welcome Britten's new work:

Reason enough to start at the end of the concert this time: rarely can the premiere of contemporary composition have been received with such rapturous applause as was Benjamin Britten's *Spring Symphony* yesterday. Britten, Eduard van Beinum and the three soloists – Jo Vincent, Kathleen Ferrier and Peter Pears – acknowledged the riot of enthusiasm hand in hand. Impressive laurel wreaths and beautiful bouquets gave added lustre to this unfamiliar sight. It seemed that no one was even thinking of going home.

Everything conspired to welcome this *Spring Symphony*: the lovely summer evening, and the presence of a number of important British guests: Field Marshal Montgomery, who was applauded on arrival; the British Ambassador, Sir Philip Nichols, and Lord Harewood. Everyone appeared to be in high spirits.

Britten's *Spring Symphony* is still, as it were, wet on the page. When springtime was due to arrive here, according to our chilly calandar, Britten, we are informed by his publishers, was still working on the symphony. They also told us in advance that the fourty-fourth oeuvre of this talented young composer was conceived for three solo voices, a mixed choir, a boys' choir and a symphony orchestra. There was also mention of a vibraphone. We heard this last instrument loud and clear, as we did templeblocks, whistling youngsters, a tam-tam and various other aural effects of which the publishers had neglected to warn us.

Britten bubbles over with enthusiasm; we knew this from his earlier works. He has an attractive energetic quality and when, on occasion, he becomes a little too earnest, he likes to send himself up. His music, including this latest composition, is always entertaining, and one of his great virtues is that he is forever young, even though he is now approaching the age of forty. A fleet-footed young colt can, however, mature into an excellent steed. Britten's compositions have a certain restlessness, a masculine vitality, an excitement, that can sometimes seem overwhelming on first acquaintance. He is a true composer, in the literal sense of the word. He takes risks and he has an astounding ear for orchestral timbres. Just one quibble though: the writing for the boys' choir is set too low for too long and misses the steely sound that boys' voices can produce.

The voices, in fact, play first fiddle in this symphony. Musicians might prefer to label the work a 'cantata'. A cantata in four movements with symphonic bits, a few solo voices and some choral bits from time to time in the background. The *Spring Symphony* consists of settings of twelve poems, old and new. Britten concludes with a splendid final, in which the famous English round 'Sumer is icumen in', dating from 1240 in the West Saxon dialect, sung by the boys' choir, is set against

PROGRAMMA

W. A. MOZART
1756-1791

Symphonie Es gr. t., K.V. 543

Adagio - Allegro
Andante con moto
Menuetto: Allegretto
Finale: Allegro

PAUZE

BENJAMIN BRITTEN
geb. 1913

Spring Symphony
(Wereldpremière)

DEEL I

Introduction	(Koor)
The Merry Cuckoo	(Tenorsolo)
Spring the Sweet Spring	(Koor, sopraan, alt en tenorsolo)
The Driving Boy	(Jongenskoor en sopraansolo)
The Morning Star	(Koor)

DEEL II

Welcome Maids of Honour	(Altsolo)
Waters above	(Tenorsolo)
Out on the Lawn I lie in Bed	(Koor en altsolo)

DEEL III

When will my May come	(Tenorsolo)
Fair and Fair	(Sopraan- en tenorsolo)
Sound the Flute	(Koor en jongenskoor)

DEEL IV

Finale	(Sopraan-, alt-, tenorsolo Koor en jongenskoor)

CONCERTGEBOUW - AMSTERDAM

Het Concertgebouworkest

DIRIGENT

EDUARD VAN BEINUM

SOLISTEN

JO VINCENT, sopraan
KATHLEEN FERRIER, alt
PETER PEARS, tenor

Met medewerking van

De samengevoegde koren van de Ned. Radio Unie en de N.C.R.V.
(ingestudeerd door Feul. Boshart)

Het Knapenkoor van de St. Willibrorduskerk te Rotterdam
(dirigent: P. de Keijzer)

DONDERDAG 14 JULI 1949 - AANVANG 8.15 UUR

Amsterdam, 14 July 1949: programme for the first performance of *Spring Symphony*

the musical backdrop. It's a sublime conceit and a salute to the ancient musical traditions of Cornwall, but was not quite articulated clearly enough. Even with the
assistance of four horns, the boys' choir could not accomplish the anticipated
effect. It seems Britten has not found the right sonority for boys' voices.

On the other hand, 'The merry cuckoo' for tenor and three trumpets was fascinating; the (unconscious?) nod in the direction of Stravinsky in 'The driving boy'
witty, and the brass in 'The morning star' beautiful. The exquisite solo for alto, with
its fluctuating octave leaps, was highly original. Britten, indeed, provides plenty of
variety. The tenor solo, 'Waters above', with the *tremolo* violins is a typical example.
That he can also be fierce, piercingly angry, highly expressive, hard and cold was
borne out in his setting of this striking passage from the poem by Auden: 'And,
gentle, do not care to know,/Where Poland draws her eastern bow,/What violence
is done'. That's Britten all over: honest, robust, concise.

This thoroughly prepared world premiere held the attention throughout and
the work cuts a fine figure in the world of contemporary music.

The excellent choir was drawn from the ensembles of the Dutch Radio Chorus
and the Dutch Christian Radio Society (NCRV) and the youthful voices of the
boys' choir were provided by the Rotterdam St Willibrorduskerk and sang with
admirable zest. The three soloists were very fine and Eduard van Beinum was a
masterly conductor. Thanks to the conductor, and of course the composer, the
symphony was a great success.

Frank Howes in *The Times* (15 July 1949) wrote a brief notice of the
premiere:

Britten's new symphony received its first performance here tonight at the hands of
Mr Eduard van Beinum and his Concertgebouw Orchestra, together with the
Netherlands Radio Chorus, a boys' choir, and three soloists (Miss Jo Vincent, Miss
Kathleen Ferrier, and Mr Peter Pears). Its subject is Spring, and it is far and away
the happiest piece of extended music that has been written for many a long day.
Maybe it is a tract for the time.

It is a vocal symphony, and, like Vaughan Williams's *A Sea Symphony*, corresponds in its four movements to the general character and speeds of a conventional
instrumental symphony. But there is nothing else conventional about it; it is more
than a setting of words, more than a song-cycle like the composer's own *Serenade*;
it is an evocation by voices from the orchestra of the spirit of Spring as it has
appealed to a dozen English poets. It employs large forces, but the texture is crystal
clear; it produces sounds that never occurred to anyone before but which are yet
perfectly apt – even the boys' whistling chorus.

Description can wait for a more ample occasion. Let it only be said now that, as
always with Britten, words kindle his imagination not to a brighter but to a hotter
flame than purely instrumental ideas. In this 'Spring' symphony words and music
have joined forces to produce something that has the brightness of spring sunshine. It was given a radiant performance, and was warmly received by an audience
that included Field-Marshal Montgomery.

Daniel L. Schorr reviewed *Spring Symphony* for the *New York Times*
(15 July 1949):

Benjamin Britten's *Spring Symphony* received a ringing ovation tonight in its world
premiere at the Holland Music Festival. The cheers of 3000 persons who jammed

Amsterdam's Concert Hall, including such celebrities as Field Marshal Viscount Montgomery of Britain, showed that this was the great event of the festival.

[...] Time will have to judge its enduring merits, but there was no doubt about the instantaneous appeal of this work, which skillfully and economically uses the vocal and instrumental forces at its command to create imagery and evoke an atmosphere of spring. It is program music at its best.

This work, which is Op. 44 of the 36-year-old British composer, is his second symphony, the first being 'The Requiem' [*Sinfonia da Requiem*] written in 1940, and his first employing voices. It is also his first large instrumental work in a long time, since he has been devoting himself lately to operas and chamber music.

Spring Symphony was commissioned by Serge Koussevitzky and its premiere was originally planned for the past season of the Boston Symphony. However, Britten's illness last winter delayed its completion until April, and the composer obtained permission from Koussevitzky to give the premiere in Holland, where Britten has often appeared in recital with Pears. The first American performance will be in August at Tanglewood.

The work can only be loosely termed a symphony, being more accurately described as a song-cycle of symphonic proportions. It is a symphony perhaps in the Mahlerian sense of *Das Lied von der Erde*. Its text consists of poems about spring by British poets from a twelfth-century anonymous verse to a contemporary poem by W. H. Auden.

This latest contribution to the musical literature on the favorite season tempts comparisons with other music about spring. But there is no comparison with either Schumann or Stravinsky, for this is a very English spring, as Britten himself made clear in an interview before the concert.

'The inspiration for the symphony is England,' he said. 'I wanted to portray spring, not the Russian primitive rites of spring, but a human spring. It is a reawakening of life as seen through an Englishman's eyes.'

There are four movements describing the various aspects of spring and the moods it creates. Each movement contains separate poems in settings of solo songs, choruses and ensembles. The introductory movement expresses the yearning of sunlight and warmth – a prayer for spring, as the composer termed it. The second is the only somber section, dealing with stormy nights and withered first flowers. The third is centered about innocent love, and the finale represents a May festival.

The whole thing is done with sparing use of the great forces at the composer's command. Only occasionally does he use the whole large orchestra, which has triple woodwinds, full brass and two harps. More often selected instruments and choirs are employed to create special colors. The voices too are treated symphonically, used often for special effects and generally playing their part in the composer's scheme rather than showing their own merits.

Because of this it is difficult to comment on individual performances, although Miss Ferrier attracted particular attention by the richness and warmth of her singing. More in point is it to say that the composer's intention was most successfully carried off by the harmonious co-operation of all the participants.

Relying only slightly on any sustained melodic lines, the composer achieved his effect by dexterous orchestration and delicate coloration. He used the three hundred instruments and voices like pastel shades, and he did it superbly well.

Dyneley Hussey in the *Listener* (21 July 1949):

The *Spring Symphony* bears witness, on the positive side, to the composer's sensitive taste in poetry and to his no less sensitive touch in the setting of them. He is particularly happy when the ideas are simple and childlike, as in Nashe's 'Spring', and happiest of all when the medium used is a chorus of boys' voices. But he can be subtle, too, and after a first hearing I would put highest among the individual songs in the cycle the setting of Auden's 'Out on the lawn I lie in bed' with its marvellous sense of troubled ease and its accompaniment of faint, nocturnal sounds borne by the breeze across the garden. Yet as a musical composition, because it at least successfully fulfils the symphonic definition, the best is the finale – a lively realization in music of an Elizabethan May Day. The use of the old Reading Rota ['Sumer is icumen in'], and especially the manner in which it is used, proved to be a stroke of genius.

The *Times* (22 July 1949) gave further space to the new work to allow Frank Howes to write more extensively about it:

Britten's new *Spring Symphony* is a work of major importance in the composer's great and unceasing productivity and therefore requires more extended comment than is possible in a short notice of its first performance.

The symphony was written last winter for Koussevitzky and the Boston Symphony Orchestra, which will play it next month at its Berkshire Festival. Its most striking characteristic is its happiness, and it therefore takes its place in a recent group of works that are animated by a determination that human folly and political muddle shall not completely obscure life's possibilities even in this mad and bad century of ours. Hence the choice of the subject of spring for its theme. The cantata, *Saint Nicolas*, and the frolic, *Let's Make an Opera*, both written for young people, belong to this same group of light-hearted pieces. But the *Spring Symphony* both in intention and effect is more serious, in that it is larger and more comprehensive in emotional appeal. The public need not complain, and no music critic staggering under the unremitting impact of major masterpieces will complain, if a composer forgets for a moment the role of major prophet, forced on him by Beethoven and the Romantic Succession, and relaxes into the eighteenth-century attitude of paid provider of entertainment by writing works intended not for immortality but for tomorrow's celebration. Britten is fertile enough to be able to spare effort for these lighter purposes. But a certain solemnity still clings to the appellation 'symphony' and critics and public must pay serious attention to anything so styled.

The main question is: how far is this purely vocal work entitled to call itself a symphony? It is constructed on an anthology of English poems from Spenser to Auden dealing with the months of May and June – April is not mentioned, though there are plenty of allusions to its natural phenomena. This method of assembling poems on a particular subject and disregarding their varied authorship and chronology was first adopted by Arthur Bliss in his *Pastoral* and *Morning Heroes*, and had already been successfully employed by Britten himself in his *Serenade*. What is unsymphonic in the method is that each poem evokes different musical imagery and though there is thus produced copious thematic material, there can be no development or recapitulation of it.

Even when, as in this symphony, the poems are chosen with sufficient skill to preserve congruity of mood within each movement, plainly nothing as musically subtle or coherent can be achieved as in a purely instrumental symphony. The nexus of thought is verbal, and it is an inevitable drawback of the reliance on words that the listener can never take in all that the composer offers him, especially in that piquant speciality of Britten's affection for words, perhaps because his is a hair-trigger imagination that catches spontaneous fire from the stimulus of poetry. The price he pays for this quick action is sometimes described as a lack of deep emotion, since not enough pressure banks up behind the imaginative flash before it is discharged.

In this symphony, however, the emotion of happiness manifests itself without the need for damming up, in quicksilver-like music that springs immediately from the words. The advantages and disabilities of the vocal symphony can be accepted, and the claims of symphonic procedure are satisfied by the adoption of the four usual movements.

Desmond Shawe-Taylor contributed a characteristically extensive notice to the *New Statesman and Nation* (23 July 1949):

Britten's Symphony contains no purely instrumental music, and I foresee that much ink will be spilled over the academic question of its right to the title. It falls into four sections, corresponding roughly to the four movements of a symphony; the composer has grouped some fourteen poems of all periods according to four moods or pictorial schemes. The first and longest group begins with an orchestral image of winter, all icicles and numbness, which the sun is invited by the chorus to dispel. In the Spenser and Nashe settings which follow, the onset of spring is felt: the cuckoo sings out (astonishingly, on the brass), but all is still rough and rude, the rhythms heavy, fingers red with the cold – until suddenly a galaxy of birdsong breaks from all three soloists, as though from a thicket (here Jo Vincent excelled herself). The next piece, a combined setting of Peele's 'When as the rye reach to the chin' and John Clare's 'Driving Boy', provided the most captivating single episode in a captivating score; it was here that the boys' choir made its first entrance. Most listeners, and most composers, too, think of boys' voices in terms of a soft, ethereal, pious, floating quality of sound – '*et ô ces voix d'enfants chantant dans la coupole*'. Years ago, in his *Ceremony of Carols*, Britten showed an unecclesiastical preference for the raw, cheeky din of trebles singing with unpursed lips low down in the scale; and both Wagner and Verlaine would have had a shock if they had heard the sound of those Rotterdam kids, the other night, as they came charging into the solemn Concertgebouw (they might almost have shinned up the wall and through the windows) with a raw, naughty, don't-care-a-rap E♭ unison tune: 'Strawberries swimming in the cream, And Schoolboys playing in the stream.' When Miss Ferrier [*recte*: Jo Vincent] took up Clare's ditty of the Driving Boy, those same boys, unless I am much mistaken, were made to whistle; and then they came splashing back again with the strawberries and cream and the larky snatch of tune. It sounds like broad farce, but it was a passage of heavenly innocence and poetry, such as only Britten could have imagined.

Not everything seemed, at a first hearing, quite so pointful and inevitable. The setting for contralto of Herrick's poem to the violets sounded too heavy for the delicate short lines, and one or two stanzas from a poem by Auden ['Out on the lawn I lie in bed'] proved recalcitrant (as his more intellectual verses are apt to be) to the sensuous demands of music: there was even a remote and in the context unsuitable reference to pre-war politics ['And, gentle, do not care to know/Where Poland draws her Eastern bow,/What violence is done;/Nor ask what doubtful act allows/Our freedom in this English house,/Our picnics in the sun.']. Both Herrick and Auden came in the second part, which was reflective and nocturnal, and contained a lovely setting for tenor of Vaughan's lines in praise of evening rain, with the vocal line surrounded by clusters of repeated notes, like raindrops, on the strings. The third movement, corresponding to the Scherzo of a symphony, was full of gaiety and impatient youthful love, expressed in rhythmic exuberance and outbursts of highly original orchestration; placed in the middle, like a Trio, was a charming A major duet for soprano and tenor to Peele's *Song of Oenone and Paris*. For his finale the composer launched boldly into a genial and extrovert C major, a piece of public jollification, with lolloping six-eight rhythms, based on the long passage from the end of *The Knight of the Burning Pestle*, which begins 'London to thee I do present the merry month of May'. The solo tenor leads off, and the musical forces gather round him, but the sense of mere thickness and overcrowding is beautifully avoided; there is none of that remorseless piling up of a climax for its own sake which is the bane of the English and German choral traditions. Everything is as clean as a whistle; the colours have a medieval gaiety, the feeling a direct Chaucerian freshness. The rhythms tighten as the banners crowd together and the Londoners set out, not in a march, but 'with scarfs and garters as you please . . . by twenty and by twenty, to Hogsdon or to Newington, where ale and cakes are plenty'. The children are there too, lusty and low down in their registers as usual, with 'Sumer is icumen in.' 'And so, my friends, I cease,' announces the tenor; and so indeed the composer does cease – with one loud, clear, tremendously unequivocal C major chord for the entire orchestra.

I won't vouch for the accuracy, in detail, of these first impressions; but I feel certain that when (the sooner the better) we get some London performances of this *Spring Symphony*, and a score, and perhaps a set of gramophone records, it will be seen to mark a new stage in the composer's career. His old power of inventing musical patterns to symbolize an intensely personal and pictorial vision is shown again, even perhaps more vividly than before; what is new is the geniality, breadth and accessibility – in a word, the maturity. It is as though the springtime of his genius – raw, brilliant and tender – were itself also about to ripen into high summer.

In an article introducing a broadcast of the UK premiere of *Spring Symphony*, *Radio Times* (3 March 1950), the music critic of the *News Chronicle*, Scott Goddard, recalled the first performance of the work:

One of the most memorable events of the Holland Festival last year was the performance of Britten's *Spring Symphony*. It was performed for the first time on that occasion, and everyone – not only the English present that night in Amsterdam – was acutely expectant. 'Shine out, fair sun' were the words with which the new work began. This much we knew in advance. But the music for the words? Of that we knew nothing, not even so much as a hint that a vibraphone was to sound its outlandish call before the voices started. That weird noise was at once to startle us and, as soon as we had assimilated it, to tell us that Britten's ear had not lost its cunning. The sun thereupon broke through the clouds and showed its 'thousand coloured lights', and so the new work started on its course.

I shall never hear it again for the first time and I envy those who come to the *Spring Symphony* on Thursday as to something new. It will be a gay and possibly a disturbing experience; but an enchanting and pleasant disturbance. The fourteen poems, from sources as old as 'Sumer is icumen in' and as new as Auden, have among them some entrancing verses. They are for me a large part of the astonishment of the work. And Britten's music, accompanying, supporting, and flashing bright light on these poems, is an exciting adventure. [. . .]

Coming out of the Concertgebouw in Amsterdam that July morning last year after listening to a rehearsal of the *Spring Symphony* I was thankful enough to see a straight street ahead of me. That was all conventional and familiar. What I had just been trying to understand was unconventional and enchantingly unfamiliar. But there again, while the street was straight and unexciting, the music still buzzing in the empty hive of one's head was exciting and adventurous. 'Fair and fair, and twice as fair' were fine words to have with one through the day, and with them came bits and pieces of music, turns of phrase and fragments of outlines from Britten's setting of those words. It was round that haunting duet that my memory began to labour. For me that was the centre of the work. At the first performance more explicit expressions began to cluster round that duet, and by the end of the second performance the whole work began to come clear. It is, in fact, clear music.

In a letter to Mary Behrend (25 July 1949), Britten was to remark: 'It was lovely to have you & Bow in Holland for the Symph., & a great encouragement that you liked it as well. I am not happy yet about a few spots, but hope to get them right soon.' There is no evidence among the source materials of any substantial revisions to *Spring Symphony* following the premiere. Perhaps Britten felt he needed to adjust the instrumentation in a few places to achieve a more satisfactory balance between voices and orchestra.

V TOWARDS *BILLY BUDD*

JULY 1949–DECEMBER 1951

CHRONOLOGY 1949–1951

YEAR	EVENTS AND COMPOSITIONS
1949	
August	Forster and Crozier working with Britten in Aldeburgh on the libretto of *Billy Budd*
13 August	Tanglewood: first US performance of *Spring Symphony*, conducted by Koussevitzky
September	COMPOSITION *A Wedding Anthem* (*Amo Ergo Sum*)
29 September	St Mark's Church, North Audley Street, London: first performance of *A Wedding Anthem* at the wedding of the Earl of Harewood and Marion Stein
13 October	Recital with Pears in Chelsea Town Hall, their last before leaving for New York
19 October–December	Major recital tour with Pears of US and Canada. In New York meets the violist William Primrose. On the West Coast Britten and Pears are reunited with Christopher Isherwood
31 October	Theatre Royal, Brighton: first performance of Ronald Duncan's play *Stratton*, with incidental music by Britten
December	Works with Forster on libretto of *Billy Budd* in Aldeburgh. Sadler's Wells Opera withdraws its commitment to premiere *Billy Budd*
1950	
January	Pears suffers from shingles
3 February	Begins composition of *Billy Budd*
13–27 February	Recital tour with Pears in Scotland
9 March	Royal Albert Hall, London: UK premiere of *Spring Symphony*, conducted by Eduard van Beinum
mid-March–April	Forster at Crag House, Aldeburgh, convalescing from a prostate operation

22 March	Attends opera-inspired fancy-dress ball in aid of the English Opera Group
22–23 April	During weekend house party at Crag House, plays through Act I of *Billy Budd* to Forster, the Harewoods and Ralph Hawkes
Spring	COMPOSITION *Five Flower Songs*
16 May	COMPOSITION *Lachrymae*
17–25 June	Third Aldeburgh Festival, which includes the first performances of Copland's *Old American Songs* (18 June; Pears and Britten) and *Lachrymae* (20 June; Primrose and Britten)
August	Approached by David Webster (Royal Opera House) concerning an operatic adaptation of *The Tempest*, which Britten declines.
October	Resumes composition of *Billy Budd*. Revises Violin Concerto
1951	
January	Begins Act III of *Billy Budd*
late March	Composing Act IV of *Billy Budd*
Spring	Collaborates with Imogen Holst on an edition of Purcell's *Dido and Aeneas* for the English Opera Group
9 April	Recital with Pears in Vienna and, on 12th, Viennese premiere of *Spring Symphony*, conducted by Clemens Krauss
1 May	Lyric Theatre, Hammersmith, London: first performance of Britten's and Imogen Holst's edition of *Dido and Aeneas*
7 May	With Pears gives first performance of Tippett's *The Heart's Assurance*
24 May	First performance (BBC broadcast) of *Five Flower Songs*
June	COMPOSITION *Six Metamorphoses after Ovid*
8–17 June	Fourth Aldeburgh Festival, which includes the first performance of *Six Metamorphoses after Ovid* (14 June; Joy Boughton)
28 July	Made a Freeman of the Borough of Lowestoft
10 August	Completes composition draft of *Billy Budd*. Scoring of the opera delayed due to illness
September	Two-week cruise with Pears and friends across the North Sea and up the Rhine
October	Discusses with William Plomer adapting Beatrix Potter's *The Tale of Mr Tod* as a children's opera
November	COMPOSITION *Billy Budd*
1 December	Royal Opera House, Covent Garden, London: first performance of *Billy Budd*, conducted by the composer

635   **To Edward Sackville-West**

4 Crabbe Street, Aldeburgh
July 27th 1949

My dear Eddy,

Returning here in the middle of a motoring exploration of East Anglia I find your lovely letter & hasten to thank you for it. I am so glad you got so good & clear impression of the work [*Spring Symphony*] even over the air & the Third Programme at that. I am pleased with it at the moment, & feel it's a bit of an advance – still, it would be pretty bad if it weren't, & I may be, like most mothers, prejudiced in favour of my youngest child! It was given a very good show – van Beinum took endless pains, & no expense was spared to get what I wanted – even the 70 little Dutch toughs, that I was glad you liked as much as me! The second performance the next day was even better. I am cross that it must wait till March before it can be done here,¹ but that is the only time the chief ingredients can come together again. The U.S.A. show happens next week or so, but I have no hopes of that altho' the orchestra (Boston) will be good.² Peter & I, flattened by this all following on the tough summer season, have been enjoying Norfolk & Suffolk churches enormously. We've been looking at them, partly spurred on by John P. [Piper] who's lyrical about them. We're even getting good about Decs. & Perps [Decorated and Perpendicular styles of architecture]. After this week I settle down with Morgan to finishing the Billy Budd libretto. So far what he's done is superb. He has a wonderful natural sense of the theatre, & his crisp pregnant dialogue will be good to set, I think.³ I am sorry you find the subject odd – certainly it's difficult, but the more we work at it, the more I feel it's built for opera. As if to bear out this view there are two other operas (not to mention a play)⁴ being written at this moment on the same subject! One in Italy, one in U.S.A.

I shall be here working all August, & then we take the operas to Denmark & Sweden⁵ – & then before we pop off to America for a tour, I have three weeks in London. It would be nice if we could meet there – perhaps even with Desmond [Shawe-Taylor]!

Peter sends his love to you both, so do I.

Yours ever,
BEN

1   See Letter 643 n. 6.

2   On 13 August Britten was to send Koussevitzky a telegram: 'MY WARMEST GOOD WISHES FOR SUCCESSFUL AMERICAN PREMIER SPRING SYMPHONY'.

   A review by Howard Taubman of the US premiere appeared in the *New York Times* (15 August 1949):

The *Spring Symphony* is filled with the spirit of an England radiant with spring. It harks back to the madrigalists of centuries ago, not literally, but in spirit. It radiates the very warmth and sunshine that were lacking in the Britten opera *Albert Herring*, which had its American premiere here last Monday.

There is no point in worrying over the academic point as to whether the work is, in the exact meaning of the word, a symphony at all. [...]

[Britten's] music has originality and ingenuity, and most of it is integrated and meaningful. Though he uses a full symphony [orchestra], a large chorus, a boys' chorus and three soloists, he avoids pretentiousness. The pastoral mood is captured in an artful blend of the archaic and modern.

Some sections seemed to be better than others. One or two, with rather literal sylvan effects, might prove to be wearing on further hearings. But one has the feeling that the piece would improve on acquaintance, especially in a smaller, more intimate hall.

The performance was a cheerful occasion in every way. Dr Koussevitzky conducted with immense relish. The Boston Symphony played in lovely and vocative fashion. The chorus, drawn from young men and women in attendance at the center, did an exceptionally fine job with the sometimes difficult music, and to Hugh Ross, who trained the group in six weeks, goes a great deal of credit.

Let us not forget the thirty-odd youngsters from nearby Camp Mah-Kee-Nac. The small boys, wearing white T-shirts and serious, shining faces, sang their music with a concentration that showed they were not unaware of the burden resting on their shoulders. And their young voices made the music of spring thoroughly authentic.

3   In BBMCPR, p. 56, Philip Reed notes that Forster

journeyed to Aldeburgh on 8 August, staying with Britten; Crozier was staying near by at a holiday home which he had rented. Whereas in March [1949] it had been Forster and Crozier who had taken the lead, Britten was now to dominate their discussions [...] Forster wrote to Bob Buckingham on the 11th: 'The work has restarted well. Eric Crozier is here and doing his stuff without jibbing, and I seem able to turn honest English prose with duetinnos [*sic*] or arias when required to do so. Luckily nothing has to rhyme. I would like to hear some musical notes from Ben, but apparently they don't start yet – only musical ideas. The conception is very ambitious in either sense (spiritually and technically) but we are both in favour of ambition. Chorus of about 100. – The last good news is that the copyright situation seems better.'

On the 22nd he added: 'Much work is done. I am all right working by myself but becoming a little stale and dazed in discussions. – Back of the libretto now broken. Have taken to Blank Verse.'

Of the changes made to the draft libretto at this period, the most significant were Britten's request for a large-scale choral climax to Act I, a scene entirely of the librettists' own invention as it does not appear in Melville, and the introduction of the character of the Novice. At this time the opera was conceived and first performed in four acts. When revised in 1960 into two acts, the concluding scene of the original Act I was omitted.

In a sequence of letters from Aldeburgh, Crozier kept Nancy Evans informed of progress on *Budd*:

15 AUGUST 1949
Picture Post want to take photos of Ben and Morgan at work on *Billy Budd* [see plates 42 and 43] and Tom Hopkinson [the editor] suggests I should write the article about it. Kind of him, and Ben and Morgan are keenly in favour, though Ben is afraid I shall minimize my own share in the collaboration.

Really the work goes very well. I believe it will be a terrific opera when finished. I had a pleasant talk with Ben this morning, and we were more relaxed than we have been for some time past and were warm and friendly to each other. He still seems to me tense, though; not specially in relation to me, but as though he were going through a prolonged internal crisis.

22 AUGUST 1949
I grow more and more fascinated by *Billy Budd* as an opera and could do with all the waking hours of every day to play my full part in the collaboration. I do not think there ever was a happier collaboration than this one between Ben, Morgan and me. We are thrilled by the work, we like each other, we respect each other's viewpoints, and yet we are all so entirely different in our experience and gifts. And when we have a good morning's work, the ideas that come seem to have a life of their own and to present themselves for testing by each of us in turn, and each one may add a little contribution to the subject under discussion and gradually a whole scene is built up from hints that have been floating in the air between us. I do hope there will be more collaborations like this [. . .]

Ben, Morgan and I worked all morning with Kurt Hutton prowling around us taking hundreds of photographs from all angles and all distances. It should prove an interesting record of the collaboration.

26 AUGUST 1949
I hope by Monday [29 August] to have written all my scenes for the opera and to be clear for other work. This week I had to write a big new chorus scene for the end of Act I, which I did with a lively sense of my own inferiority to Morgan as a writer. But he was delighted with what I had done and complimented me generously on it.

4   A letter from Anthony Gishford to Britten (8 October 1949) setting out the copyright situation in respect of Melville's *Billy Budd* mentions a play by 'Messrs Coxe and Chapman' and that 'an autumn production of the play in London, for which rehearsals were scheduled to begin this month, has been indefinitely postponed'. This stage adaptation of *Billy Budd* by Louis Osborne Coxe and Robert Chapman, produced by Chandler Cowles and Anthony B. Farrell, was to run on Broadway from 10 February to 12 May 1951. While the *New York Times* reported that the 'opera cannot be performed in this country without the permission of Cowles and Farrell', it was, in any case, a position that was open to interpretation. In June 1951 Betty Bean of Boosey & Hawkes's New York office secured the release from those responsible for the play to any claims on the operatic version. Gishford's memorandum notes only one opera, Giorgio Ghedini's one-act adaptation, which was first produced in Venice in September 1949. The composer of the other opera remains unidentified.

As Philip Reed writes in BBMCPR, p. 57:

Just before Britten's return from the States, both Forster and Crozier had shown natural curiosity about [. . .] Ghedini's [. . .] *Billy Budd* [. . .] A copy of the libretto by Salvatore Quasimodo was obtained by Boosey & Hawkes for Crozier. He passed it on to Forster who wrote about it in a letter to Crozier on 5 December: 'I thought Quasimodo good for his purpose, and the introduction of Molly Bristol as a vision most ingenious. I believe we could have done with her.' ('Molly Bristol' was Billy's sweetheart, who appears in Melville and who is introduced [. . .] in the final scene of their opera, the 'Ballata per Billy'.)

Erwin Stein held a different opinion as to the merits of Quasimodo's libretto for Ghedini. He told Britten (27 November 1949): 'It is rather threadbare which might give the music some scope to fill in, but it is all so indirect, most of the story being told or described by the speaking "corifer".' Apart from the spoken role for narrator who functions as a Greek chorus, there are only eight principal singers in the cast.

Marion Thorpe recalls that Britten and Ghedini met somewhere in Italy, possibly during 1949, and that the Italian composer mentioned his opera. Britten, however, was so taken aback that he could not bring himself to talk about his own opera on the same subject.

5 *Recte*: Denmark and Norway. The EOG gave performances of *Albert Herring* and *The Rape of Lucretia* in Copenhagen (12–16 September) and Oslo (19–23 September).

636 To Eric Crozier

4 Crabbe Street, Aldeburgh

August 27th 1949

Dear Eric,

I am so sorry not to have answered your letter before, but I am afraid I've had to consider your request very thoroughly.[1] I don't want to appear stingy, but I've had a lot of very heavy expenses recently (entertainment has been very heavy, dry-rot & painting the house, & helping E.O.G. over a few stiles) and so I have to examine this new financial commitment exhaustively before deciding to help you – which I know you know I want to. It looks now as if it will be possible, on one or two conditions. I must have a letter from the Bank saying that they will not demand the £400 before two years is up (say to summer 1951). And Boosey & Hawkes have most generously offered to let me have first claim on your royalties from them in this period, although the advances you have had from them might seem to demand the reverse. This they will put in a letter to me. I don't know when Periton[2] is back, but I believe next week. I think it would be best if he arranges the letters, since, as you say, he is friendly both personally & financially to us both.

I am sorry to appear so careful & selfish, but at the moment there are so many worries that I don't think I'd better add a financial one – for any of our sakes.

In haste,
Yours ever,
BEN

1 Crozier's letter to Britten, which elicited this response from the composer, has not survived. However, a letter Crozier sent to Nancy Evans, dated 18 August 1949, gives some indication of what he must have requested of Britten:

> [. . .] Billy Budd will still require a lot of work from me, and especially more collaboration with Morgan, for we have masses of stuff to rewrite and reshape. I think I must take my courage in both hands and tackle the question of a guarantee with Ben, so that I can arrange a big loan from my bank and clear myself of financial worry for a month or two. The security of my future royalties is perfectly safe, and it is not as if he would have to lend me the money. The bank would do that, I would pay them interest on it, and the repayment of capital should be clear inside of two years. So, distasteful though it is, I think I must approach Ben soon with the request.

Following receipt of Britten's letter, Crozier was to write to Britten on 4 September 1949 about his financial difficulties:

> I was delighted to have your most generous reply to my letter about the guarantee, but I have been worried ever since about how to answer. I feel that if I accept your willingness to help, for which I am sincerely grateful, I shall be escaping my immediate financial problems only by increasing the burden of responsibility that already weighs too heavily on you.
>
> And the last thing I want to do is to make things difficult for you or to increase your existing worries. I should so much prefer to do just the opposite, and to lighten them instead!
>
> There is only one way by which I can do that – by repaying the £200 I already owe you as soon as possible, and by withdrawing the request for a guarantee – and after thinking the whole thing over many times, I feel that I must try to do that and avoid taxing your generosity by another demand on it.
>
> I think that someone at Boosey & Hawkes has painted my royalty position blacker than it really is. Including the recent advance on Let's Make an Opera, my total indebtedness to them is £223. Against this sum has to be set all royalties for the current year on Herring, Nicolas and Let's Make (including four broadcasts), and I shall be very surprised if these do not amount to more than the sum I owe.
>
> I was counting on this when I suggested giving you first claim on my royalties for 1950 and 1951, and I still think it is probable that my 1950 royalties will begin to collect themselves free of debt.
>
> I want to suggest that you have first claim on these 1950 royalties for repayment of my £200 debt to you, and I will give Mr Periton an assurance that I won't touch any part of them until you are repaid. Since Boosey's only settle their accounts once yearly, that won't happen till December 31st, 1950, and I am sorry it has to take so long.
>
> Please forgive me for having troubled you with this whole business at a most busy time, but I feel it has not been entirely wasted since it has brought me to a

realization of the need for repaying a debt I have owed you for far too long. And if there's any hope of repaying it sooner than the end of 1950 (tho' honestly I can't see any likelihood of that), of course I shall do so.

2   Leslie Almond Periton (1908–1983), Britten's accountant, who was to become a very close friend and esteemed adviser. He qualified in 1929 and joined A. & T. Chenhalls in 1942, becoming senior partner, where he had many clients in the arts. Periton was later invited by Britten to be an executor of his will. See also Letter 383 n. 3, and PFL, plate 417.

637   To Basil Coleman

4 Crabbe Street, Aldeburgh
[Postmarked 7 September 1949]

My dear Basil,

Your letter has given me great pleasure – please forgive the usual slackness in replying, but I've been as usual drowned in work! It has been really splendid working with you this summer – & your work has been first-class.[1] I really look forward (if you are agreeable!) to many collaborations in the future. I am so sorry that some of our plans have fallen through so disappointingly – but believe me, my dear, they will happen in the future if I have any say in the matter. I have terrific faith in "Love in a Village".[2]

Please forgive the shortness of this, but I wanted to thank you for your kindnesses, tact and skill throughout an often difficult summer! And the best of luck for Coventry.[3]

Yours ever,
BEN

1   Coleman had been responsible for the first production of *Let's Make an Opera*.

2   Arthur Oldham's version of the eighteenth-century ballad opera *Love in a Village*, produced by Basil Coleman and with designs by Osbert Lancaster, was to be first performed by the EOG in the Jubilee Hall, Aldeburgh, on 16 June 1952. The conductor was Norman Del Mar, and the cast included Norman Lumsden (Woodcock), Nancy Evans (Lucinda), Gladys Parr (Deborah) and Peter Pears (Hawthorn). The dance in Act III was choreographed by John Cranko who, the following year, was to choreograph the *Choral Dances* that open Act II of *Gloriana*, and who was subsequently to collaborate with Britten on the three-act ballet *The Prince of the Pagodas*.

3   Where Coleman was to work with the Midland Theatre Company.

638   To Imogen Holst

as from: 4 Crabbe St, Aldeburgh
[Postmarked 4 October 1949]

My dearest Imogen,

So sorry not to have seen more of you on Thursday – but weddings aren't usually conducive to long conversations! It was a nice occasion, wasn't it?[1] Marion and George were really thrilled with your present – it was a sweet idea, & they will treasure the MS.[2]

My dear – this letter is really to reintroduce the R.A.F. boy, whom I am so keen to come & work with you at Dartington. You know he decided he wanted to go to some ordinary college to get his groundwork better. Now he has changed his mind, & cannot face such a place. I saw him the other day and he is really in rather a bad state – needing encouragement & confidence, all of his having been squashed by the R.A.F. He has promise in both piano & composition – I don't pretend that he'll ever be a world-beater, but he is extremely musical, & tho' young, prepossessing in a way, and <u>might</u> develop into the kind of person we all want to see helping amateurs & organising music. I don't know – could you see him some time & judge for yourself, my dear? I have to go off to U.S.A. now, but I asked him to write direct to you. He <u>might</u> come down & see you if most convenient. Money – he hasn't a bean, but there are various grants which might be organised, & I might try & help myself, if all else fails . . . I am fond of the boy, & furious that the stuffing has been knocked out of him by this bloody conscription – because he might have been (& still may be, with the aid of an angel like you) a first-rate musical citizen.

Do what you can, my dear, but if he really isn't what you want, don't hesitate to say no –

In haste, with a great deal of love,
Yours ever,
BEN

Ass that I am – forgotten the most important thing: His name: Jim Butt.[3] His address: 44 Hallswell Road, Northwood, Middlesex!!

Peter sends Imogen his love.

1   Lord Harewood and Marion Stein were married on 29 September 1949, at St Mark's, North Audley Street, London, in the presence of King George VI and Queen Elizabeth. An account of the occasion appeared in *The Times* (30 September 1949), 'A Musical Occasion'. Britten's *Wedding Anthem (Amo Ergo Sum)*, a setting of words by Ronald Duncan, was written specially for the occasion, and was performed by the choir, with Pears and Joan Cross as soloists, under the composer's direction. Once again Britten made

appropriate use of canon in the soprano and tenor duet, 'These two are not two/Love has made them one'.

In RDBB, pp. 107–8, Duncan recalled writing the *Wedding Anthem*:

When the engagement was announced, Ben telephoned me and said that he would like to write something for the wedding, and that obviously I should write the words [. . .] I then wrote a small cantata [. . .] He set it, but then we ran into snags that we could hardly believe. They were that somebody in authority saw that I had written an aria which was a plea to the Virgin Mary to bless the couple. Since the Royal Family had been invited to the wedding, it was thought that this reference to the Virgin Mary was most inappropriate as it was a Catholic gesture. I was asked by the Prime Minister's office to alter this immediately. I could not understand why, and eventually a Bishop wrote to me on the subject. Once I had understood the point, I changed it, and instead of asking the Virgin Mary to bless the couple, I asked her to intercede. The intercession was allowed [. . .] During the performance of this little Cantata the couple sat on chairs behind the composer. I could see that George was as interested, or rather more interested in the Cantata than he had been in any part of the ceremony. I could also see that his uncle, George VI, was bored. But it was well known that the King was particularly unmusical.

That was, oddly enough, not the end of *Amo Ergo Sum*. At this time the [Royal] Festival Hall was being constructed and Herbert Morrison, who was then the Home Secretary, was asked to lay the foundation stone. It was suggested that three objects should be put beneath the stone: a copy of *The Times*, an umbrella; and the third was the [copyist's] manuscript of *Amo Ergo Sum*. When Morrison laid the foundation stone and saw the manuscript he said, 'I see the intellectuals have crept in rather early.'

The autograph manuscript of the *Wedding Anthem* is in the possession of Lord Harewood.

2   Imogen Holst gave the Harewoods the autograph manuscript of Gustav Holst's 'I'll love my love', No. 6 of *Nine Folk Songs* (H. 84), as a wedding present. This manuscript was given to BPL by Marion Thorpe in 1995.

3   See Letter XXI n. 1.

639   To Edith Sitwell[1]

[*Incomplete*]

4 Crabbe Street, Aldeburgh, Suffolk
Oct. 6th 1949

Dear Miss Sitwell,

I don't know whether you will remember meeting me at Sheffield with your brother some time ago.[2]

We are holding again our Aldeburgh Festival next year in June – a small intimate festival concentrating on local associations, and works which do not fit into the usual repertoire. We were planning to perform Façade next year and wonder whether you would be interested to come down and

speak your poems in it,[3] and perhaps give a lecture on the following afternoon. Our programmes are not finally settled yet, but the probable days
would be June 21st & 22nd. We would leave the subject of the lecture to
you of course, but if you could find an East Anglian figure which appeals
to you we should be delighted. (Morgan Forster is speaking on Skelton[4] –
would Nashe or Surrey[5] attract you?)

Needless to say we should be honoured and delighted if you could [. . .]

1   Edith Sitwell (1887–1964), English poet and critic, who, with her brothers
    Osbert (1892–1969) and Sacheverell (1897–1988), made a unique contribu-
    tion to English artistic and literary life, especially during the 1920s and
    1930s. The scandal that surrounded the first public performance of *Façade*,
    for speaker(s) and chamber ensemble, with music by the then unknown
    William Walton (a protégé of the Sitwells) and verse by Edith Sitwell,
    marked a significant moment in both their respective careers, while the
    critics' unanimous condemnation of the 'entertainment' did nothing to
    deflect the emergence of a highly individual poetic voice. Although
    Façade's technical innovations had demonstrated Edith Sitwell's original
    use of dance rhythms, the collections she published later in the 1920s reveal
    her predisposition to what John Lehmann has described as her 'elegiac,
    romantic vein' (*Dictionary of National Biography, 1961–70*, p. 950). Her
    poetry of the 1940s had a strong spiritual quality which Britten found par-
    ticularly appealing and which moved him to set her 'Still Falls the Rain' as
    his *Canticle III* in 1954. A warm friendship between poet and composer
    developed, and Britten returned to Sitwell's verse when creating *The Heart
    of the Matter* in 1956. In 1959 Sitwell dedicated to the composer her poem
    'Praise We Great Men', written at Britten's request for that year's Purcell and
    Handel anniversary celebrations. The manuscript is at BPL, and the text
    was included in TBB, pp. 124–5. Some time in the mid-1960s Britten con-
    templated a setting of 'Praise We Great Men'; however, it was not until 1976,
    during the final months of his life, that Britten began work on this piece,
    which remained unfinished at his death. The fragment was edited for per-
    formance and orchestrated in 1977 by Colin Matthews, who had had the
    opportunity to discuss the work with the composer.

    See also Geoffrey Elborn, *Edith Sitwell: A Biography*, Victoria Glendin-
    ning, *Edith Sitwell: a Unicorn among Lions*; John Lehmann and Derek
    Parker (eds.), *Edith Sitwell: Selected Letters*; Richard Greene (ed.), *Selected
    Letters of Edith Sitwell*; John Pearson, *Façades: Edith, Osbert and Sacheverell
    Sitwell*, and the exhibition catalogue *The Sitwells and the Arts of the 1920s
    and 1930s*.

2   This occasion was probably when Britten and Pears gave a joint recital with
    the Griller String Quartet on 6 June 1944, at the Sheffield Philharmonic
    Chamber Music Club, City Hall, Sheffield; the programme included
    Britten's First String Quartet, Schubert lieder and Vaughan Williams's

song-cycle *On Wenlock Edge*. It is apparent from a letter Edith Sitwell wrote to Colin Hampton, cellist of the Griller String Quartet, on 3 November 1943 that she already knew and admired Britten's quartet: 'The Britten has an extraordinary explosive force. In spite of the fact that I've just had a most debilitating cold, it is still exploding in my head with a blinding light followed by new ideas, points of view, even new vision.'

3   The performance of Walton's *Façade* was to take place in the Jubilee Hall, Aldeburgh, on 22 June 1950. Edith Sitwell and Pears were to record *Façade*, with the EOG Ensemble conducted by Anthony Collins, in 1954 (Decca LXT 2977).

4   Forster delivered his lecture on the Norfolk-born poet John Skelton (*c*.1460–1529) on 22 June 1950, in the Baptist Chapel, Aldeburgh.

5   Sitwell in fact spoke on 'Modern Poetry' on 23 June 1950, in the Baptist Chapel, Aldeburgh. Thomas Nashe (1567–1601), like Britten born in Lowestoft, was represented in *Spring Symphony*. Henry Howard, Earl of Surrey (*c*.1517–1547), was among the first to introduce Renaissance poetic modes into English and was the first to use blank verse, in his translation of Books 2 and 3 of the *Aeneid*. A casualty of the rivalry between the Howards and the Seymours, he was the last person to be executed during the reign of Henry VIII.

640   To Erwin Stein

HOTEL WINDSOR, 100 WEST 58TH STREET, NEW YORK 19, N.Y.[1]

Oct. 29th 1949

Dearest Erwin,

No time for long letter – hopelessly busy rushing round – I notice that you're too busy to write too, so we are quits!

I hope you & Sophie are better & rested by Aldeburgh. We saw Lesley Bedford in Washington yesterday so we know you went there.

We both hate this place & yearn to come back home – although people are very, very kind & seem to appreciate what we do. The concerts are being very successful,[2] & already pressure is being put on us to return next year – which is, needless to say, being resisted!

I suppose that you've got Marion & George back now – I do hope they enjoyed Capri as much as they did Venice. Give them both lots of our love & say we engage them for Dec. 13th concert, please![3]

Very little news of the Children's Opera season,[4] which we are hoping is good news. I know they are all busy, but one can't help worrying –

Please tell Tony Gishford that I'd much rather not issue the Stratton music[5] commercially – you know what I think about it! If Ronnie is pleased with it, that's fine!

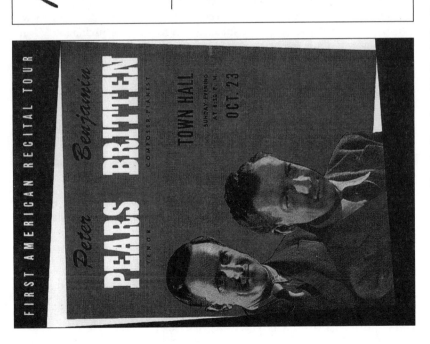

Flyer for Pears's and Britten's New York recital, 23 October 1949

I've talked to Ralph about the B & H situation[6] & he is most understanding. He's not too well, but who <u>could</u> rest or take things easy in
N. York – this terrible, nightmare city! Excuse scribble, & shortness of
this – but it's only to send lots of love to you & Sophie, from Peter &

BEN

<u>Please</u>, <u>please</u> get Eric to do something about Billy Budd script. It is
maddening not to have it with all these train journeys. Even the old one
would be better than nothing.[7]

1   Britten and Pears arrived in New York on 19 October, probably on the
    Queen Mary, to undertake their first recital tour of North America, which
    had been postponed from the previous year. In just over four weeks they
    gave twenty concerts in the United States and Canada. Shortly after their
    arrival Britten wrote to Elizabeth Sweeting (24 October):

    Our news in detail must wait till we get back (not so long now!), because I haven't
    alas time to write a long letter. What with concerts, rehearsings, meeting of friends
    & acquaintances, personal & business, old & new – there's no opportunity to stop
    & think (perhaps a good thing!) Briefly: the journey over was horrible, rough, 24
    hours delayed – but <u>terribly</u> boring. It's a horrible boat, too big, ugly, & vulgar. We
    arrived & were completely bewildered by New York & New Yorkers, but are getting
    a bit more settled now. We did our first recital at Town Hall here, last night, & it was
    (thank God) very successful; a big audience seemed to enjoy itself a lot, & Peter
    really sang beautifully. We have a day or so off now, then we start branching out
    from here (this hotel is our centre for 2 or 3 weeks) & then in mid-November off to
    the [West] Coast. It will be a relief to get away from this awful city, where one can't
    think, sleep or relax because of the heat (tropical) & noise (jingle). I couldn't feel
    more European!

    Britten's and Pears's recital on 23 October at the Town Hall, New York,
    was incorrectly billed as their first in the United States; it included songs by
    Purcell and Dowland, Britten's *Michelangelo Sonnets* and folksong arrange-
    ments.

2   The recital in New York on 23 October was followed by concerts at Dum-
    barton Oaks, Georgetown, Washington DC (27th) and Princeton University,
    New Jersey (29th).

3   Lord Harewood introduced a recital of operatic music (including duets
    from *The Beggar's Opera*) at Friends House, London, on 13 December 1949,
    performed by Joan Cross, Pears and Britten, under the auspices of the EOG.

4   A tour of *The Little Sweep*, culminating in a run at the Lyric, Hammer-
    smith, during Christmas and the New Year, 1949–50. See Letter 642 n. 1.

5   Britten's incidental music for Ronald Duncan's play *Stratton* was recorded
    by the EOG Orchestra, conducted by Norman Del Mar. According to
    Duncan (RDBB, p. 6), only six copies of the disc were pressed, four of them
    being used in the theatre production. One of the spare copies is in the

possession of the Ronald Duncan Literary Foundation, while the other is owned by Lord Harewood. *Stratton* opened at the Theatre Royal, Brighton, on 31 October 1949 in a production directed by John Fernald. The text was published by Faber and Faber in 1950. Britten's copy is inscribed: 'for Ben / with deep gratitude / for the exquisite music / love / Ronnie / 1590 [*sic*]'. See also RDBB, pp. 104–6 and 131.

6 Probably tension with Ernst Roth, who was known to be unenthusiastic about *Billy Budd*.

7 After a working session during August 1949 at Aldeburgh, when a new draft libretto was prepared, Crozier agreed to undertake a complete retyping of the text in order that Britten would have something to work on. Copies of the new libretto draft were sent to Forster and Britten on 23 October. See also Letter 643, and BBMCPR, pp. 56–7.

641 To Percy Grainger[1]

HOTEL WINDSOR, 100 WEST 58TH STREET, NEW YORK 19, N.Y.

Oct. 29th 1949

Dear Percy Grainger,

It was most kind of you to greet Peter Pears & myself with that kind letter, & it was also a great pleasure to see Mrs Grainger at our concert.[2]

I hope your concerts in Canada were a great success, & that you are now returned to New York because we much hope that there will be a chance of seeing you. This is our centre for the next two weeks, although we must travel around (we also go to Canada – tomorrow)[3] quite a lot. Would lunch on either Nov. 4, or Nov. 9th suit you both? As we only arrive back here on the morning of the 4th, perhaps you could let us have a note to the hotel saying whether or not either of these dates would be suitable. Perhaps we could meet at the hotel & then go out to a nearby restaurant?[4]

It would be a great honour & pleasure for us both if we could meet.

Many thanks again for writing,

Yours sincerely,

BENJAMIN BRITTEN

P.S. I enclose a copy of our "farewell" concert in London, which ended with three well-tried favourites of ours & our audience![5]

1 Australian-born composer, pianist, editor, folksong collector, writer and teacher (1882–1961), who became an American citizen in 1918. Grainger's earliest musical training was with his mother, with whom he had an unusually close relationship until her suicide in 1922. He subsequently studied in Frankfurt, from 1895 until 1899, and took piano lessons from

Busoni. In 1901 Grainger settled in England and launched his performing career. He became a highly active member of the English Folk Song Society and began collecting folksongs on wax cylinders. In the early 1900s he formed important friendships with Grieg and Delius, and began to secure a reputation as a composer.

In 1914 Grainger visited New York, took US citizenship four years later, and settled in White Plains, New York, where, in spite of prolonged trips abroad (notably to Denmark and Australia) he remained. He married the Swedish poet and artist Ella Viola Ström (1889–1979) in 1928.

Britten's admiration for Grainger's folksong settings dates from at least 1933 – on 3 March he noted in his diary, 'two brilliant folk-song arrangements of Percy Grainger [. . .] knocking all the V. Williams and R. O. Morris arrangements into a cocked-hat' (see also Donald Mitchell, 'Benjamin Britten: the "Arranger", liner note to the complete recording of Britten's folksong arrangements (Collins Classics, 70392, 1995)) – and Britten was to take Grainger as the exemplar for his own collections of folksong arrangements. Britten and Pears championed Grainger's original compositions and arrangements in their concert programmes at Aldeburgh and elsewhere and, together with the conductor Steuart Bedford, made a pair of remarkable gramophone recordings of Grainger's music, which played a significant role in his rehabilitation (Decca sxl 6410 and sxl 6672).

Although Pears had met Grainger in 1936 (see CHPP, p. 157), Britten did not meet him until 1958, although they occasionally corresponded. See also Malcolm Gillies and David Pear (eds.), *The All-Round Man: Selected Letters of Percy Grainger*, and John Bird, *Percy Grainger*, to which Britten and Pears contributed a prefatory note:

To have met Percy Grainger even as an old man is a cherished memory. His warmth, his originality, his charm were unforgettable, and his genial energy had already become a myth. The masterly folksong arrangements with their acutely beautiful feeling for sound were our first musical introduction, and later the preparation of a record of his music was an exciting and revealing experience. Repeated performances strengthened our respect for his work, and our few meetings confirmed our affection and admiration for the man.

Pears gave a lecture on Grainger at the British Institute of Recorded Sound on 16 February 1970, the text of which was published in *Recorded Sound* (January–April 1972), pp. 11–15. A revised version was included under the title 'A Personal Introduction' to Lewis Foreman (ed.), *The Percy Grainger Companion*, pp. 23–30.

2   Presumably the recital in New York on 23 October.

3   Britten and Pears were to give concerts in Ottawa (31 October), Toronto (1 November, with a broadcast of *Saint Nicolas* by CBC on the 2nd), and Montreal (3 November).

4   Grainger's response to Britten has not survived, but Britten was to write again on 10 November 1949:

Thank you very much for your kind letter, but it looks very much as though we shall miss you on this trip to the States and Canada, which is most disappointing.

We have to leave for the [West] Coast next Monday the 14th, on tour until the 7th of December. Then we shall only spend two days in New York before flying back to England, on the 9th of December. And I see from your letter that you cannot be in New York on those two days. Please believe me when I say how sad we both are that this is so.

When will you next be coming to Europe, because I am afraid it will be a long time before we will be able to come back to this country again? My address in England is: 4, Crabbe Street – Aldeburgh – Suffolk, England.

Would you please be sure and get in touch with me when you next come?

5 The recital, on 13 October 1949 at Chelsea Town Hall, concluded with Grainger's 'The Sprig o' Thyme', 'The Jolly Sailor' and 'Six Dukes went a-fishin''. The recital had also included the premiere of Arthur Oldham's *Five Chinese Lyrics*.

642 To Elizabeth Sweeting

HOTEL WINDSOR, 100 WEST 58TH STREET, NEW YORK 19, N.Y.

Nov. 4th 1949

My dear Elizabeth,

Peter & I are just back from a hectic, but pleasant, four days in Canada & find your two letters & telegram awaiting us. <u>Thrilled</u> that 'Let's Make' has gone so well, & is so well booked.[1] I do congratulate you most heartily, my dear, in getting it on. I realise what a struggle it was what with re-casting, re-rehearsing, & getting the new stuff out of E.C.;[2] but it is lovely that you've succeeded. I never doubted you would – but I did worry for you all the same! I've also read the first part; but alas – it is so long & wordy & terribly cliché'd. Perhaps if I could have sat over him while he did it, it would have been better – but things weren't allowed to work out like that. Still, with Basil [Coleman]'s cutting, it probably 'comes off'. What a good idea about Anne![3] I hope she's enjoying it. Give them all my love. And Norman [Del Mar] too.

No time – as usual for a letter – hopeless rush. I don't fit in at <u>all</u> in this country; really hate it. But Canada was moving & exciting. I have been talking to R. Hawkes about a tour (for the E.O.G.) there, & he's excited about the idea. Winter 1951–2 would be best.[4] We heard a recording of the Canadian P. Grimes, which was truly magnificent; it made us horribly homesick[5] as did the [*illegible*] you sent us! Still, not much more than a month more, & mostly away from New York – thank God.

I <u>don't</u>, I'm afraid, like the idea of the Stratton music recorded. It won't stand up on its own legs, & it's no advertisement for the E.O.G. orchestra to be associated with it.

Glad about your Aldeburgh visit – & that things are calm. Everyone here knows about the Festival – I think we might advertise a bit here for next year. I think I landed William Primrose[6] (the viola-player – a great one) for a recital – but more of that later.

My dear – things will be sobered down & a little more automatic by now, I hope, & you'll have a chance to relax. I can't thank you enough for the letters which keep up our spirits <u>enormous</u>ly! Please go on writing if ever there's a chance. And lots of love from Peter & me.

(Excuse the haste.)

BEN

1 Sweeting had arranged an EOG tour of *Let's Make an Opera*, starting in Brighton (6–11 November) and then continuing to Torquay (13–18 November), Cambridge (20–25 November), Birmingham (27 November–2 December) and the Lyric, Hammersmith, London (4 December – 27 January 1950).

2 Eric Crozier, who had revised the play that precedes the opera. As the letter reveals, Britten was disappointed by the new version.

3 Anne Wood shared the role of Mrs Baggott with Gladys Parr.

4 This proposal did not materialize, probably because of Hawkes's death in 1950. The EOG, however, was to take *The Turn of the Screw* to the Stratford Festival, Ontario, in August 1957.

5 Britten wrote a postcard to his sister Barbara on 14 November: '[. . .] glad you still like Grimes – I do, it makes me feel homesick away from Aldeburgh!'

6 Scottish violist (1903–1982), who studied violin in Glasgow, London, and in Belgium with Ysaÿe, who advised him to change to the viola. Primrose pursued a career as a chamber musician with the London String Quartet and as a soloist during the 1930s, before being selected by Toscanini as Principal Violist of the NBC Orchestra (1937–42). Primrose formed his own string quartet in 1939 and returned to solo work in the 1940s. In 1944 he commissioned Bartók to write a viola concerto of which Primrose gave the first performance after Bartók's death (the concerto was completed by Tibor Serly). Other composers who wrote works for Primrose include Edmund Rubbra, Peter Racine Fricker and Iain Hamilton, as well as Britten, whose *Lachrymae*, for viola and piano, was premiered by Primrose and the composer on 20 June 1950, at the Aldeburgh Festival, in a programme of 'Chamber music featuring viola' that also included a performance of Mozart's E♭ Trio (K. 498) and Arthur Benjamin's Viola Sonata.

Primrose wrote to Britten on 24 October 1949, a few days after their first meeting:

I hasten to thank you most warmly for two very gracious experiences. First of all for your concert of a few hours ago which I found a very rewarding experience. It was all so beautifully accomplished [. . .] Secondly, for your heartwarming compli-

26 Tanglewood, 1946: Benjamin Britten and Serge Koussevitzky, who commissioned *Peter Grimes* and *Spring Symphony*, at the US premiere of *Grimes*
27 Britten with W. H. Auden

28 The curtain call: the cast of *Peter Grimes,* led by conductor Leonard Bernstein, acknowledge Britten and Eric Crozier

29 On the Meare at Thorpeness, near Aldeburgh, August 1950:
George Behrend rows George and Marion Harewood and Peter
Pears, with Britten in the bow
30 Britten the hardy swimmer in the North Sea off Aldeburgh

31 Round the piano at Crag House, 1947: Peter Pears, Ronald Duncan and Arthur Oldham,
with Britten playing

32 Literary visitors to the first Aldeburgh Festival, June 1948: Christopher Isherwood,
E. M. Forster and William Plomer
33 With friends in the garden at Crag House, during the first Aldeburgh Festival: *clockwise from
bottom left* Peter Pears, Imogen Holst, E. M. Forster, Britten and Arthur Oldham

34 Britten and Pears buying vegetables from Jonas Baggott in Aldeburgh High Street, 1948

35 *Saint Nicolas* in the Parish Church during the first Aldeburgh Festival, 1948
36 Props arriving at the stage door of Aldeburgh's Jubilee Hall for the premiere of *Let's Make an Opera* in 1949: Sammy's bath follows the rocking horse up the steps

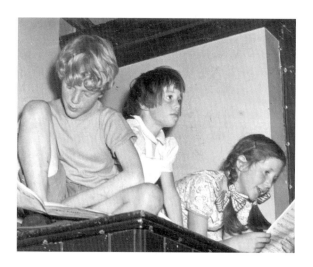

37 Hugh Gathorne-Hardy (aged eight), one of the dedicatees of *The Little Sweep*, with Britten's nieces, Roguey and Sally Welford (aged four and six), perched above the Jubilee Hall's entrance door at a rehearsal for *Let's Make an Opera*
38 Members of the audience at *Let's Make an Opera*, required to provide an *ad hoc* chorus, attempt to master their parts

39 The rehearsal scene for *The Little Sweep*, within *Let's Make an Opera*: Gladys Parr as Mrs Parworthy and Norman Lumsden as Mr Chaffinch with the unfortunate Sammy part-way up the chimney

40 *The Little Sweep* in performance: Black Bob (Norman Lumsden) and Clem (Max Worthley) menace Sammy (John Moules)
41 'The Coaching Song': the *Little Sweep* company transformed into a coach and its occupants with the help of a post horn and a couple of sweep's brushes

42 Working on the libretto of *Billy Budd* at Crag House,
August 1949: E. M. Forster, Benjamin Britten and Eric Crozier

43 Co-librettists Eric Crozier and E. M. Forster

44 *Billy Budd*, Covent
Garden, 1951: Peter Pears
as Captain Vere

45 *Billy Budd*, Act I scene 1: on the deck of the *Indomitable*, the pressganged Billy bids farewell to his old ship, the *Rights o' Man*

46 Billy in the Darbies, Act IV scene 1: the American baritone Theodor Uppman
47 *Billy Budd*, Act II scene 3: Claggart (Frederick Dahlberg) discovers the fight between Billy (Theodor Uppman) and Squeak (David Tree)

48/49 Britten the conductor in rehearsal

50 In the green room after the first performance of *Spring Symphony*, Amsterdam Concertgebouw, 1949: Britten, soprano Jo Vincent, conductor Eduard van Beinum, contralto Kathleen Ferrier and tenor Peter Pears

ment the other evening at the Hawkes' when you said I was 'needed' at Aldeburgh. Believe me I would regard it as a privilege, without a viola piece from you, but with it my cup would indeed overflow!

See also William Primrose, *Walk on the North Side: Memoirs of a Violist*, p. 185.

Primrose was to return to two subsequent Aldeburgh Festivals: in 1951, when he played Mozart's *Sinfonia concertante* in E♭ (K. 364), with Manoug Parikian (violin) and the EOG Orchestra, conducted by Britten, and participated in a chamber recital; and in 1952, when he performed *Lachrymae*, with Noel Mewton-Wood (piano), and Priaulx Rainier's Sonata, Bach's Sixth Brandenburg Concerto (conducted by Britten), and Holst's *Lyric Movement* for viola and strings (conducted by Imogen Holst). In 1976, Britten was to arrange *Lachrymae* for viola and small string orchestra (*senza* first violins).

643 To Erwin Stein

HOTEL WINDSOR, 100 WEST 58TH STREET, NEW YORK 19, N.Y.

Nov. 5th 1949

My dear Erwin,

As you can imagine – there is never enough time for more than a scribble so here are a few jottings –

Thanks for your letter. We're back in horrible New York after a few exciting and moving days in Canada. Heard recording of P. Grimes[1] – very good. A really good conductor – Waddington[2] – & on the whole an understanding & skilful cast. Thanks for the Children's Opera play – new version. Glad it's a success in Cambridge, but I find the new version as embarrassingly wordy & cliché as the old – lack of courage and simplicity. With cuts it will be better – but oh – oh and WHERE is BILLY BUDD?? I am getting really desperate about it – I'd hoped to start writing in December, but this delay makes that quite unlikely.[3]

"Spring Symphony" in Rome – can you <u>imagine</u> the Italians' English . . . ?!!! "Spring-a the sweet-a Spring-a". No, I think we'd better try for another & more gifted Italian. What about George Foa[4] of the BBC? Could you try him? I didn't know Mucci's Lucretia.[5]

"Spring Symphony" in London.[6] Could you please tell Borsdorf[7] that as I can't have Dutch boys, I want Jo Vincent?[8] And how is the John Lowe plan about urchins from L.C.C. schools going?[9] Sorry to bother you with this, but I'm so far away – alas – alas – alas. Also, please, my dear, can you send to Herbert Bardgett[10] of the Leeds Festival Choir the M.M. [metronome] markings of the chorus bits of it?[11] I suggest Joan, Anne & Peter for soloists.[12]

Must rush now – for rehearsal of Illuminations[13] – have lost <u>that</u> battle, as many others. How we <u>hate</u> this place – but that's a long story.

Lots of love to Sophie, Marion, George & lots to yourself. Back <u>soon</u>.

BEN & Peter too

P.S. Thank you so much for having the letters sent on so promptly – but the enclosed arrived by accident!

1   Presumably a recording of the CBC Opera Company's recording of the broadcast performance of *Peter Grimes*.

2   Geoffrey Waddington (1904–1966), English-born Canadian conductor, administrator and violinist, who worked extensively with the CBC orchestras from the mid-1920s and who founded in 1948 the CBC Opera Company whose broadcasts of *Peter Grimes* and *Albert Herring* were widely acclaimed. Waddington was appointed Music Director of the CBC in 1952, and was founder and Music Director of the CBC Symphony Orchestra, 1952–64.

3   Britten was not to begin work on the composition draft of *Billy Budd* until January 1950: see BBMCPR, p. 58.

4   Stein was to report to Britten on 27 November 1949 that 'the Italian translation is well on the way, if not finished. Foa is doing an excellent job with it.'

5   Presumably an Italian translation of *The Rape of Lucretia*.

6   The UK premiere of *Spring Symphony* was given on 9 March 1950 at the Royal Albert Hall, London, with Joan Cross (soprano), Anne Wood (contralto) and Peter Pears (tenor), the London Philharmonic Choir, a boys' choir from the London Schools' Music Association (Lambeth Branch), and the London Philharmonic Orchestra, conducted by Eduard van Beinum. See also Letter 657.

There was some press coverage of this important premiere, notably from *The Times*, 'The *Spring Symphony*: Britten's New Work' (10 March 1950), in which Frank Howes discussed the piece – the vocal score had just been published – before turning to the performance itself:

Benjamin Britten's *Spring Symphony*, having already enhanced its composer's reputation in Holland and America, was enthusiastically received by a large audience at its first English performance at the Albert Hall last night, when Mr Eduard van Beinum, who launched it in Holland, had charge of the London Philharmonic Choir and Orchestra, a boys' choir from the London Schools' Music Association, and Miss Joan Cross, Miss Anne Wood, and Mr Peter Pears as soloists.

Whether or not 'symphony' is the most apt designation for this orchestrally accompanied cycle of solo and choral songs is a moot point; however, of one thing there could be no doubt – the composer is a connoisseur of poetry. His reactions to his poems are sometimes unexpected (as in Blake's 'Sound the Flute' and Barnefield's 'When will my May come'), but every poetic image finds a musical counterpart as cunning as it is vivid. Last night's performance made that much very clear. Though the large orchestra is always subservient to the voices, to it falls the duty of illumining the text, not with a flood of light but with 'thousand coloured light'.

Both singers and orchestral players appeared to know their way about the score and to appreciate its subtle cleverness, but what they failed to discover, or at any rate to convey, was that spiritual radiance which made a striking impression at the work's first performance in Holland. Hushed expectancy was there, but only in the finale did the buds really break and the birds sing. Here the little boys, who had sung and whistled so gallantly earlier on, failed to cut through the general rejoicing with their 'Sumer is icumen in'; the choral singing as a whole needed much clearer articulation of consonants. All three soloists discharged their duties as a labour of love, though Miss Anne Wood's sensitive singing of the alto numbers sometimes lacked the necessary volume of tone.

Richard Capell, *Daily Telegraph*, 'Britten's New "Symphony": Dazzling Score' (10 March 1950), wrote:

This so-called symphony is rather a garland of spring flowers – including plenty of prickly blackthorn. The text is a little anthology of spring poems, principally of the 16th and 17th centuries. The one lapse from consistency is a poem by Auden, which brings in thoughts inappropriate to the rest; but, even so, the admirable music (the slow movement of the 'symphony') remains consistent enough.

More than ever in this dazzling score, the style of which is fundamentally diatonic, coloured by audacious dissonance, Britten is deft, light-handed, inventive and infallible in bringing off his puckish intentions.

The boys' choir (which is also called upon to whistle) is one of his telling resources. A duet, 'Fair and Fair', culminating in a spirited canon, is among the brilliant things Britten produces like a conjurer.

7 Presumably a London concert agent.

8 Jo Vincent did not take part. Stein was to write to Britten on 27 November, 'There seems to be a muddle [over] who is to sing the soprano solo in London.'

9 In the same letter Stein was to write to Britten, 'There is still no definite news about L.C.C. [London County Council] boys, but Lowe is confident that it will be all right. A meeting has been [held] a few days ago & we should hear about it tomorrow or Tuesday.'

10 Scottish conductor and chorus master (1894–1962), who was chorus master of the Huddersfield Choral Society (1932–62) and the Leeds Triennial Music Festival. Bardgett was preparing the Leeds Chorus for their performance under the composer's direction at the 1950 Leeds Festival, on 6 October. After this performance, Britten wrote a detailed letter to Bardgett: see Letter 678. See also R. A. Edwards, *And the Glory: A History in Commemoration of the 150th Anniversary of the Huddersfield Choral Society*.

11 Stein's letter to Britten of the 27th: 'I was in touch with the conductor of the Huddersfield Choir & sent him metronome marks; I also arranged for him to hear the records [of the first performance] which George has in Harewood.'

12 Cross, Wood and Pears were the soloists at Leeds, with the Hallé Orchestra
    under Bardgett's direction.

13 On 7 November 1949, Pears and Britten (as guest conductor) appeared with
    the Little Orchestra Society at the Town Hall, New York, in a programme of
    mainly English music in which Pears and Britten performed Britten's
    edition of Purcell's *Suite of Songs* from *Orpheus Britannicus* and Britten's
    Rimbaud cycle *Les Illuminations*. The concert was repeated on the 11th at
    Swarthmore College, Pennsylvania.

644 To Elizabeth Sweeting

HOTEL WINDSOR, 100 WEST 58TH STREET, NEW YORK 19, N.Y.

[11 November 1949]

Dearest Elizabeth,

In the wildest of hastes – just off for yet another concert in Pennsylvania, in fact 2, then one more in New York[1] & then out to the [West]
Coast. If you want anything urgent – continue to address to Mrs Mayer,
please – that will eventually catch up with us, but there will be delays from
now on. But we are halfway through & will be back <u>very</u> soon – Thank
God!! Thanks for your nice letters. Got one this morning about the Lyric
booking, & that sounds excellent. I hope you've won your battle about
3 casts [for *Let's Make an Opera*] – which sounds dotty. But from this
distance one can't judge; but I should have thought, at least for all parts
except Gladys, that <u>one</u> main with a cover would have worked.

I expect you got my cable re Holst – I'm in the dark about this. I have
always [pressed], & shall continue to press for the Wandering Scholar.
It's not a great piece, but can be quite an effective curtain raiser for the
dark, dramatic & exciting (we hope!) Easdale.[2] It's good to have an older
work & besides will work well with Cheltenham. I suggest for Aldeburgh
W. Scholar/Easdale[3] & for Cheltenham that again perhaps, and another
evening W. Scholar/Sāvitri, the latter which must & should be cheap, &
should please the Cheltenonians [*sic*].[4] If it's not long enough, we might
add an instrumental piece – also by Holst. Why then do we (& how could
we) afford a new, 4th piece??? The next year with Dido, yes. I'd like one
from Arthur [Oldham]. There is no one I know, anyhow, who could write
one in the time, or who isn't up to his eyes in opera anyhow – unless we
go to the hacks Tony Hopkins, Gordon Jacob, William Alwyn[5] – et al.;
of those Hopkins has most surprise value, at any rate. Eric will of course
faint at this suggestion. But when there is not a repertoire, we can't expect
to perform (or find) masterpieces at every turn – & that's why we must
make the best of what we've got – hence the Holst.

Sorry dear – you can't imagine the rush, or strain – we hate it, both,
although people are kind & like us. This town is hell.

So glad that you're doing so very well with the kids. Give them my love –
I'd send them a p.c. if I'd find the time. But no chance.

Love to all – & to Anne especially: I do hope her Miss Baggott works. I
think it's a splendid & plucky idea.

Lots of love – lots –

BEN

1 Britten and Pears gave recitals at Swarthmore College and Lehigh University, Bethlehem, Pennsylvania, on 11 and 12 November 1949 respectively,
before returning to New York for a reception given in their honour by the
League of Composers.

2 Holst's *The Wandering Scholar* and the premiere of Easdale's *The Sleeping
Children* were presented as a double bill by the EOG at Cheltenham on
9 July, in productions by Basil Coleman. Both operas were conducted by
Norman Del Mar.

3 Neither was performed at Aldeburgh in 1951.

4 The all-Holst programme was not presented in Cheltenham, Holst's birth-
place.

5 The English composers Antony Hopkins, whose opera *Lady Rohesia* was
produced at Sadler's Wells in 1948, Gordon Jacob (1885–1984), and William
Alwyn (1905–1985).

645 To Eric Crozier

THE TOWER HOUSE, LOS ANGELES 5
[30 November 1949]

My dear Eric,

I heard yesterday from Esther N.-S. [Neville-Smith] two bits of lovely
news about you, & although (as usual!) there's no time for a real letter
I felt I <u>must</u> write at once & say how happy I am. I gather you'll marry
Nancy round Christmas time.[1] That is really wonderful, & I am certain
that you & she will be really happy at last. Tell the darling girl how really
delighted we both are, & give her oceans of our love. Also about
Bournemouth – that this job (I presume it's the same that was supposed
to have fallen thro'?) has materialised is excellent. Although it mayn't be
exactly what you want, at least it will be interesting & a great help financially, & I hope it will re-establish an economic confidence in yourself!

I am delighted that 'Let's Make' is such a success, which I gather from
Elizabeth's notes & wires. I was also delighted that you were able to get the
revision done in time – being very aware of the rush it was for you. I am
sure it is a great improvement, & I am so happy that the general talk
about opera-planning is now so successfully in. With luck Peter & I will

see a show at the Lyric when we get back on Dec. 10th. The interest here in
it is really enormous, & the battle for it is well under way. I go tomorrow
to see a rehearsal of Herring with Ebert.[2] He has been very sweet to us – &
is terribly keen on the piece. We have St Nic. [*Saint Nicolas*] tonight,[3] so
Crozier is much in Los Angeles minds! I couldn't begin to describe the
agony, the rush, the excitement, often the great thrills, & the homesickness
of this tour. Anyhow it is soon over, & we both look forward to seeing
you. Will you be near London 10–14? Thank you so much for getting
Budd sent. I am full of it, & long to plunge into it!

   Lots of love to you both from Peter as well & very best of luck for new job.

                                                                    Yours ever,
                                                                    BEN

1   They were married on Boxing Day (26 December) 1949.

2   Ebert had originally agreed to direct the premiere of *Albert Herring* at
    Glyndebourne in 1947. His production for the University of Southern
    California, Los Angeles, was one of the earliest in the US.

3   A performance at the University of Southern California, Los Angeles.
    Britten wrote from Los Angeles to Lesley Bedford, 'Our concerts here are
    nice – good orchestra, friendly people – different from beastly, hateful,
    sinister, stupid, snobbish, unimportant New York – (I don't like New York).'
       Stravinsky, who was living in Hollywood at this time, was to write to
    Nicolas Nabokov, on 15 December 1949, a characteristically barbed com-
    ment about Britten's and Pears's Los Angeles concerts: 'All week here I've
    listened to Aunt Britten and Uncle Pears, but we will discuss that later.
    Britten himself makes quite a favourable impression, and he is very
    popular with the public. He undoubtedly has talent as a performer, espe-
    cially at the piano' (Robert Craft (ed.), *Stravinsky: Selected Correspondence*,
    vol. 2, p. 376). See also, Bayan Northcott, 'The Fine Art of Borrowing: Britten
    and Stravinsky', in the 1994 Aldeburgh Festival programme book, pp. 14–19.
       Britten and Pears were on the West Coast of the US from 14 November
    until 7 December. Among the people they met there was Christopher
    Isherwood, whom they had seen in England in 1947 and 1948 (Isherwood
    and his then partner Bill Caskey had spent a few days at the first Aldeburgh
    Festival in June, see plate 32). Isherwood's *Lost Years*, a frank, third-person
    memoir of his life from 1945 until 1951, pp. 212–15, gives an account of the
    time he spent with Britten and Pears:

    On November 20, Christopher had supper with Benjamin Britten and Peter Pears,
    who had just arrived in Los Angeles to give two or more concerts. The reunion was
    most cordial. Indeed, they both treated Christopher as the one real friend with
    whom they could relax from the strain of official hospitality. Christopher at once
    arranged to give a party, at which, he promised, they would meet as many attractive
    boys as he could manage to collect. The party was held on November 22 [Britten's
    thirty-sixth birthday]. [...]

The party wasn't an unqualified success. The house was certainly crammed with young men who were most of them fairly attractive. They danced together or went upstairs and necked. When invited, many had told Christopher that they were eager to meet the guests of honour, Britten and Pears – but, having done so, they quickly lost interest in them. In this gay setting, where celebrity snobbery was replaced by sex snobbery, Ben and Peter were just a pair of slightly faded limey queens, who were, furthermore, too shy and too solidly mated to join in the general kissing and cuddling. The party wasn't really for them, though they politely pretended to believe that it was.

The account resumes on 24 November:

That evening, he [Christopher] and Jim [Charlton] went to a concert given by Britten and Pears, downtown. I believe it was after this concert that Ben and Peter told him that they longed to get away to the country for a couple of days and be quiet. So Christopher arranged to take them on a short trip and he asked Jim Charlton to come along. On the 26th, they drove to Palm Springs and then on to the AJC Ranch, where they saw John van Druten [the playwright and novelist, who in 1951 was to write the stage play *I Am a Camera* based on Isherwood's Berlin novels]. They spent the night at the Rancho Mirage, ten miles outside Palm Springs. On the 27th, they drove southwest to Mount Palomar (the day-to-day diary doesn't actually say they visited the observatory but I assume they did), then out to the coast at Oceanside, then up to Laguna Beach, where they had supper with Chris Wood and slept at a motel nearby. On the 28th, they drove back to Los Angeles.

I don't have many memories of Ben and Peter during their visit or of this trip Christopher and Jim took with them. Once, when he was alone with Ben, Christopher asked (I suppose in a more or less tactful manner) if Ben ever had sex with other people. Ben said no, he was faithful to Peter, adding, 'I still feel the old charm.' Another memory is of Ben requesting Christopher, quite pleasantly, to stop singing. Christopher would do this for hours on end when he was by himself, repeating the same song over and over. A great favourite was Cole Porter's 'Ev'ry time we say goodbye . . .' because he loved attempting the transition in, 'But how strange / The change / From major to minor.' This was what Ben must have found particularly painful, because Christopher had almost no ear. Also I remember that Jim asked Ben how he composed – maybe he didn't put the question so crudely. Anyhow, Ben didn't snub him but replied: 'Well – I think I'll begin with some strings, and then I think I'd like to bring in some woodwind, and then I think I'll put a bit of percussion under that. . . .' (This may well be inaccurately reported and nonsense musically, but it conveys the effect which Ben's practical, unromantic attitude had upon Christopher – who had seen so many Hollywood films about composers that he had lapsed into accepting the notion that they get their ideas by hearing a lark, or church bells, or waves on the shore.)

The trip itself was undoubtedly a success. Ben and Peter loved the desert and the mountains. They became quite schoolboyish, laughing and joking. By the time they had got to Laguna Beach and had had supper with Chris Wood, they were so relaxed that they went over to his piano of their own accord and played and sang for a couple of hours. They both liked Jim. Peter may have found him physically attractive. Anyhow, I suspect that Christopher thought he did – for, when Peter knocked on the door of their two-bed motel room next morning, Christopher exhibitionistically called to him to come in (despite Jim's embarrassment) so that

Peter should see Jim and himself naked in Christopher's bed, where they had just finished having sex.

On November 30, Jim and Christopher went to another concert given by Ben and Peter, at the University of Southern California. [...]

On December 2, Christopher had lunch with Ben and Peter, just before they left Los Angeles.

Following Britten's and Pears's visit to California, Isherwood wrote to them on 15 December:

Thank you so much for your letter and the cheque; and thank you for coming to this neck of the woods. Your visit was about the nicest thing that has happened to me this year, and I will never forget that trip. Only, it should have been longer. And, thinking it over, I realize how uncomfortable you two sweet martyrs must have been on that back seat. I sat on it the other day, almost for the first time, and bounced and bounced and hit the ceiling! Everybody here adored you, as I suppose they do everywhere you go: you have a genuine springlike quality which makes buds burst and fruit appear – the pun is unintentional, and anyway let me hope you don't know what 'fruit' means in this wicked land. Now my only consolation is one of your Rossini albums, just acquired. Not the one with 'my' tune, but wonderful.

Actually, what I would like to say, and then I'll spare your blushes, is that I don't know when I've been so deeply moved by the sense of a relationship between two people. It is so right, and so simple and obvious, and so astronomically rare in this world of lies and vanity and half-promises and emotional cowardice. Jim felt this as strongly as I did. So – thank you for being together!

I was rather dismayed to find how much Gerald Heard would have liked to have seen you. I hadn't realized. He sends an urgent appeal to you both to consider seriously a cantata or an opera or something about Gandhi. Maybe it's an idea.

So glad you like Hardy.

Gerald Heard (c. 1885–1971), Irish writer, broadcaster, philosopher and religious teacher, whom Isherwood had first met in 1932. He had emigrated to Los Angeles in 1937 and it was through him that Isherwood became a disciple of Swami Prabhavananda. The mention of a piece to commemorate Gandhi is of interest: it was a project that Britten had very sympathetically considered with Ronald Duncan but finally did not pursue (see Letters 570 and 575).

It was from a volume of Hardy's *Collected Poems* given to Britten by Isherwood in 1949 that the composer selected the majority of the texts for his song-cycle *Winter Words* (1953). The volume is inscribed by Isherwood: 'For Ben & Peter / from Christopher, / with happy memories of our / week-end / Nov. 1949'.

646 To Nancy Evans and Eric Crozier

4 Crabbe Street, Aldeburgh
[December 1949]

My dearest Nancy and Eric,

The calendar is not a Christmas present – just a reminder of Suffolk, that you should occasionally remember us in your travels & new lives!

Also Peter & I won't be sending you a present yet for your wedding, until we know where you'll be living & what you most want for the household. We just send you our love for what I know will be the happiest Boxing Day of both your lives. How happy we all are! That you know.

Thank you, Eric my dear, for the long letter about the Group & Bournemouth.[1] A most happy suggestion I think; & as soon as we get settled with a new manager, we must try & see if it would work. I don't see why not. Morgan & I work on hard[2] – & hope to have lots of improvements to show you soon. I feel sure you'll approve. Morgan is in splendid form, & very inclined to overwork me!! Two queries for you, please (i) The ship at the start is hove to – hadn't we better start her? How does one do this? Could you put this on a p.c. perhaps for us & also (ii) the provisional list of chorus, & chorus-division, I think you had? Morgan is in touch with the Admiralty about Articles of War.

Lots of love to you both from Peter too, & all the happiness in the world for your new life.

Yours ever,

BEN

1 Crozier's letter has not survived but it evidently concerned a suggested arrangement whereby he divided his time between his new responsibilities at Bournemouth and those to the EOG.

2 Britten wrote to Mary Behrend on 16 December 1949: 'I am down here now with E. M. Forster – working terrifically hard on Billy Budd. It is going very well, & most exciting to work on. I think it's going to be quite a piece! But surprising.' In an unpublished letter written to Crozier on 1 December (at BPL), Forster had explained to his co-librettist what he and Britten intended to do during this pre-Christmas period: 'I propose to write in the "articles of war" speech [see Letter 713] and fill in any other gaps, with Ben's help. And no doubt I shall be discussing a producer with him; I wish he would consider Kenneth Green.' Forster must surely have meant designer rather than 'producer'; Green had been responsible for the decor and costumes for *Peter Grimes* in 1945. John Piper was to design the sets and costumes for *Budd*. See BBMCPR, p. 57, and plates 44–7.

647 To Lennox Berkeley

4 Crabbe Street, Aldeburgh
Jan. 11th 1950

My dear Lennox,

Thank you so very much for the score of the Stabat Mater[1] – I am so glad Chester's have done you so proud, with such a lovely cover. The piece really deserves it too. I hope it will have lots & lots of performances, & bring you the fame that it merits – it got off to a jolly good start in Holland I heard. Most unfortunately we can't get it into our Aldeburgh Festival this year, as we have to run on a tight budget & it is very expensive to put on. But in 1951, in our grand recapitulation year, when we shall repeat all our best pieces, it will certainly be got in.[2] I hope all the same that you & Freda will want to come this year. We are planning some pretty scrumptious programmes, with lots of Bach & Mozart & we hope the new Easdale–Guthrie opera.[3] How's your opera going?[4]

Are you going to allow me a peep at it soon? I hope to be able to pay you a visit, <u>and</u> see my godchild[5] again, next week or the week after. I pack Peter off to Switzerland soon to get well in the sun, & shall be up in London for some days. He's getting back some strength now, but it's a wearisome & painful business.[6]

My dear, I hear rumours that Freda is again 'expecting' – or whatever the polite phrase is – I never remember. That is very exciting. I am so glad that Michael will have a bro. or sis. not too far separated from him. Give her my love, please, & say I hope she's not feeling too rotten. The beginning can be nasty I remember.

Please excuse the scribble, but what with being a nurse-maid, a housekeeper (domestic arrangements are a bit haywire), a musico-business man, <u>and</u> a composer – letter-writing doesn't get a fair chance.

And <u>thanks</u>, my dear, for the lovely piece,

Yours ever,
BEN

1 Berkeley had sent Britten a full score of his *Stabat Mater* on the occasion of its first publication by J. & W. Chester in 1950, with an inscription to the work's dedicatee on the title page: 'For Ben with love Lennox. Jan: 1950'.

2 Berkeley's *Stabat Mater* had to wait until 1953 before it was heard at Aldeburgh (see Letter 553 n. 1).

3 A performance of Bach's *St Matthew Passion* was given in Aldeburgh Parish Church on 17 June 1950, to mark the 200th anniversary of Bach's death. The soloists included Pears (Evangelist) and Carel Wilhum (Christus), with Dora van Doorn-Lindeman (soprano), Nancy Evans (mezzo-soprano),

Wiebe Drayer (tenor) and Hermann Schen (bass), and the choir and orchestra of the Rotterdam Volks-Universiteit and the choir of Spangen, conducted by Bertus van Lier. It was with these largely amateur choristers and orchestra that Pears sang the Evangelist in the *St Matthew Passion* for many years in Rotterdam. The planned Mozart concert was postponed until the following year. Easdale's *The Sleeping Children* (libretto by Tyrone Guthrie) was first performed by the EOG at Cheltenham (not Aldeburgh) on 9 July 1951.

4 Berkeley's one-act opera *A Dinner Engagement*, which was first performed by the EOG at the 1954 Aldeburgh Festival.

5 Michael Berkeley.

6 Pears had begun the New Year with an attack of shingles; an Austrian tour with Britten was cancelled, and Pears went off to Switzerland instead, to convalesce (see Letter 650 n. 1). The singer wrote to his friend Liz Johnson, on 1 January 1950:

It [the New Year] starts special for me – as being the first time I've been struck by anything but laryngeal complaints for a long time. Do you know The Shingles? A nasty family. A deranged nervous system breeds them, I understand; and they have attacked me on the head and face, which is very painful and curiously bemusing. For a week, I hated everything – now I grow more amiable. I have been told to rest – what sympathetic orders! – so we have cancelled everything for six weeks & more, & I shall take it easy!

648 To David Bedford

4 Crabbe Street, Aldeburgh
Jan. 12th 1950

My dear old Dave,

At last a letter from me! So very sorry I haven't written you a letter before to thank you for the lovely scarf, but I have been so terribly, terribly busy that letter-writing was quite out of the question.

I love the scarf and wear it always. It is a lovely colour, & keeps me beautifully warm, even in the cold east winds which blow along the beach here. Thank you very much. Peter loved your letter, & thanks you very much for it. He is feeling a little better, & hopes to be well enough to go to Switzerland soon for some sun & mountains which should make him quite well again. I shall probably be taking him to London on Tuesday – will you be still there or back at school? I'd love to see you, & play you at ping-pong, although I expect you've been practising so hard that you'd beat me easily! I've been playing squash once or twice; do you play that? It's a lovely game – very fast. I think you'd be awfully good at it. How go the cricket coachings?

The sea defences are progressing very well – but very noisily, just outside our house. The pile-driver works all day, & so do the concrete mixers, and a giant scooper which takes up great buckets of shingle & waves them around in the air (often over our garden) before plonking them down somewhere else.

Here are a few stamps – not many but I'll try & save some more.

Please give my love to Stewy & the enclosed note to Peter [Bedford].

With lots of love & thanks again,

from

BEN

649 To Eric Walter White
[*Typed*]

4 Crabbe Street, Aldeburgh, Suffolk

18th January, 1950

Dear Eric,

I think it is my turn to hit the ball back to you over the Billy Budd commission. I am still not clear whether your Chairman's hope that the opera should be first performed at Sadler's Wells is a condition or not. Until I have seen George Chamberlain[1] and Ian Hunter[2] it will be very difficult for me definitely to make up my mind. The queries which worry me are as follows:

1. Even, given the willingness of Sadler's Wells to grant my smallest wish of casting, etc. could they afford it?

2. If the answer is no, is the Edinburgh Festival, the only alternative, the right place to launch a new opera? I do not demand great ceremonies, in fact, the reverse, I am scared of an international snob audience.

Anyhow, can we hold up the final decision on the commission until these queries are settled?[3]

Thank you also for your later letter. It is exciting that you are writing a book on English opera[4] and I look forward to reading it.

The only portraits of mine which come into consideration are the Henry Lamb (not a double one with Peter that the Harewoods have, but a single one of a slightly earlier date) and a Kenneth Green of slightly before Grimes time.[5] Perhaps you might like to inspect these some time.

I am afraid I have not the Neher sketch for Grimes at the Scala.[6] Have you asked Tony Gishford of Boosey & Hawkes? It must be somewhere since it was exhibited at Aldeburgh two years ago.

What a hot-tempered man Gordon Craig[7] seems! I do not understand his remark about "queering" the artists.[8] Actually, friendly as we are, I hesitate to call in Martin Shaw[9] to our production, although I should like to pay him the compliment considering he has done much for Purcell.

The trouble about Purcell is that he always becomes the personal property of each person who performs him! It was certainly this with Boyce[10] (viz. his extraordinary rearrangements of the Te Deum, etc.), Vincent Novello,[11] not to mention that old horror, E. J. Dent.[12]

I have my own strong views of Dido and Aeneas, and am going to follow these, rightly or wrongly.

I shall be most interested to see what you have written about all this.

Best wishes to the book and to all of you,

Yours ever,

BEN

[*Handwritten:*] Please excuse the typing & errors of this – it was dictated in a mad rush before I left Aldeburgh. Peter is much better – in fact off to Switzerland today to get sun & snow.

1   The General Manager of the Sadler's Wells Company.

2   English music administrator (1919–2003). Hunter began his career in 1938–39 as Busch's assistant at Glyndebourne, where, among more unorthodox duties, he appeared in the silent role of Fleance in Verdi's *Macbeth*. Following war service he was Bing's assistant for the first three Edinburgh Festivals, assuming artistic control for the next six (1950–55) following Bing's departure for the Met. In 1955 Hunter became Managing Director of the artists agency Harold Holt Ltd. He had played a role in the founding of the Bath Festival in 1948, and in the 1960s initiated several arts festivals, including those of the City of London (1962), the Commonwealth Arts Festival (1965) and Hong Kong (1973). He was knighted in 1983. See also the obituary in *The Times* (10 September 2003).

3   In December 1949 news had broken of the cancellation of the proposed venue for the first production of *Billy Budd*. It had been intended that the Sadler's Wells company (which had premiered *Peter Grimes*) should give the first performance of the new opera at the 1951 Edinburgh Festival. But disagreements over financial matters led to the withdrawal of Sadler's Wells and an offer from Covent Garden to stage the new work in September or October 1951. (In the event, *Budd* was not heard until December.)

The history of the commissioning and placing of the first production of *Billy Budd* is complex. On 1 June 1949 Norman Tucker, Director of Opera at Sadler's Wells, wrote to Britten:

I have been speaking to Eric White and I gather that there is a possibility that your next opera will be on a scale suited to a smaller theatre than Covent Garden which I believe you originally had in mind. I think I need hardly say that we would welcome with open arms the prospect of having your new opera performed by our

Company here at Sadler's Wells in the festival season of 1951 if in fact the opera will be ready by then.

Eric White told me that apart from any other considerations you had misgivings about the size of the orchestra at Sadler's Wells. The orchestra is at present 48 in number. The orchestral pit is being enlarged this summer but we shall not be able immediately to increase the size of the orchestra as we had hoped. We hope, however, that by the season after next we may be in a position to increase it to about 60 players. This may answer one of your doubts.

On 12 October 1949, anxious that some doubts had been cast over the *Budd* commission, Britten wrote to White to explain his position:

[. . .] I cannot tie myself to <u>where</u> it will be done yet for reasons you already know; but I incline towards Sadler's Wells, <u>if</u> I am given a free hand re casting, size of orchestra (not enormous). I shall try to get it done by 1951; but if there is no commission attached, I shall not feel myself committed to completing it by the time of the Festival, nor shall I feel myself committed to having it done necessarily first in England. But of course I should be happy & honoured to receive a commission & feel myself bound to produce something by 1951 Festival.

After consultation with the Chairman of the Arts Council, Sir Ernest Pooley, White was able to respond in a positive vein. In a letter of 4 January 1950 he indicated that the commission could be associated with Sadler's Wells rather than with Covent Garden, and that there were no reasons why 'you should not be free to make your conditions regarding casting, size of orchestra, etc., provided these are not unreasonable'. The same letter documents the terms of the commission:

As I have explained to you before, the commissioning fee we have in mind is £500, which would be payable in two equal instalments, the first on receipt of your acceptance of the commission, and the second on completion of the score. Your copyright would, of course, in no way be affected. We should merely have bought the right to nominate the first performance of the work [. . .]

Six days later, on 10 January, the Edinburgh Festival made its first move: Ian Hunter wrote to the composer indicating that the Festival 'would be very pleased and honoured if the first performance of this opera could be given at the 1951 Festival'. Hunter offered between six and nine performances at Edinburgh, with the practical suggestion that the opera should be given in London immediately afterwards. Sadler's Wells was to provide the fundamental company but with the 'best possible cast' of principals to be assembled in Edinburgh. Hunter recognized that the interests of so many disparate elements – Edinburgh, Sadler's Wells, the Arts Council, and, not least, Britten himself – might prove difficult to resolve.

Following a meeting with Norman Tucker, Britten wrote to White on 18 February:

I expect you have already heard from Tucker that we had an entirely negative meeting. [The] reason I think was a mutual lack of enthusiasm. I realise that it was partly my fault, because I am so loathe (loth?) to sell a work not yet written, & also

I'd seen Falstaff the night before & am worried by the lack of central musical responsibility at the Wells. So I think the next thing is to see Ian Hunter when I return from Scotland (beginning of March) & if nothing satisfactory happens there, please may we call it a day & forget any commission or commitments & just see what happens? The work cannot be ready for production before the autumn of 1951 – even that with luck – so Edinburgh is the first possible opportunity for putting it on. This is realised, isn't it? I do want to have an opera ready for the 1951 Festival, & I hope everyone realises that. But the reason I'm 'sitting on the fence' (!) comes from a reluctance to promise a work, terribly difficult to write, for a date, uncomfortably close, in theatres, which alas I have no great confidence in! But I'll do my best, & I hope Edinburgh will be the solution.

White responded on 23 February, attempting to allay Britten's concerns:

I'm sure nobody at the Arts Council or Festival of Britain wants you to be teased by this offer of a commission – particularly at a time when you must bend all your energies to the composition of a particularly long and arduous opera. My only regret, if the offer drops, is that a production in this country outside the Festival period will have to be carried on the present opera companies' normal budgets, whereas a certain amount of *extra* money is definitely available for opera productions during the Festival period, and we had naturally hoped that part of this could be devoted to your *Billy Budd* so as to make its production something outstanding.

If you agree, I think it will be best not to take any definite decision about the commission offer for the moment, but to review the position sometime later.

In the same letter, White informed Britten, in confidence, that, while the Edinburgh Festival was a possible alternative venue for the *Budd* premiere, the first performance of Stravinsky's *The Rake's Progress* was also under negotiation for the 1951 Edinburgh Festival. (Stravinsky's opera was in fact premiered at Venice in 1951: see Letter 712 nn. 4 and 6.)

In the meantime Edinburgh continued to press for the premiere of *Budd*: Hunter wrote to Britten in early April confirming Ralph Hawkes's agreement to an Edinburgh premiere. On the 21st Hunter again contacted the composer, this time with – as far as Britten was concerned – the unfortunate proposal that 'Glyndebourne should be invited to present this opera along with two others during the season'; consequently, he thought it best if Britten and Moran Caplat (Glyndebourne's General Administrator) negotiated direct. Hunter was presumably unaware of Britten's split with John Christie after the premiere of *Albert Herring* (see Michael Kennedy, 'How Albert became our kind of thing'). The minutes of a meeting of the Programme Committee of the Edinburgh Festival Society (14 November 1950) record that Hunter had further explored the possibility of Glyndebourne's involvement with *Budd*, but, as the minutes note, 'Britten declined to agree to this proposal.'

A letter from Norman Tucker to Britten (22 June 1950) was to press further the case for Sadler's Wells. A meeting between Tucker, Britten and White was arranged at which it was decided that Sadler's Wells would give the first performance at Edinburgh followed by the production transferring to London. But even at the end of August Britten was writing to White asking for clarification of the situation:

About the Opera Commission – I'm not quite clear what the position is. You know the situation – It seems likely now that it will first be done by Sadler's Wells at Edinburgh, & then afterwards, immediately Tucker hopes, at Sadler's Wells Theatre in London. Does that make the commission applicable from the Arts Council point of view? And what percentage of it goes to the librettists? – or is that for me to fight out with them? If all these points are in order I'm happy to accept the commission of course.

He added: 'Billy progresses apace – I've done Act I & am launched into Act II. Quite pleased.'

Britten acknowledged the formal commission from the Arts Council in a letter of 13 October 1950 to the Secretary-General, Mary Glasgow:

Thank you for your letter with its formal offer of a commission to write 'Billy Budd', an opera, with E. M. Forster and Eric Crozier. I am happy to accept this, and have already, as you request, offered the first performance of the work to Sadler's Wells Opera. This, we all hope, will take place during the Edinburgh Festival, September 1951.

I will let you know how the work progresses from time to time.

I should be happy if you would tell the Arts Council how happy I am to accept such a commission.

Ernst Roth (of Boosey & Hawkes) wrote on Britten's behalf to Mary Glasgow on 23 October to acknowledge receipt of a cheque for £250, the first instalment of the commission fee:

Benjamin Britten and we have noted the conditions attached to the commission, namely that *Billy Budd* should be offered to Sadler's Wells Opera Company for the first performance during the Festival of Britain on terms to be agreed between the said Company, Benjamin Britten and ourselves.

Will you please accept this letter as a formal acceptance of the commission by Benjamin Britten.

Three weeks later, on 17 November, the Chairman of the Governors of Sadler's Wells, James Smith, wrote to Hunter withdrawing the company from its Edinburgh commitment:

The Governors of Sadler's Wells Foundation met this afternoon to discuss the financial difficulties arising out of the proposed production of *Billy Budd* at the Edinburgh Festival in 1951. They also had before them the overall financial situation of the Foundation which is so unfavourable that they decided with reluctance that it was impossible to entertain any further the production of the Opera in question at Edinburgh.

In addition to the grant of £11,500 for which we should have to ask the Edinburgh Festival Council, Sadler's Wells would be involved in further expenses of some £10,000 which would bring the total cost of production up to a sum of not less than £21,000, and the Governors agreed unanimously that under the circumstances they must withdraw altogether.

I feel I should add that even if you had found it possible to increase your original offer of £7,000 by a substantial amount we should have still been compelled to withdraw.

Hunter was still anxious to secure *Billy Budd* for Edinburgh, either by drawing on additional funds or by trying to persuade Britten to agree to Glyndebourne's involvement; the latter, according to Hunter's letter to Britten (3 November 1950) would have meant the composer's 'acceptance of Busch and Ebert' as conductor and director, although Britten would retain the right of veto over casting. But an Edinburgh premiere was not to be, and Covent Garden stepped in with an offer for a London premiere in October 1951. David Webster confirmed his offer on 29 November 1950. The wording of the press release announcing the withdrawal of Sadler's Wells from the project proved to be a sensitive issue with the Arts Council and Sadler's Wells, and resulted in a heated exchange of correspondence between Sir Steuart Wilson (Deputy General Administrator at Covent Garden), Eric White, Britten and Norman Tucker. The composer wrote to White on 1 February 1951:

After a week of telephone conversations, carbon copies and press announcements all to do with 'Billy Budd', and the general operatic situation in England, there seems to have fallen a blissful silence. I hope this means that the situation is now settled and that one can get on writing the work. I was grieved, when over the telephone, the Daily Express was inclined to credit me as having anti-Festival of Britain feelings and that many correspondents have credited me with abandoning the idea of 'Budd' altogether. Also, the general tone of the press announcements have been that the work has gained in elaborateness and extravagant demands since I started writing it. This is of course, in spite of what Norman Tucker may say, entirely untrue. Nor can the letter that Tucker wrote to the Edinburgh Festival, which squeals about lack of financial resources, be taken too seriously. The situation seems mad. What the truth is I have no idea, but as I said before, I hope the matter is now closed and I can get on with writing the work itself.

This letter needs no answer and is only an effort to put down my own humble opinion in the august files of the Arts Council to further bewilder the historians of the future.

With no possible reflection on yourself, and thanking you for your endless sympathy & trouble!

Yours ever,
BEN

P.S. I am not sending a copy of this letter to Covent Garden, Sadler's Wells Theatre, Boosey & Hawkes, the Edinburgh Festival or keeping a copy myself.

4   White's *The Rise of English Opera*, for which Britten provided an intro- duction. A set of proofs for this volume was sent by the author to Britten who in turn gave them to Rosamund Strode. They are now at BPL. White revised and expanded his original text as *A History of English Opera*.

5   White was seeking a portrait of Britten for his *The Rise of English Opera*. He wrote to the composer on 10 January 1950: 'I don't like the Henry Lamb oil

sketch of you and Peter that Harewood showed me the other day – nor, I gather, does he.' The English artist Henry Lamb (1883–1960) was commissioned by the Behrends, two of his most loyal patrons, to paint a portrait of Britten in 1944. This was executed in 1944–45, immediately before the immense success of *Peter Grimes*, and was followed by a double portrait of Britten and Pears. The latter caused a slight embarrassment between Lamb and Mary Behrend, as is made clear in a letter from the artist to Britten dated 23 September 1945:

And two days ago in a London shop I saw my portrait of you on the floor and in an uncongenial frame and felt how sadly inadequate it was to the occasion [. . .] Anyway we shall see it on the wall in my show, the colour of the frame somewhat mitigated; perhaps it will be possible to judge [. . .] Not another line or stroke to the composition of a double picture of you and Peter. To tell you the truth Mary [Behrend] has rather damped my spirits by quite unmistakable signs of resentment at what she calls a 'duplicate' of Kenneth Green's picture [another double portrait: commissioned by Mary Behrend; it is now in the National Portrait Gallery, London]. As we had all openly discussed the idea of my doing a double portrait I had no suspicion that it might offend her and now of course I rather hate to proceed, although she has very kindly procured me a full-face photograph of Peter, and although there is of course no question of 'duplication' in my composition. But apart from the practical difficulties of ever bringing it off on the scale I should like, I think it would be wise at this stage just to amuse myself with the design on quite a small scale. And that was what I was doing, only to find how badly I remembered Peter's genial dial [i. e. face].

Lamb's 1945 portrait of Britten was exhibited at the Leicester Galleries in the autumn of that year. It was purchased from the Behrend family by Peter Pears in 1977, after Britten's death, and now forms part of the Britten–Pears Foundation's art collection (for a reproduction, see PFL, plate 234). The Lamb double portrait is in the possession of Marion Thorpe. See also Letter 494 n. 2, and Paul Banks and Philip Reed, *Painting and Music*, p. 9. Both Green's oil portrait of Britten (in the possession of the Britten–Pears Foundation, reproduced in PFL, plate 235) and his double portrait of the composer and Pears (National Portrait Gallery, reproduced in PFL, plate 231) date from 1943. See also Letters 443 and 473.

6   Caspar Neher (1897–1962), German theatre designer closely associated with the work of Bertolt Brecht, had been responsible for the designs for the first production of *Peter Grimes* at La Scala, Milan, in March 1947. Some of his sketches for this production were exhibited at the 1948 Aldeburgh Festival. See also John Willett, *Caspar Neher: Brecht's Designer*.

7   English artist and stage designer (1872–1966) who in 1900 designed and directed at the Hampstead Conservatoire of Music Purcell's *Dido and Aeneas*, described in the *Dictionary of National Biography* by J. C. Trewin as a 'startlingly original production in terms of light and colour'.

8   White had written to Britten on 10 January 1950:

Remembering that you might be preparing a version of *Dido* for the EOG for production in 1951 – just half a century later – I wrote to Gordon Craig and asked him
for further particulars about his *Dido* production. He searched and found the notebook he had used at the time [. . .] There are [. . .] passages from a long rambling
letter that I received [. . .] that may interest you.

> [. . .] that 'notebook' which has 'just turned up'. Yes – it's a bit long winded but
> seems a truthful statement of how admirable a fellow worker was Martin Shaw.
> I do hope that people will do him some honour at this jubilee of *Dido* – for he
> brought back Purcell into England. If anyone dares to mention my name in
> connection with that event – just squash them . . . They say Britten's music is all
> right – (you mention him) but I dare say the English Opera Group [. . .] will
> manage to queer all the artists may attempt to do in 1951 [. . .]

9 English composer (1875–1958), who founded the Purcell Operatic Society
   in 1900. It was Shaw who engaged Craig as director of the Society's production of *Dido* in 1900.

10 William Boyce (1711–1779), English composer and organist.

11 English editor, publisher and composer (1781–1861).

12 Dent's edition of *Dido and Aeneas*, the first to be based on the Tenbury
   manuscript, was published in 1925.

650 To Peter Pears

GREY HOUSE, BURGHCLERE, NEWBURY
Saturday [21 January 1950]

My dearest,

The weather today here is ideal mountain weather – you really needn't
have gone away! Sun & cold, with snow just round the corner. I hope
you've got the same. I thought about you all yesterday – rather to the
detriment of my behaviour at the various functions – & pictured you
arriving at the clinic & the quick eye roving round for the blonds! I so
wonder what it is like – but don't bother to write & say, just remember to
tell when you get back.[1]

The day with me was to schedule. I packed. Met Mr Henry Foy,[2] was
not enthusiastic about his personality, but feel he may be right for the
Group. He's a flowery cove, moustache & curly hair (how I hate curls).
But musical, & a good business man.

The Directors' meeting [of the EOG] was abortive (not enough directors
for a quorum!) but we discussed well; Elizabeth was maddeningly vague, &
Eric maddeningly precise as usual. But James Lawrie[3] & Erwin good. I
think we'll get Foy. No Arts Council news yet.

I seized a sandwich & then caught 2.35 at Paddington with sister
Barbara. Rather a distracting journey with the train full of young

Pangbournians.[4] Saw a heavenly meeting between two flowers on Reading Station – such pleasure at re-uniting after the holidays was heart warming – the Greek Anthology level.

It is lovely here – quiet, comfortable & interesting talk as always with Mary & Bow [Behrend]. Barbara a little piano, & rather nervous, but I hope she'll settle down today. It is pathetic the thought of them leaving here – they were built for this house, & it for them.[5] Perhaps it's superstition, but I can't picture them lasting long in the new cottage. Tomorrow Pipers, & Tuesday Dartington.

All my love, get better & better.

Dein

B.

P.S. If you can get me a kids' Diary – Pestalozzi,[6] without difficulty, I'd be obliged! Love.

1   Pears wrote to the composer from Les Hirondelles, Leysin, the same day:

This is really a sweet place, the village is typical Swiss, not as nice as Zermatt, but very pretty with lots of snow about. This clinic seems after 16 hours to be very well run and pleasant. All rooms face south & one has a balcony in which one gets just all the sun. The rooms are very simple and institutional but quite adequate. Food, good average not de-Luxe Swiss-li. View very fine with a fierce mountain just opposite called Les Dents du Midi – very appropriately.

One has breakfast at 7.15(!) though I am not washed before (others are) – I am allowed to make my toilet at my leisure. Lunch is at 12 – one rests from 1–3 and sleeps. That is all I know so far. Otherwise one is left blissfully alone. In bad weather it could be hideously dull, I imagine – but I seem to have brought the sun with me. It snowed for two days just before I came. Even now it's not going to be exciting, but then I'm not here to be excited – ! There's a movie which has performances on Saturday and Sunday. At the moment, I feel as if 10 days here will fill the bill – till Monday week 30th – and then a little wandering [. . .]

Give everyone my love – but keep the major part of it for yourself, my old fudge. Je t'aime.

Pears was to write again on the 24th after receiving Britten's letter:

Your letter arrived today. It was heavenly to have it – I was frightfully pleased. Letters only seem to take 2 days getting here. I hope they don't take any longer from here to you – because I've decided, Fudggie, that I don't want to stay on here. I'm perfectly well again, and am really only miserable not to be with you – and I want to get back to some gentle work too. If you were here, it would be different, 'cos you would be getting a holiday, which might be good for you. But now I just don't want any more of Switzerland, or of anywhere else much but England. So I hope to fly back on Saturday 28th and come down to Lancing for the weekend! So there! I want to be with you. (There aren't any blonds here either but that wouldn't matter anyway!) I shall leave here (which is all very nice but frightfully boring – & the sun hasn't appeared for two days – & the food is v. dull & it's essentially for sick people

& I'm <u>not</u> sick any more) on Friday – shall go to Bern for the night, & then fly back from Geneva on Saturday. I don't know when you will get this letter, but I shall send a wire on Thursday evening, I expect.

[...]

I can't tell you how I'm looking forward to coming back!!!

2   Appointed General Manager of the EOG in March 1950, Foy was asked to resign in October because of unsatisfactory managerial skills and financial irregularities.

3   James Lawrie (1907–1979), English businessman and financier, Managing Director of the National Film Corporation (1948–53), and subsequently an independent film producer and theatrical manager (1953–65). Lawrie was a member of the board of the EOG from its early years and Chairman from 1950 until 1960. His other musical interests included the National School of Opera of which he was Chairman from 1948 until 1963. Lawrie was the dedicatee of Britten's realization of *The Beggar's Opera*.

4   Pupils from Pangbourne Nautical College near Reading, Berkshire, who wore Royal Navy officer cadet uniforms.

5   Britten wrote to Mary Behrend on 26 January 1950, after he and his sister Barbara had spent the weekend with her and her husband:

I am so glad to have seen you once again in your lovely house, but also glad to have seen your new home, & to like it. I am sure you will make it as Mary & Bowish as the Grey House, and we'll all be pestering you for invitations to come and see you as we have done in the past to Grey House.

6   Britten used children's pocket diaries until the end of his life. Here he was referring to the 'Almanach Pestalozzi', which was crammed with information about, for example, national flags, the night sky and great painters.

651   To Eric Crozier

22 MELBURY ROAD, KENSINGTON, W.14
Jan 28th 1950

My dear Eric,

This is the note I mentioned to you – afraid it's going to be boring and sketchy but it's only a series of ideas I've had about L. M. an O. [*Let's Make an Opera*] while correcting the proofs. I feel we've got something so good in it that I think it's worth taking a wee bit more trouble with before delivering it into the big, cold world.

One snag – to start with; on sending the dedication to Fidelity I got a sweet grateful note back, but saying <u>Johnny</u> is not spelt like that – but Jonny – being short for Jonathan!! A bore, but worthwhile just changing in order not to hurt the boy, & also quite useful as a differentiation from the John of the play ... ???

I am still worried about Rowan's 'wet with weeping' in no. 2. I know I've been bad & set it too high, but I think it's awkward going at any pace at all, with three w's coming on top of each other, especially with 3 out of 4 vowels being short?? 'Faint with terror' or 'Faint and hungry'?[1]

I've been thinking a lot about the vexed repetition of 'When he comes back, boy – He'll be a black boy!', and I think one reason for one's embarrassment is that for the first time a sentence is broken between the two. Would it therefore be a good idea for me to rewrite that verse for them to sing together all the time? Otherwise, I've no suggestion. We've played around thinking of rhymes for '–ack, boy!' but it's jolly difficult. If one drops the rhyme – 'leave him up there, boy!' Give him a scare, boy! might do. But it's a new idea; however it might suggest something to you.[2]

The words of Rowan's aria still strike me as being stilted for a sympathetic character, even if one takes her as governess rather than a maid. The verses about her mental picture of the little boy escaping are fine – the ones I worry about are the others – & I am sure one of the reasons one can't hear the words of some of the big phrases is that they aren't easily graspable – especially for the young – 'Cruel men will soil', etc. – even if one has as you originally wrote 'Cruel Bob' – much worse to sing, incidentally. I thought perhaps I was carrying over a prejudice from E. Parry,[3] & so I asked John & Myfanwy [Piper], but they saw my point. M. suggested for this line 'See his angry features darken, Rage will make him more unkind' – which could be sung with more conviction, at any rate. Do consider this, my dear.[4] Are you happy about, How I wish that I could aid you?[5] But I see the enormous difficulty of the rhymes.

Would you mind a change in the 'How can I laugh for joy'? I have heard it many times now, & I think the double f & 'or' sound troubles the kids too much. The Ipswich boy is never as convincing, & the London boy quite inadequate, in a moment which should be most touching. I can't think of any alteration which keeps the 'joy' rhyme, but 'I cannot laugh & play' or 'How can I laugh & play' – is easier to sing, much – & gives an ABAA scheme to the whole.[6]

What are your feelings about the Miss Baggott 'scena'? After repeated hearings I feel we were right in our original ideas – that the tidying of the room should be her main train of thought which leads her inevitably to the cupboard. If one could have a reference to the opening of the door somewhere. What about 'Open the door & stack them neatly' in the penultimate line?[7] That impresses on the children (& audience) that she's just about to see inside it. We'll talk about this when we meet, & of course reconsider your new version if you still prefer it.

That finishes my queries about the musical side – by the way I have been through the piece very carefully, and in several places rewritten the voice parts to simplify, and add alternative notes to very high or low bits. In a piece like this, when it's obviously going to suffer in the hands of unsophisticated singers, I think it's best to give them an easier way round a difficulty (unless it's an essential thing) than to make them struggle with something they may do, but do it unconvincingly.

One or two points over the dialogue. After the 'Morning Sammy!' number I feel the dialogue isn't rushed & excited enough from the children. After all it's quite a moment of thrill for them! I feel Sammy should be tumbled in, strapped up with the minimum of 'Goodbyes'. Couldn't we shorten it considerably?[8]

The other point is the 'Mummy, Daddy, Harwich' bit after the 'dear Rowan' bit. Was the Harwich boat really going in 1810; surely Mummy & Daddy is very modern in sound. This section now rings untrue to me every time I hear it.[9]

I have put in shortened stage directions into the proofs which you can see when you're back in London, & correct if you wish of course. Could you also please write a <u>longer</u> one for the 'Hide Sammy, Tidy the room' pantomime.[10] I think it should be spread over more of the music. See what you feel when you see how it looks.

By the by it is byroad rather than bye-road – surely?

That ends my nuisances, I think. Sorry there are so many, but it comes of having so many long train journeys!

I had a nice lunch with J. Lawrie. He is a very nice, helpful man. Hope you had a nice weekend at Burghclere.

I am just back after a nice weekend at Lancing. They are looking forward to seeing you both next weekend. I was hearing a lot about your Chapel plans.[11] A grand idea!

Love to you, & Nancy of course,
Yours ever,
BEN

P.S. I'm just off to Aldeburgh, where I shall be for about a week. Would you comment on these queries by letter or phone, & then perhaps we could meet at the end of next week?

1 'Faint with terror' was adopted: see No. II, fig. 6^{+9}.

2 No changes were made to No. III, the duet for Black Bob and Clem: see fig. 11^{+2}.

3 Elizabeth Parry (b. 1920), English soprano, who sang the role in the original EOG production. Parry made her debut with the EOG in the 1947 revival of

The Rape of Lucretia at Glyndebourne, taking over the role of Lucia at five days' notice following the inexplicable departure of the soprano originally engaged for the part. In an interview with Richard Fawkes, 'Thirty Men and a Girl', *Classical Music* (17 June 2000), pp. 48–9, Parry recalled:

I sang the role for the first time at the dress rehearsal and I was terrified. The music was unbelievably difficult for most of us and Ben wasn't always very patient. He knew the moment someone was a double dot out. He was always very hard on poor Richard Lewis, who was doubling for Peter Pears, whenever he made mistakes.

    I'd only sung the part of Lucia with a piano before and couldn't find my note in the orchestra. Margaret Ritchie, who had created the role the year before, told me the only thing to do was get it in the wings during the interlude, shut my eyes, ignore everything else and keep humming.

Her association with the EOG continued as Cis, one of the village children, in *Albert Herring*, and, in addition to *The Little Sweep*, Britten's realization of *The Beggar's Opera*. Fawkes remarks that

It was during a performance of *Herring* that the younger members of the company decided to play a joke on Peter Pears. Just before he had a fiendishly difficult aria as the tipsy Albert, they replaced his lemonade with neat gin. Although his eyes glazed over, he didn't miss a note. And they fixed the brakes of Denis Dowling's bike so that when he entered as Sid, instead of stopping, he carried straight on into the wings from where an almighty crash was heard.

Parry remembers Britten's reaction: 'Ben was conducting that night and there were clouds of rage emanating from the pit.'

    About *The Beggar's Opera*, she told Fawkes:

We had all been promised parts and found ourselves playing the women and men of the town. Ben gave us one solo line each so that he could say we were not the chorus. It was a lovely production by Tyrone Guthrie [. . .] I didn't like Ben's arrangement at all but the production was very effective, stark and back to basics with no trimmings at all.

Parry's interview with Fawkes included one final memory of the EOG's 1947 season:

When Frederick Ashton came to Glyndebourne to produce *Albert Herring*, everybody jolly well had to act for him. I remember the singer playing Mrs Herring at one stage turning to him and saying, 'For God's sake let me stand still to count.'

On leaving the EOG in 1950 Parry and the pianist Phyllis Thorold founded the London Opera Players to present small-scale opera in schools and music clubs.

4   Crozier adapted Myfanwy Piper's suggestion to 'See his angry features blacken! Rage and fury make him blind!': see No. VIII, fig. 25[+5]. He was to write to Erwin Stein on 13 February:

Here are the new words for Rowan's song, and oh! what a trouble they have been for a negligible result! But I think they will be better for singing at Ben's extreme range. I would like to have another look at them when the second proof is ready.

Britten was himself to write to Stein on 20 February:

Thank you for sending on Eric's words – o, the old, old, difficulty again! It was sweet of Tony [Gishford] to try his hand at it, & while a lot of it is an improvement it doesn't really fit the music well enough. What we must do is to get a 'possible' version, with as little alteration as we can, just removing the impossibilities. I return Eric's own copy with one or two essential emendations. Line 2. – 'Run with all your might and main' gets rid of the idea that the pain is the object of the running in Eric's own version! I don't like 'mad' nor 'sharp' but cannot think of any other words. Perhaps 'clear' for 'sharp' – but Eric might have another idea. 'Sharp' cannot be sung legato. I agree the two 'Blacks' in verse 3 are slightly ridiculous – a sweep's face can't get any blacker, can it? Peter suggests – line 3 – 'Hear his footsteps swift behind' – but that might mean a change in the music – which I'll do when I've got it by me. Otherwise, the other idea of 'angry features darken' might be best. I don't like Tyrants – nor Torments (verse 4) but have no suggestion – Bad men is rhythmically weak, & deprave not really 'true'. If we can't think of any other versions we'd better leave it. Can you let Eric know about this – or shall it wait till I get back next week?

Crozier was not unaware of Britten's irritation with him. He told Stein (13 February):

I feel that my short period of usefulness to his genius is past and that our paths, which have run happily alongside for six years, have now come to a point where they must separate, as I always half-knew they would one day. He climbs on to heights where I can't follow – but it has been a wonderful time while it lasted, and an enormous privilege to work with such a marvellous person.

Britten and Pears were to send an amusing postcard to Anthony Gishford from St Andrew's on 27 February 1950, full of puns and in-jokes, as thanks for his help with the libretto of The Little Sweep:

Come, dear Tony, come less slowly;
    Leave the low Roth,[i] take the high.
Fear not Quilter, Gibbs or Rowley[ii]
    Envious of your liberty.

Sonorous their echoes beckon –
    Tyrant Hawk(e)s or g(L)awrie[iii] EOG![*]
Run poor boy! not lightly reckon
    (S)tiny[iv] stones or (b)oozy[v] bog!

How we thank you that you aid us
    in this Crazier poetry!
Rhyme, sense, reason – all – evade us
    ever yours P.P. – B.B.

[*]Fierce northern bird (cf. Auk) immediately recognisable through its ceaseless and dreary cry, Br-ō-ō-ke! Br-ō-ō-ke! endlessly repeated.

[i, Ernst Roth; ii, All Boosey & Hawkes composers: Roger Quilter (1877–1953), C. Armstrong Gibbs (1889–1960) and Alec Rowley (1892–1958); iii, James Lawrie; iv, Erwin Stein; v, Lesley Boosey]

5   This was modified to 'How I wish that I could save you!': see No. VIII, fig. 26.

6   Sammy's line was changed to 'How can I laugh and play': see No. X, fig. 31^{+4}.

7   Modified to 'Open the door and pack them neatly': see No. XII, fig. 40^{+8}.

8   Revisions were made to the dialogue between Nos. XVI and XVII in accordance with Britten's suggestion.

9   The dialogue between Nos. VIII and IX was revised and simplified:

JULIET: ... we can't possibly tell mama, 'cos she's away ...
GAY: Seeing papa off to join his ship!

10   No. XI.

11   It has proved impossible to identify what these plans were, but they may have been in connection with *Saint Nicolas*.

652 To Henriëtte Bosmans

4 Crabbe Street, Aldeburgh
Feb. 3rd 1950

My dear Jetty,

Please don't be cross! I know you have every reason to be, but I have lots of excuses! First of all Peter & I had this long, dreary, horrible, but I suppose worthwhile, American tour. Then when we got back, & I was preparing to work again, poor old Peter got very ill with shingles and that confused all our arrangements, & he came down here to relax & rest instead of us dashing all over the Continent. Then our man Robinson,[1] who housekeeps & all for us, went mad – quite literally! It was very weird, & not good for an invalid to be in that atmosphere. However all that is cleared now – the man is gone, Peter is better, & I have today written the first notes of the new opera [*Billy Budd*], & so I feel I can write to you my dear. First, I was very moved to hear of your mother's death. I do understand the terrible mixture of relief & sorrow that you must feel. I hope that you have now lots of work to do to fill the great gap. Work, especially when you love your work, is the best healer in cases like this. All my love & sympathy, my dear.

And then, thank you for the lovely parcel, which was most welcome, & came at a time when every luxury was most important – when we were all depressed by Peter's illness & Robinson's madness. It was a lovely parcel, & we eat the contents thinking of you. But, you simply mustn't send us any more, you know. I feel so guilty that you spend so much of your precious rations on us – you are just as short as we are. So please be a good girl, and less generous in the future. We hope to start on a concert tour the week after next if Peter's well enough. We are going to Scotland[2] – ought to be pretty cold if this weather continues. We aren't coming to Holland till May[3] & then only for a few days – I hope you will be there, & not travelling.

The children's opera I wrote was a wild success – it is strange how these little works often make a greater impression than the monster works on which one sets such great hopes! It is not running in London now, but the plan is to have it at each holiday period. The children who act in it are charming, & so are the audiences who go & see it. I wish you could see it sometime. It's very pathetic!

Billy Budd calls me now so I must stop. This comes with Peter's & my love & sympathy.

Let's know what you are doing.

Yours ever,

BEN

1   See Letter 621 n. 2.

2   Pears and Britten gave recitals in Edinburgh (13 February), Glasgow (15th), Helensburgh (16th), Milngavie (17th), Kilmarnock (20th), Dundee (21st), Aberdeen (24th), Bridge of Allen (25th) and St Andrew's (27th).

3   They were in the Netherlands from 5 to 12 May.

653   **To Ronald Duncan**

4 Crabbe Street, Aldeburgh

Feb. 3rd 1950

My dear Ronnie,

Thank you & Rose Marie so very much for the eggs. I am so sorry not to have written before, but they arrived just before we went away (we took some of them away with us, the ones we'd not immediately consumed!), and when one is travelling you know there's no time for letters. They were <u>most</u> welcome – came at a time when we were very depressed, & there's nothing like a good old egg for cheering one up! But you know, <u>please</u> let us know how much they cost! Because otherwise we shall feel guilty if we even hint for them, much more if we ask direct as we usually do! So, a nice little bill by return, please!

Peter is better now. He went off to Switzerland, to a clinic, but was back in 6 days! He was neither well enough to ski & enjoy the snow, nor ill enough to put up with the hospital atmosphere. But all the same, he must go carefully as it is such a beastly illness. We hope to start concerts again the week after next, if he's up to it.

So glad you're having Arthur to do the music for the comedy. I think he'll do you proud, as he is developing all the time & beginning to turn out nice stuff now. I was a bit alarmed at you choosing 'Le Jongleur de Notre Dame' as a subject for his opera. The Massenet is such a very 'pro' [professional] work and one which will show him up badly in his first opera.[1] Couldn't you think of something else? I think it's excellent for him to write a piece with you, if you have time for him. He is a nice young man, & really worthwhile.

My love to Rose Marie – I hope she progresses up to standard! – and the kids too if with you. I'd love to come & see you sometime – but Billy Budd (just started) takes all my time now.

Lots of love, & thanks again,

Yours ever,

BEN

1 The Oldham–Duncan opera, based on the same subject as Massenet's *Le Jongleur de Notre Dame*, would appear to have been transformed into Duncan's play *Our Lady's Tumbler*, for which Oldham provided incidental music. The play was commissioned by the Salisbury and District Society of Arts as part of the Festival of Britain celebrations, and was first performed in Salisbury Cathedral on 5 June 1950. Cecil Beaton designed the production. See also Letter 655 in which Britten mentions another Duncan–Oldham collaboration.

654 To Ned Rorem[1]

4 Crabbe Street, Aldeburgh

Feb. 6th 1950

Dear Ned Rorem,

Thank you very much for your friendly letter.[2] Peter Pears & I were only too happy to do what little we could for such a sympathetic cause in N. York.[3] We met many extremely nice people in doing so, too.

I have here some music of yours which you sent me many months ago. Please forgive me for not replying nor acknowledging it. I am a very bad correspondent, I know, but also I was hoping that a chance might come along one day & that I could help you a bit with your work. Being a fearfully busy person that chance never seemed to present itself – but perhaps one day when you come to this country, if ever, we could meet & talk a bit. Let me know to this address, which always finds me.

I met some nice & promising young composers in the U.S.A. – more promising than many of their seniors, I felt – but perhaps that is the same everywhere!

I hope your work is going well.

With thanks again, & every good wish,
Yours sincerely,
BENJAMIN BRITTEN

1 American composer and diarist (b. 1923), who studied at the Curtis Institute, Juilliard School and privately with Virgil Thomson and David Diamond. In 1949 after an award of a Fulbright scholarship, Rorem left the United States to study with Honegger in Paris. After a few months he moved to Morocco where he remained for two years. Rorem contributed a perceptive review of the 1974 New York premiere of *Death in Venice*, 'Britten's Venice' to *New Republic*, 172/6 (8 February 1975), pp. 31–2, a revised version of which appeared in DMDV, pp. 186–91.

2 This letter has not survived. The few letters that have indicate that Rorem and Britten were in very occasional touch with one another.

3 This cause remains unidentified.

655 To Ronald Duncan

as from: 4 Crabbe Street, Aldeburgh
Feb. 20th 1950

My dear Ronnie,

Yours has followed me up to Scotland where Peter & I are doing a very damp tour. He's better, thank God, but must still be careful. George Behrend is here driving us around which makes things pleasanter & easier. (This can't be more than a note, because we're a bit rushed.) Please tell Rose Marie that the idea of being guardian to her dear little brats fills me with pride, & alarm. Please don't die yet awhile, Ronnie dear – but of course I accept. Give the little dears my love. I enclose the black, black cheque[1] – if I can find my chequebook.

Thank you for the lovely poem – it is a beauty. Peter's got the Jones songs[2] & says the music's as good. I must have a look.

Arthur told me the Saint Spiv story[3] & a bit about your treatment & it sounds a most moving & intriguing story. Good luck to it, & to him. I hope he'll do it well.

Lots of love to all,
Yours ever,
BEN

1 The meaning of this is unclear.

2 Duncan wrote to Britten on 7 February 1950:

Do you know *The Muses Garden of Delights* published 1601 – songs by R. [Robert] Jones [*c.*1570–*c.*1615] for Base vyoll, Lute & the voice?? If I've time before the post goes I'll copy out a gem of a song I found there which is lovely. It lays behind Donne's sonnets, I think.

3 Oldham composed incidental music for Duncan's *Saint Spiv*, first produced in 1950 at the Watergate Theatre, London, by Kenneth Tynan.

656 To Serge Koussevitzky

BAY HOTEL, STONEHAVEN, [Kincardine, Scotland]
As from: 4 Crabbe Street, Aldeburgh, Suffolk
Feb. 23rd 1950

My dear Serge,

I only received your kind letter[1] about the 'Spring Symphony' just as I was leaving U.S.A. for Europe. Since I arrived back here my life has been hectic and complicated in the extreme; so that is why I have not replied before.

I was so happy that you had pleasure in presenting the Symphony in Tanglewood; I should much have liked to have been present. We also had a good performance, with much warmth of reception, in Amsterdam. We were extremely fortunate in our solo singers, & in a remarkable choir of small boys! Now, next month, is the premiere in England, and it will be interesting to see how this novel kind of symphony fares in this rather conservative country! There are quite a few other performances scheduled I hear,[2] so 'our' symphony may have quite a long life. I was surprised and charmed to read in your letter of the honorarium, and most grateful. Actually, if you don't mind, I would like it paid direct to the little Aldeburgh Festival, which some friends & I run in my home town, & which specialises in fine (if small) music. It is always desperately hard up, especially because the town – being almost washed away by the sea – is very poor. So unless I hear to the contrary I will ask Mr Boosey to pay this money to its funds.

I was sorry that our paths did not cross in U.S.A. – but I hope they may when you pay a welcome visit to Europe this summer.

With every good wish,
Yours sincerely,
BENJAMIN BRITTEN

1 This letter has not survived.

2 The UK premiere was to take place on 9 March 1950: see Letter 643 n. 6 and Letter 657.

657 To Thomas Russell[1]
London Philharmonic Orchestra

4 Crabbe Street, Aldeburgh
March 13th 1950

Dear Tom,

I know we are all happy that so many people came to last Thursday's concert, & that it was a good success. But I feel I must say that everyone would have been happier & the performance much better had the rehearsal organisation been better. The orchestra knew it well & played excellently, but good as the choir was, most of the rehearsal time with van Beinum was spent in teaching them their leads (& often actual notes as well), instead of polishing their singing, balancing & giving the perform-ance the authority the occasion demanded. They are a good choir, but my impression was (& it was confirmed by conversation with several of the singers) that they had had far too much to do before this concert, & simply did not know the notes well enough before these vital final rehearsals. The joint rehearsal the evening before the concert was practically useless, & I sympathised deeply with van Beinum's despair. Incidentally that situation would have been infinitely easier had there been someone in actual (L.P.O.) authority present. I appreciate the difficulty of finding a rehearsal hall big enough for such forces, but I do suggest in the future that another hall be found, if the singers cannot be persuaded to be present at a full rehearsal in the Albert Hall itself. I know that the prediction that it would be "all right on the night" was accurate – but surely we must aim at something more than "all right".[2]

Apart from my natural concern as composer, this letter is written out of interest & sympathy with your admirable orchestra – and also as a plea that the chorus can have another rehearsal before March 20th![3]

With best wishes,
Yours sincerely,
BENJAMIN BRITTEN

1 Chairman and Managing Director of the London Philharmonic Orchestra (1902–1984): see Letter 491 n. 9. Britten's letter spells out difficulties encountered in the rehearsals for the UK premiere of *Spring Symphony*.

2 Russell wrote to the composer on 16 March, addressing his criticisms. His letter details the financial constraints under which the LPO operated, as well as countering Britten's specific comments about the chorus and the first combined rehearsal.

3 A BBC Third Programme studio broadcast of *Spring Symphony*. As a con-sequence of Britten's anxieties, an additional chorus rehearsal was arranged to prepare for this broadcast performance.

ORDER NOW, SPRING 1950, the BRITTEN NUMBER of

MUSIC SURVEY

A QUARTERLY REVIEW

Edited by DONALD MITCHELL and HANS KELLER

All Main Articles are devoted to aspects of Benjamin Britten's work, and are contributed by Paul Hamburger, Arthur Hutchings, Hans Keller, Donald Mitchell, Hans Redlich and Charles Stuart.

The Composer contributes a Note about THE SPRING SYMPHONY

Usual Review Section of Music, Books, Concerts, Opera and Records

2s. 6d.

Annual subscription 11s.

Published by

MESSRS. NEWMAN WOLSEY, 6 HOLBORN PLACE, W.C.1

Advertisement for the 'Britten Number' of *Music Survey*
from the programme for the UK premiere of *Spring Symphony*

658   To Peter Pears

4 Crabbe Street, Aldeburgh
March 17th 1950

My darling,

La Travy[1] has just arrived – & I am terribly thrilled with it! What a lovely present – you could have hardly (Gainsborough[2] perhaps excepted!) have given me something which pleased me more. I have already wasted far too long in browsing over it, but it didn't matter because I'm in a bit of a muddle over Billy & not ready to start on him again yet. Anyhow one learns so much from Verdi so B.B. will be a better opera for your present, I've no doubt![3]

I'm going over to Braintree [in Essex] tomorrow morning to fetch back the car – running on 3 brakes (don't worry, I'll drive carefully!) – & then Wards[4] here will take it to pieces & see what's wrong. They can't get the hub off because they've not got the right tools, yet.

Morgan is going on well[5] – a bit of a leaky problem still, but cheerful & keen to work. May[6] is [a] sweet person who is nice to have around.

I hope all the work goes well this week. I hope at least the new wavelengths will improve the 3rd prog. reception. It was maddening last night.

Are you working with Madame?[7] But rest, as much as possible, dearest, even tho' it's boring!

This is only a scribble, to send my love, & warmest thanks for the Verdi. A great thrill!

Love, lots of it,

Your devoted old

BEN

1   A score of Verdi's *La traviata*, a work that Britten already knew and admired from the many performances given by the Sadler's Wells Opera in the early 1940s, in which Pears sang the role of Alfredo.

2   Thomas Gainsborough (1727–1788), English painter of portraits and landscapes, who was born in Sudbury, Suffolk.

3   See BBMCPR, pp. 161–2, n. 24, in which Philip Reed outlines some of the Verdian influences on *Billy Budd* and on Britten's music in general. *La traviata* was to be mentioned by Britten a year later, in a tribute article – 'Verdi – A Symposium' – to commemorate the fiftieth anniversary of Verdi's death (*Opera*, 2/3 (February 1951), pp. 113–15; reprinted in PKBM, pp. 102–3). Britten writes:

To analyse a devotion to an art is beyond me, but here are a few observations, which I hope will explain a little why I love the music of Verdi so much.

The variety and strength of his melodies. Verdi can, of course, write the obvious square tunes, which use many repetitions of the same little phrase and work to an effective climax. These abound in the earlier operas, and are immediately endearing: I think particularly of *Parigi o cara* in *Traviata*. But he can also write the long casual lines, a succession of apparently unrelated phrases, which repeated hearings discover to have an enormous tension deep below the surface. The wonderful 'conversational' duet at the end of Act I of *Otello* is a case in point.

The perpetual 'unobviousness' of his harmonies. Verdi has the gift, which only the very greatest have had: that of writing a succession of the simplest harmonies in such a way as to sound surprising and yet 'right'. The accompaniment to the Egyptian trumpet tune in *Aida* is an extreme example of this. Then later in his life he developed a new kind of harmonic originality, which I can most easily describe by reminding the reader of the astounding string accompaniment to the bell strokes in the last scene of *Falstaff*, and the obscure *Ave Maria* 'on an enigmatic scale' from the *Quattro Pezzi Sacri*.

His attitude to the voices on the stage and the orchestra. This seems to me to be perfectly right. The voices dominate, and the orchestra is the background – but what a background! In the later works especially, the orchestra has a range of colours wider than with any other composer. For soft shading, the Nile scene in *Aida* is inimitable, and no one has ever made the orchestra roar so terrifyingly as at the beginning of *Otello*.

In the construction of his later works Verdi seems to have discovered the secret of perfection. At the beginning of his life he accepted the convention of the times in the sharp definition of the numbers, and he balanced these numbers brilliantly. Fundamentally, he never changed this attitude, but later on the numbers melt into

each other with a really astonishing subtlety. The fact that the most famous composer alive today [i.e. Stravinsky] dismisses *Otello* and *Falstaff* 'because they are not
written in numbers' shows, it seems to me, that he does not know the works very well.

And so on. I have no space to write about his vitality, his breadth of humanity,
his courage, his extraordinary career which developed into an almost divine
serenity. I should like to end with a personal confession. I am an arrogant and
impatient listener; but in the case of a few composers, a very few, when I hear a work
I do not like I am convinced it is my own fault. Verdi is one of these composers.

See also Letter 682.

4 The garage in the High Street, Aldeburgh.

5 In January 1950 Forster had undergone a second prostate operation.
According to Forster's biographer, P. N. Furbank, 'May Buckingham volun-
teered to come in to the nursing home and act as his nurse. The gesture
touched and delighted him and became another bond between them. It
was also fortunate, for – or so his doctor told him afterwards – by her quickness in reporting some symptom she saved his life' (see *E. M. Forster: A Life*,
vol. 2, p. 285). Britten had invited Forster to Aldeburgh to convalesce.
Forster told Robert Trevelyan (4 April 1950): 'After leaving the nursing
home [. . .] I stayed for a while at the Buckinghams, and then Ben Britten
drove me, and May Buckingham, direct here by car' (see Mary Lago and
P. N. Furbank (eds.), *Selected Letters of E. M. Forster: Volume Two, 1921–70*,
p. 239).

6 May Buckingham (1908–?), whom Forster's friend Robert Buckingham
(1904–1974) had married in 1932. In spite of initial resentment because of
Forster's and Robert Buckingham's close relationship, a strong friendship
sprang up between Forster and Mrs Buckingham. May Buckingham's
training as a nurse was to prove invaluable as Forster grew more infirm in
the 1960s. It was at the Buckinghams' Coventry home that the writer died
in 1970.

7 Eva de Reusz, Pears's singing coach from 1950.

659 To Marion Harewood

4 Crabbe Street, Aldeburgh
March 24th 1950

My dearest Marionli,

Thank you so much for the enormous care & trouble you took over the
great Ball![1] It was, judging by raving comments I have heard, the greatest
success; & even I, not good as you know on such things, enjoyed it hugely.
You were a sweet and tactful hostess too. Please thank Caroline[2] when you
see her for the work she did. These things don't fling themselves on, & I
know a great deal of hard work was done.

I shan't see you for some time, which is a pity, but have a nice (and rest-ful!) Easter up at Harewood. If you & George ever want a few quiet days of sea air, do come here. Morgan is better, but it would do him the world of good to have you here to cheer him up. You could also see how Billy Budd goes on. Towards the end of April perhaps?[3]

I thought your little speech yesterday very nice – a dreadful thing to have to do, but you did it graciously!

Love to you both – & I can't say enough how happy I was to hear the news the other day – in some stupid way I feel connected, even with that![4] But perhaps I'm getting sentimental in my old age.

Lots of love,
BEN

1 An opera-inspired fancy-dress ball, held at 6 Stanhope Gate on 22 March 1950 in aid of the EOG, was organized by a committee chaired by Marion Harewood. The cabaret included Frederick Ashton and Moira Shearer dancing the tango from the ballet *Façade*, as well as entertainment by other members of the Sadler's Wells Ballet and Joan Cross. A pictorial record of the event can be found in the *Tatler and Bystander* (12 April 1950), pp. 62–5.

2 *Recte*: Catherine Shanks, a friend of Marion Harewood. Shanks and Harewood were the pianists in the first performance of *The Little Sweep*.

3 Forster reported to Eric Fletcher from Aldeburgh (26 April 1950):

The Harewoods have been here for the weekend [21–24 April]. *What* a nice chap he is – so gay, friendly, and straight. I wish he hadn't shut himself up at King's, I expect that people whom we needn't mention tried to exploit him – while people like our-selves kept away. The weekend before we had the Steins and Bob [Buckingham] – also a great success. [Mary Lago and P. N. Furbank (eds.), *Selected Letters of E. M. Forster, Volume Two, 1921–70*, p. 240.]

4 The Harewoods were expecting their first child: see Letter 680.

660 To Peter Pears

Aldeburgh
March 30th 1950

My darling,

Only to send my love – nothing more. I hope all is well with you – that the journey up & the flight were good & that you are now happily estab-lished in the American Hotel, flirting with all our blond young friends, drinking sociable Bols, seeing nice people & singing as only you, my dearest, <u>can</u> sing![1]

We go on here. Morgan seems better. He's dry today, thank goodness, & therefore more cheerful. He came to the Boyd Neel last night,[2] & like me enjoyed some of it. They played most of a dull programme with really great brilliance & verve. It is nice to hear people play as if they minded. The Suk Serenade (drab piece if ever there was one) was delivered with great conviction & obviously impressed. Alas, the Byrd & Mozart were as you'd expect – without any knowledge or authority, & so the ravishing & moving pieces made no effect, that is, comparable to the others. It was a great success, & everyone who came (about 100–120) enjoyed themselves. But probably as a result there'll be no 2nd concert – there being no funds. I had a tiny party after – about 15 people – including all the usual, and as well the Smiths (sister & bro. in law of Christopher Wood)³ who seemed nice. The Blake & Cotman⁴ made sensations – as well they should. The former looks terrific on the fireplace. And everyone asked tenderly after & sent their love to you, & congratulated you on your taste!

It's heavenly that you'll be here next Saturday week – I hope the interval isn't too hard – but, I know you'll sing well, & give loads of people real pleasure.

My love to you, my dearest. It was an interlude of heaven to have you with me. Billy Budd progresses.

All of me
to you,
B.

Love of course, to Peter & Jetty etc. etc.

1 Pears wrote to Britten after his 31 March British Council concert in Amsterdam:

Things go all right here. The Songs at the British Council on Friday were well appreciated, and Jetty's song ['The artist's secret'] had really quite a success. She is feeling happy now, because some songs she wrote for Noemie Perugia had a great success 10 days ago, it appears. Anyway on Friday all was happy [. . .]

Saturday was the first Concertgebouw Mat. Pas. [St Matthew Passion], and it wasn't too wonderful. E. van B. [Eduard van Beinum] has really no understanding of Bach at all, and, what was surprising, no feeling for the stimmung [mood] of it. I spoke to him about it, and yesterday's performance was noticeably better, but I am very bored by it – and I look forward to Rotterdam (rehearsal this evening). Peter [Diamand] is being very helpful and kind – driving me everywhere [. . .] Jo [Vincent] seems to be in rather a nervy state – she made a passionate attack on Peter for using foreign singers in the Holland Festival, & it was all rather embarrassing. Her singing is very tense, too. I wonder if you heard the broadcast. We only had 40 minutes interval, which in many ways is better than a huge lunch break – but maybe not for Aldeburgh! I've picked up a book by a Suffolk chap I wot not of. Arthur Young's Travels in France & Italy (1788) – a great agriculturist from nr Lavenham. A really lovely lively account, & a breath of fresh Suffolk sweet air, which I need v. badly, my pussy-cat.

2 A concert given by the Boyd Neel Orchestra, conducted by Boyd Neel, in

Aldeburgh Parish Church. For a short period, the Aldeburgh Festival tried to promote concerts during the winter. No programme has survived at BPL.

3 See Letter 645 n. 3. Con and Eric Smith were friends of Joan Cross.

4 The English artist and poet William Blake (1757–1827) and the Norwich-born painter John Sell Cotman (1782–1842). Pears purchased Blake's *St Paul and the Viper* (*c.* 1803–5) in 1949; it is now at BPL. See also Paul Banks and Philip Reed, *Painting and Music*, p. 18, and M. Butler, *The Painting and Drawings of William Blake*, no. 510. Pears's Cotman oil, entitled *Draining Mills at Crowland* (also known as 'Croyland') was purchased at Sotheby's on 20 July 1949. It is now thought not to be by Cotman, although copies of this composition are known, including a pencil drawing by Miles Edmund Cotman in 1846. J. S. Cotman made at least five watercolours and paintings of Croyland Mill. See Banks and Reed, p. 8, in which the painting is erroneously attributed to Cotman.

661 To Barbara Britten

4 CRABBE ST, ALDEBURGH, SUFFOLK

April 30th 1950

Dearest old thing,

Thanks for your letter. I'm sorry not to have replied before, but life has been hectic. Poor old Morgan has been taken bad again, & tomorrow he goes back to London & to the nursing home again to be re-examined. It's a great curse for the poor old man – & he's madly depressed. But I think it's best he should go & get it all coped with as we're all getting a bit worn![1]

My dear – I'm afraid next weekend ain't no good. Peter & I are off to Holland on 5th for a week or so. But later in the month 20th or 27th would do. Even if the house is full, there's always room for you, such a little one! – but I don't think it will be – except for inspiration, I hope.

So glad you enjoyed Schöne Müllerin.[2] It was better I think than usual – but we weren't all that pleased. I did enjoy Aunt Flo's comments. No one could ever pretend the Brittens were musical, could they? I shall never forget her Lucretia comments – wildly funny.[3]

How are you, my dear? What are your plans for the summer. Switzerland? But I hope I'll see you before long.

I hope to go over to see Beth with Peter on Tuesday. She seems cheerful on the telephone.

Excuse wild scribble, but as usual am in a panic of hurry!

lots of love, & to Helen [Hurst],

BEN

Do give Louise⁴ my love when you see her. Poor dear, to get shingles at her age. Hope she's better. Will this do?

1 P. N. Furbank relates that Forster left Aldeburgh not for reasons of continuing ill health, as Britten's letter to his sister suggests, but because 'minor frictions' had developed between composer and librettist, fuelled by

> Britten's breaking off [composition of *Billy Budd*] at every moment to play in concerts or attend conferences [*sic*] [. . .] Soon afterwards, on a visit of Britten's to Cambridge, he got it into his head that Britten had treated him off-handedly and told him so very sharply. (Crozier, who was present, was astonished at his fierceness; 'he berated him [Britten] like a schoolboy,' he related.) [Furbank, *E. M. Forster: A Life*, vol. 2, p. 285.]

The matter of Britten's ability to undertake professional engagements while deep in the composition of a major new piece was to be mentioned on several other occasions in the composer's correspondence during 1950 (see, for example, Letter 673), and was remarked on by Forster in an unpublished letter to the composer of 27 August 1950:

> Mind you plan rigidly for the next eight months, remembering that concertings, conferencings &cet. all take longer in reality than in the engagement book, since you have to allow time to get back from them into the right state for work. Probably more and more time has to be allowed as one grows older.

However, it was after a play-through of Act I of *Budd*, during the weekend of 22–23 April 1950, at which the Harewoods and Ralph and Clare Hawkes were also present, that Forster raised a criticism of Britten's music. It may well have been this difference of opinion that caused a rupture in the friendship for a time and precipitated, together with his continued ill health, Forster's premature departure from Aldeburgh. Forster wrote to Bob Buckingham on 23 April:

> Ben has played us most of the 1st Act of *Billy* – it should run to 40 minutes. I have had my first difference of opinion with him – over the dirge for the Novice [Act I, scene 1: 'Come along, kid!', with an expressive lament for alto saxophone and bass clarinet, supported by *pizzicato* cellos]. He has done dry contrapuntal stuff, no doubt original and excellent from the musician's point of view, but not at all appropriate from mine. I shall have a big discussion when the act is finished.

Forster believed that his criticisms of the dirge had been taken well by Britten (Forster to Crozier, December 1950). See also Letter 688.
    A further – and more serious – disagreement between Britten and Forster was to occur in December 1950: see Letter 679 n. 1.

2 Pears and Britten had broadcast Schubert's song-cycle in the Third Programme on 24 April 1950.

3 Beth Welford recalls (EWB, p. 189):

> Aunt Flo tried her hardest to understand Ben's music, but being so utterly unmusical

it was a struggle. She said the singers screeched. Once [...] I took her to dinner with Ben at Crag House [...] and then to a performance of *The Rape of Lucretia* [...] At the end of Act I scene 2, Aunt Flo whispered to me : 'Why can't Benjamin let the maids go to bed, and not keep them up so late?' Afterwards, however, she said she had enjoyed most of it.

Sadly, her comments on the Schubert broadcast have not survived.

4   Probably Britten's aunt, Louise Fernie (née Britten): see Letter 22 n. 3.

662 To Ronald Duncan
[*Postcard: Aldeburgh Beach*]

Aldeburgh
[Postmarked 1 May 1950]

So very glad that Stratton will come off soon;¹ I'm hoping to attend, & shan't mourn the absence of C.B.² Also glad the pomes³ [*sic*] are out at last thank you so much for sending them. Poor Morgan is not at all well – can't quite get well. He's gone back to London, & specialists, today.

Love to all,

BEN

1   The Mercury Players presented Duncan's *Stratton* at the Mercury Theatre, London, during the spring–summer season of 1950, under the direction of Stuart Latham.

2   Clive Brook (1887–1974), English actor, who had played the part of Sir Cory Stratton in the original 1949 production. In the revival the role was taken by William Devlin, who had played Michael Ransom in the Group Theatre production of *The Ascent of F6* in 1937.

3   *The Mongrel and Other Poems*. Britten's copy is inscribed: 'for Ben / love / Ronnie / '50'.

663 To Eric Crozier
4 CRABBE STREET, ALDEBURGH
May 4th 1950

My dear Eric,

What a muddle! So sorry – & now I have got to leave in a few moments for Holland – & I can't write a new Prelude to the Fugue, or double Fugue, which you return to me.¹

Briefly, then, Morgan asked me, from his depression & illness, to deal with the contract for him. He is satisfied that the general amount paid by B & H to the authors (by that I mean composer & librettists of course) is

adequate. I pointed out that the production of an opera by a publisher is
a very costly business. Anyhow, all music publishers have the same kind of
arrangements with their authors. Secondly, the division between composer
& librettist, a matter for themselves to fight out, I am now convinced is a
fair one ⅔–⅓. I was worried by your letter, because you had suggested this
was not fair ('parsimonious' Albert Herring ⅔–⅓, and 'relative largesse'
Let's make an opera – ½–½) – so I rang B & H, & found that Strauss–von
Hofmannsthal's arrangement was ¾–¼ for 'grands droits' and nothing for
sale of music! Now I am <u>not</u> suggesting that kind of arrangement – but
using it as a defence against the charge of 'doing' you – & here we came in!²
Let's forget it. Morgan is satisfied with the terms – and insists of course
on 50/50 with you – & imagines that the other points in the contract are
O.K. since you didn't comment on them.

   Please forgive the muddle & carelessness on my part – it only comes
from too much to do. I'm trying hard to write a piece for Primrose³ to
reward him for coming to the Festival – but keeping it quiet from Morgan
who doesn't like me taking a moment off Billy Budd!

Love to you & Nancy,\
Yours ever,\
BEN

Morgan is going back to nursing home – trying to find out what it is that
prevents him healing.

What are you back in NW3 for!

1 This new prelude requested by Crozier remains unidentified.

2 In April 1950 Ralph Hawkes wanted to finalize the contractual arrangements between Britten, Forster and Crozier in respect of *Billy Budd*. Forster
reported from Aldeburgh to his co-librettist on 23 April, 'He and I agreed
that you and I should divide equally any moneys payable for the libretto.'
Crozier responded in a now missing letter in which he must have protested
about an equal division of royalties between himself and Forster, and in
which he raised the general issue of the division between author–composer
and publisher. In a postcard to Crozier of 30 April, Forster was '<u>Adamant</u>
about ½ and ½ division' with his fellow librettist, but felt he could turn to
Britten for advice only about Crozier's querying of the principle of royalty
distribution between author–composer and publisher. It was against this
background, with all its inevitable misunderstandings, that Britten was to
write the businesslike communication to Crozier on 4 May, in which he
spelled out the usual disposition of such payments and the reasons for it.
Crozier, for his part, was to explain his objection to the Boosey & Hawkes
contract in a letter to Britten of 5 May:

I entirely agree with your view that ⅔/⅓ is right between composer and author. More than right! It's <u>generous</u> – but the distribution between author and composer has never seemed anything else than generous to me in the work we have done together.

My sole point was the sharing between Publisher & (Author–Composer). To illustrate my hesitation about this, I enclose the terms of a standard book-publisher's contract made with me last year for a first book [. . .]

[. . .] You will see that the Author's share in the b-p's contract is <u>much</u> higher than the combined Author–Composer's Share in a Boosey & Hawkes' contract. But if you are satisfied that this disparity is due to the higher costs of the music publisher, I have no more to say; & Morgan & I will sign the enclosed draft agreement as it stands.

3 *Lachrymae*, the first performance of which William Primrose and Britten gave on 20 June 1950 at Aldeburgh Parish Church. 'Our Special Correspondent' – Frank Howes? – wrote in *The Times* (22 June 1950):

Lachrymae, or 'Reflections on a Song of Dowland', for viola and piano, is not an easy piece to assimilate at first hearing without a score, partly because the listener has to wait till the last few bars for an overt reference to Dowland's 'If my complaints could passions move', which constitutes the main theme, easily missed on its first furtive appearance in the piano bass beneath atmospheric muted *tremolo* references to it from the viola. An extract from the same composer's 'Flow, O my tears' is heard during the ten continuous variations, but the fertility of Britten's invention again enables him to make a very little thematic material go a very long way, while the introspective, undemonstrative character of the music will no doubt make a deeper impression at each successive performamce.

'Diapason' (Hank Spruytenburg), *East Anglian Daily Times* (21 June 1950):

The work, as far as could be judged at first hearing, contains some very fine material, and with its passionate outbursts alternating with moments of deep quietude seems evocative of that passionate melancholy so strongly overlying most of the artistic expressions of the Elizabethan period. Mr Primrose's masterly technique, coupled with Mr Britten's absorption of the art of ensemble playing, gave a most persuasive reading of this jewel.

Desmond Shawe-Taylor, *New Statesman and Nation* (1 July 1950):

A short, but very striking, new work by Britten was introduced during a chamber concert at which William Primrose was the principal performer. This was *Lachrymae*, for viola and piano, described as 'Reflections on a Song of John Dowland'. The opening of the song ('If my complaints') is adumbrated with whispering recitatives for the muted viola and strange blurred passages for both instruments which a painter might liken to scumbling [the softening or reduction of the effect of otherwise brilliant colours]; in the later variations, after some bare but muscular writing in soft octaves, a wonderful slow crescendo is built up, flowering at last into a quiet statement of Dowland's own ending. The whole piece, though not at first hard to grasp, is held together by the same 'tension' of which Sir Kenneth Clark had spoken in describing Moore's forms: the listener is led irresistibly forward, and the end brings release and emotional fulfilment. It may be that *Lachrymae* heralds a new

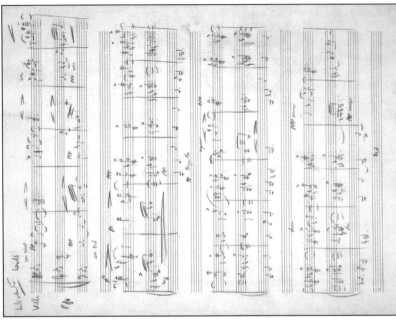

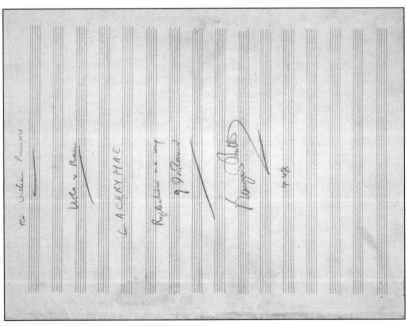

Lachrymae ('Reflections on a Song of John Dowland'), composed for William Primrose:
the title page and opening in Britten's composition draft

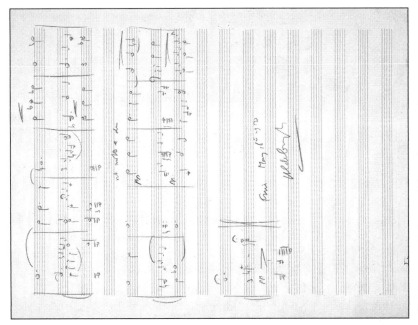

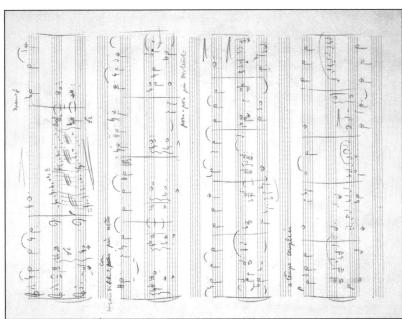

The final pages of *Lachrymae*, in which Dowland's 'If my complaints could passions move', which has formed the basis of the variations, is fully revealed

direction of Britten's pure and brilliant talent, one of the sources of which was suggested to us, on the next day, by the fine woodwind *Divertimento* (1938) of his teacher, Frank Bridge. Here, the clarity of form and texture, even the decorative loops and festoons, reminded us constantly of passages from *The Rape of Lucretia* and *Albert Herring*.

664 To Eric Crozier

4 CRABBE STREET, ALDEBURGH

May 15th 1950

Dear Eric,

This is only a scribble in haste because I am sure you'll be wanting to send off the article.[1] I have read it through, and it seems fine & sympathetic. I only query two things – the paragraphs I've marked. I <u>think</u> I see what you mean at the bottom of page 2 – but I believe it could be clearer, especially the last sentence. I don't think "composers' <u>descriptions</u>" is good. Why not ". . . as our own; the music evokes worlds beyond our world, conjured up by the addition of music itself/the new medium" – or simply "the music adds a new dimension . . ."?

Also, I don't think it's right to suggest that the first stages of libretto writing resemble writing a play. The libretto initially may <u>look</u> like a play (especially Billy because of the special case of E.M.F. not being a poet) – but I think with all our operas we consider it from <u>musical</u> angles right from the beginning. We don't, for instance, consider subjects or actions or characters which could be <u>anti</u>-musical, do we? Perhaps I'm exaggerating – but I think it's a little misleading to bring in the <u>play</u> idea. I know the composer takes a back seat at the beginning – but the librettist is always planning an opera not a play.

Forgive haste & consequent muddle-headedness, but I want you to get the thing back.

Can we talk about the contracts on Friday? Thanks for them by the way.

With love,

BEN

1 It has not been possible to identify Crozier's article but it may have been his 'Writing a Britten Opera', which appeared in *Music Parade*, 2/6 (1951), pp. 14–16.

665   To Walter Hussey

as from: 4 CRABBE ST, ALDEBURGH, SUFFOLK

June 1st 1950

My dear Walter,

You <u>are</u> a one! What a nice letter, and what a wicked present. I feel myself already gathering speed on the slippery slope, with the vision of my relatives before me (did I ever tell you the story of my relatives?),[1] & largely helped by you, dear Walter! We shall drink your health when we open the precious bottle. Thank you very much indeed.

Now petrol is free [of rationing] Peter & I hope we shall see much more of you – either you coming to us, or us to you . . . It is <u>far</u> too long. We miss sadly our trips to you, & Mrs Cotton's[2] splendiferous meals! Certainly we would love to do a concert for you next year, and may we pencil Sept. 22nd 1951?[3] We cannot say <u>definitely</u> at the moment about it, since our opera plans for that time are still in the melting pot; but we will do our best to keep it, and if not <u>that</u> date, another certainly. Donne Sonnets & the Quarles Canticle [I] are possibilities for the programme. I don't honestly think there's a chance for the Mass for 1951.[4] You see I have to finish Billy Budd (only just started) for the Festival at Edinburgh, and I have also to prepare Dido & Aeneas[5] for the Aldeburgh Festival – so my work is pretty well cut out! But if the moment arrives (& the right notes!) I will certainly do it for you. It is a thing I am determined to do.

I hope the Arnold[6] piece turns out well. I hear he's very gifted. I'd like Arthur Oldham (a protégé of mine) to do a piece for you some time – he's very lively & promising.[7]

No more now – in great haste – usual London rush! – but I wanted to write at once about your <u>smashing</u> present.

Much love,

BEN

1   Britten refers to his uncle William Hockey and William's mother Rhoda, Britten's grandmother, both of whom were alcoholics: see Letter 277 n. 1.

2   Hussey's housekeeper.

3   Pears was to write to Hussey on 15 September 1951, proposing a recital programme for 27 September 1951, comprising: 'Alleluia', 'Morning Hymn' and 'Evening Hymn' by Purcell; three arias from Handel's *Jephtha*; 'Der Einsame', 'Du bist die Ruh'' and 'Der Musensohn' by Schubert; 'Eia Mater' from Lennox Berkeley's *Stabat Mater*; Arthur Oldham's *Two Lyrics by Richard Rolle*; 'Thou hast made me' and 'Death, be not proud' from Britten's *Donne Sonnets*; and 'Folk Songs & Carols'.

4   For over twenty years, Hussey tried to persuade Britten to compose an

English-language setting of the Mass for congregational use within the Anglican tradition. Although Britten was to make settings of the canticles *Jubilate Deo* in C (1961) and *Venite exultemus Domino* (composed 1961, but not published or performed until 1983), he never fulfilled Hussey's repeated requests, which gathered urgency during the late 1960s. In 1968, an unspecified new work by Britten was listed in a Southern Cathedrals Festival brochure for first performance in July (Hussey was by this time Dean of Chichester Cathedral, one of the cathedrals participating in the festival), but this commission – very probably the English Mass setting – remained unfulfilled owing to Britten's illness earlier that year. The scheme was revived for 1971, when it was again postponed. Britten's poor health in the years after heart surgery in 1973 put paid to a further revival of this project.

Britten did, however, compose a Latin *Missa Brevis in D*, for boys' voices and organ (1959), for George Malcolm and the boy choristers of Westminster Roman Catholic Cathedral, by whom it was to be first performed at a celebration of the Mass at the Cathedral on 22 July 1959.

5   Britten's and Imogen Holst's edition of Purcell's *Dido and Aeneas* was to receive its first performance by the EOG at the Lyric Theatre, Hammersmith, on 1 May 1951, in a production directed by Joan Cross, designed by Sophie Fedorovitch and conducted by Britten. Nancy Evans and Bruce Boyce played the title roles, with Pamela Woolmore (Belinda) and Flora Nielsen (Sorceress). George Malcolm was the harpsichord continuo-player. The opera was staged at the Aldeburgh Festival on 8 June (Cross as Dido; Malcolm conducting) and the 16th (Pears as Aeneas; Britten conducting). The Britten–Holst edition provides three additional numbers, borrowed from other works by Purcell, to 'complete' the tonal circuit of Act II, as well as a complete realization by Britten of the continuo part. See also Letter 698 n. 3.

6   Malcolm Arnold (b. 1921), English composer. He studied composition and trumpet at the Royal College of Music and in 1941 began his professional career as principal trumpet with the London Philharmonic Orchestra. In the late 1940s he gave up his post at the LPO in favour of full-time composition. Among his works are nine symphonies, many concertos and smaller orchestral pieces, the latter including the popular suites of Cornish, English, Scottish and Irish dances, and more than eighty film scores, notably the incidental music for *The Bridge on the River Kwai* for which he won an Oscar.

Arnold was born in Northampton and his *Laudate Dominum*, Op. 25, a setting of Psalm 150 for chorus and organ, was commissioned by Hussey for St Matthew's, Northampton, and first performed there at the annual patronal festival.

Arnold conducted the first performance of his Concerto, Op. 67, for guitar (soloist: Julian Bream) and eight instruments at the 1959 Aldeburgh

Festival. The first performances of his Second Flute Concerto and Second String Quartet were also given at the Aldeburgh Festival, in 1973 and 1976 respectively. See also Paul Harris, *Malcolm Arnold: Rogue Genius* and Tony Palmer's documentary film, *'Towards the Unknown Region': Malcolm Arnold – a Story of Survival.*

7   Oldham did not write a piece for St Matthew's, although James Butt, another Britten protégé, did.

666   **To Benjamin Zander**[1]

4 CRABBE ST, ALDEBURGH, SUFFOLK

June 4th 1950

Dear Benjie,

Of <u>course</u> you should go on writing.[2] It is like everything else, cricket or swimming, you must get used to it. You will of course need some help, but that can come later. Write as much as you possibly can. I hope to be able to see you & talk to you soon – when my present rush of work is over. Perhaps your mother can bring you to Aldeburgh in August[3] & then you can bathe & play on the beach as well as talking & playing the piano to me.

With love from

BENJAMIN BRITTEN

1   Benjamin Zander (b. 1939), English conductor, who as a child was encouraged in his musical studies by Britten and who, in 1952, was to receive some lessons from Imogen Holst. Zander's mother had written to the composer early in January 1950 and Britten responded on 22 January: 'I was enchanted by your small son's poem. He sounds a gifted & charming child, & I should like to meet him.' A first meeting took place, after which the composer wrote once again to Mrs Zander (21 April 1950):

Thank you for your letter, & for Benji's little song. That's <u>much</u> better. I was glad indeed that he'd had the patience to cope with the writing of it himself. The other song (the Whale) was amusing, but difficult to judge because at that age improvisation comes so easily – real creation is more difficult!

Britten continued to keep in touch with the Zanders until the end of his life.
    In recent years Zander has achieved prominence as a conductor of Mahler, some of whose symphonies he has recorded. See also Sue Fox, 'Art of the possible', *Independent* (28 March 1997), pp. 16–17.

2   Zander had been told by an adjudicator at a local arts festival at Gerrards Cross, where his family lived, that he should not continue to compose until he had begun composition and harmony lessons.

3   Britten was to write to Mrs Zander on 23 August 1950:

Thank you for your letter. I am afraid we have left it a bit late for your & Benji's coming to Aldeburgh – I have to leave here early next week, & shall not be back for some weeks.

I will do my best to come to Gerrards Cross, when next in London, or if that is not possible perhaps you'd bring the boy to London. But there is no hurry: he is very young as yet, & if he can have got harmony & counterpoint lessons, as well as 'cello, this winter, he can come to no harm, & when we meet he'll be more developed as a person, & it'll be easier to see how his future looks.

667 To Lennox Berkeley

4 CRABBE ST, ALDEBURGH, SUFFOLK

June 27th 1950

My dear Lennox,

Thank you so much for your nice letter of good wishes, & for sending the Spring Symphony article.[1] You are nice to have written so sympathetically about it, & I am delighted that it is to your taste. In another way I am equally delighted that you write so harshly of the Albert Hall! Was there ever such a place? One day I hope you'll hear it properly done in a respectable hall. I'm doing it in Leeds in October[2] – what nice memories I have of 'Jonah' there![3]

We had a nice Festival here – a lot of nice music, I hope respectably done. People seemed to enjoy themselves, while we rushed madly round in small circles. The Matthew Passion was really well done[4] – a pity you both missed it. Please give Freda my love, & tell her I'll be thinking of her, & waiting expectantly for the great news.

Please excuse this scribble, but I've got to rush off to Holland[5] in 10 minutes (what a life this is!) – & I wanted to send my love to you, and my godson.

BEN

1 Berkeley's 'Britten's *Spring Symphony*', *Music & Letters*, 31/2 (July 1950), pp. 216–19, an appreciation of the symphony and a review of its UK premiere, given at the Royal Albert Hall on 9 March 1950. Berkeley explained to Britten in a letter dated 18 June 1950:

I wrote a short article on the *Spring Symphony* for *Music & Letters* mainly because I like it very much (the *S.S.*, not *Music & Letters*), though it was not my idea. I hope I haven't talked utter rot – I find that sort of thing quite dreadfully difficult.

In his article Berkeley writes:

Seldom can the acoustical shortcomings of [the Royal Albert Hall] have been more unfortunate. The publication of the symphony (by Boosey & Hawkes) will be particularly welcome to those who, like myself, have heard it only there. The extremely contrapuntal nature of the music makes it essential for the listener to hear the part-writing clearly; the moment the parts are blurred or indistinct it loses its meaning. Only on reading this beautiful but rather disconcerting work did I realize how little I had heard on March 9th and how inaccurately.

The *Spring Symphony* is by no means an easy work, and one can understand that, at first hearing, if many people appreciated it at once, others were somewhat bewildered. This was due to various reasons but chiefly, I think, to the fact that recently the composer has greatly developed his style, and his admirers have an effort to make to keep up with him [...]

But if I am right in thinking that a development of Britten's technique and personality has been a difficulty, there are others. The spirit of the work and its 'climate' are highly unconventional. It is about the spring; but it does not correspond to most people's preconceived ideas on the subject, derived, as they so often are, rather from pictures they have seen and poems they have read than from a direct, personal apprehension of Nature. The feeling for Nature here is of an unusual kind; it is far removed from Wordsworth's appreciation of Nature's moral or religious significance, and it is equally distant from the serene classical landscapes of Claude and Poussin. To my mind it is more nearly akin to Bruegel than any other artist; there is something of the same full-blooded identification of Nature with ordinary human life, the same sympathy with humanity. This breadth of feeling has always been an important part of Britten's music, and largely accounts for his success as an operatic composer [...]

I have said that the *Spring Symphony* shows a further development of Britten's idiom, but there is little in it that was not implicit in his previous works. His genius has always lain not in innovation but in masterly and valid adaptation of traditional methods to his own purpose. He has never rejected tonality, but his use of it becomes increasingly removed from diatonic harmony. Even in this work the tonal centres are very clearly defined. If the impression of bitonality or polytonality is often felt it is produced more by the simultaneous use of different scales having the same root or keynote than by such use of two or more different keys. This very free employment of notes that are foreign to the key in an idiom that is nevertheless tonal is pushed farther here than in Britten's previous music, and the ear has to get accustomed to it.

The methods of construction are as firmly classical as ever, and are used with the customary dexterity. The setting of George Peele's poem 'Fair and fair', for example, is not only a lovely tune but also a wonderful piece of craftsmanship. The melody has a rare freedom of rhythm; it is in 6/8 time, with the natural accent of the phrase appearing in each bar in a different place and forming a subtle and delightful rhythm. To this is added a counter-melody having a shape of its own but falling very neatly into place. At the recapitulation both the main melody and the counter-melody appear in canon, so that the piece moves in double canon through the whole of this section [see also Letter 545 n. 1] [...]

In general shape, too, the work is original. I can think of nothing similar. It is divided into four parts, each part except the last being subdivided [...]

The whole weight of the work is borne by the voices; indeed, the orchestra's function is chiefly to accompany and it is seldom heard alone, a fact that has caused some people to boggle at the title, the word symphony having generally been used for instrumental compositions or, in the seventeenth and eighteenth centuries, for instrumental movements occurring in vocal works. The word, however, has already served to describe music of such utterly different character and form that its use here is likely to upset none but the pedantic. Britten, for that matter, has surely earned the right to his own interpretation of words, for he has here re-created in a new and entirely individual language the very spirit of the poems of his choice.

2 Ill health was to force Britten to withdraw from the Leeds Festival performance. Herbert Bardgett, the festival's chorus master, conducted in Britten's
   place: see Letter 676.

3 Berkeley's oratorio (subsequently withdrawn), a performance of which
   Britten heard Berkeley conduct at the 1937 Leeds Festival: see Letter 11 n. 7.

4 See Letter 647 n. 3.

5 On 30 June 1950 in the Kleine Zaal of the Concertgebouw, as part of the
   Holland Festival, Pears and Britten gave a recital of songs by Purcell,
   Schumann's *Dichterliebe* and the Dutch premiere of Copland's *Old
   American Songs*.

668 To Imogen Holst

4 CRABBE ST, ALDEBURGH, SUFFOLK
July 25th 1950

My dearest Imogen,

It is about time you stopped thanking us, & high time that the boot was on the other leg. We have so much to thank you for, apart from the Schütz[1] which will be an everlasting joy to us. You have brought so much happiness into our world, the true happiness which comes from affectionate critical appreciation, & really true friendship, artistic & personal. I feel there is nothing I could not talk to you about, & to which you would not give an honest, sympathetic ear to.

I feel dreadful about the Schütz – it is just too much. But you always know where it is, & it can be a common property between us. We are already starting delving into its wonders, & planning performances for the future. We must talk about these.

I wanted to write a long letter to you about your lovely B minor Mass,[2] but the moment doesn't yet present itself. I have been up to my eyes in things important & unimportant, musical & unmusical, & only next week will I have time to stop & think. Peter & I go off today to Denmark,[3] but return here for the month of August, next Tuesday – thank God, to get back to peace & Billy Budd.

So, my dear, expect a long, warm, probably maddening, ramble about your intelligent, skilful, provocative performance of that adorable master-piece, within a week or so.

Lots of love, & more thanks than I can begin to express – about everything. Don't work too hard & don't forget a holiday from time to time!

Your devoted

BEN

1 Imogen Holst had given Britten and Pears a volume of Schütz's *Symphoniae sacrae*, edited by Philipp Spitta (now at BPL).

2 A performance given at Dartington on 9 July 1950 in memory of Christopher Martin and in commemoration of the 200th anniversary of Bach's death, by the Dartington Singers and Players conducted by Imogen Holst, with soloists Joan Cross, Rosamund Strode, Noel Barker, Alfred Deller, Peter Pears, Maurice Bevan and Cecil Cope. The performance was, as Imogen Holst later recollected, the result of three years' rehearsal and study. See Peter Cox and Jack Dobbs (eds.), *Imogen Holst at Dartington*, pp. 19, and 68–70.

3 Pears and Britten gave a recital of Purcell realizations, the *Michelangelo Sonnets* and a group of folksong arrangements in Copenhagen on 27 July 1950.

669 To Jane Clark[1]

4 CRABBE ST, ALDEBURGH, SUFFOLK

August 4th 1950

My dear Jane,

I entirely forgot, when we met at Covent Garden on Monday, to thank you for sending the bottle of gin! It was stupid of me, please forgive me, & believe that we really appreciated the present enormously – especially after the amount of liquor which was consumed in the house in Festival week! I am so glad that you & Kay enjoyed being here the two days – next year you must come for longer & taste some of our other dishes![2] We are thrilled at the moment because the accounts show that the Festival didn't lose any money this year – such a thing can never have happened before.

I hope you enjoyed the Robbins–Blitzstein ballet[3] more than we did. I thought the music very ungifted. But I think the Americans are very enterprising in the number of new things they are doing.

Thank you again very much for the gin, & apologies for the lateness of this note.

Yours ever,

BEN B.

1 The wife of Sir Kenneth ('Kay') Mackenzie Clark (1903–1983), English art historian, who was Director of the National Gallery, 1934–45, and Chairman of the Arts Council, 1953–60. One of the first directors of the English

Opera Group, Clark frequently lectured at the Aldeburgh Festival. See also Letter 432 n. 2.

2   The Clarks had attended the Aldeburgh Festival; Kenneth Clark had lectured on Henry Moore on 21 June in the Jubilee Hall. The Festival included an exhibition in the Church Hall of Moore's drawings, models and sculptures.

3   The New York City Ballet performed Marc Blitzstein's and Jerome Robbins's ballet *The Guest* when the company visited Covent Garden during the summer of 1950. According to Blitzstein's biographer, Eric A. Gordon,

> The critics divided sharply over the work: the snobbish ones absolutely could not appreciate it. Even more than in America, they fled from works with social themes. One sour reviewer said that Blitzstein's music 'sounds like Soviet music at its worst combined with American music at its worst; pretentious but well scored'. But another wrote that: 'the solos and *pas de deux* are as beautiful and expressive as anything the Americans have given us, full of tender youthful gestures of diffidence and awakening love [. . .] Blitzstein's music, which tends to the use of brass and low strings, has some attractive dissonances which help to produce an atmosphere of tension and mystery.' [*Mark the Music: The Life and Work of Marc Blitzstein*, p. 343.]

670   To David Webster

Royal Opera House, Covent Garden

4 CRABBE ST, ALDEBURGH, SUFFOLK

August 8th 1950

Dear David,

    I have been thinking over your very exciting proposal of the Tempest with Gielgud[1] at Covent Garden next August–September, & reluctantly come to the conclusion that it won't be possible. It isn't a job that could be thrown off; there's too much music, & that music must be of a most subtle nature.[2] I shall have this opera to finish, & then the production & realisation of 'Dido', & then the production of 'Billy' itself; these will take me right up to the middle of August, with literally no time for working on the 'Tempest' or for the production. I am so very sorry. Perhaps it'll come off another time. I write at once because I know you'll be wanting to plan this most important date.

    I enjoyed my talk with you. You were very accommodating (however you spell it!), & I feel we can now go forward on a fine footing. Let me know as soon as you can what dates you will want me for in October 1951.[3] I was right in thinking it will be the 2nd half of October & not November? I say this as the Group is planning a Continental tour in November,[4] & that affects not only me but Joan & Peter as well.

    I am sure we were right about taking Grimes out for this season. Everyone can then come to it fresh, & that includes the public!

Best wishes to you; have a good holiday, when you do – you'll need it!

Yours ever,

BEN

P.S. We went over to see Fred Ashton on Saturday. It really looks as if we'd better release him from Dido, as he is so terribly busy. It is a great pity from our point of view, but his schedule really looks full enough without that extra task.⁵

1 John Gielgud (1904–2000), English actor and director, a member of the theatrical Terry dynasty with a classically modulated vocal delivery. He was regarded as one of the finest Shakespearean actors of his generation, and his performances as Hamlet, Richard II and Prospero are particularly remembered. His introverted, cerebral, almost spiritual style was in sharp contrast to the physical energy and passion of his near contemporary Laurence Olivier. In the 1950s and 1960s, when his approach had fallen somewhat out of fashion, Gielgud toured the world with *The Ages of Man*, a one-man recital of passages from Shakespeare based on an anthology by George Rylands. He was admired for his roles in Wilde's *The Importance of Being Earnest*, Sheridan's *The School for Scandal* and Chekhov's *The Seagull*, and appeared frequently on television and in films. In his eighties and nineties, like Olivier, he found fresh success in contemporary stage plays by Harold Pinter, David Storey and Charles Wood and undertook cameo roles in often lightweight films where his impeccable technique, comedy timing and ultra-English vowels could serve him well. Substantial and courageous film roles included the dying writer in Alain Resnais's *Providence* (1977), scripted by David Mercer, and Prospero in what *Variety* described as Peter Greenaway's 'intellectually and erotically rampaging meditation' on *The Tempest*, *Prospero's Books* (1991). His opera productions included Berlioz's *The Trojans* (Covent Garden, 1957) and the London premiere of Britten's *A Midsummer Night's Dream* (Covent Garden, 1961). He was knighted in 1953, created a Companion of Honour in 1977, and admitted to the Order of Merit in 1996.

Gielgud made a single appearance at the Aldeburgh Festival, on 9 June 1968 in the Jubilee Hall, performing his *Ages of Man* programme. Pears wrote in the Aldeburgh Festival programme book that Gielgud 'first taught us how to speak Shakespeare, and nobody since has done it better. If we cannot expect to have him acting at Aldeburgh, we are proud to welcome him as the perfect speaker of Shakespeare.'

Britten and Gielgud were to discuss working together on *The Tempest* intermittently over the next twenty years. See Letter 672 n. 3.

In October 1953, during a vehemently anti-homosexual period instigated by the then Home Secretary Sir David Maxwell-Fyfe, Gielgud was arrested in Chelsea for soliciting and fined; see Richard Mangan (ed.), *Gielgud's Letters*, pp. 171–2. Later that autumn Britten was questioned by Scotland

Yard. As Percy Elland, editor of the *Evening Standard*, told Lord Beaver-brook in a letter of 15 January 1954, 'Scotland Yard are definitely stepping up their activities against the homosexuals. Some weeks ago they interviewed Benjamin Britten. This week I am told they have interviewed Cecil Beaton. No action is to be taken against either' (see HCBB, pp. 334–5). See also Introduction, pp. 7–9.

See the obituaries in *The Times* (23 May 2000) and by Alan Strachan and Gilbert Adair, *Independent* (23 May 2000); Thomas Sutcliffe's appreciation, with a contribution from Peter Hall, *Independent* (23 May 2000), and Richard Mangan (ed.), *Gielgud's Letters*. Although Mangan's edition comprises some eight hundred letters, none of those to Britten (held at BPL) appears in his selection.

2 See Letter 672 n. 3.

3 For rehearsals of *Billy Budd*.

4 This tour did not materialize.

5 The EOG might have approached Ashton, who had already directed the first production of *Albert Herring*, because of the significant element of dance in Purcell's opera. Gielgud was also invited to direct this production, but declined (letter from Gielgud to Britten, 23 August 1950). It was Joan Cross who eventually directed the production when it was staged in 1951.

671 To Kenneth Harrison[1]

4 CRABBE ST, ALDEBURGH, SUFFOLK
August 19th 1950

Dear Kenneth,

We are just shooting off north, & thence to Italy for a week or so – & your letter with most interesting enclosures has just arrived, so I hasten to send a note of acknowledgement & very great thanks. Thank you more than I can say for your trouble in copying & translating the excerpts from Ralph of Coggeshall.[2] As you say, I am up to the eyes in Billy Budd – but these sweet stories will go into the old subconscious & I hope bring forth fruit before too long. If you ever had time I'd love to see the Newburgh version of the Green children[3] – but I hate to bother you more than you've already been bothered.

Thank you again – in great haste.

Many greetings,
Yours ever,
BENJAMIN B.

1 Kenneth Harrison (1912–1994), a fellow of King's College, Cambridge (1938–60), where he served as Dean (1945–48). In 1960 he took up the post

of Professor of Biochemistry at the University of Tehran. He was a friend of Forster, whose rooms adjoined Harrison's, and it was Forster who introduced him to Britten. Harrison and Forster jointly hosted a party for the EOG on 30 July 1948, during a tour to Cambridge. It was Harrison who was to provide a solution to the problem of the shanty texts sung by the crew in Act II of *Billy Budd*: see Letters 688 n. 5 and 704.

2 Harrison had copied out and translated for Britten an excerpt from *Radulphi de Coggeshale Chronicum Anglicanum*, edited by J. Stevenson (Rolls series, 1875). Ralph of Coggeshall, a twelfth-century Cistercian abbot, recounted the story of the 'green children', a boy and a girl, who were discovered at Woolpit near Stowmarket in Suffolk. They claimed to have lived in an underground twilit country where they tended their flocks. Attracted by the sound of bells, they entered a cave, eventually emerging into daylight, which they found almost unbearable, weeping bitterly. Their skin was tinged with green and all they would eat was beans. The boy was listless and soon died, while the girl served out her life in the household of Sir Richard de Caine. Similar folk stories appear in other cultures and locations, for instance at the village of Banjos in Spain.

3 Britten had written to Harrison on 17 August 1950:

Thank you very much for the William of Newburgh news – some time I should love the complete story, against a rainy day, but Billy Budd's taking all my operatic time these days. Would the story be in Latin & difficult Latin too?

Harrison copied out and translated for Britten an excerpt from Willelmi de Novoburgo, *Historia Rerum Anglicanum*, edited by R. Howlett (Rolls series, 1884). Harrison's manuscript survives at BPL. William of Newburgh (or Newbridge) dates the story to the reign of Stephen and claims the children reported that their native country, 'St Martin's Land', was Christian; that the sun never rose there but that bright lands could be seen beyond a wide river. Some commentators hold that they came from the village of Fordham St Martin and that their skin discoloration was due to malnutrition.

The composer thanked Harrison on 13 October:

I simply cannot remember whether I thanked you for sending the William of Newburgh account of our two Woolpit children. I think it arrived just before Peter & I went away to Edinburgh, thence to Sicily, & then back to England to work, & alas got ill. If I did acknowledge it, please forgive the redundancy of this – but I have just read it again with great pleasure, & want to thank you for troubling to render it into English & copying it all out for me. What can be done with it musically, if anything, I don't yet see. But at the back of my mind there seems to be some dim scheme. Perhaps when Billy Budd is born the scheme will show itself & let's hope it'll be a good one.

The legend was not set by Britten. However, in 1990 Nicola LeFanu was to write an opera on this subject, *The Green Children*, to a libretto by Kevin Crossley-Holland.

672 To Ralph Hawkes

THE ENGLISH OPERA GROUP LTD
25, WIGMORE PLACE, LONDON, W1
August 23rd 1950

Dear Ralph,

Thank you so much for your letter; glad to get all your good news. This isn't really a letter, but only a quick reply to some of your <u>outstanding</u> queries!

1) Very glad about your recommendations to London for Oldham; I hope they'll follow it.[1] I wasn't, alas, able to introduce him to [Lincoln] Kirstein, as he had to leave, but I spoke to him about Arthur, & I think it sank in.[2]

2) The Tempest is shelved pending the completion of Budd, but Peter & I are going to Stratford to see Gielgud after our Edinburgh performances next week, & will talk about this most exciting idea.[3] Budd, by the way, is getting on well – Act I is satisfactorily done, & Act II beginning well. Nothing much can be done about casting, but I hope to see Tucker[4] (of Sadler's Wells Opera) soon & discuss it all with him.

3) Aldeburgh Festival 1951 plans exciting & shooting ahead. You & Clare must <u>certainly</u> be here then!

4) I don't know anything at all about Blitzstein[5] as a producer. But he must certainly be musical (an advantage!) & if he's nice with children, that would mean a great deal. I'm afraid I must leave it to you. <u>If you</u> think Norman Del Mar not too English, get him – but I'm scared that the work will appear very whimsy & old-world. That's why I'd like the <u>first part</u> to be adapted to the local atmosphere. I must also add that, here, other conductors have [been] & are doing it, & it is no longer Norman's property – but I don't want to detract from his undeniable charm in it. What about E. Chappell?[6]

<u>Really</u>, old Kous[sevitzky] makes me angry! He really <u>can't</u> have the score unless he coughs up that money. You'll remember I wrote to him (in January [*recte*: February]) saying that I'd like the money sent to Aldeburgh Festival, & at Leslie Boosey's request, I returned (to L.A.B.) the cheque already sent personally to me. I've never had an answer – but shall start agitating soon![7] Secretly, though, it's nice to know that there are actually worse correspondents than me!

I must stop this now, & dash to post. I'm expecting the Pipers any moment – John's coming especially to discuss the Budd sets. It looks like Ashton producing now.[8]

Hope your weather's better than ours. Terrific rain. Be good, & go slow as much as possible.

Love from Peter & me to you both,

Yours ever,

BEN

P.S. J. Fassett of C.B.C. was here last Sunday, & I arranged a smashing broadcast (recording) for him about the Festival, ranging from a Countess to a fisherman!⁹ He was pleased.

1   Hawkes, now permanently based in the New York office of Boosey & Hawkes, had suggested to Britten that there was a need in the United States for more choral works along the lines of Oldham's recent setting *My Truest Treasure*.

2   Arthur Oldham had been Musical Director of the Ballet Rambert, 1945–48, and had composed three ballets for the company as well as conducting repertory works. See his autobiography, *Living With Voices*, pp. 33–5. Britten had clearly hoped to interest Kirstein in Oldham's work in this field.

3   Anthony Gishford had written to Hawkes following a meeting between David Webster and Britten. Hawkes wrote to the composer on 16 August (unaware of Britten's decision to postpone this operatic project):

I cannot tell you what memories this evoked with me since I think it was one of the first things we discussed some six years ago when the [Covent] Garden scheme was being started. I can only say that the consummation of this would be the fulfilment of one of my dearest wishes [. . .] to settle this for say 1952 winter might be something which would be tremendously important [. . .]

Gielgud, however, had written to the composer on 23 August, prior to Britten's and Pears's visit to Stratford, proposing not an operatic but a film adaptation of *The Tempest*:

I would like to talk to you about *The Tempest*. Michael Powell [English film director (1905–1990)] wrote to me last week suggesting a film of it in the spring. I answered I could not do it before next *autumn* and perhaps he would like to approach you about a score? Would that horrify you? I think, if one had a strong say in the treatment, it might have great possibilities – but maybe the idea of recording nauseates you and you are too busy anyhow. I'm awfully flattered anyway that you should want to work with me – of course I should love it – but I am *very* ignorant about music.

But whether it was to be an operatic or cinematic *Tempest*, the composition of *Billy Budd* and the realization of *Dido and Aeneas* were fully to occupy Britten's composition schedule for the immediate future.

There the matter rested until the mid-1950s when Gielgud, now working with the innovative director Peter Brook, proposed that Britten write incidental music for a production of the play, possibly at Stratford (Gielgud's letter is unclear), in which the role of Ariel would be played by a boy who could sing and act. This suggestion was declined and the matter of a

Tempest project once again fell silent until January 1961, when Gielgud, now directing the London premiere of Britten's *A Midsummer Night's Dream* at Covent Garden, wrote to the composer on 23 January 1961: 'What about *The Tempest* as an opera, with Prospero left (*for me*) as sort of compère– raconteur, with some of the big speeches left in?' Gielgud reported to Kitty Black, 30 January 1962: 'I asked Britten if he wouldn't do a *Tempest*, leaving me to speak my text as Prospero. He seemed rather intrigued with the idea, but don't know if anything may ever come of it'; see Richard Mangan, *Gielgud's Letters*, p. 279. In November 1965 Gielgud was once more suggesting a *Tempest* film to Britten, with Orson Welles now directing and playing the role of Caliban.

It was not, however, until the late 1960s that the idea of a cinematic adaptation of *The Tempest*, with Richard Attenborough as director, became a serious possibility for Britten. A letter from Gielgud to the composer (15 July 1969) indicates that Britten made a positive response to the proposal. Gielgud's letter mentions that an abridged version of the play would be used (Gielgud himself would be responsible for the cuts), and that shooting would commence in autumn 1970, with some of the filming done in Japan. In a letter to Hugh Wheeler (4 December 1969), Gielgud writes:

No, I didn't go to Japan, but Attenborough still says Paramount are mad to do *The Tempest*. [Albert] Finney is toying with the idea of playing Caliban, and Britten is OK and says he thinks Bali would make a better location than Japan. His [i.e. Attenborough's] brother [David Attenborough] (who is a big noise in TV production) is soon to show me some documentaries he made there (in Bali). Might be more exciting. Pray God it all works out sooner or later.'

It was probably around this period that Gielgud sent to the composer an annotated copy of the play showing the cuts, as well as an indication of the proposed treatment. (This volume, the 1967 impression of S. C. Boorman's edition of the text, survives at BPL.) Donald Mitchell recalls that as a result of discussions about the *Tempest* enterprise Britten asked him to meet Richard Attenborough and, on his behalf, talk about the possibilities and practicalities, which he did. Mitchell had been left in no doubt that it was Bali that was uppermost in Britten's mind when returning to reconsider a passion for Shakespeare's play that had been with him for many years. Incidentally, it was not only the gamelan that was part of Britten's love for the island. He told Mitchell, when encouraging him to make his own first visit, that the people of Bali 'were the most beautiful in the world'.

In addition to the play text, BPL also possesses a typescript dated 17 June 1969, one sheet of which is entitled 'Opening sequence' and which indicates that the actor playing Caliban should be young (Albert Finney and Alan Bates are the suggestions given). Another typescript entitled 'Scheme for a film of Shakespeare's <u>The Tempest</u>' indicates that the island in the play would be Japanese, and that there was a possibility of using Japanese, Balinese or Thai ('Siamese') actors. It contains some thoughts about the score:

The music should be most important – the two storms, the plot of the wicked men, the coarse songs and horseplay of the comic characters with a hint of sinister powerful ugliness in the depictions of Caliban. Ariel's songs, his appearance as Harpy at the magic banquet, and the masque of Goddesses. All these scenes give fine opportunities both for orchestral symphonic accompaniment and some beautiful singing.

The project, which was made public in the early 1970s, foundered due to Britten's ill health in the final years of his life.

Gielgud told Humphrey Carpenter in 1990:

I never knew Ben or Peter at all well, although of course I met them many times – they used always to come round when they came to see me act. I had an ambitious desire to film *The Tempest*, and Ben promised he would compose the music, which was a most thrilling idea. [HCBB, p. 396.]

Britten's assimilation of the techniques of the musics of the Orient and South-East Asia in works such as *The Prince of the Pagodas* (1957) and the sequence of three Church Parables, beginning with *Curlew River* (1964), would undoubtedly have demonstrated in the interim Britten's unique creative response and commitment to the musics of the East.

4 Norman Tucker (1910–1978), English opera administrator and translator, who was joint Director of Sadler's Wells Opera, 1947–54, and sole Director, 1954–66. His autobiography, *Norman Tucker: Musician* was published in the year of his death.

5 Marc Blitzstein (1905–1964), American composer whose output was characterized by a commitment to topics of social and political comment, in which he was influenced by the example of figures such as Brecht and Weill. He forged a music-theatre idiom that, in the view of Copland, made indigenous American opera possible. Among his many stage works are *The Cradle Will Rock* (1936–37), a 'play in music' originally to have been mounted by the Federal Theater Project but in fact staged by Orson Welles and John Houseman, and the opera *Regina* (1946–48). See also Letter 669 n. 3.

The project under discussion in this letter was a production of *Let's Make an Opera*, given at the John Golden Theatre on Broadway, New York, on 13 December 1950, which closed after only five performances. The production had been seen at the Shubert Theatre, New Haven, 22–25 November, and at the Wilbur Theatre, Boston, as part of an out-of-town preview tour. According to his biographer, Blitzstein 'made slight changes [. . .] he merged the first two acts into one, leaving only one intermission, and for obvious reasons he changed the name of the bully master of the little sweeps from Black Bob to Big Bob' (Eric A. Gordon, *Mark the Music: The Life and Work of Marc Blitzstein*, p. 349). Norman Del Mar, who had conducted the premiere at the 1949 Aldeburgh Festival, was engaged for the performances (see Letter 684 n. 1).

Gordon notes (p. 350) that at the first night in Boston

[...] the entire cast of Cole Porter's new musical *Out of This World* joined the audience, as a dress rehearsal of their show had been cancelled. But their added voices hardly helped. Though offering benign compliments to Blitzstein's know-how as a director, the critics generally panned the work. For one thing, they found Britten's tunes not the easiest to sing. An emphatic Elliott Norton reported that Norman Del Mar behaved 'like a completely silly ass'.

It would seem that things were received even less favourably in New York. The impresario Peter Lawrence, who was backing the show under the auspices of his Show-of-the-Month Club, invited drama critics to review the production, but excluded the musical press. According to Gordon,

[...] a few reviewers found the piece zestful and captivating, and timely for the Christmas season; but most thought it juvenile, self-conscious, pretentious, and thin [...] Howard Barnes, reviewer for the *Herald Tribune*, criticized the odd turn of the music and cited cumbersome lyrics [...] He summed up the audience's reaction succinctly: 'Let's make an opera? Let's not.'

Blitzstein, who had publicly declared that he believed the work to be 'the best opera Britten has written', told Mina Curtiss, 'I have done an honorable, even imaginative job, with something less than slight material.' (See Gordon, pp. 348–50.)

Leslie Boosey attended the first night on Broadway and wrote to the composer on 29 December:

I must say I thought it was very good, quite equal to anything that has been done in England. It did not run for the simple reason that a Broadway audience is far too hard-boiled for a work of that kind, and I could never make out what possessed our friends to produce it. Norman Del Mar worked like a Trojan, and even made the Broadway First-Nighters sing, but when the *Herald Tribune* came out against it, it was impossible for it to carry on long enough to enable it to find its true level.

6   Unidentified.

7   A condition of the commission of *Spring Symphony* was that the Koussevitzky Music Foundation would be entitled to the autograph full score of the work. This manuscript had yet to be forwarded to Koussevitzky for the reasons Britten gives. See Letter 656. Donating a commission fee to the Aldeburgh Festival continued to be one of several ways in which Britten gave financial assistance to the organization. For example, he and Pears gave their services gratis and, in the late 1960s, the £10,000 fee the composer received from the BBC for *Owen Wingrave* was redirected to the fund to rebuild Snape Maltings following its destruction by fire in 1969.

8   Basil Coleman, not Ashton, was to direct *Billy Budd*.

9   No information has come to light about this CBC radio documentary, although it may be surmised that the 'Countess' and the 'fisherman' were Marion Harewood and Billy Burrell.

673   To Eric Crozier

4 CRABBE STREET, ALDEBURGH

August 29 1950

My dear Eric,

Peter & I were hoping that you'd be back from your sail on Sunday
early enough to come along & have a drink, & we could have had a
ceremonial opening of your present. But it didn't work out that way, &
I hadn't opened the exciting package when we took you in to Sax.[1]

Many thanks indeed for the beautiful diary (I can never distinguish
between dates & milk!) – fascinating & gossipy reading, as well as a great
convenience at this point when one can't get 1951 diaries. Thank you also
for what you say about Billy. I am, on the whole, pleased with Act I. It was
after all the act that we were least emotionally interested in, & I think it
was the most difficult to bring off. But I don't minimise the daunting job
ahead! Let's meet when more is done, & also when I've seen Norman
Tucker & further discussed the production. Thank you for your great
help in the design discussions. I thought they went promisingly. What
a dear John [Piper] is.

As you probably know I'm having a bit of a worry with Morgan, who
can't quite understand my method of work! Please tell him, if you get a
chance, that I always do twenty things at once, & that there'll be a good
chance of the opera being done in time!

Please excuse the horrible scribble but we're dashing off, & I wanted to
thank you for the diary.

Love to Nancy. I hope you're both better for the holiday.

With love,

BEN

1   Saxmundham, approximately seven miles inland from Aldeburgh.

674   To Erwin and Sophie Stein

From Peter Pears and Benjamin Britten
[*Postcard: Taormina – Giardino pubblico*]

[Messina][1]

Thursday

[Postmarked 14 September 1950]

Wunderschön ist es hier, das Land wo die Citronen geblüht haben.[2] Und
das Meer ist so warm und blau, obwohl unsere Hotel ist sehr hohe und
wir mussen spazieren darunter zum Seebad (meine arme Beine!). Die

Sonne brennt uns furchtbar. Taormina is ein ganz reizenden Stadt, es giebt viel Schweizer im Hotel, so alles ist wie im Himmel!

viele liebe grüsse,
PETER

Wenn Peter's Italienisch nur fliesst wie seinen Deutsch. Aber es ist wirklich zu heiss zu denken! Unglaublich – nicht? Ma questa beltà è molto buono per noi, e dolce far niente!

Con molt'amor,
Vostro
BENIAMINA

[It's lovely here, the land where the lemon trees have bloomed. And the sea is so warm and blue, although our hotel is very high and we have to walk downhill to the resort (my poor legs!). The sun burns us dreadfully. Taormina is a really charming town. There are lots of Swiss staying at the hotel so it's like being in heaven!

Many loving greetings,
PETER

If only Peter's Italian was as fluent as his German. But it's really too hot to think. Incredible, isn't it? But this loveliness is very good for us, and the delightful idleness!

With lots of love,
Your
BENIAMINA]

1　Britten and Pears were on holiday. Their German and Italian is verbatim.

2　An allusion to Goethe's 'Kennst du das Land [wo die Zitronen blühn]', set by Beethoven, Schubert, Schumann, Wolf et al.

675　To John Nicholson

as from: 4 CRABBE ST, ALDEBURGH, SUFFOLK
Sept. 29th 1950

My dear John,

Thank you so much for your letter – I've been travelling around a bit & so that is why it's not been answered before.

I am most flattered & happy that Lowestoft would like to give me its 'Freedom'.[1] It sounds a most signal honour, but I've no idea what it means (tho' I have a sneaking desire to be allowed to go on the South Pier without paying).

I cannot get down to Suffolk before Oct. 10th, but then I am there, working madly, all the winter. Could you & Pat[2] come over to dinner one evening, & explain all about the matter to me? If it's difficult for you to get over, I'll try & come to you – but as I said I'll be up to my eyes in overdue work, & it would be very nice to welcome you to Aldeburgh.

I am, of course, quite sure I shall accept the Freedom – only I'd like to know what it means exactly, and to know if I'll have to make any <u>very</u> long speeches – which I abhor![3]

I hope you are both well, & your parents too. Give them my love please.

Yours ever,
BEN (BRITTEN)

1 The ceremony at which Britten was made a Freeman of the Borough of Lowestoft was to take place on 28 July 1951.

2 Nicholson's wife, Patricia. At the end of Britten's life, she used to come to Aldeburgh and play piano duets with the composer – 'mostly Mozart', she recalled to Humphrey Carpenter – in an attempt to help him regain the use of his right hand, which had been impaired after his heart operation in 1973. According to Mrs Nicholson, ' I was somebody who, not being a professional, he felt he could play with.' See HCBB, pp. 561–2.

3 Britten's speech of thanks was widely reported in the press and published in full in *Tempo*, 21 (autumn 1951), pp. 3–5; reprinted in PKBM, pp. 108–11. Britten's Lowestoft speech touched on themes that were to be explored more fully in his 1964 speech, *On Receiving the Aspen Award*, notably the idea that as an artist Britten wanted to serve the community in which he lived: 'It is not a bad thing for an artist to try to serve all sorts of different people [...] it isn't a bad thing for an artist to have to work to order.'

676 To Peter Pears
[*in pencil*]

Melbury Road
[Postmarked 5 October 1950]

My darling P.,

Thanks everso for your nice comforting letter. Fearfully glad that Moore wasn't too Moorish,[1] & that you Madam'd away[2] – knew all the time you just have to be separated from your old boring accompanist! So now you're probably closeted with Bardgett[3] – with Anne [Wood] too, I

hope (do remind her, not too heavy glissandi in the Herrick).[4]

It is sweet of you, & I'm sorry to be a bloody nuisance. But I'm afraid the old Doctor was right – I couldn't have done it. The temp. & throat are all right, but I feel absolutely done in, & depressed. It's these filthy pills & injections, I suppose. But they're stopping now, thank Heaven. I don't really think I'll go to Aldeburgh yet – want to see you, & besides there's all this hopeless EOG muddle. Another bomblet from Elizabeth [Sweeting] about it this morning. He's a very silly little man.⁵

I hope all is nice & comfy with you, & that you don't have to see too much of those old Christies. (Glad to miss them I must say!) Marion's been in a lot, & is terribly sweet – gave me a bottle of St Emilion 1943, which the Doctor's ordered – in a big way!! – got to drink & drink – shades of Southend pier & all. Barbara's been in too & is very kind & chatty, & Lesley [Bedford] comes this morning – which is nice – Because I like being talked to, & can't read much.

Love, or whatever's suitable, to whoever's suitable. Did the fish arrive?

Must stop now – because I sweat so when I write! Longing to see you – lots of love. I'll listen tomorrow.

Love you,

B.

1 Gerald Moore (1899–1987), English pianist and accompanist, in which capacity he worked with virtually every distinguished solo singer and instrumentalist from the mid-1920s until his retirement in 1967. His musical partnerships with Dietrich Fischer-Dieskau, Elisabeth Schwarz-kopf and Victoria de Los Angeles in concert and on record were especially noteworthy. His publications include *The Unashamed Accompanist*, and his memoirs, *Am I Too Loud?* and *Farewell Recital*.

   Moore took Britten's place at the piano (as this letter makes clear, the composer was ill) for Pears's Leeds Festival recital on 4 October 1950. Pears wrote to Britten that afternoon:

   This morning was as good as could be hopefully expected. Certain things went quite well & he didn't spoil the whole thing [. . .] I don't actually think I shall do a Dominions tour with Gerald Moore this winter! Not actually, B., but you get better see?

2 A reference to the Princess Royal (1897–1965), Lord Harewood's mother and the only daughter of King George V.

3 Herbert Bardgett, the chorus master of the Leeds Festival Chorus, who, because of Britten's indisposition, was to conduct the performance of *Spring Symphony* (broadcast live in the BBC Third Programme) on 6 October. See Letter 678.

4 The setting of 'Welcome, maids of honour', the first number in Part II of *Spring Symphony*. The published score contains no indication of any glis-sandi, presumably in an attempt to discourage singers from making them.

5 Henry Foy, the General Manager of the EOG, who was obliged to resign soon after, but not before the EOG was plunged into a serious financial crisis that was not fully resolved until the end of the year. On 21 October Britten wrote to Pears:

The E.O.G. situation remains sordid & confused. Elizabeth has unearthed more & nastier troubles, but I suppose it'll be cleared away one day. Basil [Douglas] has decided to come to us, but I'm worried about whether the situation is clear enough for him to resign from the BBC for it. However he's in touch with [James] Lawrie & Elizabeth, & should know the worst. I feel we'll go on, but with curtailed activities – which <u>may</u> suit him as it would only come out as part-time.

By the end of November the Arts Council had come forward with some additional financial support for the EOG, in addition to which the Elmhirsts had offered to support the forthcoming production of *Dido and Aeneas* (see Letter 689).

677 To Elizabeth Sweeting

Melbury Road
Oct. 5th 1950

My dear Elizabeth,

Only by the grace of a vile attack of throat infection which keeps me chained to bed instead of being feted in Leeds, did I get your letter today, which is just as well. I've immediately written a sharp note to Foy, which I hope'll have some result. Please keep the Jubilee Hall pacified, if necessary pay it for the Festival, because I think this weekend will see things change in EOG considerably (managerly [*sic*]). It's all hectic with Anne, Basil [Douglas], Peter away & me in bed, but all the same I'm pretty sure that there's going to be a drastic solution. So cheer up!

I imagine the fish arrived safely up in Harewood & are now being eaten by Princely mouths – but I haven't heard.

I think Dorothy Sayers[1] is a <u>very</u> good idea – do you think better than Day Lewis[2] – perhaps?

Love,
BEN

1 Dorothy L. Sayers (1893–1957), English novelist and playwright, whose popular reputation rests on the sequence of detective stories featuring the aristocratic, erudite and nonchalant sleuth Lord Peter Wimsey. Sayers was, however, also a considerable scholar and translator (of Dante, for example) and was the author of a highly original and, in its time, controversial sequence of radio plays on the life of Christ. Entitled *The Man Born to Be King*, this series was first broadcast in 1942 in a production by Val Gielgud (brother of John). Britten contributed incidental music to two of the programmes: 'Bring me garlands, bring me wine' in the tenth episode, 'The Princes of this World'; and Mary Magdalene's song, 'Soldier, soldier, why will you roam?', in the eleventh episode, 'King of Sorrows'. See PRIM, pp. 609–11 and 623–4.

2 Cecil Day-Lewis (1904–1972), English poet and writer, associated with
   Auden, Spender and MacNeice during the 1930s. He succeeded John Masefield as Poet Laureate in 1968. Neither Sayers nor Day Lewis appeared at the
   1951 Aldeburgh Festival.

678 To Herbert Bardgett

THE ENGLISH OPERA GROUP LTD
25, WIGMORE PLACE, LONDON, W1
4 Crabbe Street, Aldeburgh
[after 6 October 1950]

My dear Herbert Bardgett,

I had wanted to write to you before to thank you, from the bottom of
my heart, for your splendid effort on behalf of the Spring Symphony &
myself![1] I am afraid this note has got delayed because of this illness, & my
journey down here, & the consequent tiredness which that caused. However, I'm glad to say that I'm now better – although still 'below par'. I can
scarcely say how sorry I was to let you all down, but I did it with a slightly
easier conscience because I knew that you were there to save the situation –
and save it, you most certainly did! I heard the broadcast, not always too
clearly, but enough to realise that you brought the performance 'off' in
no uncertain manner. The whole seemed to make a fine effect, & many
details were most lovely. Since you expressed to Mr Stein your willingness to
have his frank comments, I will presume you will extend that willingness
to include me – & so I write now a few comments on what I remember
of the performance. I realise, too, that you have the Hallé performances
coming off soon.[2] You will, you say, have the advantage then of a younger
& more flexible choir. The intonation of the Leeds choir was a little disappointing in the first, & the 'Out on the lawn' – wasn't it? Perhaps not
quite such a slow tempo for the Introduction (No. I) might help them –
only a slightly more moving tempo. Between ③ & ④ there can be a
'stringendo' for the orchestra – not a big one, but making the choral entry
at ④, the 'animato', less sudden. The balance throughout was rather odd,
but that I suspect was a lot to do with the position of the microphone.
The strings generally were much too ethereal. Can you get them to play
more firmly even in the most pp passages? How was the balance in 'Spring
the sweet spring' – did the solo voices predominate sufficiently? I wasn't
too happy over the tempo. It seemed a little rushed to me. It should be
enthusiastic, but leisurely at the same time! The boys were excellent of
course – do thank them, & Mr Gordon. Will they be the same for the
Hallé performances? The Milton ['The Morning Star'] was fine; if anything a little on the heavy side, but I'm not complaining!

I think you did the next three solos very well, considering that you must have been so new to them. They will get a little more freedom as you become familiar with them – the Herrick ['Welcome, maids of honour'] in particular, especially in the string parts. Those, as I said before, need playing a little more <u>firmly</u>, and in the 'Waters above' as well. You could give Peter a little more time in this one, as well – especially in the 3rd bar of ⑤. In the 'Out on the lawn' – the bass-flute, and -clarinet parts need

playing more flowingly – the figures   were too stiff. I

think the semichorus, for this number, is a good idea. More remote. The ensemble in the next two is difficult – but you know that as well as I do! Throughout the 'Fair & fair' the strings need, as before, to play more firmly. The Blake ['Sound the Flute'] came along well – but here the younger choir will help it to move more joyfully! The end, in particular, could fall over itself more! You held the Finale together splendidly – I do congratulate you. The Allegro started a little too slowly, but righted itself well. The percussion, timpani, need curbing a lot at ㉑ – I could scarcely hear the chorus. The cow-horn was <u>really</u> a bit too unreliable. Perhaps you'll have a better player for this in Manchester. For 'Sumer is icumen in' – the horns were too loud – but I meant to have mentioned that after my rehearsal, but forgot, I'm afraid. If the percussion is reduced, & the brass a bit too, I'm sure the wee boys won't have trouble in dominating the scene as they should! Please don't take this criticism as being in any other spirit than is meant – comments from a grateful composer on an already fine performance! I'm sending this for Mr Stein to look at, as you asked him to comment, & I don't want him to risk duplicating my remarks.

I hope you are well, & having a well-deserved rest after your triumphs last week. How is your son doing in his new school? Give him my greetings – & your wife too.

With many thanks & best wishes,
Yours sincerely,
BENJAMIN BRITTEN

1 See Letter 676 n. 3. The performance was given on 6 October 1950 by Joan Cross, Anne Wood and Peter Pears, with the Hallé Orchestra, the Leeds Festival Chorus, and 'a choir of 100 boys'.

2 A further performance of *Spring Symphony* was given at King's Hall, Belle Vue, Manchester on 5 November 1950 with Joan Cross, Anne Wood and Peter Pears, the Hallé Choir, the Chorus of Manchester Schoolboys and the Hallé Orchestra, conducted by Herbert Bardgett.

679   To Eric Crozier

October 20th 1950

Dear Eric,

The Arts Council have at last coughed up the 'Billy' commission & sent me cheque no. 1 of £250 – & so I've divided it among us according to the contract & so here's a cheque for the awkward sum of £41 13s 4d (I hope my maths is correct).

I'm getting on splendidly with Act 2 – very pleased with life. I'll be calling on you soon, I'm afraid, for one or two things, & probably also going over to King's to see Morgan.[1]

Please thank Nancy for her nice letter, & tell her I'll answer it as soon as possible, but every moment spare from work is taken up with the ghastly Foy mess. It's the most sordid muddle ever. Luckily Elizabeth is squeezing EOG matters in with her Festival work, & with the help of an accountant gradually getting the matters straighter. I hope we'll be able to go on – but that was the worst thing we ever did to engage that irresponsible ass!

Hope you're well, & work's progressing.

Love from

BEN

P.S. Sorry to have forgotten the book project. I'm afraid I'm madly against pre-performance projects like this. An ordinary libretto, O.K., but I'd like to wait for such an idea till the demand grows. Sorry, my dear, but my whole being revolts against anything at this moment about the work other than that which is only practical for the performance.

1 Britten and Crozier were to join Forster in Cambridge for the night of 23/24 November to discuss *Billy Budd* and to play over what had thus far been composed. Claggart's monologue – 'O beauty, o handsomeness, goodness' – was criticized by Forster on that occasion and his objections were to be further expounded in an undated letter to Britten from early December:

It is *my* most important piece of writing and I did not, at my first hearings, feel it sufficiently important musically. The extensions and changes you suggest in the last lap may make the difference for me, besides being excellent in themselves.
With the exception of it, all delighted me. Most wonderful.
Returning to (it), I want *passion* – love constricted, perverted, poisoned, but nevertheless *flowing* down its agonizing channel; a sexual discharge gone evil. Not soggy depression or growling remorse. I seemed turning from one musical discomfort to another, and was dissatisfied. I looked for an aria perhaps, for a more recognizable form. I liked the last section best, and if it is extended so that it dominates, my vague objections may vanish. 'A longer line, a firmer melody' – exactly.

(See Mary Lago and P. N. Furbank (eds.), *Selected Letters of E. M. Forster:*

Billy Budd, Act II scene 2 (four-act version): Claggart's 'O beauty,
o handsomeness, goodness!' in Britten's composition draft

Volume Two, 1927–70, p. 242. Forster's letter is evidently in response to one from Britten which is now lost.)

Philip Reed comments in BBMCPR, p. 61:

Such a reaction was catastrophically debilitating to Britten who sought advice immediately from Pears and Erwin Stein. He also invited Crozier to Aldeburgh to discuss the work and to play to him this particular section, and it was left to Crozier to tackle Forster on Britten's behalf and attempt to prevent any further deterioration in their relationship. Forster replied to Crozier's entreaties with appropriate humility, explaining how he had made criticisms of the Dirge in Scene 1 which were apparently taken well by the composer; he had felt therefore that it was perfectly acceptable to raise a doubt about Claggart's monologue. In the meantime, Crozier persuaded Britten not to reconsider the monologue until after he had finished Act III.

See also Reed's 'On the Sketches for *Billy Budd*', in Reed (ed.), *On Mahler and Britten: Essays in Honour of Donald Mitchell on His Seventieth Birthday*, pp. 240–46, for a discussion of Britten's revisions to Claggart's monologue.

680 To Marion Harewood

4 CRABBE ST, ALDEBURGH, SUFFOLK
October 22nd 1950

My dearest Marion,

Because it'll probably be a few days until we can talk on the telephone, or before I can get to London to see you, I thought I'd scribble a few words to tell you how <u>very very</u> pleased I am about it all.[1] Pleased that you are both well, that the son has good lungs (<u>obviously</u> going to be <u>the</u> Billy Budd baritone in a few years' time), but moved, seriously, that you and George have a son. I could write reams describing my feelings on realising that you two whom I admire & love so much have this continuation, but since I can't write, it would only come out pompously in clichés, & so I won't say it. You know anyhow what I feel.

If Billy will allow it, I'll be up in a few days to see you & him, but Billy's being quite a tyrant – fascinating problems, difficult but rewarding. It is a strange business this, creating a world which finally ends by dominating oneself.

If not – if I can't get up – will you be able any time to come here? – you know the house is aching to receive you – we've plenty of room, nurse & all of course. It is highly important that my acquaintance with my godchild should start <u>soon</u> – these first few days are important in a person's development! Thank you, both of you, for asking me to be this. I'm thrilled to do it, & will take my responsibilities seriously!

I'm now going to drive Michael Tippett to see a house near Sudbury.

He's thinking of moving here, into Suffolk. A nice thought, that he'll be near, & a nice acquisition for Suffolk music![2]

Lots, lots of love to you all three. See you all soon I hope.

Yours ever,

BEN

I wired Peter the news.[3]

1 The Harewoods' first child, David Lascelles, had been born on 21 October.

2 Tippett did not move to Suffolk, but eventually settled in Wiltshire.

3 Pears was singing in the Netherlands and Germany. Among his Dutch engagements was a performance of Handel's *Messiah* attended by Queen Juliana of the Netherlands.

While in Amsterdam Pears spent time with Peter Diamand and his wife Maria:

I've seen a lot of Peter & Maria. Lunch there Thursday – drinks there (with Henk Keining) & supper on Saturday, tea again yesterday, & a farewell visit this morning. She's a very remarkable creature – so brave, so intelligent & so honest. A great believer in us & a pillar of support. I went with Peter this morning to look over the "Kleine Comoedie" – a quite charming little theatre near the Munt, which we might have for "Dido" in the [Holland] Festival. I think it's wholly suitable – 500 people, tiny stage (like [the Jubilee Hall,] Aldeburgh) v. nicely equipped. I was very taken.

681 To Albert Goldberg[1]

4 CRABBE ST, ALDEBURGH, SUFFOLK

October 23rd 1950

Dear Albert,

It was nice to get your letter & news of you – even though it means a little work to do! I will certainly tell you now the very little to say that there is about the Violin Concerto.

It was written in 1939, & although it has been played quite a lot here & abroad I have never been happy about the form of it. The fact that Heifetz[2] was going to play the work spurred me on to looking [at] it again from this point of view, & that I have just done. There is no structural change in the work – a shortening here & a rewriting there is all I've done. There is no new material at all, although a complete rewriting of a violin passage in the last movement is a new development of existing stuff. The cadenza is shortened, & a rather embarrassing chord for orchestra in the middle of it is removed. I hope what I have done is to leave the work as it would have been had I been able to write it in 1939 with my present experience. I think I bit off then a bit more than I could chew! – especially in the last movement.[3]

I hope that's the kind of thing you wanted to know – if you've got the piano reduction, you'll know more about the work's structure than I do.

It would be lovely if you could manage to get over to one of our Festivals here – why not next year? It'll be a big year. I'll get our Manager to send you the details as soon as they're ready. We had a lovely time this year, better than ever, I think.

It has been a fearfully busy year for us both – practically without holidays. But now I am firmly stuck here for the whole winter with Billy Budd on the stocks, to be finished in time to be presented to the world in Edinburgh 1951 by the Sadler's Wells.

Peter is at this moment touring on the Continent – I think he's in Germany, but may still be in Holland. He's singing better than ever. He'd send his greetings to you if he knew I was writing.

I hope, in spite of all your terrific work, that you're well. We often talk of you & our time in Los Angeles – quite the nicest time we had in all our tour.

With every good wish,

Yours,

BEN

1   American critic, pianist, conductor and music administrator (1898–1990), whom Britten first met in 1940 when Goldberg, as Illinois State Director of the Federal Music Project (part of Roosevelt's Works Progress Administration), invited the composer to give the US premiere of his Piano Concerto, with the Illinois Symphony Orchestra conducted by Goldberg (see Letter 241 nn. 2 and 3). Goldberg's enthusiasm and encouragement led to a series of performances in Illinois under the auspices of the Works Progress Administration, and a warm friendship between Britten and Goldberg developed. They were occasionally in touch in the post-war years, and met in 1949 in Los Angeles, by which time Goldberg had joined the music staff of the *Los Angeles Times*. See Letter 229 nn. 1 and 2; Donald Mitchell's interview with Goldberg (23 May 1989, Pasadena, California; tape and transcript at BPL) and the collection of Goldberg–Britten papers, including the text of Goldberg's 'Vignette' of Britten at BPL. See also the obituary by Burt A. Folkart, *Los Angeles Times* (6 February 1990).

2   Jascha Heifetz (1901–1987), American violinist of Russian birth, renowned for his prodigious technical virtuosity, among whose commissions was the Walton Concerto. No information has come to light at BPL about any performances of Britten's Violin Concerto by Heifetz.

3   Paul Banks notes in his *Benjamin Britten: A Catalogue of the Published Works*, p. 49:

> The first batch of revisions was made in October 1950, and included some minor structural changes (e.g. the outer movements are both shortened by one bar and the second movement by three) and more extensive alterations to the violin part.

In 1954 further revisions to the violin part (removing much of [Antonio] Brosa's editing and simplifying some of the figuration) were made with the help of Manoug Parikian. In spring 1965, during editorial work on the proofs of the miniature score, the longer version of the last movement was reinstated.

Brosa was the violinist who gave the premiere of the concerto in New York in 1940, and who edited the solo violin part for the concerto's publication.

682 To George Harewood

4 CRABBE ST, ALDEBURGH, SUFFOLK
Oct. 26th 1950

My dear George,

So very glad to have continued good news about Marion & David(?). I am champing to come & see them both, but I think the delay (caused by duty) probably will improve the boy's beauty – not that you or Marion probably think that's possible. I <u>very much</u> approve of the choice of David, & if a mere Godfather has any sway in such matters, hope you'll stick to it. It seems a good start to me (you won't agree) that he cried during 'Turandot'.[1] Puccini obviously gets him down – unless it was Stanford Robinson; perhaps on the whole more likely.

About your queries. I'll certainly do the pieces for you.[2] It would be amusing & instructive to write the prefaces to the operas. I envisage notes on the character of the pieces, & also how to perform them – a thing I feel strongly about. About who should write the articles on Lucretia, etc. I'm not sure – do you want them <u>as well as</u> the prefaces, incidentally, or isn't that really too [much] Britten? If you really do want them S-Isserstedt[3] is a good idea – what about Tietyens[4] (however he's spelt)? <u>if</u> he ever gets down to Herring; if not, certainly Schüler[5] – [Hans] Zimmerman might do 'Let's Make', or one of the Oslo chaps, who judging by photos have done a splendid job there (perhaps we'd better <u>not</u> ask the conductor, although he had a great personal success – because of his name, Mr Stein Bugge).

The Verdi idea is splendid – I only feel we might improve the list of composers. V.W.,[6] if he'll do it, would be good if provocative, ditto Michael T. [Tippett]. Willy [Walton], I thought you said, won't or can't write; Lennox [Berkeley] happens to be articulate, & adores Verdi, & as he's in the middle of an opera becomes eligible, I'd have thought. I think Bush[7] would be valuable – his views might be surprising, but certainly interesting. Bliss[8] is the best other, gloomy tho' the thought is – he's at least written & had performed an opera. The dateline fills me with alarm – but maybe I'll get something done by then. My feeling about the title is to leave the approach to Verdi to individual choice, & to subtitle. "Verdi – a Symposium" – & then "My experiences of" – by R.V.W.; – "my study of" –

by L. Berkeley; my "stealing from" – by A. Bliss; the "social significance" of
– by Bush; "the psychological importance of" – by Tippett; "my abject
humility in front of" – by self – in other words how the chaps react personally to the old boy. Do you agree?[9]

I expect there'll be a Directors' meeting at end of next week, when I'll
be up, & will come & call if I may. Billy Budd shoots ahead; Act 2 Sc. 1 is
done, & I'm in the middle of the Interlude. Life seems endlessly complicated here but the sea's so beautiful & Miss Hudson's[10] cooking so satisfying & Billy Budd so absorbing, that I sail callously over all difficulties.

Your fishermen friends send respects & best wishes to Marion & the
babe. I told them, maybe, you'd be bringing them down before too long –
I hope I wasn't deceiving them. Do try.

Lots of love to you all,
Yours ever,
BEN

1 A broadcast of *Turandot*, with Joan Cross in the title role and Walter
  Midgely as Calaf, conducted by Stanford Robinson.

2 Harewood had founded *Opera* magazine in 1950 and proposed that Britten
  contribute to two forthcoming issues: a commemoration of the fiftieth
  anniversary of Verdi's death in January 1951, and a celebration of the EOG's
  London season in May 1951. For the latter Harewood told Britten, 'We
  wanted a number of distinguished foreign musicians (or perhaps producers) to write about the chamber operas. I have made various suggestions on the enclosed bit of paper about possible writers, and suitable
  photographs of foreign productions.' In addition, Harewood also invited
  Britten to contribute prefaces to his own operas, as part of a continuing
  series by various composers – 'what one's theories about the nature of
  opera and the writing of opera and opera of the future amounts to'.

  In the event, Britten did not contribute any 'prefaces' to his operas, nor
  his thoughts on the operatic tradition. The May 1951 issue however did
  include four articles on the chamber operas: Hans Schmidt-Isserstedt on
  The Beggar's Opera in Hamburg, where he had conducted the German premiere on 23 June 1950 at the Hamburg Staatsoper; Walter Hapke on *Albert
  Herring* at the Hanover Opera; Hans Zimmermann on *Let's Make an Opera*
  at the Zurich Opera House; and Roger Lalande, who was responsible for
  the design and production, on *The Rape of Lucretia* at Mulhouse.

  The same issue also contained a profile of Pears (pp. 287–92) by Hans Keller.

3 Hans Schmidt-Isserstedt (1900–1973), German conductor, who held
  appointments at the Hamburg Staatsoper (1935) and the Deutsche Oper,
  Berlin (1943). He founded the North German Radio Symphony Orchestra
  in 1945 and remained its conductor until 1971.

4 Probably Heinz Tietjen (1881–1967), German conductor and opera director,

who was Adminstrator of the Berlin Städtische Oper (1925–27, 1948–55). From 1931 to 1944 he was Artistic Director of the Bayreuth Festival, where he also conducted.

5 Britten is probably referring to the pre-eminent Swiss music critic Willi Schuh; see Letter 556 n. 4.

6 Ralph Vaughan Williams (1872–1958), English composer, with whom Britten had an uneasy relationship. He had little enthusiasm for Vaughan Williams's works and remembered what he took to be a generally unsympathetic attitude on Vaughan Williams's part during his student years. See Diary for 22 July 1931, n. 1.

7 Alan Bush (1900–1995), English composer, who maintained an unswerving adherence to Marxist principles. In March 1936 Bush conducted the first performance of Britten's *Russian Funeral* for brass band, and he was prominent in organizing the 'Festival of Music for the People' in which Britten's *Ballad of Heroes* was premiered. See also Letter 87 n. 1; and obituaries by Rupert Christiansen, *Independent* (3 November 1995), Hugo Cole, with an afterword by John Amis, *Guardian* (3 November 1995), and in *The Times* (4 November 1995).

8 Arthur Bliss (1891–1975), English composer of American descent. He was Director of Music at the BBC from 1942 to 1944, and Master of the Queen's Music from 1953 until his death. See also Arthur Bliss, *As I Remember*.

Britten and Bliss were never particularly close, though in 1966 Britten sent Bliss a warm letter of congratulations on the occasion of his seventy-fifth birthday (reproduced in *As I Remember*, p. 292). At the 1970 Aldeburgh Festival Britten conducted the premiere of Bliss's Cello Concerto, with Mstislav Rostropovich as soloist (see also *As I Remember*, p. 293), and in 1971 he was one of twenty-three composers who contributed to an album of short compositions presented to Bliss by the Composers' Guild. A photograph of Bliss looking at Britten's contribution, *Scherzettino 'A. B.'*, is reproduced in Bliss's autobiography.

9 'Verdi – A Symposium' was published in *Opera*, 2/3 (February 1951), pp. 111–17, reprinted in PKBM, pp. 102–3, with contributions from Vaughan Williams, Bliss, Britten and Berkeley.

10 Elizabeth ('Nellie') Hudson (1898–1982), Britten's housekeeper from 1948 until 1973. She retired to a bungalow in the grounds of the Red House, which Britten had specially built for her. Miss Hudson – neither Britten nor Pears used her first name – knew the composer in the late 1930s, as it was from an uncle of hers that Britten purchased the Old Mill at Snape. An interest in music led her to listen out for radio broadcasts in which Britten was to take part. During her twenty-five years' service at Crag House and later at Red House, she prepared the composer's meals – 'nursery food . . . milk pudding . . . spotted dick' – and ran his home with great efficiency. See also Alan Blyth, *Remembering Britten*, pp. 96–8. A portrait of Miss Hudson

Britten's sketch for his *Scherzettino 'A. B.'* (1971), to honour
Sir Arthur Bliss on the occasion of his eightieth birthday

by Mary Potter is reproduced in PFL, plate 230. She made a memorable contribution to TP. See also David Matthews, *Britten*, p. 124.

683 To Imogen Holst

4 CRABBE ST, ALDEBURGH, SUFFOLK
Oct. 31st 1950

My dear Imogen,

What a delightful surprise! I was just about to write you a note to
remind you about the female voices & harp idea, & to beseech you to do
something – and along come six little treasures.[1] Peter happened to be
here for a day or so when they arrived, & we played them over with the
greatest pleasure. I think they'll sound quite beautiful. Now, my dear, a
great request. You couldn't be persuaded to come & conduct the first
performance, could you? June 9th – Jubilee Hall? The singers, conductor
Peter Burges, come from Ipswich, called Northgatean; and will work very
hard to get them right for you. As soon as I have your reply, I'll get in
touch with Burges & arrange it all, but I know he'll be thrilled for you to
do it yourself. He'll do the rest of the programme – & we hope to get your
father's two (Spring & Summer)[2] little ones in – but I'm not sure what

ideas he'll have about the choir learning new works. I can't thank you enough, for doing these lovely pieces. Enid Simon[3] will be thrilled to tackle something big like this.

Yes, I quite agree, one gets something <u>very</u> special & simple & fresh from Joan's students. I remember Act 2 of Figaro at the Studio[4] with piano – it gave me infinitely more than Glyndebourne at Edinburgh.[5] I believe that it's something to do with humility which usually works in reverse ratio with gift & experience – & something, also, to do with Joan!

Thank you so very much too about Dido.[6] I was going to suggest a weekend here before you depart for India[7] to discuss this. I suppose late November or early December wouldn't be possible for you to come – you see there are some <u>very</u> important points I'd love to discuss with you before we get down to putting it into rehearsal. I'd hate suggesting this long trek, but I know journeys have no terrors for you! Why not bring young Jim[8] along too? – he might be useful in discussions – besides I'd love to see what he's been doing recently.

Please forgive the scribble – work is pressing, but I wanted to write at once & say how happy we are with Keats Imogen!

Lots of love –

BEN

What shall we do about copies of the part-songs? Have you got a publisher – or shall I try Boosey & Hawkes?[9]

1 Imogen Holst's six part-songs *Welcome Joy and Welcome Sorrow* (words by John Keats), for female voices and harp, which were given their first performance at a 'Serenade Concert' at the Jubilee Hall, Aldeburgh, on 9 June 1951 by the Northgatean Singers (Director: Peter Burges) and Enid Simon (harp) under the direction of the composer.

2 Gustav Holst's *Two Eastern Pictures* (H. 112) for female voices and harp or piano. They were not performed in the 'Serenade Concert'.

3 Harpist of the English Opera Group Orchestra, whom Maureen Garnham recalls as a 'gentle, rosy-faced creature who astonished strangers when she produced and proceeded to smoke a pipe. "A pipe!" exclaimed one visitor to a BBC session, "and such a sweet face!"' See Garnham, *As I Saw It: Basil Douglas, Benjamin Britten and the English Opera Group, 1955–1957*, p. 16.

4 The Opera Studio (later National Opera School), founded in 1948 by Joan Cross and Anne Wood. It ceased to function in 1963 with the foundation of the London Opera Centre. Imogen Holst wrote to Britten from Dartington on 28 October:

It has been such a *great* joy for us all to have the English Opera School here with us. Their performance of *The Magic Flute* is really beautiful: it was so lovely to hear it sounding effortless and the right sort of light, with no messing about with tempo, and no suggestion of 'putting in the expression' [. . .] they've got *much* more than just freshness and youth – they sound like real musicians, every one of them.

5 Glyndebourne Opera had given performances of Mozart's *Le nozze di Figaro* at the 1950 Edinburgh Festival in August and September, conducted by Ferenc Fricsay. Presumably Britten had attended a performance when he and Pears were in Edinburgh, or had perhaps heard a broadcast.

6 A reference to Britten's and Imogen Holst's edition, with a continuo realization by Britten, of Purcell's *Dido and Aeneas*, to be performed by the EOG in 1951. Imogen Holst was copying out a manuscript full score (now at BPL) in which Britten could then inscribe his realization and add dynamic markings.

7 Imogen Holst was resident as a 'student-teacher' at Santiniketan University from December 1950 until January 1951. See Letter 698 n. 1.

8 Imogen Holst and James Butt came to Aldeburgh for the weekend on 19 November.

9 The part-songs were published by Oxford University Press.

684 To Norman Del Mar

4 CRABBE ST, ALDEBURGH, SUFFOLK
Nov. 8th 1950

My dear Norman,

This is a brief note just to wish you the best of luck for the performances. I am keen to know how they go, & how the cast develops. It is very helpful that you like & trust Marc Blitzstein so much. Greet him from me – we did once meet many years ago. I am afraid, short of a miracle, that I can't get over to see it – Billy Budd is completely absorbing, & then I have Dido to cope with – apart from the ghastly mess that Henry Foy has bequeathed to us in the E.O.G. I won't say too much about that, partly because it isn't good for my temper (!), and because he's your manager.¹ But his irresponsibility & carelessness has let us in for a packet of every kind of trouble. Luckily he's gone & we have prospects of a really first-class manager now – but of course the plans for next year have all gone haywire. When they get straightened out I'll let you know. How long are you scheduled to stay in U.S.A.?

The programme of your orchestral concert at Aldeburgh looks a little like this at the moment: Siegfried Idyll, Berg double concerto² (with Noel [Mewton-Wood], & [Manoug] Parikian perhaps?) & the Carnival des Animaux.³ The latter I'd like to play with Noel, with you conducting – because I think it needs holding together more than one first imagined. Can you think of a nice English piece to start off with? There's no

particular hurry. (There wasn't, alas, a chance of getting Primrose into
this concert, after all.)

I hope you'll have excellent news of Pauline soon[4] – I do hope she is all
right. It'll be a worry for you so far away, I'm afraid. Marion's babe is fine –
I've seen him quite a lot, & he's very gay.

This comes with our very best wishes for a successful run. The
Brighton opening of our winter's tour was good last night, I gather.[5]

I hope you are flourishing & enjoying the madnesses of New York!

Yours ever,
BEN

1   Del Mar was to write to Britten on 5 January 1951, after his return from
    the US, pointing out that Foy was not his manager and expressing some
    concern that his own position with the EOG's Executive Committee was in
    some way coloured by this misapprehension. The same letter refers to his
    recent involvement in the Broadway production of *Let's Make an Opera*:

    It has been good experience even though the outcome was disappointing. I saw
    Erwin yesterday and he said that you all felt that it was a mistake to put it on on
    Broadway at all and a mistake for me to go. In the light of my present knowledge of
    the circumstances and the set-up into which I was plunged I am somewhat inclined
    to agree (!), and wish there could have been some way in which I could have found
    out what I was letting myself in for.

    See also Letter 672 n. 5 and Letter 694.

2   *Recte*: Berg's Chamber Concerto.

3   The programme given at the Jubilee Hall, Aldeburgh, on 17 June 1951 by the
    EOG Chamber Orchestra conducted by Norman Del Mar, with Manoug
    Parikian (violin) and Noel Mewton-Wood (piano), comprised: Boyce's
    Symphony No. 3 in C; Schoenberg's Chamber Symphony No. 1, Op. 9;
    Chausson's Concerto for piano, violin and string quartet, Op. 21; Wagner's
    Siegfried Idyll; and Saint-Saëns's *Le Carnaval des animaux*.

4   The Del Mars were expecting a baby.

5   *Let's Make an Opera* opened at the Theatre Royal, Brighton, on 6 November;
    between then and January 1951 it was seen in Torquay, Cambridge,
    Birmingham and London.

685   To Lesley Bedford

4 CRABBE ST, ALDEBURGH, SUFFOLK
Nov. 26th 1950

My darling Lesley,

Sweet of you to send me the Lowes Dickinson.[1] I had been re-reading
E.M.F.'s book[2] on him recently, & this comes most opportunely, & I look
forward to reading it a lot. He was a great man.

I had a quiet birthday[3] – work in the morning, & in the afternoon I took Beth & her children out to Shingle Street[4] for tea – gay & wild. Now Peter is down here, singing Nicolas at Ipswich & Bury [St Edmunds],[5] so we are belatedly celebrating the great day!

I had sweet letters from Dave & Stewy. I am glad they seem well & cheerful. I hear great things via Peter [Bedford] of Dave's scholarship papers. When is the exam?

I did so admire you in the Monteverdi.[6] Your performance was just right for the wonderful work it is. I hope you were pleased too.

Lots of love to you all, & thanks,

Yours affectionately,

BEN

1 Goldsworthy Lowes Dickinson (1862–1932), Fellow of King's College, Cambridge, and author of *The Greek View of Life*, who was a dominant figure at King's during E. M. Forster's student years there. Dickinson accompanied Forster on his first visit to India.

2 Forster's *Goldsworthy Lowes Dickinson*.

3 Britten's thirty-seventh birthday had fallen on 22 November 1950.

4 A tiny hamlet approximately twelve miles south along the coast from Aldeburgh, on a shingle bank where the river Ore finally emerges into the North Sea after running parallel to it for some five miles, separated by a narrow spit.

5 Performances by the St Edmundsbury and Ipswich Bach Choir, with a girls' choir from the Silver Jubilee Secondary Modern School, and the Alexander Orchestra, conducted by Percy Hallam. In addition to *Saint Nicolas*, Pears also sang two arias from *Messiah* and the *Benedictus* from Bach's B minor Mass.

6 Lesley Bedford (as Clorinda) had joined Pears (Testo) and Maurice Bevan (Tancredi), with members of the London Harpsichord Ensemble, in a performance of Monteverdi's *Il combattimento di Tancredi e Clorinda* at the Friends House, Euston Road, London, on 14 November 1950. This EOG-promoted concert also included music by Schütz and Bach, and the first performances of Robin Orr's *Four Romantic Songs* for tenor, oboe and string quartet, and Grace Williams's arrangements of *Three Traditional Welsh Ballads* for tenor, flute, oboe and string quartet. Britten wrote to Mary Behrend on 26 November, 'I am so glad that you enjoyed the Monteverdi as much as I did. It is a great masterpiece & I do feel Peter's performance was worthy of it.'

686 To Barbara Britten

4 CRABBE ST, ALDEBURGH, SUFFOLK
Nov. 26th 1950

Darling Barbara,

Please forgive this very late 'thank-you' letter – but I've had a more than usually hectic few days, with a very great amount of work done, a visit to Cambridge, a general meeting (with speech!) here, & a concert as well. Anyhow – the socks are splendid. I am wearing them now, & they feel warm & comfy, & fit beautifully. I haven't tried the sweets, but I'm sure they'll fit just as beautifully!

I am so glad the Christmas arrangements are all right. Peter's told you we must go up to Harewood [House] on 26th so that fits nicely. If you can get down before the Saturday do – the longer the better. You don't mention Helen [Hurst] – does she want to come? . . . It doesn't make any more trouble for us, so do try & persuade her to come with you!

I am so glad you are feeling better now. You have had a rotten patch. It is all a sign that you must leave London as soon as possible. Any more luck about houses? But I suppose you've been too seedy to go & have a look.

Peter's down here. He sang St Nicolas at Ipswich last night, & will again tomorrow at Bury. Nice to have him. I had a nice, if quiet, birthday; went with Beth & all the kids to Shingle Street.

Well, my dear, lots of love & thanks again.

See you soon.
BEN

687 To Eric Walter White

4 CRABBE ST, ALDEBURGH, SUFFOLK
Nov. 27th 1950

My dear Eric,

What a nice poem! I am very happy that the honey-tongued Cecilia should follow the example of so many friends & become 'angla'-phile – or perhaps 'angla-filia' is better. I am sure that there is much locally which she will enjoy, but the Ipswich performance of St Nicolas on Saturday would have made her smile rather wryly I'm afraid. But being an 'Angela' she could have seen into the warm hearts, & not be put off by the rather breathy voices of the Suffolk pickled boys.

It's a great relief that, after all, the chapter of your book[1] which is so nice & complimentary about the E.O.G. will not be obsolete. I feel very optimistic now, & I think, after his talk with you, so does Lawrie. There may have to be a curtailment of the season, but go forward I'm sure we can. Not so – our friends Sadler's Wells. I gather at least in the Billy Budd direction.² What a funny business?!! But it leaves me rather unmoved. The work is going to be written, come what may, & will be done somewhere some time. By the way, a little bird (albeit with rather grand plumage) told me that the reason Sadler's Wells was not going to do B. Budd was because it isn't (& won't be) ready. If you hear that story, please sit on it hard – because I cannot add a libel action to my chores at the moment.

Greetings to you, & thanks again,

Yours ever,

BEN

1   *The Rise of English Opera*, with an introduction by Britten. White extensively revised and expanded this book in 1983, when it was published by Faber and Faber as *A History of English Opera*.

2   See Letter 688.

688 To E. M. Forster

4 CRABBE ST, ALDEBURGH, SUFFOLK

Dec. 14th 1950

My dear Morgan,

Sorry not to have answered your note before, but I've been up to my eyes in Buddery.* It was just as well that you didn't come to the audition, but went holly-picking instead, because the boy wasn't well, & although he sang most beautifully gave a rather sick impression, which I hope isn't chronic.¹

I wasn't going to tell you about the Edinburgh–Sadler's Wells upset until something happened definitely, but as I gather it's in the Times today (<u>not</u> in the Manchester Guardian, I'm glad to say), I think I'll tell you very briefly what is up. The two august bodies, the Edinburgh Festival & Sadler's Wells Opera, can't apparently agree over money, or something, & so the Sadler's Wells have thrown it all up. Very annoying, except that I'm so involved in the work, I can't be annoyed, & the 1951 Festival takes a very dim view of the Sadler's Wells action. Anyhow we have now offered it to the Covent Garden Opera, who received the idea most enthusiastically (we are now on excellent terms – them & me) – so in spite of my original objections to the size of the house, state of company, lack of co-operation (the last two now being removed anyhow), it looks as if it will be there after all – in September 1951 or latest October.² I've had one very good talk with David Webster – & he's coming here soon to talk it over again with me. There are still to-ings & fro-ings, & will continue to be so, but I suspect this arrangement will be final.

Act II is nearly done. I've had some trouble with Novice & Billy, but got
that one solved, & want to talk my solution over with you some time.
Perhaps you'll come here early in the New Year?[3]

I see Billy a lot (the other Billy B.);[4] he's well, so's Brian,[5] but they split
after Christmas.

Love to you as always,

BEN

What's your reaction to Eric's shanty???[6]

*(sorry, I didn't realise till re-reading how awful that sounds!)

1 An audition of a singer for the role of Billy Budd – possibly the Welsh baritone Geraint Evans (1922–1992), with whose voice in mind Britten wrote
   much of the opera. In BBMCPR, p. 161, n. 22, Philip Reed notes: 'Evans prepared the part but, with refreshing honesty, was forced to admit to Britten
   that its tessitura lay too high for him and withdrew. He did, however, take
   part in the premiere, singing the role of the Sailing Master, Mr Flint.' (See
   also Sir Geraint Evans and Noel Goodwin, *Sir Geraint Evans: A Knight at
   the Opera*, pp. 56–7.) The role of Billy was to be created by the American
   baritone Theodor ('Ted') Uppman. For an account of Uppman's involvement, see Gary Schmidgall, 'The Natural: Theodor Uppman *is* Billy Budd',
   Opera News, 56/14 (28 March 1992), pp. 13–16. See also BBMCPR, p. 55.

2 Forster wrote to Britten on 16 December 1950: 'What a do you are having
   with the opera houses. I am a little nervous of Covent Garden, because of the
   delicacy of the monologues, but am glad it is likely to be done in London.'

3 Forster visited Britten in Aldeburgh 26–31 January, with Crozier joining
   them from the 28th until the 30th.

4 Billy Burrell (1925–1999), an Aldeburgh fisherman and friend of Britten
   from 1947 when the composer moved into Crag House, facing the North
   Sea. Britten took Burrell to see *Billy Budd* at Covent Garden and gave him
   an inscribed vocal score (now at BPL). Forster was also friendly with
   Burrell, and often stayed with him and his wife Barbara at their home in
   Aldeburgh. See also HCBB, pp. 285–6; Paul Heiney, 'Old Salts: Aldeburgh
   Fishermen', *Country Living*, 15 (March 1987), pp. 134–9, and the obituary by
   Brad Jones in the *East Anglian Daily Times* (25 June 1999).

5 Unidentified; probably a fellow fisherman working with Burrell temporarily.

6 A reference to the text of the shanties sung by the crew of the *Indomitable*
   in Act II (four-act version) of *Billy Budd*. The difficulty of devising a suitable text had been troubling the librettists as early as March 1949 when
   Forster had invited William Plomer to contribute a 'bawdy shanty', and a
   contribution from the writer and librettist Paul Dehn survives among the
   libretto drafts at BPL. In early December 1950 Forster told Britten (in an

undated letter), 'I carry the shanty-rhythms about in my pocket book. Nothing has hatched so far.'

Forster tactfully responded to Crozier's attempt, entitled 'Black Belinda', on 14 December 1950:

Your homework fills me with envy and admiration. I have done *nothing at all*, and how you managed to start & sustain the required rhythm, I cannot think. I hoped I might hear from Ben about it – perhaps you have. I like the general lay out of boarding a girl very much, but am less content with some of the details. (The verse I least like is no. 5.)

Could the girl be Moll (Mollie) Bristol (o' Bristol) do you think, with appropriate and less violent epithets attached to her? Could the man be 'Tom Bowling' instead of 'John Thomas'? – who moves towards the wrong realism, I think, and is not in use before 1840, the Dictionary of Slang informs me. When we have heard from Ben, we must meet and discuss – make him do it himself if we can't please him: I thought his Doldrums example full of appropriate fantasy.

To the composer, Forster was disarmingly frank in his criticisms (letter of 16 December):

Black Belinda is lamentable in my judgement. I have written to Eric as unawkwardly as I could, and hinted it wouldn't do as it was, and that it must either be done anew or be altered, and that we must await, my poor Ben, your decision between these two courses. If you decide on alterations only, I have made some preliminary suggestions to Eric: 'Black Belinda' to be changed to Moll/Molly/Moll o' Bristol, with adjectives appropriate to a pleasant quayside lass, and 'John Thomas' to be changed (and how much!) to Tom Bowling. A shanty about a girl is reasonable, but not when it is spattered with large cold dead smuts. Cannot you – perhaps with Peter's help – run up some fantasy words as an alternative? Your example of We all went to the Doldrums / And saw a big fish in the sky was perfect.

Anyhow let us know whether we, or rather Eric, should scrap or should alter.

The shanties were finally written by Kenneth Harrison (see Letter 704 and BBMCPR, pp. 64–5).

689 To Dorothy Elmhirst

As from Aldeburgh
HAREWOOD HOUSE, LEEDS
[between 27 and 31 December 1950]

My dear Dorothy,

I have just spoken to our General Manager, Basil Douglas, on the telephone, & he has told me the glorious news of your Trustees' decision – how you will be able to help us so magnificently towards our Dido production.[1] I find it impossible to find the right words to say 'thank you' for this enormous generosity; but I'm sure you realise the gratitude we all, everyone concerned, feel towards you, and the Trustees. I only hope that when you see the production you will feel glad that you helped so much to make it possible! I am happy about the plans for it – Joan Cross has exciting ideas for the production, & I think will have a first-rate cast. The first performance will, we hope, take place on May 1st at the Lyric, Hammersmith. Will you please make a note of that in your diary?

I am having a few days holiday up North here – combining it with the christening of my newest godchild[2] – but I return to Aldeburgh & 'Billy Budd' on New Year's Day.

Wishing you & Leonard every good wish & good health for the New Year, & in infinite gratitude,

Yours ever,
BEN

1 The financial crisis at the EOG following the involvement of General Manager Henry Foy, a crisis that, judging by Letters 684 and 687, was a genuine threat to the company's continuation. The Elmhirsts were approached by EOG Chairman James Lawrie for financial assistance for the planned new production of *Dido and Aeneas*, in support of which Britten had lunched with Dorothy Elmhirst earlier in December. On 20 December, the composer had written to Mrs Elmhirst:

> I will happily give you any more details if you want them, & I know he [Lawrie] would answer any questions that might be troubling you or them. As I said I don't want to bother you, especially as a letter from the Trustees may be at this moment in the post, held up by the Christmas rush – but if we <u>are</u> going to do Dido it will be necessary to get in touch immediately with the artists, designers and all. Anyhow whatever happens, thank you so much, dear Dorothy, for listening so sympathetically to my troubles, & for a very nice lunch indeed.

2 The christening of David Lascelles, which took place on 27 December. Britten reported to Lesley Bedford on 31 December: 'My godchild is very sweet & was christened in great style. Marion is adorable with him – an excellent mother.'

690 To Peter Pears

4 CRABBE ST, ALDEBURGH, SUFFOLK
Jan. 5th 1951

My darling,

Just a scribble to send my love & to tell you all my thoughts will be with you this evening (Sat.).[1] How lovely that you are excited by it all, & even, in a way, looking forward to it. I'm so glad also that Kleiber[2] turns out to be so sympathetic & good. I hope this will be only the first of many shows you do together.

Nancy & Eric are coming over for lunch & I shall do a bit of work on the great Battle scene[3] with him. It needs greatly tidying up. I've started Act III & am quite excited by it. It's nice to be rid (temporarily) of Act II about which I'd got quite a thing.

The wallpaper is arrived, & looks <u>awfully</u> nice! I'm very pleased with it – it's nice & nursery for me! Thank you so very much for coping with it all. I'm sorry to have been such a bore about it, only the men were rather marking time and I've got a bit bored with having them around, nice as they are.

I'll meet you in Ipswich on Sunday – can't say how I'm looking forward to that. If you could get Erwin or Sophie to ring me on Sunday morning (you won't have time to bother about trains before) saying <u>when</u> you are arriving in Ipswich – please?

Well, sweetheart; enjoy yourself, think of Mozart, & that incredible music. It's so nice to think of you happy in a performance of this kind.

All my love, as ever,

B.

1 Pears was appearing as Tamino in a production of Mozart's *Die Zauberflöte* at Covent Garden, conducted by Erich Kleiber. It was a role the tenor had previously sung at Sadler's Wells in the 1940s. The anonymous critic of *The Times* wrote in his notice of the performance (8 January 1951):

> Mr Peter Pears's voice is hardly one of Covent Garden proportions, but the fluency of his tone and, above all, the countless small nuances in his phrasing provided some of the chief delights of the evening. His make-up, it should be noted, was anything but delightful.

Britten was to write to Pears on 28 January: 'I hear your M. Flute was better than ever on Friday. I'm so glad', and again, on 20 February, 'So very happy that last night was so good; a lovely way to end your first Cov. Garden season.'

2 Erich Kleiber (1890–1956), Austrian conductor, who in his teens attended performances at the Vienna Court Opera during the last years of Mahler's tenure as Director. After holding posts at opera houses in Prague, Wuppertal and Düsseldorf, Kleiber was appointed Generalmusikdirektor of the Berlin Staatsoper in 1923, where among other repertory he conducted Janáček's *Jenůfa* (in 1924), the premiere of Berg's *Wozzeck* (1925) and Milhaud's *Christophe Colombe* (1930). He resigned from his Berlin post in December 1934 after conducting the premiere of Berg's *Lulu* Suite, as he was unwilling to sacrifice his integrity to the oppressive cultural policies of the Nazi regime. Kleiber was not to return to Berlin until 1951. Between 1937 and 1949 he was resident in Buenos Aires, where he was in charge of the Teatro Colón. After the war, he revived his European career, appearing at Covent Garden regularly between 1950 and 1953 where he played a key role in the company's development. Perhaps his most memorable Covent Garden appearance was conducting the UK stage premiere of *Wozzeck* in 1952, which, according to David Webster, 'inspired Berg's publishers to cable some Viennese authorities to come to Covent Garden to see how the

work should be done'. See Webster, 'Kleiber: An Appreciation', *Tempo*, 39 (spring 1956), pp. 5–6.

3   Act III, scene 1 (four-act version); Act II, scene 1 (two-act version). Forster had to be persuaded by Britten and Crozier to include Billy in this scene, a point he conceded in an undated letter written later in January. As Forster noted, Billy 'could be nicely seen fighting for his country instead of fighting his countryman, and could be grouped with other characters one likes – Dansker, Donald'.

691   To Robert Britten

4 CRABBE ST, ALDEBURGH, SUFFOLK

Jan. 11th 1951

Dear Robert,

Thank you for your nice letter. I was delighted that the family enjoyed the opera[1] – it was nice to see them all there. Alan[2] was a very gay companion & made a great hit with my friends whom he met.

I met last evening a master from Radley[3] who is producing a play about the Spithead Mutiny[4] next term – & he asked me down to see it. But, alas, I shall be abroad, so can't. He spoke warmly about Alan – a nice man, called Christopher Ellis.

If I can find a suitable envelope I'll include the long overdue tie – I hope it's schoolmastery & grand enough – if not, give it away!

Please thank the family for the scrumtious (spelling??) chocolates. They continue to delight us & the innumerable guests here!

Love to you all –

BEN

Best wishes for your birthday in case I forget!

1   *Let's Make an Opera*, performed by the EOG at the Lyric, Hammersmith.

2   Britten's nephew (b. 1938), Robert Britten's younger son.

3   Radley College, the public school in Abingdon, Oxfordshire.

4   Melville set his fictional *Billy Budd* in the same year – 1797 – as the Spithead Mutiny of 15 April and the Nore Mutiny of 20 May, and both are mentioned in Britten's opera in the scene in Vere's cabin:

> FIRST LIEUTENANT: Oh, the Nore! The shame of it! I remember. I served there, those days are clear in my mind. I saw the disgrace and the sorrow. I saw wickedness and its merited punishment. O God preserve us from the Nore!
> SAILING MASTER: The Nore!
> FIRST LIEUTENANT AND SAILING MASTER: The floating republic!

VERE: Ay, at Spithead the men may have had their grievances, but the Nore – what had we there? Revolution, sedition, the Jacobins, the infamous spirit of France [...] That was the Nore. Ay, we must be vigilant. We must be on our guard.

See also BBMCPR, p. 17.

692 To George and Marion Harewood

4 CRABBE ST, ALDEBURGH, SUFFOLK

Jan 13th 1951

My dearest George & Marion,

The very grand invitation for next Thursday has just arrived, & of course I'll come, thank you very much! But this letter isn't really to accept, because I think you knew that already, but to thank you both, more than I can say, for giving this party for us, for going to all that trouble & expense.[1] It is the most wonderful thing you could do for the E.O.G. Now that the financial situation is sound again, the main thing to be repaired is the lack of good will, which had come about because of the recent mess; & your party will be the most wonderful antidote to that. You are really angels.

I hope you've escaped the 'flu germ. It has hovered over & around me all this week, & I've had to spend a day or so in bed; but Billy B. hasn't suffered, & is slowly (but I think soundly) getting on.

Thank you also for the lovely holiday in Harewood. I enjoyed it enormously. And for the wine, which is really delicious. And now I think I've done saying thank you – & send lots of love to all three.

BEN

1 Britten's diary has the entry 'Harewood party' for 18 January. The same day also has two other entries: '[EOG] Executive meeting' and 'PP Persephone [by Stravinsky] 6.50'.

693 To Sir Howard Roberts

Clerk to the London County Council

[*Typed*]

4 CRABBE STREET, ALDEBURGH, SUFFOLK

31st January, 1951

Dear Sir Howard,

When I lunched with you in March of last year, you were so good as to suggest that I should become associated in an advisory capacity with the Festival Hall Sub-Committee of the London County Council. I was happy to accept your invitation and honoured that you should think I might be useful. My acceptance, along with the acceptances of Sir George Dyson[1] and Dr Vaughan Williams, was made public in the press soon after.

For about three months we were in constant touch over several matters relating to the Concert Hall. I was only able to attend one of your meetings, the one that dealt with the all-important decision to proceed with Mr Ralph Downes' specification for the new organ, but I did on several occasions write my opinions very fully to you.

Since that June (if I remember rightly) up to now, I have heard nothing either from yourself or from anyone connected with the Sub-Committee. I have, however, much to my surprise been shown by a friend a printed prospectus of concerts,[2] [*handwritten insertion:* to take place next May at the Festival Hall] sponsored I believe by the London County Council. I have heard nothing whatsoever from you on the details of these concerts. I regret to say that I do not approve of them and I cannot allow the public to connect my name with them.[3] Nor can I approve of the decision to discontinue the grant to the London Philharmonic Orchestra.

Under these circumstances, I desire to resign all connections whatsoever with your Sub-Committee and should be grateful if you could communicate this decision to them without delay.

I may have got some of the above details wrong but, having heard nothing, I am not in a position to be accurate.

Yours sincerely,

1 English composer (1883–1964), Director of the Royal College of Music 1938–52.

2 The series of inaugural concerts at the Festival Hall was conducted by Beecham, Boult and Sargent, none of whom Britten much admired.

3 Britten's resignation was accepted. Vaughan Williams and Dyson also resigned but for a different reason: they disagreed with the LCC's decision to adhere to the specification for the organ, designed by Ralph Downes, a decision that Britten had fully supported; see Letter 606.

694 To Elizabeth Mayer

4 CRABBE ST, ALDEBURGH, SUFFOLK
February 2nd 1951

My darling Elizabeth,

At last, at last, I sit me down to write to you. I <u>am</u> sorry to have been so lazy about writing, & as usual have no excuse except that I have at the moment got a secretary & so get all my letters off <u>that way</u>, which leaves me no time to write letters by hand, which is the only way I want to write to you . . .

There is so much to say, to thank you & dear William for, that I really don't know where to start. Your parcels have been a joy. The lovely Birthday one, filled with excitements & surprises – we are even now eating the sweets still; you were a darling to put so much thought into making it up, & so generous too. And then the <u>ham</u> which has just arrived. That is going to be wonderfully useful. Meat, as you probably have read, is almost non-existent with us now, & so a present like this is a real treat. But you <u>mustn't</u> send any more now, I know how difficult life is for you too, & you must deny yourself your sweet generosity! Miss Hudson was thrilled to bits with her bag. I don't know if she is too shy to write herself (there is an unwritten law in Suffolk about not saying 'thank you' for presents – a smile, & 'I don't mind it at all' is the most one dare hope for!) but I can tell you she was touched tremendously that you remembered her, & so sweetly. You are an angel, my dear Elizabeth.

Your visit here is still talked about – by so many in Aldeburgh of course, & Beth & your godchild,[1] by George & Marion, & of course the Steins! I'm sorry you were just too soon to meet my new godchild – who is a dear, but a little young yet! We all trooped up to Harewood for the Christening, all rather formal; but after it I stayed on there for a nice holiday over the New Year – most comfortable & sweet people.

The rest of the news – well for me this season, no concerts, just working hard on Billy Budd. We've had a great financial crisis in the Opera Group – a hopelessly incompetent manager who lost us a mint of money – & that all had to be coped with; but luckily we are now straight, with an excellent new one – guess who! Basil Douglas has left the BBC & come to work for us! He is excellent, efficient, serious, & honest. We once didn't get on well, but now that is all over, & we all love working with him. Our plans for this year go well – London in May: Aldeburgh, Holland, & Wiesbaden in June; Cheltenham, Liverpool in July; Scandinavia in the autumn;[2] – any possible hope of you and William catching up any of these dates?

As I said, no concerts for me this year, so Peter is solitary – travelling a lot (he has rung up, five minutes ago, from Sheffield!)[3] but manages to get down here fairly often. He's been in Holland & Germany, & soon off to Switzerland, Holland again and Austria (where I will join him). His main job has been Magic Flute in the Covent Garden opera house – a lovely performance, beautifully sung & understood. He has liked working there too – with Kleiber, who's good. I think it's done him a lot of good – given him back confidence – & people have loved him too. Billy Budd is going to be there after all – Edinburgh Festival fell through – some intrigue I didn't quite follow – but it's probably a good thing. Who will conduct or sing I don't know, but Frederick Ashton will produce,[4] & John Piper design. Probably November.[5] It's going well, I think – terribly hard & often depressing work. The subject's so big, & the problems of setting something almost entirely in prose (so <u>many</u> naval commands!!) are often teasing. But I think it'll be all right. Erwin & Peter are so far pleased. Morgan hasn't been over-well, & there has been some anxiety in his mind lest he should die before it's finished – there was a patch in the summer when he resented any moment I spent away from work. But he's better now, & I think happy about it. He hasn't been living here, but often comes for short periods. (He only left two days ago actually.)

Have you been well – all of you? Beata & her two little ones, as well? We've had this 'flu epidemic – not serious, but a bore, & held up work. Peter & I have both escaped although it's been all round us – but poor Beth, & all the family, & all the Cranbrooks too, have had nasty times.

The house is the same – some nice new pictures – the sea is a little nearer, actually sounding <u>very</u> near tonight, as there is an East wind! The house is cold, as we are economising madly over fuel; but we keep warm, if not too clean, since baths are rather rare! It is lovely to think you know it, & know where I am writing, at my desk in my study, after a terrific day's work – which is why my writing's so bad as my hand's a bit tired, & my brain none too clear!

I hope you weren't too upset about the failure of 'Let's Make' in New York. It was inevitable, just as its impact in Europe is also inevitable. I don't say this out of conceit or that anyone's right or wrong. It is just that audiences are in different stages of development. It embarrasses U.S.A. audiences to be simple, just as it's a relief for European. I only hope you didn't go. William did, & wrote very sweetly about it. Please thank him, & for all his nice little notes, & tell him all our news. I know he understands how difficult letter-writing is. This comes with love from all your friends here, to all of you dear ones,

especially from
your devoted
BEN

1 Sally, Beth's second child.

2 The EOG was to give a season in May at the Lyric Theatre, Hammersmith (Monteverdi: *Il combattimento di Tancredi e Clorinda*; Purcell: *Dido and Aeneas*; *Albert Herring*; *Let's Make an Opera*; *The Rape of Lucretia*); two performances of *Lucretia* at Wiesbaden (31 May and 1 June); *Let's Make an Opera* at Lowestoft and the Monteverdi–Purcell double bill and *Herring* at the Aldeburgh Festival in June, with further performances of the double bill in the Netherlands later that month; in July the company repeated the

Monteverdi–Purcell double bill at the Cheltenham Festival, with Brian
Easdale's *The Sleeping Children* and Holst's *The Wandering Scholar*. This
repertory was performed in Liverpool in July and August, as well as further
performances of *Herring* and *Let's Make an Opera*. The proposed visit to
Scandinavia was cancelled.

3 On 2 February Pears had performed Britten's *Serenade* with Dennis Brain
   (horn) and the Hallé Orchestra, conducted by Paul Kletzki.

4 Ashton did not direct the premiere of *Budd*; this task fell to Basil Coleman.

5 The premiere was eventually to take place at the Royal Opera House,
   Covent Garden, on 1 December 1951, but an entry in Britten's pocket diary
   for 22 November (the composer's thirty-eighth birthday) – 'Budd?' – confirms what Britten was telling Mrs Mayer in this letter.

695 To Douglas Cleverdon[1]
BBC
[*Typed*]

4 Crabbe Street, Aldeburgh
9th February, 1951

Dear Mr Cleverdon,

   Mr Meyerstein[2] has sent me a copy of your letter to him about
Chatterton's "The Revenge".[3] I am very pleased that you should want me
to do the music for this and had I been less occupied with my new opera,
I should have been delighted to have done it; but the time factor makes it
out of the question. Please realise how disappointed I am about this
because it is something I would much liked to have done.

Yours sincerely,
BENJAMIN BRITTEN

1 English publisher and radio producer (1903–1987), who for over twenty-
   five years was a BBC Radio features producer, principally with the Third
   Programme. Cleverdon produced the work of some of the most distinguished authors of the day working in radio, including Henry Reed, Ted
   Hughes, Stevie Smith and Dylan Thomas, whose *Under Milk Wood* Cleverdon produced in January 1954, just over two months after Thomas's death.
       Cleverdon was the producer responsible for Henry Reed's witty play *The
   Private Life of Hilda Tablet*, first broadcast in the Third Programme in
   May 1954, and its successors about the fictitious composer and her singer
   companion Elsa Strauss. While Reed modelled Tablet on two female composers, Dame Ethel Smyth and Elisabeth Lutyens (the latter considered
   suing Reed), at a superficial level it was intended as a mildly satirical parody
   of the composer–singer partnership of Britten and Pears. For example,

Tablet's all-female opera *Emily Butter* (music by Donald Swann, Tablet's alter ego), set in a department store, was clearly meant as a dig at *Billy Budd* (all-male cast), and even included a character, played by Anna Pollak, called Clara Taggart (the name derives from the master-at-arms, John Claggart, in Britten's opera). According to Humphrey Carpenter, Reed originally wanted to make the source of his spoof even more transparent by calling it *Milly Mudd*. See Carpenter, *The Envy of the World: Fifty Years of the BBC Third Programme and Radio 3, 1946–1996*, pp. 138–9, 145 and 147.

2   Edward Harry William Meyerstein (1889–1952), poet, novelist, biographer and writer on music (he was, for example, a contributor to *Music Survey*, edited by Donald Mitchell and Hans Keller). Meyerstein had edited collections of Chatterton's writings and published a biography (1930) of the eighteenth-century writer. Britten wrote to him on 9 February 1951: 'I must reluctantly send your copy of Chatterton [i.e. *The Revenge*] back and once again say how grateful I am for your having drawn my attention to it. I shall, incidentally, continue my search for your Life of him.'

Among Meyerstein's youthful friends were Donald Mitchell – Meyerstein's letters and postcards to him (about two hundred in number) are lodged in the archive of Hull University – the historian Lionel Butler, and John Wain, who was to achieve fame with his first novel, *Hurry On Down* (1953), one of the first manifestations of the writings of the loosely connected group of novelists and playwrights who came to be known as 'Angry Young Men'. (The phrase was coined by a press officer at the Royal Court Theatre in London describing the character of Jimmy Porter in John Osborne's *Look Back in Anger* (1956).) Wain was to become Professor of Poetry at Oxford University (1973–78) and contributed a lengthy article marking the tenth anniversary of Meyerstein's death to *Encounter*, 'Meyerstein: An Oxford Memoir', 107 (August 1962), pp. 27–42.

3   Thomas Chatterton, *The Revenge: a burletta* (1770).

696 To E. M. Forster
[*Incomplete*]

4 CRABBE ST, ALDEBURGH, SUFFOLK
Feb. 11th 1951

Dearest Morgan,

Only a scribble in the middle of an intense bit of work – very happy, I mean harpaparpy,[1] with your letter & with Kenneth's shanties.[2] Most promisingly mad – I think we've got the basis of something good there. The rhythm is fine (with the exception of 'On a halter at Malta'). But we must be careful <u>not</u> to have important points in the last line because they get lost occasionally.

Tune, fitted to Kenneth's 1st shanty:

1 An example of the schoolboy word game Roger Duncan recalls in JBBC:

He played this game of a special language which was putting 'arp' before every vowel, so, for example, 'I want to play tennis' is 'Arpi warpant tarpo plarpay tarpennarpis', and we would hold long conversations in the car in this language.

2 A reference to the second of the shanties, 'We're off to Samoa', sung below decks by the crew of the *Indomitable* (four-act version: Act II scene 2; two-act version: Act I scene 3), the original text of which was written by Kenneth Harrison. See also BBMCPR, plates 5a and 5b, pp. 67–8, for a facsimile of Harrison's text, annotated by Britten. Forster, who had been carrying around the rhythmic outline of this shanty in his pocket book since December 1950, had enlisted Harrison's assistance when both he and Crozier had failed to produce a convincing text.

697 To Eric Crozier
[*Postcard: Slaughden Quay, Aldeburgh*]

[Postmarked 12 February 1951, Aldeburgh]

So glad about the test – congratulations![1] Was it very beastly? Just off to
London for a few days.[2] I'll get in touch with you when I'm back. Billy's
been going quite well – finished Act III sc. I & am now launching into
sc. II! Afraid the Interlude[3] can't be more than 2½ minutes, which will
mean a problem for John P. [Piper] scenically, I'm sure.
    Love to Nancy if she's with you still.

BEN

1 No further information about Crozier's 'test' has come to light.

2 On 13 February Pears and Britten gave a performance of Schubert's *Die
   schöne Müllerin* at the Friends House, Euston Road.

3 The orchestral postlude to Act III scene 1 (two-act version: Act II scene 1,
   figs. 50–57), a passage built out of the chromatic 'mist' motif heard in the
   preceding battle scene.

698 To Imogen Holst

4 CRABBE ST, ALDEBURGH, SUFFOLK
Feb 12th 1951

My dear Imogen,
    I don't know if you're back from India yet – if you're not home then
this can wait & welcome you back! Anyhow, I hope it was all the greatest
success, & that you come home treasuring many lovely & valuable experiences.[1] I long to hear all about it, & am madly jealous of Peter that he's
going to see you so soon & will have your first-hand account.
    I meant all the time to send you a note out there, but life has been end-
lessly complicated, & somehow letters to go abroad need even more effort
than letters for home: one can't just sit down & scribble 'hullo' if they're
to go so many hundreds of miles. Yet another of your wildly generous
presents has given Peter & me so much pleasure, & not a little sense of
guilt in depriving you of one more treasure. The Purcell are wonderful to
have, but like the Schütz[2] they will only be regarded as 'shared'; for you to
have & to use exactly when you want. In the meantime they are happily
on our shelves, & being delved into at odd moments with fascination. I
haven't yet decided on a dance for 'Dido',[3] but when I get nearer to a decision I'll write to you, or even better, hope to see you & discuss it together.
    The other, & even greater, delight was the arrival of your book on your

father's music.⁴ You cannot imagine, my dear Imogen, what deep pleasure
that has given me. The dedication, your touching letter, & the joy of having
it all the time around & reading & re-reading it. It is so good. So wise, &
just, & so deeply sympathetic. I feel he himself (from my knowledge of
him which comes through you, his music, & one ride on a 31 bus with
him when I was a boy) would have loved it & agreed with it. What is most
remarkable, & perhaps most valuable, about it, is that it sends one straight
back to the music itself. How unlike most critical surveys! It is because of
the love (which our dear Morgan Forster so truly says is the only critical
approach) which shines through every page. I do thank you dearly for it,
& congratulate you on it.

By the way, we are at last doing the Wandering Scholar⁵ this year, first
performance early July in Cheltenham Festival. That's going to be a great
thrill, & I look forward to discussing casting etc. with you. Most unfortunately the rehearsal period comes during our performing period of Dido
in Holland, so we shan't be able to take part ourselves, but we'll do it as
well as we possibly can. Peter'll talk to you about this.

Budd goes on apace – Act III Sc. I is now completely sketched – but I
have had agonies over it. Every bar is written with depression & insecurity
looking over my shoulders – but somehow I believe it's coming out well.
It's a terrific job.

This comes with all my love, repeated & sincere thanks again for all
you've given us spiritually & practically too, & hoping to see you very soon.

With love,

BEN

1 From December 1950 to January 1951 Imogen Holst was resident at Santiniketan University, India, as a 'student-teacher', learning about Indian
   music and teaching Indian students Western music. See Jack Dobbs,
   'Imogen as "Student-Teacher" in India', in Peter Cox and Jack Dobbs (eds.),
   Imogen Holst at Dartington, pp. 71–3. Her continued enthusiasm for Indian
   music was subsequently occasionally reflected in Aldeburgh Festival programming. She described her experiences at Santiniketan in 'Indian Music',
   her contribution to TBB, pp. 104–10.

2 See Letter 668 n. 1. Imogen Holst had supplemented Britten's own collection of the Purcell Society's edition with a number of volumes, including
   volume III, *Dido and Aeneas*, which had formerly belonged to her father.

3 Britten and Imogen Holst were collaborating on an edition of Purcell's
   Dido and Aeneas, the most singular feature of which, apart from Britten's
   realization of the harpsichord continuo, was the solution they found to the
   problem of the missing music from the closing scene of Act II, the text of
   which survives in the first printed libretto. Britten and Holst made three

interpolations from other works by Purcell: a trio (from *The Indian Queen*) – 'Then since our charms have sped'; a chorus (from *Birthday Song for King James, 1687*) – 'A dance that shall make the spheres to wonder'; and a dance (from the Overture to *Sir Anthony Love*), which, as the present letter indicates, Britten was yet to choose.

In a statement (dated 4 April 1951), Britten argued his reasons for 'completing' the second act:

Anyone who has taken part in, or indeed heard a concert or stage performance, must have been struck by the very peculiar and most unsatisfactory end of this Act II as it stands; Aeneas sings his very beautiful recitative in A minor and disappears without any curtain music or chorus (which occurs in all the other acts). The drama cries out for some strong dramatic music, and the whole key scheme of the opera (very carefully adhered to in each of the other scenes) demands a return to the key of the beginning of the act or its relative major (D minor or F major). What is more, the contemporary printed libretto [. . .] has perfectly clear indications for a scene with the Sorceress and her Enchantresses, consisting of six lines of verse, and a dance to end the act. It is my considered opinion that music was certainly composed to this scene and has been lost. It is quite possible that it will be found, but each year makes it less likely. [Cited by Eric Walter White in his essay 'New Light on *Dido and Aeneas*', p. 25; Purcell's music has yet to be found.]

Britten's statement must have taken the form of a press release from the English Opera Group, for excerpts of its text appeared in a brief report, under the title '*Dido and Aeneas*: Mr Benjamin Britten's Alterations', in *The Times* (27 April 1951), p. 8. In response to this report, composer Geoffrey Bush wrote to the paper (3 May 1951, p. 5) taking issue with Britten's conclusions concerning Purcell's intentions for the close of Act II of *Dido*:

What is not clear (and what Mr Britten does not explain) is how this one short musical section came to be lost when all the rest was carefully preserved. The most probable explanation is that it was deliberately destroyed by the composer himself. When the opera came to actual performance he must have found that Aeneas's solitary and heartbreaking recitatives made a far more effective ending to the act than the conventional witches' chorus previously planned, and the resulting excision was an undoubted stroke of genius. As for Nahum Tate, he seems to have anticipated Sheridan's Mr Puff: 'To cut out this scene! – but I'll print it – Egad, I'll print it every word.'

Britten responded with a letter of his own to *The Times* (8 May 1951), p. 8; reprinted in PKBM, pp. 106–7:

In his letter of May 3 Dr Geoffrey Bush states that Purcell's music to *Dido and Aeneas* has been 'carefully preserved'. That is not quite the case. The only surviving manuscript of the music seems to be one written by John Travers 25 years after the death of Purcell and 40 years after the only contemporary performance of the work. Travers was not born at the time of this performance, and judging by obvious copying errors in the manuscript he cannot have been very familiar with the work, and it can never have been used for performance. The source for Dr W. H. Cummings's Purcell Society edition was written 'probably in Purcell's time' (Dr

Cummings's words). This came to light in the 1880s and has since disappeared (according to Professor E. J. Dent). It differs widely from the above Travers manuscript which is preserved in the library of St Michael's College, Tenbury. There was apparently yet another manuscript consulted by [Sir George] Macfarren for his edition of the work for the Musical Antiquarian Society in 1841, which again differs from the above version, actually being considerably shorter. It seems that there is no trace of this manuscript today. 'Carefully preserved' is, therefore, a scarcely accurate phrase to use.

The musical scheme of *Dido and Aeneas* is remarkable: each scene is a complete unit containing many numbers in closely related keys following each other without pause, and ending in the same tonality or its relative major or minor as it started in (very much like his own verse-anthems and sonatas in fact). That Purcell, as Dr Bush suggests, should suddenly at the last moment abandon this plan for one of the scenes seems to me inconceivable. For one thing, it is completely foreign to the aesthetic attitude of the time. For another, it suggests that he rated the part played by tonality in form as low as many composers do today. No, I am afraid that I accept the verdict of the one piece of contemporary evidence we have – the libretto – and judge that the work still remains, alas, incomplete. Until such a happy event as the discovery of the missing numbers occurs, I believe it is better to restore the original symmetry of the work with Purcellian material than to leave this wonderful musical building with a large hole in it.

For further discussion of Britten's and Holst's edition of *Dido*, see George Malcolm's contribution to DMHK, '*Dido and Aeneas*', pp. 186–97, in particular pp. 189–90; Imogen Holst's liner note to the 1978 Decca recording of the Britten–Holst edition of the opera (SET 615), and Eric Roseberry, 'The Purcell Realizations', in CPBC, pp. 360–66.

The EOG gave the first performance of Britten's and Holst's edition of *Dido and Aeneas* in a double bill with Monteverdi's *Il combattimento di Tancredi e Clorinda* on 1 May 1951 at the Lyric, Hammersmith (see Letter 694 n. 2). *The Times* reviewed *Dido* on 2 May 1951:

The English Opera Group opened its London summer season at the Lyric Theatre, Hammersmith, last night with Benjamin Britten's edition of Purcell's *Dido and Aeneas*, preceded by Monteverdi's *Combattimento di Tancredi e Clorinda*, with Mr Britten himself at the conductor's desk.

The innovation which he has made in rounding off the second act with a chorus and a curtain tune proved not to be artistically controversial, however the argument may go about Purcell's original intentions, second thoughts or sheer losses in the gulf of time. Mr Britten has chosen appropriate music from other sources in Purcell, and has made the opera more symmetrical thereby.

He chose tempi slower than is usual in most of the performances one hears, which are usually by amateurs. Miss Joan Cross, responsible for the stage production, took her cue from this slower speed and from the stylized Restoration costumes of Miss Sophie Federovitch to provide the chorus and principals with restrained movements and attitudes. Of the elegant formality thus engendered the only ill effect was that occasionally the actual singing became mannered to match, and so robbed Purcell of that 'energy of English words' of which Playford spoke in posthumous praise of him.

THURSDAY, MAY 3rd

THE ENGLISH OPERA GROUP

PRESENTS

COMBATTIMENTO DI TANCREDI E CLORINDA

Music by CLAUDIO MONTEVERDI

Words by Torquato Tasso, translated by Peter Pears

Choreography by WALTER GORE

Scenery & Costumes designed by JOHN PIPER

Narrator:	PETER PEARS
Tancredi:	sung by MAX WORTHLEY
	danced by TUTTE LEMKOW
Clorinda:	sung by VIVETTE HENDRIKS
	danced by SARA LUZITA

Conductor:—BENJAMIN BRITTEN

INTERVAL (15 minutes)

Combattimento di Tancredi e Clorinda.

Il Combattimento di Tancredi e Clorinda is a setting of some stanzas from Tasso's huge epic of the Crusade, Jerusalemme Liberata. Tancredi, a Christian Knight, has fallen in love with Clorinda, a Saracen maiden. She is a brave and skilful warrior, and, dressed in man's armour, has assaulted and burnt, with one companion, a Christian fortification. As she is returning from this victory she is seen and pursued by Tancredi. He thinks her a man and challenges her to mortal combat.

They prepare to fight, and the Narrator invoke the aid of Night in his description of the story. The fight begins, and grows furious. The combatants pause, and Tancredi begs to know the name and rank of his foe. She answers scornfully, and in the continuing battle he kills her. She, in her last words, begs for baptism, and as he baptises her, and as he does so recognises her as his beloved Clorinda. But it is too late, and she dies, confident of salvation in Christ.

In his introduction to this work, published in Venice in 1638, Monteverdi describes the first performance, twelve years earlier, in the Palazzo of Signore Girolamo Mocenigo, his "particular Signor," during Carnival. After some Madrigals had been sung, Clorinda, his introduction (Clorinda armed, on foot, appeared, followed by Tancredi, armed and on a Cavallo Mariano, and then the Text began his song. Clorinda and Tancredi acted the story in the way demanded by the words, observing diligently all the details of expression (as also did the instrumentalists), keeping exactly in time with the words and music. They must sing their parts when the moment comes, and the Text is instructed to sing clearly and firmly and to articulate well. He must not decorate the music except in the Stanza to Night; the rest he must narrate a semimindine delle passion del'orator. At the end, says Monteverdi, the audience was moved to tears and applause at this new sort of entertainment.

FOLLOWED BY

DIDO AND AENEAS

An opera in Three Acts by HENRY PURCELL

In a new realisation by BENJAMIN BRITTEN

Produced by JOAN CROSS. Scenery and Costumes designed by SOPHIE FEDOROVITCH

The English Opera Group gratefully acknowledges the co-operation of WILLIAM CHAPPELL with the dances and PETER BROOK with the lighting.

Belinda	PAMELA WOOLMORE
Dido	NANCY EVANS
Aeneas	BRUCE BOYCE
Sorceress	FLORA NIELSEN
First Witch	GLADYS WHITRED
Second Witch	MARY GRIMMETT
Spirit	VIVETTE HENDRIKS
Sailor	MAX WORTHLEY

Courtiers, Witches, Sailors sung by:—

CECILIA CARDOZO	TERRENCE CONOLEY
LILY KETTLEWELL	ANDREW GOLD
DOREEN ORME	JOHN HAUXWELL
ESME SANFORD	SCOTT HERBERT
PAULINE TINSLEY	GLYN JENKINS
PAMELA WOOLMORE	GEORGE NEIGHBOUR
	GEORGE PRANGNELL
	FREDERICK WESTCOTT

Conductor:—BENJAMIN BRITTEN

CARTHAGE

DIDO AND AENEAS

Act I, Scene 1—Dido's Court.

Dido is sad—she fears that her love for her royal guest Aeneas is not returned. Belinda and the court endeavour to reassure her, and Aeneas enters with his followers and declares his love. The scene ends with a triumphing chorus and dance.

Act I, Scene 2—The Witches' Cave.

The Sorceress and her Witches are plotting the downfall of Dido and Carthage, and conjure up a storm "to mar their hunting sport."

INTERVAL (12 minutes)

Act II—A Grove.

Dido and Aeneas are resting after the hunt. A storm bursts upon them and drives them back to town. Aeneas is detained by the Spirit of the Sorceress, who appears in the likeness of Mercury and commands him in the name of Jove to leave Dido and Carthage immediately. Aeneas is sad but proposes to obey, and the scene ends with the witches' triumphing chorus and dance. (Note: Here the music to this section of the libretto is missing and has been supplied from other music of Purcell.)

Pages from the programme for the performance of the EOG double bill of Monteverdi's *Il combattimento di Tancredi e Clorinda* and the Britten–Holst edition of Purcell's *Dido and Aeneas* at the Lyric, Hammersmith, on 3 May 1951

Philip Hope-Wallace, *Manchester Guardian* (3 May 1951), wrote:

Last night we heard Benjamin Britten conduct his sensitive and scholarly edition of Purcell's *Dido and Aeneas*, himself playing the continuo and extracting from the small means at his disposal the essence of this miniature masterpiece (as it here becomes). The production by Joan Cross and the setting by Sophie Fedorovitch aim, with fair success, at a stylized manner and a Renaissance–Classical mode.

Many difficulties were overcome, but the trouble with small-scale opera is that one looks for detail which one would not seek in a grand-opera production, and the effort to invent detail which will not interfere with the general outlines tends to an anxious fussiness – an effect, often, of simpering gentility. With the exception of Bruce Boyce, a regal Aeneas, much of the singing, too, sounded inhibited by the desire to sound at all costs 'musical', when paradoxically a fuller if coarser vocal line would have achieved better results. The trouble is exaggerated by the fact that the singers probably find it hard to hear so delicate an accompaniment and thus fear that they are singing out of tune – as once or twice they were. Nancy Evans looked a noble Dido, but her singing was loose and much less shapely than this lovely music requires.

Desmond Shawe-Taylor, *New Statesman and Nation* (5 May 1951), wrote:

Dido is a jolly little work, lasting an hour or so, with lilting songs, saucy choruses, poignant recitatives, and at the end one astonishing emotional climax, which lifts it clean out of the school-entertainment class: 'When I am laid in earth' and the lovely concluding choral threnody. Except for supplying, from other works of Purcell, a possibly lost ending to the second act, Britten's version differs little from what one generally hears in modern performances. Sophie Fedorovitch has supplied handsome Restoration costumes and sets, against which Joan Cross stages an effective, if occasionally awkward, production. Among the singers, Bruce Boyce, a resonant and upstanding Aeneas, carried off the honours; both Belinda (Pamela Woolmore) and Dido (Nancy Evans) were, on the first night, vocally uncomfortable and inclined to sing off pitch. The prime requisite for a Dido is the ability to sing that last 'Remember me!' easily and beautifully. So now – bring on more Didos.

William Mann, who attended the second performance on 3 May, wrote in *Opera* (August 1951):

Benjamin Britten made his own version of the score for the English Opera Group's production. If anyone went expecting *Beggar's Opera* treatment, he cannot have understood the difference between the works for, while the music of that is a hotchpotch of tunes culled from traditional and fashionably popular sources fitted to words and so fair game for an arranger, *Dido* is of course a finished artistic creation (save in one respect), needing no more than a few decisions as to who is to sing what, and a continuo realization. Apart from making these, Britten filled a gap in the music, at the end of the second act, with appropriate passages from Purcell, thus bringing it to a satisfactory close dramatically and tonally. He had a string band of ten players whom he conducted from the harpsichord, improvising the keyboard continuo himself with an insight that seemed to be exemplary – the part was neither dully chordal, not cluttered up with gratuitous counterpoints; this was among the most satisfying features of the EOG's performance.

The design had to fit the character of the theatre in question. At the Lyric Sophie Fedorovitch used a plain stage, with a pillar near the footlights on one side, and a ramp with steps at the back. Behind it a ship could be seen and in the harbour scene nets were hung about the stage on which the witches cavorted. Curtains were draped across the stage in the hunt scene, rather awkwardly it seemed to me, and a large tiger-rug spread on the floor to give a comically exotic effect. The ladies and Aeneas were beautifully dressed; not so the male courtiers who wore ugly knee-breeches, or the Sorceress who had a sort of bantam palm tree in her hat and looked like a local worthy opening the bring-and-buy sale (perhaps a rather sinister worthy).

Joan Cross's production was elaborate and detailed, but never fussy and always musical; the eye was immediately caught by the chorus' movement at salient musical points in 'Shake the cloud', so as to keep exquisite tableaux on the move (forgive the Irishism); one could admire too the psychological insight that made Belinda move after Aeneas' last exit, not Dido. One *clou* point is the last chorus; Cross places Dido on the ramp and, round her, makes the ladies-in-waiting twine long strips of black net whose lengths flow, supported on their arms, down to the front of the stage, like branches of mourning stemming from a trunk of death-devoted grief, or like a bridal train, the bride now of death, or like deadly fetters – infer what you will, the effect was deeply impressive.

At Hammersmith, the roles of Dido and Aeneas were shared; I heard Nancy Evans and Bruce Boyce, who made a remarkably handsome pair, dignified and statuesque yet affectingly romantic. Boyce sang with the thorough musicianship we have come to expect and his acting, never a strong suit, had been well looked after so that he never appeared stiff. Everything about Evans's performance was moving except her voice and, as she was on the verge of a sick-bed, it would be unfair to complain of that; one must just reserve comment. Pamela Woolmore, an enchanting Zerlina and Despina not long ago, seemed to have lost her talent for classical singing, and allowed her voice to spread; her Belinda was charmingly acted, phrased and pointed, so that the quality of tone was a matter for real regret. Flora Nielsen's Sorceress was a gripping study, despite her attire, magnificent in attack, rich in articulation of the text. The choral singing was absolutely first class – excellently co-ordinated and ravishingly interpreted with concise timbre and finely controlled, virtuosically varied, tone.

4   *The Music of Gustav Holst*, the first significant study of Gustav Holst's oeuvre, which Imogen Holst had dedicated to Britten.

5   Gustav Holst's one-act chamber opera (1929–30), with a libretto by Clifford Bax, was given by the EOG as part of a double bill with Brian Easdale's *The Sleeping Children*, at the Cheltenham Festival on 9 July 1951, in a production directed by Basil Coleman and conducted by Norman Del Mar. As Imogen Holst observed in her programme note for the Cheltenham performances: 'I feel sure that [my father] would have enjoyed the brilliant economy of the arrangement of the orchestral score [. . .], which Britten has made to suit the needs of the English Opera Group.' Although in the *Thematic Catalogue* Imogen Holst records the 1951 Cheltenham performance as the first of Britten's arrangement of Holst's opera, there had been, in fact, at least one earlier performance, a BBC Third Programme broadcast by the EOG on 5 January 1949, described in the *Radio Times* as 'arranged for chamber orchestra by Benjamin Britten', in which Pears sang the title role and Ivan Clayton was the conductor. See also Letter 592 n. 4.

699   To Elizabeth Mayer
[*Telegram*]

[Aldeburgh, 20 February 1951]

COULD YOU PLEASE ASK WYSTAN IF ANY CHANCE HIS BEING IN
ENGLAND IN JUNE. COULD HE READ POEMS ALDEBURGH FESTIVAL
17TH. BE PERSUASIVE. LOVE

BEN

1   Britten was to write to Pears on 1 March, 'Wystan can't come, so we're trying Stephen [Spender].' Auden was eventually to appear at the Aldeburgh
Festival in 1953, the only occasion he was to do so. Spender also declined
Britten's invitation and his place was filled by the poet, art historian and
critic Herbert Read.

700   To Douglas Cleverdon
BBC
[*Typed*]

4 CRABBE STREET, ALDEBURGH, SUFFOLK
23rd February 1951

Dear Mr Cleverdon,
    Thank you for your letter. I will certainly keep in mind the idea of the
Chatterton Burletta and if I see a clear period and plenty of ideas around,
I will let you know.
    Yes, I certainly have set quite a few of Auden's light Lyrics.[1] In fact, the
one you mention, "Tell me the truth about love", and many others were
written especially for me to set. I have not actually got copies of these but
Mrs MacNeice (Hedli Anderson) has certainly got copies. I have not got
her address in Greece but I am sure someone at the B.B.C. will have.
Should you care to, write to her asking if she could lend them to you.
Incidentally, they are the kind of songs which Rose Hill would do quite
brilliantly.

Yours sincerely,
BENJAMIN BRITTEN

1   The *Cabaret Songs*, composed 1937–39, of which the four surviving
examples (including 'Tell me the truth about love') were first published by
Faber Music in 1980.

701 To Peter Pears

4 CRABBE ST, ALDEBURGH, SUFFOLK
Feb. 25th 1951

My darling,

Your two sweet notes have given me lots & lots of pleasure. Sweet of
you to write so fully & sweetly. I am hugely glad you are enjoying yourself
so – it must be lovely.[1] I'm afraid the good weather hasn't lasted – it rains
a lot here. But you will have lots to keep you amused indoors. Fancy you
playing the viola! I wonder if you were as fine as I was at it – but you can't
compete with my vibrato ⌇⌇⌇⌇⌇⌇ !

No time for a long letter. The weekend is going quite nicely.[2] All getting
on well. We went over to Pammy's[3] yesterday for tea, & for drinks to the
Cranbrooks. This morning Eddy went to Mass, I worked with Morgan, &
then played them Act I. They sleep downstairs, & I'm just off to post
before getting them tea. Eddy loves the house, & says most comfortable –
so you needn't apologise about not having got it more ready – but if you
hadn't done so much I can't think what it would have been like under my
direction! You've been an angel.

Covent Garden descends on us tomorrow,[4] and then, I hope, back to
work!

All my love, & to Imo & Peter,[5]
Your devoted
B.

P.T.O.

Peggy Ashcroft[6] can't, alas, come & read. Any suggestions? Isaac Stern,[7]
neither, so Manoug will play – in some ways a good thing, I think, don't you?
Love to Dorothy & Leonard [Elmhirst] if they are there.

1 From 20 February until 2 March Pears was teaching the resident musicians
of the Arts Department, Dartington Hall, Devon, at the invitation of
Imogen Holst and Peter Cox. He appears to have concentrated mainly on
Schütz and Monteverdi, possibly because he was exploring new repertoire
for himself. He described his activities in a letter to Britten dated 21
February:

This morning I attended a harmony class of Imo's where we studied a Bach chorale.
She is quite brilliant – revealing, exciting. Then she came to lunch here & talked all
about India. Then this evening from 6–7, I played the viola (!!) in the orchestra
rehearsing "St Paul's Suite" [by Gustav Holst], greatest fun. Tomorrow Schütz!

In a further letter, written two days later, Pears continued the account:

Lots of rehearsals etc. with Imo & the chaps. She's in tremendous form & quite
brilliant at her job. I talked & sang Monteverdi last night – I hope it was all right,

but I hadn't got very much to say – so I sang instead! We're working at the Schütz solo cantatas with sweet chaps – & v. keen. Lovely music.

In a further letter from Dartington (25 February), Pears wrote:

Everything goes on lovely here – lots of Schütz & Monteverdi – am teaching the young and adore it. Imo in tremendous form [...]

See also Letter 703.

In a private communication (28 March 2003) Rosamund Strode, a student at Dartington in 1950, recalled a visit of Britten's there in the spring of 1950:

Ben [...] came briefly about then [...] and played Mozart piano quartets with staff and senior students. And I remember him joining me among the violas for a run-of-the-mill weekly orchestral practice conducted by Imogen Holst [...] So visits of 'real' musicians to the music department were not altogether unknown, and had the double advantage of giving visitors (such as Peter Pears) the chance to try out repertoire [...] and show the 'audience' [the performances were informal and not open to the public] what performing is all about. Mini-masterclasses, you might say.

2 In a letter of 20 February Britten had told Pears of his plans for a weekend house party at Aldeburgh:

I'm having a wild weekend here – Tony Gishford has written to say, can he come with Eddy [Sackville-West] (he knows him) & just now came a wire from Morgan wanting to come too (very upset by Gide's death – probably that's the reason). [André Gide, the openly homosexual French writer, whose works, like Forster's, often centred on moral tension.] One only now needs the threat of Menotti to materialise, of coming down to Aldeburgh to see me, for the weekend to be thoroughly gay! I think I shall retire upstairs & let them fight it out themselves alone.

3 Lady Pamela Cadogan, a Suffolk friend of Britten and Pears.

4 David Webster, General Administrator of Covent Garden, who joined the house party.

5 Peter Cox, Administrator of the Arts Department at Dartington.

6 English actress (1907–1991), who made her stage debut in 1926. Ashcroft's career embraced an impressively wide range of plays, including Sheridan, Shaw, Chekhov, Beckett and Pinter, though she was perhaps most renowned for her many Shakespearean roles. She was created DBE in 1956. Although Ashcroft was unable to accept the 1951 Festival engagement (Sybil Thorndike took her place), she was to appear at several later Aldeburgh Festivals, often in partnership with the guitarist and lutenist Julian Bream.

7 American violinist of Ukrainian birth (1920–2001), who made his recital debut in 1935 in San Francisco, and his European debut in 1948. Stern's repertory embraced the great concertos from Bach to Bartók and chamber music with, among others, Pablo Casals. Among the composers who wrote

concertos for Stern were Penderecki, Dutilleux and Maxwell Davies. In 1960 Stern was to play a major role in organizing a group to save the threatened Carnegie Hall in New York.

Britten had invited Stern to Aldeburgh to partner the violist William Primrose in a performance of Mozart's *Sinfonia concertante* in E♭ (K. 364). The performance, with Manoug Parikian taking Stern's place and Britten conducting the EOG Orchestra, was given at the Jubilee Hall, Aldeburgh, on 10 June 1951, as part of the Aldeburgh Festival.

702　To Peter Pears

4 CRABBE ST, ALDEBURGH, SUFFOLK
[27 February 1951]

Darling P –

In haste, I hope this reaches you before you leave. The enclosed notes have just come. I wasn't aware of having written a rather 'sad' letter to John [Piper], but maybe I was depressed unconsciously (not surprising considering my darling is so far away) when I wrote & it shone through.

Well, all my guests are departed & I hasten to add, thank God. It was a wild weekend, with a climactic luncheon to which Eddy & Tony stayed, tho' Morgan went. I played Billy thro', & all said nice things. I think Act II Sc. I [four-act version] is excellent, but o how the rest worries me! Webster cried a little & embraced me (–!) & is generally nice about everything. I was dead when they all went, but fine today & back at work. No more now – just off to Lowestoft to audit 40 children!![1] Hope you're still enjoying your dear self.

All my love & all,
B.

1　Britten was auditioning children for the forthcoming revival of *Let's Make an Opera*.

703　To Benjamin Britten
From Peter Pears

ARTS DEPARTMENT, DARTINGTON HALL, TOTNES, DEVON
Thursday [1 March 1951]

My Sweetest old pot of honey –

I am slowly coming to the end of my stay here. We did the 7 last words & a cantata by Schütz on Tuesday, yesterday 2 more solo cantatas, a Purcell song with violin, & Holst's Voice & Violin Songs – & today comes Tancredi & other Monteverdi bits & a Buxtehude cantata.[1] What wonderful music & really what a heavenly week it's been. Imo has been in tremendous form, & has adored it & she has had the sweetest lot of students, madly keen – & one or 2 v. promising players, & all adoring the music – 17th-century music – very exciting. It has also been very rewarding for me – & I am quite sure that somehow we have got to use Imo in the biggest way – as editor, as trainer, as teacher, etc. – she is <u>most</u> impressive.[2]

I go back to London, Schumann & Brahms tomorrow – oh dear![3]

How are you, my honey? It has been heavenly having your letters – thank you so much for them all & for sending things on. So glad the weekend & Webster were a success.

I'm coming up to London tomorrow, Fri. – may ring you before – anyway – v. much love my fudge –

P.

1 Some of the music Pears is referring to in this letter can be identified: '7 last words' = Schütz's *Die Sieben Worte unsers lieben Erlösers und Seligmachers Jesu Christi*; Holst's 'Voice & Violin Songs' = the Four Songs for voice and violin, Op. 35 (H. 132); 'Tancredi' = Monteverdi's *Il combattimento di Tancredi e Clorinda*.

2 After Imogen Holst left Dartington in the summer of 1951 to resume a free-lance career, Pears and Britten were soon to encourage her involvement at Aldeburgh. In September 1952 she accepted Britten's invitation to work with him on *Gloriana* as his first full-time amanuensis, a role she continued to fill until 1964; and, following her arrival in Suffolk, Pears asked her to form and direct a chamber choir of young professional singers, the Purcell Singers (1953–67), based in London. As an Artistic Director of the Aldeburgh Festival from 1956, she made her own individual contribution to the programming, notably in the field of early music and her father's works.

   She undoubtedly encouraged Britten and Pears in their interests in seventeenth-century music, especially that of Schütz (see Letter 698), of whose vocal works Pears was to become an admired interpreter. (It was the notation of the recitatives in Schütz's Passions, in which the pitches but not the rhythms are given, that provided Britten with the model for the notation of Aschenbach's recitatives in his last opera, *Death in Venice*. Coincidentally, the tercentenary of Schütz's death fell in 1972, the very year in which Britten completed his opera.)

   The special atmosphere at Dartington, which is evident in these letters from Pears to Britten, probably provided inspiration for the Britten–Pears School for Advanced Musical Studies, founded at Snape in 1972. The School was a venture in which Imogen Holst was also closely involved.

3 No further information about this has come to light.

704 To Kenneth Harrison

4 CRABBE ST, ALDEBURGH, SUFFOLK
March 2nd 1951

My dear Kenneth,

Your shanty proposals have been the greatest success. I have laughed a lot over them, & so have my friends who have seen them too. They fit the music extraordinarily well, most ingeniously so. Thank you more than I can say for doing them. When Morgan was here last weekend we did a lot of work on them, arranging them in a more suitable order – according to the characters singing them – & making some slight changes. The order we provisionally decided on is as follows:

a. Verse I – Donald
b. III – Red Whiskers
c. VI – Billy
d. VII – Donald
e. V – Red Whiskers
f. IV – Billy
g. II – Donald – which starts slowly, making mock love to Billy,
  & then cheers up considerably at – 'for all he's a catch on the eye!'

I'd like to wait a bit before telling you the proposed changes of phraseology which the music & characters suggest – they are not major, & are certainly fluid. The beginning we thought should start more simply, & reasonably, & suggest:

Let's sail off to Goa (or: We sailed off to Goa)
From oily Genoa,
Roll on Shenandoah
And heave . . . etc.

What do you think?

As you seem to have such a flair for shanties, would you try your hand at this one? As gloomy, homesick and nostalgic as you like – repeated indefinitely.[1]

Maybe I'll squeeze a moment to pop over to Cambridge to discuss them all with you – that'd be better than letter-writing.

Many thanks,
Yours ever,
BEN

1   The melody of the shanty 'Blow her to Hilo', sung by the crew of the *Indomitable* at the beginning of Act I scene 3 (two-act version); Act II scene 2 (four-act version). It is this melody that also forms the basis of the immediately preceding orchestral interlude.

The text Harrison supplied had some problems, which Britten took up with him on 19 March:

Thank you for your Shanty II verses. I'm sorry you're having difficulty with the rhythm. In your verses the stress usually lies on the <u>last</u> syllable of each line, whereas in the tune it's more on the <u>penultimate</u> one. The verse we first thought of, but didn't think had much to it, was something like:

That, as you see, isn't so hot – but it's the kind of thing, depressed, homesick. One verse is really enough, if it's the kind of stuff that can stand repetitions!

In the same letter Britten returned to the other shanty, the text of which Harrison had already supplied:

Glad you didn't mind us tinkering with Shanty I. Have you any suggestions for the first line. Something more definite than your original 'From Oily Genoa' & more evocative than our 'Let's sail off to Goa'. 'Farewell to Genoa'??

The final version of the first stanza reads:

DONALD: We're off to Samoa
          By way of Genoa
          Roll on Shenandoah
          And up with the line and away,
          [*With chorus*] Up with the line and away.

See also Letter 708, which suggests that it was Britten (or Pears?) who wrote the final version of this stanza.

705 To Basil Coleman

4 CRABBE ST, ALDEBURGH, SUFFOLK
March 15th 1951

My dear Basil,

Many thanks for your letter of this morning, with its good news about the Lucretia sets,[1] & disturbing news about Krips' plan of cuts & playing of the work without break.[2] I have written to him fully, frankly, but friendly, disagreeing with him. Saying that the plan of the work is classical & not melodramatic, with events & comments on them happening separately – mountains & valleys – of which the largest valley is the Interval. It is also, I think, from whatever angle, too much to expect any audience to sit, at a constant level of intensity, in a theatre for nearly two hours. I have deliberately avoided mentioning the impossible <u>practical</u> difficulties which this plan would entail – that's for Basil D. [Douglas] to bring up later. But even then I'm convinced it's a bad idea. Also the cut – which would make the Intro. to Act. II have no climax & no reason – no core – & be miles too short. I've said that the music is effective (which I maintain it is!!) especially when backed up by the movements of Joan & Peter, & the drop-curtain. He may take more convincing about this point – but I'm determined to do it, if only for the reason that the work's pretty well known now, & to do it without one of its main features would be to disappoint some of the audience.

<u>Let's Make</u>[3] – kids are now chosen – Basil D. came to the final selection yesterday. He was a bit perturbed by their naïve singing, but I've heard them in a hall & they're <u>much</u> better; even so I think we shall have to plan for some music lessons (vocal lessons) – he's going to manage that in mornings, I think. But I think you'll like them – nice fresh little creatures. We've got a fine Sammy – dark with longish uncontrollable hair & hypnotic dark eyes – also a tiny impediment which stops him saying his 'r's properly – most engaging!

I too get cold feet when I think of what's to be done – but I'm sure it'll all even out – there are finally lots of hours in the day! Budd progresses well.

With love to you,
Yours ever,
BEN

1 In an earlier letter of 7 March to Coleman, Britten had expressed his anxieties about the forthcoming performances in May by the English Opera Group at the Lyric Theatre, Hammersmith, with special reference to the 'present makeshift arrangement' of the sets. The serious financial difficulties of the EOG were also part of the problem. The five London performances and the ensuing two performances in Wiesbaden were conducted by Josef Krips.

2 Josef Krips (1902–1974), Austrian conductor. His career with the Vienna
   State Opera began in 1933 and was interrupted by the rise of Fascism and
   the war but he resumed his post from 1945 to 1950 when he was appointed
   Chief Conductor of the London Symphony Orchestra. He also conducted
   post-war at Salzburg until 1950, and it was at one of the Festivals during
   this period that he performed *Lucretia*, with Julius Patzak in the role of the
   Male Chorus. Hans Keller was present and recalled that as a probable consequence of Krips's famously poor eyesight he adopted a bizarrely fast
   tempo for Lucretia's lullaby in Act II. It was Krips's poor eyesight that was
   to lead to the last-minute cancellation of his conducting of the premiere
   of *Billy Budd* at Covent Garden. A disappointed Britten reluctantly undertook the assignment. See BBMCPR, pp. 69–72.

   There is no evidence to suggest that any of Krips's suggestions with
   regard to cuts in *Lucretia* were ever adopted in performance.

3 In the same letter of 7 March to Coleman, Britten had written:

> First of all, "Let's Make" – I am very much in favour of cutting it down to two
> scenes. I have felt always that the introduction to the opera is too long and every
> comment I have heard from the young intensifies that feeling. I hope that this
> new version cuts a great deal of the rehearsal scenes. Those, while a rather nice idea,
> seem to me to fail in actual performance and also emphasize a fact that ought not to
> be emphasized – that the conductor is not the composer as he obviously ought to be.
>
> I have a feeling that Eric [Crozier] will agree to this if it does not radically alter
> any of his writing. He suggested recently to me that the life of the first part was
> nearly over and would we consider putting another little opera with the Little
> Sweep instead. I think it is best if you write to him direct and then when I see him
> as I am certain to do fairly soon, I will back you up strongly. He is in a very good
> mood these days and I am sure that we shall not get any unhappy reactions.

It is of interest in this context to read in the schedules of EOG performances
of *Let's Make an Opera* at Liverpool in August 1951, 'No audience songs –
cuts made in play accordingly and Bath Song sung by cast on stage.'

To date no new text has become established itself as an 'authorized'
first part.

706 To Peter Pears

4 CRABBE ST, ALDEBURGH, SUFFOLK
March 16th 1951

Darling Peter,

Just a scribble to send you the tenderest love, & good wishes for everything. It was lovely to hear your voice & an unspeakable relief to know
you'd arrived safely although you'd obviously had a beastly journey. I
hope all is going as well as possible. The Passions, at least the Concertgebouw ones, can't be very good I'm afraid – most <u>irritating</u> of them to
have this dreary conductor for you.[1] I'll be listening on Sunday of course.

I've had to put Piers [Dunkerley] off this weekend as Dr Acheson has said I mustn't talk more than absolutely necessary. It is only laryngitis (however you spell it) & not serious, but unless I stop talking & stay in it'll go on and on. So I'll try & arrange for Piers sometime next weekend. Basil & Martyn² may come down with you on Sunday, but we'll be talking about all that.

Weather has gone back to bloody again – after a heavenly, nostalgic spring day yesterday – so I don't feel so bad about not going out. Work is going on slowly but steadily towards the end of the Act [*Billy Budd*, Act III], & I'm on the whole pleased. It was lovely to play it to you, & you gave me back my confidence which had been slowly ebbing away. In a work of this size & tension that is one of one's greatest problems. I believe that is yours too – if one aims high (& you achieve your aims so often) one is so desperately ashamed when one knows one is missing them.

My love of course to Peter, Bertus & all friends whom you see. And come home quick & safe, & we'll have a lovely week of you here.

All my love, my sweet.

It was a heavenly oasis to have you here this week.

B.

[*In pencil:*] The enclosed cutting will come as a shock – poor, poor Toby!³

1 Pears was in Amsterdam singing the Evangelist in performances of Bach's *St Matthew Passion* at the Concertgebouw. He wrote to Britten on 18 March:

Here I am almost halfway through my visit. I shall be off in an hour to the Concertgebouw for my 3rd & last Passion there, and then comes Bertus [van Lier]. Mr Jordaens is a competent dull little bourgeois conductor, slightly more Bach-like than van Beinum perhaps but duller and the soloists drag and get very Dutch. I am sick of this performance. The chorus makes a huge ugly noise, the orchestra doesn't know how to play Bach, & the overall effect is dismal. I look forward to Bertus. I have told Peter [Diamand] I won't do this Concertgebouw performance next year. Maybe I'll come for Bertus. Let's see –

On 18 March Britten listened to a broadcast of the *Passion* from Amsterdam and responded immediately:

I've just come upstairs to my desk, having finished listening to Part II – only Part II I'm afraid since I stayed in bed all this morning (only just popping up to switch on Hilversum to hear your first sweet notes). Most unfortunately the stupid Radio Times gave the wrong time – damnable of it because it now costs 3d – of the start of Part II so I missed the Petrus episode [Peter's denial of Christ] – but I heard all the rest, & my darling yours is a great performance. The voice sounds so full & so rich, & with so much variety, & this glorious musical phrasing. But above all there is this noble conception of the part, this dignity, this felt but sublimated emotion. There can never have been an Evangelist like you – it's wonderful to be born in your lifetime to hear you do it.

But what a curious performance? Why all the cuts? Surely there must have been a revolution among the old Dutchies at their yearly ceremony being so truncated. Hard for you too, to go on sometimes with so little breaks. One sees too, how right Bach's form is – how one misses the musical, purely musical, comments. Some of Jordaens I prefered to van Beinum, he seemed sometimes to know the work better, & some was more sensitively phrased. How I loathe the accelerandi at the end of the choruses though. And poor Jo [Vincent] – more in tune, but <u>how</u> slow off the mark. The windows here rattled when she breathed. How is the old dear tho' – give her my bestest love. [Annie] Hermes as Friesian as ever, & o, what a Tenor! [Laurens] Bogtman less exaggerated (what I heard) but sounding to me 101, & I don't think of Jesus as an old man.

The letter concludes with a report on the progress of *Billy Budd* – 'I've finished Act III (tho' not quite satisfied with the very end) & I'm well into Act IV!' Britten's throat was improving and he was trying to talk 'very little', though there were guests in the house, Paul Dehn and James Butt. The visit from Piers Dunkerley, however, was delayed.

2   Basil Douglas's partner, Martyn C. Webster.

3   Unidentified.

707 **To John Lowe**
     BBC

                                        4 CRABBE STREET, ALDEBURGH
                                        March 19th 1951

Dear John Lowe,
– If it is you who wrote me a nice (unsigned) letter four days ago about the Flower Songs –
Sorry there's not a hope of me getting up to the Midlands this summer – dates press on me all the time to the practical exclusion of my real work – but I'm very glad you're doing the new songs.[1]
They were written for the 25th Wedding Anniversary of two very good friends of mine, Leonard & Dorothy Elmhirst, of Dartington Hall & numerous other philanthropic causes. They were written about flowers because they are both keen amateur botanists. That's all there is to say – except that some of the Crabbe lines[2] are taken from the 'Borough' whence, years ago, I took the subject of P. Grimes.
I hope very much to be free to listen to either or both of the broadcasts. Good luck to them.

                                        In haste,
                                        Yours,
                                        BEN BRITTEN

1 The BBC Midland Chorus, conducted by John Lowe, was to give the first
   broadcast performance of Britten's *Five Flower Songs*, in the BBC Midland
   Home Service on 24 May 1951. The final paragraph of Britten's letter indicates there was more than one broadcast of the songs scheduled. In the
   event the broadcast was repeated on 12 June and 4 July 1951.

2 The setting of George Crabbe's 'Marsh Flowers', the third of the *Five Flower
   Songs*.

708 To E. M. Forster
[*Incomplete*]

4 CRABBE ST, ALDEBURGH, SUFFOLK

April 4th 1951

Dearest Morgan,

   Just off to Vienna, by way of Zurich,[1] so I thought I'd write you a note.
I am well satisfied with the progress of Billy. Billy in the Darbies[2] is now
finished – so, apart from tidying Claggart's Monologue,[3] I have only the
last scene to finish. I'm not worried about that since my ideas are fairly
clear, & I hope to get down to it when back in London in about 2 weeks'
time. If convenient to you I'd like to come down to Cambridge for a night
to see you, & play you what's done. The First Act is now engraved & looks
nice.[4] The Chorus parts are wanted by Covent Garden in July, so things
are moving ahead.

   I've written to Kenneth Harrison suggesting some changes, and am
awaiting his reply. Would you suggest to him – if you see him – the
following first verse of Shanty:

   We're off to Samoa
   By way of Genoa
   Roll on Shenandoa
   It's up with the line and away!

1 At the Mozart Saal, Vienna, on 9 April, Pears and Britten gave a recital of
   songs by Dowland, Purcell, Handel and Arne, a group of Schubert lieder,
   Britten's *Canticle I* and a group of his folksong arrangements.
      On 12 April 1951 the first Vienna performance of *Spring Symphony* was
   given by Clemens Krauss conducting the Vienna Philharmonic Orchestra,
   with Hilde Zadek (soprano), Else Schürhoff (contralto) and Pears as
   soloists. The chorus of the Staatsoper and a boys' chorus comprised the
   choral forces. The first half of the programme consisted of the *Serenade*,
   with Pears and Gottfried Freiberg (horn). The following paragraphs are taken
   from a review, signed 'Kr.', that appeared in *Die Presse* (14 April 1951):

With the performances of the *Serenade* and *Spring Symphony*, Benjamin Britten has completely captured the hearts of the Viennese public. What is this fine, distinguished, transparent, shining music that this extraordinarily sympathetic and highly gifted English composer produces? Both works are vocal compositions. The indications of instrumental form – 'serenade', 'symphony' – are given a very broad and free interpretation. In this way he follows the example of Gustav Mahler who, about half a century ago, wrote his 'Wunderhorn' Symphonies, the 'Eighth' and *Das Lied von der Erde*. Our view of the world and the composition of our music has in the meantime changed dramatically. Even so there occur remarkable analogies and points of contact. Furthermore, like Mahler, Britten also composes as poet-composer, and there is the common ground of the arrival of spring – 'sei kommen über Nacht' ('has come overnight' [a quotation from 'Der Trunkene im Frühling' in *Das Lied*]) – of Pan awaking and summer drawing near, of the cuckoo calling, and of the romantic sound of the horn evoking an atmospheric evening blessing.

[...]

Spring Symphony demands much larger forces than the *Serenade*: soprano, contralto and tenor soloists, chorus and boys' chorus as well as a large orchestra. The poems are collected in groups and movements and thoughtfully arranged, so that the whole is almost a dramatic structure. From the moods depicting nature at the beginning, the development leads to a colourful, merry and extravagant spectacle of a summer's day in the city of London. In between are numerous sharply characterized poetic numbers and the ardent fantasy of the poet-composer pervades with equally loving involvement both the timeless and contemporary aspects. In comparison with the *Serenade*, the *Symphony* has not quite the same unity and balance. The *Symphony* has many strong, gripping moments; with the *Serenade* it is not only individual moments but the entire work that achieves its impact.

2 Act IV scene 1 (four-act version); Act II scene 3 (two-act version), Billy's ballad 'Through the port comes the moon-shine astray!', the text of which was taken directly from Melville's poem 'Billy in the Darbies'. This poem was the catalyst for Melville's novella *Billy Budd*. (See BBMCPR, p. 18.)

Britten reported to Lord Harewood on 25 March:

Budd goes on apace – finished Act IV Scene II – only one more scene! But I have had to put it aside for the moment in order to cope with Dido [*Dido and Aeneas*] – quite a good break because I was going a bit too fast I think!

3 See Letter 679 n. 1.

4 The engraved first-act score was the first of five separate fascicles of a complete pre-publication vocal score, prepared by Boosey & Hawkes from Britten's composition draft under the supervision of Erwin Stein. It was never available for sale, but produced for the principals and chorus to learn the opera. It acted as the basis for the later published vocal score (1952), in which a number of significant details were changed, including the opus number allotted to the opera. The pre-publication score shows the incorrect 'Op. 49' instead of the correct number, 'Op. 50'.

09 To Eric Walter White

4 CRABBE ST, ALDEBURGH, SUFFOLK
April 6th, 1951

My dear Eric,

Please forgive the long silence, but I haven't been back long, & anyhow I've found it difficult to make up my mind about 'Paul Bunyan'. I have finally got hold of the score from B & H (before I had only the roughest sketches) & I must say the whole thing embarrasses me hugely. One trouble is that there are two unresolved versions – changes Auden & I started making, & then gave up. If ever the piece were to be brought out into the open, an enormous amount of work would have to be done by him & me – & I don't know that either of us is keen enough.[1]

I think that if Keller[2] & Donald Mitchell[3] want to have the book[4] really complete the only possible reference to P.B. could be an eyewitness account of the 1st performances at Columbia University – & I suggest the person to do that would be Elizabeth Mayer, a friend of Auden's & mine, who was in on all the rehearsals & performances, writes well & could, I think, be relied upon to give an objective account of the whole affair. That I think would be the only way – & would relieve you from a good deal of embarrassment & bewilderment which I'm sure would follow if you looked at that glorious hotch-potch, the score!

In haste,
Yours ever,
BEN

1   Auden died in 1973; the following year Britten allowed eight 'songs and ensembles' and the three 'ballads' from *Paul Bunyan* to be performed during the Aldeburgh Festival. He then revised the score prior to the operetta's first complete performance since its premiere, a BBC broadcast on 1 February 1976 in Radio 3, with Peter Pears in the role of Johnny Inkslinger and George Hamilton IV as the Narrator, with the BBC Northern Symphony Orchestra conducted by Steuart Bedford. It was after hearing a playback of the broadcast at the Red House, Aldeburgh, that Britten, much moved, remarked to Mitchell that he 'hadn't remembered that it was such a strong piece'. The broadcast was to be followed by a fully staged production of *Bunyan* at the 1976 Aldeburgh Festival, at which Britten himself was present.

2   Hans Keller (1919–1985) was born in Vienna. (The first volume of this series of *Letters from a Life* was dedicated to his memory.) He fled from Nazi persecution to England in 1938, was interned on the Isle of Man, and was to achieve international fame as a writer, editor, critic, teacher, translator, analyst, and senior member of the BBC's Music Department for twenty years, from 1959. Keller was a man of such exceptional gifts, to each of

which he brought high originality of a kind rarely encountered before in British musical culture, that it is virtually impossible to encompass them within a brief paragraph. His list of published works speaks for itself, and reveals an extraordinary range of response and knowledge. Who else could have written a magisterial account of Haydn's string quartets on the one hand and on the other a volume of studies of criticism, a major section of which is entitled 'Phoney Musical Professions', among them, 'the music critic', 'the musicologist' and 'the professional broadcaster', and many others? His translations for works by Britten included *The Poet's Echo*, *The Prodigal Son*, *Children's Crusade*, and *Death in Venice* (with Claus Henneberg). In 1961 he married the artist Milein Cosman, who is particularly known for her drawings of composers and performers. Some of the earliest and most telling graphic images of Britten as conductor have become widely known through her work, many examples of which are to be found at BPL. Together with Keller, who wrote the text, she published in 1962 a volume of sketches, *Stravinsky at Rehearsal*, and there were other and diverse published collaborations during their marriage.

It was undoubtedly Keller's unique capacity to provoke that was prominent during his freelance years, and nowhere more so than in the years he jointly edited *Music Survey* with Donald Mitchell. A feature of that short-lived journal (1949–1952) was not just its rigorously (sometimes mischievously) anti-Establishment character but the attention it paid, in two special issues, to Schoenberg and Britten, the two composers to whom Keller was wholly committed throughout his post-war life. In both cases this was the first time in the British press that either composer had been celebrated in such a fashion. In Britten's case this was to lead to the Mitchell–Keller *Commentary* on Britten in 1952 (DMHK), which certainly aroused much hostile criticism but at the same time undeniably resulted in a change of critical attitude to the composer and his music. Thereafter it was less easy for sceptical critics to attribute his genius to 'cleverness'.

Britten had much respect for Keller and was himself especially interested in and impressed by a particular mode of analytic approach, so-called 'Functional Analysis', which Keller invented and which became an ever increasing preoccupation of his as the years advanced. It was, inevitably, a mode that makes no use of (phoney!) words but instead articulates what it is that lends a work its unity by means of the composer's – the composition's – own materials; it is a form of analysis, one might think, that gets as close as is humanly possible to the creative process itself. At the heart of all of this was Keller's own musicality. No one who knew him could ever doubt the love and passion that generated his phenomenally multiple musical activities.

The cadenzas Britten composed in 1966 for Mozart's Piano Concerto in E♭ (K. 482) – the soloist was to be Sviatoslav Richter – were influenced by Keller's analytic method. But it was perhaps in another field that Britten demonstrated his (sometimes amused and baffled) admiration of Keller's importance. For many years Keller had dispatched postcards and letters reminding Britten that his String Quartets Nos. 1 and 2 awaited a successor. Keller had to wait a long while but eventually No. 3 was composed and completed only a year before Britten's death. The dedicatee, as it had to be, was Hans Keller, who was one of the first to write with his customary insight of what many regard to be Britten's final masterpiece.

In 1961 Keller had been commissioned to 'compose' a functional analysis of Mozart's F major String Quartet (K. 590), for performance at that year's Aldeburgh Festival. He recalled in *Music and Musicians* (December 1984):

> When I asked [Britten] why he had commissioned me, he told me that the analysis of his own work [the Second String Quartet] contained his pre-compositional thought, partly conscious and partly unconscious, and that, so far as he could hear, it had contained nothing else. I watched his face when my Mozart analysis was performed at Aldeburgh, and saw from his multiple grins, often two or three a second, that he got every single point.

Among his many major and varied publications and those dedicated posthumously to his work are: *1975 (1984 minus 9)*; *Criticism* (edited by Julian Hogg); *Music and Psychology* (edited by Christopher Wintle), and *Essays on Music* (edited by Wintle). See also *Music Survey*, original series, six issues (1947–48), edited by Mitchell, for the last of which Keller wrote a highly detailed albeit almost wholly negative review of *Figaro* at Covent Garden under the title 'An experiment in concrete criticism'; and new series (1949–52), edited by Mitchell and Keller; A. M. Garnham, *Hans Keller and the BBC: The Musical Conscience of British Broadcasting, 1959–79*, and Donald Mitchell, 'Remembering Hans Keller', in DMCN.

3 Donald Mitchell (b. 1925), English musicologist, critic and publisher. In 1947 he founded and edited the polemical journal *Music Survey* (with Hans Keller from 1949) until it ceased in 1952, the year in which his and Keller's *Benjamin Britten: A Commentary on His Works from a Group of Specialists* (DMHK) was published. During the 1950s he regularly contributed to the musical press, edited the Boosey & Hawkes house magazine, *Tempo* (1958–62), published the first of his volumes of Mahler studies, *Gustav Mahler: The Early Years*, and was a member of the music staff of the *Daily Telegraph* (1959–64). His long association with the publishers Faber and Faber dates from his appointment as Music Books Editor in 1958; in 1964, following a suggestion from Britten who was at that time disillusioned with his publishers, Boosey & Hawkes, Mitchell founded Faber Music (Managing Director, 1965–76; Chairman, 1977; President, 1988–95), where, in addition to publishing all Britten's new works, beginning with *Nocturnal after John Dowland* and *Curlew River*, he developed an impressive list of younger composers, including George Benjamin, Oliver Knussen, Colin and David Matthews and Nicholas Maw. (See also Peter du Sautoy, 'Donald Mitchell as Publisher: A Personal Recollection', in Philip Reed (ed.), *On Mahler and Britten: Essays in Honour of Donald Mitchell on His Seventieth Birthday*, pp. 167–9.) Elected a Publisher Director of the Performing Right Society in 1971, Mitchell served as Chairman of the PRS from 1989 to 1992.

While still managing Faber Music, Mitchell was appointed founding Professor of Music at the University of Sussex (1971–76); he has held visiting professorships at York University and King's College, London. He was a close adviser and friend of Britten, and the composer dedicated *The Burning Fiery Furnace* to Mitchell and his wife, Kathleen. As one of Britten's four executors, and later as a senior Trustee of the Britten–Pears Foundation and Chairman of the Britten Estate Ltd, Mitchell has played a significant role in promoting Britten's music worldwide through performances, recordings, lectures and publications.

Mitchell's writings have almost exclusively concentrated on the twentieth century, though with H. C. Robbins Landon he edited and contributed to *The Mozart Companion*. His first Mahler volume has been succeeded by two more in the series – *Gustav Mahler: The Wunderhorn Years*, and *Songs and Symphonies of Life and Death* – and other writings on the composer include *The Mahler Companion* (jointly edited with Andrew Nicholson). In addition to the first two volumes of *Letters from a Life: The Selected Letters and Diaries of Benjamin Britten* (edited with Philip Reed), Mitchell's most significant Britten publications include (with John Evans) *Benjamin Britten, 1913–1976: Pictures from a Life* (PFL); *Britten and Auden in the Thirties, the Year 1936* (originally given as the 1979 T. S. Eliot Memorial Lectures at the University of Kent, Canterbury) and a handbook on *Death in Venice* (DVDM). In 1963 he published *The Language of Modern Music*; a revised edition, with an introduction by Edward W. Said, was published in 1993. His fascination for the culture of South-East Asia has been an abiding passion, and has informed his understanding of both Mahler and Britten. See Mitchell's collection of writings on music, *Cradles of the New* (DMCN). For a full bibliography, see Maureen Buja, 'A Bibliography of Donald Mitchell's Writings, 1945–1995', in Reed, *On Mahler and Britten*, pp. 299–330.

He was appointed CBE in 2000 for his services to music.

4   This was to be published in 1952: *Benjamin Britten: A Commentary on His Works From a Group of Specialists* edited by Donald Mitchell and Hans Keller (DMHK), to which White contributed a pioneering 'Bibliography of Benjamin Britten's Incidental Music', pp. 311–13. The editors had hoped to include a chapter on Britten's and Auden's operetta of 1941. When published, however, the *Commentary* had no chapter on *Paul Bunyan*. The first account of the opera, the history of its composition and premiere in New York in 1941, was to appear in the revised edition (1970) of White, *Benjamin Britten*. See also W. H. Auden, *Paul Bunyan: The Libretto of the Operetta by Benjamin Britten*, with an Essay by Donald Mitchell.

710 To Boyd Neel

4 CRABBE ST, ALDEBURGH, SUFFOLK
July 6th, 1951

Dear Boyd,

Many apologies for the delay in answering your letter – usual excuses, work, travelling, & now, blast it, illness.[1] I am afraid I can't be in London, for more than an hour or two, for ages. But I can write what little there is to be written about the Simple Symph.

As you probably know starting at a hideously early age I poured out reams & reams of music – songs, piano works, chamber music, orchestral works, oratorios (not operas), only slowing down when I reached the age of wisdom, or rather, when I left the age of innocence. Bits of these works were used as the basis of the S.S. which I organised in 1934 (I think). The themes come mostly from piano sonatas (I wrote 12 before I left my private school!) or songs. The development of these is sometimes quite new, but often left as it was – except for the rescoring for strings – as far as I can remember most of the Pizz. movement, the scherzo i.e., is echt ['authentic', i.e. as it was originally composed].[2]

Mrs L. [Lincolne] Sutton [Audrey Alston][3] used to teach me the viola in Norwich – she was, maybe still is, one of the leading lights of music in Norfolk. Used to run a string quartet led by our old friend [André] Mangeot! I feel particularly grateful to her because it was she who introduced me to Frank Bridge, & Harold Samuel[4] – with whom she'd been at College. Her son, by the way, now music master at Lancing (John Alston) was my early music-boy-rival in the Eastern Counties . . .

That's all I can think of about that early masterpiece! Hope it'll do.

Yours ever,
BEN

1 Britten was suffering from cystitis; see Letter 712.

2 In the miniature score published by the Oxford University Press in 1935, Britten identifies the sources of each movement in a series of footnotes:

1 Boisterous Bourrée: from Suite No. 1 for piano (1926) and Song (1923)
2 Playful Pizzicato: from Scherzo for piano (1924) and Song (1924)
3 Sentimental Saraband: from Suite No. 3 for piano (1925) and Waltz for piano (1923)
4 Frolicsome Finale: from Piano Sonata No. 9 (1926) and Song (1925)

In a prefatory note to the score Britten remarks:

Although the development of these themes is in many places quite new, there are large stretches of the work which are taken bodily from the early pieces – save for the rescoring for strings.

See also Paul Banks (compiler and editor), *Benjamin Britten: A Catalogue of the Published Works*, p. 20.

3 English violinist and viola-player (1883–1966), a member of the Norwich String Quartet; she was the dedicatee of *Simple Symphony*. See also Diary for 16 February 1931, note 3.

4 English pianist and teacher (1879–1937). Britten had private lessons with Samuel between November 1928 and March 1930. See also Letter 11 n. 1.

711 To William Plomer[1]

4 CRABBE ST, ALDEBURGH, SUFFOLK
August 22nd 1951

Dear William,

I wonder if you were able to get a copy of B. Potter's 'Mr Tod',[2] & if so how you react to the idea. I can't say how much I hope you still consider working with me, & how thrilled I was that your first reaction was so friendly.

This letter is just to give you my plans for the next months in case you can come down here to talk further about it. I am here solidly till September 16th then away for 2 weeks or so – then back here on and off for October. Any time (with a little warning) would be all right for you to come (with the possible exception of next week which is rather full with Peter's relations young & old). Just send a card.[3]

The plan I thought of (as a basis for discussion) was something like this:

Act I
Scene 1. Scene in the Rabbit hole – Flopsy bunnies playing around – Mr Bouncer asleep – Tommy Brock comes in – smoking with Mr B. & stealing of bunnies.

Scene 2. Drop curtain – the way to Mr Tod's house with Benjamin Bunny meeting Peter Rabbit & planning etc. possible meeting with Rabbit relations.

Scene 3. Mr Tod's house – don't know how much here, but anyhow the depositing of the bunnies in the oven, T. Brock going to bed, & B. Bunny & P. Rabbit burrowing their hole – possible arrival of Mr Tod.

Act II
Scene 1. The Pail episode – the Fight & escape of bunnies with B. & P.

Scene 2. The journey back in front of drop curtain.

Scene 3. Rejoicings in the Burrow, but (?) sounds of the marathon struggle up above perhaps?

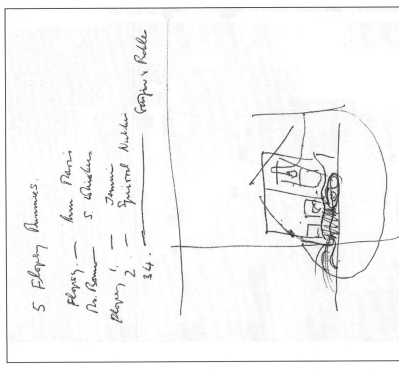

Britten's incomplete libretto synopsis for *The Tale of Mr Tod*

What you think?

In haste. It was lovely to see you here. Come again soon.

Yours ever,

BEN

1   South African-born poet, novelist and librettist of English ancestry
    (1903–1973), who was educated in South Africa and England. His early
    novel, *Turbot Wolfe* (1926), reflects his awareness of the colour prejudice in
    his homeland – the novel explores love and marriage across the racial
    divide – and gave offence in South Africa (and elsewhere) on publication.
    Leaving South Africa in the 1920s – he did not return for another thirty
    years – Plomer travelled to Japan, where he spent three years teaching. His
    knowledge of Japanese culture, particularly of Nō Theatre, made him the
    natural choice as the librettist for Britten's first Church Parable, *Curlew
    River*, which is based on the Nō play *Sumidagawa*.

    Plomer moved to London in 1929 to pursue a literary career, becoming a
    literary consultant to the firm of publishers Jonathan Cape, for which com-
    pany he secured the James Bond novels of Ian Fleming. While working for
    Cape he remained on the fringes of the Bloomsbury circle of Virginia
    Woolf and E. M. Forster. His own work included a three-volume edition
    (1938–40) of the diaries of Francis Kilvert, as well as several volumes of
    poetry (his *Collected Poems* appeared in 1960, and was enlarged in 1973) and
    two volumes of autobiography, *Double Lives* (1943) and *At Home* (1958).

    Discreetly homosexual, Plomer shared the last thirty years of his life in
    Sussex with Charles Erdman, a German refugee. He was appointed CBE in
    1968. Plomer's extensive archive of papers and correspondence is in the
    library of Durham University.

    Plomer and Britten probably first met in 1937 on the occasion of the
    opening night of Auden's and Isherwood's *The Ascent of F6*, but it was not
    until the post-war years that their friendship blossomed. Plomer attended
    the first Aldeburgh Festival in 1948, where he lectured on the Suffolk man
    of letters Edward Fitzgerald, and he was thereafter a regular and much
    appreciated contributor to the annual Festival programme. Although his
    earliest collaborations with Britten, *The Tale of Mr Tod* and *Tyco the Vegan*
    (1952) foundered, Plomer was to write the librettos for *Gloriana* (1953) and
    the three Church Parables of the 1960s – *Curlew River*, *The Burning Fiery
    Furnace* and *The Prodigal Son*. In 1963 Plomer contributed a 'Preface' to the
    celebrated Decca recording of *War Requiem* (SET 252/3), conducted by the
    composer. He advised Britten about the anthology of sentences for *Voices
    for Today* (1965) – Forster, Pears and Donald Mitchell also assisted the
    composer – and was consulted by Colin Graham concerning the latter's
    libretto for *Anna Karenina*, an operatic project that was ultimately aban-
    doned by Britten. Britten dedicated his *Canticle V: 'The Death of Saint
    Narcissus'* 'In loving memory of William Plomer'.

    See also Peter F. Alexander, *William Plomer*; Philip Reed, 'The Creative

Evolution of *Gloriana*', in PBBG; and MCBFE, pp. 115–16, 137–53 *passim*, 190–96 *passim* and 206–11 *passim*.

2 *The Tale of Mr Tod*, a projected children's opera for which Plomer was to write the libretto after the stories and characters created by Beatrix Potter, intended by Britten as a companion piece to *The Little Sweep*.

A letter from D. Billington, Managing Director of Potter's publishers, Frederick Warne, to Ernst Roth of Boosey & Hawkes, 28 May 1951, indicates that Britten was already considering this operatic project and had agreed with remarks in an earlier letter of Warne's (17 May) that there would be 'no question of any caricature or essential alteration to Miss Beatrix Potter's original work'. The same letter mentions that Britten would show Warne a 'rough of the libretto as soon as it is prepared'. The project foundered in December 1951 on copyright difficulties with Potter's publishers: specifically, agreement could not be reached in respect of royalties. An incomplete libretto synopsis in Britten's hand, probably dating from October 1951, survives at BPL.

The minutes of the meeting of the Executive Committee of the EOG on 16 December 1951, which Britten attended, gives some indication of the composer's intentions for the work. *The Tale of Mr Tod* was to be premiered at the 1952 Aldeburgh Festival (three performances), before transferring to Cheltenham and subsequently to London's West End, in a production to be directed by Basil Coleman, with – according to the minutes of previous EOG meetings (24 October and 19 November 1951) – designs 'after Beatrix Potter' by Charles Bravern under John Piper's supervision. The provisional cast list comprised soprano, tenor and bass-baritone soloists, and six children's voices; the orchestra was to be a chamber ensemble of flute, oboe, clarinet, violin, viola, cello, piano and percussion.

See also Peter Alexander, *William Plomer: A Biography*, pp. 268–70; PKSB, pp. 107–8, and Andrew Plant, *Rumours and Visions*, exhibition catalogue, pp. 28–9.

3 The illness of Plomer's father prevented the librettist accepting Britten's invitation to visit Aldeburgh until October: see Letter 714.

712 To Eric Walter White

4 CRABBE ST, ALDEBURGH, SUFFOLK
August 22nd, 1951

My dear Eric,

It was only in the faintest hope of you coming that we sent you the invitation for Saturday; so it wasn't a surprise to get your letter from Thorpe-le-Soken [Essex] saying you couldn't. But all the same we were very sorry. It was quite a gay & incredibly mixed affair[1] – from the local Squire (Vernon Wentworth) to the girl from the telephone exchange, &

my little fisherboy friend (the 'Nipper'²) – comprising all the locals who
help in the Festival. George & Marion [Harewood] were sweet to everyone, & Peter & I didn't forget too many names! No definite news yet
about last Festival finances – but we're hoping (with some additional
sympathy of the Arts Council!) to avoid calling on our guarantors.

So very sorry about all your woes – it is sickening for you.³ But if it
ensures a rest, perhaps even a blessing in disguise. I've also been ill on &
off for two months – a loathsome & depressing cystitis (??) – but getting
over it now. Are you a good patient? I'm not. I always think the end of the
world [is] at hand when I feel ill.

No, I'm not going to the 'Rake's Progress'.⁴ George & Marion are, so I
shall get reliable reports from them. Work here is too urgent, & when I get
time I'm going to have a real holiday (I'm planning a trip by boat from
here to Switzerland (sic!) – for the end of September).⁵ The Fenice, by the
way, by approaching Otakar Kraus, Peter, & John Piper to take part (in the
Stravinsky) seems to be recognising the E.O.G.! But the first only was able
to accept.⁶

Billy Budd has been held up quite a bit by my wretched illness (&
M & B)⁷ – but will be done all right, I think. The sketches have been
complete some time, the vocal score is nearly finished – & already more
than half in print – the orchestral score going on well – but o, o, what an
awful lot of notes.⁸ I'm sure it's laziness to prefer writing operas for the
Group (the one reason Frank Howes⁹ hasn't thought of!)

Basil Douglas is away for the moment, but when he gets back we hope
to be able to give you some E.O.G. plans. They include a German tour
(& Holland & possibly Denmark) in the spring, 'Love in a Village' for the
B.B.C. with the possibility of doing a production some time, a small 2nd
children's opera from me on Tale of Mr Tod¹⁰ (B. Potter) which I find an
exciting idea, & a wonderful relief after the Tale of Mr Budd! That could
probably be in Aldeburgh in June, & York & Cheltenham after – perhaps!

I hope you're enjoying Thorpe-le-Soken. I have the most glamorous
memories of that part of the world, since I used to spend the occasional
summer holiday in the rectory at Great Holland with a friend¹¹ from my
private school. I remember fetes with obstacle [races] – bicycle rides – &
tennis tournaments there – hot summer days & always success! Ay – me . . .

Get well quick – & hope to see you before long.

Yours ever,

BEN

P.S. Really the old serpent¹² excelled himself in the current Tempo – some
quite memorably inane remarks!

1   Probably a party to thank the volunteer workers of the Aldeburgh Festival.

2   The nickname of Robin Long, then aged twelve, whom Britten knew
    through his friendship with the Aldeburgh fisherman Billy Burrell. The
    Nipper appears with Britten, Forster and Burrell in photographs taken in
    Burrell's boat, which were published in *Picture Post* to illustrate a feature by
    Eric Crozier, 'An Opera Team Sets to Work' (15 October 1949), about the
    creation of *Billy Budd*. The Nipper was to be among the crew led by Burrell,
    which sailed across the North Sea and up the Rhine in September. For
    Burrell's memories of the Nipper, see HCBB, p. 286. The schoolboy Long's
    diary of the voyage was published in the *Leistonian*, 17 (1952).

3   White was convalescing from a fractured ankle when other illnesses beset
    him.

4   Stravinsky's opera, with a libretto by W. H. Auden and Chester Kallman
    after Hogarth's series of paintings (1732–33), first performed at the Teatro
    La Fenice, Venice, on 11 September 1951. Britten was to write to Ronald
    Duncan on 31 August:

    I'm afraid I don't want much to see Rake's Progress. I've seen the score, & not with-
    standing the excellence of Strav. & Auden as creators I'm not awfully interested in
    what they think about opera – not judging by what they write anyhow! – quite
    agree with your indictment of W.H.A. [writing] in Tempo. Opera's my life, & it's
    obviously not theirs.

5   For two weeks from mid-September, Britten, Pears, Basil Coleman and
    Arthur Oldham were passengers on the boat trip skippered by Billy Burrell.

6   Otakar Kraus created the role of Nick Shadow in *The Rake's Progress*. Pears
    would have been approached presumably to play Tom Rakewell, or pos-
    sibly Sellem the auctioneer. Pears, who could have been a remarkable
    Rakewell, was never to sing the role, though he was, in October 1951 at
    Cologne, to sing the title role in *Oedipus Rex* under Stravinsky's direction:
    'Oedipus seems to have gone fairly all right I think,' he told Britten in an
    undated letter (10 October 1951), from Amsterdam. While in Cologne,
    Pears sent a postcard to the editors of *Music Survey* on 6 October reacting
    to Frank Howes's 'Two Revolutionaries: Schoenberg and Stravinsky', *The
    Times* (5 October 1951). His text was published in *Music Survey*, 4/2
    (February 1952):

    Sirs, – You will have seen Our Music Critic's article in yesterday's *Times*, in which
    he finally buries both Schoenberg and Stravinsky (prematurely in the latter case, as
    I, writing from lively rehearsals of *Oedipus Rex* with the composer, can happily
    testify). This is the second major interment conducted recently by the *Times*'s
    Music Critic; he can now have no serious rivals for the title of the Grand Under-
    taker of Music.
        In this connection, might it not be suitable and rewarding for *Music Survey* to
    devote an early number to an 'Inquest on Inquests', or might this seem premature?

See also Donald Mitchell, 'Mythic Pears: Idomeneo and Oedipus', in PPT, pp. 67–8.

It was Stravinsky himself who had recommended John Piper as set designer for *The Rake's Progress*: see the composer's letter to Auden (18 July 1951) and Auden's reply (25 July) in Robert Craft (ed.), *Stravinsky: Selected Correspondence*, vol. 1, pp. 319–20.

In 'The *Rake* in progress', Stephen Walsh notes that in May 1947 Ralph Hawkes

> had just sent Stravinsky the EOG's prospectus, and he indicated that Britten was keen to have an opera by Stravinsky for the Group's repertoire. That June, Stravinsky attended a Los Angeles performance of Britten's *The Rape of Lucretia* with Aldous Huxley. Who, he asked Huxley, would be a good librettist for an English-language opera, if he were to compose one? The fact that Huxley's suggestion – W. H. Auden – was an old associate of Britten's was no doubt accidental, and may even have been unknown to the novelist. But it remains an intriguing thought that *The Rake's Progress* might have turned into a chamber opera in the *Lucretia* mould with a libretto by the author of Britten's first stage work, *Paul Bunyan*. In September 1947, when Auden was approached, Hawkes had discussed the Hogarth subject with Stravinsky and still considered an EOG work a possibility, but not – he thought – if a chorus were to be required. More to the point for Stravinsky, perhaps, was the fact that no specific commission was mentioned. Admittedly *The Rake* never was commissioned by anyone, but at least by writing it for conventional forces he would keep it within the orbit of the world's opera houses, rather than consigning it to the hazards of a small touring company with little money and an uncertain future.

In the same article Walsh suggests that the string-quartet prelude to the graveyard scene in Act III – the first music from the opera to be composed (December 1947) – may owe its scoring to the EOG idea still being a possibility. Was Britten's hostility to *The Rake's Progress* perhaps coloured by the fact that it might once have been destined for the EOG?

7   A Sulphonamide, one of the group of antibiotics discovered during the war and used in powdered form to protect open wounds from infection. It was manufactured by May and Baker, hence its nickname 'M. and B.'. As well as pain and frequency, cystitis can also cause feelings of depression, which might have been amplified by this medication.

8   Britten had finished the composition draft of *Billy Budd* on 10 August, and he played through the opera for the Harewoods when they stayed with him in Aldeburgh later that month. Harewood wrote to Britten from Austria on 31 August:

> It was tremendously exciting to hear the end for the first time, and third act and the first scene of Act IV for the second. Each time I hear it, I can only compare its emotional impact to that of *Otello*, which I think is, without exception, the most shattering piece in existence. I can't see that *Billy* is going to be far behind.

Forster had also visited Aldeburgh; he wrote to Bob Buckingham (undated letter), 'I have heard the remainder of *Billy*; very fine.'

9   The chief music critic of *The Times* (1943–60): see Letter 31 n. 3.

10 Very few of these ambitious plans were to be realized. The EOG revived
    Let's Make an Opera at the Lyric, Hammersmith (December 1951 – January
    1952), with further performances at the New Theatre, Hull (February 1952)
    and in Wimbledon (March), and gave three performances of *Love in a
    Village*, the 1762 ballad opera, in a new musical version by Arthur Oldham,
    designed by Osbert Lancaster and conducted by Norman Del Mar. It was
    broadcast in the BBC Third Programme on 9 May 1952 (repeated on 12 May).

11 Piers Dunkerley.

12 Auden's 'Some Reflections on Opera as a Medium', in *Tempo*, 20 (1951),
    reprinted as 'Notes on Music and Opera', in *The Dyer's Hand*, pp. 465–74.

713   To Erwin Stein

4 CRABBE ST, ALDEBURGH, SUFFOLK

Sept. 9th 1951

My dearest Erwin,

One or two notes about Act IV [of *Billy Budd*]. The 1st Lieut.'s reading
should now stand: "According to the Articles of War, it is provided as
follows: 'If any officer, mariner, soldier or other person in the fleet shall
strike any of his superior officers, he shall suffer death. It is further provided that if any of the fleet commit murder it shall be punished by death.'

William Budd you have been found by the Court Martial guilty of
striking your superior officer. You have further been found guilty of
murder: in accordance with the aforesaid Articles of War you are condemned to death by hanging from the yard arm."

Towards the end of the Epilogue, Vere should sing, instead of: "Yes, I
have erred . . . by the heavenly laws I have erred."

Brass – O What have I done? O What, what have I done? etc.

But he has saved me –

And in the penultimate – 'ad lib' bar please add after "long ago now" –
this – (now) years ago, centuries ago – when I etc.[1]

Hope this is all clear – if not, I'll be in, if you ring.

Not very happy with E.M.F. here. He's in a funny abstracted mood,
rather selfish in demanding lots of treatment and extra consideration
unreasonably. He's done some work with me, & demanded to have the
work played to him – but cannot remember at all what he's previously
heard of it! I've played him Acts II, III & IV – & apart from excitement
about Claggart's Monologue (rather ironical that!),[2] no comment at all,
not even of disapproval! He doesn't seem able to grasp it at all – or [be]
really interested in the musical side of the opera! Still, I must be grateful

for a wonderful libretto (with the one exception),³ & not demand anything else I suppose.

In haste, with lots of love. It was lovely to have you here.

Love to Sophie,

BEN

P.S. Thank you very much for having done all the visa business for me.

1 These late modifications to the libretto of *Billy Budd* appear in the published score.

2 See Letter 679 n. 1.

3 It remains unclear to which passage Britten is referring.

714 To William Plomer
[*Typed*]

4 CRABBE STREET, ALDEBURGH, SUFFOLK

11th September, 1951

My dear William,

I was delighted to get your letter and to learn that you are still happy
about the idea of our Potter collaboration. I am looking forward to your
coming to Aldeburgh early in October to plan her a bit. We can then start
breaking scenes down into recitatives, arias, duets, choruses, and all the
rest of the technical paraphernalia. Don't let that put you off, as the whole
thing is very easy to grasp, once one tackles it. I couldn't feel happier that
you consider working with me and have absolute confidence in your ability
to produce a libretto really worthy of the subject!¹

I have not read the life of Miss Potter² and, if you have a copy you could
lend me, I should be very happy indeed to read it. I have been looking
round a little for the book, but without success.

Peter and I leave on Sunday for our trip up the Rhine, scheduled to take
about two weeks. When I get back I shall hope to find a note from you,
saying when you can come to Aldeburgh.

[*Handwritten:*] Love from

BEN

1 Plomer worked with Britten at Aldeburgh in October. The composer wrote
to his new librettist on 4 November:

I enjoyed our two days' Toddery a great deal, & am enormously pleased with
what we accomplished. I feel confident it will make a most alarming evening's
entertainment!

2 Margaret Lane's 1946 biography, *The Tale of Beatrix Potter*; Britten's copy

of the 1949 reprint is at BPL. Plomer did indeed lend Britten his own copy when he came to Aldeburgh in October. Britten told Plomer (letter of 4 November),

I have read through the Lane Biography with great interest. I enjoyed the early part no end; but I was rather alarmed to find that the affection I had conceived for B. P. slowly slipping away through the last pages. I suppose Margaret Lane's own dislike was peeping through the sentences.

715 To Elizabeth Sweeting

From Peter Pears
[*Postcard: Aerial view of Sacré Coeur*]

Paris
13 September 1951

Paris est très très gai et très très chaud, but one eats superbly. Last night Esther [Neville-Smith], Iris [Holland Rogers] & I saw "Phèdre", a terrifying piece.[1] Tomorrow we go to Chartres for 48 hours, & then back here for 1 night. Notre Dame & Sacré Coeur are all very well but give me the Parish Church every time. I hope Chartres will not let me down. Everyone's wearing charcoal. Skirts are not much longer. Hats small!

Love,
PETER

1 Racine's final play for the professional theatre (1677). In the summer of 1975 Britten was to select passages from Robert Lowell's verse translation *Phaedra: Racine's Phèdre* as the text for his dramatic cantata *Phaedra*, for mezzo-soprano and small orchestra, which was first performed in June 1976 at the Aldeburgh Festival in the presence of Britten and Lowell, whom the composer had met in New York in 1969.

716 To Edith Sitwell

4 CRABBE ST, ALDEBURGH, SUFFOLK
Sept. 15th, 1951

Dear Dr Sitwell,

I have been wanting to write to you for many weeks, but I have had such a pressure of work – coloured by a nasty illness which will not leave me – that there hasn't been a moment. Thank you so very much for sending me the 'Canticle of the Rose' poems.[1] I find them, the later ones especially, profoundly moving. There is a grandeur of conception in them which is heartening, & a lack of sentimentality most remarkable when dealing with such contemporary subjects. Several of them appeal to me for music – if

ever the ideas blossomed would you allow me to set them?[2] I'd do my best
for them.

It was a great pleasure to meet you in Liverpool.[3] I hope to be able
to accept your kind invitation to luncheon when I am in London in
November or December. Will you be there any time then? I shall have to
be there all that time for rehearsals & performances of 'Billy Budd' which
starts at Covent Garden on Dec. 1st.

Peter & I are just starting (in spite of the atrocious weather) on our trip
up the Rhine in a boat – two weeks away from telephone & work & in
glorious scenery!

Thank you so much again for the poems, on which I send you my
heartiest congratulations.

Yours sincerely,
BENJAMIN BRITTEN

1   Sitwell's *The Canticle of the Rose: Selected Poems 1920–1947*, Britten's copy of
    which is inscribed: 'To/Benjamin Britten/with Great admiration/from/
    Edith Sitwell'.

2   Britten was to set Sitwell's 'Still falls the Rain – The raids, 1940, Night and
    Dawn' as his *Canticle III* for tenor, horn and piano in November 1954, and
    three further poems for the Sitwell sequence *The Heart of the Matter*, in 1956.

3   While Britten and Pears were in Liverpool on tour with the EOG (30 July –
    4 August 1951), Pears and Sitwell were narrators in a performance on
    2 August of Walton's *Façade*, conducted by the composer. Sitwell wrote to
    Pears on 7 August in terms that suggest she had to withdraw from the
    performance – or, at least, ask Pears to narrate a greater number of poems
    than was his usual practice:

    I can never forget your *great* kindness to me in Liverpool. I do indeed appreciate
    it. It was extraordinarily good of you to recite all those *Façade* items (and how
    beautifully!).

717 To George and Marion Harewood

4 CRABBE ST, ALDEBURGH, SUFFOLK
Oct. 2nd 1951

My dear George & Marion,

Please forgive my writing to you both together like this, but what I'm
writing about concerns you both. It is Billy Budd, & I want to dedicate
him to you. I'm hopeful that you'll agree because you've both been so nice
about him while he was being written. It is by far the biggest, & I think the
best, piece I've written for some time & in this time you have both been
such very great friends, helpful in every way artistic & personal, and

generous to a degree, that he really belongs to you, & if it will give you
pleasure I hope you will have him! I was going to say it on the telephone
last night, but the line was so unhelpful that I thought it better to wait &
write about it. Morgan, by the way, is very happy too that I should want to
dedicate him to you.[1]

I look forward to seeing you, & hearing all your Venice news,[2] & telling
you all our Rhine gossip. Thank you so much for your long & newsy letter
from Salzburg, George; you certainly had a packet of trouble, but I hope
that at least a few of the performances were worth the car & passport
troubles! Very disappointing about Wozzeck.[3] You'll have to work hard to
convince me about the Stravinsky. I feel miserably disappointed (I have
done since I first saw the libretto & first few pages of the score) that easily
the greatest composer alive should have such an irresponsible & perverse
view of opera (of the voice & of the setting of words & of characterisation
in particular). Of course I am sure it will contain a lot of beautiful music,
& it will be throughout original & distinguished, but I'm not yet convinced
that it helps opera to keep alive one little bit – & I feel Auden to be largely to
blame, being the cleverer & more sophisticated of the two. What these two
could have produced . . . ! But the subject seems quite wrong for them both.

Lots of love to you both,

Yours ever,

BEN

1 *Billy Budd* is dedicated 'To George and Marion, December 1951'. Britten
   presented the Harewoods with his manuscript full score of the opera, now
   at BPL.

2 The Harewoods had attended the first night of *The Rake's Progress* in
   Venice. Harewood was to write to Britten on 3 October 1951:

   I think we are really agreed about the Stravinsky [. . .] Of course, it is a chicken-
   hearted attempt at the form, but, being a real composer, he has achieved rather
   more than one feels he deserved to. I hate the word 'reactionary', but it can describe
   an attitude of mind sometimes rather conveniently . . . Stravinsky's is perhaps that.

   Harewood contributed an extensive notice of the first performance of *The
   Rake's Progress* to *Opera*, 2/12 (November 1951), pp. 610–18, the magazine he
   had founded the previous year.

3 The Harewoods had visited the Salzburg Festival where, among other performances, they had attended Berg's *Wozzeck* – 'cruelly under-cast, under-
   conceived, and certainly under-sold and appreciated' (Harewood to
   Britten, 31 August 1951) – in a production directed by Oscar Fritz Schuh as
   'nightmarish fantasy'. Harewood told Britten, 'Poor Helene Berg [Alban
   Berg's widow] sat in front of us at one of the two performances we saw and
   was very unhappy about it.'

718 To E. M. Forster

4 CRABBE ST, ALDEBURGH, SUFFOLK
Dec. 7th 1951

My dear Morgan,

I have received the second instalment of the Arts Council commission (B. Budd) and here is the share owing to you.[1]

I didn't really see you during the rehearsals nor after the performance to thank you for having worked on it with me. Apart from the great pleasure it has been, it has been the greatest honour to have collaborated with you, my dear. It was always one of my wildest dreams to work with E.M.F. – & it is often difficult to realise that it has happened. Anyhow, one thing I am certain of – & that's this; whatever the quality of the music is, & it seems people will quarrel about that for some time to come,[2] I think you & Eric have written incomparably the finest libretto ever. For wisdom, tenderness, & dignity of language it has no equals. I am proud to have caused it to be.

My love to you – hope the ankle progresses. By the way, the elderly doctor who attended you immediately after the catastrophe (name unknown) stopped me along Crag Path to ask after you, & was sorry to hear that it was not completely healed.

Please excuse the 'Biro'[3] – but I have to admit they are quicker to write with – so I've acquired one to help me acknowledge the sheaf of wires (well into three figures) that sit here on my desk.

Your very grateful & affectionate
BEN

1 Britten wrote to W. E. Williams at the Arts Council on 5 December:

Thank you very much for the cheque of £250, the final instalment of the Arts Council's commission fee for Billy Budd. I am very happy to have this, & am sending on the librettists' share to them, & I am sure they will be delighted too.

We all felt disappointed that the original plan of doing it in the Festival [of Britain] period was not possible – but I hope you & your Council feel that the current production at Covent Garden is as fine as I do, & worthy of the Festival.

2 There was a notably extensive press following the premiere of *Billy Budd* at Covent Garden on 3 December 1951. Desmond Shawe-Taylor in the *New Statesman and Nation* (1 December 1951), previewed the production:

Billy Budd was the last of Herman Melville's stories. He had written no fiction for thirty years, and he finished this tale only a few months before his death in 1891; it was not published till 1924. Benjamin Britten is not the first composer to have been attracted by the subject: a one-act version by Giorgio Ghedini was produced at Venice in 1949. Britten's opera, a large-scale affair in four acts, receives its first performance at Covent Garden tonight; the libretto, by E. M. Forster and Eric Crozier, follows Melville with unusual fidelity.

The entire action of the opera, as of the story, takes place on board HMS

Indomitable in 1797. The date is significant, England is at war with revolutionary France; it is also the year of the great mutinies at Spithead and the Nore. Consequently naval discipline, barbarous enough already, has been redoubled in severity. Billy Budd (baritone), a young sailor handsome of body and of soul, is a universal favourite among his fellows; but his very innocence and goodness arouse the jealous enmity of Claggart (bass), the master-at-arms. When falsely accused by Claggart of fomenting mutiny, Budd is rendered speechless by his one physical defect, a paralytic stammer at moments of stress; in his helplessness, he lashes out at his accuser with his fist. The blow proves fatal; but in any event, whatever the result and whatever the provocation, it was a capital offence. Captain Vere (tenor), the third leading personage in the story, though aware of the sailor's innocence, feels obliged to put naval law and duty before mercy. Billy Budd is hanged at dawn from the mainyard; and Melville describes his end in a strangely oblique and moving phrase: 'Watched by the wedged mass of upturned faces, Billy ascended; and ascending, took the full rose of the dawn.'

The objection can fairly be raised that this is not tragedy in the accepted sense of the term, but only a harrowing tale of undeserved misfortune. Certainly the flaw which destroys Billy is no flaw in his character. He is not naturally violent; on the contrary, he is the embodiment of goodness and innocence, 'Adam before the Fall'. Similarly, Claggart is the personification of what Melville calls 'natural depravity'; he is Satan eternally banished from felicity, enviously aware (as an ordinary man would not be) of the beauty and goodness which lie beyond his reach. But if Melville's fable is not tragedy, it is poetry; on a small scale, a kind of epic. The innocence of Budd and the iniquity of Claggart; the mysterious 'fate' which binds their destinies together; the enigmatic figure of the Captain, all-powerful yet powerless to adjust human and divine right; the vision of the ship as a microcosm: all this gives to Melville's story something of the pure quality of a ballad; and the poetic, almost mystical quality persists even through the crabbed dissertations and explanations in which the old author sometimes indulges. At the end he gives us an actual ballad: some artless lines put into the mouth of poor Billy as he lies in irons awaiting his end, lines supposedly made by the 'tarry hands' of one of his mates in the foretop of the *Indomitable*.

The music, like the libretto, is remarkably faithful to the spirit of the story; and Melville's ballad has been used, with a most poignant effect, in the first scene of the final act. Billy Budd is lying as in a trance; serene, almost resigned, his former tension and agony of spirit mysteriously healed. The rough, tender words are set to music of a simplicity and sweetness very rare in modern music; on a hint from Melville, Britten has cast the scene in the gently rocking six-eight rhythm of a cradle-song, reverting to the F major tune which we heard from a solo violoncello in a previous act, when Budd was lying half asleep in his hammock. But now it is the condemned sailor himself who sings the tune, *pianissimo*; at the end of each line the voice is left holding a note in solitary juxtaposition against the ocean-deep pedal C of the horn: first the vocal line comes to rest on B♭, then on G, then on E, then on C: always lower, more peaceful, more dreamy. What wonderful things can still be done with common chords and plain dominant sevenths! This music is almost as simple as a ballad; so direct, so true to the uncomplaining and uncomplicated character of the sailor, that one could almost fancy the composer to have written it first of all in a fever of inspiration, just as Tchaikovsky flung himself straight into Tatiana's Letter Song in *Eugene Onegin*. Not that there is anything

ROYAL OPERA HOUSE
COVENT GARDEN

SATURDAY, 1st DECEMBER, 1951

THE ROYAL OPERA HOUSE, COVENT GARDEN LTD.

General Administrator : DAVID L. WEBSTER

presents

The first performance of

"BILLY BUDD"
AN OPERA IN FOUR ACTS

Libretto by E. M. Forster and Eric Crozier
after the story by Herman Melville

Music by Benjamin Britten

Scenery and Costumes by John Piper

Lighting by Michael Northern

Guest Conductor   :   BENJAMIN BRITTEN

Producer   :   BASIL COLEMAN

Royal Opera House, Covent Garden, 1 December 1951:
programme for the first performance of *Billy Budd*

Characters in Order of Appearance

CAPTAIN VERE ...	PETER PEARS
FIRST MATE ...	RHYDDERCH DAVIES
SECOND MATE ...	HUBERT LITTLEWOOD
MR. FLINT, Sailing Master ...	GERAINT EVANS
BOSUN ...	RONALD LEWIS
FOUR MIDSHIPMEN ...	BRIAN ETTRIDGE, KENNETH NASH, PETER SPENCER, COLIN WALLER
DONALD ...	BRYAN DRAKE
MAINTOP ...	EMLYN JONES
NOVICE ...	WILLIAM McALPINE
SQUEAK, Ship's Corporal ...	DAVID TREE
MR. REDBURN, First Lieutenant ...	HERVEY ALAN
MR. RATCLIFFE, Lieutenant ...	MICHAEL LANGDON
CLAGGART, Master-at-arms ...	FREDERICK DALBERG
RED WHISKERS ...	ANTHONY MARLOWE
ARTHUR JONES ...	ALAN HOBSON
BILLY BUDD ...	THEODOR UPPMAN
NOVICE'S FRIEND ...	JOHN CAMERON
DANSKER ...	INIA TE WIATA
CABIN BOY ...	PETER FLYNN

Ratings, Officers, Midshipmen, Marines, Powder-monkeys, Drummers.

The Childrens' chorus are members of the Kingsland Central School
and have been trained by Mr. George Hurren.

(Hervey Alan appears by permission of the Governors of Sadler's Wells)

CHORUS MASTER . DOUGLAS ROBINSON
COVENT GARDEN ORCHESTRA, LEADER . THOMAS MATTHEWS

perfunctory in the rest of the score. The whole subject has evidently taken hold of the composer's imagination; the role of the chorus is as vital and various as it was in *Peter Grimes* and the part of Captain Vere, in particular, is elaborated into a creation of great musical and dramatic significance. But the mainspring of the opera, as of the story, is the innocence and heroic goodness of its central character. The idea of innocence and simplicity has always aroused a peculiar sympathy in Britten: we feel it in the *Ceremony of Carols*, in the character of Lucretia, in the 'schoolboys playing in a stream' of the *Spring Symphony*; it sweetens the absurdity of Miss Wordsworth, and it has enabled the composer to penetrate compassionately, in *Rejoice in the Lamb*, into the mad fantasies of poor Christopher Smart.

Fortunately, innocence is a subject naturally suited to music. There is a curious difference in this respect between the two arts, music and literature. While novelists have difficulty in making their good characters convincing, composers have similar trouble with their villains; in opera it cannot be said that the devil has all the good tunes. In *Billy Budd*, Britten has seized the problem of operatic villainy firmly by the horns, and given to Claggart a long, formal aria – a sort of Iago's Creed – expressive of his twisted mentality; it will be interesting to see how effectively, in performance, the character will be thereby established.

It is noticeable, by the way – and evidence perhaps of Britten's increasing ease and maturity as an opera composer – that, while the arias and monologues of *Billy Budd* are generally about twice as long as those of *Peter Grimes*, they produce no sense of dramatic stagnation. In the treatment of background and minor episodes, especially in the tautening and slackening of tension, Britten shows his customary skill and certainty of touch. Sea-shanties, in varying depths of perspective, supply an emotional background and link scenes and episodes together; bugle fanfares, whistles, drums, flying figuration of all sorts (mainly for brass and woodwind) keep the shipboard atmosphere alive and suggest the perpetual bustle of the main deck; the texture looks as clean as though a sea gale had swept through spars and rigging. All this, of course, is no more than a first impression gleaned from a study of the vocal score. Believing as I do that Benjamin Britten has more genius in his little finger than most of his contemporaries in their whole bodies, I make no apology for writing at some length about this exciting work before I have heard it performed or even rehearsed. It is possible that details which seemed vivid on paper will fail to tell in the theatre, and it may be that what I have found moving others will find sentimental. One thing is unlikely: that *Billy Budd* will strike anyone as dull, cold, or lifeless. It was written from the heart; and to the heart it will surely go.

Shawe-Taylor returned to *Billy Budd* in the *New Statesman and Nation* a week later (8 December 1951) with a review of the opera:

Throughout a long evening, the immediate theatrical effectiveness of *Billy Budd* was never in doubt. The libretto, though marred by a central fault, is a shapely piece of work in detail; and the composer, besides writing a good deal of fine music, shows his old unfailing skill in establishing and sustaining atmosphere. This was a man-o'-war, surrounded (if the stage picture had not contradicted our belief) by sky and sea; these were sailors, not a male-voice chorus; most important of all, this was Billy Budd himself, the 'sweet, pleasant fellow' of Melville's imagination, trans-lated simply and unerringly into the language of music. The audience was gripped, surprised, stirred; at moments deeply moved. No scene quite lacks the impress of genius; and one whole act – the second – strikes me as a masterpiece of dramatic veracity going hand in hand with musical beauty. No question: *Billy Budd* will be widely performed, and later performances may reveal qualities now obscured. Yet I must confess that the opera as a whole does not quite fulfil the hopes I had built on it; with all its brilliance and fascination, it falls some way short of success as an integral work of art.

Whence comes this feeling of dissatisfaction? Partly, I believe, from the dramatic and musical treatment of Captain Vere. With some justification in Melville, composer and librettists have attempted to place Vere at the centre of the action; and in the process they have turned him from credible naval officer into moralizing lay preacher. He is most alive in the beautiful scene in which he sits reading Plutarch in his cabin; and there is a welcome flash of vigour at 'John Claggart, beware!' with its slashing D major chords and rhythmically decisive vocal line. Elsewhere we find it hard to recognize in Vere the idolized leader, the man of action. When he addresses the crew at the end of Act I, his part is marked *eroico*, but there is really nothing very inspiring or heroic in his music here; it shows, in fact, a slight family resemblance to the patriotic speech of Lady Billows at Loxford May Day. Nor does the big aria after the court-martial, 'I accept their verdict', make much impact. At that point, our sympathy has been expended on Budd, and we have little left over for Vere; he has done his disagreeable duty according to his principles, and that is that. The situation is hard to sum up in an aria, and it is not surprising that Britten should have fallen back on an arioso-recitative vocal line, punctuated by sharp, isloated chords from the muted trumpets, a familiar pattern in his work. What is really fine, moving and original in this scene is its conclusion: the thirty-four plain triads, distantly related but converging towards F major, scored and spaced in every kind of colour and position, which accompany the interview between Budd and his Captain behind a closed door; the mysterious sequence slowly passes from conflict and agony of mind to acceptance and reconciliation. As the curtain falls on a still empty stage the point is made more explicit by the appearance of the six-eight cradle-song rhythm which has been heard before, and is to be heard again at the beginning of Act IV as the accompaniment to Billy's farewell ballad.

That haunting ballad, about which I wrote last week, emphasizes by its heartfelt beauty the relative bareness of some other parts of the score. Too often – and this is the second cause of our disappointment – the music seems to lack either melodic or symphonic continuity. Sometimes, no doubt, this is an illusion caused by unfamiliarity; but page after page consists of recitative, or quasi-recitative, accompanied only by a series of brilliant orchestral gestures. Even in the interludes the composer shows a curious unwillingness to use the full orchestra, as he did so effectively in *Peter Grimes*. True, operatic music must needs be dramatic, and these bare passages can be of value in advancing the action or creating tension. But they should surely be rationed. The greatest composers of opera are those who have learned the secret of dissolving action in music; those who can afford to give the music its head without loss of dramatic tension. If we doubt the truth of this, we need only think of the supreme masters at their greatest – of Mozart pouring the full flood of his inventiveness into the intrigues of *Figaro*, of Wagner counterpointing and exfoliating to his heart's content during the assembly of the Mastersingers, of Verdi elaborating the immense finale to the third act of *Otello*. Britten possesses a rich fund of lyrical invention; like his own Billy Budd, he 'can sing' – none better in our day: think only of the *Ceremony of Carols* or the *Serenade*

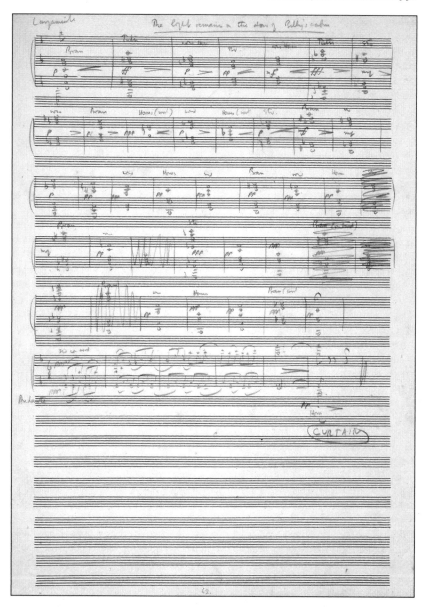

Britten's composition draft for the celebrated sequence of chords at the end
of Act III (four-act version) of *Billy Budd*: this passage represents
the interview between Vere and Billy after the court-martial

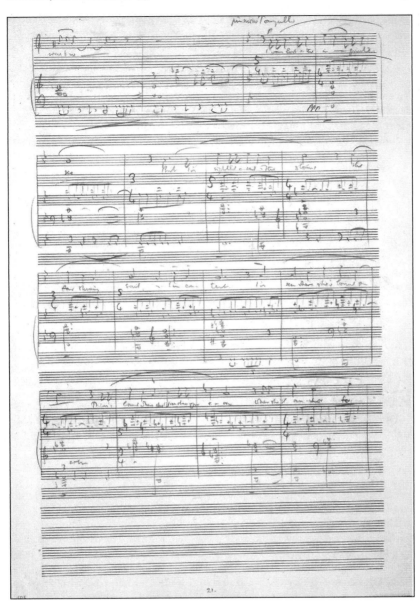

The Epilogue to *Billy Budd* in Britten's composition draft.
Vere: 'I was lost on the infinite sea but I've sighted a sail in the storms,
the far-shining sail, and I'm content.'

or the *Spring Symphony*. But at times a strange constraint hampers his lyricism. It seems a kind of shyness or pride, this obstinate refusal to make more 'music', in the disparaging sense in which the French speak of '*littérature*'.

Richard Capell in the *Daily Telegraph* (3 December 1951):

For the best part of two hours *Billy Budd* seems episodical and almost purposeless, despite the extraordinary resource and aptness of Britten's musical illustrations. Then the climax comes, and it is harrowing in its pathos. No one can fail to be moved, any more than admiration can be grudged for the vivacity of the score. But the long piece is pathetic rather than truly tragic, and the attempt made to draw a universal significance from the hero's doom is not brought home.

The subject comes from a painful story – a kind of elaborate anecdote – by Herman Melville [...]

This action has been dramatized for Britten by E. M. Forster and Eric Crozier – more or less dramatized, a phrase that means rather less than more. The fact is that neither of the chief characters, the inexplicable or, at least, unexplained Claggart and the enigmatic Captain Vere, is fully realized. The difference between life and art is that art must not be inexplicable, whatever life may be.

In Act II Claggart sings a counterpart of Iago's 'Credo in un Dio', but we do not really know why. As for Vere, he stands by like a waxwork while Billy, at the court-martial, is accused of murder, though knowing perfectly well that the act was mere manslaughter.

Yet it is Vere who, at the end, is 'redeemed' by Billy's sterling qualities. He is, in fact, the Amfortas to Billy's Parsifal. But all this is obscurely, and not dramatically, suggested.

Britten's score cannot be called much of a structure, but the incidental felicities are innumerable, and many things are in his best vein – the lower-deck songs and dances, the brilliant ensemble of the battle scene and Billy's affecting farewell to life in the condemned cell. There is matter for study in the variety and certainty of the orchestral effects.

Capell's *Daily Telegraph* review was followed by:

Twenty-one boys of Kingsland Central School, Dalston, were transformed into powder monkeys, midshipmen or drummer boys for *Billy Budd*.

They are members of a 'pool' of Kingsland boys and girls on whom Covent Garden now relies to provide its resident children's chorus. The school was recommended to Sir Steuart Wilson, Deputy General Administrator of the Opera House. 'The concert programmes the children do in their school are wonderful,' he said. 'They are a lesson to every L.C.C. [London County Council] school on what can be done.'

Frank Howes reviewed *Billy Budd* in *The Times* (3 December 1951):

Anticipation, though running high, had been qualified by doubts about the fitness of Herman Melville's curiously evasive story to make a drama, let alone a tragedy, and the ability of an all-male cast to make an opera. Ghedini has already made a one-act opera on the subject, but Britten's, being extended to four acts, undoubtedly ran the risk of producing a dark tonal monotony comparable to the *Quoniam* of the B minor Mass expanded into two acts of *Siegfried*. This doubt, however, was swept right away, in spite of a pervasive dark orchestral ground tone, by the marked contrasts of the constituent elements. The other doubt was half resolved: here was undoubtedly drama, but not tragedy. Melville comes near to providing a truly tragic clash between law and morality but misses it because the motivation of his characters is too sketchy. Here the composer has been well served by his librettists, E. M. Forster and Eric Crozier, who have filled out the personification of evil in Claggart, the master-at-arms, by giving him a *Credo* to sing, like Iago's apostrophe 'Evil be thou my good' in *Otello*, and by shifting (perhaps more questionably) the interest from innocent Billy Budd to Starry Vere, the ship's captain, who in Melville died of wounds but in the opera meditates as an old man on the problem of evil in a Prologue and an Epilogue.

Britten has himself also strengthened the plot by two strokes of genius. As in *Peter Grimes* the chief actor is not a *dramatis persona* but public opinion, so in *Billy Budd* the protagonist is not Vere nor Budd but the sea. In the first act the shrill wind, the salt tang and the eternal swell and surge of restless water envelop the listener so that whatever happens aboard the *Indomitable* he can never forget this relentless conditioning of sailors' lives. The other is the wonderful realization in a passage of antiphonal chords of what passed between the two victims of fate's malignancy, from which Melville hedges away. But the central weakness, the division in Vere's mind, cannot quite be made good in the scene of the court-martial. Yet if the opera just misses tragedy it reveals the emergence of something latent, or only revealed in glimpses, in Britten's other work, a deep emotion informing that astounding skill of his, the emotion of compassion. To those of the composer's admirers who have wondered whether and when he would sound the deeper music of humanity, *Billy Budd* provides the answer.

Colin Mason, *Spectator* (7 December 1951):

Claggart's 'natural depravity', implausibly and hazily defined by Melville, is made more explicit, if not more credible, in a monologue. In the trial scene the Captain, instead of speaking in Budd's favour, while insisting on the necessity of observing the letter of the law by hanging him so as not to endanger naval discipline, remains harshly silent, as though the librettists had preferred to follow up Melville's passing suggestion that he was momentarily seized by a kind of visionary insanity. Since he makes his real feelings clear in various other parts of Act III, this is a justifiable course to take.

The music throughout equals in beauty and far outstrips in originality anything that Britten has written before. His use of distinctive musical 'motives' is very telling. Some, such as those associated with Billy's stammer, with the *Rights o' Man* and naval discipline in general, and the theme of the Novice's subjection to Claggart, are easily picked out. Less quickly noticed is the characteristic group of musical symbols, hardly 'motives', associated with Claggart's determination to destroy Billy – the chord of F minor, the rising semitone from G to $A\flat$, and the simultaneous sounding of B and $C\sharp$. Such devices are not new, either in opera or in Britten. To define, even to identify, what it is that seems so completely new in the music is difficult. A fragment here and there recalls *Peter Grimes* or *Les Illuminations*, and the gentle clash of different common chords within the same key in both Billy's and the Captain's last soliloquies suggests Stravinsky. Perhaps the broken thirds that open the opera provide a clue to the development that Britten's idiom has undergone. Just as this opening clash of conflicting harmonies, of $B\flat$ and $B\natural$, is attenuated in these broken chords, so those spurts of concentrated harmonic beauty in which Britten's earlier music is so rich are constantly merged with the severer harmonies, and dissolved into fluid, subtle melodic lines, of which the impact, as in Wagner, is still harmonic, not contrapuntal.

There are still little pockets of ravishingly poignant harmony, but they are less frequent. The exuberant invention has been stemmed and transformed by mature thought; the former facility deliberately forsaken for the labour of elimination. Not that facility has forsaken Britten. The masterly solution of the technical problems involved in ensuring variety in a work on this scale for male voices only is a feat of virtuosity that surpasses anything he has ever done. But one is never conscious of it, so completely are technique and content identified. Everything, even the orchestral virtuosity, the marvellously descriptive noises, is now thematically worked in. The result is a consistency and concentration of musical language such as are not to be found in anything Britten has previously written.

Stephen Williams, who had already contributed a review to the *Stage* (6 December 1951), also wrote a long review for the *New York Times* (9 December 1951), which not only scrutinized the general press reception *Budd* had received but also reflected the hostility with which the established press had received the co-called 'Britten Issue' – the first ever of its kind – of *Music Survey*, 2/4, published in the spring of 1950, the year before the premiere of *Budd*:

Mr Britten is in a class by himself. He is the golden boy of British music: 'Hear Britten first' might be the slogan of any English musical tourist agency. He is phenomenally clever and phenomenally lucky. Everything he writes is performed almost immediately throughout the world, broadcast, recorded and critically compared with the works of Bach, Mozart, Verdi and Wagner, often to those gentlemen's disadvantages. As an elderly and less successful composer once said to me, 'Benjamin Britten has only to blow his nose and they record it.'

He has an astute and enterprising publisher who blazes his trail with blinding and deafening advance publicity. He has also fanatical disciples such as those who before the production of *Billy Budd* solemnly assured us that the libretto was to be compared only with Boito's *Otello* and the score only with the last works of Verdi.

Now all this kind of thing is very damaging. No one survives being overestimated, and the immediate effect of such hysterical pronouncements is to put one's back up, so that one goes to the first performance of work like this with a feeling of resentful prejudice. [...]

To sum up, *Billy Budd* is a challenging, stimulating work of art quite able to stand on its own merits without a lot of hysterical ballyhoo. In fact, one might say that with *Billy Budd* Britten has conquered not only his enemies but also his friends – a far more difficult feat.

Among further coverage in the US press of the UK premiere were reviews by Farnsworth Foule in the *New York Times* (3 December 1951) and Jack Tait in the *New York Herald Tribune* (9 December 1951).

Philip Hope-Wallace wrote in the *Manchester Guardian* (3 December 1951):

Turning again to full-scale opera of the size of *Peter Grimes*, [Britten] shows a new mastery of that essential craft of managing operatic 'attention', and with it an originality, effectiveness, and fineness of musical creation altogether magnificent. If only one could laud the distinguished librettists, E. M. Forster and Eric Crozier, in similar terms, one might be saluting a masterpiece instead of a qualified success of esteem. [...]

It is the collaborators' hard task to convert a pathetic incident into a four-act tragedy, and one has to say that their solution, however conscientious and emotionally responsive, seems to give rise to a cardinal defect in the opera, considered as a work for the stage: 'seems' because critical first reactions to opera (where so many elements are involved) are notoriously insecure. Until the music has fully flowered in the mind the bare tree stumps impede our view of the whole wood. But where a defect sticks out so clearly it should be spoken of, even if the sheer musical virtues of the score finally 'carry' the opera.

Briefly, it is that the effort to turn a pathetic incident to tragedy has been entrusted to a third character – the moralizing tenor part, sung by Peter Pears, Captain 'Starry' Vere, the much hero-worshipped and nice-minded arbiter of Budd's fate, whose stern duty it is to string up the trusting seaman. Captain Vere is identified with the narrator in a Prologue and an Epilogue and is given a heavy burden of philosophical disquisition, together with prayers for that light which distinguishes right from wrong.

This gives the opera a core of almost German earnestness and is a brave effort to find an equivalent for Melville's voice in the proceedings, but it has the effect of weakening the 'natural' hero, Budd, and the villain, Claggart, in spite of their monologues and self-revelations, into little more than abstractions of good and bad, far less sharply and humanly characterized even than Scarpia and Cavaradossi, let alone Peter Pan and Hook: while Captain Vere, in a false position dramatically, fails to catch our sympathy for his dilemma of conscience to a notable degree, appearing rather as a sanctimonious, not to say priggish, character nearer to the perplexed prefect of some story by Dean Farrar than to Melville.

Perhaps the music redeems the flaw, so immediate and telling is the poetic atmosphere (not, fortunately, matched by the dark, claustrophobic settings by John Piper or the dull production). But Mr Britten makes us sniff the salt air with a single cunningly spaced arpeggio; he holds a scene on a single rocking chord. The first scene of the second act is a masterpiece and as nearly as anything – would things had been left at that – springs the captain's dilemma in our minds. A chord and the whole ominous calm of the ship is imaginatively projected. The officers drink (trio); from the orchestra the dreaded word 'mutiny' creeps into the conversation; then, with one of those effects of which only opera is capable, the answer is given – far off – by the happy singing below decks.

The ensuing scene, below decks, is no less brilliant. The song and games, the brawl, the irruption of the villain, his Iago-like monologue (otiose, strictly speaking); the rousing of Budd from his sleep and his temptation by a suborned shipmate, the whole scene overlaid with the drowsy reminiscence of Budd's dream (which recurs in his farewell ballad in the fourth act) and ending with the fast, free, catchy duo with the elderly sailor – here, indeed, is mastery. But the climactic third act shows up the flaw. The opening, with the mist lifting and the ship going into action ('This is our moment') is superb; so, too, the change of atmosphere as the mist descends and, in rancour of disappointment, the false accusation is made. But from there to the end of the act events move jerkily. The 'accident'; the drumhead court-martial (quartet); Budd's plea for mercy, especially the captain's solo self-accusations, a quasi-Verdian outburst, are curiously implausible.

It is only when the captain leaves the stage empty to break the news of his fate to the poor seaman that the composer, freed from the fumbling libretto, can bring off a really effective operatic stroke: the reiteration, on the darkening stage, of a ponderous succession of related chords, like bell strokes (or 'ear tests'). On paper, dubious; on the stage, how triumphantly successful! They are like the ripples widening out from a marine disaster, and nothing could touch the imagination at that crucial point more effectively. What follows is anticlimax in the sense that it holds no chance of a surprise. But Britten reserves for it his most poignant music, the ballad of farewell and resignation for the prisoner and the mute, shambling procession towards execution, pierced by his cry of blessing on his captain. Then the decks are cleared of murmuring men, the mists come down, and we are back with the old narrator again. It may not have been the tragedy of conscience aimed at, but it has certainly left its emotional mark.

The *Evening Standard* (20 December 1951) reported:

American singer Theodor Uppman, who plays Billy Budd in Benjamin Britten's new opera (one of his songs is the condemned man's Farewell to the Grand Rough World), sang to 300 prisoners last night at Wormwood Scrubs.

The 300 were good-conduct men and first offenders.

Having already seen the opera on stage, J. F. Waterhouse in the *Birmingham Post* (17 December 1951) reviewed the subsequent radio broadcast:

An operatic broadcast [. . .] always has the effect of throwing a searching spotlight on the music. I found that *Billy Budd* stood the test very well indeed. It still seems to me Mr Britten's best opera, by a big margin.

[. . .] Sometimes it seems as though, in his attempt to catch in music the natural inflections of a spoken phrase, the composer has let musical values go hang while failing, after all, to secure anything like the precise equivalent he seems to be seeking. And whether the thing is really worth doing at all – whether it would not be better to descend by means of a musical 'ramp' to actual spoken dialogue – I am not perfectly sure. Nevertheless, I think that in *Billy Budd* Mr Britten has come nearer than ever before to justifying his procedure. Time and time again one recognizes with novel satisfaction a co-existence of authentic speed and live music. I can call to mind no more striking instance than the chuckling phrases ('No, gentlemen, no, no! I feel as you do!') with which Captain Vere, in the first scene of Act II, endorses his officers' comments on the French.

What impressed me anew most forcefully, at this second hearing, was the unity and stylistic integrity of the whole. *Billy Budd* is really Mr Britten's least 'patchy' opera.

He has never been a *Leitmotiv* man, and no element in this score would clearly warrant the term: not even the flickering five-note figure which accompanies Billy's stammer and which is anticipated in the Prologue when Vere refers to the 'imperfection in the divine image'; nor that curve of fifth and minor second which is first established in the haunting, melancholy shanty of the sailors holystoning the deck, and which asserts itself again and again – in Billy's farewell to the *Rights o' Man*, in the officers' bitter reference to 'the floating Republic' (Act II scene 1), in the mutinous murmur at Billy's hanging, and in countless other contexts. Also, *Billy Budd* has nothing resembling the 'symphonic development' which, rather than the *Leitmotiv* principle as such, is the special glory and power of Wagnerian opera. Mr

Britten, like Mozart and Verdi, has always directed primary attention to the stage and the voices.

Yet the whole of this magnificent opera is bound together, its separate scenes unified within themselves and its principal characters individualized, by innumerable recurrences and cross-references, melodic shapes and harmonic turns, which are often glimpsed rather than analytically recognized. There is a particularly beautiful instance in the Epilogue. Vere's vision of the 'far-shining sail' brings nothing like a musical reprise of Billy's execution-ballad, 'Billy in the Darbies', where the boy had the same vision. But the thematic and harmonic points of resemblance are just sufficient to underline the spiritual kinship between the two without formal artifice.

As for the individualizing of the characters, let us take the case of the villain, John Claggart. Now his master-at-arms is not the Claggart of the original story: it would have been impossible in any case to transfer to the stage Melville's probings into the mystery of evil and of 'natural depravity'. But in his somewhat Iago-like way the operatic Claggart is a very real and rounded and convincing personage; and he is established not by any elaborate orchestral psychologizing but principally by a 'tone of voice'. At his first appearance there are the repeated brutal, formidable rising fourths of his interrogation of the 'impressed' sailors; and, shortly afterwards, the phrase (with two falling fourths in it) of his domineeringly sarcastic reply to the First Lieutenant: 'I heard your honour!' This latter is dwelt on for a time, adopted by the orchestra, inverted. But it never becomes anything like a regular 'Claggart motive'. He has many substantial passages where it does not recur at all, though other kindred features do and the 'manner' is continuously preserved. And in his big monologue in Act II, as his resolve to destroy Billy mounts to its climax, both the rising fourth and (near the end) the falling fourth figure strongly assert themselves. It is in the very absence of any systematic working-out, in the natural spontaneity of the recurrences and echoes, that the extraordinary organic vitality of this score principally resides.

Eric Blom in the *Observer* (2 December 1951):

He has been well served by his librettists, E. M. Forster and Eric Crozier, who, we may take it, represent roughly the literary and the theatrical elements of the work. The adaptation is very skilfully made and kept closely to the original, which it not only condenses well but certain incidents of which it sometimes telescopes. Claggart's savagely ironical compliment paid to Billy, for instance, occurs after a fight that makes a dramatic point, whereas in the novel it follows Billy's spilling of soup on the deck, which would have been theatrically ineffective. A weakness seems to be that Claggart's hatred of Billy is not sufficiently accounted for to come to such a fearful issue and that he could never have made so ill-founded an accusation plausible to a man of such integrity and intelligence as Captain Vere; but the same criticism applies to the original.

The cinematographic 'throwback', on the other hand, is a new device of the librettists, and I confess that at first sight it struck me as rather cheap. But on studying the music I came to the conclusion that it must have been asked for by the composer, not only because the Prologue and Epilogue admirably round off his scheme thematically, but also because it enabled him to make a particularly subtle musical point. For when in the Prologue Vere says: 'The good has never been perfect. There is always some flaw in it . . . some imperfection in the divine image', we first hear the music afterwards associated with Billy's stammer, that fatal defect which precipitates the tragedy.

This motif – there are no *Leitmotive* in the Wagnerian sense, but a number of very interesting thematic allusions and cross-references – is one of those inventions for which Britten is famous by now: quite a simple thing, but one which nobody had thought of before (and one wonders why not?), a thing that clings to the memory and is apt to haunt it at unexpected moments, as imaginative composers' notions will do – such a thing, indeed, as distinguishes genius from talent. Britten can make this sort of indelible impression with a mere three chords, quite ordinary chords but succeeding each other in a new way, as at the end of the poignant episode after the flogging of the Novice. But whether the succession of thirty-four plain and harmonically disconnected triads in slow semibreves at the end of the third act justify themselves I am not sure yet, though I can see that they foreshadow Billy's last resolve to die without weakening.

Much else could be written about the music, but that will keep, though it may be said at once that among the things that were most immediately telling were the skilful mixtures of tonalities (harsh but always cogent), the shantyings of the sailors (so authentic, yet so individually Brittenish), shapely concerted movements like the scherzoid 'Don't like the French', the long quasi-chaconne on the ground-bass of 'Jemmy Legs is down on you', which closes the second act, and Billy's sudden loquacity at the trial, so ironically tragic because it comes too late after his being tongue-tied at the critical moment.

In 1990 Peter Gellhorn, who shared the conducting of *Billy Budd* at Covent Garden with the composer, recalled seeing Blom's *Observer* review in Pears's dressing room during the third interval at the first night. (It was possible then, as now, to purchase Sunday papers late on Saturday evening in London's West End.) Blom's notice had clearly been written after attending the final dress rehearsal, to which the press had been invited. See BBMCPR, pp. 163–4, n. 32.

Ernest Newman in the *Sunday Times* (9 December 1951):

As far as I was concerned the new work was a painful disappointment. This seems to me the least notable of Mr Britten's four operas; I can see no such musical advance in it as I had hoped for.

He has been ill served by his librettists. [...]

The prime trouble with the opera, as I see it, is that hardly anywhere do the three principal characters come to real musical life. Melville's task was easy; availing himself of the novelist's privilege to speak in his own person, he gives us a searching analysis of each of the three. But to translate these psychological subtleties into operatic terms is a difficult problem, and it is hardly to be wondered at that the librettists have failed to solve it. Claggart's brief soliloquizing shows him only as an ineffectual cross between the Iago of the 'Credo' and Pizarro [in *Fidelio*], without a Verdi or a Beethoven to back him up musically in his confession of a natural bent towards evil. Captain Vere, by means of a good deal of moralizing in a sort of recitative, does to some extent reproduce the character as Melville has drawn it. But the fundamentally negative rather than positive Billy has defied the efforts of the collaborators to endow him with real stage life.

He is less the innocent untutored barbarian of Melville's imagination than an ordinary simpleton. He talks far too much, in my opinion, and to too little effect; there were times, indeed, when I found myself wishing he would talk less and stutter more, for I found his occasional stuttering more psychologically and dramatically convincing than some of his talk.

The action would have gone better in two acts than in four [see Letter 722]; by that means we would have been spared a good deal of repetition and padding and one or two scenes that are too 'operatic' in the unflattering sense of the term, the worst example being the ensemble of the ship's company in praise of Captain Vere at the end of the first act. I could imagine something of this sort happening on the deck of H.M.S. *Pinafore* but hardly on that of H.M.S. *Indomitable*. Another piece of bad structure is to work us up in anticipation of Claggart's poisonous story to Captain Vere – the nodal point of the action – interrupt it, after a few sentences, to stage a long episode in which the crew prepare the ship for a fight (which does not materialize) with a French frigate, and then bring Claggart back to resume where he had left off.

Inexpert as the dramatic handling often is, for it keeps falling between the two stools of conventional 'opera' and modern psychological music-drama, the music, to me, is a greater disappointment still. It has several fine and some great moments, particularly in the third act; but for the most part it indulges too much for my liking in a dry speech-song in the voices and disjointed 'pointings' in the orchestra, and Mr Britten has done all this much better elsewhere. What he seems to me to need is a libretto that will give the talented musician in him more scope.

The 'London Music Critic' of the *Scotsman* (3 December 1951):

The music is more advanced in idiom than before, and more convincing in musical syntax. Britten is courageous and not content to rest on his laurels. The music of *Budd* is less obviously lyrical than the earlier operas: there is more to admire but less to be touched by. [. . .]

The librettists have fashioned with plain words and plenty of violence four acts with Vere as an old man in Prologue and Epilogue introducing and closing the story. The music is at its best in the magnificent third act when the action gets going. The first act, which introduces the ship and its characters, is by far the least convincing, and much of the music in it seems undistinguished, with the exception of the episode when a flogged novice is brought on to quite heart-rending music.

Like *Grimes*, this is a tale of the sea, but, being actually on the sea, we hear little direct evidence of it. There is no storm, only a mist. The orchestration divides the burden between wind and brass, with the strings quite unprominent. The texture is always effective, though the brass became tired and nervous on the first night on Saturday at Covent Garden.

As in the previous operas, *Budd* is held together by the use, re-use, and metamorphoses of themes. Britten, in his music, matches the symbolism that is evident in Melville's tale of the forces of good and evil. The most extraordinary page of the score is a slow series of thirty-four chords which are played to an empty stage, Vere having left to tell Budd that he has been condemned to death. This is a daring piece of writing which almost comes off.

The lack of female voices is not felt, which is a hint of Britten's mastery of self-imposed problems. How he avoids monotony is worthy of a serious study. It may have something to do with the fact that the melodic line is emphasized in the orchestra a good deal more than is usual with Britten.

A short review, credited to 'A.F.', appeared in the *Daily Mirror* (3 December 1951) under the headline, 'WHAT A NIGHT FOR THE MEN':

At last a really satisfying modern British opera – without women and without spectacle!

In *Billy Budd*, composer Benjamin Britten comes his nearest yet to greatness and his music its nearest yet to popular taste.

Seventeen curtain calls at Covent Garden showed what the audience thought of this drama of the Royal Navy's press-gang days.

A new American star, Theodor Uppman, 26 [*recte*: thirty-one] as the tragic Billy, sang like an angel.

See also BBMCPR, pp. 135–40, and Donald Mitchell, 'More Off than On Billy Budd', *Music Survey*, 4/2 (February 1952), pp. 386–408, reprinted in DMCN, pp. 365–92.

3 The trade name (after its Hungarian inventor, Ladislao Biró) of the ballpoint pen, which gained currency in the UK during the early 1950s.

719 To Eric Crozier

4 CRABBE STREET, ALDEBURGH

Dec. 7th 1951

My dear Eric,

Here is the share of the 2nd Arts Council commission. Thank you so much for having taken all this trouble over the work, & for your encouragement during the agonising weeks of rehearsal[1] – <u>that</u> is something I hope'll never reoccur in my life!! I've written to E.M.F. & told him that I think you & he have produced the finest libretto I've ever heard or read. And I think many people realise it too.

I hope to see you before long – please excuse the brevity & scribble of this – but I'm snowed under with letters to answer, & want to fight my way out before getting down seriously to writing again!

With love to you both,

Yours ever,

BEN

1 The late withdrawal of Josef Krips, who had been engaged to conduct *Billy Budd*, meant that Britten himself had to step into the breach, conducting many rehearsals and the first night himself, and then sharing the run of performances with Peter Gellhorn, Head of Music Staff at Covent Garden. See BBMCPR, pp. 69–72.

720 To David Webster
Royal Opera House, Covent Garden

4 CRABBE ST, ALDEBURGH, SUFFOLK
Dec. 7th 1951

My dear David,

Only the briefest of notes, to thank you for your telegram, but even
more for your great patience & encouragement during the most difficult
rehearsal weeks. I have been delighted with the atmosphere of the company,
& also its remarkably high quality. You said you hoped it was only the
beginning of our collaboration, & so do I. I wish, when the alarms have
somewhat died down, we could have a talk to discuss in what way I could
be a help to you, because I most sincerely would like to be.

I hope everyone in the company knows how happy I was to work with
them – I think they must – but not least I hope you know how happy I
always was in my relations with you.

Yours ever,

BEN

721 To Lennox Berkeley

4 CRABBE ST, ALDEBURGH, SUFFOLK
Dec. 14th 1951

My dear Lennox,

Thank you for your nice letter about 'Billy'[1] – for the welcome telegram
(at a horrid moment!) & finally the gay little critics' comments. I haven't
seen many of the latters' efforts (I avoid them like the plague – since they
make me angry for at least 2 hours – much too long!) but they have been
obviously up to standard! What a race – vermin, living off others' leavings!
But luckily, they don't really affect the public much – only those dreary
middlebrows who don't know what to think till they read the New
Statesman!

Yes, it would be lovely if you'd both come here, with Nelson,[2] for a
weekend – New Year's best – January? Shall I write & suggest a day?

Lots of love to you all,
In haste,
BEN

1 Berkeley had written to Britten on 2 December 1951, the day following the
premiere of *Billy Budd*:

Many congratulations on a splendid work that you alone could have written – full
of beauty and in places deeply moving. I think the long succession of common

chords at the end of Act III is the finest moment. I was particularly impressed –
apart from the pathos – with the dignity of the music. That is a very rare quality,
I think.

In a further letter (9 December), Berkeley writes:

I hope this makes you laugh as much as it did me: 'He has been ill served by his
librettists' *Sunday Times*. 'The composer has been well served by his librettists,
E. M. Forster and Eric Crozier' *Listener*. So what? A special kind of Bedlam for
musical critics seems necessary.

Another composer who was among the first-night audience was John
Ireland, Britten's former composition teacher at the Royal College of
Music, who gave his initial response in a letter to John Longmire:

All the music is extremely efficient, and some of it quite fine, in its way. But there
are no big tunes, and the libretto is unsatisfactory [. . .] on the whole I was rather
disappointed, for the opera is not nearly so strong and gripping as Melville's short
novel. Probably the librettists were to blame for this. There was a lack of continuity
and concentration, as regards the action and general design [. . .] However, it was
all rapturously received, and a great personal success for Britten. No other British
composer could have written the music, all of which was personal and characteristic
and at times, reached a very high level. The orchestration was masterly [. . .]

Ireland completed this letter on 13 December, by which time he had caught
sight of a copy of the (pre-publication) vocal score:

Last evening I went to dinner with Julian Herbage and his wife, Anna Instone [. . .]
Much of the evening was spent in discussing Britten's new opera. Herbage has the
vocal score, and on paper the music looks very much more 'odd' than it actually
sounds. In fact, played in the piano arrangement, most of it would be quite silly
and unintelligible. There are no 'tunes'. There are all sorts of odd-looking things –
passages in 2nds, 'bi-tonal' passages, quite a lot of plain common chords and
Dom. [dominant] 7ths, some with dissonant notes added (such as F in the chord
of C major), and so on. [See Longmire, *John Ireland: Portrait of a Friend*, pp. 122–3.]

Ireland wrote to Britten on 24 December 1951 in somewhat different
terms:

Knowing you would be overwhelmed with a deluge of letters about *Billy Budd*, I
have delayed writing to tell you I was present at the first performance at Covent
Garden. Melville's story was well known to me, and I was deeply moved by your
splendid musical expression of the profound emotion of it all. Your opera is indeed
a masterpiece, and embodies music which is entirely characteristic of your own
genius, not a phrase or even a *bar* of which could have been written by any other
composer.
    The clarity, the economy of means – the invariable certainty of touch – the
spontaneity, the invention – all constituted a perfect joy to me.
    I believe I recognized the unique quality of your gifts when you came up for
your scholarship at the R.C.M. If only Frank Bridge could have heard *Billy Budd*.
He too would have rejoiced, as I do.

2 Berkeley's three-act opera *Nelson* (1949–54), first performed by the Sadler's
   Wells Opera on 22 September 1954. See also Peter Dickinson, *The Music of
   Lennox Berkeley*, pp. 128–40.

722 To E. J. Dent

4 CRABBE ST, ALDEBURGH, SUFFOLK
Dec. 18th 1951

Dear Professor Dent,

Please forgive this brief note (& the horrid but convenient Biro!) in
reply to your nice long one[1] – but I am snowed under with letters, & also
with work which has got held up seriously by Billy Budd. I am so glad that
you got so much pleasure from it. I have now heard it twice myself, &
must confess myself more or less satisfied with it – until of course I write
another opera! I don't honestly feel that the brass in anyway overweighs
the voices, in fact (allowing for the fact that I know the piece) there wasn't
a moment when the voices seemed obscured to me. The all-maleness of
the cast doesn't worry me, or any of my serious friends – since one doesn't
expect the female sound at any point – ; actually the only complaints on
that account that have come to my ears are all from a certain kind of person
(male & over 40) which makes me giggle a little!

I'm sorry it seems long to some people – but there it is; it has to be that
way. If we could get the 1st & 3rd intervals down a bit, it would be better
(I originally meant it to be in 2 parts Acts I & II, & Acts III & IV only) but
that seems impossible in Covent Garden.[2] I didn't see what dear old
Ernest Newman wrote, but I don't often read criticisms. I have frank &
intelligent friends, & am a sufficiently severe self-critic, I think!

Thank you for the nice things you say about my conducting – I wish
I could say I enjoyed doing it!

I hope you are well.

With every good Christmas wish,
Yours sincerely,
BENJAMIN B.

1 Dent had written to Britten on 10 December, congratulating him on the
   success and achievement of *Billy Budd*, which he had seen on three occasions (including the dress and other rehearsals). However, he criticized
   Britten's writing for the brass, which he felt overpowered the voices, though
   he tempered his remarks by blaming his ear-trumpet for probably distort-
   ing the balance. He goes on to say, 'I am always very moved by the scene
   where the Novice is brought back after his flogging; it is a remarkable piece
   of music and extremely skilfully made.'

2 In his letter of 10 December, Dent suggested that Britten should cut the
   opera as he felt it made too long an evening with three intervals, though he
   added 'but do *not on any account* make the "obvious" cut after Vere goes
   into the dark room', i.e. the famous sequence of common chords played
   during Vere's and Billy's unseen interview.
       Circumstantial evidence suggests that subsequent performances of *Billy
   Budd* by the Covent Garden Company in 1952 divided the opera into two
   halves with only one interval, as indicated in Britten's letter. This division
   was also followed at the German premiere at Wiesbaden in 1952; see
   BBMCPR, p. 74. One of Britten's principal revisions to the score in 1960 was
   to refashion the four-act structure into a two-act shape.

BIBLIOGRAPHY

Alexander, Peter F., *William Plomer*, Oxford: Oxford University Press, 1990

Alston, Richard, *Norman Del Mar*, London: Thames Publishing, 2000

Amis, John, *Amiscellany*, London: Faber and Faber, 1985

Anonymous, 'Pervigilium Veneris' ('The Vigil of Venus'), translated by Cecil Clementi, Oxford: Blackwell, 1911

Ansermet, Ernest, 'Benjamin Brittens zweite Oper', *Welt von Heute*, 4 December 1946, *rp* in *Revue Musicale Suisse*, 6 (June 1947), pp. 230–32

Auden, W. H., *Look, Stranger!*, London: Faber and Faber, 1936

- *The Age of Anxiety*, New York: Random House, 1947, and London: Faber and Faber, 1948

- *Paul Bunyan: The Libretto of Operetta by Benjamin Britten*, with an Essay by Donald Mitchell, London: Faber and Faber, 1988

- *The Sea and the Mirror: A Commentary on Shakespeare's* The Tempest, edited and with an introduction by Arthur Kirsch, Princeton: Princeton University Press, 2003

- 'Some Reflections on Opera as Medium', *Tempo*, 20 (1951), *rp* as 'Notes on Music and Opera', *The Dyer's Hand*, pp. 465–74

- and Christopher Isherwood, *Journey to a War*, London: Faber and Faber, 1939

- *The Dyer's Hand*, London: Faber and Faber, 1988

- and Chester Kallman, *Libretti and Other Dramatic Writings by W. H. Auden, 1939–73* edited by Edward Mendelson, London: Faber and Faber, 1993

Ault, Norman (ed.), *Elizabethan Lyrics from the original texts*, London: Longmans, 1925

Banks, Paul (ed.), *Britten's 'Gloriana': Essays and Sources*, Aldeburgh Studies in Music vol. 1, Woodbridge: Boydell Press/Britten–Pears Library, 1993 (PBBG)

- (ed.), *Benjamin Britten: A Catalogue of the Published Works*, Aldeburgh: The Britten–Pears Library, 1999

- (ed.), *The Making of Peter Grimes*, Aldeburgh Studies in Music vol. 6, Woodbridge: Britten Estate Limited/Boydell Press, 2000 (PBMPG)

- 'Bibliographic Notes and Narratives', in PBMPG, pp. 167–228

- *Plymouth Town* programme note, Royal College of Music, 27 January 2004

- and Philip Reed, *Painting and Music: Exhibition Catalogue*, Aldeburgh: The Britten–Pears Library, 1993

- and Rosamund Strode, 'Gloriana: A List of Sources' in PBBG, pp. 95–170

Barnfield, Richard, *The Poems of Richard Barnfield*, London: Fortune Press, n.d.

Beck, Conrad (ed.), *Dank an Paul Sacher*, Zurich: Atlantis Musikbuch-Verlag, 1976

Beddoes, Thomas Lovell, *The Works of Thomas Lovell Beddoes*, London: Oxford University Press, 1935

Bedford, Steuart, 'The Struggle with the Word', in PPT, pp. 5–7

- 'Composer and Conductor: Annals of a Collaboration', *Opera Quarterly* 4/5 (autumn 1986), pp. 60–74

Bennett, C. E. (ed.), *Horace: the Odes and Epodes*, London: Heinemann, 1934

Berkeley, Lennox, 'Britten's *Spring Symphony*', *Music & Letters*, 31/2 (July 1950)
    pp. 216–19
Berkeley, Michael, 'We lived in a secret, intoxicating world', *Guardian*, 10 February 2003
Bing, Rudolf, *5000 Nights at the Opera*, London: Hamish Hamilton, 1972
Bird, John, *Percy Grainger*, London: Faber and Faber, 1982
Bliss, Arthur, *As I Remember*, London: Thames, 1990
Blunt, Wilfrid, *John Christie of Glyndebourne*, London: Geoffrey Bles, 1968
Blyth, Alan, *Remembering Britten*, London: Hutchinson, 1981
— 'Nancy Evans: "The Comely Mezzo"', liner note, Dutton's 'Singers to Remember' CD
    series, Dutton Laboratories, CDBP 9723, 2002
Bowen, Meirion (ed.), *Tippett on Music*, Oxford, Clarendon Press, 1995
Boys, Henry, 'The Younger English Composers: V. Benjamin Britten', *Monthly Musical
    Record*, 68/800 (October 1938)
— 'Musico-Dramatic Analysis', in RLEC, pp. 75–101
Brett, Philip (ed.), *Benjamin Britten: Peter Grimes*, Cambridge, Cambridge University Press,
    1983 (PGPB)
— 'Eros and Orientalism in Britten's Operas', in Brett, Wood and Thomas (eds.), *Queering
    the Pitch*, pp. 235–56
— '*Peter Grimes*: The Growth of the Libretto', in PBMPG, pp. 53–78
Brett, Philip, Elizabeth Wood and Gary Thomas (eds.), *Queering the Pitch: the new gay and
    lesbian musicology*, London: Routledge, 1994
Bridcut, John, 'The boys who loved Britten', *Daily Telegraph*, 29 May 2004, pp. 8–9
— 'Britten's real young Apollo', *Daily Telegraph*, 31 May 2004, p. 19
Britten, Benjamin, *Themes for improvisation*, *Tempo*, 12 (1945), p. 15
— 'Foreword', in RLEC, pp. 7–8
— 'A Note on the *Spring Symphony*', *Music Survey*, 2/4 (spring 1950), p. 237
— 'Verdi – A Symposium', *Opera* 2/3 (February 1951), pp. 113–15; rp PKBM, pp. 102–3
— 'Some notes on Forster and music', in Stallybrass (ed.), *Aspects of E. M. Forster*; rp PKBM,
    pp. 316–20
Britten, Beth, *My Brother Benjamin*, Bourne End: The Kensal Press, 1986 (EWB)
Browne, E. Martin (ed.), *Three European Plays*, Harmondsworth: Penguin, 1958
Büchner, Georg, *Danton's Death*, translated by Stephen Spender and Goronwy Rees,
    London: Faber and Faber, 1939
Bucknell, Katherine, and Nicholas Jenkins (eds.), *W. H. Auden: 'The Language of Learning
    and the Language of Love'*, Auden Studies 2, Oxford: Clarendon Press, 1995
Budd, F. E. (ed.), *A Book of Lullabies 1300–1900*, London: Eric Partridge Scholaris Press, 1930
Buja, Maureen, 'A Bibliography of Donald Mitchell's Writings, 1945–1995', in Reed (ed.), *On
    Mahler and Britten*, pp. 299–330
Burden, Michael, '"Gallimaufry" at Covent Garden: Purcell's *The Fairy-Queen* in 1946', *Early
    Music*, May 1995, pp. 268–84
Burra, Peter, 'The Novels of E. M. Forster', *The Nineteenth Century and After*, 116 (1934), pp.
    581–94
— 'The Barcelona Festival', *Monthly Musical Record*, 66 (June 1936), pp. 107–8
Burton, Humphrey, *Leonard Bernstein*, London: Faber and Faber, 1994
— and Maureen Murray, *William Walton: The Romantic Loner*, Oxford: Oxford University
    Press, 2002
Butler, M., *The Painting and Drawings of William Blake*, New Haven and London: Yale
    University Press, 1981
Butt, James, 'Lord Britten: some recollections', *East Anglian Daily Times*, 5 December 1978

Cadbury-Brown, H. T., 'Notes on an Opera House for Aldeburgh', 1957 Aldeburgh Festival
    programme book
Campion, Paul, *Ferrier – A Career Recorded*, London: Julia MacRae, 1992

Caplan, Isador, 'Recollections of Benjamin Britten', a transcript of an informal talk,
  Richmond, 24 October 1993 (BPL)
Carpenter, Humphrey, *W. H. Auden: A Biography*, London: Allen & Unwin, 1981
– *Benjamin Britten*, London: Faber and Faber, 1992 (HCBB)
– *The Envy of the World: Fifty Years of the BBC Third Programme and Radio 3, 1946–1996*,
  London: Weidenfeld and Nicolson, 1996
Carter, Miranda, *Anthony Blunt: His Lives*, London: Macmillan, 2001
Chandos, Lord [Oliver Lyttelton], *The Memoirs of Lord Chandos*, London: The Bodley
  Head, 1962
Chatterton, Thomas, *The Revenge: a burletta*, London: T. King, 1795
Church, Michael, '"My task is to liberate pianists"' (interview with Maria Curcio),
  Independent, 2 February 2001
Cobbold, Richard, *The History of Margaret Catchpole: a Suffolk Girl*, London: Henry
  Colburn, 1845
Coleman, Basil, 'Staging first productions 2', in DHOBB, pp. 34–43
Cooke, Mervyn, *Britten and the Far East*, Aldeburgh Studies in Music vol. 4, Woodbridge:
  Boydell Press, 1993 (MCBFE)
– 'Herman Melville's *Billy Budd*', in BBMCPR, pp. 15–26
– *Benjamin Britten: War Requiem*, Cambridge: Cambridge University Press, 1996 (WRMC)
– (ed.), *The Cambridge Companion to Benjamin Britten*, Cambridge: Cambridge
  University Press, 1999 (MCCCBB)
– and Philip Reed, *Benjamin Britten: Billy Budd*, Cambridge: Cambridge University Press,
  1993 (BBMCPR)
Copland, Aaron, 'A Visit to Snape', in TBB, pp. 71–3
– and Vivian Perlis, *Copland Since 1943*, New York: St Martin's Press, 1989
Coulton, Barbara, *Louis MacNeice in the BBC*, London: Faber and Faber, 1980
Cox, Peter, and Jack Dobbs (eds.), *Imogen Holst at Dartington*, Dartington: The Dartington
  Press, 1988
Craft, Robert (ed.), *Stravinsky: Selected Correspondence*, vols. 1 and 2, London: Faber and
  Faber, 1982, 1984
Cranbrook, The Earl of, 'The Suffolk Countryside', TBB, pp. 21–38
Crawford, Michael, *Parcel Arrived Safely: Tied with String*, London: Century, 1999
Crozier, Eric (ed.), *Benjamin Britten: Peter Grimes*, Sadler's Wells Opera Books no. 3,
  London: John Lane/The Bodley Head, 1945
– 'Benjamin Britten's Second Opera: "The Rape of Lucretia"', *Tempo*, 1/14 (March 1946),
  pp. 11–12
– 'Foreword' to *Albert Herring*, London: Hawkes & Son, 1947; *rp* in DHOBB, pp. 137–8
– 'Foreword to *Albert Herring*', *Tempo*, 4 (summer 1947), pp. 10–14
– (ed.), *The Rape of Lucretia: A Symposium*, London: The Bodley Head, 1948 (RLEC)
– '*Lucretia*: 1946', in RLEC, pp. 55–60
– *The Life and Legends of Saint Nicolas, Patron Saint of Children*, illustrated by Douglas
  Rolf, London: Duckworth, 1949
– 'An Opera Team Sets to Work', *Picture Post*, 15 October 1949
– 'Writing a Britten Opera', *Music Parade*, 2/6 (1951), pp. 14–16
– 'Staging First Productions 1', in DHOBB, pp. 24–33
– 'The Writing of *Billy Budd*', *Opera Quarterly*, 4/3 (autumn 1986)
– and Nancy Evans, 'After Long Pursuit', *Opera Quarterly*, 10/3–11/3 (1994–95); also
  unedited, complete typescript at BPL
Curtis, Antony, 'BBC MacNeice', *Financial Times*, 24 May 1980

Del Mar, Norman, 'The Chamber Operas III: *The Beggar's Opera*' in DMHK, pp. 163–85
De-la-Noy, Michael, *Eddy: The Life of Edward Sackville-West*, London: Arcadia Books, 1999
Dickinson, Peter, *The Music of Lennox Berkeley*, 2nd edn, Woodbridge: Boydell Press, 2003

Dictionary of National Biography
    1951–1960, edited by E. T. Williams, Oxford: Oxford University Press, 1971
    1961–1970, edited by E. T. Williams and C. S. Nicholls, Oxford: Oxford University Press, 1981
    1971–1980, edited by Lord Blake and C. S. Nicholls, Oxford: Oxford University Press, 1986
    1986–1990, edited by C. S. Nicholls, Oxford: Oxford University Press, 1996
Dinglinger, Wolfgang, et al., *De Matthäus-Passion, 100 Jahr Passietraditie van het Koninklijk Concertgebouworkest*, Amsterdam: De betreffende auteurs en Uitgeverij THOTH, 1999
Dobbs, Jack, 'Imogen as "Student-Teacher"', in Peter Cox and Jack Dobbs (eds.), *Imogen Holst at Dartington*, pp. 71–3
Doig, Allan, 'Architecture and Performance: Dean Walter Hussey and the Arts', *Theology*, 94/787 (January/February 1995)
Downes, Ralph, *Baroque Tricks: Adventures with Organ Builders*, Oxford: Positif Press, 1983
Duncan, Ronald, 'The Libretto: The Method of Work', in RLEC, pp. 61–6
– *The Mongrel and Other Poems*, London: Faber and Faber, 1950
– *Working with Britten: A Personal Memoir*, Welcombe: The Rebel Press, 1981 (RDBB)

Edwards, R. A., *And the Glory: A History in Commemoration of the 150th Anniversary of the Huddersfield Choral Society*, Leeds: Maney and Son, n.d.
Einstein, Alfred, *Mozart: His Character, His Work*, London: Cassell, 1946
Elborn, Geoffrey, *Edith Sitwell: A Biography*, London: Sheldon Press, 1981
Ellis, Vivian, entry on C. B. Cochran, in *Dictionary of National Biography, 1951–1960*
Evans, Sir Geraint, and Noël Goodwin, *Sir Geraint Evans: A Knight at the Opera*, London: Michael Joseph, 1984
Evans, James Roose (ed.), *Joyce Grenfell Darling Ma: Letters to her Mother, 1932–1944*, London: Sceptre, 1997
Evans, John, 'Profile: Nancy Evans', *Aldeburgh Soundings*, 2 (spring 1985)
Evans, Peter, *The Music of Benjamin Britten*, London: Dent, 1979; rev. pbk edn, Oxford: Clarendon Press, 1996

Falkner, Julia, *Keith Falkner: 'Ich habe genug'*, London: Thames Publishing, 1988
Fallowell, Duncan, 'The Spies Who Loved Me', *Sunday Times Magazine*, 8 April 1991
Fawkes, Richard, 'Thirty Men and a Girl', *Classical Music*, 17 June 2000, pp. 48–9
Fetthauer, Sophie, *Musikverlage im 'Dritten Reich' und im Exil*, Hamburg: von Bockel, 2004
Fifield, Christopher (ed.), *Letters and Diaries of Kathleen Ferrier*, Woodbridge: Boydell Press, 2003
Foreman, Lewis (ed.), *The Percy Grainger Companion*, London: Thames Publishing, 1981
– *From Parry to Britten: British Music in Letters*, London: Batsford, 1987
Forster, E. M. [Edward Morgan], *Aspects of the Novel*, London: Edward Arnold, 1927
– *Goldsworthy Lowes Dickinson*, London: Edward Arnold, 1934
– 'George Crabbe: The Poet and the Man', *Listener*, 29 May 1941
– *Two Cheers for Democracy*, London: Edward Arnold, 1951
Forsyth, James, *Tyrone Guthrie: A Biography*, London: Hamish Hamilton, 1976
Fox, Sue, 'Art of the possible' (on Benjamin Zander), *Independent*, 28 March 1997, pp. 16–17
Fraser, Hugh, entry on Oliver Lyttelton [Lord Chandos], in *Dictionary of National Biography, 1971–1980*
Furbank, P. N., *E. M. Forster: A Life*, 2 vols., London: Secker & Warburg, 1978
– review of Mitchell Leaska, *Granite and Rainbow: The hidden life of Virginia Woolf*, *Times Literary Supplement*, 11 December 1998, p. 9

Garnham, A. M., *Hans Keller and the BBC: The Musical Conscience of British Broadcasting, 1959–79*, Aldershot: Ashgate Publishing, 2003
Garnham, Maureen, *As I Saw It: Basil Douglas, Benjamin Britten and the English Opera Group, 1955–1957*, London: St George's Publications, 1998
Gillies, Malcolm, and David Pear (eds.), *The All-Round Man: Selected Letters of Percy Grainger*, Oxford: Clarendon Press, 1994

Gilmour, J. D. (ed.), *Sir Thomas Beecham: Fifty years in the 'New York Times'*, London: Thames Publishing, 1988

Gishford, Anthony (ed.), *Tribute to Benjamin Britten on His Fiftieth Birthday*, London: Faber and Faber, 1963 (TBB)

Glendinning, Victoria, *Edith Sitwell: A Unicorn among Lions*, London: Weidenfeld and Nicolson, 1981

Glock, William, *Notes in Advance*, Oxford: Oxford University Press, 1991

Goddard, Scott, [review of Mahler's *Das Lied von der Erde*], *News Chronicle*, 12 September 1947

Godfrey, Paul, *Once in a While the Odd Thing Happens*, London: Methuen, 1990

Goldbeck, Frederick, *The Perfect Conductor*, London: Dennis Dobson, 1960

Gordon, Eric A., *Mark the Music: The Life and Work of Marc Blitzstein*, New York: St Martin's Press, 1989

Green, Andrew, 'Rites of Passage' (on Basil Douglas), *Classical Music*, 22 August 1992

– 'Twentieth century voice' (on Roy Henderson), *Independent*, 2 July 1999

Greene, Richard (ed.), *Selected Letters of Edith Sitwell*, London: Virago, 1997

Gregory, Horace (ed.), *The Triumph of Life: Poems of Consolation for the English-Speaking World*, New York: Viking Press, 1943

Grenfell, Joyce, *Joyce Grenfell Requests the Pleasure*, London: Macmillan, 1976

Haltrecht, Montague, *The Quiet Showman: Sir David Webster and the Royal Opera House*, London: Collins, 1975

Hamilton, G. Rostrevor (compiler), *The Latin Portrait*, London: Nonesuch Press, 1929

Handford, Basil, *Lancing College: History and Memories*, Chichester: Phillimore, 1986

Harding, James, *Cochran*, London: Methuen, 1988

Hardy, Thomas, *Collected Poems*, London: Macmillan, 1923

Harewood, The Earl of, 'The Man', in DMHK, pages 1–8

– (ed.), *Kobbé's Complete Opera Book*, London: Putnam, 1954, 1976; London, Putnam and Company, 1987; (with Antony Peattie), London: The Bodley Head, 1997

– 'Foreword', 1957 Aldeburgh Festival programme book

– *The Tongs and the Bones*, London: Weidenfeld and Nicolson, 1981

Harris, Paul, *Malcolm Arnold: Rogue Genius*, London: Thames Publishing, 2004

Hayes, Malcolm (ed.), *The Selected Letters of William Walton*, London: Faber and Faber, 2002

Hayman, Ronald, *Brecht: A Biography*, London: Weidenfeld and Nicolson, 1983

Headington, Christopher, *Britten*, London: Eyre Methuen, 1981 (CHB); rev. edn, London: Omnibus Press ('The Illustrated Lives of the Great Composers'), 1996

– *Peter Pears: A Biography*, London: Faber and Faber, 1992 (CHPP)

Heiney, Paul, 'Old Salts: Aldeburgh Fishermen', *Country Living*, 15 (March 1987), pp. 134–9

Herbert, David (ed.), *The Operas of Benjamin Britten*, London: Hamish Hamilton, 1979 (DHOBB)

Herbert, George, *The Works of George Herbert*, edited with a commentary by F. E. Hutchinson, Oxford: Clarendon Press, 1941

Holloway, Robin, 'The Church Parables II: Limits and Renewals', in CPBC, pp. 215–26

Holroyd, Michael, *Bernard Shaw: Volume 3: 1918–1950: The Lure of Fantasy*, Harmondsworth: Penguin Books, 1993

Holst, Gustav, *The Wandering Scholar*, edited by Benjamin Britten and Imogen Holst, London: Faber Music, 1968 (vocal score); 1971 (full and study scores)

– *Collected Facsimile Edition of Autograph Manuscripts of the Published Works*, vol. 1: *Chamber Operas*, London: Faber Music/G. & I. Holst Ltd, 1974

Holst, Imogen, *The Music of Gustav Holst*, London: Oxford University Press, 1951

– (ed.), *Henry Purcell 1659–1695: Essays on His Music*, London: Oxford University Press, 1959

– 'Indian Music', in TBB, pp. 104–10

– 'Introduction: *The Wandering Scholar*', in Gustav Holst, *Collected Facsimile Edition of Autograph Manuscripts of the Published Works*, vol. 1: *Chamber Operas*, London: Faber Music/G. & I. Holst Ltd, 1974

– *A Thematic Catalogue of Gustav Holst's Music*, London: Faber Music/G. & I. Holst Ltd, 1974
– liner note to Purcell, edited by Britten and I. Holst, *Dido and Aeneas*, Decca (SET 615), 1978
Hopkins, Antony, *Beating Time*, London: Michael Joseph, 1982
Howes, Frank, 'Two Revolutionaries: Schoenberg and Stravinsky', *The Times*, 5 October 1951
Hughes, Spike, *Glyndebourne: A History of the Festival Opera Founded in 1934 by Audrey and John Christie*, Newton Abbot: David & Charles, 1981
Hürlimann, Bettina, *Seven Houses: My Life with Books*, translated by Anthea Bell, London: The Bodley Head, 1976
Hürlimann, Martin, *Laudatio auf Benjamin Britten*, Munich: Callway, 1976
Hussey, Walter, *Patron of Art: The Revival of a Great Tradition among Artists*, London: Weidenfeld and Nicolson, 1985

Isherwood, Christopher, 'Christopher's jungle book: Christopher Isherwood discusses his autobiography with Christopher Ford', *Guardian*, 30 March 1977
– *Christopher Isherwood: Diaries, Volume One 1939–1960*, edited by Katherine Bucknell, London: Methuen, 1996
– *Lost Years: A Memoir 1945–1951*, edited with an introduction by Katherine Bucknell, London: Chatto & Windus, 2000

Jenkins, David Fraser, *John Piper: The Forties*, London: Philip Wilson Publishers, 2000
Johnson, Graham, 'Benjamin Britten – The Unwilling Accompanist', liner note for BBCB 8011–2

Kavanagh, Julie, *Secret Muses: The Life of Frederick Ashton*, London: Faber and Faber, 1996
Keller, Hans, *1975 (1984 minus 9)*, London, Dennis Dobson, 1977
– *Criticism*, edited by Julian Hogg, London, Faber and Faber, 1987
– *Music and Psychology*, edited by Christopher Wintle with Alison Graham, London, Plumbago Books, 2003
– *Essays on Music*, edited by Christopher Wintle with Bayan Northcott and Irene Samuel, Cambridge: Cambridge University Press, 1994
Kemp, Ian, *Tippett: The Composer and His Music*, London: Eulenberg Books, 1984
Kempers, K. Ph. Bernet, and Marius Flothuis, *Eduard van Beinum*, Harlem: Antwerp Vitgeverij J. H. Gottmer, n.d.
Kennedy, Michael, *Adrian Boult*, London: Hamish Hamilton, 1987
– 'How Albert became our kind of thing', 1990 Glyndebourne Festival Opera programme book, pp. 121–7
– *Britten*, London: Dent (Master Musicians series), 1981; rev. pbk edn, 1993
– liner notes for Violin Concerto, EMI, CDM 5 66053 2, 1997
Kenyon, Nicholas (compiler), *Musical Lives: Dictionary of National Biography Entries from 1901*, Oxford: Oxford University Press, 2002
Kildea, Paul, 'Three 20th-century English Masters', liner note for BBCB 8007-2 (Holst: *Egdon Heath, c* BB)
– *Selling Britten: Music in the Market Place*, Oxford: Oxford University Press, 2002 (PKSB)
– (ed.), *Britten on Music*, Oxford: Oxford University Press, 2003 (PKBM)
Kolodin, Irving, *The Story of the Metropolitan Opera 1883–1950: A Candid History*, New York: Alfred A. Knopf, 1953

Lago, Mary (compiler), *Calendar of the Letters of E. M. Forster*, London: Mansell Publishing, 1985
– and P. N. Furbank (eds.), *Selected Letters of E. M. Forster*, 2 vols., London: Collins, 1984 and 1985
Lane, Margaret, *The Tale of Beatrix Potter*, 1946; rp London: Frederick Warne, 1949
Laughton, Bruce, *William Coldstream*, Yale: Yale University Press, 2004
Lebrecht, Norman, *Covent Garden: The Untold Story: Dispatches from the English Culture War, 1945–2001*, London: Pocket Books, 2001

Lees-Milne, James, *Ancestral Voices and Prophesying Peace*, London: John Murray, 1995
– *Caves of Ice*, London: Faber and Faber, 1984
LeGrove, Judith, 'Aldeburgh', in MCCCBB, pp. 306–17
Lehmann, John, and Derek Parker (eds.), *Edith Sitwell: Selected Letters*, London: Macmillan, 1970
Leonard, Maurice, *Kathleen: The Life of Kathleen Ferrier*, London: Hutchinson, 1988
Loppert, Max, liner note, *Clifford Curzon: Decca Recordings 1949–64*, vol. 1, Decca Original Masters, 2003
Low, Rachael, *Documentary and Educational Films of the 1930s*, London: Allen & Unwin, 1979
Lucas, John, 'Goodall and Britten, *Grimes* and *Lucretia*', liner note to CMS 7 64727 2, EMI, 1993
– *Reggie: The Life of Reginald Goodall*, London: Julia MacRae Books, 1993
Lycett Green, Candida (ed.), *John Betjeman Letters*, vol. 1, 1926–51, London: Methuen, 1994; vol. 2, 1951–1984, London: Methuen, 1995
Lyon, James K., *Bertolt Brecht in America*, New Jersey: Princeton University Press, 1980

Macdonald, Kevin, 'The composer who scored' (on Brian Easdale), *Guardian*, 20 March 1992
McDonald, Peter, [review of W. H. Auden, *The Sea and the Mirror: A Commentary on Shakespeare's The Tempest*, edited and with an introduction by Arthur Kirsch], *Times Literary Supplement*, 2 January 2004
MacNeice, Louis, *The Dark Tower and Other Radio Scripts*, London: Faber and Faber, 1947
– *Collected Poems 1925–1948*, London: Faber and Faber, 1949
MacRae, Julia, *Ferrier – A Career Recorded*, London: Julia MacRae Books, 1992
Malcolm, George, 'Dido and Aeneas', in DMHK, pp. 186–97
Mangan, Richard (ed.), *Gielgud's Letters*, London: Weidenfeld and Nicolson, 2004
Mann, William, 'The Incidental Music', in DMHK, pp. 295–310
Matthews, David, *Britten*, London: Haus Publishing, 2003
Maupassant, Guy de, translated by Marjorie Laurie, *Madame Husson's Rose King*, Harmondsworth: Penguin, 1940
Mendelson, Edward, *Later Auden*, London: Faber and Faber, 1999
Mertz, Margaret S., *History, Criticism and the Sources of Benjamin Britten's Opera 'The Rape of Lucretia'*, PhD dissertation, Harvard University, 1990
Metzelaar, Helen, 'Who sent Benjamin Britten hundreds of eggs from Holland?', *Keynotes*, September 1997, pp. 17–21
– *Zonder musiek het leven onnodig, Henriëtte Bosmans (1895–1952) een biografie*, Zutphen: Walberg Pers, 2002
Mitchell, Donald, *The Language of Modern Music*, 1963; rev. edn, with an introduction by Edward W. Said, London: Faber and Faber, 1993
– *Gustav Mahler: The Wunderhorn Years*, London: Faber and Faber, 1975
– *Gustav Mahler: The Early Years*, London: Faber and Faber, 1980
– *Britten and Auden in the Thirties, the Year 1936*, London: Faber and Faber, 1981
– *Gustav Mahler: Songs and Symphonies of Life and Death*, London: Faber and Faber, 1985
– 'Montagu Slater (1902–1956): who was he?', in PGPB, pp. 22–46
– 'Mythic Pears: Idomeneo and Oedipus', in PPT, pp. 67–8
– 'Benjamin Britten', in *Dictionary of National Biography, 1971–1980*, pp. 83–86; rp Kenyon, *Musical Lives*
– 'The Serious Comedy of *Albert Herring*', 1986 Glyndebourne Festival programme book, pp. 352–64; rp DMCN, pp. 352–64
– (ed.), *Benjamin Britten: Death in Venice*, Cambridge: Cambridge University Press, 1987 (DVDM)
– 'Down There on a Visit: A Meeting with Christopher Isherwood', *London Magazine* 32/1–2, (April/May 1992), pp. 80–87; reprinted in DMCN, pp. 441–9
– '*The Beggar's Opera*: An Introduction', liner note for *The Beggar's Opera*, Argo 436 850–2, 1993
– 'Benjamin Britten: the "Arranger"', liner note, Collins Classics, 70392, 1995

- *Cradles of the New: Writings on Music 1951–1991*, selected by Christopher Palmer, edited by Mervyn Cooke, London: Faber and Faber, 1995 (DMCN)
- 'Britten's Revisionary Practice: Practical and Creative', in DMCN, pp. 393–406
- 'Remembering Hans Keller', in DMCN, pp. 461–80
- '*Peter Grimes*: Fifty Years On' in PBMPG, pp. 125–65
- 'Britten and the Viola', 1997 Aldeburgh October Britten Festival programme book, pp. 12–13
- 'Violent Climates', in MCCCBB, pp. 188–216
- 'The Truth About Così', programme essay for Mozart, *Così fan tutte*, English National Opera, 2002
- *Memories, Commitment, Communication: A lecture marking the 25th anniversary of the death of Benjamin Britten*, London: Royal College of Music, 2003
- 'Benjamin Britten', in *The Oxford Dictionary of National Biography*, 2004
- 'Peter Pears', in *Dictionary of National Biography, 1986–1990*; rp Kenyon, *Musical Lives*; rp *The Oxford Dictionary of National Biography*
- and John Evans, *Pictures from a Life: Benjamin Britten 1913–1976*, London: Faber and Faber, 1978 (PFL)
- and Hans Keller (eds.), *Benjamin Britten: A Commentary on His Works from a Group of Specialists*, London: Rockcliff, 1952 (DMHK)
- and H. C. Robbins Landon (eds.), *The Mozart Companion*, Westport: Greenwood, 1956
- and Andrew Nicholson (eds.), *The Mahler Companion*, Oxford: Oxford University Press, 2002
- and Philip Reed (eds.), 'An *Albert Herring* Anthology', 1985 Glyndebourne Festival programme book, pp. 114–15
- and Philip Reed (eds.), *Letters from a Life: Selected Letters and Diaries of Benjamin Britten*, vol. 1: 1923–39; vol. 2: 1939–45, London: Faber and Faber, 1991; rev. pbk edn, 1998
- and Philip Reed, 'Documents' and 'A commentary on the music', liner notes for *The Beggar's Opera*, Argo 436 850–2, 1993
- and Philip Reed, '"For Hedli": Britten and Auden's Cabaret Songs', in Katherine Bucknell and Nicholas Jenkins (eds.), *W. H. Auden: 'The Language of Learning and the Language of Love'*, Auden Studies 2, Oxford: Clarendon Press, 1995, pp. 60–68
Monk, Ray, *Ludwig Wittgenstein: The Duty of Genius*, Harmondsworth: Penguin, 1991
Moore, Gerald, *The Unashamed Accompanist*, London: Aschenberg, Hopwood & Crew, 1943; 3rd edn, 1984
- *Am I Too Loud?*, London: Hamish Hamilton, 1962
- *Farewell Recital*, London: Hamish Hamilton, 1978
Mörike, Eduard, *Mozart on the Way to Prague*, translated by Walter and Catherine Phillips, New York: Pantheon, 1947
Motion, Andrew, *The Lamberts: George, Constant and Kit*, London: Chatto & Windus, 1986
Mundy, Simon, 'Curcio in Camera', *Classical Music*, 11 March 1989, p. 49

Neel, Boyd, 'The String Orchestra', in DMHK, pp. 237–44
Northcott, Bayan, 'The Fine Art of Borrowing: Britten and Stravinsky', in 1994 Aldeburgh Festival programme book, pp. 14–19

Oldham, Arthur, *Living With Voices*, London: Thames Publishing, 2000
Oliver, Michael, *Benjamin Britten*, London: Phaidon (20th Century Composers), 1996
Osborne, Charles, *W. H. Auden: The Life of a Poet*, London: Eyre Methuen, 1980
Oxford Book of Medieval Latin Verse, The, Oxford: Clarendon Press, 1928
Oxford Dictionary of National Biography, The: From the Earliest Times to the Year 2000, edited by H. C. G. Matthew and Brian Harrison, 60 vols., Oxford: Oxford University Press, 2004
Palmer, Christopher (ed.), *The Britten Companion*, London: Faber and Faber, 1984 (CPBC)
Parker, Peter, *Isherwood: A Life*, London: Picador, 2004

Partridge, Frances, *Diaries 1939–1972*, edited by Rebecca Wilson, London: Lund Humphries Weidenfeld and Nicolson, 2000

Pascal, Valerie, *The Disciple and his Devil*, London: Michael Joseph, 1971

Peacock, Carlos, *John Constable: the man and his work*, London: John Baker, 1965; rev. edn, 1971

– *Samuel Palmer: Shoreham and after*, London: John Baker, 1968

Pears, Peter, 'Neither a Hero nor a Villain', *Radio Times*, 8 March 1946

– Letter to the Editors (on Frank Howes and Stravinsky), *Music Survey*, 4/2 (February 1952)

– 'A Personal Introduction', in Lewis Foreman (ed.), *The Percy Grainger Companion*, pp. 11–15

– unpublished interview with Peter Heyworth, 17 January 1984 (BPL)

– 'The New York *Death in Venice*', in PRPP, pp. 181–200

Pearson, John, *Façades: Edith, Osbert and Sacheverell Sitwell*, London: Reprint, 1980

Piper, John, 'The Design of *Lucretia*', in RLEC, pp. 67–73

– catalogue for retrospective exhibition, London: Tate Gallery, 1983

Plant, Andrew, *Rumours and Visions*, exhibition catalogue, Aldeburgh: The Britten–Pears Library, 2004

Plomer, William, under the pseudonym William D'Arfey (ed.), *Curious Relations*, London: Jonathan Cape, 1945

– 'Preface', sleeve note for *War Requiem*, Decca, SET 252/3, 1963

Potter, Julian, *Stephen Potter at the BBC: 'Features' in War and Peace*, Orford: Orford Books, 2004

Primrose, William, *Walk on the North Side: Memoirs of a Violist*, Utah: Brigham Young University Press, 1978

Purcell's The Fairy Queen as presented by The Sadler's Wells Ballet and the Covent Garden Opera, London: John Lehmann, 1948

Quasimodo, Salvatore, *Billy Budd, Foretopman*, Milan: Edizioni Suvini Zerboni, 1949

Ralph of Coggeshall, *Radulphi de Coggeshale Chronicum Anglicanum*, edited by J. Stevenson (Rolls series, 1875)

Reed, Philip, 'Aschenbach becomes Mahler', in DVDM, pp. 178–83

– *The Incidental Music of Benjamin Britten: A Study and Catalogue of His Music for Film, Theatre and Radio*, PhD dissertation, University of East Anglia, 1988 (PRIM)

– 'Britten's Folksong Arrangements', liner note, EMI, CMS 7 64727 2, 1993

– 'The Creative Evolution of *Gloriana*' in PBBG

– 'From first thoughts to first night: a *Billy Budd* chronology' in BBMCPR, pp. 42–73

– 'Britten's Folksong Arrangements: Documentation', liner note, Collins Classics 70392, 1995

– (ed.), *The Travel Diaries of Peter Pears 1936–1978*, Aldeburgh Studies in Music vol. 2, Woodbridge: Boydell Press/Britten–Pears Library, 1995; rev. rp, 1999

– (ed.), *On Mahler and Britten: Essays in Honour of Donald Mitchell on His Seventieth Birthday*, Aldeburgh Studies in Music vol. 3, Woodbridge: Boydell Press/Britten–Pears Library, 1995

– (compiler), 'Peter Pears and *The Bartered Bride*', 1995 Aldeburgh October Britten Festival programme book

– 'Finding the Right Notes', in PBMPG, pp. 79–115

– 'A *Peter Grimes* Chronology, 1941–1945', in PBMPG, pp. 21–50

– 'The *War Requiem* in progress', in WRMC, pp. 20–48

– 'Britten, Menuhin and Gendron play Beethoven, Mozart and Bridge', liner note, BBC Legends BBCL 4134–2, 2003

Robertson, Alex J., *The Bleak Midwinter 1947*, Manchester: Manchester University Press, 1987

Rorem, Ned, 'Britten's Venice', *New Republic*, 172/6 (8 February 1977), pp. 31–2

Roseberry, Eric, 'The Purcell Realizations', in CPBC, pp. 356–66

– 'Old songs in new contexts: Britten as arranger', in MCCCBB, pp. 297–300

Rosenthal, Harold, *Two Centuries of Opera at Covent Garden*, London: Putnam, 1958

Röthlin, Dr Niklaus, et al., *80 Jahre Paul Sacher: Erinnerungen an den Geburtstag*, Basel: Editions Roche, 1986

Runciman, Rosie, 'Gordon Craig, Moiseiwitch and Chagall', *Opera Now*, September/October 1998, pp. 76–9

Rupprecht, Philip, *Britten's Musical Language*, Cambridge: Cambridge University Press, 2001

Sackville-West, Edward, '*Peter Grimes*: The Musical and Dramatic Structure' in Crozier (ed.), *Benjamin Britten: Peter Grimes*, pages 27–55

– (compiler), *And So To Bed*, London: Phoenix House, 1947

– 'Noel Mewton-Wood: A Recollection', programme, Wigmore Hall, London, 28 January 1955

Sadie, Stanley (ed.), *The New Grove Dictionary of Music and Musicians*, 20 vols., London: Macmillan, 1980; (with John Tyrrell) 2nd edn, 29 vols., 2001

– *New Grove Dictionary of Opera, The*, 4 vols., London: Macmillan, 1992

Sautoy, Peter du, 'Donald Mitchell as Publisher: A Personal Recollection', in Reed (ed.), *On Mahler and Britten*, pp. 167–9

Schafer, Murray, *British Composers in Interview*, London: Faber and Faber, 1963

Schmidgall, Gary, 'The Natural: Theodor Uppman *is* Billy Budd', *Opera News*, 56/14 (28 March 1992), pp. 13–16

Schütz, Heinrich, *Symphoniae sacrae*, edited by Philipp Spitta, Leipzig: Breitkopf und Härtel, 1888

Schwarz, Boris, *Music and Musical Life in Soviet Russia, 1917–1970*, London: Barrie & Jenkins, 1972

Searle, Adrian, 'Me, myself and eye', *Guardian* G2, 28 August 1998, pp. 2–3

Shakespeare, William, *The Tempest*, edited by S. C. Boorman, London: University of London Press, 1957

Shawe-Taylor, Desmond, 'Discography', in DMHK, pp. 352–60

Sinden-Evans, Rosy, '*The Making of a May King*' or *The Creation of* Albert Herring: *a Comic Opera by Benjamin Britten and Eric Crozier*, MMus dissertation, Goldsmiths College, University of London, 1995

Sitwell, Edith, *The Canticle of the Rose: Selected Poems 1920–1947*, London: Macmillan, 1950

Sitwells and the Arts of the 1920s and 1930s, The (exhibition catalogue), London: National Portrait Gallery, 1994

Slonimsky, Nicolas, *Music Since 1900*, 4th edn, New York: Scribner, 1971

Smith, Christopher (ed.), *Aldeburgh and Around*, Norwich: Yare Valley Publishers, 1993

Snowman, Daniel, *The Hitler Emigrés: The Cultural Impact on Britain of Refugees from Nazism*, London: Chatto & Windus, 2002

Stallworthy, Jon, *Louis MacNeice*, London: Faber and Faber, 1995

Stallybrass, Oliver, *Aspects of E. M. Forster*, London: Edward Arnold, 1969

Steane, John, 'The First Performance of the *Spring Symphony*', liner note, Decca 440–0632–2 DM, 1994

Stein, Erwin, 'Opera and *Peter Grimes*', *Tempo* (old series), 12 (September 1945), pp. 2–6

– *Orpheus in New Guises*, London: Rockcliff, 1953

Strode, Rosamund, 'A *Death in Venice* chronicle', in DVDM, pp. 26–44

Sutcliffe, Tom, 'Parental Concerns', programme book for *The Turn of the Screw*, Théâtre de La Monnaie, Brussels, 1998; revised and expanded for programme book for *The Turn of the Screw*, Welsh National Opera, 2000

Sutherland, John, *Stephen Spender: The Authorised Biography*, London: Viking, 2004

Sweeting, Elizabeth, *Theatre Administration*, London: Pitman, 1969

– *Beginners Please: Working in the Theatre*, Reading: Educational Explorers, 1971

– 'Let's Make a Festival! The Early Years of the Aldeburgh Festival, 1948–1955', unpublished memoir (BPL)

Tadié, Jean-Yves, *Marcel Proust*, translated by Euan Cameron, London: Viking, 2000

Tappolet, Claude (ed.), *Ernest Ansermet: Correspondances avec des compositeurs Européens (1916–1966)*, vol. 1, Geneva: Georg Editeur, 1994

Taylor, John Russell, *The Penguin Dictionary of the Theatre*, Harmondsworth: Penguin, 1966

Thorpe, Marion (ed.), *Peter Pears: A Tribute on his 75th Birthday*, London: Faber Music/The Britten Estate, 1985 (PPT)

Tippett, Michael, *Those Twentieth Century Blues: An Autobiography*, London: Hutchinson, 1991

Tooley, John, *In House: Covent Garden – 50 Years of Opera and Ballet*, London: Faber and Faber, 1999

Trevelyan, George Macaulay, *England Under the Stuarts*, London: Methuen, 1904

Tucker, Norman, *Norman Tucker: Musician*, London: Ellison, 1978

Vickers, Brian, 'All rising to great place is by a winding stair: The difficulties of being fair to Sir Francis Bacon', *Times Literary Supplement*, 10 June 1998, pp. 12–14

Vignoles, Roger, 'Empathy and Understanding: A Britten–Pears Song Collection', liner note for BBCB 8015–2

Vincent, Jo, *Zingend door het leren*, Amsterdam, Elsevier, 1956

Wain, John, 'Meyerstein: An Oxford Memoir', *Encounter*, 107 (August 1962), pp. 27–42

Wake-Walker, Jenni (compiler and editor), *Time & Concord: Aldeburgh Festival Recollections*, Saxmundham: Autograph Books, 1997

Walsh, Stephen, 'The *Rake* in progress', English National Opera programme book, edited by Philip Reed, 2001

Waterhouse, John F., 'Soirée Musicale', *Birmingham Post*, 18 November 1963

Webster, David, 'Kleiber: An Appreciation', *Tempo*, 39 (spring 1956), pp. 5–6

Whinyates, Seymour, 'Music and the British Council', *Tempo*, 44 (summer 1957), pp. 7–10

White, Eric Walter, *Walking Shadows*, London: Hogarth Press, 1931

– *The Little Chimney Sweep*, Bristol: White & White, 1936

– *Benjamin Britten: eine Skizze von Leben und Werk*, Zurich: Atlantis Verlag, 1948

– *The Rise of English Opera*, London: John Lehmann, 1951

– 'Bibliography of Benjamin Britten's Incidental Music', in DMHK, pp. 311–13

– 'New Light on *Dido and Aeneas*', in Imogen Holst (ed.), *Henry Purcell 1659–1695: Essays on His Music*

– *Stravinsky: The Composer and his Works*, London: Faber and Faber, 1966; 2nd edn, 1979

– 'Britten in the Theatre: a Provisional Catalogue', *Tempo*, 107 (1973), pp. 2–8

– *Tippett and His Operas*, London: Barrie & Jenkins, 1979

– *A History of English Opera*, London: Faber and Faber, 1983

– *Benjamin Britten: His Life and Operas*, 2nd edition, edited by John Evans, London: Faber and Faber, 1983 (EWW)

Whitesell, Lloyd, 'Britten's Dubious Trysts', *Journal of the American Musicological Society*, 56/3 (fall 2003), pp. 637–94

Whittall, Arnold, *The Music of Britten and Tippett: Studies in Themes and Techniques*, Cambridge: Cambridge University Press, 1982; rev. edn, 1990

Wilcox, Michael, *Benjamin Britten's Operas*, Bath: Absolute Press, 1997

Willett, John, *Brecht in Context*, London: Methuen, 1984

– *Caspar Neher: Brecht's Designer*, London: Methuen, 1986

Willett, John, and Ralph Manheim (eds.), *Bertolt Brecht Collected Plays*, London: Eyre Methuen, 1976

William of Newburgh [Willelmi de Novoburgo], *Historia Rerum Anglicanum*, edited by R. Howlett (Rolls series, 1884)

Witts, Richard, *Artist Unknown, An Alternative History of the Arts Council*, London: Little, Brown, 1998

Wood, Thomas, *True Thomas*, London: Jonathan Cape, 1936

Zelger-Vogt, Marianne, and Andreas Honegger (eds.), *Stadttheater Opernhaus: Hundert Jahre Musiktheater in Zürich*, Zurich: Verlag Neue Zürcher Zeitung, 1991

TELEVISION AND RADIO BROADCASTS

An Opera is Planned, discussion on *Albert Herring* between Britten, Eric Crozier and John
   Piper, written and produced by Stephen Potter, BBC Third Programme, 19 June 1947
Evaluations and Comparisons, a sixtieth birthday tribute to BB, presented by John Amis,
   BBC Radio 3, 25 November 1973
A time there was . . .: A Profile of Benjamin Britten, a documentary film for the *South Bank
   Show*, London Weekend Television/Tony Palmer, 1980 (TP)
'Towards the Unknown Region': Malcolm Arnold – a Story of Survival*, a documentary film
   for the *South Bank Show*, by Tony Palmer, 2004
Britten's Children, a documentary film by John Bridcut, BBC Television/Mentorn, 2004
   (JBBC)

INTERVIEWS

The tapes and transcripts of the interviews marked with an asterisk are available at BPL.

Alston, John, with Donald Mitchell, Aldeburgh, 20 June 1988*
Boys, Henry, with Donald Mitchell, London, November 1986*
Coleman, Basil, with Donald Mitchell, Aldeburgh, 29 October 2000*
Crozier, Eric, with Humphrey Burton, *Remembering Bernstein*, Aldeburgh Festival,
   10 June 1991*
Diamand, Peter, with John Drummond, BBC Radio 3, 17 August 1992
Duncan, Roger, with John Bridcut, in JBBC
Easdale, Brian, with Donald Mitchell, London,22 July 1992*
Goldberg, Albert, with Donald Mitchell, Pasadena, California, 23 May 1989*
Hardy, Alistair and Mrs George Hardy, with Donald Mitchell, Horham, 10 April 1999*
Lindsay, John, with Donald Mitchell, London, 10 July 1990*
Maud, Humphrey, with Donald Mitchell, London, 11 September 1998
Menuhin, Yehudi, with Donald Mitchell, for TP, London, 1979*
Pears, Peter, with Donald Mitchell, for TP, Aldeburgh and London, 1979*
Pounder, John, with Donald Mitchell, Aldeburgh, June 1989*
Redcliffe-Maud, Jean, with Elizabeth Sweeting, London, 1984*
Reiss, Stephen, with Donald Mitchell, Horham, 18 July 1998*
Rothman, Bobby, with Donald Mitchell and Philip Reed, Aldeburgh, 23 October 1992*
Woolford, John, with Donald Mitchell, London, 15 September 1989*

REVIEWS AND MEDIA COVERAGE OF BRITTEN AND HIS WORKS

Benjamin Britten   Ferruccio Bonavia, article on formation of the English Opera Group,
   Daily Telegraph & Morning Post, 20 July 1946; Interview with Britten, *Life*, 26 August
   1946; Frederick Goldbeck, 'L'Angleterre qui fut privée longtemps de compositeurs originaux a aujourd'hui ses jeunes maîtres', *Le Figaro*, 23 August 1947; 'Arpeggio', 'Music
   Festival at Aldeburgh: Plans announced at Ipswich concert', *East Anglian Daily Times*,
   18 December 1947; 'Opera's New Face' (interview with Britten), *Time*, 6 February 1948;
   The Money Programme, BBC2, transmitted 1 January 1970; Alan Blyth, 'Britten returns to
   composing', *The Times*, 30 December 1974
PP–BB recitals, concerts and tours   'Music in the Making', *Tempo*, 1/14 (March 1946), p. 15
Albert Herring   Richard Capell, 'Britten's New Opera: *Albert Herring*', *Daily Telegraph*,
   21 June 1947; [Frank Howes], '*Albert Herring*: Benjamin Britten's New Comic Opera', *The
   Times*, 21 June 1947; Dyneley Hussey, *New York Times*, 21 June 1947; Ernest Newman,
   Sunday Times, 22 June 1947; Charles Stuart, *Observer*, 22 June 1947; William McNaught,
   Manchester Guardian, 23 June 1947; Martin Cooper, *Spectator*, 27 June 1947; William
   Glock, *Time and Tide*, 28 June 1947; Desmond Shawe-Taylor, *New Statesman and Nation*,
   28 June 1947, p. 473; Ernest Newman, 'Mr Britten and *Albert Herring* – I', *Sunday Times*,

29 June 1947; Ernest Newman, 'Albert Herring – II', Sunday Times, 6 July 1947; William McNaught, 'Opera at Glyndebourne', Musical Times, July 1947, pp. 234–5; Herman van Born, 'Première van Britten's Albert Herring', Het Parool (Rotterdam), 23 July 1947; Lex van Delde, 'Britten in een vrolijke bui', Het Parool (Amsterdam), 23 July 1947; J. Kasander, 'Albert Herring Brittens nieuwste opera', Het Vrije Volk, 23 July 1947; 'P.T.' [Piet Tiggers], 'Bekoorlijke opera van Britten', Algemeen Handelsblad, 23 July 1947; 'v.E.', 'Continentale première in Kurzaal', Het Binnenhof, 23 July 1947; 'W.G.', 'English Opera Group: Albert Herring', Het Dagblad, 23 July 1947; 'P.P.', 'Albert Herring Nieuwe opera van Benjamin Britten', De Volkskrant, 24 July 1947; E. Bekius, 'Albert Herring van Benjamin Britten', Utrechtsch Nieuwsblad, 29 July 1947; Karel Mengelberg, 'Englese humor van het beste gehalte en originele muziek', Het Vrije Volk, 29 July 1947; Frederick Goldbeck, 'Comment l'esprit vient à un Parsifal de sous-préfecture', Le Figaro, 2 August 1947

Amo Ergo Sum Report of the wedding of the Earl of Harewood and Marion Stein, 'A Musical Occasion', The Times, 30 September 1949

The Beggar's Opera 'H.H.H.', 'Virtually a New Beggar – But Not Quite So Gay?', Cambridge Daily News, 25 May 1948; Frank Howes, The Times, 25 May 1948; Frank Howes, 'Beggar's Operas and Odious Comparisons', The Times, 28 May 1948; Charles Stuart, 'Britten in Newgate', Observer, 30 May 1948; Edward Sackville-West, New Statesman and Nation, 5 June 1948

Billy Budd Desmond Shawe-Taylor, New Statesman and Nation, 1 and 8 December 1951; Eric Blom, Observer, 2 December 1951; 'A.F.', Daily Mirror, 'What a Night for the Men', 3 December 1951; Richard Capell, Daily Telegraph, 3 December 1951; Farnsworth Foule, New York Times, 3 December 1951; Philip Hope-Wallace, Manchester Guardian, 3 December 1951; Frank Howes, The Times, 3 December 1951; Scotsman, 3 December 1951; Stephen Williams, Stage, 6 December 1951; Colin Mason, Spectator, 7 December 1951; Ernest Newman, Sunday Times, 9 December 1951; Jack Tait, New York Herald Tribune, 9 December 1951; Stephen Williams, New York Times, 9 December 1951; J. F. Waterhouse, Birmingham Post, 17 December 1951; Evening Standard, 20 December 1951; Donald Mitchell, 'More Off than On Billy Budd', Music Survey, 4/2 (February 1952), pp. 386–408

Canticle I Frank Howes, The Times, 3 November 1947

Dido and Aeneas 'Dido and Aeneas: Mr Benjamin Britten's Alterations', The Times, 27 April 1951, p. 8, based on EOG press release; Letter to the Editor, Geoffrey Bush, The Times, 3 May 1951, p. 5; Letter to the Editor, BB, The Times, 8 May 1951, p. 8; reprinted in PKBM, pp. 106–7

The Duchess of Malfi 'British director signed by Czinner', New York Times, 22 August 1946; Sam Zolotow, New York Times, 28 August 1946; Brooks Atkinson, New York Times, 16 October 1946

Four Sea Interludes and Passacaglia from 'Peter Grimes' Robert Bagar, New York World-Telegram, 14 March 1946; Olin Downes, 'Opera by Britten heard at concert', New York Times, 14 March 1946; Irving Kolodin, 'New English music by Koussevitzky', New York Sun, 14 March 1946

The Little Sweep (Let's Make an Opera) [Frank Howes], The Times, 15 June and 9 July 1949; J. F. Waterhouse, Birmingham Post, 8 July 1949; Daily Telegraph, 8 July 1949; Desmond Shawe-Taylor, New Statesman and Nation, 23 July 1949; Elizabeth Mullan, Music Survey, 2/4 (spring 1950)

Occasional Overture The Times, 1 October 1946

Paul Bunyan Olin Downes, New York Times, 6 May 1941

Peter Grimes [Frank Howes], The Times, 8 February 1946; Desmond Shawe-Taylor, New Statesman and Nation, 16 February 1946; Robert L. Jacobs, 'The Significance of Peter Grimes', Listener, 7 March 1946; Robert Bagar, 'Bostonians Give Britten Opera Fine Performance', New York World-Telegram, 14 March 1946; Dyneley Hussey, Listener, 21 March 1946; Ernest Newman, 'Peter Grimes and After – I', Sunday Times, 24 March 1946; National-Zeitung (Basel), 7 May 1946; The Times, 7 May 1946; Neue Zürcher Zeitung und Schweizerisches Handelsblatt, 3 June 1946; Robert Bagar, 'Peter Grimes Hailed in Berkshire bow', *New York World-Telegram*, 7 August 1946; John Briggs, 'Britten's *Peter Grimes* Hits You Between the Eyes', *New York Post*, 7 August 1946; Olin Downes, 'Britten's *Grimes* unveiled at Lenox', *New York Times*, 7 August 1946; Irving Kolodin, '*Peter Grimes* opera is heard', *New York Sun*, 7 August 1946; Francis D. Perkins, '*Peter Grimes* Has Premiere At Tanglewood', *New York Herald Tribune*, 7 August 1946; Douglas Watt, '*Peter Grimes* has Operatic Greatness in Lenox Premiere', *Daily News*, 7 August 1946; *Time*, 19 August 1946; *Life*, 26 August 1946; Miriam de Kika, 'Berkshire Festival', *Music Business*, September 1946; Frank Howes, *The Times*, 7 November 1947; Neville Cardus, *Manchester Guardian*, 12 November 1947; Louis Biancolli, 'Met Bravely Sounds Bleak *Peter Grimes*', *New York World-Telegram*, 13 February 1948; Olin Downes, 'Opera by Britten in Premiere Here', *New York Times*, 13 February 1948; Irving Kolodin, 'An Impressive *Peter Grimes* at the Opera', *New York Sun*, 13 February 1948; Virgil Thomson, *New York Herald Tribune*, 13 February 1948; Robert A. Hague, 'The Met Does Poorly By Britten's *Grimes*', *P.M.* (New York), 15 February 1948; *Opera News*, 12/21, 8 March 1948; *The Times*, 15 January 1949

Piano Concerto   *The Times*, 3 July 1946

Plymouth Town   Montagu Montagu-Nathan, *Radio Times*, 31 July 1953, p. 29

The Rape of Lucretia   Ferruccio Bonavia, 'New Britten opera heard in England', *New York Times*, 13 July 1946; [Frank Howes], 'Glyndebourne Opera', *The Times*, 13 and 19 July 1946; Cecil Gray, *Observer*, 14 July 1946; Eric Blom, *Birmingham Post*, 15 July 1946; Philip Hope-Wallace, 'Opera at Glyndebourne', *Manchester Guardian*, 15 July 1946; Ferruccio Bonavia, *Daily Telegraph*, 20 July 1946; Desmond Shawe-Taylor, *New Statesman and Nation*, 20 July 1946; Ernest Newman, *Sunday Times*, 21 and 28 July 1946; Frank Howes, 'Words for Music! Operatic Experiments', *The Times*, 8 November 1946; Letter to the Editor, *Manchester Guardian*, 4 August 1947; Alec Robertson, review of abridged recording, *Gramophone*, March 1948; *The Times*, 30 March 1948; *Monthly Musical Record*, May 1948; Olin Downes, 'At the Theatre', *New York Times*, 30 December 1948; John Beaufort, 'The Best of Two Worlds', *Christian Science Monitor, Boston*, 8 January 1949; Cecil Smith, *New Republic*, 24 January 1949

The Rescue   John Burrell, 'A Landmark in Radio Creation', *Radio Times*, 27 February 1948; Edward Sackville-West, 'A melodrama based on The Odyssey', *Radio Times*, 7 September 1951

Saint Nicolas   'Lancing College Centenary: Britten's Cantata', *The Times*, 26 July 1948; Desmond Shawe-Taylor, 'Lancing and Saint Nicolas', *New Statesman and Nation*, 31 July 1948; Charles Stuart, '[Vaughan] Williams and Britten', *Observer*, 1 August 1948

Spring Symphony   [Frank Howes], *The Times*, 15 July and 22 July 1949; Daniel L. Schorr, *New York Times*, 15 July 1949; Piet Tiggers, *Algemeen Handelsblad*, 15 July 1949; Dyneley Hussey, *Listener*, 21 July 1949; Desmond Shawe-Taylor, *New Statesman and Nation*, 23 July 1949; Howard Taubman, *New York Times*, 15 August 1949; Scott Goddard, *Radio Times*, 3 March 1950; Richard Capell, 'Britten's New "Symphony": Dazzling Score', *Daily Telegraph*, 10 March 1950; [Frank Howes], 'The *Spring Symphony*: Britten's New Work', 10 March 1950; Lennox Berkeley, 'Britten's *Spring Symphony*', *Music & Letters*, 21/3 (July 1950); 'Kr.', *Die Presse* (Vienna), 14 April 1951

The Young Person's Guide to the Orchestra   'P.T.', *Algemeen Handelsblad*, 4 November 1946; 'L.H.', 'From Pedagogy to Art', *De Tijd*, 4 November 1946; *De Waarheid*, 4 November 1946

OBITUARIES

Alston, John   J. F. Bell, *Lancing College Magazine*, Advent 1996

Bernstein, Leonard   Peter Dickinson, *Independent*, 16 October 1990; Edward Greenfield, 'Everyman's musician', *Guardian*, 16 October 1990; *The Times*, 16 October 1990

Bing, Rudolf   *Daily Telegraph*, 4 September 1997; *The Times*, 4 September 1997

Bowles, Paul   John Calder, *Independent*, 19 November 1999; Gary Pulsifer, *Guardian*, 19 November 1999; *The Times*, 19 November 1999

Burra, Peter   *Lancing College Magazine*, June 1937

Burrell, Billy   Brad Jones, *East Anglian Daily Times*, 25 June 1999

Bush, Alan   Rupert Christiansen, *Independent*, 3 November 1995; Hugo Cole and John Amis, *Guardian*, 3 November 1995; *The Times*, 4 November 1995

Butt, James   John Howard, 'Respects paid to a Suffolk composer', *East Anglian Daily Times*, 6 March 2003

Caplan, Isador   Donald Mitchell, *Independent*, 23 January 1995; Marion Thorpe, *Guardian*, 10 February 1995

Cross, Joan   Elizabeth Forbes, *Independent*, 14 December 1993; Frank Granville Barker, 'A leading role in the opera', *Guardian*, 14 December 1993; *Daily Telegraph*, 14 December 1993; *The Times*, 15 December 1993; Colin Graham, 'Joan Cross – "so rare a soprano"', *Opera*, February 1994, pp. 164–9; Ava June, *Opera*, February 1994, pp. 169–70

Crozier, Eric   John Calder, *Independent*, 8 September 1994; Donald Mitchell, *Guardian*, 8 September 1994; Blake Crozier, *Guardian*, 10 September 1994; Philip Reed, 'Let's make an opera', *Guardian*, 8 September 1994; *Daily Telegraph*, 8 September 1994; *The Times*, 9 September 1994; Alan Blyth, *Opera*, November 1994

Del Mar, Norman   Edward Greenfield, and Alexander Goehr, *Guardian*, 7 February 1994; Robert Ponsonby, *Independent*, 7 February 1994; *Daily Telegraph*, 7 February 1994

Diamand, Peter   John Calder, 'A diplomat at the festival', *Guardian*, 19 January 1998; *Daily Telegraph*, 19 January 1998; *The Times*, 20 January 1998; Richard Demarco, *Independent*, 21 January 1998

Douglas, Basil   Maureen Garnham, *Independent*, 10 November 1992

Dowling, Denis   Alan Blyth, 'From farmyard to Figaro', *Guardian*, 24 September 1996; Elizabeth Forbes, *Independent*, 25 September 1996; *Daily Telegraph*, 26 September 1996; Alan Blyth, *Opera*, December 1996

Downes, Ralph   *Daily Telegraph*, 30 December 1993; Marc Rochester, *Independent*, 1 January 1994

Easdale, Brian   Kevin Macdonald, with Moira Shearer and Blue Johnson, 'Music with a touch of magic', *Guardian*, 31 October 1995; *The Times*, 18 November 1995

Evans, Nancy   John Calder, *Independent*, 22 August 2000; *Daily Telegraph*, 23 August 2000; *The Times*, 23 August 2000; Jim McDonald, *Guardian*, 24 August 2000

Falkner, Keith   *The Times*, 20 May 1994; *Daily Telegraph*, 27 May 1994; Elizabeth Forbes and Michael Gough Matthews, *Independent*, 3 June 1994

Gishford, Anthony   *The Times*, 25 January 1975; 'J.H.A.' [John Andrews], *Tempo*, March 1975

Goldberg, Albert   Burt A. Folkart, *Los Angeles Times*, 6 February 1990

Headington, Christopher   *The Times*, 25 March 1996; Philip Reed, 'A friend of Aldeburgh', *Guardian*, 1 April 1996

Henderson, Roy   Elizabeth Forbes, *Independent*, 17 March 2000; *The Times*, 17 March 2000

Hewit, Jackie   *The Times*, 3 January 1998; *Daily Telegraph*, 8 January 1998

Hill, Rose   Anthony Hayward, *Independent*, 1 January 2004; Elizabeth Forbes, *Independent*, 5 January 2004

Hunter, Ian   *The Times*, 10 September 2003

Isherwood, Christopher   *The Times*, 6 January 1986; Stephen Spender, 'The Secret of Issyvoo', *Observer Review*, 12 January 1986

Kirstein, Lincoln   Dale Harris, 'New York's lord of the dance', *Guardian*, 6 January 1996; Marilyn Hunt, *Independent*, 6 January 1996; *Daily Telegraph*, 8 January 1996; *The Times*, 11 January 1996

Knollys, Eardley   Michael Parkin and Frances Partridge, *Independent*, 11 September 1991; *The Times*, 13 September 1991

Lewis, Richard   Elizabeth Forbes, *Independent*, 14 November 1990; *The Times*, 14 November 1990; Edward Greenfield, 'A very British hero-tenor', *Guardian*, 16 November 1990; Alan Blyth, 'Richard Lewis (1914–1990)', *Opera* 42/1 (January 1991), pp. 33–6

Lowe, John   *The Times*, 27 January 1996

Moiseiwitsch, Tanya   *Daily Telegraph*, 20 February 2003; *The Times*, 20 February 2003; Alan Strachan, *Independent*, 22 February 2003; Raymond Ingram, *Stage*, 27 February 2003

Oldham, Arthur   Tim Bullamore, *Independent*, 13 May 2003; Conrad Wilson, *Guardian*,
    14 May 2003; *The Times*, 23 May 2003
Piper, John   James Richards and John Russell, *Guardian*, 30 June 1992; John White,
    Guardian, 8 July 1992; *Daily Telegraph*, 30 June 1992; Henry Thorold, *Daily Telegraph*,
    30 June 1992; *The Times*, 30 June 1992; Colin Amery, 'The Master of Pleasing Decay',
    Financial Times, 6 July 1992
Shacklock, Constance   Alan Blyth, *Guardian*, 1 July 1999; Alan Blyth, *Opera*, September 1999
Shawe-Taylor, Desmond   *The Times*, 3 November 1995; Michael De-la-Noy, *Independent*,
    4 November 1995; Patrick O'Connor, *Guardian*, 4 November 1995; David Cairns, *Sunday
    Times*, 5 November 1995
Spender, Stephen   Frank Kermode, 'Grand Old Man of Letters', *Guardian*, 17 July 1995;
    Peter Porter, *Independent*, 18 July 1995; *Daily Telegraph*, 18 July 1995; *The Times*, 18 July 1995
Sweeting, Elizabeth   Paul Iles, *Guardian*, 11 December 1999; David Freud, *Independent*,
    17 December 1999
Tippett, Michael   Meirion Bowen, *Guardian*, 10 January 1998; Andrew Clark, *Financial
    Times*, 10 January 1998; Paul Driver, *Independent*, 10 January 1998; *Daily Telegraph*,
    10 January 1998; *The Times*, 10 January 1998; Nicholas Kenyon, *Observer*, 11 January 1998
Waters, Stephen   Mark Sellen, *Independent*, 25 July 1989
White, Eric Walter   Douglas Cleverdon, *The Times*, 17 September 1985
Wood, Anne   Alan Blyth, 'Opera champion', *Guardian*, 23 June 1998; *The Times*, 24 June
    1998; Rodney Milnes, *Opera*, August 1998, pp. 921 and 953

INDEX OF BRITTEN'S WORKS

For details of index style and abbreviations used in this index, see Editorial Method, p. xx.

Abelard and Héloïse (proposed opera or cantata), 366–7

Advance Democracy (1938), composition, 57

Advance Democracy (film music, 1938), composition, 172

The Agamemnon of Aeschylus (theatre music), 112

Albert Herring, Op. 39, 125, 285: anti-Establishment attitude of, 10; BB on, 211, 272–4, 305, 470; broadcasts, 292, 296, 369, 552; character names, 200–201, 250; as comedy, 11; companies and casts, 140, 148, 235, 266, 277, 308, 316, 322, 356, 369, 431, 456, 483, 486, 507, 574, 604; composition, 138, 232, 250–51, 259, 267, 271–4, 279, 282, 285, 286, 288–9, 438; dedication, 287, 363; film proposal, 328; and Glyndebourne, 244, 273; libretto (Eric Crozier after Maupassant), 19, 200, 212, 246, 248–51, 259, 267, 286–7, 292, 294–8, 309, 315, 539, 590; manuscripts, 176, *275*, *283*; *Opera* magazine preface, 623, 624; performances: Glyndebourne (premiere, 1947), *plates 9–15*, 138, 150–51, 261, 277, 292, *293*, 294–300, 302, 308, 316, 322, 328, 339, 364, 438, 465, 507, 556, 565, 574; EOG tour (Netherlands and Switzerland; summer 1947), 305–6; Covent Garden (EOG, October 1947), 300, 355; EOG tour (Newcastle, Bournemouth, Oxford; autumn 1947), 303; BBC studio performance (1948), 314; EOG (1948), 354–5, 375; Sadler's Wells (September 1948), 375, 407, 411, 412; AF (1948), 357, 359, 368, 396; Brussels (June 1948), 392, 501, 507; EOG (1949), 440–41; AF (1949), 414, 416, 514; Tanglewood (US premiere; August 1949), 501, 507; Los Angeles (1949), 556; Lyric, Hammersmith (1951), 641; Liverpool (1951), 642; Hanover, 624; Rome, 493–5, 502; Oxford University Opera Society, 413; publication and scores, 289, 338, 363; reception and reviews, 133, 170, 292–9, 302, 303, 305–6, 309–10, 374, 392, 396, 412, 421, 518, 536, 594, 686–7; royalties, 590; theme of family relationships, 11; title, 251; and *The Virtuous Isidore*, 249

Alla Quartetto Serioso (1933): composition, 56

A.M.D.G. (1939): composition, 57

American Overture, An (1941; formerly 'An Occasional Overture', Op. 27): composition, 58; manuscript, 441

Amo Ergo Sum, see Wedding Anthem (Amo Ergo Sum)

Anna Karenina (unrealized): libretto (Graham), 672

Around the Village Green (film music), 261, 368; see also *Irish Reel*

The Ascent of F6 (theatre music), 211: and Hedli Anderson, 72; composition, 57, 78, 362; manuscript, *77*; revision, 76

Ballad of Heroes, Op. 14: 'It's farewell to the drawing room's civilised cry', 72; composition, 57; premiere (1939), 57, 80, 81, 625; texts, 45, 72

The Ballad of Little Musgrave and Lady Barnard (1943): composition, 58

ballet project for de Basil (unrealized, 1938), 71

ballet project for Sadler's Wells (unrealized, 1938), 71

Basque ballet (unfinished project, 1932): composition, 69

Beggar's Opera, The, Op. 43: BB on, 393, 396; broadcast, 407, 415; companies and casts, 148, 235, 322, 333, 348, 350, 357, 369, 430, 431, 456, 486, 516, 574; composition, 274, 313, 314, 350, 351, 354, 365, 366, 370, 384, 389, 396, 421, 438; dedication, 571; film proposal and rights, 328, 365, 367, 374; manuscript, *395*; *Opera* magazine preface, 624; performances: Arts Theatre, Cambridge (premiere; 1948), *plates 16–21*, 14, 322, 333, 350, 357, 370, 393, 396–7, *398*, 399–401, 431, 516; EOG (1948), 355, 375; Holland Festival (summer 1948), 314, 396, 397; Sadler's Wells (September 1948), 375, 407, 411; EOG (1949), 440, 456, 458; Hamburg (1950), 624; Sadler's Wells (1960s), 413; programme notes, 393, 396; publication, 365; reception and reviews, 396–7, 399–401, 414–15, 650

Billy Budd, Op. 50, 9: commission, 436–8, 468, 562–7, 618, 698; companies and casts, 516, 610, 633, 640–42, 660, 698; composition, 373, 374, 495, 502, 520, 533–4, 536–7, 551–2, 559, 566, 576, 578, 582, 585–6, 588, 590, 595, 600, 602, 604–7, 622, 624, 628, 632–3, 635, 638, 640–42, 645–6, 659, 661–4, 674, 676, 677–8; and Covent Garden, 436–8, 563–5, 567, 632; dedication, 475, 680–81; and Edinburgh Festival, 439, 562–7, 595, 622, 630, 640; libretto (E. M. Forster and Eric Crozier, after Herman Melville), *plates 42–3*, 19, 68, 197, 212, 363, 374, 407–8, 409, 410, 438, 479–80, *481–2*, 495, 499–501, 503, 520, 533, 535–7,

539, 546, 547, 551, 556, 559, 566, 582, 618, 620,
633–5, 637–8, 641, 643–4, 653, 657–8, 677–9,
682–98, 700; manuscripts, 619, 644, 657, 658, 681,
688–9; parental absence, motif of, 15; parody by
Henry Reed, 643; performances: pp, 534, 588,
655, 676, 677–8; Covent Garden (premiere;
December 1951), plates 44–7, 439, 516, 534, 559,
604, 610, 632–3, 640, 642, 660, 663, 680,
682–702; Wiesbaden (1952), 702; Covent
Garden (stage premiere of two-act version;
1964), 355; BBC Television (1966), 516; Chicago
(US premiere of two-act version), 355; San
Francisco, 355; publication and scores, 663, 664,
678, 681; reception and reviews, 133, 547, 611,
655, 682–701; revisions, 620, 677–8, 701–2; royalties, 589–91; and Sadler's Wells, 438–9, 533,
562–7, 606, 622, 632; shanties, 605, 633–4, 643–4,
657–8, 663, 686
'The Birds' (1929): composition, 55
Birthday Song for Erwin (1945; Duncan setting):
composition, 105; performance: PP (pp), 105;
publication (The Red Cockatoo), 105
'Boogie-woogie' (1945; This Way to the Tomb; arr.
Runswick): performance (AF, 1990), 171;
recording, 171
A Boy was Born, Op. 3: ad lib. organ part
(Downes), 463; BB on, 61; BBC try-out, 56;
broadcast, 474; composition, 56; performances:
premiere, 56, 61, 474; New York (1947), 267, 270;
reception, 61
Bridge Variations, see Variations on a Theme of
Frank Bridge, Op. 10
'Bring me garlands, bring me wine', see Man Born
to Be King, The
Britain to America (radio music), 112
The Burning Fiery Furnace, Op. 77: dedication, 668;
libretto (Plomer), 672; theme of exclusion, 9

Cabaret Songs (1937–39), 251: 'Tell me the truth
about love', 652; and Hedli Anderson, 72, 652;
composition, 652; publication, 652; texts, 78
Cadenza for Mozart's Piano Concerto in E♭
(K. 482), 666
Canadian Carnival (Kermesse Canadienne), Op. 19:
composition, 57, 103; performance: Cheltenham (c BB; 1945), 102, 103; programme note,
102, 103–4
The Canterbury Tales (unrealized opera project),
232
Cantata academica, carmen basiliense, Op. 62:
commission, 487; premiere (c Sacher; 1960), 487
Cantata Misericordium, Op. 69: dedication, 384
Canticle I: 'My beloved is mine', Op. 40, 595:
broadcast, 339; composition, 313, 315, 319, 321,
330; dedication, 319; manuscript, 319; performances: Dick Sheppard Memorial Concert
(PP–BB, premiere, Central Hall, Westminster;
November 1947), 313, 319; AF (PP–BB; 1948),
359; Vienna (PP–BB; 1951), 663; reception and
reviews, 319; text, 319
Canticle II: 'Abraham and Isaac', Op. 51: performers, 147, 502
Canticle III: 'Still falls the Rain – The Raids, 1940,
Night and Dawn', Op. 55; composition, 543;
manuscript, 162; performance: Wigmore Hall
(PP, Dennis Brain horn; BB piano; premiere,
1955), 162; text, 543, 680
Canticle IV: 'Journey of the Magi', Op. 86: compo-
sition, 33; text, 319, 332

Canticle V: 'The Death of Saint Narcissus', Op. 89:
dedication, 672; text, 332
Ceremony of Carols, A, Op. 28, 96: 'That yongë
child', 98; 'This little Babe', 276; Interlude, 98;
'Winter', 98; 'Deo Gracias', 98; canon, 276;
composition, 58, 98; performances: premiere,
58; premiere of revised version, 475; publication, 98; reception and reviews, 302, 686–7;
revision, 98, 475
Charm of Lullabies, A, Op. 41: broadcasts, 344, 417,
418, 428; composition, 313, 343; dedication, 343,
418; and Nancy Evans, 149, 343–4, 352, 417, 418,
428; manuscript, 343–4; performances, 352–3:
The Hague (Evans–de Nobel, premiere; 1948),
313, 343; texts, 343; title, 343
Children's Crusade, Op. 82: composition, 32; translation, 666
Chopin: Les Sylphides: orchestration (lost), 89;
premiere (1941), 89
Choral Dances from 'Gloriana': broadcast, 183;
choreography, 540; performance: premiere
(1954), 183
Chorale after an Old French Carol (1944):
composition, 132
Christmas Oratorio (uncompleted): composition,
132; text, 99, 100, 268–9; see also Chorale after an
Old French Carol and A Shepherd's Carol
Christ's Nativity (Thy King's Birthday) (1931):
composition, 56
Church Parables: and Benjamin Britten Memorial
Window, 177; Far Eastern dimension, 609;
identification of character and instrumenta-
tion, 125; transcendence of, 9; see also Curlew
River, The Burning Fiery Furnace and The
Prodigal Son
'Civil War' project (unrealized opera), 287–8, 438,
457
Coal Face (film music): composition, 56, 172
'Come, silly Babe' (additional song excluded from
A Charm of Lullabies), 344
The Company of Heaven (radio music): composi-
tion, 57
'Cradle Song', see 'Sleep, my darling, sleep'
Curlew River, Op. 71: dedication, 368; Far Eastern
dimension, 609; libretto (Plomer), 672;
parental absence, motif of, 16; publication, 667

The Dark Tower (radio music), 112: broadcasts,
134, 137, 143; casts, 72, 143; composition, 58, 134;
radio productions, 143; reception, 143
The Dark Valley (radio music): composition, 58
Death in Venice, Op. 88: companies and casts, 88;
composition, 33, 35, 656; dance sequences, 507;
family, motif of, 16–17; libretto (Myfanwy Piper
after Thomas Mann), 32–4, 47, 176, 197; non-
Western musics, 17; notation of recitatives, 656;
outside/inside motif, 17; performances and
productions: premiere (Snape, 1973), 33 413;
Covent Garden (1973), 33, 34, 413; New York
Met (1974), 88, 579; Tadzio, supposed prototype
for, 31, 34–6, 38, 44; translation, 666; vibra-
phone-writing, 17
Deus in adjutorium meum (1945; This Way to the
Tomb): publication, 171; recording, 171
Diversions, Op. 21: composition, 58; premiere
(Philadelphia; 1942), 58, 93; recording
(Katchen, c BB), 204
Donne Sonnets, see The Holy Sonnets of John
Donne, The, Op. 35

Double Concerto in B minor: composition, 14, 56; viola-writing, 14

The Duchess of Malfi (theatre music; lost), 267: composition, 137, 226, 228–31, 259; performances, 229; royalties, 229; and *Serenade*, 229–30

The Eagle Has Two Heads (1946, theatre music; Cocteau–Duncan): composition, 137
Einladung zur Martinsgans (1957): composition, 48, 461; manuscript, *462*
Elegy (1930): composition, 55
Evening, Morning, Night (1945; *This Way to the Tomb*): publication, 171; recording, 171

Fanfare for D.W., A: performance: Royal Opera House (premiere; 1970), 290; programme note (BB), 290
Festival Te Deum, Op. 32: composition, 58; performance: St Gallen (1946), 182
'film-opera' (unrealized project), 407, 428
'Fish in the Unruffled Lakes' (1938): performances, 436: Amsterdam (PP–BB; 1946), 255; European tour (PP–BB; 1947), 278; Concertgebouw (PP–BB, 1948), 454
Five Flower Songs, Op. 47: 'Marsh Flowers', 662–3; dedication, 662
Folk Song Arrangements: British Isles (vol. 1): 'The Salley Gardens', 182; 'The Bonny Earl o' Moray', 453; 'The trees they grow so high', 90; 'The Ash Grove', 276, 453; French Folk Song Arrangements (vol. 2), 282, 440; 'La noël passée' ('The Orphan and King Harry'), 166, 441; 'Voici le printemps', 166; 'Fileuse', 166; 'Le roi s'en va-t'en chasse', 166; 'La belle est au jardin d'amour', 166; 'Eho! Eho!', 166; 'Quand j'étais chez mon père' ('Heigh-ho! Heigh-hi!'), 166, 453; British Isles (vol. 3): 'The Plough Boy', 326, 'There's none to soothe', 453, 454; 'Sweet Polly Oliver', 260, 276, 453; in *Tuppence Coloured* (revue), 331; 'The Foggy, Foggy Dew', 326, 456, 457–8, 461, 463; 'O Waly, Waly', 260; 'Come you not from Newcastle?', 260; Moore's Irish Melodies (vol. 4), 326: broadcasts, 182; and canon, 276; composition, 58, 138, 166, 260, 326, 384, 440; dedications, 90, 165, 326; manuscripts, 166; orchestrations, 166, 441; performances, 166, 364, 436, 454, 601: Netherlands (PP–BB; 1946), 255, 259, 260; European tour (PP–BB; 1947), 278; UK recitals (PP–BB), 319, 339, 359; North American tour (PP–BB, 1949), 546; Vienna (PP–BB; 1951), 663; publications, 165, 282, 326; reception and reviews, 453, 457–8, 517; recordings (PP–BB), 166, 182, 326, 452–4, 457–8; translations, 166
Four Sea Interludes from 'Peter Grimes', Op. 33a: BB on, 103; performances: Cheltenham (*c* BB, premiere; 1945), 103, 106; Boston (*c* Koussevitzky, US premiere; 1946), 137, 211; Edinburgh Festival (*c* Susskind; 1947), 325, 329; Los Angeles (*c* BB; 1949), 441; programme note, 103; recordings, 86, 202, 345, 348–9, 510; reception and reviews, 211–12
Friday Afternoons, Op. 7: 'Jazz-Man', 61; 'Old Abram Brown', 276; canon, use of, 276; composition, 56, 51; educative element, 29; texts, 61
Fry, Elizabeth (subject for unrealized project), 520, 521

Gandhi requiem (unrealized project), 356, 373, 375, 558

Gloriana, Op. 53, 9: companies and casts, 140, 235, 391, 392, 431, 516, 540; composition, 27, 656; and Imogen Holst, 656; libretto, 672; performances: Covent Garden (premiere; 1953), 391, 392, 431, 516; reception and reviews, 133; on tour, 308; *see also Choral Dances from 'Gloriana'*
Grand Sonata No. 4 (1925): manuscript, 48, 450

Hadrian's Wall (radio music): composition, 57
Harvest Reel (unrealized ballet project), 261
Haydn: Harpsichord Concerto in D major (H. XVIII:11): cadenzas, 190
Heart of the Matter, The (sequence): devising and texts, 543, 680
Holiday Diary, Op. 5 (formerly *Holiday Tales*): composition, 56; manuscripts, 190, 450; premiere, 56; programme note (BB), 190; score, 190
Holst: *The Wandering Scholar* (Holst edition, with Imogen Holst), *see* Index of Other Composers
The Holy Sonnets of John Donne, Op. 35, 595: 'Thou hast made me', 595; 'Death, be not proud', 104, 595; BB on, 104; broadcast (PP–BB), 153; composition, 58, 104; dedication, 104; performances: Wigmore Hall (PP–BB, premiere; 1945), 58, 105, 107; St Gallen (PP–BB; 1946), 182; Amsterdam (PP–BB; 1946), 255; UK tour (PP–BB; 1947), 339; reception and reviews, 107; recording (PP–BB), 138, 326; texts, 122
Hymn to St Cecilia, Op. 27: composition, 58; opus number, 441; premiere, and broadcast (1942), 58, 99, 111, 474; reception and reviews, 99; recording, 96, 97, 99; structure, 300; text, 78
Hymn to the Virgin, A (1930): broadcast, 474; composition, 55; manuscripts, 48, 450; first performance, 56

I saw three ships (*The Sycamore Tree*) (1930): composition, 55; manuscripts, 48, 450, *451*; performance, 56
'If thou wilt ease thine heart' (1942; Beddoes setting): composition, 121; publication (*The Red Cockatoo*), 121; text, 121
Les Illuminations, Op. 18: 'Marine', 81, 83; 'Being Beauteous', 81, 83; assignment, 82, 83; BB on, 96, 97–8, 129, 144–5; broadcasts, 81, 83, 320; composition, 57, 83, 84; dedication(s), 97, 119; performances: premiere (London; 1940), 58, 83, 97; New York (US premiere, PP, *c* BB; 1941), 83, 130; National Gallery (voice and piano version, 1943), 96; Leeuwarden (PP; 1946), 254; Zurich (PP; 1946), 184, 198; Amsterdam (PP, *c* Münch; 1947), 144, 145, 153–4, 306; Edinburgh Festival (PP; 1947), 313, 315, 320, 325; Zurich (PP, *c* BB, Zurich; 1948), 356; New York (PP, *c* BB; 1949), 551, 554; prefatory note (Sackville-West), 129–30; programme note (BB–PP, 1941), 130; publication, 83, 129; reception and reviews, 198, 332, 691; recordings, 83, 304, 451, 453–4; off-air, 120, 128; and Edward Sackville-West, 128–9; voice and piano version, 97–8; and Sophie Wyss, 97–8
Instruments of the Orchestra (film): commentary, 174; music recording, 137, 172; scenario, 172–3
Introduction and Rondo alla burlesca, Op. 23 No. 2: composition, 58; dedication, 190; manuscripts, 190; performance: Zurich Radio (BB–Braus; 1946), 182; score, 190
Irish Reel (1936): publication, 261; recording, 261; *see also Around the Village Green*

Johnson over Jordan (theatre music): composition, 57
Jubilate Deo in C (1961): composition, 596
Jubilate Deo in E♭ (1934): composition, 56

Kermesse Canadienne, see Canadian Carnival
King Arthur (radio music): composition, 57; and Piano Concerto, 158
The King's Stamp (film music): composition, 56

Lachrymae, Op. 48: arrangement for viola and small string orchestra, Op. 48a, 551; composition, 534, 550, 590; manuscripts, 190, *592–3*; performance: AF (Primrose *vla*, BB, premiere; 1950), 161, 550, 591; AF (Primrose *vla*, Mewton-Wood; 1952), 551; Wigmore Hall (1955), 162; reception and reviews, 591, 594
Let's Make an Opera, 287, *515*; playtext, 514, 549–51, 555, 590, 660; royalty arrangement, 590; *and see Little Sweep, The*
Letters to William (proposed opera), 232, 234: draft casting, 234; draft libretto (Ronald Duncan), 232, *233*, 234; synopsis by PP, 232
Little Sweep, The, Op. 45: audience participation, 501, 517–18; BB on, 660; and children, 12; companies and casts, 27, 28, 408, 431, 492, 516, 540, 549–50, 574, 655, 659; composition, 287, 407–8, 440, 441, 506–9, 512; dedication, 11, 19, 384, 571; as 'family' work, 11, 14; libretto and play (Eric Crozier), 11, 19, 212, 353, 501, 512, 518, 539, 549–51, 555, 571–6, 590, 660; parental absence, motif of, 15; performances: AF (*c* Del Mar, premiere; 1949), *plates 36–41*, 408, 416, 486, 492, 501, 514, 516–17, 585, 609; EOG (1949), 440–41, 501, 517–18, 540, 544, 550–51; New Haven, Boston, New York (1950), 609–10, 641; Lyric, Hammersmith (1950–51), 519, 550–51, 554, 556, 637, 641; Lowestoft (June 1951), 641; Liverpool (August 1951), 642, 660; Lyric, Hammersmith (1951–52), 677; Hull (February 1952), 677; Wimbledon (March 1952), 677; La Scala, London (1955), 27; Zurich, 624; preface for *Opera*, 623; publication, 506; reception and reviews, 514, 516–19, 526, 549, 551, 555, 577; royalties, 590; and *The Tale of Mr Tod*, 673
Love from a Stranger (film music): composition, 57, 343; recording, 343

'Mad Bess', see Purcell realizations
Man Born to Be King, The (incidental music): 'Bring me garlands, bring me wine', 615; 'Soldier, soldier, why will you roam?', 615
Mansfield Park (unrealized opera), see *Letters to William*
The Mark of Cain (unrealized ballet), 115
Mass (for St Matthew's, Northampton, unrealized), 165, 389, 595–6
Matinées Musicales, Op. 24: composition, 58, 89; and *Divertimento* (ballet), 89
Mazurka Elegiaca, Op. 23 No. 1: composition, 58; performance: Zurich Radio (BB–Braus, 1946), 182; score, 190
Mea Culpa (unrealized): and BBC, 155, 158; concept, 155–8; and Ronald Duncan, 155, 158, 163, 351; text, *157*
Men of Goodwill: The Reunion of Christmas (1947): broadcast, 313, 345; composition, 313, 345; publication, 346
A Midsummer Night's Dream, Op. 64: companies and casts, 149, 431; dedication, 31; libretto, 197;

performances and productions: AF (premiere; 1960), 31, 149, 431; Covent Garden (1961), 603, 608; Glyndebourne (1981), 151; recording, 149
Missa Brevis in D, Op. 63: composition, 389, 596
Mont Juic, Op. 12 (with Berkeley): composition, 57, 64, 69

'Night covers up the rigid land' (1937): composition, 65
Night Mail (1936; film music): composition, 57; text, 78
Nocturnal after John Dowland, Op. 70: publication, 667
Nocturne, Op. 60: 'The Wanderings of Cain', 15; Mahlerian instrumentation, 15; parental absence, motif of, 15; texts, 121
'Not to you I sighed. No, not a word' (Spender setting, lost), 72
'Now sleeps the crimson petal' (1943; Tennyson setting; discarded from *Serenade*): Lennox Berkeley on, 118
Noye's Fludde, Op. 59: and children, 12; companies and casts, 28, 149, 486; dedication, 10, 25, 488; family, theme of, 10, 14; libretto, 197, 287; premiere, 149; recording, 149, 486

Occasional Overture in C, Op. 38: BB on, 231; and BBC, 138, 235–6, 441; broadcasts, 236; composition, 137, 231, 234, 236, 238; manuscript. 236; orchestral parts, 236; performances: BBC broadcast (*c* Boult; 1946) 138, 236, 241; Boston, US (*c* Boult; mid-1980s), 236; Chicago (*c* Leppard; 1983), 237; publication, 237; recording, 237; *see also American Overture, An*
On the Frontier (theatre music): BB on, 76; composition, 57, 78; performance, 73
On This Island, Op. 11: 'Let the florid music praise', 254, 278, 436; 'Nocturne', 252; broadcast (PP–BB), 339; composition, 57; performances: premiere, 57, 97; Amsterdam (PP–BB; 1946), 255; European tour (PP–BB; 1947), 278; UK tour (PP–BB; 1947), 339; texts, 252, 410
Organ Concerto (unrealized), 464
Our Hunting Fathers, Op. 8: *Messalina*, 66–7; *Dance of Death*, 269–70; Berkeley on, 66; composition, 56, 62–3; performance: Norwich (premiere, *c* BB; 1936), 57, 62, 66–7, 97, 148, 368, 435, 458; programme note (BB), 66; publication, 66; reception and reviews, 66–7; text, 8, 66, 78, 269
Out of the Picture (theatre music), 112: composition, 57
Owen Wingrave, Op. 85: commission and commission fee, 35, 158, 610; composition, 32, 35; dedication, 424; libretto (Myfanwy Piper after Henry James), 32, 35, 176; pacifist element, 158; parental absence, motif of, 15; recording, 33; stage performances: Covent Garden (stage premiere; 1973), 413, 431; Britten–Pears School (1984), 516; television production: BBC2 (premiere; 1970), 32–3, 35, 42–3, 158, 413, 431, 516; theme of family, 10

Pageant of Empire (theatre music): composition, 57; performances, 68
Passacaglia from 'Peter Grimes', Op. 33b: performances: Boston (*c* Koussevitzky, US premiere; 1946), 137, 211; New York (*c* Koussevitzky, 1946), 211–12; planned performance, 161; reception and reviews, 211–12; recordings, 86, 348–9, 510;

and Edward Sackville-West, 131–2; and Erwin Stein, 132; viola-writing, 17, 131–2

Paul Bunyan, Op. 17, 46, 668, 676: availability, 125, 665; broadcast, 665; companies and casts, 87, 207, 665; composition, 58, 84, 86; extracts in performance, 665; heterophony, 276; libretto, 78; performances, 46: Columbia University (premiere; 1941), 58, 86, 87, 210, 240, 441, 665; AF (premiere of revised version; 1976), 413, 665; reception and reviews, 87; revised version, 665

Peace of Britain (film music): composition, 57

Peter Grimes, Op. 33, 125, 195, 199, 357; BB on, 128, 185, 225, 390–92, 422, 476, 550; broadcasts (and commentary), 141–2, 552; commission, 58, 100, 101, 103; companies and casts, 85, 103, 128, 140, 149, 188, 235, 355, 375, 387, 390–92; composition, 58, 100, 101, 117, 121, 128, 132; concert and recital extracts, 170, *175*, 319; dances (possible suite), 102, 104; design, 100, 363, 559; film proposal, 324–5, 327; libretto and translations, 91, 92, 123, 186, 188, 362, 378, 392, 498, 504–5, 662; outsider motif, 14; PP on Grimes, 141–2; performances and productions, 268: Sadler's Wells (premiere, *c* Goodall, 1945), 51, 58, 61, 100, 101, 132, 140, 149, 151, 167–9, 188, 212, 250, 392, 439, 559, 563; New York (*pp*; November 1945), 207–8; Sadler's Wells (revival; February 1946), 137, 139, 140–42, 143, 176, 180; Stockholm (Swedish premiere; March 1946), 137, 167, 202; Basel (German language premiere; May 1946), 167, 181, 182, 185, 186–8, 192, 194, 199; Antwerp (Belgian premiere, in Flemish; May 1946), 167, 391, 392; Zurich (June 1946), 167, 181, 182, 184, 185, 188, 192, 194, 197–9, 208; Tanglewood (*c* Bernstein; US premiere; August 1946), *plates 26–8*, 85, 87, 101, 137, 146, *204–5*, 206–11, 225–7, 237, 239, 261, 281, 379, 455; Amsterdam (1947), 254; Hamburg (German premiere; March 1947), 138, 268, 270; La Scala, Milan (March 1947), 562, 568; Berlin (May 1947), 268, 270; Covent Garden (*c* Rankl/ Goodall; November 1947, and revivals), 203, 282, 284–5, 290, 308, 313, 325, 333, *334*, 335, 338, 355, 390–92, 437, 439, 476, 602; New York Metropolitan Opera (February 1948, and tour), 261, 314, 325, 329, 371–3, 375–80, 441, 455; Covent Garden tour (Brussels and Paris; June 1948), 335, 390–92; Strasbourg (1949), 392; Tanglewood (1996) 212; projected Broadway production, 210–11; publication and scores, 104, 421; and 'Quand j'étais chez mon père', 166; reception and reviews, 61, 105–6, 112, 133, 140–42, 166, 168, 186–7, 192, 197–8, 202, 209–11, 215, 218, 219, 222, 238, 240, 263, 295, 296, 303, 333, 335–6, 376–80, 401, 437, 504–5, 517, 550, 568, 686–7, 691; recordings and plans to record, 86, 149, 201–3, 210, 308, 425–7, 549, 551–2; and Sadler's Wells Opera Book, 130–32; and Schoenberg, 423; television recording, 516; theme of social exclusion and persecution, 8–9; viola-writing, 14, 17; *see also Four Sea Interludes*, Op. 33a, and *Passacaglia*, Op. 33b

Phaedra, Op. 93: performance: AF (premiere, Baker *ms*, *c* Bedford; 1976), 413, 679; text, 679

Phantasy in F minor (1932): composition, 56; and Cobbett Prize, 56

Phantasy quartet, Op. 2: broadcasts, 80, 259–60, 270; composition, 56; performance: ISCM (1934), 56, 67

Piano Concerto, Op. 13: *Recitative and Aria*, 158;

Impromptu, 158–60, *159*, 190; BB on, 415, 460; and BBC, 155, 160; broadcasts, 416, 417, 419, 460; composition, 57; and Clifford Curzon, 158–60; dedication, 64; and *King Arthur*, 158; manuscripts, 190; performances, 84: premiere, 57, 73; Brussels (1939; BB *piano*), 78; Illinois (US premiere, *c* Goldberg; 1940), 622; Cheltenham (Mewton-Wood, *c* Britten; premiere of revised version; 1946) 137, 155, 158, 161; BBC Prom (Curzon, 1952), 161; playthrough (for Copland), 87; publication and scores, 415; reception and reviews, 161; revised version, 137, 415; two-piano arrangement (Easdale), 458

The Picture of Dorian Gray (unrealized ballet project), 115

Plymouth Town: composition, 56, 69–70; performance, 70; viola-writing, 14

Poet's Christmas, A (radio music): composition, 58; performance, 475

Poet's Echo, The, Op. 76: translations, 666

Praise We Great Men (unfinished fragment, 1976): composition, 543; orchestration (C. Matthews), 543

Prelude and Dances from 'The Prince of the Pagodas', Op. 57b, see *Prince of the Pagodas, The*, Op. 57

Prelude and Fugue, Op. 29, for eighteen-part string orchestra: composition, 58, 343; performance: Zurich (*c* BB; 1948), 356

Prelude and Fugue on a Theme of Vittoria (1946): composition, 137; performances: St Matthew's, Northampton (premiere, 1946), 138, 165; Central Hall, Westminster (1946), 260

Prince of the Pagodas, The, Op. 57: choreography, 540; Far Eastern dimension, 609; *Prelude and Dances from 'The Prince of the Pagodas'*, Op. 57b (Del Mar suite), 486

Prodigal Son, The, Op. 81: composition, 32; libretto, 672; theme of family, 10, 13–14; translation, 666

Psalm 69, *see Deus in adjutorium meum* (1945; *This Way to the Tomb*)

Psalm 70, *see Deus in adjutorium meum* (1945; *This Way to the Tomb*)

Quartettino (1930): composition, 55, 446; motto, 446

Quatre Chansons Françaises (1928): 'L'enfance', 16; composition, 16, 55; dedication, 16

The Rape of Lucretia, Op. 37, 9, 125, 210, 240, 248, 285, 366: BB on, 272, 480, 493–5; broadcasts, 138, 147, 228, 254, 422, 478; Christian elements, 178–80, 217–22, 224, 237–8; companies and casts, 137, 140, 144, 147, 148, 149, 160, 185, 187, 235, 266, 308, 322, 355, 430, 431, 448, 483, 486, 502, 514, 659–60; composition, 137, 138, 139, 144, 146, 158, 163, 167, 171, 172, 174, *175*, 196, 273–4, 438; dedications, 186, 189; design, *175*, 180; extracts in performance, 422; and Glyndebourne, 242, 244, 277; libretto, rights and translations, 49, 139, 177–9, 179, 194–7, 200, 214, 215, 217–24, 226, 231, 253–5, 258, 282, 332, 477–8, 504–5, 552; manuscripts, 189; performances and productions: Glyndebourne (premiere, *c* Ansermet/Goodall; 1946), *plates 3–8*, 137, 144, 147–51, 160, 180, 185, 193, 196, 199, 203, 206–8, 211, 212, 213–15, *215–16*, 217–24, 232, 235, 238, 242, 247, 261, 273, 277, 304, 308, 322, 355, 363, 431, 448, 477; UK tour (Manchester, Liverpool,

Edinburgh, Glasgow, Sadler's Wells, Oxford; 1946), 137, 147, 151, 206–7, 213–14, 224, 227, 230–31, 237–9, 245; Netherlands tour (1946), 138, 147, 151 182, 228, 258; Brussels (April 1947), 255, 268, 392; Basel (Swiss premiere; June 1947), 138, 200, 227, 255, 258, 268, 282, 286; Glyndebourne (premiere of revised version; July 1947), 138, 255, 263, 282, 299, 300, 573–4; EOG tour (Netherlands and Switzerland; summer 1947), 305–6, 308; EOG tour (Newcastle, Bournemouth, Oxford; autumn 1947), 303; New York: Broadway (1949), 418, 440, 441, 447–8, 455, 476–8, 480, 501; Los Angeles (1947), 676; Covent Garden (EOG; November 1947), 300, 355; EOG (1949), 440–41; AF (1949), 414, 416, 440, 514; Lyric, Hammersmith (May 1951), 641, 659; Wiesbaden (May and June 1951), 641, 659; Mulhouse, 624; AF (1954), 187; PP on, 214; proposed ballet, 260; publication and scores, 197, 227, 254, 255, 258, 282, 332, 338; reception and reviews, 133, 146, 170, 211, 214–24, 237–8, 239, 240, 263, 292, 294–9, 303, 392, 477–8, 480, 493, 501, 504–5, 518, 587, 589, 594; recordings, 138, 149, 254, 255, 302, 303–5, 351, 478; revisions, 138, 253–5, 256–7, 282, 284; and Sadler's Wells, 144; *Symposium* (RLEC), 407, 427, 428–9; tour plans, 144, 181, 182, 198–200, 226, 231, 261, 354–5; in US, 261
The Red Cockatoo & Other Songs: prefatory note, 122; publication, 105; *see* individual songs: 'Wild with passion', 'If thou wilt ease thine heart', 'Birthday Song for Erwin'
Rejoice in the Lamb, Op. 30: commission, 163; composition, 58, 132; performances: St Matthew's, Northampton (1946), 165; Central Hall, Westminster (1946), 260; reception and reviews, 302, 686
Rescue, The (radio music): and Hedli Anderson, 72, 128; BB on, 128; companies and casts, 125; composition, 58, 111, 113–17, 123, 126–7, 131, 132; identification of character and instrument, 125; manuscript, *127*; performances, 45: broadcast premiere (1943), 117, 122, 123, 128; broadcast (1948), 124–5; broadcast (1951), 124; broadcast (1956), 124; broadcast (1962), 124
Rhapsody (1929), for string quartet: composition, 55
Rossini Suite (1935): and *The Tocher*, 467
Russian Funeral (1936): composition, 56; premiere (1936), 625

Saint Nicolas, Op. 42, 576: amateur performances, 200; artists, 433; BB on, 473; broadcasts, 428, 433, 471–2, 476, 548; commission, 299, 300; composition, 299, 300, 313, 314, 315, 321–3, 344, 346, 348–51, 393, 396; performances: AF (PP, *c* BB, premiere; 1948), *plate 35*, 300–301, 314, 355, 357, 359, 475; Lancing College (PP, *c* BB; July 1948), 300–301, 314; Amsterdam (PP, *c* BB; December 1948), 414, 415, *466*, 473; Dartington (PP, *c* BB; April 1949), 435, 436, 502, 507; AF (1949), 414, 416, 485; Los Angeles (1949), 556; Ipswich and Bury St Edmunds (PP; 1950), 630–31; programme note, 460; publication and scores, 302, 409, 410, 419, 420, 471, 475; reception and reviews, 301–2, 506, 526; royalties, 590; text (Crozier), 19, 212, 300, 315, 321–3, 428, 539
Scherzettino 'A.B.': manuscript, *626*; publication, 625

Scottish Ballad, Op. 26: broadcast, (Clifford Curzon–BB) 190; composition, 58, 89–90; manuscripts, 190; performance: premiere (Cincinnati; 1941), 90; Royal Albert Hall (first UK performance; Clifford Curzon–BB), 190; and Edward Sackville-West, 123
'Sea Symphony' (unrealized): texts, 121–2
Serenade, Op. 31: 'Pastoral' (Cotton), 117; 'Nocturne' (Tennyson), 117; 'Elegy' (Blake), 117; 'Dirge' (Lyke-Wake Dirge), 102, 117, 229; 'Hymn' (Jonson), 117; 'Sonnet' (Keats), 117; BB on, 123, 181; broadcast, 182; composition, 58, 96, 98, 117, 132; dedication, 110, 112, 119; manuscript, *110*; performances: Wigmore Hall (premiere, PP, Brain *horn*; 1943), 58, 98, 123, 124; European tour (PP, *c* BB; 1947), 278; Basel (PP, *c* Sacher; 1948), 356; Amsterdam (PP, *c* van Beinum; 1948), 416; Lausanne (PP, *c* Sacher; November 1948), 464; Los Angeles (PP, *c* BB; 1949), 441; Hallé Orchestra (PP, Brain *horn*, *c* Kletzki; 1951), 642; Vienna (PP, Freiberg *horn*, *c* Krauss; 1951), 663; publication, 129; reception and reviews, 332, 524, 526, 664, 687; recording, 102; structure and texts, 112, 117–19, 123; title, 98, 118, 123; *see also* 'Now Sleeps the Crimson Petal'
Seven Sonnets of Michelangelo, Op. 22, 423: BB on, 122, 123; broadcast (PP–BB, 1946), 259; composition, 58, 84; performances: *pp* (PP–BB), 113; premiere (PP–BB, Wigmore Hall; 1942), 58, 99, 111, 113; Services Quiet Club, Liverpool (1944), 102; Concertgebouw (PP–BB; January 1946), 153; New York (Halban; October 1946), 254; European tour (PP–BB; 1947), 278; Italian tour (PP–BB; April 1947), 268, *281*; New York (PP *pp*; 1948), 443; New York (PP–BB; 1949), 546; Copenhagen (PP–BB; 1950), 601; reception and reviews, 98, 99, 113
A Shepherd's Carol (1944): composition, 132
Simple Symphony, Op. 4, 518: arrangement for two pianos, 443; BB on, 669; composition, 56, 669; dedication, 670; educative element, 29; premiere (1934), 56, 80; publication, 669
Sinfonia da Requiem, Op. 20: Dies irae, 269–70; BB on, 84, 495; broadcasts, 86, 182, 495–6; commission, 86, 211; composition, 58, 84; form: performances: premiere (*c* Barbirolli, New York; 1941), 58, 86, 269; first UK performance (BBC Prom; 1942), 111; Zurich (*c* BB; 1946), 182; Los Angeles (*c* BB), 441; publication, 96, 97; reception, 84, 495, 525; recording, 86, 304
Sinfonietta, Op. 1: broadcast, 56; composition, 56; performances: premiere, 56; Zurich (*c* BB; 1948), 356
Six Metamorphoses after Ovid, Op. 49: composition, 534; premiere: AF 1951 (Boughton; 1951), 534
'Sleep, my darling, sleep' (projected MacNeice setting), 112, 122
Soirées Musicales, Op. 9: composition, 56, 89; and *Divertimento* (ballet), 89; two-piano arrangement (Easdale), 458
'Soldier, soldier, why will you roam?', *see* Man Born to Be King, The
'Somnus, the humble god' (song excluded from A Charm of Lullabies), 344
Spring Symphony, Op. 44: 'Shine out, fair sun, with all your heat', 420–21, 528; 'The merry Cuckoo', 421, 456, 523, 527; 'Spring', 442, 456, 526, 527, 544, 616; 'The Driving Boy', 230, 454, 455, 509, 523; 'The Morning Star', 454, 523, 616;

'Welcome, maids of honour', 455, 457, 527–8, 613, 614, 617; 'Waters above', 455, 457, 523, 528, 617; 'Out on the lawn', 78, 410, 523, 526, 527–8, 529, 553, 616–17; 'When will my May come', 552; 'Fair and fair', 509, 510, 528, 553, 599, 617; 'Sound the Flute', 552, 617; 'London, to thee I do present', 528; 'Sumer is icumen in', 522, 526, 528, 529, 617; BB on, 535, 616–17; broadcasts, 535, 581, 614; commission and rights to first performance, 101, 231, 237, 279–80, 299, 347, 374, 525, 526, 610; composition, 279–80, 299, 313, 315, 373, 407–8, 414, 416–20, 435, 439, 440, 442, 449, 452, 455, 457, 459, 464, 465, 479, 495–500, 502–3, 513; dedication, 237, 511; performances: Amsterdam (Concertgebouw Orchestra, c van Beinum, premiere; 1949), *plate 50*, 347, 408, 440, 499, 500, 510, 511, 521–9, *523*, 535, 553, 580; Tanglewood (US premiere; August 1949), 374, 439, 465, 500, 511, 525, 533, 535, 580; Royal Albert Hall, London (c van Beinum, UK premiere, March 1950), 276, 533, 551, 552–2, 580–82; Leeds (c Bardgett; October 1950), 553–4, 598–9, 613–14; Manchester (c Bardgett, November 1950), 617; Vienna (c Krauss; April 1951) 534, 663–4; publication and scores, 280, 500, 598; reception and reviews, 133, 518, 521–9, 535, 552–3, 598–600, 664, 686, 690; recordings, 431, 521, 553; revisions, 529; soloists, 147, 521, 431, 502, 509, 510, 551, 617; texts and translations, 78, 279–80, 409, 410, 551–2; title, 415

'Stay, O sweet, and do not rise' (incomplete Donne setting), 105, 122

Stratton (theatre music), 533, 544, 546, 549, 589

'Street Cries' (manuscript fragment), 468

String Quartet in D (1931): composition, 56

String Quartet No. 1, Op. 25, 667: composition, 58; performances: Los Angeles (premiere; 1941), 58; Sheffield (1944), 543; reception, 202, 544

String Quartet No. 2, Op. 36, 667: composition, 58; dedication, 214; premiere (Wigmore Hall; 1945), 58, 107; reception and reviews, 133, 222

String Quartet No. 3, Op. 94, 667: composition, 667; dedication, 667

Suite No. 3, for cello, Op. 87: composition, 33

Suite, Op. 6, for violin and piano, *447*: BB on, 445–6; composition, 56, 446; motto, 446–7; performances: 445: ISCM (1936), 57; and Szigeti, 446

Suite on English Folk Tunes ('A Time There Was . . .'), Op. 90: premiere (AF; 1975), 413; recording, 86

Sword in the Stone, The (radio music): broadcast, 474; composition, 57

Sycamore Tree, The, see *I saw three ships* (1930)

The Tale of Mr Tod (unrealized opera), 534, 674, 678–9: libretto (Plomer after Potter), 670–73; rights, 197, 673; synopsis and sketch, *671*

Te Deum in C major (1934), 412: composition, 56; orchestral version, 151; performances: (c Goodall; 1936), 151; St Matthew's, Northampton (1946), 165

'Tell me the truth about love', see *Cabaret Songs*

Tema 'Sacher' (1976): composition, 487

Tempest, The (unrealized): 602–3, 606–9

Temporal Variations (1936): composition, 57

Themes for improvisation (1945): broadcast, 183; composition, 183; publication, 183

There is a willow grows aslant a brook (1932; Bridge arrangement), 366, 368

This Way to the Tomb (theatre music; 1945), 270: broadcasts, 171; composition, 58; performance: Cambridge (1946), 170, 443; publications, 171; recordings, 171; *see also* 'Boogie-woogie', *Evening, Morning, Night* and *Deus in adjutorium meum*

Three Two-part Songs (1932): composition, 56; premiere, 56; publication, 56

The Turn of the Screw, Op. 54, 133: auditions, 27; commission, 380; companies and casts, 27, 28, 140, 431, 516; composition, 26, 35, 274; dedication, 287; letter scene, 232; libretto, 27, 176; parental absence, motif of, 15, 25; performances and productions: Oxford, 24; Venice (c Britten, premiere; 1954), 25, 26, 380, 431, 516; Stratford, Ontario (1957), 550; Scottish Opera, 25; recording, 431; television broadcast, 25

Twelve Variations (1931): composition, 56

Two Ballads (1936): 'Underneath the abject willow', 78; composition, 56

Two Insect Pieces (1935): composition, 56

Two Part-songs (1933): broadcast, 474; composition, 56

Two Portraits (1930): composition, 55

Tyco the Vegan (unrealized): libretto (Plomer), 672

'Underneath the abject willow', see Two Ballads

Variation on an Elizabethan Theme (1953): performance: (AF 1953), 342

Variations on a Theme of Frank Bridge, Op. 10: composition, 57; performances: Salzburg Festival (c Neel, premiere; 1937), 57, 75, 343; (c Sacher), 487; revisions, 75

Venite exultemus Domino (1961): composition, 596

Village Harvest, see *Around the Village Green*

Violin Concerto, Op. 15: BB on, 621–2; and Antonio Brosa, 254, 487; composition, 57, 84; dedication, 338; and Manoug Parikian, 487; performances, 622: New York (Brosa *vln*, c Barbirolli; premiere, 1940), 58, 84, 347, 623; New York (Lywen *vln*, c Bernstein; 1946), 254; Cheltenham Festival (Olof *vln*, c Barbirolli; 1947), 347; publication, 623; reception, 254; recordings, 347; revisions, 487, 534, 621

Voices for Today, Op. 75: ad lib. organ part (Downes), 463; commission, 87, 158; pacifist element, 158; premieres (1965), 87; texts, 672

War Requiem, Op. 66: commission, 177, 184; composition, 375; dedication, 471; Owen texts, 10, 375; pacifist element, 51, 158, 270; soloists, 431

The Way to the Sea (film music): composition, 57

A Wealden Trio (1930): composition, 55

Wedding Anthem (Amo Ergo Sum), Op 46: composition, 533; manuscript, 542; performance: St Mark's (Cross *sop*, PP, c BB, premiere; September 1949), 533, 541–2; text, 541–2

Who are these Children?, Op. 84: composition, 32; texts, 120

'Wild with Passion' (1942; Beddoes setting): composition, 121; publication (*The Red Cockatoo*), 121; text, 121–2

Winter Words, Op. 52: dedication, 176; performances (PP–BB), 13; texts, 558

The World of the Spirit (radio music; 1938): broadcast, 276; composition, 57

Young Apollo (1939): composition, 57; premiere, 57

The Young Person's Guide to the Orchestra, Op. 34: and children, 12; commentary (Eric Crozier), 246–7; composition, 29, 58, 172–4; dedication, 11, 12, 19, 24, 271–2, 448; educative element, 11, 28–9; and *Instruments of the Orchestra* (film), 29, 172–4; performances: Liverpool (*c* Sargent, premiere; 1946), 138; Concertgebouw (Britten *narrator*; 1946), 138, 246–7, 247, 248, 258; Zurich (1947), 278; Edinburgh Festival (*c* Sargent; 1947), 325, 329; Hunter College (1948), 443; publication and scores, 271, 300, 421; reception and reviews, 248; recording (for *Instruments of the Orchestra*), 172; title, 329

'Your body is stars whose millions glitter here' (Spender setting, incomplete), 72

PURCELL REALIZATIONS

Chacony in G minor (z. 730): performances, 356, 436, 441; AF (1948), 359

Dido and Aeneas (with Imogen Holst), 534, 569, 595–6, 602, 607, 627–8, 645–8, 664; BB on, 231, 647–8; choreography, 604; companies and casts, 148, 596, 603, 634–5; financial support, 615, 634–5; and Glyndebourne, 231, 232, 234; and Holland Festival, 621; performances, 554: Lyric, Hammersmith (premiere; May 1951), 534, 596, 603, 628, 634–5, 641, 648–51; AF (1951), 596, 641; Netherlands (1951), 641, 646; Cheltenham Festival (1951), 642; Glyndebourne (1966), 151; reception, 648, 650–51; recording, 648

The Fairy Queen (concert version devised by PP; edited and realized by BB and Imogen Holst): recording, 149, 431

Harmonia Sacra: The Blessed Virgin's Expostu- lation (z. 196), 308, 345, 347; *Saul and the Witch at Endor* (z. 134), 416; *Three Divine Hymns*: 'We sing to him' (z. 199), 182; 'Evening Hymn' (z. 193), 348, 595; *Two Divine Hymns and Alleluia*: 'A Morning Hymn' (z. 198), 595; 'Alleluia' (z. 514; music by John Weldon), 454, 595; composition, 308; dedications, 308; performances, 182, 345, 347, 348, 359, 416; publication, 347; recording, 348

Ode for St Cecilia's Day (1692): Overture, 356

Orpheus Britannicus: The Queen's Epicedium (z. 383): performances (PP–BB), 278, 339; recording, 326; *Seven Songs*: 'If music be the food of love' (3rd version) (z. 379c), 339, 345, 347; performances, 339, 345, 347; *Six Duets*: 'Sound the trumpet' (z. 323/3), 339; performances (PP–BB), 339; *Six Songs*: 'Mad Bess' (z. 370):dedication, 170; performance: (Joan Cross, BB) 170; 'If music be the food of love' (first version) (z. 379A), 326; 'There's not a swain of the plain' (z. 587), 326; 'Sweeter than roses' (z. 585/1), 326; recordings, 326; *Suite of Songs*, for high voice and orchestra: 'Let sullen discord smile' (z. 321/6), 260; 'Why should men quarrel?' (z. 630/4D), 260; 'So when the glittering Queen of Night' (z. 333/11), 260; 'Thou tun'st this world' (z. 328/6), 260; ''Tis holiday – Sound Fame thy brazen trumpet' (z. 627/22), 260; composition, 258, 260; performances: Leeuwerden (PP, 1946), 258–60; Zurich (PP, 1948), 326; Los Angeles (PP, *c* BB; 1949), 441; New York (PP, *c* BB, 1949), 554

'When Myra sings' (z. 521): performance (PP–BB), 339; broadcasts, 182

INDEX OF OTHER COMPOSERS

For details of index style and abbreviations used in this index, see Editorial Method, p. xx.

Arne, Thomas: songs (PP–BB), 663
Arnold, Malcolm: *The Bridge on the River Kwai* (film music), 596; Concerto for guitar and eight instruments, 596; *Laudate Dominum*, Op. 25, 595–6; Second Flute Concerto, 597; Second String Quartet, 597

Bach, Johann Sebastian: Brandenburg Concerto No. 6 (BWV 1051) (*c* BB), 551; cantatas, 382, 414, 422; Cantata 151, 416, 483, 487; Cantata 156, 416, 483, 487; Cantata 159, 416, 483, 487; Cantata 161, 416, 487; *Jesu meine Freude*, 238; keyboard music, 359; Mass in B minor, 183, 238, 600–601, 690: *Benedictus*, 630; Passions, 8, 384, 510; preludes and fugues, 323; *St John Passion*, 185, 383, 384, 389; *St Matthew Passion*, 148, 255, 375, 382–7, 460, 484, 508–10, 560–61, 586, 598, 600, 660–62: Atkins–Elgar edition, 383; Sonata for viola da gamba and keyboard, No. 1 in G (BWV 1007); Sonata for viola da gamba and keyboard, No. 2 in D minor (BWV 1008)
Bartók, Béla: *Contrasts*, 446; *Divertimento*, 487; *Music for Strings, Percussion and Celesta*, 80, 487; Rhapsody No. 1, 446; Sonata for two pianos and percussion, 161; Viola Concerto, 550; Violin Concerto No. 2, 446
Bax, Arnold: Nonet, 306
Bedford, David: *Because he liked to be at home* (PP, Ellis *harp*; AF 1974), 412; *The Tentacles of the Dark Nebula* (PP, *c* Bedford, London Sinfonietta; 1969), 412
Beethoven, Ludwig van: *Fidelio*, 696; Symphony No. 6 ('Pastoral'), 212
Bellini, Vincenzo: *Norma*, 491: 'Casta diva', 491; *I puritani*, 456–7
Benjamin, Arthur: Viola Sonata, 550
Berg, Alban: Chamber Concerto, 628–9; Four Pieces for clarinet and piano (BB *piano*, AF), 347; *Lulu*, 188, 457; *Lulu* Suite, 636; Violin Concerto, 75; *Wozzeck*, 188, 212, 419–20, 423, 636, 681
Berkeley, Lennox: *Castaway*, 64; Cello Concerto, 81–2; *A Dinner Engagement*, 64, 560; Five Short Pieces, Op. 4, 80; *Introduction and Allegro*, 64; *Jonah*, 62–3, 598, 600; 'Lay your sleeping head, my love', 65; *Mont Juic* (with BB), 57, 69; *Nelson*, 699, 701 'Night covers up the rigid land', 65; Piano Sonata, 359, 366, 368; *Ruth*, 64, 212;

Serenade, Op. 12, 81; *Stabat Mater*, Op. 28, 64, 306–8, 560: AF (1953), 560; 'Eia Mater' (PP–BB), 339, 454, 595; 'There was neither grass nor corn', 132
Berlioz, Hector: *Messe des Morts*, 155; *The Trojans*, 603
Bernstein, Leonard: *Candide*, 85; *Chichester Psalms*, 85; *Mass: a Theater Piece for Singers, Players and Dancers*, 85; *On the Town*, 85, 87; symphonies, 85; Symphony No. 2 ('The Age of Anxiety'), 85; *West Side Story*, 85, 87
Bizet, Georges: *Carmen*, 150, 152, 209, 210, 284–5; *The Pearl Fishers*, 177; Symphony in C, 80
Bliss, Arthur: Cello Concerto, 625; *Elegiac Sonnet*, 162; *Morning Heroes*, 526; *Music for Strings*, 235; *The Olympians*, 438; *Pastoral*, 526
Blitzstein, Marc: *The Cradle Will Rock*, 85, 609; *The Guest*, 602; *Regina*, 609
Bosmans, Henriëtte: 'The artist's secret', 586
Boyce, William: Symphony No. 3 in C, 629
Brahms, Johannes: Piano Concerto No. 1 in D minor, 190; Piano Concerto No. 2 in B♭, 189; Serenade in A, Op. 16, 87
Bridge, Frank: *Divertimento*, 366, 368, 594; *Phantasy* in F♯ minor for piano quartet, 313, 339; Piano Quintet, 161; Piano Trio, 313, 339; songs (PP–BB), 436, 454; *There is a willow grows aslant a brook* (arr. Britten), 366, 368
Bush, Alan: *Autumn Poem*, Op. 45, 162; *Trent's Broad Reaches*, Op. 36, 162; *Voices of the Prophets*, 161
Bush, Geoffrey: Oboe Concerto, 301
Busoni, Ferruccio: Piano Concerto, 485
Buxtehude, Dietrich: cantatas, 655; *O fröhliche Stunden* (BuxWv 84) (PP–BB), 339
Byrd, William: *Ave Verum*, 319

Chausson, Ernest: Concerto for piano, violin and string quartet, Op. 21, 629
Chopin, Fryderyk: Ballade No. 4, 444; piano music, 359
Copland, Aaron: Clarinet Concerto, 443; *In the Beginning*, 88; *Old American Songs* (PP–BB), 88, 534, 600; Piano Quartet, 88; *Quiet City*, 88; *The Second Hurricane*, 87; *Two Pieces for String Orchestra*, 88
Crosse, Gordon: Violin Concerto, 487

Debussy, Claude: *En blanc et noir* (Lefebure–BB), 309, (PP–BB, *pp*), 423; *Pelléas et Mélisande*, 212; *Six épigraphes antiques* (Curzon–BB, AF 1962), 190–91; songs, 344; *Suite pour le piano*, 359

Delius, Frederick: *Idyll*, 148; *Mass of Life*, 148; *Sea Drift*, 148

Dowland, John: 'If my complaints could passions move', 591; songs (PP–BB), 268, 359, 663

Dvořák, Antonín: Piano Quintet (BB *piano*; 1939), 80

Easdale, Brian: *Bengal River* (AF 1949), 458; *The Sleeping Children* (EOG), 456, 458, 554–5, 560–61, 642, 651

Eccles, ?Henry: violin sonata (BB *piano*; 1936), 80

Elgar, Edward: *The Dream of Gerontius*, 355

Fauré, Gabriel: Barcarolle in A minor, Op. 26, 191; piano music, 423

Festing, Michael: violin sonata (BB *piano*; 1936), 80

Franck, César: Piano Quintet (BB *piano*; 1939), 80; *Prelude, Aria and Finale*, 319

Frankel, Benjamin: Sonata, Op. 13, 162

Gardner, John: *The Visitors*, 413

Gay, John, and John Christopher Pepusch: *The Beggar's Opera*, 350, 393, 394: version by Frederick Austin, 397, 399, 400; version by E. J. Dent, 396, 397; *see also* realization by BB (Index of Britten's Works)

Gerhard, Roberto: Piano Concerto, 161

Ghedini, Giorgio: *Billy Budd*,, 537–8, 682, 690

Gluck, Christoph Willibald: *Orfeo ed Euridice*, 184, 186, 266, 273, 277

Goehr, Alexander: Violin Concerto, 487

Gounod, Charles: *Faust*, 453–4

Grainger, Percy: folksong arrangements, 454; 'The Jolly Sailor' (PP–BB), 549; 'Six Dukes went a-fishin'' (PP–BB), 549; 'The Sprig o' Thyme' (PP–BB), 549

Greene, Maurice: songs (PP–BB), 359

Grieg, Edvard: *Holberg Suite*, 400; songs (PP–BB, *pp*), 423

Handel, George Frideric: *Jephtha*, 595; *Messiah*, 167, 231, 267, 340, 341, 344, 463, 621, 630; *Ode for Saint Cecilia's Day*, 339, 416, 485; Organ Concerto, Op. 7 No. 4, 359; songs (PP–BB), 359, 663

Haydn, Joseph: *The Creation*, 321, (*c* BB) 323; *The Seasons*, 31; string quartets, 666; symphonies, 332; violin concerto, 80

Headington, Christopher: *The Healing Fountain*, 337; *Qui habitat*, 337; *Variations*, 412

Hindemith, Paul: *Die Harmonie der Welt*, 487; Horn Sonata, 161; *Kammermusik No. 2*, 161; *Mathis der Maler*, 187, 387

Holst, Gustav: *Egdon Heath*, Op. 47 (H. 172), 434, (*c* BB) 435; Four Songs to medieval texts for voice and violin (H. 132), 655–6; 'How mighty are the Sabbaths', 436; 'I'll love my love' (*Nine Folk Songs* (H. 84)), 542; *Lyric Movement*, 551; *The Planets*, Op. 32 (H. 125), 434, 435: 'Neptune', 434, 435; Psalm 86, 485; *St Paul's Suite*, 653; *Sāvitri*, 413: and EOG, 554–5; songs (PP–BB), 436, 454; *Two Eastern Pictures* (H. 112), 626, 627; *The Wandering Scholar*, Op. 50 (H. 176), 413, 428, 430, 434–6, 503: BB and I. Holst edition,

430, 434, 651; and EOG, 430, 434, 440, 456, 476, 486, 554–5, 642, 646, 651

Holst, Imogen: *Welcome Joy and Welcome Sorrow*, 108, 627

Honegger, Arthur: *Jeanne d'Arc au bûcher*, 316; Symphony No. 2, 487; Symphony No. 4, 487

Hopkins, Antony: *Lady Rohesia*, 555

Humperdinck, Engelbert: *Hänsel und Gretel*, 169

Ireland, John: *Amberley Wild Brooks*, 485; 'Hawthorn Time' (PP–BB), 342; 'I have twelve oxen' (PP–BB), 485; *The Land of Lost Content* (PP–BB), 342; 'Love and Friendship' (PP–BB), 342; 'My true love hath my heart' (PP–BB), 342; Service in C, 165; 'The Trellis' (PP–BB), 342

Janáček, Leoš: Concertino for piano and chamber orchestra, 309; *Jenůfa*, 636

Jones, Robert: *The Muses Garden of Delights*, 579–80

Krenek, Ernst: *Karl V*, 284

Lambert, Constant: Piano Sonata, 359

LeFanu, Nicola: *The Green Children*, 605

Lehár, Ferencz: *The Merry Widow*, 149

Lehmann, Liza: *In a Persian Garden*, 364

Leoncavallo, Ruggero: *Pagliacci*, 491

Lier, Bertus van: *Het hooglied* (*The Song of Songs*), 387, 460

Liszt, Franz: Piano Sonata in B minor, 359

Mahler, Gustav: 'Ich atmet' einen linden Duft' (PP–BB), 339; *Das Lied von der Erde*, 10, 276, 280, 355, 458, 525, 664: (PP), 313, 315, 320–21, 325; 'Rheinlegendchen' (PP–BB), 339; songs, 255, 278, 344; Symphony No. 1, 276; Symphony No. 2, 485; Symphony No. 4, 254; Symphony No. 5: *Adagietto*, 6; Symphony No. 8, 664; Symphony No. 9, 320, 485; 'Der Tamoursg'sell' (PP–BB), 339; 'Um schlimme Kinder artig zu machen' (PP–BB), 339

Martin, Frank: *Petite symphonie concertante*, 487; *Sechs Monologe aus 'Jedermann'* (PP–BB), 370, 454

Massenet, Jules: *Le Jongleur de Notre Dame*, 578; *Manon*, 290–91

Mendelssohn, Felix: *Elijah*, 148

Menotti, Gian Carlo: *The Consul*, 413; *The Medium*, 477

Mewton-Wood, Noel: *As ye came from the Holy Land*, 162

Milhaud, Darius: *Christophe Colombe*, 636; *La Création du monde*, 487

Moeran, E. J.: folksong arrangements, 364

Monteverdi, Claudio: duets, 339; *Il combattimento di Tancredi e Clorinda* (EOG), 630, 641–2, 648, 655–2; *L'incoronazione di Poppea*, 495; *Il ritorno d'Ulisse in patria*, 495; 'Zefiro torna' (PP–BB), 339

Morley, Thomas: songs, 268

Morris, R. O.: folksong arrangements, 548

Mozart, Wolfgang Amadeus: *La clemenza di Tito*, 489; *Così fan tutte*, 149, 169–70, (PP Ferrando) 248; *Don Giovanni*, 152, 177, 245, 299, 358; *Die Entführung aus dem Serail*, 192, 193, 254, 490, 491–2; fantasias for piano, 508; *Idomeneo*, 355, 413; *Misero! O Sogno!* (K. 431) (PP), 260, 278; *Le nozze di Figaro*, 151, 245, 325, 328–9, 627–8, 687; operas, 421; piano duets, 613; piano concertos

(PP–BB, *pp*), 423; piano quartets, 654; Piano Sonata in A (κ. 331), 319; Quintet in E♭ (κ. 452) for piano and wind (BB *piano*), 416; quintets, 414; Sonata in D, for two pianos (κ. 488) (Curzon–BB), 191; *Sinfonia concertante* in E♭ (κ. 364): (BB *vla*, PP *piano*; *pp*), 105; (Parikian *vln*, Primrose *vla*, *c* BB), 487, 551, 655; String Quartet in F (κ. 590), 667; Trio in E♭ (κ. 498), 347, 550; Variations on 'Ah vous dirai-je, maman' (κ. 265), 421; violin sonata, 105; *Die Zauberflöte* (*The Magic Flute*), 150, 177, (PP *Tamino*) 636, 640

Musorgsky, Modest: *Boris Godunov*, 212, 336, 376

Offenbach, Jacques: *Tales of Hoffmann* (PP *Hoffmann*), 95, 96

Oldham, Arthur: *Five Chinese Lyrics* (PP–BB), 549; *Le Jongleur de Notre Dame* (proposed opera), 578; *Love in a Village* (EOG), 486, 540, 674, 677; *My Truest Treasure*, 607; *Our Lady's Tumbler* (incidental music), 578; Piano Trio, 443; *Saint Spiv* (incidental music), 580; *Summer's Lease* (PP, *c* Oldham), 423; *Two Lyrics by Richard Rolle* (PP–BB), 595; *Variations on a Carol Tune*, 368, 421

Orr, Robin: *Four Romantic Songs*, 630

Pears, Luard [Peter Pears]: 'When within my arms I hold you', 276

Ponchielli, Amilcare: *La Gioconda*, 379

Porter, Cole: 'Ev'ry time we say goodbye', 557; *Out of This World*, 610

Poulenc, Francis: *Aubade*, 487; *Sinfonietta*, 184; *Trois Poèmes de Ronsard*, 149

Puccini, Giacomo: *La Bohème*, 150; *Madama Butterfly*, 217, 328; *Manon Lescaut*, 328; *Tosca*, 328; *Turandot*, 308, 333, 623, 624

Purcell, Henry: *Birthday Song for King James, 1687*: 'A dance that shall make the spheres to wonder', 647; cantatas, 414; Chacony in G minor, 356; *Dido and Aeneas*, 151, 231, 234, 493–5, 502, 563, 568: editions and manuscripts, 569, 645–8; Tenbury manuscript, 569, 648; *see also* edition by BB and I. Holst (Index of Britten's Works); *The Fairy Queen*, 25, 149, 199, 203, 391, 494; *Evening Hymn*, 319; *Harmonia Sacra*, 107–8, 108; *The Indian Queen*: 'Then since our charms have sped', 647; *Job's Curse*, 359; *King Arthur*, 431; *My Beloved Spake*, 416; *Ode for St Cecilia's Day*, 260, 356; *Orpheus Britannicus*, 356; *Saul and the Witch at Endor*, 416; *Sir Anthony Love*: Overture, 647; songs, 255, 268, 600, 655, 663; *Te Deum*, 563; violin sonata (BB *piano*), 80; *see also* realizations by BB (Index of Britten's Works)

Quilter, Roger: songs, 364

Rainier, Priaulx: Viola Sonata, 551

Rankl, Karl: *Deirdre of the Sorrows*, 284

Ravel, Maurice: *L'Heure espagnole*, 309; *Introduction and Allegro*, 366, 368; piano music, 359; Suite: *Mother Goose*, 248

Rooper, Jasper: Chorale Prelude for strings, 301

Rossini, Gioacchino: *William Tell*, 212

Runswick, Daryl: 'Boogie-woogie' (BB arr.), 171

Saint-Saëns, Camille: *Le Carnaval des animaux* (Mewton-Wood and BB pianos), 161, 628–9

Schoenberg, Arnold: Chamber Symphony No. 1, Op. 9, 629; *Die glückliche Hand*, 329; *Moses und Aron*, 355

Schubert, Franz: 'Am See' (PP–BB), 453; 'Arpeggione' Sonata (Rostropovich–BB), 22; 'Du bist die Ruh" (PP–BB), 595; 'Der Einsame' (PP–BB), 595; 'Die Forelle' (PP–BB), 453; *Der Hirt auf dem Felsen*, 345, 347; 'Der Musensohn' (PP–BB), 595; 'Nacht und Träume' (PP–BB), 453, 459, 490; Octet in F, 366, 368; piano duet, 105; piano music, 359; piano sonatas, 323; *Die schöne Müllerin* (PP–BB), 291, 325, 341, 342, 435, 436, 587–9, 645; (Haefliger) 510; songs, 255, 259, 278, 359, 370, 436, 543, 663; String Quintet, 414, 416; *Die Winterreise* (Haefliger), 510

Schumann, Robert: *Davidsbündler*, 359; *Dichterliebe* (PP–BB), 113, 600

Schütz, Heinrich: *Christmas Story*, 346; *Der Herr ist mein Licht* (swv 359) (PP–BB), 339; Passions, 656; *Die sieben Worte unsers lieben Erlösers und Seligmachers Jesu Christi*, 655–6; *Symphoniae sacrae*, 600, 645

Searle, Humphrey: *Hamlet*, 342; *Nocturne (Adagio)*, 342; *Put away the flutes*, 342

Seiber, Mátyás: *To Poetry*, 161

Shaw, Martin: *God's Grandeur*, 359

Smetana, Bedřich: *The Bartered Bride*, 212, 248; (PP *Vašek*), 100, 101, 149, 248

Smyth, Ethel: songs, 364

Somervell, Sir Arthur: *Maud*, 122–3

Strauss, Richard: *Arabella*, 185, 187; *Ariadne auf Naxos*, 150; *Metamorphosen*, 487; *Vier letzte Lieder*, 195

Stravinsky, Igor: *Apollo musagètes*, 75; Concerto in D, 487; *L'histoire du soldat*, 189; *Orpheus*, 422, 494; *Persephone* (PP), 638; *Pulcinella*, 189; *The Rake's Progress*, 235, 355, 422, 565, 674–5, 681; *Renard*, 189; *The Rite of Spring*, 237; *A Sermon, Narrative, and a Prayer*, 487

Suk, Josef: Serenade, 586

Sutermeister, Heinrich: *Romeo und Julia*, 189

Tchaikovsky, Piotr Ilyich: *Eugene Onegin*, 232, 683; Piano Concerto No. 1 in B♭ minor (BB *pp*), 76; Piano Concerto No. 2 in G, 248

Tippett, Michael: *Boyhood's End*, 161, 162, 368; Concerto for Orchestra, 368; *Crown of the Year*, 372; *Divertimento on Sellinger's Round*, 487; *The Heart's Assurance*, 161, 162, 368, 534: 'Remember your lovers', 162; *King Priam*, 355; *The Midsummer Marriage*, 224, 235, 355, 370, 486; Piano Sonata No. 1, 161; String Quartet No. 2, 368; Suite for the Birthday of Prince Charles (Suite in D), 414; 'The Weeping Babe', 132

Traditional: 'Early One Morning', 27

Vaughan Williams, Ralph: *Dona nobis pacem*, 148; *Five Tudor Portraits*, 148; folksong arrangements, 364, 548; *Job*, 70, 177; *On Wenlock Edge*, 544; *A Sea Symphony*, 148, 523; *Serenade to Music*, 235; *The Valiant for Truth*, 319

Verdi, Giuseppe: *Aida*, 583; *Falstaff*, 189, 212, 248, 309, 565, 583–4; *La forza del destino*, 328; *Macbeth*, 151, 336, 563; *Otello*, 189, 212, 583–4, 676, 687, 690–91, 696; *Quattro Pezzi Sacri*, 583; *Rigoletto*, 325, 328; *La traviata*, 212, 325, 328, 582–3

Vittoria, Tomás Luis de: 'Ecce Sacerdos Magnus', 165

Vivaldi, Antonio: violin concerto, 80

Wagner, Richard: *Die Meistersinger*, 379, 687; *Parsifal*, 690; *Siegfried*, 690; *Siegfried Idyll*, 628–9; *Tristan und Isolde*, 210, 282, 283, 284, 423
Walton, William: *Façade*, 177, 542–4, 585, 680; *The Quest*, 177; String Quartet, 202; *Troilus and Cressida*, 235, 355, 370; Violin Concerto, 622
Warlock, Peter: *Corpus Christi Carol*, 276
Weelkes, Thomas: 'Hosanna to the Son of David' (PP), 436

Weill, Kurt: *Die Bürgschaft*, 329; *Die Dreigroschenoper*, 396–7
Williams, Grace: *Six Welsh Oxen Songs*, 495–6; *Three Traditional Welsh Ballads*, (PP; 1950) 496, 630
Williamson, Malcolm: *The Growing Castle*, 149; *Six English Lyrics*, 149
Wolf, Hugo: 'Im Frühling', 357, 358; *Mörike-Lieder*, 357, 358; songs (PP–BB) 358–9, 423; *Three Poems of Michelangelo* (Shirley-Quirk–BB), 359

For details of index style and abbreviations used in this index, see Editorial Method, p. xx.

7 & 5 Society, 176

Abbey Road Studios, London, 303, 326, 426
Aberdeen: PP–BB recital, 577
Abraham, Gerald, 113
Acheson, Dr P., 469, 490, 661
Ackerley, Joe, 461
Adair, Gilbert, 604
Adès, Thomas, 319
Adler, Kurt, 379
Advance Democracy (film), 172
Aeolian String Quartet, 418
Aeschylus: *The Agamemnon*, 112
'A.F.' (critic), 698
Agenzia Lirica Conartistica Internazionale
   (ALCI), 469
Ages of Man, The (one-man show), 603
Albert, Prince, 437
Albert Hall, London, *see* Royal Albert Hall,
   London
Albion Opera, 96
Aldeburgh, 25, 68, 249, 389
Aldeburgh: Alde House, 363
Aldeburgh: Baptist Chapel, 359, 544
Aldeburgh Cinema, 359
Aldeburgh Festival: 1948: 8, 314, 316, 317, 357–9,
   360–61, 366, 368, 381, 383, 396, 402, 408, 410, 463,
   568, 672; 1949: 414, 416, 440–41, 443, 458, 484–7,
   489, 492, 507, 513–14, *515*, 516; 1950: 88, 385,
   483–5, 534, 542, 544, 549–50, 560, 590, 598; 1951:
   108, 161, 487, 534, 551, 560, 595, 596, 606, 616, 622,
   627, 641, 652, 654–5; 1952: 161, 540, 551, 673; 1953:
   133, 161, 308, 342, 560, 652; 1954: 133, 176, 187, 561;
   1956: 388, 487; 1958: 309; 1959: 596–7; 1960: 31,
   88, 191, 431, 443; 1961: 435, 487, 667; 1962: 191;
   1966: 323; 1967: 30; 1968: 603; 1969: 30; 1970: 30,
   625; 1971: 359; 1972: 359; 1973: 597; 1974: 412, 665;
   1975: 86; 1976: 86, 597, 665, 679; 1984: 349;
   administration, 30–31, 39–40, 43–6, 212, 383,
   449, 479, 675; artists, 149, 161, 176, 347, 477, 485,
   603; calendar (1954), 176; commissions, 359;
   Council, committees and officers, 44, 46, 316,
   318, 384, 457; directorate, 107, 413, 656; exhibitions, 363, 402, 414, 602; fiftieth anniversary, 7;
   finances and fund-raising, 317, 327, 465, 483,
   514, 580, 601, 606, 610, 674; genesis, 212, 315, 316,
   318, 344; lectures and readings, 8, 359, 362, 414,
   543, 602, 652; out-of-Festival promotions,

483–4, 587; press and media coverage, 607;
   programme books, 36, 317, *360–61*, 363, 383, 507,
   556, 603; supporters, 214; 'theatre project'
   (1954/57), 36, *37*, 38, 346; *see also* Blythburgh
   Church, Snape Maltings Concert Hall
Aldeburgh Festival Choir, 359, 418
Aldeburgh Festival Orchestra, 387
Aldeburgh Festival–Snape Maltings Foundation,
   36
Aldeburgh: Jubilee Hall, *plates 36–7; 30*, 171, *175*,
   315, 319, 359, 363, 443, 458, 485, 544, 602, 603, 615,
   626, 627, 629, 655; and opera, 31, 317, 396, 486,
   515, 517–18, 540, 621
Aldeburgh Lodge preparatory school, 37, 470, 471
Aldeburgh: Moot Hall, 357, 363
Aldeburgh October Britten Festival 1997, 14
Aldeburgh Parish Church, *plate 35*; 7, 37, 357, 359,
   360, 484, 485, 487, 560, 587, 591, 679; Benjamin
   Britten Memorial Window, 177; Hall, 602
Aldeburgh: Prior's Hill, 363
Aldeburgh: Sandhills, 363
Aldeburgh: Wentworth Hotel, 36, 476, 477
Aldeburgh: White Lion Hotel, 363, 364
Aldeburgh Soundings, 149
Alexander, Peter F., 672, 673
Alexander Orchestra, 630
Alford Violet, 69
Algemeen Handelsblad (Amsterdam), 248, 522
Alkestis, 219
All Souls, Oratory of (Sandham Memorial
   Chapel), 67
Allchin, Basil, 355
'*Allo, 'Allo* (television comedy), 431
Alsace, 306
Alston, Audrey, 55, 80, 472, 669, 670
Alston, John, 471, 472, 669
Alston, Richard, 486
Alwyn, William, 554, 555
Amadeus String Quartet, 409
American Ballet, School of, 88
American Ballet Company, 88–9
American Overseas Airlines, 418
Amis, John, 153, 161–2, 309, 486, 625
Amityville, Long Island, 103
Amsterdam, Netherlands, 153–4, 354 375, 384, 388,
   417, 675: *Albert Herring*, 305–6, 308, 324, 397;
   performances by PP and/or BB, 88, 137, 144,
   246–7, 253, 262, 370, 382, 414, 509, 586, 621; *Peter*

Grimes, 254, 258; *The Rape of Lucretia*, 144, 147, 305–6, 308, 324; *Saint Nicolas*, 407, 415, *466*
Amsterdam: American Hotel, 369, 381, 385, 386, 585
Amsterdam: Concertgebouw, *145*, 247, 374, 380, 508, 527: Concertgebouw Orchestra, 145, 153, 247, 345–9, 375, 382, 416, 453–4, 510, 521, 523; *Les Illuminations*, 144, 153–4; PP–BB recitals, 255, 314, 370, 407, 415, 452, 600; *St Matthew Passion*, 255, 510, 586, 660–62; *Spring Symphony*, plate 50; 347, 408, 511, 521–9; *Young Person's Guide* (1946), 138, 247–8, 258
Amsterdam: Hotel des Pays-Bas, 385, 386
Amsterdam: Kleine Comoedie, 621
Amsterdam: Kunstkring, 414, 415
Amsterdam: Lutherskerk, 415
Amsterdam: Munt, 621
Amsterdam: Oude Kerk, 387
Amsterdam: Stadsschouwburg (Municipal Theatre), 147
Amsterdam Tonkunst Choir, 375
Amsterdam: Victoria Hotel, 154
Amsterdam: Zuiderkerk, 415
Amyot, Etienne, 235–6
And So To Bed (radio series), 114
Anderson, Hedli, 71, *72*, 112, 122, 128, 652
Anderson, Maxwell, 230
André (opera director), 168
André, Franz, 78
Andrewes, John, 326
Ankara, Turkey, 200
Annie (Swiss au pair), 417, 419, 476
Anouilh, Jean, 356
Anschluss, 97, 150, 195
Ansermet, Ernest, 152–3, 160, 185, *189*, 218, 251, 261–2, 263, 272–3, 278, 288, 495–6, 501; 'Benjamin Brittens zweite Oper', 263; and *The Rape of Lucretia*, plates 4 and 8; 137, 152–3, 160, 199, 203, 214, 222, 304
Ansermet, Madame, 262, 272, 273
Anton Dolin Ballet, 355
Antwerp, Belgium: *Peter Grimes*, 167, 391
Arcklow, Ireland: Shelton Abbey Hotel, 340
Ardingly College, 300, 346
Arfey, William D', *see* Plomer, William
Argo (record label), 342
Arlberg Express, 289, 290
Arne, Thomas: *see* IOC
Arnhem, Netherlands: PP–BB recital, 254
Arnold, Malcolm, 595, *596–7*; *and see* IOC
Around the Village Green (film), 261, 368
Arts Council of Great Britain, 170, 213–14, 372, 374, 437, 468, 485, 564–7, 569, 601, 618, 682, 698; funding of Aldeburgh Festival and Snape Maltings Concert Hall, 30, 317, 674; funding of EOG, 244, 259, 265, 282, 284, 354, 501, 503, 615; Music Panel, 485; Opera Panel, 437; Prize, 284
Arts Council of South Australia, 383
Arts Theatre Club, London, 383: *Abelard and Héloïse*, 177
Arundel, Dennis, *128*
Ashby St Ledgers, Rugby, 201
Ashcroft, Peggy, 653, *654*
Ashmole, Silvia, 332
Ashton, Frederick, 70, 203, *507*, 585, 603–4, 606, 610, 640, 642; and *Albert Herring*, plate 10; 291, 294, 303, 501, 507, 574, 604; and *Death in Venice*, 507; and *The Rape of Lucretia*, 277
Ashton, Roy, *plate 10*; 295

Aspen Festival, 436
Astle, Ethel, 55, 192, 193, 385
Astor, Nancy, 22
Astor family, 21
Atkins, Ivor, 383
Atkinson, Brooks, 229
Atlantis Verlag, 372, 461, 506
Attenborough, David, 608
Attenborough, Richard, 608
Auden, Dr G. A. (George Augustus), 98–9, *99*
Auden, Constance Rosalie, 269
Auden, W. H. (Wystan Hugh), *plate 27*; 72, 73–4, 75, *78*, 86, 91, 93, 99, 120, 172, 208, 211, 226, 227, 252, 267–8, 616, 652, 665, 674, 676, 681; *The Age of Anxiety*, 85, 267–70; *The Ascent of F6* (with Isherwood), 72–3, 74, 76, *77*, 78, 211, 362, 589, 672; *Cabaret Songs*, 251; *Coal Face*, 172; *For the Time Being* ('A Christmas Oratorio'), 99, 267–8; 'It's farewell to the drawing room's civilised cry', 71–2; *Journey to a War* (with Isherwood), 73–4; 'Lay your sleeping head, my love', 65; 'Litany and Anthem for St. Matthew's Day', 163, *164*, 165, 267–8; *Look, Stranger!*, 410; 'Night covers up the rigid land', 65; *Night Mail*, 78; 'Nocturne', 252; *On the Frontier* (with Isherwood), 71, 73, 74, 76, 78; *Our Hunting Fathers*, 78; 'Out on the lawn', 78, 410, 523, 525, 526–8, 553; *Paul Bunyan* (libretto), 78, 665; *The Rake's Progress* (libretto; with Kallman), 674–6, 681; 'The Sea and the Mirror', 268; 'Some Reflections on Opera as a Medium' ('Notes on Music and Opera'), 677; 'Three songs for St. Cecilia's day' (*Hymn to St Cecilia*), 78, 99, 114; 'Tell me the truth about love', 78; 'Underneath the abject willow', 78; BB, relationship with, 56, 65, 75, 78; in China, 73–4; at GPO Film Unit, 78; Isherwood, Christopher, work with, 67; and Merchant Marine, 99; at Swarthmore, 99–100, 269; and Webster–Brecht: *The Duchess of Malfi*, 226, 228–30, 267
Ault, Norman, 410
Austen, Jane, 151, 232; *Mansfield Park*, 151, 232, 234
Austin, Frederick, 397, 399–401
AXIS, (magazine) 176
Ayors, Ann, 277
Ayrton, Michael, 203

Bach, Johann Christian, 448
Bach, Johann Sebastian, 12, 76, 356, 358, 484, 509, 510, 560, 601, 630, 654, 661, 692; *and see* IOC
Bach Choir, 384
Bachardy, Don, 67, 68; drawing of PP, 67
Bacon, Francis, 6, 18
Bad Oeynhausen, Germany: Yehudi Menuhin–BB recital, 183
Bagar, Robert, 211–12
Baggott, Jonas, *plate 34*
Baker, Janet, 413
Baker-Smith, Malcolm, 203
Balanchine, George, 89
Balcon, Michael, 328, 354, 367, 440
Balfe, Michael, 169
Bali, 276, 608
Balinese music, 88, 608
Ballet Rambert, 421, 443–4, 607
Ballet Society (later New York City Ballet), 88, 260–61
Ballets Russes, 73, 188, 189
Ballets Russes de Monte Carlo, 73

Banjos, Spain, 605
Banks, Paul, 14, 304, 364, 465, 568, 587, 622–3, 670
B.A.O.R. (British Army of the Rhine), 181, 182, 183, 411
Barbirolli, John, 84, 86, 347, 440, 502
Barcelona, 62–4, 69, 80; and ISCM Festival, 57, 62–3
Bardgett, Herbert, 551, 553–4, 600, 613, 614, 616–17
Barker, Noel, 601
Barnes, George, 235–6, 340, 341, 342–3, 369
Barnes, Howard, 610
Barnfield, Richard: 'When will my May come that I may embrace thee', 410, 552
Barrutia, Andoni, 73
Bartlett, Ethel, 89, 90
Bartók, Béla, 79, 550, 654; and see IOC
Basel, Switzerland, 185, 186, 189, 193, 199, 351, 487; PP–BB recital, 351
Basel Chamber Orchestra (Kammerorchester), 356; Serenade, 356
Basel Conservatory, 187, 487
Basel Radio, 306
Basel Stadttheater, 188: Peter Grimes (1946), 137, 167, 181, 182, 185–8, 192; The Rape of Lucretia (1947), 138, 200, 255, 286, 289
Basil, Colonel Wassily de, 71, 73
Bates, Alan, 608
Bath Festival, 563
Bax, Arnold: see IOC
Bax, Clifford, 430, 651
Bayreuth, 47, 188
Bayreuth Festival, 625
BBC (British Broadcasting Corporation): auditions and artists, 78, 149, 448; commissions, 231, 413–14, 441; documentaries, 13; personnel, 155, 183–4, 235, 337, 342, 413, 454, 551, 615, 625, 642 665; publications, 71; and music by BB: Albert Herring, 314; A Boy was Born, 56; Cabaret Songs, 652; The Dark Tower, 137; Hymn to St Cecilia, 111; Men of Goodwill, 344; Peter Grimes, 142; Phantasy, 56; Phantasy in F minor, 56; Sinfonietta, 56
BBC, Academy of the, 486
BBC Choral Society, 433, 474
BBC Chorus, 63
BBC Drama Department, 112, 124, 134
BBC Features Department, 112, 124, 132, 642
BBC Home Service, 123, 132, 134, 143, 235, 329, 345, 384, 435
BBC Legends (record label), 50, 191, 339, 359, 435
BBC Light Programme, 171, 235, 345, 47; This Way to the Tomb, 171
BBC Maida Vale Studios, 235–6, 370
BBC Midland Chorus, 183, 663
BBC Midland Home Service, 663
BBC Music Department, 665
BBC National Service, 81
BBC Northern Symphony Orchestra, 665
BBC Orchestra, 63, 190
BBC Promenade Concerts, 111, 149; Piano Concerto, 57, 71, 72, 155, 161; Sinfonia da Requiem, 111
BBC Radio 3, 7; Evaluations and Comparisons, 309; Paul Bunyan, 665
BBC Scottish Symphony Orchestra, 485, 486
BBC Singers, 276, 346
BBC Sound Archive, 359
BBC Symphony Orchestra, 128, 235, 343, 414, 435, 496

BBC Television, 413, 431
BBC Theatre Chorus, 426
BBC Third Programme, 183, 184, 235–6, 252, 292, 329, 339, 340, 342, 344, 346, 411, 414, 417, 495, 582, 642; Albert Herring, 292, 296, 369; The Beggar's Opera, 415; A Charm of Lullabies, 417, 418; Love in a Village, 677; Occasional Overture, 138, 235–6, 441; An Opera is Planned, 252, 296, 370; PP–BB recitals, 259, 342, 370, 588; The Rape of Lucretia, 147; The Rescue, 124; Saint Nicolas, 433; Sinfonia da Requiem, 495–6; Spring Symphony, 521, 535, 581, 614; Stabat Mater (Berkeley), 307; The Wandering Scholar, 430, 651
BBC WorldWide 'The Britten Edition' (CD series), 50
BBC2 Television: Owen Wingrave, 25, 42, 413, 431
Bean, Betty, 443, 447, 448, 537
Beaumont, Francis, and John Fletcher: 'London, to thee I do present' (The Knight of the Burning Pestle), 528
Beaton, Cecil, 578, 604
Beaverbrook, Lord, 604
Beckett, Samuel, 654
Beddoes, Thomas Lovell: 'A Crocodile', 121; 'Dirge for Wolfram', 118, 121; 'A Dream' ('Thou pale Cupid'), 121; 'Dream of Dying', 121; 'Dream-Pedlary', 121; 'The Masque in the Moon', 121; 'Song from the Ship' ('To sea! To sea! The calm is o'er'), 121–2; 'Song on the Water', 121–2; The Works of Thomas Lovell Beddoes, 121
Bedford, David, 322, 412, 449, 468, 561–2, 630; and see IOC
Bedford, Lesley, plates 6 and 13; 321, 322, 349, 410, 416, 448, 449, 468, 544, 556, 614, 629–30, 635
Bedford, Leslie, 349, 449, 468
Bedford, Peter Lehmann, 412, 449, 562, 630
Bedford, Steuart, 319, 322, 412–13, 449, 468, 516, 548, 562, 630, 665
Bedford family, 410
Beecham, Sir Thomas, 79, 80, 144, 150, 476, 478–9, 485, 639
Beer, Sydney, 160
Beethoven, Ludwig van, 12, 63, 189, 443, 510, 526, 612, 696; and see IOC
Behr, Therese, 189
Behrend, George, plate 29; 214, 224, 306, 324, 333, 579
Behrend, John Louis ('Bow'), 214, 333, 529, 568, 570, 571
Behrend, Mary, 214, 333, 464, 465, 484, 529, 559, 568, 570, 571, 630
Beinum, Eduard van, plate 50; 247, 250, 255, 347, 349, 382, 386, 387, 408, 416, 509, 510, 521, 523, 535, 552, 581, 586, 662
Belgian Radio Symphony Orchestra, 78
Belgium, 81, 550: The Beggar's Opera, 456; concerts and recitals (1947), 138, 273; The Holy Sonnets of John Donne, 153; Peter Grimes, 167, 391; The Rape of Lucretia, 253; tour plans, 145, 391
Bell, Anthea, 461
Bell, J. F., 472
Bellini, Vincenzo, 457; and see IOC
Bellerivestrasse, 38, Zurich, 199
Belsen concentration camp, 51, 183; Yehudi Menuhin–BB recital, 183
Benjamin, Arthur, 55, 144, 146, 355; and see IOC
Benjamin, George, 667
Bennett, Billy, 80
Bennett, C. E., 280

Berg, Alban, 75, 76, 97, 187, 210, 338, 376, 420, 446, 457, 472, 636; *and see* IOC

Berg, Helene, 681

Bergner, Elisabeth, 228, 229

Berkeley, Freda, 64, 335, 560, 598

Berkeley, Lennox, 54, 63, 64–5, 66–7, 73, 79–80, 81–2, 118, 132, 149, 308, 335, 337, 412, 560, 598, 623–5, 699; and BBC, 124, 335; Lennox Berkeley Estate, 64; relationship with BB, 64–7, 69, 79–81; *see also* IOC

Berkeley, Michael, 22, 64, 335, 560, 561, 598

Berkshire Festival, US, 103, 279, 526; *see also* Tanglewood

Berkshire Festival Chorus, 49

Berkshire Music Center, *see* Tanglewood

Berkshire Music Center, Friends of, 227

Berlin, 636: *Peter Grimes*, 268, 270

Berlin: Charlottenburg Opera, 150

Berlin: Deutsche Oper, 624

Berlin: Deutsches Theater, 234

Berlin: Kroll Opera, 284

Berlin: Staatsoper, 636

Berlin: Städtische Oper, 188, 234, 329, 625

Berlin: State Opera, 270

Berlin Opera, 188, 284, 329

Berlin University, 46

Berlioz, Hector, 486; *and see* IOC

Bernac, Pierre, 459

Bern, Switzerland, 182, 192, 571

Berners, Lord, 70

Bernstein, Leonard, 54, 84–5, 85–6, 87, 137, 254; and *Peter Grimes, plate 28*; 206–9, 211; *see also* IOC

Betjeman, John, 177, 234, 340, 341–2; *Shell Guide to Oxfordshire* (ed.), 177

Bevan, Maurice, 601, 630

Biancolli, Louis, 378

Bible, 287, 383, 458

Bideford, Devon: PP–BB recital, 370

Billington, D., 673

Billows, Johanni, 271–2

Billows, June, 201, 359

Billows, Lionel, *plate 9*; 186, 199, 200–201, 250, 271, 282, 315, 340, 359

Biltmore, Frinton, 62, 70–71

Bing, Rudolf, 144, 150–53, 198, 213, 231, 242, 244, 247, 254, 263–4, 273, 320–22, 325, 563

biography, concepts of, 3–7

Bird, John, 548

Birkbeck College, London, 174

Birmingham, 74, 99, 183, 508: *Ascent of F6*, 74; BBC, 81; *Let's Make an Opera*, 550, 629

Birmingham, University of, 75

Birmingham: Alexandra Theatre: *Albert Herring*, 375; *The Beggar's Opera*, 375

Birmingham: King Edward Grammar School for Girls, 383

Birmingham Post, 75, 99; reviews, 220, 518, 694–5

Birmingham Repertory Theatre, 76; *The Ascent of F6*, 76

Birtwistle, Harrison, 88, 319

Biró, Ladislao, 698

Bishops' Committee, 351

Bishopstone Manor, 252

Bizet, Georges, 79; *and see* IOC

Björling, Gösta, 168

Björling, Sigurd, 168

Black, Mrs (Lowestoft), 192, 193

Black, Kitty, 608

Black Narcissus (film), 458

Black Panthers, 85

Blades, James, 134

Blake, Lord, 46

Blake, William, 343, 586–7; 'O Rose, thou art sick', 118; 'Night', 118; *St Paul and the Viper*, 586–7; 'Sound the Flute', 552, 617

Bliss, Arthur, 161, 162, 235, 303–4, 438, 623–4, 625; *As I Remember*, 625; *and see* IOC

Blitzstein, Marc, 601–2, 606, 609–10, 628; *and see* IOC

Blom, Eric, 75, 98, 99; reviews, 220, 695–6

Bloomsbury group, 362, 672

Bloxham School, Oxfordshire, 470

Blunt, Wilfrid, 150, 151

Blyth, Alan, 149, 213, 276, 332, 356, 392, 431, 516, 625

Blythburgh Church, Suffolk, 31, 88

Boehm, Andreas, 188

Bogtman, Laurens, 382, 387, 662

Boito, Arrigo: *Otello* (libretto), 692

Bonavia, Ferruccio, 219, 220

'Booming Culture', *see The British: Are They Artistic?*

Boorman, S. C., 608

Boosey, Leslie A., 82, 83–4, 158, 160, 365, 367, 369, 374, 514, 575–7, 580, 606, 610

Boosey & Hawkes, 82, 83, 97, 98, 158, 160, 167, 171, 176, 194, 195, 197, 236, 271, 284, 304, 326, 327, 329, 365, 367, 422, 428–9, 479, 538, 544, 562, 566–7, 598, 606, 627, 664, 665, 667, 673; as book publisher, 372, 506; as concert promoter, 98; contracts with BB, 56, 538, 589–91; cover designs, 465; and Eric Crozier, 513–14, 538–9; and EOG, 365, 501; hire library, 415; in Los Angeles, 147; in New York, 83, 144, 146–7, 229, 448, 537, 607; publications, 410

Boosey, Hawkes, Belwin, Inc., 195

Borsdorf (concert promoter), 551, 553

Bosmans, Henriëtte (Jetty), 387, 414–15, 415–16, 417, 419, 459–60, 498–9, 502, 508–10, 576–7, 586; *and see* IOC

Boston, Massachusetts, US, 12–13, 281: *The Duchess of Malfi*, 229; *Four Sea Interludes* and *Passacaglia from 'Peter Grimes'*, 137, 211–12

Boston Symphony Orchestra, 101, 236, 309, 511, 525, 526, 535, 536

Boston: Wilbur Theatre: *Let's Make an Opera*, 609

Bostridge, Ian, 171

Boudin, Eugène, 464, 465; *Les Crinolines*, 465

Boughton, Joy, 244

Boughton, Rutland, 54, 105–6, 106, 143

Boulanger, Nadia, 64, 67, 190, 387, 409

Boult, Adrian, 235, 236, 414, 434, 435, 495, 639

Bournemouth, 302; EOG tour, 303; and Festival of Britain, 520

Bowen, Meirion, 368

Bowles, Jane, 84, 87

Bowles, Paul, 84, 87

Boyce, Bruce, 596, 650–51

Boyce, William, 563, 569; *and see* IOC

Boyd Neel Orchestra, 83, 102, 343, 423, 453, 586

Boys, Henry, 196, 338, 339, 340; 'Musico-Dramatic Analysis', 429

Brahms, Johannes, 169, 656; *and see* IOC

Brain, Dennis, 102, 161, 162, 485, 642

Brains Trust (radio programme), 171, 174

Brannigan, Owen, *plate 6*; 144, 149–50, 168, 218, 222, 234, 337, 439

Bratislava Opera, 235

Braus, Dorothea, 182
Bravern, Charles, 673
Bray, Joan, *see* Caplan, Joan
Bream, Julian, 596, 654
Brecht, Bertolt, 372, 396–7, 568, 609; *The Duchess of Malfi* (adaptation), 228–30; *Mother Courage*, 288
Breisach, Paul, 477
Breton, Nicholas: 'Come, silly Babe', 344
Brett, Philip, 5, 10, 92
Brian (?Aldeburgh fisherman), 633
Brice, Carol, 237
Bridge, Ethel, 79, <u>80</u>, 81, 103
Bridge, Frank, 55, 75, 79, <u>80</u>, 81, 339, 472, 669, 700; and *Variations on a Theme of Frank Bridge*, 75; *and see* IOC
Bridge of Allen, Scotland: PP–BB recital, 577
Bridge on the River Kwai, The (film), 596
Bridgewater: PP–BB recital, 370
Brighton, Sally, 76
Brighton, Sussex: *Let's Make an Opera*, 550, 629
Brighton: Theatre Royal, 533, 547, 50
Brill, Charles, 261
Brill Orchestra, *see* Charles Brill Orchestra
Bristol, 177: Company of Four, 170
Britain, Festival of (1951), 284, 374, 342, 437, 564–5, 567, 578, 682
Britain to America (radio series), 112
British: Are They Artistic?, The (film), 47
British Army of the Rhine, *see* B.A.O.R.
British Broadcasting Corporation, *see* BBC
British Control Commission, 270
British Council, 186, 191, 200–202, 244, 246, 250, 259, 278, 288, 289, 303–6, 308, 317, 373, 415, 586; European Section, 152; Music Advisory Committee, 303–4; in Rome, 493, 495
British Forces Network (BFN), 182, 411
British Institute of Recorded Sound, 548
British Library, 111; Curzon Collection, 190
British Museum, 448
Britten, Alan (BB's nephew), <u>637</u>
Britten, Benjamin, **508–9**, 655–6; and air travel, 259; and Aldeburgh Festival, 31, 36, 42, 45–7, 327, 502; on apologizing, 422; appearance and clothing, 75, 211, 417; and Auden, 65, 172, 665; and Bach, 76, 382–7; and Balinese music, 88; and Bartók, 79; and BBC, 124, 125, 154–5, 235–6, 339–40, 413; and Beethoven, 20, 63; and Berg, 75, 76, 419–20, 423; and Bernstein, 85–6; and biography, 3; birthdays, 143, 338, 339, 352, 358, 368, 464, 556, 630, 642; broken relationships, 46–7, 521, 575; canon, use of, 276, 376, 381, 384, 542; and cars, 79, 80, 239–40, 241, 252, 267, 306, 324; and CEMA, 12; childhood of, 4, 18, 55; and childhood games, 14, 644; children and young people, relationships with, 12–13, 20–29, 43, 644; and Chopin, 113; and Christianity, 50; church visiting, 535; as collector of art and books, 349, 392, 402–3, 410, 464–5, 586–7, 601; composition practice, 250–51, 447–8, 504; concentration camps, visit to, 104, 106; and conservation, 10; counterpoint, use of, 274, 276; and critics and the press, 113, 169, 239–40, 306, 324, 335, 366, 370, 373–4, 399, 456–7, 478, 486, 504–6, 514, 646, 699, 701; dance of death, concept of, 269–70; dedications and inscriptions to BB, 64, 65, 368, 402, 543, 547, 558, 560, 589, 646, 651, 680; diaries of, 3, *241*, *266*, 570, 571, 611; domestic arrangements, 25, 57, 61, 64, 72, 117, 132, 140, 186, 191, 315, 321–3, 352, 381, 423, 442; as editor, 383;

and education, 11; and English Opera Group, 47, 151, 198–9, 327, 353–4, 489, 502, 538, 554–5; estate, executors and trustees, 5, 326, 424; Europe, attitude to, 154; families, relationships with, 12–13, 20–24, 29, 38, 41, 43; family, motif of, 10, 13–16, 19; as father figure, 24–6, 488; finances and financial arrangements, 144, 153, 324, 326, 327, 365, 366, 416, 538–40, 541, 610; fund-raising, 12, 154; and Gainsborough, 582; and the gamelan, 608; on girls' voices, 344; godchildren, 11, 25, 166, 623, 635; on 'hack work', 211; and Haydn, 332; health: sprained ankle (1937), 67, 68; flu (1939), 79; streptococcal infection (1940), 58; flu (1942), 113; measles (1943), 58; flu (1944), 100; reaction to vaccination (1945), 105, 106; sleeping pills (1946), 139; depression and suspected ulcer (1948), 407–8, 461, 468–71, 476, 490, 491, 495, 497, 498, 500, 511, 525; throat infection (1950), 613, 615, 616; flu (1951), 638, 641; laryngitis (1951), 661; cystitis (1951), 669, 674, 676, 679; bursitis (1953), 27, 166, 464; diverticulitis (1966), 327; heart surgery (1973), 86, 332, 597, 613; heterophony, use of, 276; holidays (and working holidays): Dublin, 313, 340, 343; France, 33; Italy, 267, 407, 484, 488–9, 491, 498, 611–12; Morocco, 327; Norfolk Broads, 410; Rhine, 534, 674, 675, 678, 680, 681; Switzerland, 181–2, 184, 271, 306, 674; homes: see entries for: Chapel House, Horham; No. 104a Cheyne Walk; Crag House, Aldeburgh; Hallam Street, London; Kirkley Cliff Road, Lowestoft; No. 22 Melbury Road, London w14; No. 7 Middagh Street, New York; Nevern Square, London; Old Mill, Snape; No. 3 Oxford Square, London w2; Red House, Aldeburgh; St John's West High Street; No. 38 Upper Park Road; honours, prizes and awards: Cobbett Prize, 56; Ernest Farrar Prize, 56; Ernst von Siemens prize, 461; Freedom of Lowestoft (1951), 48, 50, 534, 612–13; Order of Merit, 332; Innocence/Experience theme, 14, 23, 28; in interview, 211, 525; and jazz, 75; juvenilia, 669; languages: French, 79; German, 460–61, 611–12; Italian, 612; Latin, 279–80, 375; on libretto-writing, 594; and Mahler, 10, 63, 76, 116, 117, 120–21; memorials, 177; and Mozart, 21, 76, 613, 636; *New Grove*, entry in, 5; on opera, 88; on organs, 463; outside/inside death, 16; pacifism and commitment to non-violence, 10, 50–52, 58, 91, 93, 120, 125, 154–8, 424, 444; parental absence, motif of, 15; parents, relationship with, 17–19; on PP, 91; and PP's voice, 98, 100, 120, 185, 285, 316, 321, 333, 356, 366, 381, 420, 455, 456, 460, 468, 490, 495, 499, 546, 630, 640, 661–2; political attitudes: on the 'iron curtain', 471; on propaganda, 68; and Spain under Franco, 23; on transatlantic relationship, 471; portraits and photographs, *plates 1–2, 4, 5, 8, 11, 14, 16–19, 26–31, 33–4, 42, 48–50; 62–4, 562, 567–8*; programme-planning, 366, 483–5, 652–5; public speaking, 344; and Purcell, 76, 107–8, 130, 493–5, 563; radio reception, 190, 346, 417, 419, 428, 460, 495, 582–3; as reader/narrator, 114, 138, 246, 258; recitals, concerts and tours: Sheffield (June 1944), 543–4; Germany (with Menuhin, 1945), 183; Netherlands (1946), 138, 153–4, 228, 246, 267; Switzerland (1946), 199, 236; UK (1946), 138, 259–60; Amsterdam (1947), 144; Switzerland, Belgium, the Netherlands, Sweden, Denmark (1947), 138,

267, 286; Italy (1947), 138, 268; UK (1947), 313, 338, 339, 341, 342; Switzerland, Italy, the Netherlands (1948), 313, 373, 396; South-West England (spring 1948), 314, 370; Amsterdam Concertgebouw (April 1948), 314, 370; Italy and Belgium (spring 1948), 408; Amsterdam Concertgebouw (December 1948), 452, 454; Italy (January–February 1949), 469–71, 479; Switzerland, Italy, Vienna, Belgium, Netherlands (spring 1949), 499, 500, 512, 513, 516; Chelsea Town Hall (October 1949), 533; US and Canada (1949), 230, 499, 500, 511, 533, 535, 541, 545, 546, 548–9, 551; Scotland (February 1950), 533, 565, 577, 579; Netherlands (June 1950), 587, 589, 598, 600; Vienna (April 1951), 534, 663; Oxford (1960s), 23; US (1969), 13; and revue, 330–31; and Schubert, 76, 113, 325, 359; Scouting movement, 471; and the sea, 315, 321, 414, 434, 442, 455, 456, 489, 491, 498, 499; sexuality, 79, 93: attraction to pre-pubescent boys, 5, 34, 90, 316; police investigation, 604; prejudice, 125; relationship with PP, 57, 115, 117, 132, 557–8; and impact on creativity, 5–9, 29, 44; smoking, 79, 209; in social situations, 75; and sports and outdoor activities: cricket, 48–9; horse-riding, 508; sailing, 409, 468, 470; ski-ing, 271, 272, 279, 280, 282, 285–6; squash, 68, 484, 504, 561; swimming, 315, 409; tennis, 20, 48, 409; and Stravinsky, 75, 76; tastes in food, drink and sweets, 42, 388, 455, 476, 595, 601, 614, 637, 638, 640; and Tchaikovsky, 22, 75–6; as teacher, 101, 421, 444, 489; and the treble voice, 527; and US: attitude to, 82, 84, 145, 154, 366, 373–4, 476, 480, 489, 500, 544, 546, 551, 554, 556, 641; residency (1939–42), 57, 73, 81–92, 95, 111, 117, 120, 122, 230, 362, 368, 418; visit (1946), 137; concert tour (1949), 88, 154, 424, 438, 440–41, 447–8, 502; fund-raising tour (1969), 154; proposed concert tour, 259, 325, 328, 366, 369, 373–4, 375; and Venice, 33; and Verdi, 21, 76, 248, 582–4; and viola, 14, 445, 654; and violence, 85; walks, 250–51; and Wolf, 358–9; work ethic, 48, 50; writings: 'Foreword', in RLEC, 429; 'A Note on the *Spring Symphony*', 280; *On Receiving the First Aspen Award*, 613; Preface to *The Rape of Lucretia*, 223; 'Some notes on Forster and music', 363; 'Verdi – A Symposium', 583; 'A Visiting Composer Looks at Us' ('An English Composer Sees America'), 84

Britten, Charlotte Elizabeth (Beth; BB's sister), *see* Welford, Beth

Britten, [Edith] Barbara (BB's sister), 71, 96, **192–3**, 193, 285–6, 417, 419, 442, 449, 450, 470, 473, 476, 520–21, 550, 569–70, **587–8**, 614, 630

Britten (née Hockey), Edith Rhoda (BB's mother), 16, 17, 48, 54, 55, 65, 450, 460; at Frinton, 62; death of, 57, 70; travels in Europe with BB, 56, 193, 195; will, 71

Britten, Florence Hay (BB's aunt), 65, 352, 587–8

Britten, John Robert Marsh (BB's nephew), 473, 474, 476

Britten, Robert Harry Marsh (BB's brother), 29, 49, 71, 473, 474, 476, **637**

Britten, Robert Victor (BB's father), 16–19, 56, 372, 450

Britten Estate Ltd, 668

Britten–Pears Foundation, 113, 424; art collection, 568; Trustees, 189, 335, 424, 668

Britten–Pears Library, 5, 364, 424

Britten–Pears School for Advanced Musical Studies, 384, 656; finances and fund-raising, 465; public performances, 516; staff and directors, 149, 656

Britten's Blues (AF event), 171

Brompton Oratory, 463

Brook, Clive, 589

Brook, Peter, 607

Brookes, Mrs (teacher), 28

Brooks Club, 241

Brosa, Antonio, 81, 84, 105, 254, 487, 623

Brosa, Peggy, 105

Brown, Doris, 442

Brown, Ian, 121

Browne, E. Martin, 170, 197, 331

Browne, Sir Thomas, 349; *Hydriotaphia*, 349; *Religio Medici*, 349

Brownlee, John, 375, 377, 379

Brussels, 78, 289, 306: *Albert Herring*, 392, 501, 507; *Peter Grimes*, 335, 390–92; PP–BB recitals, 137, 512, 516; Piano Concerto, 78; *The Rape of Lucretia*, 144, 255; *The Turn of the Screw*, 24

Brussels: Théâtre de la Monnaie, 392, 507

Brussels Radio: *The Holy Sonnets of John Donne*, 153

Bryanston School, Dorset, 409

Bryanston Summer School of Music, 409–10

Buchan, John, 21

Büchner, Georg, 73; *Dantons Tod*, 73

Buckingham, May, 582, 584

Buckingham, Robert (Bob), 410, 536, 584, 588, 676

Bucknell, Katherine, 72, 93

Budd, F. E., 343

Buenos Aires, 636: Teatro Colón, 636

Bugge, Stein, 623

Buja, Maureen, 668

Bullamore, Tim, 421

Burden, Michael, 203

Burges, Peter, 626, 627

Burgess, Guy, 78

Burghclere, 67, 573

Burns, Robert, 343

Burra, Peter, 54, 62, 63, 64, 66, 67, 68, 69, 71; 'The Novels of E. M. Forster', 67

Burrell, Barbara, 633

Burrell, Billy, 363, 610, 633, 675

Burrell, John, 124–5; 'A Landmark in Radio Creation', 125

Burton, Humphrey, 85, 86, 201, 208

Bury St Edmunds, Suffolk: *Saint Nicolas*, 630, 631

Busch, Fritz, 151, 166, 235, 325, 329, 563, 567

Bush, Alan, 162, 623–4, 625; *and see* IOC

Bush, Geoffrey, 647–8; *and see* IOC

Busoni, Ferruccio, 161, 485, 548; *and see* IOC

Butler, Lionel, 643

Butler, M., 587

Butt, James, 101, 442, 541, 597, 627–8, 662

Butts, Anthony, 509

Buxtehude, Dietrich, 323; *and see* IOC

Byrd, William, 586; *and see* IOC

Byron, George Gordon, Lord: 'She Walks in Beauty', 118

Cabaret (film), 68

Cadbury-Brown, H. T., 36

Cadogan, Lady Pamela, 653, 654

Caesar and Cleopatra (film), 328

Caine, Sir Richard de, 605

Cairns, David, 457

Calder, John, 87, 149, 213, 246
California, 500
Camargo Society, 70
Cambridge, 74, 92, 167, 181, 410, 588, 630, 658, 663
Cambridge Arts Theatre: *The Beggar's Opera*, 128, 314, 350, 357, 389, 393, 397, 398, 399–401; *Let's Make an Opera*, 550–51, 629; *On the Frontier*, 73, 74; song recital (Joan Cross, PP, BB), 170; *This Way to the Tomb*, 170
Cambridge Arts Theatre Trust, 17
Cambridge Daily News, 399
Cambridge: Fitzwilliam College, 424
Cambridge: Guildhall: PP–BB recital, 339
Cambridge: King's College, 362, 410, 585, 604, 617, 630
Cambridge Philharmonic Orchestra and Chorus, 183
Cambridge University, 23, 168, 488
Camden Hippodrome: *The Rape of Lucretia*, 147
Camden Theatre, London: *The Beggar's Opera*, 407
Cameron, Basil, 161, 190
Cameron, Euan, 4
Cameron, Ken, 174
Camp Mah-Kee-Nac, 536
Campion, Paul, 147, 278
Campion, Thomas: 'Winter Nights', 118
Canada, 80, 81, 87, 376, 488, 516: PP–BB tour, 547, 549, 551
Capell, Richard, 292; reviews, 294, 553, 690
Caplan, Isador, 191, 326, 419, <u>424</u>, 452; 'Recollections of Benjamin Britten', 424
Caplan, Joan, 424
Caplat, Moran, 151, 196, 565
Capri, 544
Cardelli, Giovanni, 418, 420, 447, 448, 478
Cardiff, Wales: Company of Four, 170
Cardus, Neville, 335–6
Carewe, John, 88
Carisch (Rome), 502
Carl Rosa Opera Company, 235, 245, 355, 436
Carmen (Zurich tea shop), 192
Carpenter, Humphrey, 5–6, 18, 28–49 *passim*, 183–4, 230, 235, 241, 260, 268, 316, 322, 356, 486, 488, 609, 613, 643; *Benjamin Britten: A Biography* (HCBB), 5–6
Carpi, Fernando, 431
Carter, Elliott, 319
Carter, Miranda, 78
Carter String Trio, 260
Casals, Pablo, 654
Casella, Alfredo, 387
Caskey, Bill, 556
Cavalcanti, Alberto, 446
Cavelti, Elsa, 186
CBC (Canadian Broadcasting Corporation), 607, 610; *Saint Nicolas*, 548
CBC Opera Company, 552; *Peter Grimes*, 552
CBC Symphony Orchestra, 146, 552
CBS, 83, 86
Cebotari, Maria, 187
CEMA (Council for the Encouragement of Music and the Arts), 12, 21, 214, 250, 317, 372, 484
Central Hall, Westminster, 260, 319
Central London Polytechnic, 383
Chamberlain, George, 562, 563
Chandos, Lord, *see* Lyttelton, Oliver
Chapel House, Horham, 38, 44, 45
Chapman, Robert, 536
Chappell, E., 606

Chappell, William, 70
Charles, Prince of Wales, 413–14
Charles Brill Orchestra, 261
Charlotte Street, London, 186
Charlton, Jim, 557–8
Chatterton, Thomas: *The Revenge*, 642–3, 652
Chaucer, Geoffrey, 528: *The Canterbury Tales*, 232
Chausson, Ernest: *see* IOC
Chávez, Carlos, 85, <u>88</u>
Chekhov, Anton, 654: *The Seagull*, 603
Chelsea Symphony Orchestra, 485
Chelsea Town Hall, 423, 549
Cheltenham, 102–3: *Canadian Carnival*, 103; *Four Sea Interludes from 'Peter Grimes'*, 103, 106; *Let's Make an Opera*, 501, 517–18; Piano Concerto, 137, 155; *The Sleeping Children*, 458–9, 554–5, 561, 651; *The Tale of Mr Tod*, 673, 674; *The Wandering Scholar*, 554–5, 646, 651
Cheltenham Festival, 106, 161, 317, 335; 1947: 347; 1948: 365, 368; 1949: 512, 517–18; 1951: 642, 646, 651
Chenhalls, A. & T., 540
Cherniavsky, Michel, 79, <u>81</u>
Chester, J. & W. (music publishers), 560
Chester Miracle Plays, 287
Chester Music Club: PP–BB recital, 339
Cheyne Walk, London SW10, No. 104a, 111, 46
Chicago, 478: *French Folk Song Arrangements*, 166; tour plans, 441
Chicago Grand Opera, 47
Chicago Symphony Orchestra, 237
Chichester Cathedral, 163, 596
Chin-dung (Chinese car-boy), 74
Chioggia, Italy, 484, 491
Chopin, Fryderyk: *see* IOC
Choveaux, Nicholas, 282, 284
Christiansen, Rupert, 625
Christie, Audrey, *see* Mildmay, Audrey
Christie, John, 144, 148, <u>150–51</u>, 152, 198, 214, 219, 231, 232, 242–6, 252, 261–3, **264–5**, 266, 273, 292, 302, 565, 614
Church, Michael, 388
Churchill, Winston, 284
Cincinnati: Music Hall, 90
Cincinnati Symphony Orchestra, 90
City of Birmingham Symphony Orchestra, 183, 237
City of London Festival, 563
Civil Rights Movement (US), 85
Civil War, English, 288
Clar, Yvonne, 193
Clare, John, 454, 456; 'The Driving Boy', 454, 456, 527
Clark, Andrew, 368
Clark, Jane, 201, 601, 602
Clark, Kenneth, 177, 201, 243, 357, 362, 591, <u>601–2</u>; 'Constable and Gainsborough as East Anglian Painters', 357, 362
Classical Music, 388, 454, 574
Claude Lorraine, 599
Clayton, Ivan, *plate 18*; 300, 354, <u>355</u>, 356, 416, 430, 473, 483, 651
Clementi, Cecil, 281
Cleveland Orchestra, 440
Cleverdon, Douglas, 372, <u>642</u>, 652
Cliveden, 21
Clough, Prunella: Aldeburgh Festival calendar (1954), 176
Coal Face (film), 172
Coates, Edith, 392, 439
Cobbett Prize, 48
Cobbold, Richard: *The History of Margaret*

Catchpole, 410, 429
Cochran, C. B. (Charles Blake), 330–31
Cocteau, Jean, 137
Cohen, Frederic, 207
Cole, Hugo, 625
Colchester Institute, 149
Coleman, Basil, 177, 430, 512, 514, 516, 540, 659, 675; and *The Beggar's Opera*, 516; and *Billy Budd*, 516, 610, 642; and *Gloriana*, 516; and *Let's Make an Opera*, 516, 540, 549, 660; and *Love in a Village*, 540; and *Owen Wingrave*, 516; and *Peter Grimes*, 516; and *The Rape of Lucretia*, 187, 514; and *The Sleeping Children*, 459, 555, 651; and *The Tale of Mr Tod*, 673; and *The Turn of the Screw*, 27, 516; and *The Wandering Scholar*, 459, 555, 651
Coleridge, Samuel Taylor: 'The Wanderings of Cain', 15
Collegiate Chorale, New York, 46, 270
Collingwood, Lawrance, 101, 348, 427
Collins, Anthony, 544
Collins, William: 'Ode to Evening', 118
Collins Classics, 166, 548; 'Britten Edition', 413
Collins' Music Hall, London, 68, 265–6
Cologne, 188, 200, 675: *Oedipus Rex*, 675
Columbia Records (record company), 345, 346, 348
Columbia Theater Associates, 441
Columbia University, 440–41, 665
Commons, House of, 177
Commonwealth Arts Festival, Liverpool, 563
Compagnie des Quinze, 195
Company of Four, 170–71
Composers' Guild, 625
Con Moto Choir, 171
Connolly, Cyril, 268
Conrad, Doda, 459
Constable, Charles Golding, 402–3
Constable, John, 280, 357, 358, 362–4, 402–3, 464; portrait of Charles Golding Constable, 402–3; *Suffolk Landscape with Cottage* (*c*. 1820), 364
Constable, John Charles, 402–3
Constance, Lake, Switzerland, 195
Contemporary Painting by East Anglian Artists (AF exhibition), 363
Contrepoints, 309
Cook, Thomas, 47
Cooke, Arnold, 48
Cooke, Mervyn, 5
Cook's (travel agency), 289, 290, 471
Cooper, Emil, 329, 375, 377, 379, 380
Cooper, Martin, 297, 506
Co-operative Society Choir of Ipswich, 492
Cope, Cecil, 601
Copenhagen: *Albert Herring*, 538; PP–BB recitals, 278, 601; *The Rape of Lucretia*, 538
Copland, Aaron, 57, 85, 87–8, 149, 209, 211, 227, 442–3, 609; 'Music in the Twenties', 443; *and see* IOC
Corder, Frederick, 61
Corelli, Arcangelo, 484
Cornford, Frances: 'There was neither grass nor corn', 132
Cornwall, 62, 66
Coronation (HM Queen Elizabeth II), 342
Cosman, Milein, 666; *Stravinsky at Rehearsal*, 666
Cotman, John Sell, 586–7; *Draining Mills at Crowland*, 586–7
Cotman, Miles Edmund, 587
Cottesloe Theatre, *see* National Theatre

Cotton, Mrs (Walter Hussey's housekeeper), 595
Cotton, Charles: 'Pastoral', 118
Cottrell, Leonard, 345
Coulton, Barbara, 143
Council for the Encouragement of Music and the Arts, *see* CEMA
Country Living, 633
Courtauld, Samuel, 70
Covent Garden Opera Company, 187, 203, 235, 284, 391–2, 632; *see also* Royal Opera House, Covent Garden
Covent Garden Trust, 479
Coventry, 177, 540, 584
Coventry Cathedral, 158, 389; Baptistery Window, 177
Coventry Festival, 184
Coward, Noël, 253, 330; *On With the Dance*, 330; *This Year of Grace*, 330
Cowles, Chandler, 537
Cox, Peter, 107, 601, 646, 653, 654
Coxe, Louis Osborne, 536
Crabbe, George, 58, 91, 92, 320; *The Borough*, 91–92, 320, 362, 662–3
Crabbe House, Aldeburgh, 315, 316
Crabbe Street, Aldeburgh, 316, 320
Craft, Robert, 556, 676
Crag House, Aldeburgh, *plates 31, 33 and 42*; 138, 260, 305, 308, 315, 320, 322, 324, 338, 345, 352–3, 357, 358, 381, 410–11, 414, 419, 423, 442, 455, 457, 470, 476, 480, 483, 489, 492, 496, 533–4, 589, 625, 633, 636, 653
Crag Path, Aldeburgh, 320, 682
Craig, Edward Gordon, 562–3, 568, 569
Cranbrook, Countess of (Fidelity), 46, 317, 381, 383–4, 452–3, 456, 457, 474, 476, 483, 571
Cranbrook, John ('Jock') David Gathorne-Hardy, 4th Earl of, 317, 456, 457, 473–4
Cranbrook family, 641, 653
Cranko, John, 540
Cranleigh: PP–BB recital, 339
Crantock, Newquay, 63, 418
Crawford, Michael, 27–8; *Parcel Arrived Safely: Tied with String*, 27
Crazy Gang, 149
Cromwell, Oliver, 288
Cronheim, Paul, 246, 247, 386
Cross, Joan, 140, 184, 184, 225, 230–32, 250, 365, 475, 486, 585, 624; accommodation, 139; *Albert Herring*, *plate 10*; 140, 248, 250–51, 273, 289, 470; autobiography, 140; *The Bartered Bride*, 149; and Berkeley, 63; and 'Civil War' project, 288; and *Così fan tutte*, 149, 248; and *Dido and Aeneas*, 596, 604, 634–5, 648, 650–51; and EOG, 198, 231, 244, 273, 602; and *Gloriana*, 140, 391; and *Letters to William*, 234; and Opera Studio (National Opera School), 276, 354–5, 627–8; and *Peter Grimes*, 103, 140–41, 168, 185, 192, 198, 202, 203, 208, 209, 282, 333, 336–8, 391, 425–7, 437–8; and *The Rape of Lucretia*, *plate 7*; 140, 144, 209, 214, 218, 222, 228, 303, 305, 659; in recital and concert, 49, 167, 170, 181, 183, 231, 319, 483–4, 601; and Sadler's Wells, 140; and *Spring Symphony*, 546, 551–2, 554, 617; and *The Turn of the Screw*, 140; and *A Wedding Anthem*, 541
Crosse, Gordon, 487; *and see* IOC
Crossley-Holland, Kevin, 605
Crown Film Unit (CFU), 172, 174
Croydon Symphony Orchestra, 485
Croyland Mill, 587

Crozier, Biddy, *see* Johns, Margaret
Crozier, Blake, 213
Crozier, Eric, 212–13, 225, 227, 230, 241, 245–6, 280, 292, 306, 313, 315, 319, 324, 341, 343, 353–4, 364–6, 370, 373, 427–8, 484, 512, 516, 520, 538–9, 555–6, 559, 571–3, 588, 589–90, 594, 611, 618, 645, 698; *Abelard and Héloïse*, 365; 'After Long Pursuit' (with Nancy Evans), 149, 191–2, 250, 363, 364; *Albert Herring* (libretto), plate 10; 138, 200–201, 212, 232, 248, 250–53, 259, 267, 273, 277, 286–8, 309, 315, 503, 539, 590; *Billy Budd* (libretto), *plate 43*; 68, 212, 362, 374, 407–8, 409–11, 438, 480–82, 484, 496–501, 503, 513, 520, 533, 536–9, 546, 547, 551, 559, 566, 589–91, 617–18, 633–5, 637–8, 644, 682–98, 700; *The Little Sweep (Let's Make an Opera)* (play and libretto), 11, 212, 287, 353, 384, 432–3, 467, 492, 501, 503, 507, 539, 549–51, 555, 571–6, 590, 660; *The Life and Legends of Saint Nicolas, Patron Saint of Children*, 433; 'Lucretia: 1946', 429; 'An Opera Team Sets to Work', 675; *The Rape of Lucretia: A Symposium* (RLEC), 196, 338, 407, 427; *Ruth* (libretto), 212; *Saint Nicolas* (text), 212, 300, 321, 322–3, 350, 365, 471, 503, 539; scenario for 'film-opera' (1948), 407; 'Staging First Productions 1', 147; 'The Writing of *Billy Budd*', 410; 'Writing a Britten Opera', 594; *The Young Person's Guide to the Orchestra* (commentary), 212, 247; and Aldeburgh Festival, 212, 317, 327, 344, 346, 449, 479; on BB, 18, 250–51; at Bournemouth, 520, 555, 559; as broadcaster, 433; and 'Civil War' project, 287–8; as director, 101, 430; domestic life and accommodation, 149, 191, 245, 259, 352–3, 449, 473, 476, 514, 555–6, 559; and EOG, 151, 152, 198, 212, 242–4, 254, 262–6, 273, 276–7, 327, 353–4, 367, 449, 456, 479, 483–4, 496, 503, 512, 514, 520, 554, 559, 569; 'film-opera' project, 428, 431–3; finances, 513–14, 520, 538–40; health, 245, 250; letter to *Times Literary Supplement*, 505; letters to Nancy Evans, 250–51, 260, 266, 277–8, 286–9, 322–3, 344, 350, 375, 384, 433, 474, 497–8, 503–4, 506–7, 512, 521, 536–7, 539; obituary of, 18–19; personality of, 18; translations, 212; and *Peter Grimes*, 128, 142, 167, 185, 188, 206–9, 212, 224, 226, 325, 327, 330; and *The Rape of Lucretia*, *plate 8*; 176, 186, 195, 212, 222, 277, 304
Cruikshank, George, 401
Crystal Palace, London, 437
Culbert, Tom, 426
Cummings, Ruth, 418
Cummings, W. H., 647–8
Cunard, Lady, 70
Curcio, Maria, 386, 387–8, 509, 621
Curtis, Antony, 143
Curtis Institute, Philadelphia, 85, 213, 579
Curtis Institute, Orchestra of, 87
Curtiss, Mina, 610
Curzon, Clifford, 21, 49, 158–61, 186, 190–91, 357, 359, 368
Cusack, Cyril, 143
Czinner, Paul, 228–9

da Ponte, Lorenzo, 151
Dacam, C. B., 49
Dahlberg, Frederick, *plate 47*
Daily Express, 567
Daily Mirror, 698
Daily Telegraph & Morning Post, 292, 667; obituaries, 72, 78, 89, 140, 149, 150, 177, 213, 246, 328, 368, 431, 463, 486, 493; reviews, 219, 294, 553, 690
Dalman, Georges, 255
Dalman, M. G., 255
Damrosch, Walter, 435
Dante Alighieri, 615
Darmstadt, 46
Darmstadt: Hessian State Theatre, 150
Darmstadt: Landestheater, 234
Dartington Hall, 101, 107, 128, 238, 244–5, 409, 541, 570, 601, 627, 653–6, 662; PP–BB performances, 370, 435, 436, 502, 507; *Saint Nicolas*, 507
Dartington Singers and Players, 601
Davenport, John, 79
David (pupil at Wellington College), 100
Davies, Peter Maxwell, 655
Davies, Walford, 7
Davis, George, 86
Day-Lewis, Cecil, 162, 615, 616
de la Mare, Walter: 'Nicholas Nye', 27
'De rosis nascentibus' (anonymous ode), 280
Death in Venice (film), 6
Debussy, Claude, 189; *and see* IOC
Decca Record Company, 97, 149, 166, 182, 202, 210, 255, 261, 277, 304, 342, 348–9, 452–4, 456, 491, 521, 544, 548, 648; 'Britten at Aldeburgh' (CD series), 50; funding of Snape Maltings Concert Hall, 30
Dehn, Paul, 633, 662
Dekker, Thomas, 401
Del Mar, Norman, 153, 172, 307, 350, 430, 480, 483, 485–6, 549, 628–9; *Anatomy of the Orchestra*, 486; and *Albert Herring*, 486, 514; and *The Beggar's Opera*, 486; and *Let's Make an Opera*, 27, 408, 416, 517–19, 606, 609–10, 628–9; and *Love in a Village*, 540, 677; and *Noye's Fludde*, 486; and *The Rape of Lucretia*, 187, 416, 486, 514; and *The Sleeping Children*, 458, 555, 651; and *Stratton*, 546; and *The Wandering Scholar*, 459, 555, 651
Del Mar, Pauline, 629
De-la-Noy, Michael, 111, 113, 114, 116, 457
Delius, Frederick, 148, 548; *and see* IOC
Della Casa, Lisa, 186, 187
Deller, Alfred, 260, 601
Demarco, Richard, 246
Denham, Sir John: 'Somnus, the humble god', 344
Denham Studios, 174
Denmark, 448, 486, 535, 538, 548; concert tours, 138, 600
Dent, E. J., 167, 168–70, 184, 188, 199, 203, 362, 396, 399, 401, 438, 563, 569, 648, 701, 702
Dent du Midi, Les (mountains), 570
Denzler, Robert F., 185, 186, 188, 192, 198
Derry, Wilfred, 471–2
Deschamps, Bernard, 249
Devlin, William, 589
Dewas State Senior, Maharaja of, 362
Diaghilev, Serge, 189
Diamand, Maria, *see* Curcio, Maria
Diamand, Peter, 246, 259, 345, 354, 386–8, 414, 440, 469, 476, 508, 586, 621, 661
Diamond, David, 579
'Diapason', *see* Spruytenburg, Hank
Dickens, Charles: *Oliver Twist*, 401
Dickinson, Goldsworthy Lowes, 91, 93, 629–30; *The Greek View of Life*, 630
Dickinson, Peter, 63, 82, 85, 701
Dictionary of National Biography (DNB), 543, 568
Dietwieler, Pauli, 192

Dignam, Mark, 143
Digney, Angus, 141
Diligentia, Netherlands: PP–BB recital, 278
Dinglinger, Wolfgang, 383
Divertimento (ballet), 89
Dobbs, Jack, 107, 601, 646
Dodd, Anthony, 171
Doig, Allan, 389
Dolin, Anton, 70
Donald, Mrs E. M., 304
Donlevy, Edmund, 147, 218, 222, 431
Donne, John, 105, 122; love poems, 122; 'Stay, O
    Sweet, and do not rise', 122
Doone, Rupert, 62, 73
Doorn-Lindeman, Dora van, 382, 385–6, 387, 560
Dordrecht, Netherlands: PP–BB recital, 228
Dorée, Doris, 333, 390, 391
Douglas, Basil, 381, 452, 454, 661–2; and AF, 363;
    and BBC, 183, 260, 615, 640; and English Opera
    Group, 45–6, 183, 615, 634, 640, 659, 674
Douglaston, US, 225, 227
Dowland, John, 546, 663; *and see* IOC
Dowling, Denis, 303, 428, 431, 434, 574
Dowling, Eddie, 208, 211
Downes, Olin, 87, 373, 480; reviews, 209–10, 212,
    376–7, 477
Downes, Ralph, 359, 463–4, 639; *Baroque Tricks:
    Adventures with Organ Builders*, 463
Drayer, Wiebe, 561
Dresden, Germany, 329: *Romeo und Julia*, 189
Driver, Paul, 368
Drowns (art restorers), 402
Drummond, John, 246
Druten, John van, 557; *I Am a Camera*, 557
Dublin, 323, 340, 341, 343; British Embassy, 340;
    Buswell's Hotel, 340; Dáil, 340; Dolphin
    (restaurant), 340; Jaumet's (restaurant), 340
Duff, John R. K., 349; *Sheep in a Meadow*, 349
Duff, Lesley, *see* Bedford, Lesley
Dumbarton Oaks, Washington DC: PP–BB
    recital, 546
Duncan, Briony, 330, 488, 579
Duncan, Roger, 10, 25, 330, 488, 579, 644
Duncan, Ronald, *plate 31*; 10, 25, 104, 105, 147–8,
    194, 195, 268, 330, 351, 385, 484, 488, 494, 541–2,
    544, 558, 577–8, 579, 589, 675; *Abelard and
    Héloïse*, 177, 232, 366; *Amo Ergo Sum*, 541–2;
    Birthday Song for Erwin, 105; *The Canterbury
    Tales* (unrealized opera), 232; *The Eagle Has
    Two Heads* (Cocteau translation), 137; *Hylas*,
    147–8; *Letters to William* (unrealized opera),
    232, 233; 'The Libretto: the Method of Work',
    196, 429; *Mea Culpa*, 155, 157, 158, 163, 351; *The
    Mongrel and Other Poems*, 148, 158, 589; *Our
    Lady's Tumbler*, 578; *The Rape of Lucretia*
    (libretto), *plate 5*; 25, 139, 158, 176, 178–80, 194–7,
    215, 217–23, 226–8, 231, 253, 255–8, 332, 429,
    477–8, 504–5; *Saint Spiv*, 579–80; *Stratton*, 148,
    232, 533, 544, 546–7, 549, 589; *This Way to the
    Tomb*, 170, 195, 220, 268, 270, 443; on BB, 147–8;
    relationship with BB, 25, 195, 232; *see also*
    Ronald Duncan Literary Foundation
Duncan, Rose Marie, 104, 194–7, 268, 270, 330, 351,
    488, 577–9
Dundee: PP–BB recital, 577
'Dundee' (psalm tune), 90
Dunham, Sir John: 'Somnus, the humble god', 47
Dunkerley, Piers, 469–70, 470–71, 661–2, 677
Dunlop, Fergus, 152

Dupré, Marcel, 183
Durham University, 672
Dutch Christian Radio Society (NCRV), 523
Dutch Radio Chorus, 521, 523
Dutch Radio Sound Archives, 147
Dutilleux, Henri, 319, 655
Duxbury, Elspeth, 75, 76
Dvořák, Antonín: *see* IOC
Dyall, Valentine, 165
Dyson, Sir George, 638, 639

Ealing Films, 367
Easdale, Brian, 73, 456, 458, 554, 560; *see also* IOC
East 49th Street, No. 24, New York, 417
East Anglian Daily Times, 344, 346, 633
Eastern Daily Press, 66
Ebert, Carl, 150, 231, 234–5, 242–45, 262–4, 273, 277,
    288, 290, 328, 329, 556, 567
Eccles, ?Henry, 80; *and see* IOC
Eccles, John, 278
Eddy, Mrs Baker, 504
Edinburgh, Duke of, Prince Philip, 414
Edinburgh, Scotland, 230, 266: PP–BB recital, 577
Edinburgh: Caledonian Hotel, 320
Edinburgh Festival Society, 565
Edinburgh: Freemasons' Hall: *Les Illuminations*, 320
Edinburgh International Festival of Music and
    Drama, 150, 245, 313, 315, 317, 322, 325, 329, 355,
    439, 475, 627–8; administration, 245, 246, 562,
    563–7, 632; appearances by BB and/or PP, 88,
    313, 315, 320, 606
Edinburgh: King's Theatre: *Le nozze di Figaro*, 329
Edinburgh: Royal Lyceum Theatre: *The Rape of
    Lucretia* (1946), 137, 147
Edinburgh: Usher Hall: *Das Lied von der Erde*, 320;
    The Young Person's Guide to the Orchestra, 329
Education, Ministry of, 12, 23, 171, 248, 407, 432
Educational Media Associates, 147
Edwards, R. A., 553
Edwards, W. E., 242
Egypt, 476, 479
Einstein, Alfred: *Mozart, His Character, His Work*,
    338, 339
Eisenberg, Maurice, 81–2
Elborn, Geoffrey, 543
Elgar, Edward, 383; *and see* IOC
Eliot, T. S., 114, 147, 196, 319, 330–31, 332; *The
    Cocktail Party*, 331; 'The Death of St Narcissus',
    332; 'Journey of the Magi', 319, 332; *Little
    Gidding*, 114; *Poems Written in Early Youth*, 332
Eliot, Valerie, 330, 332
Elizabeth, Princess (later Queen Elizabeth II),
    413–14, 475; and Aldeburgh Festival, 30
Elizabeth, Queen (later Queen Elizabeth The
    Queen Mother), 541
Elizabethan Singers, 418
Elland, Percy, 604
Ellington, Duke, 75
Ellis, Christopher, 637
Ellis, Osian, 412
Ellis, Vivian, 330
Elmhirst, Dorothy, 244, 615, 634–5, 653, 662
Elmhirst, Leonard, 244–5, 615, 635, 653, 662
EMI (recording company), 166, 304, 347, 427
Empire Theatre, Leicester Square: *Instruments of
    the Orchestra*, 138
English Folk Song Society, 548
English National Opera (ENO), 169, 341
English Opera Group (EOG), 186, 321, 322, 575,

605, 631, 674; *Albert Herring*, 138, 244, 248, 265, 273, 294, 300, 303–4, 306, 322, 354, 431, 440–41, 514, 574, 641; *The Beggar's Opera*, 314, 322, 328, 354, 393, 397–401, 413, 431, 440, 546, 574; *Castaway*, 64; *Il combattimento di Tancredi e Clorinda*, 630, 641, 648, 649; *Dido and Aeneas*, 231, 534, 554, 569, 596, 634–5, 641, 646, 648, 649, 650–51; *A Dinner Engagement*, 64, 431, 561; *Idomeneo*, 413; *King Arthur*, 431; *Let's Make an Opera*, 440–41, 486, 501, 519, 544, 546, 549–50, 574, 637, 641, 677; *Love in a Village*, 148, 431, 486, 540, 674, 677; *The Rape of Lucretia*, 138, 244, 265, 273, 276, 300, 303–4, 306, 322, 354, 431, 440–41, 478, 514, 574, 641, 659; *Ruth*, 64; *Sāvitri*, 554–5; *The Sleeping Children*, 458–9, 554–5, 561; *Stabat Mater* (Berkeley), 64, 306–7; *The Tale of Mr Tod*, 673; *The Turn of the Screw*, 27, 431, 550; *The Visitors*, 413; *The Wandering Scholar*, 428, 430, 440, 459, 486, 554–5, 646; board and management, 12, 30, 47, 183, 212, 243–4, 276, 284, 326, 327, 332–3, 383, 424, 449, 454, 479, 514, 559, 569, 571, 601–2, 614–15, 618, 624, 628–9, 634–5, 640, 673; company members, 25, 41, 148, 203, 235, 308, 316, 322, 338, 347, 356, 410, 413, 431, 436, 439, 480, 483, 485, 514, 516, 520, 573–4; and Covent Garden, 203, 259, 438; finances and fund-raising, 244, 259, 265, 327, 354, 356, 367, 491, 501, 503, 520, 533, 538, 584–5, 614–15, 618, 634–5, 638, 640, 659; genesis and formation, 134, 138, 144, 151–52, 198, 212, 213, 231, 242–6, 254, 259, 262–6, 273, 279, 282, 438; Holland Festival (1947, 1948), 138, 305, 314; London season (May 1951), 624, 641, 659; and National Opera School, 354–5; recitals and concerts, 64, 306, 496, 546, 630; repertory, 186, 244, 248, 554; supporters, 214, 244, 605, 638; tours and tour plans, 151, 306, 317, 324, 535, 549–50, 602, 604–5, 640–42, 674, 677, 680; *see also* EOG Ensemble and EOG Orchestra
ENSA (Entertainments National Services Association), 149, 182
Entschede, Netherlands: PP–BB recital, 228
EOG, *see* English Opera Group
EOG Chamber Orchestra, 629
EOG Ensemble, 544
EOG Orchestra, 347, 359, 368, 487, 546, 549, 551, 627, 655
Epenhuysen, Jan van, 260
Erdman, Charles, 672
Escondido, California, 58, 90
Etoile (restaurant), 330
Eton, 20, 21
Euripides, 196
'European Spirit' Conference (Geneva, 1946), 261–2
Evans, Edwin, 70
Evans, Geraint, 633
Evans, Dr Harold, 192, 193
Evans, John, 149, 372
Evans, Myfanwy, *see* Piper, Myfanwy
Evans, Nancy, 49, 148–9, 250, 252, 260, 266, 277, 278, 286–9, 306, 310, 316, 322–4, 341, 343, 344, 350, 352–3, 354, 366, 375, 384, 433, 474, 497, 503–4, 506, 509, 512, 521, 536, 539, 555, 559, 560, 573, 590, 611, 617, 635, 645; and *Albert Herring*, plate 15; 148, 250–51, 296, 297; and *The Beggar's Opera*, plate 20; 148, 348, 350, 393, 397, 399, 401; and *A Charm of Lullabies*, 148, 343–4, 352, 417, 418, 428; and *Dido and Aeneas*, 148, 596, 650–51; domestic life, 149, 213, 352–3, 364–5, 473, 475

555–6, 559; and EOG, 244, 520; and *Letters to William*, 234; and *Love in a Village*, 148, 540; and *The Rape of Lucretia*, plates 6 and 8; 144, 147, 148, 222, 303, 304, 422, 441
Evans, Peter: *The Music of Benjamin Britten*, 4
Evening Standard, 156, 158, 604, 694
Ewert, Brita, 168

Faber and Faber, 148, 268, 332, 547, 632, 667
Faber Music, 326, 332, 667–8; publications, 14, 105, 237, 261, 346, 383, 430, 652
Falkner, Keith, 493–5, 502
Falkner, Julia, 493
Fallowell, Duncan, 78
Falls, Julia, 332
Farjeon, Eleanor, 61; 'Jazz-Man', 61
Farjeon, Harry, 54, 61
Farrar, Dean, 693
Farrell, Anthony B., 537
Fascism, 8, 660
Fassett, J., 607
Faull, Ellen, 507
Fauré, Gabriel: *see* IOC
Fawkes, Richard, 574
Federal Music Project (US), 622
Federal Theater Project (US), 609
Fedorovitch, Sophie, 596, 648, 650
Fedricks, Bill, 161
Fenice, La, Venice, 25
Fernald, John, 547
Fernandel, 249
Fernie, Louise (BB's aunt), 588, 589
Ferrier, Kathleen, 49, 144, 147–8, 150, 183, 214, 218–19, 222, 230–32, 234, 247, 276, 277, 300, 304, 316, 320, 345, 348, 384, 410; planned work for, 500, 502; and *Canticle II*, 502; and *The Rape of Lucretia*, plates 3 and 8; 440–41, 502; and *Spring Symphony*, plate 50; 456, 502, 521–3, 525, 527
Festing, Michael: *see* IOC
Festival Hall, *see* Royal Festival Hall, London
Festival Hall Sub-Committee, 638–9
Festival of Britain 1951, *see* Britain, Festival of (1951)
Festival of Music for the People (1939), 80
Fifield, Christopher, 147
Figaro, Le, 309–10
Financial Times: articles, 143; obituaries, 177, 368
Finland, 471–2
Finney, Albert, 608
Fischer-Dieskau, Dietrich, 49, 614
Fitzgerald, Edward, 362, 672
Fleet Street Choir, 97, 98, 99
Fleming, Ian, 672
Fletcher, Eric, 585
Florence, Italy, 235, 280; and ISCM Festival, 56, 92, 390, 401, 446; PP–BB recital, 268
Flothuis, Marius, 510
'Flowers of the Forest' (folk tune), 90
Foa, George, 551–2
Folkart, Burt A., 622
Fonteyn, Margot, 203
Forbes, Elizabeth, 140, 148, 356, 387, 431, 493
Fordham St Martin, Suffolk, 605
Foreign Service, 12
Foreman, Lewis, 203, 438
Forster, E. M., *plates 32–3*; 30, 67, 68, 130, 268, 287, 357, 362–3, 410–11, 427–9, 449, 455, 461, 476, 491, 543–4, 582, 584–5, 587–9, 594, 605, 611, 617–18, 630, 632–3, 643–4, 646, 654–5, 663, 672, 675–7,

681, **682**; *Abinger Harvest*, 362; *Aspects of the Novel* (Clark Lectures, 1927), 411; *Billy Budd* (libretto), 68, 212, 362, 407–8, 409–11, 479–82, 496–501, 503, 513, 533, 535, 536, 538–9, 547, 559, 566, 582, 589–91, 617, 633–4, 637–8, 641, 643–4, 653, 657, 676, 682–98, 700; 'George Crabbe and Peter Grimes', 359; 'George Crabbe: The Poet and the Man', 362; *Goldsworthy Lowes Dickinson*, 91, 93, 629; *Howards End*, 362; *The Longest Journey*, 362; *Maurice*, 68; *A Passage to India*, 362; 'The *Raison d'être* of Criticism', 410; *A Room With a View*, 362; *Two Cheers for Democracy*, 359, 362; *Where Angels Fear to Tread*, 362; disagreements with BB, 587, 611, 617–18; and *Voices for Today*, 672
Forsyte Kerman (solicitors), 424
Forsyth, James, 328
forza del destino, La (film), 328
Foule, Farnsworth, 692
Fox, Sue, 597
Foy, Henry, 569, 571, 614–15, 618, 628–9, 635
France, 306, 325; tour plans, 145, 391
Francis, John, 244, 260
Franck, César: *see* IOC
Franco, General Francisco, 23
Frankel, Benjamin, 162; *and see* IOC
Frederick Warne (publishing house), 673
Freiberg, Gottfried, 663
Fresnay, Pierre, 354, 356
Freud, David, 383
Fricker, Peter Racine, 550
Fricsay, Ferenc, 628
Friends House, Euston Road, London, 291, 308, 496, 546, 630, 645
Fry, Christopher, 331
Fry, Elizabeth, 520, <u>521</u>
Furbank, P. N., 30, 363, 461, 584, 585, 587, 618

Gainsborough, Thomas, 280, 357, 363, 416, <u>583</u>
Gallone, Carmine, 325, <u>328</u>
Galsworthy, Mrs W. H. M., 381, 383
Gamble, Rollo, 73
Gandhi, Mohandas Karamchand, 354, <u>356</u>, 558
Gardner, John, 149; *and see* IOC
Garnham, A. M., 667
Garnham, Maureen, 454, 627
Garrett, Newson, 316
Garris, John, 380
Gathorne-Hardy, Christina (Tina), 11, 384
Gathorne-Hardy, Gathorne (Gay), 11, 384, 433
Gathorne-Hardy, Hugh (Hughie), *plate 37*; 11, 384
Gathorne-Hardy, Jonathan (Jonny), 11, 384, 433, 571
Gathorne-Hardy, Juliet, 11, 384, 483, 484
Gathorne-Hardy, Samuel (Sammy), 11, 384, 433
Gathorne-Hardy, Sophia (Sophie), 11, 384, 433
Gay, John, 350, 393; *and see* IOC
Gellhorn, Peter, 151, 153, 696, 698
Gendron, Maurice, 260
Geneva, 182, 199, 262, 272, 273, 278, 288, 372, 491, 571
Geneva Festival, 251
Geneva: Grand Théâtre, 46, 213
Genoa, Italy, 489, 498: PP–BB recital, 516
George V, King, 475, 614
George VI, King, 345, 541, 542
Gerhard, Roberto, 486; *and see* IOC
Ghedini, Giorgio, 537–8, 682; *and see* IOC
Gibbs (Decca Record Co.), 453
Gibbs, Armstrong, 458, 575–6
Gide, André, 338, <u>339</u>, 654

Giehse, Theresa, 288
Gielgud, John, 228, 602, <u>603–4</u>, 606–9, 615
Gielgud, Val, 124, 615
Gigli, Beniamino, 490, <u>491</u>
Gilliam, Laurence, <u>134</u>, 143, 155, 345
Gillies, Malcolm, 548
Gilmour, J. D., 479
Gishford, Anthony, 324, <u>326–7</u>, 392–3, 504, 536, 544, 562, 575–6, 607, 654–5
Glasgow, Mary, 566
Glasgow, Scotland, 550: PP–BB recital, 577
Glasgow: Theatre Royal: *The Rape of Lucretia* (1946), 137, 147
Glass Mountain, The (film), 41
Glendinning, Victoria, 543
Globe Theatre, London, 331
Glock, William, 189, 223, 409; *Notes in Advance*, 409; reviews, 298–9
Gluck, Christoph Willibald, 169; *and see* IOC
Glyndebourne English Opera Company, 151
Glyndebourne Festival Opera, 150, 187, 236, 245, 247, 278, 355, 413; administration and practices, 134, 144, 150–53, 198, 203, 213–14, 224, 231–2, 235, 239, 242–3, 245, 259, 261–6, 383, 439, 563, 565, 567; Chorus, 149, 151; concerts, 150; and EOG, 151–2, 203, 242–6, 254, 259, 262–6, 273, 276, 288, 438; *Albert Herring*, 138, 150, 151, 252, 277, 294, 438, 507, 574; *Ariadne auf Naxos*, 150; *Così fan tutte*, 150; *Dido and Aeneas*, 151; *Don Giovanni*, 177; *Idomeneo*, 355; *Macbeth*, 151; *A Midsummer Night's Dream*, 151; *Le nozze di Figaro*, 148, 150, 329, 627–8; *Orfeo ed Euridice*, 266, 273, 277; *The Rake's Progress*, 355; *The Rape of Lucretia*, 134, 137, 144, 150–51, 160, 193, 206, 208, 212–17, 238, 242–3, 253, 263, 276–7, 431, 574
Glyndebourne Productions Ltd, 170
Gobbi, Tito, 47
Goberman, Max, 84, <u>87</u>
'God rest ye merry, Gentlemen', 345
Goddard, Scott, 292, 303, 320, 528
Godfrey, Paul: *Once in a While the Odd Thing Happens*, 7
Goehr, Alexander, 486, 487; *and see* IOC
Goehr, Walter, 96, 98, 124, 134, 143, 260, 345
Goethe, Johann Wolfgang von: 'Kennst du das Land?', 612
Goldbeck, Celine, 309, 386, 387
Goldbeck, Frederick, 309–10, 387; *The Perfect Conductor*, 309
Goldberg, Albert, 621–2, <u>622</u>
Goldovsky, Boris, 507
Golf Lane, Aldeburgh, 308
Goodall, Reginald, 144, <u>151</u>–2, 244, 291, 308; and *Albert Herring*, 308, 356; and *Peter Grimes*, 103, 140–41, 151, 308, 333, 335, 338, 391–2, 426; and *The Rape of Lucretia*, 138, 147, 151, 300, 303–6, 308
Goodman, Benny, 443
Goodwin, Noel, 633
Goossens, Eugene, 90, 454
Goossens, Leon, 260
Gordon (choir trainer), 616
Gordon, Eric A., 602, 609–10
Gordon, Michael, 172, 174
Gore, Spencer, 464; *The Haystacks, Richmond*, 465
Gore, Walter, 70
Gounod, Charles, 453; *and see* IOC
GPO Film Unit, 29, 56, 78, 172, 174, 446, 458, 467
Gradenwitz, Dr P., 97
Graf, Herbert, 206–8, <u>213</u>

Graham, Colin, 140, 672; *Anna Karenina* (libretto), 672

Grainger, Eileen, 339, 547

Grainger, Ella, *see* Ström, Ella Viola

Grainger, Percy, **547**, 547–8; *and see* IOC

Gramophone, 305

Gramophone Co. Ltd, *see* HMV

Granville Barker, Frank, 140

Grassina, Italy, 401

Gray, Cecil, 219–20

Great Exhibition (1851), 437

Greece, 362; tour plans, 145

Green, Andrew, 148, 454

Green, Kenneth, 100, 363, 559, 562, 568

Greenaway, Peter, 603

Greene, Eric, 381, 384

Greene, Maurice: *see* IOC

Greene, Richard, 543

Greene, Robert, 343

Greenfield, Edward, 85, 356, 486

Gregory, Dr H. A. C., 363, 364

Gregory, Horace, 319

Grenacher, Karl, 182

Grenadier Guards, 326

Grenfell, Joyce, 22, 331–2; *Joyce Grenfell Requests the Pleasure*, 331–2

Gresham's School, Holt, 54, 64

Grey House (Behrend home), 571

Grieg, Edvard, 400, 548; *and see* IOC

Grierson, John, 29, 172, 341

Griller String Quartet, 543–4

Groninger Orkestervereeniging, 260

Grotrian Hall, London, 276

Group Theatre (UK), 56, 62, 73, 76, 112, 176, 177, 413, 458; *The Agamemnon of Aeschylus*, 112; *The Ascent of F6*, 76, 362, 589; *Out of the Picture*, 112; *Trial of a Judge*, 177

Group Theatre Paper, 62

Grünewald, Matthias de: Isenheim altarpiece, 386, 387

Guardian, 6, 18, 68 49; articles, 458; obituaries, 72, 85, 87, 89, 140, 149, 177, 213, 246, 276, 337, 356, 368, 383, 392, 421, 424, 431, 457, 458, 486, 625; *see also* Manchester Guardian

Guay, André du, 332

Gucht, Jan van der, 63

Gulbenkian Trust, 30

Guthrie, Tyrone, 128, 277, 323, 328, 330, 332, 357, 362; *The Sleeping Children* (libretto), 456, 458, 560–61; 'The Theatre Today', 362; and *The Beggar's Opera*, plates 16 and 19; 128, 328, 333, 345, 350, 365, 393, 396, 397, 399–401, 516, 574; and EOG, 243; and *Peter Grimes*, 128, 325, 330, 333, 336–8, 391

Gyde, Arnold, 165

Gyde, Humphrey, 165, 166

Habington, William: 'Nox Nocti Indicat Scientiam', 118

Hadley, Patrick, 184

Haefliger, Ernst, 382, 509, 510

Haggard, Rider, 21

Hague, The, Netherlands: *A Charm of Lullabies*, 313, 343; *Les Illuminations*, 153; PP–BB recitals, 137, 368, 499, 516; *The Rape of Lucretia*, 147

Hague, Robert A., 379–80

Halban, Desi, 254

Hall, Peter, 604

Hallam, Percy, 630

Hallam Street, No. 67, London w1, 57

Hallé Orchestra, 347, 554, 616–17, 642

Haltrecht, Montague 290, 438

Hambleton, Wilfred, 368

Hamburg, Germany, 181, 182, 320, 411, 419, 50

Hamburg: Staatsoper, 624; *The Beggar's Opera*, 624; *Peter Grimes*, 138, 268, 270

Hamburg Symphony Orchestra, 412

Hamilton, G. Restrevor, 280

Hamilton, Iain, 550

Hamilton, Jean, *see* Redcliffe-Maud, Jean

Hamilton IV, George, 665

Hampton, Colin, 544

Hampstead Conservatoire of Music, 568

Handel, George Frideric, 235, 393, 454, 484, 543; *and see* IOC

Handford, Basil, 300

Hanover, Germany, 270

Hanover Opera: *Albert Herring*, 624

Hapke, Walter, 624

Hardie, Revd (Lowestoft), 192, 193

Hardie family, 192, 193

Harding, James, 330

Hardy, Alistair, 38–40, 42–3, 45–6, 51

Hardy, George, 36–42, 44–6

Hardy, Mrs George, 38–41, 46, 51

Hardy, Thomas, 558; *Collected Poems*, 558

Harewood, George Lascelles, 7th Earl of, *plate 29*; 88, 147, 189, 339, 474, 475, 508, 522, 533, 534, 541–2, 544, 546–7, 552, 553, 562, 568, 585, 588, 614, 620–21, 623–4, 638, 640, 664, 674, 676, 680–81; *The Tongs and the Bones*, 475; and Aldeburgh Festival, 36; and Edinburgh Festival, 246, 475; and *Opera*, 623–4

Harewood, Marion, *see* Thorpe, Marion

Harewood House, 553, 585, 615, 630, 638, 640

Harley Place, London, 186

Harold Holt Ltd, 563

Harper, Mr (Music Teachers' Association), 306

Harris, Dale, 89

Harris, Paul, 597

Harris, Robert, 123

Harrison, Kenneth, 410, 604–5, 634, 643–4, 657–8, 663

Harry Ransom Humanities Research Center, Austin, Texas, *see* Humanities Research Center, Texas

Hartford, US: *The Duchess of Malfi*, 229

Hartogs, Eduard, 193

Harvard University, 85, 255

Harvey (friend of Isherwood), 91, 93

Harvey, Trevor, 181, 182, 184, 454

Harvey's of Bristol, 509

Hasketon, Suffolk, 417

Hauser, Frank, 383

Haverford, Pennsylvania, 92, 93

Hawkes, Clare, 145, 154, 199, 225, 230, 259, 324, 374, 417, 440, 443, 448, 480, 499, 500, 514, 588, 606

Hawkes, Ralph, 82, 83, 84, 97, 144–6, 147, 153, 154, 198–9, 200, 203, 206–9, 225–9, 230–31, 234, 253–4, 258–9, 260–61, 278, 290, 324–5, 326, 327, 351, 369, 373–4, 375–6, 380, 417, 418, 420, 424, 434, 439–40, 441–3, 479–80, 499–502, 513–14, 575–6, 606–7, 607; and *Billy Budd*, 501, 534, 546, 565, 588, 590; death, 550; and Decca, 452–3; and EOG, 243, 501, 549; health, 515–16, 550; and *The Rape of Lucretia*, 455, 476, 478; social events, 448, 551; and *Spring Symphony*, 511; and Stravinsky, 676; and Tanglewood, 489, 511;

US tour management, 447, 502

Haydn, Joseph, 150, 323, 400; *and see* IOC

Hayes, Malcolm, 201

Hayman, Ronald, 230

Hays, H. R., 228

Hayward, Anthony, 431

Hazel (Amsterdam friend), 508

Hazelhurst, Marjorie, 76

Headington, Christopher, 5, 191, 272, 335, 337, 411–12; *and see* IOC

Heard, Gerald, 558

Hearn, Mrs (housekeeper), 79, 81

Heawood, John, 332

Heifetz, Jascha, 621, 622

Heine, Heinrich, 123

Heinsheimer, Hans, 194, 195, 196, 208, 226, 227

Heinson, Mrs, 193

Helensburgh: PP–BB recital, 577

Helpmann, Robert, 203

Hely-Hutchinson, Victor, 142, 154, 155, 158, 236

Hemmings, David, 24–8

Henderson, Roy, 144, 148, 428, 431

Henneberg, Claus, 666

Henry VIII, King, 544

Henry Wood Promenade Concerts, *see* BBC Promenade Concerts

Henze, Hans Werner, 319

Hepworth, Barbara, 176

Herald Tribune, 610

Herbage, Julian, 700

Herbert, A. P. (Alan Patrick), 331; *Tantivy Towers*, 47

Herbert, George, 104, 122; *The Works of George Herbert*, 122

Herlitschka, Herberth E., 186

Hermes, Annie, 386, 387, 662

Herrick, Robert, 456, 527; 'The Nightpiece: To Julia', 118; 'Welcome, maids of honour', 456, 527–8, 617

Hess, Dame Myra, 304

Hesse, Prince Ludwig of, 88

Hewit, Jackie, 78

Heyworth, Peter, 153, 382

'H.H.H.' (critic), 399

Highcock, John, 428, 431

Hill, David, 171

Hill, Rose, *plate 20*; 393, 399, 401, 428, 431, 434, 456, 652

Hilversum, Netherlands (radio station), 344, 416–19, 433, 460, 499, 661

Hilversum Radio Philharmonic Orchestra, 416, 460

Hindemith, Paul, 186, 219, 270, 409, 472, 485; *see also* IOC

Hines, Jerome, 380

Hirondelles, Les, Leysin, Switzerland, 570

Hiroshima, Japan, 155

Hitler, Adolf, 202

HMV (record company), 324, 326, 346, 425–6

Hockey, Rhoda (BB's grandmother), 595

Hockey, William (BB's uncle), 595

Hockney, David, 68

Hofmannsthal, Hugo von, 590

Hogarth, William, 401, 676; *The Rake's Progress*, 675

Hogg, Julian, 667

Holland, *see* Netherlands, the

Holland, A. K., 102

Holland, Mrs A. K., 102

Holland Festival, 138, 246–7, 396–7, 489, 511, 518, 521, 523, 528, 586, 600, 621

Holloway, Robin, 10

Holroyd, Michael, 327

Holst, Gustav, 428, 430, 555, 646, 651, 656; *and see* IOC

Holst, Imogen, *plate 33*; 7, 106–7, 107, 237–8, 434–5, 436, 541, 542, 600–601, 626–7, 645–6; *The Music of Gustav Holst*, 651; *A Thematic Catalogue of Gustav Holst's Music*, 430, 651; as conductor, 600–601, 654; and *Dido and Aeneas*, 534, 627–8, 645–8; as editor and arranger, 150, 383, 429, 656; friendship with BB and PP, 106–7, 601, 645–6; as teacher, 101, 597, 653–4, 656; and *The Wandering Scholar*, 428, 651–2; *and see* IOC

Homer, 124; *The Odyssey*, 112

Homerton College, Cambridge, 183

Hommages à Paul Sacher, 487

homophobia, 7–8

Honegger, Andreas, 200

Honegger, Arthur, 149, 185, 487; *and see* IOC

Hong Kong, 470

Hong Kong Arts Festival, 563

Hook of Holland, 324

Hope-Wallace, Philip, 220, 650, 692–4

Hopkins, Antony, 128, 143, 554, 555; *Talking About Music*, 128; *and see* IOC

Hopkins, Gerard Manley: 'God's Grandeur', 359

Hopkinson, Tom, 536

Horace, 47

Horder, Mervyn, 243

Hordern, Michael, 203

Horham, *see* Chapel House, Horham

Horne, William, 210

Horsley, Colin, 319

Hour with Benjamin Britten, An (radio broadcast), 182

House Un-American Activities Committee (US Congress), 423–4

Houseman, John, 609

Howard family, 544

Howes, Frank, 140–41, 292, 399, 674, 675, 677; reviews, 218–19, 294, 319, 336–7, 397, 399, 516–18, 524, 526–7, 552–3, 591, 690–91

Howlett, R., 605

Huber, Monika, 184

Huddersfield, 344

Huddersfield Choral Society, 553

Huddersfield Music Club: PP–BB recital, 339

Hudson, Nellie, 624, 625–6, 640

Hughes, Spike, 150, 277, 329

Hughes, Ted, 51

Hull: New Theatre: *Let's Make an Opera*, 677

Humanities Research Center, Austin, Texas, 148

Humperdinck, Engelbert, 169; *and see* IOC

Hunt, Marilyn, 89

Hunter, Ian, 439, 562, 563–5, 567

Hunter College (US), 443

Hurley, Mrs (housekeeper at Oxford Square), 191

Hürlimann, Martin, 372, 460, 461; *Laudatio auf Benjamin Britten*, 461

Hürlimann-Kiepenheuer, Bettina, 372, 461; *Seven Houses: My Life with Books*, 461

Hurst, Helen, 193, 286, 442, 449, 587, 630

Hurstpierpoint College, 300, 346

Hussey, Dyneley, 142, 504, 506; reviews, 295

Hussey, Walter, 85, 100, 163, 165, 292, 388–9, 411, 412, 525–6, 595, 596–7

Hutchinson, F. E., 122

Hutton, Kurt, 537

Huxley, Aldous, 676

Hyperion (record label), 171

I am a Camera (film), 68
Iacopi, Valetta, 141, 168
Ibbs & Tillett, 385
Iken Hall, Snape, 11, 316, 317, 516
Iken Rectory, 308
Iles, Paul, 383
Imperial College of Science and Technology, 437
Incorporated Society of Musicians (ISM), 478
Independent: articles, 148, 388; obituaries, 72, 85, 87, 89, 133, 140, 148, 149, 213, 246, 328, 356, 368, 383, 421, 424, 431, 454, 457, 463, 486, 493, 604, 625
India, 356, 458, 627, 630, 645, 653
Indian Government, 174
Indiana University, 420
Information, Ministry of (MOI), 172, 173
Ingram, Michael, *see* Crawford, Michael
Ingram, Raymond, 328
Instone, Anna, 700
Instruments of the Orchestra (film), 29, <u>172–4</u>, 342
Intelligence Corps, 326
International String Quartet, 80
Ipswich, Suffolk, 40, 251, 267, 417, 456, 473, 492, 501, 514, 626, 636; chamber concert (1939), 79; *Saint Nicolas*, 630, 631
Ipswich Chamber Music Society, 80
Ipswich: Christchurch School, 346
Ireland, John, 55, 341, 342, 368, 483, 484–5; *see also* IOC
ISCM (International Society for Contemporary Music), 67, 168, 396
ISCM Festivals: Florence (1934), 56, 67, 92, 390, 401, 446; Barcelona (1936), 57, 63, 67 45; London (1938), 57, 87; New York (1941), 83, 130; London (1946), 218–19; Palermo (1949), 401
Isherwood, Christopher, *plate 32*; 54, <u>67–8</u>, 72–4, 78, **91**, 93, 362, 533, 556–8; *Goodbye to Berlin*, 68; *Lost Years*, 556–7; *Mr Norris Changes Trains*, 68; *and see* Auden, W. H.
Italy, 351, 362, 49: concert tours and plans, 138, 145, 313, 351, 354, 356, 358, 469, 470, 479; holidays, 267, 484, 489, 498, 499

J. Arthur Rank Organization, 328
Jackson, Miss (Boosey & Hawkes), 365
Jacob, Gordon, 203, 554, <u>555</u>
Jacobs, Robert L., 142
Jacques, Reginald, 320, 384, 483, 484
Jacques Orchestra, 320, 384, 484
Jacques String Orchestra, 433
Jaffe, Rhoda, 211
Jagel, Frederick, 375, 377, 379, 380
Jamaica, 193
James, George, 393, 397, 399, 428, <u>430</u>, 434
James, Henry: *Owen Wingrave*, 35; *The Turn of the Screw*, 26
Janáček, Leoš, 457; *and see* IOC
Japan, 608, 672; and *Sinfonia da Requiem*, 86, 211
Jenkins, David Fraser, 46
Jenkins, Nicholas, 72
Joad, C. E. M., 174
John, Augustus, 70
Johns, Margaret, 366, 514, 520
Johnson, Blue, 458
Johnson, Brian, 453
Johnson, Edward, 325, <u>329</u>
Johnson, Graham, 171, 359
Johnson, Liz, 561
Jonathan Cape (publishing house), 672
Jones, Brad, 633

Jones, Geraint, 260, 433
Jones, Gwynn, 409
Jones, Inigo, 203
Jones, Robert, 579–80; *and see* IOC
Jones, Roderick, 430
Jonson, Ben: 'Hymn to Diana', 118
Jordaens (conductor), 661–2
Joyce, Eileen, 248
Jubilee Hall, Aldeburgh, *see* Aldeburgh: Jubilee Hall
Juilliard School, New York 579
Juliana of the Netherlands, Queen, 621
June, Ava, 140

Kainer, Ludwig, 188
Kallman, Chester, 230, 675; *and see* Auden, W. H.
Karlsruhe: Staatstheater, 187
Kasander, J., 47
Kastendieck (music critic), 49
Katchen, Julius, 204
Kauffman-Meyer, Barbara, 193
Kauffman-Meyer, Bethley, 192–3, 286
Kauffman-Meyer, Hansi ['Flansi'], 192–3
Kavanagh, Julie, 294, 507
Keats, John, 108, 627; 'Sonnet to Sleep', 118
Keele University, 343
Keining, Henk, 621
Keller, Hans, 117, 624, 660, <u>665–7</u>; *1975 (1984 minus 9)*, 667; *Criticism*, 667; *Essays on Music*, 667; *Music and Psychology*, 667; and 'Functional Analysis', 666–7; and *Music Survey*, 121, 643
Kemp, Ian, 414
Kempers, K. Ph. Bernet, 510
Kennedy, Jack, 88
Kennedy, John Fitzgerald, 85
Kennedy, Michael, 5, 236, 347, 439, 565
Kent, University of, 668
Kenyon, Nicholas, 368
Kermode, Frank, 72
Khrennikov, Tikhan Nikolayevich, <u>472–3</u>
Kildea, Paul, 214, 284, 435
Kilmarnock: PP–BB recital, 577
Kilvert, Francis, 672
Kimble, Mr (teacher), 28
King's College, London, 668
Kingsland Central School, Dalston, 690
Kingsley, Charles, <u>467</u>; *The Water Babies*, 467
Kingsway Hall, London, 33
Kirkley Cliff Road, No. 21, Lowestoft, 20, 193
Kirsch, Arthur, 269
Kirsta, George, 96
Kirstein, Lincoln, 85, <u>88–9</u>, 259, 260–61, 606–7
Kleiber, Erich, 635, <u>636–7</u>, 640
Klemperer, Otto, 284
Kletzki, Paul, 642
Knaben Wunderhorn, Des, 461
Knollys, Eardley, <u>133</u>, 134, 457
Knussen, Oliver, 319, 667
Kobbé's Complete Opera Book, 475
Kolodin, Irving, 329; reviews, 210, 212, 378–9
Korda, Alexander, 174
Koster, Ré, 387
Koussevitzky, Natalie, 103
Koussevitzky, Serge, *plate 26*; 85, 87, 100, <u>101</u>, 103, 137, **206–7**, 208, 210, 211, 227, **279**, 280, 309, 325, 374, **465**, 479–80, 511, **580**; and *Spring Symphony*, 237, 299, 325, 440, 479, 500, 511, 521, 525, 526, 533, 535, 536, 580, 606
Koussevitzky Music Foundation, 58, 237, 347, 610
Kraft, Victor, 225, 227, 230, 443

Krannhals, Alexander, 185, _187_, 199
Kraus, Otakar (Otto), *plate 8*; 218, 222, 231, _235_, 244, 366, 369, 393, 399, 401, 414, 434, 674, 675
Krauss, Clemens, 534, 663
Kraut, Harry, 86
Krenek, Ernst, 472; *and see* IOC
Krips, Josef, 659, _660_, 698
Kubelik, Rafael, 250

'L.H.' (critic), 248
Labour Party, 424
Lago, Mary, 363, 584, 585, 618
Lalande, Roger, 392, 624
Laloir, Edmond, 464
Lamb, Henry, 562, 567–8
Lambert, Constant, 70, 148, 199, _200_, 203; *and see* IOC
Lancaster, Osbert, 540, 677
Lancing College, 140, 299, 300–301, 314, 337, 346, 351, 412, 452, 457, 459, 468, 471–2, 570, 573, 669
Lancing College Magazine, 62, 472
Landon, H. C. Robbins, 668
Landowska, Wanda, 12
Lane, Margaret: *The Tale of Beatrix Potter*, 678–9
Langley, Mark, 171
Lascelles, David, 620, _621_, 623, 629, 635, 640
Latham, Sir Paul, 116
Latham, Stuart, 589
Laurie, Marjorie, 248
Lausanne, 464: *Serenade*, 464
Lausanne: Théâtre Municipal, 464
Lavenham, Suffolk, 586
Lawrence, T. B., 96, 98
Lawrence, Peter, 610
Lawrie, James, 327, 569, _571_, 573, 575–6, 615, 631, 635
Lawson, Catherine, *plate 6*, 141, 347
LCC (London County Council), 463, 551, 553, 638–9, 690
League of Composers (US), 555
League of Nations, 372
Leaska, Mitchell: *Granite and Rainbow: The hidden life of Virginia Woolf*, 30
Lebrecht, Norman, 8, 284, 290, 391
Lee, Gypsy Rose, 86
Leech, Dick, 373
Leeds Festival Choir, 551
Leeds Festival Chorus, 553, 614, 616–17
Leeds Triennial Music Festival, 475, 553, 600, 613–15
Lees-Milne, James, 113
Leeuwarden, Netherlands: PP–BB recital (1946), 255
LeFanu, Nicola, 605; *and see* IOC
Lefebure, Yvonne, 309
Left Theatre, 67, 68, 69
Legge, Walter, 149, 182
LeGrove, Judith, 319
Lehár, Ferencz: *see* IOC
Lehigh University, Pennsylvania, 555
Lehmann, John, 543
Lehmann, Liza, 364; *and see* IOC
Leicester Galleries, London, 180, 402, 568
Leiden, Netherlands: PP–BB recital, 358
Lenchner, Paula, 379
Leonard, Maurice, 277
Leoncavallo, Ruggero: *see* IOC
Leppard, Raymond, 237
Lewis, Richard, 300, 333, 354, _355–6_, 390–91, 574
Leyden Orchestra, 415
Liberal Party (UK), 189
Lier, Bertus van, 382, 384, _460_, 509, 561, 661; *and see* IOC

Lindemann, Dora, 387
Lindo, Olga, 143
Lindsay, John, 170, 342, 421–3, 442, _443–5_, 449
Lipton, Martha, 379, 380
Lisle, Lucille, 143
Listener, 69, 71, 504; articles, 142, 362; reviews, 142, 525–6, 700
Lister, Laurie, 331
Liszt, Franz, 169; *and see* IOC
Little Orchestra Society (US), 554
Liverpool, 148, 150, 290; EOG tour, 680; *Façade*, 680; *Let's Make an Opera*, 642, 660; *Young Person's Guide*, 138
Liverpool Daily Post, 102
Liverpool: Old Vic Theatre, 328
Liverpool Philharmonic Orchestra, 329, 487
Liverpool Philharmonic Society, 290
Liverpool: Royal Court Theatre: *The Rape of Lucretia*, 137, 147
Liverpool University, 498
Living Spirit of France, The (radio feature), 124
Livy, 217
Lloyd, David, 507
Lloyd, Roderick, 141
London Bach Choir, 484
London Choir School, 433
London County Council, *see* LCC
London Films, 174
London Harpsichord Ensemble, 496, 630
London Library, 330
London Magazine, 68
London Opera Centre, 627
London Opera Players, 574
London Philharmonic Choir, 552
London Philharmonic Orchestra (LPO), 80, 103, 161, 190, 208, 510, 552, 581, 596, 639
London Schools' Music Association, 552
London Sinfonietta, 412
London String Quartet, 550
London Symphony Orchestra, 161, 172, 174, 204, 345, 348, 435, 454, 660
London University, 383
London venues, *see* individual theatres
Long, Robin, 674, _675_
Long Crichel House, Wimborne, 133–4, 240, 303, 457
Long Island, 90, 117
Long Island Home, Amityville, 82
Longmire, John, 700
Lopokova, Lydia, 70
Loppert, Max, 191
Los Angeles, US, 147, 502, 557, 558, 622; *Albert Herring*, 556; Purcell–BB concert (*c* BB), 440–42; *Peter Grimes*, 376; *The Rape of Lucretia*, 676; *Saint Nicolas*, 556
Los Angeles, Victoria de, 614
Los Angeles Philharmonic Orchestra, 510
Los Angeles Times, 622
Louden Avenue, No. 123, Amityville, 91, 92
Louisville Philharmonic Society, 500, 502
Love from a Stranger (film), 343
Love is the Devil (film), 6
Low, Rachel, 468
Lowe, John, 181, _183–4_, 551, 553, **662**, 663
Lowell, Robert, 679; *Phaedra: Racine's Phèdre*, 679
Lowestoft, 25, 192, 193, 267, 385, 442, 449–50, 472, 655; fish market, 449–50; Freedom of, 612–13; *Let's Make an Opera*, 641
Lowestoft Public Library, 407, 410, 450, 451;

Benjamin Britten Collection, 450
Lowestoft Choral Society, 56
Lowestoft Musical Society, 308
Lowestoft: Sparrow's Nest Theatre, 467
Lowry, L. S., 465
Luc, Jean-Bernard, 356
Lucas, John, 153, 291, 304, 308, 392, 427
Lucas, Leighton, 50
Lucerne, Switzerland, 187, 188, 305–6, 317, 324
Lucerne: Stadt-Theater, 306: *Albert Herring*, 138;
    The Rape of Lucretia, 138, 308; Berkeley: *Stabat
    Mater*, 138
Lucerne International Music Festival, 251, 306, 324
Lugano, Switzerland, 182
Lumsden, Norman, *plates 13, 39 and 40*; 303, 540
Lush, Ernest, 418
Lutoslawski, Witold, 319
Lutyens, Elisabeth, 486, 642
Lyke-Wake Dirge, 118, 229–30
Lyon, Alan, 49
Lyon, James K., 230
Lyric Theatre, Hammersmith, 170, 383, 396–7, 519:
    Albert Herring, 641; *Il combattimento di
    Tancredi e Clorinda*, 641, 648, 649; *Dido and
    Aeneas*, 596, 641, 648, 649, 650–51; *Let's Make an
    Opera*, 546, 550, 554, 629, 637, 641, 677; *The Rape
    of Lucretia*, 641, 659
Lyttelton, Oliver, 243, <u>284</u>
Lywen, Werner, 254

Maastricht, Netherlands: PP–BB recital, 254
McBean, Angus, 180
MacCann, Mercy, 122
McCarthy, Joseph, 424
McCullers, Carson, 86
McDonald, Jim, 149
MacDonald, Kevin, 458
Macfarren, George, 648
McKechnie, James, 25
Mackerras, Charles, 27
McNaught, William, 294–5, 297–8
Macnaghten, Anne, 80
Macnaghten–Lemare concerts, 56, 80, 475
MacNeice, Hedli, *see* Anderson, Hedli
MacNeice, Louis, 72, 75, 86, 98, <u>112</u>, 122, 134, 616;
    The Agamemnon of Aeschylus (translation), 62,
    112; *Collected Poems*, 122; *The Dark Tower*, 72,
    112, 134, 137, 143; 'The nearness of remoteness
    like a lion's eye', 122; *Out of the Picture*, 112; *The
    Revenant*, 122; 'Sleep, my darling, sleep', 112, 122
McPhee, Colin, 85, <u>88</u>, 276
MacWatters, Virginia, 47
Madama Butterfly (film), 328
Madras, 200, 457
Madrid: British Embassy, 23
Maggio Musicale (Florence, 1947), 268
Mahler, Gustav, 3, 47, 63, 76, 97, 116, 117, 120–21,
    276, 320–21, 329, 338, 486, 510, 597, 636, 664, 668;
    see also IOC
Maine, US, 226
Major Barbara (film), 328
Makerere University College, Kampala, 200
Malcolm, George, 348, 389, 596, 648
Malta, 470, 471
Maltings, Snape, 316
Manchester, 46, 50
Manchester Guardian, 632; letter to the editor,
    222–3; reviews, 220, 294, 335–6, 650, 692–4; *see
    also Guardian*

Manchester: King's Hall, Bellevue: *Spring
    Symphony*, 617
Manchester Opera House, 46: *The Rape of
    Lucretia* (1946), 137, 147, 206, 207, 223, 227
Mangan, Richard, 603, 604, 608
Mangeot, André, 79, <u>80</u>, 669
Manheim, Ralph, 230
Mann, Erika, 86
Mann, Golo, 34, 86
Mann, Katia, 34
Mann, Klaus, 86
Mann, Thomas, 372: *Death in Venice*, 6, 32, 34;
    Dr Faustus, 34
Mann, William, 117, 230, 650
Manning, Florence, 210
Manon Lescaut (film), 328
Marc (friend of Lennox Berkeley), 79
Markova, Alicia, 70
Marrakesh, 327
Marriner, Neville, 339
Martin, Christopher, 128, 601
Martin, Cicely, 128
Martin, David, 339
Martin, Frank, 370, 387, 487; *and see* IOC
Martinez, José, 91, 93
Martinů, Bohuslav, 487
Marx, Chico, 211
Marx, Karl, 504
Marx Brothers, 230, 458
Mary, Queen, 475
Masefield, John, 616
Massenet, Jules, 169; *and see* IOC
Mathieson, Muir, 172, 342
Matterhorn, Switzerland, 271, 279, 285
Matthews, Colin, 543, 667
Matthews, David, 626, 667
Matthews, Michael Gough, 493
Maud, Humphrey, *plate 23*; 11–12, 19–23, 25, 28–9,
    51, 271, 300, 315, 341, 410, <u>448</u>
Maud, Jean, *see* Redcliffe-Maud, Jean
Maud, John, *see* Redcliffe-Maud, John
Maupassant, Guy de, 248, 294; *Le Rosier de
    Madame Husson*, 248–9, 249
Maw, Nicholas, 486, 667
Maxwell-Fyfe, Sir David, 603
May and Baker (M. & B.), 674, 676
Maybury, John, 6
Mayer, Beata, 226, 254, 417, 641
Mayer, Christopher, 226, 254, 258, 478
Mayer, Elizabeth, <u>82</u>, 105, 119, 146, 207, 208, <u>225–6</u>,
    228–30, 234, 236, 252, <u>253–4</u>, <u>267–8</u>, 270, 294,
    357–8, 364, 416–18, 420, 442, 450, 455, 459, 476,
    480, 489–90, 501, 554, <u>639–41</u>, 642, <u>652</u>, 665; and
    The Rape of Lucretia, 200, 227–8, 231, 253–5, 478
Mayer, Michael, 226, 254, 478
Mayer, William, <u>82</u>, 88, 225, 226, 230, 254, 267–8,
    357, 417, 420, 443, 459, 478, 489, 640–41
Mayer family, 57, 117, 191, 453
Mead, Kathleen, 61
Meadow Players, 383
Medley, Robert, 73
Meili, Max, 339, 340, 341, <u>342</u>
Melbourne Conservatory, 161
Melbury Road, No. 22, London w14, 357, 364, 454,
    479
Melville, Herman: *Billy Budd, Foretopman*, 362,
    407, 411, 429, 480, 500, 536, 637, 682, 683, 686–7,
    690–91, 693, 695–7, 700
Mendelson, Edward, 72, 230, 270

Mendelssohn, Felix: *see* IOC
Mengelberg, Rudolf, 347
Mengelberg, Willem, 87, 347, 387, 510
Menotti, Gian Carlo, 472, 654; *and see* IOC
Menuhin, Yehudi, 50–51, 58, 106, 183
Menzies, Angus, 332
Mercer, David, 603
Mercer, R., 329
Mercury & Pilgrim Players, 170
Mercury Players, 589
Mercury Theatre, Notting Hill Gate, 171, 331, 589
Merrick, Frank, 443
Merritt, Kathleen, 429–30
Mertz, Margaret, 140, 255
Messiaen, Olivier, 472
Metropolitan Opera, New York (the 'Met'), 46, 47, 48, 49
Metropolitan Opera Orchestra, 48
Metzelaar, Helen, 415
Mewton-Wood, Dulcie, 162
Mewton-Wood, Noel, 155, 158, 161–2, 359, 628–9; memorial concert, 162; *and see* IOC
Mexico, 87
Meyerbeer, Giacomo, 220
Meyerstein, E. H. W., 642, 643
Michelangelo Buonarroti , 120
Middagh Street, No. 7, New York, 58, 85, 86, 87
Midgeley, Walter, 624
Midland Theatre Company, 540
Milan, Italy, 235, 264, 370, 489: PP–BB recitals, 268, 356, 516
Mildmay, Audrey, 151, 152, 232, 243, 245, 246, 614
Milhaud, Darius, 446; *and see* IOC
Mille, Agnes de, 477–8
Milnegavie: PP–BB recital, 577
Milnes, Rodney, 276
Milton, John, 48; 'The Morning Star', 48
Milville (Basel cantonal representative), 46
Ministry of Education, *see* Education, Ministry of
Ministry of Information (MOI), *see* Information, Ministry of
Minton, John, 465
Mitchell, Donald, 54, 332, 643, 667–8, 676; *Benjamin Britten: A Commentary on His Works from a Group of Specialists* (DMHK), 117, 665; *Benjamin Britten: Pictures from a Life*, 667; *Britten and Auden in the Thirties: the Year 1936*, 667; *Death in Venice* handbook, 667; *Gustav Mahler: The Early Years*, 667; *Gustav Mahler: Songs and Symphonies of Life and Death*, 668; *Gustav Mahler: The Wunderhorn Years*, 667; *The Language of Modern Music*, 667; *The Mozart Companion*, 668; on BB, 76, 85, 169–70, 255–6, 320–21, 326, 445, 450, 608, 665; and Boosey & Hawkes, 326; as conductor, 28; conversations and interviews, 34, 36, 39, 46, 90, 182–3, 248–9, 443–4, 472, 516, 622; as executor, 424; and *Music Survey*, 643, 666–7; obituaries by, 18–19, 213, 424; references, 72, 252, 269, 350, 548; and *Voices for Today*, 672
Mitchell, Kathleen, 38, 668
Moeran, E. J. (Ernest John), 364, 366, 368, 458, 483; *and see* IOC
Moiseiwitsch, Benno, 328
Moiseiwitsch, Tanya, *plate 17*; 325, 328, 333, 350, 363, 393, 399, 401
Momento, Il (Rome), 493–5
Monet, Claude, 465
Money Programme, The (BBC documentary), 13

Monk, Ray, 18, 19
Monsieur Vincent (film), 354, 356
Mont Juic Festival, 63
Montagu-Nathan, Montagu, 70
Montagu-Pollock, W. H., 304
Monteverdi, Claudio, 342, 630, 653–4; *and see* IOC
Montgomery, Field Marshal Viscount, 522, 523, 525
Monthly Musical Record, 63, 305, 338
Montreux, 50
Moore, Gerald, 51, 98, 613, 614; *Am I Too Loud?*, 614; *Farewell Recital*, 614; *The Unashamed Accompanist*, 614
Moore, Henry, 176, 591, 602
Moot Hall, Aldeburgh, *see* Aldeburgh: Moot Hall
Mörike, Eduard, 357, 358; *Mozart on the Way to Prague*, 357, 358
Morley, Thomas: *see* IOC
Morley College, London, 260, 428, 433
Morocco, 327, 579
Morris, R. O., 548; *and see* IOC
Morris, Stuart, 444
Morrison, Angus, 12
Morrison, Herbert, 542
Mortimer, Raymond, 124, 133, 134, 457
Moszkowski, Moritz, 484
Motion, Andrew, 203
Moules, John, *plate 40*
Mozart, Wolfgang Amadeus, 3, 47, 76, 97, 114, 148, 149, 150, 151, 158, 169, 190, 235, 400, 448, 452, 454, 484, 560, 586, 613, 636, 692, 695; *and see* IOC
Mucci (translator), 551
Mudie, Michael, 153
Muffat, Georg, 278
Mulhouse, 187, 624: *The Rape of Lucretia*, 624
Mullan, Elizabeth, 519
Mullinar, Michael, 76
Mullins, Frank, 336
Münch, Charles, 144, 145, 153–4, 306, 309, 310
Mundy, Clytie, 207–8, 227, 417, 418, 420, 424, 442, 450, 455, 476, 501
Mundy, John, 417, 418
Mundy, John (jnr), 417
Mundy, Meg, 41, 417, 418, 420
Mundy, Simon, 388
Munich Hochschule für Musik, 189
Murrill, Herbert, 339, 340, 413
Murray, John, III, 288
Murray, Maureen, 201
Murray Guides, 288
Music and Musicians, 667
Music in Miniature (BBC radio series), 260, 454
Music Survey, 121, 280, 519, 582, 643, 666–7, 675, 692
Music Teachers' Association Assembly, 310
Musica Antiqua, 382
Musical Antiquarian Society, 648
Musical Times, 297–8
Musorgsky, Modest, 210, 212; *and see* IOC

Nabokov, Nicolas, 556
Nagasaki, Japan, 155
Nancy, France, 306
Naples, Italy: PP–BB recital, 268, *281*
Nash, John, 363
Nashe, Thomas, 442, 456, 527, 543–4; 'Spring', 442, 456, 526, 527
National Council for Social Service, 372
National Film Corporation, 571

National Gallery, London, 96, 98, 601
National Opera School, 276, 354–5, 627–8
National Portrait Gallery, 568
National School of Opera, 571
National Service, 23, 101, 411, 444
National Sound Archive (British Library), 147, 521
National Symphony Orchestra, 174
National Theatre, London (later Royal National Theatre), 284; Cottesloe Theatre, 7; Lyttelton Theatre, 284; Studio, 7
National Trust, 133
National Union of Townswomen's Guilds, 428–30, 513, 521
National Youth Orchestra, 11
National-Zeitung (Basel), 186–7
Nazi regime, 235, 246, 270, 329, 387, 448, 636, 665
NBC Orchestra, 550
Neel, Boyd, 83, 341, <u>343</u>, 585–6, **669**; *see also* Boyd Neel Orchestra
Neher, Caspar, 562, <u>568</u>
Netherlands, the, 352–3, 356, 552; concerts and recitals, 138, 226, 228, 236, 246–7, 258, 267, 273, 309, 313, 341, 351, 357, 382–4, 414, 464, 467, 468, 473, 525, 577, 587, 589, 621–2, 640; EOG tours, 305, 317, 640, 646; *The Rape of Lucretia* (1946 tour), 138, 228; tour plans, 145, 357
Netherlands Opera (Nederlands Oper), 246, 247, 387
Netherlands Radio Chorus, *see* Dutch Radio Chorus
Nettleship, Ethel, 418
Nettleship, Ursula, 63, 140, 359, <u>418</u>, 419, 433, 473
Neudegg, Egon, 188
Neue Zürcher Zeitung und Schweizerisches Handelsblatt, 197–8, 326
Nevern Square, No. 43, London sw5, 57, 72, 390
Neville-Smith, Esther, 139, 140, 300–301, 452, 471–2, 555, 679
Neville-Smith, H. A. N., 140
New College, Oxford, 87
New English Singers, 384
New Grove Dictionary of Music and Musicians, 387
New Grove Dictionary of Opera, 491
New Haven, US: *The Duchess of Malfi*, 229; *Let's Make an Opera*, 609
New London Orchestra, 346
New Queen's Hall Orchestra, 435
New Republic, 477–8
New Statesman and Nation, 112, 113, 133, 457, 475, 699; reviews, 141, 220–21, 298, 301–2, 400–401, 517–18, 527–8, 591, 594, 650, 682–3, 686–7
New Symphony Orchestra, 454
New York, US, 57, 100, 207, 227, 407, 440, 441, 452, 459, 548–9, 551, 554–6, 578, 628–9, 679; BB residency, 84; and Boosey & Hawkes, 144, 195; fund-raising trip, 12; and ISCM Festival (1941), 83, 130; tour plans, 145, 441; and Violin Concerto, 58, 84
New York: Broadway, 210–11, 418, 441, 448, 478, 480, 537
New York: Carnegie Hall, 655: *Four Sea Interludes* and *Passacaglia from 'Peter Grimes'*, 211–12; *Sinfonia da Requiem*, 86
New York City Ballet, 88, 602
New York City Opera, 391, 478
New York: Ethel Barrymore Theatre: *The Duchess of Malfi*, 229
New York: Hekscher Theatre, 46, 261
New York Herald Tribune, 377–8, 692

New York: Hotel Windsor, 49
New York: John Golden Theatre: *Let's Make an Opera*, 50, 609–10, 628–9, 641
New York: Mecca Auditorium, 435
New York Metropolitan Opera ('Met'), 150, 187, 211, 213, 329, 391, 448, 478, 563: *Death in Venice*, 88; *Peter Grimes*, 261, 314, 325, 372, 375–8, 455
New York Metropolitan Opera Orchestra, 418
New York Philharmonic Orchestra, 84, 85, 86, 440, 448
New York Public Library, 441
New York Scola Cantorum, 87
New York Sun: reviews, 210, 212, 378–9
New York Symphony Orchestra, 435
New York Times, 84, 229, 376, 478–9; reviews, 209–10, 212, 219, 295, 477, 524–5, 535–6, 692, 692
New York: Town Hall: PP–BB performances, 545, 546, 548, 554
New York World-Telegram: reviews, 211–12, 378
New York: Ziegfeld Theatre, 477: *The Rape of Lucretia*, 476–8
Newcastle upon Tyne; EOG tour, 303, 306
Newman, Mr (Boosey & Hawkes), 282
Newman, Ernest, 142, 214–16, 296–7, 457, 696, 701
News Chronicle, 292, 320, 528
Nichol, Aimy, 417
Nicholls, C. S., 46
Nichols, Norah, 419, 423, 442, 449
Nichols, Sir Philip, 522
Nichols, Robert, 276, 423; 'When within my arms I hold you', 276
Nicholson, Ben, 176, 50
Nicholson, John, 509, <u>510</u>, 612–13
Nicholson, Patricia, 612, <u>613</u>
Nicholson, Sheila, 332
Nicolas, St, 300
Nicolson, Vita, *see* Sackville-West, Vita
Nielsen, Flora, 222, 244, 303, 393, 397, 399, 401, 596, 651
Nineteenth Century and After, The, 67
'Nipper', *see* Long, Robin
Nixa (record label), 348
Nō Theatre, 672
Nobel, Felix de, 343
Nobel Prize for Literature, 339
Nolan, Sidney, 38
Nono, Luigi, 412
Nore Mutiny (1797), 637–8, 683
Norfolk, 366, 368
Norfolk Broads, 321, 322, 410, 470
Norfolk and Norwich Triennial Festival (1936): *Our Hunting Fathers*, 57, 62, 66
North German Radio Symphony Orchestra, 624
Northampton, *see* St Matthew's, Northampton
Northcott, Bayan, 556
Northgatean Singers, 626, 627
North-West German Radio Symphony Orchestra, 182
Norton, Elliott, 610
Norville, Hubert, 391
Norway, 448, 538
Norwich, 66, 368, 669
Norwich String Quartet, 80, 670
Nottingham Oriana Choir, 148
Novak, Joseph, 379
Novello, Vincent, 563, <u>569</u>
Novotná, Jarmila, 447, <u>448</u>
Nuremberg rallies, 9

Obey, André, 194, 195, 196–7, 220; *Loire*, 195; *Le Viol de Lucrèce*, 195, 215, 217
Observer, 68, 113, 219–20; obituaries, 368; reviews, 296, 301, 400, 695–6
O'Connor, Patrick, 457
Offenbach, Jacques: *see* IOC
Old Mill, Snape, 30, 57, 64, 71–3, 80–81, 87, 106, 111, 133, 138, 144, 166, 193, 228, 239, 259, 288–9, 305, 308, 324, 352, 357, 359, 372, 419, 470, 625
Old Vic Theatre, London, 73, 328, 332
Oldham, Arthur, *plates 31 and 33*; 149, 170–71, 342, 366, 368, 410, 419–20, 421–3, 442, 443, 449, 540, 554, 578, 579, 595, 597, 606–7, 675, 677; *Living With Voices*, 421, 423, 607; *and see* IOC
Oliver, Michael, 5
Olivier, Laurence, 141, 345, 603
Olof, Theo, 345, 346–7
Opera, 475, 623–4; EOG 1951 London season issue, 623–4; obituaries, 140, 213, 276, 356, 392, 431; reviews, 650–51, 681; Verdi anniversary issue, 623–5
'Opera as a Profession' (course), 245
Opera News (US), 380
Opera Quarterly, 149
Opera Studio, *see* National Opera School
Oppenheim, Hans, *plate 18*; 147, 152–3, 292, 294
Orchestre de la Suisse Romande, 188, 464
Orff, Carl, 189
Orford Parish Church, Suffolk, 435, 486
Ormandy, Eugène, 93
Orr, Robin: *see* IOC
Osborn, Franz, 101, 443
Osborne, John: *Look Back in Anger*, 643
Oslo: *Albert Herring*, 538; *Let's Make an Opera*, 623; *The Rape of Lucretia*, 538
Otley, Suffolk, 228
Ottawa: PP–BB concert, 548
Owen, Wilfred, 10, 48; 'The Parable of the Old Man and the Young', 10
Owl's Head Inn, Maine, 230
Oxfam, 163
Oxford, 23, 333, 397; EOG tour, 303
Oxford, Lady, 70
Oxford Book of English Verse, 118
Oxford Book of Medieval Latin Verse, The, 280–81
Oxford: New Theatre: *The Rape of Lucretia*, 137, 147
Oxford Playhouse, 383
Oxford: St Catharine's College, 383
Oxford Square, No. 3, London w2, 137, 140, 191, 226, 231, 238, 239, 245–6, 250, 286, 289, 305, 337, 352–3, 354, 357, 424, 444, 452, 459, 476
Oxford University, 304, 463, 485, 643; Extramural Studies Department, 337; past students, 64, 72, 75, 326
Oxford University Musical Society, 12
Oxford University Opera Society, 413
Oxford University Press, 628, 669
Oxford: Worcester College, 413

'P.T.' (Piet Tiggers), 248
Padua, Italy, 484, 488
Palermo, Italy: ISCM Festival (1949), 401
Palm Springs, California, 557
Palmer, Samuel, 402–3; *Sleeping Shepherd*, 403; *View of Lynmouth, Devon* (attrib.), 403
Palmer, Tony, 50, 51, 597
Pam H.J. (Amsterdam friend), 508
Pan American (airline), 206–7, 227
Pangbourne Nautical College, 570

Paramount, 608
Paramount–British Productions, 174
Parikian, Manoug, 484, 487, 551, 623, 628–9, 653, 655
Paris, 66, 70, 81, 189, 309, 679; *Peter Grimes*, 335, 390, 391; as place of study, 64, 80; tour plans, 144, 147
Paris: Notre Dame, 679
Paris: Palais Garnier, 391
Paris: Sacré Coeur, 679
Paris: Théâtre des Champs-Elysées, 187
Park Crescent, London w1, 140
Parker, Miss (secretary), 381, 383, 419, 447, 449, 452
Parker, Barbara, 260, 267, 285, 316, 321, 324, 381, 383, 417, 428, 442, 452, 473–4, 476, 492
Parker, Derek, 543
Parkin, Michael, 133
Parkinson, C. N., 498
Parr, Gladys, *plates 13 and 39*; 393, 399, 401, 540, 550, 554
Parr's Cottage, Cliveden, 21
Parry, Elizabeth, 572, 573–4
Parry, Hubert, 235
Parsons, William, *plate 10*; 63, 295, 384
Partridge, Frances, 113, 133, 134
Pascal, Gabriel, 324–5, 327, 328
Pascal, Valerie, 327
Patrick, Father, 351
Patzak, Julius, 660
Peace Pledge Union, 319
Peacock, Carlos, 402, 402–3; *John Constable: the man and his work*, 402; *Samuel Palmer: Shoreham and after*, 402
Pear, David, 548
Pearce, Stella Mary, 170
Pears, Arthur Grant (PP's father), 191–2, 226, 267, 364
Pears, Jessica (Jessie) Elizabeth de Visnes (PP's mother), 191–2, 226, 267, 320, 364
Pears, Peter, 78, 81, 139, 315–16, 321–2, 340–41, 344–5, 381–2, 385–6, 416–17, 419–20, 442, 447–8, 449–50, 452–3, 456–7, 459, 469, 473–4, 475–6, 490, 491, 492, 496, 569–70, 585–6, 613–14, 635–6, 653, 655, 660–61; and air travel, 417–18; and Aldeburgh Festival, 31, 36, 42, 45–67, 317, 603, 610, 652, 674; and BBC, 124, 183; and Britten works: *Albert Herring* (Albert), *plates 10, 13 and 15*; 248, 251, 273, 295, 298, 339, 354, 470; *The Beggar's Opera* (Macheath), *plate 20*; 350, 354, 357, 393, 397, 399, 401, 546; *Billy Budd* (Vere), *plate 44*, 480, 620, 641, 658, 693, 696; *Canticle I: 'My beloved is mine'*, 313, 319, 339; *Death in Venice* (Aschenbach), 88; *Dido and Aeneas* (Aeneas), 596; *Holy Sonnets of John Donne*, 138, 339; *Les Illuminations*, 83, 119, 144, 153, 198, 306, 313, 320, 325; *Letters to William*, 234; *On This Island*, 255, 278, 339; *Paul Bunyan* (Johnny Inkslinger), 665; *Peter Grimes* (Peter Grimes), 103, 106, 141, 185, 198, 202, 203, 208, 227, 282, 285, 298, 333, 336–8, 391, 425–7, 437–8; Purcell arrangements and realizations, 339; *The Rape of Lucretia* (Male Chorus), *plate 7*; 144, 218, 222, 227, 258, 303–5, 354, 448, 659; *Saint Nicolas* (Nicolas), 300–302, 323, 359, 407, 433, 472, 630–31; *Serenade*, 102, 123, 181, 182, 642, 663; *Seven Sonnets of Michelangelo*, 84, 99; *Spring Symphony*, 521–3, 551–2, 554, 617, 663; *Voices for Today*, 672; *A Wedding Anthem*, 541; and Britten–Pears School for Advanced Musical Studies, 149, 516; as collector of books and art,

288, 338, 349, 364, 402–3, 465, 568, 586–7, 601;
compositions (as 'Luard Pears'): 'When within
my arms I hold you', 276; domestic arrangements and social life, 38, 42–3, 57, 58, 139, 140,
186, 191, 315, 321–2, 364, 423, 479; as editor and
deviser, 104, 150, 383; and English Opera Group,
47, 152, 198, 244, 273, 354, 483, 496, 520, 602, 615,
674; estate and executors, 424; as Evangelist in
Bach Passions, 8, 255, 282, 375, 381, 385, 460,
508–9, 560–61, 660–62; and family, 8, 456–8, 521;
in Glyndebourne Chorus, 149, 151; health:
blood pressure, 496; depression, 447, 455; hay
fever, 193; throat problems and colds, 245, 333,
386, 409, 508; shingles, 533, 560–61, 563, 569,
576–8; holidays, see entry for BB; in interview,
248–9; in oratorio, 183, 231, 267, 340, 341, 344,
346, 462–3, 621; personality, 444–5; portraits
and photographs, plates 2, 8–9, 29, 31, 33–4, 50;
67, 567–8; press profiles: Opera, 624; programme-
planning, 365; and Purcell, 106–7; repertoire
and performances (not including those with
BB), 47, 48, 88, 95, 100, 101, 113, 278, 282, 291, 313,
320–21, 325, 339, 341, 342, 407, 414, 423, 428, 496,
534, 540, 544, 583, 601, 621, 622, 630, 638, 651,
653–4, 656, 675; see also entries in Index of
Britten's Works and Index of Other Composers;
and Schubert, 282, 325; sexuality, 7; and
Stravinsky, 674, 675; as teacher, 653–4; teachers
and vocal coaches, 189, 418, 496, 584; and texts,
365, 367, 383, 575, 658; as translator of Bach
Passions, 383; US: residency in (1939–1942), 81,
82, 86, 87, 90, 92, 111, 189; visit (1948), 416–18,
420, 424, 428, 434, 440–41, 452, 459, 464; visit
(1949), 87, 424; and viola, 653; and The
Wandering Scholar (Holst), 428, 430, 434
Pears, Steuart, 456, 457–8
Pearson, John, 543
Pease, James, 210, 507
Peckham, London, 193
Peele, George, 454, 527; 'Fair and fair' (Song of
Oenone and Paris), 454, 528, 599; The Old Wives'
Tale, 230; 'When as the rye reach to the chin',
230, 527
Pemaquid Point, Maine, US, 226, 230
Penderecki, Krzysztof, 655
People (newspaper), 7
People's Palace, London, 375
Pepusch, John Christopher, 350, 393, 394, 400
Performing Right Society, 668
Periton, Leslie, 326, 424, 538–9, 540
Perugia, Noemie, 586
'Pervigilium Veneris' (anonymous ode), 280–81
Pestalozzi, Almanach, 570, 571
Philadelphia Academy of Music, 93
Philadelphia Orchestra, 93
Philip, Prince, see Edinburgh, Duke of
Philip, John, 343
Phillips, Catherine, 358
Phillips, Walter, 358
Phipps, Sue, 45
Phoenix Opera, 276
Picard, Olivier, 255
Picture Post, 537, 675
Pijper, Willem, 415, 460
Pilgrim Players, 171
Pilgrim Trust: Recording Britain project, 177
Pinter, Harold, 603, 654
Piper, John, 73, 176–7, 288, 340, 341, 358, 364, 370,
464, 535, 570, 571, 611, 655, 674, 676; Albert

Herring: Drop cloth of Loxford, 364, 465;
Benjamin Britten Memorial Window, 177; 'The
Design of Lucretia', 429; and Albert Herring,
plate 10; 252–3, 273; and Aldeburgh Festival, 175,
363; and Billy Budd, 559, 606, 611, 640, 645, 693;
and Death in Venice, 33; and EOG, 243, 244, 259,
262, 265, 273, 276; and Owen Wingrave, 175; and
Peter Grimes, 282; and The Rape of Lucretia, 175,
218, 220, 222, 224, 240, 429, 477, 478; and The Tale
of Mr Tod, 673; and The Turn of the Screw, 175
Piper, Myfanwy, 176, 341, 570, 571, 574, 606; on BB,
18; Death in Venice (libretto), 32–3; The Turn of
the Screw (libretto), 27, 175
Pissarro, Camille, 465
Plant, Andrew, 673
Playford, John, 648
Plomer, William, plate 32; 342, 362, 461, 509, 633,
670–72, 672–3, 678, 679; At Home, 672; The
Burning Fiery Furnace (libretto), 672; Collected
Poems, 672; Curious Relations (under pseudo-
nym William D'Arfey), 508, 509; Curlew River
(libretto), 672; Double Lives, 672; Gloriana
(libretto), 672; The Prodigal Son (libretto), 672;
The Tale of Mr Tod (adaptation), 534, 670–72,
678–9; Turbot Wolfe, 672; Tyco the Vegan
(libretto), 672; and Voices for Today, 672
P.M. (US), 379–80
Poet's Christmas (radio feature), 132
Pollak, Anna, plate 3; 218, 234, 643
Ponchielli, Amilcare: see IOC
Ponselle, Rosa, 490, 491
Ponsonby, Robert, 486
Pooley, Sir Ernest, 564
Porte, Betsy de la, plate 13
Porter, Cole, 557, 610; and see IOC
Porter, Peter, 72
Portland Place, London, 140
Portofino, Italy, 484, 491, 498
Potter, Beatrix, 197, 534, 670–74, 678–9
Potter, Julian, 124, 253
Potter, Mary, 124, 488; Aldeburgh Festival calendar
(1954), 176; portrait of Roger Duncan, 488;
portrait of Mary Potter, 626
Potter, Stephen, 123–4, 241, 252–3
Poulenc, Francis, 149, 184, 459, 485, 487; and see
IOC
Pound, Ezra, 196
Pounder, John, 389–90, 390
Poussin, Nicolas, 599
Powell, Michael, 458, 607
Prabhavananda, Swami, 558
Prague, 235, 358, 436, 636; tour plans, 145
Prague: German Opera, 436
Prague: Neues Deutsches Theater, 284
Prausnitz, Frederik, 12–13
Prausnitz, Maja, 13
Prausnitz, Margaret, 13
Prausnitz, Sebastian, 13
Prentice, Herbert M., 76
Pressburger, Emeric, 458
Presse, Die (Vienna), 663
Priestley, J. B., 438; Johnson over Jordan, 438; The
Olympians (libretto), 438
Primrose, William, plate 24; 161, 533, 550–51,
590–91, 629, 655; Walk on the North Side:
Memoirs of a Violist, 551
Princess Royal (Princess Mary), 613, 614
Princeton, New Jersey: The Duchess of Malfi, 229
Princeton University: PP–BB recital, 546

Proctor, Norma, 148
Prokofiev, Sergey, 472
Prokosch, Frederic, 121
Prospero's Books (film), 603
Proust, Marcel, 3–4; *A la recherche du temps perdu*, 3
Providence (film), 603
Providence, Rhode Island, US: Metropolitan Theatre: *The Duchess of Malfi*, 138, 229
Psalm 69, 170–71
Puccini, Giacomo, 219, 623; *and see* IOC
Pulitzer Prize, 268
Pulsifer, Gary, 87
Punch, 331
Purcell, Henry, 76, 130, 149–50, 170, 235, 244, 278, 319, 339, 393, 429, 493, 543, 546, 563, 645–8; and *The Young Person's Guide to the Orchestra*, 27; *and see* IOC
Purcell Operatic Society, 569
Purcell Singers, 656
Purcell Society, 646–8
Pye (gramophone manufacturer), 425
Pygmalion (film), 328

Quarles, Francis, 315, 319, 321, 323; *Emblems*, 330; 'Ev'n like two little bank-divided brooks', 319, 330
Quarryfield, *see* Crantock, Cornwall
Quasimodo, Salvatore: *Billy Budd* (Ghedini) libretto, 538
Quebec, 57, 103
Queen Elizabeth (passenger liner), 441
Queen Mary (passenger liner), 441, 546
Queen's Hall, London, 80, 435; *Ballad of Heroes*, 80
Quiller-Couch, Arthur, 118
Quilter, Roger, 364, 575–6; *and see* IOC

Raalte, Albert van, 416, 460
Racine: *Phèdre*, 679
Radcliffe Hospital, Friends of, 23
Radio Berlin, 183
Radio Beromünster, 184
Radio Times: articles, 70, 124, 141-2, 492, 528–9; billings, 80, 123, 171, 235, 433, 651, 661
Radley College, 637
RAF Central Band, 485
Rafaelli, José, 79, 80–81
Rainier, Priaulx: *see* IOC
Raleigh, Walter, 162
Ralph of Coggeshall, 604–5; *Radulphi de Coggeshale Chronicum Anglicanum*, 605
Rambert, Marie, 70
Randolph, Thomas, 343
Random House (publishers), 268
Rankl, Karl, 203, 282, 284–5, 333, 335–7, 437–8, 476, 478; *and see* IOC
Ransome, Arthur, 416
Rapallo, Italy, 489, 498
rationing, 232, 286, 452, 453, 595
Rattle, Simon, 237
Ravel, Maurice, 189, 446; *and see* IOC
Ravizza (?critic, Rome), 493–4
Rawsthorne, Alan, 184, 486, 487
Raybould, Clarence, 63, 128, 190
RCM Sinfonietta, 70
Read, Herbert, 652
Reading Rota, 526
Realist Film Unit, 172
Record Guide, 457
Recorded Sound, 548

Red House, Aldeburgh, 45, 88, 308, 625, 665
Red Shoes, The (film), 458
Redcliffe-Maud, Caroline, 11, 19, 22, 271
Redcliffe-Maud, Humphrey, *see* Maud, Humphrey
Redcliffe-Maud, Jean, 11–12, 19–21, 24, 271, 272, 299–300, 341, 448
Redcliffe-Maud, John, 11–12, 22–3, 29, 271, 342, 448, 492
Redcliffe-Maud, Pamela, 11, 19, 271, 272
Redcliffe-Maud, Virginia, 11, 19, 22, 23, 271, 272
Redcliffe-Maud family, 19, 43, 303, 315, 476, 480
Redlich, Hans F., 96
Reed, Henry, 642–3; *The Private Life of Hilda Tablet*, 642–3
Reed, Philip, 5, 42, 169, 191, 200, 271, 344, 536, 537, 583, 620, 633; interviews, 90; obituaries by, 213, 337; references, 72, 101, 166, 201, 252, 339, 350, 364, 375, 465, 568, 587
Rees, Goronwy, 73; *and see* Spender, Stephen
Regent Street Polytechnic, London, 106
Rehfuss, Heinz, 188
Reinhardt, Max, 234
Reiniger, Lotte, 372, 467–8
Reinshagen, Victor, 187
Reiss, Beth, 31
Reiss, Stephen, 30–31, 33, 36, 38–41, 44–7, 51
Renan (singer; Junius), 49
Renishaw Hall, Derbyshire, 177
Residentie Orkest, 47
Resistance (in occupied Europe), 388
Resnais, Alain, 603
Resnik, Regina, 375, 377, 379, 380
Reusz, Eva de, 496, 584
Revue Musicale, 309
Revue Musicale Suisse, 263
Reyntiens, Patrick, 177
Rhine, river, 534, 674, 675, 678, 681
Richards, Bernard, 339
Richmond, Surrey, 424
Richter, Sviatoslav, 49, 666
Rickett, Denis, 243
Rigoletto (film), 328
Rimbaud, Arthur, 81, 120, 129, 130, 554
Ritchie, Margaret ('Mabel'), *plates 3 and 10*; 218, 222, 234, 244, 248, 260, 295–6, 303, 305, 308, 322, 344–6, 348, 430, 434, 456, 574
Robbins, Jerome, 601–2; *The Guest* (ballet), 602
Robert Shaw Chorale, 270
Roberts, Sir Howard, 638–9
Roberts, Winifred, 104, 105
Robertson, Alec, 305
Robertson, Rae, 89, 90
Robinson, Mr (domestic servant at Crag House), 491–2, 576
Robinson, Stanford, 300, 623, 624
Rochester, Marc, 463
Rodgers, W. R.: 'Put away the flutes', 342
Rodzinski, Artur, 85, 439, 440–41
Rogers, Iris Holland, 166, 184, 186, 487, 679
Rogier, Frank, 222
Rolf, Douglas, 433
Rome, Italy, 358; PP–BB recitals, 268, 516; *The Rape of Lucretia*, 493–5, 502
Rome Opera, 495
Rommel, Erwin, 92
Ronald, Landon, 61
Ronald Duncan Literary Foundation, 547
Rooper, Jasper, 381; *and see* IOC

Roosevelt, Franklin Delano, 622
Rootham, Jasper, 344, 346, 471–2
Rorem, Ned, 578–9, 579
Roseberry, Eric, 350, 648
Rosenthal, Harold, 203
Rosewell, Michael, 70
Ross, Hugh, 84–5, 87, 207, 536
Rossini, Gioacchino, 558; and see IOC
Rostropovich, Mstislav, 22, 49, 319, 473, 487, 625
Roth, Ernst, 167, 194, 195, 196, 199, 326, 352, 479,
   493, 494–5, 501, 502, 547, 566, 575–6, 673
Roth, George, 359
Roth, Nicholas, 387
Roth Trio, 50
Rothermere, Lord, 70
Röthlisberger, Max, 188, 198
Rothman, Bobby, 89, 90, 95
Rothman, David, 89, 90, 95, 100
Rothman, Joan, 89
Rothman, Ruth, 89, 95
Rothmüller, Marko, 187
Rotterdam, Netherlands, 381, 509; Albert Herring,
   397; concerts (PP/BB), 414; St Matthew Passion
   (PP), 381, 384, 561, 586
Rotterdam Conservatory, 51
Rotterdam: St Willibrorduskerk, Boys' Choir of,
   521, 523, 527
Rotterdam Volks-Universiteit, 384, 415, 561
Rowley, Alec, 575–6
Royal Academy of Music, London: staff, 61; former
   students, 61, 148, 161, 337, 412–13, 431
Royal Air Force (RAF), 442, 541
Royal Albert Hall, London, 160, 161, 384, 428, 435,
   437, 518, 581, 598; Scottish Ballad, 190; Spring
   Symphony, 533, 552
Royal Ballet, 507
Royal College of Music, London, 437; BB as a
   student at, 55, 56, 211, 338, 341, 355, 700; Cobbett
   Prize, 56, 443; former students, 12, 87, 338, 355,
   368, 431, 443, 458, 463, 475, 485, 596; and
   Plymouth Town, 70; and Sinfonietta, 56; staff,
   146, 342, 486, 493, 639, 700; and see RCM
   Sinfonietta
Royal Court Theatre, Sloane Square, London, 193,
   643
Royal Family, 542
Royal Festival Hall, London, 161, 464, 638–9;
   organ, 463–4, 638–9; see also Festival Hall Sub-
   Committee
Royal Marines, 470
Royal National Theatre, see National Theatre
Royal Navy, 571
Royal Opera House, Covent Garden, 282, 285, 287,
   601–2, 607, 633; administration, 47, 150, 199,
   203, 290, 330, 333, 390–91, 438, 478, 567, 653; and
   EOG, 244, 259, 438; personnel, 7–8, 308, 328,
   355, 636; Albert Herring, 300; Billy Budd, plates
   44–7; 355, 374, 436–8, 564, 642, 680, 682–98,
   684–5, 699, 701–2; The Fairy Queen, 199, 203,
   391, 494; Gloriana, 235, 308, 431; Hamlet, 342;
   King Priam, 355; Manon, 290–91; The
   Midsummer Marriage, 355; A Midsummer
   Night's Dream, 608; Moses und Aron, 355; Le
   nozze di Figaro, 667; Peter Grimes, 128, 235, 282,
   308, 313, 325, 355, 390–91, 437; The Queen of
   Spades, 22; The Rape of Lucretia, 300, 355;
   Troilus and Cressida, 235, 355; Turandot, 308;
   Wozzeck, 187, 235; Die Zauberflöte, 177, 636
Royal Opera House Benevolent Fund, 290

Royal Opera House Orchestra, 426
Royal Philharmonic Orchestra, 150, 246, 485
Rubbra, Edmund, 550
Runswick, Daryl, 171; and see IOC
Ruskin, John, 4
Russell, John, 46
Russell, Thomas, 581
Russia, 471; see also Soviet Union
Rylands, George, 228, 603

Sacher, Paul, 356, 464, 483, 487
Sackville-West, Edward, plate 25; 54, 111–34
   passim, 162, 239–40, 241, 302, 303, 350, 457, 535,
   653–5; And So To Bed (compilation), 350;
   'A melodrama [The Rescue] based on The
   Odyssey', 124; 'Noel Mewton-Wood: A
   Recollection', 162; 'Peter Grimes: The Musical
   and Dramatic Structure', 130–31; BBC commitments, 123–4; as pianist, 113; The Rescue, 72,
   111–17, 122–8, 126, 131; reviews, 239, 400–401; on
   Peter Grimes, 17
Sackville-West, Vita, 303
Sadler's Wells Theatre Ballet (later Royal Ballet),
   71, 290, 355, 485, 585; Job, 177; The Quest, 177
Sadler's Wells Opera Company (later English
   National Opera), 103, 105, 182, 285, 332; admin-
   istration, 105, 140, 144, 152, 181, 475, 533, 562,
   563–7, 606, 609, 632; artists, 149, 151, 392, 431;
   chorus, 188; Albert Herring, 375, 407, 411, 412;
   The Bartered Bride, 101, 149, 248; The Beggar's
   Opera, 375, 407, 411; Così fan tutte, 248; Falstaff,
   565; Lady Rohesia, 555; Nelson, 701; The Pearl
   Fishers, 177; Peter Grimes, 103, 105, 137, 140–41,
   167, 188, 212; The Picture of Dorian Gray, 115;
   The Rape of Lucretia, 137, 144, 147, 224, 238, 245;
   La traviata, 583; Die Zauberflöte, 636
St Andrew's, Scotland, 575; PP–BB recital, 577
Saint-Denis, Michel, 195
St Edmundsbury and Ipswich Bach Choir, 630
St Felix School, Southwold, 79, 81
St Gallen, Switzerland, 182, 194, 195; Cathedral, 195
St Gallen Concert Society, 187
St Gallen Kammerchor, 182
St John's Church, Lowestoft, 193
St John's Wood High Street, No. 45a, London NW8,
   58, 97, 106, 111, 146
St Louis Symphony Orchestra, 436
St Mark's, North Audley Street, London, 183, 533,
   541; A Wedding Anthem, 533, 541
St Matthew's Church, Northampton, 138, 163, 165,
   388–9, 411, 412, 596–7; Choir, 165
St Michael's College, Tenbury, 648
St Michael's School, Petworth, 300, 344, 346
Saint-Saëns, Camille: see IOC
Salisbury Cathedral, 578
Salisbury and District Society of Arts, 578
Salzburg, 47, 235, 262, 489, 491, 660
Salzburg: Conservatorium Mozarteum, 355
Salzburg Festival (1937), 57, 343, 681; Wozzeck, 681
Samuel, Harold, 12, 55, 669, 670
San Francisco, 448
Sandberg, Herbert, 168
Sandham Memorial Chapel, see All Souls, Oratory of
Santiniketan University, India, 628, 646
Sargent, Malcolm, 171–3, 174, 329, 348, 473, 474,
   495, 639
Sarton, Harold, 453
Sartre, Jean-Paul, 197; Huis-clos, 194, 197
Sautoy, Peter du, 667

Saxmundham, Suffolk, 611
Sayers, Dorothy L., 615, 616: *The Man Born to Be King*, 615
Scala, La, Theatre, London, 25, 27
Scandinavia, 51; concerts and recitals, 273, 290
Schafer, Murray, 76
Schaffhausen, Switzerland, 182, 185, 189
Schen, Hermann, 561
Scherchen, Gustel, 92, 166–7, 168, 169, 171, 181
Scherchen, Hermann, 92, 169, 181, 184, 278, 460
Scherchen, Wulff, *see* Woolford, John
Scherman, Thomas, 443
Scheveningen, Netherlands, 262; *Albert Herring*, 397; EOG tour, 305–6, 308, 310, 324; *Spring Symphony*, 522
Scheveningen: Kurzaal, 308, 310
Schey, Hermann, 387
Schiøtz, Aksel, 222, 447, 448
Schipa, Tito, 490, 491
Schirmer, G., Inc., 195
Schmid-Bloss, Karl, 187, 193, 199, 200
Schmidt-Isserstedt, Hans, 623, 624
Schnabel, Artur, 12, 21, 161, 186, 189–90, 246, 387, 409–10
Schoeffler, Paul, 187
Schoenberg, Arnold, 34, 97, 131, 209, 284, 342, 401, 423, 675; *and see* IOC
Schofield, Margaret, 433
Schorr, Daniel L., 523–4
Schouwenberg, J. W. de Jong, 345, 346, 347, 387
Schubert, Franz, 12, 76, 97, 123, 186, 189, 190, 339, 359, 453, 454, 612; *and see* IOC
Schuh, Oscar Fritz, 681
Schuh, Willi, 324, 326, 623, 625
Schumann, Robert, 525, 612, 656; *and see* IOC
Schürhoff, Else, 663
Schütz, Heinrich, 342, 600, 630, 645, 653–4; tercentenary (1972), 656; *and see* IOC
Schwarz, Boris, 472
Schwarz, Rudolf, 183
Schwarzkopf, Elisabeth, 614
Scotland Yard (Metropolitan Police headquarters), 604
Scotsman, 697
Scott, Miss (friend of E. J. Dent), 169
Scottish Orchestra (later Scottish National Orchestra), 329, 436
Scouting movement, 471–2
Searle, Adrian, 6
Searle, Humphrey, 341, 342, 423; *and see* IOC
Second Viennese School, 409
Seiber, Mátyás, 101, 485, 487; *and see* IOC
Serly, Tibor, 550
Sewell, Captain, 49–50, 52
Seymour family, 544
Shacklock, Constance, 391–2
Shakespeare, William, 217; *Hamlet*, 603; *Much Ado About Nothing*, 294; *Richard II*, 603; sonnets, 423; *The Tempest*, 269, 534, 602–3, 606–9
Shakespeare Memorial Theatre, Stratford upon Avon, 328
Shanks, Catherine, 584–5
Shapero, Harold, 443
Sharp, Anne, *plate 13*; 507
Sharp, Frederick (Jimmy), *plate 15*; 147, 295, 303, 428, 430, 431, 434
Shaw, Alexander, 171, 174, 428, 432
Shaw, Bobbie, 22–3
Shaw, George Bernard, 70, 325, 327, 328, 654;
Androcles and the Lion, 325, 327, 328; *Caesar and Cleopatra*, 327, 328; *Major Barbara*, 327; *Pygmalion*, 327; *St Joan*, 325, 328
Shaw, Martin, 48, 563, 569; *and see* IOC
Shaw, Robert, 267, 270
Shaw II, Robert Gould, 22
Shawe-Taylor, Desmond, 133–4, 167, 203, 303, 349, 456, 457, 491, 535; reviews, 141, 220–21, 298, 301–2, 517–18, 527–8, 591, 594, 650, 682–3, 686–7
Shearer, Moira, 458, 585
Shebalin, Vissarion, 472
Sheffield, 542, 640
Sheffield: City Hall, 543
Sheffield Philharmonic Chamber Music Club, 543
Shell Guides, 177, 341
Shelley, Percy Bysshe: 'The Moon', 118; 'Night', 118; 'Remorse', 118
Shelton, Lucy, 121
Sheppard, Dick, 319; Memorial Concert, 319
Sheridan, Richard Brinsley, 603, 654; *The Critic*, 647; *The School for Scandal*, 603
Shilling, Eric, 171
Shingle Street, Suffolk, 630–31
Shirley-Quirk, John, 148, 359
Shostakovich, Dmitry, 472–3
Shrubbery, Hasketon, Suffolk, 228
Shubert Theatre, New Haven, 50
Sibelius, Jean, 210
Sickert, Walter, 465
Sidney, Sir Philip: 'His Lady's Cruelty', 118
Sigriswil, Switzerland, 181, 192
Silver Jubilee Secondary Modern School, 630
Simon, Enid, 627
Sinden-Evans, Rosy, 252
Singher, Martial, 166
Sitwell, Edith, 162, 542–3, 543, 544–5, 679–80; *The Canticle of the Rose*, 679–80; *Façade*, 542–4; 'Modern Poetry' (lecture), 544; 'Praise We Great Men', 543; 'Still Falls the Rain', 162, 543, 680; 'The Weeping Babe', 132
Sitwell, Osbert, 71, 73, 177, 543
Sitwell, Sacheverell, 543
Skelton, John, 543, 544
Slade School of Art, 465
Slater, Montagu, 68, 115, 130, 174, 372; *The Mark of Cain* (ballet scenario), 115; *Pageant of Empire*, 68; *Peter Grimes* (libretto), 92, 123, 186, 336, 337, 378
Smart, Christopher, 686
Smetana, Bedřich: *see* IOC
Smith, Cecil, 477–8
Smith, Christopher, 197
Smith, Con, 587
Smith, Eric, 587
Smith, James, 566
Smith, James F. A., 243
Smith, Leonard, 348, 425–6, 427
Smith, Oliver, 261
Smith, Stevie, 642
Smithwick, Cecily, 492
Smithwick, Walter, 492
Smyth, Ethel, 364, 642; *and see* IOC
Snape, Suffolk, 40, 43, 46, 250, 322; *see also* Old Mill, Snape
Snape Maltings Concert Hall, 154, 358–9, 418; administration, 31–3, 36, 40–43; construction (1967) and reconstruction (1969), 30–32, 38, 610; fire (1969), 30, 41, 610; recording for television, 516
Snape Maltings Foundation, 290

Snowman, Daniel, 150, 284
Société des Auteurs Compositeurs et Editeurs de Musique (SACEM), 197
Solti, Georg, 290
Somervell, Sir Arthur, 122; *and see* IOC
Songs of Benjamin Britten (broadcast recital), 339
Song of Solomon, 319
Sophocles, 195
Sotheby's, 465
Sound of Music, The (musical), 392
Soutar, William, 120
South Lodge Preparatory School, Lowestoft, 48–9, 55, 390, 470, 510
Southern California, University of, 502; PP–BB recital, 556, 558
Southern Cathedrals Festival (1968), 596
Southern Philharmonic Orchestra, 277
Southold, Long Island, 89, 95
Southolme pre-preparatory school, 193
Southwold, Suffolk, 81, 353, 450, 503
Soviet Union, 472–3
Spangen, choir of, 561
Spanish Civil War, 8
Speaight, Robert, 416
Spectator, 297
Spencer, Stanley, 67, 214
Spender, Stephen, 54, 71–2, 72, 73, 616, 652; *Danton's Death* (Büchner translation, with Goronwy Rees), 73; 'Not to you I sighed. No, not a word', 72; *Trial of a Judge*, 177; 'Your body is stars whose millions glitter here', 72
Spenser, David, *plate 10*; 315, 316
Spenser, Edmund, 456, 526, 527; 'The merry Cuckoo', 421, 455, 527
Spessivtseva, Olga, 70
Speth, Werner, 278
Spithead Mutiny (1797), 637–8, 683
Spitta, Philipp, 601
SPNM (Society for the Promotion of New Music), 88
Spring-Rice, Margaret (Margery), 315, 316, 317, 381, 453, 456
Spruytenburg, Hank ('Diapason'), 591
Stage, 328, 692
Stallworthy, Jon, 122, 143
Stallybrass, Oliver, 363
Stanhope Gate, No. 6, London, 585
Star (Bournemouth), 520
Stars of the Old Vic and Sadler's Wells (compilation record box set), 427
Steane, John, 522
Steen, Jac Van, 343
Steer, Philip Wilson, 465
Stefan, Pete, *see* Martinez, José
Stein, Erwin, *plate 22*; 54, 96, 97, 102–3, 104, 111, 160, 167–8, 184–6, 191, 196, 227, 228, 235–6, 252–4, 259, 271, 272, 282, 284–6, 294, 305–6, 365, 409, 419, 422–3, 428, 479, 544–6, 551–2, 575–6, 611–12, 677–8; 'Opera and *Peter Grimes*', 131–2; *Orpheus in New Guises*, 104; BB, first meeting with, 56; and *Billy Budd*, 538, 541, 664, 677–8; and Decca, 452; and EOG, 243, 483, 569; family life, 475, 585, 636, 640; health, 491; and *The Little Sweep*, 506, 512, 574–5, 629; and Mahler, 121; as music editor, 119, 130; and Schoenberg, 131; sixtieth birthday, 105; and *Spring Symphony*, 500, 553, 616–18; and Suite, for violin and piano, 446; as teacher and lecturer, 101, 409, 443–4; in Vienna, 284

Stein, Marion, *see* Thorpe, Marion
Stein, Sophie, 96, 97, 186, 191, 282, 286, 289, 409, 474, 544, 546, 552, 585, 611–12, 636, 640, 678
Stein family, 104, 111, 267, 351, 358, 364, 424, 452, 479
Stellman, Maxine, 379
Stephen, King, 605
Stern, Isaac, 653, 654–5
Stevenson, J., 605
Steward, A. V., 450
Stiedry, Fritz, 277, 325, 329
Stockholm: *Peter Grimes*, 137, 167–8; PP–BB recital, 278
Stoll Theatre, London, 160
Storey, David, 603
Strachan, Alan, 328, 604
Strand Films, 174
Strasbourg, 187, 391, 392
Strasfogel, Ignatz, 229
Stratford Festival, Ontario, 49
Stratford-upon-Avon, Warwickshire, 186, 328, 606–7
Strauss, Richard, 184, 185, 222, 326, 485, 486, 590; *and see* IOC
Strauss Festival (1948), 485
Stravinsky, Igor, 63, 75, 76, 147, 149, 161, 186, 189, 235, 372, 422, 446, 472, 523, 525, 556, 584, 676, 691; *and see* IOC
Strode, Rosamund, 34, 45, 122, 567, 601, 654
Ström, Ella Viola, 548
Stuart, Sir Campbell, 326
Stuart, Charles, 295–6, 301, 400
Stubenrauch, Freddy, 188
Sturmdorf, Regina, 95, 100–101
Sudbury, Suffolk, 583, 620
Suddaby, Elsie, 384
Suffolk County Record Office, 450
Suffolk Rural Music School, 175, 316, 319, 456
Suffolk Rural Music Schools Association, 344, 346
Suk, Josef: *see* IOC
Sumidagawa (Nō play), 672
Sunday Times, 457; letter to the editor, 142; obituaries, 457; reviews, 142, 215–16, 296–7, 696–7, 700
Sunday Times Magazine, 78
Sundström, Inga, 168
Surfling, Anne, 51
Surrey, Henry Howard, Earl of, 543–4
Sussex, University of, 76, 668
Susskind, Walter, 96, 329, 434, 436, 440
Sutcliffe, Thomas, 604
Sutcliffe, Tom, 24, 26
Suter-Schlotterbeck, Lisel, 192, 193
Sutermeister, Heinrich, 185, 189; *and see* IOC
Sutherland, Graham, 388, 389; *Christ in Glory in the Tetramorph*, 389; *Crucifixion*, 389
Sutherland, John, 72
Sutton, Mrs Lincolne, *see* Alston, Audrey
Svanholm, Set, 168
Swann, Donald, 643
Swarthmore College, Pennsylvania, 99, 269, 554–5
Sweden, 448, 486: concert tour (1947), 138; tour plans, 145, 535
Sweeting, Elizabeth, 12, 260, 383, 442, 457, 479, 483–4, 546, 549–50, 554–5, 615, 679; *Beginners Please: Working in the Theatre*, 383; 'Let's Make a Festival!', 383; *Theatre Administration*, 383; and Aldeburgh Festival, 36, 319, 381, 383, 479, 483–5, 618; and EOG, 36, 383, 479, 483–5, 512, 520, 549–50, 554–5, 569, 614–15, 618

Swiss Radio, 46
Switzerland, 92, 196, 199–200, 264, 271, 277, 279, 286, 288, 357, 506, 560, 587; concerts and recitals, 137, 138, 267, 273, 313, 464, 640; convalescence (PP), 560, 561, 563, 570, 577; EOG tour, 317; holidays, 137, 174, 181, 306; *Peter Grimes*, 167, 208; *The Rape of Lucretia*, 253
Syben, Magrit von, 188
Sylvester, David, 6
Synge, J. M.: *Deirdre of the Sorrows*, 284
Szell, Georg, 329, 436
Szigeti, Joseph, 445–6, <u>446</u>

Tadié, Jean-Yves, 4
Tait, Jack, 692
Takemitsu, Toru, 319
Tale of Tanglewood: Peter Grimes Reborn, A (film), 212
Tanglewood, 85, 87, 101, 213, 237, 270, 278, 280–81, 443, 465, 479, 480; *Albert Herring*, 501; *Peter Grimes* (1946), 47, 146, 204–5, 206–7, 225–7, 229, 379, 455; and *Spring Symphony*, 500, 511, 533; *see also* Berkshire Festival
Taormina, Italy, 612
Tappolet, Claude, 189, 262
Tate, Nahum, 647
Tate Gallery (now Tate Britain), London, 364, 402; John Piper retrospective exhibition (1983), 177
Tatler and Bystander, 585
Taubman, Howard, 535
Taylor, John Russell, 197
Tchaikovsky, Piotr Ilyich, 31, 75–6, 154; *and see* IOC
Tehran, University of, 605
Tempo, 26, 84, 153, 183, 326, 327, 613, 667, 674, 675
Tenison Singers, 170
Tennent Plays Ltd, 170
Tennyson, Alfred Lord: *Maud*, 122–3; 'Now sleeps the crimson petal', 118; 'The Splendour Falls', 118
Terry family, 603
Teyte, Maggie, 144–5, 148, 154
Theology, 389
This Modern Age (film), 328
'This Modern Age' Film Unit, 328
Thomas, Dylan, 642; *Under Milk Wood*, 642
Thomas, Gary, 5
Thomas of Celano, 270
Thompson, Eric, 236
Thompson, Hugh, 380
Thompson, Leonard, 185, 188
Thomson, Virgil, 377–8, 579
Thoran, M. C., 255
Thorndyke, Sibyl, 654
Thorold, Phyllis, 574
Thorpe, Jeremy, <u>189</u>
Thorpe, Marion, *plate 29*; 97, 105, 186, <u>189</u>, 191, 232, 282, 306, 351, 409, 411, 424, 443, 475, **507–8**, 533, 534, 538, 541–2, 544, 552, 562, 568, **584–5**, 588, 610, 614, **620–21**, 623, 629, 635, **638**, 640, 674, 676, **680–81**
Thorpe-le-Soken, Essex, 673, 674
Tietjen, Heinz, 4, 623, <u>624–5</u>
Tiggers, Piet, 522; *see also* 'P.T.'
Tijd, De, 24
Tillett, Emmie, 381, <u>385</u>
Time, 210–11, 237, 370, 371, 372, 374
Time and Tide, 298–9
Time There Was . . ., A (film), 50
Times, The, 62, 63, 68, 117, 260, 270, 292, 419, 542, 632, 677; articles, 332, 541, 647; letters to the edi-

tor, **213**, 647–8; obituaries, 72, 78, 85, 87, 89, 133, 140, 148, 149, 150, 177, 213, 246, 276, 326, 328, 337, 356, 368, 372, 421, 458, 493, 563, 604, 625; reviews, 140–41, 161, 218–19, 294, 301, 305, 319, 336–7, 397, 399, 439, 516–18, 523, 526–7, 552–3, 591, 636, 648, 690
Times Literary Supplement, 18, 269, 504
Tippett, Michael, 132, 161, 184, 223–4, 255, 319, 366, <u>368</u>, 369–70, 372, 414, 433, 486, 620–21, 623–4; *and see* IOC
Tiverton, Devon, 381: PP–BB recitals, 370, 385
Tiverton: Blundell's School, 385
Tobin, John, 148
Tocher, The (film), 467
Tooley, John, 290
Top of the World (Crazy Gang show), 149
Torquay: *Let's Make an Opera*, 550, 629
Toronto: PP–BB concert, 548
Toronto Symphony Orchestra, 436
Tosca (film), 328
Toscanini, Arturo, 550
Townswomen's Guild, *see* National Union of Townswomen's Guilds
Travel and Industrial Development Association, 261
Travers, John, 647–8
traviata, La (film), 328
Treasury: and capital transfer tax, 424; currency restrictions, 417, 419
Tree, David, *plate 47*
Trevelyan, George Macaulay: *England Under the Stuarts*, 288
Trevelyan, Robert, 584
Trewin, J. C., 568
Tribunal for the Registration of Conscientious Objectors, 50, 51, 91, 93, 94, 111, 120, 444
Trieste: PP–BB recital, 356
Tryon House, No. 11, Mallord Street, London sw3, 96
Tucker, Norman, 439, 563–7, 606, 609, 611; *Norman Tucker: Musician*, 609
Tuppence Coloured (revue), 331, 383
Turin, Italy: PP–BB recitals, 268, 516
'Turn Ye to Me' (folk tune), 90
Turner, Claramae, 379
Turner, Joseph Mallord William 358, 364, 464; *Coastal scene* (attrib.), 364
Tynan, Kenneth, 580

UN General Assembly Hall, New York, 87
Unicorn Kanchana (record label), 171
United Nations, 87, 158
United States of America, see America, United States of
Unity Theatre, London, 71
Universal Edition (music publisher), 195, 329
University College, London, 72
University College, Oxford, 12, 23
Upper Park Road, No. 38, 458
Uppman, Theodor ('Ted'), *plate 46*; 633, 694, 698
Utrecht, Netherlands, 228: *Albert Herring*, 397; concert (PP), 415

Valois, Ninette de, 70
Vancouver, 144, 146
Variety, 603
Vaughan, Henry, 456, 528; 'Waters above', 456, 528
Vaughan Williams, Ralph, 87, 148, 149, 184 241, 364, 458, 475, 485, 548, 623, <u>625</u>, 639; *and see* IOC
Venice, Italy, 33, 356, 407, 412, 484, 488–9, 491, 498, 544, 681, 682: *The Rake's Progress*, 235, 565, 674,

681; *The Turn of the Screw*, 380, 431
Venice Biennale (1952), 27
Venice: Teatro La Fenice, 674, 675
Venice Festival, 374, 380
Verdi, Giuseppe, 76, 97, 169, 189, 235, 309, 329, 623–4, 692, 695–6; BB on, 582–4; *Opera* magazine anniversary issue, 623–4; *and see* IOC
Verlaine, Paul, 527
Verona, Italy: PP–BB recital, 268
Vickers, Brian, 18
Victoria and Albert Museum, London, 180
Vienna, Austria, 47, 56, 195, 320; as place of study, 187, 342; PP–BB recitals, 516, 663; *Spring Symphony*, 663
Vienna Court Opera, 636
Vienna: Mozart Saal, 663
Vienna Philharmonic Orchestra, 150, 320, 663
Vienna: Staatsoper, chorus of, 663
Vienna State Opera, 660
Vienna Volksoper, 329
Vignoles, Roger, 359
Vilasse, Andrée, 225, 227, 230
Vincent, Henry, 170
Vincent, Jo, *plate 50*; 509, <u>510</u>, 521–3, 527, 551, 553, 586, 662; *Zingend door het leren*, 510
Vincent de Paul, St, 356
Virgil, 196; *Aeneid*, 544
Virtuous Isidore, The (film, 1932), 249, 252
Vischegonov, Lubomir, 188
Visconti, Luchino, 6
Vishnevskaya, Galina, 49
Vittoria, Tomás Luis de: *see* IOC
Vivaldi, Antonio: *see* IOC
Vlachopoulos, Zoë, 277
Vogel (translator), 226, 227, 231
Volkskrant, De (Amsterdam), 47
Vosper, Margery, 330
Vrije Volk, Het (Amsterdam), 47
Vroons, Frans, 382, 386, <u>387</u>
Vyvyan, Jennifer, 355, 428, <u>431</u>, 456

Waarheid, De, 248
Waddell, Helen: *The Wandering Scholar*, 430
Waddington, Geoffrey, 551, <u>552</u>
Wade, Martyn: *The Ceremony of Innocence*, 7
Wadham, Dorothy, 66–7
Wadham College, Oxford, 326
Wagner, Richard, 47, 169, 188, 219, 329, 377, 527, 692, 694, 696; *and see* IOC
Wain, John, 643: *Hurry On Down*, 643
Waley, Arthur, 223
Wallace, Ian, 430
Wallace, Lucille, 190
Wallace, Vincent, 169
Wallenstein, Alfred, 441
Walling, Metcalfe, 227, 459
Walsh, Stephen, 676
Walter, Bruno, 85, 150, 316, <u>320</u>–21, 325, 329, 458
Walton, Richard, 134
Walton, Susana, 201
Walton, William, 184, 199–200, <u>201–2</u>, 235, 304, 369–70, 622, 623; *and see* IOC
War Cabinet, 284
War Resisters' International, 291
Wards (garage), 582, 584
Warlock, Peter: *see* IOC
Warrell, Ian, 364
Washington, US, 544
Watergate Theatre, London, 580

Waterhouse, John F., 74, <u>75–6</u>, 77, 518, 694–5
Waterhouse, Mrs John F., *see* Duxbury, Elspeth
Waters, Stephen, 244, 345, <u>347</u>, 365, 366, 483
Watford Town Hall, 174
Watson, Clare, *see* Hawkes, Clare
Watt, Douglas, 46
Waugh, Evelyn, 177; *Brideshead Revisited*, 177
Weber, Annie, 187
Webern, Anton, 284, 342
Webster, David, 150, 203, 289–90, <u>290</u>, 390–91, 436–7, 456, 467, 476, 534, 567, 602–3, 607, 632, 636, 654–6, **699**
Webster, John, 137; *The Duchess of Malfi*, 137, 226, 228–30
Webster, Martyn C., 661, 662
Weelkes, Thomas: *see* IOC
Weill, Kurt, 230, 396–7, 609; *and see* IOC
Weingartner, Felix, 329, 487
Welford, Mrs, 450
Welford, Beth, <u>65</u>, 71, 79, 250, 315, 452, 456, 459, 470, 490, 491, 588–9; *My Brother Benjamin*, 65; family life, 20, 95, 101, 193, 225, 226, 228, 231, 239, 267, 286, 352, 357, 381, 384, 417, 449–50, 473–4, 476, 587, 630–31, 640–41; in London, 65; sharing flat with BB, 61; and Women's Institute, 139
Welford, Christopher ('Kit'), 65, 228, 286, 417, 470
Welford, Elizabeth Ellen Rosemary (Roguey), *plate 37*; 10, 381, 384, 417, 449, 470, 630–31
Welford, Sarah Charlotte (Sally), *plate 37*; 10, 101, 381, 384, 417, 449, 470, 630–31, 640, 641
Welford, Thomas Sebastian, 10, 79, <u>80</u>, 95 381, 449, 470, 473, 630–31
Welford family, 267, 315, 357, 641
Welles, Orson, 608, 609
Wellesz, Egon, 475
Wellington College, 99, 100
Wells, H. G., 70
Welsh National Opera, 24: *The Turn of the Screw*, 24
Welt von Heute, 263
Wembley Town Hall, 172
Wentworth, Vernon, 673
West Berlin: Städtische Oper, 235
West Cottage Road, London NW6, 45
Westby's (garage), 79
Westminster Cathedral, 596
Westminster Cathedral Choir, 171, 389
Westminster Hospital, London, 48
Westminster School, 326
Weston super Mare: PP–BB recital, 370
Westrup, Jack, 304
Wheeler, Hugh, 608
Wheeler, Pamela, 51
Whinyates, Seymour, 191, 200, 495
Whistler, Rex, 70, 113
White, Eric Walter, 35, 230, 370, <u>372</u>, **460–61**, 467, 468, 504, 506, 562–3, 564–9, 631–2, 647, **665**, 673–4, 675; *Benjamin Britten: eine Skizze von Leben und Werk*, 372, 407, 460–61; *Benjamin Britten: His Life and Operas*, 372, 504–6; 'Bibliography of Benjamin Britten's Incidental Music', 668; *A History of English Opera*, 372, 567, 632; *The Little Chimney Sweep*, 467; *The Rise of English Opera*, 562, 567, 631–2; *Stravinsky: The Composer and his Works*, 372; *Tippett and His Operas*, 372; *Walking Shadows*, 372
Whitesell, Lloyd, 5
Whitred, Gladys, 430
Whittall, Arnold: *The Music of Britten and Tippett*, 4

Wicklow, Earl of, 340, 341
Wiesbaden: *The Rape of Lucretia*, 641, 659
Wigmore Hall, London, 341: *Canticle III*, 162; *Holy Sonnets of John Donne*, 105, 107; *Serenade*, 98, 123; *Seven Sonnets of Michelangelo*, 99, 111; String Quartet No. 2, 107
Wilcox, Michael, 7, 24; *Benjamin Britten's Operas*, 7
Wilde, Oscar: *The Importance of Being Earnest*, 603; *The Picture of Dorian Gray*, 115
Wilder, Thornton: *The Happy Journey*, 287
Wilhum, Carel, 560
Wilkinson, G. A. M., 103
Will, Hans, 278
Willett, John, 230, 568
Willi (Amsterdam friend), 381, 385
William of Newburgh, 604–5; *Historia Rerum Anglicanum*, 605
Williams, Grace, 224, 241, 474, 475, 495–6; *and see* IOC
Williams, Harold, 384
Williams, Stephen, 692
Williams, Tennessee: *The Glass Menagerie*, 211
Williams, Tom, 337, 439
Williams, W. E., 682
Williamson, Malcolm, 149; *and see* IOC
Williamson, Reginald Ross, 340, 341
Wills, John, 433
Wilson, Conrad, 421
Wilson, Steuart: at Arts Council, 214, 284; as conductor, 346; at Covent Garden, 7, 567, 690; as Evangelist, 12, 382–3; 'The Future of Music in England', 362
Wimbledon: *Let's Make an Opera*, 677
Windsor Castle, 177
Winterthur, 181, 182
Winterthur Musikkollegium, 184
Winterthur: Stadthaussaal: PP–BB concert, 278
Wintle, Christopher, 667
Wirén, Arne, 168
Wittgenstein, Ludwig, 18, 19
Wittgenstein, Paul, 93
Witts, Richard, 8
Wolf, Hugo, 113, 357, 612; *and see* IOC
Wolfsgarten, Schloss, Germany, 33
Wolverhampton, 508, 509: *Let's Make an Opera*, 501
Women's Institute (W.I.), 139, 140
Wood, Anne, 276, 367; and EOG, 273, 276, 289, 305, 322, 353–5, 365, 366, 383, 483, 485, 496, 520, 549–50, 615; and Opera Studio (National Opera School), 276, 354–5, 627; and *Spring Symphony*, 276, 551–4, 613, 617
Wood, Charles, 603
Wood, Chris, 557
Wood, Christopher, 586
Wood, Elizabeth, 5
Wood, Thomas, 483, 485; *True Thomas*, 485
Woodard Schools, 346

Woodbridge, Suffolk, 228, 470
Woodgate, Leslie, 276, 359, 416, 433, 473, 474–5, 476
Woodger, Cissie, 250
Woolf, Virginia, 30, 130, 672
Woolford, John, 65, 72, 91, 92–3, 119, 166–7, 181, 182–3
Woolford, John R., 500, 502
Woolford, Pauline, 183
Woolmore, Pamela, 596, 650–51
Woolpit, Suffolk, 605
Wordsworth, William: 'Evening on Calais Beach', 118
Works Progress Administration (US), 622
Wormwood Scrubs prison, 694
Worthley, Max, *plate 40*; 430
Wosniak, Bislaw, 187
Wright, Basil, 171, 172, 174
Wyss, Sophie, 97–8, 165–6; and *French Folk Song Arrangements*, 166; and *Les Illuminations*, 83, 96, 119; recital partnership with BB, 49

Yale Dramatic Workshop, 270
Yale University, 270
Yannopoulos, Dino, 375, 379
Yeend, Frances, 49
York, 340: *The Tale of Mr Tod*, 674
York University, 668
Yorkshire Symphony Orchestra, 485
Young, Arthur: *Travels in France and Italy*, 586
Yoxford, Suffolk, 40, 249
Ysaÿe, Eugène, 550

Zadek, Hilde, 663
Zander, Benjamin, 597–8
Zander, Mrs, 597–8
Zelger-Vogt, Marianne, 200
Zermatt, 271, 272, 279, 285, 570
Zimmermann, Hans, 186, 188, 198, 623, 624
Zollner, Clare, *see* Hawkes, Clare
Zolotow, Sam, 229
Zorian String Quartet, 162, 260, 339, 368
Zurich, Switzerland 11, 184, 186, 193, 199, 272, 288, 351, 356, 370, 487, 663
Zurich: Collegium Musicum: PP–BB concert, 351, 354, 356
Zurich Conservatory, 188
Zurich Opera, 187, 188, 213, 624: *Let's Make an Opera*, 624; *Lulu*, 188, 198; *Mathis der Maler*, 187, 188, 198
Zurich Radio, 182, 306
Zurich: Stadttheater (Municipal Theatre), 167, 200, 285; *Arabella*, 187, 200; *Die Entführung aus dem Serail*, 193, 200; *Peter Grimes* (1946), 137, 167, 181–2, 184, 185, 192, 194, 197–8, 208
Zurich: Tonhalle: EOG concert, 306, 307; *Serenade*, 278; *Sinfonia da Requiem*, 182
Zurich Tonhalle Orchestra, 182